Industrial Organization

THE ADDISON WESLEY SERIES IN ECONOMICS

Industrial Organization

THEORY AND PRACTICE

THIRD EDITION

Don E. Waldman
Colgate University

Elizabeth J. Jensen
Hamilton College

PEARSON

Addison
Wesley

Boston San Francisco New York
London Toronto Sydney Tokyo Singapore Madrid
Mexico City Munich Paris Cape Town Hong Kong Montreal

To our families,
Lynn, Abigail, and Gregory
Bob, Ben, and Annie

Publisher: Greg Tobin

Editor in Chief: Denise Clinton

Acquisitions Editor: Adrienne D'Ambrosio

Editorial Assistant: Margaret Beste

Managing Editor: Nancy H. Fenton

Senior Production Supervisor: Kathryn Dinovo

Senior Design Manager: Chuck Spaulding

Senior Marketing Manager: Roxanne Hoch

Marketing Assistant: Kate MacLean

Rights and Permissions Advisor: Shannon Barbe

Senior Manufacturing Buyer: Carol Melville

Cover Design and Text Design: Henry Rachlin

Production Coordination: Elm Street Publishing Services, Inc.

Composition and Illustrations: WestWords, Inc.

Cover photo: © 2006 Marlene Healey, healeyartgroup.com

For permission to use copyrighted material, grateful acknowledgment is made to the copyright holders on p. 712, which is hereby made part of this copyright page.

Many of the designations used by manufacturers and sellers to distinguish their products are claimed as trademarks. Where those designations appear in this book, and Addison Wesley was aware of a trademark claim, the designations have been printed in initial caps or all caps.

Library of Congress Cataloging-in-Publication data

Waldman, Don E.
 Industrial organization : theory and practice / Don E. Waldman, Elizabeth J. Jensen.— 3rd ed.
 p. cm. — (Addison-Wesley series in economics)
 Includes bibliographical references and index.
 ISBN 0-321-37610-2
 1. Industrial organization (Economic theory) 2. Industrial organization. 3. Industrial policy. I. Jensen, Elizabeth Jane. II. Title. III. Series

HD2326.W349 2007
338.9—dc22 2006047529

2 3 4 5 6 7 8 9 10—CRW—10 09 08 07

ABOUT THE AUTHORS

DON E. WALDMAN is the Richard M. Kessler Professor of Economic Studies at Colgate University. He has taught at Colgate since 1981 and has served as chair of the economics department and director of the division of social sciences. Before arriving at Colgate, he received outstanding teaching awards at Cornell University and the University of Maryland, Baltimore County. Professor Waldman received a B.A. in mathematics from Temple University, an M.A. in economics from Brown University, and a Ph.D. in economics from Cornell University. He is the author of three other books, *Microeconomics, Antitrust Action and Market Structure,* and *The Economics of Antitrust: Cases and Analysis,* as well as numerous articles, comments, and book reviews. Professor Waldman has also served as a consultant and expert witness on legal cases, specializing in antitrust, for both the government and private firms.

In addition to teaching a wide variety of courses at Colgate, on three occasions Professor Waldman has led a group of honors students to study economics for a semester in London. He has been teaching courses on industrial organization and public policy for more than 30 years. Professor Waldman lives in Hamilton, New York, with his wife. They have two children.

ELIZABETH J. JENSEN is Professor of Economics at Hamilton College. She has taught at Hamilton since 1983, and served as chair of the economics department. She has been honored for her teaching, receiving an award for outstanding teaching from Hamilton College in 2002. Professor Jensen received a B.A. in economics from Swarthmore College and a Ph.D. in economics from the Massachusetts Institute of Technology. Before coming to Hamilton, she worked at the Council of Economic Advisers. She has recently been investigating the determinants of students' interest in economics and students' course choices.

Professor Jensen, who fondly remembers her first course in industrial organization at Swarthmore College as being the course that made her decide to become an economist, has been teaching courses on industrial organization since she came to Hamilton College. She lives in Clinton, New York, with her husband. They have two children.

BRIEF CONTENTS

CONTENTS

CHAPTER **3** **Competition and Monopoly** 51

CHAPTER **6**

Market Power and Performance: The Empirical Evidence 161

PART II | MODERN INDUSTRIAL ORGANIZATION:
GAME THEORY AND STRATEGIC BEHAVIOR

CHAPTER **7** | **Game Theory: A Framework for Understanding
Oligopolistic Behavior** 207

CHAPTER **8** | **The Development of Oligopoly Theory** 230

CHAPTER 12

Oligopoly Behavior: Entry and Nonpricing Strategies to Deter Entry 372

PART III BUSINESS PRACTICES

CHAPTER **15**

Price Discrimination 515

CHAPTER **16**

Vertical Integration and Vertical Relationships 562

PREFACE

Just as eating against one's will is injurious to health, so study without a liking for it spoils the memory, and it retains nothing.

—Leonardo da Vinci

We wrote this book to help students learn about industrial organization. As the field of industrial organization has changed over the past 25 years, the industrial organization courses we teach at Colgate University and Hamilton College have evolved as well; this book reflects much of what we have learned by teaching. Industrial organization has moved from being primarily empirically oriented to relying more extensively on sophisticated theoretical models. In keeping with this change, this text uses game theory as a unifying method of analysis of firm and industry conduct. Yet, as the transition from an empirical to a theoretical orientation has occurred, we have feared a loss of the valuable empirical tradition on which the field was built. Over time we have become convinced that our students learn best when we present them with both the modern theory of industrial organization and an array of empirical examples of industry behavior and performance.

Our ultimate goal has been to write a comprehensive text that would be theoretically up-to-date and sophisticated yet rich in empirical examples of interest to students. In this third edition we have added many new applications and set them off from the text. We also continue to present competing views of the field and to encourage students to compare and contrast differing interpretations. In *Industrial Organization,* third edition, we believe we have accomplished these goals.

We believe that more than any other text on the market, *Industrial Organization,* third edition, is written for undergraduates. We have not tried to write a book that can be used as a primary graduate text; instead, the book is aimed squarely at undergraduates who have completed at least a one-semester microeconomics course. The level of technical mathematics necessary to understand virtually all of the material is equivalent to the mathematics necessary to understand a standard intermediate microeconomics text. We continue to avoid calculus except in footnotes; whenever possible, we have used numerical examples rather than more generalized and abstract mathematical forms to make a point. Over the years we have been amazed at how much more quickly our students comprehend a numerical example. For our students at least, a linear demand curve such as $p = 100 - q$ is much less intimidating than a demand curve written as $p = a - q$.

Industrial Organization, third edition, can also be used as the primary text in undergraduate policy-oriented economics or business courses, and might serve as an easy background reference text for graduate courses in industrial organization or public policy toward business.

We want to highlight several features of the text. First we begin by analyzing the theory of firm behavior, perfect competition, and monopoly. We move on to examine

why market structures evolve so differently in different markets. Monopoly practices are then examined and the problems associated with monopoly power are identified.

The analysis of oligopolistic conduct begins with Chapter 7, which is entirely devoted to the essentials of game theory. Following that chapter, we employ a simple game theory approach as the primary, but not the sole, framework for the remaining chapters on oligopolistic conduct. Using game theory as a basic framework helps our students understand the common relationships between different models of oligopolistic behavior. Without this framework, students have often told us that the differing models of oligopolist behavior appear disjointed and confusing.

Another strength of the text is the detailed discussion of many cases, including a wide variety of antitrust cases. Industrial organization is a field full of good stories and informative case studies. Throughout this book we present many examples to help students understand the close connection between theory and the real world. We use certain industries repeatedly, including the oil, automobile, airline, computer, and food distribution industries. As a result, students should gain not only an understanding of theory and empirical work in industrial organization, but also an appreciation of the importance of case studies in expanding our knowledge of the field.

We hope that incorporating many stories in the text will ensure that the book reads easily and that it will hold the interest of most undergraduate students. Despite its accessibility, the text should equip students with the necessary theoretical sophistication to enable them to gain a great deal of insight into firm behavior and public policy issues such as antitrust, regulation, deregulation, and international trade.

The study of industrial organization can be organized in many different ways. We have divided this text into three main parts:

I. The Basics of Industrial Organization

In Chapter 1 we present a brief history of the field and explain the differences between the two generally accepted approaches to industrial organization: the structure-conduct-performance approach and the Chicago School approach. Antitrust policy in The United States is also introduced in this chapter. Chapter 2 examines alternative theories of the firm, including a discussion of the boundaries of the firm and the firm's costs. Chapter 3 reviews the basic microeconomic theory of perfect competition and monopoly and examines U.S. antitrust policy toward monopoly. Chapter 4 considers the structure of markets in the United States, market entry and exit, and mergers, including a discussion of the impact of mergers on market structure and antitrust policy toward mergers. Chapter 5 examines three important models associated with monopoly. In Chapter 6 we review the major conclusions regarding the relationship between market structure and economic performance and consider the interpretation of the empirical regularities established by industrial organization scholars over the past 50 years.

II. Modern Industrial Organization: Game Theory and Strategic Behavior

Chapters 7–12 are the core chapters, examining conduct, primarily, but not entirely, from a game theory perspective. We have worked hard to make even sophisticated game theory models accessible to undergraduate students. We have devoted all of Chapter 10 to case studies of collusion and Chapter 12 to nonpricing strategies to

deter entry, such as raising rivals' costs and product proliferation. Appendices to Chapters 11 and 12 delve into more advanced game theory models.

III. Business Practices

Chapter 13 explores product differentiation and advertising, and Chapter 14 investigates the relationship between market structure and the rate of technological advance. Chapter 14 also includes a fairly detailed look at Schumpeter's theory of creative destruction and considers the United States patent system. Chapters 15 and 16 explore price discrimination and vertical integration, respectively, from a theoretical perspective. We have included in appendices several more advanced topics, such as the welfare effects of price discrimination with nonlinear demand curves and the problem of input substitution in the absence of vertical integration. Finally, Chapter 17 presents the traditional theory of public utility regulation as well as recent developments in the area of deregulation. The book concludes on the note that the history of regulation and deregulation in the United States suggests that competition rather than regulation is usually the best method of achieving economic efficiency.

Changes to the Third Edition

We are gratified by the response to both the first and second editions of *Industrial Organization*. But we are also pleased to have the opportunity to make improvements. We have made several changes to the third edition, based on feedback from colleagues and students as well as our own experiences in using the book in class.

Major changes have been made involving the placement of material. First, we have moved the antitrust material from Chapters 18 and 19 into the appropriate theoretical chapters. Chapter 16 has been moved to Chapter 6 to end the discussion of the traditional SCP paradigm earlier in the text and transition more smoothly toward the modern industrial organization approach. Chapter 17, Using the Tools, has been cut entirely, yet some of its discussion has been included in several sections on the *Microsoft* case. Additionally, the major sections on limit pricing and excess capacity have been completely reformulated for clarity. A new Chapter 5 on monopoly practices repositions material that appeared in Chapters 5 and 7 in the second edition and adds a new section on network economies.

Next, we have added a significant amount of material to each chapter in the form of new applications, new sections, and end-of-chapter questions and problems. Most major topics have an application which, in most cases, also includes data.

Our Web site, www.aw-bc.com/waldman_jensen, introduced with the Second Edition, has been a great resource for students and instructors. It has been updated to include information from the third edition and to follow the new organization. Professor Rochelle Ruffer of Youngstown State University has designed special web exercises for our site that enable students to apply their newly acquired knowledge of industrial organization to "real world" situations.

We have tried to write a flexible text that can be covered in full or in part in a variety of ways. Ideally, the entire book would be covered in one semester or two quarters. An instructor teaching a one-quarter course will probably have to decide whether to emphasize theory or policy. The following are possible course outlines:

In a two-quarter course, cover Chapters 1–10 in the first quarter and Chapters 11–17 in the second quarter.

In a one-quarter course emphasizing theory, cover Chapters 1–9 and 10–16 and selectively delete some sections on antitrust policy.

In a one-quarter course emphasizing policy, in a one-quarter course on public policy toward business, or in business school courses, cover Chapters 1–6, 9–10, and 12–17.

To facilitate review and learning, we have included a summary at the end of each chapter to recap the important points. Compared to the second edition, each chapter offers many additional questions for discussion as well as problems. The answers to the odd-numbered problems are presented at the end of the book. A glossary is included at the end of the text in case a student forgets, for example, the difference between *certain information* and *complete information*.

Acknowledgments

We wish to thank many for their help in preparing this book. John Greenman of HarperCollins worked with us throughout the preparation of the first edition of the text and showed great wisdom and patience in his approach toward the project. We owe a great deal to Jack. Denise Clinton and Adrienne D'Ambrosio at Addison Wesley have been tremendously helpful and encouraging, and Kathryn Dinovo and Jennifer Moquin cheerfully kept track of materials and reminded us of deadlines. Brandi Nelson did a wonderful job during the final production stages of the text. Sheri Aggarwal did a great job checking several chapters for accuracy. We are indebted to Rochelle Ruffer for her work on the Web site.

We owe our gratitude as well to the many first, second, and third edition reviewers who offered fine guidance at various stages of the evolution of the manuscript. They are:

Sheri Aggarwal, University of Virginia
Donald L. Alexander, Western Michigan University
Gary Biglaiser, University of North Carolina, Chapel Hill
Erwin A. Blackstone, Temple University
James W. Brock, Miami University of Ohio
Michael R. Butler, Texas Christian University
Kathleen A. Carroll, University of Maryland, Baltimore County
Indranil Chakraborty, University of Oklahoma
Yongmin Chen, University of Colorado, Boulder
Maryanne Clifford, Eastern Connecticut State University
Coldwell Daniel III, University of Memphis
Marc Dudey, Rice University
Patrick Emerson, University of Colorado, Denver
Robert M. Feinberg, American University
Gary M. Galles, Pepperdine University
Devra Golbe, Hunter College/CUNY
Charles M. Gray, University of St. Thomas
Carl R. Gwin, Babson College
Claire Hammond, Wake Forest University
David Kamerschen, University of Georgia

Alan Kessler, Providence College
Philip King, San Francisco State University
Dan Kovenock, Purdue University
Ping-Sing Kuo, Academia Sinica, Taipei
Luther D. Lawson, University of North Carolina, Wilmington
Jim Lee, Fort Hays State University
Li Way Lee, Wayne State University
Daniel Levy, Emory University
Nancy A. Lutz, Virginia Polytechnic Institute and State University
Richard L. Manning, Brigham Young University
David E. Mills, University of Virginia
Iwuagwu Oguledo, Florida A&M University
Randal Reed, Morgan State University
Stanley S. Reynolds, University of Arizona
David Ridley, Duke University
David Rosenbaum, University of Nebraska, Lincoln
Leola B. Ross, East Carolina State University
Rochelle Ruffer, Youngstown State University
Nicholas Rupp, East Carolina University
Frank A. Scott Jr., University of Kentucky
Sergei Severinov, University of Wisconsin, Madison
Joseph Shaanan, Bryant College
Doris F. Sheets, Southwest Missouri State University
John M. Vernon, Duke University
Natalie J. Webb, Naval Postgraduate School
Everett E. White, Loyola University of New Orleans
Dr. E.F.M. Wubben, Erasmus University, Rotterdam

Our students at Colgate University and Hamilton College deserve our thanks, not only for tolerating partial early drafts as their only textbook, but also for suggesting many fine improvements and pointing out more than one error. Our colleagues and friends—economists and noneconomists alike—gave us much tangible and intangible help. Finally, our spouses, Lynn Waldman and Robert Turner, and our children, Abigail and Gregory, and Ben and Annie, deserve the greatest praise for their support and patience.

D. E. W.
E. J. J.

Introduction

In the beginning there was perfect competition. And economists saw that it was good. So they assumed perfect competition.

A nyone who has studied microeconomics at the introductory level can appreci-
ate the preceding statement, as can anyone who has taught an introductory
microeconomics course. In the authors' introductory courses students often ask
why we assume perfect competition when we analyze the automobile, computer, or
cellular phone industries. Students ask: How can you assume that there are a large
number of sellers in those industries? How is it possible that no firm or group of firms
has any control over price? How can you assume a homogeneous product in the auto-
mobile industry? When those questions arise, we tell our students that they are asking
excellent questions and that economists use the perfectly competitive model as an
approximation of the real world, but that it is obvious that those industries do not
conform strictly to the assumptions of the model. We also tell students interested in
learning more about such issues to take a course in industrial organization.

The field of industrial organization developed as an offshoot of traditional micro-
economics. Microeconomics courses examine the interactions among consumers,
producers, and government, with an emphasis on two traditional models: *perfect
competition* and *monopoly*. While some courses also touch on models of **monopolistic
competition** and **oligopoly,** most traditional courses pay relatively little attention to
these models.

The perfectly competitive model assumes a large number of buyers and sellers,
each of which is a price taker. The monopoly model assumes the opposite: one seller
with complete control over price. While these models are easy to work with theoreti-
cally, neither is an accurate depiction of most real-world markets. Perfect competition
accurately describes some markets, such as agriculture, retailing, some service indus-
tries, and the stock market. However, perfect competition is rare in manufacturing
and mineral extraction.

Monopoly is also rare in the real world. Examples include public utilities such as
your local distributor of electricity or natural gas; in most communities, the supplier
of cable television; and, in small isolated towns, the local food market or gasoline sta-
tion. In its pure form, however, monopoly is even less prevalent than perfect competi-
tion. Structurally, most markets are neither perfectly competitive nor monopolistic but

fall somewhere in between. Such "in between" industries are classified as either oligopolies or monopolistic competition. *Oligopoly* refers to a market structure where a relatively small number of firms control the market. The prevalence of oligopoly is indicated by the fact that in 1997 the U.S. Bureau of the Census calculated that the top four firms controlled at least 20 percent of national sales in 81.6 percent of the 947 government-defined manufacturing industries.[1]

Industrial organization economists recognize that the models of perfect competition and monopoly do not accurately depict most real-world markets. Nevertheless, the field has its roots in the traditional theory of the firm developed by Adam Smith in the eighteenth century and Alfred Marshall in the nineteenth century. The first important theoretical advances in the area of oligopoly theory were made by Augustin Cournot and Joseph Bertrand in the nineteenth century.[2]

Historically, a very important theoretical advance was made with the development of the theory of monopolistic competition by Edward Chamberlain in the early twentieth century.[3] *Monopolistic competition* is characterized by a large number of buyers and sellers, easy entry, and a differentiated product. Examples of monopolistically competitive markets include furniture, costume jewelry, textiles, and restaurants. Chamberlain's theory differed from the theories of Smith and Marshall by focusing attention on product differentiation and the study of the *firm* instead of the *industry*. One of the driving forces behind Chamberlain's work was a belief that previous models were poor representations of the real world. Chamberlain believed that real-world firms competed not only on the basis of price but also on the basis of product differentiation. The theory of monopolistic competition was a major breakthrough because it helped to fill the glaring gap between theory and empirical observations of how markets operated. It was quickly incorporated into mainstream economic thought, and within a decade the theory of monopolistic competition was included in every microeconomics theory textbook.

Unfortunately, the model of monopolistic competition turned out to have as many problems as the models of perfect competition and monopoly. The model has very limited predictive capability, and its few predictions are susceptible to serious criticisms. Despite its drawbacks, monopolistic competition introduced into economic theory the concepts of product differentiation and a downward-sloping demand curve associated with product differentiation, and highlighted the crucial role of entry. Chamberlain's model provided the first theoretical link between perfect competition and monopoly and ultimately led to renewed interest in oligopoly theory and development of the traditional industrial organization paradigm connecting structure, conduct, and performance.

In his seminal work, Chamberlain also discussed oligopoly, but in far less detail than he discussed monopolistic competition. Examples of oligopoly are numerous and include manufacturing industries such as automobiles, steel, pharmaceuticals, cereals, soft drinks, and beer. Early theoretical work on the relationship between oligopoly and economic performance resulted in few strong conclusions but led economists, among them Joe Bain, to test the relationship empirically.[4] Early empirical studies found that increased market control by a few firms in an industry was associated with higher industry profits; this was interpreted as an indication that the firms had colluded to raise price.

The evolution of industrial organization into a major area of economics has also been closely linked to the development of the modern theory of the firm. In the stan-

dard models of perfect competition and monopoly the firm has no discretion over its behavior. In both models, *all* firms maximize profits, and *all* firms increase price in response to an increase in costs. Industry case studies in the 1920s, however, suggested that real-world firms did not respond in such mechanistic ways. To the contrary, case studies indicated that firms had considerable discretion over price, output, and advertising expenditures. Berle and Means, for example, found that oligopolists followed behavioral objectives other than profit maximization.[5] The recognition that oligopolists had discretion over key economic variables led to a new series of questions. Could oligopolists engage in strategic behavior with regard to pricing, research and development, advertising, merger activity, and collusion to influence future market structure and economic performance?

Once economists recognized that *firms* have discretion over key choice variables, the primary focus for analyzing the relationships among structure, conduct, and performance shifted away from the industry and toward the firm. Economists who emphasized the discretionary freedom of firms often rejected the profit-maximizing hypothesis and placed great emphasis on the ability of firms to select alternative behavioral objectives.

As the above discussion implies, courses in microeconomic theory usually emphasize theoretical rigor at the expense of real-world accuracy. Industrial organization courses tilt the balance in the opposite direction, emphasizing an accurate depiction of the real world. As you will learn, however, industrial organization courses do not ignore theory. In fact, in recent years theory has played an increasingly important role in the field. Industrial organization economists, however, will not analyze the cereal industry by assuming it is perfectly competitive or monopolistic. Instead, the industrial organization economist recognizes that the best way to analyze the cereal industry, both theoretically and empirically, is as an oligopoly.

1.1 Two Approaches to the Study of Industrial Organization

There are two major historical approaches to the field of industrial organization: the structure-conduct-performance approach and the Chicago School approach. In this section we compare and contrast these two approaches and see why the two have converged in recent years.

1.1.1 The Structure-Conduct-Performance (SCP) Approach

In the last two decades, the field of industrial organization has become much more theoretical. The **structure-conduct-performance (SCP)** industrial organization paradigm, however, was primarily empirical in its orientation. The SCP paradigm was developed by Edward Mason and Joe Bain in the 1940s and 1950s.[6] Mason, Bain, and their followers hypothesized that there is a direct relationship between *market structure, market conduct,* and *market performance.* Microeconomics courses emphasize this link without *overtly* recognizing it. Consider, for example, the link between structure and performance in microeconomic theory. In perfectly competitive markets, an atomistic *market structure* results in efficient *economic performance* with price equal to

marginal cost, inefficient firms driven from the market, and long-run economic profits equal to zero. With a monopolistic market *structure,* economic *performance* is poor: Price exceeds marginal cost, inefficient firms can survive in the long run, and economic profits are greater than zero.

The SCP paradigm extends the structure-conduct-performance relationship to oligopoly. Figure 1.1 depicts the paradigm. The heavy arrows on the right show the pri-

FIGURE 1.1 The Structure-Conduct-Performance Paradigm

In the SCP approach to the study of industrial organization, the heavy arrows show that basic market conditions determine market structure, market structure determines conduct, and conduct determines performance. On the right side, we see that government impacts structure, conduct, and performance. The thin arrows on the left show how there can be feedback effects of performance on conduct and structure, and of conduct on structure.

mary relationships: Basic market conditions determine market structure; market structure determines conduct; and conduct determines performance. In addition, government policies have a direct impact on structure, conduct, and performance. The thin arrows on the left depict the feedback effects of conduct on structure and of performance on conduct and structure.

An example may help explain Figure 1.1. Consider the ready-to-eat cereal industry. In terms of *market structure,* the cereal industry is an oligopoly, with Kellogg's, General Mills, Kraft Foods (Post), and Pepsico (Quaker Oats) dominating the market. In 1997 these four firms controlled 82.9 percent of ready-to-eat cereal sales.[7] There are a small number of sellers, and product differentiation through the production of many different brands is extremely important. The significance of product differentiation results in *conduct* that includes a great deal of advertising and a product strategy where each firm is constantly attempting to develop new brands. In 2004 General Mills spent $912,500,000, or 9.7 percent of its sales revenues, on advertising.[8] As a point of comparison, in 2003 total advertising expenditures in the United States were just over 2.2 percent of the gross domestic product (GDP).[9] This conduct results in *performance* that is characterized by price being greater than marginal and average cost, with the cereal industry consistently ranked among the most profitable industries in the United States.[10]

The cereal industry analysis becomes more complicated when the feedback arrows on the left of Figure 1.1 are considered. Performance includes high profits, and these profits may result in increased advertising and increased investment in new product development. In this way *performance* may have an impact on *conduct.* In addition, the high advertising expenditures may make entry into the market more difficult (i.e., increase **entry barriers**) and reduce the number of sellers. In this way *conduct* may have an impact on *structure.* When analyzing the cereal industry, industrial organization economists consider all these effects.

In the 1960s and 1970s SCP industrial organization economists studied the relationships suggested by Figure 1.1 in detail. A majority of this work was empirical. Many case studies as well as numerous statistical studies utilized data across industries. Common questions addressed in these studies included the following:

1. Is there a relationship between market structure and profitability?

2. Do increased entry barriers result in increased profits?

3. What are the most important entry barriers?

4. How does market structure affect the rate of technological advance?

5. What market structure(s) are associated with effective collusion?

6. How does market structure affect pricing strategies?

7. How does government regulation affect economic efficiency?

8. What is the impact of mergers on economic efficiency?

9. Does increased market power result in increased advertising, or does increased advertising result in increased market power?

10. Should the law permit collusion?

11. Should the government regulate monopolies?

1.1.2 The Chicago School Approach

The SCP paradigm provides one important approach to the study of real-world markets, but it is not the only valid way to approach the study of industrial organization. Economists associated with the **Chicago School of economics** have long argued that price theory models should be the primary tool for analyzing markets.*[11] Followers of the Chicago School rely heavily on price theory models to make predictions about expected conduct and performance and to design empirical tests of their theories. We have already noted that in the nineteenth century economists used theoretical models to analyze oligopoly behavior long before the development of the SCP paradigm. The Chicago School's theoretical approach to oligopoly, therefore, predates the SCP approach to the field.

In the 1960s and 1970s Chicago School economists questioned many of the major empirical conclusions reached by followers of the SCP approach. For example, SCP economists claimed that there was strong empirical evidence suggesting a positive relationship between monopoly power and profits. According to the SCP economists, increases in market power resulted in increased profits. Chicago School economists, however, argued that the true relationship might well be that increased *efficiency* led to increased market power and increased *profits*. Similarly, SCP industrial organization economists provided empirical studies suggesting that increased advertising raised entry barriers and resulted in increased profits. Chicago School economists, however, used theory and empirical evidence to suggest that advertising often provided information and that this improved information resulted in lower prices. SCP adherents also argued that high capital costs associated with entering a market erected entry barriers, but Chicago School economists argued that capital markets functioned efficiently, and therefore all potential entrants had equal access to capital. The debate between the followers of the two schools has been extremely beneficial to the development of the field. Both camps have had a major influence by introducing many important new concepts into the economics profession.

Over the past 25 years a good deal more consensus has developed among economists who specialize in industrial organization.[12] The set of ideas embodied in this consensus is often called the *new industrial organization*. A key part of the new industrial organization is the use of **game theory** to model the behavior of firms within an oligopoly. Game theorists view competition among oligopolists as a game. Of course, the game's outcome depends on its assumptions, and economists have attempted to devise oligopoly games that come closer and closer to approximating the real world. This text relies heavily on the use of game theory to provide a theoretical framework for understanding oligopoly. We believe, however, that the empirical tradition of industrial organization is important; we make extensive use of empirical evidence to support the theoretical conclusions, including the New Empirical Industrial Organization (NEIO), which relies heavily on the detailed empirical study of the behavior of individual firms within industries to understand market conduct and economic performance.

*The Chicago School refers to a school of thought rather than a geographic location. Chicago School economists believe in the efficiency of markets in the absence of government intervention. Generally, Chicago School economists argue that markets take on structures that are efficient. Academic centers for the followers of this tradition include the University of Chicago, UCLA, and the University of Rochester, but followers are found at most major universities.

1.2 Static versus Dynamic Models

Another important distinction between microeconomics courses and industrial organization courses is the emphasis industrial organization places on **dynamic performance.** Most microeconomics courses emphasize **static models** that deal with a moment in time. Short-run marginal and average cost curves shown in a textbook figure represent a snapshot of the industry at a precise moment in time. *Dynamic models* deal with changes *over time.* Dynamic models are strategic and tend to emphasize technological change more than static models do.

Static efficiency requires price to equal marginal cost and long-run average cost. Dynamic efficiency requires an optimal rate of technological advance and can exist even if price exceeds marginal and average cost. Courses in industrial organization tend to place considerable emphasis on dynamic models and dynamic efficiency. While this makes industrial organization analysis more complex and intricate than traditional microeconomic analysis, it provides valuable insight into what really constitutes efficient economic performance. Most economists recognize that even if an industry achieves static efficiency, its performance may be poor if it fails to invest in research and development at an optimal rate.

1.3 Theory and Empiricism

Many of the major questions in industrial organization yield ambiguous theoretical conclusions. For example, economic theory hypothesizes that increased advertising could have a positive economic impact by providing increased information or that increased advertising could have a negative economic impact by making entry more difficult. There is no way to use theory to prove which relationship is dominant. Under such circumstances the only way to provide insight into the economic impact of increased advertising is to rely on empirical studies.

Industrial organization relies heavily on the use of both case studies and statistical analyses. Case studies provide detailed examinations of specific industries. Studies of the beer, cereal, eyeglass, and soup industries have shed important light on the economic impact of advertising. Statistical studies of the advertising-competition relationship have also provided important evidence. Statistical studies suggest, for example, that the relationship is different depending on the types of goods being considered. Empirical evidence on the advertising-competition relationship is presented throughout the text, and an overview of the relationship is presented in Chapter 13.

As you begin the study of industrial organization, it is important to bear in mind that the field requires a thorough understanding of both theory and empirical work. In the 1950s, 1960s, and 1970s, traditional industrial organization economists tended to rely too heavily on empirical findings, while the Chicago School economists typically relied too heavily on standard price theory. The modern approach to industrial organization tries to balance theory and empirical evidence, and we follow this approach throughout this book.

1.4 Government and Industrial Organization

Throughout this book we analyze the potential problems associated with market power. In fact, if no problems were associated with increased market power there would be far less reason to study industrial organization as a subfield in economics. Governments often attempt to limit the negative effects of market power. In the United States these attempts have centered on two broad policies—antitrust and direct regulation. Regulation will be examined in detail in Chapter 17. Antitrust policy will be explored throughout the text, with specific areas of antitrust policy covered in the relevant chapters. As we examine specific aspects of the antitrust laws, it is important to understand the laws that established the current standards for U.S. enforcement of antitrust policy.

It is relatively easy to understand the political pressures that led to the passage of the first U.S. antitrust law, the **_Sherman Act_**, in 1890.[13] Before the Civil War, the United States was mainly an agrarian society in which high transportation costs kept the geographic size of most industrial markets small. After the Civil War, the organization of American industry changed dramatically. The rapid growth of national markets in many products developed from a combination of (1) mass production, introduced by the Industrial Revolution, which resulted in significant economies of scale;* (2) a national railroad system, which greatly increased the size of the geographic market for many products; (3) the development of modern capital markets; and (4) the liberalization of the laws of incorporation in many states. With the growth of national markets, many small regional manufacturers faced competition for the first time. The larger national firms, which took advantage of economies of scale, were often able to invade local markets that were formerly insulated from competition and charge significantly lower prices. As the national producers captured a larger and larger share of many local markets, they threatened to eliminate many local producers.

During the 1888 national elections both the Democrats and the Republicans offered platform planks to fight the trusts, and immediately before the election Republican Senator John Sherman introduced the first Senate antitrust bill. On July 2, 1890, President Harrison signed the measure, an act he probably thought would be little remembered by history.

1.4.1 The Content of the Antitrust Laws

The major provisions of the Sherman Act are Sections 1 and 2, which read in part:

> _Section 1:_ Every contract, combination in the form of a trust or otherwise, or conspiracy, in restraint of trade or commerce among the several states, or with foreign nations, is hereby declared to be illegal. Every person who shall make any such contract or engage in any such combination or conspiracy, shall be deemed guilty of a misdemeanor, and, on conviction thereof, shall be punished by fine not

*Economies of scale refer to a decrease in the long-run average cost of production and will be discussed in detail in Chapter 2.

exceeding five thousand dollars, or by imprisonment not exceeding one year, or by both said punishments, in the discretion of the court. . . .

Section 2: Every person who shall monopolize, or attempt to monopolize, or combine or conspire with any other person or persons to monopolize any part of the trade or commerce among the several States, or with foreign nations, shall be deemed guilty of a misdemeanor. . . .

On a first reading, the Sherman Act sounds quite strong. Certain problems with regard to the legal implications of the wording of the Act arose soon after its passage, however. Section 1 made it illegal for competitors to combine to fix prices and created an incentive for firms to get around the law by *merging* with competitors. Paradoxically, therefore, the first major merger wave in the United States at the turn of the century was encouraged and fueled by the Sherman Act.

Another major problem developed from the somewhat ambiguous wording of Section 2. During the 1890s, Section 2 was completely ineffective in dealing with the monopolization problem. In 1911 two major decisions, the *Standard Oil* and *American Tobacco* rulings, provided both hope for enforcement and confusion with regard to what constituted a violation of Section 2. In its famous *Standard Oil* decision the Supreme Court ruled that only *unreasonable* attempts to monopolize violated the Sherman Act. This interpretation made only the verb "to monopolize" illegal, while permitting the noun "monopoly" to exist as long as the monopoly did not result from an aggressive attempt to monopolize. This precedent has come to be known as the ***Rule of Reason.***

Partly as a result of the handing down of the Rule of Reason, and partly as a result of a lack of clarity in the wording of the Sherman Act with regard to certain types of specific business conduct, by 1912 there were calls for new legislation. What emerged in 1914 were two pieces of major antitrust legislation, the ***Clayton Act*** and the ***Federal Trade Commission Act.***

The Clayton Act aimed to prevent certain specific types of business conduct. It contained the following four substantive sections:

Section 2 forbade price discrimination "where the effect of such discrimination may be to substantially lessen competition or tend to create a monopoly in any line of commerce." The section provided for three defenses: discrimination based on the quantity sold; the different costs of selling or transportation; or the need to meet a competitor's lower price. These defenses, particularly the quantity defense, turned out to be large loopholes in Section 2.

Section 3 forbade ***tying contracts,*** which forced a purchaser to buy good X to obtain good Y, and ***exclusive dealing arrangements,*** which forced a buyer to purchase its entire supply of a commodity from one seller.

Section 7 forbade the acquisition of the *stock* of another corporation if the acquisition would "restrain commerce in any section or community or tend to create a monopoly of any line of commerce." The section was directed at the merger wave that had developed after the passage of the Sherman Act and was limited to horizontal mergers between direct competitors.

Section 8 forbade interlocking directorates between any two competing corporations. This prevented the same individual from sitting on the boards of directors of competing companies.

The Federal Trade Commission Act established the *Federal Trade Commission (FTC)* as an independent antitrust agency to enforce the Clayton Act. The FTC Act also contained one major substantive provision, Section 5, which reads in part:

> The commission is hereby empowered and directed to prevent persons, partnerships, or corporations, except banks, and common carriers subject to the Acts to regulate commerce, from using unfair methods of competition in commerce.

One can hardly imagine a broader mandate. "Unfair methods of competition" could include just about any business practice. Furthermore, many practices considered "unfair" by competitors may have a positive effect on competition. The FTC had little power in its early days. In fact, its only available remedy was to issue cease and desist orders.

The next major antitrust statute was the *Robinson-Patman Act* of 1936, which dealt with price discrimination. The Robinson-Patman Act amended Section 2 of the Clayton Act to include the following major provisions:

> *Section 2(a):* That it shall be unlawful for any person engaged in commerce, in the course of such commerce, either directly or indirectly, to discriminate in price between different purchasers of commodities of like grade and quality, . . . where the effect of such discrimination may be substantially to lessen competition or tend to create a monopoly in any line of commerce, or to injure, destroy or prevent competition with any person who either grants or knowingly receives the benefit of such discrimination, or with customers of either of them:
>
> PROVIDED, That nothing herein contained shall prevent differentials which make only due allowance for differences in the cost of manufacture, sale, or delivery resulting from the differing methods or quantities in which such commodities are to such purchasers sold or delivered.
>
> *Section 2(b):* PROVIDED, HOWEVER, That nothing herein contained shall prevent a seller rebutting the *prima facie* case thus made by showing that his lower price or the furnishing of services or facilities to any purchaser or purchasers was made in good faith to meet an equally low price of a competitor, or the services or facilities by a competitor. . . .
>
> *Section 2(f):* That it shall be unlawful for any person engaged in commerce, in the course of such commerce, knowingly to induce or receive a discrimination in price which is prohibited by this section.

The Robinson-Patman Act contained three additional sections that declared specific types of price discrimination illegal per se. An action is illegal per se if there is no acceptable legal justification for undertaking the action. In antitrust law most restraints of trade come under the Rule of Reason interpretation and can be justified by a "reasonableness" defense; a few actions, however, are illegal per se and cannot be justified as being "reasonable" restraints of trade. The sections of the Robinson-Patman Act pertaining to specific types of price discrimination attempted to close potential loopholes in the Act. *Section 2(c)* forbade the payment of any brokerage commission except for services actually rendered by an independent broker. This section was intended to prevent large grocery chains such as A&P in the 1930s from setting up their own brokerage agencies that would then "charge" their suppliers a

brokerage "fee" for the act of transferring goods from A&P to A&P. *Section 2(d)* forbade a supplier from paying its buyers for promotional services, unless the payments were made available to all buyers on "proportionally equal terms." Finally, *Section 2(e)* forbade the supplier from providing promotional services to any buyer unless the services were made available to all buyers on "proportionally equal terms."

The Robinson-Patman Act is extremely controversial because it has often been used to protect individual competitors rather than the competitive process. The potential problems are easily seen in a careful reading of Section 2(a), which extended the Clayton Act's wording "where the effect of such discrimination may be substantially to lessen competition or tend to create a monopoly," to include the words "where the effect may be substantially . . . to injure, destroy, or prevent competition with any person. . . ." The addition of this last clause justified using the Robinson-Patman Act in cases in which price discrimination injured just one competitor, even if the discrimination actually increased effective competition and improved economic efficiency.

The final major amendment to the Clayton Act occurred in 1950 with the passage of the **Celler-Kefauver Act.** In 1926 the Supreme Court emasculated Section 7 of the Clayton Act when it ruled that corporations could legally avoid the law by acquiring the *assets* rather than the *stock* of another corporation. It wasn't until 1950 that this loophole was plugged. The Celler-Kefauver Act amended Section 7 of the Clayton Act to include mergers through asset as well as stock acquisition. The Celler-Kefauver Act also extended Section 7 to reach all mergers rather than only mergers between direct competitors. With the passage of the Celler-Kefauver Act, Section 7 of the Clayton Act finally had some clout in dealing with anticompetitive mergers. It took 36 years, however, to plug this loophole.

1.4.2 Enforcement Procedures

Antitrust enforcement typically begins with an action by either the Antitrust Division of the Justice Department or the Federal Trade Commission. Most cases are precipitated by either a complaint from a competitor or a report in the business press. Occasionally a case begins with a staff report from a government agency.

Once a Justice Department case is in the federal court system, it proceeds to trial and a decision in the District Court. Either side can appeal the District Court's decision to one of 11 Circuit Courts of Appeal. Once the Circuit Court rules, either side can appeal to the Supreme Court. The Supreme Court will hear the case (grant *certiorari*) if at least four justices agree that the legal issues warrant a hearing. Otherwise, the Supreme Court refuses to hear the case (*certiorari* denied) and the Circuit Court's decision stands. The entire process is typically long and drawn out, with litigation periods averaging over five years and some major cases lasting several decades.

The workings of the FTC are different from those of the Antitrust Division. The FTC is headed by five commissioners who are appointed by the President to serve seven-year terms. Although some Commissioners have been well trained in economics, many others have little understanding of economics because they are primarily political appointees. Initially most FTC cases go before an administrative law judge who works for the FTC.* Based on a hearing that is very similar to a District Court

*Merger cases are appealed directly to the District Court.

trial, the administrative law judge makes a ruling. The judge's opinion can be appealed to the full commission by either the respondent or the FTC staff. The five-member commission hears the appeal and makes a decision, which only the respondent can appeal to the Circuit Court of Appeals. After the Circuit Court decision, either the FTC or the respondent can appeal to the Supreme Court.

Antitrust suits can also be filed by private parties. In fact, in most years private antitrust cases have greatly outnumbered government cases. From 2000–2004, for example, 93.7 percent of all antitrust cases were filed by private parties.[14] Furthermore, for many firms the threat of a large private suit is much greater than the threat of a government action because private cases can result in treble damage awards that can dwarf the fines imposed in government cases.

Remedies

In the event of a government victory, there are several possible penalties or remedies. In criminal cases fines and jail sentences may be imposed. The original Sherman Act set a maximum fine of $5000 per violation. This limit was increased to $50,000 in 1955, to $1,000,000 in 1974, and to $10,000,000 in 1992. The Antitrust Criminal Penalty Enhancement and Reform Act of 2004 increased the maximum Sherman Act corporate fine to $100 million per violation, the maximum individual fine to $1 million per violation, and the maximum jail sentence to 10 years per violation. The FTC also has the power to impose a fine of $10,000 per day on any respondent who refuses to abide by an FTC order. To America's largest and most powerful corporations, these fines are likely to look insignificant. A $1,000,000 fine imposed on Microsoft is likely to have about as much effect as a $500 fine imposed on Donald Trump.

In civil cases, only remedies, not penalties, can be imposed. The distinction between a remedy and a penalty is purely semantic because many antitrust remedies provide more of a threat to violators than the maximum criminal penalties do. Civil remedies may include conduct or structural changes. In cases in which conduct is believed to be the major problem, injunctions are often issued forbidding a certain type of conduct, such as forbidding price discrimination or tying. Injunctions change future behavior without penalizing the defendant for past behavior.

Occasionally the courts may adopt structural remedies such as the breakup of AT&T in 1984. Structural remedies include divestiture, dissolution, and divorcement. These remedies have been used most commonly in merger cases.

Even this brief overview of the antitrust laws indicates the potential reach of the law is quite long. Modern U.S. corporations operate within the guidelines established by antitrust laws, not only in the United States, but in the rest of the industrialized world, where foreign antitrust authorities enforce their own antitrust laws.

1.5 The Global Economy and Industrial Organization

Until recently courses on industrial organization typically ignored international trade theory, and courses on international trade characteristically ignored industrial organization theory and dealt strictly with models of perfect competition. The

recent trend toward a global economy, where American companies produce and sell abroad and foreign companies produce and sell in the United States, has dramatically changed this view. Industrial organization economists can no longer treat the international sector as a minor sidelight. Fortunately conditions have changed rapidly in both fields in the past 25 years with the introduction of many industrial organization models applied to situations of international competition. We integrate these new international realities throughout the text.

1.6 General Approach of This Book

The study of industrial organization can be organized in several different ways. In this text we combine the structure-conduct-performance and price theory approaches to the field, with an emphasis on game theory. Chapter 2 explores the theory of the modern firm, including costs concepts. Chapter 3 reviews the economic theories of perfect competition and monopoly and examines antitrust policy toward monopoly. Chapter 4 discusses the structure of markets in the United States, market entry and exit, and mergers, including antitrust policy toward mergers. Chapter 5 examines several important models of monopoly behavior. Chapter 6 explores some of the major issues and findings of the empirical literature on the relationship between market structure and economic performance. Chapters 7 through 12 examine conduct, mostly, but not entirely, from a game theoretic perspective. Chapter 13 explores product differentiation and advertising, and Chapter 14 investigates the relationship between market structure and the rate of technological advance. Chapters 15 and 16 explore price discrimination and vertical integration, respectively, from a theoretical perspective. Finally, Chapter 17 surveys recent developments in the areas of regulation and deregulation.

SUMMARY

1. The field of industrial organization developed as an offshoot of microeconomic theory.

2. Industrial organization emphasizes the behavior of firms as compared with the behavior of industries more than does traditional microeconomic theory.

3. The two traditional approaches to the study of industrial organization are the structure-conduct-performance approach and the Chicago School approach. The structure-conduct-performance approach originally was primarily empirical in its orientation, whereas the Chicago School approach emphasized the use of price theory.

4. Modern industrial organization emphasizes the use of game theory to explore oligopoly behavior.

5. Industrial organization economists place great emphasis on dynamic efficiency, or the optimal rate of technological advance.

6. The antitrust laws developed in response to the Industrial Revolution, which resulted in significant economies of scale and greatly increased the size of the geographic market for many products. The laws were also spurred by the development of modern capital markets that enabled firms to raise large amounts of capital in the equity market and the liberalization of the laws of incorporation in many states.

7. The Sherman Act was signed into law in 1890. Section 1 banned "restraints of trade" such as price fixing, and Section 2 banned "attempts to monopolize." Monopoly per se was not a violation of the Sherman Act.

8. In 1911, Chief Justice White laid down the Rule of Reason precedent in the *Standard Oil* decision. The Rule of Reason declared that only unreasonable attempts to monopolize violated the Sherman Act.

9. In 1914 the Clayton Act and Federal Trade Commission Act were signed into law. The Clayton Act outlawed specific types of economic behavior, such as tying agreements and price discrimination. The Federal Trade Commission Act established an independent commission to prevent "unfair methods of competition."

10. In 1936 the Robinson-Patman Act was passed to tighten the loopholes in the Clayton Act with regard to price discrimination.

11. In 1950 the Celler-Kefauver Act closed a major loophole in Section 7 of the Clayton Act that had permitted firms to acquire a firm's assets instead of its stock to avoid violating the law.

KEY TERMS

Celler-Kefauver Act

Chicago School of economics

Clayton Act

dynamic performance

entry barriers

exclusive dealing
 arrangements

Federal Trade Commission
 (FTC)

Federal Trade Commission Act

game theory
monopolistic competition
oligopoly
Robinson-Patman Act
Rule of Reason

Sherman Act
static models
structure-conduct-
 performance
(SCP) paradigm

tying contracts

DISCUSSION QUESTIONS

1. Why do you think traditional microeconomics courses emphasize the perfectly competitive and monopoly models and pay relatively little attention to oligopoly?

2. In what important way(s) does the structure-conduct-performance approach to industrial organization differ from the Chicago School approach?

3. Can you suggest a few industries where it appears that performance has had a feedback effect on structure?

4. What two types of empirical studies are used in industrial organization? Why do you think it is important to use both types of studies?

5. How can the study of industrial organization help policymakers arrive at better decisions?

6. What historical circumstances resulted in the passage of the Sherman Act in 1890?

7. In antitrust law, what does the term *Rule of Reason* mean?

8. Why is the Robinson-Patman Act often controversial?

9. What made Section 7 of the Clayton Act ineffective and how did Congress act to strengthen this aspect of the antitrust laws?

10. Do Department of Justice and Federal Trade Commission cases proceed exactly the same way through the federal court system?

11. What were the original maximum penalties in criminal antitrust cases? What are the current maximum penalties? Do you believe these maximum penalties act as an effective deterrent against violation of the law?

12. Why do you think that, compared to the typical microeconomics course, the typical industrial organization course places far more emphasis on dynamic efficiency compared to static efficiency?

NOTES

1. Authors' calculations based on U.S. Bureau of the Census, *1997 Census of Manufacturers, Concentration Ratios in Manufacturing*, www.census.gov/prod/ec97/m31s-cr.pdf.

2. Adam Smith, *An Inquiry into the Nature and Causes of the Wealth of Nations* (New York: Modern Library edition, 1937); Alfred Marshall, *Principles of Economics*, 8th ed. (London: Macmillan, 1920); Augustin Cournot (1938) *Recherches sur les principes mathematiques de la theorie des richesses*. Paris: M. Riviere & Cie., 1938. Translated in *Researches into the Mathematical Principles of Wealth* (New York: A.M. Kelly, 1960); and Joseph Bertrand, book review of "Recherches sur les Principes Mathematiques de la Theorie des Richesses," *Journal de Savants* 67 (1883): 499–508.

3. Edward H. Chamberlain, *The Theory of Monopolistic Competition* (Cambridge, MA: Harvard University Press, 1933).

4. Joe S. Bain, *Barriers to New Competition* (Cambridge, MA: Harvard University Press, 1956); Joe Bain, *Industrial Organization* (New York: John Wiley & Sons, 1959); Richard Caves, *American Industry: Structure and Performance* (Englewood Cliffs, NJ: Prentice-Hall, 1964); and Willard F. Mueller, *A Primer on Monopoly and Competition* (New York: Random House, 1970).

5. Adolf A. Berle and Gardiner Means, *The Modern Corporation and Private Property* (New York: Macmillan, 1932).

6. Edward S. Mason, "Price and Production Policies of Large-Scale Enterprise," *American Economic*

Review 29 (March 1939): 61–74; Edward S. Mason, "The Current State of the Monopoly Problem in the United States," *Harvard Law Review* 62 (June 1949): 1265–1285; and Joe S. Bain, *Barriers to New Competition* (Cambridge, MA: Harvard University Press, 1956).

7. U.S. Bureau of the Census, *1997 Census of Manufacturers, Concentration Ratios in Manufacturing,* www.census.gov/prod/ec97/m31s-cr.pdf.

8. *Advertising Age,* 100 Leading National Advertisers Supplement, June 27, 2005, www.adage.com/images/random/lna2005.pdf.

9. Newspaper Association of America, "U.S. Advertising Expenditures—All Media," www.naa.org/info/facts04/expenditures-allmedia.html; and *Statistical Abstract of the United States,* www.census.gov/statab/www/.

10. F.M. Scherer, "The Breakfast Cereal Industry," in Walter Adams, ed., *The Structure of American Industry* (New York: Macmillan, 1986), pp. 192–193.

11. See George J. Stigler, *The Organization of Industry* (Homewood, IL: Richard D. Irwin, 1968). Also see Richard A. Posner, "The Chicago School of Economic Analysis," *University of Pennsylvania Law Review* 127 (April 1979); and Melvin W. Reder,

"Chicago Economics: Permanence and Change," *Journal of Economic Literature* 20 (March 1982).

12. Jean Tirole, *The Theory of Industrial Organization* (Cambridge, MA: MIT Press, 1988), Chapter 1.

13. For background historical information see Hans B. Thorelli, *The Federal Antitrust Policy: Origination of an American Tradition* (Baltimore: Johns Hopkins Press, 1955); John D. Clark, *The Federal Trust Policy* (Baltimore: Johns Hopkins Press, 1931); Albert H. Walker, *History of the Sherman Law* (New York: Equity Press, 1910); Jessie W. Markham, "Survey of the Evidence and Findings on Mergers," in National Bureau of Economic Research, *Business Concentration and Price Policy* (New York: Arno Press, 1975), pp. 141–212; Simon N. Whitney, *Antitrust Policies: American Experience in Twenty Industries* (New York: Twentieth Century Fund, 1958), Chapter 1; and A.D. Neale and D.G. Goyder, *The Antitrust Laws of the U.S.A.* (Cambridge, England: Cambridge University Press, 1980).

14. Andrew E. Abere, "Trends in Private Antitrust Litigation: 1980–2004," Princeton Economics Group, accessed February 28, 2006, www.econgroup.com/news_view.asp?newid=19.

 INTERNET EXERCISES

Visit **www.aw-bc.com/waldman_jensen** for this chapter's web exercises. Answer our real-world economics problems by searching the Internet for solutions!

The Firm and Its Costs

T hroughout this book, we will spend much time analyzing the actions of firms in oligopolistic industries and examining the consequences of those actions for market behavior and performance. How does an oligopolistic firm like Kellogg's set the price of its products? What factors determine Procter & Gamble's expenditures on advertising? How does Nabisco decide how many varieties of Oreos it will make? Before considering these questions, it is necessary to think about modern firms and look carefully at the important assumption of profit maximization. Economists typically assume that firms maximize profits, but does this assumption make sense for real-world firms? We turn to this issue first in this chapter.

After we have looked at the organization and objectives of firms, we examine their costs. Costs are a key determinant of firm behavior such as pricing. Think, for example, about the decision faced by a pharmaceutical firm that has discovered a new drug. What is the relationship between the costs of research and testing and the price charged for the new drug? How are the costs of production factored in? Clearly, we have to understand various types of costs in order to predict firm behavior.

Costs are also an important determinant of market structure. The four largest breweries account for over 85 percent of sales in the U.S. beer market, while the four largest manufacturers of footwear account for some 30 percent of sales. As we think about such differences in market structure, we need to look at the underlying costs. This chapter explores some key cost concepts which we will need for our analyses.

2.1 The Neoclassical Firm

S uppose that at the beginning of your first microeconomics course, your professor had asked you to name some firms. Your list might have included Wal-Mart, General Motors, Microsoft, Comcast, Coca-Cola, and Procter & Gamble. All of these firms are among the largest U.S. industrial corporations as ranked by *Fortune*. You probably noticed in your microeconomics course that a "firm" in economic theory appeared to be quite different from these real-world large corporations.

Microeconomists usually model a firm as a single entity with a clear goal that it pursues without any wasted effort. The traditional neoclassical firm is represented by a production function that summarizes the relationship between inputs and output given

the current technology. Regardless of industry structure, each firm is assumed to maximize profits, making it possible to precisely predict its output and pricing decisions. Real-world firms are much more complex than the neoclassical firm of microeconomic theory, however. Firms today often operate in many different product and geographical markets and are characterized by many operating divisions and levels. Recognizing the complex structure of present-day firms, economists have begun to think more carefully about the firm.[1]

We look first at work on the theory of the firm and the boundaries of a firm. Then we examine the structure of modern firms, exploring the reasonableness of the profit-maximizing assumption for these firms. Some critics of profit maximization have focused on the role of corporate managers in daily business decisions, asking what motivates these managers. Other critics have pointed out the implications of large size and structural complexity for the realism of the assumption of profit maximization. Analyzing firm conduct becomes much more complicated without the assumption of profit maximization. Once this assumption is abandoned, for example, analyzing firm decisions such as pricing and advertising strategies requires an examination not only of market structure but also of the objectives of the firm, and the already challenging task of predicting strategies of oligopolistic firms becomes even more formidable. Consequently, we will also consider what forces, both carrots and sticks, exist to keep managers from deviating from profit-maximizing behavior.

2.2 The Theory of the Firm

A number of economists have focused attention on the theory of the firm, recognizing that the firm, unlike the consumer, is not an individual decision maker. Rather, the firm can be regarded as a series of contracts between a number of parties, including the workers, the managers, and the suppliers of capital. Some of these contracts are explicit; an example is the contract between Ford and the United Automobile Workers. Other contracts are implicit, reflecting managers' and workers' understandings about the conditions of work. As you can imagine, contracts vary widely across different types of firms. The theory of the firm examines the reasons for different types of explicit and implicit contracts and considers how these types of contracts affect the operation of the firm.

What factors determine whether production takes place within or outside of a firm? Why are some activities coordinated by the price signals of the market and others by the managers of firms? The modern theory of the firm tries to answer questions such as these.

2.2.1 A Firm's Boundaries

As early as 1937, Ronald Coase recognized that the firm and the market were alternative ways of organizing production.[2] Consider, for example, the decisions faced by Dell or Apple when producing computers. One possible way to produce a computer is to have a firm perform only one stage of production, such as assembly. Such a firm would buy all the necessary parts—from the hard disc drives to Firewire and USB ports

to monitors—from independent suppliers, assemble the computer, and then turn the completed product over to another firm for marketing. At the other extreme, production of all parts, assembly, and marketing could be done within one large firm. How does Dell or Apple decide when it will produce a necessary input internally and when it will rely on the marketplace?

Coase argued that a firm would expand until the costs of undertaking a transaction internally were just equal to the costs of using the market to handle that transaction. The costs of using the market to conduct business are called ***transaction costs.*** Williamson has built upon Coase's point, writing extensively on the importance of transaction costs and the types of organizational structures that have been developed to minimize transaction costs.[3]

Advantages of the Market

Williamson points out three production cost advantages of using the market.[4] First, suppose production of some input is subject to substantial *economies of scale,* yet suppose also that an individual firm requires only a relatively small quantity of that input. By aggregating the demands of many such small firms for that input, a single producer can realize economies of scale and produce at a lower average cost. Similarly, markets may aggregate related demands, allowing realization of *economies of scope* not available to a single firm.* A third production cost advantage associated with the market is reduction of risk. If there are uncertainties in demand for a single firm's product, a market can reduce risk by pooling demands over many firms.†

Using the market also enables a firm to take advantage of competitive pressures to control its costs; a competitive market allocates resources efficiently and results in production at the lowest possible cost. In Williamson's words, "Markets promote high-powered incentives and restrain bureaucratic distortions more effectively than internal organization."[5] Assuming there are a number of potential suppliers, a firm can search for the lowest-cost producer by purchasing rather than making an input.

Advantages of the Firm

Given the advantages of using the market to procure inputs, why would a firm ever choose to produce some inputs internally? Coase and Williamson point out that there are also costs of using the market, and that in certain circumstances, these costs are high enough to outweigh the production cost advantages of markets. Specifically, if transaction costs are high, firms are likely to turn to internal production.

Transaction costs arise from activities such as searching for a supplier, negotiating with the supplier about contract terms, arranging for delivery, and monitoring the quality of the input. Two assumptions are important in transaction cost economics. The first is ***bounded rationality.*** The assumption of bounded rationality recognizes that limits on knowledge, foresight, skill, and time constrain individuals' ability to

*Economies of scope occur when it is less costly to produce two products together than to produce each separately. Economies of scope are discussed in detail in Section 2.6.

†The risk reduction benefit of pooling occurs as long as the individual firms' demands are not perfectly correlated.

solve complex problems.[6] Because of bounded rationality, a firm cannot write a contract ahead of time that covers all contingencies. That is, in the terminology of the theory of the firm, bounded rationality implies that contracts are of necessity incomplete.

Williamson notes, however, that even an incomplete contract that does not cover all possible outcomes could be used to carry out transactions if it were not for the second assumption of transaction cost economics: the presence of ***opportunism.*** In Williamson's words, opportunism is "self-interest seeking with guile."[7] Opportunism builds upon the usual behavioral assumption that individuals act to maximize their utility. Opportunism postulates in addition that economic agents will try to mislead, disguise, and confuse others if it is to their advantage to do so and if they think such activities cannot be detected easily. Because of opportunism, economic agents are not completely trustworthy.

As noted earlier, a firm is likely to rely on internal production rather than use the market when transaction costs are high. This is likely to occur when it is difficult to write a contract that eliminates the potential for opportunistic behavior. Three dimensions of transactions are important in identifying these circumstances: their frequency, the amount of uncertainty associated with transactions, and the degree of asset specificity.[8]

FREQUENCY Imagine a firm negotiating for the services of a machine. If these services will be needed only once or a few times, the firm can use the market. On the other hand, if these services will be needed repeatedly, the transaction costs of using the market will be high because of the frequent renegotiation costs. The more frequent a firm's need for an input, the more the firm can save on transaction costs by internal production.

UNCERTAINTY Williamson discusses three kinds of uncertainty. Primary uncertainty arises because circumstances can change and no one can predict the future perfectly. Secondary uncertainty is caused by lack of communication. One decision maker may simply not know what plans are being made by others, and transferring information accurately and completely is a difficult task. Finally, Williamson recognizes a third kind of uncertainty, behavioral uncertainty, that can result from strategic—or opportunistic—decisions about disclosure of information.

Whatever the nature of uncertainty, the conclusion of transaction cost economics is that the higher the degree of uncertainty, the higher are the transaction costs. A firm can adapt to changing circumstances at lower cost than can the market.

ASSET SPECIFICITY *Asset specificity* refers to the degree to which some assets are of value primarily to one firm. Assets can be specific as a result of geographic location, physical characteristics, or specialized human capital. A professor who can teach industrial organization well is of value to any college or university (or "firm") that wants to offer that course. However, a computer classroom set up on a specific campus is of value only to that institution because it cannot be transported elsewhere. Other examples of specialized assets are a pipeline from an oil refinery to an isolated distribution terminal, the giant presses used to stamp out automobile body parts, and brand-name capital.

Transactions that involve highly specialized assets are likely to be costly. Once the investment in a specialized asset has been made, buyer and seller are in a bilateral relationship in which each side has few other options. This is likely to lead to difficult and expensive negotiations, possibly involving considerable bargaining and bluffs on each side. Consider, for example, automobile dies (the presses used to stamp out automobile body parts). The dies are specific to a particular car: Toyota needs Camry dies in order to make bodies for its Camrys, so the owner of the dies has bargaining power. Yet the dies cannot be used to make other models, so the owner of the dies is also dependent upon Toyota. In this case, it might make sense for Toyota to own the dies. In general, ownership of the specialized asset by the user reduces the incentive for opportunistic behavior and lowers the associated transaction costs.

In summary, Williamson's expansion of Coase's original insight still maintains the usual assumption that a firm is interested in minimizing costs. The addition is that costs are recognized as the sum of the usual production costs and transactions costs. The more frequent a transaction, the greater the uncertainty, and the higher the degree of asset specificity, the more likely it is that an activity will be performed internally.

2.3 The Structure of Modern Firms

Having thought about the theoretical aspects of external versus internal procurement, we now turn our attention to the way in which modern firms are actually organized. Firm ownership takes several forms, with the most common in the United States being sole proprietorships, partnerships, and corporations.* Until the end of the nineteenth century, almost all firms were organized as sole proprietorships or partnerships. Two characteristics of proprietorships and partnerships became increasingly disadvantageous as technology and industry structure began to change in the years between the end of the Civil War and the beginning of the twentieth century.[9] One was *unlimited* liability. If a proprietorship or a partnership fails, the owner(s) can lose *all* assets, both business and personal. Also, proprietorships and partnerships both have *finite lives*. If one member of a partnership leaves or dies, the entire firm is automatically dissolved and a new partnership must be formed to continue the business.

By number, sole proprietorships and partnerships are still the dominant form of organization of firms in the United States. About 80 percent of businesses today are proprietorships or partnerships. These firms, however, are typically small, accounting for only 11 percent of total sales in the United States.[10] In addition, the rate of turnover among proprietorships and partnerships is high.

The vast majority of sales in the United States today are made by corporations. A corporation is a separate legal entity, created by government charter and given certain powers, privileges, and liabilities. Table 2.1 gives you a sense of the magnitude of some of today's largest corporations.

An important advantage of a corporation is that its owners have limited liability. Ownership of a corporation takes the form of holding of shares of stock which can be

*Other forms of ownership include labor-managed firms and not-for-profit firms.

TABLE 2.1 Ten Largest U.S. Industrial Corporations in 2005

Firm	Industry	2005 Sales ($ millions)	2005 Assets ($ millions)
Wal-Mart Stores	General merchandisers	288,189.0	120,624.0
Exxon Mobil	Petroleum refining	270,722.0	195,256.0
General Motors	Motor vehicles & parts	193,517.0	479,603.0
Ford Motor	Motor vehicles & parts	172,233.0	292,654.0
General Electric	Diversified financials	152,363.0	750,330.0
ChevronTexaco	Petroleum refining	147,967.0	93,208.0
ConocoPhillips	Petroleum refining	121,663.0	92,861.0
Citigroup	Commercial banks	108,276.0	1,484,101.0
American Intl. Group	Insurance: P & C (stock)	98,610.0	800,000.0
IBM	Computers, office equipment	96,293.0	109,183.0

Source: Data from www.fortune.com/fortune/fortune500

bought or sold. The owners, the shareholders, are liable only for the amount they paid to buy the shares of stock initially. This limit on the amount an owner can lose makes it less risky to invest in the firm than if the owner could also lose his or her personal assets. Also, a corporation has an infinite life; it is not automatically dissolved when an owner dies or decides to leave the business. Because of these advantages, corporations can raise large sums of money more easily than can proprietorships or partnerships. The ability to raise large sums of money became increasingly important in the late 1800s as the minimum efficient size of firms grew.* Since then the corporate form of organization has gained steadily in prominence.

2.3.1 Separation of Ownership and Control

Before the 1900s, when most firms were organized as sole proprietorships or partnerships, ownership and control of the firm were combined in the hands of one or a few people. The person who made the day-to-day decisions was also the person who received any profits from the firm's operations. As corporations developed, however, ownership and control became increasingly separated.

The owners of a corporation are its stockholders, and a large corporation typically has many, many owners. While there are many owners in the modern corporation, the day-to-day corporate business decisions are made by a relative handful of professional managers. In theory, the stockholders elect a board of directors to oversee the managers, ensuring that the owners' interests are represented. In practice, however, the candidates for the board of directors for the vast majority of corporations are

*Minimum efficient size, or minimum efficient scale, is the smallest level of output for which long-run average cost is at its lowest level. This concept and its importance are considered further in Chapter 4.

selected by the managers. Few stockholders typically attend a corporation's annual meeting. Instead they give the managers their proxies, or permission to vote on behalf of the nominated candidates. Consequently, many corporate boards of directors are more of a rubber-stamping body than an independent group vigilantly examining the decisions made by management and protecting the interests of the owners.[11] In fact, over 80 percent of the largest 200 nonfinancial corporations in the United States today are considered to be controlled by management.[12]

2.3.2 Managerial Objectives

Why does it matter whether a firm is controlled by its owners or by managers? Let's start by accepting a central assumption of microeconomic theory: Individuals act to maximize their own utility, the total satisfaction or benefit from consuming a good. This principle applies to people when they are operating firms as well as when they are behaving as consumers. The people who run firms will maximize profits *as long as* profit maximization is in their best interest. When the firm is run by its owners, profit maximization and utility maximization are consistent goals, because the main source of income for the owners is the firm's profits.*[13]

When ownership and control are separate, however, profit maximization and utility maximization may conflict as managers pursue objectives other than maximizing profits. For example, in an early alternative to profit maximization, William Baumol hypothesized that managers attempt to maximize sales revenue.[14] Managers may focus on sales rather than on profits if managing a "large" company adds to their sense of status and prestige. Rankings such as the Fortune 500 are typically made on the basis of sales. Also, salaries may be more closely tied to sales or to the growth rate of sales than to profits. Commissions based on sales, for example, provide an incentive to focus on maximizing revenues rather than profits.

APPLICATION 2.1
Executive Compensation: Pay for Performance?

When Charles K. Gifford retired as chairman of the Bank of America early in 2005, his retirement package included a cash payment of $16.36 million, additional "incentive payments" of as much as $8.67 million for work during the 13 months prior to his retirement, and guarantees of $3.1 million per year for life. Other pieces of the package: provisions for his wife in the event that Mr. Gifford dies before she does ($2.3 million per year for life), guaranteed consulting fees of $50,000 per year, 120 hours of free flight time each year on the company's jet, an office, and a secretary. And, perhaps most amazing of all for those of us who are Red Sox fans: Mr. Gifford's retirement package offered him the right to buy 60 Red Sox tickets each year from the bank for the rest of his life.

Other recent examples of sweet retirement deals include Home Depot's package for Robert L. Nardelli, its chief executive since December 2000. A payment of $20 million awaits Mr. Nardelli if he loses his job without cause; this payment will be supplemented by stock and deferred compensation worth around $48.7 million. John F. (Jack) Welch Jr.

*If owner-managers also value nonpecuniary benefits, economic theory predicts that, in equilibrium, some expenditures will be made on benefits.

received retirement perks from General Electric that included the use of an apartment in Manhattan (complete with wine, food, laundry services, toiletries, and newspapers), free New York Knicks tickets, tickets for the U.S. Open, and satellite television at Mr. Welch's four homes.

Retirement packages are one dimension of a running debate about executive compensation. Bebchuk and Fried argue that corporate boards deliberately design compensation plans to obscure their total value. They also charge that many executives receive excess compensation that "deviates from what best serves shareholders' interests." If they are correct, then corporate boards of directors are, in fact, not acting as independent groups that examine the decisions made by managers and protect the interests of the owners.

On the other hand, some argue that the market for corporate managers dictates the compensation that must be paid. For example, several airline companies have recently lost key managers because of compensation issues. A senior executive at AMR Corporation, the parent firm of American Airlines, stated, "We're just not competitive on salaries within our own industry."* And according to a US Airways spokesperson "the management team . . . is fleeing" at US Airways, which lost 331 middle and senior managers in 2004.[†] Core, Guay, and Thomas have sharply criticized the arguments made by Fried and Bebchuk. They argue that providing "interesting examples of bad apples" does not "show that the entire barrel is bad." Furthermore, they see many settings where contracts with managers anticipate and try to minimize the costs of managerial power. And they note that executives' stock and option portfolios are important parts of managers' compensation—parts that provide strong incentives to pay attention to the performance of the firm. In the end, then, the debate about whether managers act to maximize firms' profits and the role played by various dimensions of their compensation packages continues.

Sources: Timothy L. O'Brien, "Mayday? Payday! Hit the Silk!" *The New York Times,* January 9, 2005; Lucian Bebchuk and Jesse Fried, *Pay Without Performance: The Unfulfilled Promise of Executive Compensation* (Harvard University Press, 2004); Joann S. Lublin, "Cost-Cutting Airlines Grapple With Issue of Executive Pay," *The Wall Street Journal,* January 25, 2005; and John E. Core, Wayne R. Guay, and Randall S. Thomas, "Is U.S. CEO Compensation Inefficient Pay Without Performance?" Vanderbilt University Law School Law & Economics Working Paper Number 05-05.

*Joann S. Lublin, "Cost-Cutting Airlines Grapple with Issue of Executive Pay," *The Wall Street Journal,* January 25, 2005, p. B1.
[†]*Ibid.* ■

Oliver Williamson has also analyzed the implications of utility-maximizing managers.[15] Williamson believes that managers' utility depends in part on profits, so managers do pay attention to profits. However, Williamson theorizes that managers also get satisfaction from executive perks such as fancy offices, executive jets, and "power breakfasts." Thus costs are higher than in the profit-maximizing model because money is spent on nice carpeting and art for the corner offices.

In a world in which managers have some discretion over costs, costs may also be higher due to *X-inefficiency.* If managers are interested in living a quiet, peaceful life, they may not continually strive to find the least costly way of organizing production, handling materials, and, in general, doing business. As a result, costs are higher than necessary. Harvey Leibenstein, the originator of the term *X-inefficiency,* defines it as "the extent to which a given set of inputs do not get to be combined in such a way as to lead to maximum output."[16]

APPLICATION 2.2

X-Inefficiency Goes Extreme: Putting Masseuses, Christmas Trees, Renoirs, and Monets on the Company Payroll

Since the fall of Enron in 2001, several former corporate executives have faced charges of white-collar crimes. These recent investigations and trials have shed interesting light on corporate executives' ability to use funds in ways that are inconsistent with profit maximization. For example, in June 2005 the 80-year-old founder of Adelphia Communications Corp., John Rigas, was sentenced to 15 years in prison for fraud and conspiracy. His son Timothy, the former chief financial officer of Adelphia, received a sentence of 20 years in prison. Testimony during the trial described a corporate culture of lying and abuse of company funds. Among other things, company funds were used to pay a masseuse $40,000 per year and to purchase 17 company cars. Witnesses described use of the company plane for golf outings and to ship Christmas trees to New York City. Prosecutors said that $26 million of Adelphia's money was used to buy 3,600 acres of timberland in order to preserve the view from John Rigas's home in Coudersport, Pennsylvania.

The Adelphia executives are not alone in their extravagant lifestyles. Dennis Kozlowski, the former CEO of Tyco International, and Mark H. Swartz, Tyco's former chief financial officer, were convicted in June 2005 of grand larceny, falsifying business records, securities fraud, and other charges. During the trial, prosecutors described improper use of an employee loan program; among other things, Kozlowski used these funds to buy artwork, including oil paintings by Renoir and Monet. This artwork was displayed in Kozlowski's Manhattan apartment along with furnishings such as a $6,000 shower curtain, bringing the price of the apartment to more than $30 million. For his wife's fortieth birthday, Kozlowski threw a toga party on the island of Sardinia; Tyco picked up about half of the tab. The ex-treasurer of Tyco testified that Mr. Swartz made changes to company policy without authorization from the compensation committee so that Tyco would pay for private schooling for the children of a small group of executives. All told, the abuses ate up more than $600 million of Tyco's funds.

Sources: Christine Nuzum, "Executives on Trial: Rigas High Life Described in Trial," *The Wall Street Journal,* March 17, 2004, p. C.6; Peter Grant, "Adelphia Insider Tells of Culture of Lies at Firm," *The Wall Street Journal,* May 19, 2004, p. C.1; Erin McClam, "Adelphia founder sentenced to 15 years in prison," *The Associated Press State & Local Wire,* June 20, 2005. Online. LexisNexis Academic. July 19, 2005; Dionne Searcey and Li Yuan, "Adelphia's John Rigas Gets 15 Years," *The Wall Street Journal,* June 21, 2005, p. A.3; "Executives on Trial: Tyco Ex-Treasurer Testifies on Benefits," *The Wall Street Journal,* March 8, 2005, p. 1; Chad Bray, "Executives on Trial: Tyco Was Billed Millions for Art Bought by Ex-CEO, Dealer Says," *The Wall Street Journal,* April 19, 2005, p. C.2; Samuel Maull, "Former Tyco executives convicted of looting company," *The Associated Press State & Local Wire,* June 17, 2005. ■

Finally, managers may care most about protecting their jobs. Does an interest in job security conflict with profit maximization? The answer is ambiguous. If a manager perceives that the best way to avoid being fired is to earn the highest possible profits, then there is obviously no conflict with profit maximization. Managers, however, probably face asymmetric returns to risky decisions.[17] The downside risk of a bad decision is extremely large—a manager can lose her or his job.[18] The reward for a good decision is far less dramatic—a manager might receive a bonus. Because of this asymmetry, managers of large corporations may avoid projects with high expected profits but also high risk.[19]

2.3.3 Feasibility of Profit Maximization

Rather than emphasizing the separation of ownership and control, some economists have focused their attention on the large size and structural complexity of modern firms. These economists have developed their theories primarily through observation of corporations and corporate decision makers.[20] Separation of ownership and control is not inconsistent with the predictions of these economists, however.

Most large corporations have thousands of employees, often organized into multiple functional components. Some specialize in production, some in finance, some in research and development, and some in environmental protection. This list could be extended almost indefinitely. Is it realistic to expect each of these thousands of employees to be striving in unison toward the goal of maximum profits? Different specialists are likely to have different goals or at least different ideas about how to achieve maximum profits. Engineers may be interested in new technological developments, while marketing staff may want to focus on products with great appeal to consumers. It is the top managers' job to choose among conflicting objectives. Managers, however, cannot know everything known by the employees under them in the chain of command. Furthermore, it is often notoriously difficult to accurately convey information. Because of these problems, top managers may simply be unable to choose the profit-maximizing strategy.

Because of organizational size and complexity, managers may opt for *"satisficing"* instead of profit maximizing. The satisficer sets a minimum acceptable level of performance below which he or she does not want to fall. Once this level is reached, the satisficer can relax. In short, the satisficer does not strive to be the best that he or she can be but settles for something less. To make decisions, a satisficing manager is likely to rely on a variety of rules of thumb. Application 2.3 explains how firms use this kind of pricing.

APPLICATION 2.3
How Do Firms Use Rule-of-Thumb Pricing?

Two primary types of **rule-of-thumb pricing** formulas have been identified by economists. The first is based on an assumed objective of earning a fixed rate of return on invested capital. Suppose, for example, a firm sets a target rate of return of R_0, where:

$$R_0 = \frac{TR - TC}{K} = \frac{Q(P - AC)}{K}$$

and K represents total invested capital. To make this pricing system workable, the firm must assume it will sell some quantity of output Q. Suppose the firm assumes it will sell 80 percent of its capacity. In that case, Q and AC are identified, and because the firm already knows K, the only remaining unknown in the above equation is P. All that remains to be done is to solve the equation for P.* If demand is particularly strong, sales will exceed 80 percent of capacity, Q will increase, AC will fall, and R_0 will exceed 10 percent. This, of course, is a preferred outcome for the firm. If demand is weak, however, Q will decrease, AC will rise, and R_0 will fall below 10 percent.

Another variation of rule-of-thumb pricing has firms setting prices as a fixed markup over invoice costs. For many years department stores such as Macy's and Bloomingdales priced by simply charging a fixed percent markup over the invoice cost

of an item. If the markup was 100 percent, then $\dfrac{P - MC}{MC} = 1$ and $\dfrac{P - MC}{P} = 0.5$.

A blouse that cost Macy's $50.00 would have a retail price of $100.00; a suit that cost $300.00 would be priced at $600.00. If all of the major department stores followed this cost-plus pricing system, it would keep them from competing too aggressively on the basis of price. The system worked well for many years until discount stores such as Marshall's, T.J. Maxx, and Loehmann's began to underprice the major department stores by 20 to 50 percent.

*For example, suppose that the target rate of return is 10 percent so $R_0 = 0.10$. If capacity is 1,000,000 units, 80 percent of capacity is 800,000 units. If $AC = 10$ for a production of 800,000 units and total invested capital $K = 100,000,000$, then:

$$R_0 = \frac{Q(P - AC)}{K} \Rightarrow 0.10 = \frac{800,000(P - 10)}{100,000,000}$$

Solving for P yields $P = 22.5$. ∎

Early empirical evidence suggested that rule-of-thumb pricing is in fact a common phenomenon. Hall and Hitch discovered that 30 of 38 British firms surveyed in the 1930s claimed to use some rules to set prices.[21] Fog found similar results for Danish firms.[22] In the United States the theory first received widespread attention when Kaplan, Dirlam, and Lanzillotti discovered that half of a sample of 20 large firms used some rules to set prices.[23] Kaplan and colleagues suggested that large corporate giants such as General Motors, International Harvester, Alcoa, DuPont, Standard Oil of New Jersey, Johns-Manville, General Electric, General Foods, US Steel, and Union Carbide all priced to achieve a target rate of return.[24] Furthermore, they concluded that "[t]arget return on investment was probably the most commonly stressed of company pricing goals."[25]

Despite the apparent strength of Kaplan and coworkers' findings, their results raised some serious questions concerning rule-of-thumb pricing techniques. Although 10 large corporations claimed to use some target rate of return to set prices, these targets varied widely from 20 percent on invested capital for Alcoa, General Electric, and General Motors down to just 10 percent for International Harvester and 8 percent for US Steel.[26] Furthermore, in most cases the firms actually earned rates of return that were significantly greater than the targets. General Motors, for example, averaged a 26 percent return between 1947 and 1955.

Why would the target rate of return used by such powerful corporations vary so widely? The simplest explanation is that because these firms faced widely differing elasticities of demand, they targeted widely differing returns on investment. The more inelastic the demand, the greater the rate of return. Along these lines, Heflebower looked at the empirical evidence available on full-cost pricing and concluded:

> [F]urther consideration of these cost explanations of prices shows that the cost rules themselves contain, or in application are modified for, demand influences. In direct relation to the height of cross elasticities of demand among rivals' products, the gross margin used by the individual firm reflects not its own indirect costs but rather the margin it finds by experience to be desirable in light of costs and market conduct of rivals.[27]

In essence, what Heflebower is saying is that firms that claim to be using a full-cost pricing method may be maximizing profits. In the words of Alfred Kahn, "In many situations, target-return pricing simply does not make sense except as an *ex post* rationalization of profit maximization."[28]

Another serious criticism of the rule-of-thumb theory is that even in industries in which surveys have revealed the existence of target pricing, more detailed studies have shown that other factors have a far greater effect on price.[29] In one such study of the Canadian cotton textile industry, McFetridge tested to see whether prices were altered by short-run changes in demand. He discovered that they were and therefore completely rejected the rule-of-thumb model.[30]

What can we conclude about the use of rules-of-thumb pricing methods and the implications for the assumption of profit maximization? First, there is little doubt that many firms claim to use such methods. Second, these methods are almost always augmented by careful consideration of demand conditions. And, finally, such rules may be fully consistent with profit-maximizing behavior if the rules merely reflect the best the firm can *expect* to achieve given current demand and cost conditions.

2.3.4 Constraints on Managers

Criticism of the assumption of profit maximization has led its defenders to assert that, in fact, both constraints and incentives keep managers from straying too far from the straight and narrow path of profit maximization. These activities are not without cost, of course. The magnitude of the costs varies from firm to firm, depending on factors such as the complexity of the operations, the tastes of the managers, and the costs of devising a monitoring system. In this section we consider the effectiveness of various constraints and incentives.

One constraint is the possibility of ***stockholder revolt.*** After all, owners always have the option of selling shares of stock if they are unhappy with a company's performance. Some argue that this form of indirect control encourages managers to treat stockholders carefully and keep their interests in mind.

A counterargument is that owners are unlikely to have complete information about alternative policies available to a firm.[31] They can try to determine whether profits are being maximized by watching how similar firms perform. Because no two firms are exactly alike, however, this kind of monitoring provides incomplete information. Available evidence confirms that indirect control through stockholder revolt is only a weak constraint on managers' behavior.[32]

APPLICATION 2.4

Stockholder Revolt at the Happiest Place on Earth: The Disney Stockholders versus Michael Eisner

These days even Mickey Mouse can't avoid corporate chaos: Late in 2003 turmoil began to brew at Disney. Roy E. Disney, nephew of founder Walt Disney, resigned from Disney's board after he learned that he was going to be forced out due to a mandatory retirement policy. His longtime business partner, Stanley Gold, also resigned, and the two began a fight against Michael Eisner, then chairman and CEO of Disney, expressing

concerns about his leadership, the governance procedures of Disney, and the financial performance and stock price over a period of seven years. As part of his fight against management, Roy Disney used a website, savedisney.com, to communicate with stockholders about their concerns.

The stockholder revolt gained momentum after two Wall Street firms, Institutional Shareholder Services and Glass Lewis & Co., joined Disney and Gold in opposition to Eisner. Several pension funds, including the California Public Employees' Retirement System and funds in New York, North Carolina, Florida, and Ohio also called for changes in Disney's management. For weeks and months, critics hammered at Eisner and other Disney board members for losing the "creative heart"* of Disney and for poor financial performance.

In an unprecedented protest against the CEO of a major company, 45 percent of Disney's shareholders withheld their votes from Mr. Eisner at a dramatic and lengthy annual meeting in Philadelphia in March 2004. In response to this clear signal of stockholder discontent, Michael Eisner agreed to step down as chairman of Disney. Eisner remained as CEO of Disney, although he announced in September 2004 that he would retire at the end of his current term.

The battle against management continued for another year, with Disney and Gold expressing unhappiness at the choice of Eisner's successor, Robert Iger. In May 2005 they filed a lawsuit against Walt Disney Co., contesting both the selection of Iger and Eisner's management. Finally, on July 8, 2005, the fight ended peacefully: The company appointed Roy Disney as a director emeritus and a consultant. Disney and Gold agreed to drop their lawsuit and Roy Disney announced intentions to shut down his website in August.

Why was stockholder revolt an effective way to bring about change in management in this case when it has so often been a weak constraint? One possible explanation is that those leading the revolt had good information: Both Disney and Gold had been on the board. Moreover, they were backed up by the pension funds, large institutional investors. Such large investors are more likely to be knowledgeable about financial strategies than are individual investors. Another key may be the Internet, which makes it much easier to communicate with large numbers of shareholders and to share information. Perhaps stockholder revolt will be a stronger constraint on managerial behavior in the twenty-first century than it was in the twentieth century.

*Bruce Orwall, Brian Steinberg, and Joann S. Lublin, "Disney's Eisner Steps Down From Chairman Post," *The Wall Street Journal,* March 4, 2004, p. A.1.

Sources: Orwall et al., *op. cit.;* Greg Hernandez, "Disney Replaces Eisner as Chairman, Keeps Him as CEO," *Daily News,* March 4, 2004. Online. LexisNexis Academic, July 19, 2005; Wendy Tanaka, "Anti-Eisner Vote at Disney Was Higher than Reported at Philadelphia Meeting," *Philadelphia Inquirer,* April 16, 2004. Online. LexisNexis Academic, July 19, 2005; Mike Hughlett, "Disney head Eisner enjoys happier annual meeting this year," *Chicago Tribune,* February 12, 2005. Online. LexisNexis Academic, July 19, 2005; "Disney, ex-directors peacefully end management battle," Kyodo News International, July 8, 2005. Online. LexisNexis Academic, July 19, 2005. ■

A more serious constraint arising from financial markets is the threat of a ***takeover.***[33] Many takeovers result from the ***market for corporate control.*** Suppose that current management is not maximizing profits. This will result in a firm's stock selling for less than it would under profit-maximizing management because stockholders are willing to pay no more than the present discounted value of the income, or profits,

earned by the firm.* In such a case, different management could purchase the firm's stock, fire the incumbent management, and begin to pursue a profit-maximizing strategy, thereby earning large capital gains as the value of the firm rises well above the purchase price. Assuming financial markets work well, such a takeover should occur whenever the potential gain in profits is greater than the costs of the takeover.†

What are the costs of a takeover bid? First, there are planning and legal costs. Also, once a poorly managed firm has become a target, its stock price may be driven up considerably both by speculative purchases by investors hoping to make a quick profit and by competition among acquiring firms.[34] In addition, transaction costs arise from information problems. Insiders, such as the current management, have the most accurate information about whether profit is being maximized. An outsider may have trouble distinguishing between low profits due to poor management and low profits due to events outside the firm's control.‡ Stockholders must also evaluate the claims of the group attempting a takeover, keeping in mind that the group has an incentive to reveal only information favorable to its attempt.

Because of these costs, the threat of takeover is unlikely to be a completely effective constraint on managers.§ However, the *product market* may also constrain managers' behavior. A firm that is not maximizing profits faces the possibility of being forced out of a competitive market as long as at least some other firms in the industry *are* striving for the highest possible profits. A highly competitive market, therefore, disciplines a firm to minimize costs and pick the profit-maximizing output level.

Finally, we note that in addition to the "sticks" of stockholder revolt and takeover threats, "carrots" may also encourage managers to maximize profits. One such incentive is to tie executive compensation to profits through bonuses or stock options. A recent study examined the compensation of the CEOs and of the five most highly compensated managers at 1500 firms, looking in part at their equity-based compensation: the value of the options and restricted stock that such managers typically receive. The researchers found that the fraction of compensation that was equity-based increased dramatically over the period from 1993 to 2003, during a period when overall compensation was also growing rapidly. This was true for firms of all sizes in the database. For example, equity-based compensation comprised 41 percent of compensation for the CEOs among the Standard & Poors 500 firms in 1993 and 59 percent in 2003. The researchers found that the equity-based compensation of the top five executives increased from 37 percent of compensation in 1993 to 55 percent in 2003 for the largest 500 firms, from 41 percent to 51 percent for the next 400 medium-sized firms, and from 34 percent to 41 percent for the next 600 smaller firms.[35] Presumably,

*Present discounted value, or simply present value, refers to the value today of money received in the future. The present value of $1 received t periods in the future is $1/(1 + i)^t$, where i is the interest rate received per period. To understand this, recognize that if you deposited this amount (the present value) in the bank today, you would have a balance of $1 in t periods. See Chapter 3 for more detail.

†Current management will be concerned about the threat of a takeover if the loss of their jobs results in loss of income or of "rents" attached to managerial jobs such as prestige or reputation.

‡Because of this kind of information problem, it is not unusual to see current or former members of a firm's management involved in a takeover attempt.

§This conclusion is reinforced when we recognize that managers have many ways of protecting themselves from hostile takeover bids. These tactics include the scorched earth, the poison pill, the staggered board, and protective acquisitions. See R.A. Walkling and M.S. Long, "Agency Theory, Managerial Welfare, and Takeover Bid Resistance," *Rand Journal of Economics* 15 (1984): 54–68.

these executives are well aware of the link between the value of their companies' stock and their own wealth.

The empirical evidence on whether firms maximize profits is extensive, yet somewhat inconclusive. Firms may do a better job of selecting the profit-maximizing price than of choosing the cost-minimizing levels of production, employment, or perks. Not surprisingly, the assumption of profit maximization is most likely to hold in the longer run and in those markets where firms face competitors. In the end, given the constraints on managers and the incentives for them to maximize profits, profit-maximizing behavior appears to be a reasonable first assumption to make in many cases. We will maintain this assumption throughout most of this book, although we recognize that many exceptions to profit maximization exist.

2.4 The Profit-Maximizing Output Level

How does a profit-maximizing firm choose its output level? **_Profits_ (π)** are defined as total revenue minus total costs. Profits depend on the quantity of output produced because both total revenue and total costs depend on output.* Suppose a firm is deciding whether to increase output by one unit. To find the effect of this increase on its profits, the firm compares its **marginal revenue (MR)**, the change in total revenue resulting from selling an additional unit of output, to its **marginal cost (MC)**, the change in total cost resulting from producing that additional unit of output. If marginal revenue is greater than marginal cost, then selling one more unit of output will increase profits. On the other hand, if marginal revenue is less than marginal cost, selling another unit of output will reduce profits, and the firm should consider cutting back on its level of output. Using this kind of incremental reasoning, the firm eventually arrives at the output level for which marginal revenue equals marginal costs. This is the profit-maximizing level of output for any firm, regardless of industry structure.[†]

Marginal cost is thus the relevant cost concept for a profit-maximizing firm _given_ that the firm chooses to produce any output at all. Why might a firm not want to produce? If demand is very weak, producing the output level for which marginal revenue equals marginal cost is likely to lead to a low price. In such a case, the revenue the firm receives might be below the costs it can save by shutting down, and the firm

*We express this mathematically as $\pi(q) = R(q) - C(q) = P(q) \cdot q - C(q)$, where P is the market price. Writing price as a function of quantity allows for the possibility that the price the firm receives might be affected by the quantity of output it sells.

[†]This result can also be shown using calculus. To find the value of q that maximizes profits, set the derivative of profits with respect to q equal to 0:

$$\frac{d\pi}{dq} = \frac{dR(q)}{dq} - \frac{dC(q)}{dq} = 0$$

so the first-order condition for a maximum is that $\frac{dR(q)}{dq} = \frac{dC(q)}{dq}$. This is simply the mathematical statement of the result that a necessary condition for maximizing profits is to choose q such that marginal revenue equals marginal cost.

would be better off producing no output. As we will see in more detail in the next chapter, this decision rule has different implications for the short and long runs.

To understand the implications of the profit-maximizing rule, we need to consider its two parts: marginal revenue and marginal cost. Because demand determines marginal revenue, it is necessary to specify the market structure before discussing marginal revenue. We therefore turn first to an examination of some relevant cost concepts; these cost concepts apply for firms in all industry structures from perfect competition to monopoly.

2.5 Cost Concepts: Single-Product Firms

2.5.1 Accounting Costs versus Economic Costs

Before discussing the theory of costs, we have to clarify what economists mean by "costs," distinguishing between *accounting costs* and *economic costs. Accounting costs* are the costs reported by firms in their financial reports following various bookkeeping conventions. The *economic cost* of an input is defined as the payment that input would receive in its best alternative employment. The definition of economic costs draws on the concept of the *opportunity cost* of a good: the value of the resources used to produce that good in their best alternative use. Consider a car. Suppose that producing computers is the best alternative use of the inputs, including labor, used in producing cars. If 10 computers could have been made from the resources used to produce one car, then the opportunity cost of a car is 10 computers. For convenience, opportunity cost is often expressed in monetary units: The opportunity cost of a car is the dollar value of 10 computers.

It is economic costs that are relevant for economic theory of firm behavior. A good way to understand the distinction between the two definitions of costs is to use each to measure the costs of various inputs.

For some inputs, the cost as measured by accountants and the cost as measured by economists are the same. An example is labor hired at some hourly wage rate. Consider a firm that hires four workers at the going wage rate of $12 per hour. An accountant would measure the cost of labor as the out-of-pocket expenditures of $48. To calculate the opportunity cost, an economist would assume that the going wage rate of $12 per hour is the amount that the labor services would earn in their best alternative employment. The opportunity cost of hiring four workers for one hour would thus also be $48.

For other inputs, accounting costs and economic costs differ considerably. Two important categories are capital and labor inputs supplied by the owners of a firm. Consider a machine that is owned by a firm. An accountant would determine how much of the original price of the machine to charge to current costs by applying a standard depreciation formula to the historical cost of the machine. Economists, however, want to know the opportunity cost of using that machine for one hour of production. This implicit cost is the *rental rate:* the amount that another firm would be willing to pay for the use of the machine for an hour. By continuing to use the machine, the firm is implicitly choosing to give up the rental income it could earn from another firm.

A similar distinction between accounting cost and economic cost arises in the case of labor services supplied to a firm by its owner. An accountant would not count

the value of the owner's services as part of cost. An economist, however, would ask what an owner (or "entrepreneur") could have earned in the best alternative employment. This opportunity cost would be included as part of economic costs.

Because accounting and economic costs differ, accounting profits and economic profits differ. Economic profits are typically smaller than accounting profits because accountants do not count the value of any labor and capital inputs supplied by the owners of the firm. In fact, it is worthwhile for a firm to continue producing in the long run as long as economic profits are equal to *zero*. If economic profits equal zero, then revenues just cover economic costs, indicating that all resources are receiving their opportunity cost.

2.5.2 Short-Run Costs of Production

As we saw above, the profit-maximizing rule tells a firm to choose the output level for which marginal revenue is equal to marginal cost, where marginal cost was defined as the addition to total costs resulting from the production of one additional unit of output. But what are "total costs"? The answer depends on the time period under consideration.

Economists customarily distinguish between the "short run" and the "long run."* Short-run total costs have two components: fixed costs and variable costs. In the short run, the level of use of some inputs, such as land, buildings, and equipment, cannot be changed. The costs of these inputs are *fixed costs (FC)*. Fixed costs do not vary with the level of output but are the same whether the firm produces a large or small amount of output. Examples include rent and property taxes.

Consider a firm that signs a contract to rent equipment for $300 per year, paid at the beginning of the year. This $300 is a fixed cost because the rental fee does not vary with the level of output. If the firm decides to go out of business at the end of the year, it would not sign a rental contract for the next year. But what would happen if the firm decides to stop production partway through the year? Could it get a refund of part of the $300 by returning the equipment? The answer depends on the terms of the contract. Suppose the rental agreement specifies that if the equipment is returned within the year, the firm will receive $100 back. The $200 is thus a *sunk cost:* It is that portion of fixed costs that is not recoverable. Because sunk costs cannot be recovered once they have been paid, they *should not* affect any subsequent decisions. The $100 that the firm could receive by returning the equipment within the year, however, *should* affect the firm's decisions; it is a recoverable cost.

APPLICATION 2.5
When Do Sunk Costs Matter to a Firm?

Economists teach their students that sunk costs are like spilled milk or like water under the bridge. Because a sunk cost cannot be recovered once it has been paid, the firm should not consider this cost in deciding how much output to produce. Students often

*Dividing time into just two periods is a simplifying assumption. In reality, there are many short runs, with increasingly more adjustment possible as we move from the shortest period toward the long run. In the very shortest run, all inputs are fixed.

struggle with this. They point to costs such as licensing fees for doctors or taxicab drivers, expenditures on specialized equipment, and money a firm spends to investigate a new market or product, arguing that these costs *must* matter to a firm.

The answer to students' confusion is to think about whether the cost is a prospective cost or one that has already been incurred. Before entering an industry or a new geographic market or developing a new product, a firm must expect to at least cover its costs. Otherwise, entry or product development would not make sense. At this point, then, a profit-maximizing firm should indeed pay attention to initial sunk costs, asking whether future profits are expected to be high enough to cover the costs. However, once the licensing fee has been paid, the specialized equipment purchased, or the market research conducted, a firm should no longer think about these costs in making decisions about how much to produce. ∎

Variable costs (VC) are the costs associated with those inputs that can be varied according to the level of output being produced.* Examples of variable inputs are labor, raw materials, and energy. The sum of variable costs and the recoverable part of fixed costs is called *avoidable costs* because the firm will not pay these costs if it produces no output.

Decisions about how much output to produce in the short run could be made using total costs. Often, however, using per-unit costs is easier. To understand the relationships among various short-run costs, we will work through a numerical example, shown in Table 2.2.

Total fixed costs are given in the second column. In this example, all fixed costs are assumed to be sunk; the firm must pay $50 per month even if it produces no output.[†]

The third column shows total variable costs. To produce more output in the short run, the firm must use more of the variable inputs such as labor, electricity, and raw materials. Because the usage of variable inputs increases with the level of output, so do variable costs.

Table 2.2 identifies five additional types of short-run costs. All of these additional measures of cost are derived from the total fixed costs and the total variable costs. The other costs are just different ways of expressing the same basic information.

Total cost (TC) is the sum of fixed costs and variable costs. For example, look at the row in Table 2.2 corresponding to an output level of 6 units per month. Fixed costs are $50 and variable costs are $124, yielding total costs of $174. Because variable costs increase with the level of output and fixed costs are constant, total costs increase as the firm produces more output.

As defined earlier, short-run marginal cost (MC) is the change in short-run total cost resulting from a one-unit change in output.[‡] When output increases from 4 to 5 units, for example, total cost increases from $130 to $150. The marginal cost of the fifth unit of output is thus $20. Because variable cost is the only part of total cost that

*Variable costs are usually written as a function of output, VC(q), to show that they change as the level of output changes.

[†]If the firm could recover part of the fixed cost if it went out of business, then only the nonrecoverable part of fixed cost would be associated with an output level of zero. For example, suppose that in order to produce and sell output, a firm needs a license that costs $50 per month. If $10 of the $50 is refundable, then the relevant cost for an output level of zero is $40; the fixed cost for any output level greater than zero is $50.

[‡]Using calculus, short-run marginal cost, $SRMC = \dfrac{dC(q)}{dq}$.

TABLE 2.2 An Example of Short-Run Costs

Output (units per month) (1)	Total Fixed Cost ($ per month) (2)	Total Variable Cost ($ per month) (3)	Total Cost ($ per month) (4) = (2) + (3)	Marginal Cost ($ per unit) (5)	Average Fixed Cost ($ per unit) (6) = (2)/(1)	Average Variable Cost ($ per unit) (7) = (3)/(1)	Average Total Cost ($ per unit) (8) = (4)/(1)
0	50	0	50				
1	50	30	80	30	50.00	30.00	80.00
2	50	49	99	19	25.00	24.50	49.50
3	50	65	115	16	16.67	21.67	38.33
4	50	80	130	15	12.50	20.00	32.50
5	50	100	150	20	10.00	20.00	30.00
6	50	124	174	24	8.33	20.67	29.00
7	50	150	200	26	7.14	21.43	28.57
8	50	180	230	30	6.25	22.50	28.75
9	50	215	265	35	5.56	23.89	29.44
10	50	255	305	40	5.00	25.50	30.50
11	50	300	350	45	4.55	27.27	31.82
12	50	360	410	60	4.17	30.00	34.17

changes with the level of output, marginal cost can also be calculated from variable costs. Variable cost rises from $80 to $100 when output increases from 4 to 5 units, again giving marginal cost of the fifth unit of output as $20. For many of a firm's decisions, marginal cost is the most important cost to consider.

Table 2.2 also shows three measures of average cost per unit of output. *Average fixed cost (AFC)* is fixed cost divided by output. Because fixed cost is constant, average fixed cost falls as output increases. For example, the average fixed cost associated with 2 units of output is $25 per month, whereas it is $5 per month for 10 units of output.

Average variable cost (AVC), shown in column seven, is variable cost divided by output. Short-run *average cost* (or average total cost) *(AC)*, shown in column eight, is total cost divided by output. Average total cost can also be defined as the sum of average fixed cost and average variable cost.* For example, total cost of 10 units of output is $305, so average cost is $305 divided by 10, or $30.50. Alternatively, for 10 units of output, average fixed cost is $5 and average variable cost is $25.50, so average total cost is the sum, $30.50.

So far we have simply defined the various measures of short-run costs and explained the arithmetical relationships among them. But what is behind the various

*Short-run average cost,

$$\frac{C(q)}{q} = \frac{VC(q) + F}{q} = \frac{VC(q)}{q} + \frac{F}{q} = AVC(q) + AFC(q).$$

cost relationships? What factors determine how cost varies with the level of output a firm produces?

A firm's costs depend both on the level of inputs being used to produce a given level of output and on the prices that the firm must pay for those inputs. The existing technology dictates what inputs must be used to produce a given level of output. The relationship between inputs and output is represented by a **production function,** a mathematical relationship that identifies the maximum quantity of a good that can be produced per time period using a specific combination of inputs. In the short run the firm cannot change the levels of the fixed inputs. The short-run production function therefore indicates the relationship between the level of output and the quantity of the variable inputs.

Figure 2.1 shows the short-run per-unit cost curves for a firm. The shapes of these curves are consistent with the data in Table 2.2 and, in fact, are the typical shapes for short-run cost curves. It is important to note first that the prices of inputs are held constant in drawing these curves; we assume that the firm can hire any quantity of an input at a given price per unit. The cost curves would shift up if the price of an input, such as labor, increased.*

Short-run marginal cost in the numerical example of Table 2.2 and in Figure 2.1 is U-shaped. At first, the cost of additional units of output falls as the firm adds more units of labor, the variable input. The firm benefits from specialization and division of labor. In the example of Table 2.2, marginal cost falls until the firm is producing 4 units of output per month. Eventually, however, the fixed plant and equipment begin to be overutilized; the workers start to get in each other's way. At this point, short-run marginal cost starts to increase.† Average fixed cost (AFC) falls over the entire range of output because the fixed amount is spread over larger and larger quantities of output. Average variable cost (AVC) is U-shaped for the same reason as marginal cost; beyond some point, the constraint of the fixed factors of production—typically assumed to be the plant and equipment—makes each additional unit of labor less productive than the previous one. Workers' tasks become redundant and it becomes more and more expensive to produce output within a given plant.

Average cost (AC) is also U-shaped. The minimum of AC occurs at a higher level of output than the minimum point of AVC because AC reflects the steadily decreasing average fixed cost in addition to AVC.

The relationship between marginal and average, a frequently used relationship in economics, is the same for all curves. Consider the case for which MC is less than AC as output expands. AC reflects the costs of all units of output produced so far, whereas MC measures the cost of producing an additional unit of output. If the cost of producing one more unit is below average cost, average cost is pulled down by producing that unit. [You can understand this relationship by thinking of performance in a

*An increase in the wage rate paid to labor would not cause the average fixed cost curve to shift up because labor is assumed to be a variable input.

†The shape of the short-run marginal cost curve is inversely related to the marginal product of the variable input. As long as the marginal product is increasing, marginal cost falls. In the short run, economists usually assume that the law of diminishing marginal returns is relevant. This law is a generalization of empirical evidence that indicates that increasing the variable input, or inputs, while holding technology and other inputs constant, will eventually result in smaller and smaller increases in total product. When the marginal product of the variable input begins to fall, short-run marginal cost increases.

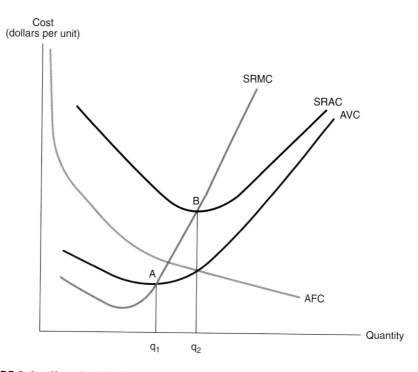

FIGURE 2.1 Short-Run Per-Unit Cost Curves for a Hypothetical Firm

This graph shows the general shapes for a firm's short-run per-unit curves: marginal cost (SRMC), average total cost (SRAC), average variable cost (AVC), and average fixed cost (AFC). The short-run marginal cost curve always intersects the AVC and SRAC curves at their minimum points, shown as points A and B, respectively. Fixed costs are constant as output increases; consequently, the AFC is always downward sloping.

course. If the grade on the most recent exam in a course (the "marginal grade") is below the average grade before the exam, the exam pulls down the course average.] Similarly, if MC is greater than AC, then average costs are increasing. If marginal and average costs are both U-shaped, the relationship between marginal and average implies that they are equal at the minimum of the average cost curve. This is shown in Figure 2.1: MC equals AVC at q_1, the minimum of AVC, and MC equals AC at q_2, the minimum of AC.

2.5.3 Long-Run Costs of Production and Economies of Scale

In the short run some inputs are fixed; the firm has to do the best it can with a given capital stock and plant size, for example. In the long run, however, the firm can buy new equipment and move into a different plant. In fact, all inputs are variable in the long run; the firm can choose that combination of inputs that allows it to produce a given level of output at the lowest possible cost.

Because all inputs are variable in the long run, there are fewer long-run cost curves to worry about. In the short run we have to distinguish among three total cost curves: fixed cost, variable cost, and total cost. Each short-run total cost curve corresponds to a short-run average cost curve. In the long run there is only one total cost curve and one average cost curve.

Figure 2.2 shows long-run marginal and average cost curves for a hypothetical firm. The relationship between average and marginal again implies that if the long-run average cost curve is U-shaped, MC equals AC at the minimum of AC, shown as q_1 in Figure 2.2.

Why would a long-run average cost curve be U-shaped? The short-run explanation—that some input or inputs are fixed—does not apply in the long run because all inputs are variable. Underlying the long-run curves is a characteristic of the firm's production function called **returns to scale.** A production function exhibits *constant* returns to scale if a proportionate increase in all inputs causes output to increase in the same proportion; for example, tripling all inputs leads to exactly three times as much output. A production function is subject to *increasing* returns to scale (or

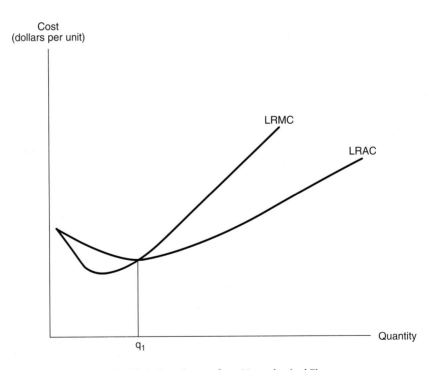

FIGURE 2.2 Long-Run Per-Unit Cost Curves for a Hypothetical Firm

Because there are no fixed costs in the long run, there are only two per-unit cost curves: the long-run marginal cost (LRMC) and the long-run average cost (LRAC) curves. The shape of the LRAC curve is determined by returns to scale. On this graph, production exhibits increasing returns to scale until q_1, the minimum of LRAC, and decreasing returns to scale as output expands beyond q_1. LRMC intersects LRAC at the minimum of LRAC.

economies of scale) if a proportionate increase in all inputs results in a more than proportionate increase in output; that is, output more than triples when all inputs are tripled. The final possibility is that a proportionate increase in all inputs leads to a less than proportionate increase in output. This third case is *decreasing* returns to scale (or *diseconomies of scale*).

Returns to scale dictate the shape of the long-run average cost curve.* If a production function is characterized by economies of scale, long-run average cost falls as the volume of output increases. Constant returns to scale imply a horizontal long-run average cost curve, while long-run average cost increases with output if the production function exhibits diseconomies of scale.[†] Long-run average cost will be U-shaped, therefore, if the firm's production function exhibits economies of scale at low levels of output and diseconomies of scale at higher levels of output. To see why this might be the case, we now consider the sources of economies and diseconomies of scale.

APPLICATION 2.6
A Measure of Economies of Scale

Economies of scale exist if average cost falls as output increases. But we know from the mathematical relationship between marginal cost and average cost that average cost falls only if marginal cost is below average cost. Conversely, there are diseconomies of scale—increasing average costs—only when marginal cost is greater than (or above) average cost. Economists have used this relationship to define a precise measure of scale economies, S, defined as the ratio of average cost to marginal cost. That is, $S = AC(q)/MC(q)$. If $S > 1$, economies of scale exist; diseconomies of scale are present if $S < 1$.

There is another useful interpretation of S. Define the output elasticity of costs in the standard way as the percentage increase in costs that results from a given percentage increase in output. Writing out this definition and simplifying, S is the inverse of the output elasticity of costs:

$$S = \frac{\dfrac{TC}{q}}{\dfrac{\Delta TC}{\Delta q}} = \frac{\Delta q}{\Delta TC}\frac{TC}{q} = \frac{\dfrac{\Delta q}{q}}{\dfrac{\Delta TC}{TC}}$$

*We continue to assume that the firm can hire any quantity of each input at a given price per unit.

[†]To see the relationship between returns to scale and long-run average cost, suppose the production function is given by $q = f(L,K)$. Choose any levels of labor L, and capital, K, say L_1 and K_1. Then $q_1 = f(L_1,K_1)$ and the long-run average cost associated with this level of output is $AC_1 = \dfrac{wL_1 + rK_1}{q_1}$. Here w represents the wage and

r represents the rental rate of capital. We can rewrite this as $(AC_1)(q_1) = wL_1 + rK_1$. Now consider a proportionate increase in L and K and let $q_2 = f(aL_1,aK_1)$. The long-run average cost associated with this level of output is

$$AC_2 = \frac{waL_1 + raK_1}{q_2} = \frac{a(wL_1 + rK_1)}{q_2} = \frac{a(AC_1)q_1}{q_2}.$$

With increasing returns to scale, q_2 is greater than aq_1 and AC_2 is less than AC_1. You should be able to show that AC is constant with constant returns to scale and that it increases with the level of output in the case of decreasing returns to scale.

What S tells us, then, is the percentage change in output arising from a given percentage increase in costs. If S is greater than 1, a firm can increase the amount of output it is producing by 1 percent for less than a 1 percent increase in costs. ■

Sources of Economies of Scale[36]

Economies of scale can exist at the *product* level, at the *plant* level, and at the *multiplant* level. At the product level, specialization is an important source of economies of scale. Often, firms can reduce the time required to produce one unit of output considerably by utilizing specialized machinery, but the setup time required for specialized machinery is usually high. Because of the extensive setup time, a firm producing relatively small quantities of output may find it cheaper to use general-purpose machinery instead of investing in specialized machinery. As the quantity of output increases, firms find it profitable to incur the larger setup time associated with the cost-reducing technology in order to realize savings in running time.

Similar savings can result from specialization and division of labor. As the number of employees producing a particular product increases, tasks can be more narrowly defined, giving workers the opportunity to become better at their tasks through repetition. Total labor time and cost will thus fall as the quantity of output increases.

At the plant level, economists have identified economies of scale resulting from increases in the size of processing units. This is important for industries such as petroleum refining, cement, and chemical manufacturing in which production requires such capital equipment as tanks and pipelines. For this type of equipment the laws of geometry tell us that doubling surface area with a consequent doubling of materials costs leads to more than double the volume. In fact, a rough rule of thumb indicates that a firm can double the capacity of a processing unit such as a pipeline for an increase in capital costs of approximately 60 percent.*

As plant size increases, economies of scale can also result from *economies of massed reserves.*[37] All firms hold inventories of some machines or important replacement parts so that production will not be interrupted by a random breakdown. However, a large firm operating several specialized machines does not need to hold reserves for *each* machine in operation. Average costs thus decrease as the cost of holding replacement parts is spread out over a larger volume of output.

Similar savings from spreading overhead over a larger volume of output can be realized in other functions performed by a firm. These include auditing, marketing, finance, personnel, and research and development.† A firm such as Intel or one that develops computer software realizes considerable economies of scale from spreading overhead over large volumes of output.

Multiplant economies appear to be particularly important in certain types of industries. One is an industry that produces a product with relatively high transporta-

*In general, if capacity is increased by a factor of x, the *two-thirds rule* indicates that capital costs will increase by a factor of $x^{0.67}$.

†There are overlaps between economies of scale at the product level and at the plant level. Some economies at the plant level, such as spreading of overhead, could be realized by a large plant that produced a single product or by a large plant producing multiple products. Especially if demand for a single product is insufficient to justify production at a large enough volume to realize plant-specific economies, a firm may choose to produce more than one product in the same plant.

tion costs relative to value, such as steel or cement (see Sources of Diseconomies of Scale below). In this case, if the geographic market is large, a firm may be able to achieve lower costs if it has several plants, each serving a single region, than if it has only one plant. A second type of industry in which multiplant economies of scale are likely to be important is one in which each firm produces multiple products. Here, specialization is again the source of economies of scale; it may be possible to achieve savings by having each plant specialize in a particular product line. Still a third type of industry is one in which multiple plants permit firms to advertise nationally instead of locally and enable firms to utilize national or world capital markets instead of local markets. Access to national advertising and capital markets can significantly reduce costs.* A firm that operates only one plant may not have access to national markets, but a firm operating several plants in different areas of the country may.

Sources of Diseconomies of Scale

Eventually, economies of scale will be exhausted. The savings in unit cost associated with spreading setup time and overhead over larger and larger volumes of output decrease as the quantity of output produced increases. Similarly, economies of massed reserves become relatively less important as firm size grows. These arguments suggest that long-run average cost curves should eventually flatten.

Further arguments suggest that, as Figure 2.2 shows, long-run average cost may increase beyond some quantity of output. At first, this may seem somewhat odd. Surely, even if there are no further gains from specialization, a firm should be able to double all inputs, reproducing exactly what it had done before, and produce twice as much output. This would imply that the long-run average cost curve should be horizontal. Economists have suggested at least two reasons for increasing average cost beyond some quantity of output.

First, even in the long run, some input may actually be fixed, or at least scarce, and therefore not able to be increased proportionately with other inputs. A common example of such an input is managerial ability or entrepreneurship. In this case, organizational difficulties associated with increasing size might lead to less than proportionate increases in output. In fact, firms have devoted considerable attention to organizational structure in an attempt to avoid diseconomies associated with large-scale management. General Motors was an early leader in moving away from a centralized structure to a multidivisional one, splitting itself into five independent divisions—Buick, Cadillac, Chevrolet, Oldsmobile, and Pontiac—in the 1920s. Such decentralization is intended to reduce the number of decisions and amount of coordination on the part of the chief executive officer. Today most large firms are multidivisional. Of course, even with decentralization, firms need an ultimate decision maker, whose talents and time can be stretched only so far.

Overall economies of scale depend not only on the production function but also on other functions of the firm. A firm may realize economies of scale in production for reasons such as those discussed above, yet still experience overall diseconomies of

*Most of the cost savings discussed in this section represent real economies as opposed to pecuniary economies. **Real economies** are those that reflect actual savings of resources, such as reduction of transaction costs. Society benefits from the realization of real economies. **Pecuniary economies** are savings that are purely redistributive, increasing the welfare of one group and reducing the welfare of another. The differential in capital costs across firms reflects both real and pecuniary savings.

scale. The most important source of diseconomies of scale at the plant level is transportation costs. As a plant expands, its requirements for raw materials increase. Also, to sell its output, the finished products must typically be shipped to a larger geographic area. As the geographic area expands, transportation costs per unit sold may increase. This is especially true for bulky, low-value products such as cement, sand, and steel. For these products, transportation costs rise quickly enough to lead to overall diseconomies of scale, limiting the geographic market that can be efficiently served by one plant.*

2.6 Cost Concepts: Multiproduct Firms

Most real-world firms are multiproduct firms, producing more than one product.[38] Think, for example, of Toyota, which produces several models of cars as well as SUVs, vans, and trucks. Or Sony with its lines of computers, printers, digital cameras, camcorders, televisions, DVD players, and more. Nabisco makes Animal Crackers, Oreos, Fruit Snacks, Ritz, and Newtons. One obvious explanation for the existence of multiproduct firms is that it may be less costly for one firm to produce several products than for the same production to occur in several single-product firms.

Economists have named the cost savings that result from producing joint products *economies of scope.*[39]† Formally, let q_1 and q_2 represent two specific quantities of two goods, such as cars and trucks; the total cost of producing these quantities is thus given by $C(q_1, q_2)$. For this two-product case, an economy of scope will exist if $C(q_1, q_2) < C(q_1, 0) + C(0, q_2)$; using our example, there are some cost savings from having cars and trucks produced by the same firm rather than by two separate firms.

What are the sources of economies of scope? One is a fixed factor of production, such as a specialized machine. As discussed earlier, such a fixed factor is a classic source of economies of scale. If demand for a single product is not great enough to exhaust the economies of scale, the firm may look for other products that can utilize the same fixed factor of production. An example is railroad track. A railroad may offer both freight and passenger service if demand for either product does not fully utilize the track.[40]

APPLICATION 2.7

A Measure of Economies of Scope

Economists have developed a measure of the degree of economies of scope analogous to the measure of economies of scale, S. Call this measure S_C:

$$S_C = \frac{C(q_1, 0) + C(0, q_2) - C(q_1, q_2)}{C(q_1, q_2)}$$

*It may be possible for a firm to overcome diseconomies of scale arising from transportation costs at least partially by operating multiple plants in different areas of the country.

†Economists have also considered how to extend the concepts of marginal and average cost to multiproduct firms.

What S_C measures is the relative increase in costs that would result from producing par-ticular quantities of two goods separately rather than together. Larger economies of scope result in larger values of S_C. ■

The sharing of an input also gives rise to economies of scope. A farmer who is rais-ing cows may choose to sell both the hide and the beef, rather than raising some cows just for the beef and others for the hide. Here, because two products can share the same input, economies of scope exist even in the absence of scale economies in any stage of production.

An important type of shared input is an intangible asset such as research knowl-edge or business know-how about production. Learning how to produce cars is likely to teach a firm much about producing trucks. As discussed earlier, transaction costs of obtaining new information initially, as well as of transferring information from one firm to another, are high. If several products require similar know-how, the high trans-action costs associated with information transfer may make it less costly to produce all products within a single firm.

Empirical evidence on the importance of economies of scope is scarce. As shown by the technical definition of economies of scope, a researcher needs to calculate the cost of producing a specific level of each of at least two products separately, as well as the cost of producing those specific levels of the products together. In one carefully done study, Friedlaender, Winston, and Wang noted that estimating multiproduct cost functions leads to "formidable data problems."[41] Nonetheless, their work indi-cates the kind of information that can be obtained from such a study.

Friedlaendaer and colleagues estimated a multiproduct cost function for each of the three largest U.S. automobile producers, using data from the period from 1955 to 1979. They found wide variability in the measures of economies of scale and scope at different levels of output, indicating the inappropriateness of broad generalizations. They did find that, for all of the firms, economies of scope could be obtained by com-bining the production of large cars with small cars and trucks. A firm that already pro-duced small and large cars, however, did not realize further economies of scope from also producing trucks. In general, they concluded that although economies of scope are undoubtedly important in some industries, it is difficult to evaluate their impor-tance using current empirical evidence.

APPLICATION 2.8

Are There Economies of Scope in Institutions of Higher Education?

What is the output of an institution of higher learning—of a college or a university? Upon first thought, your answer might be "educated students." But further reflection suggests that institutions of higher education are multiproduct firms. There are at least two types of teaching output: undergraduate and graduate training. And faculty members at institu-tions of higher education produce an array of research output, including publications in scholarly journals, research reports, patents, and public lectures. As we know, economies of scope often arise when particular outputs share common inputs. The fact that under-graduate education, graduate education, and research share the common input of faculty members suggests that economies of scope may exist in colleges and universities.

As you can imagine, estimating multiproduct cost functions for institutions of higher education is not easy. Researchers must decide on measures of both teaching and research output and also measure faculty input. Also, calculating average cost is complicated because there is no one clear measure of quantity to use in the denominator of the average cost formula. However, a careful study using data on more than 1800 institutions of higher education suggests that teaching and research may be complementary—that cost savings may result when faculty members produce multiple outputs. In fact, the evidence suggests that for private-sector schools in particular, "complex" institutions of higher education where faculty teach both undergraduate and graduate students and also engage in research are considerably less costly than more specialized institutions. Sharing the common input among different outputs seems to lead to lower costs.

Source: Elchanan Cohn, Sherrie L. W. Rhine, and Maria C. Santos, "Institutions of Higher Education as Multi-Product Firms: Economies of Scale and Scope," *The Review of Economics and Statistics* (May 1989): 284–290. ■

SUMMARY

1. Many modern firms bear little resemblance to the traditional firm of microeconomic theory. They are large, complex entities that often operate in many different product and geographical markets.

2. The modern theory of the firm builds on Ronald Coase's fundamental observations that the firm and the market are alternative ways of organizing production and that costs are associated with either way of organizing production.

3. Advantages of using the market include the ability to aggregate demands of many small firms, allowing a producer to realize economies of scale or economies of scope. In addition, using the market can reduce production costs by reducing risk.

4. When transaction costs are high, firms are likely to rely on internal production rather than using the market. Three dimensions of transactions are important in identifying circumstances when transaction costs are likely to be high: their frequency, the amount of uncertainty associated with them, and the degree of asset specificity.

5. In firms that are organized as sole proprietorships or partnerships, ownership and control of the firm are combined in the hands of one or a few people. In a corporation, however, ownership and control are typically separated.

6. The separation of ownership and control in corporations gives managers the freedom to pursue objectives other than profit maximization. Possible managerial goals include sales maximization, pursuit of a high growth rate, utility maximization, and a focus on job security.

7. Some economists argue that the size and complexity of modern firms make it difficult for managers to choose the profit-maximizing strategy. They hypothesize that managers opt for satisficing behavior rather than profit-maximizing behavior. Managers who adopt satisficing behavior may use a variety of rules of thumb to make their day-to-day business decisions.

8. Defenders of the assumption of profit maximization argue that managers are both constrained and encouraged to maximize profits. Among the constraints are the possibility of stockholder revolt, the threat of takeover, and competitive pressure from the product market. Incentives such as bonuses and stock options encourage managers to pay attention to profits.

9. Any profit-maximizing firm, regardless of industry structure, will choose the quantity of output for which marginal revenue equals marginal cost. Average costs are important for firms' decisions about whether to continue production or remain in the industry.

10. It is important to distinguish between accounting costs and economic costs. Although accounting costs are reported by firms in their financial reports, economic costs are the relevant costs for a firm's decisions.

11. A firm's cost curves differ depending on the time period under consideration. In the short run, at least one of the firm's inputs is held constant; total short-run cost

can thus be divided into fixed cost and variable cost. Fixed costs which cannot be recovered once they have been paid are sunk costs.

12 In the long run, all inputs are variable and the firm can choose whatever combination of inputs allows it to produce a given level of output at the lowest possible cost. The shape of a firm's long-run average cost curve depends on the returns to scale. Increasing returns to scale, or economies of scale, imply a negatively sloped long-run average cost curve, whereas a positively sloped long-run average cost curve corresponds to decreasing returns to scale.

13 Economies of scale can exist at the product, plant, and multiplant levels. Sources of economies of scale include specialization, increases in the size of processing units, economies of massed reserves, spreading of overhead, and access to national capital or advertising markets.

14 Cost concepts have to be modified for firms that produce more than one product. A key concept for a multiproduct firm is economies of scope, the cost savings that result from producing multiple products. Economies of scope can arise from the use of fixed factors of production or from the sharing of an input; when economies of scope exist, firms have a strong incentive to realize the cost savings by producing more than one product.

KEY TERMS

accounting cost
asset specificity
average cost (AC)
average fixed cost (AFC)
average variable cost (AVC)
avoidable cost
bounded rationality
diseconomies of scale
economic cost
economies of scale
economies of scope
fixed cost (FC)

marginal cost (MC)
marginal revenue (MR)
market for corporate control
opportunism
opportunity cost
pecuniary economies
production function
profits
real economies
rental rate
returns to scale

rule-of-thumb pricing
satisficing
separation of ownership and
 control
stockholder revolt
sunk cost
takeover
total cost (TC)
transaction costs
variable cost (VC)
X-inefficiency

DISCUSSION QUESTIONS

1. Ronald Coase won the Nobel Prize in economics in 1991 for his insights about the factors that influence the organization of firms. Suppose your friend, who is very bright but who has not studied economics, asks you to explain Coase's theory to her. What would you say?

2. Explain how using the market can help a firm control its costs.

3. Explain what is meant by "bounded rationality." What role does this assumption play in the theory of the firm?

4. Does the presence of opportunistic behavior contradict the assumption of utility maximization? Explain your reasoning.

5. U.S. automobile manufacturers have traditionally been highly vertically integrated, not only assembling parts into automobiles but also producing the parts. Japanese automobile manufacturers, in contrast, are much less highly integrated. They rely on a network of supplier firms for parts.

 a. Discuss the advantages and disadvantages of the U.S. system in comparison with the Japanese system.

 b. Japanese firms sometimes share technical personnel with their suppliers. Can you explain this using the theory of the firm? What concerns would motivate the firms to share personnel?

 c. Recently U.S. automobile manufacturers have turned to "outsourcing," relying on suppliers for parts rather than producing the parts internally. Not surprisingly, this move has caused tension with the United Automobile Workers union. Explain why automobile manufacturers are willing to risk labor disputes in order to rely on outside suppliers for parts.

6. Give some examples of job-specific skills and explain why transactions costs are higher if workers have job-specific skills.

7. Suppose you are writing the contract for a manager of a large corporation. How might you structure the contract to take the owners' interests into account?

8. A 1985 study of 130 stock purchase plans found that on average, these plans offered about 8 percent of the corporation's stock to its managers at a discount of 12 to 15 percent off the market price.* Typically, the plans allowed the managers to borrow funds at very low interest rates to buy the shares.

 a. Explain the purpose of these stock purchase plans.

 b. The stock market generally views the institution of such a plan positively. Following the announcement of a plan, the value of a firm's shares rose, on average, 3 percent above the market trend. What does this say about the stock market's evaluation of the effectiveness of the stock purchase plan?

9. "Insider trading" refers to stock transactions that allow individuals with insider knowledge of a firm (such as its managers) to profit. Many people regard this as an unfair advantage and argue that insider trading should be illegal. Can you make an argument *in favor of* insider trading?

10. Your inquisitive friend (from question 1) is back. She has read something about the "market for corporate control" and asks you to explain what that is and how it helps enforce profit-maximizing behavior on firms. What do you say to her?

11. The owner of a small flower shop is a highly trained certified public accountant and does her own accounting work. Discuss how to value the cost of her time.

12. Explain why the purchase price of a machine is not the relevant price for a firm trying to decide how much labor and how much capital to use in producing output.

*Sanjai Bhagat, James A. Brickley, and Ronald C. Lease, "Incentive Effects of Stock Purchase Plans," *Journal of Financial Economics* 14 (June 1985): 195–215.

PROBLEMS

1. a. Fill in the blanks in the following table.
 b. Draw a graph that shows marginal cost, average variable cost, and average total cost.

Q	FC	TVC	TC	MC	AFC	AVC	ATC
0			50				
1			62				
2				10			
3						10	
4		9					
5							21

2. A firm finds that at an output level of 7 units, its total cost is $1834; at 8 units of output, its total cost is $2048.
 a. Read Application 2.6 on measuring economies of scale, and then calculate the value of S for this firm at 8 units of output.
 b. Are there economies of scale at 8 units of output? Explain your reasoning.
 c. Explain what the value of S tells you about the relationship between increasing output and increasing costs for this firm. Be as specific as possible in your answer.

3. A firm builds shipping crates out of wood. If wood costs $1 per square foot, how much will the wood for a 1-cubic-foot square crate (1 ft. × 1 ft. × 1 ft.) cost? How much would it cost to buy wood for an 8-cubic-foot square crate? Relate this calculation to economies of scale.

4. The Q & H Company produces a number of products including shampoo, q_S, and toothpaste, q_T. Suppose that the cost functions for these products are given by

$$C(q_S, 0) = 4 + q_S^2$$
$$C(0, q_T) = 4 + \sqrt{q_T}$$
$$C(q_S, q_T) = 7 + q_S^2 + \sqrt{q_T}$$

 a. Does the production of shampoo exhibit economies of scale? Explain your reasoning.
 b. Does the production of toothpaste exhibit economies of scale? Explain your reasoning.
 c. Are there economies of scope associated with producing shampoo and toothpaste? Explain your reasoning.

5. A firm produces cars, q_C, and trucks, q_T. Its costs are given by

$$C(q_C, q_T) = 50q_C + 60q_T - \frac{3q_Cq_T}{2}.$$

 Calculate the measure of economies of scope (see Application 2.7) for 20 cars and 10 trucks. What does this answer tell you about the production of cars and trucks?

NOTES

1. Surveys include Beth V. Yarbrough and Robert M. Yarbrough, "The Transactional Structure of the Firm," *Journal of Economic Behavior and Organization* 10 (1988): 1–28; Paul Milgrom and John Roberts, "Economic Theories of the Firm: Past, Present, and Future," *Canadian Journal of Economics* 21 (August 1988): 444–458; and Roger Clarke and Tony McGuinness (eds.), *The Economics of the Firm* (Oxford: Basil Blackwell, 1987).

2. Ronald H. Coase, "The Nature of the Firm," *Economica* 4 (November 1937): 386–405.

3. References include Oliver E. Williamson, "Transaction Cost Economics," in Richard Schmalensee and Robert D. Willig (eds.), *Handbook of Industrial Organization* (Amsterdam: North-Holland, 1989); *The Economic Institutions of Capitalism: Firms, Markets, Relational Contracting* (New York: Free Press, 1985); "The Modern Corporation: Origins, Evolution, Attributes," *Journal of Economic Literature* 19 (December 1981): 1537–1568; "Transaction-Cost Economics: The Governance of Contractual Relations," *Journal of Law and Economics* 22 (October 1979): 3–61; and *Markets and Hierarchies—Analysis and Antitrust Implications: A Study in the Economics of Internal Organization* (New York: Free Press, 1975). See also Armen A. Alchian and Harold Demsetz, "Production, Information Costs and Economic Organization," *American Economic Review* 62 (1972): 777–795 and Benjamin Klein, Robert G. Crawford, and Armen A. Alchian, "Vertical Integration, Appropriable Rents, and the Competitive Contracting Process," *Journal of Law and Economics* 21 (October 1978): 297–326.

4. See, for example, p. 1547 in Williamson, "The Modern Corporation: Origins, Evolution, Attributes."

5. Oliver E. Williamson, "Transaction Cost Economics," p. 150.

6. The notion of bounded rationality is attributed to Herbert A. Simon. References include Herbert A. Simon, *Models of Man* (New York: John Wiley and Sons, 1957) and "Theories of Decision-Making in Economics and Behavioral Science," *American Economic Review* 49 (June 1959): 253–283.

7. Oliver E. Williamson, *The Economic Institutions of Capitalism: Firms, Markets, Relational Contracting* (New York: Free Press, 1985), p. 47.

8. This discussion draws upon Williamson, "Transaction Cost Economics," pp. 142–144.

9. See the discussions in Glenn Porter, *The Rise of Big Business, 1860–1920,* second edition (Arlington Heights, IL: Harlan Davidson, 1992), and Alfred D. Chandler, Jr. *The Visible Hand: The Managerial Revolution in American Business* (Cambridge, MA: Harvard University Press, 1977).

10. Data for 2001 from the *Statistical Abstract of the United States,* Table 716, 2004, p. 483.

11. Robert Larner, *Management Control and the Large Corporation* (New York: Dunellen, 1970), p. 3.

12. Edward S. Herman, *Corporate Control, Corporate Power* (Cambridge: Cambridge University Press, 1981): pp. 58–64. Newer work by Gompers, Ishii, and Metrick shows that firms whose boards give shareholders more control generate greater shareholder value than firms whose boards restrict shareholder control. See Paul Gompers, Joy Ishii, and Andrew Metrick, "Corporate Governance and Equity Prices," *Quarterly Journal of Economics* 118 (February 2003): 107–155.

13. R. Joseph Monsen, Jr., and Anthony Downs, "A Theory of Large Managerial Firms," *The Journal of Political Economy* 73 (June 1965): 221–236.

14. William J. Baumol, *Business Behavior, Value and Growth* (New York: Macmillan, 1959).

15. Oliver E. Williamson, *The Economics of Discretionary Behavior: Managerial Objectives in a Theory of the Firm* (Chicago: Markham, 1967).

16. Harvey Leibenstein, "Competition and X-Efficiency," *Journal of Political Economy* 81 (May 1973): 766.

17. William Fellner, *Competition Among the Few* (New York: Knopf, 1949), pp. 172–173.

18. A manager's performance may be judged by looking at the trend of profits over recent years. Evidence suggests that corporate presidents' tenure is shortened if profits deviate from trend. See W.M. Crain, Thomas Deaton, and Robert Tollison, "On the Survival of Corporate Executives," *Southern Economic Journal,* vol. 43 (January 1977): 1372–1375; Michael S. Weisbach, "Outside Directors and CEO Turnover," *Journal of Financial Economics* 20 (January/March 1988): 431–460; and Jerold B. Warner, Ross L. Watts, and Karen Wruck, "Stock Prices and Top Management Changes," *Journal of Financial Economics* 20 (January/March 1988): 461–492.

19. See R. Schramm and R. Sherman, "Profit Risk Management and the Theory of the Firm," *Southern Economic Journal* 40 (January 1974): 353–363; and Kenneth J. Boudreaux, "Managerialism and Risk-Return Performance," *Southern Economic Journal* 39 (January 1973): 366–372.

20. Important contributions include R.M. Cyert and J.G. March, *A Behavioral Theory of the Firm* (Englewood Cliffs, NJ: Prentice-Hall, 1963); Herbert A. Simon, "Rational Decision Making in Business Organizations," *American Economic Review* 69 (September 1979): 493–513; K.J. Cohen and R.M. Cyert,

Theory of the Firm (Englewood Cliffs, NJ: Prentice-Hall, 1965); and J.C. March and H.A. Simon, *Organizations* (New York: John Wiley, 1958).

21. R.L. Hall and Charles J. Hitch, "Pricing Theory and Business Behavior," *Oxford Economic Papers* 2 (May 1939): 12–45.

22. B. Fog, *Industrial Pricing Policies* (Amsterdam: North-Holland, 1960), p. 217.

23. A.D.H. Kaplan, J.B. Dirlam, and R.F. Lanzillotti, *Pricing in Big Business* (Washington, DC: Brookings Institution, 1958); see also R.F. Lanzillotti, "Pricing Objectives in Large Companies," *American Economic Review* 48 (December 1958): 921–940.

24. Kaplan et al., *ibid.,* pp. 130–165; and Lanzillotti, *ibid.,* pp. 924–927.

25. Kaplan et al., *ibid.,* p. 130.

26. Lanzillotti, "Pricing Objectives in Large Companies."

27. R.B. Heflebower, "Full Costs, Cost Changes, and Prices," in National Bureau of Economic Research conference report, *Business Concentration and Price Policy* (Princeton: Princeton University Press, 1955), p. 366.

28. Alfred E. Kahn, "Pricing Objectives in Large Companies: Comment," *American Economic Review* 49 (September 1959): 674.

29. Heflebower, *Supra* note 27: 374–375.

30. D.G. McFetridge, "The Determinants of Pricing Behavior: A Study of the Canadian Cotton Textile Industry," *Journal of Industrial Economics* 22 (December 1973): 141–152.

31. Monsen and Downs, "A Theory of Large Managerial Firms," p. 25.

32. Oliver Williamson, *Corporate Control and Business Behavior* (Englewood Cliffs, NJ: Prentice-Hall, 1970); and Brian Hindley, "Separation of Ownership and Control in the Modern Corporation," *Journal of Law and Economics* (April 1970): 185–210.

33. References include Robin Marris, "A Model of the 'Managerial' Enterprise," *Quarterly Journal of Economics* 77 (May 1963): 185–209; Marris, *The Economic Theory of "Managerial" Capitalism* (London: Macmillan, 1964); Henry G. Manne, "Mergers and the Market for Corporate Control," *Journal of Political Economy* 73 (April 1965): 110–120; and the Symposium on Takeovers in *The Journal of Economic Perspectives* 2 (Winter 1988): 2–82.

34. Ravenscraft and Scherer offer evidence that, on average, acquiring firms lose money on their acquisitions. See David J. Ravenscraft and F.M. Scherer, *Mergers, Sell-offs, and Economic Efficiency* (Washington, DC: Brookings Institution, 1987) and "Life After Takeover," *Journal of Industrial Economics* 36 (December 1987): 147–156.

35. Lucian Bebchuk and Yaniv Grinstein, "The Growth of Executive Pay," NBER Working Paper 11443 (Cambridge, MA: National Bureau of Economic Research, June 2005).

36. This section draws upon work done by F.M. Scherer and his colleagues. References include F.M. Scherer, "Economies of Scale and Industrial Concentration," in Harvey J. Goldschmid, H. Michael Mann, and J. Fred Weston (eds.), *Industrial Concentration: The New Learning* (Boston: Little, Brown, 1974): 16–54; F.M. Scherer, Alan Beckenstein, Erich Kaufer, and R.D. Murphy, *The Economics of Multi-Plant Operation: An International Comparison Study* (Cambridge, MA: Harvard University Press, 1975); and F.M. Scherer and David Ross, *Industrial Market Structure and Economic Performance,* third edition (Boston: Houghton Mifflin, 1990), Chapter 4.

37. The phrase comes from E.A.G. Robinson, *The Structure of Competitive Industry,* rev. ed. (Chicago: University of Chicago Press, 1958): 26–27.

38. See John C. Panzar and Robert D. Willig, "Economies of Scale in Multi-Output Production," *Quarterly Journal of Economics* 91 (1977): 481–493; and William J. Baumol, John C. Panzar, and Robert D. Willig, *Contestable Markets and the Theory of Industry Structure* (New York: Harcourt Brace Jovanovich, 1982) for an extensive discussion of multiproduct firms.

39. Elizabeth E. Bailey and Ann F. Friedlaender, "Market Structure and Multiproduct Industries," *Journal of Economic Literature* 20 (1982): 1024–1048; Baumol, Panzar, and Willig, *op. cit.;* John C. Panzar and Robert D. Willig, "Economies of Scale in Multi-Output Production," *Quarterly Journal of Economics* (1977): 481–493.

40. This discussion is drawn from Bailey and Friedlaender, pp. 1026–1028.

41. Ann F. Friedlaender, Clifford Winston, and Kung Wang, "Costs, Technology, and Productivity in the U.S. Automobile Industry," *The Bell Journal of Economics* 14 (1983): 2.

INTERNET EXERCISES

Visit **www.aw-bc.com/waldman_jensen** for this chapter's web exercises. Answer our real-world economics problems by searching the Internet for solutions!

Competition and Monopoly

A standard microeconomic theory course or textbook emphasizes the economics of firms in perfectly competitive and monopolistic industries. In these markets, strategic interaction is of little or no importance. Because each firm in a perfectly competitive market is so small, nothing one firm does affects other firms. In a pure monopoly, there is only one firm. As we will see, very few—if any—industries in the real world fall into either of these extreme market structures. Therefore, we direct most of our efforts in this book at examining firms' behavior in industries that are neither perfectly competitive nor monopolistic—industries in which strategic interaction plays a big role. Yet it is important to understand the perfectly competitive model because it will serve as a valuable reference point for examining other industry structures. Similarly, the monopoly model highlights how a firm with market power chooses its price and output level, as well as the welfare consequences of that choice.

This chapter begins by reviewing the economics of a perfectly competitive market. We introduce welfare concepts that are key for economists and policymakers, then turn to an examination of a monopoly market. The importance of perfect competition as a reference is highlighted in a welfare comparison between perfect competition and monopoly. We discuss present value and discounting and, finally, turn to a discussion of antitrust policy toward monopolization.

3.1 The Economics of Perfect Competition

The material discussed in Chapter 2 applies to all firms, regardless of the market structure in which they operate. Any firm striving to maximize profits will choose to produce the level of output for which marginal revenue equals marginal cost. And nothing in our review of cost concepts depends on the market structure. The underlying determinants of costs are input prices and production functions for any firm.

To complete the model of output determination, we need to specify the demand conditions facing the firm. The demand conditions determine the revenues the firm can earn by selling various quantities of output. Unlike costs, the demand conditions depend on the market structure. We begin by considering the economics of perfect competition. Even though real-world markets rarely, if ever, exhibit all the characteristics of a perfectly competitive market, this model is important as an ideal against which other markets can be compared.

3.1.1 The Assumptions of Perfect Competition

In everyday usage, competition refers to intense rivalry among firms, such as that between the Coca-Cola Company and Pepsico or between Toyota and Ford. Firms that are competitors in this sense recognize that their decisions affect other firms. We would certainly expect, for example, that when Kellogg's decides how much output to produce or what advertising campaign to adopt, it considers the effect on General Mills and Kraft Foods (Post cereals) and their likely responses.

Perfect competition as modeled by economists is quite different from the everyday view of competition. Each firm in a perfectly competitive market recognizes that its effect on the overall market is insignificant. Therefore, perfectly competitive firms do not view other firms as rivals; they make business decisions without considering the actions or reactions of other firms in the industry. Each firm views the market price as independent of its own level of output. A wheat farmer in Nebraska, for example, does not expect his decision about how much wheat to grow to affect the market price. Another example of a "small" firm in a competitive market is a broker on the New York Stock Exchange.

Formally, the long-run characteristics of perfect competition are as follows:

1. *Large number of buyers and sellers.* A perfectly competitive market contains many buyers and sellers, each small relative to total purchases or sales.

2. *Homogeneous product.* Firms in a perfectly competitive market produce a homogeneous, or identical, product. Because consumers cannot distinguish one firm's product from another's, they are indifferent about their supplier.

3. *Perfect information.* All economic agents (firms and consumers) have all of the information they need to make economic decisions. Consumers know the price and quality of the product produced by each firm, and firms know their production functions and the prices of all inputs and outputs.

4. *No transaction costs.* Transaction costs are the costs of using the market, such as the costs of negotiating and monitoring a contract. In a perfectly competitive market, transaction costs are zero for both buyers and sellers.

5. *Free entry and exit.* Adjustments to changing market conditions require that resources enter or leave the industry. In a perfectly competitive market these adjustments occur without firms having to incur any special costs; there are no barriers to entry or exit.

The characteristics of a perfectly competitive market ensure that firms and consumers are *price takers.* Because consumers are indifferent about their supplier, have perfect information about price, and incur no transaction costs in switching to a different seller, any firm that raises its price above the market price will immediately discover that it cannot sell any output. On the other hand, no perfectly competitive firm has any incentive to price below the market price because it can sell as much output as it wants at the going price. Therefore, buyers view the market price as beyond their control; they cannot find any firm willing to sell output at a price below the market price.

Figure 3.1 shows the demand curve facing a perfectly competitive firm. The vertical portion of the demand curve reflects the firm's belief that it will sell nothing if it

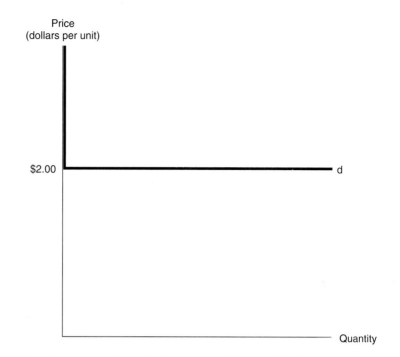

FIGURE 3.1 **The Demand Curve Facing a Perfectly Competitive Firm**

A perfectly competitive firm takes the equilibrium market price of $2 as fixed; it faces the horizontal and perfectly elastic demand curve shown as d. For a perfectly competitive firm, the demand curve is also equal to the marginal revenue curve.

charges a price higher than the market price, $2 in this case. The horizontal portion of the demand curve shows that the firm can sell whatever amount it wants if it charges the market price. It is important to emphasize that this figure shows the demand curve facing an *individual* firm in a perfectly competitive market. The market demand curve, which shows the relationship between the market price and the *total* amount of output demanded by consumers, is still assumed to be downward sloping.

The **price elasticity of demand**, often called simply the *elasticity of demand*, is a measure of how sensitive quantity demanded is to a change in price. It is defined as the percentage change in quantity demanded divided by the percentage change in price. The higher the absolute value of the elasticity of demand, the larger the change in quantity resulting from a change in price.* For example, an elasticity of −0.3 indicates that a 10 percent increase in price will reduce quantity demanded by only 3 percent (−3 percent/10 percent = −0.3). We would say that demand is inelastic since $|-0.3| < 1$. If the elasticity is −3, a 10 percent increase in price will reduce quantity demanded by 30 percent (−30 percent/10 percent = −3). In this case demand is elastic since $|-3.0| > 1$.

*For any downward-sloping demand curve, the elasticity of demand is negative because a decrease in price will lead to an increase in quantity demanded.

The elasticity of demand can be calculated as

$$\frac{\frac{\Delta Q}{Q}}{\frac{\Delta p}{p}} = \left(\frac{\Delta Q}{\Delta p}\right)\left(\frac{p}{Q}\right).$$

Note that when demand is graphed as $P = a - bQ$, $\dfrac{\Delta Q}{\Delta p}$ is the inverse of the slope of this demand curve: $\dfrac{-1}{b}$. For a horizontal demand curve, $\Delta p = 0$ everywhere, implying that $\dfrac{\Delta Q}{\Delta p} = \dfrac{\Delta Q}{0}$ and therefore that theelasticity of demand is infinity. The demand curve facing an individual firm in a perfectly competitive market is thus said to be *infinitely elastic* or *perfectly elastic*.

3.1.2 The Firm's Supply Curve

The profit-maximizing rule tells a firm to produce that quantity of output for which marginal revenue equals marginal cost. In the special case of a firm in a perfectly competitive industry, marginal revenue always equals price. To understand why, remember that a perfectly competitive firm can sell another unit of output without having to lower its price. For example, consider a firm that is selling 10 units of output at a price of $2. Its total revenue is $20. If this firm sells 11 units of output at a price of $2, total revenue increases from $20 to $22; marginal revenue is $2, the market price.*

Combining the profit-maximizing rule with the fact that price equals marginal revenue for a perfectly competitive firm, we conclude that if a perfectly competitive firm wants to produce any output, it will choose the level for which price equals marginal cost. Sometimes, however, a firm may choose not to produce any output. To understand why, it is necessary to analyze the firm's supply decision in both the short run and the long run.

Short Run

A firm should produce in the short run if its total revenue is greater than or equal to its avoidable costs, defined earlier as the sum of variable costs and the recoverable part of fixed costs. Consider first the case in which *all* fixed costs are *sunk*—that is, the firm's only avoidable costs are its variable costs. Even if a firm produces no output in the short run, it must still pay its fixed costs. In the short run, therefore, a profit-maximizing firm will choose to produce some output as long as the revenue it gets from selling that output—its **total revenue (TR)**—is greater than or equal to the costs of the variable inputs it must hire to produce that output—its VC. If the firm more than covers its VC, it can apply the revenues above variable costs toward its fixed costs so that its short-run loss will be less than FC. Stating this result in another way: A profit-maximizing firm will produce some output in the short run as long as price is greater than or equal to

*Mathematically, marginal revenue $= MR(q) = \dfrac{d[P(q) \cdot q]}{dq} = P + q \cdot \dfrac{dP}{dq}$. Because a perfectly competitive firm's actions do not affect the market price, $\dfrac{dP}{dq}$ equals 0, and $MR = P$.

average variable cost.* To summarize, in the short run, a perfectly competitive firm will produce the output for which price equals marginal cost *as long as that price is greater than or equal to average variable cost.* The point at which P = AVC is called the ***shutdown point.*** Because of the relationship between marginal and average, the point at which P = AVC = MC is the minimum point on the AVC curve.

Figure 3.2 shows the firm's short-run supply curve. P_0 is the shutdown price for the firm; above P_0 the short-run supply curve is the marginal cost curve. Note that for prices below P_1 but above P_0 the firm produces output in the short run even though its economic profits are negative.[†] Economic profits are shown as the area of a rectangle with length equal to the quantity of output being produced and width equal to the difference between price and average cost at that quantity. For example, profits at q_2 equal the red rectangle in Figure 3.2.

Now consider the case in which some fixed costs are *not* sunk costs. For example, assume that a firm rents equipment for $300 per year but can return the equipment

FIGURE 3.2 **A Perfectly Competitive Firm's Short-Run Supply Curve**

The firm's short-run supply curve is vertical at an output of zero for all market prices less than P_0, the minimum of AVC. For prices above P_0, the supply curve is identical to the firm's short-run marginal cost curve, SRMC.

*TR > TVC implies that $(q \cdot P) - (q \cdot AVC) > 0$. This can be rewritten as $q(P - AVC) > 0$, or P > AVC.

[†]Profits = TR − TC, where TR is total revenue and TC is total costs. Because TR = P · q and TC = AC · q, profits can be written as $q(P - AC)$. In Figure 3.2, if price is above P_0 but below P_1, P < AC, implying that economic profits are negative.

within the year and receive $100 back. The fixed cost is $300; the sunk cost is $200. The firm's avoidable costs equal its variable costs *plus* $100, the recoverable portion of its fixed costs. To produce in the short run, total revenues must be greater than or equal to avoidable costs, raising the shutdown price.

In general, the higher the recoverable portion of fixed costs, the further the shutdown price is above average variable costs. In the extreme case all fixed costs are avoidable, and price must equal average cost in order for a firm to produce in the short run.

APPLICATION 3.1

Short-Run Losses in the Airline Industry

The airline industry was hit hard in 2001. In the aftermath of a recession and the events of September 11, American Airlines reported a loss of $1.8 billion in 2001, Delta Airlines a loss of $1.2 billion, and US Airways a loss of $2.1 billion. The losses forced US Airways to file for bankruptcy protection in 2002; despite that protection and subsequent reorganization, the successor company continued to lose money. After losing $174 million for the nine months ending on December 31, 2003 and $611 million in 2004, US Airways filed again for bankruptcy protection in September of 2004. Things also did not improve for American or Delta. American's reported losses amounted to $3.5 billion in 2002, $1.2 billion in 2003, and $761 million in 2004; Delta lost $1.3 billion in 2002, $773 million in 2003, and $5.2 billion in 2004. Finally, in September 2005, Delta also filed for bankruptcy protection.

The early years of the twenty-first century were hardly the first years of losses for the airline industry. In 1992, American Airlines reported a loss of $475 million, Delta Airlines a loss of $565 million, and US Airways a loss of $601 million. To make matters worse, because of the economic recession of the early 1990s, 1992 was the third consecutive year of large losses in the airline industry. The industry had also suffered losses from 1980 through 1982. Despite these years of consecutive economic losses, major carriers like American, Delta, and US Airways kept selling tickets and carrying passengers.

Why don't the major carriers shut down in years when they report substantial net losses? If they do shut down, they would still lose their fixed costs, with the largest fixed costs for the airlines being the interest payments on loans they made to purchase equipment such as airplanes and ground machinery. Unless they could resell these planes and equipment (an unlikely scenario in a highly competitive industry in which several firms were reporting losses), the airlines would have to pay these fixed costs even if they closed down. By operating, the airlines are able to more than cover their total variable cost, so it makes sense for them to continue to fly in the short run. Of course, as we move from the short run to the long run, we expect that some airlines will go out of business if the net losses continue. ∎

Long Run

In the long run, all inputs are variable and a firm will leave an industry if it is earning negative economic profits. In the long run, therefore, a profit-maximizing firm will produce only if total revenue is greater than or equal to total costs; that is, the firm produces in the long run only if price is greater than or equal to long-run average costs. The firm's long-run supply curve is simply its marginal cost curve above the minimum point on the long-run average total cost curve. For any price above the

minimum point on the average total cost curve, the firm will earn positive economic profits. For any price below this minimum, the firm will not produce in the long run.

3.1.3 The Market Supply Curve and Equilibrium

The short-run market supply curve is derived by choosing a price and adding up the quantities of output produced by each firm at that price. (Remember that the number of firms in the industry in the short run is fixed.) Market equilibrium is the intersection of the market demand and market supply curves. At the equilibrium price, the quantity supplied by producers is equal to the quantity demanded by consumers. Figure 3.3 shows short-run equilibrium for the market and for a representative firm. In this figure, P_0 is the minimum of the firm's average variable cost and P_1 is the short-run equilibrium price. The equilibrium quantity produced by each firm is q_1 and the equilibrium quantity for the market is Q_1.*

In the short run a perfectly competitive firm may be making positive, negative, or normal (zero) economic profits. In Figure 3.3, for example, the firm is earning excess (above normal) economic profits: Price is greater than average total costs. Profits are shown as the red rectangle in Figure 3.3(a).

Because resources are mobile, however, no firm can make either positive or negative economic profits in the long run. Positive profits induce entry, which increases supply and reduces price, whereas negative profits cause firms to leave. Exit decreases supply and increases price. In long-run equilibrium, therefore, price must equal average

(a) Firm (b) Market demand and supply

FIGURE 3.3 **Short-Run Equilibrium for a Representative Firm and the Market**

In panel (b), the market equilibrium price is P_1. In panel (a), a representative firm takes the market price, P_1, as given and maximizes profit by producing q_1, where price equals marginal cost. In this case, price exceeds average total cost at q_1, so the firm earns positive economic profit of $q_1(P_1 - ATC_1)$, which equals the red area.

*$Q_1 = nq_1$, where n is the number of firms in the industry.

cost so that economic profits equal zero. But remember that price is also equal to short-run *and* long-run marginal cost at the profit-maximizing level of output for the perfectly competitive firm. The long-run equilibrium price must thus equal P*, where short-run marginal cost, long-run marginal cost, short-run average cost, and long-run average cost are all equal. Figure 3.4 shows long-run equilibrium.

3.1.4 Properties of Competitive Equilibrium

The perfectly competitive model serves as a valuable reference point because of the desirable properties of long-run equilibrium. The equilibrium resource allocation in a competitive economy is *efficient,* meaning that no possible reallocation of resources will make one market participant (consumer or firm) better off without hurting another. All mutual gains from trade have been achieved.

One important type of efficiency concerns the level of output being produced and purchased. Efficiency in the level of output, called **allocative efficiency,** requires that the marginal benefit of producing another unit of output equal its marginal cost. If the marginal benefit is greater than marginal cost, too little of the good is being produced; if marginal benefit is less than marginal cost, too much is being produced. In competitive equilibrium, price, a measure of the value a consumer places on the *last* unit bought, equals the marginal cost to society of producing that last unit. This ensures that the socially optimal quantity of the good is produced.

Competitive equilibrium also exhibits *efficiency in production.* Figure 3.4 indicates that in long-run equilibrium each firm is producing at the minimum point on its

FIGURE 3.4 **Long-Run Equilibrium for a Representative Firm and the Market**

In long-run equilibrium, no firm can make either positive or negative economic profits; price must equal average cost so that economic profits equal zero. But a perfectly competitive firm chooses to operate where price equals marginal cost. Consequently, the long-run equilibrium for the firm occurs at the minimum of LRAC where LRAC = LRMC = SRAC = SRMC. P* is the long-run equilibrium price; each firm produces q*. At this price and output level, there is no incentive for entry into or exit from this market.

long-run average cost curve. Output is produced using the least costly combination of inputs. Furthermore, high-cost firms will be forced to exit the market.

A third characteristic of competitive equilibrium is that each perfectly competitive firm earns zero economic profits in long-run equilibrium. Therefore, productive resources receive only their opportunity cost and nothing more.

3.2 Introduction to Welfare Economics

The perfectly competitive model serves as an important reference point for industrial organization economists. To study the economic cost of a departure from perfect competition, economists use the two related concepts of *consumer surplus* and *producer surplus*. For example, economists often evaluate the welfare effects of changes in market structure or of government policies by looking at changes in consumer and producer surplus.

Consumer surplus is the difference between the maximum amount consumers are willing to pay for a good and the amount they actually pay. Suppose a consumer is willing to pay a maximum of $50 for a sweater but is actually able to purchase the sweater for $40. She would receive $10 in consumer surplus. In general, the demand curve indicates the value to consumers of consuming additional units of a good. We thus measure consumer surplus by the area bounded above by the market demand curve and below by the market price, as shown by triangle ABC in Figure 3.5. Note that no consumer surplus is associated with the fiftieth unit of output; that unit of output would not be purchased at any price higher than $40. For the demand curve pictured in Figure 3.5, consumer surplus equals $1000: $\frac{1}{2}(50 \times \$(80 - 40))$.

Producer surplus is analogous to consumer surplus. *Producer surplus* is the difference between the market price the producer receives for selling a unit of output and its reservation supply price, the lowest price for which firms would be willing to produce. For example, if it costs $20 to produce the first sweater and the market price is $40, the producer surplus on that sweater is $20. Since marginal cost increases with output, the producer surplus will be smaller for output after the first sweater. For example, if the marginal cost of the twenty-fifth sweater is $30, then the producer surplus on that unit would be $10. Because the supply curve represents the marginal cost of producing, producer surplus is the area to the left of the supply curve, bounded above by the market price. This is shown in Figure 3.5 as triangle BCD; producer surplus equals $500, the area of this triangle: $\frac{1}{2}(50 \times \$(40 - 20))$.

APPLICATION 3.2

Consumer and Producer Surplus
and the Basic Theory of the Gains from Trade

Economists realize that there are important links between the material covered in international trade courses and the material covered in industrial organization courses. We can highlight one of the links using consumer and producer surplus to examine the gains from international trade.

Suppose that the United States is initially closed to all foreign trade in good X and that good X is produced in perfectly competitive markets in both the United States and

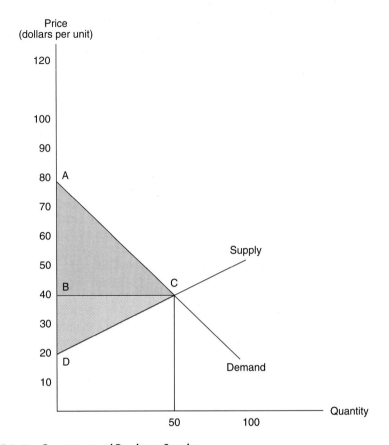

FIGURE 3.5 Consumer and Producer Surplus

At the competitive price of $40 and output of 50, consumers enjoy a consumer surplus equal to triangle ABC, which is $\frac{1}{2}(80 - 40)50 = 1000$. This surplus is the difference between the maximum amount consumers are willing to pay for a good and the amount they actually pay. Producer surplus at this price and output level is the area of triangle BCD, $\frac{1}{2}(40 - 20)50 = 500$; this measures the difference between the amount the seller actually receives from selling a unit of output and the reservation supply price, the lowest price for which firms would be willing to produce. Consumer and producer surplus are used to assess how well-off consumers and firms are in any given market outcome.

the rest of the world. There are many ways to prevent trade, the most common being prohibitive tariffs or import restrictions. The Japanese, for example, have long restricted rice imports in this manner. The graph on the next page depicts the two markets: on the left is the market in the United States, and on the right is the market in the rest of the world (ROW). In the absence of trade between the United States and the rest of the world, the equilibrium price will be P_4 in the United States and P_2 in the rest of the world. Total consumer surplus in the United States equals the light red triangle A, and total producer surplus in the United States equals the sum of gray areas B and D.

Suppose the United States decides to permit trade in good X. Because the price of good X in the United States, P_4, is greater than the price in the rest of the world, P_2, firms in the rest of the world will want to export good X to the United States. To determine how much these foreign firms will be willing to export at prices greater than P_2, take the horizontal difference between the supply curve in the rest of the world, S_{ROW}, and the demand curve in the rest of the world, D_{ROW}. For example, at a price of P_3, foreign firms are willing to export $q_3 - q_1$ units of good X (represented by the distance of the red line segment) to the United States. By adding the amount that foreign firms are willing to export to the United States at every price above P_2 to the United States supply curve without trade, S_{US}, we obtain the United States supply curve with trade, S_{US+FOR}.

If trade is permitted, the price in the United States will decline to P_3, where the supply curve with trade, S_{US+FOR}, equals the demand curve in the United States. With trade, American firms will supply Q_1 units of good X to the United States market, and foreign firms will export $Q_3 - Q_1$ units of good X, which by construction must equal $q_3 - q_1$ units of good X. The equilibrium price in the United States and the rest of the world must be equalized by free trade at P_3 or else there would be an incentive to sell more in the market with the higher price. As a result of trade, total consumer surplus in the United States has *increased* by the sum of areas B and C, so that total consumer surplus is equal to the sum of areas A, B, and C. However, total producer surplus earned by American firms equals the light gray area D and has *declined* by the dark gray area B.

What is the net welfare effect of the decision to permit trade? Consumer surplus increased by the areas B and C, but producer surplus among American firms has decreased by the gray area B. Because the area B represents a gain to American consumers and a loss to American producers, it has no net impact on American welfare. The dark red area C, however, represents a net welfare gain to American consumers. The net impact on American consumers and producers of permitting trade is positive. This increase in welfare is called the ***gains from trade.***

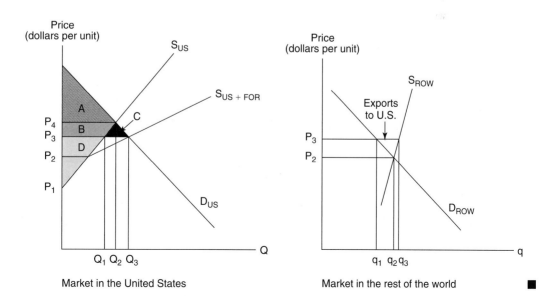

Market in the United States Market in the rest of the world

3.3 The Economics of Monopoly

3.3.1 The Relationship Between Marginal Revenue and Price

A *monopoly* is the sole producer of a good for which there are no close substitutes. Thus, a monopolist *is* the industry and faces the market demand curve for its product. That demand curve, like any market demand curve, slopes downward, and the monopolist can operate at any point along that market demand curve. It can choose a high price and sell a relatively small quantity of output, or it can choose a lower price and sell more output.

A monopolist, like any profit-maximizing firm, will choose to produce the quantity for which marginal revenue equals marginal cost. Unlike a perfectly competitive firm, however, marginal revenue for a monopolist does *not* equal price. To understand why, recall the definition of marginal revenue: the additional revenue a firm obtains from selling one additional unit of output. Because a monopolist faces the downward-sloping market demand curve, the only way it can sell an additional unit of output is by lowering the price on *all* units.* Although it gains revenue from the additional unit of output, it loses revenue on those units previously sold at a higher price. Figure 3.6 shows the trade-off faced by a monopoly. At P_1 the monopoly sells Q_1 units of output, and total revenue is the area of the rectangle OP_1AQ_1. To sell $Q_1 + 1$ units of output, the monopolist must lower price to P_2; total revenue becomes the area $OP_2B(Q_1 + 1)$. The monopoly gains area $Q_1CB(Q_1 + 1)$ in total revenue. The width of this rectangle is 1 and its height is P_2, so the area of the gain in revenue is P_2. However, by lowering price, the monopoly also loses area P_1ACP_2, which is the original quantity sold, Q_1, times the change in price. Marginal revenue is the sum of the two areas. Thus for a monopoly marginal revenue is always less than price. The precise relationship is given by:[†]

$$MR = P + Q\frac{\Delta P}{\Delta Q} = P\left(1 + \frac{Q}{P}\frac{\Delta P}{\Delta Q}\right). \qquad [3.1]$$

Because

$$e_D = \frac{\Delta Q}{\Delta P}\frac{P}{Q}, \qquad [3.2]$$

we have
$$MR = P\left(1 + \frac{1}{e_D}\right) = P\left(1 - \frac{1}{|e_D|}\right), \qquad [3.3]$$

where e_D is the price elasticity of demand.

Graphically, the marginal revenue curve lies below the market demand curve for each level of output. Figure 3.7 shows that Q_M is the profit-maximizing quantity of

*This argument assumes that the monopolist is not able to practice price discrimination. Price discrimination is considered in detail in Chapter 15.

[†]To derive this relationship, begin with TR = PQ. For a small change in quantity,

$$\Delta TR = P\Delta Q + Q\Delta P, \text{ so } MR = \frac{\Delta TR}{\Delta Q} = P + Q\frac{\Delta P}{\Delta Q}.$$

$$\text{Using calculus, } MR = \frac{dTR}{dQ} = P + Q\frac{dP}{dQ} = P\left(1 + \frac{Q}{P}\frac{dP}{dQ}\right).$$

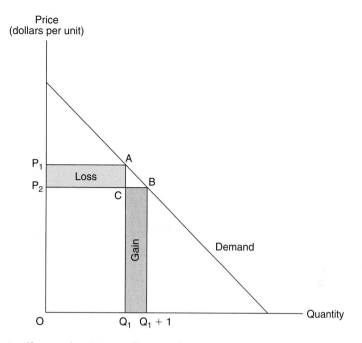

FIGURE 3.6 **Changes in a Monopolist's Total Revenue Resulting from a Price Cut**

If output increases by one unit from Q_1 to $Q_1 + 1$, the monopoly gains area $Q_1CB(Q_1 + 1)$ in revenue, which equals $P_2\Delta Q = P_2$. However, on the units produced up to Q_1, the monopolist loses revenue equal to area P_1ACP_2, which equals $Q_1\Delta P$. Marginal revenue is the sum of these two areas, or $P_2 + Q_1\Delta P$. Because $\Delta P < 0$, this is clearly less than P_2; marginal revenue for a monopolist is less than price.

output for the monopolist; here MR = MC. The profit-maximizing price corresponding to this quantity is P_M, which is found from the market demand curve.

Figure 3.7 also illustrates a relationship that we will use extensively later in this book. If the demand curve is linear, then the marginal revenue curve is also linear. Furthermore, the marginal revenue curve has the *same vertical intercept* as the demand curve but is *twice as steeply sloped,* so that the horizontal intercept of the marginal revenue curve is half the horizontal intercept of the demand curve.

To see the relationship between a linear demand curve and its marginal revenue curve, begin with the formula for marginal revenue given in Equation 3.1:

$$MR = P + Q\frac{\Delta P}{\Delta Q}.$$

If the linear demand curve is given by the equation $P = a - bQ$, then:*

$$MR = (a - bQ) + Q\frac{\Delta P}{\Delta Q}.$$ [3.4]

*Using calculus, TR = $(a - bQ)Q = aQ - bQ^2$ so $\dfrac{dTR}{dQ} = a - 2bQ$.

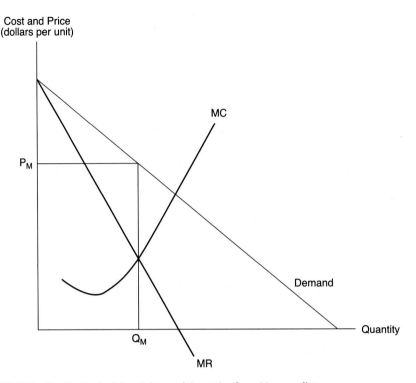

FIGURE 3.7 Profit-Maximizing Price and Quantity for a Monopolist

The monopolist maximizes profit by producing the quantity of output for which marginal revenue equals marginal cost, Q_M. The profit-maximizing price, P_M, is found from the market demand curve. This graph also illustrates the fact that the marginal revenue curve corresponding to a linear demand curve has the same vertical intercept as the demand curve but is twice as steeply sloped.

Since $\dfrac{\Delta P}{\Delta Q}$ is the slope of the linear demand curve, it equals $-b$ and:

$$MR = (a - bQ) + Q(-b) = a - 2bQ. \hspace{2em} [3.5]$$

If, for example, the demand curve is $P = 100 - 3Q$, then $MR = 100 - 6Q$. In later chapters we will refer to this relationship between demand and marginal revenue as the "twice as steep rule."

3.3.2 Elasticities, the Degree of Market Power, and the Lerner Index

Throughout this book we make use of the concepts of elasticity, market power, and the Lerner Index. This section shows how these concepts relate to one another.

Any firm that has the ability to set price above marginal cost, the perfectly competitive equilibrium price, is said to have **market power** or *monopoly power*. While we know that the monopolist will choose the profit-maximizing price-quantity combina-

tion on the market demand curve, we do not know how high the monopoly price will be in relation to marginal cost. How much can the monopolist raise price above marginal cost? What constraints does it face on raising price significantly above marginal cost?

We can answer these questions using the relationship between marginal revenue and price introduced in Equation 3.3:

$$MR = P\left(1 - \frac{1}{|e_D|}\right).$$

Combining the formula for marginal revenue with the fact that marginal revenue equals marginal cost at the optimum price-quantity combination and rearranging terms yields a measure of the degree of market power called the **Lerner Index**, or the monopoly markup:*

$$\text{Lerner Index} = \frac{P - MC}{P} = \frac{1}{|e_D|}. \qquad [3.6]$$

The Lerner Index indicates that even a monopolist has only limited control over price. If the price elasticity of demand is high, as illustrated in Figure 3.8(a), then a monopolist's profit-maximizing price is still relatively close to its marginal cost. A less elastic demand curve such as that shown in Figure 3.8(b) results in a larger monopoly markup. If the elasticity equals -10, for example, the Lerner Index equals 0.1 and the gap between price and marginal cost is quite low. If the elasticity equals -1.5, however, then the Lerner Index is 0.67 and the gap is considerably larger.

3.4 Welfare Comparison

Earlier we noted that equilibrium in a perfectly competitive market exhibits several highly desirable characteristics. How does monopoly compare? Why do economists worry about market power? The major concern is that monopoly misallocates resources by producing the "wrong" amount of a good, where price does not equal marginal cost. In other words, monopoly is *always* allocatively inefficient. Figure 3.9 compares a market under perfect competition and under monopoly, assuming costs are the same under both industry structures. In this figure the perfectly competitive output is Q_{PC} and the perfectly competitive price is P_{PC}. Consumer surplus under perfect competition is shown by ABC. Producer surplus under perfect competition is area CBD. What happens to these surpluses if the industry is monopolized? Under monopoly, with profit-maximizing quantity Q_M and price P_M, consumer surplus is the much smaller triangle AEF. Producer surplus under monopoly increases to area EFGD. (Note

*For profit maximization MR = MC:

$$MR = P\left(1 - \frac{1}{|e_D|}\right) = MC$$

$$P - \frac{P}{|e_D|} = MC \Rightarrow P - MC = \frac{P}{|e_D|} \Rightarrow \frac{P - MC}{P} = \frac{1}{|e_D|}.$$

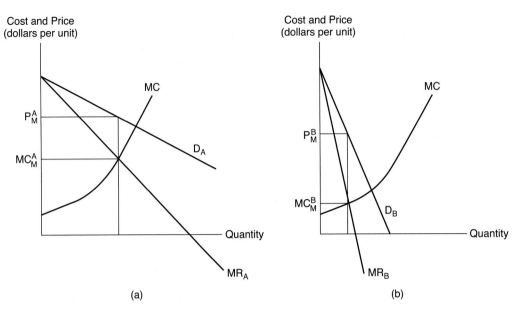

FIGURE 3.8 Effect of Price Elasticity of Demand on the Gap Between Profit-Maximizing Price and Marginal Cost

The monopolist's ability to raise price above marginal cost depends on its elasticity of demand. If the market demand curve is relatively elastic, such as the curve shown in panel (a), the monopolist's profit-maximizing price is relatively close to its marginal cost. A less elastic demand curve, such as that shown in panel (b), results in a relatively larger gap between price and marginal cost.

that, by cutting back on quantity and increasing price compared to the competitive outcome, the monopolist does give up area HBG in surplus but gains a larger area, CEFH.) The part of excess monopoly profits equal to area CEFH represents a transfer from consumers of the good to the owner(s) of the monopoly. Thus, this area is *not* a loss from society's point of view, although we may be concerned about the effects of this transfer on the distribution of income. The area of the triangle FBG, however, represents a loss of social welfare; it reflects the potential surplus that would have gone to some group—consumers or producers—under perfect competition. This area, called the *deadweight loss,* thus measures the misallocation of resources due to monopoly. By producing where price is greater than marginal cost, the monopoly produces too few units of the good.

It is very important to understand that this problem arises because the monopoly price is *greater* than the marginal cost of the good. The demand curve indicates the prices that consumers are willing to pay for output beyond Q_M, while the supply curve shows the marginal cost of producing this additional output. Even though consumers would be willing to pay more for an additional unit of the good than it would cost society to produce that unit, the monopolist does *not* produce it. This is the fundamental problem associated with monopoly power.

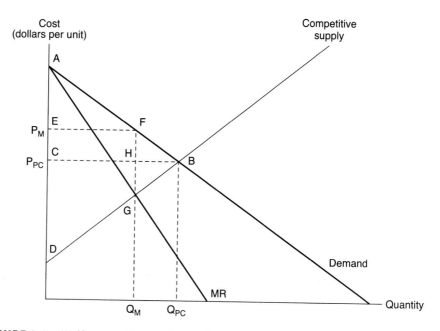

FIGURE 3.9 **Welfare Loss Due to Monopoly**

Under perfect competition, output is Q_{PC} and price is P_{PC}; consumer surplus is area ABC and producer surplus is area CBD. The monopolist produces Q_M priced at P_M; consumer surplus is AEF and producer surplus is EFGD. The deadweight loss resulting from monopoly is area FBG.

3.4.1 Measurement of the Costs of Market Power

How large is the welfare loss due to the misallocation of resources resulting from market power? The first economist to attempt to measure the magnitude of the deadweight loss was Arnold Harberger.[1] He recognized that, assuming constant LRMC = LRAC, the deadweight loss (DWL) could be measured by the formula $DWL = \frac{1}{2}r^2Se_D$, where $r = \dfrac{P_M - P_{PC}}{P_{PC}}$, $S = P_{PC} \cdot Q_{PC}$ (revenue), and e_D is the elasticity of demand.* Using data on profit returns on capital from 73 manufacturing industries from 1924 through 1928, Harberger estimated that the deadweight loss due to monopoly power in the United States was less than 0.1 percent of GNP.

*With constant marginal cost:

$$DWL = \tfrac{1}{2}(P_M - P_{PC})(Q_{PC} - Q_M) = \tfrac{1}{2}r^2Se_D$$

$$= \frac{1}{2}\left(\frac{P_M - P_{PC}}{P_{PC}}\right)\left(\frac{P_M - P_{PC}}{P_{PC}}\right)(P_{PC} \times Q_{PC})\left(\left|\frac{(Q_{PC} - Q_M)\,P_{PC}}{(P_M - P_{PC})\,Q_{PC}}\right|\right).$$

Everything cancels in the far right-hand term on the last line above, except:

$$DWL = \tfrac{1}{2}(P_M - P_{PC})(Q_{PC} - Q_M).$$

As you might imagine, Harberger's conclusion that deadweight loss was such a small percent of GNP resulted in much criticism and many further calculations.[2] Economists have examined Harberger's assumptions and his calculations, arguing that they led to an underestimate of the magnitude of deadweight loss. Critics assert that Harberger's assumed price elasticities of demand were too low* and that his assumed competitive rate of profit was too high.[†] Additionally, using industry profit rates causes an aggregation bias by averaging high monopoly profit rates with losses of other firms in the industry. Some of the revised estimates put the deadweight loss as high as 4 to 7 percent of GNP.[3]

Economists have identified other important possible costs of monopolization in addition to the deadweight loss, arguing that significant rent-seeking costs are involved in trying to gain and maintain monopoly power. A monopoly, for example, may spend "too much" on advertising, product differentiation, or investment in excess production capacity. Tullock and Posner argue that the welfare costs of monopoly include expenditures on lobbying and campaign contributions intended to obtain tariff protection, patent protection, and other preferential government treatment.[4] In the extreme, a firm would be willing to spend an amount up to the potential monopoly profits to become a monopolist. Such rent-seeking activities would increase the welfare costs of a monopoly.

Two economists who considered this issue carefully, Keith Cowling and Dennis Mueller, used advertising expenditures to approximate the costs of monopolization to society.[5] Adding these costs to their estimate of deadweight loss, they estimated that the welfare cost of monopolization may be as high as 13 percent of GNP.

APPLICATION 3.3
Monopoly Rent-Seeking in the Pharmaceutical Industry

Unlike the governments of most other countries, the government of the United States does not regulate prescription drug prices. Not surprisingly, then, prescription drug prices are higher in the United States than in other countries. For example, in late 2004, a month's supply of 20-milligram Lipitor, a cholesterol-lowering drug made by Pfizer, cost a customer in the Bronx about $118 while PharmacyinCanada.com, a Canadian online pharmacy, sold the same amount of the drug for $79.* This is typical: Prescription medications from U.S. suppliers often cost 40 to 70 percent more than in Canada. Because of this price differential, and because consumers are increasingly concerned about the high cost of their prescription medications, pressure has been building to

*Harberger assumed that price elasticities of demand in all industries were equal to 1 (in absolute value). This assumption implies that the firm is not maximizing profits because a profit-maximizing monopoly will always operate at a level of output for which the elasticity of demand is greater than 1.

†Harberger used the average profit rate of his sample industries as a measure of the competitive profit rate. Critics contend that this method automatically led to an underestimate of the deadweight loss because of the characteristics of Harberger's sample. His sample was limited to manufacturing industries, a sector that tends to have a higher rate of return than other sectors, such as agriculture, retail, and service. According to Harberger's critics, because many manufacturing industries are somewhat monopolistic, averaging profit rates across manufacturing industries would lead to an overstatement of the "competitive" profit rate.

change U.S. law to allow pharmacists and wholesalers in the United States to import cheaper drugs from Canada and from other countries.

The pharmaceutical industry has been fighting hard against legislation that would make reimportation of drugs from other countries easier. In July of 2000, for example, when the House of Representatives passed legislation barring the Food and Drug Administration from enforcing a 1988 law banning reimportation of drugs, the pharmaceutical industry launched a major lobbying effort, sending lobbyists to Capitol Hill and running full-page newspaper ads warning that consumers' safety would be threatened by counterfeit or substandard imports. In 2003, Congress was again considering legislation to allow importation of less expensive drugs from other countries; the Pharmaceutical Research and Manufacturers Association of America, the industry's trade group, spent $8.5 million in lobbying against the bill. Individual pharmaceutical firms also devoted funds to lobbying. Overall, the industry spent more than $29 million in lobbying in the first half of 2003, with Eli Lilly & Co. anteing up $2.9 million, Bristol-Myers Squibb Co. spending $2.6 million, and Johnson & Johnson kicking in $2.2 million. So far, the fight has been successful; no federal legislation has been passed, although many state legislatures are currently considering drug importation laws. The pharmaceutical companies continue the battle, running ad campaigns designed to raise concerns among consumers about the safety of imported drugs.

Clearly, pharmaceutical industry executives are concerned about increased price competition from abroad and the loss of their economic profits. The expenditures on lobbying and advertising are a good example of rent-seeking costs by firms trying to protect their market power.

*Eduardo Porter, "Importing Less Expensive Drugs Not Seen as Cure for U.S. Woes," *New York Times,* October 16, 2004, A.1.

Sources: Laurie McGinley, "Drug Industry Seeks to Prevent Importation of Cheaper Medicines," *The Wall Street Journal,* July 19, 2000, p. 1; "Drug Firms Spend Millions to Battle Importation Plan," *The Wall Street Journal,* October 13, 2003, p. A.15; Sarah Lueck and Anna Wilde Matthews, "Drug Makers Not Out of Woods," *The Wall Street Journal,* April 13, 2004, p. A.4; Eduardo Porter, "Importing Less Expensive Drugs Not Seen as Cure for U.S. Woes," *New York Times,* October 16, 2004, A.1; "Warnings Regarding Safety of Imported Drugs Force Americans to Buy in Homeland," PR Newswire US, June 15, 2005. Online. LexisNexis Academic, July 26, 2005. ∎

Finally, we noted in Chapter 2 that in less competitive markets, there is less pressure on firms to use inputs efficiently. Inefficient monopolists may not be driven out of the market even in the long run. This X-inefficiency results in higher costs for a monopoly. Figure 3.10 illustrates the welfare implications of a monopolist operating under higher costs than a competitive industry. If monopolization raises costs, the deadweight loss triangle is larger. In addition, the costs of producing the monopoly output level are higher. The important welfare point is that if increasing competition in monopolized markets would lead to reduced costs, then estimates of welfare losses based on deadweight loss triangles such as Harberger's will be far too low.[6]

While the controversy over the welfare cost of market power has not been resolved, it is possible to step back and make three observations. First, even a relatively small percent of GNP represents a considerable amount of resources. In a $12 trillion economy, 1 percent is $120 billion! Second, any strategic behavior on the part of firms intended to obtain or protect their monopoly positions raises the costs of

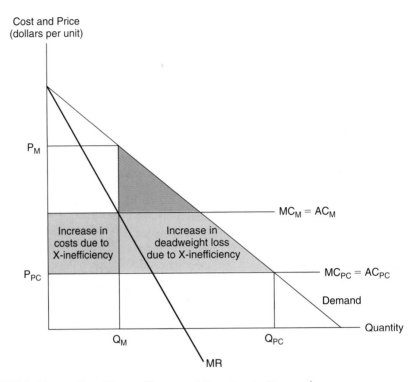

FIGURE 3.10 Welfare Effects of Increased Costs Due to Monopoly

If monopolization of an industry raises costs, the deadweight loss is larger because the monopoly restricts output further. In addition, the costs of producing the monopoly level of output are higher.

monopolization substantially. Third, in some industries, the potential gains to society from decreasing monopoly power are large.

3.4.2 Cautions

So far we have reviewed the theories of perfect competition and monopoly. We have also looked at the welfare comparison between perfect competition and monopoly. At this point it is useful to consider certain complicating factors—reasons why policymakers might not want to attack firms with market power as aggressively as simple theory might suggest.

One important reason for allowing a firm to possess at least some degree of market power is the existence of economies of scale in production. If a firm's long-run average cost curve decreases significantly as the quantity of output it produces increases, then it would be inefficient to have output produced by many small firms. In the extreme case, called a ***natural monopoly***, one firm can serve the market at lower average cost than can multiple firms. We return to the importance of economies of scale in Chapter 4.

A second reason to hesitate before recommending that policymakers stamp out all monopoly power is concern about the rate of technological change. Our simple welfare comparison of perfect competition and monopoly is a static comparison—a comparison at one specific point in time. As we shall discover, theory suggests that firms possessing market power may be more innovative than perfectly competitive firms. Perfectly competitive firms, for example, may lack the resources necessary to invest in research and development (R&D). Consider farmers, who do not typically do agricultural research. If there is a connection between market power and innovation, we might willingly accept some deadweight loss today in return for the considerable benefits associated with new products and new production techniques in the future. Recent antitrust policy has given increasing weight to concerns about technological change. Technological change is discussed in much greater detail in Chapter 14.

Finally, our comparison of perfect competition and monopoly must be reconsidered in light of the second-best theorem. There are many instances in the real world in which perfect competition is not feasible or even desirable. Inputs such as raw materials and managerial talent may be scarce, so that there cannot be many firms in an industry. Substantial economies of scale may dictate an industry structure in which firms possess at least some market power. Lipsey and Lancaster examined the welfare considerations of imposing perfect competition in some but not all markets in the economy.[7] Their second-best theorem states that overall welfare *may* improve by selectively achieving perfect competition—but it may not. In a second-best world, it is impossible to give general advice to policymakers.

3.5 Present Value and Discounting

In our consideration of the models of competition and monopoly, we distinguished between two time periods, the short run and the long run. In the short run, the firm could not adjust all inputs and no entry into or exit from the industry could occur. When we arrived at the long-run equilibrium, entry or exit had occurred, resulting in zero economic profits, and the firm had adjusted the level of all inputs optimally. Yet this long run was like the short run in that it was envisioned as a single market period.

However, as we begin to consider strategic interaction among firms, it makes more sense to think of the long run as a series of individual, finite periods. In this case, a firm may need to choose between an action that yields some profits soon and an action that yields larger profits in some future period. How does a firm evaluate the trade-off between current and future profits? We consider this question in this section.

We begin by noting that, with multiple time periods, firms want to maximize *long-run*, not short-run, profits. Understanding long-run profit maximization requires understanding the economic concepts of **present value** and **discounting**. Because X dollars invested today at an interest rate i would increase in value to $X(1 + i)$ dollars in one year, $X(1 + i)(1 + i) = X(1 + i)^2$ in two years, and $X(1 + i)^t$ in t years, the present value of $X(1 + i)^t$ dollars received t years from today is X dollars.* By

*If X = $100 and i = 10%, then the present value of $110 received in one year is $100 because it is necessary to invest $100 today to receive $110 in one year. Similarly the present value of $121 received in two years is $100 today.

similar reasoning, the promise to pay X dollars t years from today has a present value of:*

$$\text{present value} = \frac{X}{(1 + i)^t}.$$

Let π_t represent a typical firm's profits in time period t, and $(1 + i)$ represent the rate at which the firm is willing to trade future for present income. The "i" in the term $(1 + i)$ is referred to as the firm's **discount rate.** π_{pv} represents the firm's **present value of profits** in the following equation:

$$\pi_{pv} = \frac{\pi_1}{(1 + i)} + \frac{\pi_2}{(1 + i)^2} + \frac{\pi_3}{(1 + i)^3} + \cdots + \frac{\pi_n}{(1 + i)^n} \qquad [3.7]$$

or:

$$\pi_{pv} = \sum_{t=1}^{n} \frac{\pi_t}{(1 + i)^t}.$$

The maximization of long-run profits implies the maximization of π_{pv}. From Equation 3.7 it is apparent that the maximization of long-run profits depends not only on the flow of economic profits, π_t, but also, and critically, on the discount rate i. Firms with short time horizons will have high discount rates and will want to earn high profits in early periods even if it means sacrificing future profits, and firms with longer time horizons and lower discount rates will want to sacrifice current profits to earn higher profits in the future.[†] Assuming n goes to infinity and π_t is constant and equal to π for all values of t, it is easy to prove that:[‡]

$$\pi_{pv} = \sum_{t=1}^{\infty} \frac{\pi}{(1 + i)^t} = \frac{\pi}{(1 + i)} + \frac{\pi}{(1 + i)^2} + \frac{\pi}{(1 + i)^3} + \cdots = \frac{\pi}{i}. \qquad [3.8]$$

The above relationship can be generalized for any sum beginning at any time t, not just for t = 1. Consider the following sum:

$$\pi_{pv} = \sum_{t=c}^{\infty} \frac{\pi}{(1 + i)^t} = \frac{\pi}{(1 + i)^c} + \frac{\pi}{(1 + i)^{c+1}} + \frac{\pi}{(1 + i)^{c+2}} + \cdots, \qquad [3.9]$$

*At an interest rate of 10 percent, the promise to pay $100 in one year has a present value of $90.91 because:

$$\text{present value of \$100 received in one year} = \frac{100}{(1.1)} = 90.909090.$$

[†]For example, a firm owned by an individual nearing retirement with no heirs might have a very high discount rate.

[‡]This result can be obtained by using simple algebra as follows:

$$\pi_{pv} = \frac{\pi}{(1 + i)} + \frac{\pi}{(1 + i)^2} + \frac{\pi}{(1 + i)^3} + \cdots$$

$$\pi_{pv} = \frac{1}{(1 + i)}\left[\pi + \frac{\pi}{(1 + i)} + \frac{\pi}{(1 + i)^2} + \cdots\right]$$

$$\pi_{pv} = \frac{1}{(1 + i)}(\pi + \pi_{pv})$$

$$\pi_{pv}(1 + i) = \pi + \pi_{pv}$$

$$\pi_{pv} = \frac{\pi}{i}.$$

where c is any number less than, equal to, or greater than zero.

Factoring out $\dfrac{1}{(1 + i)^{c-1}}$ yields:

$$\pi_{pv} = \frac{1}{(1 + i)^{c-1}} \left[\frac{\pi}{(1 + i)} + \frac{\pi}{(1 + i)^2} + \frac{\pi}{(1 + i)^3} + \cdots \right] = \frac{\pi}{i(1 + i)^{c-1}}. \qquad [3.10]$$

For example, consider the following three infinite sums. The first sum begins at $t = 1$:

$$\frac{100}{(1 + .1)} + \frac{100}{(1 + .1)^2} + \frac{100}{(1 + .1)^3} + \cdots = \frac{100}{.1} = 1000.$$

The second sum begins at $t = 4$:

$$\frac{100}{(1 + .1)^4} + \frac{100}{(1 + .1)^5} + \frac{100}{(1 + .1)^6} + \cdots$$

$$= \frac{100}{.1(1 + .1)^3} = \frac{100}{.1(1.1)^3} = \frac{100}{.1(1.33)} = 751.88.$$

The third sum begins at $t = -4$:

$$\frac{100}{(1 + .1)^{-4}} + \frac{100}{(1 + .1)^{-3}} + \frac{100}{(1 + .1)^{-2}} + \cdots$$

$$= \frac{100}{.1(1 + .1)^{-5}} = \frac{100}{.1(1.1)^{-5}} = \frac{100}{\dfrac{.1}{(1.1)^5}} = \frac{100(1.1)^5}{.1} = 1610.$$

Knowing these summation formulas will prove to be extremely useful as we proceed through the remainder of the text.

3.6 Antitrust Policy Toward Monopolization

As we've seen, monopoly power is associated with inefficiencies, measured by the deadweight loss. However, in section 3.4.2, we explained that monopoly power may be economically justified if it is based on economies of scale or necessary for invention and innovation. Chapter 1 introduced the pieces of antitrust legislation in the United States; here, we consider the evolution of policy toward monopolization, cases brought under Section 2 of the Sherman Act. Our purpose is not to provide a comprehensive survey of cases over the past hundred-plus years but to help you understand the difficult task faced by policymakers who try to distinguish between cases of justified monopoly and cases of unjustified monopoly. Enforcement of Section 2 has ebbed and flowed with political trends, sometimes becoming fairly tight and sometimes becoming considerably looser. An understanding of antitrust policy, therefore, requires a historical as well as an economic perspective. We begin with an examination of early court interpretations and then show how these interpretations have changed over time.

3.6.1 Early Cases

STANDARD OIL OF NEW JERSEY CASE[8] (1911)—The *Standard Oil* case is unquestionably one of America's most famous legal cases. The case dealt with Standard's control of the oil refining industry during the last quarter of the nineteenth century. All of Standard Oil's actions seemed to be aimed at one objective: maintaining control over the oil refining business in the United States. Standard managed to maintain a 90 percent share for a long period by acquiring over 100 competitors through merger; controlling the major oil pipelines, which permitted it to cut off crude oil supplies from its competitors; obtaining freight rebates from railroads on not only its own shipments but its *competitors'* shipments as well; and, perhaps, using localized price cutting to drive its more stubborn competitors out of the market.*

The Supreme Court ruled unanimously against Standard Oil. As noted in Chapter 1, in his landmark decision Chief Justice White laid down his famous Rule of Reason doctrine, which declared that only unreasonable attempts to monopolize violated Section 2.

Chief Justice White emphasized Standard's intent and positive drive as being the key necessary to any conviction under Section 2. The significance of the *Standard Oil* decision from a legal and economic standpoint cannot be overstated. The decision firmly established the precedent that market power, in and of itself, is insufficient to condemn a firm under Section 2. Power must be combined with some effort to obtain and abuse that power. Standard Oil violated Section 2 not simply because it controlled 90 percent of the market, but because it went beyond the use of "normal methods of industrial development" to maintain control.

The Rule of Reason has resulted in cases that require proof of both the existence of market power and some effort to obtain that power through other than normal methods of business competition.

Immediately after the *Standard Oil* ruling, the Supreme Court handed down a companion decision in the *American Tobacco* case.[9] The points of law in the *American Tobacco* case were virtually identical to those in the *Standard Oil* case. Given American Tobacco's behavior, discussed in Application 3.4, it is not surprising that the Court condemned its conduct and ruled against the Tobacco Trust.

APPLICATION 3.4

American Tobacco's "Attempt to Monopolize"

Before 1890, five companies dominated the cigarette segment of the tobacco industry: W. Duke, Allen and Ginter, Kinney Tobacco, W.S. Kimball, and Goodwin. These firms, which accounted for 95 percent of domestic cigarette production, merged in January 1890 to form the American Tobacco Company, with James B. Duke as the key player in the consolidation. Shortly after the consolidation, the new corporation closed Goodwin, one of its own members. According to the government, this was just the beginning of a series of aggressive acquisitions followed by aggressive dismantlings.

*An interesting question is whether Standard Oil pursued predatory pricing—aggressively expanding output and cutting price to drive out competitors. We consider predatory pricing in Chapter 11.

American Tobacco's behavior in the plug tobacco market is typical of its behavior overall. (Plug tobacco is chewing tobacco pressed into a round container.) In 1893 American approached several plug manufacturers to suggest possible mergers. When the plug producers refused, American embarked on a strategy designed to give it control of the competitors. As part of its pricing strategy, American created "fighting brands"—brands that were sold at prices below average total cost. Appropriately, one of these brands was named Battle Axe. Battle Axe, a small and relatively unimportant brand before the price war, sold for 50 cents per pound in 1891. During the so-called "Plug War" of 1895 to 1898, American cut the price of Battle Axe to 13 cents per pound. American also undertook massive advertising campaigns.

This was an expensive strategy in the short run: Between 1893 and 1898, American lost more than $4 million in the plug market. It did, however, gain control over the major plug manufacturers, shutting down its competitors after acquiring them when they were struggling. In 1899 American Tobacco had captured more than 90 percent of the market and earned a profit of 56 percent on sales.

Sources: United States v. American Tobacco Company, 221 U.S. 106 (1911); Don E. Waldman, *The Economics of Antitrust Cases and Analysis* (Boston: Little, Brown, 1986), pp. 47–48; Malcolm R. Burns, "Outside Intervention in Incumbentic Price Warfare: The Case of the 'Plug War' and the Union Tobacco Company," *Business History Review* 56 (Spring 1982). ∎

After the *Standard Oil* and *American Tobacco* precedents, the government won several additional victories during the next decade. In 1920, however, the next major Supreme Court ruling took a different turn, greatly affecting subsequent antitrust policy.

US STEEL CASE[10] (1920)—In the 1890s, the steel industry was characterized by periods of aggressive price competition. In fact, as the United States Steel Corporation was taking shape in 1900, steel prices were falling. US Steel was formed in 1901 through the consolidation of 12 major steel companies; at the time of its formation, US Steel accounted for over 65 percent of the industry's output. Unlike American Tobacco, US Steel chose not to undercut its competitors' prices but followed a path of cooperation.

US Steel cooperated through a variety of devices, including pools, associations, trade meetings, and most famously (or infamously), from 1907 until 1911, the "Gary dinners." At these dinners, Judge Elbert Gary, president of US Steel, invited competitors to "dinner" for the more or less expressed purpose of fixing and stabilizing prices.[11] The government brought a Section 2 case against US Steel, alleging illegal monopolization of the market.

By a 4–3 ruling, the Supreme Court acquitted US Steel and, in so doing, considerably weakened Section 2 for years to come. The four-Justice majority believed that US Steel could not control steel prices. The court reasoned that because US Steel had to conspire with its competitors to fix prices, it did not have monopoly power. This line of reasoning ignored the fact that if US Steel had chosen to discipline its competitors, it almost certainly could have maintained and even increased its market share.

Between 1920 and 1945 the *US Steel* precedent protected dominant firms that refrained from predatory actions from Section 2 attack. This policy changed abruptly, however, in 1945 with the handing down of the *Alcoa* decision.

3.6.2 The Alcoa Era

ALCOA CASE[12] (1945)—In 1937 the Justice Department charged the Aluminum Company of America (Alcoa) with monopolizing the aluminum ingot market. The District Court relied heavily on the *US Steel* precedent and dismissed the case, but the Justice Department appealed. The Supreme Court could not obtain a quorum of six justices to hear the case because four justices had previously been involved in the litigation of the case. As a result, the New York Court of Appeals served as the highest appeals court and under the leadership of Judge Learned Hand overturned the District Court ruling. Judge Hand's ruling established the major precedent for Section 2 cases for the next 25 years.

The correct market definition was the first issue addressed by Judge Hand.* The District Court had defined Alcoa's market share in 1937 as 33 percent by including secondary ingot (ingot produced from scrap aluminum) in the same market as primary ingot. Furthermore, the District Court had eliminated from the relevant market all ingots that Alcoa produced and then used in its vertically integrated fabrication operations. The Court of Appeals, however, ruled that because Alcoa produced virtually all primary aluminum, it indirectly controlled the secondary scrap market. According to the Court, Alcoa's market share was 90 percent of the relevant "primary aluminum ingot" market.

Once Judge Hand established that Alcoa had a 90 percent market share in 1937, he turned to the issue of Alcoa's intent. In keeping with typical judicial procedure, Judge Hand went to great lengths to make his ruling consistent with the *Standard Oil* Rule of Reason precedent. Yet in Alcoa there was little evidence of aggressive practices such as existed in the *Standard Oil* or *American Tobacco* cases. In fact, Alcoa's market power originated from a cost advantage associated with patents rather than predatory behavior. And its continued market domination resulted from high barriers to entry (especially economies of scale in the conversion of bauxite ore into aluminum oxide or alumina), vertical integration into all four stages of production, and a limit pricing policy that kept profits at moderate levels.†

Judge Hand's decision greatly reduced the government's burden in Section 2 cases. Essentially Hand ruled that once the government had proved that Alcoa had a monopoly, the government had gone far enough, *unless* Alcoa could prove that the monopoly was "thrust upon it" because of the existence of large economies of scale or patents. Hand went on to state that "unchallenged economic power deadens initiative, discourages thrift and depresses energy; that immunity from competition is a narcotic, and rivalry is a stimulant, to industrial progress; that the spur of constant stress is necessary to counteract an inevitable disposition to let well enough alone."

The *Alcoa* decision seemed to reverse the *US Steel* precedent and set a new one: A monopolist with an overwhelming market share violated Section 2 unless that market power had been thrust on it and was virtually unavoidable.

UNITED SHOE MACHINERY CASE[13] (1954)—In 1954 the Supreme Court supported the *Alcoa* precedent in its *United Shoe Machinery* decision. United Shoe was a classic

*Issues involving market definition are discussed in detail in Chapter 4.

†Limit pricing refers to a policy of keeping prices low to deter entry. Limit pricing is discussed in detail in Chapter 11.

"good trust." Profits were normal, prices were uniform, its machines were reliable and efficient, service was provided free, and the cost of machinery was kept down to only 2 percent of the average wholesale price of shoes.

Despite United's good behavior, the Justice Department charged that its power resulted from an illegal long-term leasing policy. United refused to sell its machines but, instead, leased them for a minimum period of ten years. Lessees could return a machine before the expiration of a lease, but only if they paid a significant financial penalty. The ten-year leases created several problems for potential entrants. The leases eliminated competition from a secondhand market (such as exists in automobiles or business machines), increased the capital requirements for entry, and greatly limited the market available to potential entrants each year (to approximately one-tenth of the total shoe machinery market).

The Supreme Court affirmed the decision of the District Court in favor of the Justice Department and in so doing endorsed the *Alcoa* precedent. The "Alcoa era" was thus a period of strict interpretation of Section 2.

3.6.3 Recent Trends in Section 2 Cases

The "Alcoa era" came to an end sometime in the mid-1970s. The Justice Department filed major suits against International Business Machines (IBM) in 1969 and American Telephone and Telegraph (AT&T) in 1974; however, during the 1970s and 1980s, a series of court and FTC decisions generally favoring fairly aggressive actions by dominant firms seemed to put an end to the approach of the *Alcoa* and *United Shoe* decisions. A few decisions are worth reviewing as examples of this change in court interpretation.

AMERICAN TELEPHONE AND TELEGRAPH COMPANY (1982)—In 1974, the Justice Department filed a suit against the American Telephone and Telegraph Company (AT&T), the largest private corporation in the world. In 1981, AT&T had assets exceeding $130 billion and a market share of 83 percent of all telephones in the United States.

AT&T was a holding company that controlled 22 local distribution telephone companies, Bell Long Lines Division, Western Electric, and Bell Labs. Its control of the telecommunications industry was built on a combination of government regulation, vertical integration, and aggressive competitive practices.

The complaint charged that AT&T had monopolized the industry by adopting two major policies. First, AT&T had shut out independent equipment manufacturers from the AT&T markets by purchasing all of its equipment from AT&T's own equipment manufacturing arm, Western Electric. Second, AT&T had prevented competition by obstructing independent equipment and independent long-distance carriers from interconnecting with the AT&T system.

Originally the complaint suggested that AT&T be permitted to keep the 22 regulated local operating companies and be divested of Western Electric, Long Lines, and Bell Labs. On January 8, 1982, however, the Justice Department and AT&T signed a consent decree with just the opposite result. AT&T was permitted to keep Western Electric, Long Lines, and Bell Labs but agreed to divest its 22 local operating companies. Furthermore, AT&T was given permission to enter nonregulated markets.

When the decree was carried out, it resulted in the largest divestiture in antitrust history, over $87 billion in assets. The impact of this decree is discussed in detail in Chapter 17.

ASPEN SKIING COMPANY CASE[14] (1985)—In 1967 Aspen Skiing Company (Aspen) gained control over three of the four ski areas in Aspen, Colorado, one of the nation's premier skiing areas. The fourth area was owned by Aspen Highlands Skiing Corporation (Highlands). From 1967 until 1978 the two companies worked in coordination to offer ski lift tickets that allowed skiers to ski all four areas during a weeklong vacation. Revenues from these four-area ski tickets were divided based on usage at each area.

Aspen complained to Highlands for several years that it did not have faith in the accuracy of the monitoring system used to measure usage at each ski area. Then, for the 1978–1979 ski season, Aspen offered Highlands a take-it-or-leave-it fixed 12.5 percent of revenues from the sale of four-area tickets. This fixed percentage was below Highlands' historical usage figures, and Highlands rejected the offer. Aspen refused to consider any counteroffer from Highlands and eliminated the four-area tickets. However, Aspen continued to offer an attractive three-area pass that was good only at its three skiing resorts.

With the elimination of the four-area ticket, Highlands attempted to introduce its own version of a four-area ticket by issuing a product it called the "Adventure Pack," which consisted of three days of skiing at Highlands and three prepaid vouchers to ski at the three areas owned by Aspen. Although Highlands had prepaid for the vouchers, Aspen refused to accept them. Highlands was then forced to include American Express traveler's checks or money orders in its "Adventure Pack" to pay for skiing at Aspen's three areas. In response to the traveler's check offer, Aspen increased the price of a one-day lift ticket to $22, "thereby making it unprofitable . . . to market [the] Adventure Pack."

Aspen's policies had a devastating financial impact on Highlands, which saw its share of ski lift ticket revenues decline from 20.5 percent in 1976–1977 to 15.7 percent in 1977–1978, 13.1 percent in 1978–1979, 12.5 percent in 1979–1980, and 11 percent in 1980–1981. Furthermore, Highlands' revenues from other ski services such as equipment rentals, schools, and restaurant facilities suffered similar declines.

A District Court jury awarded Highlands $2.5 million in actual damages and $7.5 million in treble damages plus court costs and attorney's fees. The Court of Appeals affirmed, ruling that the all-area ticket was an "essential facility" that Aspen had an obligation to market jointly with Highlands.

The Supreme Court also ruled in favor of Highlands. The Court noted that "the record in this case comfortably supports an inference that the monopolist made a deliberate effort to discourage its customers from doing business with its smaller rival. . . . The refusal to accept the Adventure Pack coupons in exchange for daily tickets was apparently motivated entirely by a decision to avoid providing any benefit to Highlands even though accepting the coupons would have entailed no cost to [Aspen] itself, would have provided it with immediate benefits, and would have satisfied its potential customers."

The *Aspen* case indicated that Section 2 cases could still succeed if the following two elements of the case are proved: "(1) the possession of monopoly power in

a relevant market, and (2) the willful acquisition, maintenance, or use of that power by anticompetitive or exclusionary means or for anticompetitive or exclusionary purposes."

KODAK[15] (1997)—In 1987 17 small companies that provided maintenance service to customers who owned Kodak photocopiers and micrographic equipment filed an antitrust lawsuit against Kodak. The suit alleged that Kodak illegally attempted to monopolize the service market by tying its service to its replacement repair parts for its copiers and micrographic equipment. It also alleged that Kodak had conspired with its outside parts suppliers to prevent these small independent service organizations (ISOs) from obtaining parts.

At the time the case was filed, Kodak had an established national network of service technicians for its copiers and micrographic equipment and many small ISOs were providing maintenance on Kodak's machines at prices that were 15 to 30 percent below Kodak's. Evidence suggested that the overall quality of the ISOs' maintenance was similar to that of Kodak. In 1985, after Image Technical Services (ITS) underbid Kodak to win a large service contract, Kodak changed its parts and maintenance policies. Kodak announced that it would no longer sell parts to ISOs for either its copiers or its micrographic equipment. Kodak also began tracking parts sales to ensure that equipment owners were not purchasing more than they needed and then reselling them to ISOs. Kodak even required prospective parts purchasers to provide proof of ownership of the machines for which the parts were needed.

Kodak asked the District Court to issue a ***summary judgment*** in its favor. A summary judgment is a court ruling in favor of one party on the grounds that there is insufficient reason to even hear the evidence. Kodak's legal position was that it had no market power in the equipment market because consumers had many alternative options. According to Kodak, if it attempted to gain extra profits on maintenance, the equipment consumers would take their business elsewhere.

The District Court judge agreed with Kodak and granted a summary judgment. The Ninth Circuit Court of Appeals, however, reversed and ordered a trial. Kodak appealed to the Supreme Court and in 1992 the Court affirmed the Circuit Court's decision. Subsequently, the case went to trial and a jury found Kodak guilty and liable for $72 million in trebled damages. In February 1996 the District Court issued a 10-year injunction requiring Kodak to sell parts to ISOs at nondiscriminatory prices. Kodak appealed, but on August 26, 1997, the Ninth Circuit upheld the verdict.

MICROSOFT[16] (2001)—The most recent important Sherman Act case is *Microsoft*. On May 18, 1998, the U.S. Department of Justice, 20 individual states, and the District of Columbia filed an antitrust action against Microsoft. In this case, the government argued first of all that Microsoft had monopoly power in the market for personal computer (PC) operating systems. This charge arose from the dominance of Windows in the operating systems market; for at least a decade, Windows has had 90 percent or more of this market. The government further alleged that Microsoft tied its browser, Internet Explorer, together with Windows in order to protect and enhance its market power. According to the government, Microsoft's bundling of Internet Explorer with Windows unfairly restricted the market for competing browsers, such as Netscape. In its defense, Microsoft argued that Windows and Internet Explorer were inextricably

linked—that the browser was an integral part of the operating system and that separating the two would damage at least one of the programs.*

The Microsoft trial received a tremendous amount of national attention. Among the more compelling evidence against Microsoft was a series of 150 e-mails provided by Netscape showing how Microsoft attempted to force Internet users to use Microsoft's Internet Explorer instead of Netscape's Navigator.[17] In June 2000, District Court Judge Thomas Penfield Jackson ruled that Microsoft was a monopolist in the market for Intel-compatible PC operating systems and should be broken up into two companies, one to produce the operating system and one to produce other software. Upon appeal, in August 2001, the Circuit Court of Appeals for the District of Columbia affirmed Jackson's findings of fact concerning Microsoft's monopolization of the operating systems market; however, the Appeals Court overturned his ruling that the company should be broken up. In a highly unusual decision, the Appeals Court disqualified Judge Jackson from any further consideration of the case because he had violated ethical guidelines by making public comments about the case while the appeal was pending. The Appeals Court then sent the case back to a new District Court judge, Colleen Kollar-Kotelly, to consider appropriate remedies against Microsoft. In November 2002, the Department of Justice reached a final settlement agreement with Microsoft. The settlement requires Microsoft to disclose more information to competitive software developers, restricts some of Microsoft's actions, and establishes a monitoring system to ensure compliance. In the end, then, behavioral remedies were chosen rather than the structural remedy initially crafted by Judge Jackson.

*The economics of Microsoft's practices of price discrimination and bundling are considered in detail in later chapters.

SUMMARY

1. While very few industries can be classified as either perfectly competitive or purely monopolistic, examining these theoretical extremes is useful. The perfectly competitive model serves as an important reference point for examining other industry structures, and the monopoly model shows how a firm with market power chooses its price and output.

2. Because of the characteristics of a perfectly competitive market, each firm takes price as given by the market equilibrium of demand and supply. The firm thus faces a horizontal demand curve for its own output, making the demand curve and the marginal revenue curve the same.

3. In the short run, a perfectly competitive firm will produce the output for which price equals (short-run) marginal cost as long as that price is greater than the average avoidable cost. If all fixed costs are sunk, average avoidable cost is identical to average variable cost.

4. In the long run, profit-maximizing perfectly competitive firms choose the output level at which price equals long-run marginal cost.

5. Market equilibrium is the intersection of the market demand and market supply curves. In the short run a perfectly competitive firm may be making positive, negative, or zero economic profits. In the long run, equilibrium price must equal average cost so economic profits are zero.

6. Economists often evaluate the welfare effects of changes in market structure or of government policies by looking at changes in consumer and producer surplus. Consumer surplus measures the difference between the maximum amount consumers are willing to pay for a good and the amount they actually pay. Producer surplus is the difference between the market price the producer receives and the lowest price for which the firm would be willing to produce a given level of output.

7. The competitive market equilibrium is allocatively efficient: It maximizes the sum of consumer and producer surplus.

8. A monopoly is the only producer of a product that has no close substitutes. Because the monopoly faces the downward-sloping market demand curve, marginal revenue is less than price. If the market demand curve is linear, the monopolist's marginal revenue curve has the same vertical intercept as the demand curve but is twice as steeply sloped.

9. Because of the difference between price and marginal revenue, price is greater than marginal cost at the monopolist's profit-maximizing level of output.

10. A monopolist's ability to charge a price that is above marginal cost depends on the elasticity of market demand. The less elastic the demand, the greater the market power the monopoly has.

11. The deadweight loss triangle is a measure of the misallocation of resources resulting from monopoly. Many economists have estimated the size of the deadweight loss. Their estimates range from as low as 0.1 percent of GNP to as high as 13 percent of GNP.

12 The simple comparison of competition and monopoly highlights the resource mis-allocation associated with market power. However, policymakers need to keep a few cautions in mind. In particular, significant economies of scale or dynamic considerations concerning technological change may warrant a more lenient attitude toward monopoly power than the simple model suggests.

13 In order to consider trade-offs over time faced by a firm, economists use the concept of present value. This chapter introduced this concept and gave summation formulas that will be useful as we consider firms' strategic decisions in the remainder of the text. A key result is that $\Pi_{pv} = \dfrac{\Pi}{(1+i)^c} + \dfrac{\Pi}{(1+i)^{c+1}} + \cdots = \dfrac{\Pi}{i(1+i)^{c-1}}$, where i is the firm's discount rate and c is any number less than, equal to, or greater than zero.

14 Section 2 of the Sherman Act bans "attempts to monopolize." In 1911, Chief Justice White laid down the Rule of Reason precedent in the *Standard Oil* decision. The Rule of Reason declared that only unreasonable attempts to monopolize violated the Sherman Act. The mere existence of monopoly power is not sufficient to establish a violation of the law; instead, violation of Section 2 of the Sherman Act requires proof of monopoly power in some well-defined market and evidence of an intent to monopolize that market.

15 The interpretation of Section 2 and the Rule of Reason has varied over time from the behavioral interpretation of the *Standard Oil* decision to a more structural interpretation expressed in the *Alcoa* decision and then back to a more behavioral interpretation in recent rulings. A historical perspective would suggest that the courts' position might change again someday.

KEY TERMS

allocative efficiency	Lerner Index	price elasticity of demand
consumer surplus	market power	producer surplus
deadweight loss	monopoly	shutdown point
discount rate	natural monopoly	summary judgment
discounting	perfect competition	total revenue
efficiency in production	present value	
gains from trade	present value of profits	

DISCUSSION QUESTIONS

1. Consumer theory tells us that, other things being equal, consumers normally buy more of a good as its price falls. Given this, explain how we can say that the demand curve facing a perfectly competitive firm is horizontal.

2. Why would a firm that is making negative economic profits in the short run choose to produce rather than shut down? Explain the relevance of fixed and sunk costs for this decision.

3. Why would a profit-maximizing firm choose to enter an industry in which it expected to earn zero long-run profits? Why would it stay in such an industry?

4. What do economists mean by the statement that perfect competition leads to efficiency?

5. Explain why the Lerner Index can be viewed as a measure of monopoly or market power. What determines the magnitude of the Lerner Index for a profit-maximizing monopoly?

6. Describe Harberger's approach to measuring the deadweight loss of a monopoly. Why might his estimate have been too low? Too high?

7. Opponents of free trade in the United States often argue that in competitive markets (for example, clothing manufacturing) free trade "exports" American jobs abroad. Is there any truth to this position? If there is any truth to this argument, does it follow that free trade should be prevented?

8. Explain the role of the discount rate in a firm's decision about sacrificing current profits in order to earn higher profits in the future.

9. Would you expect the managers of a corporation to have a higher or lower discount rate than the owner-manager of a small firm? Why?

10. It has been suggested that the *Standard Oil* and *US Steel* decisions taken together defined an "era of dastardly deeds." Discuss what the person who said this might have meant.

11. Do you think that the issue of aggressive actions should be important in monopoly cases? Why or why not? How would enforcement of the Sherman Act differ if the courts had ruled that aggressive actions are not important in monopolization cases?

12. In monopolization cases the defense typically argues that divestiture will result in a significant loss of economies of scale. Some argue that the loss of economies of scale should be an absolute defense against a charge of monopolization. That is, they argue that if a monopolist could prove that there would be a significant loss of economies of scale if it were broken up it could not be found to have violated Section 2 of the Sherman Act. Do you agree with this argument? Explain your reasoning.

PROBLEMS

1. Consider the owner of a small lawn-mowing service. She can use one of two methods to mow lawns. Method 1 is to purchase a tractor that costs $200 a year to own and then spend $1 (for labor and gas) for every acre of grass cut. Method 2 is to spend $40 on a used push mower that will last one year and then spend $5 (for labor) for every acre of grass cut.
 a. Write down the total cost functions for the two methods, letting q represent the number of acres of grass cut per year.
 b. Find the average cost function and the marginal cost for each of the two methods.
 c. Assume first that the tractor and the push mower have no resale value. What is the smallest number of acres of grass cut per year for which she should buy the tractor?
 d. Now assume that the tractor has a positive resale value but that the push mower has no resale value. How does this change affect the decision about which method of mowing lawns should be chosen?

2. A perfectly competitive firm has the following short-run cost function:

$$SRTC = q^2 + 30q + 400.$$

The corresponding short-run marginal cost function is given by:

$$SRMC = 2q + 30.$$

 a. If the market price is $50, how much output will this firm produce? Is $50 a long-run equilibrium price? Explain your reasoning.
 b. Find the equation of this firm's short-run supply function.

3. Consider a perfectly competitive firm with the following short-run total costs:

$$SRTC = 150 + 2q^2.$$

The corresponding short-run marginal cost is given by:

$$SRMC = 4q.$$

 a. If the market price is $80, how much output will the firm produce?
 b. What will the firm's profits be at a price of $80?
 c. Find the quantity of output for which marginal cost equals average variable cost. What does this information tell you about this firm's decision about whether to shut down in the short run rather than produce a positive quantity of output?

4. A competitive firm has a short-run total cost function given by:

$$SRTC = q^2 + 100.$$

The corresponding short-run marginal cost function is:

$$SRMC = 2q.$$

 a. If the market price is $60, how much output will the firm produce?
 b. Find the firm's profits at this level of output.
 c. Find the equation of the firm's short-run supply curve.
 d. If there are 100 identical firms in the market, find the equation of the industry supply curve.

5. Assume that the watch industry is perfectly competitive. Market demand is given by:

$$Q_D = \frac{12,000 - 100P}{9}.$$

There are 100 firms in the industry, each with long-run total and marginal costs as follows:

$$LRTC = q^2 + 10q + 100$$
$$LRMC = 2q + 10.$$

 a. Find the equation of each firm's supply curve. (This will be an equation expressing q_S as a function of P.)
 b. Find the equation of the industry supply curve.
 c. Solve for the equilibrium market price and quantity.
 d. How much does each firm produce at this equilibrium?
 e. Is this industry in long-run equilibrium? Explain your reasoning.

6. Assume the market for oil is perfectly competitive, with the following market demand and supply curves:

$$Q_D = 100 - P$$
$$Q_S = -50 + 2P.$$

 a. Find the equilibrium price and quantity for this market.
 b. Calculate consumer and producer surplus in this competitive equilibrium.

7. A monopoly can produce at constant average and marginal costs of AC = MC = 5. The market demand curve is given by:

$$P = 53 - Q.$$

 a. Use the twice-as-steep rule to find the equation of the marginal revenue curve corresponding to the market demand curve.
 b. Calculate the profit-maximizing quantity of output for the monopoly. What price will it charge?
 c. Find the monopolist's profits.
 d. Find the consumer surplus under monopoly.
 e. What level of output would be produced by this industry under perfect competition? What would the perfectly competitive price be?
 f. Find the consumer surplus under perfect competition.
 g. What is the value of the deadweight loss from monopolization of this industry?
 h. Verify that the sum of consumer surplus under monopoly, monopoly profits, and deadweight loss is equal to consumer surplus under perfect competition.

8. A monopoly has long-run total cost and long-run marginal cost given by:

$$TC = Q^2 - 5Q + 100$$
$$MC = 2Q - 5.$$

The market demand curve is given by:

$$P = 55 - 2Q.$$

 a. Use the twice-as-steep rule to find the equation of the marginal revenue curve corresponding to the market demand curve.
 b. Find the profit-maximizing quantity of output for the monopoly and the price the monopolist will set.
 c. Calculate the monopolist's profits.
 d. Calculate the consumer surplus under monopoly.
 e. What quantity of output would be produced if the monopolist acted like a perfect competitor and set MC equal to P?
 f. Calculate profits and consumer surplus corresponding to the competitive equilibrium.
 g. Find the deadweight loss due to the monopoly.

9. Consider a monopolist with the following long-run costs:

$$TC = 2Q^2$$
$$MC = 4Q.$$

The market demand curve is given by:

$$P = 96 - 6Q.$$

 a. Use the twice-as-steep rule to find the equation of the marginal revenue curve corresponding to the market demand curve.

 b. Determine the price the monopolist will charge and the quantity of output it will produce.

 c. Find the monopolist's profits.

10. (This problem is based on Application 3.2. You will need a calculator to answer this question.) Suppose the widget industry is perfectly competitive. Currently, imports of widgets into the United States are prohibited. The U.S. demand for widgets is given by:

$$P = 100 - Q$$

and the supply of domestic producers of widgets is:

$$P = 25 + q_{US}.$$

If trade were permitted, foreign firms' supply of widgets to the United States would be:

$$P = 25 + 2q_f.$$

What are the welfare gains to the United States of permitting trade?

11. a. Find the present value of a promise to pay $1000 in two years at a discount rate of 10 percent.

 b. Find the present value of a promise to pay $1000 for the next 100 years (starting next year) at a discount rate of 10 percent.

 c. What would happen to your answers to parts a and b if the discount rate were 5 percent? Why does a lower discount rate affect present values in this way?

12. Suppose you own a vacant lot worth $50,000. You are considering whether to build an office building on the lot; the construction cost of the building would be $300,000. You expect a shortage of office space next year, which would enable you to sell the new building for $400,000 in a year if you build it. Your decision is thus whether it makes sense to invest $350,000 this year in order to earn $400,000 next year.

 a. Explain why the investment this year is $350,000 rather than simply the $300,000 construction cost.

 b. If the interest rate is 7 percent, should you build the office building? Explain your reasoning.

 c. If the interest rate is 15 percent, should you build the office building? Explain your reasoning. What role is the interest rate playing in the decision?

13. This problem asks you to think about some strategies similar to those allegedly used by Standard Oil. Suppose that SO is a large petroleum refinery that dominates the Cleveland market but that does have one competitor, ABC Oil. Currently, SO earns a profit of $200,000 per year.

 a. One option is for SO to cut its prices to costs in order to drive ABC Oil out of the market. Doing so, of course, would mean that SO would earn no profits in the current year; afterwards, assuming ABC Oil is gone from the market forever, SO could earn $220,000 per year. At an interest rate of 11 percent, is driving ABC Oil out of the market a good investment? Explain your reasoning.

 b. Is it realistic to assume that once ABC Oil has been driven out of the market, it will be gone forever? Explain.

c. An alternative strategy for SO is to buy ABC Oil for $180,000 today and then operate as a monopoly, earning $220,000 for every future period. Is this a good business strategy? Explain.

NOTES

1. Arnold C. Harberger, "Monopoly and Resource Allocation," *American Economic Review,* Papers and Proceedings, 44 (May 1954): 77–87.

2. A summary of the methodological and empirical controversies surrounding the calculation of welfare loss is found in Frederic Jenny and Andre-Paul Weber, "Aggregate Welfare Loss Due to Monopoly Power in the French Economy: Some Tentative Estimates," *The Journal of Industrial Economics* 22 (December 1983): 113–129. See also James R. Hines Jr. "Three Sides of Harberger Triangles," *Journal of Economic Perspectives,* 13 (Spring 1999): 167–188.

3. David R. Kamerschen, "An Estimation of the Welfare Losses from Monopoly in the American Economy," *Western Economic Journal* 4 (Summer 1966): 221–236; and Keith Cowling and Dennis C. Mueller, "The Social Costs of Monopoly Power," *Economic Journal* 88 (December 1978): 724–748, with comment by S.C. Littlechild, *Economic Journal* 91 (June 1981): 348–363, and reply by Cowling and Mueller, *Economic Journal* 91 (September 1981): 721–725.

4. Gordon Tullock, "The Welfare Costs of Tariffs, Monopolies and Theft," *Western Economic Journal* 5 (June 1967): 224–232, and Richard A. Posner, "The Social Costs of Monopoly and Regulation," *Journal of Political Economy* 83 (August 1975): 807–827.

5. Cowling and Mueller, *Supra* note 3.

6. Comanor and Leibenstein (William S. Comanor and Harvey Leibenstein, "Allocative Efficiency, X-Efficiency and the Measurement of Welfare Loss," *Economica* 36 (August 1969): 304–309), estimate that the pure X-inefficiency effect of monopoly may be as high as 9 percent of net national product.

7. R.G. Lipsey and Kelvin Lancaster, "The General Theory of Second Best," *Review of Economic Studies* 24 (1956): 11–32.

8. *United States v. Standard Oil Co. of New Jersey, et al.,* 221 US 1 (1911).

9. *United States v. American Tobacco Co.,* 221 US 106 (1911).

10. *United States v. United States Steel Corporation, et al.,* 251 US 417 (1920).

11. Don E. Waldman, *The Economics of Antitrust: Causes and Analysis* (Boston: Little Brown and Company, 1986), p. 49.

12. *United States v. Aluminum Company of America, et al.,* 148 F.2d 416 (1945).

13. *United States v. United Shoe Machinery Corporation,* 110 F. Supp. 295 (1953), affirmed 347 U.S. 521 (1954).

14. *Aspen Skiing Company v. Aspen Highlands Skiing Corporation,* 472 US 585 (1985).

15. *Image Technical Service, Inc. v. Eastman Kodak Co.,* 504 US 452 (1992). See also *Image Technical Service, Inc. v. Eastman Kodak Co.,* C 87-1686 (January 18, 1996); and *Image Technical Service, Inc. v. Eastman Kodak Co.,* 1997–2 Trade Case (CCH), para. 71, 908 (9th Cir. 1997).

16. For the legal record, see *U.S. v. Microsoft* 253 F. 3d 34 (D.C. Cir., 2001) and *U.S. v. Microsoft,* 231 F. Supp. 2d 144 (D.D.C. 2002). For a discussion of the economic issues, see Daniel L. Rubinfeld, "Maintenance of Monopoly: *U.S. v. Microsoft* (2001)" in J.E. Kwoka and L.J. White, eds., *The Antitrust Revolution: Economics, Competition, and Policy* (4th edition) (Oxford: Oxford University Press, 2004).

17. "U.S. Releases E-Mail to Back Up Testimony," *Washington Post,* October 24, 1998, p. D4.

INTERNET EXERCISES

Visit **www.aw-bc.com/waldman_jensen** for this chapter's web exercises. Answer our real-world economics problems by searching the Internet for solutions!

Market Structure

Chapter 2 looked at the firm, considering its structure and objectives. Recall from microeconomics that firms are grouped together into markets. The structure of markets—the number of firms and their size distribution—varies widely from one theoretical extreme, perfect competition, to the other, monopoly. Some industries, such as automobiles, disposable diapers, or breakfast cereals, contain only a few large firms, while others, such as agriculture, women's clothing, or shoes, have many more firms.

The traditional structure-conduct-performance paradigm starts with a given market's structure, using that structure to make predictions about firms' conduct. Newer work recognizes that strategic choices made by firms affect market structure and examines this link. In both lines of work, however, structure is a key element. To put the theory we will learn in the next several chapters into perspective, we look first at market structure in this chapter.

Because of concerns about monopoly or market power and a firm's resulting ability to set price above marginal cost, policymakers usually focus on the structure of individual markets. Recall from the welfare comparison of perfect competition and monopoly in Chapter 3 that pricing above marginal cost leads to a misallocation of resources: At the profit-maximizing output level, the value to society of another unit of output, price, is greater than the cost of producing that extra unit of output, marginal cost. This allocative inefficiency is a key reason why economists and policymakers are concerned about firms with market power.*

Traditionally, a measure of market share or concentration has been used as a proxy for market power, although recent work has shown that it is important not to associate market share with market power blindly. Other factors such as barriers to entry and exit and potential competition may be more important than market share in determining market power. Consequently, after looking at market concentration, this chapter turns to a discussion of entry and exit. Following that, we look at one important factor that has affected market structure: the level of merger activity. The chapter presents evidence on merger history and considers the motives for mergers.

*Allocative efficiency is only one dimension of performance. Other important dimensions include the distribution of income and the possibility of X-inefficiency, discussed in Chapter 2, and technological progress, discussed in Chapter 14.

Finally, we think about the effects of mergers on competition and welfare and discuss antitrust policy toward mergers.

4.1 Concentration in Individual Markets

A s we saw in the previous chapter, markets work well when they are competitive. In the idealized perfectly competitive market, each firm is such a small part of the market that its actions have no effect on price. Consequently, antitrust authorities who worry about "competitiveness" often look first at the structure of specific markets, examining how closely a given structure resembles the structure of a perfectly competitive market. They are, for example, more likely to challenge mergers in a "concentrated" market than in an unconcentrated one. Because of the importance of structure for policymakers and because of the role measures of structure play in empirical work, we will look at measures of concentration in some detail.

4.1.1 Structure-Based Measures

Several statistical measures of seller concentration within an individual market are available. No measure is perfect; which one is used in any given situation depends on data availability and the questions being examined.

One possible measure of seller concentration is simply the number of firms in an industry. Economic theory indicates that if everything else is equal, competition ought to increase as the number of firms within an industry increases. A monopolistic industry, of course, consists of only one firm, whereas perfectly competitive or monopolistically competitive industries contain many firms. In between are oligopolies, with a few firms.

The number of firms is most useful as a measure of concentration in the extreme cases of perfect competition and monopoly. If there are a few firms in the industry, however, a measure of concentration that also reflects market share is desirable. Imagine two industries, each containing five firms. Suppose that in one industry, the market is equally divided and each firm has a market share of 20 percent. In the second industry, suppose that one firm controls 80 percent of the market and the remaining four firms each have market shares of 5 percent. It seems likely that pricing and other behavior will be different in these two industries, suggesting that a good measure of concentration should somehow account for inequality of market shares.

Two measures of concentration take both the number of firms and the distribution of market shares into account. The first is the ***concentration ratio (CR).*** The concentration ratio is the cumulative share of the K largest firms in the market, where typical values of K are 4, 8, and 20. Thus, the four-firm concentration ratio (CR4) is the sum of the market shares of the largest four firms in the industry. The most common measure of market size is sales, although concentration ratios can also be calculated using other measures of size such as value added, employment, or assets.

Concentration ratios have the advantage of being relatively easy to understand. They range from a value of slightly greater than 0 for a perfectly competitive industry to a value of 100 for a monopoly. Furthermore, for the manufacturing sector at least, data on concentration ratios are readily available.

Because the concentration ratio has been so widely used in empirical studies and in antitrust cases, it is important to understand its limitations. First, any given concentration ratio describes the percentage of market shares held by a specific number of firms. Because of this, the concentration ratio will not be affected by changes in market share outside the largest firms. Also, the concentration ratio will not necessarily give consistent rankings of the degree of competition within an industry. It is possible, for example, that one industry appears to be more concentrated than a second using the four-firm concentration ratio but less concentrated using the eight-firm concentration ratio.*

Another problem is that the concentration ratio provides no information about the distribution of market shares *among* the top firms. Knowing that the top four firms control, for example, 60 percent of the market tells us something but does not indicate whether there is one dominant firm with 40 or 50 percent of the market or four fairly large firms each with approximately 15 percent. Similarly, changes in market share among the top firms will not change the reported concentration ratio.

An index called the ***Herfindahl-Hirschman Index (HHI)*** takes into account both the number of firms and the inequality of market shares.[†] The HHI was originally defined as the sum of the squares of the market shares of all of the firms in the industry, expressed mathematically as

$$\text{HHI} = S_1^2 + S_2^2 + S_3^2 + \cdots + S_K^2 = \sum_{i=1}^{K} S_1^2, \qquad [4.1]$$

where K is the number of firms in the industry.

While the original definition of the HHI used market shares, antitrust practitioners have typically moved the decimal point two places to the right, using percentages of the market instead.[‡] We will follow this practice. Using this convention, the HHI approximates 0 for a perfectly competitive industry and equals 10,000 for a monopoly.

APPLICATION 4.1

Aggregate Concentration

Aggregate concentration statistics measure the role played by large companies such as Exxon Mobil in the economy as a whole rather than measuring the extent to which, for example, Kellogg's dominates the breakfast cereal industry. Policymakers often worry about possible abuses of the political system by very large firms. The largest firms, with sales and assets amounting to hundreds of billions of dollars, may have considerable political influence and may use this influence to gain legislative favors.

*A simple example illustrates this possibility. Suppose the market share of each of the largest eight firms in Industry A is 10 percent; let the distribution of market shares of the largest eight firms in Industry B be 20, 20, 5, 5, 2.5, 2.5, 2.5, and 2.5 percent. The CR4 for Industry A is 40 compared to a CR4 of 50 for Industry B. By contrast, the CR8 shows Industry A to be more concentrated: 80 for Industry A compared with 60 for Industry B.

[†]The HHI was invented independently by two economists, Albert Hirschman and Orris Herfindahl. See A. O. Hirschman, "The Paternity of an Index," *American Economic Review* (September 1964), p. 761, for historical detail.

[‡]Current antitrust policy, beginning with merger guidelines issued by the Justice Department in 1982, is based on the HHI.

Despite political concern about large size and aggregate concentration, data for the entire economy are scarce. Typically, evidence is anecdotal or pertains to individual sectors. Furthermore, any conclusions about aggregate concentration are affected by the variable used to measure size. Candidates include value added,[§] employment, payroll, plant sales, and new capital expenditures. While value-added data are perhaps the least biased measure, these data are available only for the manufacturing sector. In looking at other sectors, a researcher must balance concerns about possible bias in the data with the reality of what is available.

What do we find when we look at aggregate concentration in the manufacturing sector? Lawrence White has done considerable work on this and gathered data from the *Census of Manufactures* for the United States, among other sources. The table below shows some of his data for the 50 largest firms, the 100 largest firms, and the 200 largest firms.

Aggregate Concentration in Manufacturing in the United States, Selected Years

Share of Value Added (percent)	1947	1958	1963	1967	1970	1977	1982	1987	1992	1997
CR50	17	23	25	25	24	24	24	25	24	24
CR100	23	30	33	33	33	33	33	33	32	32
CR200	30	38	41	42	43	44	43	43	42	40

These data show that aggregate concentration in manufacturing increased from 1947 until 1958 but has not changed much since then. Using the best available data for other sectors of the economy, White concluded that aggregate concentration in the U.S. economy decreased during the 1980s and early 1990s but increased somewhat in the late 1990s. Despite this recent increase, the levels of aggregate concentration in the economy as a whole are comparable to the levels in the late 1980s or early 1990s and considerably below the levels of aggregate concentration in the early 1980s. In White's words, "the giants of the economy have not expanded their shares of aggregate economic activity."[†] Of course, this does not mean that these firms do not wield significant political power; it is a statement about trends over time.

[§]*Value added* is basically revenues minus the outside cost of materials, fuel, and power.

Source: Lawrence J. White, "Trends in Aggregate Concentration in the United States," *Journal of Economic Perspectives,* Fall 2002, pp. 137–160.

[†]*Ibid.,* p. 145. ■

In general, the more firms there are in an industry, the lower is the value of the HHI, *ceteris paribus.** One way to see this is to use the fact that, in an industry with N firms of equal size, the value of the HHI is 10,000/N. The value of N is referred to as the **numbers equivalent.** For example, the HHI for an industry containing three firms

Ceteris paribus is Latin for "all other things equal." Economists frequently make this assumption in order to isolate the effects of a change in one specific factor.

each with one-third of the market is 3333, while an industry with four firms of equal size has an HHI of 2500.

The numbers equivalent relationship is sometimes used to give insight into the meaning of a particular value of the HHI. An HHI of 1000, for example, has a number equivalent of 10:

$$N = \frac{10,000}{1000} = 10.$$

A market with 10 firms of equal size would thus have an HHI of 1000.

The HHI increases as the market shares of a given number of firms become less equal. The simple example shown in Table 4.1 illustrates this property of the HHI and shows the advantage of the HHI compared to the concentration ratio. Although both hypothetical industries have a four-firm concentration ratio of 90, the HHI for Industry B is higher, reflecting the less equal distribution of market shares among the four largest firms in each industry. Note that in calculating the four-firm concentration ratio, data on only the four largest firms are used, whereas data on all firms in the industry are used to calculate the HHI.

Finally, we note that the HHI is very sensitive to the market shares of the largest firms, due to the squaring of market shares. For example, $50^2 = 2500$ while $25^2 + 25^2 = 1250$. For this reason, it is very important to have accurate data on the market shares of the largest firms in an industry, but it is of much less concern if accurate data on the smallest firms are not available.

Since 1982, the Census Bureau has reported the HHI for U.S. manufacturing industries. Table 4.2 shows four-firm concentration ratios and HHI's for some selected manufacturing industries.* This table suggests that there is a high correlation

TABLE 4.1 Calculation of Four-Firm Concentration Ratio and HHI for Two Hypothetical Industries

Market Share (percent)	Industry A	Industry B
Firm 1	30	70
Firm 2	25	10
Firm 3	20	5
Firm 4	15	5
Firm 5	4	4
Firm 6	3	3
Firm 7	2	2
Firm 8	1	1
CR4	90	90
HHI	2180	5080
Numbers equivalent	4.59	1.97

*Market definition is discussed shortly. Table 4.2 uses industry definitions developed by the Bureau of the Census.

TABLE 4.2 1997 Concentration Ratios and HHI of Selected Industries*

Industry Name	Four-Firm Concentration Ratio	HHI for 50 Largest Companies
Ice cream and frozen desserts mfg.	32.3	444.7
Frozen fruit, juice, & vegetable mfg.	34.3	349.5
Breakfast cereal mfg.	82.9	2445.9
Cookie, cracker, & pasta mfg.	41.7	602.0
Breweries	89.7	N/R[†]
Cigarette mfg.	98.9	N/R
Textile mills	13.8	94.4
Paper mfg.	18.5	173.3
Petroleum refineries	28.5	422.1
Pharmaceutical & medicine mfg.	32.3	446.3
Soap & other detergent mfg.	65.6	1618.6
Tire mfg.	68.4	1517.8
Cement mfg.	33.5	466.6
Iron & steel mills	32.7	445.3
Computer & peripheral equipment mfg.	37.0	464.9
Household refrigerator & home freezer mfg.	81.5	2025.1
Automobile mfg.	79.5	2349.7
Sporting & athletic goods mfg.	21.4	161.1
Aircraft mfg.	84.8	N/R

*Using value of shipments.

[†]Not reported.

Source: "Concentration Ratios in Manufacturing," U.S. Bureau of the Census, 1997 Census of Manufacturing, June 2001.

between the two measures of market power. Industries with high four-firm concentration ratios tend to have high HHIs, and low four-firm concentration ratios are typically associated with low HHIs. Kwoka confirmed this relationship, finding a correlation of +0.929 between CR4 and the HHI and of +0.961 between CR2 and the HHI.[1] While this evidence suggests that the choice of concentration measure might not matter, Kwoka has also shown that even if they are highly correlated, different measures of market power can have considerably different explanatory power when used in statistical studies of the effects of market power.[2] In summary, it is fair to say that no single measure of seller concentration is best for all purposes. The choice depends on the availability of data and on the questions being asked.

4.1.2 Definition of the Relevant Market

A more crucial issue than the choice of concentration measure may well be the definition of the market. Many antitrust cases center around market definition. A properly defined market includes all firms that compete with each other but excludes all non-competitors. To identify competitors, substitutability on the part of both consumers and producers should be considered. If two products are used for similar purposes by consumers, the firms making those products ought to be regarded as competitors. Also, if two goods are produced using similar production processes, then their producers are also potential competitors.*

A market definition that is too narrow results in too few firms being included; as a result, measures of market power are overstated. A too-broad definition, on the other hand, includes too many firms, with the result that reported measures of market power tend to be biased downward. In both cases, reported measures of market power are not very useful for purposes of prediction or of evaluation of performance.

Most researchers examining the United States use market definitions developed by the U.S. Bureau of the Census. Until 1997, the basic system for classifying the output of manufacturing firms was the **Standard Industrial Classification (SIC).** In April of 1997, the Clinton Administration announced that the United States would begin to use a new industrial classification system, the **North American Industry Classification System (NAICS),** reflecting standardization by Canada, Mexico, and the United States.

Although the two classification systems differ, the general outlines are the same. The Bureau of the Census first assigns the output of business units in the United States into 20 broad *sectors* of the economy, such as mining, manufacturing, finance and insurance, and educational services. Each sector in the NAICS is assigned a two-digit code. For example, codes 31 through 33 are used for the manufacturing sector. Sectors are divided into three-digit *subsectors*, which are then further subdivided into four-digit, five-digit, and six-digit levels representing increasingly narrower categories. Table 4.3 shows an example of the NAICS divisions. The six-digit NAICS level defines a national (Canadian, Mexican, or United States) industry; among publicly available

TABLE 4.3 An Example of NAICS Categories

NAICS Code	NAICS Level	Description
51	Sector	Information
515	Subsector	Broadcasting (except Internet)
5151	Industry group	Radio and television broadcasting
51511	Industry	Radio broadcasting
515112	U.S. industry	Radio stations

*Consider two firms, one producing dog biscuits and one producing children's animal crackers. Assume that the production processes are very similar, although consumers do not view dog biscuits and children's animal crackers as substitutes. If the manufacturer of dog biscuits begins to earn excess profits, the manufacturer of children's animal crackers is likely to switch to producing dog biscuits also. Thus, the two firms are competitors. (Thanks to Sheri Aggarwal for suggesting this example.)

data sources, this level corresponds most closely to economic markets, although we consider problems with market definition shortly. The 2002 Economic Census defined 1179 industries.

Most firms, of course, produce more than one product; many operate in more than one industry. Statisticians at the Bureau of the Census assign any given plant according to the primary product of that plant, as measured by sales. Once plants have been assigned, the statisticians can use total sales and firm shares for each level to calculate measures of concentration. The Bureau of the Census publishes both concentration ratios and HHI regularly. (Refer again to Table 4.2 for data on the concentration indices for some well-known industries.)

In defining markets, the NAICS groups establishments that use similar production processes together. While substitutability on the production side is relevant for market definition, we would also like goods that consumers view as closely substitutable to be grouped together in a market. Because of the focus on production processes, some markets defined by the Census Bureau are too narrow and some are too broad.

Examples of industry pairs that are too narrowly defined include plastic bottles (326160) and metal cans (332431); cane sugar refining (311312) and beet sugar refining (311313); and snack food manufacturing (31191) and cookie, cracker, and pasta manufacturing (31182). In each of these pairs of industries, the products compete with each other in many uses, yet the manufacturers are classified as being in noncompeting industries. As noted earlier, measures of concentration in such industries will overstate actual market concentration; effective market concentration is less than the published statistics indicate.

Other NAICS industries are clearly too broadly defined. A good example is pharmaceutical preparations (325412). Included in this industry are a wide range of therapeutic groups such as anesthetics, anticancer agents, antibiotics, and cardiovascular hypotensives. Clearly these products are not substitutes from the consumer's point of view. The reported 1997 concentration ratio of 35.6 and HHI of 462.4 therefore understate actual market concentration; the manufacturers of products in different therapeutic goods are not truly competitors.

The issues of market definition discussed so far concern proper definition of the *product market*. Concerns about the *geographic market* are also relevant. The two main issues here are the exclusion of imports and exports from Census calculations and the assumption that the geographic market is national.

Publications from the Bureau of the Census report only information for manufacturers located in the United States. This causes an upward bias in measures of market concentration in those industries in which competition from imports is important. A classic example of such an industry is U.S. automobiles. The reported four-firm concentration ratio for their industry in 1997 was 79.5. For consumers, however, imported automobiles are a very close substitute for automobiles produced by U.S. firms and, thus, there is more competition than the reported concentration ratio suggests.* Other examples of industries in which imports are important include textile machinery, women's shoes, and consumer audio and video equipment.

*Output produced by a foreign manufacturer in a plant located in the United States is counted in the value of shipments for that industry. Thus, the trend toward production of cars in the United States by foreign companies such as Toyota and Volkswagen has decreased the bias in concentration ratios associated with ignoring imports.

The Census calculations implicitly define the geographic market as national. If the relevant market is regional or local, the reported measures understate the actual market concentration. This is most likely to be the case for products with a high ratio of transportation costs to value, such as cement, and petroleum refining, or for products that are highly perishable, such as ice cream and fluid milk.[3] In such cases, the nationwide concentration ratio may be quite low, while individual firms have considerable market shares within their particular markets.

In summary, we note that industrial organization economists must make use of the best data available. This frequently means accepting government figures and market definitions but using these data with care. For broad cross-sectional studies, government concentration ratios can sometimes be adjusted to reduce the bias or extremely biased observations can be eliminated. For detailed industry analyses such as those used in antitrust cases, however, researchers often conduct their own studies.

4.2 Entry and Exit

Entry and exit conditions are important determinants of existing firms' market power. A firm with a large market share may not be able to set price much above marginal cost if entry into the industry is relatively easy. Additionally, microeconomic theory predicts that entry and exit are important for ensuring an efficient flow of capital between industries. New capital is attracted to an industry by the prospect of earning economic profits. Old, inefficient capital is forced to leave an industry due to losses. Both barriers and incentives affect entry into and exit from an industry.

4.2.1 Patterns of Entry and Exit

Before looking in detail at possible determinants of entry and exit, let's examine some evidence about actual patterns of entry and exit of firms in the U.S. economy. In 1988 Dunne, Roberts, and Samuelson published one of the most detailed studies of entry and exit available.[4] They used Census data on firms in manufacturing industries in the years 1963, 1972, 1977, and 1982 to identify entrants into an industry and follow their growth or decline over time. They found several interesting results. First, on average, turnover among firms in manufacturing industries was fairly substantial. In each census year almost 39 percent of the firms producing in each industry were new entrants since the previous census year.* The statistics on exit are similar: An average of approximately 31 percent to 39 percent of existing firms left each industry between one census year and the next.[5]

The statistics on entry and exit are slightly misleading, however. Looking more closely at their data, Dunne, Roberts, and Samuelson noted that both the entering and exiting firms were, in general, considerably smaller than existing firms. Entering

*Not all of these firms had been created in the time since the previous census. Some firms entered by diversification, either building a new plant or changing the outputs produced in existing plants. On average, slightly more than half the total number of entrants in each industry were new firms entering by constructing new plants.

firms produce only 17 percent of the output level of existing firms while exiting firms produce 20 percent of the output of the average exisiting firm. In addition, new firms had high rates of failure. More than 60 percent of all entrants, on average, left an industry within five years of the census in which they first appeared, and almost 80 percent exited within 10 years.* Thus, successful entry seems to be more difficult than the statistics on the percent of an industry comprising new firms indicate. In Dunne, Roberts, and Samuelson's sample, at least, entrants tended to be small relative to all firms in an industry, and they failed at a high rate. These facts suggest considerably more movement on the fringes of an industry than at its center.

Disaggregation of the data reveals a considerable variation in entry and exit patterns across industries. An average of 60 percent of firms in the instruments industry were new entrants, whereas only 20.5 percent in the tobacco industry were new. Despite the variation across industries, the correlation between average entry and exit rates is high. Industries with high entry rates tend to have high exit rates, and low entry rates are associated with low exit rates.

How can we explain the observed patterns of entry and exit? The answer is complicated, and we begin with a discussion of entry.

4.2.2 Entry

Theory tells us that entry into an industry can facilitate adjustment to changes in demand and input prices, increase competition, and put pressure on existing firms to operate as efficiently as possible. New products or new technology may also be introduced through entry. In considering the determinants of entry, it is necessary to think about both factors that make entry difficult and factors that increase the incentives for entry. We consider impediments, or barriers to entry, first.

Barriers to Entry: Definitions

There are several alternative definitions of barriers to entry.[6] Literally, a barrier to entry is any factor that prevents instantaneous entry. For practical purposes, such a definition is unworkable. As we saw in Chapter 3, even firms in a perfectly competitive industry can earn positive economic profits in the short run. It is only in the long run that profits encourage firms to enter, driving economic profits to zero. Thus, in talking about barriers to entry, we are in fact considering *long-run* factors.

Bain, one of the first economists to do considerable work in industrial economics, defined barriers to entry as market conditions that allow incumbent firms to raise prices above the competitive level without attracting entry.[7] According to Bain's definition, a barrier to entry exists if a new firm cannot achieve the same level of profits after entry that an incumbent earned before entry occurred.[†]

*The size of the surviving entrants increased relative to all firms in the industry over time.

†Bain's definition is complicated by the fact that not all potential entrants are equally advantaged. Bain suggested considering those barriers that would face the "most advantaged" potential entrant. These barriers would then serve as a minimum estimate of the height of barriers facing *any* entrant. (Bain, *Barriers to New Competition* [Cambridge: Harvard University Press, 1956], pp. 9–11).

Other economists do not accept Bain's definition of barriers to entry. Stigler defined a barrier to entry as "a cost of producing (at some or every rate of output) which must be borne by firms which seek to enter an industry but is not borne by firms already in the industry."[8] For Stigler, an entry barrier exists only if the conditions of entry are more difficult for new entrants than for established firms.

For our purposes, a key distinction between Bain's and Stigler's definitions is whether economies of scale constitute a barrier to entry. Bain argued that economies of scale can and sometimes do act as an important barrier to entry into an industry. Stigler does not regard economies of scale as an entry barrier as long as both incumbents and potential entrants can operate on the same cost curve; he views the cost disadvantage faced by an entrant forced to produce at suboptimal levels as a consequence of demand conditions. In Stigler's words, "Some economists will say that economies of scale are a barrier to entry meaning that economies explain why no additional firms enter. It would be equally possible to say that inadequate demand is a barrier to entry."[9]

Other definitions have also been proposed. Von Weizsacker qualified Stigler's definition by requiring that a barrier to entry must lower consumer welfare: A barrier to entry exists if a cost differential between incumbents and entrants "implies a distortion in the use of economic resources from the social point of view."[10] According to Gilbert, a barrier to entry is the additional profit a firm can earn due solely to being an incumbent.[11] Gilbert's definition is similar to Bain's, although it focuses only on the incumbent firm.*

Our discussion of entry barriers uses Bain's determinants of the conditions of entry as a starting point. Bain basically considered *structural barriers to entry,* barriers related to structural or technical characteristics of an industry. Firms within the industry have no control over such structural barriers to entry. Most structural barriers involve cost differences of some kind between incumbents and potential entrants.

The literature on entry and exit has evolved considerably over the past 50 years, becoming increasingly complex. Economists have introduced the concepts of exit barriers, impediments to firms leaving an industry, and of behavioral barriers to entry. Behavioral or *strategic barriers to entry* are based on the notion of strategic entry deterrence; economists have realized that existing firms might deliberately behave in ways that decreased the probability of entry by other firms.[12] Exit barriers are considered later in this chapter, and strategic entry deterrence is considered in Chapters 11 and 12 following the development of a game theoretic framework for use in the analysis.

4.2.3 Static or Structural Barriers to Entry

Bain identified four elements of market structure that act as barriers to entry: economies of scale, absolute cost advantages, capital cost requirements, and product differentiation advantages. Each of these is considered in turn, although product differentiation is sufficiently important and complex to warrant further attention later.

*Gilbert's analysis also emphasizes the behavior of incumbents and their strategic responses to entry or the threat of entry.

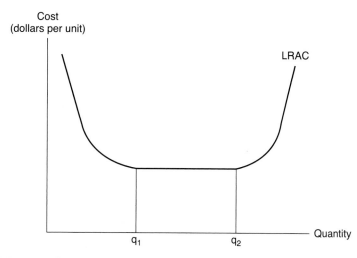

FIGURE 4.1 **Hypothetical Long-Run Average Cost Curve**

Economies of scale exist for output levels less than q_1, the minimum efficient scale (MES). The MES is the smallest level of output for which average cost is at its minimum. Between q_1 and q_2 returns to scale are constant; increasing output brings no change in average cost. For output levels greater than q_2, there are diseconomies of scale.

Economies of Scale

THEORY

As we saw in Chapter 3, economies of scale exist if the long-run average cost falls as the volume of output increases. This relationship is illustrated in Figure 4.1 for output levels below q_1. In this figure, q_1 is the ***minimum efficient scale (MES).*** This is the smallest level of output for which average cost is at its minimum. Figure 4.1 also illustrates the two further theoretical possibilities of constant returns to scale and decreasing returns to scale, or diseconomies of scale. Between q_1 and q_2, increasing output brings no changes in unit cost; the long-run average cost curve is horizontal. For output levels greater than q_2, average cost rises with increases in output.

How do economies of scale act as a barrier to entry?* Assume for the moment that capital markets work perfectly so that entrants can raise sufficient capital to finance entry as long as entry is profitable. Also, assume that all firms have access to the same technology. Under these conditions, economies of scale act as a barrier to entry if there is room in an industry for only a small number of firms, each of which produces enough output to minimize average cost. If each firm has the long-run average cost curve shown in Figure 4.1, it must produce and sell at least q_1 units of output, the MES, to produce at the lowest possible cost. The number of firms of at least the MES that can exist in an industry depends on the position of the market demand curve.

*Remember that some economists do not consider scale economies as barriers to entry. Stigler and others have argued that barriers to entry do not exist if there is no *postentry* difference between firms. This would be the case once an entrant had built an MES plant.

Figure 4.2 shows three possible market demand and long-run average cost curves. In Figure 4.2(a) demand is sufficiently low that one firm can satisfy demand and still not reach MES. In Figure 4.2(b), however, several firms could produce and sell enough output to minimize average cost. Figure 4.2(c) shows a situation where the MES is very small relative to industry demand. Thus, economies of scale are a more significant barrier to entry in the first case than in the second; the third case depicts a much more competitive market.

The key to understanding the argument about economies of scale as a barrier to entry is to recognize that existing, or incumbent, firms have already built MES plants. When the MES is large relative to demand, potential entrants must think carefully about the effect of entry on the market price of the product. They must guess how incumbent firms will react to entry.

Bain assumed that incumbent firms would choose to hold output constant at preentry levels even after entry. This "output maintenance assumption" is highly controversial among economists today, but we will maintain it for now.*

If incumbents continue to produce the same amount of output after entry as they did before entry, entry of another firm at the MES may well drive price below average cost, leading to economic losses. The losses will be large if the MES represents a large percent of the output of the relevant market and if a firm incurs a significant cost disadvantage by producing at a suboptimal scale. If a firm incurs higher average cost when it produces at a suboptimal scale, its LRAC will be steep and suboptimal scale firms will produce with much higher average costs than optimal scale firms. In addition, if a firm has to incur substantial sunk costs to enter an industry, the possibility of sustaining economic losses may deter entry.

APPLICATION 4.2

How Do Economists Estimate Economies of Scale?

Economists use three techniques to estimate economies of scale: statistical cost analysis, survivor studies, and engineering analysis. Not surprisingly, each methodology has its advantages and disadvantages.

In a **statistical cost analysis,** the researcher runs a statistical test to test for a relationship between average cost and output. To control for the effects of other factors that influence costs, variables such as the age of the equipment, the capacity utilization rate, and input prices must also be included in these statistical tests. These studies are appealing because the researcher can employ high-powered statistical techniques. Unfortunately, such studies require extensive data that are often hard to obtain. Because of the constraint imposed by data availability, statistical cost analyses have primarily been done for regulated industries for which regulatory agencies require firms to report detailed and fairly uniform accounting data. Examples include electric power, railroads, and telecommunications. But these are the industries that typically have been regulated precisely *because* they were believed to be natural monopolies with the average cost curve decreasing over a large quantity of output. Consequently, it is

*Bain's model, the limit pricing model of entry deterrence, is considered carefully in Chapter 11, along with criticisms and modifications.

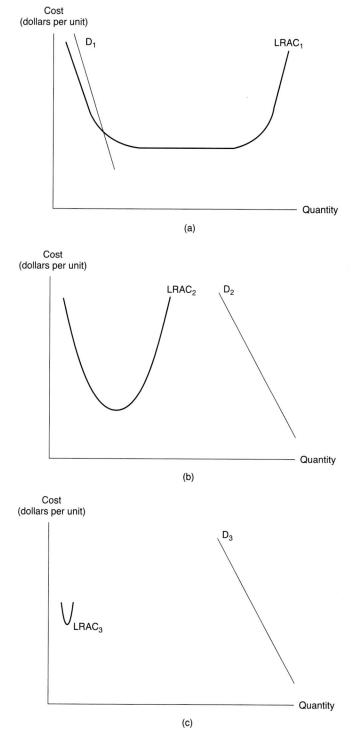

(a)

(b)

(c)

FIGURE 4.2 Different Demand Curves in Relation to Long-Run Average Cost

The number of firms of at least the MES that can exist in an industry depends on the position of the market demand curve. In (a) demand is so low that one firm can satisfy demand and still not reach MES. In (b) several firms could produce and sell enough output to minimize average cost. Panel (c) shows a market that is potentially much more competitive: The MES is very small relative to industry demand.

hard to make generalizations about the importance of economies of scale to other nonregulated industries.

The **survivor test,** developed by George Stigler, is an intuitively appealing method for estimating economies of scale. The idea underlying the survivor test is simply that, over time, the firms that "survive," supplying constant or increasing fractions of an industry's total output, must be efficient. A decreasing share of output over time is evidence of relative inefficiency; firms or plants of this size are not surviving.

As Stigler notes, the survivor test covers more than just efficiency in production; survival entails dealing successfully with a range of problems, such as relationships with labor and the government. The appeal of this method is its simplicity and the availability of necessary data. Because of this, many studies since Stigler's have used the survivorship technique. However, interpreting the results of survivor studies is somewhat tricky. For one thing, factors other than size, such as input costs, product mix, and age of equipment may differ across firms. But economies of scale refers to decreases in costs as output increases *with all other factors held constant.* Also, the results are sometimes ambiguous and confusing, with different researchers finding different patterns of survival or different results depending on the exact technique used. Sometimes the smallest and largest firms in an industry "survive," while the fraction of output produced by intermediate-size firms decreases over time. It is hard to know what such a result says about economies of scale.

Because of problems with both statistical cost analyses and survivor studies, some economists have used **engineering studies** to estimate economies of scale. This approach uses interviews, questionnaires, and surveys to gather information from engineers who are responsible for designing and planning new plants. These industry experts are asked how costs vary with the amount of output produced and what factors lead to economies or diseconomies of scale. Their responses are used to estimate the minimum efficient scale (MES) plant. Then, in order to examine whether a plant needs to produce a large fraction of total industry output to realize economies of scale, the MES plant is compared to total demand for the relevant industry.

Largely because of the enormous amount of work involved in conducting a careful engineering study, relatively few have been done. The results of these studies generally show that most industries in the United States can support a fairly large number of MES firms. Exceptions include turbogenerators, diesel engines, and civilian aircraft production. In other industries, such as synthetic rubber, cigarettes, and transformers, each MES plant accounts for somewhere between 5 and 10 percent of total national output. Overall, however, the conclusion of engineering studies is often that least cost production is not inconsistent with an industry structure containing many firms. In other words, we don't have to sacrifice competition to achieve production efficiency in many cases.

Sources: George J. Stigler, "The Economies of Scale," *Journal of Law & Economics* 1 (October 1958): pp. 54–71; William G. Shepherd, "What Does the Survivor Technique Show About Economies of Scale?" *Southern Economic Journal* 34 (July 1967): pp. 113–122; C.F. Pratten, *Economies of Scale in Manufacturing Industry* (Cambridge, England: Cambridge University Press, 1971); F.M. Scherer, Alan Beckenstein, Erich Kaufer, and R.D. Murphy, *The Economics of Multi-Plant Operation: An International Comparison Study* (Cambridge, MA: Harvard University Press, 1975); and Leonard W. Weiss, "Optimal Plant Size and the Extent of Suboptimal Capacity," in Robert T. Masson and P.D. Qualls (eds.), *Essays on Industrial Organization in Honor of Joe S. Bain* (Cambridge, MA: Ballinger, 1975).

Absolute Cost Advantages

A second barrier to entry identified by Bain is an ***absolute cost advantage.*** Such an advantage is illustrated in Figure 4.3. For simplicity we have assumed that average cost is constant for both incumbent firms and potential entrants but that a typical established firm can produce at a lower average cost for any given level of output. Consider any price above $10 but below $15. At such a price an established firm makes positive economic profits, ordinarily an inducement for new firms to enter the industry. With its higher average cost curve, however, a potential entrant cannot make a profit unless price rises above $15. Thus, the absolute cost advantage of incumbent firms acts as a barrier to entry.

What factors could lead to a gap between the average costs of established firms and potential entrants? Firms already in the industry may control a crucial input, may be able to borrow investment funds at lower interest rates than potential entrants, or they may have access to superior production technologies, perhaps protected by patents. They may have built plants in the most desirable locations, forcing new firms to ship raw materials or the final product greater distances. Also, entrants may have

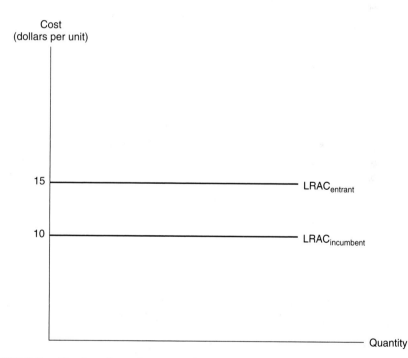

FIGURE 4.3 **Absolute Cost Advantage of an Incumbent Firm**

The incumbent firm can produce any level of output for $10 but the average cost for a potential entrant is $15. Consequently, any price above $10 but below $15 will result in positive economic profits for the incumbent firm but no entry. The cost advantage of the incumbent firm acts as a barrier to entry into this industry.

to pay more for scarce inputs, such as raw materials, managerial talent, or research personnel.*

As with each of Bain's original structural determinants of barriers to entry, recent theoretical work has considered how strategic decisions by incumbents affect cost asymmetries. Firms may, for example, try to prevent entrants from gaining access to inputs by negotiating contracts with suppliers or by buying existing supplies of a scarce raw material.[†] Another example is incumbents' use of "sleeping patents," which are held by a firm on a particular technology even though it is not using the technology. Such patents are valuable to incumbents because they prevent competitors from using a specific technology. This kind of strategic behavior is considered carefully in Chapter 12.

The empirical evidence on absolute cost advantages is scarce. Studies on the determinants of entry across industries typically do not include a variable to measure this barrier because of a lack of data. What we are left with, therefore, are some stories about industries in which established firms are at an advantage because of their ownership of the best (i.e., most easily accessible, lowest-cost, or highest-quality) supplies of an important input. Examples include ownership of ore deposits by Alcoa and International Nickel, control of supplies of tobacco leaf by the American Tobacco Company, Kodak's ownership of important patents, and Microsoft's ownership of the most widely used operating system software.[13] Perhaps not surprisingly, stories of absolute cost advantages often come from antitrust cases in which the government charges firms with monopolization of an industry. While absolute cost advantages are undoubtedly a barrier to entry in some industries, it is difficult to generalize about their overall importance. As we will see shortly, however, they tend to be important in industries where patents are significant or where capital costs are very high.

Capital Costs

High capital costs, the third structural barrier to entry, could have been included with the absolute cost advantage barrier discussed above. By focusing on high capital costs separately, we can emphasize a distinction from the absolute cost advantages discussed so far. As Figure 4.3 shows, the other absolute cost advantages are not necessarily associated with the scale of production. The horizontal average cost curves indicate that

*Gilbert ("Mobility Barriers and the Value of Incumbency" in R. Schmalensee and R. Willig [eds.], *Handbook of Industrial Organization* [New York: North Holland, 1989], pp. 494–495) argues that any scarce factor of production has an opportunity cost that should be included in the calculation of economic profits accruing to incumbents. Access to a scarce input by established firms, therefore, creates a barrier to entry only if the existing firm earns positive economic profits *after accounting for the opportunity cost of the resource*. For example, consider a firm with a key patent, such as Xerox's patent on xerography. Gilbert points out that such a patent is not necessarily a barrier to entry if the value of the resource in its next best use (i.e., its opportunity cost) is equal to its value to the holder of the patent. In this case, the patent should be sold, making the technology available to any firm willing to pay the price. However, if resources are specific to firms, then a patent may have a higher value to its holder than to any other firm, creating an absolute cost advantage for the patent holder.

[†]A classic example of such strategic behavior is Alcoa's alleged deliberate attempt to acquire deposits of bauxite ore to make it more difficult for new firms to produce aluminum. *U.S.* v. *Aluminum Company of America*, 148 F.2d 416 (1945).

the per-unit advantage of established firms is the same at small and large quantities of output. Capital costs, by contrast, are closely connected with economies of scale.

In general, the larger the minimum efficient scale, the larger will be the amount of financial capital required to enter at the MES. The higher the capital costs associated with entry, the less likely it is that one entrepreneur (even with a little help from her or his friends) can finance entry out of savings. A potential entrant in an industry with high capital costs must therefore turn to the capital market for funds.*

Now comes the connection to an absolute cost advantage.[†] If new firms have to pay a higher interest rate on borrowed funds than established firms, then they face a barrier to entry. Furthermore, the effect of this differential in interest rates will be greater the more capital investment a firm needs to finance to enter at the efficient size.

Why might new firms have to pay more for borrowed funds than established firms? Economists have identified at least three reasons for such a differential: risk, transaction costs, and loan market imperfections. Creditors may charge new firms a higher interest rate to compensate for a higher risk of bankruptcy and default on loans. Remember that Dunne, Roberts, and Samuelson found that the failure rate of new firms is indeed high.[‡] Their evidence also shows that entrants tend to be small relative to all firms in an industry. A relationship between risk and firm size would thus be another reason for financial markets to charge entrants a risk premium. Theory suggests such a relationship: Larger firms are more likely to be able to spread risks, protecting themselves from adverse events such as a price war, an increase in the cost of an important input, or a drop in demand. Larger firms spread the risk in several ways, including multiplant production and diversification across geographic and product markets.

Transaction costs are also related to firm size. Smaller firms pay a higher interest rate than larger firms. Fixed transaction costs are associated with issuing new securities. Large firms can spread these fixed costs over a larger volume of securities because they tend to issue new securities in relatively large amounts. Spreading fixed costs over a larger quantity reduces the per-unit cost.

Theory suggests that market power in the loan market may also lead to an interest rate differential between small and large firms. Two assumptions are needed for this to occur. First, assume that concentration in local and regional banking markets is higher than in the national market. Especially in the past, this was likely to be true because of regulatory restrictions on interstate branching. Second, assume that large firms tend to borrow in the national or international market, whereas small firms are more likely

*The deterrent effect of high capital costs is greater for some potential entrants than for others. Consider entry by two firms into the steel industry: General Motors and Waldman and Jensen's newly-formed steel company. Capital costs would be a considerably more formidable barrier for the second of these companies than for the first.

[†]In fact, Bain stated that one implication of the absence of an absolute cost advantage for an established firm is "that established firms should have no price or other advantages over entrants in purchasing or securing any productive factor (*including investible funds*)" (Bain, 1956, p. 12; italics added).

[‡]Some potential entrants, of course, will be able to enter a market successfully. However, as discussed in Chapter 2, it is difficult to convey information accurately. Poor risks are likely to behave opportunistically, distorting information about the risk of default. Because lenders cannot easily distinguish between potential entrants who have the ability to succeed from those who will fail, the cost of capital is higher for *all* new firms.

to look for funds in the local market. To the extent that these assumptions are true, local banks will use their market power to charge small firms interest rates somewhat higher than the competitive rates available to large firms.

The available empirical evidence mostly examines interest rate differentials across firms of different sizes. Evidence from the 1960s and 1970s suggests that small firms do pay a higher interest rate than larger firms and that this differential persists even when comparing relatively large firms. For example, Scherer and his colleagues found that corporations with assets of $1 billion could borrow funds at an average interest rate 0.34 percentage points lower than firms with assets between $200 million and $1 billion. At the time, this was a significant difference relative to average long-term interest rates.[14] Some, but not all, of this differential can be explained by risk; small firms seem to pay a higher premium on their loans than is warranted by their higher risk of default.[15]

Studies of the banking industry support the predictions of the loan market imperfections hypothesis. The more concentrated a local banking market is, the higher the interest rate paid by small firms. As theorized, concentration in a local banking market does not affect the interest rate paid on business loans to large firms because they are able to borrow in the national market.[16]

The bottom line is that small firms undoubtedly pay a higher interest rate on business loans than do large firms. Because new firms tend to be smaller and because of the greater uncertainty associated with new firms, entrants also pay a premium on borrowed funds. The greater the capital investment needed to operate a minimum efficient scale plant, the higher the barrier to entry will be.

The welfare implications of this differential in the cost of raising funds are complicated. The differential reflects both real and pecuniary savings. Real economies reflect actual savings of resources, while pecuniary economies are savings that are purely redistributive, increasing the welfare of one group and reducing the welfare of another. A small firm pays a bank a higher interest rate for its capital, and an investor in the bank earns a higher rate of return. Loan market imperfections create largely pecuniary economies.

Product Differentiation

The final element of market structure identified by Bain as a barrier to entry is product differentiation. Consumers view products as imperfect substitutes for a variety of reasons, including differences in quality, performance, or reputation. In addition, costs may be associated with switching from one brand to another, in which case products that are initially seen as identical become differentiated once a consumer has purchased a particular brand. We consider product differentiation in much more detail in Chapter 13. For now the relevant issue is how product differentiation can act as a barrier to entry.

Product differentiation gives individual producers some market power because each firm can raise its price without losing all of its customers. Product differentiation, however, does not necessarily allow incumbent firms to raise prices above the competitive level without attracting entry. Even though entrants cannot imitate the products of established firms perfectly, they may still be able to attract buyers. Product differentiation does not, therefore, necessarily create an advantage for established firms relative to newcomers.

Although product differentiation does not *necessarily* result in positive long-run economic profits for established firms, evidence suggests that it often does. Indeed, Bain's early evidence frequently identified product differentiation as the single most important factor in determining whether incumbents could earn excess profits. More recent theoretical and empirical work supports Bain's results.

Product differentiation activities by firms can take many forms, including advertising, efforts by sales forces, offering service contracts and warranties, and making style changes. Our discussion focuses on advertising, although it can be extended to other product differentiation activities as well.

Economists have identified at least three ways in which advertising can create an advantage for incumbents.* These three channels are familiar ones: (1) advertising can contribute to an absolute cost advantage of existing firms; (2) advertising may exhibit economies of scale; and (3) advertising can increase the capital costs of entry.[17]

ABSOLUTE COST ADVANTAGE

The key to whether advertising can create an absolute cost advantage for incumbents is whether the effects of advertising carry over from one period to the next. If *past* advertising does not affect *current* demand, then all firms have to start over each period in terms of advertising, and an entrant faces no disadvantage relative to incumbents.

Suppose, on the other hand, that advertising is cumulative and its effects last over time. A winter advertising campaign might still be generating sales in the summer or fall. This could be the case, for example, if a specific ad persuades a consumer to try a product and if the consumer then develops brand loyalty toward the product. Another explanation for a carryover or lagged effect is that a consumer may need to hear or see a series of ads, say 10, before deciding to purchase a product. In this case, although the tenth ad triggers the sale, it is not wholly responsible.

If the effects of advertising last over time, then advertising can be viewed as an investment. In this case a new firm will have to spend more on advertising than an established firm in order to reach a comparable demand curve. Even if the established firm spends *nothing* on advertising in the current period, it still "inherits" some stock of advertising from previous periods. An entrant has to spend advertising dollars in the current period to catch up to the established firm. To the extent that past advertising affects current demand, advertising creates an absolute cost advantage for incumbents.

We can use a simple example to show the advantage to an incumbent of advertising carryover. Suppose that each established firm in a market spends $15 million on advertising and that the established firms have equal sales. Assume that the carryover effect of advertising expenditures is 0.2 so that having spent $15 million on advertising *last* year is equivalent to spending $3 million *this* year (0.2 × $15 million) and having spent $15 million on advertising *two* years ago is the same as spending $0.6 mil-

*It is important to note that advertising can be procompetitive rather than anticompetitive. After all, for a competitive market to function, consumers must have good information. In some cases, advertising can be an effective way for a new firm to let consumers know about its product. Our discussion of the circumstances under which advertising is likely to be procompetitive as well as an examination of the empirical evidence about advertising is postponed until Chapter 13.

lion this year $(0.2 \times 0.2 \times \$15$ million). The total value of advertising per year for an established firm is thus $15m + $3m + $0.6m + 0.12m + \ldots$, which is equal to $18.75 million.*

What this simple example shows is that a new firm would have to spend $18.75 million during its first year to match the effect of a $15 million expenditure by an established firm. Even if the established firms spend nothing on advertising in a particular year, an entrant would have to spend $3.75 million on advertising. For the first year, at least, the entrant's advertising costs per unit of sales will be greater than the established firms' costs per unit of sales at every level of sales.

Of course, the advantage to the established firms depends on the extent of carryover. A higher rate of carryover in the simple example above would lead to higher total annual value of advertising expenditures for established firms. How much carryover exists from one period to the next varies across industries and across types of products.[18] For low-priced, frequently purchased products, advertising depreciation rates seem to be fairly high. One study found that 90 percent of the cumulative effect of advertising on sales for such products takes place within three to nine months of the advertisement.[19] For other types of products, however, the cumulative effects of advertising on sales continue to occur for two to three years. This is especially true for higher-priced, infrequently purchased products such as automobiles, appliances, and tires. The greater the carryover effect, the larger the advantage for established firms.

ECONOMIES OF SCALE IN ADVERTISING

Advertising can also create an advantage for incumbents if economies of scale in advertising are important. Economies of scale in advertising may exist for several reasons. First, there may be a threshold below which advertising has no effect on sales. The cost of this minimum amount of advertising, like any other *sunk* fixed cost, leads to decreasing average cost as the quantity of output increases. A threshold exists if consumers have to hear a message several times in order to be affected by it or if a firm must buy a specified minimum amount of advertising. For example, consider a firm that wishes to buy advertising on national television, perhaps because its market is national. Such a firm faces a considerably higher fixed cost than one that can use local media to enter a regional market, but the cost per viewer is likely to be lower for the national advertiser.

Increasing returns to advertising over some range also occur if volume discounts are given for advertising. The evidence on this is somewhat mixed, although some discounts do exist. Magazine advertisers are often offered volume discounts, and the cost per second of a television commercial decreases as the length of the time bought increases.[† 20] Again, the cost per viewer of a television ad is much less at the national level than at the local level. One study found that "[n]etwork rates range from approximately 10 to 70 percent of the sum of individual station rates, with the discount varying by time of day and season. This means that a potential entrant cannot effectively utilize spot advertising in a limited area to counter network advertising."[21]

*$15(1 + 0.2 + 0.2^2 + 0.2^3 + \ldots) = \$15\left(\dfrac{1}{1 - 0.2}\right) = \18.75

†Note that this discount may particularly benefit producers of more than one product who can divide a 30-second spot into commercials for two distinct products.

The importance of economies of scale in advertising is difficult to estimate. Undoubtedly, the magnitude differs across industries. Products for which repetition contributes to the effectiveness of advertising and products that must be advertised nationally are likely to exhibit economies of scale.

EFFECT ON CAPITAL COST OF ENTRY

The third way in which advertising can create an advantage for incumbents is connected to the first two. If the effects of advertising carry over substantially from one period to the next or if economies of scale in advertising are important, entry costs will include not only the cost of physical plant and equipment but also funds for advertising. Capital markets are likely to regard investment in advertising as sunk costs and particularly risky. It is difficult to predict the success of an advertising campaign, and advertising does not typically result in tangible assets that could be resold if the firm failed.[22] The riskiness of investment in advertising would result in entrants paying a high interest rate for such funds.

APPLICATION 4.3

What Does the Evidence Say About Barriers to Entry?

The earliest work on entry focused on a relatively small number of industries, using questionnaires and other evidence on past entry to identify and evaluate individual barriers to entry. This method was pioneered by Bain, who classified an industry as having very high barriers to entry, substantial barriers to entry, or moderate to low barriers. He focused on the ability of firms to raise price above the competitive level without attracting entry: An industry had very high barriers to entry if existing firms could raise price 10 percent or more, substantial barriers if existing firms could raise price 7 percent, and moderate to low barriers if firms could raise price no more than 4 percent.

The table below shows Bain's evidence for 20 major U.S. manufacturing industries during the late 1940s and early 1950s. This table shows that product differentiation was the most important barrier to entry, closely followed by capital costs. Bain found economies of scale to be very high barriers in three industries and substantial in seven. Absolute cost barriers were moderate to low in most industries, with the exception of copper, gypsum products, and steel. It is interesting to look at this list of industries and think about whether their structure has changed significantly over the past 50 years.

Bain's Evidence on Relative Heights of Specific Entry Barriers in 20 Industries (Higher Numbers Denote Higher Entry Barriers)

Industry	Scale Economy	Product Differentiation	Absolute Costs	Capital Requirements
Automobiles	3	3	1	3
Canned goods	1	1 to 2	1	1
Cement	2	1	1	2
Cigarettes	1	3	1	3
Copper	n.a.	1	3	n.a.
Farm machinery	2	1 to 3	1	n.a.

Flour	1	1 to 2	1	0
Fountain pens	n.a.	1 to 3	1	1
Gypsum products	n.a.	1	3	1
Liquor	1	3	1	2
Meat packing	1	1	1	0 or 1
Metal containers	n.a.	2	1	1
Petroleum refining	2	2	1	3
Rayon	2	1	1	2
Shoes	2	1 to 2	1	0
Soap	2	2	1	2
Steel	2	1	3	3
Tires and tubes	1	2	1	2
Tractors	3	3	1	3
Typewriters	3	3	1	n.a.

More recent evidence on entry barriers comes from a survey by Karakaya and Stahl of executives from 49 major U.S. corporations about the entry opportunities in 32 hypothetical market situations. The survey assessed the importance of six barriers to entry:

1. cost advantages of incumbents, including both economies of scale and absolute production cost advantages
2. capital requirements associated with entry
3. product differentiation advantages of incumbents due to brand loyalties
4. customer switching costs
5. limited access to distribution channels
6. government policy, such as licensing requirements or regulations

The barrier to entry ranked as important by the highest percentage of executives in the surveyed corporations was cost advantages of incumbents. Capital costs were ranked as important by the second highest percentage, while product differentiation was in third place. Note that these rankings differ from Bain's rankings in terms of what are the most important barriers to entry.

Sources: Joe S. Bain, *Barriers to New Competition* (Cambridge, MA: Harvard University Press, 1956); Fahri Karakaya and Michael J. Stahl, "Barriers to Entry and Market Entry Decisions in Consumer and Industrial Goods Markets," *Journal of Marketing* (April 1989): pp. 80–91.

4.2.4 Incentives to Enter

Economists recognize that entry decisions depend on incentives as well as barriers. Much less work, both theoretical and empirical, has been done on incentives than on impediments, however. Empirical work on entry has focused primarily on two incentives: expected profitability and market growth.

Expected Profitability

Microeconomic theory predicts that profit-maximizing firms will enter an industry if the net present value of expected profits, appropriately adjusted for risk, is positive.

Entry decisions thus depend on expected post-entry revenues, expected entry costs, and expected post-entry operating costs. A key part of understanding entry is, therefore, understanding how firms form expectations. The simplest model—one you learned in microeconomics—is that potential entrants look at the current economic profits of incumbents and enter if those profits are positive.

Some economists have developed more complex models of the formation of expectations. Highfield and Smiley hypothesized that potential entrants look not just at the level of current profits but also at the trend in profits over recent years.[23] Falling profits may discourage entry even in an industry in which incumbents' current profits are high. Still more sophisticated models require potential entrants to consider not only the effect of their own entry on prices and profits, but also the possible reactions of rivals to entry.[24] This kind of modeling gets quite complicated; most of the empirical work on entry, therefore, uses some fairly simple measure of past industry profits as a proxy for expected profitability.

Market Growth

Market growth is generally hypothesized to be positively related to entry. The higher the rate of growth of market output, the more "room" there is in the industry for an entrant and the less price will be driven down by the entrant's production, given a specific rate of supply expansion by established firms.* Also, potential entrants may expect it to be easier to sell their product to new customers than to take sales away from an incumbent in a market in which demand is stable or decreasing. Finally, new firms may have more flexibility, and thus lower costs, in adjusting to increased demand than do established firms.[25]

4.2.5 Exit

Economic theory tells us that exit also plays an important role in influencing market structure and performance. Firms that earn negative economic profits should be able to leave an industry. Doing so will make resources available for production of goods in other industries.

Considerably less work has been done on exit than on entry. As with entry, both barriers and incentives should affect the rate of exit from an industry.

Barriers to Exit

Any cost that a firm must incur to leave an industry is an ***exit barrier.*** For example, suppose workers' contracts stipulate that the employer must pay a month's wages if workers are fired even as a result of the firm leaving that particular market. These severance fees are an exit barrier.[26]

Exit barriers are generally thought of as some type of sunk costs. Remember that sunk costs can never be recovered; an asset whose cost is sunk cannot be resold. Sunk costs typically arise from investments in assets that are durable and specific to the firm

*It is possible that incumbents might respond more aggressively to entry in a market in which demand growth is high, however, since they would have more to lose in such a market. As noted before, we ignore this kind of strategic consideration in this chapter.

or the product. Examples include a patent combined with complementary physical or human capital* and investments in advertising and marketing.

Economists hypothesize that exit should be slower from markets in which capital costs cannot easily be recovered than from markets in which assets are readily resold. Having committed funds to nonrecoverable assets, the incumbents are tied to their markets by their inability to divest. Firms with relatively large sunk costs will stay in an industry longer than firms with fixed costs that can be recovered in an attempt to generate sufficient returns from their investment. A good example of an industry with large sunk capital costs is the railroad industry. Because of the large amount sunk in rails, railroad companies have been slow to leave the industry even when they are losing money.

Incentives to Exit

Incentives to exit from an industry can be viewed as another side of incentives to enter. Just as positive economic profits encourage entry, negative profits ought to lead to exit. Also, while a high rate of growth is an inducement to enter, a permanent decrease in demand may lead to exit. This reasoning suggests that variables measuring profits and market growth should be included in any empirical studies concerning exit.

Empirical Evidence on Exit

Relatively few studies of exit have been done.[27] These are the main results:

1. The evidence on the link between low profitability and exit is mixed. Some models of gross exit support the hypothesis that low profitability leads to exit. However, models of net exit and more complex statistical studies of gross exit have not found a statistically significant relationship between exit and profitability.

2. Evidence generally indicates that firms exit at a higher rate from slow-growth industries than from industries with a faster rate of growth.

3. Tangible durable specific assets, such as investment in plant and equipment, seem to act as a barrier to exit. Some studies find that intangible durable specific assets, such as those associated with research and development and advertising, deter exit, whereas others find no relationship to exit.

4.2.6 The Interaction of Entry and Exit

Evidence on patterns of entry and exit across industries shows a high correlation between the two. Industries with high rates of entry tend to have high rates of exit, while those with relatively few entrants also have relatively few firms exiting. This suggests that entry barriers and exit barriers may be highly correlated.

At least two hypotheses predict a high correlation between entry barriers and exit barriers. First, common determinants may exist: Something that creates an entry barrier may also create an exit barrier. In fact, Caves and Porter, two economists who were

*The complementary physical or human capital combines with the patent to create an asset whose value to the holder is greater than its value in the next best alternative. It is not profitable for other firms to pay the holder enough to part with the patent (Gilbert, *Handbook of Industrial Organization,* p. 522).

among the first to recognize the importance of exit barriers, stated, "Each source of entry barriers identified by Bain can also erect a barrier to exit by going firms."[28]

A very important factor common to both entry barriers and exit barriers is sunk costs. Because such assets have limited, if any, scrap value, sunk costs increase the losses associated with unsuccessful entry. This raises the barriers to entry into the industry by increasing the riskiness of entry.* As we saw earlier, sunk costs also create barriers to exit.

A second reason for the high correlation between entry and exit rates across industries is possible interdependencies between the two.[29] For one thing, new firms may push some established firms out of the industry. In this situation, entry causes exit so that industries with high rates of entry will tend to have high rates of exit as well. A second possibility is that barriers to exit actually *are* barriers to entry. As discussed above, sunk costs create barriers to exit for established firms. Therefore, investment in durable and specific assets by incumbent firms sends a signal to potential entrants that the incumbents intend to remain in the market. This signal is discouraging to potential entrants; there is little room for them in the industry. Thus, high exit barriers lead to low rates of exit and to low rates of entry.

Economists have only recently begun to examine the interaction between entry and exit barriers empirically.[30] A study by Shapiro and Khemani emphasizes the importance of taking into account interdependencies between entry and exit rates. Their results support the hypotheses that barriers to exit are barriers to entry and that much exiting is due to displacement of established firms by entrants. Rosenbaum and Lamont suggest that markets without sunk capital costs do have higher exit rates than markets with sunk capital costs.[31] Their study, however, does not find evidence that exit barriers act as entry barriers. While the two market phenomena of entry and exit are related, the nature of the relationship is still unclear.

4.3 Mergers

One important factor affecting market structure throughout the last century has been the level of merger activity. There are three broad categories of mergers: horizontal, vertical, and conglomerate. **Horizontal mergers** involve firms that are *direct* competitors. The firms must compete in both the same product market and the same geographic market so that buyers regard the firms' products as substitutes. Examples of recent horizontal mergers include the 1996 merger of the Union Pacific Railroad with the Southern Pacific Railroad and the merger of Bell Atlantic and NYNEX in 1997.

Vertical mergers involve firms that produce at different stages of production in the same industry. A vertical merger thus combines a previous customer with its supplier. Simple examples would be a merger between a supermarket and a baking factory or between an oil producer and a petroleum refiner.

*Gilbert points out that in a world of perfect foresight, potential entrants would be able to correctly calculate their profits after entry and would avoid entering unprofitable markets. In such a world, the direct cost of exit would be irrelevant. In the real world of imperfect foresight, however, "the cost of potential mistakes is likely to be a major factor in the decision to enter markets and in the availability of external financing" (Gilbert, *Handbook of Industrial Organization,* p. 521).

Conglomerate mergers involve companies that operate in either different product markets or the same product market but different geographic markets. Conglomerate mergers can be subdivided into three types. A *product extension merger* involves firms that produce different but related products; examples of such mergers would be Procter & Gamble's purchase of Gillette in early 2005 and Hershey's 2005 purchase of Joseph Schmidt Confections, a maker of premium chocolates and specialty cookies. *Geographic extension mergers* take place between companies that produce the same product in different locations. An example is US Airways' 2005 bid to merge with America West: US Airways is focused heavily along the East Coast of the United States while America West is stronger in travel from the East Coast to western cities such as Las Vegas and Phoenix. A *pure conglomerate merger* puts together firms that operate in entirely separate markets. ITT became famous in the 1960s for buying literally hundreds of companies in unrelated industries, ranging from auto parts to hotels to Wonder Bread.

4.3.1 Merger History

Figure 4.4 combines data from several sources on the number of mergers in the United States since approximately the beginning of the twentieth century. The figure shows that five merger waves have influenced the structure of American industry.*

Spurred by the passage of the Sherman Act, the first merger wave occurred around the turn of the century. Most of the mergers during this period were horizontal, often involving several firms. In fact, 75 percent of firm disappearances during this wave resulted from mergers involving at least five firms.[32] Many of today's large firms were formed in this period, including Standard Oil of New Jersey (Exxon Mobil), Goodyear, US Steel (USX), General Electric, Nabisco, and Eastman Kodak. As one economic historian stated, "It is no exaggeration to say that the structure of the modern American economy has been reshaped by the end of the first decade of the twentieth century."[33]

The second major merger wave took place in the 1920s. Stigler has called this wave the *merger to oligopoly* movement, as compared with the first *merger to monopoly* wave.[34] Mergers of this period typically combined fewer firms than the mergers of the first wave and, rather than creating the industry leader, often resulted in the formation of the second or third largest firm in an industry. Whereas most of the mergers during the first wave took place in manufacturing and mining, during the second wave, considerable merger activity occurred in other sectors, such as utilities, banking, and retailing. Horizontal mergers again were prevalent during this wave, although product extension and vertical mergers were also common.[35]

Figure 4.4 shows little merger activity from the beginning of the Great Depression until the third merger wave began sometime in the mid-1950s. More than 25,000 mergers took place in the years 1960 to 1970, with slightly more than half taking place in mining or manufacturing.[36] In large measure because passage of the Celler-Kefauver Act in 1950 made horizontal mergers subject to effective legal challenge, this merger wave differed from the earlier two waves in that the vast majority were con-

*The number of mergers reported for the early years is biased downward because early data sources reported only mergers between "large" firms.

FIGURE 4.4 **Annual Number of Mergers and Acquisitions**

This figure shows that five major merger waves have influenced the U.S. economy. The first occurred near the turn of the century, the second peaked in the late 1920s, the third took place in the 1960s, and the fourth was in the 1980s. The fifth wave began in the 1990s and is continuing into the twenty-first century.

Notes: Nelson: Data derived by Nelson (1959) for manufacturing and mining. Thorpe: Data derived by W. Thorpe, reported in Nelson (1959, 166) for manufacturing and mining. FTC: Continuation of Thorpe series by the Federal Trade Commission. Mergerstat: *Mergerstat Review* (2005).

Source: Adapted from Golbe and White (1988). Figure 9.6 in Alan J. Auerbach, ed., *Corporate Takeovers*. Copyright 1988 by the National Bureau of Economics Research. All rights reserved.

glomerate mergers. From 1963 to 1972 approximately 80 percent of the assets acquired were the result of conglomerate mergers. Pure conglomerate mergers, in particular, were widespread during this period.[37]

 The fourth merger wave took place in the 1980s, with a slowdown in the early 1990s. Mergers picked up again in the mid-1990s; this wave is still ongoing, although activity slowed somewhat following the terrorist attacks of September 11, 2001. A record number of mergers—over 9700—occurred in 2004. As Figure 4.4 shows, the number of mergers in most years of this most recent wave exceeds the number of mergers in the previous waves. Furthermore, many of these mergers involved giant

TABLE 4.4 **Some Recent Large Mergers**

Buyer	Seller	Year	Price Offered ($ billions)
Pfizer	Warner-Lambert	1999	116.7
America Online	Time Warner	2000	101.0
Exxon	Mobil	1998	81.4
SBC Communications	Ameritech	1998	75.2
Vodafone	AirTouch Communications	1999	62.8
Bell	GTE	1998	60.5
Pfizer	Pharmacia	2002	58.3
British Petroleum	Amoco	1998	56.5
AT&T	Tele-Communications	1998	52.5
Viacom	CBS	1999	48.8

corporations: Table 4.4 shows the dollar values of 10 of the largest recent mergers. These recent mergers have received considerable attention, in part because of the huge sums of money involved. Also, some of the mergers of the 1980s resulted from hostile takeovers; even though hostile takeovers accounted for less than 14 percent of the mergers in the 1980s, they still made for dramatic news reports. Nearly half of the mergers in the most recent, on-going merger wave occurred in industries that had recently been deregulated, such as airlines, banks and thrifts, utilities, and telecommunications. This evidence suggests that deregulation played an important role in restructuring and consolidation of industries.[38]

Even though the number of mergers in the most recent wave is unparalleled and the sums of money are vast, we need to remember that the economy has grown considerably throughout the past century. In fact, measured by the number of mergers per dollar of real GNP, the first merger wave dwarfs the others. Eckard, for example, investigated the impact of the 1980s merger wave and concluded that the wave "may have caused at most very slight increases in manufacturing industry concentration."[39]

4.3.2 Motives for Merger

In one sense all mergers occur for the same reason: One group believes that the acquired company is worth more than the acquired company's owners believe the company is worth. No merger will take place unless this condition is fulfilled. Several major reasons are commonly advanced to explain mergers.[40] Seven of the most commonly advanced reasons are discussed below.

Market Power

All three types of mergers can increase market power, and the next section of this chapter analyzes the potential anticompetitive effects in detail. Horizontal mergers are more likely than either vertical or conglomerate mergers to have serious anticompetitive effects.[41] Because horizontal mergers always increase concentration, the possibil-

ity exists that market power will increase. If General Motors acquired Ford, it is very likely that prices and profits would increase in the automobile market, even given competition from the Japanese and Europeans. Vertical mergers may result in increased entry barriers, or an increased likelihood of collusion. Finally, although other negative effects are possible, the most likely negative impact of a conglomerate merger is a reduction in the level of potential competition.

Efficiency Gains

Mergers are often motivated by a desire to increase economic efficiency, and some mergers result in significant efficiency gains. Economies of scale may result from any merger but are most common in horizontal mergers. A horizontal merger may enable the consolidated firm to reduce its production or marketing costs. In one documented example, three British bearing manufacturers were able to increase their output per employee by 40 percent after a merger.[42] A merger can also result in cost-savings due to economies of scope. Vertical mergers also may result in real economies by reducing the transactions costs associated with coordinating the different stages of production, and conglomerate mergers may improve efficiency by taking advantage of synergies in production or distribution.

All three types of mergers may improve efficiency by eliminating *X-inefficiencies*. Recall from Chapter 2 that in a world in which managers have some discretion, costs may not be minimized because of X-inefficiency. If managers are interested in living a quiet, peaceful life, they may not continually strive to find the least costly way of organizing production, handling materials, and, in general, doing business. As a result, costs are higher than necessary. Inefficient firms suffering from X-inefficiencies may be the most likely targets of takeover bids because these firms have the greatest potential for improving their profitability by replacing current managers with more efficient managers.

Although horizontal mergers may result in real economies of scale or a reduction in X-inefficiencies, one must be careful to distinguish *real* economies from *pecuniary* economies. Pecuniary economies result when increased market power gives a firm the ability to obtain inputs, including capital, at lower prices than its competitors. Such pecuniary economies lead to a change in the distribution of income but do not lower the opportunity costs of production. Recent evidence suggests that although many mergers, particularly horizontal mergers, result in some cost reductions, the cost savings are often small.[43]

Financial Motives

A motive for merger may be speculation that the "whole is worth more than the sum of its parts." When a large conglomerate is on a roll of good purchases, its stock value will rise, and so will its price/earnings ratio. If this successful conglomerate purchases another profitable company with a lower price/earnings ratio, and finances the purchase by exchanging its stock for the acquired firm's stock, all parties may gain financially in the short run. The owners of the acquired firm gain if the conglomerate pays a premium for their stock, that is, if the conglomerate pays more than the stock is worth on the open market. In addition, the owners of the conglomerate gain because earnings per share rise when the acquired firm's profits are added to the conglomerate's profits.

Suppose for example that a large conglomerate firm, hypothetically named GEAKO, has a price/earnings ratio for its stock of 20, but a small target firm, hypothetically named WEAKO, has a much lower price/earnings ratio of 10. If the annual profits (earnings) of WEAKO are $10 million, then its current stock value is 10 × $10 million = $100 million. If the annual profits of GEAKO *before* the merger are $500 million, its stock value is 20 × $500 million = $10 billion. If GEAKO acquires WEAKO, GEAKO's earnings rise to $510 million and its stock value rises by $200 million to $10.2 billion. Suppose GEAKO offers to pay $125 million for WEAKO. The WEAKO stockholders receive $25 million more than the stock is valued by the stock market, and the stockholders of GEAKO still come out ahead: The price of $125 million is considerably below the $200 million increase in the value of GEAKO's stock.

This analysis may seem complicated but it boils down to a simple phenomenon: Because of stock market myopia, even in the absence of any real benefits from the merger, the stock market behaves as if the acquired firm will fare better under the conglomerate's ownership. The potential problem is that if investors stop believing in the conglomerate's ability to keep growing and keep increasing its profitability, then its stock value will tumble, and existing stockholders will sustain large capital losses. By that time many of the original stockholders will have sold their stock for large short-run capital gains. This financial motive for merger was probably strongest during the merger wave of the late 1960s, when acquisitions were financed largely through stock exchanges. Evidence suggests that, in fact, many of the diversification mergers of the 1960s were ultimately failures.

Risk Reduction

It is often argued that mergers, particularly conglomerate mergers, reduce risk, and there is some truth to the old saying: It's foolish to put all your eggs in one basket.* For a merger to reduce risk, the acquiring firm's profits must not be perfectly correlated with the acquired firm's profits. Although this technical condition is met in most mergers, a merger will not reduce risk significantly if the acquired firm operates in an industry that is highly interdependent with the acquiring firm's other business activities. In the case of considerable interdependence, when one part of the acquiring firm's business flounders, so will the acquired part.

Pure conglomerate mergers are the most likely mergers to reduce risk. Few horizontal, vertical, product extension, or geographic extension mergers significantly reduce risk, however, because they usually involve markets that are interdependent with the firm's other operations. If two coal companies merged and then the market for coal became depressed, both firms would suffer, and the merger would have done little to reduce risk. Similarly, if a hotel firm purchased a rental car company, and then because of a recession the demand for vacation travel declined, both the hotel and car rental businesses would suffer.

Empire Building

A factor encouraging some mergers is the desire of an individual to build a financial empire. Strange as it may seem, some mergers are primarily the result of an individ-

*It is important to realize that diversification by a firm lowers the *firm's* risk, but *individual investors* can always select their optimal combination of returns and risk by diversifying their investment holdings.

ual's effort at self-aggrandizement. Perhaps the two best examples were the efforts of Harold Geneen as the chief executive officer (CEO) at ITT, and Charles Bluhdorn as the CEO at Gulf & Western. To these individuals, growth, pure and simple, was often sufficient motive for a merger.

Failing Firm

A firm on the verge of bankruptcy may attempt to find a buyer to bail it out. The Penn-Central railroad merger, which ultimately ended in bankruptcy, was a classic example. Few large mergers appear to be motivated by the existence of a failing firm, however. Defining a large merger as a merger in which the acquired firm had at least $10 million in assets, Boyle found that in only 4.8 percent of all large mergers was the acquired firm suffering from economic losses before the merger.[44]

Aging Owners

In some cases, a motive for merger is the age structure of the company's ownership. If a company is privately owned or controlled by an individual without heirs, or without heirs who have a desire to operate the business, then the owner will sometimes search for a buyer. A merger permits the owner to retire on the anticipated future earnings of the firm because these earnings are capitalized into the present value of the firm.

APPLICATION 4.4

Can Pixar Save Disney?

As the creator of characters Mickey Mouse and Donald Duck, the Walt Disney Company once dominated the world of animation movies. And even as recently as a decade ago, Disney was reaping the fruits of its revival of traditional hand-drawn animation films with movies such as *Mulan* and *The Lion King*. At that time, Disney was partially financing films produced by Pixar, a small firm working in the then-new world of computer animation.

How times change! Pixar has now had a string of major hits, including *Finding Nemo, Toy Story,* and *The Incredibles,* while Disney has been struggling, producing animation films that were modest successes, at best, at the box office. Three years ago Disney decided to make the transition from hand-drawn animation to computer animation, a difficult task. Because many of Disney's employees were skilled at hand animation rather than computer animation, they had to be retrained, and the process was far from smooth.

Now Disney has decided to acquire Pixar for $7.4 billion. This move will combine the animation studios of Disney and Pixar and, Disney hopes, revive its animation efforts. The merger is not without its risks, especially because Pixar is recognized for having a unique culture—a highly collaborative environment that includes an in-house educational system that allows its employees to take classes ranging from sculpture to screen-writing to tai chi. Can this culture survive the merger with Disney's animation studio? Will the merger achieve its objective of kick-starting Disney's animation? Time will tell.

Sources: "Pixar to the Rescue?" *The Wall Street Journal,* January 20, 2006, p. A.9; "Disney Sets $7.4 Billion Pixar Deal," *The Wall Street Journal,* January 25, 2006, p. A.3; "A Techie's Task: Drawing Pixar's Magic to Disney," *The Wall Street Journal,* January 30, 2006, p. B.7. ∎

4.3.3 The Effects of Mergers on Competition and Welfare

Horizontal Mergers

Horizontal mergers may result in both an increase in market power and a reduction in costs because of increased economies of scale. The positive effects of increased economies must be balanced, therefore, against the negative effects of increased market power.[45] Williamson's model to explain this trade-off is analyzed in Figure 4.5.* Before the merger, the industry performed competitively, with output equal to q_1 and price equal to P_1, which equals marginal cost MC_1. The merger results in the creation of a monopoly. After the merger, marginal costs are reduced to MC_2, but because of monopoly, output declines to q_2, the level at which $MC = MR$, and price increases to P_2. The merger reduces consumer surplus by the dark gray and light gray areas P_2ABP_1,

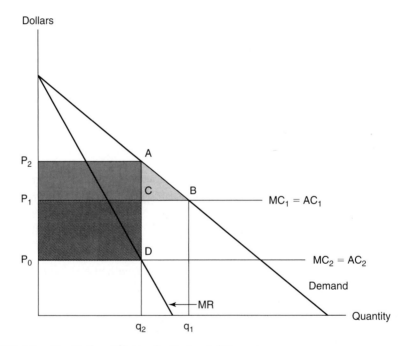

FIGURE 4.5 The Welfare Effects of a Horizontal Merger

Before the merger, the industry performed competitively, with output of q_1 and price P_1, which equals marginal cost MC_1. The merger results in the creation of a monopoly with lower marginal costs of MC_2 but with lower quantity of q_2 and higher price P_2. If the deadweight loss triangle ABC is larger than the rectangle P_1CDP_0, the merger has a net negative effect on society. If the deadweight loss triangle is smaller than the rectangle, then the merger has a net positive effect.

*The model was developed in O. E. Williamson, "Economies as an Antitrust Defense: The Welfare Tradeoffs," *American Economic Review* 58 (March 1968): pp. 18–36. Williamson's analysis is static and ignores the potential dynamic impacts of mergers on the rate of technological advance. As we will see in Chapter 14, these dynamic impacts may be more important than the static impacts analyzed by Williamson.

but also reduces the costs of producing the q_2 units by the red area P_1CDP_0. The dark gray rectangle P_2ACP_1 represents the transfer from consumer surplus to producer profits that results from the merger. The light gray triangle ABC represents the deadweight loss resulting from the merger. If the light gray deadweight loss triangle ABC is larger than the red rectangle P_1CDP_0, then the merger has a *net* negative effect. If the light gray deadweight loss triangle ABC is smaller than the red rectangle P_1CDP_0, then the merger has a *net* positive effect.

Figure 4.6 shows a numerical example in which a merger takes place in an industry with demand curve $P = 100 - 0.25Q$. Before the merger, the industry performed competitively, with output equal to $q_1 = 280$ and price equal to marginal cost $MC_1 = 30$. After the merger, marginal costs fall to $MC_2 = 10$, but output declines to $q_2 = 180$, the level at which $MC = MR$, and price increases to $P_2 = 55$. The merger reduces consumer surplus by the dark gray and light gray areas $P_2ABP_1 = 180(25) + (1/2)(25 \times 100) = 5750$, but it also reduces the costs of producing the q_2 units by the

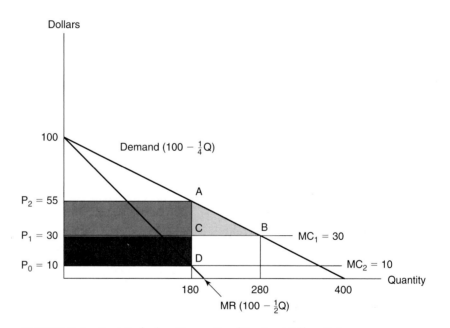

FIGURE 4.6 Cost-Reducing Merger Resulting in a Welfare Gain

In this example, the competitive industry produced 280 units of output with price equal to marginal cost of 30. After the merger, marginal costs fall to 10, but output declines to 180 and price increases to 55. The merger reduces consumer surplus by the sum of the dark gray and light gray areas $P_2ABP_1 = 180(25) + (1/2)/(25 \times 100) = 5750$, but it also reduces the costs of producing the 180 units by the red rectangle $P_1CDP_0 = 180 \times 20 = 3600$. The dark gray rectangle $P_2ACP_1 = 180 \times 25 = 4500$ represents a transfer from consumer surplus to producer profits. The light gray triangle $ABC = 1/2(25 \times 100) = 1250$ represents the deadweight loss resulting from the merger. Because the light gray deadweight loss $ABC = 1250$ is smaller than the red cost-savings area $P_1CDP_0 = 3600$, this merger has a net positive effect.

red rectangle $P_1CDP_0 = 180 \times 20 = 3600$. The dark gray rectangle $P_2ACP_1 = 180 \times 25 = 4500$ represents a transfer from consumer surplus to producer profits. The light gray triangle $ABC = 1/2(25 \times 100) = 1250$ represents the deadweight loss resulting from the merger. Because the light gray deadweight loss $ABC = 1250$ is smaller than the red cost-savings area $P_1CDP_0 = 3600$, this merger has a net positive effect.

To understand the implications of Figures 4.5 and 4.6, it is necessary to understand the trade-off of market power for cost reduction. If the effects of the cost reduction exceed the effects of the market power increase, the merger has on balance a positive effect, whereas if the effects of the market power increase exceed the effects of the cost reduction, the merger has on balance a negative effect.

Vertical Mergers

The economic and legal thinking concerning vertical mergers continues to change. As we discussed in Chapter 2, firms have to decide when to use the market and when to undertake an activity internally. Vertical integration can allow a firm to take advantage of technological complementarities or reduce transactions costs. A firm might have better information about a production process or the quality of an input if it is vertically integrated. Society can benefit from vertical mergers for these reasons.

But vertical integration can also increase entry barriers into an industry. In these cases, vertical mergers serve to create or enhance market power. Because of the complexity of the economics concerning vertical relationships, we defer a fuller discussion until Chapter 16, outlining here only the major legal theories used by the government to oppose vertical mergers in earlier periods.

One major legal theory used by the government to oppose vertical mergers is *foreclosure,* which is controversial among economists but has been accepted by the courts in the past. Consider this hypothetical example: Suppose McDonald's purchased a large producer of restaurant equipment. McDonald's would then buy its equipment from its own subsidiary, and therefore, the merger would foreclose other equipment suppliers from selling to McDonald's. In theory, such a merger might result in the demise of restaurant equipment suppliers that had previously supplied McDonald's, and as a result, market structure might deteriorate in the equipment industry. Furthermore, after the merger, McDonald's fast-food competitors might be forced to pay higher equipment prices, and this could ultimately result in higher fast-food prices to consumers.*

Vertical mergers can raise the capital barrier to entry, facilitate collusion, and result in a *price squeeze.* A price squeeze exists when a vertically integrated dominant manufacturer of a final good and an important input simultaneously increases the price of the input and decreases the price of the finished good. It has been argued, for example, that before 1930, Alcoa increased the price of aluminum ingots (the input) while simultaneously reducing the price of aluminum sheets and fabricated products.[46] Because Alcoa had a monopoly on ingots, this policy resulted in serious problems for unintegrated fabricators, such as Reynolds. Reynolds saw its input prices

*In Chapter 16, we will see that the anti-competitive foreclosure story is dependent on the existence of significant market power in at least one of the markets, either the restaurant equipment market or the fast-food market in the example. Under other conditions, foreclosure can have neutral or even positive effects on efficiency.

rising and its fabricated goods' prices falling. Alcoa was able to weather the reduction in profits on fabricated goods because its profits in the ingot market increased. Vertical mergers, therefore, can have a negative economic impact.

Conglomerate Mergers

Theoretically, conglomerate mergers also may increase market power.[47] Attacks on conglomerate mergers have been based on four arguments: (1) the elimination of potential competition, (2) reciprocal buying, (3) cross-subsidization, and (4) economic forbearance.

The classic *potential competition* argument was advanced when Procter & Gamble, the nation's leading detergent producer, purchased Clorox, the leading bleach producer. In a precedent-setting antitrust case, the government argued that Procter's existence as a potential entrant into the liquid bleach market served as a check on the pricing behavior of existing liquid bleach manufacturers, because existing producers were aware that high prices and profits would encourage Procter to enter. According to this argument, once Procter purchased Clorox, this potential competition was eliminated and the price of bleach would increase.

Reciprocity refers to the possibility that a large conglomerate can encourage its suppliers to purchase inputs from another of the conglomerate's divisions. If a large food wholesaler purchased a major spice manufacturer, it might "request" that its food suppliers purchase their spice requirements from its spice division. As a result, the market power of the acquired spice manufacturer might increase, and small independent spice manufacturers might be forced to withdraw from the market.

Cross-subsidization is another argument that has been advanced against conglomerate mergers. According to this theory, conglomerates will attempt to gain an increased market share in one market by using profits earned in another market to subsidize short-run losses. It has been argued that when Philip Morris purchased Miller Beer it chose to subsidize Miller's extensive advertising campaign with profits earned in Philip Morris's other markets.[48] This practice may be both rational and anticompetitive if it results in higher concentration and increased long-run prices and profits. It is likely, however, that few conglomerate mergers result in substantial subsidization; unless entry barriers are high, the short-run losses associated with subsidization will usually be greater than any potential long-run profit gains.

Some economists have also theorized that conglomerate mergers will result in *economic forbearance* between the nation's leading firms, a situation in which no conglomerate firm will rock the boat in any market because it fears retaliation in another market.[49] For instance, suppose Toyota purchased Dell, and Ford bought Gateway Computers. Ford might discourage Gateway from competing too aggressively against Dell for fear of retaliation by Toyota in the automobile market. As a result, Toyota and Ford might compete less aggressively in both markets.

4.3.4 Empirical Evidence on the Effects of Mergers

Economists have relied on three types of evidence to determine whether mergers improve economic efficiency. *Event studies* examine the impact of a proposed merger on the stock market valuation of the firm around the time of the merger. If merger

targets often suffer from severe X-inefficiencies, investors should believe new owners will replace the inefficient management team with a more efficient one. As a result, the stock market evaluation of the acquired firm should increase at the time of the announcement of the merger because the anticipated higher *future* earnings should be capitalized into the value of the stock.

Some empirical evidence suggests that around the time of a merger the acquired firm experiences a significant increase in the value of its stock, which results in large capital gains for the stockholders of the acquired company. Jensen and Ruback found that positive returns at the time of the merger ranged between 16 and 30 percent for tender offers before 1980.[50] Similarly, DeAngelo, DeAngelo, and Rice found an average 27 percent gain for leveraged buyouts between 1973 and 1980.[51] Several other studies have found similar results, including an examination of returns for the 1990s.[52] Because these studies generally find that the stock values of the acquiring companies did not experience any significant change at the time of merger, they conclude that the anticipated net effect of these mergers on efficiency must be positive. This follows because a positive gain for acquired firms plus a zero change for acquiring firms sums to a positive net change.

A second type of study examines the *premerger profitability* of acquired and acquiring firms. If mergers enhance efficiency, acquiring firms should be more profitable than other firms, and acquired firms should be less profitable. This follows if the acquired firms suffer from X-inefficiencies and are therefore less profitable. Acquiring firms, by contrast, should be full of highly efficient managers and should be more profitable. One careful study of the profitability of acquired firms was carried out by Ravenscraft and Scherer, who found that acquired firms tended to be more profitable than their competitors.[53] Table 4.5 summarizes one of their major findings. In each year the acquired firms tended to be more profitable than the benchmark firms. Ravenscraft and Scherer concluded, "When would-be acquirers 'fished' among the population of relatively small manufacturing enterprises for noncoercive acquisitions, they tended to haul in mainly the specimens with superior profit records."[54] The evidence regarding acquiring companies suggests that the acquiring firms are relatively large and tend to be growing quickly, but there is little evidence that they are particularly profitable compared with the typical firm.[55]

TABLE 4.5 Profitability of Acquired Firms

Acquisition Period	Number of Firms	Average Profits (%)	FTC Profit Benchmark (%)
1968	392	20.8	11.3
1971	113	19.6	8.6
1974	129	18.9	11.6
All three years	634	20.2	10.9

Source: David J. Ravenscraft and F. M. Scherer, *Mergers, Sell-Offs, and Economic Efficiency* (Washington, DC: Brookings Institution, 1987), p. 60.

A third kind of evidence comes from postmerger studies of profitability and productivity. Postmerger studies test directly whether mergers result in improved economic performance on the part of the acquired firms. One influential study, the Ravenscraft and Scherer study, found that the target lines of business suffer a loss in profitability following a merger. They also found that just under 50 percent of all mergers eventually resulted in divestiture of the acquired operation.[56] This sell-off phenomenon was heavily emphasized by Ravenscraft and Scherer, who noted that the sell-offs were generally preceded by a period of low and declining profitability.

Another key study reached a different conclusion about the gains from mergers. Healy, Palepu, and Ruback looked at postmerger operating performance for the 50 largest mergers between 1979 and 1984.[57] When they compared the merged firms to their industry medians, they found that postmerger performance improves relative to the industry benchmark. This study highlights the importance of using an industry-based benchmark to capture the effects of any shocks hitting all firms within an industry. Healy, Palepu, and Ruback's results were supported by a study looking at approximately 2000 mergers from 1973 to 1998 that found improved performance of firms following a merger.[58]

What can we conclude from the empirical work on mergers? Perhaps the key point is that policymakers should view mergers on a case-by-case basis, assuming neither positive nor negative effects. The effect of most mergers on competition and efficiency is probably quite small. In other words, most mergers are more or less neutral with regard to real economic impacts.[59]

4.3.5 Public Policy Toward Mergers

Mergers raise some of the more intriguing policy questions in industrial organization because many mergers have positive as well as negative effects on competition and efficiency. As a result, there is a continuing debate among economists as to whether mergers generally promote greater efficiency or greater market power. Moreover, there has been something of a revolution in antitrust policy over the past 40 years, with increasing attention paid to industrial organization economics. Economic reasoning helps determine which cases the Justice Department and the Federal Trade Commission pursue, shapes the issues being examined, and plays a larger role within the reasoning of the courts. Consequently, as we will see, the application and interpretation of the antitrust laws toward mergers have changed rather dramatically over time.

Horizontal Mergers: Policy Before 1950

Section 1 of the Sherman Act actually encouraged mergers by forbidding price fixing and other restraints of trade. It was not until 1914 that Congress acted to tighten the law with the passage of the Clayton Act. Unfortunately, although the Clayton Act outlawed mergers by stock acquisition, it made no mention of asset acquisitions, in which one firm purchased the physical plant and equipment of another firm. The courts could have interpreted Congress's intent as including asset acquisitions, but on November 23, 1926, the Supreme Court seriously weakened Section 7 when it handed down three simultaneous rulings. The most significant of these was a simple two-page decision in the *Thatcher Manufacturing* case.

THATCHER MANUFACTURING CASE[60] (1926) Thatcher was a major glass manufacturer that acquired the stock of three direct competitors, Lockport Glass, Essex Glass, and Travis Glass. After purchasing the stock, Thatcher purchased the assets of all three companies, so that as of January 13, 1921, the three firms ceased to exist. On March 1, 1921, the FTC staff filed a complaint charging Thatcher with violating the Clayton Act. The Commission ordered Thatcher to divest all of its assets that were formerly held by the three acquired firms.

The Supreme Court overturned the Commission and ruled, "The Act has no application to ownership of a competitor's property and business obtained prior to any action by the Commission, even though this was brought about through stock unlawfully held." This ruling effectively meant that as long as a firm acquired the assets, rather than the stock, of a competing company, there was nothing the government could do under the Clayton Act.

Horizontal Mergers: The Celler-Kefauver Act of 1950

Recall from Chapter 1 that the final major amendment to the Clayton Act occurred in 1950 with the passage of the *Celler-Kefauver Act.* The Celler-Kefauver Act amended Section 7 of the Clayton Act to include mergers through asset as well as stock acquisition, thereby closing the large loophole opened by the Supreme Court's interpretation of the original Section 7. The Celler-Kefauver Act also extended Section 7 to reach vertical and conglomerate mergers as well as horizontal mergers. With the passage of the Celler-Kefauver Act, Section 7 of the Clayton Act finally had some clout in dealing with anticompetitive mergers. The first Supreme Court ruling came in 1962 in the *Brown Shoe* decision.

BROWN SHOE CASE[61] (1962) The *Brown Shoe* case established major precedents for both horizontal and vertical mergers. In 1955 Brown Shoe purchased Kinney. Each firm was both a manufacturer and retailer of shoes. Brown was the fourth largest manufacturer with a 4 percent market share, and Kinney was the twelfth largest manufacturer with a 0.5 percent share. In retailing, Kinney was the nation's largest chain retailer, operating over 400 family shoe stores, and it ranked eighth among all shoe retailers in sales. Brown was the nation's third largest shoe retailer by sales volumes.

The shoe industry was highly competitive in both sectors. In manufacturing, the top 24 firms controlled only 35 percent. In retailing, there were virtually no entry barriers, and thousands of independents competed successfully against the large chains. Despite the almost perfectly competitive nature of the shoe retailing industry, the Supreme Court handed down a strong ruling against Brown Shoe. The decision was an obvious attempt to deter future horizontal mergers, even in competitive industries in which the potential negative effects of such mergers would be minimal or nonexistent.

The Court ruled that because in 118 cities the combined market shares of Brown and Kinney exceeded 5 percent, the merger violated the Clayton Act. Chief Justice Warren wrote:

> If a merger achieving 5% control were now approved, we might be required to approve future merger efforts by Brown's competitors seeking similar market shares. The oligopoly Congress sought to avoid would then be furthered and it would be difficult to dissolve the combinations previously approved.

The *Brown Shoe* decision established the ***incipiency precedent*** with regard to horizontal mergers. The incipiency precedent suggested that horizontal mergers should be banned even in competitive markets to prevent future increases in concentration.

PHILADELPHIA NATIONAL BANK CASE[62] (1964) In November 1960, the Philadelphia National Bank (PNB) attempted to acquire the Girard Trust Corn Exchange Bank (Girard). The two banks ranked second and third, respectively, among Philadelphia's 42 commercial banks, and the merger would have created the largest bank in the area. Had the merger been approved, the four-firm concentration ratio in Philadelphia would have risen to 78 percent. Unlike the *Brown Shoe* case, the *PNB* case involved a highly concentrated market.

The Supreme Court held that the 30 percent combined market share of PNB and Girard Trust went well beyond the legal limit for a horizontal merger. The Court suggested that unless there were highly mitigating circumstances a horizontal merger between two large firms in a concentrated market would be considered a violation of Section 7. The *PNB* decision, combined with the *Brown Shoe* decision, made horizontal mergers almost per se illegal under the Supreme Court leadership of Chief Justice Warren during the 1960s. A more conservative Supreme Court under the leadership of Chief Justice Warren Burger in the 1970s, however, took a more lenient attitude.

GENERAL DYNAMICS CASE[63] (1974) The *General Dynamics* case revolved around the activities of one of General Dynamics' acquisitions, Material Service Corporation. Material Service was a large midwestern producer of building materials, concrete, limestone, and coal. All of Material Service's coal production was from deep-shaft mines. In 1954 Material Service began purchasing the stock of United Electric Coal. By 1959 it had acquired 34 percent of United Electric's stock, enabling Material Service to control United Electric. When General Dynamics acquired Material Service in 1959, it acquired the nation's fifth largest coal producer.

The Justice Department's complaint contended that Material Service's acquisition of United Electric substantially reduced competition in two geographic markets: the "Eastern Interior Coal Province Sales Area," consisting of Illinois and Indiana and parts of Kentucky, Tennessee, Iowa, Minnesota, Wisconsin, and Missouri; and the State of Illinois. At the time of the merger, Material Service ranked as the second largest producer in both submarkets, with a 7.6 percent share in the "Eastern Province," and a 15.1 percent share in Illinois. United Electric ranked sixth in the "Eastern Province," with a 4.8 percent share, and it ranked fifth in Illinois with an 8.1 percent share.

The defense argued that despite these market share figures, the merger was justified on two grounds. First, United Electric had only a small quantity of reserves, and therefore, without a buyer, United would cease to be a significant competitive factor in the future. Second, because United Electric operated only strip mines, it competed in an entirely different market from Material Service, which operated only deep-shaft mines.

The Supreme Court accepted both defenses and found for General Dynamics. The decision signaled that a more conservative Supreme Court would no longer side automatically with the government in all Section 7 cases. By 1984 the courts had moved

even farther away from their strict interpretation of the 1960s, as indicated by the Second Circuit Court of Appeals decision in the *Waste Management* case.*

WASTE MANAGEMENT CASE[64] (1984) In 1980 Waste Management acquired Waste Resources. The two firms provided waste disposal services in many states, but the case revolved around the effect of the merger in Dallas, Texas. The District Court found that the two firms had a combined 48.8 percent share of the relevant waste disposal market in Dallas and that under the *PNB* precedent the merger should be dissolved. The Court of Appeals reversed based on an argument that entry barriers were so low that even a firm with a 48.8 percent market share could not permanently raise prices above competitive levels. The *General Dynamics* and *Waste Management* decisions represented major shifts away from the incipiency precedent.

STAPLES[65] (1997) Staples opened the world's first office superstore (OSS) in 1986. A few months later Office Depot opened its first store, and shortly thereafter other OSSs started opening all over the country. At one time there were 23 competing office superstore chains in the United States. After a period of intense competition, however, by 1996 there were only three remaining OSSs: Staples, Office Depot, and Office Max. On September 4, 1996, Office Depot and Staples, the two largest OSSs in the United States, announced they had reached a merger agreement. The FTC argued that the merger would decrease competition in the market for "consumable office supplies that were sold through office superstores." The FTC's market definition excluded consumable office supplies that were not sold in office superstores. For example, office supplies sold at Wal-Mart, Kmart, and small office supply stores were excluded from the FTC's market definition. Based on this market definition, after the merger Office Depot and Staples would have a dominant market share of between 45 and 100 percent in many geographic markets. The FTC recognized that because of increased economies of scale and scope, prices might decrease after the merger; however, the Commission argued that prices would decrease even more in the absence of the merger. The FTC presented a great deal of evidence comparing prices of the same product sold under different competitive conditions. For example, file folders were priced at $1.95 in Orlando, Florida, where Office Depot competed with Office Max and Staples, but the same files sold for $4.17 just 50 miles away in Leesburg, Florida, where Office Depot competed only with Office Max.

In March 1997 the Federal Trade Commission voted 4–1 to oppose the merger because it would harm competition and lead to higher prices. After the FTC vote, the FTC staff negotiated a tentative settlement with Office Depot and Staples whereby the merged companies would agree to divest 63 of their stores to Office Max in cities where Office Depot and Staples were the only two OSSs. The settlement, however, was rejected by the full Commission. Office Depot appealed the FTC ruling, but on June 30, 1997, Judge Thomas F. Hogan of the United States District Court for the District of Columbia granted a preliminary injunction to prevent the merger. This put an end to Office Depot's and Staples' attempt to merge.

*The courts were not the only institution changing their attitude toward horizontal mergers. As discussed later in this chapter, the guidelines toward mergers issued by the U.S. Department of Justice also evolved over this period.

Despite the *General Dynamics* and *Waste Management* decisions, horizontal mergers remain an area in which the antitrust laws hold some punch. It is doubtful that the Supreme Court would permit a merger between two dominant firms in a highly concentrated market. However, the modern trend in the lower courts today (and in the government's guidelines, discussed later in this section) is to recognize cost-saving efficiencies as a defense in horizontal mergers. The approach is a more flexible one, allowing consideration of more factors that are relevant to an analysis of competitive effects. Moreover, the government could not win a case similar to the *Brown Shoe* case today. There is no longer a Supreme Court majority that believes in the *incipiency* argument, and a merger between two small firms would be permitted today.

Vertical Mergers

As noted earlier, the economic and legal thinking concerning vertical mergers continues to change. For some time, however, economists, antitrust authorities, and courts have recognized that vertical mergers are less likely to have anticompetitive effects than horizontal mergers. Yet they can increase entry barriers and the probability of collusion. From a legal standpoint, vertical merger cases have dealt primarily with one issue: *foreclosure.*

DU PONT–GENERAL MOTORS CASE[66] (1957) The first major vertical merger case to reach the Supreme Court involved two of America's corporate giants, General Motors (GM) and Du Pont. In 1917, before General Motors became the dominant automobile producer, Du Pont began to acquire General Motors' stock, until by 1919, Du Pont controlled 23 percent of GM. Thirty years later, in 1949, the Justice Department filed a complaint under the Clayton Act charging that Du Pont's stock interest in GM foreclosed other firms from the market for paints and fabrics used by General Motors.

Du Pont contended that the government's market definition was incorrect, because automobile and appliance paints and fabrics made up a very small percentage of the total paint and fabric market. Furthermore, Du Pont argued that despite the stock link, General Motors often bought paints and fabrics from other companies besides Du Pont. Finally, Du Pont raised the obvious issue of timing. Could the government file a Section 7 case 30 years after the alleged violation?

In 1957, 40 years after the stock acquisition, the Supreme Court ruled that the link between Du Pont and General Motors violated the Clayton Act. The majority emphasized that Du Pont always supplied the largest portion of GM's requirements for paints and fabrics and that this dominant position "was not gained solely on competitive merit."

In 1961 the Supreme Court ordered Du Pont to divest its General Motors stock. By then 44 years had elapsed since the original stock acquisition. It is not surprising, therefore, that the case came to be known by a phrase used in Justice Burton's dissenting opinion as "The Sleeping Giant Case."

BROWN SHOE CASE REVISITED[67] (1962) The *Brown Shoe* case involved a merger between the nation's fourth largest shoe manufacturer, Brown, and one of the nation's leading retailers, Kinney. Evidence suggested that after the merger Kinney had significantly increased its purchases of Brown shoes. In a highly competitive

market, however, it is doubtful that this had any significant economic impact. Nevertheless, the Supreme Court ruled that the vertical elements of the merger violated the Clayton Act.

The Court's majority stated:

> [W]e cannot fail to recognize Congress' desire to promote competition through the protection of viable, small, locally owned businesses. Congress appreciated that occasional higher costs and prices might result from the maintenance of fragmented industries and markets. It resolved these competing considerations in favor of decentralization.

In this portion of the decision, the Court made a purposeful choice in favor of maintaining a large number of firms regardless of the effect on prices and costs. Such a decision seems to place a priority on social goals (a large number of small firms) over efficiency goals (lower prices and costs).

The *Du Pont* and *Brown Shoe* precedents suggested that vertical mergers violated Section 7 as long as a *reasonable probability* of foreclosure existed. A 1989 Court of Appeals ruling in the *Fruehauf* case, however, suggested a change in court interpretation.

THE FRUEHAUF CASE[68] (1989) In the 1970s Fruehauf was the nation's leading producer of truck trailers with a 25 percent market share. The four-firm concentration ratio in the truck trailer market was 49. Fruehauf acquired Kelsey, a leading manufacturer of "heavy-duty wheels" used in the manufacture of truck trailers. Kelsey held a 15 percent market share, and the market for heavy-duty wheels was highly concentrated with a four-firm concentration ratio of approximately 70. The Federal Trade Commission ruled that the merger foreclosed a maximum of 5.8 percent of the heavy-duty wheel market and that the percentage violated Section 7 of the Clayton Act.

The Court of Appeals recognized the likelihood of some foreclosure, but reversed the FTC. According to the Appeals Court, no evidence showed that as a result of the merger competing buyers of heavy-duty wheels would be unable to obtain supplies from Kelsey or its competitors at competitive prices, or that entry into the truck trailer market would require simultaneous entry into the heavy-duty wheel market. Furthermore, the Court concluded that Fruehauf was never a serious potential entrant into the manufacturing of heavy-duty wheels.

The *Fruehauf* decision suggests that under a more recent interpretation of Section 7, the courts are likely to look at far more than the percentage of the market foreclosed by a vertical merger. In the *Fruehauf* case the Court closely examined all of the expected competitive impacts of the merger and concluded that there was a very small probability of significant anticompetitive effects.

Conglomerate Mergers

Conglomerate mergers have been treated more cautiously by the courts than either horizontal or vertical mergers. The government has based its relatively few legal attacks on one issue: the elimination of ***potential competition.***

POTENTIAL COMPETITION CASES
PROCTER & GAMBLE CASE[69] (1967) In 1957, Procter & Gamble, the nation's leading producer of soaps and detergents, acquired Clorox, the nation's leading producer of

liquid bleach. Both firms held dominant positions: Procter had a 54.4 percent share of the detergent market, and Clorox had a 48.8 percent share of the liquid bleach market. The four-firm concentration ratio was over 80 in both markets; therefore, the merger involved the leading firms in two highly concentrated and complementary markets.

The government complaint charged three major negative effects of the merger. First, the merger eliminated Procter & Gamble as a potential competitor in the liquid bleach market. Second, it further entrenched Clorox as the industry leader, because Procter, as the nation's leading advertiser, could greatly increase the advertising expenditures of Clorox. Finally, the FTC argued that smaller competitors would be hesitant to compete aggressively against large, diversified Procter & Gamble.

The Supreme Court ordered the merger dissolved because Procter was the most likely potential entrant into the liquid bleach market. The Court noted, however, that if Procter & Gamble had acquired a small bleach producer, and then competed aggressively with Clorox, such a *toehold* merger might have significantly increased the level of effective competition. A few years later, the FTC addressed the issue of a *toehold* merger in the *Bendix* case.

BENDIX CASE[70] (1970) In 1967, Bendix, a large, diversified firm specializing in the aerospace, automotive, automation, and scientific industries, acquired Fram, a leading producer of automotive, aerospace, and water filters. The complaint revolved around the automobile filter market, which was highly concentrated, with General Motors controlling 32.4 percent, Purolator 21.7 percent, and Fram 17.2 percent. Bendix held a very small 0.35 percent market share and decided that it wanted to expand into the market on a much larger scale. After some deliberation, Bendix decided it would only expand through merger, not through internal expansion.

The FTC staff argued that the Bendix-Fram merger eliminated potential competition. The full Commission agreed but, in the process, handed down an important ruling which stated that the FTC would be inclined to permit toehold mergers between a large potential competitor and a small nondominant firm.

In 1971, the Sixth Circuit Court of Appeals overturned the Commission's ruling, not on substance, but on a legal technicality.[71] The Appeals Court ruled that because the FTC had failed to inform Bendix of its intention to use the toehold theory in its case, Bendix had not been given the opportunity to prepare an adequate defense. The Appeals Court did not rule on the legitimacy of the toehold theory.

YAMAHA MOTORS CASE[72] (1981) In the late 1970s, Brunswick, a large, diversified manufacturer, was the second largest seller of outboard motors in the United States with a market share that ranged between 19.8 and 26 percent. Despite its position as the leading seller, Brunswick did not *manufacture* outboard motors. Brunswick decided to enter into a *joint venture* with Yamaha Motors of Japan to manufacture outboard motors in the United States. Yamaha produced outboard motors in Japan but did not sell outboard motors in the United States. Under the terms of a joint venture, two firms agree to engage in a commercial activity and share in the profits. Functionally, joint ventures have been treated as mergers under the antitrust laws because the two firms combine to engage in a joint activity exactly as they would if they merged.

The Eighth Circuit Court of Appeals affirmed an FTC ruling that the joint venture violated Section 7. The Court noted that for the joint venture to violate the law it was necessary for the FTC to show that Brunswick or Yamaha had "available feasible

means" for entering the American outboard motor market, and "that those means offer[ed] a substantial likelihood of ultimately producing deconcentration of that market or other significant procompetitive effects." The Appeals Court concluded that the evidence supported a finding that the joint venture significantly reduced potential competition and therefore violated Section 7.

TENNECO CASE[73] (1982) A year after the Eighth Circuit Court of Appeals handed down the *Yamaha* decision, the Second Circuit Court of Appeals handed down a far different ruling in the *Tenneco* case. In the late 1960s and early 1970s, Tenneco had wanted to enter the shock absorber market, and it had contacted major European manufacturers concerning possible patent licensing arrangements. Tenneco went so far as to acquire a small manufacturing company that held a shock absorber patent. Tenneco then decided abruptly to change strategy and entered the shock absorber market by acquiring Monroe, a major manufacturer of shock absorbers. The FTC ruled that the acquisition violated Section 7, but the Second Circuit Court of Appeals, by a split 2–1 vote, overturned.

The Second Circuit Court ruled that there was insufficient evidence that Tenneco would have entered the market *de novo* in the absence of its purchase of Monroe. Despite the Appeals Court's finding that "[t]he record contains abundant evidence that Tenneco had both the interest and the incentive to enter the market for replacement shock absorbers," the Court ruled against the FTC. Ultimately, the Second Circuit ruling emphasized that Section 7 deals with "probabilities," not "ephemeral possibilities," and the Court found an insufficient probability that Tenneco would have entered the market either *de novo* or through a toehold acquisition.

4.3.6 Merger Guidelines and the Hart-Scott-Rodino Act

Having looked at some of the courts' decisions, we now turn to the criteria used by the government to decide which mergers to challenge. In 1968 the Justice Department issued its first set of merger guidelines. The guidelines were meant to help reduce the uncertainty regarding the legality or illegality of a particular merger. Especially with regard to *horizontal mergers*, the 1968 guidelines tended to be quite strict. In an industry with a four-firm concentration ratio of over 75, the guidelines suggested that the antitrust authorities would challenge any of the mergers in Table 4.6.

With regard to *vertical mergers*, the 1968 guidelines suggested that a challenge would be forthcoming if the buyer of an input made 6 percent of the total purchases

TABLE 4.6 Mergers Challenged Under the 1968 Guidelines*

Acquiring Firm's Market Share (%)	Acquired Firm's Market Share (%)
4	4
10	2
15	1

*assuming CR4 ≥ 75.

of the input *and* the supplier of the input made 10 percent of total input sales; if the supplier of the input made 20 percent of total input sales; if the buyer of the input controlled 10 percent of its market; or if there was a significant trend toward vertical integration in the industry.

With regard to *conglomerate mergers*, the 1968 guidelines suggested that a merger would be challenged if the merger eliminated a main potential entrant; if the merger created a substantial possibility of reciprocal buying arrangements; if the merger created increased leverage for the acquired firm, such as an increased advertising advantage; or if *any* of the largest 200 firms tried to acquire any other significant firm.

The 1968 guidelines were in keeping with the main line of economic thinking during the 1960s and the fairly tough policy toward mergers of the Supreme Court under Chief Justice Earl Warren. When President Reagan took office in 1980, both economic thinking and the Supreme Court's position under the leadership of Chief Justice Warren Burger had changed. Economists and the Courts had become more accepting of the economic advantages associated with mergers and less suspicious of the potential negative impacts, particularly with regard to vertical and conglomerate mergers. As a result of this new attitude, Assistant Attorney General William Baxter presided over a major rewriting of the merger guidelines in 1982.

The new guidelines were released in June 1982 and revised slightly in 1984. Instead of basing the standard on traditional concentration ratio measures, the 1982 guidelines were based on the Herfindahl Index.* [74]

The 1982 horizontal merger guidelines suggested that the Justice Department would not challenge a merger if the postmerger industry Herfindahl would be less than 1000. If the postmerger Herfindahl would fall between 1000 and 1800, mergers causing an increase in the Herfindahl of less than 100 were unlikely to be challenged, but mergers causing an increase in the Herfindahl of more than 100 were likely to be challenged, subject to an analysis of the effects of the merger on entry barriers, the probability of collusion, and other competitive conditions. If a merger resulted in a postmerger Herfindahl greater than 1800 and caused an increase in the Herfindahl of 100, it was very likely to be challenged. If a merger resulted in a postmerger Herfindahl of more than 1800 and caused an increase in the Herfindahl of between 50 and 100, it was likely to be challenged subject to a consideration of its competitive effects. Finally, if a merger resulted in a postmerger Herfindahl of over 1800 and caused an increase in the Herfindahl of less than 50, it was unlikely to be challenged.

The 1982 guidelines were significantly more lenient than the 1968 ones. Under the old guidelines, the Brown Shoe–Kinney merger would have been a borderline case for challenge. Under the 1982 guidelines, the Brown Shoe merger would not have come close to being challenged.

With regard to vertical mergers, the 1982 guidelines eliminated all mention of specific market share limitations. Instead the new guidelines listed three requirements for *consideration* of a challenge to a vertical merger. First, the merger had to make it unlikely that any entrant would enter one market (the primary market) without entering the other market (the secondary market) involved in the merger. Second, the merger had to make entry into the primary market much less likely. Third,

*Recall that the advantages of the Herfindahl Index were discussed earlier in this chapter.

entry barriers and other characteristics of noncompetitive performance had to exist in the primary market. The combined effect of these requirements was to make a challenge to any vertical merger unlikely. Under these guidelines, the Brown Shoe–Kinney Shoe merger and the Du Pont–General Motors merger would certainly have been permitted.

The 1982 guidelines mentioned only one reason for challenging a conglomerate merger—the elimination of potential competition. With regard to potential competition challenges, the 1982 guidelines created a tough standard. First, the market had to be highly concentrated, with a Herfindahl of over 1800. This requirement alone put most conglomerate mergers beyond the reach of the guidelines. Second, entry into the market had to be difficult. Third, there had to be only a few other potential entrants into the market. Fourth, the market share of the acquired firm had to be at least 5 percent. Under these guidelines, few conglomerate mergers would be challenged.

Compared with the 1968 guidelines, the 1982 guidelines left relatively few mergers open for challenge. The 1982 guidelines suggested a retreat from an aggressive anti-merger policy.

In 1984, the Department of Justice revised the 1982 guidelines. The 1982 guidelines stated that the Department generally would *not* consider potential efficiency gains before deciding whether to challenge a merger. The 1984 guidelines explicitly recognized efficiency gains as a relevant factor in the Department's decision-making process but made it clear that efficiencies were not to be considered an absolute defense but merely one factor to be considered before a final decision was reached on a particular merger.

In 1992 the guidelines were revised again to further deemphasize the importance of simple concentration measures and to further emphasize the impact of the merger on price and entry conditions. The 1992 guidelines made it clear that the Justice Department would not rely on simple changes in concentration measures without evidence that the merger would result in higher prices or a greater likelihood of effective collusion. Furthermore, even a merger that was likely to result in higher short-run prices would be permitted as long as the higher prices were likely to induce entry within two years. Under the 1992 guidelines very few mergers will be challenged. In 1997 the guidelines were revised slightly to clarify when the Justice Department would consider economies a valid defense. This revision had little if any effect on actual enforcement procedures.

It is important to note one other major change in antitrust enforcement that went into effect in 1976 with the passage of the ***Hart-Scott-Rodino Act*** (also known as the Antitrust Improvements Act). The Hart-Scott-Rodino Act amended Section 7 of the Clayton Act to require advance notification to the Justice Department and the FTC of any major merger. Any merger in which one firm has sales or assets of at least $100 million and the other firm has sales or assets of at least $10 million must be reported to the government at least 30 days in advance. The act requires the provision of extensive data concerning the proposed merger and gives the government time to report to the potential merger partners whether a challenge will be forthcoming.

Although compliance with the Hart-Scott-Rodino Act is expensive, it has resulted in improved enforcement by enabling the government to act quickly and before the fact against proposed mergers. In fact, it is no mere coincidence that no major merger case has worked its way to the Supreme Court since the passage of the Hart-Scott-Rodino Act.

SUMMARY

1. Most work within industrial organization looks at the structure of individual markets. Traditionally, a measure of market share has been used as a proxy for market power. Although recent work has shown that it is important not to associate market share with market power blindly, measures of market concentration still play an important role in public policy.

2. Several statistical measures of seller concentration within an individual market are available. The two most commonly used measures are the concentration ratio and the Herfindahl-Hirschman Index. The concentration ratio is the cumulative share of the K largest firms in the market, with typical values of K being 4, 8, and 20. The Herfindahl-Hirschman Index is the sum of the squares of the market shares of all of the firms in the industry.

3. Regardless of which measure of concentration is used, an important issue is the definition of the relevant market. A properly defined market includes all firms that compete with each other but excludes all noncompetitors. The market definitions used by the Bureau of the Census are less than perfect.

4. Entry and exit conditions are important determinants of existing firms' market power. Both barriers and incentives affect entry into and exit from an industry.

5. Data on entry and exit patterns show a high rate of turnover among firms in manufacturing industries; both the entering and exiting firms are considerably smaller than existing firms, on average. Disaggregation of the data shows a considerable variation in entry and exit patterns across industries, although the correlation between average entry and exit rates is high.

6. We examined structural barriers to entry, conditions facing a firm over which it has no control. The four categories of structural barriers to entry are (1) economies of scale, (2) absolute cost advantages, (3) capital costs, and (4) product differentiation.

7. Economies of scale can act as a barrier to entry if an industry has room for only a small number of firms, each of which is producing at the minimum efficient scale. If incumbent firms act as a perfect cartel and choose to hold output constant at pre-entry levels even after new firms enter the industry, entry may well drive price below average cost.

8. A number of factors can create an absolute cost advantage for existing firms. Among these are control of a crucial input, access to investment funds at a lower interest rate than that facing potential entrants, superior production technologies, and the ability to pay less for scarce inputs such as raw materials or personnel.

9. Capital costs can create a barrier to entry in industries with large minimum efficient scales if new firms have to pay a higher interest rate on borrowed funds than do established firms.

10. Advertising can create an advantage for incumbents through three channels: (1) absolute cost advantages, (2) economies of scale, and (3) high capital costs of entry.

11. Entry decisions depend on incentives as well as barriers. Two incentives of particular note are expected profitability and market growth.

12 Both barriers and incentives affect the rate of exit from, as well as the rate of entry into, an industry. Exit barriers are generally thought of as some type of sunk cost. Profits and market growth influence exit as well as entry.

13 One important factor affecting market structure throughout the last century has been the level of merger activity. The three types of mergers are horizontal mergers, which involve firms that are direct competitors; vertical mergers, involving firms that produce at different stages of production in the same industry; and conglomerate mergers, which involve companies that operate in either different product markets or the same product market but different geographic markets.

14 Five major merger waves have taken place in the United States. The first four occurred at the turn of the century, in the 1920s, in the 1960s, and in the 1980s. The fifth wave began in the mid-1990s and is continuing into the twenty-first century.

15 The primary motives for merger include increasing market power, efficiency gains, financial gains to stockholders, risk reduction, empire building, failing firms, and aging owners.

16 Horizontal mergers are most likely to result in increased market power, but they also may result in efficiency gains due to economies of scale.

17 Vertical mergers can benefit society if they allow a firm to take advantage of technological complementarities or reduce transactions costs. But vertical mergers can also increase entry barrier into an industry or raise rivals' costs.

18 Conglomerate mergers are least likely to reduce actual competition, but they may reduce *potential* competition.

19 Public policy toward horizontal mergers was lax until 1950, then strict for 25 years until the mid-1970s. Since then, the modern trend in the lower courts is to recognize cost-saving efficiencies as a defense in horizontal mergers. However, major horizontal mergers with significant effects on market structure still are subject to antitrust enforcement.

20 Public policy toward vertical mergers centers on the issue of foreclosure. Policy was strict in the 1950s and 1960s but has loosened up considerably since then as economic and legal thinking concerning vertical mergers continues to change.

21 Recent public policy toward conglomerate mergers has centered on the issue of potential competition. Some conglomerate mergers were successfully challenged in the 1960s, 1970s, and 1980s, but few cases would be challenged under the current Department of Justice guidelines.

22 Since 1968 the Department of Justice has established merger guidelines suggesting which mergers the Department is likely to challenge. The guidelines were amended in 1982, 1984, 1992, and 1997. The changes resulted in fewer mergers that would be challenged. Under current guidelines very few vertical or conglomerate mergers are likely to be challenged. The 1992 guidelines increased the importance of price effects and entry conditions in horizontal merger cases and reduced the likelihood of challenges to horizontal mergers as well.

KEY TERMS

absolute cost advantage
aggregate concentration
Celler-Kefauver Act
concentration ratio (CR)
conglomerate merger
cross-subsidization
economic forebearance
engineering studies
event studies
exit barrier
foreclosure

geographic extension mergers
Hart-Scott-Rodino Act
Herfindahl-Hirschman Index (HHI)
horizontal mergers
incipiency precedent
minimum efficient scale (MES)
North American Industry Classification System (NAICS)
numbers equivalent
potential competition

price squeeze
product extension mergers
pure conglomerate mergers
reciprocity
Standard Industrial Classification (SIC)
statistical cost analysis
strategic barriers to entry
structural barriers to entry
survivor test
vertical mergers

DISCUSSION QUESTIONS

1. Read Application 4.1. Should policymakers be worried about the level of aggregate concentration in the economy? Think about both theoretical reasons and the available empirical evidence.

2. Discuss the relative advantages and disadvantages of four-firm concentration ratios compared to Herfindahl-Hirschman indexes.

3. The case of *United States v. Continental Can Company* involved a merger between Continental Can, the nation's second largest manufacturer of metal containers, and Hazel-Atlas Glass Company, the third largest producer of glass containers in the country. The two largest can manufacturers accounted for about 55 percent of can and bottle sales.

 Market definition was a crucial issue in this case. Three alternative market definitions were considered:
 a. a narrow definition that considered metal containers and glass containers as separate markets
 b. a broad definition that combined metal and glass containers
 c. a still broader definition that included paper and plastic as well as metal and glass

 What evidence would you examine to decide which of these three definitions is the best? Explain your reasoning.

4. Discuss the principal biases introduced by using Census data to measure market concentration. If a researcher used the following NAICS definitions, which biases would apply?
 a. 311511 Fluid Milk
 b. 51111 Newspaper Publishers
 c. 325412 Pharmaceutical Preparations Manufacturing
 d. 32616 Plastic Bottles Manufacturing
 e. 316213 Men's Footwear Manufacturing, except Athletic
 f. 33431 Household Audio and Video Equipment

5. Discuss the difference between Bain's definition of barriers to entry and Stigler's definition. Would each of the following factors be a barrier to entry using Bain's definition? Using Stigler's? Explain your reasoning.
 a. economies of scale
 b. a brand name
 c. exclusive ownership of a key input

6. Explain how an increase in the market demand for a product can reduce the importance of economies of scale as a barrier to entry.

7. In thinking about economies of scale as an entry barrier, Bain assumed that incumbent firms would hold output constant at pre-entry levels even after entry. Do you think this assumption is reasonable? Why or why not?

8. In addition to estimating the MES, economists studying economies of scale also estimate the steepness of the average cost curve

at output levels less than the MES. Why is this relevant when thinking about economies of scale as a barrier to entry?

9. Suppose an economist compares the interest rates charged to established firms and the interest rates charged to new firms and finds that established firms pay a lower rate. He concludes that this is evidence of imperfections in the loan market. Do you agree with him? Explain your reasoning.

10. Explain why the question of whether the effects of advertising carry over from one period to the next is important for determining whether advertising creates a barrier to entry. Do you think the effects of advertising last over time? Can you think of particularly memorable advertising campaigns?

11. Why might firms look at the trend in profits over recent years in deciding whether to enter an industry?

12. Explain why exit is likely to be affected by sunk costs. Can you think of industries other than the railroad industry in which large sunk costs might have slowed down exit even though firms are losing money?

13. Recent years have seen record numbers of mergers. Choose one and explain what type of merger it was. Discuss possible motives for that particular merger.

14. Suppose Kellogg's, the nation's largest ready-to-eat cereal manufacturer, purchased a leading manufacturer of cardboard boxes. Should the government challenge this merger?

15. In 1986 the Federal Trade Commission challenged the mergers of Coca-Cola with Dr Pepper and Pepsico with Seven-Up but then permitted the merger of Dr Pepper with Seven-Up. Did these decisions make economic sense?

16. Suppose McDonald's attempted to acquire Burger King. Should the Federal Trade Commission challenge the merger?

17. Explain how elimination of a large potential entrant could have a significant effect on a market.

18. In major merger cases, the defendant almost always argues that a tremendous increase in costs will result if the merger is prevented. Is such a defense justified in most cases? Explain your reasoning.

19. Suppose a particular horizontal merger results in realization of some economies of scale. Does it follow that the merger should be permitted? What other evidence might you look at in evaluating this merger?

PROBLEMS

1. Consider an industry that has eight firms with the following market share percentages: 30, 20, 12, 10, 10, 8, 7, and 3.
 a. Calculate the four-firm concentration ratio for this industry.
 b. Calculate the Herfindahl-Hirschman index for this industry.

2. Consider an industry that has eight firms with the following market share percentages: 20, 20, 16, 16, 9, 8, 6, and 5.
 a. Calculate the four-firm concentration ratio for this industry.
 b. Calculate the Herfindahl-Hirschman index for this industry.

3. Use your answers to questions 1 and 2 to discuss the advantages of the HHI over the four-firm concentration ratio.

4. Suppose you know only the market shares for the largest six firms in an industry. Although you cannot compute the HHI for this industry, you can find an upper bound and a lower bound for its values. Explain and calculate these bounds.

5. Calculate the numbers equivalent for each of the following values of the HHI.
 a. 1000
 b. 1250
 c. 1428
 d. 2500

 Explain what the numbers equivalent tells us about a market. What information is *not* conveyed by the numbers equivalent?

6. Let a firm's total cost function be TC = 800 + 8q + 8q². Its marginal cost is then given by MC = 8 + 16q.
 a. Derive an expression for the firm's average cost function.
 b. Find the range of production characterized by economies of scale.
 c. Do you think that economies of scale constitute a serious barrier to entry into this industry? Explain your reasoning.

7. a. An industry is currently performing competitively with price equal to marginal cost. If demand is P = 200 − Q and LRMC = LRAC = 50, what are output and price?
 b. If a series of mergers monopolizes the industry *and* results in lower costs such that LRMC = LRAC = 40, what happens to industry output and price?
 c. Does this series of mergers improve welfare?
 d. If the mergers reduced the monopolist's costs to LRMC = LRAC = 20, would the mergers improve welfare?

NOTES

1. John E. Kwoka Jr., "The Herfindahl Index in Theory and Practice," *Antitrust Bulletin* 30 (Winter 1985): 915–947.
2. John E. Kwoka Jr., "Does the Choice of Concentration Measure Really Matter?", *Journal of Industrial Economics* 29 (June 1981): 445–453; see also John E. Kwoka Jr., "Herfindahl Concentration with an Import Fringe and Supply Constraints," *Review of Industrial Organization* 13 (1998): 401–407; and Charles R. Laine, "The Herfindahl-Hirschman Index: The Consumers' Point of View," *Antitrust Bulletin* 40 (Summer 1995): 423–432.
3. See David Schwartzman and Joan Bodoff, "Concentration in Regional and Local Industries," *Southern Economic Journal* 37 (January 1971): 343–348.
4. Timothy Dunne, Mark J. Roberts, and Larry Samuelson, "Patterns of Firm Entry and Exit in U.S. Manufacturing Industries," *Rand Journal of Economics* 19 (Winter 1988): 495–515.
5. A recent article provides further evidence on turnover. See Richard E. Caves, "Industrial Organization and New Findings on the Turnover and Mobility of Firms," *Journal of Economic Literature* 36 (December 1998): 1947–1982.
6. See R. Preston McAfee, Hugo M. Mialon, and Michael A. Williams, "When Are Sunk Costs Barriers to Entry?" *American Economic Review* 94 (May 2004): 461–465 for a discussion of seven principal definitions of entry barriers and four additional proposed definitions.
7. Joe S. Bain, *Barriers to New Competition* (Cambridge: Harvard University Press, 1956), p. 3.
8. George J. Stigler, "Barriers to Entry, Economies of Scale and Firm Size," Chapter 6 in *The Organization of Industry* (Homewood, Illinois: Richard D. Irwin, 1968), p. 67.
9. *Ibid.*
10. C. von Weizsacker, "A Welfare Analysis of Barriers to Entry," *Bell Journal of Economics* 11 (1980): 400.
11. Richard J. Gilbert, "Mobility Barriers and the Value of Incumbency," in R. Schmalensee and R. Willig (eds.), *Handbook of Industrial Organization* (New York: North Holland, 1989), p. 478.
12. Some early studies emphasized behavioral foundations more than Bain did. References include A.G. Papandreou and J.T. Wheeler, *Competition and Its Regulation* (Englewood Cliffs: Prentice-Hall, 1954), Chapter 12, and H.R. Edwards, "Price Formation in

Manufacturing Industry and Excess Capacity," *Oxford Economic Papers* 7 (February 1955): 94–118.

13. *United States* v. *Aluminum Company of America,* 148 U.S. 416 (1945); for nickel—Robert D. Cairns, "Changing Structure in the World Nickel Industry," *Antitrust Bulletin* (Fall 1984): 561–575; for tobacco—*American Tobacco Co. et al. v. United States,* 328 U.S. 781 (1946).

14. Scherer et al., *Multi-Plant Operation,* pp. 284–287; Marc R. Reinganum and Janet K. Smith, "Investor Preference for Large Firms: New Evidence on Economies of Size," *Journal of Industrial Economics* 32 (December 1983): 213–227.

15. G. William Schwert, "Size and Stock Returns, and Other Empirical Regularities," *Journal of Financial Economics* 12 (June 1983): 3–12; Marc R. Reinganum and Janet K. Smith, "Investor Preference for Large Firms: New Evidence on Economies of Size," *Journal of Industrial Economics* 32 (December 1983): 221–225; K.C. Chan, Nai-fu Chen, and David A. Hsieh, "An Exploratory Investigation of the Firm Size Effect," *Journal of Financial Economics* 14 (September 1985): 451–471; Ted Mallett and Anindya Sen, "Does Local Competition Impact Interest Rates Charged on Small Business Loans? Empirical Evidence from Canada," *Review of Industrial Organization,* December 2001, vol. 19, No. 4, pp. 437–452; and James H. Rauch and Jill M. Hendrickson, "Does Bank Consolidation Hurt the Small Business Borrower?", *Small Business Economics,* October 2004, vol. 23, No. 3, pp. 219–226; and Charles W. Calomiris and Thanavut Pornrojnangkool, "Monopoly-Creating Bank Consolidation? The Merger of Fleet and Bank Boston," NBER Working Paper: 11351, 2005, www.nber.org/papers/w11351.pdf.

16. References include F.R. Edwards, "Concentration in Banking and Its Effect on Business Loan Rates," *Review of Economics and Statistics* 46 (August 1964): 294–300, and Paul A. Meyer, "Price Discrimination, Regional Loan Rates, and the Structure of the Banking Industry," *Journal of Finance* (March 1967): 37–48.

17. William S. Comanor and Thomas A. Wilson, *Advertising and Market Power* (Cambridge: Harvard University Press, 1974), Chapters 3 and 4; Comanor and Wilson, "Advertising and Competition: A Survey," *Journal of Economic Literature* 17 (June 1979): 453–476.

18. References include Jean J. Lambin, *Advertising, Competition and Market Conduct in Oligopoly over Time* (Amsterdam: North-Holland Publishing Company, 1976); and Darral G. Clarke, "Econometric Measurement of the Duration of Advertis-

ing Effect on Sales," *Journal of Marketing Research* 13 (November 1976): 345–357.

19. Clarke, *op. cit.,* p. 355.

20. Julian L. Simon, *Issues in the Economics of Advertising* (Urbana: University of Illinois Press, 1974), p. 15, and Michael E. Porter, "Interbrand Choice, Media Mix and Market Performance," *American Economic Review* 66 (May 1976): 402.

21. Porter, *op. cit.,* p. 403.

22. Comanor and Wilson, "Advertising, Market Structure and Performance," *Review of Economics and Statistics* 49 (November 1967): 426.

23. Richard Highfield and Robert Smiley, "New Business Starts and Economic Activity," *International Journal of Industrial Organization* 5 (1987): 51–66.

24. Paul A. Geroski, Richard J. Gilbert, and Alexis Jacquemin, *Barriers to Entry and Strategic Competition* (Chur, Switzerland: Harwood Academic Publishers, 1990).

25. The discussion in this paragraph is based on John J. Siegfried and Laurie Beth Evans, "Empirical Studies of Entry and Exit: A Survey of the Evidence," *Review of Industrial Organization* 9 (April 1994): 127.

26. The discussion in this paragraph and this example are based on Gilbert, *Supra* note 11, p. 520.

27. The first careful empirical study of exit behavior is Richard E. Caves and Michael E. Porter, "Barriers to Exit," in P. David Qualls and Robert Masson (eds.), *Essays on Industrial Organization in Honor of Joe S. Bain* (Cambridge: Ballinger, 1976). Other references include Larry L. Duetsch, "An Examination of Industry Exit Patterns," *Review of Industrial Organization* 1 (1984): 60–68; James M. MacDonald, "Entry and Exit on the Competitive Fringe," *Southern Economic Journal* 52 (1986): 640–652; Timothy Dunne and Mark J. Roberts, "Variation in Producer Turnover Across U.S. Manufacturing Industries," in P.A. Geroski and J. Schwalback (eds.), *Entry and Market Contestability* (Oxford: Basil Blackwell, 1991), pp. 187–203; and John J. Siegfried and Laurie Beth Evans, "Entry and Exit in United States Manufacturing Industries from 1977 to 1982," in David W. Audretsch and John J. Siegfried (eds.), *Empirical Studies in Industrial Organization: Essays in Honor of Leonard W. Weiss* (Dordrecht: Kluwer Academic Publishers, 1992): 121–155.

28. Caves and Porter, *Supra* note 27, p. 44.

29. This paragraph is based on the discussion in Daniel Shapiro and R.S. Khemani, "The Determinants of Entry and Exit Reconsidered," *International Journal of Industrial Organization* (March 1987): 16.

30. Shapiro and Khemani, *op. cit.,* pp. 15–26; David I. Rosenbaum and Fabian Lamont, "Entry, Barriers,

Exit, and Sunk Costs: An Analysis," *Applied Economics* 24 (1992): 297–304.

31. Rosenbaum and Lamont, *op. cit.*

32. Ralph L. Nelson, *Merger Movements in American Industry, 1895–1956* (Princeton, NJ: Princeton University Press, 1959), p. 29.

33. Glenn Porter, *The Rise of Big Business, 1860–1920,* 2nd edition (Arlington Heights, IL: Harlan Davidson, 1992), p. 84.

34. George J. Stigler, "Monopoly and Oligopoly by Merger," *American Economic Review* 40 (May 1950): 23–34; reprinted in *The Organization of Industry* (Homewood, IL: Irwin, 1968), pp. 95–107.

35. Carl Eis, "The 1919–1930 Merger Movement in American Industry," *Journal of Law & Economics* 12 (October 1969): 280–284.

36. Federal Trade Commission, *Economic Report on Corporate Mergers* (Washington, DC: U.S. Government Printing Office, 1969).

37. Bruce T. Allen, "Merger Statistics and Merger Policy," *Review of Industrial Organization* (Summer 1984); and David J. Ravenscraft and F.M. Scherer, *Mergers, Sell-Offs, and Economic Efficiency* (Washington, DC: Brookings Institution, 1987), pp. 198–199.

38. The discussion in this paragraph draws on Gregor Andrade, Mark Mitchell, and Erik Stafford, "New Evidence and Perspectives on Mergers," *Journal of Economic Perspectives* 15 (Spring 2001): 103–120.

39. E. Woodrow Eckard, "The Impact of the 1980s Merger Movement on U.S. Industrial Concentration," *Antitrust Bulletin* (Summer 1995): 397–398.

40. Cynthia Benzing, "Mergers—What the 'Grimm' Data Tell Us," *Review of Industrial Organization* 8 (December 1993): 747–753. For a relatively new explanation for vertical mergers see Benjamin Klein and Kevin M. Murphy, "Vertical Integration as a Self-Enforcing Contractual Arrangement, *American Economic Review* 87 (May 1997): 415–420.

41. John E. Kwoka Jr., "The Private Profitability of Horizontal Mergers with Non-Cournot and Maverick Behavior," *International Journal of Industrial Organization* 7 (September 1989): 403–411.

42. F.M. Scherer, Alan Beckenstein, Erich Kaufer, and R.D. Murphy, *Multiplant Operation: An International Comparison Study* (Cambridge: Harvard University Press, 1975), p. 169.

43. Dennis C. Mueller (ed.), *The Determinants and Effects of Mergers* (Cambridge, UK: Oelgeschlager, Gunn & Hain, 1985); and Geoffry Meeks, *Disappointing Marriage: A Study of the Gains from Merger* (Cambridge, UK: Cambridge University Press, 1977).

44. Stanley E. Boyle, "Pre-Merger Growth and Profit Characteristics of Large Conglomerate Mergers in the United States: 1948–1968," *St. Johns Law Review, Special Edition* (Spring 1970): 160–161. For a theoretical model, see Mark A. Dutz, "Horizontal Mergers in Declining Industries," *International Journal of Industrial Organization* 7 (March 1989): 11–33.

45. See Kenneth D. Boyer, "Mergers that Harm Competition," *Review of Industrial Organization* 7 (1992): 191–202; and Laurence Schumann, "Patterns of Abnormal Returns and the Competitive Effects of Horizontal Mergers," *Review of Industrial Organization* 8 (December 1993): 679–696.

46. *United States* v. *Aluminum Company of America,* 148 F.2d 416 (1945).

47. John T. Scott, "Purposive Diversification as a Motive for Merger," *International Journal of Industrial Organization* 7 (March 1989): 35–47; and Thomas A. Wilson, "An Analysis of the Profitability of Business of Diversified Companies," *Review of Industrial Organization* 7 (1992): 151–185.

48. Kenneth G. Elzinga, "The Beer Industry," in Walter Adams (ed.) *The Structure of American Industry,* 8th edition (New York: Macmillan Publishing Company, 1990), p. 146; and "Miller's Fast Growth Upsets the Beer Industry," *Business Week* (November 8, 1976): 58–67.

49. See Willard F. Mueller, "Conglomerates: A 'Nonindustry'" in Walter Adams (ed.), *The Structure of American Industry,* 7th edition (New York: Macmillan Publishing Company, 1986), especially pp. 377–381.

50. Michael C. Jensen and Richard R. Ruback, "The Market for Corporate Control: The Scientific Evidence," *Journal of Financial Economics* 11 (1983): 5–50.

51. Harry DeAngelo, Linda DeAngelo, and Edward M. Rice, "Going Private: Minority Freezeouts and Stockholder Wealth," *Journal of Law and Economics* 27 (1984): 367–402.

52. See also Gregg A. Jarrell, James A. Brinkley, and Jeffrey M. Netter, "The Market for Corporate Control: The Empirical Evidence Since 1980," *Journal of Economic Perspectives* 2 (1988): 49–68; and Andrei Schleifer and Robert W. Vishny, "Value Maximization and the Acquisition Process," *Journal of Economic Perspectives* 2 (1988): 7–20; Matthew J. Hergott, "Airport Concentration and Market Power: An Event Study Approach," *Review of Industrial Organization* 12 (1997): 793–800; Judith A. Chevalier, "Capital Structure and Product Market Competition: Empirical Evidence from the Supermarket Industry," *American Economic Review* 85 (June 1995): 415–435; and Andrade et al., *Supra* note 38.

53. David J. Ravenscraft and F.M. Scherer, *Mergers, Sell-Offs and Economic Efficiency* (Washington, DC: Brookings Institution, 1987); and David J. Raven-

scraft and F.M. Scherer, "The Profitability of Mergers," *International Journal of Industrial Organization* 7 (March 1989): 101–116. See also Avi Dor and Bernard Friedman, "Mergers of Not-for-Profit Hospitals in the 1980s: Who Were the Most Likely Targets?" *Review of Industrial Organization* 9 (August 1994): 393–407; Laurence Schumann, "Patterns of Abnormal Returns and the Competitive Effects of Horizontal Mergers," *Review of Industrial Organization* 8 (December 1993): 679–696; William W. Alberts and Nikhil P. Varaiya, "Assessing the Profitability of Growth by Acquisition: A 'Premium Recapture' Approach," *International Journal of Industrial Organization* 9 (March 1989): 133–149; Ralph Bühner, "The Success of Mergers in Germany," *International Journal of Industrial Organization* 9 (December 1991): 513–532; and Richard E. Caves, "Mergers, Takeovers, and Economic Efficiency," *International Journal of Industrial Organization* 7 (March 1989): 151–174.

54. David J. Ravenscraft and F.M. Scherer, *Mergers Sell–Offs and Economic Efficiency, Supra* note 53, p. 74.

55. See Dennis C. Mueller, *Determinants and Effects of Mergers* (Cambridge: Oelgeschlager, Gunn & Hain, 1980); Geoffrey Meeks, *Disappointing Marriage: A Study of the Gains from Mergers* (Cambridge: Cambridge University Press, 1977); for evidence from the United Kingdom see Alan Hughes, "The Impact of Merger: A Survey of Empirical Evidence for the UK," in James A. Fairburn and John A. Kay (eds.), *Mergers and Merger Policy* (Oxford: Oxford University Press, 1989).

56. David J. Ravenscraft and F.M. Scherer, *Mergers Sell–Offs and Economic Efficiency, Supra* note 53, p. 190.

57. Paul M. Healy, Krishna G. Palepee, and Richard S. Ruback, "Does Coporate Performance Improve After Mergers?" *Journal of Financial Economics* 31 (1992): 135–175.

58. Andrade et al., *Supra* note 38.

59. For a recent survey of many of the studies on the effects of mergers and acquisitions, see Dennis C. Mueller, "Merger Policy in the United States: A Reconsideration," *Review of Industrial Organization* 12 (1997): 655–685. See also Chulho Jung and Barry J. Seldon, "The Degree of Competition in the Advertising Industry," *Review of Industrial Organization* 10 (1995): 41–52.

60. *Thatcher Manufacturing Company* v. *Federal Trade Commission,* 272 US 554 (1926).

61. *Brown Shoe Company* v. *United States,* 370 U.S. 294 (1962).

62. *United States* v. *Philadelphia National Bank et al.,* 374 U.S. 321 (1964).

63. *United States* v. *General Dynamics Corporation et al.,* 415 U.S. 486 (1974).

64. *United States* v. *Waste Management, Inc. and EMW Ventures Inc.,* 743 F.22d 976 (1984).

65. *Federal Trade Commission* v. *Staples, Inc.,* No. 97–701 (1997).

66. *United States* v. *E.I. du Pont de Nemours & Co. et al.,* 353 U.S. 586 (1957).

67. *Brown Shoe Company* v. *United States,* 370 U.S. 294 (1962).

68. *Fruehauf Corporation* v. *FTC,* 603 F.2d 345 (1989).

69. *Federal Trade Commission* v. *Procter & Gamble Co.,* 386 U.S. 568 (1967).

70. *In the Matter of The Bendix Corporation et al.,* 77 F.T.C. 731 (1970).

71. *In the Matter of The Bendix Corporation et al.,* see 450 F.2d 534 (1971).

72. *Yamaha Motors Company* v. *FTC,* 657 F.2d 971 (1981); *certiorari denied* by the Supreme Court 456 U.S. 915 (1982).

73. *Tenneco, Inc.* v. *FTC,* 689 F.2d 346 (1982).

74. For a discussion of some potential problems with using the HHI, see Jack Nickerson, "Durable Goods and Horizontal Merger Analysis," *Review of Industrial Organization* 10 (April 1995): 209–220.

INTERNET EXERCISES

Visit www.aw-bc.com/waldman_jensen for this chapter's web exercises. Answer our real-world economics problems by searching the Internet for solutions!

Monopoly Practices

Chapter 3 considered the economics of a pure monopoly. Here, we extend that discussion in three ways. First, we look at industries which are "almost" monopolies. In some industries, one firm has less than 100 percent of the market, but is still large enough to dominate the industry and set the price. After examining the dominant-firm model, we turn to the theory of contestable markets. This theory emphasizes the importance of potential competition and suggests that there are some circumstances in which even a completely monopolized market may perform as if it were perfectly competitive in structure. Our final topic for this chapter is network effects. Strong network effects can enhance monopoly power and enable extension of monopoly power from one product line to another.* In contrast to contestable markets, therefore, competition is less viable in markets with network effects.

5.1 Dominant-Firm Price Leadership Model[1]

Few industries are truly monopolies. In practice, it is much more common to find industries in which there is a dominant firm as well some number of smaller fringe firms. Think, for example, of the market for microprocessors, the central processing unit of a computer system. Intel has dominated this market for two decades, although recent news reports suggest that competitor Advanced Micro Devices (AMD) is gaining market share. Still, Intel holds an 80 percent share of the PC microprocessor market. Other historical examples of dominant firms include IBM in PCs in the early 1980s and in mainframe computers in the 1960s and 1970s, Kodak in photographic film, and Boeing in commercial jet aircraft. In a market with a dominant firm, it makes sense to assume that the dominant firm will set the industry price and the fringe firms will take that price as given. In other words, the fringe firms behave exactly like perfectly competitive firms in the sense that they are price takers and maximize their profits by equating price to marginal cost. We will examine the pricing behavior carefully after considering some reasons for the rise of a dominant firm.

*Another important topic related to monopoly power is price discrimination. This pricing technique allows a firm with a downward-sloping demand curve to increase its profits. Chapter 15 considers price discrimination in detail.

5.1.1 Sources of Dominance

Two factors can lead to a dominant firm–competitive fringe market structure:

1. The dominant firm may have a *significant cost advantage* compared to its rivals. This cost advantage can arise from superior efficiency. For example, a firm might have superior technology or it might have better management. As a result, the dominant firm can produce any given level of output at a lower cost than other firms. The dominant firm may also have been an early entrant into the industry. In this case, the cost advantage over later entrants might arise because the early entrant has had time to benefit from learning by doing or to grow large enough to realize economies of scale.

2. The dominant firm may have a *superior product*. For example, Intel's microprocessors were traditionally the fastest and most advanced microprocessors available.

5.1.2 Pricing by a Dominant Firm

The **dominant-firm price leadership model** can be explained by using the steel industry as an example. During the first half of the twentieth century the American steel industry had this structure with United States Steel (US Steel) acting as the dominant firm. In Figure 5.1, the steel industry demand curve D is $P = 100 - Q$ (in Figure 5.1, the industry demand curve is the dashed red line for $\$25 \leq P \leq \100 and the black line for $0 \leq P < \$25$), the fringe's supply curve S_f is $P = 25 + 2q_f$, and the dominant firm's marginal cost curve (US Steel's MC curve) is $MC_u = 25 + (1/3)q_u$. To obtain US Steel's residual demand curve, subtract the fringe supply curve from the total demand curve at every price greater than $P = \$25$. For example, if $P = \$75$, total *industry* quantity demanded would equal 25 units, and the fringe would supply the entire industry demand of 25. If $P = \$75$, therefore, the residual demand for US Steel would be zero. If $P = \$25$, total industry quantity demanded would equal 75 units, and the fringe would supply zero. The residual demand for US Steel would then be 75 units.

Similar calculations can be done to obtain US Steel's residual demand for any price between $\$25$ and $\$75$.* Such calculations yield the black linear residual demand curve that connects the two points (0, 75) and (75, 25). The equation of this demand curve is:

$$P = 75 - \tfrac{2}{3}q_u \quad \text{for } \$25 \leq P \leq \$75. \tag{5.1}$$

By the "twice-as-steep rule," marginal revenue is:

$$MR_u = 75 - \tfrac{4}{3}q_u \quad \text{for } \$25 \leq P \leq \$75. \tag{5.2}$$

*For any price, to obtain US Steel's *residual demand*, it is necessary to subtract q_f from the total quantity demanded Q.

We have $P = 100 - Q$, so $Q = 100 - P$. In addition:

$$P = 25 + 2q_f \quad \text{or} \quad q_f = \tfrac{1}{2}P - 12.5.$$

Because $q_u = Q - q_f$,

$$q_u = (100 - P) - (\tfrac{1}{2}P - 12.5) = 112.5 - \tfrac{3}{2}P.$$

Solving for P yields:

$$P = 75 - \tfrac{2}{3}q_u.$$

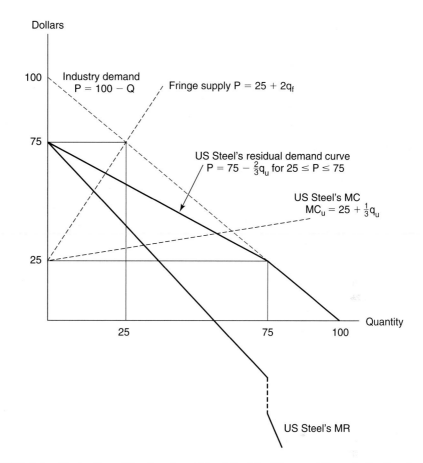

FIGURE 5.1 Derivation of the Dominant Firm's Residual Demand Curve in the Dominant-Firm Price Leadership Model

The market demand for steel is given by $P = 100 - Q$. Because US Steel, the dominant firm, knows that the fringe firms' supply curve is given by $P = 25 + 2q_f$, it can calculate its residual demand by subtracting the fringe supply curve from the total demand curve for every price. For prices below \$25, the fringe firms supply no output, and the dominant firm faces the entire market demand curve. Once price is greater than \$25, the fringe begins to supply output to the market. For example, if $P = \$75$, the fringe would supply the entire industry demand of 25, leaving a residual demand of zero for the dominant firm. The black line connecting $(0, 75)$ to $(75, 25)$ shows US Steel's residual demand for $\$25 \leq P \leq \75.

For prices between 0 and \$25, US Steel's demand curve is identical to the industry demand curve and equals $P = 100 - q_u$. US Steel's residual demand curve, therefore, has a kink at $q_u = 75$, and the MR_u curve has a gap at $q_u = 75$. The residual demand curve and the MR_u curve are drawn in black in Figure 5.1.

Once the residual demand curve of US Steel is identified, the profit-maximizing output for US Steel can be calculated. Recall that the marginal cost curve for US Steel is:

$$MC_u = 25 + \tfrac{1}{3}q_u. \qquad\qquad [5.3]$$

To maximize profits, US Steel equates MC_u to MR_u and produces 30 units.* To obtain price, go up vertically to point Z on US Steel's residual demand curve and P = \$55.00.

Once price is known, the fringe firms act as perfectly competitive price takers and supply the quantity at which the fringe supply curve intersects the horizontal line P = \$55.00. In this case, $q_f = 15.$† Total industry output is simply the sum of US Steel's output and the fringe's output, or Q = 30 + 15 = 45.

One of the major implications of the dominant-firm price leadership model is that the dominant firm's market share declines continuously over time. Worcester explained this tendency using the following dynamic model.[2] If the competitive fringe firms earn above-normal economic profits, there will be an incentive for the fringe supply to increase over time as new firms enter and existing fringe firms expand output. As a result, the residual demand for the dominant firm will shift to the left (decrease), and the dominant firm's relative share of output will decline.

Suppose in our previous example profits existed for the competitive fringe, inducing new firms to enter the industry. Figure 5.3 shows what would happen if the number of fringe firms doubled. The fringe's supply curve would then double so that S_f would be P = 25 + q_f. To obtain US Steel's new residual demand curve, subtract the fringe supply curve from the total demand curve at every price greater than P = \$25. In Figure 5.3, if P = \$62.50, total *industry* quantity demanded would equal 37.5 units, and the fringe would supply the entire industry demand of 37.5. If P = \$62.50, therefore, the residual demand for US Steel would be zero. As in Figures 5.1 and 5.2, if P = \$25, total industry quantity demanded would equal 75 units, and the fringe would supply zero. The residual demand for US Steel would then be 75 units. For prices between \$25 and \$62.50, US Steel's demand curve is a linear demand curve that connects the two points (0, 62.5) and (75, 25). The equation of this curve is:

$$P = 62.50 - \tfrac{1}{2}q_u \quad \text{for } \$25 \le P \le \$62.50. \qquad\qquad [5.4]$$

By the "twice-as-steep rule," marginal revenue is:

$$MR_u = 62.50 - q_u. \qquad\qquad [5.5]$$

Just as in Figure 5.1, for prices between 0 and \$25, US Steel's demand curve is identical to the industry demand curve and equals P = 100 − q_u. US Steel's demand curve, therefore, has a kink at $q_u = 75$, and the MR_u curve has a gap at $q_u = 75$.

*
$$MR_u = 75 - \tfrac{4}{3}q_u = 25 + \tfrac{1}{3}q_u = MC_u.$$

Solving for q_u yields $q_u = 30$.

†The competitive fringe firms set P = 55.00 equal to S_f or:

$$P = 55 = 25 + 2q_f = S_f.$$

Solving for q_f yields $q_f = 15$.

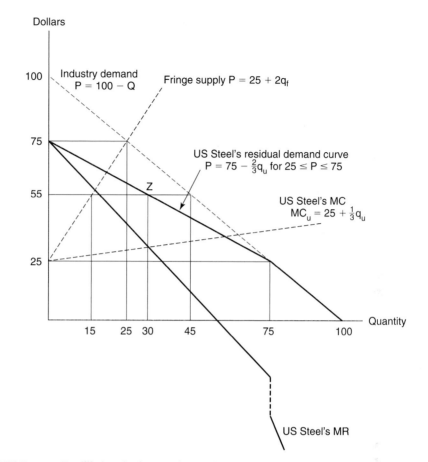

FIGURE 5.2 Equilibrium in the Dominant-Firm Price Leadership Model

Once the residual demand curve for US Steel is known, the marginal revenue curve can be found using the "twice-as-steep rule." Because the residual demand curve has a kink at (75, 25), the corresponding marginal revenue curve has a gap at this quantity. The residual demand curve and the marginal revenue curve for US Steel are shown in black in this figure. US Steel calculates its profit-maximizing level of output by equating its marginal cost to marginal revenue and produces 30 units of output. To obtain price, go up vertically to point Z on US Steel's residual demand curve; the equilibrium price is $55.00. The fringe firms act as price takers and produce 15 units of output, giving a total industry output of $30 + 15 = 45$.

Recall that the marginal cost curve for US Steel, as shown in Equation 5.3, is:

$$MC_u = 25 + \tfrac{1}{3}q_u.$$

To maximize profits, US Steel equates MC_u to MR_u and produces 28.125 units.* To obtain price, go up vertically in Figure 5.3 to point Z on US Steel's residual demand curve and $P = \$48.4375$.

*

$$MR_u = 62.5 - q_u = 25 + \tfrac{1}{3}q_u = MC_u.$$

Solving for q_u yields $q_u = 28.125$.

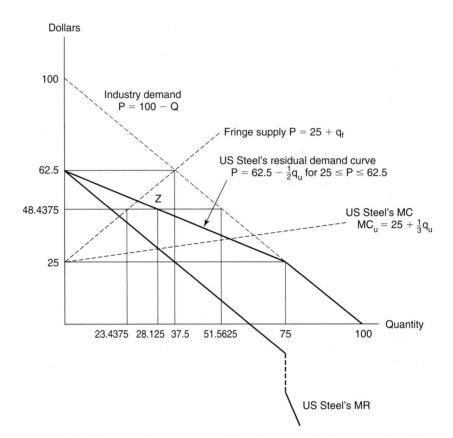

FIGURE 5.3 Equilibrium with an Increased Fringe Supply in the Dominant-Firm Price Leadership Model

If the fringe firms earn above-normal profits at the price set by the dominant firm, there is an incentive for new firms to enter the market. Entry shifts the supply curve of the fringe to the right, causing the residual demand curve for the dominant firm to shift to the left. In this figure, the number of fringe firms has doubled compared to Figure 5.2; the fringe supply is now given by $P = 25 + q_f$. With the same market demand, the dominant firm's profit-maximizing quantity falls to 28.125 units; it sets a lower price of $48.44. As a result of entry, the dominant firm's market share decreases.

Once price is known, the fringe firms act as perfectly competitive price takers and supply the quantity at which the fringe supply curve intersects the horizontal line $P = \$48.4375$. In this case, $q_f = 23.4375$.* Total industry output is the sum of US Steel's output and the fringe's output, or $Q = 28.125 + 23.4375 = 51.5625$.

Because of the expansion of the competitive fringe, US Steel's market share has declined from 66.7 percent (30/45) to 54.5 percent (28.125/51.5625). After this expan-

*The competititve fringe firms set $P = 48.4375$ equal to S_f or:

$$P = 48.4375 = 25 + q_f = S_f.$$

Solving for q_f yields $q_f = 23.4375$.

sion, if the competitive fringe is still earning excess profits, the dominant firm's share will continue to decline.

The dominant firm is remarkably passive in this model. This passivity is often cited as one of the major weaknesses of the model. As we will see in Chapters 11 and 12, a dominant firm can adopt certain strategies to help to maintain its market power in the face of potential entry. However, it sometimes makes sense for a dominant firm to sacrifice market share to its competitors.

APPLICATION 5.1

Banks and Credit Unions: Dominant Firms and Fringe Suppliers?

Some types of loans are not widely available through a national market. For such products, it is reasonable to think of the appropriate market as local. And some of these local markets turn out to be dominated by one or two banks or S&Ls, with credit unions in the markets having considerably smaller shares. A recent study examined 77 such small local consumer lending markets throughout the United States over a five-year period, asking whether the dominant-firm price leadership modeled explained behavior in these markets. In the markets included in the sample, the average market share of the top two depository institutions was 50 percent, while credit unions had an average share of deposits of 9.2 percent. This structure is, of course, consistent with the dominant-firm model. Moreover, a key empirical result from this study is that an increase in the market share of credit unions had a strong price-reducing effect on the cost of loans. Looking at Figures 5.2 and 5.3, we see that this is exactly the result we would expect using the dominant-firm price leadership model: Expansion by the fringe firms over time lowers the market share of the dominant firm and the price of the product.

Source: Robert M. Feinberg, "Credit Unions: Fringe Suppliers or Cournot Competitors?", *Review of Industrial Organization* 20 (March 2002): 105–113. ∎

5.1.3 Empirical Evidence of the Decline of Dominant-Firm Price Leaders

Some empirical evidence suggests that dominant firms' market shares often decline substantially over time. As we noted in the previous section, US Steel behaved as a classic dominant firm after its formation in 1902. At the time of its creation, US Steel's market share was 65 percent; by 1920 its share had declined to 50 percent.[3] In the low-volume segment of the copier industry, Xerox behaved as a classic dominant-firm price leader.[4] Xerox set high profit-maximizing prices in this sector and conceded market share to its smaller rivals.

Few examples of dominant firm price leadership resulting in a decline in market share are more dramatic than the case of the Reynolds International Pen Corporation, which invented an improved ball-point pen that operated on gravity. Reynolds began selling the pens in 1945.[5] Initially the pens cost approximately 80 cents each to produce and Gimbel's department stores sold them for $12.50. Gimbel's sold 10,000 pens the first day they went on sale. By early 1946, Reynolds was producing 30,000 pens a day and earning large economic profits. But Reynolds's high prices encouraged the competitive fringe to enter. By Christmas 1946, many firms were in the industry and prices had fallen as low as 88 cents. By 1948 prices had declined further to 39 cents, and by 1951 they had declined still further, to as low as 19 cents. By then Reynolds

was long gone from the industry. Reynolds came and went quickly, but for one brief, shining moment it was a dominant-firm price leader and earned very large economic profits. This example points out clearly the risks associated with dominant-firm price leadership. By being completely passive toward its competitors, Reynolds found itself booted out of the market in just a few years.

Other examples of dominant-firm price leaders have included International Harvester in farm equipment, Goodyear in tires, RCA in color televisions, General Electric in appliances, and IBM in mainframe computers.[6] Most of these firms lost significant market share to competitors as a result of a high-price policy with little concern for the entry or expansion of competitors, consistent with the predictions of the model.

5.2 Contestable Markets: A Check on Market Power?

In 1982, Baumol, Panzar, and Willig advanced a new theoretical framework for thinking about entry and exit—the theory of contestable markets.[7] The **contestable markets** hypothesis contends that potential competition may be more important than actual competition and that even a completely monopolized market may perform as if it were perfectly competitive in structure. When it was introduced, this theory represented a dramatic departure from the conventional wisdom of economists, and, therefore, it drew a great deal of attention and scrutiny.

Like the theory of perfect competition, the theory of perfectly contestable markets begins with a set of three basic assumptions:

Assumption 1: Entry is free. Free entry means that incumbent firms have no inherent advantages vis-à-vis potential entrants. There are no cost advantages, no patents, and no product differentiation advantages. Entrants are on completely equal footing with established firms, even with an established monopolist.

Assumption 2: Entry is absolute. Absolute entry implies that if a potential entrant enters the market and charges a price below the incumbent's price, then the entrant will *completely* displace the incumbent. This is a very strong assumption with the implication that the incumbent has no time or ability to respond to entry.

Assumption 3: No sunk costs are associated with entry. The assumption of no sunk costs permits "hit-and-run" entry. Firms can enter a market, extract profits for a period of time, and then withdraw with zero sunk cost losses. It is important to note that this assumption does not eliminate *fixed* costs but only *sunk* costs.

Consider the implications of these three assumptions. Suppose that a perfectly contestable market is also a natural monopoly; suppose also that potential entrants exist. Such a situation is depicted in Figure 5.4. What price must the monopolist charge? If it charges the monopoly price P_M and earns a positive economic profit, then the potential entrant will have an incentive to enter the market and charge a price below P_M, because *by assumption* it can enter with identical costs (assumption 1), displace the monopolist (assumption 2), and leave with no sunk cost losses (assumption 3). The only price that the monopolist can sustain is P_C = LRAC, the price at which the LRAC curve intersects the demand curve. A price equal to average cost is the only *sustainable* price because any higher price attracts entry, whereas any lower price results in economic losses.

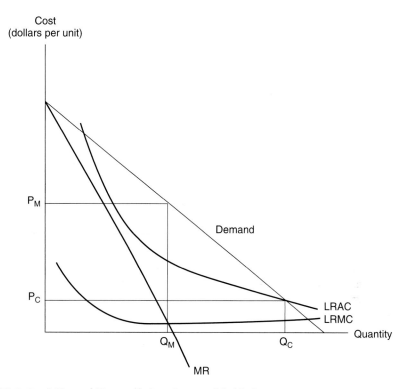

FIGURE 5.4 **A Natural Monopoly in a Contestable Market**

The monopoly price for this market is P_M. However, under the strong assumptions of the contestable market hypothesis, this price is not sustainable. If the monopolist charges P_M and earns a positive economic profit, a potential entrant would enter the market and charge a price below P_M. The entrant would then displace the monopolist. Consequently, the only price that the monopolist can sustain is $P_C = $ LRAC, the price at which the long-run average cost curve intersects the demand curve. Any higher price attracts entry, whereas any lower price results in economic losses.

The implications of the theory are remarkably strong. To achieve a zero-profit result, all that is required is the existence of *one* potential entrant. In this model potential competition is more important than actual competition, and even a natural monopolist may earn zero economic profits. The originators of the theory recognized that any movement away from the three basic assumptions would result in dramatically different results. If sunk costs were greater than zero, for example, then hit-and-run entry would be impossible and incumbents could earn excess profits without attracting entry.

Baumol and colleagues pointed to the airline industry, which had recently been deregulated, as an example of a perfectly contestable market. This choice made some sense in 1982 because there had been a great wave of entry into the industry in the years 1979 to 1981. According to the proponents of the theory of contestability, entry into the airline industry required little more than a pilot and the leasing of an old

plane. The firm could enter whatever market happened to yield the highest profit at the moment. In December, for example, the plane could fly from New York to Miami. If a World Series were being played between the Yankees and the Dodgers, the plane could simply fly back and forth between New York and Los Angeles. In this market, hit-and-run entry could truly evolve into a highly computerized art form. Any carrier charging a price above average cost would be displaced and new airlines would rule the skies. If Baumol and colleagues had been right, we would all be flying on original low-fare carriers such as People Express and Midway instead of Southwest and JetBlue.

Is the airline industry a good example of a contestable market? Consider the assumptions of a perfectly contestable market. Assumption 1 contends that entry is free in the sense that potential entrants and incumbents face identical costs. It is extremely unlikely that assumption 1 holds in the airline industry because potential entrants are likely to have difficulty obtaining gate slots for their planes. Also, they will be forced to spend significant amounts on advertising to penetrate any new market. Assumption 2 claims that entry is absolute and that a low-priced entrant will displace a high-priced incumbent. The assumption of complete displacement is highly questionable in any market, and is certainly not true in the airline industry, in which incumbents always have sufficient advance notice of any impending entry to permit them to respond with competitive price reductions. Assumption 3 contends that there are no sunk costs. This assumption is refuted by the necessity of advertising to enter a new market: Advertising certainly establishes sunk costs for any entrant. Thus none of the assumptions appear to be valid in the airline industry; therefore, it is unlikely that the industry would behave in a manner consistent with the theory of contestable markets.

A significant amount of empirical evidence now suggests that the airline industry is not perfectly contestable. Some of the evidence is anecdotal. The major airlines, for example, did not roll over and disappear when low-price carriers such as People Express, Midway, and Air West entered the industry. There was clearly no absolute displacement of the major carriers.

Better evidence is provided by a number of good statistical studies. In one study, Call and Keeler examined the effects of several variables on airline fares, using data on 89 city pairs.[8] According to the contestable markets hypothesis, *actual* entry should have no effect on fares because potential entry should constrain fares to be equal to average costs. Similarly, the contestable markets hypothesis implies that concentration should have no significant effect on fares because, even in a monopolized market, fares should be forced down to average costs.

Call and Keeler's test of the contestable markets hypothesis revolves around the statistical significance of three variables on fares: a measure of market concentration and two measures of entry. Their results show that all three variables have statistically significant effects on airline fares. Higher concentration results in significantly *higher* fares, while entry by either trunk or nontrunk carriers results in statistically significant *lower* fares. These results strongly suggest that concentration and entry have a significant impact on fares, yet in a *perfectly* contestable market neither concentration nor *actual* entry should have any impact on fares. These results, therefore, strongly refute the argument that the airline industry is perfectly contestable.

In another study that was highly critical of the contestable markets hypothesis, Moore found that the number of airline carriers on a route had a statistically significant

effect on fares in 1983.[9] In particular Moore found that routes with five or more carriers had much lower fares than routes with fewer than five competitors. Once again, such a result runs contrary to the contestable markets hypothesis.

Although the airline industry appears not to be a contestable market, the theory has had a major impact on the industry. The contestable markets hypothesis provided a rationale for the Reagan administration not to be concerned with concentration in the airline industry because, according to the theory, even a monopolized airline market would have to price at average cost. The contestable markets hypothesis with regard to the airline industry, therefore, was consistent with a policy that permitted virtually all mergers in the industry and resulted in higher market concentration.

Experimental economists have been able to simulate perfectly contestable markets and achieve the predicted results. But one of the major tests of any theory has always been its ability to predict and explain real-world phenomena, and according to this test, the contestable markets hypothesis has not fared very well.[10] It is possible that the theory may ultimately find its greatest use in the field of international trade, where it might be used to explain the impact of potential foreign competition on domestic markets. Also, just as perfect competition serves as a benchmark even though no real-world industries are truly perfectly competitive, contestability can serve as a useful theoretical benchmark when thinking about a multiproduct environment.

5.3 Network Economics[11]

Recently, economists have realized that in markets for certain types of goods, a competitive equilibrium is unlikely to exist. The special characteristics of these **network industries** often lead to market failure and the emergence of a firm with monopoly power. Many industries exhibit the characteristics of network industries, including airline services, banking services, telephone services, e-mail, the Internet, computer software, music players, and DVD players. In this section, we examine the characteristics of these industries and think about how these characteristics work against the development of a competitive market.

Four main characteristics distinguish network industries from other industries:

1. Complementarity, compatibility, and standards
2. Consumption externalities
3. Switching costs and lock-in
4. Significant economies of scale in production

Let's examine each of these characteristics and its effect on competition in turn.

5.3.1 Complementarity, Compatibility, and Standards

Some products must be consumed together with other products: Trains must run on tracks and digital cameras are not useful without memory cards. Similarly, a DVD player is used in combination with DVDs, and a computer and software are used together. Such products are called **complements.** Because of complementarity, consumers often shop for systems; they buy computers with software installed and stereo

receivers along with speakers.* Consequently, firms have to think about how to compete with other firms: Should a firm, for example, design a product that can be used with a product produced by one of its competitors?

In order to work together, components must exhibit **compatibility**, which implies that they must operate on the same **standard.** An early example of problems that arise when complementary products are not compatible comes from American economic history. In 1860, there were more than 30,000 miles of railroad track in the United States. However, at least five different gauges—the distance between rails—with at least 1000 miles of track each were in use. Southern railroads had a five-foot gauge, while many railroads in the North used a four-foot-nine-inch gauge. Some other railroads used six-foot gauges or five-foot-six-inch gauges. This multiplicity of gauges made it difficult and expensive to transfer traffic from one railroad to another.[12] A more modern example would be accessories for an iPod. If you are looking for a universal dock or a rechargeable battery pack for your iPod, you need to be sure that the device you purchase will be compatible with your iPod.

Clearly, when compatibility is required, some *coordination* is necessary to make sure that components work together. Coordination across firms may be difficult for at least two reasons: (1) transactions costs associated with communicating across firms; and (2) concern about violating antitrust laws by sharing information. For both of these reasons, a firm may choose to produce multiple components itself. This, combined with consumers' tendency to shop for systems, can increase the entry barriers for new firms.

5.3.2 Externalities

The value of goods or services produced in network industries to a potential customer depends on the number of consumers already owning that good or using that service. For example, think of a telephone service or e-mail. You would not use either service unless you knew that other people also used it. And the more people you know who use the service, the more valuable it is to you. This kind of side effect is an **externality**, and the externalities arising from network effects are referred to as **adoption** or **network externalities.**

Network externalities affect the adoption of a new technology. Early on, only a few consumers will subscribe to a new service or purchase a new good. However, after a specific percentage of consumers, called the **critical mass,** has subscribed to the service or bought the product, its value increases to become greater than or equal to the price. After this point, all potential consumers subscribe to the service or buy the good.[†] This pattern is illustrated by the use of e-mail: Although the first e-mail was sent in 1969, it wasn't until sometime in the mid-1980s that it was widely used. And now most of us cannot imagine life without e-mail.

In the presence of network externalities, an early entrant often gains a competitive advantage. For example, consider the story of Mirabilis, the Israeli start-up that

*Some complementary products are much more likely to be purchased together as a system than are others. DVDs, for example, are typically bought separately from DVD players.

†Of course, it is not possible to continue increasing the number of subscribers to a service indefinitely. At some point, the addition of another user pushes the existing system beyond capacity, decreasing the value obtained by every other user.

developed instant messaging ("IM").* Mirabilis gave its product away for free to increase the number of users. Mirabilis also prevented interoperability between its client software and other products to deny competitors access to its customers. By using these strategies, Mirabilis was able to dominate the market for instant messaging. Network externalities played an important role: New IM users were much more likely to join Mirabilis's system than a competing system.

5.3.3 Switching Costs and Lock-In

Most users don't like learning features of a new operating system, a new word-processing program, or a new spreadsheet. Just imagine, for example, telling a dedicated Macintosh user that he will have to switch to a Windows machine. Similar *switching costs* arise in service industries such as banking.[†] Switching costs can arise in a variety of forms, including the costs of breaking a contract, the costs of training and learning a new system, the costs of converting data from one software program to another, the costs of searching, and the costs associated with giving up loyalty benefits such as frequent-flyer miles.[13]

In the presence of significant switching costs, consumers are *locked in* to using a specific service or product. Once this occurs, firms know that they have some room to raise price without losing consumers. Of course, firms understand the value of locking in consumers, so they may use strategies such as discounts and free services to attract consumers who are not yet locked in. This explains the fact that competition for consumers can be intense even in a market where firms have market power.

5.3.4 Significant Economies of Scale

Production of goods or services in network industries often involves significant economies of scale. Think about the development of a new word-processing program or a new computer game. It takes hundreds or thousands of hours of programming time to develop the program, and the costs of this development time are sunk. However, once the program has been written, the marginal cost of producing an additional copy (on a CD or on a website to be downloaded) is almost zero. This type of cost structure—very high fixed sunk cost combined with very low marginal cost—exists whenever the product involves information. As we discussed in Chapter 3, the presence of significant economies of scale often leads to a market dominated by one or a few firms.

5.3.5 Summary of Network Effects

Network effects do not *have* to lead to one firm dominating the market. A key is whether standards are established that allow multiple firms to produce competing products. For example, strong competition exists within the market for long-distance

*Mirabilis was later bought by America Online.

[†]This is clear to one of the authors of this textbook. Even though she is annoyed at her bank for charging a monthly fee for online banking, she has not switched to another bank. Clearly, the costs of changing banks outweigh the annoyance costs for her.

telephone service within the United States. No one firm has a proprietary protocol that it can use to dominate the market. However, in other cases, network effects can be used to enhance monopoly power. Application 5.2 discusses the importance of network effects for Microsoft's dominance of operating systems and computer software.

APPLICATION 5.2
Microsoft and Network Effects

For over 10 years, the Microsoft Corporation has controlled about 90 percent of the market for operating systems for personal computers. In addition, Microsoft applications such as Microsoft Word and Excel dominate the word-processing and spreadsheet markets. What role have network effects played in Microsoft's dominance? Think first about the connection between the operating system and software applications: In order to work with a particular operating system, the code for an application such as a word-processing program or a computer game has to include an application programming interface (API). Because Windows dominates the operating system market, it is critical for developers of alternative operating systems and software to have access to the APIs for Windows. The complementarity between the operating system and the software applications has given Microsoft's application software an advantage over competitive software. Thus Lotus 1-2-3, a hugely popular spreadsheet program in the mid-1980s written for an IBM operating system called OS/2, gradually lost out to Excel with the rise of Windows in the operating systems market.

The complementary relationship between applications and Windows feeds back into the dominance of Windows operating systems. Manufacturers of hardware and software write their programs to be compatible with Windows in order to gain access to the large number of Windows users. The continuing increase in the number of applications written for Windows then strengthens its dominant position in the operating systems market. In order for a rival operating system to take market share away from Windows, it would have to have software applications to compete with Microsoft's applications. But who would write applications for an operating system that does not have a substantial share of the market?

In addition, important network externalities are in effect. For consumers choosing an application such as a word-processing program or a spreadsheet, an important consideration is how easy it will be to share documents or presentations with other users. The more users there are of a particular application, the more it makes sense for any individual to adopt that application. Both authors of this textbook, for example, formerly were fans and users of WordPerfect. However, as use of Word became increasingly widespread, they bowed to the inevitable and switched word-processing programs. Similar reasoning applies to employers deciding which office suite to purchase or standardize on. If employees are already trained in Microsoft applications, it makes sense for an employer to adopt Microsoft Office as its office suite. Again, this is the case at both colleges where the authors teach. Microsoft has clearly reaped huge benefits from network externalities.*

*Many computer professionals believe that Microsoft has taken strategic actions to maintain its monopoly in operating systems and extend that monopoly power to other markets. We consider strategic actions in detail beginning in Chapters 11 and 12. ■

SUMMARY

1. In the dominant-firm price leadership model, the dominant firm sets the industry price subject to the supply of the competitive fringe of firms. The dominant firm's cost advantage allows it to be the price leader but is typically not great enough to allow it to act as a monopolist.

2. If the competitive fringe earns positive economic profits at the price set by the dominant firm, there is a tendency for the fringe to expand and the dominant firm's market share to decline over time.

3. Empirical evidence from several industries supports the theoretical prediction about the decline in a dominant firm's market share over time.

4. Throughout the 1980s, economists explored the implications of a new theoretical framework for thinking about entry and exit: contestable markets. This hypothesis contends that potential competition may be more important than actual competition and that even a completely monopolized market may perform as if it were perfectly competitive.

5. The theory of contestable markets is built upon three strong assumptions: (1) Entry is free; (2) entry is absolute; and (3) no sunk costs are associated with entry.

6. Some economists initially pointed to the airline industry as an example of a perfectly contestable market. However, none of the assumptions has proven to be valid, and a significant amount of empirical evidence now suggests that the airline industry is not perfectly contestable.

7. Another recent theoretical development is consideration of network industries. Examples of such industries include the markets for banking services, the Internet, computer software, and DVD players.

8. Four characteristics distinguish network industries from other industries: (1) complementarity, compatibility, and standards; (2) consumption externalities; (3) switching costs and lock-in; and (4) significant economies of scale in production.

9. The special characteristics of network industries work against the development of a competitive market. This is especially true if a firm can use network effects to enhance its monopoly power and to extend that power to another product.

KEY TERMS

adoption externalities
compatibility
complements
contestable markets

critical mass
dominant-firm price
 leadership model
externalities

network externalities
network industries
standards
switching costs

DISCUSSION QUESTIONS

1. In the dominant-firm price leadership model, the dominant firm is extremely passive toward its competitors. Why might firms with dominant market shares permit competitors to continually chip away at their market shares?

2. For decades, the 3M Company has ruled the transparent-tape market, with a market share of more than 90 percent. In 1999, a tiny Pennsylvania-based competitor, LePage, sued 3M for antitrust violations. Use the Internet to find information about this case. What are the reasons for 3M's dominance of the transparent-tape market? Do 3M's actions seem to be consistent with the assumptions of the dominant-firm price leadership model? Explain your reasoning.

3. Global Gillette controls over 70 percent of the global wet-shaving market. Use the Internet to find information about Global Gillette and the wet-shaving market. What are some possible reasons for Gillette's dominance in this market? Do you think Gillette's actions are consistent with the assumptions of the dominant-firm price leadership model? Explain your reasoning.

4. Can you think of other examples of dominant firms? Use the Internet to see if you can find market shares of these firms.

5. In many ways, the airline industry looks like a good example of a contestable market. Explain why. Other characteristics of this industry, however, make the assumptions of contestability seem less applicable. Consider each of the following features and explain how they might contradict the assumptions of the contestability theory:

 a. Part of an airline's capital is invested in terminal facilities.

 b. Many people prefer to fly on a specific airline, particularly if they are members of a frequent-flyer club.

 c. Airports like O'Hare in Chicago and Reagan National in Washington, DC, are operating very close to capacity.

 d. Due to deregulation, the major carriers have changed the way they organize their flights, developing hub-and-spoke designs.

6. On February 6, 2006, the Department of Justice indicated that it would allow Blackboard Inc. to take over WebCT Inc. Both companies sell content-management software to academic, corporate, and governmental organizations; estimates place Blackboard's share of the college course-management market at 45 to 50 percent and WebCT's share at 35 to 40 percent. Because of some overlap, the newly merged company is expected to have 65 to 75 percent of the college course-management market.

 a. Do you think the newly merged firm will be a dominant firm in this market? If so, why might the Department of Justice have allowed the merger to take place?

 b. Industry analysts believe that the course-management market is easy to enter, and that potential entrants include big software companies, such as Microsoft or Oracle, as well as open-source projects, such as Sakai and Moodle. Does this suggest that this market is perfectly contestable? Keep the assumptions of the contestability theory in mind as you think about this question.

7. This chapter gave several examples of network industries. Pick one and explain in what ways that industry exhibits the special characteristics of network industries.

8. Can you think of other examples of network industries? Explain why your example(s) fit into this category.

PROBLEMS

1. Suppose the market demand curve for widgets is given by:

$$Q_T = 800 - 3P,$$

where $Q_T = Q_F + Q_D$ and Q_T is the total quantity, Q_F is the quantity supplied by fringe firms, and Q_D is the quantity supplied by the dominant firm. The dominant firm's total costs are given by $TC_D = 80Q_D$ and the competitive fringe's supply curve is given by $Q_F = -200 + 2P$.

 a. Graph the market demand curve and the fringe firms' supply curve. Label the vertical intercepts of each.

 b. Find the dominant firm's marginal and average costs. Show these costs on your graph.

 c. Find the price at which the fringe firms will supply the entire quantity demanded by the market. Call this price P_1.

 d. Find the price at which the fringe firms will choose to supply no output. Call this price P_2.

 e. Find the dominant firm's residual demand curve for prices between P_1 and P_2. Show the residual demand curve on your graph.

 f. Find the dominant firm's profit-maximizing quantity of output.

 g. Find the price level the dominant firm would set.

 h. Why are the fringe firms willing to accept the price as set by the dominant firm?

 i. Find the profits of the dominant firm.

 j. If the dominant firm sets price at P_2, what will its profits be? Might this pricing strategy ever make sense? Explain your reasoning.

2. (You need a calculator to answer this question.) A domestic monopolist exists in the American zonker market. The U.S. demand for zonkers is $P = 100 - Q$ and the American monopolist's costs are $AC = MC = 20$. Currently there is an import ban on zonkers into the United States.

 If trade were permitted, a group of small international firms would enter the U.S. zonker market, and the American monopolist would act as a dominant-firm price leader. The supply in the United States of the international fringe firms would be:

$$P = 20 + q_f.$$

 What would be the net welfare effect on the United States of permitting trade? Would American consumers benefit? Would the American monopolist benefit?

NOTES

1. This model is sometimes referred to as the Forchheimer Model because it was derived in Karl Forchheimer, "Theoretisches zum unvollstandegen Monopole," *Schmollers Jahrbuch* (1908): 1–12; A.J. Nichol, *Partial Monopoly and Price Leadership* (Philadelphia: Smith-Edwards, 1930). See also Dean A. Worcester, "Why Dominant Firms Decline," *Journal of Political Economy* 65 (August 1957): 338–347.

2. Worcester, *ibid.*

3. See *United States* v. *United States Steel Corporation* 251 US 417 (1920).

4. Erwin A. Blackstone, "Limit Pricing and Entry in the Copying Machine Industry," *Quarterly Review of Economics and Business* 12 (Winter 1972): 57–65.

5. Thomas Whiteside, "Where Are They Now?" *New Yorker* (February 17, 1951): 39–58.

6. For evidence of the decline of each of these price leaders, see Richard T. Pascale, "Perspectives on Strategy: The Real Story Behind Honda's Success," *California Management Review* 26 (1984): 47–72.

7. W.J. Baumol, J.C. Panzar, and R.D. Willig, *Contestable Markets and the Theory of Industrial Structure* (San Diego: Harcourt Brace Jovanovich, 1982).

8. G.D. Call and T.E. Keeler, "Airline Deregulation Fares and Market Behavior: Some Empirical Evidence," in A. Daughety (ed.), *Analytical Studies in Transport Economics* (New York: Cambridge University Press, 1985), pp. 222–247.

9. T.G. Moore, "US Airline Deregulation," *Journal of Law and Economics* 29 (April 1986): 1; for further evidence on the contestability hypothesis and the airline industry, see S.H. Baker and J.B. Pratt, "Experience as a Barrier to Contestability in Airline Markets," *Review of Economics and Statistics* 71 (May 1989):

352–356; and Margaret A. Peteraf, "Sunk Costs, Contestability and Airline Monopoly Power," *Review of Industrial Organization* 10 (1995): 289–306.

10. Criticisms have also been raised concerning the theory of contestability. See, for example, Robert D. Cairns, "Asymmetry of Information and Contestability Theory," *Review of Industrial Organization* 9 (1994): 99–107.

11. This section draws on material in Oz Shy, *The Economics of Network Industries* (Cambridge: Cambridge University Press, 2001).

12. Jeremy Atack and Peter Passell, *A New Economic View of American History,* 2nd edition (New York: W.W. Norton & Company, 1994), p. 429.

13. The categorization of switching costs comes from Carl Shapiro and Hal Varian, *Information Rules: A Strategic Guide to the Network Economy* (Boston: Harvard University Press, 1999).

INTERNET EXERCISES

Visit www.aw-bc.com/waldman_jensen for this chapter's web exercises. Answer our real-world economics problems by searching the Internet for solutions!

Market Power and Performance: The Empirical Evidence

As discussed in Chapter 3, pricing above marginal cost leads to a misallocation of resources. Price measures the value to society of an additional unit of output, and marginal cost measures the resource cost of producing that extra unit of output. If price is greater than marginal cost, then too little of the good is being produced from society's viewpoint. Allocative inefficiency is a key reason for policymakers' concerns about market power. This chapter examines the available empirical evidence on the relationship between market power and efficiency. *Is* there a problem with market power?

Detecting market power and measuring its effects on performance have been the focus of much empirical work in industrial organization over many years. Comprehensively surveying the voluminous empirical work in the area would be nearly impossible for us; reading such a survey might be nearly impossible for you! We'll focus instead on helping you understand both how economists approach the topic of market power and what stylized facts have emerged from their work.

Economists have used several different methodologies in their search for firms with market power. The most extensively used technique for many years was broad cross-section studies that examine the determinants and effects of market power across different industries. This methodology underlies literally hundreds of empirical studies, and we begin our examination of the empirical evidence with this work. Along the way, we consider a variety of criticisms of cross-section studies. These criticisms fall into two broad categories: (1) concerns about data problems and measurement and (2) concerns about the methodology and the interpretation of results.

More recently, economists have turned to case studies in an attempt to avoid some problems associated with cross-section work. Case studies focus on market power in single industries or in closely related industries. Additionally, recognizing that cross-section and case studies tend to be largely static, some recent work has focused attention on dynamic issues. The last part of the chapter briefly examines the most recent approaches to the empirical study of market power.

6.1 Structure-Conduct-Performance

Now that we have explored briefly the market structure of American industries, we are ready to ask an important question: Should we be concerned about economic inefficiency in the vast majority of U.S. and world markets that are not perfectly competitive in terms of their market structures? This was the most important issue examined by the early followers of the SCP paradigm in the tradition of Edward Mason and Joseph Bain.[1] Mason and Bain theorized that an understanding of market structure could be used to predict conduct and performance. The implications for public policy of the answer to the above question are enormous. If there is no relationship between market structure and performance, that is, if monopolies and oligopolies perform just as efficiently as perfectly competitive markets, then there is no justification for government intervention into the structure or conduct of markets simply because structurally the markets are less than perfectly competitive. On the other hand, if monopolies and oligopolies consistently perform worse than perfectly competitive markets, then there is far more possible justification for government intervention.

As noted in Chapter 1, the structure-conduct-performance (SCP) paradigm searches for a link between various elements of market structure and some measure of performance. The traditional SCP approach hypothesized that certain elements of market structure increase the likelihood of collusive behavior and that collusive behavior results in higher prices and profits.* Because collusive behavior is not directly observable, SCP studies use evidence on the relationship between performance and various characteristics of market structure to make inferences about market power. If, for example, a researcher finds that higher concentration is associated with higher industry profits, the SCP explanation is that firms in highly concentrated industries are better able to collude, leading to higher prices and profits and allocative inefficiency.

The economists who developed and first used the SCP approach did not base it on formal models of oligopoly behavior like those we will explore in the next sections of this book. Instead, the original followers of the SCP tradition simply looked for empirical associations and statistical relationships between market structure, conduct, and performance. Yet we will see in later chapters that models of oligopoly behavior can be used to develop a second interpretation of the standard empirical SCP studies—an interpretation that is not based on overt collusion.[†] This second interpretation works as follows: Assuming a link between market structure, conduct, and performance, there should be a relationship between industry profit and some measures of industry concentration corresponding to a set of profit-maximizing industry actions that lead to a choice of price or output that ultimately determines profit. According to this interpretation of the early SCP paradigm, whether or not there is overt collusion, prices are raised above marginal costs in an "apparently collusive" manner.[2] The job of the economist,

*That a story of collusion underlies the SCP paradigm can be seen in Bain (1956, p. 191): "This predicted influence of the condition of entry on the size of price-cost margins and profits is clearly subject to the concomitant influence of the degree of seller concentration within the industry. Specifically, it is expected to be evidenced in a verifiable simple association of the condition of entry on profits *mainly as far as seller concentration throughout is high enough to support effective collusion* in industries with both high and medium entry barriers." [Emphasis added.]

[†]The standard SCP statistical analysis is discussed in detail later in this chapter.

therefore, is to look for the empirical relationships between market structure and prices or profits. If there is a positive relationship between market concentration and prices or profits, it implies that firms behave "as if" they are colluding regardless of whether or not they actually are.

6.2 Statistical Tools Used to Test the SCP Paradigm

To study the relationship between market structure and economic performance, economists turn to statistical techniques. The most widely used statistical technique in economics is **regression analysis.** This is a way of quantifying economic relationships and using economic data to test hypotheses about the relationships between economic variables.

Suppose that an economist wants to investigate the relationship between market structure and profits. The theories of perfect competition and monopoly suggest a simple hypothesis: Economic profits increase as markets become more concentrated.* Let X_1 stand for a measure of market structure and Y for a measure of economic profits.

We can graph a simple relationship between these two variables using a scatter diagram. Each point in this diagram represents an observation for a firm or an industry. Because our simple hypothesis is that an increase in concentration leads to an increase in economic profits, values of X_1 are plotted on the horizontal axis and values of Y are graphed on the vertical axis. If the hypothesis about the relationship between market concentration and economic profits is correct, a scatter diagram of data on X_1 should look like Figure 6.1(a): As the value of X_1 (market concentration) increases, so does the value of Y (profits). If the hypothesis is not correct, a scatter diagram might look like Figure 6.1(b), where there is no relationship between the values of X_1 and Y.

We can also express the hypothesis about the relationship between market structure and profits using a simple linear equation:†

$$Y = \alpha_0 + \alpha_1 X_1. \qquad [6.1]$$

Here Y is called the **dependent variable,** X_1 is the **independent** or **explanatory variable,** and the αs are the **parameters** of the equation. In this equation of a straight line, α_0 is the vertical intercept and α_1 is the slope. If the hypothesis about the relationship between market structure and profits is correct, α_1 should be positive.

If no other factors affected profits, then all of the observations of X_1 and Y would lie exactly on the line. Profits, however, are likely to depend on many other variables, including some unobservable factors such as management skills. These unobservable factors are represented in the equation by ϵ, an error term:

$$Y = \alpha_0 + \alpha_1 X_1 + \epsilon.$$

*Remember that measures of market concentration were discussed in Chapter 4.

†At this point we are assuming a linear relationship between the variables. This is a convenient assumption but not the only possibility. Nonlinear relationships are discussed on p. 166.

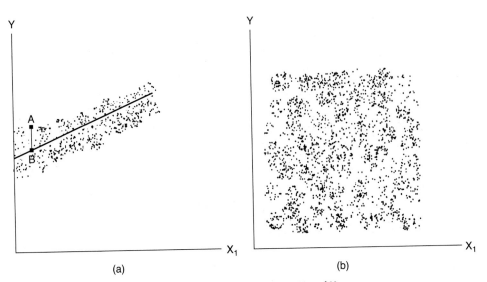

FIGURE 6.1 Hypothetical Scatter Diagrams of Data on Y and X

If X_1 measures market concentration and Y measures profit, the scatter diagram in panel (a) shows a positive relationship between the two: As market concentration increases, so does profit. The upward-sloping line in (a) shows the best-fitting line that minimizes the sum of square residuals. The scatter diagram in panel (b) shows no relationship between market concentration and profit.

Because of the omitted factors, actual observations do not lie on a straight line but around it, as Figure 6.1(a) shows. The vertical distance between each data point and a straight line fitted through the observations is called the *residual*. AB shows the residual for the observation located at point A.

It is possible to sketch more than one line through the observations. Therefore, we need to decide which of these lines is "best." The most common method for fitting the line through data points is least squares regression. This technique chooses values of α_0 and α_1 such that when all the residuals are squared and added together, the resulting sum is minimized. Note that least squares treats positive errors (where the actual observation lies above the fitted line) and negative errors (where the actual point lies below the fitted line) symmetrically. It also gives greater weight to larger residuals.

Least squares regression can also be used when theory suggests that more than one independent or explanatory variable exists, although graphing such relationships quickly becomes very difficult. For example, economies of scale may be a second important determinant of profitability. Letting X_2 represent economies of scale, the equation becomes:

$$Y = \alpha_0 + \alpha_1 X_1 + \alpha_2 X_2 + \epsilon.$$

Now, α_1 measures the effect of an increase in market concentration on profits with the effect of economies of scale held constant. Similarly, α_2 measures the effect of an increase in economies of scale on profits with the effect of market concentration held constant. To get meaningful results, it is important to include all relevant variables in

the model. Otherwise, some effects that are due to an omitted variable might be mistakenly attributed to the included variable(s). For example, if economies of scale were left out of the estimated equation, the least squares estimate of α_1 would reflect not only the effects of market concentration on profits but also the effects of economies of scale on profits. Economic theory is the guide in deciding which variables should be included in a model.

Economists typically do not have data on an entire population, such as all of the firms within an industry. They therefore use data from a sample—a fraction of the relevant population—to calculate estimates of various parameters. The least squares estimates of the parameters of the model depend on the particular sample of observations used for the estimation. Using a different sample of firms would give different estimates of the parameters. Because of this, we want to know how close the estimates from any sample are to the true values—those that would be obtained from using the entire population—of the parameters. We want to be able to reach conclusions about the contribution of each independent variable to changes in the dependent variable and about how well the estimated equation fits the data.

Fortunately, simple statistical tests allow us to answer these questions.* Suppose that we have estimated a regression equation and want to know whether our estimate of α_1 indicates a true relationship between market concentration and profits, or whether the estimated coefficient is an artifact of the sample. Roughly speaking, we want to know whether α_1 is zero or whether it is greater than zero, as theory suggests. To test the hypothesis that a true parameter is actually equal to zero, we can look at a test statistic called the *t-statistic*.† The t-statistic is defined as:

$$t = \frac{\hat{\alpha}}{\text{standard error of } \hat{\alpha}},$$

where $\hat{\alpha}$ is the least squares estimate of α and the standard error of $\hat{\alpha}$ is a measure of the dispersion of estimates of α around its mean.

High absolute values of t-statistics (a rough rule of thumb is a t-statistic greater than or equal to 2 in absolute value) indicate that it is unlikely that the true value of α is zero. In such a case, we would have evidence for a true relationship between the explanatory variable and the dependent variable, and we would say that α is statistically significant. Low absolute values of t-statistics, however, provide evidence that the true value of α may well be zero, indicating that the independent variable does not help explain variation in the dependent variable. Coefficients with small t-statistics are said to be not statistically significant.‡

In addition to examining the effect of a specific independent variable on the dependent variable, we may want to know how closely the estimated regression line fits the data. A statistic that provides information about the overall goodness-of-fit of

*The validity of these tests depends on certain assumptions about the error term. A course in econometrics examines these assumptions in detail and considers the implications of violations of the assumptions.

†Economists typically use one of several standard statistical computer packages that estimate least squares parameters and report information about the regression, including the t-statistics.

‡In some cases estimated coefficients have large standard errors, and thus low t-statistics, even though the true values of the parameters are not zero. This occurs as a result of a problem called ***multicolinearity***, in which two or more of the independent variables are very highly correlated, meaning that they tend to move together. This makes it hard to separate the independent effects of the variables.

the regression is called R-squared, written R^2. This statistic measures the percentage of the total variation of the dependent variable around its mean value that is explained by all of the independent variables included in the model. Its value ranges from 0, meaning that the independent variables account for none of the variation in the dependent variable, to 1, indicating that the independent variables completely explain the variation in the dependent variable.

As an example, suppose we collected data on profits and a measure of market concentration and ran a regression, obtaining the following results:

$$Y = 2.65 + 0.567X_1$$
$$(3.46)$$
$$R^2 = 0.27$$

The number in parentheses is the t-statistic for the coefficient $\alpha_1 = 0.567$. These results would suggest that there is a positive and statistically significant relationship between market concentration and profits. The R^2 of 0.27 indicates that market power explains only 27 percent of the total variation in profits.

Because it is so easy to look at the R^2 as a summary statistic, we caution against putting too much emphasis on R^2. A high R^2 is not sufficient evidence to conclude that the variables included in the model are the appropriate ones. For example, even if a regression of sales of new homes on the price of soda happened to yield a high R^2, our knowledge of economics should lead us to question the validity of the results. In fact, adding additional explanatory variables will increase R^2, regardless of the economic importance of the variables. Economic theory should always serve as a check on the interpretation of empirical results.

Finally, several issues should be kept in mind when looking at the results of any regression. First, is the specification of the model correct—that is, does the model leave out any variables that theory suggests should be included? Earlier we noted that omitting a relevant variable biases the estimation. A second issue concerns the functional form of the equation. The equations discussed thus far assume that all of the explanatory variables affect profits in a linear fashion. While this is a convenient assumption, it is not the only possibility. The relationship between an independent variable and the dependent variable may be nonlinear. Figure 6.2 shows two common nonlinear shapes. To estimate a relationship of the form shown in Figure 6.2(a), a researcher can use a log-linear functional form, estimating a regression in which the dependent variable is log Y rather than Y. A relationship such as that shown in Figure 6.2(b) can be estimated using a quadratic functional form, in which both X and X^2 are included as explanatory variables. A third issue is the quality of the data. As we will show shortly, industrial organization data are often of less than ideal quality. Problems with data include market definitions that are too broad or too narrow from an economic perspective, accounting data that do not accurately measure the relevant economic variables, and measurement errors due to various incentives facing those filling out the forms to inflate or deflate reported figures.

6.2.1 Exogenous and Endogenous Variables

The variables in a regression model are classified into two types, and the distinction is always important. An *exogenous variable* is one whose numerical value is determined "outside" the model. That is, the model is not intended to explain how the variable is

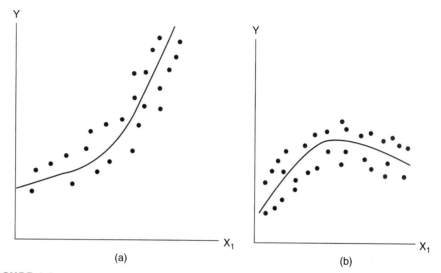

FIGURE 6.2 **Examples of Nonlinear Relationships**

Panel (a) shows one common nonlinear functional form used in regression analysis where the dependent variable is log Y instead of Y. Panel (b) shows another common nonlinear estimation technique using a quadratic form in which X and X^2 are both included as explanatory variables.

determined, or to predict when or how it might change. Exogenous variables are simply given, and used as data. An *endogenous variable,* by contrast, is determined "inside" the model. Indeed, a key goal of building any model is to predict the values of endogenous variables and to explain when and how they might change.

In our simple regression model there is one endogenous variable, profit, and one exogenous variable, market structure. Our model does not attempt to explain how market structure is determined. On the contrary, the measure of market structure is taken as given data. If and when market structure changes, there is a new piece of data to work with. Whether a particular variable is exogenous or endogenous is not an intrinsic trait of the variable, but rather a consequence of how that variable is used in a particular model. A variable can be exogenous in one model, yet endogenous in another. In another model some of the roles could be reversed: Profit could become an exogenous variable, and market structure could become endogenous. For example, one might specify a model where research and development expenditures are a function of profit. In this case, profit is an exogenous variable. In another model, market structure might be a function of advertising expenditures. In this model, market structure is an endogenous variable. The choice of which variables are endogenous and which are exogenous in a model is very important and defines the skill of the economist and econometrician.

6.3 Measurement Issues

One major problem faced by economists in the early SCP studies was how to measure performance. Furthermore, we saw in Chapter 4 that measures of market structure can present serious difficulties because of the problems associated with correctly

defining markets. In the next two sections, we first consider alternative measures of performance and then discuss the key structural variables used in studies examining the relationship between market structure and economic performance.

6.3.1 Measures of Performance

Market power permits a firm to raise price above the competitive level. This suggests that a good way to measure market power might be to look directly at prices. Unfortunately, looking at prices makes sense only for a given product. To make comparisons across industries or even across firms that produce a variety of products, a common denominator is necessary.

One possible common denominator is costs. The Lerner Index, defined in Section 3.3.2 as $\dfrac{P - MC}{P}$, is theoretically appealing because it directly measures the increase of price above marginal cost. Unfortunately, the Lerner Index is difficult to estimate because data are lacking on firms' marginal costs. Four different measures have been used as a proxy for the Lerner Index in SCP studies: *excess return on sales, profit rate, price-cost margin,* and *Tobin's q.* Not surprisingly, none of these measures is ideal.

Excess Return on Sales

Closely related to the Lerner Index, the **excess return on sales** is the ratio of economic or excess profits to sales revenue $\left(\dfrac{TR - TC}{TR}\right)$. Let's see why this measure is related to the Lerner Index. Assuming that firms are in long-run equilibrium and are operating in the range of their production functions with constant returns to scale, the excess profit rate on sales will, on average across all products produced by the firm, equal the Lerner Index. To see this, begin with the Lerner Index $\dfrac{P - MC}{P}$ and recognize that if a production function exhibits constant returns to scale, MC = AC. Substituting MC = AC into the Lerner Index yields $\dfrac{P - AC}{P}$. Multiplying $\dfrac{P - AC}{P}$ by $\dfrac{q}{q}$ yields $\dfrac{Pq - ACq}{Pq}$. Because AC equals $\dfrac{TC}{q}$, this is equal to $\dfrac{TR - TC}{TR}$, which is economic profits over sales.

Despite its theoretical appeal, few studies have used the excess profit rate on sales to measure performance. A difficulty arises in the calculation of economic profits, which can be broken down into sales revenue minus noncapital costs minus depreciation minus annual capital costs. Theoretically, annual capital costs equal the total capital stock multiplied by the competitive cost per unit of capital, that is, the annual rental fees if capital were rented in a competitive market. Accounting data, however, do not report the competitive rate of return on capital; to measure the excess profit rate of return, a researcher must make a judgment about what the appropriate competitive rate of return is. One study, for example, used 6 percent as the "normal" or competitive rate of return, arguing that this rate of return closely approximates the after-tax rate of return on equity over the long run in competitive industries.[3] Researchers who want to avoid the problem of estimating the competitive rate of return on capital turn to one of the other measures of performance.

Profit Rate

Many researchers use accounting profits as a measure of relative performance. These data are readily available from standard sources and do not require a judgment about the competitive rate of return. For purposes of comparison across firms, profits are divided by some base figure to yield a ***profit rate,*** or a rate of return. Earning positive economic profits is equivalent to earning a rate of return that is greater than the competitive rate of return. Suppose, for example, that a firm earns a 9 percent rate of return. If investment in a competitive industry yields a 6 percent rate of return, then 9 percent is an *excess* rate of return, and we can conclude that the firm is earning *positive* economic profits.

Most early SCP studies used the ***rate of return on stockholders' equity after tax*** to measure profitability. This is calculated as $\frac{\pi - T}{E}$, where π is profits, T is the tax on profits, and E is stockholders' equity. This measure is attractive because it corresponds with what individual investors are trying to maximize.* Also, competitive industries with the same risk will have the same rate of return on equity in the long run.†

There are many potential problems with this measure of profits. First, the rate of return on equity is sensitive to variations in the debt/equity ratio across firms. Issuing both debt (bonds) and equity (stocks) results in two groups having claims on the assets of the firm, with debtholders getting paid before stockholders if a firm gets into financial trouble. The risk to stockholders of not getting paid increases as the debt/equity ratio increases. To compensate for the higher risk, stockholders will require a higher rate of return from a firm with a high ratio of debt to equity than from a firm with a low debt/equity ratio.

To reduce the problems associated with variations in the debt/equity ratio, some researchers use the ***rate of return on assets after tax.*** This is calculated as $\frac{\pi - T + I}{A}$, where π and T are as defined above, I is interest payments to debtholders, and A is total assets.‡ Although this measure differs from the rate of return on equity, the two profit rates are highly correlated.[4]

A serious problem with both the rate of return on equity and the rate of return on assets is that the numerator and denominator tend to move together. To see this, consider a firm that has some asset, such as a brand name or ownership of a scarce input, that gives it market power. If the firm that owns this asset is sold, the purchaser is likely to pay a higher price for the acquisition than it would pay if there were no market power. The higher price reflects the acquiring firm's expectations of earning positive

*Note that investors care about the after-tax rate of return rather than the pre-tax rate of return. Firms in two different industries may have very different pre-tax rates of return but identical after-tax rates of return if they face different tax rates on their assets.

†Investors must be compensated for bearing risk: The higher the risk, the higher is the expected rate of return. Two competitive firms will have different rates of return, therefore, if they are pursuing projects with different degrees of risk. A firm is earning an excess rate of return if the actual rate of return is higher than the ***risk-adjusted rate of return,*** which is the return a competitive firm would earn if its projects carried the same level of risk as the firm being examined.

‡Interest payments must be added to the numerator because debtholders are paid interest; profits are paid to stockholders. Total assets measures the value of both equity and debt capital.

economic profits. After the merger, therefore, the profit rate may appear to be competitive because the denominator, the value of equity or assets, has been written up to reflect the potential to earn positive economic profits. Even a firm that does not change hands may sometimes revalue an asset. In particular, a firm may write down the value of an asset that turns out to be less profitable than was expected. By increasing the equity of the more profitable firms and decreasing the equity of the less profitable firms, such revaluation tends to bias all firms toward equal profit rates.

Second, profit rates may be mismeasured because of problems with reported profits.[5] Although economic theory makes predictions about *economic* profits, reported profits are *accounting* profits. Using accounting data can lead to biased estimates of rates of return because economic profits and accounting profits differ in several key ways. Theoretically, economic profits are revenues minus the opportunity costs of inputs. Reasonably good data exist on revenues, labor costs, and the costs of materials. However, accurately measuring the annual costs of long-lived assets such as plant and equipment, advertising, and research and development is difficult, if not impossible.

In calculating the annual capital costs of a firm, two problems arise with accounting data. First, capital should be valued at its **replacement cost,** which is the long-run cost of buying a capital asset of comparable quality. The rate of return calculated using replacement cost indicates whether entry or exit should occur. If the rate of return is greater than the competitive rate of return, then new capital should enter the industry. If the rate of return is less than the competitive rate of return, the industry should contract and capital should leave the industry.

Accounting data, however, use **book value,** which is calculated using the historical value of an asset. To illustrate the problem with this method, consider an asset that was inexpensive at the time of its purchase but whose price has increased significantly. In this case, the rate of return calculated using historical cost will be considerably greater than the rate of return using replacement cost, overestimating the profitability of investment in the industry.

A second problem with accounting data is the calculation of **depreciation.** Any durable asset, such as a machine, wears out over time; depreciation measures the decrease in economic value that occurs during the period the asset is used. Suppose, for example, that a landlord rents a building for $1500 per year and has to spend $300 per year to maintain the building. The $300 is depreciation, and the landlord's net annual rental is $1200. It is the return after depreciation has been deducted that matters to the landlord or, in general, to the investor.

Accountants calculate depreciation using one of several fixed formulas, such as **straight-line depreciation.** This method assumes that an asset lasts for some fixed period and decreases in value in equal increments over that fixed period. If, for example, a machine that costs $1000 is assumed to last for five years, the annual depreciation would be $200 for the first five years. If the machine happens to last more than five years, there would be no further depreciation.

Unfortunately, depreciation as calculated by an accounting formula does not necessarily correspond to the true decline in an asset's economic value. Using the reported rate of depreciation, therefore, may lead to a biased estimate of a firm's profitability, an estimate that is either too high or too low.

Third, further problems with accounting data arise for expenditures on advertising and on research and development (R&D). Like expenditures on plant and equipment, money spent on advertising or on R&D may create effects that last over time. A

successful advertising campaign in one year can affect demand in subsequent years if consumers remember the campaign. Similarly, R&D expenditures in one year can affect demand or costs in future years. A common accounting procedure is to deduct the entire costs of advertising or R&D in one year and then deduct nothing in subsequent years. If this practice is followed, the rate of return will be underestimated in the first year and overestimated in future years.

A fourth problem with accounting data arises from inflation. Researchers must be careful when comparing rates of return to ensure that all rates are either nominal rates, which include the effects of inflation, or real rates, which have been adjusted for inflation. To calculate a real rate of return, the values in both the numerator and denominator must be adjusted to account for the increase in prices that result from inflation.

Any one of these problems could be serious, but the combination of all of them makes it difficult to have great confidence in the profit rate as a measure of economic performance. See Application 6.1.

APPLICATION 6.1

Does the Method of Calculating Profit Rates Matter?

Given all of the possible problems associated with correctly calculating profit rates across firms and industries, one might hope that the choice of methodology would have little impact on the results in economic studies. To test this hypothesis, J. K. Kapler examined the impact of correcting for many of the problems identified in Section 6.1.2 on her ability to explain differences in profit rates across firms.* She began with the traditional measure of accounting rates of return (ARR) for 562 U.S. manufacturing firms for the years 1985–1990. She then made four corrections to the ARR and developed what she called the *economic accounting rate of return* (EARR) for the same firms. These adjustments were as follows:

1. The ARR reports pre-tax income net of interest paid by the firm because interest on debt is treated as an expense. This creates a problem because the ARR does not distinguish between firms with high debt-to-equity ratios and those with low debt-to-equity ratios. Kapler added back net interest paid so that the measure of EARR would not be distorted by differences in the debt-to-equity ratio across firms.

2. The ARR reports pre-tax income net of depreciation as measured by the federal tax code. This method is based on the legal rather than economic definition of depreciation and is based on the book value rather than the replacement value of the firm's assets. Kapler added the tax code–based depreciation back into pre-tax income and then deducted a measure of depreciation derived from data from the U.S. Department of Commerce Bureau of Economic Analysis that is much more in line with the economic measure of depreciation.

3. The ARR reports pre-tax income net of research and development expenditures. Kapler added the firms' R&D expenditures back into pre-tax income and then adjusted the firms' assets for the creation of new intangible assets that were derived from their R&D spending.

4. The ARR is based on a measure of the book value (or original cost) of assets, not the replacement value of assets. Kapler used data from the Bureau of Economic

Analysis to adjust the book value of assets to be in line with the replacement value of assets.

Kapler then ran regressions using first ARR and then EARR as the dependent variable. If both profit measures performed equally well in these regressions, then it would not matter which measure a researcher used in statistical studies. However, if one measure performed significantly better in explaining variations in profit rates across firms, then that measure would be preferred in empirical studies.

Kapler ran her regressions for the sample of 562 firms from 1985 to 1990 with firm and industry characteristics as independent variables. The simple model was as follows:

profit rate = f(firm characteristics, industry characteristics).

Such a model is called a fixed-effects model because it controls for the variation in firm and industry characteristics over time. The table below shows Kapler's results.

Dependent Variable: Profit Measure	Independent Variable: Firm Effects Only, Adjusted R^2	Independent Variable: Industry Effects Only, Adjusted R^2	Independent Variables: Firm and Industry Effects, Adjusted R^2
ARR	35.4	11.1	44.3
EARR	44.0	13.7	58.0

Firm effects alone explained 44.0 percent of the variation in EARR compared to only 35.4 percent of the variation in ARR. Industry effects alone explained relatively little of the variation in profit rates, only 11.1 percent of the variation in ARR and 13.7 percent of the variation in EARR. Using both firm and industry effects, Kapler was able to explain 58 percent of the variation in EARR, but only 44.3 percent of the variation in ARR. As Kapler noted, "[t]his constitutes a substantial increase in explanatory power compared to studies based upon unadjusted ARR." Kapler's results imply that any explanation of the variation in firm profit rates that uses the ARR to measure profit would underestimate the combined impact of firm and industry characteristics on profit. Studies utilizing a measure of firm profit rate, therefore, should adjust the ARR to reflect the potential problems associated with the use of standard accounting profit measures.

*J.K. Kapler, "Measuring the Economic Rate of Return on Assets," *Review of Industrial Organization*, 17, (December 2000): 457–463. ■

Price-Cost Margins

Another measure of performance used in numerous studies is the ***price-cost margin.*** The main advantage of using the price-cost margin rather than profit rates arises from the level of aggregation at which data are reported. Because profit rates are calculated from firm-specific data, reported profits for any diversified firm reflect profits from several industries.* Hence, it is difficult to match profits with industry-specific measures

*Firm-specific data are often classified into industries using the primary industry method. In this method the entire accounting values of variables such as profits are assigned to a firm's primary industry—that industry in which its percentage of its total sales is the highest.

of structure, such as the concentration ratio. In contrast, the price-cost margin is cal-culated from data available in the *Census of Manufactures*. Census data are reported at the level of the individual plant, which is typically much less diversified than are firms.* Therefore, using *Census* data makes the fit between the measure of perform-ance and the measures of structure much better.

Unfortunately, the same feature that makes census data attractive can also be seen as a drawback. Because each plant shares certain joint costs with other plants in the firm, researchers cannot use accounting profits to calculate rates of return. Instead they typically estimate a price-cost margin.[6]

To understand the rationale for using the price-cost margin as a measure of per-formance, start again with the Lerner Index, $\dfrac{P - MC}{P}$. Because data on marginal costs are usually not available, economists often assume long-run constant returns to scale so that long-run average cost equals long-run marginal cost.[7] With this assumption, the Lerner Index can be written as

$$\frac{P - MC}{P} = \frac{Q}{Q}\left(\frac{P - v - (\rho + \delta)p_K(K/Q)}{P}\right) = \frac{PQ - vQ}{PQ} - (\rho + \delta)p_K\frac{K}{PQ} \qquad [6.2]$$

where v = variable cost per unit, p_K = the price of a unit of capital, δ = depreciation rate of capital, ρ = competitive rate of return, P = price, Q = output, and K = dollar value of capital employed. The first term on the right in Equation 6.2, (total revenue − variable cost)/total revenue, is the price-cost margin. Under competitive conditions, price should equal long-run average (and marginal) cost, so $\dfrac{P - MC}{P} = 0$. This implies that the first term on the right side of Equation 6.2 should on average equal the sec-ond term on the right side of Equation 6.2 if the industry is competitive. A common practice, therefore, is to use the price-cost margin (the first term) as the dependent variable in a regression and to include the ratio of assets to sales as one of the inde-pendent variables. Equation 6.2 shows that this approach amounts to assuming that both the competitive rate of return, ρ, and the rate of depreciation, δ, are the same for all industries in the sample, an assumption that may not be valid.

Researchers typically calculate variable costs, v, as the cost of materials plus pay-roll. This calculation omits several possible variable costs, including advertising, cen-tral office expenses, taxes, and research and development.[8] Recognizing this problem, some researchers include industry aggregates for these factors as independent vari-ables in their regression equations to control for their effects.

Tobin's q

Problems with accounting rates of return and price-cost margins have led many econ-omists to measure profitability by *Tobin's q*, the ratio of the market value of a firm to the replacement value of its assets.[9] In a perfectly competitive industry in long-run equilibrium, the value of q would be 1; the market value of the firm would just equal

*Census data are reported at the six-digit NAICS level.

what it would cost to rebuild it. If q is greater than 1, the market value of the firm is greater than its replacement cost. In this case, other firms would want to enter the industry, anticipating that the market value of their investment will be greater than its cost. Thus, in the absence of barriers to entry and exit, q will be driven to 1; it will persist above 1 if entry is barred.

Tobin's q has several advantages over rate of return measures.[10] The numerator of q, market value, reflects expected future profits, whereas accounting data reflect only past profits. Also, the market value of a firm depends partly on risk, so q incorporates an adjustment for risk.* In addition, q is much less sensitive to errors in measuring its components than are profits.†

Unfortunately, q is not without problems. Like rate of return measures, q reflects the operations of the entire firm, creating problems for diversified firms. Also, because accounting data are used to calculate the replacement cost, some of the objections to accounting rates of return also apply to estimates of q.‡

These problems involve the measurement of a firm's capital assets. Accountants' use of depreciation schedules that do not reflect true economic depreciation is a problem for calculation of q, as it was for calculation of accounting rates of return. Also, replacement costs should include the value of intangible assets resulting from expenditures on advertising and research and development. If a researcher ignores these intangible assets, the denominator of q will be too low, leading to an estimate of q that is greater than one even for competitive firms. In fact, one study estimated average Tobin's q over the period 1960 to 1976 for a sample of U.S. industries, finding a median value of q of 1.35.[11] This could indicate either that firms typically earn positive economic profits or that measurement errors biased q upwards. Without more information, it is not possible to distinguish one explanation from the other.

6.3.2 Correlations Among Measures of Performance

Before turning to measures of structure, it is worth pausing to look at how closely related one measure of performance is to another. As discussed in Application 6.1, a close relationship between two measures would suggest that the choice of which to use is not an important decision. If two measures are not closely related, however, empirical evidence for the link between structural variables and performance may depend on the choice of measure, and the researcher would have to decide whether one measure of profitability is theoretically more appealing than another.

A commonly used statistical measure of the strength of the relationship between two variables is the ***correlation coefficient***, r. The correlation coefficient ranges from 1 to −1. If r equals 1, there is a perfect positively sloped linear relationship between the

*Profit rates can be compared using an estimate of the risk-adjusted required rate of return. To do so, however, a specific asset pricing model has to be chosen; q is attractive because it contains the correct risk adjustment, regardless of the true asset pricing model.

†Suppose, for example, that revenues are 110 and costs are 100, giving profits of 10. If costs are measured with a 1 percent error, profits will be mismeasured by 10 percent. (Costs are mismeasured as 101, leading to an estimate of profits of 9.) By contrast, if a firm's capital stock is overestimated by 1 percent, q will be misestimated by only 1 percent.

‡For any publicly traded firm, market value, the numerator of q, is measured by the value of any securities the firm has issued, such as stocks and bonds.

two variables: The value of one variable increases as the value of the other variable does. A correlation coefficient equal to −1 also indicates a perfect linear relationship; in this case the relationship is negative. If r equals 0, no relationship exists between the two variables.

Correlations among the accounting rates of return, such as the rate of return on equity and the rate of return on assets, are high. Liebowitz, for example, finds correlations between one rate of return and another almost always above 0.8.[12] Regression results are usually not sensitive to which measure of rate of return is chosen, so the choice is not critical.

The correlation of accounting rates of return with the price-cost margin, however, is lower. In fact, after calculating correlations among price-cost margins and other measures of profitability, Liebowitz concluded "None of the correlations seems high enough to warrant the conclusion that the census price-cost margin is a close substitute for non-census price-cost margins of any ilk or for other measures of profitability."[13] This low correlation of the price-cost margin with other measures of profitability thus makes the choice more critical. In light of this, Fisher criticized using the price-cost margin to infer monopoly power. He argued that it is an unreliable estimate of the Lerner Index and that the measurement error associated with the price-cost margin can be large.[14]

What about the relationship between accounting rates of return and q? For the purpose of comparison, Salinger estimated regressions using both the rate of return on assets and q as the dependent variable.[15] He found that the results in the profitability regressions are significantly different from the results in the q regressions. Shepherd, however, notes that the profit rate and q are highly correlated with each other; he finds "similar patterns" in regressions using profit rates and those using q to measure profitability.[16] Further evidence on the reliability of alternative measures of profitability comes from a set of simulation experiments conducted by McFarland.*[17] McFarland's results suggest that, although measurement error exists both for estimates of q and for accounting rates of return, estimates of q are more closely related to the true value. Reassuringly, however, McFarland concluded that accounting measures of both q and the rate of return are useful measures of profitability, although they should be used with care.[18]

6.3.3 Summary of Measures of Profitability

We have covered a considerable amount of difficult ground, raising many questions about alternative measures of firm profitability. At this point it is reasonable to ask whether the flaws in accounting data are so serious that these data should not be used at all. This is the view of some economists.[19] Others, however, believe that the data can be used with caution.[20] We agree with those who believe that these data contain useful information, provided that researchers identify biases and correct for them whenever possible. At a minimum, if correcting for biases is not possible, the direction and likely magnitude of the bias should be considered in the interpretation of empirical results.

*These experiments were done using Monte Carlo methods. In these experiments, a universe of firms with known values of q and the rate of return is constructed, allowing the researcher to know "the truth." Then accounting estimates of the two measures of profitability are calculated and compared with the true values.

6.4 Measures of Market Structure

A structure-conduct-performance study searches for a link between various elements of market structure and a measure of performance. In this section we consider the measures of structure commonly used in these studies. Fortunately, we already covered much of this material in Chapter 4.

6.4.1 Measures of Concentration

A key variable in most SCP studies is a measure of market concentration. As we saw, there are several possible measures of market concentration. Ideally, oligopoly theory would indicate which measure of concentration is appropriate.* Several authors have, in fact, used oligopoly theory to argue for a particular measure of concentration. In an early article, Stigler advocated the Herfindahl-Hirschman Index (HHI), arguing that it can be used to detect cheating on collusive agreements.[21] Cowling and Waterson also favored the HHI; they showed that if firms behave as classic oligopolists, the HHI is related to the weighted average of firms' price-cost margins.[22]

Under alternative behavioral assumptions, however, the concentration ratio is the appropriate measure. Thomas Saving modeled an industry consisting of a dominant group of firms and a competitive fringe. Using this model, profits of the industry and of the dominant firms increase with CR_n, the share of sales produced by the n dominant firms.[23] Unfortunately, therefore, theory does not give us an unambiguous choice of concentration ratio. Furthermore, given that some of the hypotheses of interest involve the effect of concentration on behavior, it is problematic to assume a particular model of behavior *ex ante*. Until theory can provide better guidance, it is advisable to view results that are sensitive to the choice of specification or of sample selection with caution.[†]

6.4.2 Barriers to Entry

For a firm to maintain its price above the competitive level over time, there must be barriers to entry into the industry. Economists who have studied the determinants of market performance have, therefore, typically included some measure of entry barriers in their studies.

*In addition to choosing a measure of concentration, a researcher must also think about the definition of the market. As discussed in Chapter 4, markets as defined by the compilers of official statistics are often flawed. Many researchers accept the markets as given. Others try to correct for problems in market definition in various ways: dropping observations from the sample for which markets do not seem to be sensibly defined (Bain, 1951), adjusting published data for the existence of regional markets (W. G. Shepherd, *The Treatment of Market Power* [New York: Columbia University Press, 1974], or including the ratio of imports to domestic production to control for foreign competition (R. E. Caves, "International Trade and Industrial Organization: Problems, Solved and Unsolved," *European Economic Review* 28 [1985]: 377–395).

†Alternative measures of concentration tend to be highly correlated. However, the choice among even highly concentrated measures of concentration can affect the results. (See the discussion in Chapter 4 as well as Leo Sleuwaegen and Wim Dehandschutter, "The Critical Choice Between the Concentration Ratio and the *H*-index in Assessing Industry Performance," *Journal of Industrial Economics* 35 [1986]: 193–198.)

Chapter 4 discussed barriers to entry in detail. We saw which elements of market structure have been identified by economists as potential barriers, and we considered the methodologies used to measure barriers. Many economists have used proxies for entry barriers as independent variables in their regression equations. The commonly used measures of barriers to entry include the following:

1. Economies of scale: often approximated by the ratio of midpoint plant sales, the sales of the plant in the middle of the size distribution of plants, to total industry sales.

2. Capital requirements: typically measured by the estimated amount of capital required by a midpoint plant.

3. Product differentiation: Several measures of product differentiation have been used in SCP studies. The most common is advertising intensity, measured by the ratio of advertising expenditures to sales.

 Some economists have estimated their regression equation separately for producer and consumer goods industries. As explained in Chapter 13, the argument for doing this is that advertising and other forms of product differentiation are expected to have less effect on concentration and on profitability in producer goods industries than in consumer goods industries, because buyers in producer goods industries tend to be large and well informed. This gives firms less room in producer goods industries than in consumer goods industries for persuasive advertising and for collusion that would increase profits.

4. Research intensity: usually measured by the ratio of R&D expenditures to sales.

6.4.3 Other Variables

Researchers have used a variety of additional explanatory variables in SCP studies. One is some measure of recent sales growth. This variable is included to control for the effects of disequilibrium.*

A second variable is the degree of unionization. This variable is included to test the hypothesis that a union may be able to capture at least some of the excess profits generated by product market power by bargaining for higher wages.

6.5 Early Structure-Conduct-Performance Studies

The first SCP empirical work primarily involved detailed case studies of individual industries.[24] These studies were extremely time-consuming and greatly limited by data constraints. Beginning with the work of Bain in the 1950s, economists employed an inter-industry, cross-section approach to examine the relationships among various measures of market structure, conduct, and performance.[25]

*Note that there is no relationship between the degree of competition within an industry and short-run profits. In each of the four industry structures—perfect competition, monopolistic competition, oligopoly, and monopoly—short-run economic profits can be positive, zero, or negative, suggesting that a researcher should try to avoid disequilibrium periods when estimating an SCP study.

By today's standards, the empirical approach Bain used to test his hypotheses is simple. He gathered data on manufacturing industries and organized these data into groups according to a structural characteristic of interest, with the main focus on market concentration. After grouping the data, Bain compared average profit rates across groups to see if they differed. Bain's measure of profits for each industry was the average of the largest firms' (up to four per industry) accounting rate of return on stockholders' equity.*

Bain conducted two pioneering studies examining the relationship between profitability and market concentration. In these works Bain hypothesized that firms in highly concentrated industries were better able to collude, which led to increased prices and profits. In his first test of this hypothesis, Bain used data for 42 manufacturing industries and divided his sample into two groups: those with an eight-firm concentration ratio above 70 percent and those with an eight-firm concentration ratio below 70 percent. As expected, Bain found that the more concentrated industries had higher average profit rates.

In his second study, Bain examined the simultaneous effect of market concentration and barriers to entry on profitability. He predicted that profits would be higher in concentrated industries with high barriers to entry than in concentrated industries with low barriers to entry. For this study, Bain used a sample of 20 manufacturing industries, noting that the amount of work needed to collect information about each industry imposed a "practical limitation" on the sample size.[26] His sample covered the periods 1936 to 1940 and 1947 to 1951.

Bain found a statistically significant difference between the average profit rates of industries with *very high* entry barriers and those in the other categories. Being in the substantial entry barriers category as opposed to the moderate to low entry barriers category, however, did not lead to a statistically significant difference in average profit rates. Although profit rates tended to increase with market concentration, Bain concluded that "*seller concentration alone is not an adequate indicator of the probable incidence of extremes of excess profits and monopolistic output restriction. The concurrent influence of the condition of entry should clearly be taken into account.*"[27] This result is consistent with oligopoly models that predict that oligopolists may set price close to the competitive level if entry barriers are low.

Using Bain's methodology, Mann got similar results for data from 1950 to 1960.[28] In Mann's sample, profits were higher in more concentrated industries. The average rate of return for sample industries with eight-firm concentration ratios above 70 percent was 13.3 percent, whereas for industries in the less concentrated group, the average rate of return was only 9.0 percent. Like Bain, Mann found a distinct difference between the average profit rates for the very high entry barriers group and the other two entry barrier groups.

6.6 Econometric Studies

Shortly after Mann's study was published, the empirical technique used to examine the structure-performance relationship changed, largely because of advances in statistical estimation techniques and computer technology. We turn now to a considera-

*Bain used the average of the largest firms' profit rates because he hypothesized that concentration and entry barriers would primarily benefit the largest firms in an industry.

tion of these regression studies, focusing first on the relationship between concentration and profitability.

6.6.1 Concentration and Profitability: Evidence from Industry-Level Studies

Because they are published on a regular basis in the *Census of Manufactures,* industry-level data are easily available. Thus, many of the econometric studies of structure-performance relationships used large cross-section samples of manufacturing industries.

Collins and Preston

An early and influential industry-level study was published by Collins and Preston in 1969.[29] Their basic hypothesis was the same as Bain's: All other things equal, more highly concentrated industries should exhibit higher average profits. To test this hypothesis, Collins and Preston regressed the price-cost margin on the four-firm concentration ratio, the capital-sales ratio, and a measure of geographic dispersion.* Their sample consisted of data for 417 industries from the 1963 *Census of Manufactures.*

Table 6.1 shows Collins and Preston's regression results using the entire sample. The main coefficient of interest for testing the hypothesis that higher concentration facilitates collusion and thus higher profits is that of the four-firm concentration ratio. As expected, the coefficient of concentration is positive and statistically significant.[†]

Weiss

After the publication of Collins and Preston's study, economists used the same general methodology but included additional independent variables to control for factors

TABLE 6.1 **Collins and Preston's Results—Overall Sample**

$$\text{PCM} = 19.54 + 0.096^a\text{CR4} + 0.092^a\text{CSR} - 0.029^b\text{DISP} \qquad R^2 = 0.19$$

Abbreviations: PCM, price-cost margin; CR4, four-firm concentration ratio; CSR, capital-sales ratio; DISP, index of geographic dispersion.

[a]Significant at 1 percent level; such an estimate would occur only once in 100 times by chance, on average.

[b]Significant at 5 percent level; such an estimate would occur only five times in 100 by chance, on average.

Source: Norman R. Collins and Lee E. Preston, "Price-Cost Margins and Industry Structure," *Review of Economics and Statistics* 51 (August 1969): 277.

*As discussed earlier, the capital-sales ratio is typically included in regressions using the price-cost margins because of the way these margins are calculated. An index of geographic dispersion is included to account for the fact, discussed in Chapter 4, that some geographic markets are primarily regional or local rather than national, as is assumed in the calculation of concentration ratios.

[†]The estimated coefficients of the capital-sales ratio and the index of geographic dispersion also have the expected signs and are statistically significant.

other than concentration that affect profitability. One representative example is shown in Equation 6.3, which is taken from a study by Weiss.[30]

$$PCM = \underset{(2.08)}{16.3 + 0.050}\ CR4\ \underset{(2.00)}{-\ 0.029}\ DISP\ \underset{(7.44)}{+\ 0.119}\ CAP/S \qquad [6.3]$$

$$\underset{(7.20)}{+\ 1.30}\ A/S\ \underset{(0.42)}{-\ 1.90}\ CAO\ \underset{(0.169)}{+\ 0.023}\ INV/S$$

$$\underset{(2.90)}{+\ 0.26}\ GROW\ \underset{(2.70)}{+\ 0.00083}\ CONSxCR4$$

$$\underset{(0.38)}{+\ 0.095}\ MID\ \underset{(1.65)}{-\ 0.033}\ PLANTCAP$$

$$N = 399,\ R^2 = 0.427$$

(The t-statistics of the estimated coefficients are shown in parentheses. A t-statistic greater than 1.97 is statistically significant at a 5 percent level.)

where PCM = price-cost margin; CR4 = the four-firm concentration ratio; DISP = an index of geographic dispersion (High values of DISP indicate low levels of dispersion of production. This variable is included to correct for poorly defined markets); CAP/S = the ratio of capital to sales; A/S = the ratio of advertising to sales; CAO = the ratio of central office employment to total employment (Like CAP/S, this variable is included because of the way price-cost margins are calculated); INV/S = the ratio of inventories to sales; GROW = past output growth; CONSxCR4 = the four-firm concentration ratio multiplied by the percentage of industry sales going to consumer goods markets; MID = the ratio of midpoint plant sales (the sales of the plant in the middle of the size distribution of plants) to total industry sales; and PLANTCAP = the estimated amount of capital required by a midpoint plant.

6.6.2 Summary of Industry-Level Results

Weiss's results are consistent with, and therefore a good example of, the many cross-section industry-level studies of the determinants of profitability done in the 1960s and 1970s. Such studies usually found the estimated coefficient of concentration to be positive and statistically significant.*

Given the general robustness of the results of cross-section industry studies done in the 1960s and 1970s, most economists accepted the structure-conduct-performance hypothesis underlying these regressions. Higher levels of concentration were thought to facilitate collusion among firms, resulting in prices above marginal cost. This relationship appeared to be particularly strong in the presence of high barriers to entry.

*Hundreds of studies have examined the robustness of the industry-level structure-performance results, using different econometric techniques, samples, and explanatory variables. Worth mentioning are studies that examine the effects of competition from foreign suppliers. As theory suggests, imports as a percent of domestic sales are negatively associated with profitability: The ability of domestic firms to exercise market power is limited by competition from foreign firms.

6.7 Effects of Other Elements of Market Power on Profits

Many variables in addition to a measure of concentration have been included in cross-section SCP studies. Several of these are intended to measure barriers to entry.

Although Collins and Preston did not include any explanatory variables to measure barriers to entry, they did estimate their regression equation separately for consumer and producer goods industries. Table 6.2 reports Collins and Preston's results for the separate subsamples, which support the hypothesis that behavior differs in consumer and producer goods industries.

The estimated coefficient of concentration is much higher and its statistical significance is stronger for consumer than for producer goods industries. In consumer goods industries, increasing the concentration ratio by 10 percentage points (e.g., from 50 to 60 percent) would increase the average price-cost margin by 1.99 percent. In producer goods industries, however, the same increase in the concentration ratio would increase the average price-cost margin by only 0.3 percent. As expected, concentration has a larger effect on profits in consumer goods industries, in which barriers to entry based on product differentiation are higher, than in producer goods industries.

Other studies also found that the effect of concentration on profits is greater in consumer goods industries than in producer goods industries. One example is the study by Weiss reported earlier. The positive and statistically significant coefficient of the interaction variable CONSxCR4 in Equation 6.3 shows that the effect of concentration increases as the percentage of industry sales going to consumer goods markets increases.

Evidence from studies that include advertising intensity as a measure of product differentiation supports the hypothesis that consumer and producer goods industries

TABLE 6.2 Collins and Preston's Results—Consumer and Producer Goods Industries

Consumer	PCM $= 17.36 + 0.199^{a}$CR4 $+ 0.103$ CSR $- 0.022$ DISP $R^2 = 0.28$
Producer	PCM $= 19.48 + 0.033^{b}$CR4 $+ 0.133^{a}$CSR $- 0.035^{a}$DISP $R^2 = 0.26$

Abbreviations: PCM, price-cost margin in percent; CR4, four-firm concentration ratio; CSR, capital-sales ratio; DISP, index of geographic dispersion.

[a]Significant at 1 percent level; such an estimate would occur only once in 100 times by chance, on average.

[b]Significant at 10 percent level; such an estimate would occur only once in 10 times by chance, on average.

Source: Norman R. Collins and Lee E. Preston, "Price-Cost Margins and Industry Structure," *Review of Economics and Statistics* 51 (August 1969): 277.

are different. A result that emerges strongly from the available empirical work, much of which is reported in Chapter 13, is that advertising intensity is positively related to average industry profitability.[31] In producer goods industries, however, advertising intensity is negatively related to profitability.[32] Thus, advertising appears to act as a barrier to entry in consumer goods industries but not in producer goods industries.

The estimated coefficients of the variables measuring economies of scale and capital costs, such as MID and PLANTCAP in Weiss's study, tend to be positive in the industry-level studies. The statistical significance of variables such as MID and PLANTCAP varies across studies; in Weiss's study, these variables are not statistically significant.

One explanation for this weak statistical significance is that measures of concentration and measures of scale-related barriers to entry are often highly correlated with each other. When two or more independent variables are highly correlated, estimating the independent effect of any one of them on the dependent variable is difficult. For example, the four-firm concentration ratio tends to increase as economies of scale increase; therefore, it is difficult to separate the effect of the four-firm concentration ratio on profitability from the effect of economies of scale on profitability.

Most evidence from cross-section studies indicates that research and development intensity has a positive effect on profitability. This effect is not as strong, however, when concentration is high. In fact, some evidence indicates that, at high levels of concentration, research intensity is negatively related to concentration.[33]

In examining the effect of factors other than concentration and entry barriers on profitability, the two most commonly included variables are measures of past industry growth and of unionization. Almost all studies find that recent growth in revenue is positively related to profitability.[34] Unionization has a substantial negative effect on profitability in highly concentrated industries, reducing the price-cost margins by between 17 and 66 percent. The effect of unionization on profitability in unconcentrated industries is much smaller, decreasing price-cost margins between 0 and 13 percent.[35]

6.8 Conceptual Problems with SCP Studies

Even as many additional industry-level studies throughout the 1970s confirmed the general structure-performance results, criticisms were raised. Skeptics pointed out a number of conceptual problems and problems of interpretation with the studies, considered below.

6.8.1 Collusion versus Efficiency

One important criticism concerns the interpretation of the observed statistical relationship between market concentration and profitability. Economists associated with the Chicago School, especially Harold Demsetz, noted that, rather than arising from collusion among leading firms, the statistical relationship between market concentration and profitability might be the result of efficiency.[36]

To understand the efficiency interpretation, suppose that there is in fact *no* relationship between concentration and firms' ability to increase price above marginal cost. Furthermore, suppose that more efficient firms earn both higher profits and a larger market share over time *as a result of* their superior efficiency. This would lead to a positive relationship between market share and profits at the firm level.

What is the connection between the supposed *true* relationship between market share and profits at the firm level and the *observed* relationship between concentration and profits at the industry level? The link is that (1) high market shares, by definition, lead to high levels of industry concentration and (2) profits of large firms (assumed in this case to be the more profitable firms) receive more weight than profits of smaller firms in the calculation of the industry average level of profits. Therefore, more highly concentrated industries would, in fact, be associated with higher average profit levels, as shown repeatedly in the industry-level structure-performance studies.

Firm-Level Studies

One way to discriminate between the collusion hypothesis and the efficiency hypothesis is to include both concentration and market share in the same equation.[37] To do this, researchers must use a data set that enables them to measure the market share of individual firms. The results of one such study by Ravenscraft are:[38]

$$\text{PCM} = -22.3 + 0.183\ \text{S} - 0.022\ \text{CR4} + \text{other variables} \qquad [6.4]$$
$$(4.95)^* \qquad (1.38)^*$$
$$N = 3186,\ R^2 = 0.208.$$

Equation 6.4 shows that S, the measure of market share, is strongly and positively correlated with profitability. A firm with a higher market share will have a higher price-cost margin, all else being equal. Note from Equation 6.4 that including market share in the estimated equation dramatically changes the estimated effect of concentration. The four-firm concentration ratio is now *negatively* associated with profitability, although its statistical significance is somewhat weak. Other firm-level studies using samples of firms from many industries have strongly supported both of Ravenscraft's results: (1) that market share is strongly correlated with profitability and (2) that the estimated coefficient of concentration is either negative or statistically insignificant.[39] Such studies suggest that the well-established connection between average industry profitability and concentration may not actually be a causal connection, but may instead be due to aggregating data from the firm to the industry level.

Can we conclude from the firm-level SCP studies that Demsetz's efficiency hypothesis has won the day? Perhaps not surprisingly, things are not that simple. Evidence from firm-level studies that focus on a specific manufacturing industry complicates the picture. If Demsetz's hypothesis is correct, the more efficient firms within an industry should be more profitable, and thus the positive relationship between market share and profitability should hold using an intra-industry as well as an inter-industry sample. This, however, is not the case. The link between profitability and market share *within* a particular manufacturing industry is not as strong as it is *across* industries,

*t-statistics

suggesting that the results of the firm-level inter-industry studies may be strongly influenced by a few unrepresentative industries.[40]

Large versus Small Firms

Given that the evidence from firm-level studies does not definitely support either the collusion or the efficiency hypothesis, can other evidence help? Demsetz argued that evidence on the rates of return of large versus small firms could be used to distinguish between the collusion and the efficiency hypotheses.[41] He reasoned that collusion should benefit all firms in an industry; therefore, if concentration fosters collusion, both small and large firms in concentrated industries should earn higher rates of return. Conversely, if concentration is due to the greater efficiency of large firms, only the large firms in concentrated industries should earn higher rates of return.

Other economists have challenged the hypothesis that collusion ought to benefit *all* firms within a concentrated industry proportionately. Indeed, as noted earlier, Bain expected that concentration would primarily benefit the largest firms in an industry. He, and others, noted that small firms might have inefficiently small plants or smaller product-differentiation advantages than larger firms. The theoretical debate about what can be inferred from profit rate differentials across firms of different sizes continues.

The evidence on the relative rates of return of large versus small firms is also unclear. Some evidence indicates that the positive association between profits and concentration holds for large firms but not for small firms; other evidence shows no systematic differences by size.[42] In a study designed to test the effects of both the concentration and the efficiency explanations on the price-cost margins of firms of different sizes, Martin found support for both hypotheses.[43] His results indicated that increases in productivity increase the price-cost margin of firms in each size group, supporting the efficiency hypothesis. However, the price-cost margins of firms in each size group also increased with the market share of the four largest firms. This result suggests that concentration fosters collusion that benefits all firms in an industry.

Efficiency or Collusion: Summary

The results of tests intended to differentiate the efficiency hypothesis from the collusion hypothesis are, as one researcher said, "discouraging in a number of respects."[44] It seems likely that some complicated firm-specific intra-industry effects have not yet been explained by economic theory.

6.8.2 Assumption of Linearity

A second issue in SCP studies is the exact form of the relationship between concentration and profits. Most studies estimate a linear relationship such as that shown in Figure 6.3(a). Some evidence suggests, however, that the relationship is nonlinear or discontinuous.[45] One example of a nonlinear relationship is shown in Figure 6.3(b). In this example, an increase in concentration has a greater effect on performance for intermediate levels of concentration than for either low or high levels. A linear approximation is appropriate if concentration ratios lie between CR_1 and CR_2 but not

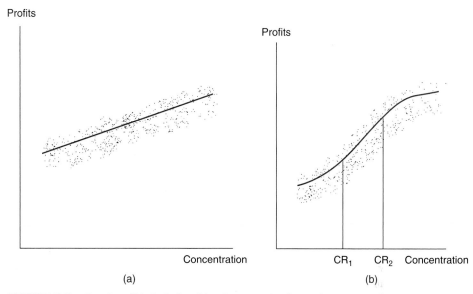

FIGURE 6.3 **Two Possible Relationships Between Profits and Concentration**

Most studies estimate a linear relationship between concentration and profits like the relationship in panel (a). But some evidence suggests the true relationship is like the one depicted in panel (b), where the positive relationship is strongest for intermediate values of concentration and much weaker at low and high levels of concentration.

for very low or very high levels of concentration. As discussed in Section 6.2, assuming linearity when the true functional form is nonlinear may lead to biased estimates.

6.8.3 Variations over Time

Fairly recent evidence suggests that the relationship between concentration and profitability may not be stable over time. Domowitz, Hubbard, and Petersen constructed a database on price-cost margins in 284 manufacturing industries between 1958 and 1981.[46] This panel data set allowed them to focus on price-cost margins both across industries and over time.

Table 6.3 shows some of the results from Domowitz, Hubbard, and Petersen's study. This table replicates the basic regression estimated by Collins and Preston for each of the years in their sample. They found that the coefficient of CR4 initially increased, stabilized during the middle years of the 1960s, and then decreased throughout the remaining years of the sample. The statistical significance of this coefficient also falls from the late 1960s. The explanatory power of the regression, as indicated by the R^2, falls throughout the sample period; by the end of the period, the simple Collins and Preston model has almost no explanatory power.

Domowitz and colleagues explored possible reasons for the changes in the relationship between concentration and price-cost margins over time. Their evidence indicates that industry price-cost margins are sensitive to fluctuations in demand and

TABLE 6.3 Annual Price-Cost Margins—Concentration Regressions, 1958–1981

Year	Constant	CR4	K/Q	Adjusted R^2
1958	.164(.010)	.100(.022)	.079(.017)	.18
1959	.168(.010)	.101(.022)	.100(.019)	.19
1960	.165(.011)	.102(.023)	.089(.019)	.17
1961	.163(.011)	.112(.024)	.077(.018)	.17
1962	.167(.011)	.116(.023)	.076(.018)	.17
1963	.174(.011)	.117(.023)	.080(.018)	.18
1964	.177(.011)	.115(.024)	.081(.019)	.16
1965	.175(.011)	.116(.023)	.096(.018)	.20
1966	.176(.011)	.116(.023)	.093(.018)	.19
1967	.187(.011)	.110(.023)	.076(.016)	.17
1968	.191(.012)	.106(.024)	.087(.017)	.17
1969	.194(.012)	.116(.024)	.068(.018)	.14
1970	.204(.012)	.099(.024)	.050(.017)	.10
1971	.207(.011)	.112(.025)	.038(.018)	.09
1972	.215(.012)	.092(.025)	.049(.018)	.08
1973	.212(.011)	.081(.024)	.079(.018)	.12
1974	.223(.011)	.050(.024)	.098(.021)	.10
1975	.218(.011)	.050(.025)	.071(.021)	.06
1976	.226(.012)	.063(.025)	.059(.023)	.05
1977	.236(.012)	.061(.025)	.042(.024)	.03
1978	.240(.012)	.066(.026)	.020(.024)	.03
1979	.240(.012)	.065(.025)	.042(.024)	.04
1980	.241(.013)	.059(.026)	.028(.025)	.02
1981	.247(.013)	.047(.026)	.021(.026)	.01

Note: Standard errors are in parentheses.

Abbreviations: CR4, four-firm concentration ratio; K/Q, capital-sales ratio.

Source: Ian Domowitz, Glenn R. Hubbard, and Bruce C. Petersen, "Business Cycles and the Relationship Between Concentration and Price-Cost Margins," *Rand Journal of Economics* 17 (Spring 1986), Table 2. Reprinted by the permission of Rand.

that margins are more procyclical in concentrated than in unconcentrated industries. Failure to control for demand and business cycle effects therefore leads to biased estimates of the effects of concentration on price-cost margins. They also found some evidence that increased competition from imports reduced the effect of domestic market concentration on price-cost margins over time.

6.8.4 Endogeneity Problem

A final conceptual problem with SCP studies is the assumption that the structural variables are exogenous. The assumed chain of causation runs from market structure to market conduct to market performance. This assumption is clearly too simple: In the long run, conduct affects structure. Mergers affect concentration, the actions of established firms influence the attractiveness of entry, and innovation changes available technologies.

Thus, in the long run, almost all, if not all, structural variables are essentially endogenous. Treating these variables as exogenous can lead to biased estimates. Some authors have estimated models that treat at least some structural variables as endogenous.[47] Most of the studies that acknowledge and try to correct for the endogeneity have yielded estimates very similar to those of the simple SCP regressions. However, the similarity of results may be largely due to the particular methods used to control for the endogeneity.[48] At this point, the most that can confidently be said is that economists have recognized the problem of endogeneity but have not yet solved it definitively.

6.9 Prices and Concentration

Some economists have examined *price* rather than *profitability*. Before we briefly review this evidence, consider the relationship between profitability and price. Remember that resources are misallocated if the price of a good is not equal to the marginal cost of that good. We want to know, therefore, if there is a direct relationship between economic profits and pricing above marginal cost.

Consider first a firm in a perfectly competitive industry. Assuming profit-maximizing behavior, price will equal marginal cost. In the short run, economic profits can be positive, zero, or negative. In the long run, however, entry and exit will occur until economic profits are zero.

A monopolistically competitive firm differs from a perfectly competitive firm in that price is set above marginal costs.* Thus, unlike a perfectly competitive industry, a monopolistically competitive industry does not produce the optimal quantity from society's viewpoint. Economic profits in the short run can be positive, zero, or negative, but again, because of entry or exit, long-run profits for a monopolistically competitive firm are zero.

Economic theory predicts that price will also be above marginal cost in oligopoly or monopoly. Short-run profits can again be positive, zero, or negative. In the long run, oligopoly or monopoly profits should be zero or positive, depending on the market demand and on the height of barriers to entry.

What do we learn from this brief summary of the predictions of economic theory? First, SCP studies should focus on long-run measures of performance rather than on short-run measures. Second, evidence that long-run profits equal zero does not imply that price equals marginal cost, as is evident from monopolistic competition. Long-run profits will be driven to zero if entry is easy, even if price is greater than

*Monopolistic competition is a market structure with product differentiation and easy entry. Firms face downward-sloping demand curves, but earn zero economic profit in the long run. Monopolistic competition is considered in detail in Chapter 13.

marginal cost. Looking directly at price, therefore, is a theoretically attractive way to measure market power.*

Looking at price rather than profitability is also attractive because it avoids the serious accounting problems of profitability studies discussed earlier in this chapter. Finally, because the focus of price studies is a single industry, bias arising from omitted market-specific variables is of less concern than in cross-section profitability studies. The drawback of price studies, however, is that the data are less readily available.

One type of concentration-price study uses data from separate geographic markets in the same industry. Such studies have been done for a variety of markets, including life insurance, banking services, cement, air transportation, newspaper advertising, radio advertising, groceries, legal services, hospital services, beer, and railroads.[49] These studies all show strong evidence of a positive relationship between concentration and the level of price. Given that price-concentration studies have fewer problems than profitability-concentration studies, these robust results provide strong support for the concentration-collusion hypothesis.

A second type of concentration-price study uses time-series data to see how price changes as concentration changes. These studies also find a positive relationship between concentration and price. Some of this evidence comes from mergers or changes in regulation. An example is Xidex Corporation, a microfilm company. Xidex began the 1970s with a market share of 46 percent and then acquired two competitors, raising its market share to 55 percent as a result of the first acquisition and to 70 percent as a result of the second. An examination of Xidex's prices showed that, as a result of these acquisitions, price increased first by 11 percent and then by an additional 23 percent.[50] Another familiar example is long-distance telephone service. The entry of companies such as MCI and Sprint reduced AT&T's market share and dramatically lowered the price of long-distance calls.

To summarize this brief discussion on price-concentration studies, "Our evidence that concentration is correlated with price is overwhelming."[51] This evidence strengthens the collusion hypothesis rather than the efficiency hypothesis.

6.10 An Alternative Approach: Sunk Costs and Market Concentration

Economists have long been aware of the myriad of problems associated with trying to accurately measure market structure and market performance. Furthermore, traditional SCP studies assumed that market structure measures like the concentration ratio were exogenous variables, that is, variables determined outside the model, when in fact the concentration ratio is almost certainly an endogenous variable determined by industry characteristics such as pricing, advertising, and research and development expenditures. In recent years economists have recognized that the problems associated with the traditional large cross-section SCP models are so severe that they have largely stopped testing these types of models. Instead, researchers have turned to new

*Positive long-run economic profits do, however, provide some information. They indicate that firms possess some degree of market power and that there are barriers to entry into that industry.

approaches to add insight into what determines market structure and how market structure impacts economic performance.

One of the important new approaches was developed by John Sutton, who theorized that sunk costs, and particularly advertising sunk costs, play a very important role in determining market structure.[52] Sutton's approach avoids many of the most serious measurement problems by completely avoiding measuring profit. Instead of focusing on profit, Sutton examined the relationship between market concentration (the endogenous variable) and market growth (the exogenous variable). Market growth is measured by the increase in sales, which is a relatively straightforward variable to measure. There are two types of industries in Sutton's model: those with exogenous sunk costs and those with endogenous sunk costs. Let's examine each of these types.

6.10.1 Markets with Exogenous Sunk Costs

Markets with exogenous sunk costs have homogeneous products, competition based solely on price, fixed exogenous sunk costs equal to F, and easy entry. Sutton considered three types of competition in these markets. Market 1 is a cartel that charges the profit-maximizing monopoly price all the time. In this market, if there are initially n firms, each firm controls $\frac{1}{n} \times$ *total market sales.* With price fixed at the monopoly level, firms enter until profit is driven down to normal levels, that is, until economic profit per firm equals zero. Market 2 is an oligopoly that charges a price less than the monopoly price but greater than the competitive price. Because price is less than the monopoly price, firms have less incentive to enter the oligopoly market than to enter the monopoly market, and therefore, fewer firms enter. In equilibrium, however, each firm again earns a zero economic profit. Market 3 is a highly competitive market, a market that is so competitive that if more than one firm enters the market (that is, $n > 1$), price is driven down to marginal cost and the firms cannot cover their fixed costs F. Therefore, the equilibrium number of firms in the highly competitive market is one and the market is a monopoly.

Sutton summarized these theoretical results in Figures 6.4 and 6.5. Figure 6.4 shows the relationship between price and the number of firms. For $n > 1$, price is highest with a cartel, lowest with competition, and in between for the oligopoly. Figure 6.5 shows Sutton's most surprising theoretical result: *For any given market size S, the greater the degree of competition, the higher the level of market concentration!* The cartel results in the lowest level of concentration, and a highly competitive market results in a monopoly. Because the cartel maintains a high price regardless of the number of firms that enter, there is an incentive for lots of entry. On the other hand, heavy competition results in a low price and discourages all but one firm from entering.

Figure 6.5 identifies Sutton's predicted relationship between market size and concentration in markets with exogenous sunk costs: *In all but the most competitive industries, there is a negative relationship between market size and market concentration.*

6.10.2 Markets with Endogenous Sunk Costs

Markets with endogenous sunk costs are markets in which firms compete along both price and nonprice quality dimensions, such as advertising and product differentiation,

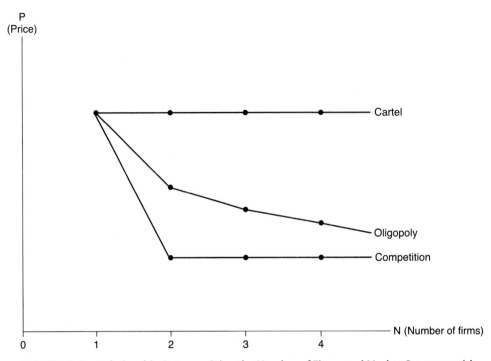

FIGURE 6.4 **Relationship Between Price, the Number of Firms, and Market Structure with Exogenous Sunk Costs**

The figure shows Sutton's prediction that, with exogenous sunk costs, a cartel charges the constant monopoly price regardless of the number of firms; a competitive market charges price equal to marginal cost for any number of firms greater than one; and an oligopoly charges a price between the monopoly price and the competitive price for any number of firms greater than one.

Source: John Sutton, *Sunk Costs and Market Structure* (Cambridge, MA: MIT Press, 1991), p. 34.

research and development activities, and reliability. In markets with endogenous sunk costs, firms decide how much to invest to improve the quality of their products. By improving quality, firms attract customers away from lower-quality goods produced by their competitors. Improving quality, however, is not without costs. Improvements in quality require sunk cost investments in things like advertising and research and development.

As the size of the market S increases, firms have an increased incentive to improve the quality of their products, but this requires an increase in their sunk costs such as advertising. Quality will improve with an increase in the size of the market, but concentration no longer decreases as it did in the case of exogenous sunk costs.

Sutton's equilibrium in the case of endogenous sunk costs has the following characteristics:

1. The largest firms are also the highest-quality firms.

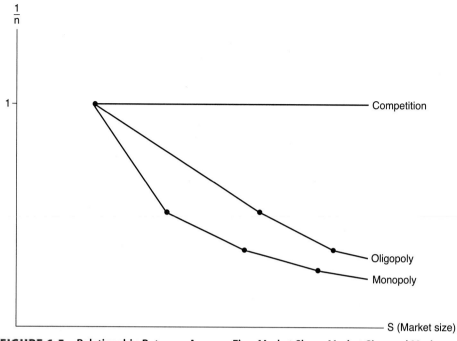

FIGURE 6.5 **Relationship Between Average Firm Market Share, Market Size, and Market Structure with Exogenous Sunk Costs**

The figure shows Sutton's prediction that, with exogenous sunk costs, competition results in monopoly regardless of the size of the market; a cartel results in the lowest average market share per firm; and an oligopoly results in a higher market share per firm than does monopoly.

Source: John Sutton, *Sunk Costs and Market Structure* (Cambridge, MA: MIT Press, 1991), p. 34.

2. An increase in market size results in an increase in overall quality, especially the quality of the highest-quality products. Furthermore, some low-quality products disappear from the market.

3. *As market size increases, the large sunk costs necessary to improve quality limit the number of firms that can afford to pay these sunk costs, and therefore, concentration does not decrease as market size increases.*

6.10.3 Sutton's Empirical Tests

Sutton used a sample of 18 industries in six countries to test his theories.* Six industries had low advertising-to-sales ratios and were placed in the category with exogenous sunk costs.† The remaining 12 industries with high advertising-to-sales ratios

*The six countries are France, Germany, Italy, Japan, the United Kingdom, and the United States.

†The six industries with exogenous sunk costs are salt, sugar, flour, bread, processed meat, and canned vegetables.

were placed in the category with endogenous sunk costs.* He used both regression analysis and detailed industry histories to examine his theoretical conclusions.

The Econometric Model

Sutton's basic regression model was:

Concentration ratio = f(market size, industry effects, country effects).

Sutton measured market size as S/σ, where S is total expenditures on the good and σ is the size of an efficient production plant. Table 6.4 shows the regression results. In the exogenous sunk costs industries with low advertising-to-sales ratios, the estimated coefficient of $\ln(S/\sigma)$ is *negative* and statistically significant. For the endogenous sunk costs industries with high advertising-to-sales ratios, the estimated coefficient of $\ln(S/\sigma)$ is very close to zero and is not statistically different from zero.

These findings are supportive of Sutton's two major theoretical predictions. First, in markets with low advertising-to-sales ratios and exogenous sunk costs, increases in market size result in statistically significant decreases in market concentration. Second, in markets with high advertising-to-sales ratios and endogenous sunk costs, increases in market size result in no statistically significant change in market concentration.

Industry Histories

In addition to econometric tests, Sutton presented detailed histories of each of the 18 industries in each of the six countries. The histories are presented in too much detail to effectively summarize in this text. But the following evidence is presented to give a feel for the types of evidence presented in Sutton's industry histories.

- The histories of the salt and sugar industries appeared to be consistent with markets with exogenous sunk costs and heavy competition.[53] The early histories of both industries were characterized by extensive price competition and price-cutting that resulted in the development of highly concentrated markets.

TABLE 6.4 **Sutton's Regression of Concentration on Market Size for Exogenous and Endogenous Sunk Costs Industries**

Dependent Variable	Industry Group	Regression Coefficient of $\ln(S/\sigma)$	Number of Observations	R^2	Statistically Significant Industry or Country Effects
Four-firm CR	Exogenous sunk costs	−0.187 (t = 3.2)	32	0.86	Sugar(−) UK(+) US(+)
Four-firm CR	Endogenous sunk costs	−0.02 (t = 0.63)	58	0.49	Sugar(−)

Source: John Sutton, *Sunk Costs and Market Structure* (Cambridge, MA: MIT Press, 1991), p. 122.

*The 12 industries with endogenous sunk costs are frozen food, soap, margarine, soft drinks, RTE cereals, mineral water, sugar and chocolate confectionary, coffee, biscuits, pet foods, baby foods, and beer.

- The history of the frozen food industry was characterized by endogenous sunk costs in both the United States and United Kingdom, with early histories in both markets of extensive and escalating advertising competition.[54] The endogenous and large sunk costs required in both of these markets eventually resulted in high market concentration with a few dominant firms controlling each market.

- The frozen-food industry history was essentially repeated in the U.S. markets for coffee, RTE (ready-to-eat) cereals, biscuits, and beer and in the UK markets for RTE cereals and pet foods, as well as in the French market for mineral water.[55]

Overall, there is a good deal of evidence presented in Sutton's industry histories to suggest that high endogenous sunk costs in the form of advertising result in high market concentration. It is also true, however, that Sutton finds that the same industries sometimes evolve in very different ways in different countries despite having similar sunk costs. This finding serves as an important caution to researchers not to make broad generalizations about the relationship between sunk costs and market structure.

APPLICATION 6.2
Applying Sutton's Theory in the Supermarket Industry

Sutton's theory can be applied not only to manufacturing industries but to retailing markets as well. In many retailing markets, there is a tendency for the market to evolve toward what has been called *natural oligopoly*. In these natural oligopolies, no matter what the size of the market, a small number of firms come to dominate. The following markets have evolved in this manner: office superstores where Office Depot, Staples, and Office Max dominate; home improvement superstores where Home Depot and Lowe's dominate; retail bookstore superstores where Borders and Barnes and Noble dominate; and supermarkets where a few large oligopolists dominate in all regional U.S. markets.

Ellickson studied the structure of the supermarket industry in all 51 "spatially defined distribution markets" in the United States.* He hypothesized that Sutton's theory applied to the supermarket industry because modern supermarkets compete by supplying an ever-increasing number of products and higher quality to consumers and this improvement in quality requires large fixed endogenous sunk cost investments in distribution. As an indication of improving quality, Ellickson noted that the number of products in a typical supermarket increased from 14,145 in 1980 to over 30,000 in 2004. As a result, market expansion requires (1) building not only more, but larger stores, and (2) larger and more technologically advanced (for example, computer inventory control) distribution networks. As existing supermarket chains expand, they incur these increasingly larger endogenous sunk costs, and these sunk costs discourage entry by all but a fringe of small firms.

The scatter diagrams on the next page summarize Ellickson's major finding. The top figure shows the relationship between market size, as measured by the ln(Sales), and the market share of the top firm in the market. The bottom figure shows the relationship between market size and the market share of the top six firms in the market. As Sutton predicted, there is no statistical relationship between the two. (Sutton also predicted that there is a *lower bound* to concentration in markets with large endogenous sunk costs, and this prediction is also supported by these scatter diagrams.)

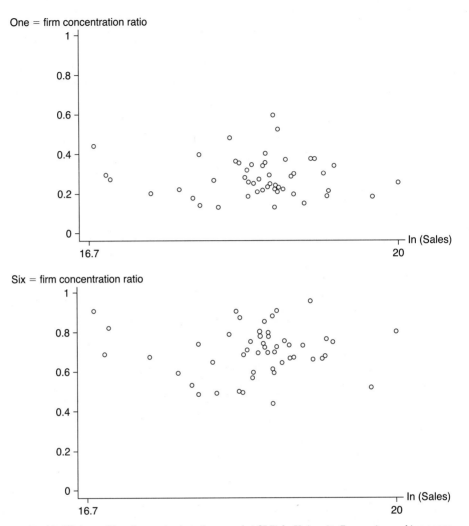

Source: Paul B. Ellickson, "Does Sutton Apply to Supermarkets?" Duke University Economics working paper #05-05, August 25, 2005, www.econ.duke.edu/~paule/DoesSuttonApply.pdf, p. 13.

The table on the next page shows Ellickson's breakdown of the 51 markets by quintiles based on market size, with Q_1 being the smallest markets and Q_4 the largest. C_i represents the i-firm concentration ratio, so C_1 is the market share of the largest firm in the market and C_4 is the four-firm concentration ratio. The results are striking. There is no observed relationship between market size and concentration as measured by either the concentration ratio or the Herfindahl. F_{70} identifies the mean number of firms that control the top 70 percent of sales in each of these market quintiles. There is no significant increase in F_{70} as market size increases. The only thing that does increase with market size is the total number of firms, but the increase in the total number of firms has no impact on concentration. These additional firms are, therefore, quite small and make up a large fringe of small firms.

	Q_1	Q_2	Q_3	Q_4
C_1	28	30	27	27
	$(11, 48)$	$(21, 59)$	$(13, 52)$	$(15, 37)$
C_2	41	46	43	44
	$(18, 70)$	$(31, 73)$	$(20, 80)$	$(29, 64)$
C_4	58	62	59	62
	$(31, 86)$	$(44, 83)$	$(33, 88)$	$(46, 89)$
C_8	72	77	73	76
	$(49, 92)$	$(53, 91)$	$(53, 92)$	$(58, 97)$
C_{20}	85	87	84	86
	$(70, 98)$	$(67, 96)$	$(70, 95)$	$(73, 98)$
Herfindahl	1345	1506	1348	1373
	$(399, 2606)$	$(796, 3769)$	$(436, 3503)$	$(700, 2452)$
F_{70}	8.8	7.6	9.1	7.6
	$(3, 20)$	$(2, 24)$	$(2, 21)$	$(3, 16)$
Firms	91	141	166	224
	$(28, 138)$	$(67, 245)$	$(74, 249)$	$(65, 449)$

Ranges in parentheses.
Source: Paul B. Ellickson, "Does Sutton Apply to Supermarkets?" Duke University Economics working paper #05-05, August 25, 2005, http://www.econ.duke.edu/~paule/DoesSuttonApply.pdf, p. 19.

Ellickson's results led him to conclude that the U.S. supermarket industry is a regional natural oligopoly with from four to six firms controlling each regional market. The results are completely consistent with those predicted by Sutton's model of markets with large endogenous sunk costs. The U.S. supermarket industry, therefore, provides an excellent example of how Sutton's theory can be applied to real-world markets.

*This application is based on the results found in Paul B. Ellickson, "Does Sutton Apply to Supermarkets?" Duke University Economics working paper #05-05, August 25, 2005, http://www.econ.duke.edu/~paule/DoesSuttonApply.pdf. ∎

6.11 The New Empirical Industrial Organization

In response to the criticisms of the SCP studies, industrial organization economists have turned to a new kind of empirical research. This approach, the "new empirical industrial organization" (NEIO), uses systematic statistical evidence in the study of single industries, rather than a cross-section of industries, in an attempt to understand firm conduct within an industry.

A review of the methodology of the NEIO studies is beyond the scope of this book. Instead, we briefly indicate the main ideas of these studies and summarize the results.[56]

The main ideas underlying the NEIO studies are the following:

1. Price-cost margins cannot be observed. A researcher, unable to *observe* a firm's marginal cost, can *infer* it from behavior or can use differences between closely related markets to identify the effects of changes in marginal cost. Alternatively, some NEIO studies measure market power without any measure of marginal cost at all.

TABLE 6.5 Lerner Estimates for Selected Industries

Author	Year	Industry	Lerner Index
Breshnahan	1981	Automobiles	0.100–0.340
Appelbaum	1982	Rubber	0.049
		Textiles	0.072
		Electrical machinery	0.198
		Tobacco	0.648
Porter	1983	Railroads (in collusive phase)	0.40
Lopez	1984	Food processing	0.504
Roberts	1984	Coffee roasting (largest/second-largest firms)	0.055/0.025
Spiller-Favaro	1984	Banks (Regulated, large/small firms)	0.88/0.21
		Banks (Deregulated, large/small firms)	0.40/0.16
Suslow	1986	Aluminum	0.590
Slade	1987	Retail gasoline	0.100
Buschena and Perloff	1991	Philippines coconut oil	0.89
Gasmi, Laffont, and Vuong	1992	Soft drinks (Coke/Pepsi post-1976)	0.64/0.056
Wann and Sexton	1992	Fruit cocktail	1.41
Ellison	1994	Railroads (in collusive phase)	0.472
Deodhar and Sheldon	1995	German bananas	0.26
Nebesky, McMullen and Lee	1995	U.S. Motor carriers (before regulation reform/after regulation reform)	0.262/0.019
Taylor and Zona	1997	Long-distance telephone service (AT&T)	0.88
Genesove and Mullin	1998	Sugar refining 1880–1914	0.05
Fischer and Kamerschen	2003	Airlines 1991–1996, 24 markets	> 0 for all markets

Sources: Timothy F. Breshnahan, "Departures from Marginal-Cost Pricing in the American Automobile Industry," *Journal of Econometrics* 17 (1981): 201–227; Timothy F. Breshnahan, "Studies of Industries with Market Power," in Richard Schmalensee and Robert D. Willig, eds., *The Handbook of Industrial Organization* (Amsterdam: North Holland, 1989); Elie Appelbaum, "The Estimation of the Degree of Oligopoly Power," *Journal of Econometrics* 19 (1982): 287–299; Robert H. Porter, "A Study of Cartel Stability: The Joint Executive Committee, 1880–1886," *The Bell Journal of Economics* 14 (1983): 301–314; R.E. Lopez, "Measuring Oligopoly Power and Production Responses of the Canadian Food Processing Industry," *Journal of Agricultural Economics* 35 (1984): 219–230; Mark J. Roberts, "Testing Oligopolistic Behavior," *International Journal of Industrial Organization* 2 (1984): 367–383; Pablo T. Spiller and Edward Favaro, "The Effects of Entry Regulation on Oligopolistic Interaction: The Uruguayan Banking Sector," *Rand Journal of Economics* 15 (1984): 244–254; Valerie Y. Suslow, "Estimating Monopoly Behavior with Competitive Recycling: An Application to Alcoa," *Rand Journal of Economics* 17 (1986): 389–403; Margaret E. Slade, "Interfirm Rivalry in a Repeated Game: An Empirical Test of Tacit Collusion," *The Journal of Industrial Economics* 35 (1987): 499–516; David E. Buschena and Jeffrey M. Perloff, "The Creation of Dominant Firm Market Power in the Coconut Oil Export Market," *American Journal of Agricultural Economics* 73 (1991): 1000–1008; F. Gasmi, J.J. Laffont, and Q. Vuong, "Econometric Analysis of Collusive Behavior in a Soft Drink Market," *Journal of Economics and Management Strategy* 1 (1992): 277–311; Joyce J. Wann and Richard J. Sexton, "Imperfect Competition in Multiproduct Food Industries with Application to Pear Processing," *American Journal of Agricultural Economics* 74 (November, 1992): 980–990; G. Ellison, "Theories of Cartel Stability and the Joint Executive Committee," *Rand Journal of Economics* 25 (1994): 37–57; Satish Y. Deodhar and Ian M. Sheldon, "Is Foreign Trade (Im)perfectly Competitive?: An Analysis of the German Market for Banana Imports," *Journal of Agricultural Economics* 46 (September, 1995): 336–348; William Nebesky, B. Starr

(continued)

McMullen, and Man-Keung Lee, "Testing for Market Power in the U.S. Motor Carrier Industry," *Review of Industrial Organization* 10 (1995): 559–576; W. Taylor and J. Zona, "An Analysis of the State of Competition in Long-Distance Telephone Markets," *Journal of Regulatory Economics* 11 (1997): 227–255; David Genesove and Wallace Mullin, "Testing Static Oligopoly Models: Conduct and Cost in the Sugar Industry, 1890–1914," *Rand Journal of Economics* 29 (1998): 355–377; and Thorsten Fischer and David R. Kamerschen, "Price-Cost Margins in the US Airline Industry Using a Conjectural Variation Approach," *Journal of Transport Economics and Policy* 37, Part 2 (May 2003): 227–259.

2. Because of institutional details, industries are so individual that researchers cannot learn anything useful from broad cross-section studies of industries.

3. NEIO studies try to specify and estimate the behavioral equations by which firms set price and quantity.

4. NEIO studies identify and estimate the degree of market power.

Evidence from NEIO studies is rapidly accumulating.[57] The work has primarily focused on the measurement of market power rather than on its causes. Two general statements, however, can be made based on the results of existing studies. First, as shown in Table 6.5, several studies have found evidence of market power in individual markets. Of course, this may be partly because an economist who develops a new method for detecting market power is likely to try it out first in those industries most likely to exhibit market power. The choice of industries has been guided by evidence from "old-fashioned" case studies or from prior knowledge of existing cartels.

The second general result of NEIO studies is that anticompetitive conduct is one important cause of high price-cost margins. Some studies find evidence of explicitly collusive behavior.[58]

The NEIO studies are appealing because they provide evidence that does not suffer from the criticisms of the SCP approach. The detail of the studies also makes rebuttal of alternative explanations possible, which is not true of SCP studies. Clearly, additional work on more industries needs to be done.

APPLICATION 6.3

Price-Cost Margins in the RTE Cereal Industry

The new empirical industrial organization focuses on measuring market power by estimating the Lerner Index; that is, estimating the price-cost margin (PCM). Theory predicts a large Lerner Index in industries with high concentration, large advertising-to-sales ratios, and the rapid introduction of new products. The ready-to-eat (RTE) cereal industry is just such an industry. Empirical studies have found that the RTE cereal industry is characterized by a high PCM and this high PCM indicates some form of collusive behavior. Collusion, however, is not the only possible explanation for the observed high PCM. Two of the other possible explanations that have been proposed are (1) product differentiation that results in market power for individual brands, and (2) multiproduct firm pricing that minimizes interbrand competition within firms.

Nevo examined which of the three theories best explains the high PCM in the RTE cereal industry.* He used data for 25 cereal brands for 65 U.S. cities from 1988 to 1992 to estimate the PCM under the following three hypothetical supply assumptions: (1) each brand is produced by one firm, in which case product differentiation between brands explains the PCM; (2) brands are produced under the current market structure

(Kellogg's and General Mills each produced nine brands, Post three, Quaker three, and Nabisco one), in which case multiproduct firm oligopoly pricing explains the PCM; and (3) perfect collusion, in which case collusion explains the PCM.

Under the first specification with each brand produced by a different firm, Nevo estimated that the PCM = 35.8% with a 95 percent confidence interval from 24.4% to 46.4%, meaning that there was a 95% probability that the actual value of the PCM was in the interval from 24.4% to 46.4%. Under the second specification with the 25 brands produced by their current firms, the estimated PCM = 42.2% with a 95 percent confidence interval from 29.1% to 55.8%. Under the third specification with collusion, the estimated PCM = 72.6% with a 95 percent confidence interval from 62.2% to 97.2%.

Nevo then compared his hypothetical estimates with Cotterill's estimate of the actual accounting PCM = 46.0%.[†] Based on his estimates, Nevo rejected the collusion model because the actual PCM = 46.0% was well outside the 95% confidence interval from 62.2% to 97.2% for the collusion model. The actual value of 46.0% is barely within the 95% confidence interval from 24.4% to 46.4% for the product differentiation model. However, Cotterill's estimate of a PCM = 46.0% fits almost perfectly with Nevo's estimate of a PCM = 42.2% for the multiproduct firm oligopoly pricing model.

Nevo concluded that "the high observed PCM[s] are primarily due to the firms' ability to maintain a portfolio of differentiated brands and influence the perceived quality of these brands by means of advertising."[‡] Perhaps of more interest, however, was Nevo's conclusion that "prices in the industry are not a result of collusive behavior."

[*]Aviv Nevo, "Measuring Market Power in the Ready-to-Eat Cereal Industry," *Econometrica*, 69, (March 2001): 307–342.

[†]R. W. Cotterill, "High Cereal Prices and the Prospects for Relief by Expansion of Private Label and Antitrust Enforcement," *Agribusiness: An International Journal*, 15, (1999): 229–245.

[‡]Nevo, "Measuring Market Power in the Ready-to-Eat Cereal Industry," p. 336. ■

SUMMARY

1 Detecting market power and measuring its effects on performance have been the focus of much empirical work in industrial organization for many years.

2 The structure-conduct-performance paradigm, introduced in the 1930s and 1940s, hypothesizes that firm performance follows directly from industry structure. According to this paradigm, certain elements of market structure increase the likelihood of collusive behavior, leading to higher prices and profits. Oligopoly models can also be used to show, under certain behavioral assumptions, a link between industrial concentration and profitability.

3 Economists typically employ regression analysis to test the statistical relationship between variables. These models attempt to explain how the variation in one variable, called the *dependent variable,* depends on the variation in other variables, called the *independent variables.*

4 Regressions look for statistically significant impacts of the independent variables on the dependent variable. Higher t-statistics for a regression coefficient for an independent variable indicate a higher degree of significance in the relationship

between the independent variable and the dependent variable. The R^2 measures the percentage of the total variation in the dependent variable that is explained by all the independent variables combined.

5 Economists have used several measures of market power in their empirical work. Among these are the Lerner Index, excess return on sales, profit rate, price-cost margin, and Tobin's q. Each of these measures has strengths and weaknesses.

6 Problems with several measures of profitability arise from the distinction between economic profits and accounting profits. Capital costs and expenditures on advertising and on research and development, in particular, are treated differently by accountants and by economists.

7 Measures of structure used in structure-conduct-performance studies commonly include measures of market concentration, economies of scale, capital requirements, product differentiation, and research intensity. Hundreds, if not thousands, of these studies have been done.

8 Studies using cross-section industry-level data typically found a strong, statistically significant relationship between market concentration and profitability. This relationship appeared to be particularly strong in the presence of high barriers to entry. Based on this evidence, the structure-conduct-performance paradigm was widely accepted by the early 1970s.

9 Even as additional industry-level studies throughout the 1970s confirmed the general structure-performance results, critics pointed out a number of conceptual problems and problems of interpretation.

10 One important criticism, raised by economists associated with the Chicago School, is that the statistical relationship between market share and profitability might be the result of efficiency rather than of collusion. According to this interpretation, high profits result from low costs rather than high prices, and market concentration is not the *cause* of collusion but the *result* of superior efficiency.

11 Economists have used firm-level data in an attempt to discriminate between the collusion hypothesis and the efficiency hypothesis. These studies suggest that the connection between average industry profitability and concentration may not actually be a causal connection, but may be caused by aggregating data from the firm to the industry level.

12 At this point, the results of the empirical research on concentration and profitability do not support one clear conclusion. Researchers have learned to be cautious about inferring the existence of market power from market structure.

13 Some economists have examined the relationship between concentration and price, rather than profitability. Concentration-price studies using data from separate geographical markets in the same industry find strong evidence of a positive relationship between concentration and the level of price. Studies using time-series data also find evidence of this relationship.

14 John Sutton developed a new approach to the study of the determinants of market structure by examining the relationship between the height of endogenous sunk costs and market concentration. He theorized that in industries with high

exogenous sunk costs, concentration would decrease with increases in market size, but that in industries with high endogenous sunk costs, concentration would not decrease with increases in market size. Dividing industries according to their advertising-to-sales ratios (a high advertising-to-sales ratio meant high endogenous sunk costs), Sutton supported his theory with both econometric evidence and industry case studies.

15 Recent work, called the "new empirical industrial organization," argues that price-cost margins cannot be observed and that industries are so individual that researchers cannot learn anything useful from broad cross-section studies. This work focuses on a single industry and tries to estimate behavioral equations to make inferences about price and quantity.

KEY TERMS

book value
correlation coefficient
dependent variable
depreciation
endogenous variable
excess return on sales
exogenous variable
explanatory variable

independent variable
multicolinearity
parameters
price-cost margin
profit rate
rate of return on stockholders'
 equity after tax

rate of return on assets after tax
regression analysis
replacement cost
risk-adjusted rate of return
straight-line depreciation
Tobin's q

DISCUSSION QUESTIONS

1. To determine if a firm is earning positive economic profits, a researcher can compare the firm's rate of return to the competitive rate of return. If you were conducting such a study, how would you determine the competitive rate of return?

2. Explain why it is important to adjust rates of return for risk and how neglecting to make such an adjustment can affect the conclusions drawn from an examination of market power.

3. Think of an example of a firm that owns a scarce asset such as a brand name. Do you think this firm has market power? Now suppose that this firm is sold. Explain how the purchase is likely to affect the value of equity or assets. What effect does this have on the reported profits? Has the acquisition reduced the market power of the acquired firm?

4. Accountants use historical cost ("book value") to value a firm's physical capital stock; economists use replacement cost, writing the value of physical capital up or down to reflect its cur-

rent market price. Discuss how this difference in the valuation of physical capital affects the measurement of market power.

5. Explain how an accountant's treatment of expenditures on advertising and research and development differs from an economist's treatment. What is the significance of this difference for estimating rates of return?

6. Explain what Tobin's q is and why values of q greater than 1 may indicate the existence of market power.

7. Economists have often looked at a sample of manufacturing industries to determine the relationship between an industry's profit rate and its structure.

 a. Based on the structure-conduct-performance paradigm, what is the expected relationship between profit and structure? Explain your answer.

 b. How do economists measure market power within a given industry? Briefly discuss the

advantages and disadvantages of alternative measures of market power.

c. Some economists have also included one or more measures of the height of entry barriers in their estimations. Explain the rationale for including measures of entry barriers.

d. What features of an industry would you consider in deciding whether entry barriers are high or low? Why?

8. Why might a researcher studying the relationship of profit measures and concentration want to control for the degree of unionization in the study? What might be the effect of leaving this variable out of a regression equation?

9. Evaluate the validity of the following statement: The robust relationship between market concentration and the average profitability of an industry is strong support for the structure-conduct-performance paradigm.

10. Explain the rationale for including both market concentration and a firm's market share in a regression equation explaining profitability.

11. Explain how a firm can charge a price above marginal cost and yet earn zero economic profits.

12. Consider the following estimated regression equation:

$$Y = 2.50 + 0.34X_1 + 5.67X_2 - 1.23X_3 + 0.04X_4$$
$$\quad\quad\quad (0.56) \quad (7.34) \quad (1.04) \quad (0.01)$$
$$R^2 = 0.17 \quad\quad N = 112$$

The numbers in parentheses are the standard errors of the regression coefficients.

Y = the industry's Lerner Index
X_1 = a measure of economies of scale; larger values indicate more significant economies
X_2 = a measure of the industry's growth in demand
X_3 = the industry's advertising/sales ratio
X_4 = the industry's four-firm concentration ratio

a. What is the most significant independent variable in this equation?

b. The sign of which coefficient is most surprising? Why?

c. What does the value of the R^2 suggest about this equation?

13. The following equation has been estimated in a hypothetical empirical study:

$$LI = 16.3 - 0.055 \text{ MS} + 2.11 \text{ CAP/S} + 1.30 \text{ A/S} + 0.26 \text{ GROW}$$
$$\quad\quad\quad (0.044) \quad\quad (1.01) \quad\quad\quad (1.34) \quad\quad (0.09)$$
$$\quad\quad + 2.35 \text{ HHI} + 1.23 \text{ STOCK}$$
$$\quad\quad\quad (0.87) \quad\quad\quad (0.33)$$
$$N = 150 \quad\quad R^2 = 0.25$$

where LI is the industry's Lerner Index; MS is the market share of the leading firm in the industry; CAP/S is the ratio of capital to sales; A/S is the ratio of advertising to sales; GROW is a measure of the growth in sales; HHI is the Herfindahl Index; and STOCK is a measure of the degree to which stockholders control decisions in the firm (a higher measure of STOCK means greater stockholder control of the firm). The numbers in parentheses are the standard errors of the regression coefficients, and N is the number of industries in the sample.

Interpret these results. What are the significant *economic* findings? Are there any major surprises in these results? Do the findings support the profit-maximizing hypothesis or an alternative theory of the firm?

14. Suppose the hypothetical estimate of the *gross rate of entry* into 156 American manufacturing industries found the following results:

$$logE = 2.45 - 0.57\pi_p - 0.98X + 2.56K - 1.23A - 0.34r + 4.78G$$
$$\qquad\quad (0.21) \quad (0.33) \quad (1.96) \quad (0.45) \quad (0.56) \quad (2.01)$$

$$R^2 = 0.65 \qquad N = 156$$

where

 E = a measure of *gross entry,* the average annual increases in the number of corporations in an industry
 π_p = average level of past industry profit rate
 X = the output of an MES (MOS) plant in an industry, divided by total industry sales
 K = capital requirements, defined as the cost of fixed capital required to establish an MES (MOS) plant
 A = advertising intensity, defined as the ratio of industry advertising expenditures to industry sales
 r = a measure of risk, calculated as the standard deviation of industry profit rates
 G = past rate of growth of industry output

 The numbers in parentheses are the *standard errors* of the regression coefficients, and N is the number of industries in the sample.

 Interpret these results. What are the significant *economic* findings? Are there any surprises in these results?

15. According to Sutton, which of the following industries would be likely to have a statistically significant negative relationship between market size and concentration, and which would be likely to have no significant relationship between market size and concentration? Explain your reasoning in each case.

 a. flour

 b. baby food

 c. soft drinks

 d. processed meats

 e. RTE cereal

16. According to Ellickson, what evidence from the supermarket industry supports Sutton's theory? What other retail markets appear to be consistent with Sutton's predictions?

17. According to Nevo, does the RTE cereal market's price-cost margin appear to be consistent with an industry that practices a form of collusion? Explain your reasoning.

18. In a 1984 study, Spiller-Favaro found that banks in regulated markets had significantly higher price-cost margins than banks in deregulated markets. What does this finding suggest about market power in regulated and deregulated banking markets? Why do you think this is the case?

19. What does it mean if an industry has a Lerner Index greater than one? Would you expect a monopolized industry to have a Lerner Index greater than one? Explain your reasoning.

20. Early econometric studies like those of Mann, Collins and Preston, and Weiss almost all found a statistically significant positive relationship between either market concentration and profits or market concentration and price-cost margins. Why didn't these findings hold up under more sophisticated econometric analysis? Did later econometric tests prove that there is no relationship between market concentration and profits?

21. What distinguishes the new empirical industrial organization (NEIO) studies from the traditional SCP studies? What is the major advantage of the NEIO?

NOTES

1. Early work includes Edward S. Mason, "Price and Production Policies of Large-Scale Enterprise," *American Economic Review* 29 (1939): 61–74; Edward S. Mason, "The Current State of the Monopoly Problem in the United States," *Harvard Law Review* 62 (1949): 1265–1285; and Joe S. Bain, *Barriers to New Competition* (Cambridge: Harvard University Press, 1956).

2. The phrase "apparent collusion" is taken from J. Cubbin, "Apparent Collusion and Conjectural Variations in Differentiated Oligopoly," *International Journal of Industrial Organization* 2 (1983): 155–164, although others before him had derived relationships between measures of concentration and measures of profitability from profit-maximizing behavior. See, for example, K. Cowling and M. Waterson, "Price-Cost Margins and Market Structure," *Economica* 43 (1976): 275–286.

3. P. David Qualls, "Concentration, Barriers to Entry, and Long Run Economic Profit Margins," *Journal of Industrial Economics* 20 (April 1972): 146–158.

4. Stanley J. Liebowitz, "What Do Census Price-Cost Margins Measure?" *Journal of Law and Economics* 25 (1982): 231–246.

5. For discussion of the problems associated with using accounting profits, see Franklin Fisher and John McGowan, "On the Misuse of Accounting Rates of Return to Infer Monopoly Profits," *American Economic Review* 73 (March 1983): 82–97. They argue that the problems with accounting profits are so severe that using "accounting rates of return to make inferences about monopoly profits is a baseless procedure" (p. 89). For rebuttals, see William F. Long and David J. Ravenscraft, "The Misuse of Accounting Rates of Return: Comment," *American Economic Review* 74 (June 1984): 494–500; Stephen Martin, "The Misuse of Accounting Rates of Return: Comment," *American Economic Review* 74 (June 1984): 501–506; J.A. Kay and C.P. Mayer, "On the Application of Accounting Rates of Return," *Economic Journal* 96 (March 1986): 197–207; Henry McFarland, "Evaluating q as an Alternative to the Rate of Return in Measuring Profitability," *Review of Economics and Statistics* (November 1988): 614–622; and Stephen Martin, "The Measurement of Profitability and the Diagnosis of Market Power," *International Journal of Industrial Organization* 6 (September 1988): 301–321.

6. Pioneering use of price-cost margins in SCP studies was by Norman Collins and Lee E. Preston, "Price-Cost Margins and Industry Structure," *Review of Economics and Statistics* 51 (August 1969): 271–286; and *Concentration and Price-Cost Margins in Manu-facturing Industries* (Berkeley: University of California Press, 1968).

7. Two studies that estimate marginal costs based on cost functions are Ann F. Friedlaender and Richard H. Spady, "A Derived Demand Function for Freight Transportation," *Review of Economics and Statistics* 62 (1980): 432–441; and Theodore E. Keeler, *Railroads, Freight, and Public Policy* (Washington, DC: Brookings Institution, 1983).

8. For criticisms of the price-cost margin as a measure of performance, see Stanley I. Ornstein, "Empirical Uses of the Price-Cost Margin," *Journal of Industrial Economics* 24 (December 1975): 105–117; S.J. Liebowitz, "What Do Census Price-Cost Margins Measure?" *Journal of Law and Economics* 25 (October 1982): 231–246; and Franklin M. Fisher, "On the Misuse of the Profit-Sales Ratio to Infer Monopoly Power," *Rand Journal of Economics* 18 (1987): 384–396.

9. See, for example, Stavros B. Thomadakis, "A Value-Based Test of Profitability and Market Structure," *Review of Economics and Statistics* 59 (1977): 179–185; Eric Lindenberg and Stephen Ross, "Tobin's q Ratio and Industrial Organization," *Journal of Business* 54 (January 1981): 1–32; Michael A. Salinger, "Tobin's q, Unionization, and the Concentration-Profits Relationship," *Rand Journal of Economics* 15 (Summer 1984): 159–170; Michael Smirlock, Thomas Gilligan, and William Marshall, "Tobin's q and the Structure-Performance Relationship," *American Economic Review* 74 (December 1984): 1051–1060; and Steven Lustgarten and Stavros Thomadakis, "Mobility Barriers and Tobin's q," *Journal of Business* 60 (October 1987): 519–537.

10. See Michael A. Salinger, "Tobin's q, Unionization, and the Concentration-Profits Relationship," *Rand Journal of Economics* 15 (Summer 1984): 159–170; and Henry McFarland, "Evaluating q as an Alternative to the Rate of Return in Measuring Profitability," *Review of Economics and Statistics* 70 (November 1988): 614–622.

11. Eric Lindenberg and Stephen Ross, "Tobin's q Ratio and Industrial Organization," *Journal of Business* 54 (January 1981): 1–32.

12. Liebowitz, *supra* note 8, p. 245.

13. Liebowitz, *ibid.*, p. 241.

14. Franklin M. Fisher, "On the Misuse of the Profits-Sales Ratio to Infer Monopoly Power," *Rand Journal of Economics* 18 (Autumn 1987): 384–396.

15. Salinger, *supra* note 10, pp. 166–167.

16. William G. Shepherd, "Tobin's q and the Structure-Performance Relationship: Comment," *American*

Economic Review 76 (December 1986): 1205–1210. See also the reply by Smirlock, Gilligan, and Marshall in the same issue, pp. 1211–1213.

17. Henry McFarland, "Evaluating q as an Alternative to the Rate of Return in Measuring Profitability," *Review of Economics and Statistics* 70 (November 1988): 614–622.

18. McFarland, *ibid.*, pp. 621–622.

19. See Fisher and McGowan, *op. cit.*, Fisher, *op. cit.*, and George J. Benston, "The Validity of Profits-Structure Studies with Particular Reference to the FTC's Line of Business Data," *American Economic Review* 75 (March 1985): 37–67.

20. See William F. Long and David J. Ravenscraft, "The Misuse of Accounting Rates of Return: Comment," *American Economic Review* 74 (June 1984): 494–500; Stephen Martin, "The Misuse of Accounting Rates of Return: Comment," *American Economic Review* 74 (June 1984): 501–506; J.A. Kay and C.P. Mayer, "On the Application of Accounting Rates of Return," *Economic Journal* 96 (March 1986): 199–207; F.M. Scherer et al., "The Validity of Studies with Line of Business Data: Comment," *American Economic Review* 77 (March 1987): 205–217; and F.M. Scherer and David Ross, *Industrial Market Structure and Economic Performance*, 3rd edition (Boston: Houghton Mifflin Company, 1990), pp. 421–422.

21. George J. Stigler, "A Theory of Oligopoly," *Journal of Political Economy* 72 (1964): 44–61.

22. Keith Cowling and Michael Waterson, "Price-Cost Margins and Market Structure," *Economica* 43 (1976): 267–274.

23. Thomas Saving, "Concentration Ratios and the Degree of Monopoly," *International Economic Review* 11 (1970): 139–145.

24. An example is D.H. Wallace, *Market Control in the Aluminum Industry* (Cambridge, MA: Harvard University Press, 1937).

25. Joe S. Bain, "Relation of Profit Rate to Industry Concentration," *Quarterly Journal of Economics* 65 (1951): 293–324; Joe S. Bain, *Barriers to New Competition* (Cambridge: Harvard University Press, 1956).

26. Bain, *ibid.*, 1956, p. 44.

27. Bain, *ibid.*, 1956, p. 201.

28. Michael Mann, "Seller Concentration, Barriers to Entry, and Rates of Return in Thirty Industries, 1950–1960," *Review of Economics and Statistics* 48 (1966): 290–307.

29. Norman R. Collins and Lee E. Preston, "Price-Cost Margins and Industry Structure," *Review of Economics and Statistics* 51 (August 1969): 271–286.

30. Leonard W. Weiss, "The Concentration-Profits Relationship and Antitrust," in Harvey J.

Goldschmid et al. (eds.), *Industrial Concentration: The New Learning* (Boston: Little, Brown, 1974), pp. 201–220 and updated in Scherer and Ross, *supra* note 20, p. 427.

31. W.S. Comanor and T.A. Wilson, "Advertising, Market Structure and Performance," *Review of Economics and Statistics* 49 (1967): 423–440; W.S. Comanor and T.A. Wilson, *Advertising and Market Power* (Cambridge: Harvard University Press, 1974); A.D. Strickland and L.W. Weiss, "Advertising, Concentration and Price-Cost Margins," *Journal of Political Economy* 84 (1976): 1109–1121; S. Martin, "Advertising, Concentration and Profitability: The Simultaneity Problem," *Bell Journal of Economics* 10 (1979): 639–647; S. Martin, "Entry Barriers, Concentration and Profit," *Southern Economic Journal* 46 (1979): 471–488; J.L. Bothwell, T.F. Cooley, and T.E. Hall, "A New View of the Market Structure-Market Performance Debate," *Journal of Industrial Economics* 32 (1984): 397–417; I. Domowitz, R.G. Hubbard, and B.C. Petersen, "Business Cycles and the Relationship Between Concentration and Price-Cost Margins," *Rand Journal of Economics* 17 (1986): 1–17; and I. Domowitz, R.G. Hubbard, and B.C. Petersen, "The Intertemporal Stability of the Concentration-Margins Relationship," *Journal of Industrial Economics* 35 (1986): 13–34.

32. R.M. Bradburd and R.E. Caves, "A Closer Look at the Effect of Market Growth on Industries' Profits," *Review of Economics and Statistics* 64 (1982): 635–645; and Domowitz et al., *supra* note 31, (1986) in *Rand*.

33. R.J. Stonebraker, "Corporate Profits and the Risk of Entry," *Review of Economics and Statistics* 58 (1976): 33–39; H.G. Grabowski and D.C. Mueller, "Industrial Research and Development, Intangible Capital Stocks, and Firm Profit Rates," *Bell Journal of Economics* 9 (1978): 328–343; R.A. Connolly and M. Hirschey, "R&D, Market Structure and Profits: A Value-Based Approach," *Review of Economics and Statistics* 66 (1984): 678–681; M.A. Salinger, "Tobin's q, Unionization and the Concentration-Profits Relationship," *Rand Journal of Economics* 15 (1984): 159–170; M. Hirschey, "Market Structure and Market Value," *Journal of Business* 58 (1985): 89–98.

34. A good example is Bothwell, Cooley, and Hall, *supra* note 31.

35. Richard B. Freeman and James L. Medoff, *What Do Unions Do?* (New York: Basic Books, 1984); Thomas Karier, "Unions and Monopoly Profits," *Review of Economics and Statistics* 67 (February 1985): pp. 34–42; and Paula B. Voos and Lawrence R. Mishel, "The Union Impact on Profits in the Super-

market Industry," *Review of Economics and Statistics* 68 (August 1986): 513–516.

36. This argument is advanced by, among others, Yale Brozen, "Concentration and Structural and Market Disequilibria," *Antitrust Bulletin* 16 (Summer 1971): 244–248; Harold Demsetz, "Industry Structure, Market Rivalry, and Public Policy," *Journal of Law and Economics* 16 (April 1973): 1–9; Demsetz, "Two Systems of Belief About Monopoly," in Harvey J. Goldschmid et al. (eds.), *Industrial Concentration: The New Learning* (Boston: Little, Brown, 1974), pp. 164–184; Richard B. Mancke, "Causes of Inter-firm Profitability Differences: A New Interpretation of the Evidence," *Quarterly Journal of Economics* 88 (May 1974): 181–193; and Almarin Phillips, "A Critique of Empirical Studies of Relations Between Market Structure and Profitability," *Journal of Industrial Economics* (June 1976): 241–249.

37. An early advocate of this test was Leonard W. Weiss, "The Concentration-Profits Relationship and Antitrust," in Harvey J. Goldschmid et al. (eds.), *Industrial Concentration: The New Learning* (Boston: Little, Brown, 1974).

38. David J. Ravenscraft, "Structure-Profit Relationships at the Line of Business and Industry Level," *Review of Economics and Statistics* 65 (February 1983): 22–31.

39. References include J.L. Bothwell, T.F. Cooley, and T.E. Hall, "A New View of the Market Structure-Market Performance Debate," *Journal of Industrial Economics* 32 (1984): 397–417; M. Smirlock, T. Gilligan, and W. Marshall, "Tobin's *q* and the Structure-Performance Relationship," *American Economic Review* 74 (1984): 1051–1060; R. Schmalensee, "Do Markets Differ Much?" *American Economic Review* 75 (1985): 341–351; and D. Mueller, *Profits in the Long Run* (Cambridge: Cambridge University Press, 1986).

40. See Richard Schmalensee, "Inter-Industry Studies of Structure and Performance," in the *Handbook of Industrial Organization,* vol. 2, pp. 984–985.

41. Demsetz, "Two Systems of Belief about Monopoly," *supra* note 36, pp. 164–184.

42. M.E. Porter, "The Structure Within Industries and Companies' Performance," *Review of Economics and Statistics* 61 (May 1979): 214–227; R.T. Masson and J. Shaanan, "Stochastic-Dynamic Limit Pricing: An Empirical Test," *Review of Economics and Statistics* 64 (August 1982): pp. 413–422; M. Marcus, "Profitability and Size of Firm," *Review of Economics and Statistics* 61 (February 1969): 104–107; Louis Amato and Ronald P. Wilder, "The Effects of Firm Size on Profit Rates in U.S. Manufacturing," *Southern Economic Journal* 52 (July 1985): 181–190;

and Louis Amato and Ronald P. Wilder, "Market Concentration, Efficiency, and Antitrust Policy: Demsetz Revisited," *Quarterly Journal of Business and Economics* 27 (1988): 3–19.

43. Stephen Martin, "Market Power and/or Efficiency?" *Review of Economics and Statistics* 70 (May 1988): 331–335.

44. Richard Schmalensee, "Collusion Versus Differential Efficiency: Testing Alternative Hypotheses," *Journal of Industrial Economics* 35 (June 1987): 420.

45. Studies examining the form of the concentration-profits relationship include Stephen A. Rhoades and Joe M. Cleaver, "The Nature of the Concentration-Price Cost Margin Relationship for 352 Manufacturing Industries: 1967," *Southern Economic Journal* 40 (June 1973): 90–102; J.A. Dalton and J.W. Penn, "The Concentration-Profitability Relationship: Is There a Critical Concentration Ratio?" *Journal of Industrial Economics* 25 (1976): 133–142; Lawrence J. White, "Searching for the Critical Concentration Ratio: An Application of the 'Switching of Regimes' Technique," in S. Goldfeld and R. Quandt (eds.), *Studies in Non-Linear Estimation* (Cambridge, MA: Ballinger, 1976); J.E. Kwoka Jr., "The Effect of Market Share Distribution on Industry Performance," *Review of Economics and Statistics* 59 (1979): 101–109; and R.M. Bradburd and A.M. Over, "Organization Costs, 'Sticky' Equilibria and Critical Levels of Concentration," *Review of Economics and Statistics* 64 (1982): 50–58.

46. Ian Domowitz, R. Glenn Hubbard, and Bruce C. Petersen, "Business Cycles and the Relationship Between Concentration and Price-Cost Margins," *Rand Journal of Economics* 17 (Spring 1986): 1–17.

47. Examples include W.S. Comanor and T.A. Wilson, *Advertising and Market Power* (Cambridge: Harvard University Press, 1974); A.D. Strickland and L.W. Weiss, "Advertising, Concentration and Price-Cost Margins," *Journal of Political Economy* 84 (1976): 1109–1121; S. Martin, "Advertising, Concentration and Profitability: The Simultaneity Problem," *Bell Journal of Economics* 10 (1979): 639–647; P.A. Geroski, "Simultaneous Equations Models of the Structure-Performance Paradigm," *European Economic Review* 19 (1982): 145–158; and R.A. Connolly and M. Hirschey, "R&D, Market Structure and Profits: A Value-Based Approach," *Review of Economics and Statistics* 66 (1984): 678–681.

48. See Schmalensee in the *Handbook of Industrial Organization, supra* note 40, pp. 953–956.

49. An incomplete list of references includes J.D. Cummins, H.S. Denenberg, and W.C. Scheel, "Concentration in the U.S. Life Insurance Industry," *Journal of Risk and Insurance* 39 (June 1972): 177–199; R.A.

Gilbert, "Bank Market Structure and Competition: A Survey," *Journal of Money, Credit and Banking* 16 (1984): 617–645; Roland H. Koller and L.W. Weiss, "Price Levels and Seller Concentration: The Case of Portland Cement," in L.W. Weiss (ed.), *Concentration and Price* (Cambridge, MA: MIT Press, 1989), pp. 17–40; E.E. Bailey, David R. Graham, and Daniel P. Kaplan, *Deregulating the Airlines* (Cambridge, MA: MIT Press, 1985), pp. 155–165; R.S. Thompson, "Structure and Conduct in Local Advertising Markets," *Journal of Industrial Economics* 33 (December 1984): 241–249; George J. Stigler, "A Theory of Oligopoly," *Journal of Political Economy* 72 (1964): 44–61; F.E. Geithman, H.P. Marvel, and L.W. Weiss, "Concentration, Price, and Critical Concentration Ratios," *Review of Economics and Statistics* 63 (1981): 346–353; Ronald W. Cotterill, "Market Power in the Retail Food Industry," *Review of Economics and Statistics* 68 (August 1986): 379–386; John R. Schroeter, Scott L. Smith, and Steven L. Cox, "Advertising and Competition in Routine Legal Service Markets: An Empirical Investigation," *Journal of Industrial Economics* (September 1987): 49–60; Monica Noether, "Competition Among Hospitals," *Journal of Health Economics* 7 (September 1988): 259–284; and James M. Mac-Donald, "Competition and Railroad Rates for the Shipment of Corn, Soybeans, and Wheat," *Rand Journal of Economics* 18 (Spring 1987): 151–163.

50. David M. Barton and Roger Sherman, "The Price and Profit Effects of Horizontal Merger: A Case Study," *Journal of Industrial Economics* 33 (December 1984): 165–177.

51. Weiss, *Concentration and Price* (Cambridge: MIT Press, 1989), p. 283.

52. John Sutton, *Sunk Costs and Market Structure* (Cambridge, MA: MIT Press, 1991).

53. *Ibid.*, pp. 136–157.

54. *Ibid.*, pp. 173–197.

55. *Ibid.*, pp. 232–244, pp. 251–256, pp. 275–282, pp. 285–299, pp. 479–481, and pp. 500–502.

56. This discussion draws on Timothy F. Bresnahan, "Empirical Studies of Industries with Market Power," in *Handbook of Industrial Organization*, pp. 1012–1057.

57. For two surveys of the NEIO studies, see R. Porter, "Recent Developments in Empirical Industrial Organization," *Journal of Economic Education* 25 (1994): 149–161; and M. Slade, "Empirical Games: The Oligopoly Case," *Canadian Journal of Economics* 28 (1995): 368–402.

58. R.H. Porter, "A Study of Cartel Stability: The Joint Executive Committee, 1880–1886," *Bell Journal of Economics* 14 (1983): 301–314; and T.F. Bresnahan, "Competition and Collusion in the American Automobile Oligopoly: The 1955 Price War," *Journal of Industrial Economics* 35 (June 1987): 457–482.

 INTERNET EXERCISES

Visit www.aw-bc.com/waldman_jensen for this chapter's web exercises. Answer our real-world economics problems by searching the Internet for solutions!

Game Theory: A Framework for Understanding Oligopolistic Behavior

In the next few chapters a number of models of oligopolistic behavior are introduced. These models attempt to explain pricing in oligopolistic industries. Trying to predict oligopolistic price or nonprice competition presents many difficult problems for economic theorists. In the past these models often appeared to have little in common, and this section of an industrial organization course sometimes seemed liked a series of unrelated and highly speculative models of behavior. Recently the application of game theory to models of oligopoly behavior has established a basic framework for understanding this section of the course. In this chapter we introduce some of the basic game theoretic approaches used to examine oligopoly behavior.[1] In the next few chapters it will become clear why game theory provides a semblance of glue for holding the different models of oligopoly behavior together.

For more than 100 years one point has been apparent to economists: Oligopolists recognize their interdependencies. General Motors understands that its actions affect Ford, Daimler-Chrysler, Toyota, Nissan, and all other automobile manufacturers. When the number of competitors is relatively small, each firm realizes that any significant move on its part is likely to result in countering moves by its competitors. In this sense oligopolistic competition can be viewed as a "game," in which one move results in a countermove by competitors. The illustrative games presented in this chapter are played by duopolists. As shown in later chapters, however, the implications of most of the results are true even when the number of players is greater than two.

7.1 What Is Game Theory?

Game theory is the study of how interdependent decision makers make choices. Game theory can be used to provide insight into many types of decision making, from political decisions such as voting to sports decisions such as whether a tennis player serves to the forehand or backhand side. In the last two decades game theory has been used by economists to analyze a wide variety of economic interactions. In industrial organization the primary concern is the interactions between

competing oligopolists, and game theory provides a useful framework to understand these interactions.

A game must include players, actions, information, strategies, payoffs, outcomes, and equilibria. Together the *players, actions,* and *outcomes* define the rules of the game. The following simple definitions will be helpful as we proceed with the text:

1. The players are the decision makers. In most of our games the players will be two or more oligopolists, or a monopolist and a potential entrant.

2. The actions include all of the possible moves that a player can make.

3. Information is modeled by defining how much each player knows at each point in the game.

4. Strategies are rules telling each player which action to choose at each point in the game.

5. Payoffs usually consist of the profits or expected profits the players receive after all of the players have picked strategies and the game has been played out.

6. The outcome of the game is a set of interesting results the modeler selects from the values of actions, payoffs, and other variables after the game has been completed.

7. An equilibrium is a strategy combination that consists of the best strategy (for example, the long-run profit-maximizing strategy) for each player in the game.

Additional definitions of terms will be introduced as needed in the games that follow.

7.2 Simple Zero-Sum Games[2]

Consider the following simple game that was actually played by ice cream truck driver Don Waldman on July 4, 1968, and repeated on July 4, 1969. On those two holidays, Waldman was driving an ice cream truck in a New Jersey suburb of Philadelphia that held an annual Fourth of July parade. Unfortunately for Waldman, the suburb also had one other ice cream truck. The two drivers had to decide where to park during the parade. The parade route was about one-half mile long, and the trucks were free to park anywhere along the route. Where did the trucks locate?

Consider three possible locations, the beginning, middle, or end of the route. Table 7.1 presents the possible sales payoffs for Waldman and the infamous "Other Truck." If both locate at the same point, the trucks split sales 50-50. But if one locates at the middle while the other locates at the beginning or end, the truck in the middle

TABLE 7.1 Sales of Ice Cream (% Waldman Sales, % "Other Truck" Sales)

		"Other Truck" Location		
		Beginning	*Middle*	*End*
Waldman Location	**Beginning**	50, 50	25, 75	50, 50
	Middle	75, 25	50, 50	75, 25
	End	50, 50	25, 75	50, 50

gets 75 percent of total sales. Both drivers faced identical choices, and Waldman reasoned as follows:

> If the other truck locates at the beginning of the parade, it is better for me to locate in the middle and gain 75 percent. If the other truck locates in the middle, it is still better for me to locate in the middle and gain a 50-50 split. Finally, if the other truck locates at the end of the parade, I should still locate in the middle. No matter what the other truck does, I should locate in the middle.

In this game, *middle* is Waldman's **dominant strategy.** A dominant strategy is a strategy that outperforms any other strategy *no matter what strategy an opponent selects*. Waldman, of course, decided to park in the middle, where he found the other truck already parked. The Other Truck had reasoned exactly as Waldman and played its dominant strategy—middle.

Looking at Table 7.1, one might ask why the trucks immediately selected middle-middle as the solution instead of beginning-beginning, end-end, beginning-end, or end-beginning. Closer inspection reveals that only middle-middle is a stable solution to the game. Suppose that because of an early morning traffic jam, both trucks were initially located at the beginning. The split is 50-50, but if Waldman believes that Other Truck will remain at the beginning of the parade, then Waldman should move to the middle and gain a 75-25 split. Other Truck should reason exactly the same way, so there is no stability to the solution beginning-beginning. Even though the result in terms of sales split is identical at beginning-beginning and middle-middle, only middle-middle is stable.

Middle-middle has one unique characteristic compared with any of the other eight cells in the payoff matrix. It is the only one of the game's cells where both players are doing the best they can *given the choice of their opponent*. Such a solution is called a **Nash equilibrium** after mathematician John Nash, who first came up with the idea.[3] The concept of a Nash equilibrium is one of the most important concepts to understand about the application of game theory to economic behavior. Although all dominant solutions are Nash equilibria, some games without a dominant solution can have more than one Nash equilibrium.

The game depicted by Table 7.1 has another important characteristic: In each and every cell the combined sales of the two trucks add up to 100 percent. For every 1 percent increase in sales for Waldman there will be a 1 percent reduction in sales for Other Truck. Such a game, in which one player's gain is always matched by another player's loss, is called a **zero-sum game.**

One dominant solution to all zero-sum games is obtained by using the so-called **minimax strategy.** If Waldman plays a strategy that minimizes the maximum possible outcome for Other Truck, Waldman will be playing his dominant strategy. Returning to Table 7.1, Waldman should surmise that if he parks at either the beginning or end, Other Truck will play middle and gain 75 percent. If Waldman selects middle, Other Truck will play middle and gain 50 percent. Waldman's minimax strategy is to play middle, which minimizes Other Truck's maximum possible outcome at 50 percent. Viewed from Other Truck's perspective, the minimax strategy is to maximize the minimum possible outcome for each possible play. Because the minimum possible result of playing either beginning or end is 25 percent, and the minimum possible result of playing middle is 50 percent, Other Truck will play middle.

APPLICATION 7.1

University Rankings and Merit-Based Financial Aid as a Zero-Sum Game

For many high school juniors and seniors, few magazine articles are more important than the *U.S. News & World Report* annual rankings of universities and colleges that appear every fall. Students, their parents and families, and universities and colleges all anticipate the new rankings with both interest and fear. Students wonder if their top choices will go up or down in the rankings. College administrators wonder the same thing and fear with true trepidation the implications of a drop in the rankings. Schools jockey for better rankings by doing many things, some good (for example, curricular innovation, more dollars for scholarship aid, increased emphasis on good teaching) and some bad (for example, rejecting qualified students who are unlikely to attend to increase their selectivity rating; basing more of their admission decisions on SAT scores that, *ceteris paribus,* tend to favor wealthier over poorer applicants; and limiting the size of their classes to fewer than 20 students only in the fall when data are collected while teaching more sections of over 50 students in the spring), to improve their ranking.

The competition between schools for the best possible *U.S. News & World Report* ranking is a zero-sum game. There is a fixed number of schools in every one of the *U.S. News & World Report* categories such as national universities, national liberal arts colleges, and regional universities. If one school goes up two positions in the rankings, it follows that some other school must go down two positions or two other schools must each go down by one position. For every gain, there is an equal loss.

The quest for a higher ranking results in another zero-sum game that colleges play in their attempts to attract students of the highest possible overall quality. Because higher-quality students as measured by SAT scores and class rank are important determinants of a college's *U.S. News & World Report* ranking, colleges have increasingly moved toward using more merit-based financial aid in place of need-based financial aid to attract better students. However, because the total number of high school graduates going to college in a given year is more or less fixed, any successful attempt by one school to attract a better student by offering merit-based aid results in one less high-quality student for some other school. If Princeton uses merit-based aid to attract a student who would otherwise have gone to Stanford, it reduces the number of high-quality students at Stanford by one. Princeton's minimax strategy in the aid game is to offer a large number of merit-aid packages that minimizes the maximum number of high-quality students going to Princeton's competitors, including the seven other Ivy League schools (Brown, Columbia, Cornell, Dartmouth, Harvard, Penn, and Yale) and schools like Stanford and MIT. Of course, each of Princeton's competitors has the same minimax solution to the game. In the end, the schools are likely to offer far more than the optimal number of large merit-aid packages relative to the packages that they could use to attract the same overall quality of students if they all agreed to offer only need-based aid. ■

7.3 The Information Structure of Games

In the ice cream truck example, each player knew all of the information in Table 7.1; *in addition,* each player knew that the other player also knew all of the information in Table 7.1. In this case information is referred to as *common knowledge.*

There are four other useful ways of categorizing the information structure of a game. In a game with *perfect information,* each player knows *every* move that has been made by the other players *before* taking any action. Given this definition, all games in which the players move *simultaneously* are games of imperfect information because the players do not know the simultaneous move of the other player. The Waldman ice cream truck game is an example of a game with imperfect information.

Many games require a *nonplayer* to take *random* actions at some point in the game. For example, in some games this nonplayer randomly determines at the beginning of the game whether one of the players will always take the same action (e.g., an established firm might *always* fight new firms) or vary its actions (e.g., an established firm might *sometimes* fight new firms and *sometimes* accommodate new firms). Game theorists refer to a nonplayer who takes such random actions as *nature.*

If a game includes nature, but nature does *not* move first, or nature's first move is observed by *all* players, the game is of **complete information.** Furthermore, if nature *never* moves after any other player moves, then the game is of **certain information.**

Finally, if all players have exactly the same information when each player moves, the game is said to be of **symmetric information.** If some players know different information when they move than other players, then the game is of **asymmetric information.**

7.4 Prisoner's Dilemma Games[4]

All zero-sum games have fairly straightforward solutions. What happens, however, when we move into the realm of non-zero-sum games?

Oligopoly games of collusion are typically non-zero-sum games. In non-zero-sum games, the total payoff in each cell varies. Consider a collusive agreement between two duopolists, General Electric and Westinghouse, to keep the price of turbine generators at the high joint profit-maximizing level. Table 7.2 represents a possible profit matrix for such a game. Note that the combined profits vary from cell to cell, from a minimum of $160 million to a maximum of $200 million. If both firms abide by the high price agreement, they each earn $100 million. If they both break the agreement, they each earn only $80 million. If only one chisels, the chiseler earns $140 million, leaving the high-price firm with only $25 million. The game is of imperfect information because GE and Westinghouse *simultaneously* select prices. This game is also a **static game** because both players move simultaneously. *Static games* are distinguished from **dynamic games,** in which players take turns moving.

Start by considering whether there is a dominant strategy to this game. If GE prices high, then Westinghouse should price low and earn $140 million. If GE prices low, Westinghouse should still price low and earn $80 million. *No matter what strategy*

TABLE 7.2	Profits (General Electric, Westinghouse)		
		Westinghouse Price	
		High Price	*Low Price*
GE Price	**High Price**	100, 100	25, 140
	Low Price	140, 25	80, 80

GE adopts, Westinghouse should price low. Low price is a *dominant* strategy for West-inghouse. Furthermore, because the matrix is perfectly symmetric, GE's dominant strategy is also low price. Both firms should price low and earn $80 million. Yet something seems amiss with this result. They could both be better off if only they would agree to play high price.

The basic form of this game is known as the ***prisoner's dilemma.*** Chapter 10 explores several possible strategies to try to solve the prisoner's dilemma, but first let's consider why this game is called the prisoner's dilemma. Suppose two members of the mob, Big Boy and Mumbles, have just been arrested for drug dealing. The district attorney knows that she needs a confession from at least one of them to get a strong conviction and stiff sentence. Police detective Tracy puts them in separate rooms for interrogation, where both are offered the same deal. If either confesses and turns state's evidence, he will receive a lighter sentence. Of course, if both confess there is no need to use either of them in court, and they will receive a somewhat smaller break in return for a confession.

The game matrix is represented by Table 7.3. Both Big Boy and Mumbles have a dominant strategy. No matter what the other does, both are better off if they confess. If Mumbles confesses, Big Boy reduces his sentence by four years by also confessing. If Mumbles stays quiet, Big Boy reduces his sentence by two years by confessing. Clearly Big Boy should confess, and so should Mumbles. Given this payoff matrix, confession is a dominant strategy. This is the classic form of the prisoner's dilemma.

Realizing this problem, the mob will work hard to find a solution to the dilemma. One solution might be to change the matrix so that it is known with virtual certainty that all "squealers" will be killed. This "slight" alteration in the matrix changes Table 7.3 into Table 7.4 and obviously changes the outcome. The dominant solution is now to play *don't confess.* The death threat actually reduces both Big Boy's and Mumbles's sentences.

TABLE 7.3 Sentences (Big Boy, Mumbles)

		Mumbles's Action	
		Confess	*Don't Confess*
Big Boy's Action	Confess	6 years, 6 years	1 year, 10 years
	Don't Confess	10 years, 1 year	3 years, 3 years

TABLE 7.4 Sentences (Big Boy, Mumbles)

		Mumbles's Action	
		Confess	*Don't Confess*
Big Boy's Action	Confess	Death, death	Death, 10 years
	Don't Confess	10 years, death	3 years, 3 years

APPLICATION 7.2

A Prisoner's Dilemma—Doctors and HMOs

The prisoner's dilemma is applicable to many types of business negotiations involving competitors. According to Dr. Joseph Bernstein of the University of Pennsylvania, it is

one of the major reasons why many doctors who would prefer to remain in their own practices find themselves with no choice but to join an HMO.*

According to Dr. Bernstein, if you are a doctor in your own practice and you compete with another doctor in the same local area, you are faced with a prisoner's dilemma when an HMO moves into your community and begins to recruit doctors. This dilemma is represented in the table below which considers the dilemma faced by two doctors Grey and Carter. An HMO recruits each to sign up. As Bernstein notes, the two doctors are prevented from communicating with each other because communication violates the antitrust laws. Therefore, because the two doctors are talking independently to the HMO, but they are not talking to each other, this situation has all of the requirements of a prisoner's dilemma. Assuming Grey and Carter currently share their market 50-50 and they both have the ability and willingness to take on many additional patients (all the available patients, according to Bernstein); then they each face the same choices.

Consider the situation facing Grey. If she joins the HMO and Carter also joins, she keeps 50 percent of the patients, but her income goes substantially down. If she joins the HMO and Carter does not, she gets 100 percent of the patients and her income goes way up. If she refuses to join the HMO and Carter joins, she loses her entire patient base and may as well move out of town. Finally, if she refuses to join the HMO and Carter also refuses, she keeps 50 percent of the patients and her current high income. Carter, of course, is faced with the exact same set of choices. If they could collude, they would both refuse to join, maintain the status quo, and earn high incomes. But it is impossible to collude, and in the game below there is a dominant solution: Both join the HMO. Regardless of what Carter decides to do, Grey always earns a higher income by joining the HMO. The outcome is not optimal for Grey and Carter, but because of the prisoner's dilemma, it is almost inevitable that the doctors will join the HMO and both their incomes will decrease substantially.

*Joseph Bernstein, "Topics in Medical Economics: Lessons of the Prisoner's Dilemma," *Journal of Bone and Joint Surgery* 82 (April 2000): 595–598. ■

7.5 Repeated Games[5]

The classic prisoner's dilemma game is played only once, but most oligopoly games are played repeatedly. Dell and Gateway compete not only in the current period, but in many future periods as well. The repeated nature of oligopoly games makes it possible for a player's current action to affect future outcomes. If GE and Westinghouse competed in the turbine market in only *one* period and the payoff matrix was the one depicted in Table 7.2, then each firm has a powerful incentive to play *low price*. In a one-period game, no matter what GE does, it makes sense for Westinghouse to play *low price*, and vice-versa.

Suppose GE and Westinghouse expect to compete in this market for a *finite* number of periods. Perhaps Westinghouse and GE anticipate that they will sell their turbine operations in 10 years, so they expect to compete for another 40 quarters. What should they do in each quarter for the next 10 years? In a ***repeated game*** like this one, a simple one-period *simultaneous* move game is repeated over and over again. In each additional round, the players know the *previous* actions undertaken by all other players. Repeated games of this form are referred to as games of *almost perfect* information. Because the moves are simultaneous, the game must be of *imperfect information*.

Consider GE's strategy in the last quarter, the 40th, which occurs in 10 years. In the 40th quarter, GE has nothing to fear regarding the future playing of the game, and therefore, in the last period (the 40th quarter), GE should play its dominant strategy— low price. This is in its best interest in the last period, no matter what Westinghouse does. Westinghouse, of course, does the same thing, so the 40th quarter results in a payoff of *low price, low price,* or $80 million.

Now what should GE do in the 39th quarter? Because the result of the 40th quarter is known, GE's action in the 39th quarter will not affect the 40th quarter outcome, and GE should play the 39th quarter as if it were the last quarter. This means it should play its dominant strategy in the 39th quarter—low price. Westinghouse does the same, and the 39th quarter results in an equilibrium of *low price, low price*. But now the 38th quarter becomes the last, and the actions undertaken in the 38th quarter will have no effect on the outcome in the 39th quarter. The equilibrium in the 38th quarter, therefore, must also be *low price, low price*. By simply continuing to work backward through time, it is obvious that the equilibrium play in *every period* is the dominant strategy in the last period—*low price, low price*. This will be true for any *finite* game: Because there is no incentive to play *high price* in the last round, there will be no incentive to play *high price* in any earlier round.

To complicate things more, it is important to realize that most games played by oligopolists are *infinite* games. GE and Westinghouse probably expect to play the turbine generator game forever. In any infinite game, there is no known last round, and players can undertake early actions in the hopes of affecting the future strategy of their competitors. In an infinite game, GE may believe that an early play of *high price* on its part may encourage Westinghouse to play *high price* in the future. As we will see in Chapter 9, the optimal strategy in this infinite game may be very different from the optimal strategy in a finite game.

7.6 Games of Mixed Strategies[6]

S o far all the games presented have resulted in one Nash equilibrium. Some games, however, fail to produce even one Nash equilibrium. Take the game depicted by the matrix in Table 7.5. McDonald's and Burger King engage in a game, but no matter what their current action, at least one of them has an incentive to change tactics in the next round of this infinite game. If the current position is McDonald's—*low price,* Burger King—*heavy advertising,* then McDonald's has an incentive to move to *heavy advertising.* But then in the cell *heavy advertising, heavy advertising,* Burger King has an incentive to play *low price.* Unfortunately, once the play is McDonald's—*heavy advertising,* Burger King—*low price,* then McDonald's has an incentive to play *low price* as well, but then Burger King has an incentive to play *heavy advertising* and we are right back where we started. As an exercise, prove to yourself that none of the status quo cells results in a stable equilibrium either, and that even if the two firms begin at *status quo, status quo,* things will quickly move toward alternating in a clockwise manner between the four corner cells.

In Table 7.5, *status quo* is a **dominated strategy.** A dominated strategy is a strategy that is *always* worse than some other strategy. *Status quo* can always be beaten by some other strategy. It is helpful to recognize dominated strategies and realize that they are not viable options. As such, dominated strategies can be eliminated as possible solutions to any game. If this is done, Table 7.5 can be transformed into Table 7.6. Even with *status quo* eliminated, there is still no simple solution to the game.

What should Ronald McDonald and the Burger King do? The answer is to play a **mixed strategy.** In an optimal mixed strategy, each player *randomly* selects its actions with given probabilities that maximize its expected payoff *given the randomly selected strategy being played by its opponent.* Although it is well beyond the mathematical rigor

TABLE 7.5 Payoff Matrix (McDonald's Profits, Burger King's Profits)

		Burger King's Action		
		Low Price	*Status Quo*	*Heavy Advertising*
McDonald's Action	Low Price	60, 35	65, 20	55, 45
	Status Quo	40, 40	60, 40	45, 55
	Heavy Advertising	55, 50	60, 30	60, 40

TABLE 7.6 Payoff Matrix with the Elimination of Dominated Strategy—Status Quo (McDonald's Profits, Burger King's Profits)

		Burger King's Action	
		Low Price	*Heavy Advertising*
McDonald's Action	Low Price	60, 35	55, 45
	Heavy Advertising	55, 50	60, 40

of this book, it can be proved that an optimal set of probabilities always exists to solve such problems.[7] For the matrix presented in Table 7.6, the optimal strategy for Burger King is to play *low price* 50 percent of the time and *heavy advertising* 50 percent of the time. For McDonald's the optimal strategy is also to play each strategy 50 percent of the time.*

To understand the remainder of this text, it is not important whether you understand the calculus in the footnote. It is important, however, to understand that one of the characteristics of all mixed strategy equilibria is that once the equilibrium is obtained, both players are indifferent between playing their equilibrium strategy and any other strategy. In Table 7.6, notice that *if McDonald's plays its optimal mixed strategy of 50 percent low price and 50 percent heavy advertising,* then Burger King's expected profits are $42.5 million *no matter what strategy Burger King selects.* You can check this result for yourself by observing that Burger King's expected profits are $42.5 million if it plays its own optimal strategy of a 50-50 split, or if it plays low price 100 percent of the time, or if it plays heavy advertising 100 percent of the time, or if it plays any other strategy.

This characteristic of optimal mixed strategies may at first seem strange, but it actually makes a great deal of intuitive sense if the optimal mixed strategy is envisioned as the strategy that makes your opponent's selection of a strategy *irrelevant* to its outcome. By playing the optimal mixed strategy, you have placed your opponent in a weak position where it simply does not matter what it does. In other words, once Burger King selects the strategy *low price* 50 percent of the time, *heavy advertising* 50 percent of the time, McDonald's will earn the same expected payoff no matter what strategy it selects, and vice-versa for Burger King.

Once this basic characteristic of all mixed strategy equilibria is understood, it is possible to solve for a mixed strategy equilibrium without using calculus. Consider the game depicted in Table 7.7. McDonald's optimal profit-maximizing mixed strat-

*Using calculus, the solution to the game represented in Table 7.6 is obtained in the following manner: In the analysis, π represents profits, and ρ represents probability. For example, ρ_{LM} represents the probability that McDonald's plays *low price,* and ρ_{HABK} represents the probability that Burger King plays *heavy advertising.* The problem for both McDonald's and Burger King is to maximize their expected value of profits. For McDonald's the problem is to maximize expected profits, $E(\pi)$, where:

$$E(\pi) = \rho_{LM}[60\rho_{LBK} + 55(1 - \rho_{LBK})] + (1 - \rho_{LM})[55\rho_{LBK} + 60(1 - \rho_{LBK})].$$

After some algebraic manipulation:

$$E(\pi) = 10\rho_{LM}\rho_{LBK} - 5\rho_{LM} - 5\rho_{LBK} + 60.$$

Assuming the existence of an interior solution, profit maximization requires:

$$\frac{\partial E(\pi)}{\partial \rho_{LM}} = 10\rho_{LBK} - 5 = 0 \quad \text{or} \quad \rho_{LBK} = \tfrac{1}{2} \quad \text{and} \quad \rho_{HABK} = \left(1 - \tfrac{1}{2}\right) = \tfrac{1}{2}.$$

For Burger King the problem is to maximize expected profits, $E(\pi)$, where:

$$E(\pi) = \rho_{LBK}[35\rho_{LM} + 50(1 - \rho_{LM})] + (1 - \rho_{LBK})[45\rho_{LM} + 40(1 - \rho_{LM})].$$

After some algebraic manipulation:

$$E(\pi) = -20\rho_{LBK}\rho_{LM} + 10\rho_{LBK} + 5\rho_{LM} + 40.$$

Assuming the existence of an interior solution, profit maximization requires:

$$\frac{\partial E(\pi)}{\partial \rho_{LBK}} = -20\rho_{LM} + 10 = 0 \quad \text{or} \quad \rho_{LM} = \tfrac{1}{2} \quad \text{and} \quad \rho_{HABK} = \left(1 - \tfrac{1}{2}\right) = \tfrac{1}{2}.$$

TABLE 7.7 Profit Matrix (McDonald's Profits, Burger King's Profits)

		Burger King's Action	
		Low Price	*Heavy Advertising*
McDonald's Action	**Low Price**	60, 35	56, 45
	Heavy Advertising	58, 50	60, 40

egy is the one that takes choices away from Burger King. In other words, McDonald's optimal strategy results in equal profits for Burger King regardless of whether Burger King plays *low price* 100 percent of the time, *heavy advertising* 100 percent of the time, or any other strategy. Let ρ_{ML} represent the optimal mixed strategy probability for McDonald's to play *low price* and $(1 - \rho_{ML})$ represent the optimal mixed strategy probability for McDonald's to play *heavy advertising*. Burger King must have the same expected value of profits regardless of whether Burger King *always* plays *low price* [expected profits = $35\rho_{ML} + 50(1 - \rho_{ML})$] or *always* plays *heavy advertising* [expected profits = $45\rho_{ML} + 40(1 - \rho_{ML})$]. Mathematically, the following condition must, therefore, hold:

$$35(\rho_{ML}) + 50(1 - \rho_{ML}) = 45(\rho_{ML}) + 40(1 - \rho_{ML})$$
$$35\rho_{ML} + 50 - 50\rho_{ML} = 45\rho_{ML} + 40 - 40\rho_{ML}$$
$$50 - 15\rho_{ML} = 40 + 5\rho_{ML}$$
$$10 = 20\rho_{ML} \Rightarrow \rho_{ML} = \frac{1}{2} \Rightarrow (1 - \rho_M) = \frac{1}{2}$$

McDonald's optimal mixed strategy is to play *low price* half of the time and *heavy advertising* half of the time.

Of course, Burger King's optimal profit-maximizing mixed strategy is the strategy that makes McDonald's indifferent about its own choice of strategy. If Burger King plays its optimal strategy, McDonald's will earn equal profits regardless of whether McDonald's plays *low price* 100 percent of the time, *heavy advertising* 100 percent of the time, or any other strategy. Let ρ_{BL} represent the optimal mixed strategy probability for Burger King to play *low price* and $(1 - \rho_{BL})$ represent the optimal mixed strategy probability for Burger King to play *heavy advertising*. McDonald's must have the same expected value of profits regardless of whether Burger King always plays *low price* or always plays *heavy advertising*. Mathematically, the following condition must, therefore, hold:

$$60(\rho_{BL}) + 56(1 - \rho_{BL}) = 58(\rho_{BL}) + 60(1 - \rho_{BL})$$
$$60\rho_{BL} + 56 - 56\rho_{BL} = 58\rho_{BL} + 60 - 60\rho_{BL}$$
$$56 + 4\rho_{BL} = 60 - 2\rho_{BL}$$
$$4 = 6\rho_{BL} \Rightarrow \rho_{BL} = \frac{2}{3} \Rightarrow (1 - \rho_{BL}) = \frac{1}{3}$$

Burger King's optimal mixed strategy is to play *low price* two-thirds of the time and *heavy advertising* one-third of the time.

Any equilibrium using a combination of strategies in some proportion is called a **mixed strategy Nash equilibrium.** A mixed strategy Nash equilibrium is inherently

unstable because profits are the same regardless of the strategy adopted by the firms, and therefore, both firms have little incentive to maintain the equilibrium.

7.7 Sequential Games[8]

So far all our games have been *static games of imperfect information* in which both players move simultaneously. Many oligopoly games, however, are sequential, in which Firm 1 moves, then Firm 2 responds, then Firm 1 responds to Firm 2's response, and so on. If one player moves first, then it would be misleading to represent the game in matrix form because that would camouflage the fact that one player knows the other player's choice before making a move. Because the next player to move knows the previous move of its competitor, sequential games of this type are games of *perfect information*. Sequential games are known as dynamic games and are represented by **game trees.** The game tree representation of the game is known as the **extensive form of a game.** Game theorists distinguish the *extensive form* of a game from the simpler strategic form of a game.* In its *strategic form,* a game is represented by a simple profit matrix such as Table 7.8.

To illustrate why it is important to represent sequential games in their *extensive form,* consider Table 7.8 and Figure 7.1. Initially, both Table 7.8 and Figure 7.1 may appear to be representing the same game, but the outcomes may be quite different. If the game is represented in its *strategic form* as a simultaneous move game such as Table 7.8, then there are two Nash equilibria: *top, left* and *bottom, right.*

Now consider the extensive form of the same game as shown in Figure 7.1. In Figure 7.1, Ben has been given the first move. Ben must choose either *right* or *left.* As Dixit and Nalebuff noted, the first rule of game theory is to "look ahead and reason back."[9] Suppose Ben does just that. Ben knows that a choice of *left* will result in a profit of $1 million no matter what Jerry does. However, a choice of *right* means that the only sensible thing for Jerry to do is play *bottom* because obviously, given a choice between earning $0 or $4 million, Jerry will select $4 million. Ben knows that a play of *right* will result in a profit of $4 million, and a play of *left* results in a profit of only $1 million. The choice for Ben is clear—play *right!* Once Ben has played *right,* Jerry will

TABLE 7.8 Payoff Matrix (Jerry's Profit $millions, Ben's Profit $millions)

		Ben's Action	
		Left	*Right*
Jerry's Action	Top	6, 1	0, −2
	Bottom	6, 1	4, 4

*The *strategic form* of the game was originally known as the *normal form* of the game, but the term "normal form" is rarely used today.

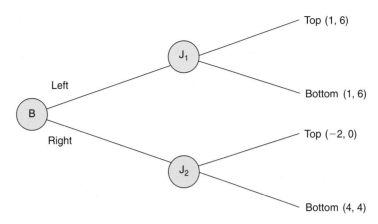

FIGURE 7.1 The Extensive Form of the Game in Table 7.8 (Ben's Profits $millions, Jerry's Profits $millions)

Ben moves first and can go *right* or *left*. Given Ben's move, Jerry selects *top* or *bottom* to maximize his profits. Because Ben knows that he will earn $1 million if he goes *left* but $4 million if he goes *right* and Jerry maximizes his profits, Ben goes *right,* and Jerry then chooses *bottom*. The only equilibrium is Ben—*right,* Jerry—*bottom.*

play *bottom* and also earn $4 million. In the extensive form of the game there is only one equilibrium—(*bottom, right*).

But wait a minute. Why should Jerry have to settle for just $4 million, when he could earn $6 million *if* Ben would just play *left?* Can't Jerry *threaten* to play *top* if Ben plays *right?* Of course, Jerry can threaten to play *top* if Ben plays *right,* but is the threat *credible?* After all, once Ben selects *right,* Jerry's choice is either earn $0 or earn $4 million. Given those choices, a rational firm would select $4 million.

The game depicted by Figure 7.1 can easily be related to a game of potential entry. Consider Ben as a potential entrant and Jerry as an established monopolist. If *left* is "stay out," *right* is "enter," *top* is "respond aggressively if entry occurs," and *bottom* is "maintain price at the current level," the game becomes easy to reinterpret.

In Figure 7.2, we have made all of the changes in the game tree. Once this is done, the game becomes an entry choice for Ben, followed by a response choice for Jerry. Given the preceding analysis, the equilibrium in this game is for Ben to enter and Jerry to maintain his current price. In the real world, many a Jerry has attempted to change this game tree by making Ben believe that it would actually choose *aggressive if entry.*

7.7.1 Credible versus Noncredible Threats and Subgame Perfect Nash Equilibria

In the game depicted in Figure 7.2, could Jerry ever manage to convince Ben that he would play *aggressive if entry* if Ben played *enter?* Surely there are ways to make this threat credible. Jerry could hire an impartial agent, perhaps a lawyer or a firm in another industry, and sign a contract that stated: If Ben ever plays *enter,* my agent will make my move for me and play *aggressive if entry.* By giving up the option of making

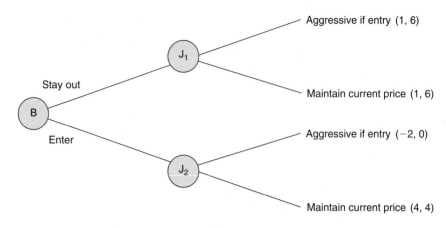

FIGURE 7.2 A Game of Entry (Ben's Profits $millions, Jerry's Profits $millions)

Ben moves first and can either *enter* or *stay out*. Given Ben's move, Jerry selects *aggressive if entry* or *maintain current price* to maximize his profits. Since Ben knows that he will earn $1 million if he stays out but $4 million if he enters, Ben enters, and Jerry maintains his current price.

the choice for himself, Jerry might convince Ben that a play of *enter* will result in a payoff of −$2 million.

But is such a threat to hire a lawyer credible? Suppose Jerry hires a lawyer to make his move for him and the lawyer is told that if Ben enters, the lawyer should play *aggressive if entry*. Now suppose that Ben enters; what should Jerry do? Jerry should immediately pick up a phone and tell his lawyer, "Wait, wait, don't *play aggressive if entry* because that move will cost me $4 million! I'm instructing you to play *maintain current price*." The threat to play *aggressive if entry* is simply not credible. Once Ben is in the market, it's too late to play *aggressive if entry*.

The game in Figure 7.2 has only one equilibrium: Ben enters and Jerry maintains current price. This strategy is called a ***perfect Nash equilibrium*** or ***subgame perfect Nash equilibrium*** because it is a Nash equilibrium in which the strategies are credible. Strategies are considered credible if a rational player would stick with that strategy in *any subgame* of the complete game. A *subgame* is a game that starts at any decision point or ***node*** in a game and continues to the end of the game. A *node* is a point in an *extensive form* of a game at which a player or nature takes an action, or the game ends. In Figure 7.2 there are three nodes: B, J_1, and J_2. Consider the subgame beginning at the node J_2. Jerry has a choice of playing *aggressive if entry* and earning a normal economic profit of zero or playing *maintain current price* and earning a positive economic profit of $4 million. Given those choices in this subgame, Jerry will *always* play *maintain current price*. In this subgame, the threat to play *aggressive if entry* is not a credible threat and the potential outcome Ben enters and Jerry plays *aggressive if entry* is not a strategy that a rational player would ever play; therefore, the outcome where Ben enters and Jerry plays *aggressive if entry* is not a subgame perfect Nash equilibrium.

There will be numerous instances where the concept of a subgame perfect Nash equilibrium is used in later chapters. The more the concept is used in specific games, the clearer the concept should become.

APPLICATION 7.3
Dr. Strangelove and Credible Threats Gone Wrong

One of the most famous fictional examples of an effective credible threat gone terribly wrong comes from Stanley Kubrick's movie *Dr. Strangelove.* For almost 50 years following World War II, the United States and the Soviet Union maintained world peace by building huge stockpiles of nuclear weapons and aiming them at each other. This strategy, known as *mutually assured destruction,* or *MAD,* resulted in a prisoner's dilemma because if either superpower attacked first, the initial attack would be met with a cataclysmic counterattack. The dominant strategy, therefore, was not to attack. But what if one side attacked by mistake? That is the premise of the movie *Dr. Strangelove* (loosely based on Peter George's book *Red Alert*).

 The movie begins with a thoroughly insane American General Ripper (played by Sterling Hayden) deciding to launch a preemptive strike on the Soviet Union. Even the American President Merkin Muffley (played by Peter Sellers, who also played Dr. Strangelove and Royal Air Force Captain Mandrake) can't call off Ripper's attack, so a war room meeting is arranged with the Soviet Ambassador Alexiy DeSadeski (Peter Bull) and the President calls Soviet Premier Demitri Kissoff. The President attempts to defuse the situation by explaining to Kissoff that the attack is a mistake and the Soviets should shoot down the American plane. He offers to help the Soviets ward off the attack, but then DeSadeski informs the horrified group of top American national security personnel that once the American attack is detected, it will trigger the detonation of the Soviet doomsday machine that will destroy all civilization. Picking up the script at this point, we can follow exactly why the Soviets' credible threat failed to work.

DeSadeski: When [the doomsday machine] is detonated, it will produce enough lethal radioactive fallout so that within 10 months, the surface of the earth will be as dead as the moon!

General Turgidson: (George C. Scott): Ah, come on DeSadeski, that's ridiculous. Our studies show that even the worst fallout is down to a safe level after two weeks.

DeSadeski: You've obviously never heard of cobalt thorium G.

Turgidson: No, what about it?

DeSadeski: Cobalt thorium G has a radioactive half-life of ninety-three years. If you take, say, fifty H-bombs in the hundred-megaton range and jacket them with cobalt thorium G, when they are exploded they will produce a doomsday shroud. A lethal cloud of radioactivity which will encircle the earth for ninety-three years!

. .

President Muffley: I'm afraid I don't understand something, Alexiy. Is the Premier threatening to explode this if our planes carry out their attack?

DeSadeski: No sir. It is not a thing a sane man would do. The doomsday machine is designed to trigger itself automatically.

Muffley: But surely you can disarm it somehow.

DeSadeski: No. It is designed to explode if any attempt is ever made to untrigger it.

Muffley: Automatically?

Turgidson: Ahh . . . it's an obvious commie trick, Mr. President. Look at the big board! They're getting ready to clobber us!

Muffley: But this is absolute madness, Ambassador. Why should you *build* such a thing?

DeSadeski: There are those of us who fought against it, but in the end we could not keep up with the expense involved in the arms race, the space race, and the peace race. And at the same time our people grumbled for more nylons and washing machines. Our doomsday scheme cost us just a small fraction of what we'd been spending on defense in a single year. But the deciding factor was when we learned that your country was working along similar lines, and we were afraid of a doomsday gap.

Muffley: This is preposterous. I've never approved of anything like that.

DeSadeski: Our source was the *New York Times.*

Muffley: Dr. Strangelove, do we have anything like that in the works?

Strangelove: A moment please, Mr. President. Under the authority granted me as director of weapons research and development, I commissioned last year a study of this project by the Bland Corporation. Based on the findings of the report, my conclusion was that this idea was not a practical deterrent, for reasons which, at this moment, must be all too obvious.

. .

Muffley: But, how is it possible for this thing to be triggered automatically, and at the same time impossible to untrigger?

Strangelove: Mr. President, it is not only possible, it is essential. That is the whole idea of this machine, you know. Deterrence is the art of producing in the mind of the enemy . . . the *fear* to attack. And so, because of the automated and irrevocable decision-making process which rules out human meddling, the doomsday machine is terrifying. It's simple to understand. And completely credible, and convincing.

Turgidson: Gee, I wish we had one of them doomsday machines, Stainsy.

. .

Strangelove: Yes, but the . . . whole point of the doomsday machine . . . is lost . . . if you keep it a secret! Why didn't you tell the world, eh?

DeSadeski: It was to be announced at the Party Congress on Monday. As you know, the Premier loves surprises.

Dr. Strangelove is, of course, correct in stating that "the . . . whole point of the doomsday machine . . . is lost . . . if you keep it a secret!" If you have the potential to use a credible threat like the mob's death threat or the doomsday machine, you must make public your intentions to use the threat. In the movie *Dr. Strangelove,* the Soviets' failure to disclose the existence of the doomsday machine ultimately led to the destruction of the world. Although in Kubrick's movie version, even the destruction of the earth is shown with satiric humor as nuclear bombs explode all over the world as the song "We'll Meet Again" plays in the background. ■

SUMMARY

1. Game theory is the study of how interdependent decision makers make choices.

2. A game must include players, actions, information, strategies, payoffs, outcomes, and equilibria.

3. In simple zero-sum games the minimax strategy is a dominant solution to the game.

4. A Nash equilibrium exists if all the players are doing the best they can given the choices of their opponents.

5. It is important to understand the information structure of a game. In a game of perfect information each player knows every move that has been made by the other players before taking any action. In games of complete information, nature does not move first or nature's first move is observed by all the players. In a game of certain information, nature never moves after another player moves. In a game of symmetric information, all players have exactly the same information when each moves.

6. The dominant solution to the classic prisoner's dilemma game results in a nonoptimal solution for the players.

7. In a game of mixed strategy there is no Nash equilibrium. Furthermore, in the mixed strategy equilibrium, both players are indifferent between playing their mixed strategy equilibrium and any other strategy.

8. In sequential games, the players take turns moving instead of moving simultaneously.

KEY TERMS

asymmetric information
certain information
complete information
dominant strategy
dominated strategy
dynamic game
extensive form of a game
game theory
game trees

minimax strategy
mixed strategy games
mixed strategy Nash
 equilibrium
Nash equilibrium
nature
node
perfect information
perfect Nash equilibrium

prisoner's dilemma game
repeated games
static game
subgame
subgame perfect Nash
 equilibrium
symmetric information
zero-sum game

DISCUSSION QUESTIONS

1. Are all dominant strategy equilibria also Nash equilibria? Are all Nash equilibria also dominant strategy equilibria?

2. Can you suggest a business strategy that is equivalent to the death threat strategy used by organized crime to prevent squealing?

3. Suppose you are playing a game and your opponent is *not* playing her Nash equilibrium strategy. Should you play your Nash equilibrium strategy?

4. It was noted in the text that mixed strategy equilibria are inherently unstable. Explain why.

5. Do you think the outcome of the movie *Dr. Strangelove* would have changed if Premier Kissoff had announced the existence of the doomsday machine *before* General Ripper implemented his plan to drop a nuclear bomb on the Soviet Union? Explain the logic of your answer.

6. Can you think of any other movies that have game theory built into their plots? (Hint: One of the most famous is about the life of John Nash, but there are many others.)

7. Suppose that Carter is considered a more experienced doctor than Grey, and therefore, if they are competing in private practices, Carter sees two out of every three patients in the area. However, if either one of them joins the HMO and the other refuses to join, the one who refuses to join loses his or her patient base because the HMO offers much better insurance coverage. Would the fact that Carter is a preferred physician compared to Grey alter the outcome of the game in Application 7.2? Explain your reasoning.

8. Suppose only one school in the United States offered merit-based financial aid while all other schools offered *only* need-based aid. Would such a situation represent an equilibrium situation in the zero-sum game in Application 7.1? Explain your reasoning and the way you would expect the other schools to respond to the school offering merit-based aid.

PROBLEMS

1. Suppose that in the Waldman ice cream truck example with a 1-mile parade route, the local police had forced Waldman to park $\frac{1}{4}$ mile from the beginning of the parade route and Other Truck to park $\frac{1}{4}$ mile from the end of the route. How would sales have been split in this case? Is this a Nash equilibrium? Is society better or worse off with this forced result?

2. Suppose that a game has the following extensive form:

A Game of Entry
(Ben's Profit, Jerry's Profit)

	Aggressive if Entry	(0, 1)
Stay Out — Jerry	Maintain Current Price	(0, 1)
Ben	Aggressive if Entry	(−0.5, −1)
Enter — Jerry	Maintain Current Price	(1, 0)

What is the equilibrium in the game? Can Jerry undertake an action to prevent this outcome?

3. Consider the following payoff matrix for McDonald's and Burger King. McDonald's profits are shown first, followed by Burger King's profits.

| | Burger King's Action | |
	High Price	Low Price
McDonald's Action		
High Price	40, 30	30, 35
Low Price	35, 25	32, 20

Is there a dominant strategy in this game? Is there a Nash equilibrium in this game? What strategy would the firms adopt in this case? Be precise in answering this last part.

4. There are two movie theaters in town. They agree to charge $9 per ticket in order to maximize joint profits. However, each theater must consider whether to "cheat" on the agreement and offer a "2-for-1" ticket price to its customers. Consider the payoff matrix below, depicting their payoffs in a game played once.

	Movie Theater X charges $9	Movie Theater X offers 2-for-1 deal
Movie Theater Y charges $9	4000 / 4000	6000 / 1000
Movie Theater Y offers 2-for-1 deal	1000 / 6000	3000 / 3000

a. Determine if either theater has a dominant strategy. Solve for the Nash equilibrium of the game.
b. Is this game a prisoner's dilemma? Why or why not?

5. Consider the extensive form of the following sequential entry game that is played once. The incumbent (I) has threatened to fight entry if the entrant (E) decides to enter.

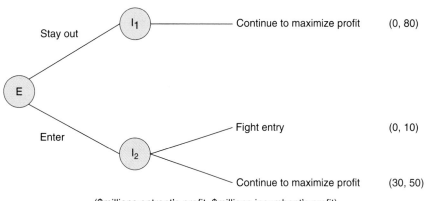

Stay out — I₁ — Continue to maximize profit — (0, 80)

E

Enter — I₂ — Fight entry — (0, 10)

Continue to maximize profit — (30, 50)

($millions entrant's profit, $millions incumbent's profit)

 a. What is the Nash equilibrium of the game? Explain.

 b. Is the incumbent's threat to "fight entry" credible? Explain.

6. Joe and Jerry are the only two hot dog vendors on the beach each summer. Each summer, they must decide where to locate on the mile-long beach. They have three choices of locations: at the beginning, middle, and end. The game is a zero-sum game because Joe and Jerry are competing for percentage of sales of hot dogs on the beach.

 a. Derive a payoff matrix that will reflect the payoffs (in terms of percentage of sales) for Joe and Jerry.

 b. Does either Joe or Jerry have a dominant strategy? If so, what is it?

 c. What is the Nash equilibrium of this game?

7. Consider the following matrix for two local grocery stores in a small town. They've each developed two strategies: offer double coupons or stay open 24 hours to help increase sales.

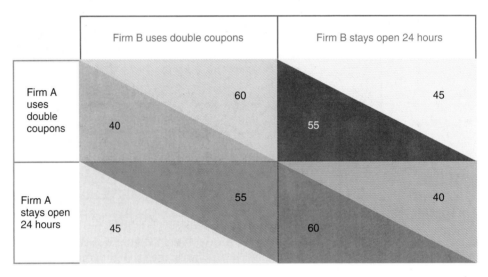

 a. Does either firm have a dominant strategy? If so, what is it?

 b. Solve for the Nash equilibrium of the game.

8. Stacey and Betsy are contestants on a game show. They each select a wrapped box from four choices. They know that one box contains $100, one contains $1000, one contains $10,000, and one contains $100,000. They each unwrap their chosen box and look inside. They then have a choice of whether or not to trade with one another. Stacey uses all the information in the game correctly. Betsy's husband has advised her to trade if her box has anything less than $100,000 inside. Betsy's box has $1000 inside. She offers to trade with Stacey. Stacey agrees to trade. Did Betsy's husband give her good advice? Explain.

9. Two local department stores in town (Store K and Store D) both advertise their upcoming sales each week in the Thursday newspaper. They must turn in their advertisements no later than noon on Tuesday. However, Store K has a "spy" who works in Store D's advertising department and reports the sale information

to Store K's advertising department. What type of information is represented in this game?

10. Consider the following game. Assume it is played one time and one time only. The game represents the collusive agreements of two countries who agree to fix the output of oil.

	Venezuela colludes (limits output)	Venezuela defects (increases output)
Saudi Arabia colludes (limits output)	900 — 600	700 — 800
Saudi Arabia defects (increases output)	1100 — 300	800 — 400

 a. Does Venezuela have a dominant strategy? If so, what is it? Does Saudi Arabia have a dominant strategy? If so, what is it?

 b. Solve for the Nash equilibrium of the game.

 c. Is this game a prisoner's dilemma? Explain why or why not.

11. Historically, Coke has been the leader in the carbonated beverage market. In that sense, Coke might be considered to play first in any games that Coke and Pepsi play. Consider the following sequential game. Coke is trying to decide whether to develop a new product. The payoff situation (in profits) is the following: If Coke does develop the product, Coke will get $600 million if Pepsi develops a new product, too, and $800 million if Pepsi chooses not to develop a new product. If Coke doesn't develop a new product, Coke will get $200 million if Pepsi does develop a new product and $400 million if Pepsi doesn't develop a new product. If Coke does develop a new product, then Pepsi will get $600 million if it develops one, too, and only $200 million if it doesn't develop one. If Coke does not develop a new product, then Pepsi will get $800 million if it develops a new product and only $400 million if it doesn't develop a new product.

 a. Create an extensive form of this game that represents the situation described.

 b. Solve for the Nash equilibrium of the game.

12. Consider Coke and Pepsi and the simultaneous game depicted in the following payoff matrix.

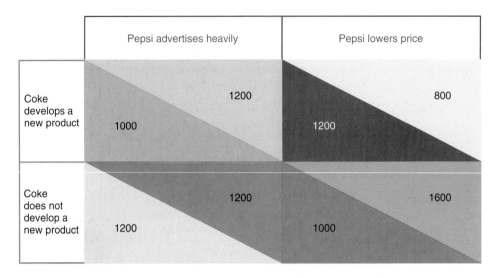

a. Does Pepsi have a dominant strategy? Explain your reasoning.
b. Does Coke have a dominant strategy? Explain your reasoning.
c. Solve for the Nash equilibrium of the game (mixed strategy equilibrium).

13. Consider Coke and Pepsi and the simultaneous game depicted in the following payoff matrix.

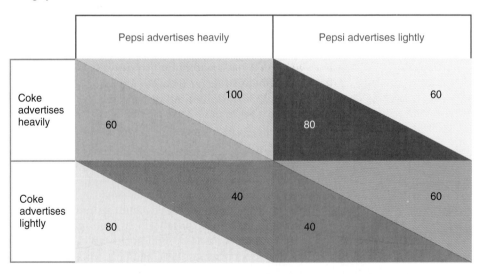

a. Does Pepsi have a dominant strategy? Explain your reasoning.
b. Does Coke have a dominant strategy? Explain your reasoning.
c. Solve for the Nash equilibrium of the game (mixed strategy equilibrium).

NOTES

1. For an excellent basic introduction to game theory, see Avinash Dixit and Barry Nalebuff, *Thinking Strategically* (New York: Norton, 1991). For the early and seminal work, see John von Neumann and Oskar Morgenstern, *Theory of Games and Economic Behavior* (Princeton, NJ: Princeton University Press, 1944); see also Thomas C. Schelling, *The Strategy of Conflict* (Cambridge: Harvard University Press, 1960). For more advanced treatments directed at economics, see Martin Shubik, *Game Theory in the Social Sciences* (Cambridge: MIT Press, 1984); James W. Friedman, *Oligopoly and the Theory of Games* (Amsterdam: North-Holland, 1977); and R. Duncan Luce and Howard Raiffa, *Games and Decisions* (New York: John Wiley and Sons, 1957). For a recent summary of the field, see Jean Tirole, *The Theory of Industrial Organization* (Cambridge: MIT Press, 1988), especially chapter 11; and Robert Gibbons, *Game Theory for Applied Economists* (Princeton, NJ: Princeton University Press, 1992). See also Morton Davis, *Game Theory: A Nontechnical Introduction* (New York, Basic Books, 1983); and Eric Rasmusen, *Games and Information* (Oxford: Basil Blackwell, 1989).

2. For a good, simple treatment of zero-sum games, see J.D. Williams, *The Complete Strategist* (New York: McGraw-Hill, 1966).

3. John Nash, "Noncooperative Games," *Annals of Mathematics* 54 (September 1951): 286–295. The middle-middle solution was first identified by Hotelling. See Harold Hotelling, "Stability in Competition," *Economic Journal* 39 (1929): 41–57.

4. The prisoner's dilemma is usually attributed to R. Duncan Luce and Howard Raiffa, *Games and Decisions* (New York: John Wiley and Sons, 1957), p. 94. For an easy-to-follow treatment, see Dixit and Nalebuff, *supra* note 1, chapter 4, pp. 89–118. For more on the prisoner's dilemma, see Robert Axelrod, *The Evolution of Cooperation* (New York: Basic Books, 1984).

5. For a basic explanation of a repeated game, see Dixit and Nalebuff, *supra* note 1, pp. 95–118; and Gibbons, *supra* note 1, pp. 83–99. See also Friedman, *supra* note 1; Axelrod, *supra* note 4; Richard Selten, "The Chain Store Paradox," *Theory and Decision* 9 (April 1978): 127–159; Drew Fudenberg and Eric Maskin, "The Folk Theorem in Repeated Games with Discounting or with Incomplete Information," *Econometrica* 54 (May 1986): 533–554; and Drew Fudenberg and Jean Tirole, "Game Theory for Industrial Organization: Introduction and Overview," in Richard Schmalensee and Robert Willig (eds.), *Handbook of Industrial Organization* (Amsterdam: North Holland, 1989).

6. For a basic explanation of mixed strategy equilibria, see Rasmusen, *supra* note 1, chapter 3, pp. 69–82. See also Dixit and Nalebuff, *supra* note 1, chapter 7, pp. 168–198; and Tirole, *supra* note 1, pp. 423–425.

7. Gibbons, *supra* note 1, pp. 29–33.

8. See Dixit and Nalebuff, *supra* note 1, chapter 5, pp. 119–141. Also Tirole, *supra* note 1, pp. 439–441; and Gibbons, *supra* note 1, pp. 55–82.

9. Dixit and Nalebuff, *supra* note 1, p. 34.

INTERNET EXERCISES

Visit www.aw-bc.com/waldman_jensen for this chapter's web exercises. Answer our real-world economics problems by searching the Internet for solutions!

The Development of Oligopoly Theory

I n this chapter we begin our consideration of oligopoly theory with the introduction of three important models developed during the nineteenth and twentieth centuries. These models were originally derived without the use of game theory and, as a result, sometimes seemed to be based on highly questionable assumptions. The application of game theory to oligopoly modeling has made it possible to obtain many of the theoretical results using what are generally regarded as more reasonable assumptions.

8.1 Models Based on Quantity Determination

8.1.1 The Cournot Model

Augustin Cournot made the first attempt at formal modeling of oligopoly behavior in 1838.[1] Cournot considered the case of a duopoly market with two identical firms. The firms face identical costs and there is no product differentiation. Under these conditions, price is a simple function of the total quantity produced by the two firms.

To make things more concrete, assume the following linear *industry* demand curve:

$$P = 100 - Q,$$

where P is price in millions of dollars and Q is total industry output. Assume further that both firms face identical constant marginal cost and average cost equal to 10 (i.e., MC = AC = 10), and that each firm believes, or conjectures, that its competitor will always maintain its current output.*

The assumption of output maintenance was critical to Cournot's result. Suppose the two firms are Boeing and Airbus.† Airbus observes that Boeing is currently producing $q_B = 45$, the industry joint profit-maximizing level of output, and price is \$55.‡

*Models of the type presented in this chapter are often called models of *conjectural variations*.

†For now Boeing and Airbus simply represent any two duopolists. Later in this chapter we consider the real-world competition between these two firms in the commercial aircraft industry.

‡The assumption that Boeing and Airbus have constant and identical marginal and average costs is made to simplify the analysis. This assumption is not true in the real world.

What output should Airbus produce? Recall that the industry's demand curve is $P = 100 - Q$. If Airbus assumes that Boeing produces 45 units, then the demand curve faced by Airbus will be $P = 55 - q_A$. Airbus's demand curve is called a ***residual demand curve,*** because it is derived by assuming that Airbus faces a demand curve that is simply left over, or residual, after Boeing has chosen its output.

To better understand the concept of a residual demand curve, consider what happens to price if Boeing produces $q_B = 45$ and Airbus begins to produce any output greater than zero. If Airbus produces one unit, total industry output equals 46 and $P = 54$. Therefore, one point on Airbus's residual demand curve is $(q_A = 1, P = 54)$. What if Airbus sells five units? Then $Q = 50$, and $P = 50$, so a second point on Airbus's residual demand curve is $(q_A = 5, P = 50)$. Note that for each unit Airbus produces, the price declines by one additional dollar below $55. The residual demand curve is, therefore, $P = 55 - q_A$.

Figure 8.1 depicts the situation from Airbus's perspective. With MC = 10, recalling again that the MR curve bisects the linear demand curve, Airbus will maximize profit by producing where $MR = 55 - 2q_A = 10 = MC$, so $q_A = 22.5$. Total industry output is now $Q = q_B + q_A = 45 + 22.5 = 67.5$, so $P = 32.5$.

Now it is Boeing's turn to respond to Airbus's output. If Boeing assumes that Airbus will maintain an output of 22.5, what is its profit-maximizing output? Figure 8.2 shows

FIGURE 8.1 **Airbus's Cournot Equilibrium When $q_B = 45$**

Airbus assumes that Boeing will produce 45 planes forever and therefore faces a residual demand curve $P = 55 - q_A$ and maximizes profit by producing 22.5 planes and charging a price of $32.5.

FIGURE 8.2 Boeing's Cournot Equilibrium When q_A = 22.5

Boeing assumes that Airbus will produce 22.5 planes forever and therefore faces a residual demand curve $P = 77.5 - q_B$ and maximizes profit by producing 33.75 planes and charging a price of $43.75.

the situation from Boeing's perspective. Assuming that q_A is constant at 22.5, Boeing's residual demand curve will be $P = 77.5 - q_B$, and its profit-maximizing output will be 33.75 units. Total industry output will be $22.5 + 33.75 = 56.25$, and $P = 43.75$.

Now Airbus discovers that it was wrong. Boeing did not maintain output at 45. What should Airbus do? You might be tempted to think that Airbus should give up its obviously false assumption that Boeing will maintain output. According to Cournot, however, Airbus will now assume that Boeing will maintain output at 33.75. As shown in Figure 8.3, Airbus's residual demand curve becomes $P = 66.25 - q_A$. Airbus will equate its new MR curve to MC = 10 and produce 28.125 units. Industry output is now $28.125 + 33.75 = 61.875$, and $P = 38.125$.

The story is still not over. Now Boeing's assumption that $q_A = 22.5$ has been violated, and Boeing must respond by changing output yet again. As an exercise, prove to yourself that Boeing's next response will be to reduce its output to 30.94 units. This will result in yet another response by Airbus.

When does all of this end? Only when both firms face identical residual demand curves, and therefore, both produce the same output. In Figures 8.1 to 8.3 the residual demand curves have been converging, and they eventually converge completely when Boeing faces a residual demand of $P = 70 - q_B$, and Airbus faces a residual demand of $P = 70 - q_A$. This equilibrium is shown in Figure 8.4. Only when each firm produces

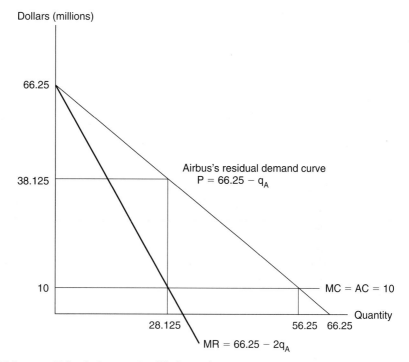

FIGURE 8.3 **Airbus's Cournot Equilibrium When q_B = 33.75**

Now Airbus assumes that Boeing will produce 33.75 planes forever, and it therefore faces a residual demand curve $P = 66.25 - q_A$ and maximizes profit by producing 28.125 planes and charging a price of \$38.125.

30 units will each firm's assumption regarding the other's output be correct. In equilibrium total industry output is 60 and $P = 40$. This is the Cournot equilibrium.

Several important characteristics are associated with the Cournot equilibrium. Note that the equilibrium output is between the joint profit-maximizing output of 45 and the perfectly competitive output of 90.* In fact, with linear demand and constant marginal costs, the Cournot equilibrium quantity with two firms is precisely equal to two-thirds of the competitive equilibrium quantity.

An important and useful concept associated with the Cournot model is that of a **reaction function.**[2] To derive Boeing's reaction function, begin with Cournot's major assumption—Boeing assumes that Airbus's output will remain constant. Given this assumption, there exists an optimal output response for Boeing associated with any *given* output produced by Airbus, and vice-versa. The functional relationship between q_B and q_A may be written as:

$$q_B = f(q_A).$$

*It is possible to determine the profit-maximizing quantity by recalling the "twice-as-steep rule" for MR from Chapter 3. For demand curve $P = 100 - Q$, $MR = 100 - 2Q$, and the industry's profit-maximizing output is where $MR = 100 - 2Q = 10 = MC$. Solving for Q, $Q = 90/2 = 45$. With $Q = 45$, the profit-maximizing price is $P = 100 - 45 = 55$.

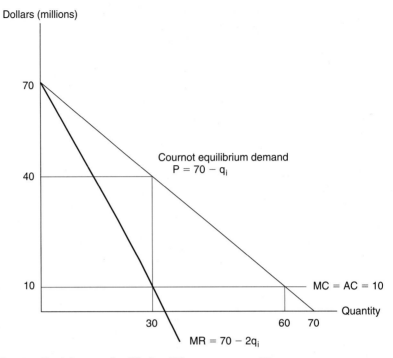

FIGURE 8.4 Final Cournot Equilibrium When $q_B = q_A = 30$

In the final Cournot equilibrium, Boeing and Airbus assume the other firm will produce 30 planes forever, and therefore, both firms face a residual demand $P = 70 - q_i$ and maximize profits by producing 30 planes and charging a price of $40 per plane.

This function is Boeing's *reaction function.*

We can use calculus to show that, given our demand and cost conditions, Boeing's reaction function is:*

$$q_B = f(q_A) = \frac{90 - q_A}{2} = 45 - \tfrac{1}{2}q_A. \qquad [8.1]$$

Without calculus, the result can be obtained by recalling from Chapter 3 that for a linear demand curve the marginal revenue curve has the same intercept but twice

*To maximize profits, Boeing must set MR = MC for any given level of Airbus's output. Total revenue for Boeing, TR_B, can be derived as follows:

$$TR_B = q_B P = q_B(100 - q_B - q_A)$$

or

$$TR_B = 100q_B - q_B^2 - q_B q_A.$$

Marginal revenue, MR_B, is simply the partial derivative of TR_B:

$$MR_B = \frac{\partial TR_B}{\partial q_B} = 100 - 2q_B - q_A.$$

Because MC = 10, we set $MR_B = 10$ and obtain:

$$100 - 2q_B - q_A = 10$$

or

$$q_B = \frac{90 - q_A}{2} = 45 - \tfrac{1}{2}q_A.$$

the slope of the demand curve. For *industry* demand curve $P = 100 - q_B - q_A$, Boeing's residual demand curve can be identified by noting that for any given level of Airbus's output, q_A, the quantity $(100 - q_A)$ is a constant. It follows that for any given q_A, Boeing's demand curve is simply:

$$p_B = (100 - q_A) - q_B. \qquad [8.2]$$

Because Equation 8.2 is a linear demand curve, with intercept $(100 - q_A)$ and slope -1, the associated marginal revenue curve is:

$$MR_B = (100 - q_A) - 2q_B.$$

To obtain Boeing's reaction function, set MR = MC for profit maximization, so:

$$MR_B = 100 - q_A - 2q_B = 10 = MC. \qquad [8.3]$$

Solving for q_B, Boeing's reaction function is:

$$q_B = 45 - \tfrac{1}{2}q_A. \qquad [8.4]$$

Because Airbus faces identical demand and cost conditions, Airbus's reaction function is:

$$q_A = 45 - \tfrac{1}{2}q_B. \qquad [8.5]$$

Figure 8.5 shows both reaction functions on the same graph. The Cournot equilibrium occurs at the intersection of the two reaction functions because only at that

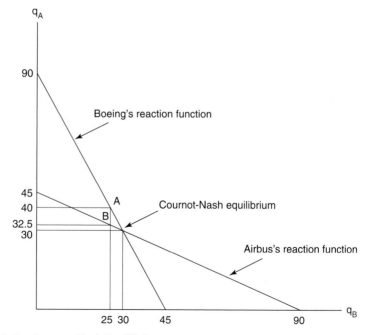

FIGURE 8.5 Cournot-Nash Equilibrium

Boeing's reaction function is $q_B = 45 - \tfrac{1}{2}q_A$, and Airbus's reaction function is $q_A = 45 - \tfrac{1}{2}q_B$. Only at the Cournot equilibrium where the two reaction functions intersect and $q_A = q_B = 30$ is there no incentive for either firm to change its output.

point are both firms' assumptions concerning the output of the other correct. When each firm produces 30 units, neither firm has an incentive to change output, and therefore, the assumption that the other will maintain output is correct.

In Cournot's original model, no other output combination could be sustained. Suppose Airbus produced 40 units. Then Boeing should produce at point A in Figure 8.5 on its reaction function, and produce $q_B = 45 - (40/2) = 25$ units. But if Boeing produced 25 units, then Airbus should operate at point B on its reaction function and produce $q_A = 45 - (25/2) = 32.5$ units. But that would result in a response by Boeing, which would result in a response by Airbus, and so on. Only when each produces the Cournot equilibrium quantity is a stable equilibrium achieved.

8.1.2 The Cournot-Nash Equilibrium

The Cournot equilibrium in Figure 8.5 is based on the questionable assumption of output maintenance by competitors. The Cournot equilibrium, however, is also a Nash equilibrium in a simple two-player game. The Cournot-Nash game is a *simultaneous* move game, and therefore, it is a game of *imperfect information*. To better understand why the Cournot equilibrium is also a Nash equilibrium, it is useful to express Boeing's and Airbus's profits as a function of both firms' outputs, that is, to express $\Pi_B = f(q_B, q_A)$ and $\Pi_A = f(q_A, q_B)$ where Π_B and Π_A represent Boeing's and Airbus's profits and q_B and q_A represent Boeing's and Airbus's outputs, respectively. Given that industry demand is $P = 100 - Q$, and $MC = AC = 10$ for both firms, each firm's profits will be:

$$\Pi_B = TR_B - TC_B = Pq_B - 10q_B \qquad [8.6A]$$

$$\Pi_A = TR_A - TC_A = Pq_A - 10q_A \qquad [8.6B]$$

where TR represents total revenue and TC represents total costs. Substituting $P = 100 - q_B - q_A$, the industry demand curve, into the firms' profit Equations 8.6A and 8.6B, we obtain:*

$$\Pi_B = (90 - q_A)q_B - q_B^2 \qquad [8.7A]$$

$$\Pi_A = (90 - q_B)q_A - q_A^2 \qquad [8.7B]$$

To better comprehend why the Cournot equilibrium is a Nash equilibrium, consider Figure 8.5. Does a Nash equilibrium exist in Figure 8.5? Recall from Chapter 7 that a Nash equilibrium exists if both players are doing the best they can *given the choice of their opponent*. In the context of the game depicted in Figure 8.5, a Nash equilibrium exists if neither firm has an incentive to change *its quantity* as long as the other firm maintains *its quantity* at its current level. In Figure 8.5, there is one, and only one, Nash equilibrium, where $q_B = q_A = 30$. If both firms produce 30, then a unilateral move to produce more or less than 30 *always* reduces profits for the firm that moves

*The algebra is as follows:

Substituting $P = 100 - q_B - q_A$ into 8.6A yields:

$$\begin{aligned} \Pi_B = Pq_B - 10q_B &= (100 - q_B - q_A)q_B - 10q_B \\ &= 100q_B - q_B^2 - q_Bq_A - 10q_B \\ &= (90 - q_A)q_B - q_B^2. \end{aligned}$$

Substituting $P = 100 - q_B - q_A$ into 8.6B yields an analogous result.

away from producing q = 30. If Airbus unilaterally moved to produce 20, for example, from Equation 8.7B, its profits would decline from $900 $[(90 - 30)30 - 30^2 = 900]$ to $800 $[(90 - 30)20 - 20^2 = 800]$. If Boeing unilaterally moved to produce 40, its profits would decline from $900 to $800 $[(90 - 30)40 - 40^2 = 900]$.

Does the Nash equilibrium maximize joint profits? If the firms arrive at the Nash equilibrium, joint profits are $1800 ($900 for each firm). Other output combinations, however, result in larger joint profits, and one combined output in particular maximizes joint profits. For demand curve P − 100 − Q in Figure 8.6, MR = 100 − 2Q, and the industry's profit-maximizing output equals 45. With Q = 45, the profit-maximizing price is $55. To maximize joint profits, the two firms must combine to produce Q = 45. Regardless of how output is distributed between the two firms, if the two combine to produce 45 units of output, then total industry profits will be maximized at $2025. If the two combine to produce 45 units of output, however, the combination will *not* be a Nash equilibrium. Each firm could, for example, produce 22.5 units and earn profits of $1012.5. But as Figure 8.5 shows, if each firm produced 22.5 units, each would have an incentive to move to its respective reaction functions by increasing output to 33.75 $(q_B = 45 - \frac{1}{2}q_A = 45 - 11.25 = 33.75)$ units and earn a profit of $1139.0625 $(\Pi_B = (90 - 22.5)33.75 - (33.75)^2 = 1139.0625)$. Alternatively,

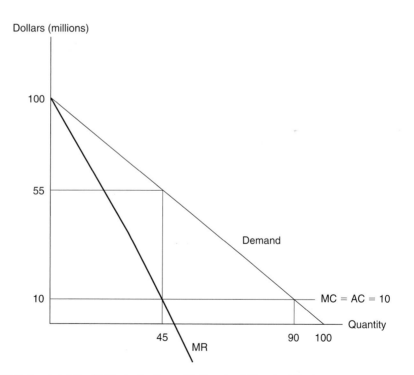

FiGURE 8.6 Joint Profit Maximization with Constant Marginal Costs

Joint profits are maximized where MR = MC at an industry output of 45 planes and a price of $55. Any combination of Boeing's and Airbus's output that equals 45 results in joint profits being maximized at $2025.

if a total output of 45 units were produced with Boeing producing 35 units and Airbus producing 10 units, then Boeing would have an incentive to increase its output to 40 $\left(q_B = 45 - \frac{1}{2}q_A = 45 - 5 = 40\right)$ units to increase its profit from \$1575 ($\Pi_B = (90 - 10)35 - (35)^2 = 1575$) to 1600 ($\Pi_B = (90 - 10)40 - (40)^2 = 1600$), and Airbus would have an incentive to increase its output to 27.5 $\left(q_B = 45 - \frac{1}{2}q_A = 45 - 17.5 = 27.5\right)$ units to increase its profit from \$450 ($\Pi_B = (90 - 35)10 - (10)^2 = 450$) to \$756.23 ($\Pi_B = (90 - 35)27.5 - (27.5)^2 = 756.23$).

Because the Cournot equilibrium is also a Nash equilibrium, the equilibrium has come to be known as a ***Cournot-Nash equilibrium.*** The Cournot equilibrium and the Nash equilibrium are identical because both occur at the point at which the two reaction functions in Figure 8.5 intersect. The Cournot equilibrium occurs at that point because only at that point are both firms' output maintenance assumptions concerning the other correct. The Nash equilibrium occurs at that point because it is the only output combination at which both players are doing the best they can given the choice of the other. The result is the same, but the Nash assumptions are much more reasonable than the Cournot assumptions and therefore provide a more solid theoretical basis for the equilibrium.

8.1.3 Cournot-Nash Model with More Than Two Firms[3]

We have developed the Cournot-Nash equilibrium for a duopoly, but the result can be generalized to any number of identical firms. Assuming N *identical* firms, each firm faces an identical reaction function. An easy method of identifying the Cournot-Nash equilibrium in this case is to calculate a representative ith firm's reaction function.* Because all N firms are identical, the equilibrium for each is symmetric, so:

$$q_i = \frac{Q}{N} \qquad \text{or} \qquad Q = Nq_i.$$

Firm i's *residual demand curve* can then be written as:

$$P = (100 - Q) = 100 - Nq_i$$

or

$$P = [100 - (N - 1)q_i] - q_i$$

*Using calculus the analysis can be simplified. The ith firm wishes to maximize profits as follows:
$$\Pi_i = TR_i - TC_i = Pq_i - 10q_i.$$
The first-order condition for profit maximization is:
$$\frac{d\Pi_i}{dq_i} = P\frac{dq_i}{dq_i} + q_i\frac{dP}{dq_i} - \frac{d(10q_i)}{dq_i} = 0.$$

Because $\dfrac{dP_i}{dq_i} = (-1)$, we have:
$$\frac{d\Pi_i}{dq_i} = P + q_i(-1) - 10 = (100 - Nq_i) - q_i - 10 = 0$$

or:
$$90 - (N + 1)q_i = 0,$$

so:
$$q_i = \frac{90}{(N + 1)}.$$

where q_j is the output of any firm other than the ith firm.

Using the "twice-as-steep" rule and remembering that Firm i views q_j as constant, Firm i's marginal revenue curve is:

$$MR_i = [100 - (N - 1)q_j] - 2q_i.$$

Setting MR = MC = 10 for profit maximization yields Firm i's reaction function:

$$MR_i = [100 - (N - 1)q_j] - 2q_i = 10 = MC.$$

This can be rewritten as:

$$q_i = 45 - \frac{(N - 1)}{2}q_j. \qquad [8.8]$$

Multiplying Equation 8.8 by 2 yields:

$$2q_i = 90 - (N - 1)q_j.$$

Recognizing that $q_i = q_j$ in equilibrium and solving for q_i yields:*

$$q_i = \frac{90}{N + 1}. \qquad [8.9]$$

From Equation 8.9, total output Q will be:

$$Q = Nq_i = N\frac{90}{(N + 1)} = \frac{N}{(N + 1)}90. \qquad [8.10]$$

According to Equation 8.10, as the number of firms in a Cournot industry increases, total output continuously approaches the competitive output of 90. In our example, a monopolist (N = 1) would produce the profit-maximizing output of 45; duopolists (N = 2) would produce Q = 60 or two-thirds of the competitive output; three firms would produce Q = 67.5 or three-fourths of the competitive output; and for N "very large," Q approaches 90, the competitive output. There is something intuitively appealing about this result.

The equilibrium output for the ith firm could also be identified graphically using the ith firm's reaction function. Because of symmetry, $q_i = q_j$, for all values of i and j. In Figure 8.7, the reaction function for firm i in an industry with three firms is identified from Equation 8.8 and symmetry as:

$$q_i = 45 - \frac{(3 - 1)}{2}q_j = 45 - q_j.$$

Equilibrium is attained where the reaction function and the 45° line (where $q_i = q_j$) intersect. From Equations 8.9 and 8.10, in the case with three firms, each would produce 22.5 units for a total industry output of 67.5 units.

*The algebra is:

$$2q_i + (N - 1)q_i = 90$$

$$(N + 1)q_i = 90$$

$$q_i = \frac{90}{N + 1}.$$

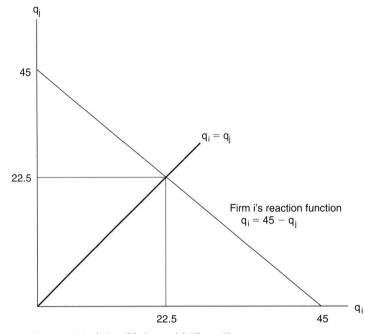

FIGURE 8.7 **Cournot-Nash Equilibrium with Three Firms**

With three identical firms in a Cournot-Nash industry, each firm's reaction function is
$q_i = 45 - q_j$. Because each of the three identical firms produces the same output at the Nash
equilibrium, the equilibrium is at an output of 22.5 where the firm's reaction function
$q_i = 45 - q_j$ intersects the 45-degree line from the origin.

APPLICATION 8.1

Empirical Evidence of Cournot-Nash Behavior—Experimental Games with Varying Numbers of Players

Empirical evidence on the likelihood of Cournot-Nash behavior is difficult to obtain because it requires showing that oligopolists select prices between the competitive price and the joint profit-maximizing price. Because of this difficulty, economists have used experimental games to try to determine the likelihood of the Cournot-Nash outcome. Typically these games are played by college students who receive information concerning their profit payoffs after making an output decision. The student participants are allowed to keep some of the profits they earn so there is a strong incentive to do well—the higher the students' profits, the more money they earn. A survey of experimental results by Huck, Norman, and Oechssler found the Cournot-Nash outcome to be fairly common in experimental games.* The survey also indicated that as the number of players increased, total output increased as well.

Huck, Norman, and Oechssler also performed a series of experiments simulating competition between two, three, four, and five firms. Each market simulation lasted 25 rounds and students were paid according to the total profits they earned in all 25 rounds. There were six simulations for each market structure. Students were given feedback after each round concerning the market's total output and their profits. They

could do simulations of their possible decisions on their computers before they made a final output choice in each round.

The table below shows the total quantities in the simulations and classifies these quantities as either (C)ollusive, (N)ash, or (R)ivalistic. The results are striking in several respects.

Classification of Sessions

		Session					
n	Cournot-Nash Quantity	1	2	3	4	5	6
2	66.67	61.28 (N)	60.40 (N)	58.44 (N)	64.86 (N)	57.36 (C)	53.80 (C)
3	74.25	74.64 (N)	72.48 (N)	83.56 (N)	63.24 (N)	69.84 (N)	77.04 (N)
4	79.20	73.00 (N)	76.00 (N)	92.82 (R)	72.12 (N)	74.24 (N)	75.36 (N)
5	82.50	89.00 (N)	93.36 (R)	80.04 (N)	76.80 (N)	93.96 (R)	83.52 (N)

Note: Classifications: (C)ollusive, (N)ash, (R)ivalistic.

The collusive result occurred only twice and both times with duopoly (two firms). With more than two firms, the competitors were never able to collude to earn higher profits. The rivalistic, or competitive outcome, occurred only three times, once with four firms and twice with five firms. The predominant outcome was the Nash equilibrium, which occurred in 19 of the 24 experimental games.

The bar graph below shows the results by breaking down the outcomes for the entire game and the last 9 rounds (rounds 17–25) of the games. Notice that the average total quantity increases consistently as the number of firms increases. With two firms the average quantity of 59.36 is, on average, less than the Nash equilibrium quantity (66.67); the average quantity with five firms (86.21) is greater than the Nash equilibrium quantity (82.50); and the average quantities with three (74.25) and four firms (79.20) are very close to the Nash equilibrium quantities (73.47 and 77.26, respectively).

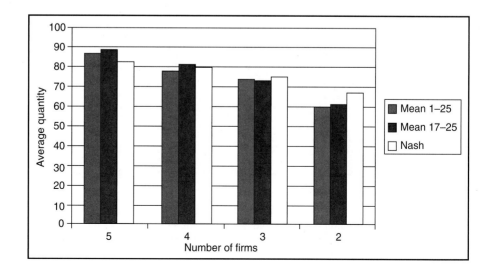

The Huck, Norman, and Oechssler simulations are remarkably consistent with the theoretical predictions of the Cournot-Nash model and suggest it is difficult for more than two firms to ever successfully collude to maximize profit.

*Steffen Huck, Hans-Theo Normann, and Jorg Oechssler, "Two are Few and Four are Many: Number Effects in Experimental Oligopolies," *Journal of Economic Behavior and Organization* 53, (April 2004): 435–446. ■

APPLICATION 8.2
The Paradox of Mergers in a Cournot-Nash Market*

One of the strange implications of the Cournot-Nash equilibrium with linear demand and constant marginal cost is that with *more than two firms,* mergers reduce the combined profits of firms that decide to merge. Consider the table below that shows how price, firm output and profits, and industry output and profits vary as the number of firms increase in a Cournot-Nash market with demand $P = 100 - Q$ and constant marginal cost $MC = 10$. These are the conditions used in Section 8.1.3.

Number of Firms	Price	Firm Output	Firm Profits	Industry Output	Industry Profits
1	55	45	2025	45	2025
2	40	30	900	60	1800
3	32.5	22.5	506.25	67.5	1518.75
4	28	18	324	72	1296
5	25	15	225	75	1125

Suppose there are currently four firms in this market. Price equals 28 and each firm earns a profit equal to 324. Total industry profits are 1296. Now suppose two of the firms merge and the remaining three continue to exhibit Cournot-Nash pricing behavior. Price increases to 32.5, and each of the remaining three firms earns a profit of 506.25. Total industry profits are 1518.75; but before the merger, each of the merger firms earned a profit of 324, so the two firms combined to earn a profit of 648. The merger has reduced the profits earned by the two merged firms by 21.9 percent, from 648 to just 506.25! Even if three of the firms merged, their combined profits would decrease from 972 (3×324) to 900 (a decline of 7.4 percent). Only if all four firms merged to form a monopoly would the merger increase combined profits for the merged firms. Cournot-Nash behavior creates an incentive for the firms *not to merge,* unless the merger itself changes the firms' behavior and moves them toward collusion.

*Stephen W. Salant, Sheldon Switzer, and Robert Reynolds, "Losses from Horizontal Merger: The Effects of an Exogenous Change in Industry Structure on Cournot-Nash Equilibrium," *Quarterly Journal of Economics* 98 (1983): pp. 185–199. ■

APPLICATION 8.3
Examples of Cournot-Nash Pricing in Real Markets

Several case studies of real-world markets suggest the possibility of Cournot-Nash pricing. One study by Iwata concluded that in the Japanese flat-glass industry, which was dominated by two firms (Asahi and Nippon), firms produced outputs that were between the Cournot-Nash and joint profit-maximizing outputs.* Iwata could not reject the possibility of Cournot-Nash behavior. In addition, Brander and Zhang found

evidence that the pricing behavior of American Airlines and United Airlines between 1984 and 1988 most closely resembled the Cournot-Nash model's predictions.[†]

Nun and Sarvary studied mobile telecommunications markets in many countries. Based on data from 10 countries (Denmark, Ecuador, Finland, Malaysia, Poland, Portugal, Sri Lanka, Thailand, Turkey, and Uruguay), each of which had oligopolies in its cellular phone industry, they could *not reject* the hypothesis that Cournot-Nash pricing tended to be used in these markets.[‡] Furthermore, they found that when a country's cellular phone market switched from being a monopoly to an oligopoly (usually a duopoly), prices declined below the monopoly level but remained well above the competitive level, perhaps at the Cournot-Nash level.

Rather than examining one industry, Aiginger examined three different large data sets for Austrian oligopolies: a firm data set developed by the Austrian National Bank of 1500 firms between 1983 and 1992; a three-digit industry data set constructed by the Austrian Census of Manufacturers of 97 industries between 1983 and 1988; and a survey data set of over 1500 firms developed by the Austrian Institute of Economic Research in 1991.[§] Aiginger analyzed the statistical relationship between price-cost margins and market shares, and price-cost margins and the elasticity of demand, to determine whether these relationships were consistent with the implications of the Cournot-Nash model. The results for two of the data sets (the Austrian Census and the Austrian Institute of Economic Research) were consistent with the Cournot-Nash model. However, the results using the Austrian National Bank data set were not supportive of the Cournot-Nash model. In fact, the results using the Austrian National Bank data were not even consistent with basic economic theory (e.g., higher *firm* market shares were associated with lower price-cost margins), probably because price-cost margins were measured poorly as the ratio of firm sales to industry sales at the *two-digit* level. Aiginger concluded, "The evidence that market shares and price elasticities do influence margins is predicted by the Cournot model and replicated by two of our three data sets. Both these findings are more compatible with this model than with its alternatives in the theory of oligopoly. . . ." Overall, empirical evidence suggests that the Cournot-Nash equilibrium is more than a theoretical construction.

*Gyoichi Iwata, "Measurement of Conjectural Variations in Oligopoly," *Econometrica* 42 (September 1974): 947–966.

[†]James A. Brander and Anming Zhang, "Dynamic Oligopoly Behavior in the Airline Industry," *International Journal of Industrial Organization* 11 (September 1993): 407–435.

[‡]Dana Nunn and Miklos Sarvary, "Pricing Practices and Firms' Market Power in International Cellular Markets, An Empirical Study," INSEAD working paper series, February 2004, http://ged.insead.edu/fichiersti/inseadwp2004/2004-16.pdf.

[§]Karl Aiginger, "Confronting the Implications of the Cournot Model with Industry and Firm Data," *Small Business Economics* 8 (October 1996): 365–378. ∎

8.1.4 Using the Cournot-Nash Model in the Context of International Trade[4]

Industrial organization and international trade economists often assume Cournot-Nash behavior when analyzing global competition between oligopolists. In recent years economists have used Cournot-Nash models to examine the potential use of *anti*–free trade policies, such as tariffs and subsidies, for improving domestic welfare in markets where economies of scale are significant. These analyses sometimes indicate that domestic welfare can be increased by the adoption of restrictive trade policies.

Government intervention is often presented as a game in which the government moves first and the domestic and foreign firms move second. One possible intervention would be to grant a direct or indirect subsidy to domestic firms. We examine the subsidy case in detail, but the same basic conclusions have been drawn using other types of government intervention such as tariffs and import quotas.

Using the Cournot-Nash framework, consider a model with one domestic American firm, Boeing, one foreign firm, Airbus, and no government intervention. To simplify the analysis, we assume that the product is sold only in the domestic market. The foreign firm, therefore, produces only for export. The demand in the American market is $P = 100 - q_B - q_A$. For both firms $MC = AC = 10$; here we set fixed costs equal to 500, so $TC = 500 + 10q$.* The existence of fixed costs does not affect marginal cost, so MC remains equal to 10.

We showed in Section 8.1.1 that these conditions yield the following reaction functions:

$$q_B = 45 - \frac{1}{2}q_A$$

$$q_A = 45 - \frac{1}{2}q_B$$

and the following Cournot-Nash equilibrium price and quantity:

$$q_B = q_A = 30$$
$$P = 100 - 60 = \$40.$$

To obtain profits for each firm, calculate $TR - TC$:

$$\Pi_B = \Pi_A = Pq - FC - MCq = (40 \times 30) - 500 - 10(30) = \$400,$$

where Π_B represents the profits for the domestic firm, Boeing, and Π_A represents the profits for the foreign firm, Airbus. Each firm produces 30 units of output and earns an economic profit of $400 million.

In Figure 8.8 the gray triangle depicts consumer surplus in the American market, which equals:

$$\text{Consumer Surplus} = \frac{1}{2}60^2 = \frac{3600}{2} = \$1800 \text{ million.}$$

Boeing earns a profit of $400, so its profits plus American consumer surplus equals $2200 million (400 + 1800).

Suppose the United States grants a subsidy, s, of $3 per unit to Boeing. Boeing's total costs become:

$$TC_B = FC + MCq_B - sq_B = 500 + (10 - 3)q_B = 500 + 7q_B.$$

Boeing's effective marginal cost is now:

$$MC_B = MC - s = 10 - 3 = 7.$$

*Recall from Application 2.6 that one method of measuring scale economies is the *function coefficient*, S, defined as the ratio of average cost to marginal cost. In Figure 8.8, $S > 1$ for all $q > 0$, and therefore, economies of scale exist for all $q > 0$.

These conditions establish sufficient but not necessary conditions for the existence of economies of scale, and they are used here to simplify the analysis. Economies of scale could, for example, also exist for some $q > 0$ if there is a fixed setup cost and increasing marginal cost or if there are decreasing marginal costs for some $q > 0$. For further clarification see Andreu Mas-Colell and Michael D. Whinston, *Microeconomic Theory* (New York: Oxford University Press, 1995), pp. 144–145.

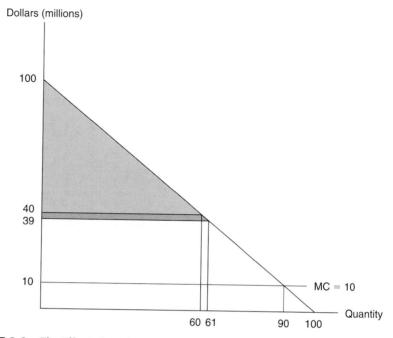

FIGURE 8.8 The Effect of a Subsidy on Consumer Surplus

In the absence of a subsidy, the Cournot-Nash equilibrium is for each firm to produce 30 planes for an industry total output of 60 planes and a price per plane equal to \$40. Consumer surplus equals the area of the gray triangle, which equals $\frac{1}{2}(60)^2 = $ \$1800 million. If the United States grants a subsidy of \$3 per plane to Boeing, the new Cournot-Nash equilibrium is for Boeing to produce 32 planes and Airbus to produce 29 for a total market output of 61. Consumer surplus increases by the red area to $\frac{1}{2}(61)^2 = $ \$1860.5 million.

Boeing's reaction function is derived as follows:

$$MR_B = 100 - q_A - 2q_B = 7 = MC$$

or:

$$q_B = 46.5 - \frac{1}{2}q_A.$$

With the subsidy, Boeing has a cost advantage over Airbus. To solve for the new Cournot-Nash equilibrium, substitute Airbus's reaction function into Boeing's reaction function and obtain Boeing's equilibrium output:

$$q_B = 46.5 - \frac{1}{2}q_A = 46.5 - \frac{1}{2}\left(45 - \frac{1}{2}q_B\right)$$

or

$$q_B = 46.5 - 22.5 + \frac{1}{4}q_B$$

so

$$q_B = \frac{24 \cdot 4}{3} = 32.$$

Airbus's output is therefore:

$$q_A = 45 - \frac{1}{2}(32) = 29.$$

Total industry output is $Q = 32 + 29 = 61$, and $P = 100 - 61 = \$39$ million.

Profits are now substantially different for each firm. Boeing produces more than Airbus and, including the subsidy, earns:

$$\Pi_B = Pq - FC - MCq + sq = (39 \times 32) - 500 - 10(32) + 3(32) = \$524 \text{ million.}$$

Airbus earns:

$$\Pi_A = Pq - FC - MCq = (39 \times 29) - 500 - 10(29) = \$341 \text{ million.}$$

With the subsidy, consumer surplus increases by the red area in Figure 8.8 and equals:

$$\text{Consumer Surplus} = \frac{1}{2}61^2 = \frac{3721}{2} = \$1860.5 \text{ million.}$$

Now the sum of consumer surplus and Boeing's profit equals $1860.5 + 524 = \$2384.5$ million. The cost of the subsidy to U.S. taxpayers, however, equals $3(32) = \$96$ million. Subtracting the cost of the subsidy from the sum of consumer surplus and Boeing's profit yields $2384.5 - 96 = \$2288.5$ million.

Recall that in the absence of government intervention total American consumer surplus plus Boeing's profits equaled $2200 million. With the subsidy, total consumer surplus plus Boeing's profits minus the cost of the subsidy equals $2288.5 million. Because $2288.5 million > $2200 million, the United States is better off as a result of the subsidy.

The existence of entry barriers and presubsidy economic rents is important for this result. If there are no entry barriers and entry is easy, then the effects of a subsidy may be quite different. If we assume economies of scale in production but easy entry, profits will be normal in both the initial and final equilibrium, and a subsidy will have dramatically different impacts on the domestic and foreign economies. This is essentially the model of monopolistic competition.

To understand this different outcome, consider a market characterized by a linear demand curve, constant marginal cost, and Cournot-Nash behavior. Suppose the demand curve for color televisions in Japan is the familiar demand curve $P = 100 - Q$. Assume fixed costs equal $256 and marginal cost equals $20, so:

$$TC = 256 + 20q.$$

In the initial equilibrium there are *two* Japanese firms (Sony and Hitachi) and *two* American firms (RCA and Zenith), or a total of four firms. We know from Equation 8.9 that the Cournot-Nash equilibrium in a market with four identical firms, linear demand, and linear marginal cost is:

$$q_S = q_H = q_R = q_Z = \frac{1}{N+1}Q_{pc} = \frac{1}{5}80 = 16,$$

where Q_{pc} is the competitive output ($P = MC = \$20$), and N is the number of firms in the industry. In this example, total output is 64 and $P = \$36$. Figure 8.9 depicts the demand curve and the relevant Cournot-Nash equilibrium.

Because fixed costs equal $256, each firm earns a normal profit:

$$\Pi_S = \Pi_H = \Pi_R = \Pi_Z = Pq - FC - MCq$$
$$= (36 \times 16) - 256 - 20(16) = 576 - 256 - 320 = 0.$$

In the absence of government intervention, Japanese consumer surplus equals the light gray area in Figure 8.9, or:

$$\text{Consumer Surplus} = \frac{1}{2}64^2 = \frac{4096}{2} = \$2048.$$

Because profits are zero, the sum of Japanese consumer surplus and the Japanese firms' profits also equals $2048.

If the Japanese government places a subsidy of $16 per unit on color televisions, this effectively reduces the marginal cost of production, MC_S, for Japanese firms from $20 to $4 ($MC - s = 20 - 16 = \4) in Figure 8.9. Because the American firms earn zero economic profits before the subsidy, they will be unable to compete after the subsidy and will leave the market entirely to the Japanese firms. In Figure 8.9, the perfectly competitive price in Japan with the subsidy would be $4, and the competitive output with the subsidy would be 96. Because entry is free, the subsidy will attract additional firms into the Japanese market. In the final equilibrium, profits must equal

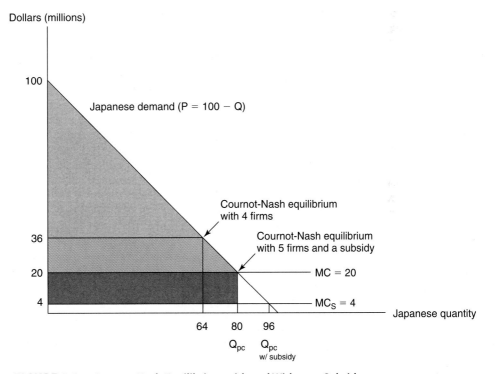

FIGURE 8.9 **Cournot-Nash Equilibrium with and Without a Subsidy**

With easy entry and no subsidy, two American and two Japanese firms each produce 16 units for a total market quantity of 64 and a price equal to $36. Consumer surplus equals the light gray area, which equals $\frac{1}{2}(64)^2 = \$2048$. With a subsidy of $16 paid to Japanese producers, the two American firms exit the market and are replaced by three Japanese firms. With five Japanese firms, each produces 16 units for a total market quantity of 80 and a price equal to $20. Consumer surplus increases by the red area and equals $\frac{1}{2}(80)^2 = \$3200$, but Japanese taxpayers must pay the subsidy, which equals the area of the dark gray rectangle ($80 \times 16 = \$1280$).

zero. This occurs when three additional firms begin producing televisions in Japan, giving a total of five firms in the Japanese market (Sony and Hitachi plus three Japanese entrants).* Suppose the three Japanese entrants are Toshiba, Matsushita, and Sharp. The Cournot-Nash equilibrium with five Japanese firms is:

$$q_S = q_H = q_T = q_M = q_{SH} = \frac{1}{N+1}Q_{pc} = \frac{1}{6}(96) = 16.$$

With five Japanese firms each producing an output of 16, total output is 80, and P = \$20. *The price declines by the exact amount of the subsidy.* Figure 8.9 shows the new Cournot-Nash equilibrium. Furthermore, because fixed costs equal \$256, each firm earns a normal profit:

$$\Pi_S = \Pi_H = \Pi_T = \Pi_M = \Pi_{SH} = Pq - FC - MCq + sq$$
$$= (20 \times 16) - 256 - 20(16) + 16(16) = 320 - 256 - 320 + 256 = 0.$$

As a result of the subsidy, Japanese consumer surplus has increased by the red area in Figure 8.9, and total Japanese consumer surplus equals:

$$\text{Consumer Surplus} = \frac{1}{2}80^2 = \frac{6400}{2} = \$3200.$$

The Japanese firms' profits still equal zero, but the Japanese government must pay a subsidy equal to the dark gray area in Figure 8.9. The cost of the subsidy equals qs = 80 · 16 = \$1280. Consumer surplus minus the cost of the subsidy equals 3200 − 1280 = \$1920. Because total consumer surplus without the subsidy was \$2048, the subsidy has resulted in a net loss for the Japanese economy.

In this example each of the five firms continued to produce the same output as each of the four firms produced before the implementation of the subsidy. Horstmann and Markusen have shown this to be a general result.[5] They proved that assuming a specific subsidy per unit, free entry, Cournot-Nash behavior, and linear demand curves, the post-entry equilibrium will be where each firm continues to produce the same output at the same average cost as firms produced before the subsidy.

In 1962 the Japanese share of the American color television market was virtually zero, but by the late 1980s the Japanese manufacturers had completely displaced the American manufacturers of color televisions. The above theoretical analysis suggests that the Japanese economy as a whole may have suffered a welfare decline as a result of the Japanese government's efforts to subsidize their domestic television manufacturers.[†] Of course, the previous theoretical model, the Boeing-Airbus example, without free entry suggests exactly the opposite.

APPLICATION 8.4

The Effectiveness of Industrial Policy: UK Subsidies and Tariffs

As we have seen, theoretical analysis yields ambiguous results regarding the welfare effects of industrial policies such as subsidies and tariffs. Several empirical studies have found that while industrial policies may yield improvements in welfare, these improvements tend to be quite small.

*Remember that two American firms, RCA and Zenith, left the market, so there is a net gain of one firm worldwide.

†This result depends on the profits the Japanese manufacturers earned on sales outside of Japan.

Venables examined the potential effect of export subsidies and import tariffs in the United Kingdom.* Using data for nine industries in 1982, he found that the potential gains from industrial policy tended to be quite small. The first table below presents Venables's results for export subsidies of 4 percent and 2 percent. In 10 of 18 cases, the subsidy reduces welfare. Furthermore, only in the "Artificial and Synthetic Fibers" industry does a subsidy yield a gain "as large as 1 percent" of the base of consumption. The second table presents the results for import tariffs. Once again the gains tend to be small, except in the "Artificial and Synthetic Fibers" industry. Venables summarized his findings by stating that "the conclusion which emerges from the simulations is that trade models of this type provide a rather weak case for policy intervention."[†]

Welfare Effects of Export Subsidies Under Oligopoly: UK Industries 1982 Data (Gain as a Percentage of Base Consumption*)

	4% Subsidy	2% Subsidy
257 Pharmaceutical products	−0.23	−0.06
260 Artificial and synthetic fibers	1.01	0.55
322 Machine tools	−1.34	−0.25
330 Office machinery	−1.09	0.23
342 Electric motors, generators	−0.38	−0.05
346 Domestic electrical appliances	0.22	0.14
350 Motor vehicles	0.92	0.66
438 Carpets, linoleum	−0.65	0.04
451 Footwear	−3.49	−0.19

*Cournot-Nash assumptions regarding competition
Source: Anthony J. Venables, "Trade Policy under Imperfect Competition: A Numerical Assessment," in Paul Krugman and Alasdair Smith (eds.), *Empirical Studies of Strategic Trade Policy* (Chicago: University of Chicago Press, 1994), p. 57.

Welfare Effects of Import Tariffs Under Oligopoly: UK Industries 1982 Data (Gain as a Percentage of Base Consumption*)

	5% Tariff	10% Tariff	15% Tariff	20% Tariff
257 Pharmaceutical products	0.59	0.96	1.15	1.20
260 Artificial and synthetic fibers	2.23	3.93	5.07	5.64
322 Machine tools	0.67	0.44	−0.20	−0.81
330 Office machinery	1.52	2.09	1.97	1.81
342 Electric motors, generators	0.76	1.04	0.96	0.65
346 Domestic electrical appliances	1.15	1.54	1.46	1.18
350 Motor vehicles	1.44	2.13	2.24	1.99
438 Carpets, linoleum	0.74	0.64	0.48	0.39
451 Footwear	0.60	0.48	0.47	0.47

*Cournot-Nash assumption regarding competition
Source: Anthony J. Venables, "Trade Policy under Imperfect Competition: A Numerical Assessment," in Paul Krugman and Alasdair Smith (eds.), *Empirical Studies of Strategic Trade Policy* (Chicago: University of Chicago Press, 1994), p. 52.

*Anthony J. Venables, "Trade Policy Under Imperfect Competition: A Numerical Assessment," in Paul Krugman and Alasdair Smith (eds.), *Empirical Studies of Strategic Trade Policy* (Chicago: University of Chicago Press, 1994).
[†]*Ibid.*, p. 63.

APPLICATION 8.5

The Effectiveness of Industrial Policy: The Commercial Aircraft Industry

In 1967 a British, French, and German government consortium provided subsidies to enable the Europeans to enter the commercial aircraft industry. In 1974 the first European aircraft appeared on the market, but they were a commercial failure. The governments then decided it was necessary to produce a complete line of aircraft to compete with Boeing. This goal was finally accomplished by Airbus, the European-subsidized company, but Airbus still faced a significant cost disadvantage because of its relatively small size. This cost disadvantage resulted in a need to supply ever larger government subsidies.

The subsidies were paid in the form of launch aid by Germany, Britain, France, and Spain to help Airbus develop new commercial aircraft. The table below shows the amount of launch aid paid by each country to Airbus in millions of U.S. dollars for each type of plane. The four countries paid over $15 billion in launch aid subsidies. These subsidies were paid regardless of whether or not a particular plane was a commercial success or failure. Boeing argued that this type of direct subsidy to Airbus created an unfair competitive advantage for Airbus, and on October 4, 2004, Boeing filed a formal complaint against Airbus with the World Trade Organization (WTO).

Country	A300/A310	A320	A330/A340	A330–200	A340–500	A380	Total
Germany	1550	702	2010	0	0	1070	5332
UK	0	567	1040	0	215	867	2689
France	2050	672	1450	58	337	1370	5937
Spain	233	87	270	0	75	426	1091
Total	3833	2028	4770	58	627	3733	15,049

Source: Data from David Greising, "Arming for Trade War: Boeing Sleuths Seek Proof of Improper Subsidies to Airbus, *Chicago Tribune,* May 20, 2005.

These subsidies undoubtedly helped Airbus compete more effectively against Boeing; however, in light of our analysis of Cournot-Nash pricing in an international duopoly, it is not theoretically apparent whether the Airbus subsidies would increase or decrease welfare. In a 1994 study, Gernot Klepper analyzed the impact of these subsides on economic welfare.* His results, presented in the table below, suggest that if Airbus's entry is compared with an alternative market structure of monopoly, presumably a Boeing monopoly, total economic welfare worldwide decreases by more than $73 billion as a result of the subsidies. Total welfare in Europe, however, increases by over $7 billion. Curiously, if Airbus's entry is considered an alternative market structure to duopoly, worldwide welfare is increased by $5.9 billion with the subsidy; however, all of the gains accrue to North American producers.

These results are consistent with our Cournot-Nash theoretical analysis. Because of the existence of large economies of scale, the optimal structure is a monopoly, and the entry of subsidized Airbus into a monopolized industry forces higher costs on society and results in greatly reduced producer surplus. Conversely, if the alternative structure is duopoly with both duopolists initially assumed to produce equal and suboptimal quantities, then the entry of subsidized Airbus at a small scale results in the exiting of one of the two original duopolists. However, it also results in the expansion of output by the remaining North American producer. Consequently, compared with duopoly, the larger scale of the one remaining North American firm leads to almost a $12 billion pro-

ducer surplus gain to the North American firm. Notice that consumers gain only compared with the monopoly situation. It is, therefore, not clear whether the subsidies to Airbus improved welfare.

Distribution of Welfare Effects of European-Supported Market Entry into Commercial Aircraft (Million 1986 $US)			
	Producer Surplus	**Consumer Surplus**	**Total**
Compared with monopoly			
Europe	−2826	10,544	7718
North America	−107,582	12,631	−94,951
Rest of world	0	13,630	13,630
Total	−110,408	36,795	−73,613
Compared with duopoly			
Europe	−2826	−905	−3731
North America	11,974	−1405	10,569
Rest of world	0	−958	−958
Total	9148	−3268	5880

Source: Gernot Klepper, "Industrial Policy in the Transport Aircraft Industry," in Paul Krugman and Alasdair Smith (eds.), *Empirical Studies of Strategic Trade Policy* (Chicago: University of Chicago Press, 1994), p. 116.

*Gernot Klepper, "Industrial Policy in the Transport Aircraft Industry," in Paul Krugman and Alasdair Smith (eds.), *Empirical Studies of Strategic Trade Policy* (Chicago: University of Chicago Press, 1994). ■

8.2 The Stackelberg Model[6]

The Cournot-Nash model is a one-period simultaneous move game. In 1934 economist Heinrich von Stackelberg questioned Cournot's assumption that both firms take their opponent's output as given by considering what would happen in a sequential game if only one of the two firms, known as the ***Stackelberg follower,*** assumed its opponent would maintain its output, while the other firm, known as the ***Stackelberg leader,*** used this knowledge about its opponent to select an output that maximized its profit. In the ***Stackelberg model,*** the leader makes a more logical assumption than the follower, and as a result, the game's equilibrium changes.

8.2.1 Firms with Identical Costs and Demand

The Stackelberg model is a sequential game where the Stackelberg leader moves first and the Stackelberg follower moves second. Returning to our Boeing-Airbus game, suppose Airbus is the leader and moves first, then Boeing, the follower, moves, and then the game ends. The demand and cost conditions are the same as they were before: Demand is $p = 100 - q_B - q_A$ and costs are $MC = AC = 10$ for both firms. As an initial simplifying assumption, suppose Airbus can select from only eight possible quantities: 20, 25, 30, 35, 40, 45, 50, or 55. Boeing observes Airbus's quantity and then selects its quantity. The game tree in Figure 8.10 identifies the possible outcomes of such a game. Once Airbus selects an output, Boeing chooses its profit-maximizing output by substituting Airbus's quantity for q_A into Boeing's reaction function (Equation 8.4). If Airbus produces

20 planes, Boeing produces $q_B = 45 - \frac{1}{2}q_A = 45 - 10 = 35$ planes; if Airbus produces 25 planes, Boeing produces $q_B = 45 - \frac{1}{2}q_A = 45 - 12.5 = 32.5$ planes, etc. In Figure 8.10, the numbers in parentheses show Airbus's and Boeing's profits, respectively.

What is Airbus's optimal move? Airbus knows that if it produces 20 planes, Boeing produces 35 planes and Airbus's profits equal $700 million; if Airbus produces 25 planes, Boeing produces 33.2 planes and Airbus's profits equal $812.5 million, and so on. Airbus selects the output that maximizes its profits, and produces 45 planes. Boeing responds by producing 22.5 planes. Airbus earns profits of $1012.5 million, and Boeing earns $506.3 million. Then the game ends. Figure 8.10 shows the Cournot-Nash equilibrium at B_3 where Airbus and Boeing both produce 30 planes, and Airbus's profits are $900 million. By moving first, Airbus is able to "force" Boeing onto its reaction function, and as a result, Airbus earns a larger profit ($1012.5 million) than in the Cournot-Nash equilibrium ($900 million).

Next, we eliminate the simplifying assumption that Airbus can produce only eight possible outputs and consider the more realistic game where Airbus can produce any output. While Airbus can select any output in this version of the game, Boeing must

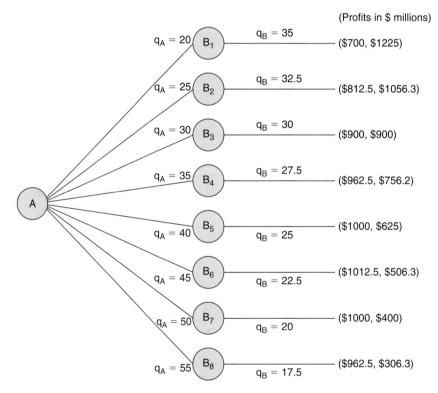

(Profits in $ millions)

$q_A = 20$	B_1	$q_B = 35$	($700, $1225)
$q_A = 25$	B_2	$q_B = 32.5$	($812.5, $1056.3)
$q_A = 30$	B_3	$q_B = 30$	($900, $900)
$q_A = 35$	B_4	$q_B = 27.5$	($962.5, $756.2)
$q_A = 40$	B_5	$q_B = 25$	($1000, $625)
$q_A = 45$	B_6	$q_B = 22.5$	($1012.5, $506.3)
$q_A = 50$	B_7	$q_B = 20$	($1000, $400)
$q_A = 55$	B_8	$q_B = 17.5$	($962.5, $306.3)

FIGURE 8.10 The Extensive Form of the Stackelberg Game (Airbus's Profits, Boeing's Profits)

If Airbus can produce only eight possible outputs between 20 and 55 planes, Boeing responds to Airbus's output by producing an output that maximizes Boeing's profits. Airbus moves first and selects $q_A = 45$, knowing that Boeing will respond by producing 22.5. Airbus produces 45 planes because that output maximizes Airbus's profits at $1012.5 million.

move on its reaction function when it takes the second move. This restriction is placed on Boeing by substituting Boeing's reaction function, $q_B = 45 - \frac{1}{2}q_A$, directly into Airbus's demand curve, which yields:*

$$p = (100 - q_B) - q_A = \left[100 - \left(45 - \frac{1}{2}q_A\right)\right] - q_A = 55 + \frac{1}{2}q_A - q_A$$

$$p = 55 - \frac{1}{2}q_A. \tag{8.11}$$

Equation 8.11 is Airbus's demand curve. Using the "twice-as-steep" rule, Airbus's marginal revenue is:

$$MR_A = 55 - q_A. \tag{8.12}$$

To maximize profits, Airbus sets $MR_A = MC$:

$$MR_A = 55 - q_A = 10$$

or:

$$q_A = 45.$$

Airbus's profit-maximizing output is 45 planes.

Once Airbus produces 45 planes, we know from Figure 8.10 that Boeing's optimal response is to substitute $q_A = 45$ into its reaction function and produce 22.5 planes $\left(q_B = 45 - \frac{1}{2}q_A = 45 - 22.5 = 22.5\right)$. Total industry output is $Q = q_A + q_B = 45 + 22.5 = 67.5$ planes, and price is $p = 100.00 - 67.5 = \$32.5$ million. The Stackelberg equilibrium yields a greater total industry output and lower price than the Cournot-Nash equilibrium.

In Figure 8.11, the Stackelberg equilibrium is identified as point A. Note that point A is on Boeing's reaction function, but it is *not* on Airbus's reaction function. In the Stackelberg model the leader selects the point on the *follower's* reaction function that maximizes the *leader's* profit.

8.2.2 The Stackelberg Model: Firms with Different Costs

Having identified the Stackelberg equilibrium in the case of completely symmetric duopolists, it is useful to address one common question: Why is Airbus, and not Boeing, the Stackelberg leader? The truth is if both firms face symmetric demands and costs, there is no theoretical reason why one firm should be the leader and the other the follower. Complete symmetry, however, is rare in real-world oligopolies. For example, General Motors and Toyota are not completely symmetric in terms of production costs or product demands. The same is true for Coca-Cola and Pepsi, Dell and Gateway, Kodak and Fuji, and Airbus and Boeing. In each of these oligopolies there is some variation between the firms in terms of costs and demands.

*Using calculus:

$$TR_A = Pq_A = \left[100 - \left(45 - \frac{1}{2}q_A\right) - q_A\right]q_A = 55q_A - \frac{1}{2}q_A^2$$

then

$$MR_A = \frac{dTR_A}{dq_A} = 55 - q_A.$$

Setting $MR = MC$,

$$55 - q_A = 10 \quad \text{or} \quad q_A = 45.$$

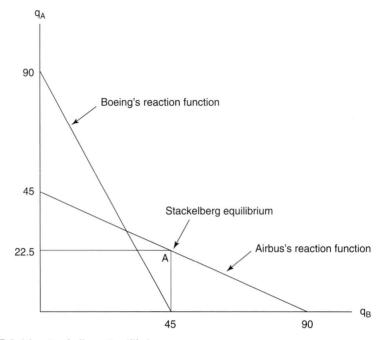

FIGURE 8.11 Stackelberg Equilibrium

The Stackelberg leader selects the point A on the follower's reaction function that maximizes the leader's profit.

Consider a case where one of the duopolists has an advantage because of lower production costs and/or greater demand. In this case, it is logical to assume that the firm with the advantage is the Stackelberg leader. Suppose, for instance, that because of government subsidies supplied by European countries, Airbus's costs are $MC_B = AC_B = 10$, but Boeing's costs are 10 percent higher, so $MC_A = AC_A = 11$. Under these cost conditions, it makes sense to assume that Airbus, the low-cost firm with the theoretical ability to drive Boeing from the market by charging a price below 11, controls the game by moving first.

Boeing's higher costs change its reaction function and the Stackelberg equilibrium. Airbus's reaction function, however, remains unchanged because its costs and demand have not changed. To calculate the new Stackelberg equilibrium, it is necessary to first identify Boeing's new reaction function and then substitute the new reaction function into Airbus's demand curve. To derive Boeing's new reaction function, we start with Boeing's demand curve:*

*Using calculus:

$$TR_B = Pq_B = (100 - q_A - q_B)q_B = 100q_B - q_Aq_B - q_B^2$$

$$MR_B = \frac{\partial TR_B}{\partial q_B} = 100 - q_A - 2q_B$$

for profit maximization MR = MC, or:

$$MR_B = 100 - q_A - 2q_B = 11 = MC \qquad \text{or} \qquad q_B = 44.5 - \frac{1}{2}q_A.$$

$$P_B = (100 - q_A) - q_B. \qquad [8.13]$$

By the "twice-as-steep" rule, Boeing's marginal revenue is:

$$MR_B = (100 - q_A) - 2q_B.$$

To obtain Boeing's reaction function, set $MR_B = MC = 11$:

$$MR_B = (100 - q_A) - 2q_B = 11 = MC_B, \qquad [8.14]$$

or,

$$2q_B = 89 - q_A. \qquad [8.15]$$

Solving Equation 8.15 for q_B, Boeing's new reaction function is:

$$q_B = 44.5 - \frac{1}{2}q_A \qquad [8.16]$$

Substituting $q_B = 44.5 - \frac{1}{2}q_A$ from Equation 8.16 into Airbus's demand curve yields:

$$p = (10.00 - q_B) - q_A = \left[100 - \left(44.5 - \frac{1}{2}q_A\right) \right] - q_A = 55.5 + \frac{1}{2}q_A - q_A$$

$$p = 55.5 - \frac{1}{2}q_A \qquad [8.17]$$

Equation 8.17 is Airbus's new demand curve, so Airbus's marginal revenue is:

$$MR_A = 55.5 - q_A. \qquad [8.18]$$

To maximize profits, Airbus equates marginal revenue to marginal cost:

$$MR_A = 55.5 - q_A = 10$$

so:

$$q_A = 45.5.$$

To obtain Boeing's profit-maximizing output, substitute $q_A = 45.5$ into Equation 8.16:

$$q_B = 44.5 - \frac{1}{2}q_A = 44.5 - \frac{1}{2}(45.5) = 44.5 - 22.75 = 21.75.$$

If Boeing's costs are 10 percent higher than Airbus's, Airbus is the Stackelberg leader and produces 45.5 planes, while Boeing is the follower and produces 21.75 planes. Total output is $45.5 + 21.75 = 67.25$ planes and $p = 100 - 67.25 = \$32.75$ million. A 10 percent increase in Boeing's costs results in:

- a 1.1 percent increase in Airbus's output from 45 to 45.5,
- a 3.3 percent decrease in Boeing's output from 22.5 to 21.75,
- a 0.37 percent decrease in total output from 67.5 to 67.25, and
- a 0.80 percent increase in price from \$32.5 million to \$32.75 million.

APPLICATION 8.6

Empirical Examples of Stackelberg Equilibrium

Several empirical case studies have found evidence suggesting the real-world use of Stackelberg quantity leadership. Gollop and Roberts studied the U.S. coffee-roasting industry in 1972 and concluded that the largest firm may have acted as a Stackelberg quantity leader.* They rejected the hypothesis that all firms in the industry adopted Cournot behavioral assumptions. In the study firms were grouped into three sizes:

(1) the largest firm; (2) the next five largest firms (medium-sized firms); and (3) the remaining smaller firms. They found that both the medium-sized and the small firms made Cournot assumptions about the small firms; that is, both the medium and small firms assumed that the small firms would maintain their current output in the face of output expansion by medium or small competitors. The largest firm, however, appeared to assume that medium-sized firms would *reduce* output in response to an output expansion by the largest firm and that small firms would *expand* output in response to an output expansion by the largest firm. Only the largest firm, therefore, anticipated that *all firms* would change their outputs in response to a change in its output. This can be interpreted as evidence that the largest firm acted as a Stackelberg quantity leader.

Pazo and Jaumandreu studied the behavior of the Spanish fertilizer industry between 1976 and 1988, an unusual period for the industry because due to high tariff and nontariff barriers to entry, the industry was a protected domestic oligopoly.[†] Three firms dominated the Spanish market for nitrogenous fertilizers; the former state-owned firm ENFERSA controlled 42 percent, and two other firms—ERT and CROS—controlled 18 and 10 percent, respectively. Pazo and Jaumandreu hypothesized that the former state monopoly, ENFERSA, might behave as a Stackelberg leader subject to some continuing government price regulation. First, they estimated the demand and costs for nitrogenous fertilizer. Once the demand and costs were estimated, it was possible to estimate the competitive and monopoly quantities and prices as well as the Cournot-Nash and Stackelberg quantities and prices. The estimated monopoly price implied a 29 percent price-cost margin; however, the actual price-cost margin was, on average, only 16 percent, well below the monopoly price-cost margin but well above the competitive price. Pazo and Jaumandreu concluded that these results were only consistent with Stackelberg behavior by ENFERSA.

*Frank M. Gollop and Mark J. Roberts, "Firm Interdependence in Oligopolistic Markets," *Journal of Econometrics* 10 (1979): 313–331.

†M. Consuelo Pazo and Jordi Jaumandreu, "An Empirical Oligopoly Model of a Regulated Market," *International Journal of Industrial Organization,* 17 (January 1999): 25–57. ■

8.3 The Bertrand Model

In 1883, Joseph Bertrand criticized Cournot's equilibrium by showing that if each duopolist assumes that its opponent holds constant its price (instead of its quantity), Cournot's logic results in an entirely different equilibrium.[7] Bertrand considered the case where the two firms produce a homogenoeous product.

Because most consumers consider a seat on any nonstop flight between the same two cities a homogeneous product, consider a game that Southwest Airlines and US Airways play on flights between Albany, New York, and Baltimore, Maryland. Suppose the demand for seats is $p = 1000 - Q$ and the marginal cost of adding an additional passenger on a one-way flight is $70. If Southwest assumes that US Airways always maintains its price at its current level, p_{US}, then Southwest's demand is dependent on the current relationship between Southwest's price, p_S, and the US Airways price, p_{US}. Because seats on any flight are a homogeneous product, passengers always purchase a ticket on the less-expensive airline. If Southwest's price is greater than US Airways' price, US Airways captures the entire market, and $q_S = 0$. If Southwest's price is less

than the US Airways price, Southwest captures the entire demand, and $q_S = 1000 - p_S$. Finally, if $p_S = p_{US}$, the two firms split the market, in which case each obtains one-half of the total industry demand, and Southwest's demand curve is:

$$q_S = \frac{1}{2}(1000 - p_S)$$

$$q_S = 500 - \frac{1}{2}p_S \text{ for } p_S = p_{US}. \tag{8.19}$$

Southwest's demand curve can therefore be identified as:

$$q_S = \begin{bmatrix} 0 \text{ if } p_S > p_{US} \\ 500 - \frac{1}{2}p_S \text{ if } p_S = p_{US} \\ 1000 - p_S \text{ if } p_S < p_{US} \end{bmatrix} \tag{8.20}$$

The **Bertrand model** with a homogeneous product is driven by the assumption that one of the airlines can capture the entire market if it charges a lower fare than its competitor. Given this assumption, if Southwest charges a fare just slightly less than p_{US}, it will virtually double its output and profit. This implies that if $p_S = p_{US} - \epsilon$, where ϵ represents a number that is *infinitesimally* greater than 0, Southwest captures the entire market. Of course, if $p_{US} = p_S - \epsilon$, then US Airways captures the entire market.

Figure 8.12 identifies Southwest's demand curve if US Airways charges a fare of $400 for a one-way ticket. If Southwest charges any fare greater than $400, US Airways sells all the tickets, Southwest sells no tickets, and Southwest's demand curve is the vertical red line along the price axis. If Southwest matches the US Airways fare and charges $400, the airlines divide the total demand of 600 tickets, and Southwest sells 300 tickets at point A. Finally, if Southwest charges any fare less than $400, US Airways sells no tickets, Southwest sells all the tickets, and Southwest's demand curve is identical to the industry's demand curve $p = 1000 - q_S$.

What is Southwest's optimal pricing strategy? If Southwest assumes US Airways maintains its price at $400, then Southwest can charge a fare *slightly* less than $400 and capture the entire market. To simplify the analysis, we assume that fares can be quoted only in whole dollar amounts. If Southwest lowers its fare by $1.00 to $399, its output will more than double, from 300 to 601 tickets. Southwest's marginal revenue associated with a fare reduction from $400 to $399 is calculated as follows. First, calculate the change in total revenue associated with the fare reduction: At $p_S = \$400$, $TR_S = pq_S = \$400(300) = \$120,000$, and at $p_S = \$399$, $TR_S = pq_S = \$399(601) = \$239,799$. Next, calculate Southwest's marginal revenue:

$$MR_S = \frac{\Delta TR_S}{\Delta q_S} = \frac{\$239,799 - \$120,000}{601 - 300} = \frac{\$119,799}{301} = \$398.00.$$

Because marginal revenue is $398 and marginal cost is $70, Southwest is better off if it reduces its fare from $400 to $399.

Should Southwest reduce its fare further in order to sell more tickets? To sell one additional ticket to the 602nd passenger, Southwest must reduce its fare to $398. The marginal revenue of reducing its fare from $399 to $398 is:

$$MR_S = \frac{\Delta TR_S}{\Delta q_S} = \frac{\$239,596 - \$239,799}{602 - 601} = \frac{-\$203}{1} = -\$203.$$

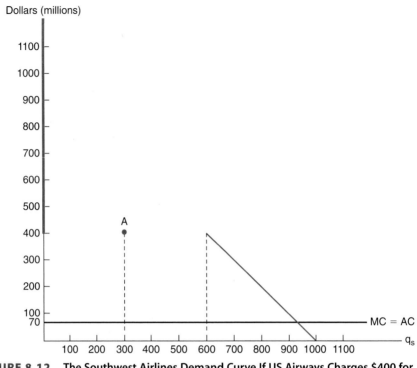

FIGURE 8.12 The Southwest Airlines Demand Curve If US Airways Charges $400 for a Ticket

If Southwest Airlines assumes that US Airways will maintain its fare at $400, its demand curve consists of three segments. If Southwest charges a fare higher than $400, it sells zero tickets. If Southwest charges a fare equal to $400, it sells half the 600 tickets demanded, or 300 tickets at point A. If Southwest charges a fare below $400, it sells all the tickets demanded.

Marginal revenue is negative (notice that Southwest is operating on the bottom half of a linear demand curve, where demand is inelastic), and therefore, any further fare reductions reduce Southwest's total revenues and profit. Southwest's optimal policy is to lower its fare to $399.

But surely, from US Airways' perspective, the game cannot end there. After Southwest lowers its fare to $399, what is US Airways' optimal pricing strategy? If US Airways assumes that Southwest will maintain its fare at $399, then US Airways can charge a fare slightly less than $399 and capture the entire market. If US Airways lowers its fare to $398, its output increases from zero at a fare of $400 to 602 at a fare of $398. US Airways' marginal revenue associated with this price reduction is:

$$MR_{US} = \frac{\Delta TR_{US}}{\Delta q_{US}} = \frac{\$239{,}596 - \$0}{602 - 0} = \frac{\$239{,}596}{602} = \$398.00.$$

Because US Airways's marginal revenue is $398 and marginal cost is $70, US Airways is better off if it reduces its fare to $398.

But now Southwest is left out of the market, unless it lowers its fare to $397, in which case US Airways will respond by lowering its fare to $396. When does the game end? Any fare greater than MC = $70 will result in one airline reducing fares, which

in turn will result in a fare reduction by the other, and so on. Equilibrium occurs only when both fares equal MC = $70, because only then will neither firm have an incentive to reduce its fare further.

Figure 8.13 identifies the reaction functions for Southwest and US Airways. Southwest's reaction function goes through the point ($70, $70), but is not identified for fares below $70, because a fare cut below $70 would result in economic losses; the fare would be below average cost. For all $p_{US} > 70, Southwest charges a fare $p_S = (p_{US} - \$1.00)$; therefore, for $p_{US} > 70, Southwest's reaction function lies at a distance $1.00 to the left of the 45-degree line. Similarly, the US Airways reaction function lies at a distance $1.00 below the 45-degree line. For $p > 70, the two reaction functions will be parallel to each other and also parallel to the 45-degree line where $p_S = p_{US}$. The Nash equilibrium occurs at the intersection point ($70, $70), because this is the only point where both firms are doing the best they can given the choice of their competitor.

We can interpret the Bertrand model as a simultaneous move game. Both firms reason: "If we set our fare at any $p > MC$, then our opponent will set its fare at $p - \epsilon$, and we will sell nothing. But, if we set our fare at $p = MC = 70, then we either capture the entire market or split the market 50-50. We should, therefore, set our fare equal to MC."

Although the implications of the Cournot model seem plausible, the implications of the Bertrand model may at first seem a bit bizarre. In a Bertrand duopoly, price falls to MC, the perfectly competitive price, and there is allocative efficiency. We will not go through the formal analysis, but this extreme result can be made much more reasonable by introducing some product differentiation into the Bertrand model, which we do in Chapter 13.[8] The introduction of product differentiation eliminates the highly implausible "all or nothing" nature of the model and results in an equilibrium price greater than marginal cost.

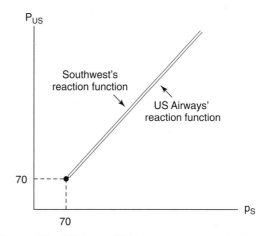

FIGURE 8.13 **A Bertrand Equilibrium with Homogeneous Products**

If Southwest charges a fare above MC = $70, US Airways responds by charging a fare $1.00 less than Southwest's fare, and the US Airways reaction function lies at a distance $1.00 below the 45-degree line. By the same reasoning, Southwest's reaction function lies at a distance $1.00 to the left of the 45-degree line. The Bertrand equilibrium is the Nash equilibrium at the intersection point ($70, $70).

The results of some experimental games support the Bertrand equilibrium. Fouraker and Siegel found that when student players selected prices rather than quantities and were given Bertrand-type profit payoffs, three-player games almost always resulted in the Bertrand outcome.[9] The Bertrand result was also common with two players as long as the players did not have perfect price information about their competitor's price.

Pricing behavior in the airline industry has often appeared consistent with Bertrand price behavior.[10] The major carriers' rationale for this behavior is consistent with the Bertrand model's assumptions. Each of the major carriers fears that if its fares are even slightly higher than the competition, it will lose virtually its entire market share. Other strategic aspects of pricing in the airline industry are discussed in detail in Chapter 11.

APPLICATION 8.7

Bertrand Pricing in the Airline Industry

Consistent with Bertrand price behavior, many airlines have followed a policy of pricing at near-marginal cost on routes where they face competition, especially from low-price carriers such as Southwest Airlines or JetBlue. The carriers' rationale for this behavior is consistent with the Bertrand model assumptions. Each carrier fears that if its fares are even slightly higher than the competition, it will lose nearly its entire market share.

Consider the following fares offered by US Airways over the Internet on August 28, 2002. The distance from Syracuse to Baltimore is almost identical to the distance from Albany to Baltimore.

US Airways competed against Southwest Airlines in the Albany market, but not in the Syracuse market. In the Albany market, US Airways essentially matched Southwest's low fares. In the Syracuse market, US Airways was a virtual monopolist on flights to Baltimore and Raleigh-Durham. US Airways' lowest advanced-purchase fare from Syracuse to Baltimore was 50.4 percent higher than its lowest advanced-purchase fare from Albany to Baltimore, and its lowest fare from Syracuse to Raleigh-Durham was 22.7 percent higher than its lowest fare from Albany to Raleigh-Durham. If Southwest charged fares close to marginal cost, then the Albany fares can be interpreted as Bertrand equilibrium fares. US Airways reasoned that if its Albany fares were higher than Southwest's, it would fly mostly empty planes out of Albany to Baltimore or Raleigh-Durham.

Route	US Airways' Lowest Round-Trip Advanced Fare	Southwest's Lowest Round-Trip Advanced Fare
Syracuse, NY to Baltimore, MD	$173.00	No flights
Albany, NY to Baltimore, MD	$115.00	$120.00
Syracuse, NY to Raleigh-Durham, NC	$216.00	No flights
Albany, NY to Raleigh-Durham, NC	$167.00	$172.00

APPLICATION 8.8

Bounded Rationality, Sluggish Consumers, Internet Pricing, and the Failure to Achieve a Bertrand Equilibrium

One of the important assumptions of the Bertrand model is that all consumers know the prices offered by all sellers. The introduction of Internet shopping sites that allow con-

sumers to instantly compare many sellers' prices on identical items brings this assumption closer to reality, and therefore, should result in closer adherence to Bertrand pricing. Consider, for example, the Internet site shopping.com that enables users to compare prices on thousands of identical items for products ranging from books and clothing to computers and automobiles. If one company's price is higher than another company's price for an identical item, the Bertrand model suggests that all consumers will buy from the lower-priced seller. Yet consider the data below for a Sony model DVP-NS575P DVD player posted at shopping.com on June 18, 2005. Prices range from a low of $51.00 at Ubid.com to a high of $149.29 at, of all places, Amazon.com. The average price at all 10 websites was $93.09.

B&H Photo-Video-Pro Audio	$138.05
Amazon.com	$149.29
eCost.com	$62.43
6ave.com	$89.06
Business-Supply	$93.03
Plasma Creations	$86.26
Everything-4-Electronics	$93.82
Ubid.com	$51.00
Boscovs.com	$69.99
OnlineSavingsDirect.com	$97.95
Average price	$93.09

Several studies of Internet pricing have confirmed that prices typically vary greatly for identical products purchased from different Internet sellers. In one study, Baye and Morgan examined data for the top 100 products sold at Shopper.com on March 26, 2001.* For every product sold by two or more sellers, there was a range of prices, that is, the Bertrand equilibrium was never achieved, even with two sellers. Furthermore, for many products there was a wide variation in sellers' prices.

Why would anyone purchase the Sony NS575P DVD player from Amazon.com for $149.29 instead of from one of the lower-priced sellers? The answer is closely related to an important concept from the theory of the firm in Chapter 2: *bounded rationality*. Recall that the assumption of bounded rationality recognizes that limits on knowledge, foresight, skill, and time constrain individuals' ability to solve complex problems, or perhaps in the case of the Sony DVD player, not-so-complex problems. Baye and Morgan developed a theoretical model in which even relatively small levels of bounded rationality on the part of sellers can result in price offers that diverge and fail to move toward the Bertrand equilibrium. While Baye and Morgan viewed the bounded rationality problem from the sellers' perspective, Hehenkamp viewed the bounded rationality problem from the consumers' perspective and assumed that "some consumers are sluggish consumers if they do not learn sellers' prices with some positive probability."[†] If, for example, some consumers automatically go first to Amazon.com to purchase a Sony DVD player, or almost anything over the Internet, then it may be in Amazon.com's interest to maintain a higher price than other Internet sellers offer for an identical product. Hehenkamp's model suggests that if consumers are not sluggish, the Bertrand equilibrium is attained. However, if consumers are extremely sluggish, meaning the rate at which they gather price information is essentially zero, then each seller charges a monopoly price for its good to those consumers who are informed about it. If consumers are only slightly sluggish, then prices move toward the Bertrand equilibrium.

On a more personal level, it is likely that most readers of this book, including the authors, have purchased an item on the Internet only to find out later that another Internet seller offered the same item for less. Bounded rationality is a problem even for fairly well-informed consumers, not to mention the many uninformed consumers who purchase goods through the Internet.

*Michael R. Baye and John Morgan, "Price Dispersion in the Lab and on the Internet: Theory and Evidence," *Rand Journal of Economics,* 35(August 2004): 450–451.

†Burkhard Hehenkamp, "Sluggish Consumers: An Evolutionary Solution to the Bertrand Paradox," *Games and Economic Behavior* 40 (2002): pp. 44–76. ∎

SUMMARY

1 In this chapter three important oligopoly models were analyzed: the Cournot-Nash model, the Stackelberg model, and the Bertrand model. Each model was built on different assumptions and resulted in different equilibrium outcomes.

2 The Cournot-Nash model is based on the assumption that a firm's competitors maintain their current outputs. The model results in an equilibrium quantity that is greater than the monopoly quantity but less than the competitive quantity.

3 The Cournot-Nash model is commonly used to link the fields of industrial organization and international trade. The Cournot-Nash model indicates that domestic welfare can be increased by the adoption of restrictive trade policies. However, under different assumptions, this model often suggests that industrial policies aimed at increasing domestic welfare by restricting trade have the opposite effect and reduce domestic welfare.

4 In the Stackelberg model, the leader assumes that the follower will respond to the leader's quantity decision by producing on its reaction function. The leader selects a quantity that maximizes profits given the follower's decision to remain on its reaction curve.

5 In the Bertrand model, firms take their competitors' prices, rather than quantities, as fixed. In the absence of product differentiation, the Bertrand model results in a price equal to marginal cost.

6 Empirical evidence and experimental games suggest that some industries behave according to each of the models analyzed in this chapter.

KEY TERMS

Bertrand model

Cournot-Nash equilibrium

reaction function

residual demand curve

Stackelberg follower

Stackelberg leader

Stackelberg model

DISCUSSION QUESTIONS

1. For any given demand and cost conditions, could a Stackelberg leader in a duopoly ever earn *lower* profits than it would earn with a standard Cournot-Nash equilibrium?

2. From the standpoint of allocative efficiency, compare the Cournot-Nash, Stackelberg, and Bertrand equilibriums.

3. The results expressed in the Bertrand model are often referred to as the "Bertrand Paradox." Why do you think this result is considered a paradox?

4. Under certain conditions the Cournot-Nash and Bertrand equilibriums are identical. One of these conditions has to do with the number of firms in the industry. What is this condition?

5. Do you agree with the following statement? Free trade is always better for domestic welfare. Domestic welfare can never be improved by interfering with free trade.

6. Why is it difficult for economists to identify the Cournot-Nash equilibrium in real-world markets? Given this identification difficulty, how do economists attempt to obtain evidence of the existence of Cournot-Nash behavior?

7. Suppose an oligopoly consists of four firms with equal 25 percent market shares. Currently Cournot-Nash behavior is the typical form of pricing behavior in the industry. If two of these firms with identical costs merge, would you anticipate the continuing use of Cournot-Nash pricing by the merged firm? Explain your reasoning.

8. What type of market structure might lead you to suspect the possible use of Stackelberg pricing? How might you expect a Stackelberg market structure to differ from a Cournot-Nash market structure?

9. Consider Application 8.8. Can you think of reasons why many consumers exhibit sluggish behavior? Is sluggish behavior necessarily irrational behavior? Explain your reasoning.

10. In the previous edition of this book, it was assumed that Boeing was the Stackelberg leader and Airbus was the Stackelberg follower in the commercial aircraft industry. In this edition, the roles are purposefully reversed, and Airbus is assumed to be the leader. Why do you think this change was believed to be necessary in 2007? What are the possible implications of this small change in the book for government policy regarding subsidization of global oligopolies?

PROBLEMS

1. Consider the general case of two firms each facing a demand curve $P = a - bq$ and a marginal cost c, where a, b, and c are positive constants. What is the Cournot equilibrium output for each firm in this general case?

2. Suppose an oligopoly consists of three identical firms. Industry demand is $P = 100 - 2Q$ and $MC = AC = 20$. What is the Cournot-Nash equilibrium output in this industry for each firm?

3. Suppose Boeing is a Stackelberg leader and Airbus is the follower in a duopoly, and industry demand and cost conditions are:

$$P = 60 - 2(q_B + q_A)$$
$$MC_B = 10 \quad \text{and} \quad MC_A = 20.$$

What are the Stackelberg equilibrium quantities? What is the Stackelberg equilibrium price?

4. Two duopolists face the following *industry* demand curve:

$$P = f(Q) = \frac{1000}{Q}.$$

$MC = AC = 20$ for each firm. What is the Bertrand equilibrium output for each firm? What is total output in the Bertrand equilibrium?

5. (You need a calculator to answer this question.) One Japanese firm produces widgets and one American firm produces widgets. Both produce with the following total costs:

$$TC = 250 + 40q.$$

The only demand for widgets is in the United States and is $P = 100 - Q$. MC $= 40$. What is the Cournot-Nash equilibrium for the duopolists?

Suppose the United States government places a tariff (tax) of 10 per widget on Japanese widgets sold in the United States, while American widgets continue to be sold tax-free.

a. Assuming Cournot-Nash behavior, what is the new equilibrium output for each firm?

b. What is the Cournot-Nash equilibrium price?

c. What is the impact of the tariff on American welfare?

6. Consider a market with two identical firms. The market demand is $P = 26 - 2Q$, where $Q = q_a + q_b$. $MC_a = MC_b = AC_a = AC_b = 2$.

a. Solve for the Cournot reaction functions of each firm.

b. Solve for the Cournot-Nash equilibrium. Calculate the quantity, price, and profit for each firm.

7. Consider a market with two identical firms. The market demand is $P = 26 - 2Q$, where $Q = q_a + q_b$. $MC_a = MC_b = AC_a = AC_b = 2$.

a. Solve for output and price with collusion.

b. Assume that the firms initially split the collusive output evenly. Show that Firm A has an incentive to increase output by 1 unit. Does Firm B also have an incentive to increase output?

8. Consider a market with two identical firms. The market demand is $P = 26 - 2Q$, where $Q = q_a + q_b$. $MC_a = MC_b = AC_a = AC_b = 2$. Now assume this market has a Stackelberg leader, Firm A. Solve for the quantity, price, and profit for each firm.

9. Consider a market with two firms. The market demand is $P = 26 - 2Q$, where $Q = q_a + q_b$. Assume Firm A has a lower MC than Firm B. $MC_a = AC_a = 2$ and $MC_b = AC_b = 2.5$. This difference in cost functions provides better justification for existence of a Stackelberg leader.

a. Which firm would you expect to be the Stackelberg leader? Why?

b. Solve for Firm B's Cournot reaction function.

c. Solve for Firm A's demand curve.

d. Solve for the Stackelberg quantity, price, and profit for each firm.

10. Consider a market with two identical firms. The market demand is $P = 26 - 2Q$, where $Q = q_a + q_b$. $MC_a = MC_b = AC_a = AC_b = 2$. Assume there is no product differentiation in this case and the firms follow a Bertrand pricing model. Solve for the Bertrand equilibrium: Calculate output for each firm, and price and profit as well.

11. In questions 6, 7, 8, 9, and 10, we have used the same demand function to solve for the Cournot, collusive, Stackelberg, Stackelberg with different costs, and Bertrand outcomes. Compare the results of these five different models in terms of price, output for each firm, total market output, profit for each firm, and total industry profits. Comment on the differences. Which outcomes are best from an economic perspective? Which are worst?

NOTES

1. Augustin Cournot, *Recherches sur les principes mathematiques de la theorie des richesses* (Paris: M. Riviere & Cie., 1938). Translated in *Researches into the Mathematical Principles of Wealth* (New York: A.M. Kelly, 1960).

2. The concept was introduced by Arthur L. Bowley, *The Mathematical Groundwork of Economics* (Oxford: Oxford University Press, 1924).

3. See William Novshek, "Cournot Equilibrium with Free Entry," *Review of Economic Studies* (April 1980): 473–486; and Jean Tirole, *The Theory of Industrial Organization* (Cambridge, MA: MIT Press, 1988), pp. 218–221.

4. Major contributions include: J.A. Brander and B.J. Spencer, "International R&D Rivalry and Industrial Strategy," *Review of Economic Studies* 50 (1983): 707–722; J.A. Brander and B.J. Spencer, "Export Subsidies and International Market Share Rivalry," *Journal of International Economics* 18 (1985): 227–242; A.K. Dixit and G.M. Grossman, "Targeted Export Promotion with Several Oligopolistic Industries," *Journal of International Economics* 21 (1986): 233–250; J. Eaton and G.M. Grossman, "Optimal Trade and Industrial Policy Under Oligopoly," *Quarterly Journal of Economics* 101 (1985): 383–406; I. Horstmann and J.R. Markusen, "Up the Average Cost Curve: Inefficient Entry and the New Protectionism," *Journal of International Economics* 20 (1986): 225–248; P.R. Krugman, "Import Protection as Export Promotion: International Competition in the Presence of Oligopoly and Economies of Scale," in H. Kierzkowski (ed.), *Monopolistic Competition in International Trade* (Oxford: Oxford University Press, 1984); and A.J. Venables, "Trade and Trade Policy with Imperfect Competition: The Case of Identical Products and Free Trade," *Journal of International Economics* 19 (1974): 1–20.

5. I. Horstmann and J.R. Markusen, "Up the Average Cost Curve: Inefficient Entry and the New Protectionism," *Journal of International Economics* 20 (1986): 225–248.

6. The original work was in Heinrich von Stackelberg, *Marktform und Gleichgewicht* (Vienna: Springer, 1934).

7. Bertrand's model was developed in a critical review of Cournot published 45 years after the original article in Joseph Bertrand, book review of "Recherches sur les Principes Mathematiques de la Theorie des Richesses," in *Journal de Savants* 67 (1883): 499–508.

8. For a fairly simple treatment of the introduction of product differentiation into the Bertrand model, see Eric Rasmusen, *Games and Information: An Introduction to Game Theory* (Oxford: Basil Blackwell, 1989), pp. 267–269.

9. Lawrence Fouraker and Signey Siegel, *Bargaining Behavior* (New York: McGraw-Hill, 1963).

10. "The Airline Mess," *Business Week* (July 6, 1992): 50–55.

 ## INTERNET EXERCISES

Visit www.aw-bc.com/waldman_jensen for this chapter's web exercises. Answer our real-world economics problems by searching the Internet for solutions!

Collusion: The Great Prisoner's Dilemma

F ew topics in industrial organization have attracted the attention of economists more than collusion. Models of overt and tacit collusion have abounded since Adam Smith declared:[1]

> People of the same trade seldom meet together, even for merriment and diversion, but the conversation ends in a conspiracy against the public, or in some contrivance to raise prices.

Intuitively, one of the best methods for solving the prisoner's dilemma should be **overt collusion,** in which a group of competitors sit down to discuss and set price. One tremendous mitigating circumstance against the effective use of overt or **explicit collusion** in the United States and Europe is that it is illegal. Of course, so is running a red light, drug possession, and prostitution; and overt price fixing, despite its illegality, has been tried from time to time with varying degrees of success. Because overt collusion is illegal in the United States, most efforts to fix prices are tacit rather than overt or explicit. **Tacit collusion** results when different firms set identical prices without ever meeting to discuss prices because of a "meeting of the minds," whereby competitors recognize that it is in all their best interests to avoid price competition.

Recently, economists have recognized that because of the **prisoner's dilemma,** it is often difficult to maintain collusive agreements for very long.[2] Yet, exceptions occur. In the past, successful collusion existed for years and even decades in some industries, including steel, cement, glucose, oil, vitamins, electrical equipment, and tobacco. Why do some attempts to fix prices work, and others fail miserably? In an effort to answer this question, this chapter explores the major theoretical approaches to collusion. We then turn to U.S. antitrust policy toward collusion. Empirical evidence of effective methods of collusion is presented in Chapter 10. We begin here with a return to the prisoner's dilemma model of Chapter 7.

9.1 The Prisoner's Dilemma Revisited

I n Chapter 7, the prisoner's dilemma was introduced. It was shown that in any finite prisoner's dilemma game, like the one depicted in Table 7.2, the players will always play the dominant strategy of *low price, low price.* Table 7.2 is basically reproduced here

as Table 9.1, except that the two options have been changed from *High price, Low price* to *Collude, Defect.*

In this chapter we use the term ***perfect collusion*** to indicate that the firms are producing the joint profit-maximizing output. Table 9.1 shows that if General Electric and Westinghouse are able to perfectly collude, they each earn a profit of 100, but if they each defect (i.e., charge a low price), they each earn 80. If only one defects, it earns 120, whereas the other firm earns 25. The dilemma for both firms is how to remain at the perfectly collusive result when each has an incentive to cheat.

Suppose General Electric and Westinghouse believe the game represented by Table 9.1 will go on forever, that is, the game is an ***infinite game.*** This is not an unreasonable assumption for modern corporations that anticipate survival for many years into the future. In an infinite game, firms can adopt strategies today to affect future outcomes. What strategies enable firms to achieve the joint profit-maximizing result? Consider the necessary characteristics of a solution to the dilemma. The firms must establish an environment in which each believes the other will stick to the collusive high-price policy. Intuitively, any solution to the dilemma has to be characterized by: (1) an ability to detect cheating and (2) an ability to punish cheaters. In the absence of these two conditions, firms will have such a strong incentive to defect that the result will almost certainly be the dominant strategy of *Defect, Defect.*

Recall from our discussion of the Mumbles–Big Boy example in Chapter 7 that an effective solution to the dilemma for the mob is to ensure that all squealers will be killed. This solution to the Mumbles–Big Boy game has both characteristics. The mob can identify the squealer (cheater) by observing the trial or the pretrial plea bargaining, and the mob has the ability to enact swift punishment. The death threat is extremely effective.

Short of a death threat, are there strategies that will enable firms to reach the cooperative solution? In an attempt to find the best solution to the prisoner's dilemma, political scientist Robert Axelrod invited world-renowned game theorists to try to solve the dilemma.[3] In Axelrod's first competition, 14 theorists submitted computer programs. Each program was run a total of 15 times: once in head-to-head competition against each of the other 13 programs, once against a random computer-generated choice, and once against itself. The entrants knew that the game would last 200 rounds. The winner of Axelrod's tournament was Anatol Rapoport, who used a relatively simple strategy known as ***tit-for-tat.****

TABLE 9.1 Profits (General Electric, Westinghouse)

		Westinghouse Action	
		Collude	*Defect*
GE Action	**Collude**	100, 100	25, 120
	Defect	120, 25	80, 80

*It is interesting to note that Axelrod later ran his tournament with one slight modification. Instead of knowing that the game would last 200 rounds, there was a probability equal to 0.00346 that the game would end on any given round. Once again Rapoport and tit-for-tat won. Eric Rasmusen, *Games and Information: An Introduction to Game Theory* (Oxford UK: Basil Blackwell, 1989), p. 120.

A tit-for-tat player adopts the following strategy:

1. Start off in the first round cooperating.

2. In every subsequent round, adopt your opponent's strategy in the previous round (e.g., in round N, adopt your opponent's strategy in round N − 1).

Despite the fact that tit-for-tat *never* beat any of the other 13 strategies in head-to-head competition, it still won the overall contest! How? By piling up relatively good showings against every other strategy.

APPLICATION 9.1

Tit-for-Tat in Baseball

Tit-for-tat is one of the oldest strategies in baseball and has been used for over 100 years by pitchers to protect their own batters from being thrown at by opposing pitchers. One classic example of tit-for-tat occurred in Game Three of the 2003 American League Championship series when Roger Clemens of the New York Yankees pitched against Pedro Martinez of the Boston Red Sox. The Red Sox scored two runs in the first inning, but the Yankees scored a run in the second inning and another run in the third to tie the game. In the top of the fourth inning the Yankees took a 3–2 lead, and immediately after the Yankees took the lead, Martinez threw a fastball at the head of Yankee batter Karim Garcia. Garcia was awarded first base because he was hit by the pitch.

The Yankees were convinced that Martinez had purposefully thrown at Garcia's head. When the Red Sox came to bat in the fourth inning, Clemens threw a fastball right over the head of Red Sox star Manny Ramirez, both benches cleared, and a brawl ensued. The most famous image of the brawl was Martinez throwing 72-year-old Yankee coach Don Zimmer to the ground by grabbing Zimmer's face. Before the game was over, with the Yankees winning 4–3, the Boston police charged two Yankee players with assaulting a member of the Red Sox ground crew.

Both Martinez and Clemens denied they were intentionally throwing at Garcia and Ramirez, respectively, but the history and tradition of baseball suggest a different story. Clemens was almost certainly playing tit-for-tat with Martinez and retaliating for Martinez's throw at Garcia's head. After Martinez threw at Garcia, everyone watching the game at Fenway Park or on television or listening on the radio knew that Clemens would throw at a Red Sox player at some point in the game.

Pitchers have known since the invention of the game of baseball that there are several major advantages associated with keeping batters concerned about the possibility of a high inside pitch. First, batters can't possibly hit a high inside pitch and sometimes even if the batter is awarded first base because the ball hits him, it causes less damage for the pitcher than throwing the batter a pitch he can hit. Second, in some rare circumstances the pitcher may actually want to cause a minor injury to a batter; for example, if the batter is an opposing pitcher who has just hit one of the pitcher's teammates. Finally, pitching "high and tight" reduces the willingness of many batters to stand close to the plate, giving the pitcher a big advantage because batters standing far away from the plate cannot hit strikes thrown on the outside part of home plate.

Pitchers have always thrown some pitches close to batters' heads. In fact, it is somewhat remarkable that, given the many advantages of throwing "up-and-in," more pitches are not thrown close to batters' heads. The reason for the relatively small per-

centage of pitches thrown close to a batter is that pitchers play a classic tit-for-tat game with each other. The rules of the game are simple: If you avoid throwing at my hitters, I will avoid throwing at yours. However, if you *ever* throw at one of my hitters, I will retaliate by either throwing at you when you bat (the preferred response in the National League, where pitchers bat) or at another hitter (the preferred response in the American League, where pitchers do not bat because of the designated hitter rule). If the Clemens–Martinez match-up had occurred in the National League in 2005 when Clemens was pitching for the Houston Astros and Martinez was pitching for the New York Mets, Clemens probably would have thrown at Martinez's head when he batted next. How well does tit-for-tat work in preventing hit batters? Data suggest that the strategy works very well because less than 1 in 100 major league at bats result in a batter getting hit. In fact, for most of baseball's history, less than 1 in 200 at bats have resulted in a hit batter.

Because National League pitchers have to hit but American League pitchers do not, it has been hypothesized that National League pitchers would be *less* likely to hit batters because they face direct retaliation when they bat. This hypothesis has recently been tested by Bradbury and Drinen using detailed batting histories from both leagues.* Controlling for batter quality, pitcher quality, retaliation situations, and game situations (for example, how many men on base, how many outs, and whether the game was close, etc.), they found that a batter was significantly more likely to be hit by a pitch when the designated hitter rule was in effect. Bradbury and Drinen also found that when a pitcher batted, he was statistically more likely to be hit with a pitch if he had hit a batter in the previous half-inning.

Tit-for-tat has been an effective method of limiting the number of hit batters for over a century; however, in 1994 Major League Baseball decided to limit the use of this strategy by changing the rules so that after a first batter is hit in a game, both teams are given a warning that the next time any pitcher hits a batter, the pitcher will be ejected from the game. This rule is known as the double-warning rule. One unintended consequence of the double-warning rule has been an increase in the number of batters hit by pitches because a team that hits a batter first has less fear of direct retaliation. Following the imposition of the double-warning rule, the incidence of batters getting hit by pitches *increased* significantly, especially in the National League, where the new rules provide some degree of protection for pitchers who bat after they hit an opposing player with a pitch. Major League Baseball was better served by the tit-for-tat equilibrium than by its attempt to limit the number of hit batters through direct regulation.

*John Charles Bradbury and Douglas J. Drinen, "Crime and Punishment in Major League Baseball: The Case of the Designated Hitter and Hit Batter," working paper, The University of the South, June 16, 2005, *bradbury.sewanee.edu/BD1_IMH.pdf.* ∎

To understand how tit-for-tat works, consider the following Jensen–Waldman Mini Tournament, where Jensen plays tit-for-tat and Waldman plays the dominant strategy. As in the Axelrod tournament, the strategies will be pitted against each other and then they will be pitted against an opponent playing the same strategy. The game will be played according to the payoffs in Table 9.2. Begin with Jensen playing tit-for-tat against Waldman playing the dominant strategy. Waldman, of course, will defect in every round. We know that Waldman must win the head-to-head competition because the dominant strategy always beats or ties against any other strategy (it ties

TABLE 9.2 Profits (Jensen, Waldman)

		Waldman Action	
		Collude	*Defect*
Jensen Action	**Collude**	100, 100	25, 120
	Defect	120, 25	80, 80

against another dominant strategy player). Based on the information in Table 9.2, we consider what happens in such a game.

Assume for simplicity that Jensen and Waldman value a dollar earned today as equivalent to a dollar earned any time in the future, so the discount rate is $i = 0$. Later in this chapter this simplifying assumption is eliminated.

A round-by-round depiction of the Jensen versus Waldman game would look as follows:

Round	Jensen Strategy (Profits) Plays Tit-for-Tat	Waldman Strategy (Profits) Plays Dominant Strategy
1	Collude (25)	Defect (120)
2	Defect (80)	Defect (80)
3	Defect (80)	Defect (80)
⋮	⋮ ⋮	⋮ ⋮
200	Defect (80)	Defect (80)
Total Profits:	Jensen = 15,945	Waldman = 16,040

In the first round Jensen uses the tit-for-tat strategy and plays *collude*. Waldman plays the dominant strategy in the prisoner's dilemma game and defects. Waldman wins the first round and earns 120. Jensen loses the first round and earns 25. In round 2, Jensen plays Waldman's round 1 strategy and defects. Waldman continues to play the dominant strategy and defects. In round 2 they each earn 80. In every subsequent round they both defect and earn 80. The 200-round totals: Waldman—16,040, Jensen—15,945. Waldman has "won," but it is surely a Pyrrhic victory because if they had reached the perfectly collusive result, they each would have earned profits of 20,000 (100×200).

In the Axelrod tournament, each strategy was also pitted against itself. Consider a game in which Jensen plays tit-for-tat against another tit-for-tat player. A round-by-round tit-for-tat versus tit-for-tat game would look as follows:

Round	Jensen Plays Tit-for-Tat	Player 2 Plays Tit-for-Tat
1	Collude (100)	Collude (100)
2	Collude (100)	Collude (100)
3	Collude (100)	Collude (100)
⋮	⋮ ⋮	⋮ ⋮
200	Collude (100)	Collude (100)
Total Profits:	Jensen = 20,000	Player 2 = 20,000

In tit-for-tat versus tit-for-tat, defections never occur, and each player earns the maximum 20,000.

By contrast, consider a game in which Waldman plays against another dominant strategy player. Defections *always* occur, and each player earns only 16,000. A round-by-round Waldman dominant strategy versus another player's dominant strategy game would look as follows:

Round	Waldman Plays Dominant Strategy	Player 2 Plays Dominant Strategy
1	Defect (80)	Defect (80)
2	Defect (80)	Defect (80)
3	Defect (80)	Defect (80)
⋮	⋮ ⋮	⋮ ⋮
200	Defect (80)	Defect (80)
Total Profits:	Waldman = 16,000	Player 2 = 16,000

Even in our greatly simplified tournament, Jensen's tit-for-tat easily defeats Waldman's dominant strategy in combined profits as follows:

Combined Profits in the Two Games for Each Strategy

Jensen's Profits Using Tit-for-Tat
 Game 1—Jensen v. Waldman
 Jensen's Profits—15,945
 Waldman's Profits—16,040
 Game 2—Jensen v. Another Tit-for-Tat Player
 Jensen's Profits—20,000
Jensen's Tit-for-Tat Combined Profits = 15,945 + 20,000 + 35,945.

Waldman's Profits Using the Dominant Strategy
 Game 1—Waldman v. Jensen
 Jensen's Profits—15,945
 Waldman's Profits—16,040
 Game 2—Waldman v. Another Dominant Strategy Player
 Waldman's Profits—16,000
Waldman's Dominant Strategy Combined Profits = 16,040 + 16,000 = 32,040.

In the Jensen–Waldman Mini Tournament, Jensen playing tit-for-tat wins 35,945 to 32,040. However, in terms of wins and losses, Jensen had a record of zero wins, one loss, and one tie; and Waldman had a record of one win, zero losses, and one tie. In the real Axelrod tournament, tit-for-tat won in exactly the same manner, by doing reasonably well against every other strategy, despite losing 7 of the 14 head-to-head competitions. Its overall record in the Axelrod Tournament was a weak zero wins, seven losses, and seven ties; yet it won.[4]

Does tit-for-tat solve the prisoner's dilemma? Not really. It does not guarantee that the collusive price will be maintained in all, or even most, rounds, yet it won by exhibiting several important properties: It is relatively *nice* toward competitors; it *punishes* all defections; and it *forgives* defectors who return to the fold. Tit-for-tat is

nice in the sense that it never initiates an aggressive action. It is aggressive in the sense that it punishes all aggressive moves, even first-time defections, and it is forgiving in that it rewards defectors who revert to cooperation by also reverting to cooperation.

According to Axelrod, the niceness characteristic was tit-for-tat's most important advantage.[5] Virtually all of the highly rated strategies submitted to Axelrod were nice. In fact, each of the top eight ranking strategies was nice in the sense that it was *never* the first to defect until very close to the end of the game. The nice entries did much better than the more aggressive entries in terms of average scores.[6]

One major lesson to be learned from the victory of tit-for-tat in Axelrod's tournament is the importance of being able to recognize and punish defectors. But it would be incorrect to generalize tit-for-tat's victory into an implication that oligopolists should simply adopt the tit-for-tat strategy in all circumstances. Tit-for-tat has some glaring weaknesses as a solution to the prisoner's dilemma. For one thing, in a single-elimination tournament, such as the NCAA basketball tournament, tit-for-tat would be knocked out early. If our simple Jensen–Waldman tournament had been a single-elimination tournament, Jensen's tit-for-tat would have been defeated and eliminated by Waldman's dominant strategy in the first round. For another thing, in a game with *uncertain* and *incomplete* information where the nonplayer nature randomly enters the game once in a while and selects *defect* as the move to be played by one of the players, two tit-for-tat players competing against each other fare very poorly.*

To understand why two tit-for-tat players fare very poorly in such a game, consider a 200-round game played by General Electric and Westinghouse where nature randomly selects *defect once for each firm* between round 2 and round 10, but otherwise both firms always play tit-for-tat. Recall Table 9.1 shows the payoff matrix. The pattern in such a game would be:

Round	GE Strategy (Profits)	Westinghouse Strategy (Profits)
1	Collude (100)	Collude (100)
2	Collude (100)	Collude (100)
3	*Nature selects* defect (120)	Collude (25)
4	Collude (25)	Defect (120)
5	Defect (120)	Collude (25)
6	Collude (25)	Defect (120)
7	Defect (120)	Collude (25)
8	Collude (25)	Defect (120)
9	Defect (80)	*Nature selects* defect (80)
10	Defect (80)	Defect (80)
11	Defect (80)	Defect (80)
12	Defect (80)	Defect (80)
⋮	⋮ ⋮	⋮ ⋮
200	Defect (80)	Defect (80)
Total Profits:	15,995	15,995

*Recall from Chapter 7 that many games require a nonplayer (nature) to take random actions at some point in a game. If a game includes nature, but nature does not move first, or nature's first move is observed by all players, the game is of *complete information*. Furthermore, if nature never moves after any other player moves, then the game is said to be of *certain information*. In the game being played here, nature moves after a move by another player, and nature's move is not observed by both players; therefore, the game is a game of *incomplete and uncertain information*.

In this game with incomplete and uncertain information, either firm would earn higher profits by playing the dominant strategy and earning either 16,040 if its opponent played tit-for-tat or 16,000 if its opponent played the dominant strategy.

If both firms behaved even more nicely and played tit-for-*two*-tats, however, they would have fared much better. Suppose that General Electric and Westinghouse play tit-for-two-tats, with nature randomly selecting *defect* once for each firm between round 2 and round 10. Such a game would have the following pattern:

Round	GE Strategy (Profits)	Westinghouse Strategy (Profits)
1	Collude (100)	Collude (100)
2	Collude (100)	Collude (100)
3	*Nature selects* defect (120)	Collude (25)
4	Collude (100)	Collude (100)
5	Collude (100)	Collude (100)
6	Collude (100)	Collude (100)
7	Collude (100)	Collude (100)
8	Collude (100)	Collude (100)
9	Collude (25)	*Nature selects* defect (120)
10	Collude (100)	Collude (100)
11	Collude (100)	Collude (100)
12	Collude (100)	Collude (100)
⋮	⋮	⋮
200	Collude (100)	Collude (100)
Total Profits:	19,945	19,945

Thus if General Electric and Westinghouse are just a bit nicer and allow for one unpunished defection, their profits increase from 15,995 to 19,945, an increase of 24.7 percent. The decision to play the more aggressive tit-for-tat strategy would cost each firm a great deal of profit. In Axelrod's first tournament, a strategy of tit-for-two-tats would have won.[7]

Just as nature randomly selects *defect* in the above games and this random defection can destroy effective collusion, in the real world of oligopolistic competition a price reduction or defection can be misinterpreted by competitors as an aggressive act, leading to a large decline in price unless competitors behave nicely.

APPLICATION 9.2

A Real-World Example of "Nice" Behavior in Response to Random or "Accidental" Defections Automobiles*

After World War II, General Motors was the dominant firm in the automobile market. Until the late 1970s, the automobile manufacturers announced price changes once each year when the new models were introduced in the fall. The typical pricing policy was for Ford and Chrysler to match General Motors' percentage price increases. Sometimes, however, Ford or Chrysler would introduce their new car models before General Motors introduced its new cars. In those years Ford and Chrysler would try to guess how large GM's price increases would be and announce their price increases accordingly. If they guessed "too high," Ford and Chrysler would lower their prices to match GM's price

increases. This is not surprising because Ford and Chrysler had to be competitive with the industry leader.

In 1956, 1970, and 1974, however, Ford and Chrysler introduced their new cars first and guessed "too low"—GM later announced higher price increases. Ford and Chrysler clearly preferred lower price increases than GM in 1956, 1970, and 1974, and Ford and Chrysler could have used those lower prices to gain market share at GM's expense. Instead, in each of those three years, Ford and Chrysler behaved "nicely" and revised their price increases upward to match GM's increases. By behaving nicely, Ford and Chrysler were able to maintain industry pricing stability and avoid a potential downward price spiral.

*U.S. Senate, Committee on the Judiciary, Subcommittee on Antitrust and Monopoly, Report, *Administered Prices: Automobiles* (Washington, DC: Government Printing Office, 1958), pp. 53–54 and 67–69; "Chrysler Increases Prices Again For '71, Following G.M. Pattern," *New York Times* (December 2, 1970): 35; and "Ford Motor Adds to Boost on '75 Models; Price Rise Will Near G.M.'s Almost 10%," *The Wall Street Journal* (August 21, 1974): 3. ∎

9.2 Another Strategy for Maintaining Effective Collusion: Trigger Price Strategies[8]

In Chapter 8 the Bertrand equilibrium in a finite game played by two firms, Boeing and Airbus, was identified as P = MC. Recall the basic conditions of the Bertrand game in Chapter 8: The firms produce a homogeneous product, industry demand is P = 100 − Q, and MC = AC = \$10 for both firms. If the firms could solve the prisoner's dilemma and engage in perfect collusion, the joint profit-maximizing quantity of 45 would be produced and price would equal \$55. However, given Bertrand behavioral assumptions, Q = 90 and P = \$10.

Now consider an infinitely repeated version of this game played with both firms following the behavioral rules listed:

1. Start by cooperating and charging the joint profit-maximizing price P = \$55.

2. Continue to charge the joint profit-maximizing price P = \$55 *unless* the other player lowers price below P = \$55, in which case charge the Bertrand equilibrium price P = \$10 forever.

The strategy in this game is referred to as a ***trigger price strategy*** because even a single deviation from cooperation ends cooperation forever. Because of the swift and aggressive punishment associated with defecting in this game, this strategy is also often called the ***grim strategy.***

Suppose Staples and Office Depot play the grim strategy game. What is the equilibrium? If the two firms engage in perfect collusion, P = \$55, $q_S = q_{OD} = 22.5$, and $\pi = Q(P - AC) = 22.5(\$55 - \$10) = \$1012.50$ for each firm. In this case the firms share the industry's jointly maximized profit of \$2025. Using the results of the discussion of present value and discounting in Chapter 3, we find that if both firms cooperate forever beginning at time t = 0, the present value of profits for each is:

$$\pi_{pv}^{collude} = \sum_{t=0}^{\infty} \frac{\$1012.50}{(1 + i)^t} = \frac{1012.50(1 + i)}{i}.$$

Suppose Staples decides to defect in period t = 0 and charge a price P = $55 − ϵ. The price P is *infinitesimally* less than $55. Staples would then capture the *entire* market (remember the product is homogeneous) in period t = 0, and Staples would earn an amount *infinitesimally* less than $2025. By the grim strategy, however, in every subsequent round P = $10 and economic profits are zero because P = $10 = AC. The present value of Staples's profits would then be:

$$\pi_{pv}^{defect} = \$2025 - \epsilon + \sum_{t=1}^{\infty} \$0 = \$2025 - \epsilon.$$

Should Staples cooperate? It makes sense to cooperate as long as the following condition is met:

$$\pi_{pv}^{collude} > \pi_{pv}^{defect}$$

or if

$$\frac{\$1012.50(1 + i)}{i} \geq \$2025 \Rightarrow i \leq 1.$$

Defecting only makes sense if i > 1. A discount rate i > 1 (or a discount rate above 100 percent), however, would imply that Staples cares little about future profits and is willing to sacrifice more than $200 in profits next year in return for just $100 in profits this year. Such a high discount rate, although not impossible, is quite improbable in the world of modern corporations. In the real world, firms' discount rates will typically be much less than 1 because firms place considerable value on future profits as well as on current profits. Economists typically assume a discount rate in the range of 5 percent to 10 percent (0.05–0.10) as being reasonable. A discount rate of 10 percent implies that Staples is willing to sacrifice $110 in profits next year in return for $100 in profits this year.

As long as i ≤ 1, the equilibrium in the grim strategy game is for both firms to *always* charge the perfectly collusive price P = $55 and share maximum joint profits in each period. Intuitively, the reason for this result is that if a firm charges a price below the monopoly price in any period, it gains *all* of the monopoly profits in that period, but for one period only; then the price cutter earns economic profits equal to zero forever. In this game even a small price cut triggers a punitive response that lowers price to marginal cost, and therefore the collusive result holds for all periods.*

9.3 Collusive Agreements as Viewed by One Firm in a Cartel

Suppose a cartel consists of many firms. How will any one firm view its best alternative given the choices of the other firms? Consider a hypothetical firm, the "MidEast Corporation." Suppose, in Figure 9.1, the cartel price has been set by an

*The grim strategy provided a formal game theoretic foundation for successful perfect collusion, but there is a problem with the result. If instead of the perfectly collusive price P = $55, the two firms began the game by charging any price between $10 and $55, and then adopted the grim strategy, the initial price would also be a valid equilibrium price. This result is known as the **Folk Theorem** because it was part of the oral tradition or "folk wisdom" among game theorists long before it was published.

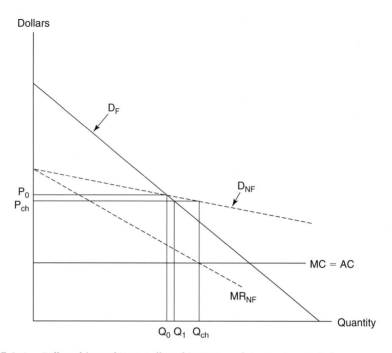

FIGURE 9.1 **Followship and Non-Followship Demand Curves in a Cartel**

If the cartel's joint profit-maximizing price is P_0 and all cartel members including MidEast abide by the price P_0, then MidEast's demand curve is D_F, which is called a *followship demand curve*. If MidEast secretly reduces its price below P_0 and the other cartel members maintain their prices at P_0, then MidEast steals buyers away and moves along its more elastic *non-followship demand curve* D_{NF}.

explicit agreement at P_0, the cartel's joint profit-maximizing price. If *all* cartel members *always* abide by the cartel price then MidEast's demand curve can be calculated as D_F, where D_F is called a ***followship demand curve*** because it assumes that MidEast is simply following the price of all other cartel members. The cartel's price, P_0, may or may not be the price for which $MR_F = MC$ for MidEast.

MidEast Corporation can consider two broad pricing options: (1) maintaining the price at P_0 or (2) attempting to *secretly* reduce its price below P_0. If MidEast is able to secretly reduce its price relative to other cartel members, then it should be able to steal buyers away and move along its ***non-followship demand curve***, D_{NF}, which is drawn under the assumption that MidEast alone changes price while all other firms price at P_0. D_{NF}, therefore, will be more elastic than D_F. For prices below P_0, D_{NF} is simply a *cheating on the cartel* demand curve. If MidEast decides to cheat, then profit maximization calls for an expansion of output to Q_{ch} and a lowering of price to P_{ch}.

Of course, if MidEast thinks it can cheat without being detected, why wouldn't every other cartel member think the same way? And if each and every member of the cartel believed that it could cheat without being detected, then each firm would lower price, and MidEast would move along its *followship demand curve* D_F. If every firm

behaved exactly like MidEast and cut price to P_{ch}, then MidEast would operate on D_F and sell only Q_1 units. Because P_0 represents the cartel's joint profit-maximizing price, industry profits must decline when the industry's price declines to P_{ch}.

The MidEast situation is simply another example of the prisoner's dilemma. A price reduction is a dominant solution for MidEast because it is MidEast's best option no matter what strategy is adopted by the other cartel members. If the other members maintain price at P_0, then MidEast should move along its non-followship demand curve and cut price to P_{ch}. On the other hand, if the other cartel members reduce price below P_0, then MidEast would experience a dramatic reduction in sales unless it matched the price reduction.

Previously we stated that "the cartel's price, P_0, may or may not be the price for which $MR_F = MC$ for MidEast." If P_0 is the joint profit-maximizing price, shouldn't it be the price for which $MC = MR_F$ for MidEast and every other member? If all firms face identical costs of production and there is no significant product differentiation, then P_0 should be the price for which $MC = MR_F$ for MidEast. If the firms have differing costs, however, or if product differentiation is significant, then P_0 will be a compromise price that is unlikely to coincide with MidEast's desired profit-maximizing price.

Figures 9.2(a) through 9.2(c) depict a situation where duopolists in retailing have differing costs. Wal-Mart is the low-cost producer and Sears is the high-cost firm. In panel 9.2(a) industry demand is:

$$P = 100 - \tfrac{1}{2}Q = 100 - \tfrac{1}{2}(q_W + q_S).$$

Therefore, by the "twice-as-steep rule," marginal revenue is:

$$MR = 100 - (q_W + q_S).$$

Assume there is no product differentiation, and therefore, if the firms charge the same price, they split the demand curve. In panels 9.2(b) and 9.2(c), the equal shares demand curves are drawn as:

$$p_W = 100 - q_W \quad \text{and} \quad p_S = 100 - q_S.$$

By the "twice-as-steep rule," the firms' equal shares marginal revenue curves are:

$$mr_W = 100 - 2q_W \quad \text{and} \quad mr_S = 100 - 2q_S.$$

In Figures 9.2(b) and 9.2(c), the firms have the following cost curves:

$$FC = \$150$$
$$mc_W = 40 + 2q_W \quad \text{and} \quad mc_S = 50 + 2q_S.$$

Equating mc and mr in panels (b) and (c) yields the following preferred profit-maximizing quantity and price for Wal-Mart and Sears, respectively:

$$q_W = 15 \quad \text{and} \quad p_W = \$85.00$$
$$q_S = 12.5 \quad \text{and} \quad p_S = \$87.50.$$

Not surprisingly, the high-cost firm, Sears, prefers a price that is higher than that of the low-cost producer Wal-Mart. Furthermore, note that the two firms have different marginal costs at their preferred profit-maximizing quantities, with $mc_W = \$70$ and $mc_S = \$75$. Because joint profit maximization requires that the marginal cost of production be equal for both firms, this outcome is clearly not the joint profit-maximizing result.

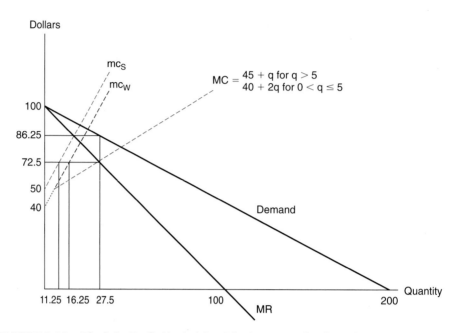

FIGURE 9.2A The Joint Profit-Maximizing Price in a Duopoly Where the Firms Have Different Costs

Suppose Wal-Mart and Sears can produce with different marginal costs $mc_w = 40 + 2q_w$ and $mc_s = 50 + 2q_s$, respectively. If they collude, they minimize the cartel's costs by producing each additional unit at the lowest possible marginal cost, which requires that marginal cost must be equal for both firms. The marginal cost of production for both firms combined is the horizontal summation of the two marginal cost curves, which is $MC = 45 + q$ for $q > 5$. If demand is $p = 100 - \frac{1}{2}Q$, marginal revenue is $MR = 100 - Q$; $MC = MR$ for $Q = 27.5$ and $p = \$86.25$, and marginal cost is $\$72.5$ in each plant. Sears produces 11.25 units and Wal-Mart produces 16.25 units.

How do these preferred prices compare with the joint profit-maximizing price? To determine the joint profit-maximizing price, the *industry* marginal cost curve must be equated to the *industry* marginal revenue curve. This is done in Figure 9.2 (a). Notice that the industry marginal cost curve is derived by adding the two individual marginal cost curves *horizontally*, not vertically, to yield:*

*For marginal costs between 40 and 50, only the low-cost firm Wal-Mart's marginal cost curve is relevant, so for industry outputs between 0 and 5 the marginal cost curve is simply $MC = 40 + 2Q$.

For marginal costs greater than 50, the industry's marginal cost curve is derived by adding the *quantities* for any given marginal cost as follows:

$$mc_w = 40 + 2q_w \quad \text{or} \quad q_w = \tfrac{1}{2}mc - 20$$
$$mc_s = 50 + 2q_s \quad \text{or} \quad q_s = \tfrac{1}{2}mc - 25$$
$$Q = q_w + q_s = \tfrac{1}{2}mc - 20 + \tfrac{1}{2}mc - 25 = mc - 45$$

or

$$mc = 45 + Q.$$

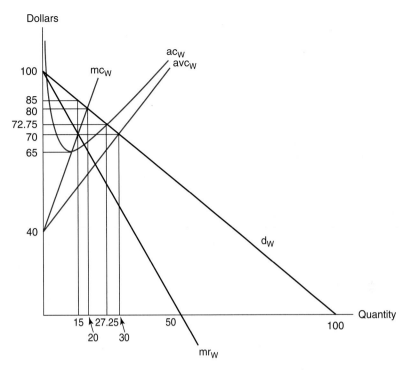

FIGURE 9.2B Profit-Maximizing Price for the Low-Cost Firm Wal-Mart

In the absence of collusion, Wal-Mart and Sears charge identical prices and split the industry demand so Wal-Mart's demand is $P_W = 100 - q_W$ and $mr_W = 100 - 2q_W$. Setting $mr_W = 100 - 2q_W = mc_W = 40 + 2q_W$, Wal-Mart's preferred output is 15 units and its preferred price is $85.

$$MC = 40 + 2Q \quad \text{for } 0 < Q \le 5$$
$$MC = 45 + Q \quad \text{for } Q > 5.$$

For joint profit maximization:

$$MC = 45 + Q = 100 - Q = MR.$$

Solving for Q yields $Q = 27.5$, and substituting back into the demand curve yields $P = 100 - 0.5(27.5) = \$86.25$.

The joint profit-maximizing price is a compromise between the preferred prices of the two firms. This creates a serious problem for the firms in their attempt to arrive at a price agreement regardless of whether the agreement is explicit or tacit.

Another serious barrier to achieving joint profit maximization with differing costs is that it requires significant differences in the outputs of the two firms. With joint profit maximization, total industry output is 27.5 units, but the division of output between Wal-Mart and Sears would have to ensure that the marginal cost of each firm was *equal*. In this example, each firm's marginal cost would have to equal the industry's marginal cost of $72.50 in panel (a). To maximize industry profits Sears would be

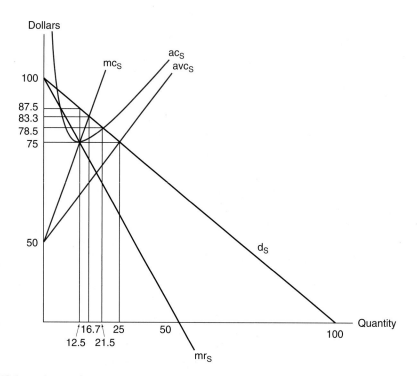

FIGURE 9.2C Profit-Maximizing Price for the High-Cost Firm Sears

In the absence of collusion, Sears and Wal-Mart charge identical prices and split the industry demand so Sears's demand is $P_S = 100 - q_S$ and $mr_S = 100 - 2q_S$. Setting $mr_S = 100 - 2q_S = mc_S = 50 + 2q_S$, Sears's preferred output is 12.5 units and its preferred price is $87.5.

forced to reduce its output to 11.25 units compared with 16.25 units for Wal-Mart.* Unless the two firms can figure out a way to share profits more equitably, it is doubtful Sears would go along with such a result.

Why doesn't Wal-Mart simply announce its desired low price, $85.00, and force Sears to go along? Although this might seem like an easy solution, it presents serious potential problems for Wal-Mart. If Sears wants to show its displeasure with P = $85.00, it might start a price war. Sears has latitude to lower price, because it could reduce price to marginal cost, P = $83.3, and still earn positive economic profits because its

*To maximize joint profits each firm must produce the output for which mc = 72.50. For Sears, this implies that:

$$mc_S = 50 + 2q_S = 72.50$$

or

$$q_S = 11.25.$$

For Wal-Mart, this implies that:

$$mc_W = 40 + 2q_W = 72.50$$

or

$$q_W = 16.25.$$

price would be above average total cost, even if Wal-Mart matched its price cut to $83.3. Wal-Mart, of course, could respond to Sears's price cut by lowering its price to P = $80.00, cover its marginal cost, and earn positive economic profits, but such a move would be risky for a number of reasons. First, if Wal-Mart reduced price to $80.00, Sears could still reduce price further. In fact, Sears could reduce price to $78.50 and still cover its average total cost. If Sears got really upset with Wal-Mart, Sears could reduce its price considerably below $78.50, all the way down to $75 and still cover its *average variable cost* (AVC). Of course, the low-cost producer Wal-Mart could more than match any cuts by Sears and could reduce price to $70 and still cover its AVC.

A price reduction by Wal-Mart below its AVC of $70, however, might result in legal trouble in the United States. The antitrust laws make it illegal to reduce prices in an effort to monopolize a market. Price reductions aimed at monopolizing a market are referred to as **predatory prices,** and a cut below AVC, which is below the firm's *shutdown price,* might be viewed as predatory and result in antitrust action.

Second, if Wal-Mart cuts price to marginal cost at $80.00, but Sears cuts only to $83.3, then Wal-Mart will have a major price advantage and customers are likely to flock to Wal-Mart. As a result the assumption of an equal shares demand curve would no longer be valid, and Wal-Mart would be faced with a much more elastic *non-followship* demand curve. The problem for Wal-Mart might then be its inability to meet this additional demand with its existing capacity. Angry customers might willingly return to buy available supplies from Sears, and Wal-Mart might end up losing much of its goodwill.

To summarize briefly, when firms face differing costs, it is much more difficult to agree on a price.

An analogous argument can be made for industries with significant product differentiation.[9] Suppose, for example, that Coke and 7-Up have identical marginal costs, but because of product differentiation, Coke's demand is greater than 7-Up's demand. Figures 9.3(a) and 9.3(b) show such a situation. In Figures 9.3(a) and 9.3(b), the following demand curves are drawn under the assumption that both firms charge an identical price:*

$$\text{Coke's demand curve: } p_C = 100 - q_C$$
$$\text{7-Up's demand curve: } p_7 = 100 - 2q_7$$

Using the "twice-as-steep rule," the marginal revenue curves are:

$$mr_C = 100 - 2q_C$$
$$mr_7 = 100 - 4q_7.$$

Suppose each firm's costs are:

$$FC = \$150$$
$$mc = 40 + 2q.$$

*The assumption of identical prices in a market with product differentiation may seem highly unlikely. This assumption is used here in part to simplify the mathematical analysis. It is, however, plausible that firms *tacitly* agree to compete strictly on the basis of product differentiation and avoid price competition. For example, Ben and Jerry's and Häagen Dazs Ice Cream may recognize that competition based on product differentiation in the form of different flavors, different fat contents, and different social images may result in greater profits than competition based on price, because it is less likely to result in a breakdown in discipline.

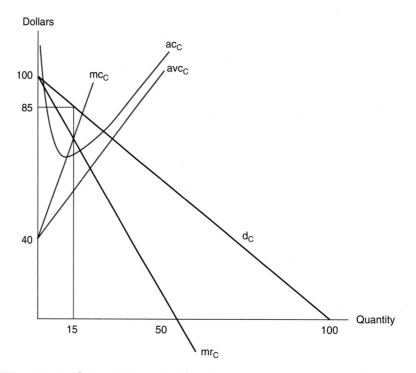

FIGURE 9.3A Profit-Maximizing Price for Coke with a Larger Demand

If Coke's demand curve is $P_C = 100 - q_C$, then $mr_C = 100 - 2q_C$. Setting $mr_C = 100 - 2q_C = mc_C = 40 + 2q_C$, Coke's preferred output is 15 units and its preferred price is $85.

Equating mc and mr in Figures 9.3(a) and 9.3(b) yields the preferred profit-maximizing quantity and price for each firm. The profit-maximizing quantities and prices for Coke and 7-Up are:

$$q_C = 15 \quad \text{and} \quad p_C = \$85.00$$
$$q_7 = 10 \quad \text{and} \quad p_7 = \$80.00.$$

In this case Coke, with a larger demand, prefers the higher price. Once again, the firms will have to compromise if they are to reach any kind of price agreement.

9.4 Factors Affecting the Ease or Difficulty of Effective Collusion

In Section 9.3, we showed that effective collusion becomes more difficult if members of a cartel face either different costs or different demands. In this section we examine what other factors influence the ability of a cartel to maintain an agreement. Recall that effective collusion entails an ability to detect and punish cheaters. In addition to

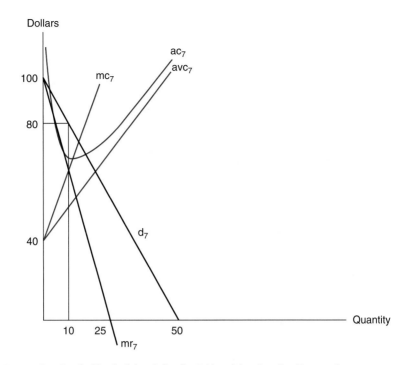

FIGURE 9.3B Profit-Maximizing Price for 7-Up with a Smaller Demand

If 7-Up's demand curve is $P_7 = 100 - 2q_7$, then $mr_7 = 100 - 4q_7$. Setting $mr_7 = 100 - 4q_7 = mc_7 = 40 + 2q_7$, 7-Up's preferred output is 10 units and its preferred price is $80.

cost and demand conditions, many other factors affect the ease or difficulty of detecting or punishing cheaters. Some of these factors are considered next.[10]

9.4.1 The Existence of Market Power

If a cartel is going to be effective in its effort to raise price above the competitive level, its members must have some degree of market power. What factors give the cartel market power? Three important factors are the existence of entry barriers, market concentration, and the elasticity of demand.

Entry Barriers

To be effective, a cartel must be protected from large-scale entry by the existence of entry barriers. In the absence of entry barriers, entry is likely to undermine the cartel's efforts to increase price and divide the market among its members. Furthermore, in the absence of entry barriers, high profits are likely to attract large-scale entry, which would result in the development of excess capacity that makes it difficult to maintain an effective collusive agreement.

Concentration[11]

Concentration should also influence the likelihood of effective collusion. High concentration should make it easier for the largest firms to behave as price leaders with smaller firms simply following. Consider two industries, each with 12 firms. If the four-firm concentration ratio is 80 in industry 1 and 30 in industry 2, then the four dominant firms in industry 1 should be able to agree on price with less concern about the response of the competitive fringe of firms.

Empirical evidence supports a positive relationship between concentration and *effective* collusion. Hay and Kelley, for example, found that most stable cartels were formed in industries with a fairly high degree of concentration.[12] According to Connor, evidence from recent global cartels in lysine, citric acid, and vitamins suggests that very high concentration was associated with each of these effective cartels.[13] Global four-firm concentration exceeded 95 percent in lysine and vitamins and 80 percent in citric acid.

Elasticity of Demand[14]

Recall that the Lerner Index suggests an inverse relationship between the elasticity of demand and market power. The more inelastic the demand, therefore, the greater the cartel's potential market power and the greater the incentive to collude because it is easier to raise price without having to significantly reduce industry output. If demand is highly elastic, even the strongest cartels will struggle to increase price, because a price increase will result in a large reduction in industry output and require significant output reductions by all cartel members.

9.4.2 The Costs of Reaching and Maintaining an Agreement

Even if market power exists, an effective cartel is unlikely if the costs of reaching and maintaining an agreement are high. Each firm wants to negotiate the best possible deal with the other members of the cartel. Negotiations are likely to be fraught with difficulty and agreements are likely to break down more often than not. Several important factors make it more difficult to reach and maintain an agreement. We have already examined several of these factors, including differing costs and demand conditions and low levels of industry concentration. The number of firms, the rate of technological advance, the rate of demand growth, and the frequency of sales also impact the effectiveness of cartel agreements.

Number of Firms[15]

Generally speaking, as the number of firms increases, reaching an agreement to fix price becomes harder because negotiating an agreement and detecting cheating become more difficult. Strong theoretical and empirical evidence supports this view. When two or three firms are involved, it is extremely unlikely that one firm can get away with a significant price reduction without being detected. Conversely, with 50 firms the likelihood of escaping detection is much greater.

Not only is detection easier with a smaller number of firms, but also the incentive to retaliate against price cutting is far greater. If one relatively small firm in a 50 firm cartel cheats, it is unlikely to have a major impact on the profits of the other 49 firms,

and it may not be worth the profit sacrifice for the others to retaliate. However, cheating by one of three firms is very likely to make a major dent in the profits of the other two, resulting in a strong incentive for retaliation.

Empirical studies of the incidence of price fixing support both these general conclusions. Connor examined 98 global cartels from 1990 to 2003; the descriptive statistics for those cartels are shown in Table 9.3. Notice that the average number of cartel members was only 7.4 and that if the Euro-Zone Banks cartel, which had 149 members, is eliminated from the data set, the average number of members in the remaining 97 cartels was only 5.9. Furthermore, the 42 global cartels averaged only 4.9 members and the 23 NAFTA (North American Free Trade Agreement) area cartels averaged only 4.5 members. Empirical evidence suggests that very few effective price-fixing agreements involve 10 or more firms.

Rate of Technological Change

A rapid rate of technological advance results in either new products or new, lower-cost methods of production. Frequent introduction of new products results in fluctuations in demand *among* firms, leading to the problems associated with differing demand curves. Constantly changing production processes leads to cost differences and their associated problems.

A contrast between two industries should help clarify this point. Reaching a price agreement in the computer industry is very difficult because technology changes both the product mix and the costs of production so rapidly. Any price agreement reached today is likely to be cheated on by the newest low-cost or new-product producer tomorrow. By contrast, in the gypsum board industry, technological change has proceeded at a snail's pace over the last 80 years, and few, if any, differences exist between firms' production methods.* Therefore gypsum board producers can relatively easily reach price-fixing agreements.

Rate of Demand Growth

Unlike the impact of the elasticity of demand, the impact of the rate of growth in demand on the likelihood of effective collusion is ambiguous. In industries in which demand is stagnant or declining, firms may sustain economic losses and turn to collusion in a desperate attempt to earn a profit. Slow rates of demand growth, therefore, may be associated with higher levels of collusion. However, declining demand may make it difficult to maintain effective collusion. Such was the case throughout the 1950s in the electrical equipment industry. Firms in the industry were quick to attempt to tighten up on collusive agreements during recessions and were just as quick to break the agreements. OPEC has also tried hard to reach agreement during recessions, but, like the electrical equipment manufacturers, OPEC has had difficulty maintaining those agreements.

Markets where demand is growing at a steady, stable rate are likely to be most conducive to effective collusion because there are fewer problems getting members to agree on market shares than with declining or rapidly growing demand. On the other hand, with rapidly growing demand, entry is more likely to undermine the cartel.

*Gypsum board is commonly known as *wallboard* and is used to build walls in most modern homes.

TABLE 9.3 Description of Data Set: International Cartels

Cartel Characteristic	Number	Companies per Cartel[b]			Global Sales Affected[b]		Regional or Global Overcharges[b]
		Min.	Max.	Avg.	Per Cartel	Total	
					$millions		Percent
Product cartelized[a]							
Food-and-feed ingredients	42	2	8	3.8	2,883	86,488	26
Organic chemicals	50	2	17	4.9	2,946	102,127	27
Graphite-based	3	2	8	6.0	6,000	6,000	—
Carbon-based	4	2	6	3.8	—	—	—
Plastic material	6	5	17	12.8	—	—	—
Metal, metallic oxides	10	2	14	5.8	742	3,710	—
Services (finance, transport, etc.)	17	2	149	14.9	1,669	6,674	—
Cement	1	42	42	42.0	61,000	61,000	
Total	98	2	149	7.4[d]	3,907	210,998	25
Geographic areas affected							
Global	42	2	8	4.9	3,716	111,468	27
NAFTA area only	23	2	9	4.5	776	10,087	29
EU only	32	2	149	15.3[d]	7,658	91,894[c]	35

[a]Categories nonexclusive.

[b]Some rows contain missing observations.

[c]Excluding cement, $2.8 billion per cartel.

[d]Excluding *Euro-Zone Banks*, average is 5.9 worldwide, 11.0 for EU regional.

Source: John M. Connor, "Private International Cartels: Effectiveness, Welfare and Anticartel Enforcement," working paper, Purdue University, June 18, 2003, Table 2, p. 10, *papers.ssrn.com/sol3/papers.cfm?abstract_id=611909*; and John M. Connor, *Global Price Fixing: Our Customers Are the Enemy* (Boston, Kluwer Academic Publishers, 2001), Appendix Table 1.

Frequency of Sales[16]

In some industries, such as light bulbs and toiletries, the frequency of sales is very rapid and orders come in at a smooth, consistent pace. In industries with a high frequency of sales, the loss of an order or two creates few problems for any firm and there is less need to turn to collusion to allocate market shares.

In other industries, such as commercial aircraft and electric turbines, the frequency of sales is slow and orders come in at a lumpy, inconsistent pace. In industries with a low frequency of sales, one order can keep a plant in operation for months, sometimes even years. Consider, for example, the importance of defense contracts in the aerospace industry or orders for multimillion-dollar electric turbines in the electrical equipment industry. In the absence of collusion, such lumpiness of orders

TABLE 9.4 Different Factors' Impacts on the Ease of Collusion

Factors Facilitating Effective Collusion	Factors Hindering Effective Collusion
1. High entry barriers	Low entry barriers
2. Identical costs for all firms	Differing costs between firms
3. No product differentiation	Significant product differentiation
4. Small number of firms	Large number of firms
5. High concentration	Low concentration
6. Slow rate of technological advance	Rapid rate of technological advance
7. Steady rate of demand growth	Slow rate of demand growth or declining demand
8. Low elasticity of demand	High elasticity of demand
9. Low frequency of sales	High frequency of sales

often makes it difficult to avoid price wars as each firm battles to maintain its market share. To avoid destructive price competition, such industries often turn to price-fixing agreements.

Table 9.4 summarizes the major factors that affect the ease or difficulty of reaching effective collusive agreements.

APPLICATION 9.3

Factors Facilitating Global Cartels: Evidence from Lysine, Citric Acid, and Vitamins A and E

During the 1990s, government antitrust agencies in the United States, Canada, and Europe uncovered a surprisingly large number of global cartels that included members from outside the investigating agencies' jurisdictions. The aggressive prosecution of these international cartels broke with previous enforcement policies that emphasized domestic cartels. According to John Connor, from 1995 to 2003, 50 to 70 percent of U.S. Department of Justice price-fixing prosecutions were of foreign companies. In the vitamin price-fixing cases alone, for example, the Swiss firm Hoffman–La Roche and the German firm BASF were fined a total of $725 million. Hoffman–La Roche was also fined $14 million in the citric acid case.

Three of the largest global cartels were in lysine, citric acid, and vitamins. These products have several important physical characteristics in common. Lysine is an amino acid that helps in the rapid development of muscle tissue. The type produced by the cartel was a powder sold as an additive to animal feed manufacturers. Citric acid is a common additive in many food products used to improve taste and prevent bacterial growth. Vitamins are a common additive in a large number of human food and animal feed products. Notice that each of these common additives is a relatively minor ingredient, with no available close substitutes, which is added to far more complex human food and animal feed products. Because lysine, citric acid, and vitamins are minor ingredients in far more complex products, the buyers of lysine, citric acid, and vitamins all have highly inelastic demands for these inputs into their production processes. All

three products are completely homogeneous and produced using essentially identical technology by all manufacturers, and therefore, the costs of production are similar, if not identical, for all producers. In addition, lysine, citric acid, and vitamins are all purchased by a large number of buyers and no individual buyer has any leverage in negotiating prices.

The table below shows Connor's analysis of the economic conditions that facilitated collusion in these markets. The list is very similar to the theoretical list presented in Table 9.4. Consistent with the list in Table 9.4, in the table below, all three markets are characterized by (1) high entry barriers; (2) a high four-firm concentration; (3) a small number of firms participating in each cartel; (4) homogeneous products with slow rates of technological advance (that is, lysine is lysine and citric acid is citric acid); (5) a steady rate of growth in demand; and (6) a low frequency of sales. As previously noted, all three markets were also characterized by highly inelastic demands.

Economic Conditions Facilitating Global Price Fixing: Lysine, Citric Acid, and Vitamin A, Early 1990s

Market Conditions	Lysine	Citric Acid	Synthetic Vitamins A and E
High seller concentration:			
Global market	CR4 > 95%	CR4 > 80%	CR4 > 95%
U.S. market	CR4 > 97%	CR4 = 90%	CR4 = 100%
Few cartel participants	4 or 5	4 or 5	3
High cartel supply control	95–99%	65–70%[b]	95–100%
Low buyer concentration	CR4 < 30%	CR4 < 40%	CR4 < 20%
Homogeneous product[a]	Perfect	High	High
High barriers to market entry:			
Large plant scales	$150 mil.	$150 mil.	Probably
Sunk investment costs	Yes	Yes	Yes
Technology secret	Yes	Yes	Yes
Building new plants slow	3 years	3 years	3 years
Transparency of market prices to buyers	None	Some	Little
Large, infrequent transactions	Yes	Yes	Yes
Major rivals have long history of strategic interaction	3 of 5	3 of 5	Yes[c]
Annual market growth	10%, steady	8%, steady	2-3%, steady
Cultural propinquity of cartel members	Low	Moderate	High[c]

Sources: John M. Connor, "Private International Cartels: Effectiveness, Welfare and Anticartel Enforcement," working paper, Purdue University, June 18, 2003, Table 1, p. 9, *papers.ssrn.com/sol3/papers.cfm?abstract_id=611909*; and John M. Connor, *Global Price Fixing: Our Customers Are the Enemy* (Boston: Kluwer Academic Publishers, 2001), Chapters 4, 7, and 10.
[a]Within well-recognized industry grades when prices were at cartel-enhanced levels. There were no substitutes when prices were within a normal range.
[b]Control by formal members of the cartel. Cargill, a major supplier with up to 20 percent of U.S. capacity, provided passive support for the cartel's pricing decisions.
[c]The vitamin conspirators were long-time rivals from Western Europe, but in most of the other vitamin cartels Japanese or Northern American companies had to be recruited to the cartels.

Connor also found that all three cartels were characterized by high cartel supply control (that is, members of the cartel controlled a large percentage of the total market); low buyer concentration; limited market price transparency for buyers (that is, prices paid by other buyers were not made publicly available); a long history of cartel members competing against each other; and close cultural relationships (propinquity) with the other members of the cartel.

Sources: John M. Connor, "Private International Cartels: Effectiveness, Welfare and Anticartel Enforcement," working paper, Purdue University, June 18, 2003, papers.ssrn.com/sol3/papers.cfm?abstract_id=611909; and John M. Connor, *Global Price Fixing: Our Customers Are the Enemy* (Boston, Kluwer Academic Publishers, 2001). ■

9.5 Antitrust Policy Toward Collusion

We have shown that whenever firms collude to fix prices, the objective is the same: to solve the prisoner's dilemma and increase or stabilize prices. In theory, all ***overt price-fixing agreements,*** where firms meet in an effort to fix prices, are attempts to widen the gap between price and marginal cost, and therefore, they should all reduce economic efficiency. It is necessary, however, to examine whether there are any valid justifications for price fixing.

Several justifications have been advanced by defendant firms. First, price fixing may prevent *cutthroat competition.* This argument is particularly popular in industries characterized by high fixed costs relative to variable costs, such as the steel and railroad industries. When demand declines in these industries, marginal cost is likely to be less than average cost because each firm operates on the downward-sloping portion of its average cost curve. Under such conditions, a firm's demand curve may be everywhere below its average cost curve. This situation is shown in Figure 9.4. The firm may attempt to attract new business by secret discriminatory price discounts to some purchasers. As long as price remains above marginal cost to *all* buyers and the firm is able to maintain its high price to all of its original customers, its losses will be reduced as it attracts additional customers by cutting prices. If a firm's discriminatory price cutting remains secret, this strategy may work because the price cutter is able to attract new customers away from its competitors. Secret price cuts, however, usually become public and lead to matching cuts by other firms. When this occurs, prices may fall to very low levels as each firm matches its competitors' lower prices. Widespread price cutting throughout the industry will lead to a downward price spiral and significant economic losses for all firms.

In Figure 9.4, suppose that price is initially stable at the firm's loss-minimizing price P_1, and the firm is sustaining an economic loss equal to area P_1abC_1 (the gray and striped areas). If cutthroat competition developed, prices might fall below P_1 on all sales. In fact, prices might decline to marginal cost P_2 and the firm would then sustain a much greater economic loss equal to area P_2xyC_2 (the red and striped areas).

A price decline to P_2 would certainly result in economic losses and serious problems for firms in the industry. The price decline, however, should not be a major cause for society's concern or used as a justification for permitting price fixing. When price equals P_2, price equals marginal cost, which is the allocatively efficient price. The profit issue is a value judgment, not an economic efficiency issue. From an economic efficiency perspective, the short-run socially optimal price is P_2. Price fixing to maintain prices above P_2 should not be permitted.

FIGURE 9.4 Cutthroat Competition with AC Above Demand

If price is initially P_1, the firm sustains an economic loss equal to P_1abC_1, which equals the sum of the gray and striped areas. With cutthroat competition, price might decline to marginal cost P_2 and the firm's economic loss would increase to P_2xyC_2, which equals the sum of the red and striped areas. However, P_2 is the socially optimal price because P = MC.

With regard to profits, the theory of competitive markets implies that long-run economic profits will be zero, or normal, but that short-run profits will vary. During expansion periods, excess profits are likely to exist (as they often did in the railroad and steel industries), whereas during recessions and depressions, economic losses are likely to occur. True competition is often cruel, and in highly competitive markets firms periodically sustain economic losses and are forced to leave. The exiting of firms suggests that the competitive process is working, not that it is failing. One can be fairly confident that in most instances when firms complain about cutthroat competition they are really complaining about just plain old competition.

Another argument is that price fixing reduces risk, resulting in a more stable economy. According to this argument, high risk discourages investment, reduces supply, and results in higher prices. By reducing risk, price fixing may encourage investment; however, collusion that *artificially* reduces risk may create a different set of economic problems. Risk artificially reduced through collusion may result in a sluggish rate of technological advance as firms lose some of their incentive to produce new products. Furthermore, artificially reduced risk may encourage entry and capacity expansion beyond the socially optimal level.[17] An artificial reduction in risk caused by collusion, therefore, is likely to result in excess capacity and economic inefficiencies.

Finally, higher profits associated with collusion may be necessary to encourage research and development. This argument seems dubious because price fixing, by

encouraging cooperation among competitors, seems unlikely to spur firms to attempt to produce new products that would make it more difficult to continue a policy of successful collusion. Furthermore, as noted in Section 9.4.2, in technologically advanced industries, in which research and development expenditures are high, price-fixing agreements rarely work, because new products are developed too rapidly. It would be virtually impossible, for example, to form an effective cartel in the computer industry because new technology is developed almost daily.

Despite the preceding analysis, a few price-fixing agreements might be justified on efficiency grounds.[18] These exceptions are so few and far between, however, that an absolute ban on direct price-fixing agreements probably is the optimal public policy.

9.5.1 Public Policy Toward Direct Price-Fixing Agreements

The first issue concerning price fixing that the courts had to decide was whether overt price fixing is illegal per se, that is, always illegal; or whether it comes under a Rule of Reason interpretation, as handed down in the 1911 *Standard Oil* case, and is sometimes legal (see Chapter 3). Two important cases decided this issue, the 1899 *Addyston Pipe* case and the 1927 *Trenton Potteries* case.

ADDYSTON PIPE AND STEEL CASE[19] (1899)—The *Addyston Pipe* case involved six large producers of cast iron pipe in the Midwest and South. Beginning in 1894, the six firms, which controlled more than 65 percent of the market, entered into agreements that divided the market into exclusive *pay* territories and *free* territories. In pay territories, it was agreed that one firm would be the low bidder on all jobs. For example, Addyston Pipe was located in Cincinnati and was awarded the pay territories of Cincinnati, Ohio; Covington, Kentucky; and Newport, Kentucky. Each of the six agreed to pay "bonuses" into a common pool on all sales made in pay territories. These "bonuses" were then divided among the six defendants.

The defense argued that prices were reasonable and prevented *ruinous competition* in an industry characterized by high fixed costs relative to variable costs. The Supreme Court ruled unanimously against Addyston Pipe but, in the process, appeared to leave open the possibility that firms could sometimes use a *reasonableness* defense. The Supreme Court stated:

> We have no doubt that where the direct and immediate effect of a contract or combination among particular dealers in a commodity is to destroy competition between them and others, so that the parties to the contract or combination may obtain increased prices for themselves, such contract or combination amounts to a restraint of trade in the commodity. . . . All the facts and circumstances are, however, to be considered in order to determine the fundamental question—whether the necessary effect of the combination is to restrain interstate commerce.

This section of the decision placed a great emphasis on *higher prices* acting as a restraint of trade. It is possible to derive a corollary from this position: Agreements that do not raise prices do not result in a restraint of trade and do not violate the Sherman Act. In 1927, however, the Supreme Court removed any doubt concerning the per se ban on direct price-fixing agreements in the *Trenton Potteries* case.

TRENTON POTTERIES CASE[20] (1927)—The *Trenton Potteries* case involved 23 members of the Sanitary Potters Association. The defendants controlled more than 80 percent of the vitreous pottery fixture market (better known as commodes and tubs). Competitors met through the association, set standard price lists, and attempted to persuade each other not to sell below list price. Evidence suggested that the agreements often broke down and that many sales took place at prices below list. The Supreme Court, however, stated its strong support for a per se ban on all price-fixing agreements.

Justice Stone delivered the majority opinion:

> The aim and result of every price-fixing agreement, if effective, is the elimination of one form of competition. The power to fix prices, whether reasonably exercised or not, involves power to control the market and to fix arbitrary and unreasonable prices. The reasonable price fixed today may through economic and business changes become the unreasonable price of tomorrow.

In the *Trenton Potteries* case the price-fixing agreements probably had little, if any, effect on price, and yet the Supreme Court majority forcefully condemned the attempt to fix prices. Despite one aberrational decision in 1933,[21] this remains the basic precedent today: Any overt attempt to fix prices is illegal per se.

Based on the *Trenton Potteries* precedent, direct price-fixing agreements are illegal per se in the United States. In antitrust law, however, most restraints of trade come under the Rule of Reason interpretation handed down by Judge White in the *Standard Oil* case. Under a Rule of Reason interpretation a firm can argue that its "restraint of trade" is economically justified because it is a reasonable restraint.

When is a "restraint of trade" between direct competitors illegal per se, and when is a "restraint of trade" considered under a Rule of Reason? The remaining sections of this chapter explore a number of restraints of trade that could fall under either a per se or Rule of Reason interpretation. These areas include price information exchanges between competitors without an explicit agreement to fix prices; oligopoly behavior in which firms charge identical prices without agreeing to fix prices; trade associations in which members agree to exchange a wide variety of firm and industry data; and agreements by groups of nonprofit colleges and universities to set the terms under which member schools' sports teams can appear on television or to set student financial aid packages.

9.5.2 Price-Exchange Agreements

While it is settled law that overt price-fixing agreements are illegal *per se,* other, subtler forms of solving the prisoner's dilemma have been left open for judicial interpretation. One open area is the question of ***price-exchange agreements*** between competitors. The Supreme Court first addressed this issue in the 1969 *Container Corporation* case.

CONTAINER CORPORATION CASE[22] (1969)—The *Container Corporation* case involved an agreement among eighteen manufacturers of cardboard containers in the southeastern United States. These firms controlled 90 percent of the relevant market. Each firm agreed to supply its competitors with price information on its most recent sales in exchange for a reciprocal agreement from each of its competitors. Despite the information exchanges, prices were generally declining throughout the period of the

price exchanges. Furthermore, there was a large increase, from 30 to 51, in the number of firms in the market.

The Supreme Court ruled for the government, but made it clear that price-exchange agreements were not illegal per se. According to the Court, price exchanges would have no effect on a truly competitive market, but because the cardboard container industry was dominated by relatively few sellers, the exchanges tended to result in "price uniformity." Justice Douglas's opinion indicated that price exchanges would violate the Sherman Act if the structural characteristics of an industry led to the conclusion that prices would be affected by the exchanges.

U.S. GYPSUM CASE[23] (1978)—The *Container Corporation* decision was modified in the 1978 *U.S. Gypsum* case. Gypsum board was sold in a highly concentrated market, with an eight-firm concentration ratio of 94. The eight leading producers had followed precisely the same price-exchange practices as the cardboard container manufacturers.

The Supreme Court majority ruled, however, that the jury had been improperly charged that "if the effect of the exchanges of pricing information was to raise, fix, maintain, and stabilize prices, then the parties to them are presumed, AS A MATTER OF LAW, to have intended that result." According to the Court, the determination of intent "must be established by evidence and inferences drawn therefrom and cannot be taken from the trier of fact through reliance on a legal presumption of wrongful intent from proof of an effect on prices."

While still leaving price-exchange agreements vulnerable under the Sherman Act, the *U.S. Gypsum* decision significantly weakened the *Container Corporation* precedent.

9.5.3 Oligopolistic Behavior—Conscious Parallelism

For rational reasons, oligopolists often find it in their best interests to avoid aggressive price competition even in the absence of collusion. This presents an extremely difficult problem for antitrust authorities because oligopolistic behavior that, on the surface, may appear to be in restraint of trade may simply represent rational independent business behavior aimed at maximizing long-run profits.

The courts have defined the term *conscious parallelism* as a group of oligopolists behaving in an identical manner but with a lack of proof that the firms ever met to agree on this parallel course of behavior. *Conscious parallelism* refers to the idea that rational business behavior in a tight oligopoly will lead firms to behave identically with regard to price and other business practices. When does conscious parallelism become illegal? As the cases below suggest, that question has proved difficult for the courts to answer.

AMERICAN TOBACCO CASE[24] (1946)—In the 1946 *American Tobacco* case, there was no evidence of an overt conspiracy or even a tacit conspiracy. Divestiture after the 1911 *American Tobacco* monopolization case resulted in the establishment of over a dozen new tobacco companies, including Liggett & Myers and R. J. Reynolds. For about a decade, the cigarette producers competed aggressively, and then, in the early 1920s, price competition suddenly ceased. The *Big 3* (as American, Liggett, and Reynolds were known) rigged the tobacco auction markets so that all three purchased tobacco at identical prices. Furthermore, they followed each other's pricing policies in lockstep.

This *consciously parallel* behavior may have been the natural outgrowth of the oligopolistic structure of the cigarette industry. Relying on strong circumstantial evidence, however, the Supreme Court ruled for the government and stated, "No formal agreement is necessary to constitute an unlawful conspiracy." Instead, the Court noted, "Where the circumstances are such as to warrant a jury in finding that the conspirators had a unity of purpose or a common design and understanding, the conclusion that a conspiracy is established is justified."

The *American Tobacco* case resulted in total fines of only $255,000 and no structural relief. This raises a serious question regarding the remedies in oligopoly cases. If a firm's behavior is the natural result of an oligopolistic market structure, then the levying of fines is unlikely to have any effect on future behavior or economic performance. In fact, behavior in the cigarette industry changed little after the 1946 decision.

The *American Tobacco* case was initially thought to be a breakthrough in antitrust policy because the Supreme Court was ruling that **tacit price-fixing agreements** were illegal.* It was followed in 1948 by several other government victories, including a major case against Paramount and four other leading motion picture producers and distributors that resulted in the divestiture of over 65 percent of the leading producers' movie theaters.[25] In 1954, however, the courts took the first major step away from the *American Tobacco* precedent in another motion picture industry case.

***THEATRE ENTERPRISES* CASE**[26] (1954)—After the 1948 *Paramount* decision, Theatre Enterprises built a new theater, the Crest, in suburban Baltimore, with the hope of attracting first-run motion pictures. Theatre Enterprises contacted eight major distributors and each refused to supply the Crest with first-run films, despite Theatre Enterprises' offer of substantial financial guarantees. Assuming that the refusals resulted from consciously parallel behavior, Theatre Enterprises sued.

In 1954 the Supreme Court ruled against Theatre Enterprises because of a lack of evidence that the eight distributors had an agreement, "tacit or express," to refuse to supply the Crest with films. The Court declared, "Circumstantial evidence of consciously parallel behavior may have made heavy inroads into the traditional judicial attitude toward conspiracy; but 'conscious parallelism' has not yet read conspiracy out of the Sherman Act entirely."

The *Theatre Enterprises* case represented a significant first movement away from the *American Tobacco* precedent. The movement continued with the 1984 *Ethyl* decision.

THE *ETHYL* CASE[27] (1984)—For many years Ethyl Corporation was a monopolist in the market for lead-based antiknock gasoline additives, but in 1948 Du Pont entered, and in the early 1960s PPG Industries and Nalco Chemical entered. In 1974 Du Pont held a 36 percent market share, followed by Ethyl with 34 percent, PPG with 17.5 percent, and Nalco with 12.5 percent.[28]

From 1974 to 1979 there were 24 list price changes in the industry. In 20 of these cases all four firms changed price on the same day. In the other four cases, all four firms had identical prices a day or two apart. Such a high degree of price uniformity required a sophisticated form of price leadership. Leadership was characterized by: (1) at least 30 days' advance notice of all price changes; (2) public press notices of all

*A tacit price-fixing agreement is a method of collusion where firms fix identical prices without ever meeting to discuss prices because of a "meeting of the minds."

price changes; (3) a delivered price system that required buyers located in the same city to pay the same price; and (4) the use of most favored customer clauses, whereby if one buyer received a lower price, all buyers would receive the same reduced price. Price leadership was clearly established to ensure both detection of all price cuts and punishment of cheaters.

The FTC ruled that the practices represented "unfair methods of competition" and therefore violated Section 5 of the FTC Act. The Court of Appeals, however, overturned the FTC ruling. Noting that the FTC had never argued that the practices "were the result of any agreement express or tacit," the Appeals Court argued that absent evidence of a tacit agreement the FTC carried a heavy burden of proof. According to the Court of Appeals, the FTC had to prove that there was "anti-competitive intent or purpose" on the part of the producers or that there was "an absence of an independent legitimate reason for [their] conduct."

Today conscious parallelism remains a practice that is for the most part beyond the reach of the antitrust laws. In the absence of an explicit agreement to fix prices, only the most extreme forms of parallel behavior can be successfully fought in court.

9.5.4 Trade Associations

Trade associations present another unique set of problems for antitrust enforcement. Trade association practices vary widely, from innocent information-gathering and disseminating activities to sophisticated attempts to force compliance with published list prices. In highly competitive industries, it is doubtful that even aggressive attempts at price fixing by associations will be successful. In concentrated markets, however, trade associations may provide a successful vehicle for price fixing.

As precedents have developed, a Rule of Reason has evolved in trade association cases. Simple information gathering and dissemination have become viewed as reasonable; however, attempts to impose prices directly or indirectly have become viewed as unreasonable.

SUGAR INSTITUTE CASE[29] (1936)—The Sugar Institute consisted of 15 manufacturers that produced more than 80 percent of the refined cane sugar in the United States. Early in its history the Institute established a Code of Ethics that distinguished "ethical" from "unethical" types of behavior. The Justice Department filed suit, contending that the Code of Ethics went beyond the simple announcement of prices. Under the code, members refused to deal with water carriers that refused to announce freight rates or who granted price concessions to any sugar refiner; wholesalers who granted any price concessions; and any trucker, broker, or warehousemen who granted secret rebates. The Institute required sugar brokers to pledge, under oath, to adhere to the Code of Ethics. Members were also prohibited from granting quantity-based price discounts, even if the discounts were justified by lower costs. Finally, F.O.B. (freight on board) pricing, whereby buyers paid the mill price plus actual freight costs, was prohibited.

The Supreme Court condemned this behavior because "[t]he unreasonable restraints which defendants imposed lay not in advance announcements, but in the steps taken to secure adherence, without deviation, to prices and terms thus announced." According to the Court, the Sugar Institute tried far too hard to eliminate price cutting, and it was this behavior that led to its condemnation.

TAG MANUFACTURERS CASE[30] (1949)—The Tag Manufacturers Institute consisted of 31 members that produced over 95 percent of all business tags. The Institute required its members to report their prices under threat of financial penalty. Relying on evidence that the required reporting of prices had no effect on actual prices, the Court of Appeals ruled in favor of the tag manufacturers.

Perhaps the most important piece of evidence in the case was the fact that the Institute's rules stated explicitly, "Nothing herein shall be construed as a limitation or restriction upon the right of each Subscriber independently to establish such price, or such terms and conditions of sale, or policies of whatever nature affecting prices or sales, as he may deem expedient." Furthermore, there was abundant evidence of continuing price competition in the industry.

The *Sugar Institute* and *Tag Manufacturers* cases represent fairly well the state of the law with regard to trade association activities. Price-reporting schemes that do little more than ask members to report prices, and which then make this information available to the public, will generally be permitted. Direct attempts to force adherence to list prices, or restrict price cutting, however, will bring an association within the reach of Section 1.

9.5.5 Nonprofit Organizations: Cases Involving Colleges and Universities

Another issue in two major Section 1 cases decided since 1984 has been whether nonprofit organizations such as colleges and universities can engage in restraints of trade that attempt to protect the missions of these institutions. In both cases, the Supreme Court ruled that restraints imposed by groups of colleges and universities typically would be decided under a Rule of Reason interpretation. Despite this Rule of Reason interpretation, however, the Court found against the schools in both cases.

THE *NATIONAL COLLEGIATE ATHLETIC ASSOCIATION* CASE[31] (1984)—The National Collegiate Athletic Association (NCAA) was created in 1905 to help support and regulate intercollegiate athletics. Beginning in 1952, the NCAA limited the total number of televised college football games and the number of television appearances per season for each college or university team.

The College Football Association (CFA) consisted of a group of large universities with major football programs that banded together to promote their interests in college football within the overall NCAA structure. In 1979 the CFA negotiated a separate television contract with the National Broadcasting Company (NBC) that allowed for more television appearances for each school than the NCAA permitted. In response, the NCAA announced it would discipline the members of the CFA. The members of the CFA then sued the NCAA under Section 1 of the Sherman Act and immediately obtained a court order, or an ***injunction,*** preventing the NCAA from taking any disciplinary action against the CFA schools. The District Court and the Court of Appeals both ruled that the NCAA television plan was a per se violation of Section 1 because the plan limited the output of televised college football games.

On appeal, the Supreme Court ruled that it was inappropriate to apply a per se rule to the case, but nonetheless concluded that the NCAA's restrictions violated Section 1 under a Rule of Reason interpretation. The Supreme Court majority used a Rule of Reason interpretation because they believed that some horizontal restraints of

trade were necessary to supply the product, college football games, at all. The Court recognized that unless the members of a football league agreed jointly to certain league rules, no games would be played. Jointly-agreed-to rules spanned the gambit from the size of the field and the number of players to the requirements that student athletes should not be paid and must attend classes. In the absence of such restrictions, colleges would not agree to play each other, and consumer choice would be restricted.

The NCAA argued that its plan was pro-competitive because it protected attendance at college football games and promoted competitive balance among NCAA member teams. The Supreme Court ruled that the NCAA did not appear to take either of these objectives too seriously. For one thing, the television plan allowed for broadcast of national games into local communities in which live games were simultaneously taking place. Furthermore, the NCAA did not limit the amount of money a school could spend on football or the amount of revenue it could collect from football-related activities, such as ticket and merchandise sales. Finally, the NCAA did nothing to limit the way in which those revenues could be spent by the colleges.

The majority Supreme Court opinion stated that "the record supports the District Court's conclusion that by curtailing output and blunting the ability of member institutions to respond to consumer preference, the NCAA has restricted rather than enhanced the place of intercollegiate athletics in the Nation's life."

***IVY LEAGUE OVERLAP GROUP* CASE**[32] (1993)—In 1958 the Massachusetts Institute of Technology (MIT) and the eight Ivy League schools formed the "Ivy League Overlap Group."* The purpose of the group was to meet to agree on the financial aid packages offered to students admitted to more than one of the schools. All nine schools offered admission based strictly on merit, but offered financial aid packages based strictly on need. Each April the nine schools met and explicitly set the award packages offered to each student. Differences of $500 or less were ignored, but if there was more than a $500 disagreement about the size of a package, the schools agreed to a compromise amount.

The Justice Department charged that the Overlap Group was engaged in a price-fixing conspiracy to set the price of tuition for every admitted student. The eight Ivy League schools decided to sign a consent decree prohibiting them from continuing to meet to set financial aid packages. MIT, however, refused to sign the consent decree and took the Justice Department to court. The District Court ruled that the Overlap Group was engaged in a price-fixing conspiracy, but that because of the nonprofit status and educational mission of the schools, the conspiracy was not illegal per se. Instead of a strict per se rule, the District Court decided to apply an ***abbreviated Rule of Reason*** to the case. The abbreviated Rule of Reason "applies in cases where per se condemnation is inappropriate, but in which 'no elaborate industry analysis is required to demonstrate the anticompetitive character' of an inherently suspect restraint." Under the abbreviated Rule of Reason, the District Court offered MIT a chance to present a pro-competitive defense and then found for the Justice Department.

*The eight Ivy League schools are Brown University, Columbia University, Cornell University, Dartmouth College, Harvard University, Princeton University, the University of Pennsylvania, and Yale University.

The Court of Appeals overturned the District Court, and remanded the case for a full Rule of Reason hearing. The Court of Appeals noted that it was possible that the Overlap Group meetings had no negative competitive impact. In its defense, MIT argued that the meetings improved the quality of education at the schools, increased consumer choice by making an Overlap Group education more accessible to a larger number of students, promoted competition among the members in areas other than price, and promoted socioeconomic diversity at the schools.

In the absence of the meetings, MIT feared that a bidding war for highly qualified wealthy students would leave less financial aid for qualified needy students. Because the resources available for aid are relatively fixed each year, this would result in fewer total students being offered aid and far fewer needy students, particularly minority students, being offered aid.

On December 22, 1993, MIT agreed to a consent decree. The settlement prohibited a return to the former practices of the Overlap Group, but permitted the colleges to agree "on general principles for determining financial aid, to award aid solely on the basis of financial need, and to exchange limited data about applicants' financial profiles."

SUMMARY

1. Firms wish to collude to maximize long-run, not short-run, profits.

2. Solutions to the prisoner's dilemma require the ability to detect and punish cheaters. Effective solutions also appear to require that the leading firms exhibit some degree of *niceness* toward competitors.

3. A tit-for-tat strategy appears to be one possible solution to the prisoner's dilemma. Another possible solution is a trigger price strategy, also called the grim strategy.

4. Differences in costs and demand increase the difficulty of solving the prisoner's dilemma and often require elaborate schemes to solve the game theoretic problems associated with collusion.

5. Low entry barriers, product differentiation, a large number of firms, low concentration, a rapid rate of technological advance, declining industry demand, a high elasticity of demand, and large frequency of sales all make effective collusion less likely.

6. The Court's tough stand against direct price-fixing agreements makes economic sense. There are so few cases of economically justified price fixing that a per se ban—thus avoiding long, complicated, and costly arguments over reasonableness—represents an optimal policy.

7. The basic issue of direct price-fixing agreements has been settled by the courts, but other more subtle forms of solving the prisoner's dilemma have been left open for judicial interpretation. One open area is price exchanges between competitors. The Supreme Court has ruled that price exchanges come under a Rule of Reason interpretation and are illegal only if there is an intent to raise prices.

8 With regard to oligopolistic behavior, the issues are far more complex. Consciously parallel behavior is likely to remain outside the reach of the current antitrust statutes. Oligopolists follow consciously parallel behavior because it is rational. In the absence of structural remedies, it is doubtful that convictions and fines will have much impact on oligopolistic behavior.

9 Unless the Courts dramatically change their current position and order structural remedies in oligopoly cases, any long-run change in policy toward conscious parallelism would require new legislation.

10 With regard to trade associations, the continuous reporting of price information to competitors can be used to discourage price cutting because few firms wish to be identified as chiselers by their competitors, who are often also their friends. Price-reporting schemes that do little more than ask members to report prices, and which then make this information available to the public, will generally be permitted. However, direct attempts to force adherence to list prices or restrict price cutting will bring an association within the reach of Section 1.

11 In two major cases, the courts ruled that nonprofit organizations such as colleges and universities also are subject to the Sherman Act.

12 Overall, the antitrust laws have been fairly successful in the area of horizontal agreements. In the absence of the Sherman Act, price fixing would undoubtedly be far more common.

KEY TERMS

abbreviated Rule of Reason

conscious parallelism

explicit collusion

Folk Theorem

followship demand curve

grim strategy

infinite game

injunction

non-followship demand curve

overt collusion

overt price-fixing agreement

perfect collusion

predatory prices

price-exchange agreement

prisoner's dilemma

tacit collusion

tacit price-fixing agreement

tit-for-tat strategy

trigger price strategy

DISCUSSION QUESTIONS

1. Is the chapter's assumption of a zero discount rate in the Waldman–Jensen Tournament reasonable? Explain.

2. If the Axelrod Tournament had been a single-elimination tournament (that is, losing once to an opponent results in elimination from the tournament), would there be a strategy that ensured you could never lose the tournament?

3. Suppose in a duopoly one firm produces with high fixed costs and low variable costs and the other firm produces with low fixed costs and high variable costs. Which firm would prefer a lower price? Will that firm be necessarily able to force the other firm to charge that lower price?

4. In which of the following industries would you expect price collusion to be easier to maintain? Explain your reasoning.
 a. Steel or ready-to-eat cereals
 b. Hotels or crude oil production
 c. Glass containers or fast food

5. What court decision examined in this chapter makes the most sense to you in terms of economic analysis? What court decision examined in this chapter makes the least sense to

you in terms of economic analysis? Explain your reasoning.

6. Discuss one economic strength and one economic weakness in the antitrust laws with regard to price fixing. Make sure you use precedents to support your position.

7. In the *Container Corporation* case the court refused to accept the argument that declining prices are a legitimate defense in price-exchange cases. Do you believe this decision made economic sense?

8. Can you identify any examples from your local neighborhood (such as gasoline stations, food stores, or restaurants) of tacit or overt collusion? Which type of collusion do you suspect? Why?

9. Why does oligopoly present a particularly difficult problem from both an economic and legal standpoint? How have the courts dealt with this problem in this century? What one precedent do you believe makes the most economic sense? Why?

10. What are the common justifications offered by defendants in price-fixing cases? Are any of these justifications valid?

11. Do you agree or disagree with the following statement: If two small producers of bread exchanged price information over the telephone, it would not be necessary to prove that they intended to increase prices to an unreasonable level to show a criminal violation of the Sherman Act.

12. Suppose a hospital always receives identical secret bids to buy antibiotics from five drug companies. Would such identical bids "prove" the existence of collusion?

13. Do you agree with the initial ruling against the Ivy League Overlap Group? What group of students would most likely emerge as winners from such a ruling? What group of students would most likely emerge as losers from such a ruling? What would likely happen to the total number of students on financial aid?

14. Suppose that, at the next national meeting of the American Economics Association, economists agreed that no new Ph.D. in economics would accept a professorship from a four-year university or college for less than $75,000 per year. Do you think such an agreement would have any significant economic impact? Would such an agreement be legal?

15. Explain why Major League Baseball's decision to crack down on pitchers who throw at batters may have caused an increase in the number of hit batters. Tie your explanation into the theory of collusion.

16. After the *Ivy League Overlap Group* case was settled, many colleges and universities in the United States began to offer more merit financial aid that was not based on a student's financial need. Explain why economists would not be surprised by this development.

PROBLEMS

1. What would the result of a competition between Jensen and Waldman have been if Jensen played the grim strategy and Waldman played tit-for-tat?

2. Suppose a duopoly faces an industry demand curve of $P = 100 - Q$. If the firms charge the same price, they share the demand so that they each face a demand curve:

$$P_i = 100 - 2q_i \quad \text{for i = 1, 2.}$$

The firms, however, face the following different marginal costs:

$$mc_1 = 10 + 2q_1 \quad \text{and} \quad mc_2 = 22 + 2q_2.$$

a. If both firms charge the same price, what is Firm 1's preferred price?
b. If both firms charge the same price, what is Firm 2's preferred price?
c. What is the joint profit-maximizing price? How much output would each firm produce if it charged the joint profit-maximizing price?

3. Would it be easy or difficult to maintain effective collusion if two duopolists faced the following profit matrix?

		Firm B's Action	
		High Price	Low Price
Firm A's Action	High Price	1000, 150	700, 100
	Low Price	800, 50	500, 75

Does there appear to be a dominant firm in this industry? Does Firm A have a dominant solution to this game? Does Firm B have a dominant solution to this game?

NOTES

1. Adam Smith, *An Inquiry into the Nature and Causes of the Wealth of Nations* (New York: Modern Library Edition, 1937), p. 128.
2. See, for example, R. Preston McAfee and John McMillan, "Bidding Rings," *American Economic Review* 83 (June 1992): 579–599; and Jonathan Cave and Stephen W. Salant, "Cartel Quotas Under Majority Rule," *American Economic Review* 85 (March 1995): 82–102.
3. Robert Axelrod, *The Evolution of Cooperation* (New York: Basic Books, 1984).
4. Axelrod, *ibid.*, p. 194.
5. Axelrod, *ibid.*, p. 33.
6. *ibid.*
7. *ibid.*
8. For an expanded discussion, see Jean Tirole, *The Theory of Industrial Organization* (Cambridge, MA: MIT Press, 1988), pp. 245–247. See also James Friedman, "Noncooperative Equilibrium for Supergames," *Review of Economic Studies* 28 (1971): 1–12; James Friedman, *Oligopoly and the Theory of Games* (Amsterdam: North-Holland, 1977); D. Fudenberg and E. Maskin, "The Folk Theorem in Repeated Games with Discounting and with Incomplete Information," *Econometrica* 54 (1986): 533–554; E. Green and R. Porter, "Noncooperative Collusion Under Imperfect Price Information," *Econometrica* 52 (1984): 87–100; R. Porter, "Optimal Cartel Trigger Price Strategies," *Journal of Economic Theory* 29 (1983): 313–338; and A. Rubinstein, "Equilibrium in Supergames with the Overtaking Criterion," *Journal of Economic Theory* 21 (1979): 1–9.
9. For game theory approaches to this issue, see Myong-Hun Chang, "The Effects of Product Differentiation on Collusive Pricing," *International Journal of Industrial Organization* 9 (September 1991): 543–569; Thomas W. Ross, "Cartel Stability and Product Differentiation," *International Journal of Industrial Organization* 10 (March 1992): 1–13; Jonas Hächner, "Collusive Pricing in Markets for Vertically Differentiated Products," *International Journal of Industrial Organization* 12 (June 1994): 155–177; and Philippe Jehiel, "Product Differentiation and Price Collusion," *International Journal of Industrial Organization* 10 (December 1992): 633–641.
10. Although these are the major factors, there are, of course, other possible factors. Scott has argued that increased product diversification makes it easier to maintain effective collusion. See John T. Scott, "Multimarket Contact among Diversified Oligopolists," *International Journal of Industrial Organization* 9 (June 1991): 225–238. Taking a different approach, Lambson has suggested that collusion is more difficult in markets where "aggregate efficiency (i.e., the ability of firms to profitably produce at prices exceeding the Cournot price) is large relative to the level of demand." See Val Eugene Lambson, "Aggregate Efficiency, Market Demand, and the Sustainability of Collusion," *International Journal of Industrial Organization* 6 (June 1988): 263–271. In addition, Feinberg has pointed out that increases in imports should reduce the effectiveness of collusion. Robert M. Feinberg, "Imports as a Threat to Cartel Stability," *International Journal of Industrial Organization* 7 (June 1989): 281–288.

11. George A. Hay and Daniel Kelley, "An Empirical Survey of Price Fixing Conspiracies," *Journal of Law & Economics* 17 (April 1974): 13–38; Arthur G. Fraas and Douglas F. Greer, "Market Structure and Price Collusion: An Empirical Analysis," *Journal of Industrial Economics* 26 (September 1977): 29–33.

12. G.A. Hay and D. Kelley, *supra* note 11, p. 26.

13. John M. Connor, "Private International Cartels: Effectiveness, Welfare and Anticartel Enforcement," working paper, Purdue University, June 18, 2003, Table 1, p. 8, *papers.ssrn.com/sol3/papers.cfm? abstract_id=611909*.

14. G.A. Hay and D. Kelley, *supra* note 11, p. 15; J.M. Clark, *Studies in the Economics of Overhead Costs* (Chicago: University of Chicago Press, 1923), pp. 434–450; L.G. Reynolds, "Cutthroat Competition," *American Economic Review* 30 (December 1940): 736–747; Samuel M. Loescher, *Imperfect Collusion in the Cement Industry* (Cambridge, MA: Harvard University Press, 1959), pp. 191–199; Almarin Phillips, *Market Structure, Organization and Performance* (Cambridge, MA: Harvard University Press, 1962), pp. 16–19 and 221–242; Ralph G.M. Sultan, *Pricing in the Electrical Oligopoly,* vol. 2 (Boston: Harvard Business School Division of Research, 1974), pp. 286–298; and Joseph L. Bower, *When Markets Quake: The Management Challenge of Restructuring Industry* (Boston: Harvard Business School Press, 1986), Chapter 4.

15. Almarin Phillips, *Market Structure, Organization and Performance* (Cambridge: Harvard University Press, 1962); Samuel M. Loescher, *Imperfect Collusion in the Cement Industry* (Cambridge: Harvard University Press, 1959); Jesse W. Markham, *Competition in the Rayon Industry* (Cambridge: Harvard University Press, 1952); James W. McKie, *Tin Cans and Tin Plate* (Cambridge: Harvard University Press, 1959); Edmund P. Learned and Catherine C. Ellsworth, *Gasoline Pricing in Ohio* (Boston: Harvard Business School Division of Research, 1959); and Oliver E. Williamson, "A Dynamic Theory of Interfirm Behavior," *Quarterly Journal of Economics* 79 (November 1965): 579–607.

16. Sidney L. Carroll, "The Market for Commercial Airliners," in R. Caves and M. Roberts (eds.), *Regulating the Product Quality and Variety* (Cambridge, MA: Ballinger, 1975), pp. 150, 163; John Newhouse, *The Sporty Game* (New York: Alfred A. Knopf, 1982); *Business Week* (May 8, 1989): 34–35; and *Business Week* (January 25, 1988): 38.

17. Don E. Waldman, "Welfare and Collusion: Comment," *American Economic Review* 72 (March 1982): 268–271.

18. This view was common during the first 25 years of this century. See J.M. Clark, *Studies in the Economics of Overhead Costs* (Chicago: University of Chicago Press, 1923), pp. 434–450. For a later statement of this position see Almarin Phillips, *Market Structure, Organization and Performance* (Cambridge, MA.: Harvard University Press,1962), pp. 221–242.

19. *Addyston Pipe and Steel Company* v. *United States,* 175 U.S. 211 (1899).

20. *United States* v. *Trenton Potteries Company et al.,* 273 U.S. 392 (1927).

21. *Appalachian Coals Inc.* v. *United States,* 288 US 344 (1933).

22. *United States* v. *Container Corporation of America et al.,* 393 U.S. 333 (1969).

23. *United States* v. *United States Gypsum Company et al.,* 438 U.S. 422 (1978).

24. *American Tobacco Company et al.* v. *United States,* 328 U.S. 781 (1946).

25. *United States* v. *Paramount Pictures et al.,* 334 U.S. 131 (1948).

26. *Theatre Enterprises, Inc.* v. *Paramount Film Distributing Corporation et al.,* 346 U.S. 537 (1954).

27. *Ethyl Corporation* v. *FTC,* 729 F.2d 128 (1984).

28. *ibid.,* pp. 204–205.

29. *Sugar Institute, Inc. et al.* v. *United States,* 297 U.S. 553 (1936).

30. *Tag Manufacturers Institute* v. *Federal Trade Commission,* 174 F.2d 452 (1949).

31. *National Collegiate Athletic Association* v. *Board of Regents of University of Oklahoma,* 486 U.S. 85 (1984).

32. *United States* v. *MIT University,* 5 F.3d 658 (1993).

INTERNET EXERCISES

Visit www.aw-bc.com/waldman_jensen for this chapter's web exercises. Answer our real-world economics problems by searching the Internet for solutions!

Cartels in Action

C hapter 9 examined both the theory of collusion and public policy toward collusion in the United States. In this chapter, our attention turns toward real-world attempts to achieve effective collusion. As you read the chapter keep in mind the two overriding principles of successful collusion laid out in the previous chapter: the need to identify cheaters and the ability to punish them. Also keep in mind the factors that affect the ease or difficulty of attaining effective collusion, including (1) the height of entry barriers, (2) the number of firms, (3) concentration, (4) the degree of product differentiation, (5) demand growth and elasticity, (6) the frequency of sales, and (7) the rate of technological change.

10.1 Attempted Methods of Achieving Effective Collusion

10.1.1 Dominant-Firm Price Leader and Benefactor

Competitors have shown great ingenuity in their efforts to overcome the prisoner's dilemma. Some of those efforts have been quite successful, while others have not. In this section we examine some of the more successful efforts to see if there are any themes associated with successful collusion.

OIL PRODUCTION: 1973–1985 Some of the best examples of overt price-fixing cartels have come from the annals of international commodity cartels, and no example is more famous, or infamous, than the international oil cartel, OPEC (The Organization of Petroleum Exporting Countries). In Chapter 9's hypothetical example of the MidEast Corporation, MidEast's alternatives closely approximated those faced by the smaller members of OPEC, as well as non-OPEC oil-producing countries such as Egypt, Great Britain, and Mexico, since OPEC gained economic power in the 1970s. Saudi Arabia has been the major player and leader of OPEC. From the viewpoint of the relatively small producers, an increase in output should have little effect on price and might result in greatly increased profits *so long as Saudi Arabia attempts to maintain the cartel's official price at a higher level.* If the Saudis hold price at the official high level,

cartel members such as Kuwait, Venezuela, Algeria, Qatar, Gabon, and Ecuador have a strong incentive to increase production to increase revenues and profits.

Put differently, a problem for OPEC's stability has been the tendency for non-OPEC oil-producing countries to take the official OPEC price as a ***parametric price*** or a price that is *fixed* by economic conditions. In Figure 10.1 suppose the official OPEC price is P_{OPEC} and the marginal cost and average cost of producing oil for a non-OPEC oil producer such as Mexico are represented by the curves MC and AC. If Mexico believes that countries such as Canada and the United States would just as soon buy Mexican oil instead of OPEC oil at identical prices, then theory suggests that Mexico should take OPEC's price as given and maximize profits by producing the *competitive* output Q_1. Under these conditions there is little or no incentive for Mexico to restrict its output below the competitive output of Q_1. As a result, Mexico would gain market share at OPEC's expense.

This is precisely what happened almost continuously after OPEC gained its economic power in the mid-1970s, and especially after the fall of the Shah of Iran in 1979 sent oil markets into turmoil and pushed official OPEC prices up to $34 a barrel in 1981. From 1974 to 1985, OPEC's share of world production fell from 55 percent to 30 percent, and non-OPEC producers (including the United States) and producers from the communist and former communist states experienced an increase in their share from 45 percent to over 70 percent.[1]

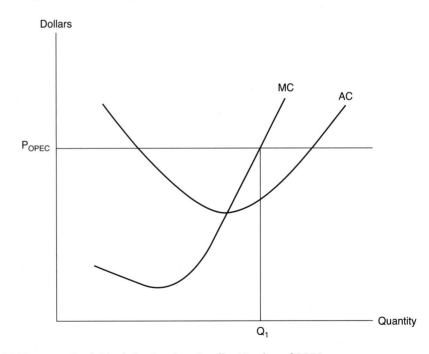

FIGURE 10.1 **Profit Maximization for a Smaller Member of OPEC**

If the official OPEC price is P_{OPEC}, then a nonmember of OPEC, such as Mexico, has an incentive to produce where P_{OPEC} = MC at the perfectly competitive output Q_1. If all nonmembers produce where P_{OPEC} = MC, OPEC's market share declines.

The biggest loser from the relative decline in OPEC's market share was Saudi Arabia. To stabilize prices, Saudi Arabia was forced to significantly reduce its output from an average of 6.5 million barrels per day in 1982 to 5.1 million in 1983, 4.7 million in 1984, and 3.4 million in 1985. When output reached a rate of about 2 million barrels per day in the summer of 1985, Saudi Arabia reached the limit of its restraint on behalf of the cartel.[2] In late 1985 the Saudis decided to assert their always-present economic power to control price. Once the Saudis decided to increase output to preserve their market share, instead of attempting to maintain a high price, industry prices plummeted to below $10 a barrel in 1986. At $10 a barrel the output of non-OPEC countries began to decline as marginal wells were shut down.[3] When the price was eventually stabilized at approximately $18 a barrel in 1986–1987, OPEC's share relative to non-OPEC countries once again began to increase.

In the early years of this scenario, Saudi Arabia did not play even a moderately aggressive strategy such as tit-for-tat, or even tit-for-two-tats. In fact, Saudi Arabia probably had no incentive to play tit-for-tat in response to "small" amounts of cheating. A hypothetical game matrix will help to explain why. Table 10.1 represents a possible game matrix for Saudi Arabia and Venezuela, which is used here to represent any small OPEC member. In Table 10.1 Saudi Arabia sets the price for the cartel—either high or low. Because Saudi Arabia produces so much more output than Venezuela, a decision to respond to a defection by cutting price actually results in a large reduction in Saudi Arabia's profits (from 9000 to 7000). In Table 10.1 the Saudis have a dominant strategy—set a high price. No matter what Venezuela does, the Saudis should keep the price high. Venezuela, of course, also has a dominant strategy—defect.

Table 10.1 suggests a possible solution to the prisoner's dilemma: Find a large price leader that has a self-interest in keeping the price high *regardless* of the actions of the other cartel members. This requires an industry structure in which one firm is strongly dominant like the dominant-firm model analyzed in Chapter 5.

Not all economists believe OPEC has operated as a cartel. One alternative theory suggests that oil-producing states have set production to generate sufficient revenues to cover their oil investment requirements. According to this theory, producing states view prices as fixed, that is, set by competitive forces; therefore, an increase in industry price permits a reduction in output to meet the country's investment requirements.[4] James Griffin attempted to test empirically whether the oil industry operated competitively or as a cartel.[5] His findings suggested that OPEC countries operated as a cartel, but that non-OPEC countries operated according to the competitive model. Overall, Griffin concluded that a "partial market-sharing cartel model dominates the competitive model."[6]

TABLE 10.1 Profits (Saudi Arabia, Venezuela)

		Venezuela's Strategy	
		Cooperate	*Defect*
Saudi Arabia's Strategy	High Price	10,000, 500	9000, 1000
	Low Price	8000, 375	7000, 450

STEEL: 1901–1920 Just as Saudi Arabia has played the role of dominant-firm price leader for OPEC, United States Steel played that role in the steel industry at the turn of the century, with much the same consequences. In the 1890s, before the formation of the United States Steel Corporation, the steel industry was characterized by periods of aggressive price competition. In fact, as the corporation began to take shape in 1900, steel prices were declining.[7] US Steel was formed in 1901 through the consolidation of 12 major steel companies. At the time, US Steel accounted for over 65 percent of the industry's output. Although US Steel almost certainly had the power to force compliance with its pricing policies, it chose a different path. Instead of aggressively cutting price to eliminate its competitors, it cooperated with them.

As we saw in Chapter 3, US Steel cooperated through a variety of devices, including pools, associations, trade meetings, and, most infamously, from 1907 until 1911, the "Gary dinners," at which Judge Elbert Gary, president of US Steel, invited competitors to "dinner" for the more or less expressed purpose of fixing and stabilizing prices.[8] Because US Steel decided to set prices at a level that attracted entry, and because it refrained from predatory practices, its market share declined continuously after its formation, and by 1920 its share had declined to approximately 50 percent.[9]

US Steel continued to provide a price umbrella for its smaller competitors even after 1911 when the explicit collusion associated with the Gary dinners ended as a result of a government antitrust investigation. After 1911 US Steel became the recognized price leader and held that role for decades until its power was permanently eroded by foreign competition.

Dominant-firm price leadership is generally only partially successful in solving the prisoner's dilemma. Because the system provides a tremendous incentive for new firms to enter and for smaller incumbent firms to expand output, downward pressure on price often ensues. Furthermore, even if cheating is easily detected, the dominant firm may have little incentive to punish price cutters.

10.1.2 Price Leadership

To solve the prisoner's dilemma, some method of communication between firms is crucial. One method is to overtly collude; another is to rely on a price leader or leaders to signal price changes, with the expectation that others will follow the leader. The ability of a price leader to force adherence depends critically on an industry's market structure. Chapter 5 developed a model of dominant-firm price leadership in which one firm had a very large market share, generally over 60 percent, and a cost advantage over fringe firms that enabled it to set its price independently. The dominant-firm price leadership model suggests that if the dominant-firm price leader sets a high price, new firms enter, existing firms expand, and ultimately the dominant firm's market share declines. As shown in the previous section, this is precisely what happened to Saudi Arabia and US Steel.

When a dominant-firm price leader loses its dominant position, a different type of leadership often evolves—*collusive price leadership.* Collusive price leadership exists when a few large firms in a concentrated industry set price and expect that the price will be followed by others.[10] It is not important for the identity of the price leader to remain the same, but it is important that price changes be followed. In the rare instance when a change is not followed, the price leader will usually rescind the

change, but if the leader fails to rescind, a price war may result in which all firms are big losers. Examples are easy to come by.

STEEL: 1911–1960 With the end of the Gary dinners in 1911, US Steel became the tacit price leader in steel and held that role for decades. The steel industry's use of tacit price leadership provided price stability that was at least as effective as the explicit attempts to fix prices through the Gary dinners, indicating that tacit collusion can be as effective as explicit collusion.

From 1920 until the early 1960s, US Steel was the acknowledged price leader in the steel industry. As Adams and Mueller noted,[11]

> During the administered price era, steel prices were characterized by remarkable rigidity and uniformity. Price stability was obtained at the expense of instability in output and employment. Unless impelled by sharp increases in direct cost or dangerous sniping by rivals, U.S. Steel generally preferred to resist both price increases and decreases and to sacrifice stability "only when the decision [was] unavoidable."
>
> After World War II, this price policy was transformed into one of "upward rigidity," that is, a pattern of stairstep price increases at regular intervals. . . . With or without resort to the conspiratorial basing point system,* the integrated giants matched each other's prices with monotonous consistency. They maintained a lockstep price uniformity by punishing any major mill that showed deviationist tendencies.

As US Steel lost its dominant position, it remained the recognized price leader even in fields in which it held a clear minority market share. In 1957, for example, US Steel held only a 26.6 percent share of capacity for cold-rolled piling compared with Bethlehem's 72.2 percent, yet US Steel was the price leader.[12] Similarly, in the Northeast, National was the output leader in cold-rolled sheets, but it followed US Steel's prices without question.[13]

In 1958 something unprecedented occurred in the steel industry: US Steel failed to lead an industry-wide price increase.[14] On July 1, 1958, a large wage increase for steelworkers went into effect. Traditionally, US Steel would increase prices following a wage increase. This time was different. When US Steel failed to respond, Armco, with a mere 4.4 percent of industry ingot capacity, announced a price increase. Other firms, including US Steel, followed, and the price increase stuck. A new chapter in the history of price leadership in steel had begun. US Steel had relinquished its position as the only price leader. Thereafter, price changes were initiated by one of several firms, most commonly US Steel, Armco, Bethlehem, or Republic.[15]

The passing of the old system created new uncertainty and less pricing stability, as became clear in a 1968 episode. After US Steel undercut Bethlehem on a major order, Bethlehem retaliated with a 22 percent price decrease on hot-rolled sheets (from $113.50 to just $88.50 per ton).[16] The other majors, including US Steel, followed Bethlehem's retaliatory price cut; however, three weeks later, US Steel suddenly increased its price to $125.00 per ton. Nine days later, Bethlehem followed with an increase, but only to $117.00 per ton. When US Steel matched the $117.00 price, the brief price

*Basing point systems are explained in detail in Section 10.1.4 of this chapter.

skirmish was over. In this instance, industry discipline had been brought about by Bethlehem's disciplinary price cut, and US Steel was actually the defector. As the once-mighty US Steel disappeared from the steel industry, Bethlehem assumed the major burden of price leadership.[17]

LEAD-BASED ANTIKNOCK COMPOUNDS: 1974–1979[18] In the days when most gasoline contained lead, only a few firms produced lead-based antiknock gasoline additives. Recall from Chapter 9 that from 1920 to 1948 Ethyl Corporation was the only American producer. In 1948 Du Pont entered, followed by PPG Industries and Nalco Chemical in the early 1960s. In 1974 Du Pont held a 36 percent market share, followed by Ethyl with 34 percent, PPG with 17.5 percent, and Nalco with 12.5 percent.[19]

The facts of this case were laid out in Chapter 9, but are repeated here for convenience. From 1974 to 1979 there were 24 price changes in the industry.[20] In 20 of these cases all four changed price on the same day. In the other four cases, all four firms had identical prices a day or two apart. Such a high degree of price uniformity required a sophisticated form of price leadership. Leadership was characterized by (1) at least 30 days' advance notice of all price changes; (2) public press notices of all price changes; (3) a delivered price system that required buyers located in the same city to pay the same price (these systems are discussed in a later section); and (4) the use of *most favored customer clauses,* whereby if one buyer received a lower price, all buyers would receive the same reduced price. Price leadership was clearly established to ensure both detection of all price cuts and punishment of cheaters.

The policy of giving at least 30 days' advance notice of price changes gave competitors ample time to respond and also gave the initiator of any change time to rescind its decision if the change was not matched by the others. If, for example, Du Pont intended to raise its price on May 1, it would announce its intention by April 1. Of course, Du Pont could also announce an intended price change more than 30 days in advance. An announcement on March 28, for example, would give its competitors three days to either announce matching changes or do nothing. If they matched the change, the new price would go into effect on May 1. If they failed to match, Du Pont could simply rescind its announcement. All of this occurring in public, through the press, guarded against secret price cuts, as did the use of a delivered price system and most favored customer clauses.[21] Furthermore, as discussed in Chapter 9, because there was no evidence of overt price fixing, the industry escaped antitrust action.

CIGARETTES: 1923–1941 One of the most famous instances of price leadership occurred in the cigarette industry.[22] As a result of the 1911 antitrust decree discussed in Chapter 3, the American Tobacco Company's monopoly over cigarettes was destroyed, and more than a dozen new cigarette companies were established, including Liggett & Myers and R. J. Reynolds. For about a decade, the cigarette producers competed aggressively, but in the early 1920s price competition suddenly ceased. Between 1928 and 1941, prices were identical and there were only eight price changes, five increases and three decreases. All five price increases were announced first by Reynolds, with American and Liggett following immediately. Of the three price decreases, American led two and Reynolds one.

In June 1931, the Big 3, as American, Reynolds, and Liggett & Myers were known, controlled 90 percent of the cigarette market. During that month, because of the

Depression, raw tobacco prices were at their lowest since 1905. In the midst of the greatest economic crisis the nation had ever seen, on June 23, 1931, Reynolds *raised* the net wholesale price of Camel cigarettes, its leading brand, from $5.64 to $6.04 per thousand. The same day, American and Liggett & Myers raised the price of their leading brands, Lucky Strikes and Chesterfield, respectively, to an identical $6.04.[23]

According to the president of Reynolds, the rationale for this action was "to express our own courage for the future and our own confidence in our industry."[24] In a perhaps more honest assessment, the president of American gave as his rationale "the opportunity of making some money."[25] Both presidents, however, greatly underestimated the cross-elasticity of demand between the leading premium brands that sold for 13 cents per pack and the lower-quality 10-cent brands. After the Big 3 increased their list prices, the 10-cent brands saw their market share increase from a mere 0.28 percent in June 1931 to 22.78 percent in November 1932. As a result, in January 1933, the Big 3 were forced to reduce the net price of their leading brands from $6.04 to $5.20 per thousand, and in February, they had to cut their price further to just $4.85 per thousand. It was estimated that at a price of $4.85 per thousand, Camels and Lucky Strikes were being sold at a loss. Despite these price cuts, the market share of the Big 3 was never again close to 90 percent.

The price increase of 1931 proved to be a monumental mistake. It led to the introduction of new brands and the establishment of new companies such as Brown and Williamson and Philip Morris, which would seriously challenge and, in some cases, actually displace the Big 3. Price leadership, however, survived. After World War II Reynolds and American remained the price leaders. In 1956 an attempt by Liggett & Myers to lead a price increase was rejected by the two leaders, and Liggett rescinded. Similarly, in 1965 Lorillard's effort to raise prices was rejected and rescinded. Finally, in the 1970s the establishment of Philip Morris's Marlboro brand as the worldwide sales leader enabled it to assert some leadership.[26]

Like dominant-firm price leadership, collusive price leadership is generally only partly successful in solving the prisoner's dilemma. Problems arise because no single firm is capable of effectively disciplining its rivals. If, for example, the firms are of more or less equal size and economic power, it may be difficult to discipline any one of the major players that becomes a price maverick.

Dominant-firm and collusive price leadership have been used effectively to try to move price toward the joint profit-maximizing level. A third type of price leadership, **barometric price leadership,** has also been used in some industries. With barometric price leadership, the price leader tends to be a small, nondominant firm that acts, as the name implies, more or less as an indicator of change. The barometric leader is relatively small; it does not have the ability to discipline rivals or enforce its will on the industry. Instead, it leads through example. When demand or cost conditions warrant a price change, the barometric price leader is the first to move. The more dominant firms then choose to either follow or reject the lead. Like collusive price leadership, barometric price leadership is a less effective method of solving the prisoner's dilemma than dominant-firm price leadership.

There is evidence of barometric price leadership in fields as diverse as gasoline, steel, cellophane, electric turbines, and cheese. In the bulk cheese market, it has been suggested that Kraft has served as a barometric price leader.[27] The previously cited example of Armco, instead of US Steel, increasing steel prices in 1958 is another

example of a barometric leader indicating that it was time for a change in an industry's pricing policy.

ELECTRIC TURBINES: 1950–1960 In electric turbines, Westinghouse and Allis-Chalmers were the price leaders on actual *transactions prices* in the 1950s even though General Electric, with approximately a 60 percent market share, led changes in *book prices*.[28] Sultan has suggested that in this case General Electric acted as a buffer to prevent larger swings in price.[29] According to this theory, in a period of falling demand, General Electric would not reduce book prices but would permit Westinghouse and Allis-Chalmers to reduce transactions prices. Similarly, in a period of rising demand, General Electric would not increase book prices but would permit Westinghouse and Allis-Chalmers to increase transactions prices. General Electric's relative market share would then fall during recessions, but it would increase during expansions when General Electric's actual transactions prices would be below Westinghouse's and Allis-Chalmers' prices. Over the entire expansion-contraction business cycle, such a policy would result in stable prices and stable market shares.

CELLOPHANE: 1941–1957 There is also evidence of barometric price leadership in the cellophane industry, with Avisco leading price changes that were often not followed by Du Pont.[30] Avisco led most price changes in the cellophane industry despite Du Pont's dominant position.

GASOLINE RETAILING IN OHIO: 1950s Standard Oil of Ohio (SOHIO) was the barometric price leader in the retail gasoline market in Ohio even though it was relatively small compared with the large national chains with which it competed.[31]

An advantage of barometric leadership is that it prevents price changes by the leaders from being misinterpreted as aggressive strategic decisions. A barometric leader's price change is less likely to result in a breakdown in industry pricing discipline than a price change initiated by a major firm under collusive price leadership. Although barometric price leadership may at first appear to be an innocent method of reading market signals, it may also be symptomatic of an attempt to raise and stabilize price.

One of the major factors necessary to solve the prisoner's dilemma, an ability to discipline, is missing in cases of barometric price leadership. Barometric price leadership, therefore, may not be very effective.

APPLICATION 10.1

A Sweet Case of Price Leadership: Dole and Del Monte in the Canned Pineapple Industry

While it is easy to tell anecdotal tales of price leadership, it is much more difficult to find reliable data to test the actual price reactions between oligopolists. Vickner and Davies, however, managed to do precisely that in the canned pineapple market, a market completely controlled by two firms, Dole with a 72 percent market share and Del Monte with the remaining 28 percent.* Point-of-purchase supermarket scanner data were obtained for all pineapple sales in the United States for 120 consecutive weeks between June 25, 1994, and October 5, 1996. Average prices for Dole and Del Monte for

each week are shown in the figure above. Note that Dole's price is almost always higher than Del Monte's price and that the two price sequences appear to move together. For the entire 120 weeks, Del Monte's average price was 74 cents per pound and Dole's was 81 cents per pound. Generally, the dominant firm, Dole, charged a price approximately 10 percent higher than Del Monte's price.

Vickner and Davies used regression analysis to analyze the pricing interactions between the two firms. They modeled the changes in Dole's and Del Monte's prices as a function of their own lagged prices, their competitor's lagged prices, and the interaction of each other's prices. The results indicated that Del Monte's price adjusted rapidly to a change in Dole's price, while Dole's price was not significantly affected by a change in Del Monte's price. Furthermore, while Del Monte's price was significantly affected by a lagged change in Dole's price, Del Monte's price was *not* significantly affected by a lagged change in its *own* price. On the other hand, Dole's price was *only* affected by a lagged change in its own price. These results suggest that Dole was the price leader in the canned pineapple market and that Del Monte pretty much followed along.

*Steven S. Vickner and Stephen P. Davies, "Estimating Strategic Price Response in a Product-Differentiated Oligopoly: The Case of a Domestic Canned Fruit Industry," *Agribusiness* 12 (April 2000): 125–140. ■

10.1.3 Most Favored Customer Clauses and "Low-Price" Guarantees[32]

Two of the more counterintuitive methods of getting around the prisoner's dilemma are to offer either a ***low-price guarantee*** or a ***most favored customer clause***. *Low-price guarantees* promise the customer that the seller "will not be undersold and will match or beat any competitor's price." Such guarantees are extremely common in retailing,

as when Sears offers appliance buyers the guarantee that if the buyer finds the same appliance sold or advertised for a lower price at another store in the next 30 days, Sears will match the other store's price plus give a further 10 percent price reduction. *Most favored customer clauses* promise that if the seller charges any future buyer a lower price than current buyers, the current buyers can receive a reimbursement to cover the price difference. Sears also uses most favored customer clauses when it sells an appliance with the guarantee that if the appliance goes on sale at Sears in the next 30 days, the buyer can receive a reimbursement to cover the difference in costs.

ELECTRIC TURBINES: 1963–1975[33] In Chapter 9 we used General Electric and Westinghouse as players in a hypothetical prisoner's dilemma game. Now consider the real-world battle between these two corporate giants. General Electric and Westinghouse compete in virtually every major segment of the electrical equipment industry. Throughout the 1950s, it was common practice for firms to fix prices through direct price-fixing agreements.[34] In 1960, however, the industry was caught red-handed breaking the antitrust laws, and the formal overt agreements fell apart as firms were fined and executives were sent to prison. Through a series of antitrust consent decrees the defendants were enjoined from entering into any further overt attempts to fix prices. One of the consent decrees, signed on October 1, 1960, required General Electric, Westinghouse, and Allis-Chalmers (the only three American producers of turbine generators) to set turbine prices independently and to publicly announce their prices.[35] As a result of the uncovering of the conspiracy and the consent decree, price competition developed in the turbine market between 1960 and 1963. In fact, competition became so intense that low prices and large discounts forced Allis-Chalmers out of the market in December 1962.[36] This left only two domestic producers, General Electric and Westinghouse.

In May 1963, General Electric introduced a new turbine-pricing policy.[37] First, General Electric announced its intention of maintaining its book prices and eliminating all discounts. Second, General Electric published a revised price book that simplified the procedure for determining prices. To determine prices under the new system, buyers simply multiplied General Electric's book price by a published multiplier. For example, if General Electric announced a multiplier of 0.80, actual prices equaled 80 percent of book prices. The third component was a *price protection clause* whereby General Electric guaranteed that if it lowered *any* product's price below its list price to *any* buyer, it would retroactively grant the lower price to any buyer that had purchased the product during the previous six months. Furthermore, to guard against secret price reductions, General Electric opened its books to public inspection.

Within days of learning about General Electric's new pricing policy, Westinghouse began using the General Electric pricing system, even *using General Electric's price book to set its prices!* Nine months later, Westinghouse introduced its own price book but continued to follow General Electric's prices. As a result of these policies, after August 1964, the two firms charged identical prices on all turbine orders.

The system worked because it ensured detection of cheating and guaranteed punishment. Detection was ensured by the open books policy that allowed anyone to check on the price either charged to any buyer. Any price reduction, therefore, would immediately be detected. Punishment was ensured because if either firm reduced a price to *any* buyer, regardless of whether it was a General Electric buyer or a Westinghouse buyer, it would have to reduce its price to *all* buyers of that product over the

previous six months. Any price cut by General Electric would therefore primarily hurt General Electric, not Westinghouse, and any price cut by Westinghouse would primarily hurt Westinghouse. The scheme was an excellent solution to the prisoner's dilemma, and it worked.

ELECTRONICS RETAILING: 1980[38] Even in highly competitive industries, low-price guarantees can help maintain discipline. Have you ever wondered why so many major appliance dealers offer low-price guarantees? Customers who believe that such guarantees ensure the lowest possible price in a highly competitive market should think again.

Crazy Eddie was a large dealer of audio equipment in New York City. Anyone who watched New York City television in the 1970s and 1980s probably knew the "crazy" Crazy Eddie commercials. Crazy Eddie claimed that his prices were "insane," because he would not be undersold. Newmark & Lewis was one of Crazy Eddie's largest competitors and also had a low-price guarantee. In fact, Newmark & Lewis promised to pay *double* the difference between its price and a competitor's lower price.

Suppose that both Crazy Eddie and Newmark & Lewis charged $1000 for a particular stereo component. One day Crazy Eddie gets "crazy" and cuts the price to $900. Will this attract customers to its store? Quite the contrary: The price cut actually drives customers to Newmark & Lewis, where they can now buy the component for $800 ($1000 minus twice the difference between Newmark & Lewis's price of $1000 and Crazy Eddie's price of $900). Furthermore, as customers come in to get the $800 bargain, they act as informants against Crazy Eddie's price cut. Crazy Eddie's price cut is identified and punishment in the form of lost sales is immediate. As a result of the low-price guarantees, the only policy that makes sense is to maintain the price at $1000. Crazy Eddie could rant and rave about low prices all he wanted to on television because the more he did, the higher prices would be. Eddie Antar, the former chairman and CEO of Crazy Eddie, wasn't so crazy after all, although he did have to flee from the United States because of charges of embezzlement. In 1997 Antar was sentenced to 82 months in federal prison after pleading guilty to racketeering and conspiracy charges.

The use of most favored customer clauses is an effective method of solving the prisoner's dilemma. Cheating is easily detected by consumer-provided information, and punishment in the form of lost customers is swift.

APPLICATION 10.2

Most Favored Customer Clauses for Medicaid, But What About Everyone Else?*

Most favored customer clauses are usually established by competing firms; however, in 1990, the United States Congress mandated a most favored customer clause for Medicaid drug purchases when it passed the Omnibus Budget Reconciliation Act (OBRA). The act included a rebate program to be paid by pharmaceutical companies to the government for drugs purchased by Medicaid.[†] Prior to the OBRA, Medicaid generally paid higher prices for drugs than did other large buyers such as hospitals, health maintenance organizations (HMOs), and some large insurance groups because Medicaid paid hospitals and pharmacies directly for individual prescriptions rather than purchasing drugs in bulk.

The OBRA required drug companies to pay rebates to state and federal Medicaid programs based on a formula that was effectively a most favored customer clause. Rebates were based on Medicaid's overpayments and the overpayments were based on the drug company's average manufacturer price (AMP) or lowest price, whichever resulted in a larger rebate. The basic plan required Medicaid to purchase branded drugs (those drugs sold under a brand name like Lipitor or Prilosec) for 87.5 percent of the AMP. If a drug manufacturer sold any drugs below 87.5 percent of the AMP, then Medicaid would pay that lower price. For example, if a pharmaceutical company charged one large buyer 75 percent of the AMP, then Medicaid would receive a rebate based on a price that was 75 percent of AMP. For generic drugs sold under a chemical compound name (for example, pseudoephedrine hydrochloride instead of Sudafed), Medicaid would pay 90 percent of the AMP.

The most favored customer clause created several new incentives for the drug manufacturers. First, the guarantee gave the manufacturers an incentive to raise their lowest discounted prices on branded drugs. Second, the average price aspect of the legislation gave the drug companies an incentive to raise their overall price levels in order to increase their AMPs and lower their rebates to Medicaid. However, if the branded drug manufacturers have market power and face downward-sloping demand curves for their non-Medicaid buyers (which is very likely), then like all profit-maximizing firms with market power, they will be pricing on the *elastic* portion of their demand curves, and therefore, raising prices will *decrease* total revenue on sales to non-Medicaid buyers.

Fiona Morton studied the impact of the most favored customer clause on wholesale prices for cardiovascular drugs sold from 1989 to 1991. Morton theorized that after the passage of the OBRA, the price of drugs with a larger Medicaid market share would increase. Furthermore, she hypothesized that the most favored customer clause would give firms an incentive to raise the price of larger packages of drugs (those with more doses) relative to smaller packages because the drug manufacturers typically offered large quantity-based discounts on larger packages before passage of the OBRA. In her study, she also controlled for market concentration in the drugstore and hospital market and for the number of generic substitutes available for a branded drug.

For branded drugs facing generic competition and sold in *drugstores,* Morton found that the Medicaid market share of a drug had a positive and statistically significant impact on the price of a drug after the implementation of the most favored customer clause and that the guarantee resulted in an approximately 4 percent price increase. She also found that package size and the number of generic substitutes available had positive and statistically significant impacts on the price of a drug after the implementation of the most favored customer clause. These results are completely consistent with the theory that the most favored customer clause resulted in higher drugstore prices.

For branded drugs facing generic competition and sold in *hospitals,* the only statistically significant relationship was that package size had a positive impact on price after the implementation of the most favored customer clause. However, Medicaid's market share of a drug did not have a significant impact on *hospital* drug prices. Because *inpatient* hospital sales of drugs to Medicaid patients did not come under the most favored customer clause in the legislation, Morton was not surprised with this finding.

Morton concluded that as a result of the most favored customer clause (1) the average *drugstore* price of a branded drug facing generic competition, and which

was commonly sold to Medicaid patients, increased significantly; and (2) drugstores increased the prices for large packages of these drugs, particularly those drugs with more generic substitutes. These findings are bad news for the vast majority of pharmaceutical users who are not on Medicaid. For those buyers, prices *increased;* and because Medicaid only covered about 13 percent of drug expenditures from 1989 to 1991, most buyers paid higher prices for these branded drugs at drugstores. As a result, the drug manufacturers' profits may have increased.

The bottom line is that while the most favored customer clause reduced government Medicaid expenditures, it also increased prices for many drugs commonly purchased by non-Medicaid buyers and may well have increased the drug manufacturers' profits. Perhaps the members of Congress should have read about the economic impact on prices of most favored customer clauses before passing the OBRA.

*The following is based on Fiona Scott Morton, "The Strategic Response by Pharmaceutical Firms to the Medicaid Most-Favored-Customer Rules," *Rand Journal of Economics* 28, (Summer 1997): 269–290.

†Medicaid is the U.S. program that pays medical bills for the poor. It is not to be confused with Medicare, which pays medical expenses for senior citizens. ∎

10.1.4 Basing Point Pricing Systems

Under a ***basing point pricing system,*** or delivered price system, one or more geographic locations are established as basing points. Buyers are charged prices that include standard freight charges from the nearest basing point, even if the seller's manufacturing plant is located far from the basing point. Basing point systems are most common in industries characterized by high transportation costs relative to value, such as steel, cement, and lumber.

STEEL: 1901–1948 The most famous basing point system was the steel industry's "Pittsburgh Plus" system.[39] From 1884 to 1924 Pittsburgh was the only basing point in the steel industry, and all steel shipments included a freight charge from Pittsburgh, even if the steel was shipped from Chicago or Birmingham. If a Chicago appliance manufacturer purchased steel from a Chicago steel mill, it paid for freight from Pittsburgh. No freight charges were actually incurred; the Chicago producer was able to pocket this ***phantom freight.*** If a Chicago mill sold steel to a Pittsburgh buyer, however, it would be forced to absorb the freight charges.

Consider the example illustrated in Figure 10.2. In 1920 the base price of steel purchased in Pittsburgh was $40 per ton. The curve ABC represents the actual basing point price of steel at various locations between Pittsburgh and Chicago, and the curve DBE represents the $40.00 per ton base price plus true freight costs from Chicago. A mill located in Chicago received phantom freight on all shipments to locations between Chicago and Toledo, Ohio, and it absorbed freight costs on all shipments to locations between Toledo and Pittsburgh. Only at Toledo would a Chicago seller receive a price that covered actual freight charges. In 1920, transportation costs from Pittsburgh to Chicago were $7.60 per ton, so the Chicago price was $47.60. If a buyer in Chicago bought from a mill in Chicago, the price was $47.60, and the Chicago seller received $7.60 in phantom freight. If a buyer in Pittsburgh purchased from a Chicago mill, it would pay only $40.00 and the seller would incur $7.60 in freight absorption charges.

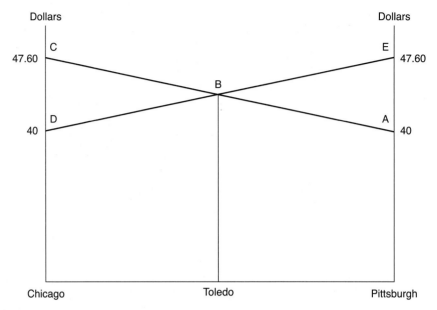

FIGURE 10.2 Phantom Freight with a Basing Point Pricing System

The curve ABC represents the basing point price of steel, which is what buyers actually pay per ton, at locations between Pittsburgh and Chicago. The curve DBE represents the $40 per ton base price plus true freight costs from Chicago. A mill located in Chicago receives phantom freight on all shipments between Chicago and Toledo and absorbs freight charges on all shipments between Toledo and Pittsburgh.

Basing point systems have two major advantages for oligopolists. First and foremost, prices are fixed for delivery anywhere in the country; the system is an excellent method for maintaining price discipline. Second, all firms do reasonably well under basing point systems. Firms located at a basing point can compete with producers located far from the basing point, and firms located far from the basing point obtain phantom freight on many shipments to cover their freight absorption on shipments close to the basing point.

A basing point system can easily be used as a method of tacit collusion to solve the prisoner's dilemma. The system establishes uniform prices in any location in the country. Furthermore, it discourages price chiseling because if chiselers are caught, the other members of the industry can establish a *punitive basing point* at the cheater's plant location, meaning that prices would be established at the punitive basing point at a level below the cheater's average cost. If a punitive basing point were established, the price cutter would sustain an economic loss on every sale and would eventually be forced to raise prices to accepted levels, to leave the market, or to sell out to a competitor. The punitive basing point would be successful in restoring price discipline because the price cheater would sustain economic losses on every sale, while its competitors would sustain losses only on sales in the price cutter's market.

The basing point system requires a method for setting the base price. In the steel industry that method was price leadership by US Steel. As discussed previously, in the

early part of this century US Steel had the ability and incentive to unilaterally set the price of steel. The basing point system simply provided a way to minimize price cutting. The system worked well until the Great Depression drove capacity utilization rates under 20 percent and led to widespread price cutting.[40]

SOUTHERN PLYWOOD: 1963–1971[41] In the 1970s the basing point system once again became a topic of interest because of the discovery of a delivered price system in the plywood industry. Until 1963 all the plywood produced in the United States came from the Northwest. A technological advance in the early 1960s, however, allowed builders to substitute southern pine for Northwestern Douglas fir. As a result the industry expanded rapidly into the South. The first southern entrants, led by Georgia-Pacific in 1963, were also the leading producers of Northwestern Douglas fir. Spurred on by the large potential freight savings associated with southern production, by 1969 there were 34 southern plywood mills, producing about 21 percent of the nation's output.[42]

Georgia-Pacific initially priced its southern plywood by using a basing point system based on shipment from Portland, Oregon. The southern pine price was adjusted slightly downward, apparently to account for some perceived, as opposed to actual, product differentiation on the part of buyers, who continued to believe that Douglas fir was a superior wood. Additional firms entering the southern market all used the same Oregon-based price system.

The basing point system was extremely functional. Beginning in 1958, two trade publications, *Crow's* and *Random Lengths,* published plywood prices on a weekly basis. These weekly price lists were used as a basis for future price negotiations in the industry. The southern manufacturers of plywood simply adopted the *Crow's* and *Random Lengths* prices and added freight charges from Portland, Oregon. This pricing system generated large phantom freight profits for the southern producers.

It is not surprising that when the first southern mill was established, Georgia-Pacific elected to charge a Portland-based price. Economic theory predicts that one southern mill would have virtually no impact on price, and therefore, that mill would act as a perfectly competitive firm and take the Portland-based price as the competitive price. What is surprising is that as capacity in the South increased to roughly 30 percent of national output in 1973, 25 southern producers operating 53 mills were *still* setting Portland-based prices.[43]

As noted previously, basing point systems can be effective methods of maintaining discipline only if a method exists to fix the basing point price. In the southern plywood industry, two trade publications located thousands of miles away were the effective method of setting price.

Basing point systems have proved to be effective methods of solving the prisoner's dilemma. Cheating is easily detected, and punishment in the form of the adoption of a *punitive basing point* can be very quick and effective.

10.1.5 Trade and Professional Associations

SUGAR: 1927–1935 Recall from Chapter 9 that in the early part of the 20th century most sugar was sold through independent brokers, who before the creation of the Sugar Institute had made it a common practice to grant discriminatory price concessions to

buyers. These concessions often led to a general breakdown in price discipline. To eliminate this price discrimination, the Sugar Institute was established. The 15 members produced 70 to 80 percent of the refined cane sugar in the United States. The Institute established a *code of ethics* that distinguished "ethical" from "unethical" types of behavior. The code required far more than the simple announcement of prices. Institute members agreed to refuse to deal with (1) water carriers who refused to announce freight rates or who granted price concessions to any sugar refiner; (2) wholesalers who granted any price concessions; and (3) truckers, brokers, or warehouse owners who granted secret rebates.

The Sugar Institute sought to force compliance with its policies through an elaborate system of punishments.[44] The main objective was to require adherence to prices that were publicly announced and to eliminate all price discrimination. The Institute required brokers to sign a written contract stating that they would not grant discriminatory price concessions and that, if they did, they would have to pay a rebate to the refiner equal to the amount of the concession. Such a contract provided a strong enforcement mechanism against price cutting by brokers. As a further enforcement mechanism, members refused to deal with any broker who would not sign the agreement.

Evidence suggests that the Sugar Institute was somewhat successful in its efforts to stabilize price. Compared with raw sugar, the number and frequency of price changes declined for refined sugar after the establishment of the Institute's code of ethics. Furthermore, despite the existence of large excess capacity, price-cost margins and profits increased after the Sugar Institute's plan was implemented.[45]

LEGAL SERVICES IN VIRGINIA: 1970s In 1971, the Goldfarbs purchased a home in Fairfax County, Virginia. To secure a mortgage, they were required to obtain title insurance. The Goldfarbs contacted 36 lawyers and were told by each that the fee would be 1 percent of the value of the property.[46] They were also told that the Fairfax County Bar Association "suggested" this 1 percent fee to its members.

The reason for the identical pricing quickly became clear to the Goldfarbs: The 1 percent figure came right from the published list of minimum fees of the Virginia State Bar. The Virginia State Bar published a suggested minimum fee schedule in 1962 and a revised schedule, with higher fees, in 1969. The Bar Association even had a special "Committee on Economics of Law Practice" that recommended the fee schedules.

To enforce its suggested prices, the State Bar threatened to investigate any lawyer charging a lower fee (higher fees were considered ethical) and warned its members that the charging of lower fees "raises a presumption that such lawyer is guilty of misconduct."[47] A lawyer found guilty of misconduct was in very serious professional trouble because, according to the rules of the Virginia Supreme Court of Appeals, all lawyers were required to be members "in good standing" of the Virginia State Bar to practice law in Virginia.[48]

Trade and professional associations have had mixed results in their efforts to solve the prisoner's dilemma. Because there are often such a large number of firms, detecting cheating can be very difficult. In addition, punishment may not be effective. The Virginia Bar Association's plan was extremely effective in solving the prisoner's dilemma, however. In this case, cheating was easily detected because many fees, such as closing costs on a home, were public, and the threat of professional sanctions and a loss of the right to practice law made punishment effective.

APPLICATION 10.3

*"Something Is Rotten in the State of Denmark"**:
The Danish Government Promotes Tacit Price Fixing

In Chapter 9 we observed that price-exchange agreements have been viewed suspiciously by the United States Department of Justice because they can be used to establish tacit price-fixing agreements. While price-exchange agreements are not illegal per se, in the 1969 *Container Corporation* case Supreme Court Justice Douglas wrote in his majority opinion that the cardboard container industry's price exchanges tended to result in "price uniformity." If all the members of a trade association agree to permit the association to publish actual transaction prices on every sale, a trade association can serve as a cover for a price-exchange agreement.

But here's a twist on the concept of a price-exchange agreement: What if a *government antitrust agency* published transaction prices on each and every sale in an industry? Could this action result in tacit pricing fixing? In October 1993, the Danish Competition Council, which oversees antitrust policy in Denmark, decided to do exactly that in the ready-mixed concrete industry. According to Albæk, Møllgaard, and Overgaard, the Danish Competition Council's decision to publish all transaction prices in the ready-mixed cement industry led to a dramatic increase in prices and resulted in tacit collusion.[†] The council decided to publish prices because it thought that the publication of price information would reduce the possibility of oligopolistic collusion or price discrimination. The council reasoned that publication of price information would make the ready-mixed concrete industry more competitive because perfectly competitive markets require perfect information for all buyers and *sellers*. Unfortunately, what was missing from the council's analysis was a realization that the Danish ready-mixed concrete industry was far from perfectly competitive. In fact, the industry was made up of a group of regional monopolies and oligopolies. Because ready-mixed concrete is shipped in large mixing trucks that can keep the concrete wet for a maximum of two hours, the relevant geographical market is quite small, approximately 20 miles (32 kilometers) in diameter. The Danish four-firm concentration ratio in 1987 was 57 percent; however, regional concentration was much higher. Many regional markets were monopolies, and in most relevant regional markets the largest firm controlled about 70 percent. Prior to the council's publication of price data, the industry had been characterized by rigid list prices with many secret large discounts.

The council published transaction prices for two types of concrete, 10 MPa, a weaker concrete, and 25 MPa, a stronger concrete, for three regions of the country, Copenhagen, Aarhus, and Northern Jutland. Albæk, Møllgaard, and Overgaard used the figure on the next page to show that during the first few months of 1994 following the publication of the council's price information, ready-mixed concrete prices increased significantly by an average of 19 percent. After October 1994, prices leveled off at this higher price plateau. The figure also shows that the price of the most important input into ready-mixed concrete, cement, *declined* during the period and the average price of all types of concrete (not just the ready-mixed variety for which prices were published) increased at a much slower rate.

Albæk, Møllgaard, and Overgaard also found that in the Aarhus region, following the publication of the council's price information, all firms increased their prices but at

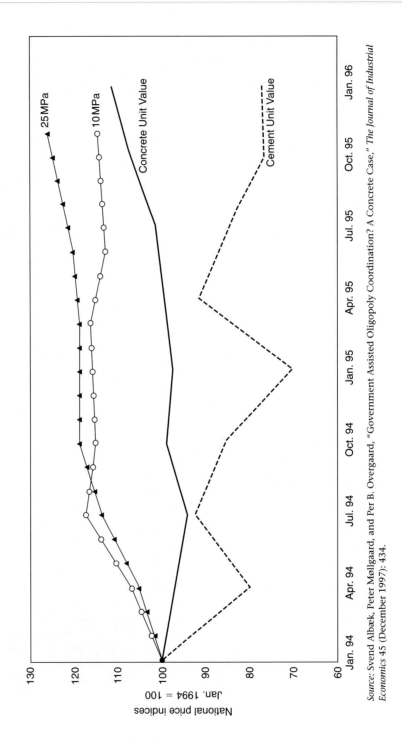

Source: Svend Albæk, Peter Møllgaard, and Per B. Overgaard, "Government Assisted Oligopoly Coordination? A Concrete Case," *The Journal of Industrial Economics* 45 (December 1997): 434.

different rates. Within a few months, however, all the firms' prices had converged toward the council's published prices, which effectively became the collusive prices in Aarhus.

Something was clearly rotten in the state of Denmark and the Competition Council eventually figured out what it was—it was the council's supposedly pro-competitive price publication policy that was leading to tacit price collusion. Searching for a better end than Hamlet met, in December 1996 the Competition Council decided to cease publishing ready-mixed concrete prices.

*Marcellus in *Hamlet* (Act I, Scene IV, Line 90).

†Svend Albæk, Peter Møllgaard, and Per B. Overgaard, "Government Assisted Oligopoly Coordination? A Concrete Case," *The Journal of Industrial Economics* 45 (December 1997): 429–443. ∎

10.1.6 Schemes to Divide Markets

SWITCHGEAR ASSEMBLIES* IN THE ELECTRICAL EQUIPMENT INDUSTRY: 1950s As previously stated in the discussion of the electric turbine market, price fixing was rampant in the electrical equipment industry in the 1950s. The five major manufacturers of switchgear assemblies, General Electric, Westinghouse, Allis-Chalmers, I-T-E, and Federal Pacific, however, faced repeated cheating in their attempts to fix prices. Many methods were used to try to fix prices, but one was so unique and ingenious that it has received a great deal of attention. On November 9, 1958, the five manufacturers reached an agreement to divide the sealed bid market as follows: GE, 39 percent; Westinghouse, 35 percent; I-T-E, 11 percent; Allis-Chalmers, 8 percent; and Federal Pacific, 7 percent. A bit later, the five firms established the *phases of the moon* pricing system.[49]

The ***phases of the moon system*** contained not only a method to set price, but also detection and enforcement mechanisms. Under the system, each company was awarded a target percentage of the switchgear market. Just as the phases of the moon rotate every week, the company in the low-bid position rotated on a periodic basis. For example, GE might occupy the low-bid position for three weeks, followed by Allis-Chalmers for a week. The firm in the low-bid position was supposed to submit the agreed-on low bid, and each of the other four firms knew exactly how much more they were supposed to bid. As a result, the purchasing agency would receive five different bids, thereby "proving" the existence of competition.

To try to enforce adherence, the conspirators met 25 times between November 1958 and November 1959. There was even a cloak-and-dagger atmosphere to the conspiracy. According to the testimony of Nye Spencer of I-T-E, for example, "It was considered discreet not to be too obvious, and to minimize telephone calls, to use plain envelopes if mailing material to each other, not to be seen together in traveling, and so forth."[50] At the meetings, a cumulative list of all sealed-bid transactions was presented and compared with the agreed-on quotas. If one firm was receiving "too much" business (or "too little"), adjustments would be made on future bids.[51]

*According to Herling, "Switchgear assemblies control and protect electrical apparatus used in the generation, conversion, transmission, and distribution of electrical energy. They consist of switching and interrupting devices in combination with control, metering, protection, and regulating equipment and their associated interconnections and supporting structures." (John Herling, *The Great Price Conspiracy* [Washington, DC: Luce, 1962], p. 353.)

The phases of the moon system is an excellent example of an attempt to fix prices by establishing quotas to divide the market. According to the following song that made its way around GE, it must have worked:[52]

(To be sung to the tune of "Moonglow")

It must have been Moonglow
Way up in the blue
It must have been Moonglow
That brought that bid to you.

I still hear them saying
As they rigged the price
The customer's paying
Too much, but it's so nice!

We've fixed the prices in the air
All of our schemes sock the buyer everywhere

If we play it cozy
And build our cartel
Our life will be rosy
Who cares—and what the hell?

In addition to the phases of the moon system, the electrical manufacturers used other devices to establish quotas.[53] In the power switching equipment* market, 15 companies established a *quadrants* system to divide the United States. Four companies were assigned to each quadrant. These companies would meet and decide how to divide the market in their region. After the meetings, companies that were not present would be contacted for approval of the agreement.

By the time the government completed its investigation of the electrical equipment industry, 20 indictments covering 22 product groups had been handed down. Every indictment resulted in a plea of either guilty or *nolo contendere*.† Eventually seven executives spent 30 days each in jail, another two dozen received 30-day or one-month suspended sentences, and fines totaling approximately $2,000,000 were imposed on firms and individuals.[54]

LYSINE AND CITRIC ACID: 1992–1995 In the 1990s, two important conspiracies concerned schemes to divide world markets and resulted in huge antitrust fines. In 1996, the Archer Daniels Midland Company (ADM) had to pay a $100 million criminal fine. ADM had conspired with Ajinomoto Co., Kyowa Kakko Kogyo Co. Ltd., Sewon America, Inc., and others to restrain trade in lysine, an amino acid used by farmers as a feed additive to help ensure proper growth of swine and poultry, and citric acid, an

*According to Herling, "Power switching equipment is used for interrupting an electrical circuit or for isolating a portion of it when changing connections, replacing equipment, repairing a fault or breakdown, or when for other reasons a completely open circuit is desired." (John Herling, *The Great Price Conspiracy* [Washington, DC: Luce, 1962], p. 354.)

†A plea of *nolo contendere* means that while the indicted party does not admit to guilt, it chooses not to contest the charges. It is a very common plea in antitrust cases.

organic acid that is used in many food products and beverages, cosmetics, medicine, detergents, chemicals, and textiles.[55] ADM and its co-conspirators held meetings and conversations in which they discussed the price and volume of sales of lysine and citric acid.[56] During these meetings and conversations the companies agreed not only to fix prices, but to allocate the volume of sales for each company in both the United States and throughout the world. The conspirators also agreed to issue price announcements and price quotations for the purpose of monitoring and enforcing the agreed-on prices and sales volumes.[57]

VITAMINS: 1990–1999 On May 20, 1999, Hoffmann-La Roche of Switzerland and BASF AG of Germany pleaded guilty to fixing vitamin prices and were fined $725 million. From 1990 until February 1999, Hoffmann-La Roche, BASF, and their co-conspirators participated in a conspiracy to restrain the world trade in vitamins.[58] Through executives, officers, and employees, the two firms conspired with other vitamin manufacturers to allocate the volume of certain vitamins in the United States and the world, and to allocate customers to specific companies in the United States. This was accomplished through a series of conversations and meetings. At these meetings agreements were reached regarding the prices at which each conspirator would sell certain vitamins and also the timing of price increases and the volume of sales for each firm.[59] Additionally the conspirators agreed to rig bids so that specific companies would be awarded contracts to supply vitamin premixes to particular U.S. customers.

10.1.7 Patent Cartels

GLASS CONTAINERS: 1924–1945[60] Patents sometimes provide a wonderful opportunity to create effective cartels that last well beyond the life of the patents. This is precisely what occurred in the glass container industry from 1924 to 1945.

A bit of history is useful. At the turn of the century, glass making was still done primarily by hand. However, in 1904 Owens-Illinois developed the first fully automated suction process machine for producing glass containers. When Owens refused to license its revolutionary machine, many glass container manufacturers were threatened with extinction. Unfortunately for Owens, a competing machine was developed that used the suspended gob feeding process. Hartford-Fairmont (the predecessor of Hartford-Empire) acquired the basic gob process patents and improved on them. At the same time, the Empire Machine Company, which was controlled by Corning Glass, owned certain gob process patent applications that interfered with Hartford-Fairmont's patents. In 1916 Hartford-Fairmont and Empire granted each other exclusive cross-licenses on their gob patents. Further negotiations led to the consolidation of the two firms as the Hartford-Empire Company on October 6, 1922.

Throughout this period Owens-Illinois also held gob process patents that were in conflict with Hartford's patent claims. On April 9, 1924, Owens and Hartford-Empire settled their conflicting patent claims. Under the agreement (1) Owens granted Hartford an exclusive license on its patents, and Hartford granted Owens a nonexclusive license to make machines under Hartford's patents; (2) Owens received half of all Hartford's royalties over $600,000 per year; and (3) Owens received a veto over any attempt by Hartford to grant a license to any company that used any of Owens'

patents. The agreement also prevented Owens from entering the pressed and blown glass field, which was reserved for Corning Glass, and left Owens in complete control of its original suction process patents.

After reaching this settlement with Owens, Hartford-Empire attempted to purchase all of the existing patents on gob feeder equipment. By 1938, Hartford had acquired over 600 glass manufacturing patents.[61] Once its patent control was complete, Hartford allocated each glass manufacturer a strict production quota on each specific type of glass container.

In 1931 Hartford's control was enhanced by the establishment of the "statistical committee" of the Glass Container Association. In consultation with the major glass manufacturers, the statistical committee assigned quotas to the association's members and through the use of patent infringement suits was aggressive in its efforts to enforce the quotas.[62] As a result of these complex agreements, in 1938, 94 percent of all glass containers were produced on machines using one or more of Hartford-Empire's patents.[63]

The use of *patent pooling* by Hartford enabled the glass container manufacturers to solve the prisoner's dilemma by simply having Hartford negotiate and set quotas. Cheating was easily detected, and the threat of punishment in the form of a lower quota on one or more glass container items was always present.

GYPSUM BOARD: 1929–1948[64] Another classic example of patent pooling is found in the gypsum board industry. Since its organization in 1901 United States Gypsum has been the dominant firm in the gypsum products market. In 1939, US Gypsum controlled 55 percent of the wallboard market, and the eight-firm concentration ratio was over 90.[65] US Gypsum's control was built primarily on one patent, the Utzman patent, for producing wallboard with closed edges. Until 1912, wallboard had been produced by sandwiching a gypsum core between two pieces of paper. Utzman's idea was to enclose the edges of the gypsum core with a paper cover so that the edges would be much less likely to crumble. Essentially, Utzman received a patent for the idea of covering the entire gypsum core (including the edges) with paper instead of enclosing just the two sides. It's hard to believe that such a minor technological advance could result in US Gypsum's domination of an industry for a quarter century, but it did.

When the Utzman patent expired in 1929, US Gypsum met with each of its licensees to work out a new set of patent agreements based on a new US Gypsum patent for producing *bubble board,* a new type of wallboard produced by introducing a soap foam into the wallboard mixture. What emerged was an agreement signed on August 6, 1929, the exact day the Utzman patent expired, that expanded US Gypsum's patent control into a full-blown cartel. Each licensee agreed to pay a royalty on "all plaster board and gypsum wallboard of every kind" whether or not made by patented processes. The agreement covered 50 patents and seven patent applications and was to run until the most junior patent expired. Through these agreements US Gypsum was able to fix the minimum price on all wallboard products.

To prevent cheating, US Gypsum set up a subsidiary, Board Survey, Inc., to check complaints that a licensee had violated the agreement. It was common practice for Board Survey to send letters to licensees requesting explanations for alleged violations and to audit a licensee's books to check that price concessions were not being made

on non–gypsum board products as a cover for negotiated secret price concessions. Frequent meetings were also held to explain provisions of the bulletins that were unclear.

Evidence suggests that the agreements resulted in increased gypsum board prices after 1929, and letters written by the licensees to US Gypsum indicated that the major objective of the agreement was to raise and stabilize wallboard prices.

An analysis of the glass container and gypsum board industries suggests that patents can be used not only as a spur for technological advance, but also as a vehicle for collusion. Patent cartels have proved to be effective methods of solving the prisoner's dilemma. Cheating is easily detected, and punishment in the form of patent infringement suits may be swift and effective.

10.2 How Successful Are the Solutions?

Section 10.1 examined some of the more successful efforts to solve the prisoner's dilemma and collude. However, considering how many industries could increase their profitability substantially by colluding, it is a wonder that collusion is not far more widespread. In this section, we explore some of the major factors mitigating against successful long-term collusion.

10.2.1 Excess Capacity Problems

One of the ironies of a successful solution to the prisoner's dilemma is that it almost invariably sows the seeds for the future demise of effective collusion.[66] Suppose an industry engages in a form of effective explicit or tacit collusion, and prices and profits rise. The increase in profits encourages the entry of new firms and the expansion of capacity by existing firms. Often, this entry and capacity expansion result in serious excess capacity problems that put great strains on any attempt to maintain discipline. It makes little difference whether the capacity expansion is by firms that join the collusive agreements or not.

Considerable evidence indicates that excess capacity has been a recurring theme in many cartels, especially during recessions.[67] For example, OPEC has been periodically plagued by such problems. OPEC's success in the 1970s and early 1980s resulted in capacity expansion both within and outside of OPEC. Because the smaller producers had a great incentive to expand output, world capacity increased dramatically. Between 1973 and 1986, crude oil production in Western Europe (North Sea oil) increased from 139 million to 1395 million barrels per year, an increase of *1256 percent*.[68] During the same period output increased by 1800 percent in communist nations and by 360 percent in Asia.[69] To maintain prices, Middle Eastern members of OPEC were forced to reduce their output from 7745 million barrels in 1973 to just 4639 million barrels in 1986.[70] In an attempt to stabilize prices, by the mid-1980s the Saudis were producing only 2.5 million barrels a day, well below their OPEC quota of over 4 million barrels per day.[71] This implied that the more successful Saudi Arabia was in stabilizing price, the greater was the development of excess capacity and the greater were the cartel's future problems.

The basing point system in the cement industry also provides evidence of the effect of collusion on capacity. The first apparent use of a basing point system in cement occurred in 1901. In 1902 the American Portland Cement Association was established as the industry's trade association, and by 1908 the Association's "Trade Relations Committee" had established a policy that "all prices quoted for Portland cement shall be the prices for delivery at the point required by the purchaser."[72] By 1915 the basing point system was firmly entrenched on a national basis.

As indicated in Table 10.2, the cement industry experienced chronic excess capacity before the Supreme Court struck down the basing point system in 1948 and much less excess capacity thereafter. Table 10.2 indicates that capacity utilization rates fell below 80 percent for 13 consecutive years between 1929 and 1941, and then again from 1943 until 1946. Declining demand during the Great Depression certainly was the major cause of the excess capacity problem. However, more than demand factors appears to have been involved. According to Loescher, "On top of the capacity idled by the depression there existed an estimated 60,000,000 barrels of practical capacity idled by excessive building—or about 25 percent of the average practical capacity of the period 1931 to 1935."[73]

Evidence indicates that during the height of explicit collusion in the electric turbine market, GE, Westinghouse, and Allis-Chalmers were all expanding capacity at a rate that exceeded any possible demand increases.[74] Capacity expansion was encouraged because the turbine producers often used the existence of large amounts of excess capacity as a bargaining chip at meetings designed to divide the market.

10.2.2 Encroachment of Substitute Products

Any successful attempt to fix price also encourages the development and marketing of substitute products, resulting in a much more elastic demand curve in the long run than the short run. Substitutes have been a continuing problem for OPEC. The dramatic price increases of the mid-1970s led many consumers to shift to wood for heating and many utilities to switch to coal for electricity generation. Furthermore, they encouraged the production of more energy-efficient automobiles, homes, and factories. As a result, world oil consumption declined by about 32.5 percent from 1975 to 1986.[75]

A similar pattern emerged in the steel industry. Between 1947 and 1967 the relative price of steel increased compared with plastic, aluminum, cement, and glass. During the same 20-year period, domestic steel production increased by just 35 percent compared with increases of 1900 percent for plastic, 500 percent for aluminum, and 100 percent for both cement and glass.[76]

10.2.3 More Effective Antitrust Strategies: The Department of Justice Corporate Leniency Program

Recent antitrust policy changes in the United States, Canada, and the EU have also made effective long-term collusion more difficult. In August 1993, the United States Department of Justice adopted a new Corporate Leniency Policy for antitrust violations that Canada and the EU later adopted in slightly modified forms.[77] Under the leniency program the first company to come forward and inform on a cartel before the Justice Department begins an investigation receives complete criminal immunity. The policy protects the corporation's directors, officers, and employees from all criminal charges. The 1993

TABLE 10.2 Practical Capacity and Production of Cement in the United States, 1909–1964 (in millions of barrels per year)

Year	Practical Capacity	Production	% Cap.	Year	Practical Capacity	Production	% Cap.
1909	84.2	65.0	77.2	1937	229.7	116.2	50.6
1910	87.9	76.6	87.1	1938	230.1	105.4	45.8
1911	101.2	78.5	77.6	1939	230.5	121.9	52.9
1912	99.8	82.4	82.6	1940	228.4	129.8	56.8
1913	104.3	92.1	88.3	1941	222.2	163.6	73.6
1914	104.3	88.2	84.6	1942	223.4	182.1	81.5

Basing point system in full force

Year	Practical Capacity	Production	% Cap.	Year	Practical Capacity	Production	% Cap.
1915	116.8	85.9	73.5	1943	217.0	132.4	61.0
1916	120.6	91.5	75.9	1944	215.0	89.9	41.8
1917	123.1	92.8	75.4	1945	215.9	101.3	46.9
1918	123.1	71.1	57.4	1946	215.8	162.3	75.2
1919	120.7	80.8	66.9	1947	221.9	184.6	83.2
1920	131.8	100.0	75.9	1948	226.5	203.0	89.6

Basing point system ends

Year	Practical Capacity	Production	% Cap.	Year	Practical Capacity	Production	% Cap.
1921	129.1	98.8	76.1	1949	231.1	207.5	89.8
1922	131.6	114.8	87.2	1950	249.7	228.8	93.2
1923	145.7	137.5	94.4	1951	251.9	241.8	96.8
1924	157.6	149.4	94.8	1952	251.9	245.2	97.3
1925	174.2	161.6	92.8	1953	258.7	260.5	100.7
1926	193.8	164.5	84.9	1954	264.9	268.7	101.4
1927	204.4	173.2	84.7	1955	280.4	293.3	104.6
1928	219.3	176.3	80.4	1956	314.5	316.4	100.6
1929	233.0	170.6	73.2	1957	342.4	298.4	87.1
1930	243.0	161.1	66.3	1958	362.5	311.5	85.9
1931	244.6	125.4	51.3	1959	378.4	339.1	89.6
1932	244.2	76.7	31.4	1960	389.6	319.0	81.9
1933	242.4	63.7	26.3	1961	398.4	324.1	81.4
1934	236.4	77.7	32.5	1962	422.0	336.5	79.7
1935	235.7	76.7	32.5	1963	429.8	352.5	82.0
1936	230.0	112.6	49.0	1964	431.5	368.6	85.4

Sources: Samuel M. Loescher, *Imperfect Competition in the Cement Industry* (Cambridge: Harvard University Press, 1959), pp. 168–169; and *Federal Trade Commission Report on Mergers and Vertical Integration in the Cement Industry* (Washington: U.S. Government Printing Office, 1966), p. 55.

leniency policy was considered such a success that it was broadened in the 2004 Antitrust Criminal Penalty Enhancement and Reform Act to limit liability in civil cases for firms that receive leniency.[78] The 2004 act also increased the maximum fines for individuals in antitrust cases from $350,000 to $1 million, increased the maximum fines for corporations from $10 to $100 million, and increased the maximum prison sentence for an antitrust violation from three to 10 years. The leniency policy has resulted in a huge increase in the number of amnesty applications received by the Justice Department, from approximately one application per year to two applications per *month*.[79]

The program has been successful in helping to break up several large international cartels, such as the vitamin and graphite electrode cartels. As discussed earlier in this chapter, the vitamin cartel was one of the more elaborate worldwide cartels in history.[80] The cartel held regular meetings to set prices and quotas: members referred to the cartel at Vitamin Inc. as if only one firm sold vitamins throughout the world. The largest fine in antitrust history, or for that matter, in any U.S. criminal case of any kind—$500 million—was handed down to the Swiss vitamin producer Hoffman-LaRoche. The German firm BASF also paid a huge $225 million fine. The vitamin cartel might never have been identified if not for the fact that the French firm Rhône-Poulenc received amnesty.

The international graphite electrodes* cartel was revealed when Carbide Graphite Group of Pittsburgh applied for leniency and received complete immunity.[81] In the graphite electrodes case, seven firms, Mitsubishi (of Japan), SGL Carbon (Germany), UCAR International (USA, but 50 percent controlled by Mitsubishi), Showa Denko Carbon (USA), Tokai Carbon (Japan), SEC (Japan), and Nippon (Japan) conspired to fix the price of graphite electrodes through a series of covert meetings and agreements. Under the cartel, Mitsubishi even served as a broker for its competitors' sales. The seven firms paid fines totaling over $400 million, and Mitsubishi, the leading firm in the cartel, paid a $134 million fine.

Domestic cartels have also been exposed because of the leniency policy. In 2000, the Justice Department uncovered a scheme to fix auction commission rates by Sotheby's and Christie's, the two dominant auction houses in New York that control the American auction market for fine art and other expensive goods. When Christie's board of directors decided to come forward under the leniency policy and admit to conspiring with Sotheby's, Sotheby's was left to take the fall. Sotheby's paid a $45 million fine and Sotheby's then-chair, Alfred Taubman, was sentenced to a year in prison.[82] In the $1-billion-a-year rubber chemical industry,† Crompton Corporation, a subsidiary of Uniroyal Chemical, applied for amnesty after another company identified Crompton as one of the members of the cartel. Crompton agreed to pay a $50 million fine for its part in the price-fixing conspiracy that cost consumers hundreds of millions of dollars between 1995 and 2001.[83] After Crompton came forward, several other members of the cartel applied for leniency and the Justice Department uncovered the vast extent of the rubber chemicals cartel.

The leniency policies, combined with larger fines and longer prison sentences, have further reduced the likely stability of cartels. Given the instability associated

*Graphite electrodes are used to make steel using electric furnaces. The electrodes are large columns that are used to create the tremendous heat required to melt scrap steel and turn the scrap into refined steel.

†Rubber chemicals are additives used to produce many important products such as tires, automotive parts, shoes, and outdoor furniture.

with excess capacity problems, the development of substitutes, tougher international law enforcement, and the basic problem of holding together prisoner's dilemma–type agreements, it is not surprising that many cartels are relatively short-lived.

SUMMARY

1. Table 10.3 summarizes the major themes running through this chapter. This is by no means a scientifically controlled sample, but the cases do represent many of the classic attempts to solve the prisoner's dilemma. A few points are striking. First, entry barriers were high in 14 of the 19 cases. Second, in 14 of 19 cases concentration was high and in only two cases was it low.

2. In one of the two cases in which concentration was low, a professional association was required to try to solve the dilemma in a more elaborate manner.

3. Product differentiation was low in 13 cases and high in only one. As our theoretical analysis in Chapter 9 suggested, solutions to the dilemma appear to be much easier when dealing with an essentially homogeneous product.

4. The rate of technological advance was slow in 13 cases and rapid in none, suggesting that it is difficult to reach agreements in industries characterized by rapid product or process changes.

5. In 17 of the 19 cases demand was inelastic.

6. Table 10.3 suggests that solutions to the prisoner's dilemma will be more effective in industries with high entry barriers, moderate to high concentration, relatively few firms, little product differentiation, a relatively slow rate of technological growth, and an inelastic demand.

7. As theorized in Chapter 9, all successful collusion appears to require a method of detecting cheaters and a threat of effective punishment.

TABLE 10.3 Summary of Industry Attempts to Solve the Prisoner's Dilemma

	Entry Barriers	Number of Firms	Concentration	Product Differentation	Demand Elasticity	Lumpiness of Orders	Rate of Technological Advance
Large firm							
OPEC	High	Medium	Medium	Low	Inelastic	No	Slow
Steel, early	High	Medium	High	Low	Inelastic	Yes	Slow
Most favored							
Turbines	High	Small	High	Medium	Inelastic	Yes	Moderate
Stereo eq.	Low	Large	Low	Medium	Elastic	No	Slow

(continued)

TABLE 10.3 *(continued)*

	Entry Barriers	Number of Firms	Concentration	Product Differentation	Demand Elasticity	Lumpiness of Orders	Rate of Technological Advance
Trade associations							
Sugar	Medium	Medium	Medium	Low	Inelastic	No	Slow
Legal services	Low	Large	Low	Medium	Inelastic	Yes	Slow
Divide markets							
Switchgear	High	Small	High	Medium	Inelastic	Yes	Moderate
Lysine, citric acid	High	Small	High	Low	Inelastic	No	Slow
Vitamins	High	Small	High	Low	Inelastic	No	Slow
Patents							
Glass containers	High	Small	High	Low	Inelastic	No	Slow
Gypsum board	High	Small	High	Low	Inelastic	No	Slow
Basing point							
Steel, 1884–1948	High	Medium	High	Low	Inelastic	Yes	Slow
Plywood	Medium	Medium	High	Low	Inelastic	No	Slow
Price leadership							
Steel, 1911–	High	Medium	High	Low	Inelastic	Yes	Slow
Antiknock	High	Small	High	Low	Inelastic	No	Moderate
Cigarettes	High	Small	High	High	Inelastic	No	Moderate
Cellophane	High	Small	High	Low	Elastic	No	Moderate
Retail gasoline	Low	Medium	Medium	Low	Inelastic	No	Slow
Turbines	High	Small	High	Medium	Inelastic	Yes	Moderate

KEY TERMS

barometric price leadership

basing point pricing system

collusive price leadership

low-price guarantee

most favored customer clause

parametric price

phantom freight

phases of the moon system

DISCUSSION QUESTIONS

1. What is the likely impact of successful collusion on the amount of excess capacity in an industry? Explain.

2. In both cases discussed in the chapter in which a large firm acted as the industry's dominant firm price leader and benefactor, the leader's market dominance eventually declined. Suggest a theoretical reason as to why this happened in each of these cases.

3. What is the difference between collusive and barometric price leadership? Is it always easy to distinguish between the two?

4. Is it possible for a cartel to set a price that maximizes short-run profits but is "too high"? Explain.

5. Can you identify an industry in your geographic area in which all the firms use a low-price guarantee? Do prices in that industry appear to vary much from store to store?

6. How does the use of a basing point pricing system result in suboptimal economic performance? Which buyers are hurt by a basing point pricing system? Why do you think *single* basing point systems were generally unstable and most industries ultimately adopted *multiple* basing point systems?

7. Would an industry with only three firms be expected to use a trade association to fix prices? Would an industry with 1000 firms use a trade association to fix prices?

8. What facts about an industry's pricing behavior might lead you to suspect that the firms were fixing prices?

9. Why is there typically so much cheating in cartels?

10. Would you suspect that price-fixing agreements would become more or less stable over time?

11. Would you be surprised to learn that in many antitrust price-fixing cases the defendants argue that the agreements were broken far more than they were maintained? Does this mean that these agreements had no negative impacts on economic performance?

12. Explain how a statistical analysis of pricing behavior in the canned pineapple market led to the conclusion that Dole was the market's price leader. What is particularly surprising about Del Monte's pricing behavior in the canned pineapple market?

13. Did all consumers benefit from Medicaid's most favored customer clause for purchasing pharmaceuticals? Currently Medicare does not have a most favored customer clause for purchasing pharmaceuticals. Suppose the government adopted such a clause for Medicare as well as Medicaid. What impact would you expect this to have on the drugstore price of pharmaceuticals? Explain your reasoning.

14. Perfect information is critical to the efficient functioning of a competitive market. Could the publication of price information in a perfectly competitive market have any negative economic consequences? Is the same true for the publication of prices in a highly concentrated oligopoly? Explain your reasoning.

15. Explain how the United States Department of Justice Corporate Leniency Program works. Why would this program be attractive to firms that are earning large economic profits in a cartel? After one firm applies for leniency, does the incentive for other firms to apply for leniency increase or decrease? Explain your reasoning.

16. Would the large increase in criminal penalties in antitrust cases enacted in 2004 increase or decrease the incentive for firms to apply for leniency under the Justice Department's Corporate Leniency Program? Would the increase in penalties have an impact on the *average* profits generated by a cartel?

17. John M. Connor has estimated that the average overcharge in the typical international cartel from 1990 to 2003 was 28 percent. Furthermore, he found that the percentage overcharges generally remained constant over time in a cartel and the overcharges varied little from geographic region to region within a cartel. What do these facts suggest about the

price-fixing methods used in these cartels? In particular, do you think that price changes were driven more by changes in costs or changes in demand?

18. It has been theorized that changing business ethics during the 1980s in the United States and Europe made price fixing a more acceptable business practice and this resulted in the creation and eventual discovery of a large number of international cartels in the 1990s. Why do you think some economists and sociologists developed this theory? Do you think business ethics have changed since the 1990s? Explain your reasoning.

19. An alternative theory to the declining business ethics theory presented in question 18 is that slowing profitability in the 1980s led to a growing number of cartels during the 1990s. Why might declining profitability result in an increase in cartel formation? And why might declining profitability in the 1980s have led specifically to the development of many international, as opposed to regional, cartels?

20. The three dominant office supply superstores, Office Depot, Staples, and Office Max, all use a low-price guarantee. Do you think these guarantees increase or decrease the prices charged for office supplies in these stores?

21. In a 1973 consent decree the Greater Pittsburgh Board of Realtors (now the Realtors Association of Metropolitan Pittsburgh, or RAMP) agreed to cease from fixing the price of real estate commissions in the Pittsburgh area. The 1973 consent decree prevented Realtors from publishing real estate commissions in advertisements. In 2005, the Justice Department decided to modify the 1973 decree to permit the publication and advertising of real estate commissions by the RAMP. Why do you think the Justice Department decided to modify the 1973 consent decree? (*Hint:* What had changed about the way in which firms would advertise their commissions between 1973 and 2005?)

NOTES

1. Stephen Martin, "The Petroleum Industry," in Walter Adams (ed.), *The Structure of American Industry,* 8th edition (New York: MacMillan, 1990), p. 50.

2. "Saudi Arabia Plays High-Stakes Game," *New York Times* (January 24, 1986): D1; "Belt-Tightening by Saudis," *New York Times* (January 28, 1986): D1; "Why the Saudis Keep Talking the Price of Oil Down," *Business Week* (March 17, 1986): 52; and "OPEC Panel to Tackle Pricing," *New York Times* (November 14, 1986): D1.

3. Martin, *supra* note 1, p. 50.

4. See Jacque Cremer and D. Salehi-Isfahani, "A Competitive Theory of the Oil Market: What Does OPEC Really Do?" Working Paper, No. 80–4 mimeo, University of Pennsylvania, 1980; Ali Ezzati, "Future OPEC Price and Production Strategies as Affected by Its Capacity to Absorb Oil Revenues," *European Economic Review* 8 (August 1976): 107–138; and David Teece, "OPEC Behavior: An Alternative View," in J.M. Griffin, *OPEC Behavior and World Oil Prices* (London: Allen & Unwin, 1982).

5. James M. Griffin, "OPEC Behavior: A Test of Alternative Hypotheses," *American Economic Review* 75 (December 1985): 954–963; see also James M. Griffin and Weiwen Xiong, "The Incentives to Cheat: An Empirical Analysis of OPEC," *Journal of Law and Economics* 40 (October 1997): 289.

6. James M. Griffin, *supra* note 5, p. 962.

7. Don E. Waldman, *The Economics of Antitrust: Cases and Analysis* (Boston: Little Brown and Company, 1986), p. 49.

8. *Ibid.*

9. *Ibid.*

10. For a somewhat different explanation based on a classic model, see V. Bhaskar, "The Kinked Demand Curve," *International Journal of Industrial Organization* 6 (September 1988): 373–384.

11. Walter Adams and Hans Mueller, "The Steel Industry," in Walter Adams (ed.), *The Structure of American Industry,* 8th edition (New York: MacMillan, 1990), p. 84.

12. Walter Adams, "The Steel Industry," in Walter Adams (ed.), *The Structure of American Industry,* 4th edition (New York: MacMillan, 1971), p. 94.

13. *Ibid.*

14. Leonard W. Weiss, *Case Studies in American Industry* (New York: John Wiley and Sons, 1980), pp. 191–192.

15. *Ibid.,* p. 192.

16. "Bethlehem Cuts Major Prices 22%," *New York Times* (November 5, 1968): 67; "Steel Industry Hit By Major Price Cut," *Business Week* (November 9, 1968): 35; "U.S. Steel Moves to End Price War," *New York Times* (November 28, 1968): 75; "New Split Opens in Steel Pricing," *New York Times* (December 7, 1968): 73; "Revolution in Steel Pricing?" *Business Week* (December 14, 1968): 41; "Bethlehem Steel Cuts Steel Sheet List," *New York Times* (February 5, 1969): 47; and "Steel Heads Up Again," *Business Week* (February 8, 1969): 27.

17. "Dr. Bethlehem's New Formula," *Business Week* (November 15, 1969): 39; "A Hold on Steel Prices," *Business Week* (November 4, 1972): 33; and "Bethlehem, National Lift Prices," *New York Times* (August 9, 1986): A29.

18. See George A. Hay, "Practices that Facilitate Cooperation: The Ethyl Case," in J.E. Kwoka and Lawrence A. White (eds.), *The Antitrust Revolution* (Glenview, IL: Scott Foresman, 1989), pp. 183–207.

19. *Ibid.*, pp. 204–205.

20. *Ibid.*, p. 195.

21. *Ibid.*, pp. 193–197.

22. *American Tobacco Company* v. *United States,* 328 US 781 (1946).

23. Richard B. Tennant, "The Cigarette Industry," in Walter Adams (ed.), *The Structure of American Industry,* 4th edition (New York: MacMillan, 1971), p. 225.

24. *American Tobacco Company* v. *United States,* 328 US 781 (1946), p. 805.

25. *Ibid.*

26. "Marketing Observer," *Business Week* (February 24, 1973): 48.

27. Willard F. Mueller, Bruce W. Marion, and Maqbool H. Sial, "Price Leadership on the National Cheese Exchange," *Review of Industrial Organization* 12 (1997): 145–170.

28. Ralph G.M. Sultan, *Pricing in the Electrical Oligopoly,* vol. I (Boston: Harvard Business School Division of Research, 1974), pp. 213–214.

29. *Ibid.*, vol. II, pp. 234–235.

30. A.D.H. Kaplan, Joel B. Dirlam, and Robert Lanzillotti, *Pricing in Big Business: A Case Approach* (Washington: Brookings Institution, 1958), pp. 100–103.

31. Edmund P. Learned and Catherine C. Ellsworth, *Gasoline Pricing in Ohio* (Boston: Harvard Business School Division of Research, 1959), pp. 23–25 and 106–107; and A.D.H. Kaplan, Joel B. Dirlam, and Robert Lanzillotti, *Pricing in Big Business: A Case Approach* (Washington: Brookings Institution, 1958), pp. 100–103.

32. See also David Besanko and Thomas P. Lyon, "Equilibrium Incentives for Most-Favored Customer Clauses in an Oligopolistic Industry," *International Journal of Industrial Organization* 11 (September 1993): 347–367.

33. Waldman, *supra* note 7, pp. 155–157.

34. See Ralph G.M. Sultan, *supra* note 28.

35. Waldman, *supra* note 7.

36. Waldman, *supra* note 7; and Don E. Waldman, "The Inefficiencies of 'Unsuccessful' Pricing Fixing Agreements," *Antitrust Bulletin* (Spring 1988): 67–93.

37. Waldman, *supra* note 7.

38. This section is adapted from Avinash Dixit and Barry Nalebuff, *Thinking Strategically* (New York: Norton, 1991), pp. 102–105.

39. James W. McKie, *Tin Cans and Tin Plate* (Cambridge: Harvard University Press, 1959), pp. 66–71.

40. Walter Adams, *supra* note 12, p. 73.

41. *In the Matter of Boise Cascade Corporation et al.* 91 FTC 1 (1978); and Samuel M. Loescher, "Economic Collusion, Civil Conspiracy, and Treble Damages Deterrents with Southern Plywood," *Quarterly Review of Economics and Business* 20 (Winter 1980): 6–35.

42. Loescher, *supra* note 41, p. 14.

43. *Ibid.*

44. *Sugar Institute* v. *United States* 297 US 553 (1936), p. 587.

45. *Ibid.*, p. 583.

46. *Goldfarb* v. *Virginia State Bar* 421 US 773 (1975).

47. *Ibid.*, p. 778.

48. *Ibid.*, p. 776.

49. John Herling, *The Great Price Conspiracy* (Washington: Luce, 1962), p. 70.

50. *Ibid.*, p. 109.

51. *Ibid.*, p. 71.

52. J.G. Fuller, *The Gentleman Conspirators* (New York: Grove, 1962), p. 66.

53. Herling, *supra* note 49, p. 88.

54. *Ibid.*, pp. 335–351.

55. *United States of America* v. *Archer Daniels Midland Company,* Criminal No.: 96-CR-00640, filed 10/15/96, p. 7.

56. *Ibid.*, p. 2.

57. *Ibid.*, pp. 2–3.

58. *United States* v. *Hoffmann-La Roche LTD,* Criminal No. 3:99-CR-184-R, Filed: May 20, 1999, p. 3.

59. *United States* v. *Hoffmann-La Roche LTD,* Criminal No. 3:99-CR-200-R, Plea agreement, p. 3.

60. *Hartford-Empire Company* v. *United States* 323 US 386 (1945); and Waldman, *supra* note 7, pp. 217–222.

61. Waldman, *supra* note 7, p. 218.

62. *Hartford-Empire* v. *United States* 323 US 386 (1945), p. 400.

63. Waldman, *supra* note 7, p. 218.

64. *United States* v. *United States Gypsum Company* 333 US 3664 (1948); and Waldman, *supra* note 7, pp. 222–225.

65. Waldman, *supra* note 7, p. 222.

66. See Margaret E. Slade, "Cheating on Collusive Agreements," *International Journal of Industrial Organization* 8 (December 1990): 519–543; and Chaim Fershtman, "Disadvantageous Semicollusion," *International Journal of Industrial Organization* 12 (June 1994): 141–154.

67. Don E. Waldman, "The Inefficiencies of 'Unsuccessful' Pricing Fixing Agreements," *Antitrust Bulletin* (Spring 1988): 67–93.

68. Stephen Martin, "The Petroleum Industry," in Walter Adams (ed.), *The Structure of American Industry,* 8th edition (New York: MacMillan, 1992), p. 51.

69. *Ibid.*

70. *Ibid.*

71. *Ibid.*, p. 62.

72. Samuel M. Loescher, *Imperfect Competition in the Cement Industry* (Cambridge: Harvard University Press, 1959), pp. 95–96.

73. *Ibid.*, p. 181.

74. Waldman, *supra* note 67, pp. 85–92.

75. American Petroleum Institute, *Basic Petroleum Data Book,* vol. 8, 1988.

76. Adams, *supra* note 12, p. 99.

77. United States Department of Justice, *Corporate Leniency Policy,* Issued August 10, 1993, www.usdoj.gov/atr/public/guidelines/lencorp.htm.

78. Scott D. Hammond, Acting Deputy Assistant Attorney General for Criminal Enforcement Antitrust Division U.S. Department of Justice, "An Overview of Recent Developments in the Antitrust Division's Criminal Enforcement Program," January 10, 2005, www.usdoj.gov/atr/public/speeches/207226.pdf.

79. *Ibid.*, pp. 8–9.

80. Stephen Labaton and David Barboza, "U.S. Outlines How Makers of Vitamins Fixed Global Prices," *New York Times,* May 21, 1999, pp. A1.

81. United States Department of Justice, Press Release, May 10, 2001, "Mitsubishi Corporation Fines $134 Million for its Role in International Price-Fixing Cartel," http://www.usdoj.gov/atr/public/press_releases/2001/8186.pdf.

82. Orley Ashenfelter and Kathryn Graddy, "Anatomy of the Rise and Fall of a Price-Fixing Conspiracy: Auctions at Sotheby's and Christie's, *Journal of Competition Law and Economics,* 1(March 2005): 2–19.

83. "Price-Fixing Probe Bags Big Boys," *InTech,* June 23, 2004, www.isa.org/InTechTemplate.cfm?Section=InTech&template=/ContentManagement/ContentDisplay.cfm&ContentID=36495.

 INTERNET EXERCISES

Visit www.aw-bc.com/waldman_jensen for this chapter's web exercises. Answer our real-world economics problems by searching the Internet for solutions!

Oligopoly Behavior: Entry and Pricing to Deter Entry

The preceding two chapters suggested that because of the prisoner's dilemma, oligopolists often have difficulty coordinating their behavior. Also, following a strict short-run profit-maximizing strategy is likely to result in the entry of new firms or the capacity expansion of smaller established firms, not to mention the loss of market share to close substitute products. This is precisely what happened in the steel and oil markets. Conversely, Microsoft in computer operating systems, Alcoa in aluminum, and Inco (International Nickel) in nickel managed to maintain their monopolies for decades. Can a pricing strategy be identified that enables some firms to maintain their market power over long periods? We begin by reviewing one of the earliest major models of dynamic behavior, the limit pricing model, and then proceed to analyze the possible use of predatory pricing.

11.1 Limit Pricing

Limit pricing theory begins with the logical assumption that rational firms should maximize *long-run*, not short-run, profits.[1] Maximization of long-run profits requires maximizing the *present value of profits*, and maximizing the present value of profits requires recognition that current pricing decisions can impact the future behavior of competitors and potential competitors. For example, a monopolist may be able to choose between (1) charging a high price today and attracting entry; or (2) charging a low price today in an attempt to deter entry. The latter policy, charging a low price to deter entry, is known as **limit pricing.** Furthermore, the highest possible price the monopolist can charge and still prevent entry is called the **limit price.** In this section, we develop a model to explain why rational firms may adopt a limit pricing policy.

11.1.1 Limit Pricing with a Cost Advantage for the Monopolist Firm

Consider a monopolist facing the hypothetical demand and cost conditions depicted in panel (a) in Figure 11.1. Total industry demand is $p = 100 - q$ and the monopolist produces with constant marginal and average costs $MC_M = AC_M = \$40$. Given these demand and cost conditions, the monopolist maximizes short-run profits by setting

FIGURE 11.1 The Monopolist's and Potential Entrant's Demand and Costs

In panel (a), the monopolist has lower costs than the potential entrant and maximizes profit by setting $MC_M = MR_M$ at $q = 30$ and $p = \$70$. A potential entrant then faces the residual demand curve equal to the line segment AC. In panel (b), the residual demand curve for a potential entrant is drawn as the line segment XZ. Given the potential entrant's costs, the potential entrant maximizes profit by setting $q = 10$, and the price falls to $60.

$MR_M = MC_M$, selling a quantity of 30 at a price of $70, and earning profits equal to $q(p - AC_M) = 30(\$70 - \$40) = \$900$.

Suppose a potential entrant is considering entering the industry; however, the potential entrant faces a cost disadvantage because the monopolist holds a patent. As a result of the patent, the potential entrant can only produce at higher costs $MC_{PE} = AC_{PE} = \$50$. If the monopolist currently is maximizing short-run profits and charging price $p = \$70$, the residual demand curve faced by the potential entrant is $p = (100 - q_M) - q_{PE} = (100 - 30) - q_{PE} = 70 - q_{PE}$, which equals the line segment AC in panel (a) and the line segment XZ in panel (b).

In the original limit pricing models, one critical assumption was the Cournot assumption that the monopolist would maintain its output even after entry occurred.[2] Of course, in the real world the monopolist might expand, contract, or maintain its output in the face of entry. The Cournot assumption of postentry output maintenance is highly questionable, but for the time being we will use it. Given the assumption that the monopolist will maintain its current output *forever*, if the potential entrant enters, it maximizes profits in panel (b) by setting $MR_{PE} = MC_{PE} = \$50$, selling a quantity of 10 at a price of $60, and earning profits equal to $q(p - AC_{PE}) = 10(\$60 - \$50) = \$100$. The monopolist must now match the entrant's price of $60; as a result, the monopolist's profits decline to $q(p - AC_M) = 30(\$60 - \$40) = \$600$. The arrival of a new entrant has resulted in a 33 percent reduction in the monopolist's profits from $900 to just $600.

To deter entry, the monopolist must lower its price sufficiently to ensure that the potential entrant's residual demand curve lies everywhere below the potential entrant's average cost curve. In Figure 11.1, if the monopolist charges any price greater than $50, the residual demand curve will have a segment that is above the potential entrant's average cost. However, if the monopolist increases output to 50 and charges price p = $50, the residual demand curve faced by potential entrants will be $p - (100 - q_M) - q_{PE} = (100 - 50) - q_{PE} = 50 - q_{PE}$, which equals the line segment BC in Figure 11.1 panel (a).

Figure 11.2 shows the residual demand curve $p = 50 - q_{PE}$ in relation to the potential entrant's costs. The AC_{PE} curve is now everywhere below the demand curve except for an output of zero. Therefore, in Figure 11.2, if the potential entrant produces any output greater than zero, it will sustain an economic loss. A monopoly price, p = $50, therefore, completely deters entry. The price of $50 is the limit price because it is the highest possible price the monopolist can charge and still prevent entry.

As noted previously, one major criticism of the early limit pricing models was their assumption of output maintenance after entry occurred.[3] Such an assumption contradicts short-run profit-maximizing behavior, which requires the monopolist to reduce its output in response to entry. We can use the monopolist's residual demand to calculate the monopolist's *postentry* profit-maximizing quantity in Figure 11.1. If the entrant produces 10 units in Figure 11.1(b), the monopolist's residual demand curve is $p = 90 - q$ and $MR = 90 - 2q$. Setting $MR = MC$, $90 - 2q = 40$, so the monopolist's profit-maximizing quantity is 25 and the industry's price is $p = 100 - (25 + 10) = $65. In other words, once entry occurs, to maximize short-run profits the monopolist should reduce its output below 30 units and increase price to $65.

Although short-run profit maximization calls for a postentry restriction in the monopolist's output, another possible logical strategy is for the monopolist to expand

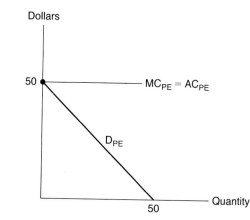

FIGURE 11.2 The Potential Entrant's Residual Demand Curve and Costs if the Monopolist Sets Price Equal to $50

If the monopolist lowers its price to $50, the potential entrant's residual demand curve is $p = 50 - q$, which lies everywhere below the potential entrant's costs. Therefore, if the monopolist is assumed to maintain its output after entry, the entrant will sustain an economic loss and entry is impossible.

its output in response to entry and reduce price below $50. If potential entrants know that the monopolist is willing to lower price to $49, for example, potential entrants know they would sustain an economic loss if they entered, and therefore no entry would occur. With p = $49, however, the monopolist would continue to earn an economic profit of $459 and the monopolist could continue to earn this profit indefinitely.* A postentry policy of either reducing output or expanding output almost always makes more sense than maintaining output.

11.1.2 Limit Pricing in the Absence of a Cost Advantage for the Monopolist Firm

Suppose that in our previous example, potential entrants could also produce with MC = AC = $40. The limit price would therefore equal 40. Of course there would then be no incentive for the monopolist to limit price because the monopolist would earn zero economic profits if it limit-priced at p = $40. In this case the monopolist would always put off limit pricing as long as there was some remaining positive economic profit to be earned. The monopolist would be better off simply maintaining output at Q = 30 and earning some economic profits for as long as possible.

This result follows from the fact that with MC = AC = $40 for both the monopolist and potential entrants, there are no economies of scale in production. We next show that if economies of scale exist, a limit pricing policy may make sense even in the absence of a cost advantage for the monopolist.

In Figure 11.3(a), significant economies of scale exist, and we assume that the monopolist and potential entrants face identical costs. Suppose that the monopolist produces with long-run average costs represented by the hypothetical curve LRAC[†] and potential entrants face no cost disadvantage and are also capable of producing with identical long-run average costs LRAC.

The total industry demand curve is given by P = 100 − 1.25Q, and the residual demand curve faced by a potential entrant will depend on the price charged by the monopolist. Given the cost curves in Figure 11.3(a), if the monopolist maximizes short-run profits, it will sell a quantity of 34 at a price of $57.50 and earn profits of $1275.[‡] The residual demand curve faced by a potential entrant will then be the line segment ABC in Figure 11.3(a), or P = 57.50 − 1.25q.

Figure 11.3(b) shows this residual demand curve in relation to the curve LRAC. Notice that the potential entrant could enter profitably because the demand curve is above the LRAC for all outputs between Q_1 and Q_2.[§] What is the limit price in this case? Making the Cournot assumption once again that the monopolist will maintain output after entry, the monopolist must lower its price sufficiently to ensure that the potential entrant's residual demand curve lies everywhere below the average cost

*Note that with p = $49, π = q(p − AC) = 51($49 − 40) = $459.

†The numbers associated with the cost curves in Figures 11.3(a)–11.3(c) are strictly hypothetical and are not associated with any real industry.

‡Profits = Q(P − AC) = 34(57.50 − 20) = $1275.

§If the demand curve were below the LRAC in Figure 11.3(b), then profitable entry would be impossible even if the incumbent maximized short-run profits. Under these circumstances entry would be *blockaded* by the existence of significant economies of scale.

FIGURE 11.3(a) Limit Pricing with Economies of Scale and No Cost Advantage

Here the monopolist and potential entrants can produce with identical long-run average costs, represented by LRAC. The industry demand curve is P = 100 − 1.25Q. The monopolist maximizes short-run profits where MR = MC with Q = 34 and P = \$57.50. Profits are \$1275. The residual demand curve faced by a potential entrant is the line segment ABC, which is the line P = 57.50 − 1.25q.

curve LRAC. If the monopolist lowers price to P = \$40 in Figure 11.3(a), the residual demand curve faced by potential entrants will be the line segment BC, or P = 40 − 1.25q. Figure 11.3(c) shows the residual demand curve P = 40 − 1.25q in relation to LRAC. Notice that the LRAC curve is just tangent to the residual demand curve at q = 10. Any price that is less than \$40, even by an infinitessimal amount, will shift the potential entrant's residual demand curve to the left in Figure 11.3(c) and deter entry. It would thus be possible for the monopolist to prevent entry by limit-pricing at P = 40 − ε, even in the absence of a cost advantage.

11.1.3 The Critique of Game Theorists

Game theorists have sharply criticized the basic limit pricing result. To understand their criticism, we begin by illustrating the situation depicted in Figure 11.3(c) as a sequential game similar to the game presented in Chapter 7 in Figure 7.2. Figure 11.4 shows a sequential game associated with the market conditions in Figures 11.3(a) and

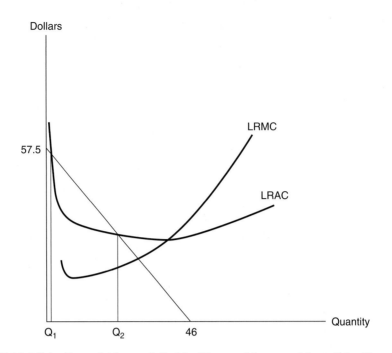

FIGURE 11.3(b) Potential Entrant's Residual Demand Curve and Costs if the Monopolist Sets Price Equal to $57.50.

Figure 11.3(b) shows the residual demand curve ABC in Figure 11.3(a) in relation to the potential entrant's average cost curve LRAC. The potential entrant could enter profitably for outputs between Q_1 and Q_2 because the demand curve is above the LRAC for those outputs.

11.3(c). Recalling from Chapter 7 that sequential games must be solved *backwards,* we find only one solution to the game in Figure 11.4. Assuming that both firms have the same information, a potential entrant would reason as follows:

1. If I stay out, I earn zero.

2. If I enter and the monopolist produces the limit price quantity $48 + \epsilon$, I sustain an economic loss and the monopolist earns $264 - \epsilon$.

3. If I enter and the monopolist shares the market and maximizes joint profits, we each earn $540.*

4. If I enter, the monopolist has a choice between sharing the market and earning $540 or producing $48 + \epsilon$ and earning $264 - \epsilon$. *Given these choices, the monopolist's only rational choice is to share the market.*

5. I will enter and earn $540, which is much better than staying out and earning zero.

*An alternative assumption would be that the two firms arrive at a Cournot-Nash equilibrium, in which each firm earns less than $540 but more than $264. This assumption would not change the implications of the game.

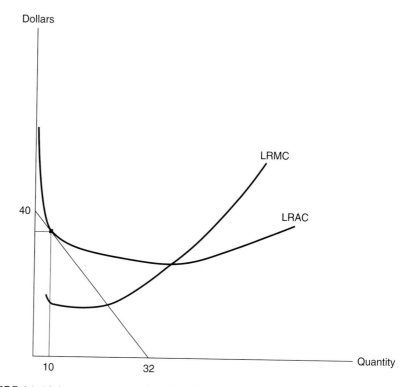

FIGURE 11.3(c) Potential Entrant's Residual Demand Curve and Costs if the Monopolist Sets Price Equal to $40

If the monopolist in Figure 11.3(a) lowers price to P = $40, the residual demand curve faced by potential entrants will be the line segment BC, or P = 40 − 1.25q. Here the residual demand curve is shown in relation to the potential entrant's LRAC and the LRAC curve is just tangent to the residual demand for q = 10. Any price that is less than $40 will shift the potential entrant's residual demand curve to the left so that the demand curve will be everywhere below LRAC and entry will be deterred.

The game has only one solution: The entrant will enter and the monopolist will share the market. Using the terminology from Chapter 7, section 7.7.1, any other threatened response is simply not a *credible threat*. But suppose that, for some unexplained reason, the potential entrant elects not to enter. The game is reduced to a choice for the monopolist of either (1) maximizing short-run profits or (2) limit pricing. A quick examination of Figure 11.4 reveals that the monopolist has only one rational choice. If entry does not occur, the choice is either earn $1275 or earn $864 − ε. Given this choice, the monopolist would choose the $1275 and maximize short-run profits. A limit pricing policy is not believable. It reduces the monopolist's profits this period and does not credibly deter entry next period because the entrant knows that the monopolist will share the market after entry occurs. The problem with the early limit pricing models is obvious: There simply is no reason for the entrant to stay out even if the monopolist charges the limit price.

$^a\pi = q(P - AC) = 34(57.5 - 20) = 1275$.
$^b\pi = q(P - AC) = 48(40 - 22) - \epsilon = 864 - \epsilon$.
cIf the monopolist shares the market, the two firms split the demand curve, so each faces a demand curve
of $P = 100 - 2.5q$. Therefore, profit maximization requires that $MR = 100 - 5q = MC$. In Figure 11.3(a), profit
maximization requires $q = 18$ and $p = 55$, so:

$$\pi = q(P - AC) = 18(55 - 25) = 540.$$

dIf entry occurs, the entrant produces $q = 10$ and the monopolist produces $q = 48 + \epsilon$; therefore, total $Q = 58 + \epsilon$
and $P = 100 - 1.25(58 - \epsilon) = 27.5 - \epsilon$. It follows that:

$$\pi = q(P - AC) = 48(27.5 - 22) - \epsilon = 264 - \epsilon.$$

FIGURE 11.4 A Game of Entry (Potential Entrant's Profit, Monopolist's Profit)

At this point it is useful to recall the concept of a *subgame perfect Nash equilibrium* from Chapter 7. Table 11.1 presents the normal form of the game shown in Figure 11.4. The player who moves second, the monopolist, has the following four possible strategies:

1. Choose Π (profit maximization) if the potential entrant chooses *stay out* (SO), and choose Π if the potential entrant chooses Enter (E). We denote this strategy as {Π, Π}.

2. Choose Π if the potential entrant chooses SO, and choose L (limit pricing) if the potential entrant chooses E, denoted by {Π, L}.

3. Choose L if the potential entrant chooses SO, and choose Π if the potential entrant chooses E, denoted by {L, Π}.

4. Choose L if the potential entrant chooses SO and choose L if the potential entrant chooses E, denoted by {L, L}.

In Table 11.1, there are three Nash equilibria: (E, {Π, Π}), (SO, {Π, L}), and (E, {L, Π}). Consider the differences between these three Nash equilibria. In the first equilibrium, (E, {Π, Π}), the monopolist's equilibrium strategy is {Π, Π}, which means that if the potential entrant chooses SO, the monopolist chooses Π, and if the potential entrant chooses E, the monopolist also chooses Π. This is exactly the solution to the game we found using backward induction above. As for the potential entrant's equilibrium strategy, we know from backward induction that entering, E, is better for the potential entrant than staying out, SO. The equilibrium (E, {Π, Π}), therefore, corresponds to the backward induction solution with one difference: Instead of just noting that the potential entrant enters in the first stage and the monopolist profit-maximizes in the second stage, we note that the potential entrant's equilibrium strat-

TABLE 11.1 Normal Form of the Game in Figure 11.4 (Potential Entrant's Profits, Monopolist's Profits)

		Monopolist's Strategy			
		$\{\Pi, \Pi\}$	$\{\Pi, L\}$	$\{L, \Pi\}$	$\{L, L\}$
Potential	**SO (Stay out)**	(0, 1275)	(0,1275)*	(0, 864)	(0, 864)
entrant's	**E (Enter)**	(540, 540)*	(loss, 264)	(540, 540)*	(loss, 264)
action					

*Nash equilibrium

egy is to enter and the monopolist's equilibrium strategy is $\{\Pi, \Pi\}$. Here we are considering the monopolist's *entire strategy* $\{\Pi, \Pi\}$, rather than just its *action* Π.

The second Nash equilibrium is (SO, $\{\Pi, L\}$). To prove that this is a Nash equilibrium, we must prove that neither firm has an incentive to move from its current position *given the current strategy of its rival*. The monopolist's strategy is $\{\Pi, L\}$, which means that the monopolist chooses Π if the potential entrant chooses SO, and the monopolist chooses L if the potential entrant chooses E. The potential entrant's profits, therefore, equal zero if it chooses SO, and the potential entrant sustains an economic loss if it chooses E. The potential entrant, therefore, has no incentive to move away from the strategy SO. Given the potential entrant's strategy of SO, the monopolist has no incentive to move from a strategy of $\{\Pi, L\}$ because profit maximization is the firm's best response to *stay out*. The problem with the monopolist's equilibrium strategy $\{\Pi, L\}$, however, is that it requires the monopolist to choose limit pricing if the potential entrant chooses *enter*. Of course, this would be foolish, and there is no reason to believe that the monopolist would ever respond to entry in this manner.

If the monopolist somehow ended up at the M_2 node in Figure 11.4, its best response would be profit maximization, not limit pricing! This is the key difference between the (SO, $\{\Pi, L\}$) Nash equilibrium and the (E, $\{\Pi, \Pi\}$) Nash equilibrium. When the monopolist's equilibrium strategy is $\{\Pi, \Pi\}$, the monopolist is behaving rationally in response to both of the potential entrant's possible strategies. When the monopolist's equilibrium strategy is $\{\Pi, L\}$, the monopolist is only behaving rationally in response to the potential entrant's choice of *stay out*, but not to the potential entrant's choice of *enter*.

We can use the concept of a subgame perfect Nash equilibrium to distinguish between these equilibria. In Figure 11.4, there are two subgames: the one beginning at the node M_1 and the one beginning at the node M_2. These two subgames are shown in Figure 11.5. Recall that a subgame perfect Nash equilibrium is a Nash equilibrium for the complete game and for every possible subgame. We have already shown that the strategy combination (E, $\{\Pi, \Pi\}$) is a subgame perfect Nash equilibrium. The monopolist's strategy of $\{\Pi, \Pi\}$ means that the firm chooses Π at the M_1 node and Π at the M_2 node. There is no rational reason for the monopolist to ever deviate from these choices. The strategy combination (E, $\{\Pi, \Pi\}$), therefore, implies rational behavior at every node of every subgame.

Similar reasoning proves that the Nash equilibrium (SO, $\{\Pi, L\}$) is *not* a subgame perfect Nash equilibrium. The equilibrium (SO, $\{\Pi, L\}$) requires that at the subgame

FIGURE 11.5 The Two Subgames in Figure 11.4 (Potential Entrant's Profit, Monopolist's Profit)

The two subgames in Figure 11.4 begin at nodes M_1 and M_2. In both these subgames, the monopolist's strategy is to profit maximize. Limit pricing, therefore, is not a subgame perfect equilibrium.

beginning at the M_2 node, the monopolist chooses limit pricing, but this is not a Nash equilibrium for that subgame. We leave it as a problem at the end of the chapter for you to show that the third Nash equilibrium in Table 11.1 (E, {L, Π}) is also not a subgame perfect Nash equilibrium.

Because the only subgame perfect Nash equilibrium is (SO, {Π, Π}), the monopolist will never use a limit pricing strategy.

The game has only one solution: The entrant will enter and the monopolist will maximize its postentry profit. But suppose that for some unexplained reason, there is a small probability that the potential entrant makes a mistake and chooses not to enter. The small probability of such a mistake (or any mistake in these games) is called a **tremble**. The game is then reduced to the monopolist's choice of either maximizing short-run profits or employing limit pricing. Figure 11.4 reveals that the monopolist has only one rational choice. If the entrant stays out because of trembling, the monopolist's choices are to earn \$1275 or earn \$864 − ϵ. Given this choice, the monopolist's only rational choice is to maximize profit and earn \$1275. A limit pricing policy would not be reasonable, because it reduces the monopolist's profit without credibly deterring entry. Even if the game were repeated, the entrant knows that the monopolist will share the market after entry occurs. There is no reason for the entrant to stay out, even if the monopolist charges the limit price.

11.1.4 Limit Pricing with Asymmetric Information

In the preceding game in Section 11.1.3, the information structure is perfect, complete, certain, and symmetric. Given this information structure, limit pricing is never a viable strategy. Milgrom and Roberts have shown, however, that if we change the information structure of the entry game to be *imperfect, incomplete, certain, and asymmetric;* limit pricing can be a reasonable profit-maximizing strategy.[4]

Figure 11.6 shows such a game with three players, nature (the pseudo-player introduced in Chapter 7), a monopolist, and a potential entrant. Both firms know the profit payoffs. The game is played as follows. First, nature, identified by N, moves and selects the monopolist to be either a high-cost or a low-cost firm. Only the monopolist knows nature's move. The game is, therefore, a game of incomplete information, because nature moves first and nature's move is unobserved by at least one of the

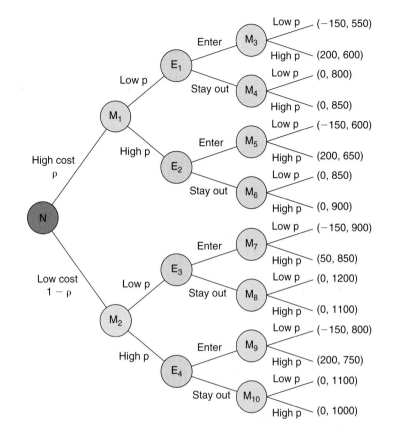

FIGURE 11.6 A Game of Entry with Asymmetric Information ($millions Entrant's Profit, $millions Monopolist's Profit)

The potential entrant knows only the probability ρ that nature selects the monopolist to be high cost, whereas the monopolist knows whether it is a high-cost or low-cost firm. A high-cost monopolist may play *low price* at the node M_1, because then the potential entrant does not know whether the game has moved to the node E_1 or E_3. The potential entrant's expected profit is therefore $E(\pi) = \rho(200) + (1 - \rho)(-150)$. If $\rho < 0.429$, then $E(\pi) < 0$, and the potential entrant's expected profit is negative, so the potential entrant stays out at node E_1. By charging a low price, a high-cost monopolist can deter entry.

players. In this case, nature's move is unobserved by the potential entrant. The probability that the monopolist is a high-cost producer is ρ, and the probability that the monopolist is a low-cost producer is $(1 - \rho)$. Because the monopolist has information that is unavailable to the potential entrant, the game is also a game of asymmetric information. In the absence of a threat of entry, a high-cost monopolist prefers to charge a high price, and a low-cost monopolist prefers to charge a low price.

After nature moves, the monopolist, identified by M, selects either a low price (high output) or a high price (low output). The potential entrant, identified by E, then decides either to enter or to stay out. After the entrant makes its decision, the monopolist moves again and sets the price either low or high.

Suppose nature selects the monopolist to be a low-cost producer, so the monopolist's first move is from the node M_2. If we look at only the bottom half of the game beginning at node M_2, we see a low-cost monopolist's dominant solution of always playing low price. If the low-cost producer is at node M_2 and plays *low p*, then the game moves to node E_3. If the entrant enters, the game moves to node M_7, and the monopolist maximizes profit at $900 million by playing *low p* once again. Unfortunately for the entrant, this results in a $150 million loss. If at node E_3 the entrant instead stays out, the monopolist still plays *low p* at node M_8, because *low p* maximizes the monopolist's profit at $1200 million. A low-cost monopolist would *never* play *high p* at node M_2, because that would move the game to node E_4, and from that node, no matter what the entrant decided to do, the monopolist would always be better off if it had played *low p* at node M_2. In other words, the monopolist is better off if the game moves to node M_7 and it plays *low p* and earns $900 million than if the game moves to M_9 and it plays *low p* and earns $800 million. Similarly, the monopolist is better off if the game moves to node M_8 and it plays *low p* than if the game moves to node M_{10} and it plays *low p*.

If the potential entrant knows with certainty that the monopolist is a low-cost producer—that is, if $\rho = 0$—then there is only one solution to the game from node M_2: the monopolist plays *low p*, and because the entrant knows that if it enters it will sustain a $150 million loss, it stays out and earns a normal profit of $0. The equilibrium, therefore, would be (*low p, stay out, low p*), which maximizes the low-cost monopolist's profits at $1200 million. Consequently, if the potential entrant knows that the monopolist is a low-cost producer, it stays out.

Now suppose that nature selects the monopolist to have high costs, so the game moves to node M_1. The potential entrant, however, does not know whether the game is at node M_1 or node M_2. If the high-cost monopolist plays *high p* at node M_1, it immediately reveals that the monopolist is a high-cost producer, because the potential entrant knows that if the monopolist were a low-cost producer at node M_2, it would never play *high p*. Therefore, if the monopolist plays *high p* at node M_1, the entrant knows the game is at node E_2. From node E_2, if the potential entrant enters, the monopolist plays *high p* and the entrant earns $200 million, which is better than the normal profit the potential entrant earns if it stays out. Therefore, from node M_1, if the monopolist plays *high p*, the game has only one solution: (*high p, enter, high p*).

There is another option for the high-cost monopolist at node M_1: It can play *low p*. If the monopolist plays *low p*, the potential entrant cannot tell whether the game has moved to node E_1 or node E_3. The potential entrant, however, knows that there is a probability ρ of being at node E_1 and a probability $1 - \rho$ of being at node E_3. We've already seen that if the potential entrant enters at node E_3, it sustains an economic loss of $150 million. On the other hand, if it enters at node E_1, then the game moves to node M_3 and the high-cost monopolist maximizes profit by playing *high p*, while the entrant earns $200 million in profit. The outcome of the game is determined entirely by the value of ρ. The larger ρ, the more likely the entrant is to earn $200 million; and the smaller ρ, the more likely the entrant is to lose $150 million. The entrant's expected profit is:

$$E(\pi) = \rho(200) + (1 - \rho)(-150)$$

If $\rho < 0.429$, then $E(\pi) < 0$, and the potential entrant's expected profit is negative, so the potential entrant stays out at node E_1. If the potential entrant stays out at node E_1, the game moves to node M_4, and the high-cost monopolist's final move is *high p*. The high-cost monopolist earns \$850 million, which is considerably greater than the \$650 million the monopolist would earn if it played *high p* at node M_1.

Suppose, for example, the potential entrant believes the probability that the monopolist is a high-cost producer is 30 percent; that is, $\rho = 0.30$. If the potential entrant enters, expected profit is $0.3(\$200) + 0.7(-\$150) = \$60 - \$105 = -\$45$. If nature selects *high-cost* and the game moves to node M_1, the optimal play for the high-cost monopolist is *low p*, and the game's outcome is (*low p, stay out, high p*). The high-cost monopolist earns \$850 million, which is much better than the alternative outcome of (*high p, enter, high p*), which results in a profit of \$650 million. The high-cost monopolist charges a low price in order to deter entry: In other words, it is using limit pricing.

Intuitively, the game can be summarized as follows. A monopolist knows with certainty whether it is a low-cost or a high-cost producer; however, potential entrants can determine only the probability that the monopolist is a high-cost producer. A high-cost monopolist therefore may find it profitable to charge a low price in order to prevent potential entrants from gaining any information regarding the monopolist's true costs. As a result, potential entrants can calculate their expected profits only after entry, based on the probabilities that the monopolist is a low-cost or high-cost producer. If the probability that the monopolist is a low-cost producer is high enough, the potential entrant's expected profit is negative. Consequently, the potential entrant is deterred from entering if the high-cost monopolist charges a low price, that is, if the high-cost monopolist adopts a limit pricing strategy.

11.1.5 Empirical Evidence of Limit Pricing

Empirical evidence on limit pricing comes from a number of case studies and a few statistical studies. The case study approach attempts to identify industries in which firms have maintained dominant positions and yet earned only normal or even below-normal profits, or industries in which large increases in output have not been associated with increased net earning. Of course, finding a dominant firm with below-normal profits does not prove the existence of limit pricing because such an outcome could occur for many other reasons. For example, demand could be low, many close substitutes could exist, or costs could be high. But some case studies reveal strong circumstantial evidence suggesting the use of limit pricing.

DU PONT IN CELLOPHANE[5] From 1924 to 1947 Du Pont held a virtual monopoly in the U.S. cellophane industry. Significant economies of scale existed in the industry, and Du Pont realized early on the advantages of moving down the average cost curve before competitors had entered. As a result, Du Pont followed a policy of continually lowering price. Prices declined by 84.8 percent between 1924 and 1940, from \$2.51 per pound to just \$0.38 per pound.[6]

During the industry's early years demand increased rapidly, and entrants might have been able to penetrate the market if Du Pont had maintained high prices. But by continually reducing its cellophane prices, Du Pont established control before new

firms had an opportunity to enter. Potential entrants undoubtedly realized that large-scale entry required either a postentry reduction in Du Pont's output or a dramatic postentry industry-wide price reduction. Du Pont's pricing between 1924 and 1940 was consistent with that of a firm attempting to deter entry. To maintain its dominant market position, Du Pont was apparently willing to accept lower prices and reduced profits on cellophane.

UNITED SHOE MACHINERY[7] Until the mid-1950s United Shoe Machinery Corporation (USM) controlled the market for virtually all shoe machinery in the United States, with a national market share between 85 and 90 percent. United Shoe has been called the classic example of a "good trust." United's rental rates were reasonable and uniform, its rate of return on invested capital was typically normal or below normal, the machines performed well, service was provided free, and the cost of shoe machinery averaged less than 2 percent of the wholesale price of shoes.

Despite USM's good behavior, in an antitrust case the government complained that USM's power resulted from its marketing conduct, and in a 1954 decision the Supreme Court ruled that USM had monopolized the industry. As part of the decree, the Court ordered that in 10 years the case would be reviewed to determine whether the industry had become more competitive.

A comparison of United Shoe's pricing policies before and after the 1954 Supreme Court decision provides some evidence of limit pricing behavior.[8] The Court's decision gave USM an incentive to raise prices and reap high short-run profits rather than keep prices down to deter entry. USM surely knew that if its market share remained around 90 percent, the government would demand a stronger structural remedy in 10 years. It seems reasonable that USM would end whatever pricing restraint it may have been practicing. Because high prices and profits would help attract entrants, the worse USM's pricing policies became for its buyers, the better those policies might appear to the courts in 10 years.

In the two years following the decree, USM's prices and profits rose dramatically. In 1954 United's net income was only $7.2 million, and its rate of return on equity was a modest 8.2 percent.[9] In 1955, however, net income soared to a company record of $18.9 million, and USM's rate of return reached an all-time high of 18.3 percent.[10] This tremendous leap resulted in part from windfall revenues generated from the sale of many machines that had been leased before 1955, but much of the jump also resulted from large increases in the rental rate for United's machinery.

As USM hiked prices, new firms entered the industry. The appearance of 56 new firms in the 10 years after the Supreme Court's decree suggests that USM's high-price policy was effective in attracting entrants or, put differently, that USM's early policy of keeping prices relatively low was effective in deterring entry.[11]

GENERAL FOODS In a study of the pricing policies of 20 major industries, Kaplan, Dirlam, and Lanzillotti found evidence that General Foods placed a greater emphasis on long-term than short-term profits.[12] On specialty items such as Minute Rice, Postum, Sanka, Jell-O, and Birds Eye frozen foods, management realized that it was unwise to set high profit margins that would shorten the lives of these products as specialty items. While recognizing the ability to set high margins on these brands, General Foods' management also understood that "a high price [would] restrict the volume and that it [would] speed up the process of developing competition."[13]

Kaplan and colleagues found that General Foods took potential competition into account in all of its pricing decisions. A former chairman of the board of directors at General Foods told the researchers that the strategy objective was aimed at a "stable franchise."[14] In other words, General Foods kept prices well below the short-run profit-maximizing level, realizing full well that any gain associated with higher prices would be more than offset by subsequent losses to new competitors.

XEROX[15] Blackstone has suggested that Xerox engaged in a complex pricing strategy that included elements of limit pricing during the early years of its dominance in the copier industry. When Xerox introduced its plain paper copiers in 1959, it had no significant cost advantage over Electrofax coated paper technology in the low-volume segment of the industry and therefore decided to price its low-volume copiers at the short-run profit-maximizing level. High profits encouraged at least 25 firms to enter the low-volume segment of the industry between 1961 and 1967.[16] In the medium-volume segment, however, Xerox had a modest cost advantage and elected to price below the profit-maximizing level but above the strict limit price. In this segment, 10 firms entered, and Xerox recognized that it would eventually give up a considerable amount of market share to competitors. Finally, in the high-volume segment, where Xerox enjoyed a significant cost advantage, it priced close to the limit price, and only three firms entered.[17]

REGULATED BANKING IN PENNSYLVANIA Timothy Hannan used data from the Pennsylvania banking industry in 1970, when the industry was still under tight regulation that limited entry and potential entry, to study the impact of potential entry on interest rates paid on passbook savings accounts.[18] In 1970, regulations prevented out-of-state banks from entering the Pennsylvania market and permitted entry into new markets only through branching by existing Pennsylvania banks and only in a "county contiguous to the county of its home office."[19] The Federal Reserve Bank of Philadelphia divided the state into 53 local markets and Hannan used these markets for his study.

Hannan examined the impact of potential entry on the passbook savings interest rates in commercial banks. He hypothesized that an increase in potential competition would have a positive impact on the passbook savings interest rate because banks would pay higher rates on saving to prevent entry. The study controlled for many factors that could impact the interest rate on passbook savings, including per capita income, the number of manufacturing establishments, total bank deposits, the number of branches in the market, the ratio of savings bank deposits to commercial bank deposits, and market concentration (using three different measures: the three-firm concentration ratio, the Herfindahl, and the number of banks in the market). Finally, Hannan observed that banks with less than $300 million in deposits almost never branched into a new market. In fact, banks with $300 million or more in deposits were 30 times more likely to branch into new markets than banks with less than $300 million in deposits. Based on this observation, Hannan controlled for potential competition by using the number of potential entrants into a market with more than $300 million in deposits.

The results showed that potential competition had a statistically significant positive impact on passbook savings interest rates regardless of which measure of market concentration was used. This study is one of the few industry studies where a specific measure of the likelihood of entry into a market is available.

APPLICATION 11.1

Limit Pricing in the Antihistamine Market

Millions of allergy sufferers in the United States used to walk around half-asleep for much of the year because of treatment with antihistamine drugs such as Benadryl and Chlortrimiton. Then, in the 1980s, the introduction of three drugs—Seldane, Hismanol, and Claritin—changed the world for many allergy sufferers. These nonsedating antihistamines made it possible to stop sneezing without falling asleep. In the early 1990s, when Seldane and Hismanol were found to increase the risk of heart problems and heart attacks, Schering-Plough's Claritin became the dominant drug in the nonsedating antihistamine market. A few years later, two other nonsedating antihistamines appeared: Pfizer's Zyrtec and Aventis's Allegra.

Claritin, Zyrtec, and Allegra remained patented prescription-only drugs in the United States until the fall of 2002, when Claritin lost its U.S. patent protection and became a nonprescription, over-the-counter drug. In Canada, however, these antihistamines lost their patent protection and became over-the-counter drugs in the 1990s. According to Pillbot.com, in September 2002, the lowest prices for a one-month supply of the three prescription drugs in the United States were $88.99 for Claritin, $65.77 for Allegra, and $58.51 for Zyrtec. In September 2002, if you were fortunate enough to live in the United States close to the Canadian border, you could drive across the border, stop at the first Shopper's Drug Mart you came upon, and purchase a one-month supply of the same drugs for the following prices: $22.22 (Can$33.33) for Claritin, $24.31 (Can$36.47) for Allegra, and $19.99 (Can$29.99) for Zyrtec (sold in Canada under the brand name Reactine).

It's not surprising that these drugs were much less expensive in Canada, due to a lack of patent protection and their over-the-counter status. What is surprising, however, is that there were few generic alternatives to Claritin, Zyrtec, and Allegra available in Canadian drugstores. For example, in September 2002, Shopper's Drug Mart in Niagara Falls, Ontario, offered one generic alternative to Claritin and no alternatives to Zyrtec or Allegra. Furthermore, on the day the Shopper's Drug Mart price data were collected, the chain was offering a "two-boxes-for-the-price-of-one special" for Claritin, and as a result, the generic drug, Loratadine, was more expensive. By comparison, Shopper's Drug Mart offered many generic alternatives to analgesics such as Bayer aspirin, Tylenol, Advil, and Motrin, and to the most popular decongestant, Sudafed. In each of these markets, the generic drugs were much cheaper than the brand-name drugs.

Limit pricing theory can explain Schering-Plough's, Pfizer's, and Aventis's Canadian pricing behavior. In the United States, patent protection and the prescription drug status of Claritin, Zyrtec, and Allegra eliminated the threat of entry. However, in Canada, without patent protection or prescription drug status, if Schering-Plough, Pfizer, and Aventis charged high prices, there would be a tremendous threat that other drug manufacturers would enter the generic antihistamine market. To prevent large-scale entry, the three manufacturers charged very low prices in Canada compared to those in the United States. By charging low prices, the companies signaled their ability to earn economic profits even at low prices, and therefore, they signaled that they could produce these drugs at low costs. Schering-Plough, Pfizer, and Aventis could have charged high prices in Canada when Claritin, Zyrtec, and Allega first became available over the counter, but they choose not to. Instead, they slashed prices. This policy succeeded in limiting entry into the generic antihistamine market. ■

Statistical Tests

It is difficult to test the limit pricing model using a large data set because it is statistically impossible to identify the actual limit price or the actual profit-maximizing price in an industry. Masson and Shaanan, however, have made two good efforts to test statistically the limit pricing hypothesis.[20] They tested for which of the following three competing limit pricing theories most accurately predicted firms' pricing behavior:

Theory 1[21]—Firms charge either the short-run profit-maximizing price or the strict limit price. In this model, when entry barriers are high, firms charge the limit price; when entry barriers are low, firms charge the profit-maximizing price.

Theory 2[22]—If no entry barriers exist, the monopolist charges the high short-run profit-maximizing price and permits entry. As entry barriers rise, the monopolist's optimal price declines. When entry barriers reach a critical level, B*, the optimal price exactly equals the strict limit price, and no entry occurs. As barriers continue to increase beyond B*, the optimal price and the limit price remain equal to each other and rise in lockstep together (obviously, the limit price rises as entry barriers rise) until the optimal price and the limit price return to the short-run profit-maximizing price for very high entry barriers.

Theory 3[23]—The optimal price is always above the limit price but converges toward the limit price for very high entry barriers. In this model some entry is permitted, but the monopolist controls the rate of entry by varying the difference between the actual price and the limit price.

Masson and Shaanan first studied a sample of 37 American manufacturing industries to determine which, if any, of these theories was consistent with observed pricing behavior.[24] Their 1982 results strongly supported theory 3 and rejected both theory 1 and theory 2.

One implication of Masson and Shaanan's 1982 results was that few firms charge either the strict limit price or the strict short-run profit-maximizing price. Instead, prices tend to lie between the two extremes, thereby encouraging some entry but discouraging a flood of entry. This finding is consistent with the theoretical belief that strict limit pricing rarely makes economic sense and with Blackstone's earlier observed pricing by Xerox in the 1960s.

In 1987 Masson and Shaanan replicated their previous study using a sample of 43 Canadian manufacturing industries.[25] The statistical results of this follow-up study were less robust than those of their 1982 study but were still consistent with theory 3.

11.2 Predatory Pricing

Limit pricing requires the monopolist to maintain a low price before entry occurs. By comparison, ***predatory pricing*** assumes that a monopolist maximizes profit until entry occurs, and that after entry, the monopolist expands output aggressively and cuts price, so that the entrant sustains an economic loss, even if this requires the monopolist to sustain an economic loss as well. What happens if a monopolist plays this predatory pricing strategy in response to every entry? It seems likely that potential entrants would eventually get the message and assume that the monopolist would

respond aggressively to all entry, and, as a result, future potential entrants would stay out. By establishing a reputation for being aggressive early, the monopolist prevents later entry. Such a result depends, however, on the information available to the monopolist and potential entrants.

11.2.1 Predatory Pricing with Perfect, Certain, Complete, and Symmetric Information

At the end of Chapter 7, we analyzed the basic predatory pricing game using perfect, certain, complete, and symmetric information, and concluded that entry could not be deterred. Figure 11.7 presents a slight variation of that game. Both players know all of the information in Figure 11.7. As you learned in Chapter 7, if this game is played once, there is only one equilibrium: The potential entrant enters and the monopolist accommodates entry. Once the potential entrant enters, it is irrational for the monopolist to fight, because fighting results in an economic loss of $1 million, whereas accommodation results in an economic profit of $4 million.

Suppose the game is repeated any finite number of times. For example, the game is repeated N times sequentially from round 1 through round N. It may seem logical to presume that a rational monopolist would fight in early rounds in order to build an aggressive reputation and deter entry in later rounds. But, as Chapter 7 showed, that is not the equilibrium outcome in this game. The equilibrium is obtained by playing the game backwards from round N (the last round) through round 1. In the last round, round N, the monopolist has no incentive to fight, because fighting cannot possibly deter entry in later rounds, because there are no later rounds. The monopolist, therefore, accommodates the entrant in the last round and earns a profit of $4 million. The potential entrant into the last round knows this and enters. The potential entrant in round N − 1 knows that the monopolist will accommodate entry in round N, and therefore knows that the monopolist has no incentive to establish an aggressive reputation in round N − 1. Why bother sustaining an economic loss of $1 million in

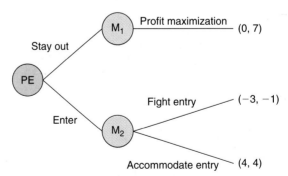

FIGURE 11.7 A Game of Entry ($millions Potential Entrant's Profit, $millions Monopolist's Profit)

If this game is played with perfect, certain, complete, and symmetric information, the only equilibrium is for the potential entrant to enter and the monopolist to accommodate entry. Both firms earn profits of $4 million.

round N − 1 when it does nothing to deter entry in the next round? In a sense, round N − 1 is now the last round of the game, so the potential entrant enters, and the monopolist accommodates entry in round N − 1. Regardless of the number of rounds, by reasoning backwards to the first round, the monopolist *never* fights; instead, it accommodates entry in each and every round from 1 through N. Economist Richard Selten first identified this result in 1978 and called it the ***chain store paradox.***[26] Selten described it as a "paradox," because even with hundreds or thousands of rounds, the implication is that entry will be accommodated in each and every round, a somewhat counterintuitive result.

The chain store paradox is consistent with an economic theory developed in 1958 by economist John McGee.[27] McGee argued that predatory pricing almost never makes economic sense, because the profit losses associated with predatory pricing can almost never be recouped by raising prices later. McGee developed his theory after studying the behavior of John D. Rockefeller's Standard Oil monopoly in the last quarter of the nineteenth century. Before McGee's analysis, the common belief among scholars was that Standard Oil used predatory pricing on many occasions to eliminate its competitors. McGee found, however, that while Standard Oil indeed eliminated many competitors, it almost always eliminated them through merger. Furthermore, McGee discovered that Standard Oil typically paid a price for its competitors' assets that was greater than the assets' market value. Rather than engage in a drawn-out and costly period of predatory pricing, Standard Oil eliminated competitors by buying them out at highly attractive prices. In most cases, the cost of acquiring competitors through merger was far less than the cost of driving them out by using predatory pricing. McGee generalized his findings by suggesting that predatory pricing is rarely used to eliminate competitors. In a world of perfect, certain, complete, and symmetric information, McGee's analysis makes a great deal of sense.

11.2.2 Predatory Pricing with Imperfect, Certain, Incomplete, and Asymmetric Information

Let's change the information structure of the predatory pricing game in Figure 11.6. In this new game, information is imperfect, certain, incomplete, and asymmetric. Now suppose nature first selects the monopolist to be either: (1) a ***strong monopolist,*** which enjoys being predatory and is always predatory; or (2) a ***weak monopolist,*** which is predatory in one market only if it believes it will increase its future profit in other markets to at least compensate for its lower current profit. Nature selects the monopolist to be strong with probability ρ and weak with probability $(1 - \rho)$. The monopolist knows whether it is strong or weak; however, the potential entrant only knows the value of ρ, the probability that the monopolist is strong. Potential entrants gain some information from observing the behavior of the monopolist, but initially, potential entrants do not know whether they are facing a strong or weak monopolist. Such a game is one of *incomplete* information, because nature moves first and nature's move is unobserved by the potential entrant. It is also a game of *asymmetric* information, because one player, the monopolist, knows more information than the other player, the potential entrant.

If the game is repeated many times, a weak monopolist may engage in predatory pricing in early rounds in order to create the impression that it is a strong firm. In this case, the weak monopolist is attempting to convince future potential entrants that

it is strong. Because strong monopolists never permit entry, if a weak monopolist accommodates entry in any round, it reveals itself to be weak. Once the monopolist is revealed to be weak, the game transforms into a game with perfect, certain, complete, and symmetric information, because all future potential entrants know that $\rho = 0$. From that point onward, all potential entrants will enter and the weak monopolist will accommodate them.

Now suppose this version of the predatory pricing game, with imperfect, incomplete, and asymmetric information, is repeated N times sequentially from round 1 through round N. Figure 11.7 gives the profit payoffs. Assume that nature selects the monopolist to be weak. In the early rounds of the game, a rational weak monopolist responds to entry by fighting entry and sustaining an economic loss of $1 million. As a result, if a potential entrant enters, it will sustain an economic loss of $3 million. By fighting entry, the monopolist increases the probability in the minds of future potential entrants that it is actually a strong monopolist and is likely to fight all entry—even entry in the last, Nth round of the game. If the monopolist can prevent entry in a few future rounds, it can earn a profit of $7 million in each of those rounds, which is 75 percent higher than the $4 million it earns by accommodating entry. Essentially, the weak monopolist decides that it is willing to accept a few $1 million losses early in the game in order to earn a few extra $7 million gains later.

11.2.3 The Kreps and Wilson Predatory Pricing Game

How exactly would such a game play out? David Kreps and Robert Wilson developed a model to answer that question.[28] They considered a game with a finite number of markets, for example, 200 markets, and the incomplete and asymmetric information structure described above. Although it is technically difficult to develop the solution to the Kreps and Wilson predatory pricing game, the equilibrium result is intuitively appealing and fairly easy to explain. Essentially, we have already shown that by behaving aggressively in early markets, a weak monopolist may prevent entry in other markets by fooling potential entrants into thinking that it is strong. A weak monopolist therefore may increase its present value of profits by behaving aggressively. As we show in the Appendix, the equilibrium in the Kreps and Wilson game has the following important characteristics:

1. In early markets such as the first 150 markets in a 200-market game, entry will *not* occur because both *strong* and *weak* firms will adopt a predatory response to all entry. This occurs because in early markets even a *weak* firm has a great incentive to build up a reputation as a *strong* firm. If, for example, entry occurred in the third market and was not met with a predatory response, then all future potential entrants would know that the monopolist was *weak,* and by the chain store paradox, there would be no deterrent to entering the fourth through 200th markets.

2. As the number of markets approaches 200, a *weak* monopolist has little incentive to continue to put forward a facade as a *strong* firm, and the monopolist will share the market.

3. Between the early and late markets, the monopolist plays a mixed strategy of predatory pricing in the nth market with a probability of μ_n and sharing the mar-

ket with a probability of $(1 - \mu_n)$, where μ_n *generally* diminishes in later rounds.* Of course, if the monopolist actually shares even *one* market, then the monopolist is identified as *weak,* and by the logic of the chain store paradox the monopolist will accommodate all future entry.

Figure 11.8 shows this basic result. In markets from N through X, a *weak* monopolist will always behave aggressively. In markets Y through 1, a *weak* monopolist will always accommodate entry. In markets X through Y, however, the monopolist adopts a mixed strategy.

Perhaps the most important implication of the asymmetric information model of predatory behavior is that as N becomes very large, even a small probability that a monopolist is strong may deter entry.[29] Suppose, for example, that initially $\rho = 0.01$; that is, there is a 1 percent probability that the monopolist is strong and a 99 percent probability that the firm is weak. Given $\rho = 0.01$, potential entrants can be fairly confident that the monopolist will accommodate entry. Now suppose in the 10th round of the game, a potential entrant enters, and the monopolist fights, so the entrant sus-ains an economic loss of $3 million. As a result, the potential entrant into the 11th und is likely to increase its estimate of ρ, the probability that the monopolist is rong. In round N, the last round, the monopolist has no incentive to fight, because hting cannot possibly deter entry in later rounds. Furthermore, as the game proaches the last, Nth round, a weak monopolist has progressively less and less entive to fight entry, because there are fewer and fewer rounds available in which arn $7 million. A weak monopolist is trying to trick potential entrants into believ-hat it is a strong monopolist and would always fight entry. One implication of the atory pricing game with asymmetric information is that even a very small proba-that a monopolist is strong—that is, a small ρ—might deter entry for a substan-riod of time, especially if the monopolist fights entry in early rounds.

rical Evidence: Predatory Pricing uilding a Tough Reputation

amples: Standard Oil and American Tobacco

s consider Standard Oil of New Jersey the classic predatory firm.[30] In the f the twentieth century, historians and economists reported that John D. forced many competitors out of the oil refining business by lowering average cost. As noted in section 11.2.1, however, in a 1959 article John ided evidence that Standard Oil rarely resorted to predatory behavior but, ded to purchase its competitors on what might be deemed reasonable the other hand, in section 3.6.1 we saw that all of Standard's actions

predatory	Play mixed strategy	Always accommodate
X	Y	N

ponse of Weak Monopolist to Entry in Markets N Through 1

g game, a weak monopolist is always predatory in rounds N through X, plays nds X through Y, and always accommodates entry in rounds Y through 1.

model presented in the Appendix explains the derivation of μ_n.

seemed aimed at one objective: maintaining control over the oil refining business in the United States.

Although Standard Oil received most of the historical attention around the turn of the century, as we showed in Application 3.4, American Tobacco was a more aggressive monopolist.[32] There is little doubt that Standard Oil to some extent, and American Tobacco to a far greater extent, engaged in predatory pricing to create a tough reputation and intimidate competitors. Several more recent cases suggest that the practice continues.

Maxwell House Coffee[33]

In 1970 General Foods held approximately a 43 percent national market share for noninstant coffee. A majority of that share was held by Maxwell House, and General Foods was the only national distributor of ground coffee. Procter & Gamble's Folgers brand, the leading brand in the West, was not sold in the East. But in 1971 Procter & Gamble began to market Folgers in the East by selling in a few test markets, including Cleveland, Pittsburgh, Philadelphia, and Syracuse. In each of these markets the Maxwell House brand commanded the lead, with a market share two to five times larger than the second-ranking brand.

In response to Folgers' entry, General Foods slashed the price of Maxwell House in the four test markets. Evidence suggested that Maxwell House was sold at prices below marginal and average variable costs. In the late winter of 1974, for example, Maxwell House was sold for $2.095 per three-pound can in Pittsburgh, whereas the price of a three-pound can of unroasted green coffee beans was $2.10.[34]

According to Hilke and Nelson, General Foods' aggressive actions had the effect of making Procter & Gamble believe that General Foods would respond aggressively to entry into any eastern market.[35] As a result, Folgers' eastern expansion lagged, and General Foods earned higher profits in the eastern market for several additional years.

Airlines

As we have discussed, until the late 1970s airline fares in the United States were regulated by the Civil Aeronautics Board (CAB). Deregulation of the industry resulted in the entry of many new airline carriers, among them Midway, People Express, and Southwest. These new airlines had significantly lower costs than established carriers, such as American, United, and Delta, and initially were able to gain a substantial market share on many routes.

Table 11.2 suggests the dramatic impact of entry on fares. In each of the four comparison cases, fares decreased considerably on routes on which entry occurred, and fares increased by more than 50 percent on routes without entry. Table 11.2 suggests that deregulation had the anticipated positive effect of reducing fares. Hidden behind these fare figures, however, is another story: the aggressive use of selective predatory pricing by established carriers in markets entered by new airlines.

To understand why Table 11.2 suggests the use of predatory tactics, consider this list of new jet carriers that entered the industry between 1979 and 1984 after deregulation:[36]

1. Midway (entered 1979)

2. New York Air (1980)

3. People Express (1981)

TABLE 11.2 Comparative Airline Fares in Markets Entered by People Express and Southwest

Market	Distance	1980 Fare	1984 Fare	Percent Change
New York–Buffalo (People Express)	282	$48	$36	–25%
Boston-Philadelphia	281	$52	$79	53%
New York–Norfolk (People Express)	284	$48	$32	–30%
Chicago-Columbus	284	$48	$98	103%
Dallas–Little Rock (Southwest)	303	$59	$49	–17%
Atlanta-Mobile	303	$56	$87	56%
El Paso–Phoenix (Southwest)	346	$74	$44	–41%
St. Louis–Tulsa	351	$60	$110	83%

Source: Daniel P. Kaplan, "The Changing Airline Industry," in Leonard W. Weiss and Michael W. Klass (eds.), *Regulatory Reform: What Actually Happened* (Boston: Little, Brown, 1986), p. 59.

4. Muse (1981)

5. Jet America (1982)

6. Pacific Express (1982)

7. Northeastern (1982)

8. Pacific East (1982)

9. American International (1982)

10. Hawaii Express (1982)

11. Air One (1983)

12. Sunworld (1983)

13. America West (1983)

14. Frontier Horizon (1984)

15. Florida Express (1984)

16. Air Atlanta (1984)

In reaction to these entrants, the established carriers, led by American Airlines, followed a practice of aggressive price cutting. In virtually every market in which a major carrier faced competition from a new carrier, the established firm responded by slashing prices to match or undercut the entrant's fares.

A classic example is Northwest's response to the entry of People Express into the Minneapolis–St. Paul market in June 1984.[37] People Express entered the Newark-to-Minneapolis market with fares of $99 weekdays and $79 weekends and evenings. People Express was a low-cost, low-service operation that charged for amenities such as meals and baggage handling. In June 1984 Northwest's standard economy fare

between Minneapolis and each of the three New York airports was $263, and the lowest highly restrictive fare available was $149. Following the entry of People Express, Northwest slashed its unrestricted fares to $95 weekdays and $75 weekends and evenings. Because Northwest flew to all three New York airports and its fares included meals, wider seats, and baggage handling, these fare reductions represented a significant undercutting of People Express fares. People Express responded by further reducing its fares to $79 and $59, but Northwest met those fares as well.

The Northwest–People Express scenario was repeated many times by different carriers during the 1990s. For example, in 1995 Spirit Airlines entered the Detroit market and offered a one-way Detroit-Philadelphia fare of $49. Northwest, the dominant carrier out of Detroit, was charging an average Detroit-Philadelphia fare of $170 when Spirit entered. After Spirit entered, Northwest reduced its Detroit-Philadelphia fare to $49 for most seats. Furthermore, Northwest dramatically increased its capacity on the route. As a result of Northwest's actions, Spirit left the Detroit-Philadelphia market. Northwest then increased its fares to $230 and reduced its capacity.[38] Northwest behaved similarly in 1998 when Kiwi entered Northwest's major Minneapolis hub. After reducing its fares and eliminating Kiwi from the Minneapolis-Newark market, Northwest raised its one-way Minneapolis-Newark fare from $69 to $588![39]

Other airlines have responded to entry in a similar manner. When AirTran entered Delta's Atlanta-Mobile market in 1998, Delta reduced its fares to match those of AirTran. After AirTran decided to leave the market, Delta increased its fare from $59 to $404.[40] Similarly, when Vanguard entered American's Dallas-Wichita market, American responded by cutting its fares in half, from $106 to $53.[41]

The aggressive response of the established airlines to new entry in the 1980s and 1990s is consistent with a predation strategy. In response to every entry, the established airlines responded with aggressive price cuts and gave the impression that they were *strong* firms (even if they were in fact weak) that would respond aggressively to all entry.

APPLICATION 11.2
Does Wal-Mart Use Predatory Pricing?

Does Wal-Mart use predatory pricing to drive competitors out of the market and prevent new competitors from entering? If you asked Wal-Mart's competitors, from the small local drugstore to giant Kmart, they would probably contend that Wal-Mart's pricing behavior is predatory. Wal-Mart's advertising slogan professes: "Always Low Prices *Always*." But are Wal-Mart's prices so low as to eliminate the competition? In 1991, three local pharmacies in Faulkner County, Arkansas, thought so, and took legal action to prove that Wal-Mart used predatory pricing in its Faulkner County store.*

Wal-Mart entered Faulkner County by building a store in Conway. The Conway Wal-Mart began selling prescription drugs in 1987. Its main competitors were a dozen small local pharmacies and several large supermarkets. Wal-Mart admitted it sold many health and beauty items and pharmaceuticals below invoice cost; that is, below the cost of the items to Wal-Mart. In fact, evidence showed that up to 30 percent of the Conway Wal-Mart's health and beauty aids and pharmaceuticals were sold below invoice cost for extended periods of time. The products sold below cost included some of the most widely used pharmaceuticals and health and beauty aids, such as the acid reducer Tagament, Efferdent, Mylanta, Oil of Olay, and Crest toothpaste. In addition to charging prices below cost, the Conway Wal-Mart monitored its competitors' prices and dis-

played a "scorecard" in the front of the store showing that its prices were lower than its competitors' prices. In addition, Wal-Mart advertised these comparison price advantages extensively throughout Faulkner County. Prices at the Conway Wal-Mart were substantially lower than in nearby Wal-Mart stores that faced less competition. This was consistent with the company's philosophy to "meet or beat" competitors' prices for all "highly competitive, price-sensitive merchandise."

On October 14, 1993, Judge David Reynolds of the Chancery Court of Faulkner County ruled that Wal-Mart's behavior violated the Arkansas Unfair Trade Practices Act. Specifically, the judge wrote:

> "The act" makes it unlawful for a business to sell, or advertise for sale "any article or product" at less than the "cost thereof." "Cost" in this instance is defined as the "invoice or replacement cost of the article to the distributor or vendor plus the cost of doing business."

The judge ordered Wal-Mart to pay $396,469 in damages to the three plaintiffs.

Wal-Mart appealed Judge Reynolds's ruling, and on January 9, 1995, the Arkansas Supreme Court by a 4–3 decision overturned the lower court's judgment. The majority accepted Wal-Mart's defense that it was simply using below-cost pricing on a few products to entice customers into the Conway store where they would buy other items priced above cost. Wal-Mart contended that the pharmaceuticals and health and beauty aids departments in the Conway store always made a profit, proving that most items were sold above Wal-Mart's invoice costs.

Did Wal-Mart practice predatory pricing in Conway? Legally, it depends on which court and set of judges is writing the decision. From an economic standpoint, it is certainly consistent with Wal-Mart's overall pricing philosophy that prices were set below cost on many items for extended periods of time. Wal-Mart's pricing policies have established its reputation as an aggressive competitor that will stop at nothing to ensure that it has the lowest prices throughout the United States. That aggressive reputation has almost certainly made other firms hesitant to enter markets where Wal-Mart competes.

*Wal-Mart Stores v. American Drugs et al., Appeal from the Faulkner County Chancery Court, No. E-92-1158, January 9, 1995. ■

APPLICATION 11.3

Don't Mess with Bill: Netscape versus Microsoft in the Internet Browser Market

On January 22, 2002, Netscape Communications Corporation, then owned by AOL Time Warner, filed a private antitrust suit against Microsoft claiming that Microsoft had illegally monopolized the Internet browser market that Netscape had founded in 1994.* The introduction of Netscape Navigator version 1.0 revolutionized the Internet by changing the way information is gathered and disseminated throughout the world. By 1995, Netscape was growing at a phenomenal rate. It won many software product awards and was installed on more than 15 million computers. Its customers included 70 of the Fortune 100 largest companies. However, a few short years later, its market had essentially evaporated in the face of an aggressive campaign by Microsoft to gain control of the browser market with Internet Explorer (IE). By June 2005, Netscape's market share was under 1 percent.[†]

In its complaint, Netscape charged that Microsoft "embarked on a series of anti-competitive and exclusionary acts so as to undermine Netscape's ability to grow into an alternative competitive platform." Microsoft's most significant act was tying its IE browser to its Windows operating system by requiring all computer manufacturers to install Microsoft's IE on all new computers that used Microsoft's Windows operating system. This meant that the marginal cost of IE to the consumer of a new computer was *zero,* while the cost of installing Netscape Navigator was much greater than zero. Because Microsoft had a virtual monopoly on personal computer operating systems, which it still maintains, by tying its IE browser to its operating system, Microsoft destroyed Netscape's dominant position in a remarkably short period of time.

The United States Department of Justice argued that a 1995 consent decree signed by Microsoft banned the tying of the IE browser to Windows and complained to the court that Microsoft was in contempt. On December 11, 1997, the District Court entered a preliminary injunction banning the tying of the Internet Explorer to Windows.[‡] Microsoft filed an appeal of this injunction, and on May 12, 1998, the Court of Appeals granted a stay of the injunction. Six days later, on May 18, 1998, the Justice Department filed a formal antitrust action charging Microsoft with attempting to monopolize the market in Internet browsers by tying the Internet Explorer to Windows.

The trial received great national attention, especially when Bill Gates testified by video deposition. Much of his testimony consisted of the government's attorneys showing Gates's e-mail messages that he had either sent or received, with Gates indicating that he had no recollection of the messages.

Among the more interesting evidence was a series of 150 e-mails provided by Netscape showing how Microsoft attempted to force users to use Microsoft's IE instead of Netscape's Navigator.[§] For example, in a June 13, 1996, message, a Netscape employee reported that Microsoft had offered a Dutch Internet service provider free browsing software and a $400,000 marketing fund. "This was extended on the understanding that [the service provider] would NOT purchase any s/w [software] from Netscape." In another message, an Internet service company tells a Netscape employee that "we have ceased distribution of Netscape. Your product is excellent but totally lacking in marketing support and we could never justify the $20 setup cost when Microsoft will fly a blimp with our name on it for free." A June 10, 1996, message to Netscape from Kurt Brecheisen, president of a company called Global Telecom, said: "Microsoft gave me a deal I couldn't refuse. Free dialer, browser, developer kit, freely distributable, etc. . . . I know Netscape is better, but $0 vs $18K is impossible to beat."

In May 2003, AOL Time Warner agreed to drop its suit against Netscape in return for $750 million and an agreement from Microsoft to work closely with AOL Time Warner on several projects, including development and support of digital media technology and digital rights management. Ironically, the settlement agreement also gave AOL the right to use Internet Explorer for free for seven years.

*In the District Court for the District of Columbia, *Netscape Communications Corporation* v. *Microsoft Corporation,* Jury Trial Demanded, Per Local Civil Rule 40.5, Related to Civil Action Nos. 98-1232 and 98-1233, filed January 22, 2002.

†Janco Associates, *Browser Market Share White Paper,* June 2005, www.e-janco.com/browser.htm, August 10, 2005.

‡*United States* v. *Microsoft Corporation* No. 98–1232 (DDC filed May 18, 1998).

§"U.S. Releases E-Mail to Back Up Testimony," *Washington Post,* October 24, 1998, p. D4. ∎

IBM

In the 1960s, well before the introduction of personal computers, IBM was a virtual monopolist in the large mainframe computer market. During this period of monopoly power, IBM provided free service to all its mainframe customers and free computers to educational institutions. IBM charged high prices for replacement equipment in order to cover the costs of providing free service to all customers and free systems to educational institutions. In November 1967 the first of many small firms began to market individual pieces of "plug-compatible IBM equipment," such as tape and disk drives, at much lower prices than those charged by IBM.

The market for plug-compatible computer equipment grew rapidly in the late 1960s. In 1966 only three firms produced plug-compatible equipment, whereas by 1972 there were approximately 100 manufacturers.[42] In the late 1960s these firms were offering IBM-plug-compatible equipment at prices well below those of IBM. As a result, IBM lost a significant share of the peripheral market.

IBM responded to these inroads with a series of aggressive actions. It selectively and dramatically reduced the price of peripheral equipment. IBM also redesigned certain equipment so that it could be connected to the IBM central processing unit only through an integrated file adapter, rather than through the traditional external disk control unit. This change made the use of non-IBM equipment much less attractive to users. In 1971 IBM announced a fixed-term leasing plan, which provided for an 8 percent price reduction for users signing a one-year lease on peripheral equipment and a 16 percent price reduction for signers of a two-year lease. Finally, at the same time that IBM announced large price reductions on peripheral equipment, it announced large price increases on its central processing units to recoup lost revenues.

IBM's actions forced the manufacturers of peripheral equipment to cut prices drastically. These actions resulted in a series of private antitrust actions by the manufacturers of peripheral equipment.[43]

One of the unanticipated effects of IBM's new pricing strategy of greatly reducing peripheral prices and greatly increasing mainframe prices was entry into the mainframe computer (CPU) market. The first major entrant was Amdahl Corporation, founded by Gene Amdahl after he left IBM. In 1975 Amdahl introduced the Amdahl 470 computer, which was fully compatible with IBM's best System 370 computer, but was much faster and priced much lower.[44] By 1978 several other firms were producing CPUs to challenge IBM's machines.[45]

Threatened with a significant decrease in its CPU market share, IBM once again responded with a series of actions. In 1977 it introduced a more powerful computer, the 3033. Later in 1977 IBM reduced prices on its System 370 computers by between 20 and 35 percent.[46] As a result, Amdahl's entry was unsuccessful.

SUMMARY

1 Firms wish to maximize long-run, not short-run, profits.

2 The theory of limit pricing suggests that firms may charge lower short-run prices to restrict future entry.

3　Game theorists have criticized basic limit pricing theory because of its lack of a credible threat of retaliation in the face of entry and because limit pricing is not consistent with a subgame perfect Nash equilibrium. Instead, they have concentrated on extending the limit pricing model so that limit pricing results in a credible threat of retaliation.

4　Empirical evidence suggests that firms may utilize limit pricing.

5　As an alternative to limit pricing, firms may charge profit-maximizing prices before entry and respond to entry by using predatory pricing policies.

6　In a game with *perfect, certain, complete,* and *symmetric* information, predatory pricing is irrational because of Selten's chain store paradox.

7　In a game with *imperfect, certain, incomplete,* and *asymmetric* information, it may be rational for weak monopolists to engage in predatory pricing to fool potential entrants into believing that they are strong.

8　Empirical evidence suggests that firms sometimes engage in predatory pricing to build a tough reputation.

KEY TERMS

chain store paradox

limit price

limit pricing

predatory pricing

strong monopolist

tremble

weak monopolist

DISCUSSION QUESTIONS

1. In an industry with no cost advantage for incumbent firms, would limit pricing become more or less viable as economies of scale become more significant? Explain, using a graph or graphs.

2. Does limit pricing improve allocative efficiency?

3. An economist estimates that one monopolist prices where the elasticity of demand equals 1.5 and another monopolist prices where the elasticity of demand equals 0.5. Which monopolist is more likely to be limit pricing? Why?

4. Suppose you suspected that a firm was engaged in predatory pricing tactics. What evidence might convince you that the firm was in fact behaving in a predatory manner?

5. What is the difference between the information structure in the Milgrom and Roberts limit pricing model and the limit pricing model presented in section 11.1.1? How does this difference in the information structure affect the outcomes in the two games?

6. Explain the difference between limit pricing and predatory pricing.

7. Explain how the existence of asymmetric information helps to justify the theoretical possibility of limit pricing.

8. In recent years in many parts of the United States there have been two or three new drugstores built literally across the street from each other along short stretches of road. How might you explain this entry using the theory of the chain store paradox?

9. Discuss the different types of strategic pricing behavior a monopolist might be able to use to deter entry.

10. Application 11.2 discusses the behavior of Wal-Mart.

a. What incentive does Wal-Mart have to price below cost for so many products? Does Wal-Mart play a finite or infinite game with its competitors?

b. Recently a new discount store, Target, entered the Utica, New York, market almost across the street from a Wal-Mart.

Many people describe Target as an "upscale version of Wal-Mart." Given the information in Application 11.2, what type of behavior might you expect from Wal-Mart given a new competitor in town? Are there issues of product differentiation that might affect Wal-Mart's behavior?

PROBLEMS

1. Suppose that the industry demand curve is given by

$$P = 200 - Q$$

and a monopolist faces the following total cost function:

$$TC_I = 50q_I$$

and potential entrants face the following cost function:

$$TC_E = 60q_E.$$

a. What is the limit price in this market?

b. If the monopolist charged its profit-maximizing price, what would its profits equal?

c. If the monopolist charged the limit price, what would its profits equal?

2. Let the rate of entry be a function of the differential between the monopolist's price and the limit price, so that:

$$E = \lambda[P_A - P_{LP}]$$

where E is the rate of entry, λ is a positive constant that measures the speed of entry, P_A is the actual price, and P_{LP} is the limit price. If λ is very small (approaches zero), do you think that limit pricing would be an attractive strategy for a monopolist? If λ is very large (approaches infinity), do you think that limit pricing would be an attractive strategy for the incumbent? What values of λ would result in a high likelihood of limit pricing? What factors might affect your answer?

3. Show that the Nash equilibrium (E, [L, Π}) in Table 11.1 is *not* a subgame perfect Nash equilibrium.

4. Suppose that in a predatory pricing game with imperfect, certain, incomplete, and asymmetric information, the probability that a monopolist is strong in period $n + 1$ is ρ_{n+1}. Suppose that $\rho_{n+1} = 0.25$. If entry occurs in period $n + 1$ and the monopolist accommodates entry, what would be the value of ρ_n?

5. Consider a monopolist with the following demand curve: $P = 390 - 2Q$. The monopolist faces $MC_M = AC_M = 30$.

a. Solve for the profit-maximizing level of monopoly output, price, and profits.

b. Suppose a potential entrant is considering entering, but the monopolist has a cost advantage. The potential entrant faces costs $MC_{PE} = AC_{PE} = 40$. Assuming the monopolist continues to profit-maximize, solve for the residual demand curve for the entrant.

 c. Assume the potential entrant follows the Cournot assumption about the monopolist's output. Solve for the potential entrant's output, price, and profits in this scenario. What are the new monopoly profits?

 d. Is there a price the monopolist could charge to deter entry? Solve for the limit price and output that will completely deter entry. What is monopoly profit at this point?

6. Consider the problem described in problem 5.

 a. Make an extensive form of the game based on your solutions in problem 5.

 b. Solve for the Nash equilibrium of the game. If the monopolist threatens ahead of time to limit price, is the threat credible? Explain.

 c. What if the potential entrant trembled? What would the monopolist choose to do? Explain.

7. Consider the entry game from problem 5 in Chapter 7. We played the game once and found that the Nash equilibrium there predicted that the entrant would enter and the monopolist would continue to profit-maximize (accommodate entry). What would be the result of this game if it were played n times with perfect, complete, certain, and symmetric information?

8. Consider problem 5 in Chapter 7. How might asymmetric information change the outcome of the game? For example, assume nature selects the monopolist to be either weak or strong, but only the monopolist knows the selection. Discuss in what ways the result of the game might be altered under this situation.

9. Suppose a monopolist has a discount rate of 10 percent and can deter entry indefinitely, but only by being predatory for 10 years in a row beginning with the current year and continuing for the next nine years. In each of those 10 years of predatory pricing, the monopolist sustains an economic loss of $2 million. Thereafter, the monopolist can earn an economic profit of $3.5 million *forever*. The alternative to being predatory is to accommodate entry, in which case, the monopolist earns the following profit flow: $4 million this year (t = 0), $3 million next year (year t = 1), $2 million in the following year (year t = 2), and $1 million every year thereafter (years t = 3 through t = ∞). Using your knowledge of present value from Chapter 3, section 3.5, does the predatory behavior make sense for the monopolist? What do the above figures suggest about John McGee's hypothesis concerning the use of predatory pricing?

For those who read the appendix, answer problem 10.

10. a. Suppose that in the Kreps and Wilson model the values of N, a, b, and δ are:

$$N = 10; a = 2; b = \tfrac{1}{2}; \text{ and } \delta = \tfrac{1}{4}.$$

 The only change in these values from the example in the Appendix is that $\delta = \tfrac{1}{4}$ instead of $\delta = \tfrac{1}{10}$; that is, there is a higher initial probability that the monopolist is strong. What changes would occur in this game compared with the game played out in Table 11.3? Provide an intuitive explanation for this change.

 b. Suppose that in the Kreps and Wilson model the values of N, a, b, and δ are:

$$N = 10; a = 2; b = \tfrac{1}{4}; \text{ and } \delta = \tfrac{1}{10}.$$

The only change in these values from the example in the Appendix is that $b = \frac{1}{4}$ instead of $b = \frac{1}{2}$; that is, the entrant's profits are smaller if the monopolist does not fight entry. What changes would occur in this game compared with the game played out in Table 11.3? Provide an intuitive explanation for this change.

NOTES

1. See J.S. Bain, *Barriers to New Competition* (Cambridge, MA: Harvard University Press, 1956); P. Sylos-Labini, *Oligopoly and Technical Progress* (Cambridge, MA: Harvard University Press, 1962); and F. Modigliani, "Developments on the Oligopoly Front," *Journal of Political Economy* 66 (June 1958): 215–232.

2. See Bain, *supra* note 1; Sylos-Labini, *supra* note 1; and Modigliani, *supra* note 1.

3. Darius W. Gaskins, Jr., "Dynamic Limit Pricing: Optimal Pricing Under Threat of Entry," *Journal of Economic Theory* 3 (September 1971): 306–322; N.J. Ireland, "Concentration and the Growth of Market Demand," *Journal of Economic Theory* 5 (October 1972): 303–305; Kenneth L. Judd and Bruce C. Peterson, "Dynamic Limit Pricing: A Reformulation," *Review of Industrial Organization* 2 (1985): 160–177.

4. P. Milgrom and J. Roberts, "Limit Pricing and Entry Under Conditions of Incomplete Information and Equilibrium Analysis," *Econometrica* 50 (March 1982): 443–460.

5. Don E. Waldman, "The Du Pont Cellophane Case Revisited: An Analysis of the Indirect Effects of Antitrust Policy on Market Structure and Economic Performance," *Antitrust Bulletin* 25 (Winter 1980): 805–830. See also *United States* v. *E. I. du Pont de Nemours,* 351 US 377 (1956).

6. Waldman, *op cit.,* p. 818.

7. Don E. Waldman, *Antitrust Action and Market Structure* (Lexington, MA: D.C. Heath, 1978), pp. 40–49. See also *United States* v. *United Shoe Machinery Corporation,* 347 US 521 (1954) and 391 US 244 (1968).

8. Waldman, *ibid.,* pp. 47–49.

9. *Ibid.,* p. 48.

10. *Ibid.*

11. *Ibid.,* p. 49.

12. A.D.H. Kaplan, Joel B. Dirlam, and Robert F. Lanzillotti, *Pricing in Big Business: A Case Approach* (Washington: Brookings Institution, 1958), pp. 214–217.

13. *Ibid.,* p. 216.

14. *Ibid.*

15. The following is taken from Erwin A. Blackstone, "Limit Pricing and Entry in the Copying Machine Industry," *Quarterly Review of Economics and Business* 12 (Winter 1972): 57–65.

16. *Ibid.,* p. 60.

17. *Ibid.,* p. 61.

18. Timothy Hannan, "Limit Pricing and the Banking Industry," *Journal of Money, Credit and Banking* 11, no. 4 (November 1979): 438–446.

19. *Ibid.,* p. 440.

20. Robert T. Masson and Joseph Shaanan, "Stochastic-Dynamic Limit Pricing: An Empirical Test," *Review of Economics and Statistics* 64 (August 1982): 413–422; and Masson and Shaanan, "Optimal Oligopoly Pricing and the Threat of Entry," *International Journal of Industrial Organization* 5 (September 1987): 323–339. For a statistical test suggesting the possible use of limit pricing in the airline industry, see Margaret A. Peteraf and Randal Reed, "Pricing and Performance in Monopoly Airline Markets," *Journal of Law and Economics* 37 (April 1994): 193–214.

21. This is the model based on Bain's assumptions, Bain, *op cit.*

22. This is the model based on Gaskins, *supra* note 3.

23. This model is based on Morton I. Kamien and Nancy L. Schwartz, "Limit Pricing and Uncertain Entry," *Econometrica* 39 (May 1971): 441–454; and David P. Baron, "Limit Pricing, Potential Entry, and Barriers to Entry," *American Economic Review* 63 (September 1973): 666–674.

24. Robert T. Masson and Joseph Shaanan, "Stochastic-Dynamic Limit Pricing: An Empirical Test," *Review of Economics and Statistics* 64 (August 1982): 413–422.

25. Masson and Shaanan, "Optimal Oligopoly Pricing and the Threat of Entry," *supra* note 20: 323–339.

26. See Richard Selten, "The Chain Store Paradox," *Theory and Decision* 9 (1978): 127–159.

27. John S. McGee, "Predatory Price Cutting: The Standard Oil Case," *Journal of Law & Economics* 1 (October 1958): 137–169.

28. David Kreps and Robert Wilson, "Reputation and Imperfect Information," *Journal of Economic Theory* 27 (August 1982): 280–312.

29. *Ibid.*

30. Alan Nevins, *Study in Power: John D. Rockefeller* (New York: Scribner's, 1953). Also *Standard Oil Company of New Jersey* v. *United States,* 221 US 1 (1911).

31. John S. McGee, *supra* note 27.

32. *United States* v. *American Tobacco Company,* 221 US 106 (1911).

33. The following analysis is taken from John C. Hilke and Philip B. Nelson, "Strategic Behavior and Attempted Monopolization: The Coffee (General Foods) Case," in John E. Kwoka Jr. and Lawrence J. White (eds.), *The Antitrust Revolution* (Glenview, IL: Scott, Foresman and Company, 1989), pp. 208–240. See also *In the Matter of General Foods Corp.,* 103 FTC 204 (1984); and Philip B. Nelson and John C. Hilke, "Retail Featuring as a Strategic Entry or Mobility Barrier in Manufacturing," *International Journal of Industrial Organization* 9 (December 1991): 533–544.

34. Hilke and Nelson (1989), *supra* note 33.

35. *Ibid.,* p. 224.

36. Daniel P. Kaplan, "The Changing Airline Industry," in Leonard W. Weiss and Michael W. Klass (eds.), *Regulatory Reform: What Actually Happened* (Boston: Little, Brown and Company, 1986), p. 58.

37. Alfred E. Kahn, "Thinking About Predation—A Personal Diary," *Review of Industrial Organization* 6 (1991): 141.

38. James W. Brock, "Industry Update: Airlines," *Review of Industrial Organization* 16: 45; and W. Zellner,

"How Northwest Gives Competition a Bad Name," *Business Week* (March 16, 1995): 34.

39. M. Conlin, "Northworst," *Forbes* (November 30, 1998): 105; and Brock, *supra* note 38.

40. M. Brannigan, "AirTran Says Rival Won't Let It Get Off the Ground," *The Wall Street Journal* (November 23, 1998): B4.; and Brock, *supra* note 38.

41. Brock, *supra* note 38.

42. *Telex Corporation* v. *International Business Machines* 510 F.2d 894 (1975).

43. See for examples, *Telex Corporation* v. *International Business Machines* 510 F.2d 894 (1975); and *ILC Peripherals Leasing Company* v. *International Business Machines* 458 F.Supp. 423 (1978); and *Memorex Corporation* v. *Inertnational Business Machines* 636 F.2d 1188 (1980).

44. "A Tyro Challenges IBM in Big Computers," *Business Week,* (May 12, 1975): 65–67.

45. "New Wave of Change Challenging IBM," *Business Week* (May 29, 1978): 92–99.

46. "I.B.M. Forsees Benefits from Price Cuts," *New York Times* (April 26, 1977): 51; and "More Tumult for the Computer Industry," *Business Week* (May 30, 1977): 58–66.

INTERNET EXERCISES

Visit www.aw-bc.com/waldman_jensen for this chapter's web exercises. Answer our real-world economics problems by searching the Internet for solutions!

Appendix

Details of the Kreps and Wilson Predatory Pricing Model

Figure 11.9 presents the payoffs for a monopolist and potential entrants in each round of the Kreps and Wilson predatory pricing game. In the Kreps and Wilson game, information is *imperfect, certain, incomplete,* and *asymmetric.* Nature first selects the monopolist to be either (1) a *strong monopolist,* in which case the firm enjoys being predatory and is always predatory, or (2) a *weak monopolist,* in which case the monopolist will be predatory in one market only if it believes it will increase its profits in future markets to compensate for its predatory response. ρ_n represents the potential entrant's subjective probability in round n that the monopolist is strong. In each additional round the potential entrant must reestimate the value of ρ based on past beliefs and observed behavior. If the monopolist behaves aggressively and fights entry in any round, it *may* increase the value of ρ in later rounds. However, if the monopolist accommodates entry in *any* round, ρ decreases to *zero* in the next round because future potential entrants know that the monopolist is weak. The game is played sequentially from round N (the *first* round entered) through round 1 (the *last* round entered).

Let's consider the rules of the game as defined by Kreps and Wilson, beginning with their definition of the function ρ_n. Define ρ_n as follows:

1. In the Nth market, the *first* market subject to potential entry, set $\rho_n = \delta > 0$. This implies that, at the beginning of the game, the potential entrant believes that there is some positive probability that the monopolist will fight entry.

2. If there is no entry in round n + 1, then $\rho_n = \rho_{n+1}$.

3. If there is entry in round n + 1, this entry is fought, and $\rho_{n+1} > 0$, then ρ_n equals the maximum of b^n or ρ_{n+1}, where b comes from Figure 11.9 and represents the entrant's profits if the monopolist does *not* fight entry. Note that $0 < b < 1$.* Fighting entry in round n + 1 therefore can increase ρ_n in the next round of the game.

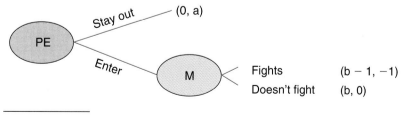

Where a > 1 and 0 < b < 1

FIGURE 11.9 **A Game of Entry with a Strong Monopolist (Potential Entrant's Profit, Monopolist's Profit)**

*The fact that the value of b is represented by a fraction does not imply that the potential profits associated with successful entry are small, because b can be measured in billions or trillions of dollars.

4. If there is entry in round n + 1 and either this entry is not fought or $\rho_{n+1} = 0$, then $\rho_n = 0$. This follows because accommodation to entry in any round reveals to *all* future potential entrants that the monopolist is a weak firm.

Given this definition of the function ρ_n, Kreps and Wilson created strategies for both players in terms of ρ_n. The following strategies define one possible set of strategies laid out by Kreps and Wilson:

Monopolist's Strategy

1. If the monopolist is *strong*, it *always* fights entry.

2. If the monopolist is *weak* and entry occurs in round n, then:

 a. If n = 1 (that is, the game is in the *last* round), the monopolist does not fight.

 b. If n > 1 and $\rho_n \geq b^{n-1}$, the monopolist fights. (Note that in each additional round, b^{n-1} gets *larger* because $0 < b < 1$, and therefore if ρ_n remains constant from round to round, a weak monopolist is less likely to fight in each additional round of the game.)

 c. If n > 1 and $\rho_n < b^{n-1}$, the monopolist plays a mixed strategy and fights with probability μ_n, where:

$$\mu_n = \frac{(1 - b^{n-1})\rho_n}{(1 - \rho_n)b^{n-1}},$$

and does not fight with probability $(1 - \mu_n)$. Notice that if $\rho_n = 0$, then $\mu_1 = 0$; and if $\rho_n = b^{n-1}$, then $\mu_n = 1$.

Potential Entrant's Strategies

1. If $\rho_n > b^n$, the potential entrant stays out.

2. If $\rho_n < b^n$, the potential entrant enters. (Note that in each additional round b^n gets *larger* because $0 < b < 1$, and therefore if ρ_n remains constant from round to round, the potential entrant is more likely to enter in each additional round of the game.)

3. If $\rho_n = b^n$, the potential entrant plays a mixed strategy of staying out with probability $\theta_n = 1/a$ and entering with probability $(1 - \theta_n) = 1 - (1/a)$. (Recall from Figure 11.8 that a > 1 is the profit earned by the monopolist if entry does *not* occur. Increases in the monopolist's potential profits therefore increase the probability that the potential entrant will enter; that is, higher industry profits make entry more likely.)

We now have sufficient information to play the game for given values of N (the total number of rounds), a (the monopolist's profits in the absence of entry), b (the entrants' profits if the monopolist does not fight), and δ (the potential entrants' initial subjective probability that the monopolist is strong).

Consider the game associated with the following values:

$$N = 10; \ a = 2, \ b = 1/2; \ \text{and} \ \delta = 1/10.$$

TABLE 11.3 Kreps and Wilson Predatory Pricing Game

Round	ρ_n	b^n	b^{n-1}	Monopolist's Action	Potential Entrant's Action
10	1/10	1/1024	1/512	Fight	Stay out
9	1/10	1/512	1/256	Fight	Stay out
8	1/10	1/256	1/128	Fight	Stay out
7	1/10	1/128	1/64	Fight	Stay out
6	1/10	1/64	1/32	Fight	Stay out
5	1/10	1/32	1/16	Fight	Stay out
4	1/10	1/16	1/8	Mixed strategy with: $\mu_4 = 7/9$ $(1 - \mu_4) = 2/9$	Stay out
3	1/10	1/8	1/4	Mixed strategy with: $\mu_3 = 1/3$ $(1 - \mu_3) = 2/3$	Enter
2 if entry was fought in round 3	1/4	1/4	1/2	Mixed strategy with: $\mu_2 = 1/3$ $(1 - \mu_2) = 2/3$	Mixed strategy with: $\theta_2 = 1/2$ $(1 - \theta_2) = 1/2$
2 if entry was not fought in round 3	0	1/4	1/2	Not fight	Enter
1 if entry was fought in round 3 and in round 2	1/2	1/2	1	Not fight	Mixed strategy with: $\theta_1 = 1/2$ $(1 - \theta_1) = 1/2$
1 if entry was fought in round 3 and there was no entry in round 2	1/4	1/2	1	Not fight	Enter
1 if entry was not fought in either round 3 or round 2	0	1/2	1	Not fight	Enter

This game would play out according to Table 11.3. Round 10 is played first. In round 10, $\rho_{10} = \delta = 1/10$; that is, the potential entrant assumes that there is a 10 percent probability that the monopolist is strong and will always fight. Because $b = 1/2$, $b^{10} = (1/2)^{10} = 1/1024$ and $b^9 = (1/2)^9 = 1/512$. Because $\rho_{10} > b^9$ [$(1/10) > (1/512)$], then by monopolist strategy 2(b), the monopolist would fight entry; and because $\rho_{10} > b^{10}$ [$(1/10) > (1/1024)$], by potential entrant strategy 1, the potential entrant stays out. The same conditions hold for rounds 9, 8, 7, 6, and 5.

In round 4, $\rho_4 < b^3$ [$(1/10) < (1/8)$], and therefore by monopolist strategy 2(c), the monopolist plays a mixed strategy of fighting entry with probability 7/9 ($\mu_4 = 7/9$)

and not fighting with probability 2/9 $[(1 - \mu_4) = 2/9]$.* Entry, however, will not occur, because $\rho_4 > b^4 [(1/10) > (1/16)]$.

In round 3, however, $\rho_3 < b^3 [(1/10) < (1/8)]$, and by potential entrant strategy 2, the firm will enter. There is a 1/3 probability (that is, $\mu_3 = 1/3$) that the monopolist will fight entry in round 3, and a 2/3 probability [that is, $(1 - \mu_3) = 2/3$] that entry will not be fought.[†]

The outcome in round 2 now depends critically on whether entry was fought in round 3. If entry was *not* fought, the monopolist is revealed to be weak, so $\rho_2 = 0$, entry will occur in round 2, and the monopolist will not fight. If entry was fought in round 3, however, then ρ_2 equals the maximum of $b^2 = 1/4$ or $\rho_3 = 1/10$; in this case the maximum is $\rho_2 = 1/4$. By fighting entry in round 3, the monopolist has greatly *increased* the potential entrant's assessment of the probability that the monopolist will fight entry in round 2. If entry was fought in round 3, then because $\rho_2 = b^2$ $[(1/4) = (1/4)]$ by potential entrant strategy 3, the potential entrant will play a mixed strategy in round 2 and enter with a probability of $\theta_2 = 1/a = 1/2$ and stay out with a probability of $(1 - \theta_2) = [1 - (1/a)] = 1/2$. Fighting in round 3 therefore may deter entry in round 2.

In round 1 a weak monopolist will never fight: However, entry may still be deterred if the monopolist fought entry in both round 3 and round 2. If entry was fought in rounds 3 and 2, then ρ_n in round 1 is the maximum of $b^n = \frac{1}{2}$ or $\rho_{n+1} = \frac{1}{4}$. Therefore, $\rho_1 = \frac{1}{2}$, and because $\rho_1 = b^1 = \frac{1}{2}$, the potential entrant plays a mixed strategy in round 1, and there is a 50 percent probability that the potential entrant will stay out *even if it is facing a weak monopolist*. Essentially, if the monopolist continues to fight entry right up until the last round, this aggressive behavior greatly increases the

*From monopolist strategy 2(c), we have:

$$\mu_4 = \frac{(1 - b^{n-1})\rho_n}{(1 - \rho_n)b^{n-1}}$$

$$= \frac{\left(1 - \dfrac{1}{8}\right)\dfrac{1}{10}}{\left(1 - \dfrac{1}{10}\right)\dfrac{1}{8}} = \frac{\dfrac{7}{8}\dfrac{1}{10}}{\dfrac{9}{10}\dfrac{1}{8}}$$

$$= \frac{\dfrac{7}{80}}{\dfrac{9}{80}} = \frac{7}{9}.$$

It follows that

$$(1 - \mu_4) = 1 - \frac{7}{9} = \frac{2}{9}.$$

[†]From monopolist strategy 2(c), we have:

$$\mu_3 = \frac{(1 - b^{n-1})\rho_n}{(1 - \rho_n)b^{n-1}}$$

$$= \frac{\left(1 - \dfrac{1}{4}\right)\dfrac{1}{10}}{\left(1 - \dfrac{1}{10}\right)\dfrac{1}{4}} = \frac{\dfrac{3}{4}\dfrac{1}{10}}{\dfrac{9}{10}\dfrac{1}{4}}$$

$$= \frac{\dfrac{3}{40}}{\dfrac{9}{40}} = \frac{1}{3}.$$

It follows that

$$(1 - \mu_3) = 1 - \frac{1}{3} = \frac{2}{3}.$$

probability in the potential entrant's mind that it is facing a strong monopolist even if the monopolist is weak! The potential entrant's belief that it may be facing a strong monopolist may effectively deter entry.

Generalizing the Kreps and Wilson model, in a game with N rounds and asymmetric information, a *weak* monopolist may be able to prevent entry in later markets by behaving aggressively in early markets. As noted earlier in this chapter, the equilibrium has the following characteristics:

1. In early rounds (here, rounds 10, 9, 8, 7, 6, and 5), entry will not occur because both strong and weak monopolists will fight all entry. This occurs because in early markets even a weak monopolist has a great incentive to establish a reputation as a strong firm. In our example, if entry occurred in round 9 and was *not* met with a predatory response, then all future potential entrants would know that the monopolist was weak, and there would be no deterrent to entering markets 8 through 1.

2. As the number of markets approaches n = 1, a weak monopolist has little incentive to continue to put forward a facade as a strong firm, and the monopolist will not fight entry.

3. Somewhere between the early and late rounds, the monopolist plays a mixed strategy of fighting in the nth market with a probability of μ_n and sharing the market with a probability of $1 - \mu_n$, where μ_n generally diminishes as n moves toward the last market where n = 1. Of course, if the monopolist does not fight in any round, then the monopolist is identified as weak, and by the logic of the chain store paradox, the monopolist will accommodate all future entry.

We saw this result in Figure 11.8. In rounds N through X (here markets 10 to 5), a weak monopolist will always behave aggressively. In markets Y through 1 (here only market 1), a weak monopolist will always accommodate entry. In markets X through Y (here markets 4 to 2), the monopolist adopts a mixed strategy.

The most important implication of Kreps and Wilson's asymmetric information model of predatory behavior is that as N becomes very large, the size of δ needed to deter entry becomes small.* In Table 11.3, for example, δ = 1/100 would deter entry in rounds 10, 9, and 8. Therefore, even a very small probability that a monopolist is strong may deter entry.

*David Kreps and Robert Wilson, "Reputation and Imperfect Information," *Journal of Economic Theory* 27 (August 1982): pp. 253–279.

Oligopoly Behavior: Entry and Nonpricing Strategies to Deter Entry

In Chapter 11 we asked the question: Can dominant firms or effective cartels engage in pricing behavior to prevent their loss of market power in the long run? We suggested that limit pricing or predatory pricing can delay or prevent a loss of market share. This chapter extends the analysis to consider nonpricing strategies that can delay or prevent entry. Nonpricing strategies may be preferable to pricing strategies from a legal and economic standpoint. From a legal viewpoint, nonpricing strategies are less likely to raise antitrust concerns, and from an economic standpoint they are less likely to be misinterpreted by competitors as aggressive acts.

This chapter includes an examination of the empirical evidence regarding which strategies are most commonly used by dominant firms.

12.1 Excess Capacity[1]

Models of entry deterrence based on the building of *excess capacity* are models in which the monopolist moves first and selects a level of capacity, then the potential entrant decides whether to enter, then the monopolist selects a capacity level and an output. The potential entrant produces a quantity of zero if it stays out.

In Figure 12.1(a), a monopolist faces a market demand $p = 100 - q$ and currently can produce up to 40 units of output at a constant marginal cost of \$20. Assuming that all of the monopolist's fixed costs were sunk costs and paid many years ago, the monopolist's current fixed costs, FC_M, equal zero. Because the monopolist has sufficient capacity to produce a maximum of just 40 units, the marginal cost of producing more than 40 units is infinite, so the MC_1 curve is vertical at $q = 40$. In the absence of a threat of entry, the monopolist maximizes profit by producing $q = 40$, setting price $p = \$60$, and earning profit:

$$\pi = q(p - MC) - FC_M = 40(\$60 - \$20) - \$0 = \$1600. \qquad [12.1]$$

Now suppose that a potential entrant appears on the scene. For a sunk cost of \$575, the potential entrant can build a plant capable of producing output at constant

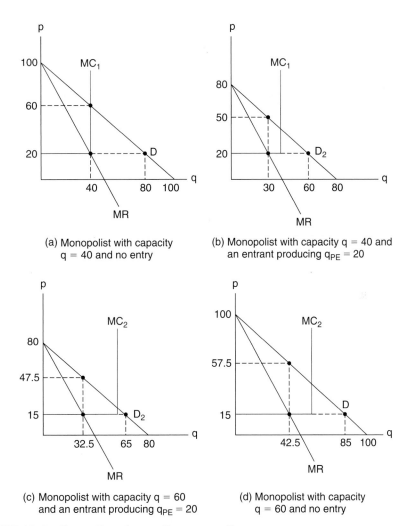

(a) Monopolist with capacity
q = 40 and no entry

(b) Monopolist with capacity q = 40 and
an entrant producing q$_{PE}$ = 20

(c) Monopolist with capacity q = 60
and an entrant producing q$_{PE}$ = 20

(d) Monopolist with capacity
q = 60 and no entry

FIGURE 12.1 Excess Capacity as a Deterrent to Entry

In panel (a), a monopolist can produce a maximum of 40 units of output at constant marginal cost of $20. In the absence of entry, the monopolist produces q = 40 at p = $60 and earns profit π_M = $1600. In panel (b), an entrant produces q$_{PE}$ = 20, so the residual demand curve is p = 80 − q, and the monopolist produces q = 30 at p = $50 and earns profit π_M = $900. In panels (c) and (d), a monopolist invests $575 in new capacity and can produce a maximum of 60 units of output at constant marginal cost of $15. In panel (c), an entrant produces q$_{PE}$ = 20, so the residual demand curve is p = 80 − q; and the monopolist produces q = 32.5 at p = $47.5 and earns profit π_M = $481.25. In panel (d), in the absence of entry, the monopolist produces q = 42.5 at p = $57.5 and earns profit π_M = $1231.25.

marginal cost of $20 up to a maximum capacity of 20 units. Assume that if the potential entrant builds the plant and enters, it produces at capacity and sells 20 units. Therefore, if entry occurs, the monopolist faces the residual demand curve p = 80 − q

in panel (b). Given this residual demand curve, the monopolist maximizes profit by setting MR = MC, producing q_M = 30, and setting p = $50. To simplify the analysis, we assume a zero discount rate so that a dollar of profit in period 1 equals a dollar of profit in period 2. Profits for the two firms are:

$$\pi_M = q(p - MC_1) - FC_M = 30(\$50 - \$20) - 0 = \$900 - 0 = \$900 \qquad [12.2]$$

$$\pi_{PE} = q(p - MC_{PE}) - FC_{PE} = 20(\$50 - \$20) - \$575$$

$$= \$600 - \$575 = \$25, \qquad [12.3]$$

where π_M represents the monopolist's profit and π_{PE} represents the potential entrant's profit.

Alternatively, in response to entry, the monopolist can increase its capacity by expanding its current production facilities. Suppose that for a sunk cost of $575, the monopolist can expand its plant so that it can produce up to a maximum of 60 units at a lower marginal cost of $15 per unit. Figure 12.1(c) shows the monopolist's new marginal cost curve, MC_2. If the monopolist builds this additional capacity in response to entry, it faces the residual demand curve p = 80 − q in panel (c). Given this residual demand curve, the monopolist maximizes profit by setting MR = MC, producing q_M = 32.5, and setting p = $47.5. With lower marginal costs, the monopolist charges a lower price p = $47.5 and the total quantity demanded by consumers is q = q_M + q_{PE} = 32.5 + 20 = 52.5. Profit is:

$$\pi_M = q(p - MC_2) - FC_M = 32.5(\$47.5 - \$15) - \$575$$

$$= \$1056.25 - \$575 = \$481.25 \qquad [12.4]$$

$$\pi_{PE} = q(p - MC_{PE}) - FC_{PE} = 20(\$47.5 - \$20) - \$575$$

$$= \$550 - \$575 = -\$25. \qquad [12.5]$$

If the potential entrant elects not to enter, and the monopolist builds the extra capacity, it faces the market demand curve p = 100 − q in panel (d), and the monopolist maximizes profit by setting MR = MC, producing q_M = 42.5, and setting p = $57.5. The monopolist's profit is:

$$\pi_M = q(p - MC_2) - FC_M = 42.5(\$57.5 - \$15) - \$575$$

$$= \$1806.25 - \$575 = \$1231.25. \qquad [12.6]$$

Beginning at node PE_2 in Figure 12.2, the bottom part of the game tree summarizes the game if the monopolist initially selects q = 40. If the potential entrant enters, the game moves to node M_4. If the monopolist maintains its current capacity of 40 as shown in Figure 12.1(b), Equations 12.2 and 12.3 identify the firms' profits: The monopolist earns a profit of $900 and the entrant earns a profit of $25. If the potential entrant stays out, the game moves to node M_5, as in Figure 12.1(a), and Equation 12.1 identifies the monopolist's profit: the monopolist earns a profit of $1600 and the entrant earns a normal profit of $0. Suppose the monopolist responds to entry at node M_4 by expanding its capacity to 60, as shown in Figure 12.1(c), in which case Equations 12.4 and 12.5 identify the firms' profits: The monopolist earns a profit of $481.25 and the entrant sustains an economic loss of −$25. Finally, suppose

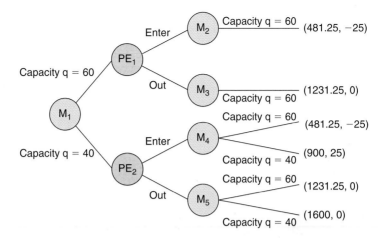

FIGURE 12.2 The Game of Excess Capacity to Deter Entry (Monopolist's Profit, Potential Entrant's Profit)

The monopolist moves first and selects a level of capacity either large $(q = 60)$, or small $(q = 40)$. The entrant then decides to enter or stay out. If the monopolist selects a large capacity, the game moves to node PE_1, and the entrant sustains an economic loss if it enters; so the entrant stays out and the monopolist earns a profit of $1231.25. If the monopolist selects a small capacity at node M_1, the game moves to node PE_2: The entrant enters, the monopolist maintains a small capacity at node M_4, and the entrant earns profit of $25, while the monopolist earns a profit of $900. In the Nash equilibrium, the monopolist selects a large capacity and the potential entrant stays out.

the potential entrant stays out, but the monopolist expands its capacity to 60, as in Figure 12.1(d). The monopolist's profit is identified in Equation 12.6 as $1231.25.

Look carefully at the game beginning at node PE_2 in Figure 12.2. If the game begins at node PE_2, the only equilibrium is: the potential entrant enters and the monopolist maintains its capacity at 40. The potential entrant knows that if it stays out, it earns a normal economic profit of $0; but if it enters, the monopolist will maximize profit by maintaining its capacity at 40. Therefore, the potential entrant enters. The monopolist earns a profit of $900 and the entrant earns a profit of $25. The monopolist can threaten to build the extra capacity after the potential entrant has already entered; however, such a threat is not credible. Once the entrant has entered, the monopolist earns $900 if it maintains its capacity or $481.25 if it expands its capacity to 60. At this point in the game, it is too late to build extra capacity. Instead, the monopolist maintains its capacity at 40 and earns $900.

The monopolist, however, is not forced to accept this outcome. Instead, the monopolist can build the extra capacity in advance of the potential entrant's decision of whether to enter. The game then moves to node PE_1 in Figure 12.2. The monopolist's early expansion of capacity would affect the profit payoffs for the two firms. If the monopolist builds the extra capacity, and the potential entrant enters, the game moves to node M_2, and the monopolist is in the situation depicted in Figure 12.1(c). Equations 12.4 and 12.5 identify the firms' profits: The monopolist earns a profit of

$481.25 and the entrant sustains an economic loss of $-\$25$. If the potential entrant stays out, the game moves to node M_3, and the monopolist is in the situation depicted in Figure 12.1(d). Equation 12.6 identifies the monopolist's profit as $1231.25.

Viewing the entire game in Figure 12.2 beginning at node M_1, there is one Nash equilibrium: The monopolist expands capacity to 60 and the potential entrant stays out. The monopolist charges p = $57.5 in Figure 12.1(d) and earns a profit of $1231.25. The entrant stays out and earns a normal profit of $0. Because the monopolist has *precommitted* to the expansion of capacity, it responds to entry by charging a low price p = $47.5 in Figure 12.1(c), which would result in a loss for the entrant. The monopolist has increased its profit from $900 if it elected not to increase its capacity at node M_1 to $1231.25 at the Nash equilibrium. By investing a fixed cost of $575 early on to increase its capacity, the monopolist has maintained its monopoly and increased its profit by 36.8 percent.

12.1.1 Investing in Research and Development to Lower Costs

In the above game, the monopolist invests in excess capacity in period 1 in order to lower its costs in period 2; more importantly, this investment lowers the monopolist's costs in relation to a potential entrant's costs in period 2. As a result, the monopolist deters entry and earns larger profits over the two periods. There are other possible investments in period 1 that will lower the monopolist's costs in period 2, and thereby also possibly deter entry.[2] One alternative investment would be in research and development. A monopolist might have a choice of either investing or not investing in cost-reducing research and development in period 1. Suppose in the absence of any threat of entry, the monopolist is better off not investing in research and development. Faced with a threat of entry, however, if the monopolist chooses *not* to invest in research and development in period 1, it earns a large profit in period 1; but, entry occurs and its profits in period 2 will be significantly reduced. Alternatively, faced with a threat of entry, the monopolist can invest in research and development in period 1 and earn a smaller profit in period 1; however, if the monopolist's lower costs in period 2 deter entry, the monopolist's profits will be significantly increased in period 2.

Such a game might play out exactly like the game in Figure 12.2. At the node M_1 the monopolist must choose to either invest in research and development and go up to node PE_1 or *not* invest in research and development and go down to node PE_2. The equilibrium in this game would be for the monopolist to invest in research and development and for the potential entrant to stay out. Furthermore, even if entry is not deterred in period 2, the investment in research and development, by lowering the monopolist's costs relative to the potential entrant's costs, might increase the monopolist's combined profits in the two periods.

12.1.2 Empirical Evidence

ALUMINUM In its landmark 1945 *Alcoa* antitrust decision, a majority of the Second Circuit Court of Appeals ruled that Alcoa had built excess capacity to deter entry into the aluminum refining industry. According to Judge Hand:[3]

> It was not inevitable that [Alcoa] should always anticipate increases in the demand for ingot and be prepared to supply them. Nothing compelled it to keep doubling

and redoubling its capacity before others entered the field. It insists that it never excluded competitors; but we can think of no more effective exclusion than progressively to embrace each new opportunity as it opened, and face every newcomer with new capacity already geared into a great organization, having the advantage of experience, trade connections and the elite of personnel.

TITANIUM DIOXIDE Hall has suggested that Du Pont built excess capacity in the titanium dioxide industry to deter entry.[4] Titanium dioxide is a chemical whitener used to make products such as paint or paper either whiter or opaque. In the 1960s three different processes were used to manufacture titanium dioxide. The first two, the sulfate process and the generic chloride process, were available to all titanium dioxide producers. The third process, however, was the proprietary chloride process developed exclusively by Du Pont. Because Du Pont's chloride process had low pollution control costs relative to the other two processes, Du Pont's costs were unaffected by tougher pollution control laws instituted in the 1970s, and Du Pont's technology was the industry's low-cost technology.

Using econometrics, Hall tested whether Du Pont's pattern of capital expansion between 1972 and 1979 was consistent with an entry deterrence policy. As Table 12.1 indicates, Du Pont expanded production capacity using its proprietary chloride process by 114 percent between 1972 and 1977. Du Pont's capacity expansions were clearly concentrated in plants using its proprietary chloride process. No other titanium dioxide producer increased capacity by nearly as large a percentage between 1972 and 1977.* The capacity expansion data in Table 12.1 suggest that Du Pont committed capital to preempt its five smaller rivals.[5]

Hall's findings were generally supportive of the theoretical implications of the capital commitment model.

SUPERMARKETS IN EDMONTON, CANADA Between 1968 and 1982, Safeway was the dominant supermarket in western Canada. West and Von Hohenbalken examined the supermarket industry in Edmonton, Alberta, and hypothesized that "[i]f [Safeway] want[ed] to maintain its dominance, it w[ould] be forced to open new stores on its own before it would pay incipient rivals to enter. In other words, it would need to preempt the market and carry excess capacity as a result."[6] As shown in Table 12.2, when Dominion, Tom Boy, and Loblaws expanded rapidly into the Edmonton market in the early 1960s, Safeway responded by building many new stores. Safeway built these new stores either near the entrants' stores or in new geographic areas where the entrants were likely to open stores. For example, note that between 1968 and 1973 Safeway opened 10 new stores in Edmonton and closed only two.

Safeway's behavior resulted in the filing of a monopolization case against the firm in 1972. In 1973 Safeway signed a consent decree that prohibited it from expanding its total square footage in Edmonton for three and a half years. Table 12.2 indicates that after signing the decree, Safeway opened only four new stores and closed seven old stores between 1974 and 1977. After the decree expired, Safeway opened five new stores

*As indicated by the asterisk in Table 12.1, SCM's large increase in generic chloride capacity is misleading because SCM purchased Sherwin-Williams' generic chloride capacity in 1974.

TABLE 12.1 Titanium Dioxide Capacity by Production Process (thousands of tons, December 1972–1977)

	1972	1973	1974	1975	1976	1977	Percent Change 1972–1977
Du Pont							
Generic chloride	25	26	27	29	30	30	20%
Proprietary chloride	185	273	340	392	395	395	114
Sulfate	55	55	0	0	0	0	−100
NL Industries							
Sulfate	180	221	223	223	225	140	−22
SCM Corp							
Generic chloride*	25	25	25	60	60	72	188*
Sulfate	50	50	50	50	55	55	10
American Cyanamid							
Generic chloride	40	40	40	45	50	50	25
Sulfate	70	70	70	60	50	50	−29
Gulf and Western							
Generic chloride	25	25	27	30	30	30	20
Sulfate	42	42	42	42	42	42	0
Kerr-McGee							
Generic chloride	45	45	45	50	50	50	11
Sherwin-Williams							
Generic chloride	27	27	27	0	0	0	−100

*SCM purchased Sherwin-Williams' generic chloride capacity in 1974. Eliminating the impact of SCM's purchase of Sherwin-Williams' capacity, SCM's capacity increased by 33 percent between 1972 and 1977.
Source: U.S. Bureau of Mines, 1972–1977, *Minerals Yearbook,* and FTC Docket No. 9108 printed in E.A. Hall "Analysis of Preemptive Behavior in the Titanium Dioxide Industry," *International Journal of Industrial Organization* 8 (September 1990): 472.

and closed only two between 1978 and 1982. Safeway, therefore, ultimately had as many stores in 1982, 35, as it did in 1973.[7] By comparison, the number of stores operated by Dominion, Tom Boy, and Loblaws declined from 21 in 1967 to 12 in 1973, and to just six in 1982. West and Von Hohenbalken also observed that "Safeway stores, on average, had market area populations greater than the break-even level, while [Dominion, Tom Boy, and Loblaws] had smaller ones, a result that is consistent with the implications of the reputation hypothesis."[8]

In the final analysis, West and Von Hohenbalken concluded that Safeway engaged in capacity expansion to deter entry by its three largest potential rivals.

TABLE 12.2 Store Count and Gross New Entry of Supermarkets in Edmonton, 1959–1982

Year	Total Number of Safeway Stores	Number of New Safeway Stores	Total Number of Dominion, Tom Boy, and Loblaws Stores	Number of New Dominion, Tom Boy, and Loblaws Stores	Total Number of Competitive Fringe Stores	Number of New Competitive Fringe Stores
1959	18	—	12	—	31	—
1960	23	5	15	5	31	12
1961	26	3	16	2	28	3
1962	24	0	20	4	26	2
1963	25	1	21	1	25	1
1964	25	3	21	1	25	3
1965	26	2	22	1	26	4
1966	27	2	23	1	26	0
1967	27	0	21	0	25	0
1968	32	5	21	0	25	1
1969	32	0	21	1	28	3
1970	33	2	21	0	30	3
1971	34	1	17	0	31	2
1972	34	1	15	0	33	2
1973	35	1	12	0	33	1
1974	35	0	11	1	32	1
1975	33	2	10	1	33	2
1976	32	1	11	1	32	5
1977	32	1	11	0	32	1
1978	33	2	9	0	30	0
1979	32	0	7	0	31	1
1980	33	1	7	0	31	0
1981	33	0	7	0	32	1
1982	35	2	6	0	33	2

Source: D. West and B. Von Hohenbalken, "Empirical Tests for Predatory Reputation," *Canadian Journal of Economics* 19 (February 1986): 172.

12.2 Raising Rivals' Costs[9]

Another strategy to which economists have devoted a great deal of attention over the last 25 years is the possibility that firms attempt to deter entry by **raising rivals' costs** of entry. Consider Figure 11.7 from the predatory pricing game analyzed in section 11.2.1. With perfect, complete, certain, and symmetric information, there is no credible way of deterring entry. In this situation, the only Nash equilibrium is for the entrant to enter and for the monopolist to accommodate. Both firms earn an economic profit of $4 million. There may be another strategic alternative available to the monopolist, however. Figure 12.3 depicts a somewhat different game. There are two

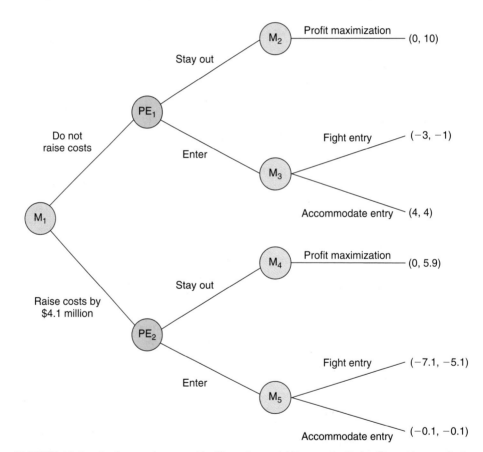

FIGURE 12.3 Profits are shown as ($millions Potential Entrant Profit, $millions Monopolist's Profit). If the monopolist does not raise costs, the game moves to node PE_1 and the Nash equilibrium is for the potential entrant to enter and the monopolist to accommodate. Both firms earn a profit of $4 million. If the monopolist takes an action that increases the monopolist's and the potential entrant's costs by $4.1 million, the game moves to node PE_2 and the equilibrium is for the potential entrant to stay out and the monopolist to maximize profit. The monopolist now earns a profit of $5.9 million.

changes in Figure 12.3 compared to Figure 11.7. The monopolist earns $10 million instead of $7 million if it does not raise costs, and the monopolist has the option of undertaking a strategic action that increases both the potential entrant's costs and its own costs by $4.1 million. If the monopolist does not raise costs, the game moves to node PE_1, the potential entrant enters, the monopolist accommodates, and both firms earn profits equal to $4 million. If the monopolist takes a strategic action that raises costs by $4.1 million for both the potential entrant and the monopolist, the games moves to node PE_2. The potential entrant now sustains an economic loss no matter what action the monopolist takes in response to entry at node M_5, and therefore the potential entrant stays out. Because the potential entrant stays out, the game moves to node M_4, and the monopolist earns an economic profit of $5.9 million, which is 47.5 percent larger than the $4 million profit it earns if it does not raise costs. The equilibrium, therefore, is for the monopolist to raise costs and the potential entrant to stay out.

The monopolist may have an even better possible outcome. It might be able to spend $1.00 to increase the potential entrant's costs by more than $1.00; perhaps, for example, it can spend $1.00 to increase the potential entrant's costs by $2.00, or $5.00, or $100.00. How can a monopolist raise its rivals' costs? Economists have suggested four primary methods: (1) lobbying the government to erect barriers to entry, (2) increasing advertising expenditures to force entrants to increase their advertising expenditures, (3) providing complementary goods and services to force entrants to also provide complementary products, and (4) sabotaging corporate competitors.

12.2.1 Lobbying to Increase Barriers to Entry[10]

In New York City, only taxicabs displaying a city-issued taxicab medallion can legally cruise the streets. To limit entry, current medallion owners lobby city officials to prevent New York City from issuing more medallions. Potential entrants are forced to purchase one of the existing medallions in order to drive a cab. What's the fixed cost of a medallion? In 2005, the price of a medallion was $250,000 per taxicab, increasing significantly the capital costs requirements of entry. Recall that increases in the capital requirements to enter an industry increase barriers to entering the New York City taxicab market. Periodically, some city politicians suggest either eliminating the taxicab medallion requirement or having New York City offer a large supply of new medallions at a relatively low price. The group that has been most opposed to such a policy change is the organized group of current taxicab medallion owners who want to keep the capital requirements of driving a cab high. Like the taxicab owners, organized groups of doctors, dentists, lawyers, plumbers, electricians, and morticians have also lobbied to raise the cost of entry by establishing educational and licensing standards to enter their respective markets. There is an almost endless list of successful and unsuccessful lobbying efforts aimed at increasing the costs of entry.

12.2.2 Increasing Advertising[11]

An increase in advertising is probably the most common method used to raise rivals' costs. Because increased advertising increases both demand and costs, it can theoretically have either a positive or negative effect on profit. Analyzing the direct effects of advertising can be complicated.* Intuitively, increased advertising creates brand loyalty

*The complicated effects of advertising are considered in the next chapter.

and makes demand more inelastic. These factors limit the likelihood of a net negative effect of increased advertising on dominant firms' profits. If the leading firms in an industry increase their advertising expenditures, this increase can deter potential entrants from entering by forcing them to at least match funds spent on advertising.

Recall from Chapter 6 that John Sutton studied the impact of increased advertising expenditures on sunk costs and entry in many industries and in many countries.[12] Sutton concluded that increased advertising expenditures deterred entry by increasing sunk costs in many markets. Leading examples included coffee, ready-to-eat cereals, biscuits, beer, prepared soups, margarine, soft drinks, chocolate candy, and baby foods.

12.2.3 Providing Complementary Goods and Services

A third method of raising rivals' costs is to provide complementary goods or services to consumers. Few markets have been more inundated with complementary services than the Internet service providers (ISP) market. First, America On-Line (AOL) offered 50 free minutes of Internet access for first-time AOL users, to entice consumers to sign up for its Internet services. It then provided 100 minutes, then 500, then 700, until in 2002, AOL was offering 1000 free minutes—that's almost 42 free days of service to convince consumers to try AOL. By giving away so many free minutes of service, AOL made it difficult for smaller ISPs to enter the market, because the new entrants would also have to offer hundreds of hours of free access. But ISPs are not the only high-tech market where firms are providing complementary goods and services. Wireless telecommunications firms constantly offer free cellular telephones, free minutes, and free premiums to entice consumers to try their service. Airlines also offer free travel through their frequent-flyer programs. Each of these programs increases the cost of entering the market.

12.2.4 Sabotaging Corporate Competitors

Occasionally a competitor resorts to rather extreme methods of raising rivals' costs by sabotaging a competitor's products or marketing efforts. Sabotage can range from spreading false rumors and filing nuisance lawsuits all the way up to corporate espionage and vandalism against physical facilities. Even the mildest forms of sabotage force firms to spend valuable resources to repair damage to their reputations. Some corporate sabotage efforts turn out to be almost humorous to everyone except the victims, who may be forced into costly legal battles to overcome the effects of the saboteur's efforts.

12.2.5 Empirical Evidence on Raising Rivals' Costs

The *first-mover advantages* associated with advertising have been important, effective methods of maintaining market share in many industries.

Canned Soups

A comparison of the history of the canned soup industry in the United States and Britain provides a particularly interesting test of the first-mover theory.[13] In the

United States, Campbell's first entered the soup market in 1869 and adopted a strategy of heavy advertising and low prices. Heinz was a late entrant and, despite heavy advertising, was unable to make a significant dent in Campbell's domination. At one time, Heinz's promotional costs exceeded 33 percent of its sales revenues, yet it could not gain a major market share. In 1986, Campbell's still held a huge 82 percent share.[14]

By comparison, in Great Britain, Heinz entered first and Campbell's second. The scenario played out exactly the same way, only with Heinz the leader. Heinz entered the British market in 1930 with ready-to-eat canned soups, as opposed to Campbell's condensed soups, and used heavy advertising to establish its market dominance. Campbell's entered the market in the 1950s with a full line of condensed soups. Heinz's initial reaction was to offer its own line of premium-priced condensed soups, but Heinz quickly switched to a low-price policy on condensed soups. The low-price strategy apparently led British consumers to view condensed soup as a poor-quality alternative to ready-to-eat soups, and Heinz was able to force Campbell's into the role of a minor player in the British market. In the mid-1980s Heinz held a 58 percent market share compared with Campbell's 12 percent.[15]

In the United States Heinz has been relegated to being a producer of private label soup, whereas in Britain, Campbell's was forced into an identical private label status. In the United States Campbell's forced Heinz out of the premium brand market, and in Britain Heinz forced Campbell's out. The advantages of the first mover are striking in this example.

Soft Drinks

One more or less given in the soft drink industry in the United States is that every few years Pepsi will launch a major advertising campaign aimed at taking away Coke's leadership. Sometimes these campaigns gain early success, but eventually Coke always seems to maintain its position. Much of Coke's advantage appears to stem from its first-mover advantage of a century ago. With a distinctive bottle and heavy advertising, Coca-Cola established its early leadership in the first two decades of the 20th century.

In 1966, Coke held a 33.4 percent share compared with Pepsi's 20.4 percent.[16] Despite a highly successful advertising campaign built around the "Pepsi Generation," Pepsi's market share fell to 19.8 percent in 1972, compared with Coke's 34.7 percent. Pepsi then launched another major advertising campaign based on consumers taking "the Pepsi Challenge" (a taste test). In 1975, however, Coke continued to maintain a 35.3 percent to 21.2 percent market share lead.

In the 1980s Coke feared some slippage in its market dominance and introduced "New Coke" in 1985. "New Coke" bombed with consumers but resulted in the reintroduction of "Coca-Cola Classic," which proved to be a great success. Ironically Coke's marketing mistake improved its market position, as it continued to dominate the market with "Coca-Cola Classic." In 1985 Coke continued to lead the industry with a 37.4 percent market share, and Pepsi continued to follow with a 28.9 percent share.[17]

Consumer Batteries

In 1986 Duracell and Eveready dominated the consumer battery market with a combined 80 percent market share.[18] When corporate giant Kodak attempted to enter the industry, both incumbents responded with expensive advertising campaigns. Eveready boasted that toys powered with its batteries "keep on going and going and going."

Duracell relied on powerful athletes to show how "tough" its batteries were. Big and powerful Kodak tried but was unable to appreciably penetrate the market. Other factors besides advertising clearly were at work here; for example, shelf space was difficult for Kodak to obtain, and Duracell and Eveready also reduced prices. Nevertheless, there is little doubt that the significant increases in advertising impeded Kodak's entry.

Internet Browsers

Economides has suggested that Microsoft raised its rivals' costs in the Internet browser market by requiring computer manufacturers to install Microsoft's Internet browser, Internet Explorer, when they installed Microsoft's Windows95 operating system on a computer.[19] According to Economides:

> If it takes time or effort for a user to install a competing browser, Microsoft has an advantage if its browser is already installed by the PC manufacturer. This advantage can be significant if Microsoft bundles IE 3.0 and IE 4.0 and Windows95, given the very large market share of Windows95 in the market for operating systems for PC's.[20]

The essential argument is that once consumers purchased their new computers with the Internet Explorer already installed, few would pay the costs associated with installing and learning to use another browser. This policy obviously had its greatest impact on Microsoft's large Internet browser rival, Netscape, whose browser market share, as we showed in Chapter 11, plummeted after Microsoft began requiring computer manufacturers to install its Internet Explorer with its Windows95 operating system.

Examples of Corporate Sabatoge

***OPERA SOFTWARE* v. *MICROSOFT*—** Consider the charges made by the Norwegian firm Opera Software against Microsoft in 2003. When Opera produced its Opera 7 web browser, it charged that Microsoft had purposefully sent Opera a style sheet that caused strange things to happen when an Opera 7 user went to the MSN.com website.[21] According to Opera, Microsoft's style sheet instructions caused two visual problems: Many lines appeared to be partially hidden, and pages showed less content than they showed using Microsoft's Internet Explorer browser. When Microsoft failed to respond to Opera's complaints, Opera responded by creating a special edition of Opera 7, the Bork edition, that turned the tables on Microsoft. When a user of the Bork edition of Opera 7 went to MSN.com, the user was greeted by a web page in the language of the *Muppet Show's* famous Swedish Chef, "Hergee berger snooger bork."[22] According to Opera product line manager Mary Lambert, "[t]his is a joke, however, we are trying to make an important point. The MSN site is sending Opera users what appear to be intentionally distorted pages. The Bork edition illustrates how browsers could distort content, as the Bork edition does."[23]

While the Opera-Microsoft saga contained elements of humor, it also raised Opera's costs by requiring Opera to defend its reputation and to pay to create the Bork browser. Microsoft's actions certainly hurt Opera's efforts to make inroads into the browser market.

***BRITISH AIRWAYS* v. *VIRGIN ATLANTIC AIRWAYS*—** Perhaps the most highly publicized and documented example of corporate sabotage in the last 20 years was the British Airways (BA) effort to drive Virgin Atlantic out of the transatlantic market.[24] In 1992, British Airways published an article in its *BA News* that accused Virgin Atlantic of making up charges of sabotage against British Airways merely for publicity. This turned out to be a foolish move on British Airways' part because Virgin Atlantic sued BA for libel and the *BA News* article opened up a Pandora's box for British Airways. In a 1993 settlement, British Airways admitted to playing a series of dirty tricks on Virgin Atlantic, all aimed at destroying Virgin Atlantic's market share on its New York to London flights. Among other actions, British Airways broke into Virgin Atlantic's computers and employees' cars and homes. British Airways also attempted to gather dirt on Virgin Atlantic's flamboyant founder and CEO, Richard Branson. In perhaps its most outrageous behavior, British Airways sent agents posing as Virgin Atlantic agents to intercept Virgin Atlantic passengers on their way to their gates at JFK airport in New York and tell the Virgin Atlantic passengers that their flights had been canceled because of scheduling problems. The agents then switched the passengers to British Airways flights. British Airways employees also called Virgin Atlantic passengers at home and offered them incentives to switch from Virgin Atlantic to British Airways flights.

British Airways eventually settled the case by agreeing to pay £500,000 to Branson and £110,000 to Virgin Atlantic. Furthermore, British Airways incurred up to £3 million in legal expenses because it had to pay both Virgin Atlantic's and its own legal costs. In a final, strange twist, Branson distributed his £500,000 award to his employees by paying each £166.

APPLICATION 12.1

Detergent Wars and the Battle of Good versus Evil:
Amway v. Procter & Gamble

Procter & Gamble (P&G) and Amway engaged in a 20-year battle of corporate charges and countercharges that each firm was spreading false rumors about the other. P&G is the world's largest producer of soaps and detergents.* Amway sells soaps and detergents in competition with P&G through an elaborate system of independent distributors. In the United States, there are approximately one million Amway distributors and there are approximately three million distributors worldwide. P&G accused Amway of spreading a false rumor that P&G was a supporter of the Church of Satan and contributed a share of its profits to the church. The rumor was sparked by P&G's former use of the man in the moon symbol as part of the company's trademark. Procter & Gamble calculated that the Satan rumors cost it millions of dollars in sales revenues.

P&G long contended that Amway had a corporate policy of fueling the Satan rumor, and in July 1997 P&G sued Amway and its agent, Randy Haugen. Haugen was a large distributor of Amway products with an estimated network of 100,000 distributors working for him. Haugen served on the Amway Distributors Association Council, and in April 1995 he posted the following message on AmVox, the company's communication system.[†]

Just talking to a guy the other night about this very subject and it just so happens that a guy brings information in and lays it on my desk this morning, so here it goes.

It says the president of Procter & Gamble appeared on the Phil Donahue Show on March 1, '95. He announced that due to the openness of our society, he was coming out of the closet about his association with the church of satan. He stated that a large portion of the profits from [P&G] products go to support his satanic church. When asked by Donahue if stating this on television would hurt his business, his reply was, "There are not enough Christians in the United States to make a difference." And below it has a list of the [P&G] products which I'll read: [the subject message then lists 43 P&G products].

It says if you are not sure about a product, look for the symbol of the ram's horn that will appear on each product beginning in April. The ram's horn will form the 666 which is known as satan's number.

Needless to say, P&G was not too pleased with the above statement and decided to sue both Haugen and Amway. According to Amway, however, P&G's retribution did not stop with the lawsuit. Amway contended that P&G also retaliated by using one of its employees, Sydney Schwartz, to establish an anti-Amway website. In a counter-lawsuit, Amway argued that P&G used the Schwartz website to circulate "vulgar, false and defamatory statements about Amway." [‡] For example, the Schwartz website accused Amway of "being a cult and screwing people over."

The lawsuits and countersuits cost P&G and Amway millions of dollars, yet in the end both suits were dismissed by the courts. The Fifth Circuit Court of Appeals dismissed the Amway suit and the Tenth Circuit dismissed the P&G suit. Amway then appealed its case to the Supreme Court, which on October 1, 2001, declined to review the Fifth Circuit's ruling that Schwartz's website was protected under the First Amendment. [§]

[*]See *Amway v. Procter and Gamble*, complaint filed U.S. District Court, Western District of Michigan, October 13, 1998; and *Procter and Gamble v. Haugen* 222 F.3d 1262 (2000).

[†]*Procter and Gamble v. Haugen* 222 F.3d 1262 (2000).

[‡]*Amway v. Procter and Gamble*, complaint filed U.S. District Court, Western District of Michigan, October 13, 1998.

[§]*Amway v. Procter and Gamble*, 242 S.Ct. 329 (2001).

12.3 Learning by Doing

As output increases, certain production processes result in lower costs because experience gained through the actual production process lowers direct labor costs.[25] A good example is the purchase of a set of outdoor chairs that come in boxes completely unassembled. The buyer reads the assembly instructions only to discover that the writer had difficulty explaining things in English. The instructions boldly state that "any child can assemble a chair in less than 30 minutes"; however, two hours into the assembly of the first chair, it still resembles a bunch of unassembled plastic pieces and hardware. Finally, four hours after beginning the process, the first chair is assembled. The consumer now understands many, but not all, of the errors made in assembling the first chair, and the second chair requires a mere two hours to put together. The third chair is finished in one hour, and the fourth is ready for use in just 45 minutes. This is an example of ***learning by doing.***

Imagine the same process on a grand scale in the aircraft industry. To assemble just a few prototypes of a new plane requires a huge investment of time and resources, but later prototypes require less and less time. Eventually, through experience, copies of the model can be produced at relatively low cost.

When learning by doing is important, early entrants into the market may be able to maintain a large market share and increase the present value of their profits by strategically producing significantly larger outputs early on than would be justified by short-run profit-maximizing behavior. By producing large quantities in early periods, the first firms into the market can significantly reduce their future costs. A new firm attempting to enter the market later will face a significant cost disadvantage because it will not yet have moved down its *learning curve*. In markets characterized by significant learning by doing, entry is likely to be difficult.

An illustration of a simple learning curve is:*

$$AC(q) = 10 + \frac{100}{2^{\lambda q}},$$ [12.7]

where $AC(q)$ represents the average unit cost of production for a cumulative output of q and λ is a constant measuring the rate at which unit costs decline with volume, or the *speed of learning*. According to Equation 12.7, if $\lambda = 1.5$ and $q \to \infty$ (i.e., if cumulative output approached infinity), the second term on the right-hand side would approach zero, and minimum average costs of 10 would be achieved. On the other extreme, if $\lambda = 1.5$ and if $q = 0$, then $2^{1.5q} = 1$ and average unit costs would be at the maximum of 110.

Consider the impact of the learning curve on competitive behavior. If λ is very large, average costs approach 10 very quickly for all firms and the industry will behave competitively, just as if it had constant long-run average costs of 10. When λ is very small, average costs will remain stuck around 110 for all firms, and the industry will reach a competitive equilibrium with long-run average costs of 110. It is for intermediate values of λ that the outcomes become interesting.

Figure 12.4 shows how the average cost curve in Equation 12.7 is related to λ. The larger the value of λ, the more quickly average costs decline to 10. For intermediate values of λ, early entrants can create a type of absolute cost entry barrier by expanding output beyond the short-run profit-maximizing output. By producing large outputs, the first firm or firms into the market are protected from some, if not all, future potential entrants and will maintain higher long-run average market shares. Models based on the existence of learning by doing have suggested that in markets with a moderate rate of learning, entry ceases with only a few firms (usually three or four).[26]

Like investments in excess capacity and research and development, learning by doing can be viewed as an investment in cost reduction. The early entrant is willing to invest in large current outputs to reduce its future costs, even if this investment significantly reduces current profits.

*Generally the learning curve can be thought of as:

$$AC(q) = m_0 + c_0 e^{-\lambda q},$$

where m_0 represents the minimum possible average cost, e is the base of the natural logarithmic function such that $\ln e = 1$, and c_0 represents the cost disadvantage of a firm that produces zero units of output.

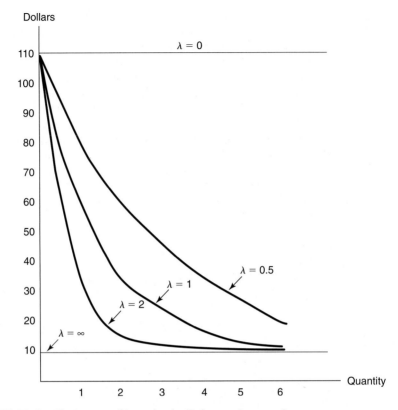

FIGURE 12.4 The Impact of Learning by Doing on Average Costs

The average cost curve is related to the value of λ in Equation 12.7. For $\lambda = 0$, the AC curve is AC = 110. The larger the value of λ, the more quickly learning takes place and the more quickly average costs decline. If learning takes place instantaneously, $\lambda \rightarrow \infty$ and AC = 10.

12.3.1 Empirical Evidence on Learning by Doing

In industries characterized by steep learning curves, early entrants can prevent future entry by moving down the learning curve. In such industries the first-mover advantage can create a permanently concentrated market.

Commercial Aircraft

The *learning curve* was first identified in the aircraft industry during World War II when it was discovered that with each 100 percent increase in *cumulative* output, direct labor costs in hours declined by 20 percent.[27] In other words, the fourth plane required only 80 percent of the labor hours needed to produce the second plane; the twentieth plane required 80 percent of the labor hours needed to produce the tenth plane; the hundredth plane required 80 percent of the labor hours needed to produce the fiftieth plane; and so forth.

During World War I the aircraft industry expanded tremendously because of military production, but only after the war did the commercial industry become important. In the 1930s four manufacturers dominated the market: Boeing, Douglas, Lockheed, and Curtiss-Wright. When Douglas developed the DC-3, it was the best commercial aircraft available and Douglas came to dominate the market. As Table 12.3 indicates, from 1937 through 1941 Douglas held a huge market share that ranged from 85 to 98 percent.

During World War II, the commercial aircraft industry effectively ceased to exist as all productive capability was turned toward the military. Lockheed, for example, was a small factor in the commercial industry before the war. Given the government's insatiable demand for planes, a few new firms became major government suppliers during the war. Chief among these were Convair and Martin. During the war, the government required cross-licensing of patent designs, and as a result, when the war ended Lockheed, Convair, and Martin had all become viable competitors for Douglas. In the absence of the war, it is likely that Douglas would have continued to move down its learning curve and would have remained the dominant firm.

From 1948 to 1955, five producers—Douglas, Boeing, Lockheed, Convair, and Martin—jockeyed for industry leadership. Given the importance of large production runs to lower costs, it is not surprising that price competition was intense in the postwar period.[28] In 1958 the industry underwent its next major technological breakthrough when Boeing introduced the 707 and Douglas introduced the DC-8. Competition now centered on which of these firms could expand production and move down its learning curve more quickly. As a result, both firms engaged in aggressive price cutting to obtain sales. The three other firms more or less dropped out of the market, and eventually, as Table 12.4 indicates, Boeing came to dominate the industry.

Boeing continued to control the market, and in 1967 Douglas was forced to merge with McDonnell, a firm that produced a military product line, to form McDonnell-Douglas.[29] Shortly thereafter, aggressive price competition between McDonnell-Douglas and Lockheed in the market for wide-body jets left Lockheed on the verge of

TABLE 12.3 Douglas's Control of the Commercial Aircraft Industry, 1936–1941

Year	Total Aircraft Manufactured	Douglas DC-3s Manufactured	Douglas's Market Share (%)
1936	42	29	69
1937	54	47	87
1938	24	21	88
1939	41	40	98
1940	112	95	85
1941	36	35	97

Source: David C. Mowery and Nathan Rosenberg, "The Commercial Aircraft Industry," in Richard R. Nelson (ed.), *Government and Technical Progress: A Cross-Industry Analysis* (New York: Pergamon Press, 1982), p. 107.

TABLE 12.4 Market Shares in the Commercial Aircraft Industry, 1947–1965

Year	Douglas	Boeing	Convair	Lockheed	Martin
1947	74.3%	0.0%	0.0%	17.1%	8.6%
1948	21.7	0.0	60.0	5.2	13.0
1949	1.7	17.2	48.3	32.8	0.0
1950	9.8	0.0	11.8	60.8	17.6
1951	47.6	0.0	0.0	23.8	28.6
1952	14.9	0.0	16.2	16.2	52.7
1953	29.1	0.0	58.3	9.4	3.1
1954	66.7	0.0	24.0	9.3	0.0
1955	38.2	0.0	3.6	43.6	0.0
1956	40.0	0.0	15.2	8.0	0.0
1957	67.0	0.0	12.8	18.4	0.0
1958	59.8	0.0	0.0	14.6	0.0
1959	10.8	30.1	0.0	57.8	0.0
1960	39.2	35.1	14.4	11.3	0.0
1961	9.6	45.6	19.2	12.0	0.0
1962	12.1	51.5	31.8	0.0	0.0
1963	8.7	69.6	21.7	0.0	0.0
1964	6.7	91.6	1.7	0.0	0.0
1965	12.6	78.5	0.0	0.0	0.0

Source: David C. Mowery and Nathan Rosenberg, "The Commercial Aircraft Industry," in Richard R. Nelson (ed.), *Government and Technical Progress: A Cross-Industry Analysis* (New York: Pergamon Press, 1982), p. 111.

financial collapse. Only a $250 million government loan guarantee averted Lockheed's bankruptcy.[30]

The history of competition in the commercial aircraft industry is consistent with the strategic use of the learning curve. The key to success is to be the first firm to introduce a major technologically superior plane and to price it low enough to take advantage of the learning curve. This strategy was the key to both Douglas's early success and Boeing's later success. More recently Boeing has been locked in a battle with the European Airbus to maintain its leadership position.*

Automobiles

From 1909 until 1926, Ford followed a strategy of lowering the price of its Model T to take advantage of the learning curve. In 1908, when the Model T was first introduced at a price of $950, the least expensive Ford was priced at $850. Henry Ford was determined to dramatically increase output and cut price even without knowing what his

*The Boeing-Airbus battle was discussed in detail in Chapter 8.

future costs would be, so he announced his plans to eventually sell cars for $400.[31] As it turned out, Ford was able to sell the Model T for just $355 in 1921 and for $290 in 1925.[32]

As Ford lowered the price of the Model T, its sales and market share increased dramatically. Table 12.5 shows that its sales increased by *12,358 percent* between 1909 and 1925 compared with an increase for the remaining firms in the industry of just 1900 percent. Furthermore, Ford's profits continued to increase as it moved down the learning curve. In 1909 it took 21 days to build a Model T, by 1913 it took 14 days, and by 1921 it required just 4 days from beginning to end of the production process.[33] During this period the labor hours required to build a Model T declined by 60 percent.[34]

The Achilles' heel in Ford's strategy turned out to be that the Model T's design remained essentially unchanged for 18 years. When General Motors began producing heavier cars with closed bodies and much greater comfort, Ford was slow to respond. As a result, Ford's market share declined from 40 percent in 1925 to 10 percent in 1927. As Alfred Sloan, the person who created the strategy that catapulted GM into the leadership position, stated:[35]

> Mr. Ford . . . had frozen his policy in the Model T, . . . preeminently an open-car design. With its light chassis, it was unsuited to the heavier closed body, and so in less than two years the closed body made the already obsolescing design of the Model T noncompetitive as an engineering design.

The story of Ford's rise and fall in the automobile industry is remarkably similar to Douglas's rise and fall in the aircraft industry. In both cases, an early technological leader maintained its dominance by reducing price in advance of cost reductions and moving down the learning curve, only to be overtaken by later technological developments. In recent years this same scenario played itself out in the semiconductor market.

TABLE 12.5 Sales of the Model T, 1909–1925

Year	Price of Model T Ford	Total Ford Sales	Total Industry Sales	Ford Market Share	Ford Profits ($mil)
1909	$950	12,000	124,000	9.7%	NA
1911	690	40,000	199,000	20.1	$21
1913	550	182,000	462,000	39.4	75
1915	440	342,000	896,000	38.2	74
1917	450	741,000	1,746,000	42.4	51
1919	525	664,000	1,658,000	40.0	140
1921	355	845,000	1,518,000	55.7	125
1923	295	1,669,000	3,625,000	46.0	193
1925	290	1,495,000	3,735,000	40.0	219

Source: Lawrence J. White, "The Automobile Industry," in Walter Adams, *The Structure of American Industry,* 5th edition (New York: MacMillan, 1977), p. 173; and William J. Abernathy and Kenneth Wayne, "Limits of the Learning Curve," *Harvard Business Review* (Sept./Oct. 1974): p. 114.

Semiconductors

The semiconductor industry is a high-tech industry in which the learning curve has long been recognized as important. New products are priced very close to manufacturing costs to take advantage of the learning curve, and the first firm into a new product line tends to gain a significant cost advantage. In 1976 Motorola executive Robert R. Heikes described the competitive environment as follows:[36]

> The frightening thing in this business is that if you're not first—or a fast second or third—you're in trouble. . . . If you come in a year late, you'd better have a much improved version or a new process that permits you to make the product more cheaply.

One example of the importance of the learning curve in the semiconductor industry is Intel's 1971 introduction of the 1024-bit random access memory (RAM) integrated circuit. The Intel 1024-bit RAM was initially priced at $28.00 per unit; by April 1974 the price had declined to between $3.00 and $4.00 per unit.[37] The learning curve has forced firms to price for market share and to anticipate dramatic cost reductions as output increases. Econometric studies of the importance of learning by doing in the semiconductor industry suggest that doubling cumulative output reduces costs by about 20 to 30 percent.[38]

According to Cabral and Leiblein, learning by doing is so rapid in the semiconductor industry that while cumulative knowledge about a previous generation of semiconductors increases the probability of developing the next generation of semiconductors, cumulative knowledge from two generations back has no significant effect on the probability of developing a new technology.[39] Cabral and Leiblein examined data on the adoption of 0.5-micron process technology from 1990 to 1995 for 152 U.S., European, and Asian semiconductor firms. They found that cumulative experience producing the previous generation of 0.6- to 0.75-micron semiconductors increased the rate of adoption of the newest 0.5-micron technology, but that cumulative experience with 0.75- to 1.0-micron technology had no impact on the rate of adoption of 0.5-micron technology. Large firms with annual sales above $1 billion and medium-size firms with sales between $200 million and $1 billion were also five to seven times more likely than small firms to rapidly adopt the latest 0.5-micron technology.[40] These results suggest that the advantages of learning by doing, while significant, diminish extremely rapidly in the semiconductor industry.

APPLICATION 12.2

Qualitative Learning by Doing in the Motion Picture Industry: The Case of the "Talkies"

Learning by doing is usually thought of as a quantity concept, that is, as a firm produces cumulatively more of a product, its average costs decrease. It is possible, however, to think of learning by doing as a quality concept as well; that is, as a firm produces cumulatively more of a product, the quality of the product improves. Such qualitative improvements would also be expected to help firms maintain or expand their market power. Charles Moul analyzed the quality aspects of learning by doing with the introduction of sound movies (talkies) in the motion picture industry.*

The first talking motion picture, *The Jazz Singer,* was released in fall 1927. As the figure below shows, after the introduction of sound pictures, the market share of silent pictures decreased very rapidly, with silent pictures virtually disappearing by July 1930. Notice that the major studios introduced sound pictures much more rapidly than independents. Moul suggested that learning by doing was primarily responsible for studios producing higher-quality sound pictures.[†]

Moul examined the impact of the introduction of sound on the studio revenues from 1925 to 1941. His hypothesis was that studios that *cumulatively* produced more sound pictures were able to produce higher-quality movies and, therefore, were able to capture a larger share of the market as measured by revenues per movie. Moul distinguished between the effect of a studio simply producing more sound pictures and a studio utilizing learning by doing to produce higher-quality sound pictures by controlling for both the impact of a studio's share of movies that used sound (the simple effect of consumers' preference for sound) and the impact of the interaction of the studio's share of sound pictures with its past experience using sound (the learning-by-doing effect) on its revenues per movie. The statistical results showed that a studio's past experience using sound had a positive and statistically significant effect on its revenues per movie independent of the simple effect of the share of sound pictures on revenues per movie.

More specifically, a studio that had already produced 100 sound movies and that only produced sound movies averaged approximately $500,000 more revenue per movie than a studio that produced only sound pictures but had no previous experience producing sound pictures.[‡] Furthermore, the industry's early leader in utilizing sound, MGM, had significantly larger revenues than its competitors. Moul concluded by noting that "it would be interesting to model the theoretical strategic considerations of this sort of learning and especially to test if (in the motion picture industry) studios 'overproduced' talkies from a static point-of-view to purposefully improve their future movies' quality and maximize some dynamic concept of profits."[§]

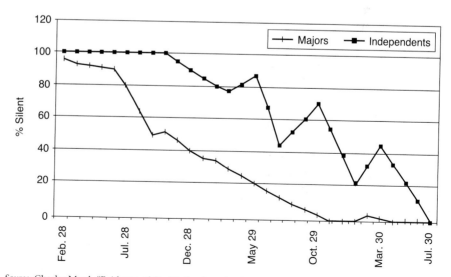

Source: Charles Moul, "Evidence of Qualitative Learning-By-Doing from the Advent of the 'Talkie'" *Journal of Industrial Economics* 49 (March 2001): 100.

*Charles Moul, "Evidence of Qualitative Learning-By-Doing from the Advent of the 'Talkie'," *Journal of Industrial Economics* 49 (March 2001): 97-109.

†*Ibid.*, p. 101.

‡*Ibid.*, p. 105.

§*Ibid.*, p. 108. ■

12.4 Product Proliferation

Product proliferation** refers to the strategic decision to preempt potential entrants by creating brands to fill every available product niche. Have you ever wondered why, for example, there are so many different varieties of cereal, almost all produced by Kellogg's, General Mills, or Kraft (Post) or so many different varieties of beer, most produced by Busch or Miller? Economists theorize that by filling many different niches in the market for cereal or beer, the incumbents are able to prevent potential entrants from gaining even a small foothold in the industry.[41]

Because even a simple game theoretic analysis of this strategy can become complicated, a detailed examination is presented in the Appendix to this chapter. The intuition behind the product proliferation model is best understood from the viewpoint of a dominant incumbent such as Kellogg's or Budweiser. Essentially, the optimal strategy for the dominant firm is to enter a new niche (such as "sugar-frosted grape-flavored corn flakes") just before it is profitable for a potential entrant to enter that niche. By entering at precisely that moment, the dominant incumbent is able to preempt entry and earn greater long-run profits than it would earn if it permitted entry.

Suppose, for example, that a potential entrant into the sugar-frosted grape-flavored corn flakes market knows that if it does not enter this market by time t = 10, Kellogg's will maximize its profits by entering at t = 10 and thereby freeze the potential entrant out of the market. The potential entrant must therefore try to preempt Kellogg's by entering at some time earlier than t = 10, say t = 10 − ε. Knowing this, Kellogg's must try to preempt the potential entrant by entering at an even earlier time, perhaps t = 10 − 2ε. Of course, such a game regresses backward to a point at which Kellogg's enters the market just infinitesimally before it is profitable for the entrant to enter at all. This is the only solution to the game. Kellogg's enters before it is profitable for the potential entrant to enter and preempts the potential entrant from the grape-flavored corn flakes market. In this manner, Kellogg's and General Mills maintain their market power.

12.4.1 Empirical Evidence on the Use of Product Proliferation

It does not take an economist to detect industries that appear full of products in every niche. Commonly cited examples include the ready-to-eat cereal, beer, safety razor, canned soup, and laundry detergent markets.

Ready-to-Eat Cereals

The ready-to-eat (RTE) cereal market is the most commonly used example of product proliferation. In this industry, the six leading manufacturers (Kellogg's, General Mills, Kraft [Post], Quaker, Nabisco, and Ralston) increased the number of brands from 26 in

1950 to 80 in 1973.[42] During that 23-year period, 84 new brands were introduced, but 30 did not survive.[43]

The rate of introduction increased somewhat over time, as follows:[44]

Period	New Brands Introduced
1950–1955	8
1956–1960	15
1961–1965	22
1966–1970	19
1971–1973	20

The new brands typically took market share away from older, established brands. Corn flakes, which accounted for 33 percent of sales in 1940, accounted for only 10.8 percent in 1972, and only 6.8 percent in 1982. Furthermore, the average market share per RTE cereal brand declined from 4 percent in 1950 to just 1.3 percent in 1972.[45]

Between 1950 and 1972, Kellogg's introduced 24 new brands, General Mills introduced 34, and Kraft introduced 21.[46] Most of these new brands achieved only small market shares. In fact, only seven new brands ever achieved market shares exceeding 2 percent.* The only attempt by new competitors to enter the RTE cereal market occurred in the early 1970s.[47] One niche that had previously gone unfilled was the "natural cereal" niche. Natural cereals or granolas were generally sold only in health food stores. In the 1970s, Pet, Pillsbury, and Colgate all entered, with some initial success. Pet's Heartland cereal reached almost a 2 percent market share in 1974.[48] The initial success of the intruders led to a response by the major firms. In 1973 Quaker responded first with the introduction of Quaker 100% Natural Cereal. General Mills followed with Nature Valley and Kellogg's with Country Morning. As a result, Heartland's sales plummeted to just 0.1 percent in 1980, and Pillsbury and Colgate left the market. In the long run only Quaker 100% Natural Cereal has left a lasting mark on the industry.[49]

One complicating factor in the cereal industry is that launching a new cereal brand requires huge advertising expenditures. It is possible, therefore, that Kellogg's was able to maintain its dominant share because of lower advertising expenditures per dollar of sales, which resulted in a first-mover advantage.[50] Table 12.6 indicates that Kellogg's had consistently lower advertising costs than its two major competitors.

In 1982, Kellogg's continued to lead the industry with a 39 percent share followed by General Mills with 21 percent, Kraft with 16 percent, and Quaker Oats with 9 percent.[51] One reasonable interpretation of the evidence is that Kellogg's initially relied on a first-mover advantage to establish its dominance in the basic brands such as Corn Flakes and Rice Krispies, and later used a brand proliferation strategy to maintain its dominant position.[52] Campbell's has followed a similar strategy in soups.[53]

Campbell's Canned Soups and Other Products

We noted earlier that Campbell's established its dominance in the American canned soup market through a policy of heavy advertising. That policy has also been augmented

*The seven brands introduced between 1950 and 1972 that achieved at least a 2 percent market share were Kellogg's Frosted Flakes (peak market share of 6.3 percent in 1971); Kellogg's Special K (4.1 percent in 1971); General Foods' Post Alpha Bits (2.7 percent in 1959); General Mills' Total (2.6 percent in 1967); Quaker Cap'n Crunch (2.4 percent in 1965); Quaker Life (2.0 percent in 1966); and General Mills' Jets (2.1 percent in 1955). *Federal Trade Commission* v. *Kellogg et al.*, Docket No. 8883, 99 FTC Reporter 8 (1982), §589.

TABLE 12.6 RTE Cereal Advertising-to-Sales Ratio, 1958–1972

Year	Kellogg's	General Mills	Kraft
1958	14.57%	18.47%	16.09%
1959	17.23	22.56	15.92
1960	16.26	17.43	14.81
1961	15.42	20.15	13.49
1962	15.21	18.43	14.71
1963	15.19	20.57	15.30
1964	15.23	20.19	16.99
1965	16.61	22.38	18.62
1966	15.72	19.81	20.98
1967	15.56	20.69	22.09
1968	12.08	17.25	18.43
1969	12.09	16.05	15.39
1970	10.60	13.23	16.34
1971	9.74	12.72	14.67
1972	9.39	14.76	13.78
15-year averages	14.06%	18.31%	16.50%

Source: Federal Trade Commission v. Kellogg et al., Docket No. 8883, 99 *FTC Reporter* 8 (1982), p. 430.

by a *product proliferation* strategy. Campbell's has tried to fill not only every national soup niche, but regional niches as well. In Texas and California, for example, Campbell's made a spicier nacho cheese soup than it did anywhere else.[54] In 1987, it marketed a Creole soup in Southern markets and a red-bean soup in some Hispanic markets. Campbell's sold a Duck-Gizzard Soup in China and a Cream of Chili Poblano soup in Mexico.

Campbell's created new brands not only in soups but introduced more than 400 new products in the five-year period between 1981 and 1985.[55] In some cases it introduced entirely new product lines, in an attempt to fill a variety of niches at once. Examples included a full line of Prego spaghetti sauces and Simply Home soups in glass jars.

Statistical Evidence on Product Proliferation

Statistical evidence on the use of product proliferation is limited. In one important study, however, John Connor investigated the use of the strategy in the food products industry.[56] Connor used data in *Advertising Age* magazine to identify all new brands in the food products industry for the years 1977 and 1978. The sample included 419 new products introduced into 102 product classes. New products and new flavor varieties were included, but new package sizes and designs were excluded. The 10 most active product lines were:[57]

Product Category	**New Products 1977 and 1978**
1. Nonalcoholic beverages and mixes	70
2. Alcoholic beverages	49
3. Pet foods	39
4. Flour mixes and baking ingredients	38
5. Frozen foods	30
6. Candy and chewing gum	27
7. Canned fruits, vegetables, and specials	26
8. Breakfast cereals	24
9. Tobacco products	23
10. Dehydrated vegetables and soup mixes	20

Of the 419 new products, 59 percent were marketed by the top 50 food or tobacco firms and 70 percent came from the top 200 firms.[58]

Connor tested a number of hypotheses, including one that the number of new products introduced in a given product category was a function of concentration, advertising, market size as measured by the value of shipments, and costs incurred for packaging materials. Connor theorized that the relationship between the number of new products introduced and concentration was *nonlinear* and tested for this by controlling for the effects of both the four-firm concentration ratio and the *square* of the four-firm concentration ratio in his statistical analysis.* He also controlled for many

*The use of the square of concentration tests whether a *linear* or *nonlinear* relationship exists between concentration and the number of new products introduced. Consider for example the following hypothetical regression result:

$$y = 12 + 2x - \frac{1}{4}x^2,$$

which graphs as:

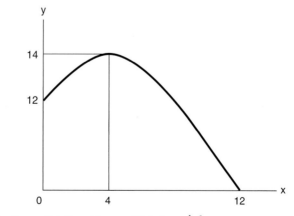

Graph of the Nonlinear Relationship $y = 12 + 2x - \frac{1}{4}x^2$

This graph shows that the relationship between the dependent variable y and the independent variable x is nonlinear because of the significant *negative* coefficient on the squared term. For values of x < 4 the relationship between y and x is *positive,* but for values of x > 4 the relationship is *negative.*

other factors that might influence the number of new products introduced, such as research and development intensity and the rate of growth of demand.

Connor found that the four-firm concentration ratio had a statistically significant positive effect on the number of new products introduced; however, the square of the four-firm concentration ratio had a statistically significant *negative* effect on the number of new products introduced. The negative effect of the square of the four-firm concentration ratio suggests that for small values of concentration, the relationship between the number of new products and concentration is positive, but for larger values of concentration the relationship between the number of new products and concentration is negative.* This suggests that when concentration becomes high, either all product niches have already been filled or product proliferation is less necessary to protect the leading firms' market shares. Advertising was used as a proxy for product differentiation and had a statistically significant positive effect on the number of new products introduced. Greater product differentiation did indeed result in greater product proliferation, holding other things equal.† Market size also had a statistically significant positive effect on the number of new products introduced, suggesting that in industries with larger demands there is "room" for more product proliferation. Finally, packaging costs had a positive effect on the number of new products introduced. Connor interpreted packaging costs as a proxy for the ease with which brands can be physically differentiated from each other through the use of packaging. None of the other control variables had a statistically significant impact on the number of new products introduced. Connor concluded by noting that:[59]

> The results reported here for the food-manufacturing industries provide empirical support for the market structure-conduct linkage suggested by [the product proliferation] model. Product proliferation is one of several forms of business conduct open to firms in oligopolistic industries with differentiated products, but it appears to be a widespread strategy in the food industries.

William Putsis tested for the significance of product proliferation in the food products market by using supermarket scanner price data from 1991 to 1992 for 135 food product categories in 59 geographic markets.[60] Consistent with basic price theory, Putsis found that an increase in the price of private label products or the market share of branded products resulted in a significant increase in the price of branded products, and an increase in the price of branded products or the market share of private label products resulted in a significant increase in the price of private label products.

Putsis tested the impact of increased brand proliferation on the price of branded and private label products using two measures of brand proliferation: the number of brands in a product category and the brand-level Herfindahl Index. The study, therefore, controlled not only for the absolute number of brands in a product category, but also the distribution of market shares for those brands. Controlling for a large number

*See the previous footnote.

†This study, and others like it, have been severely criticized by some economists because of the use of advertising to proxy product differentiation, and the resulting conclusion that increased advertising and increased product differentiation *cause* increased product proliferation. This ignores the distinct and at least as likely possibility that increased product proliferation *causes* increased advertising and increased product differentiation.

of other factors, Putsis found that the absolute number of brands in a product category had a statistically significant positive effect on the prices of branded *and* private label food products. This is consistent with the theory that increased product proliferation results in greater market power by both reducing the elasticity of demand for each brand (consumers are willing to pay higher prices for brands that more closely match their tastes) and deterring entry; and as a result, increased product proliferation is associated with increased prices. These data showed that increasing the number of brands from the mean number of 36 to approximately 43 increased branded prices by about 2.33 cents, or about 1 percent.[61]

Putsis also found that the Herfindahl Index had a statistically significant *negative* effect on the prices of branded products and a statistically significant *positive* effect on the prices of private label food products. In a product category with a large Herfindahl Index, one or a couple of brands dominated the market, and in a product category with a small Herfindahl Index, many brands had significant market shares. The Herfindahl Index, therefore, measured the distribution or dispersion of market shares across brands: the *higher* the Herfindal Index, the *lower* the brand dispersion. Putsis interpreted the negative effect of the Herfindahl Index on the prices of branded products as evidence of the existence of economies of scale or economies of scope in those markets, which result in lower prices.

Putsis concluded that:[62]

> Brand proliferation has the primary effect of increasing the number of brands offered in the market, and thereby raising prices. However, the net effect of brand proliferation strategies will depend upon the distribution of market shares that result from additional brands. If new brand introductions increase the dispersion of brands, there will be a secondary effect enhancing the ability of branded manufacturers to raise prices; if the new introductions increase the concentration of brands, manufacturers' ability to raise prices will be reduced accordingly.

Putsis's results suggest a much more complex relationship between product proliferation and market power. Firms considering introducing new brands should consider not only the impact of that brand on the number of brands, but the impact on brand dispersion as well.

12.5 Empirical Evidence on the Use of Price and Nonprice Strategies to Deter Entry

Chapter 11 and this chapter have suggested a number of strategic methods of maintaining long-run market dominance, including:

1. Limit pricing

2. Establishing a "tough" reputation (the threat of predatory pricing)

3. Creating excess capacity

4. Raising rivals' costs (e.g., advertising costs)

5. Utilizing learning by doing

6. Product proliferation (filling product niches)

Robert Smiley devised a business questionnaire to examine how often each method of deterrence was used. Smiley's results were based on 294 responses from product managers of major corporations.[63] The product managers were asked to rate on a scale from 1 to 5 the degree to which different entry-deterring strategies were used in their product markets. Smiley's results are shown in Table 12.7.[64]

TABLE 12.7 Smiley's Entry Deterrence Strategy Study, Frequency of Use of Different Strategies

	New Products				
	Frequently	*Occ./Freq.*	*Occasionally*	*Never/Occ.*	*Never*
1. Excess capacity	6%	16%	20%	22%	36%
2. Advertising	32	30	16	17	5
3. R&D strategies	31	25	15	12	17
4. Tough reputation	10	17	27	24	23
5. Limit pricing to prevent all entry	2	4	17	34	44
6. Limit pricing to "slow" rate of entry	3	8	21	33	35
7. Use learning by doing	9	17	29	27	18
	Existing Products				
	Frequently	*Occ./Freq.*	*Occasionally*	*Never/Occ.*	*Never*
1. Excess capacity	7%	14%	17%	32%	30%
2. Advertising	24	28	26	14	7
3. R&D strategies	11	20	16	31	23
4. Tough reputation	8	19	22	31	21
5. Limit pricing to prevent all entry	7	15	21	32	25
6. Limit pricing to "slow" rate of entry	6	14	21	32	27
7. Product proliferation—filling niches	26	31	22	14	6
8. Hide profits	31	28	20	10	12

Source: Robert Smiley, "Empirical Evidence on Strategic Entry Deterrence," *International Journal of Industrial Organization* 6 (1980): p. 172.

The most striking finding was that the strategic use of advertising and product proliferation was common in both new and existing product markets. For both new and existing product lines, 78 percent of respondents claimed that advertising was used at least occasionally to deter entry. Limit pricing and excess capacity appeared to be the least used strategies, but even these were used in a substantial number of markets. For example, 36 percent of the new product respondents and 53 percent of existing product respondents reported at least occasional use of limit pricing.[65] Smiley also reported that 54 percent of new product respondents and 58 percent of existing product respondents reported frequent use of at least one strategy, and that 89 percent of new product and 98 percent of existing product respondents reported at least occasional use of some strategy.[66]

Respondents were also asked the following open-ended question, "Have you observed any other activities that appear to be designed primarily to prevent or slow entry?" In order of frequency of response, respondents noted the following strategies:[67]

1. Sign long-term contracts with customers, middlemen, or wholesalers.

2. Have product specifications or controlling regulations designed so that only your product qualifies.

3. React aggressively when a new entrant is in the promotion stage, especially with wholesalers and retailers, thereby denying them reliable information about their new product's steady-state profitability.

4. Keep products or processes secret as long as possible.

5. Make preemptive purchases of all available raw materials or supplies.

6. Make early sales to critical buyers–opinion leaders.

7. Announce the product long before it is ready.

Smiley's study suggests that entry deterrence should be of more than theoretical interest to economists. In fact, fully 54 percent of respondents rated entry deterrence as "at least as important" as other strategic marketing and production decisions in the "grand scheme of things."[68]

One final point with regard to Smiley's study is worth noting. Modern industrial organization is sometimes criticized because different theoretical models that, appear to be quite similar on the surface yield dramatically different results. For example, compare the outcome in the basic Cournot quantity game with the outcome in the basic Bertrand price game in Chapter 8. The Smiley study provides evidence that in the real world firms use many different methods to deter entry, and at least two of these methods appear to be diametrically opposed: keeping products or processes secret as long as possible, and announcing the product long before it is ready. Both of these strategies were used by real-world firms to achieve the same end. Here is an example of an empirical survey supporting the proliferation of theory in industrial organization. In the real world slightly different circumstances result in very different strategies, and so it is in theory as well.

SUMMARY

1. Game theorists have concentrated on models that result in credible threats of retaliation. These models suggest that there are several ways of credibly deterring entry, including predatory pricing, the building of excess capacity, raising rivals' costs, product proliferation, and first-mover advantages associated with the learning curve.

2. Excess capacity can create a credible entry deterrent, but it may result in large profit sacrifices for the incumbent.

3. A number of methods of raising rivals' costs have been suggested. One is to lobby the government to impose an increase in costs. Others include increasing advertising to force competitors to advertise more, providing complementary goods and services, and sabotaging competitors.

4. If learning by doing is important, early entrants into the market may be able to maintain a large market share and increase their present value of profits by strategically producing significantly larger outputs early on than would be justified by short-run profit-maximizing behavior.

5. By filling many different niches in the market, incumbents may be able to prevent potential entrants from gaining even a small foothold in an industry. This practice is called *product proliferation.*

6. Empirical evidence suggests that firms use many different types of entry deterrence strategies. The most common strategies appear to be heavy advertising, product proliferation, and investment in research and development. Far fewer firms use limit pricing or the building of excess capacity.

KEY TERMS

excess capacity

first-mover advantage

learning by doing

location game

product proliferation

raising rivals' costs

uniform density

DISCUSSION QUESTIONS

1. As a firm's discount rate *increases,* is it more or less likely to build excess capacity to deter entry? Explain.

2. The Federal Aviation Administration (FAA) sets safety standards for commercial airlines in the United States. Would you expect the most profitable carriers, such as Southwest and Jet Blue, to fight the FAA's attempts to require costly additional safety features on commercial aircraft? Explain your reasoning.

3. Can you identify a case of learning by doing in your life experience? Was the speed of learning slow or fast?

4. Identify three markets in which product proliferation appears to be important. Would you categorize concentration in these markets as low, moderate, or high? What does this suggest about the effect of product proliferation?

5. Sometimes a dominant firm fails to fill an important niche in an industry before a competitor does. Can you identify a dominant firm that lost considerable market share because it failed to fill an important market niche?

6. Based on Smiley's findings, which strategies appear to be most commonly used by firms to deter entry? What strategies are least com-

monly employed? A [obscured] with the theory [obscured] and this chapter?

7. A recent perusal [obscured] found a minimum [obscured] bonated beverages [obscured] (not to mention b[obscured] products etc.). On [obscured] Cola announced i[obscured] which was intro[obscured] The press release [obscured] ture a new tropic [obscured] of Sprite and will [obscured] graphic treatme[obscured] logo." Sprite Rer[obscured] the incredible [obscured] Mist. Discuss th[obscured] depicted in this [obscured]

8. Economists have theorized that firms in technologically advanced industries like pharmaceuticals and computers might engage in so-called "patent races" to beat their competitors to patents. Using the information from this chapter, how might you explain the rationale behind patent races?

9. In his book *Freakonomics* Steven Levitt showed that in the 1980s a street-level crack cocaine dealer who worked for four years had about a 25 percent probability of being murdered by another drug dealer. What impact would this statistic have on the crack-cocaine market? Using the information from this chapter, how might you explain Levitt's finding?

10. Suppose a monopolist sells in two periods in a market where learning by doing is important.

[obscured] the monopolist's profit-maximizing price [obscured] be greater than, less than, [obscured] e in the second period? [obscured] oning. Can you think of a [obscured] y where learning by doing [obscured] this result?

11. [obscured] by doing by one firm has positive "spillover effects" on competitive firms, that is, one firm's cumulative experience is quickly acquired and transferred to other firms with [obscured] umulative experience. What impact might [obscured] hese spillover effects have on the competitive [obscured] equilibrium in an industry?

12. Over the past [obscured] 0 years, there has been a con[obscured] of franchise expansion in the [obscured] fessional sports leagues (base[obscured], football, and hockey) in the [obscured] For example, in Major League baseball [obscured] were only 16 teams in 1960, but there are now 30. In the National Football League there were only 12 teams in 1960, now there are 32. Can you suggest a strategic economic explanation for this significant franchise expansion? (Hint: What would happen if these leagues did not expand?)

For those who read the appendix, answer the following questions:

13. What is the information structure in the product proliferation game?

14. In the product proliferation game, if the demand for all types of cereals continued to increase, would you expect that eventually the incumbent would produce little sweetness, medium sweetness, and great sweetness corn flakes? Why?

PROBLEMS

1. Consider the extensive form of a game of entry on the next page. The numbers in parentheses represent the potential entrant's profits and the dominant firm's profits, respectively.
 a. What is the current solution to this game?
 b. Suppose the dominant firm knows that for every dollar it spends on net advertising costs, an entrant would have to spend 2 dollars to maintain its relative market position. How much would the incumbent have to spend on advertising to prevent entry? What would be the solution to this new game?

2. Suppose q represents cumulative firm output and λ is a positive constant measuring the speed of learning. Long-run average costs are:

$$LRAC(q) = 50 + \frac{100}{10^{\lambda q}}.$$

 a. If λ = 0, what would be the long-run equilibrium price in this industry?
 b. If λ = ∞, what would be the long-run equilibrium price in this industry?
 c. Would you anticipate that there would be more firms in this industry if λ = 0 or if λ = 1? Explain.

3. Consider a monopolist with the following demand curve: P = 210 − Q. Assume the fixed costs of the monopolist are equal to 0 ($FC_M = 0$) because the monopolist has been in business so long. The monopolist has a constant $MC_M = 30$ for levels of output ≤ 90. If $q_M > 90$, MC_M is infinite.
 a. Solve for the profit-maximizing level of output, price, and profit for the monopolist.
 b. Suppose a potential entrant has an option to enter the market for a sunk cost of $3000. If it enters, the potential entrant's $MC_{PE} = 30$ for output ≤ 45 units. If $q_{PE} > 45$, MC_{PE} is infinite. If the entrant does enter, it produces $q_{PE} = 45$. Assuming that the monopolist accommodates entry, solve for the output and profits to the monopolist and the potential entrant.
 c. Suppose the monopolist has the option to increase its capacity up to a maximum of 135 units and lower its marginal cost to 25 (infinity after $q_M = 135$) for a sunk cost of $1600. If the monopolist chooses to make this investment and then accommodates entry of the potential entrant with $q_{PE} = 45$, solve for the output, price, and profits to the monopolist and the potential entrant.
 d. Assume the entrant chooses not to enter, but the monopolist spends the $1600 to expand as described in part c. Solve for the monopolist's output and profit.
 e. Consider the game just described. Construct a game tree depicting this situation. What is the Nash equilibrium of the game?

4. Consider a monopolist with the following demand curve: P = 140 − 2Q. Assume the fixed costs of the monopolist are equal to 0 ($FC_M = 0$) because the monopolist has been in business so long. The monopolist has a constant $MC_M = 20$ for levels of output ≤ 30. If $q_M > 30$, MC_M is infinite.

a. Solve for the profit-maximizing level of output, price, and profit for the monopolist.

b. Suppose a potential entrant has an option to enter the market for a sunk cost of $775. If it enters, the potential entrant's $MC_{PE} = 20$ for output ≤ 15 units. If $q_{PE} > 15$, MC_{PE} is infinite. If the entrant does enter, it produces $q_{PE} = 15$. Assuming that the monopolist accommodates entry, solve for the output and profits to the monopolist and the potential entrant.

c. Suppose the monopolist has the option to increase its capacity up to a maximum of 45 units and lower its marginal cost to 15 (infinity after $q_M = 45$) for a sunk cost of $400. If the monopolist chooses to make this investment and then accommodates entry of the potential entrant with $q_{PE} = 15$, solve for the output, price, and profits to the monopolist and the potential entrant.

d. Assume the entrant chooses not to enter, but the monopolist spends the $400 to expand as described in part c. Solve for the monopolist's output and profit.

e. Consider the game just described. Construct a game tree depicting this situation. What is the Nash equilibrium of the game?

5. Suppose in a two-period model Firm 1 is a monopolist in the first period and prices to maximize monopoly profits. In period 2 an entrant, Firm 2, is going to enter this market. Industry demand equals $P = 10 - Q$ or $P = 10 - q_1 - q_2$, where q_1 and q_2 represent Firm 1's and Firm 2's outputs, respectively. In period 1 (the monopoly period), the monopolist's total cost function is $TC = 4q_{11}$, so $MC = 4$. Here q_{11} represents Firm 1's output in period 1. In the second period, the monopolist's total cost function is $TC = (4 - \frac{1}{2}q_{11})q_{12}$, where q_{12} represents Firm 1's output in period 2. Firm 2's total cost function is $TC = TC = 4q_{22}$, where q_{22} represents Firm 2's output in period 2.

a. If the monopolist ignores the entry that is about to take place in period 2, what is Firm 1's monopoly output, price, and profit in period 1?

b. If the monopolist produces the output you found in part a in period 1, what is the Cournot-Nash equilibrium in period 2? Calculate the monopolist's total profits in the two periods. For simplicity, assume a discount rate equal to zero.

c. Now suppose the monopolist produces one more unit of output in period 1, that is, the monopolist in period 1 produces $(q_{11} + 1)$ units. Calculate the new Cournot-Nash equilibrium in period 2. Once again assume a zero discount rate. What are the monopolist's total profits in periods 1 and 2? Is the monopolist better or worse off than in part b? What lesson can you learn about learning by doing from this simple problem?

For those who read the appendix, answer the following question:

6. (You will need a calculator for this problem.) Consider the model of product proliferation presented in the appendix. If the fixed costs of producing sickeningly sweet corn flakes were 225 instead of 75, would product proliferation still be a rational strategy? If so, would the monopolist enter the sickeningly sweet market earlier, later, or at the same time as that depicted in Figure 12.7?

NOTES

1. For an early treatment see John T. Wenders, "Excess Capacity as a Barrier to Entry," *Journal of Industrial Economics* 20 (November 1971): 14–19; John T. Wenders, "Collusion and Entry," *Journal of Political Economy* 79 (Nov./Dec. 1971): 1258–1277. For later treatments see A. Michael Spence, "Entry Capacity, Investment and Oligopoly Pricing," *Bell Journal of Economics* 8 (Autumn 1977): 534–544; Avinash Dixit, "A Model of Duopoly Suggesting a Theory of Entry Barriers," *Bell Journal of Economics* 10 (Spring 1979): 20–32; Jeremy Bulow, John Geanakoplos, and Paul Klemperer, "Holding Idle Capacity to Deter Entry," *Economic Journal* 95 (March 1985): 178–182; Marius Schwartz and Michael Baumann, "Entry-Deterrence Externalities and Relative Firm Size," *International Journal of Industrial Organization* 6 (June 1988): 181–197; David I. Rosenbaum, "An Empirical Test of the Effect of Excess Capacity in Price Setting, Capacity-Constrained Supergames," *International Journal of Industrial Organization* 7 (June 1989): 231–241; Pankaj Ghemawat, "The Snowball Effect," *International Journal of Industrial Organization* 8 (September 1990): 335–351; Elizabeth A. Hall, "An Analysis of Preemptive Behavior in the Titanium Dioxide Industry," *International Journal of Industrial Organization* 8 (September 1990): 469–484; and Beth Allen, "Capacity Precommitment as an Entry Barrier for Price-Setting Firms," *International Journal of Industrial Organization* 11 (March 1993): 63–72. For conclusions that run against conventional wisdom see Jean-Pierre Benoît and Vijay Krishna, "Entry Deterrence and Dynamic Competition," *International Journal of Industrial Organization* 9 (December 1991): 477–495; and A.M. McGahan, "The Effect of Incomplete Information about Demand on Preemption," *International Journal of Industrial Organization* 11 (September 1993): 327–346.

2. The seminal article on the strategic use of research and development is James Brander and Barbara Spencer, "Strategic Commitment with R&D: The Symmetric Case," *Bell Journal of Economics* 14, no. 1 (Spring 1983) 225–235. For good surveys of the early pathbreaking research see Wesley M. Cohen and Richard C. Levin, "Innovation and Market Structure," in Richard Schmalensee and Robert D. Willig, eds., *Handbook of Industrial Organization,* vol. 2. (Amsterdam: North-Holland, 1989), pp. 1059–1107; and Jennifer F. Reinganum, "The Timing of Innovation: Research and Development, and Diffusion," in Richard Schmalensee and Robert D. Willig, eds., *Handbook of Industrial Orga-*

nization, vol. 2. (Amsterdam: North-Holland, 1989), pp. 849–905.

3. *United States* v. *Aluminum Company of America,* 148 F.2d 416 (1945).

4. Elizabeth A. Hall "An Analysis of Preemptive Behavior in the Titanium Dioxide Industry," *International Journal of Industrial Organization* 8 (September 1990): 469–484.

5. *Ibid.,* p. 483.

6. D. West and B. Von Hohenbalken, "Empirical Tests for Predatory Reputation," *Canadian Journal of Economics* 19 (February 1986): 162.

7. *Ibid.,* p. 172.

8. *Ibid.,* p. 175.

9. See Thomas G. Krattenmaker and Steven C. Salop, "Anticompetitive Exclusion: Raising Rivals' Costs to Achieve Power Over Price," *Yale Law Journal* 96 (1986): 209–293; Steven C. Salop and David T. Scheffman, "Cost-Raising Strategies," *Journal of Industrial Economics* 36 (1987): 19–34; Scott M. Fuess, Jr., and Mark A. Lowenstein, "On Strategic Cost Increases in a Duopoly," *International Journal of Industrial Organization* 9 (June 1991): 389–395.

10. For an example taken from the United States margarine market see John Sutton, *Sunk Costs and Market Structure: Price Competition Advertising, and the Evolution of Concentration* (Cambridge, MA: MIT Press, 1991) pp. 213–214.

11. John Cubbin, "Advertising and the Theory of Entry Barriers," *Economica* 48 (April 1981): 289–298; Richard Schmalensee, "Product Differentiation Advantages of Pioneering Brands," *American Economic Review* 72 (June 1982): 349–365; and A. Michael Spence, "Notes on Advertising, Economies of Scale, and Entry Barriers," *Quarterly Journal of Economics* 56 (November 1980): 472–475.

12. Sutton, *supra,* note 10.

13. *Ibid.,* pp. 207–209.

14. *Ibid.,* p. 209.

15. *Ibid.,* p. 210.

16. The market shares in this section are taken from Sutton, *ibid.,* p. 220.

17. Lawrence J. White, "Applications of the Merger Guidelines: The Proposed Merger of Coca-Cola and Dr. Pepper," in John E. Kwoka Jr. and Lawrence J. White (eds.), *The Antitrust Revolution* (Glenview, IL: Scott, Foresman and Company, 1989), p. 82.

18. See "Battery Makers See Surge in Competition," *The Wall Street Journal* (November 30, 1987): 8; and *The Wall Street Journal* (April 10, 1990): B1 and B5.

19. Nicholas Economides, "Raising Rivals' Costs in Complementary Goods Markets: LEC's Entering

into Long Distance and Microsoft Bundling Internet Explorer." Paper presented at TPRC conference, October 1997, 1–26, p. 17. For more information go to http://raven.stern.nyu.edu/networks/ms/top.html.

20. *Ibid.*, p. 17.
21. Paul Festa, "Opera Cries Foul Against MSN—again," news.com.com/Opera+cries+foul+against+MSN—again/2100–1023_3–983500.html.
22. Opera Press Releases, "Opera Releases 'Bork' edition, The Swedish Chef Goes After Microsoft," opera.com/pressreleases/en/2003/02/14/.
23. *Ibid.*
24. Martyn Gregory, *Dirty Tricks: British Airways' Secret War against Virgin Atlantic* (London: Virgin Books, 2000); and Paula Dwyer, "British Air: Not Cricket," *Business Week*, January 25, 1993.
25. For explanations of the theory see Jack Hirshleifer, "The Firm's Cost Function: A Successful Reconstruction?" *Journal of Business* 35 (July 1962): 235–255; Kenneth J. Arrow, "The Economic Implications of Learning by Doing," *Review of Economic Studies* 29 (April 1962): 155–173; L.E. Preston and E.C. Keachie, "Cost Functions and Progress Functions: An Integration," *American Economic Review* 54 (March 1964): 100–106; Sherwin Rosen, "Learning by Experience as Joint Production," *Quarterly Journal of Economics* 86 (August 1972): 366–382; Karl F. Habermeier, "The Learning Curve and Competition: A Stochastic Model of Duopolistic Rivalry," *International Journal of Industrial Organization* 10 (September 1992): 369–392; and Clement G. Krouse, "Market Rivalry and Learning-by-Doing," *International Journal of Industrial Organization* 12 (December 1994): 437–456.
26. A. Michael Spence, "The Learning Curve and Competition," *Bell Journal of Economics* 12 (Spring 1981): 62.
27. Frank J. Andress, "The Learning Curve as a Production Tool," *Harvard Business Review* 32 (Jan./Feb. 1954): 87–88.
28. David C. Mowery and Nathan Rosenberg, "The Commercial Aircraft Industry," in Richard R. Nelson (ed.), *Government and Technical Progress: A Cross-Industry Analysis* (New York: Pergamon Press, 1982), pp. 109–113.
29. *Ibid.*, p. 113.
30. *Ibid.*
31. William J. Abernathy and Kenneth Wayne, "Limits of the Learning Curve," *Harvard Business Review* 52 (Sept./Oct. 1974): 112.
32. Lawrence J. White, "The Automobile Industry," in Walter Adams (ed.), *The Structure of American Industry* (New York: MacMillan, 1977), p. 173.

33. William J. Abernathy and Kenneth Wayne, *op.cit.*, p. 113.
34. *Ibid.*
35. *Ibid.*, p. 114.
36. "New Leaders in Semiconductors," *Business Week* (March 1, 1976): 43.
37. "The Complexities of Electronics Pricing," *Business Week* (April 6, 1974): 44–45.
38. Harold Gruber, "Learning by Doing and Spillovers: Further Evidence for the Semiconductor Industry," *Review of Industrial Organization* 13 (1998): 697–711; D.W. Webbink, *The Semiconductor Industry: A Survey of Structure, Conduct, and Performance.* Staff Report to the FTC (Washington: U.S. Government Printing Office, 1977); and A.R. Dick, "Learning by Doing and Dumping in the Semiconductor Industry," *Journal of Law & Economics* 34 (1991): 133–159.
39. Ricardo Cabral and Michael J. Leiblein, "Adoption of a Process Innovation with Learning-by-doing: Evidence from the Semiconductor Industry," *Journal of Industrial Economics* 49, no. 3 (September 2001): 269–280.
40. *Ibid.*, p. 277.
41. See Richard Schmalensee, "Entry Deterrence in the Ready-to-Eat Breakfast Cereal Industry," *Bell Journal of Economics* 9 (1978): 305–327; Bruce L. Benson, "Increasing Product Variety and Rising Prices," *Review of Industrial Organization* 5 (1990): 31–52; Chong Ju Choi and Carlo Scarpa, "Credible Spatial Preemption Through Reputation Extension," *International Journal of Industrial Organization* 10 (September 1992): 439–447; and Ruth S. Raubitschek, "Hitting the Jackpot: Product Proliferation by Multiproduct Firms Under Uncertainty," *International Journal of Industrial Organization* 6 (December 1988): 469–488.
42. *Federal Trade Commission v. Kellogg et al.,* Docket No. 8883, 99 FTC Reporter 8 (1982) §581.
43. *Ibid.*
44. *Ibid.*
45. *Federal Trade Commission v. Kellogg et al.,* Docket No. 8883, 99 FTC Reporter 8 (1982), §582; and F.M. Scherer, "The Breakfast Cereal Industry," in Walter Adams (ed.), *The Structure of American Industry,* 7th edition (New York: MacMillan, 1986), p. 178.
46. *Federal Trade Commission v. Kellogg et al.,* Docket No. 8883, 99 FTC Reporter 8 (1982), §585.
47. F.M. Scherer, "The Breakfast Cereal Industry," in Walter Adams, *The Structure of American Industry,* 7th edition (New York: MacMillan, 1986), pp. 181–182.
48. *Ibid.*, p. 182.
49. *Ibid.*
50. Sutton, *supra* note 10, pp. 235–236.

51. F.M. Scherer, *supra* note 39, p. 176.

52. Sutton, *supra* note 10, Chapter 10, pp. 227–247.

53. "Marketing's New Look: Campbell Leads a Revolution in the Way Consumer Products Are Sold," *Business Week* (January 26, 1987): 64–69.

54. *Ibid.*, p. 64.

55. *Ibid.*, p. 67.

56. John M. Connor, "Food Product Proliferation: A Market Structure Analysis," *American Journal of Agricultural Economics* 63 (November 1981): 607–617.

57. *Ibid.*, p. 613.

58. *Ibid.*

59. *Ibid.*, p. 615.

60. William P. Putsis Jr., "An Empirical Study of the Effect of Brand Proliferation on Private Label–National Brand Pricing Behavior," *Review of Industrial Organization* 12, no. 3 (June 1997): 335–354.

61. *Ibid.*, pp. 361 and 367.

62. *Ibid.*, p. 368.

63. Robert Smiley, "Empirical Evidence on Strategic Entry Deterrence," *International Journal of Industrial Organization* 6 (1980): 170.

64. Note in Table 12.7 that "hiding profits" was cited by many respondents as an entry-deterring strategy. For an explanation of this strategy see Nils-Henrik Mørch von der Fehr, "How Entry Threats Induce Slack," *International Journal of Industrial Organization* 10 (June 1992): 231–249.

65. Smiley, *supra* note 63, p. 174.

66. *Ibid.*, p. 174.

67. *Ibid.*, pp. 174–175.

68. *Ibid.*, p.177.

INTERNET EXERCISES

Visit www.aw-bc.com/waldman_jensen for this chapter's web exercises. Answer our real-world economics problems by searching the Internet for solutions!

Appendix

Product Proliferation Revisited

The game theoretic analysis of **product proliferation** can become complicated, but it is possible to present the basic model in a fairly simple framework.* The product proliferation game is often presented as a **location game,** in which firms choose between different locations for their plants.† In fact, we can begin by returning briefly to the first game presented in Chapter 7—the ice cream truck game. Recall that the solution to the ice cream truck game was for both firms to locate in the middle of the parade route. Now consider a similar example.

The product proliferation game is one of common knowledge with perfect, certain, symmetric, and complete information. In Figure 12.5, suppose that a monopolist produces only corn flakes with no sugar but that consumers are spread out with **uniform density** over the five preferences in Figure 12.5. *Uniform density* simply means that consumers are equally spaced over the preferences. Suppose there are 10 consumers: Two consumers prefer unsweetened corn flakes, two consumers prefer a little sweetness, two consumers prefer medium sweetness, two consumers prefer great

*The following analysis is based on Jean Tirole, *The Theory of Industrial Organization* (Cambridge, MA: MIT Press, 1988), pp. 346–349.

†The seminal paper was by Harold Hotelling, "Stability in Competition," *Economic Journal* 39 (March 1929): 41–57. See also Donald A. Hay, "Sequential Entry and Entry-Deterring Strategies in Spatial Competition," *Oxford Economic Papers* (July 1976): 240–257.

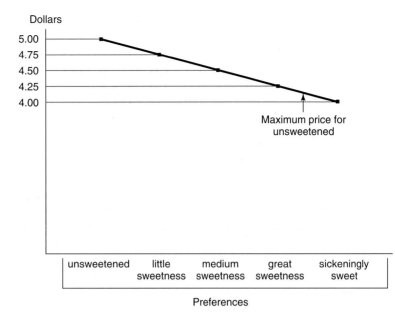

FIGURE 12.5 Maximum Price for a Box of Unsweetened Corn Flakes for a Consumer Preferring Unsweetened Corn Flakes

If the monopolist produces only unsweetened corn flakes and consumers are spread out with uniform density over the following five preferences (unsweetened corn flakes, little sweetness, medium sweetness, great sweetness, and sickeningly sweet), the figure shows the maximum price each type of consumer will pay for a box of unsweetened corn flakes. A consumer preferring unsweetened corn flakes is willing to pay $5.00 for a box of unsweetened corn flakes, but a consumer preferring sickeningly sweet corn flakes will only pay $4.00 for a box of unsweetened corn flakes.

sweetness, and two consumers prefer sickeningly sweet corn flakes.* For a perfectly sweet box of cereal, each consumer will pay a price of $5. But for *each* step away from perfection, the maximum price the consumer is willing to pay declines by $0.25. Figure 12.5 shows the maximum price that each consumer would be willing to pay for a box of unsweetened corn flakes. In Figure 12.5, the consumer located at sickeningly sweet will pay only $4.00 for an unsweetened box, and the consumer in the middle would pay $4.50 for a box.

Suppose that at time t = 1, a monopolist, hypothetically called the Big K Corporation, produces only unsweetened corn flakes at a marginal cost of $1.00 per box (MC = $1.00). For simplification, further assume that the only alternative to producing unsweetened corn flakes is to produce sickeningly sweet corn flakes, also at MC = $1.00, and that at any moment another plant can be built to produce only sickeningly sweet corn flakes at a fixed cost of $75.00.

Consider the profit possibilities for monopolist Big K. If it continues to produce only unsweetened corn flakes, and maximizes profits by selling one box to each

*If six of the 10 consumers preferred medium sweetness and only one consumer preferred each of the other four alternatives, then consumers would be spread out with *nonuniform density* over the five preferences.

consumer at its profit-maximizing price of $4.00, its flow of profits, ignoring fixed costs, in each period would be:*

$$\pi_{un} = PQ - Q(MC) = \$4.00(10) - 10(\$1.00) = \$30.00,$$

where π_{un} represents Big K's profit if it produces only unsweetened corn flakes. If Big K's discount rate is 10 percent, and assuming constant demand, Big K's present value of profits is:

$$\pi_{pv}^{un} = \frac{\$30.00}{0.10} = \$300.00.$$

Now suppose that at t = 1, Big K builds a second plant to produce sickeningly sweet corn flakes at a fixed cost of $75.00. Because of product differentiation, its new profit-maximizing price will increase to $4.50.[†] Four consumers, those preferring no sweetness and a little sweetness, will buy unsweetened corn flakes. Four consumers, those preferring great sweetness and sickeningly sweet, will buy sickeningly sweet corn flakes. And two consumers, those preferring medium sweetness, will be indifferent between the two types at a price of $4.50. Assume that the two consumers preferring medium sweetness divide randomly, with one buying unsweetened and the other buying sickeningly sweet corn flakes. Big K will then sell one box to each of the 10 consumers, and in each period its flow of profits, again ignoring fixed costs, would be:

$$\pi_{unss} = \$4.50(10) - 10(\$1.00) = \$35.00,$$

where π_{unss} represents Big K's profits if it produces both types of corn flakes. Assuming again a discount rate of 10 percent and constant demand, and recognizing the fixed cost of $75.00 to build the second plant, Big K's present value of profits with two plants would be:

$$\pi_{pv}^{unss} = \frac{\$35.00}{0.10} - \frac{\$75}{1.1} = \$350.00 - \$68.18 = \$281.82.$$

If there is no threat of entry, Big K maximizes its present value of profits by producing *only* unsweetened corn flakes because $\pi_{pv}^{un} = \$300.00 > \$281.82 = \pi_{pv}^{unss}$.

*Big K's profit-maximizing price is $4.00 because the marginal revenue curve is as follows:

Quantity	Price	Marginal Revenue
2	$5.00	—
4	$4.75	$4.50
6	$4.50	$4.00
8	$4.25	$3.50
10	$4.00	$3.00

Because the marginal cost is $1.00 per box, profit maximization requires expanding output to 10 units and selling all units at the same price of $4.00.

[†]A price of $4.50 now maximizes profits because any price above $4.50 would prevent the medium sweetness consumers from buying corn flakes, whereas a price below $4.50 would not increase total sales. The demand curve for both types of corn flakes is:

Quantity	Price	Marginal Revenue
4	$5.00	—
8	$4.75	$4.50
10	$4.50	$3.50

Because marginal revenue is above marginal cost of $1.00 per box, Big K should set the price at $4.50 and produce 10 boxes of corn flakes.

Given this monopoly market, is there a current threat of entry? Consider the options for a potential entrant, hypothetically called Big G Corporation. Big G can build a plant for $75.00 to produce sickeningly sweet corn flakes with MC = $1.00 and compete with Big K. Suppose that if Big G produces sickeningly sweet corn flakes, Big K and Big G compete through price and product differentiation. Figure 12.6 shows the maximum price each consumer would be willing to pay for each type of corn flakes. The little sweetness consumers would pay a maximum of $4.75 for unsweetened but only $4.25 for sickeningly sweet corn flakes. The little sweetness consumers therefore would be willing to pay a premium of $0.50 a box for unsweetened corn flakes compared with sickeningly sweet cornflakes.

If Big G enters, assume that Big K and Big G play a Bertrand game with product differentiation.* Given symmetry, in equilibrium both firms must charge the same price and neither firm has an incentive to change price given the choice of its competitor. In equilibrium, therefore, Big K and Big G would split the demand and each would sell five boxes of cereal. To solve for the equilibrium price, we make one additional assumption: The minimum possible price increase or decrease is assumed to equal $0.25. This is consistent with the demand curve depicted in Figure 12.5.

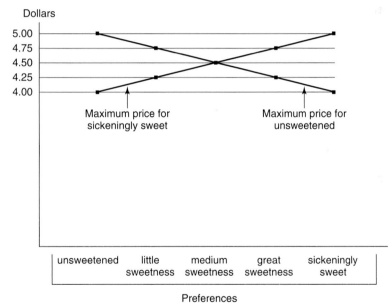

FIGURE 12.6 **Maximum Price for a Box of Corn Flakes by Consumer Preferences and Sweetness of Cereal**

If Big K produces only two types of corn flakes, unsweetened and sickeningly sweet, the figure shows the maximum price each type of consumer will pay for each type of corn flakes. A consumer preferring unsweetened corn flakes is willing to pay $5.00 for a box of unsweetened corn flakes and a consumer preferring sickeningly sweet corn flakes will pay $5.00 for a box of sickeningly sweet corn flakes. Notice that consumers preferring medium sweet corn flakes would be willing to pay $4.50 for a box of either unsweetened or sickeningly sweet corn flakes.

*This game is analyzed in Chapter 13.

Let p be the equilibrium price. In equilibrium the firms are better off selling five units rather than increasing price by $0.25 and selling four units, or decreasing price by $0.25 and selling six units. Mathematically, the following conditions must hold:

$$[(p - \$0.25) - MC]6 < (p - mc)5 \quad \text{and} \quad [(p + \$0.25) - mc]4 < (p - mc)5.$$

If both of these conditions are met, the firms would be worse off if they either increased or decreased price by $0.25. For MC = $1, the two inequalities are solved for $2 < p < \$2.5$. Therefore, p = $2.25 is the equilibrium price because this price leaves the firms indifferent between maintaining price and either increasing price or decreasing price by $0.25.

If Big G enters at t = 1 and price declines to $2.25, Big G's flow of profits will be:

$$\pi_G = PQ - Q(MC) = \$2.25(5) - 5(\$1.00) = \$6.25.$$

With constant demand, fixed costs of $75.00, and a 10 percent discount rate, Big G's present value of profits would be:

$$\pi_{pv}^G = \frac{\$6.25}{0.10} - \frac{\$75}{1.1} = \$62.50 - \$68.18 = -\$5.68 < 0.$$

Because Big G's present value of profits is negative, it would *not* enter. Big K would remain a monopolist and produce only unsweetened corn flakes; its present value of profits would be $300.00.

Now relax one assumption. Suppose that at time T_{3d} the density of the demand function suddenly triples, so that there are exactly six consumers of every type instead of two. To simplify the discussion, we will define the time T_{3d} as t = 1. This implies that the present period is t < 1. To simplify further, suppose that this is the only time that demand will ever increase. If the demand density triples and Big G produces sickeningly sweet corn flakes at t = T_{3d} = 1, its flow of profits after T_{3d} would exactly triple to:

$$\pi_{G3d} = PQ - Q(MC) = \$2.25(15) - 15(\$1.00) = \$33.75 - \$15.00 = \$18.75.$$

With a 10 percent discount rate, Big G's present value of profits would be:

$$\pi_{pv}^{G3d} = \frac{\$18.75}{0.10} - \frac{\$75}{1.1} = \$187.50 - \$68.18 = \$119.32. \qquad [A1]$$

Entry is now profitable. In the absence of any strategic move by Big K, Big G would enter at time t = T_{3d} = 1, earn present value profits equal to $119.32, and split the market with Big K. As noted previously, Big G's entry would reduce price to $2.25, so that Big K's profits would also decline to a flow of $18.75 (3 × $6.25) per period.

Can Big K do anything to prevent such an outcome? Consider the following strategic move: Big K could preempt Big G by moving to produce sickeningly sweet corn flakes first.* If Big G has not entered at t = 1, consider Big K's options at that time when demand triples. At time t = T_{3d} = 1, Big K could either continue to produce only unsweetened corn flakes or produce both types. If Big K is still a monopolist, its new profit flows if demand density tripled would also triple to:

*See Jean Tirole, *The Theory of Industrial Organization* (Cambridge, MA: MIT Press, 1988), pp. 346–349.

$$\pi_{un} = \$90.00 \quad \text{and} \quad \pi_{unss} = \$105.00.$$

The present value of Big K's profits if Big K produced only unsweetened corn flakes beginning at time $t = t_0 < 1$ would become:

$$\pi_{pv}^{un} = \sum_{t=t_0}^{0} \frac{\$30}{(1.1)^t} + \sum_{t=1}^{\infty} \frac{\$90}{(1.1)^t}. \qquad [A2]$$

If Big K entered the sickeningly sweet corn flakes market at time $t = T_{3d} = 1$ and produced both types of corn flakes, the present value of Big K's profits would be:*

$$\pi_{pv}^{unss} = \sum_{t=t_0}^{0} \frac{\$30.00}{(1.1)^t} + \sum_{t=1}^{\infty} \frac{\$105.00}{(1.1)^t} - \frac{\$75.00}{(1.1)^1}. \qquad [A3]$$

Because the first terms in Equations A2 and A3 are identical, to compare the two equations, it is necessary to compare only the last term in A2 with the last two terms in A3, which yields the following:

$$\sum_{t=1}^{\infty} \frac{\$105}{(1.1)^t} - \frac{\$75}{(1.1)^1} = \$1050 - \$68.18 = \$981.82 > \sum_{t=1}^{\infty} \frac{\$90}{(1.1)^t} = \$900.$$

Therefore, $\pi_{unss}^{pv} > \pi_{un}^{pv}$, and it now makes sense for Big K to produce *both* types of corn flakes.

Now the game becomes interesting. In the absence of entry by the other firm, each firm would choose to produce sickeningly sweet corn flakes at $t = T_{3d} = 1$. However, once one firm produces sickeningly sweet corn flakes, the other firm has no incentive to produce them because if both produced sickeningly sweet corn flakes, Bertrand competition with a homogeneous product would drive price to marginal cost of $1.00 for consumers with preferences at medium sweetness, great sweetness, and sickeningly sweet, and the second firm to enter would not recover its fixed costs. In other words, there is room for only one profitable producer of sickeningly sweet corn flakes, and the first firm in will prevent the other firm from entering.

The key to solving the "who will enter when" game is to recognize that there *must* exist some time $t < 1 = T_{3d}$ at which the potential entrant is indifferent between entering and not entering the market for sickeningly sweet corn flakes. If $t_G < 1$ is the time of Big G's entry into the sickeningly sweet corn flakes market, then the present value of profits for Big G is given by:

$$\pi_{pv}^{G} = \sum_{t=t_G}^{0} \frac{\$6.25}{(1.1)^t} + \sum_{t=1}^{\infty} \frac{\$18.75}{(1.1)^t} - \frac{\$75.00}{(1.1)^{t_G}}$$

$$= \sum_{t=t_G}^{0} \frac{\$6.25}{(1.1)^t} + \$187.50 - \frac{\$75.00}{(1.1)^{t_G}}.$$

*The first term on the right-hand side of Equation A3 represents Big K's profits if it produces only unsweetened corn flakes beginning at time $t = t_0$ before demand triples. The second and third terms represent Big K's profits if it enters the sickeningly sweet market at time $t = 1$ when demand triples.

On a computer a straightforward calculation shows that for $t_G = -31$, $\pi_G^{pv} = \$5.03$; for $t_G = -32$, $\pi_G^{pv} = -\$6.96$.*

In Figure 12.7, the present values of profits associated with Big G's entry at any time t are identified as curve π_{pv}^G. Notice that at some critical time $t^* < 1$, $\pi_{pv}^G = 0$, and Big G is indifferent between entering and not entering.

Figure 12.7 identifies two other curves. These curves represent Big K's possible present values of profits. The higher curve, π_{KF}, represents Big K's profits if it enters the market for sickeningly sweet corn flakes first; the lower curve, π_{KNE}, represents Big K's profits if Big G enters the sickeningly sweet corn flakes market first, in which case Big K does *not* enter the sickeningly sweet market. The present value of Big K's profits if it enters the sickeningly sweet market first at $t = t_K$ is given by:[†]

$$\pi_{KF} = \sum_{t=t_{un}}^{t_K-1} \frac{\$30.00}{(1.1)^t} + \sum_{t=t_K}^{0} \frac{\$35.00}{(1.1)^t} + \sum_{t=1}^{\infty} \frac{\$105.00}{(1.1)^t} - \frac{\$75.00}{(1.1)^{t_K}}, \qquad [A4]$$

where t_{un} represents the time at which Big K entered the unsweetened corn flakes market. If Big G enters the sickeningly sweet market first at $t = t_K$, Big K stays out of the sickeningly sweet market, and Big K's profits are given by:

$$\pi_{KNE} = \sum_{t=t_{un}}^{t_K-1} \frac{\$30.00}{(1.1)^t} + \sum_{t=t_K}^{0} \frac{\$6.25}{(1.1)^t} + \sum_{t=1}^{\infty} \frac{\$18.75}{(1.1)^t}. \qquad [A5]$$

Comparing the right-hand sides of Equations A4 and A5, notice that for *any given time of entry* t_K, the first terms are equal, but the second and third terms are much larger in Equation A4 than in Equation A5. Therefore, unless the negative fourth term (which represents the discounted fixed costs of entering the sickeningly sweet market) in Equation A4 is very large, $\pi_{KF} > \pi_{KNE}$. This implies that in virtually all circumstances, Big K will prefer entering the sickeningly sweet corn flakes market first.

Given the curves in Figure 12.7, consider the game from Big G's standpoint. Big G knows that if it does not enter at $t = T_{3d} = 1$, Big K will. Therefore, Big G must try to preempt Big K by entering at some time earlier than $t = T_{3d} = 1$; let's call it $t = 1 - \epsilon$. Understanding this, Big K must try to preempt Big G by entering at some time earlier, perhaps $t = 1 - 2\epsilon$. Of course, the game regresses to the point at which Big K enters the market for sickeningly sweet corn flakes just infinitesimally before t^*. This is the only solution to the game. Big K enters before the increase in demand and in time to

*The calculations are as follows:

$$\pi_G = \sum_{t=t_G}^{0} \frac{\$6.25}{(1.1)^t} + \sum_{t=1}^{\infty} \frac{\$18.75}{(1.1)^t} - \frac{\$75}{(1.1)^{t_G}}$$

$$= \sum_{t=t_G}^{0} \frac{\$6.25}{(1.1)^t} + \$187.5 - \frac{\$75}{(1.1)^{t_G}};$$

for $t_G = -31$, $\pi_{pv}^G = \$1257.11 + \$187.5 - \$1439.58 = \5.03,

and for $t_G = -32$, $\pi_{pv}^G = \$1389.07 + \$187.5 - \$1583.53 = -\6.96.

Of course, similar calculations could be done for any value of t_G.

[†]The first term on the right-hand side of Equation A4 represents Big K's profits if it produces only unsweetened corn flakes beginning from time $t = t_{un}$ until time $t = t_K - 1$. The second and fourth terms represent Big K's profits if it produces *both* types of corn flakes from time $t = t_K$ until time $t = 0$. The third term represents Big K's profits if it continues to produce both types of corn flakes after demand triples at $t = 1$.

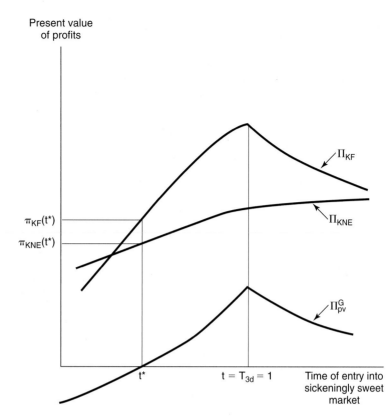

FIGURE 12.7 **Present Value of Big G's and Big K's Profits by Time of First Entry into Sickeningly Sweet Market**

The present values of profits associated with Big G's entry at any time t are identified by the curve Π_{pv}^{G}. At some critical time t* < 1, $\Pi_{pv}^{G} = 0$ and Big G is indifferent between entering and not entering. The curve Π_{KF} represents Big K's profits if it enters the market for sickeningly sweet corn flakes first and the curve Π_{KNE} represents Big K's profits if Big G enters the sickeningly sweet corn flakes market first. Big K's equilibrium is to enter at a time just before t = t*. In equilibrium, Big K's profits equal $\Pi_{KF}(t*)$ and are greater than the $\Pi_{KNE}(t*)$ profits Big K earns if Big G enters first at t = t*.

preempt Big G. In Figure 12.7, Big K's profits after entry will be $\pi_{KF}(t*)$, and Big G will be prevented from entering. Big K earns higher profits, $\pi_{KF}(t*)$, than if it allowed Big G to enter at t* and earned $\pi_{KNE}(t*)$. In this way Big K maintains its monopoly.

Product Differentiation and Advertising

Product differentiation and advertising have been recurring topics throughout this text. Recall that product differentiation and advertising are associated with possible advantages for incumbent firms. These advantages include increased economies of scale, possible cost advantages for incumbents, and an increase in the capital barrier to entry. Chapter 12 explored the theory of product proliferation and showed that incumbents might use product proliferation to strategically prevent entry. This chapter expands on our previous analysis and emphasizes the impact of product differentiation and advertising on economic welfare.

13.1 Forms of Product Differentiation

The objective of product differentiation is to increase profits by increasing demand and decreasing the price elasticity of demand. Sellers attempt to differentiate their products in many ways. Common forms of differentiation include location, service, physical characteristics, and subjective image differences.

Here is an example of location differentiation:[1] In Syracuse, New York, one cinnamon bun franchiser had two identical stands located in different malls. One stand was in an upscale mall and was usually busy. The other stand was located in a lower-quality mall and rarely seemed to be crowded. One franchise appeared to be a great success while the other floundered and went out of business. Such examples are common and support the adage that business success depends first and foremost on "location, location, location." Professional sports franchises are another good example of the importance of location. Franchises in big television markets are worth more than franchises in smaller markets.[2]

In addition to location, products are differentiated by service. Some firms offer high-quality service, usually at a high price. Others offer little or no service at low prices. If a consumer purchases a computer from a local computer store and something goes wrong, the dealer may send a representative to fix the problem. If a consumer purchases the same computer from a discount warehouse such as Sam's Club or BJ's and has a problem, she may be on her own with an 800 telephone number as her only source of help. Many consumers are willing to pay a price for better service.

Sears has dominated the market for major household appliances, not because the company sells better washers, dryers, and refrigerators, but because "Sears Services What It Sells." IBM's market power in computers from 1960 to 1985 was also built on the company's reputation for solving its customers' problems quickly and efficiently. Other examples of high-price, high-quality-of-service stores include Banana Republic, Williams-Sonoma, and Brookstones.

A third form of differentiation is based on physical characteristics. Water-based paints are different from oil-based paints. Wool suits are different from polyester suits. Fresh-squeezed orange juice is different from Hi-C fruit drink with 10 percent fruit juice. Because consumers value variety and because they have different tastes, it is not surprising that firms attempt to pry consumers away from their current products by offering physically differentiated products.

Finally, product differentiation is often based on efforts to create subjective image differences between products. A famous example is Clorox bleach. Clorox is fundamentally the same product as any other liquid bleach, yet Clorox has been able to create a premium image that has enabled it to consistently sell for higher prices than competitive products.[3] Cigarette advertising is infamous for attempting to create an image for a product that brings financial and sexual success when, in fact, all of the objective evidence suggests the contrary. McDonald's has long used Ronald McDonald to create an image as a great place to take young children, by ignoring the quality and price of the food and emphasizing the image of Ronald McDonald and toys in kids' meals.

Economists distinguish between two broad categories of product differentiation based on the attributes or characteristics of products: ***horizontal differentiation*** and ***vertical differentiation.*** *Horizontal differentiation* refers to differences between brands based on different product characteristics but not on different overall quality. Horizontal differentiation is common in the fast-food industry. A McDonald's Quarter Pounder is somewhat different from a Burger King Whopper or a Wendy's Single, but the overall quality of the three burgers is similar. By comparison, *vertical differentiation* refers to differences in the actual quality of two brands. Ben & Jerry's ice cream and Häagen-Dazs ice cream have a higher fat content than Breyers ice cream, which has a higher fat content than the typical store brand of ice cream. A Lexus is a higher-quality car than a Taurus. However, differences between similar models, such as a Toyota Camry and a Ford Taurus, represent horizontal differentiation.

13.2 Theoretical Analysis of Product Differentiation

Economists have approached the theoretical issues associated with product differentiation by developing extensions of other models, models that are hybrids of other models, and models that incorporate asymmetric information. This section examines each of these approaches. In the first section, we explore how incorporating product differentiation into the Bertrand model completely changes the implications of the model. In the second section, the hybrid model of monopolistic competition, which is based partly on the theory of perfect competition and partly on the theory of monopoly, is introduced and analyzed. Finally, in the third section, we investigate how asymmetric information affects markets with product differentiation.

13.2.1 The Potential Impact of Product Differentiation on Price: The Bertrand Model Revisited

In Chapter 8 we derived the Bertrand equilibrium in a model with a homogeneous product. Recall that the equilibrium resulted in price equal to marginal cost. As a first theoretical step toward analyzing the possible impact of product differentiation on price, we analyze a Bertrand model with a *differentiated product.*

Suppose that, because of brand loyalty, two Bertrand firms, Ben & Jerry's and Häagen Dazs, face the following symmetric demand curves:

$$q_B = 96 - 2p_B + p_H \qquad [13.1A]$$

$$q_H = 96 - 2p_H + p_B, \qquad [13.1B]$$

where $q_B, q_H \geq 0$ and $p_B, p_H \leq 48$.

The restriction that $q_B, q_H \geq 0$ prevents quantities from becoming negative, and the restriction that $p_B, p_H \leq 48$ prevents output from becoming infinite as an opponent's price increases. Equation 13.1A shows that Ben & Jerry's demand is an inverse function of p_B and a *positive* function of p_H. Notice that even if $p_B > p_H$, Ben & Jerry's still has a positive quantity demanded: Some consumers will buy Ben & Jerry's even if it is more expensive than Häagen-Dazs. Furthermore, in Equation 13.1A, an increase in p_H results in an increase in q_B; that is, an increase in the price of Häagen-Dazs will increase the quantity demanded of Ben & Jerry's.

Assume MC = 12, so that in the absence of product differentiation, the Bertrand equilibrium price would equal MC of 12. Using calculus, it is fairly simple to derive Ben & Jerry's reaction function $p_B = f(p_H)$ as:*

$$p_B = 30 + \frac{1}{4}p_H. \qquad [13.2]$$

The reaction function shown in Equation 13.2 can also be derived by using the "twice-as-steep rule." In the following derivation of Ben & Jerry's reaction function,

*To obtain marginal revenue for Ben & Jerry's begin by solving Equation 13.1A for p_B and proceed as follows:

$$2p_B = 96 + p_H - q_B \Rightarrow p_B = 48 + \frac{1}{2}p_H - \frac{1}{2}q_B$$

$$TR_B = p_B q_B = \left[48 + \frac{1}{2}p_H - \frac{1}{2}q_B\right]q_B = 48q_B + \frac{1}{2}p_H q_B - \frac{1}{2}q_B^2$$

$$MR_B = \frac{\partial TR_B}{\partial q_B} = 48 + \frac{1}{2}p_H - q_B.$$

To find the reaction function, set $MR_B = MC = 12$:

$$MR_B = 48 + \frac{1}{2}p_H - q_B = 12 = MC.$$

Solving for q_B yields:

$$q_B = 36 + \frac{1}{2}p_H.$$

Substituting $q_B = 96 - 2p_B + p_H$ into the above equation and solving for p_B yields the reaction function:

$$q_B = 36 + \frac{1}{2}p_H = 96 - 2p_B + p_H \Rightarrow 2p_B = (96 - 36) + p_H - \frac{1}{2}p_H \Rightarrow 2p_B = 60 + \frac{1}{2}p_H$$

or

$$p_B = 30 + \frac{1}{4}p_H.$$

remember that the function $p_B = f(p_H)$ is in terms of prices, not quantities, and Ben & Jerry's assumes p_H is constant throughout. First solve Equation 13.1A for p_B:

$$2p_B = 96 + p_H - q_B \Rightarrow p_B = \left(48 + \frac{1}{2}p_H\right) - \frac{1}{2}q_B.$$

Because p_H is assumed to be constant, by the "twice-as-steep rule" MR_B is:

$$MR_B = \left(48 + \frac{1}{2}p_H\right) - q_B.$$

Profit maximization requires MC = MR, so:

$$MR_B = \left(48 + \frac{1}{2}p_H\right) - q_B = 12 = MC$$

or

$$q_B = 36 + \frac{1}{2}p_H. \qquad [13.3]$$

To obtain the reaction function in terms of *prices*, that is, $p_B = f(p_H)$, substitute $q_B = 96 - 2p_B + p_H$ from Equation 13.1A into 13.3, which yields:

$$96 - 2p_B + p_H = 36 + \frac{1}{2}p_H \Rightarrow 2p_B = 60 + p_H - \frac{1}{2}p_H$$

or

$$p_B = 30 + \frac{1}{4}p_H. \qquad [13.4]$$

By analogous reasoning, Häagen-Dazs's reaction function is:

$$p_H = 30 + \frac{1}{4}p_B. \qquad [13.5]$$

At the Nash equilibrium, $p_B = p_H$. Substituting $p_H = 30 + \frac{1}{4}p_B$ from Equation 13.5 into Equation 13.4 and solving for p_B yields the Nash equilibrium:

$$p_B = 30 + \frac{1}{4}\left(30 + \frac{1}{4}p_B\right) = 37.5 + \frac{1}{16}p_B$$

or

$$\frac{15}{16}p_B = 37.5$$

or

$$p_B = 40.$$

By analogous reasoning, $p_H = 40$.

Figure 13.1 shows the two reaction functions and the Nash equilibrium. The Bertrand equilibrium with product differentiation yields a price of 40. In the absence of product differentiation, the Bertrand equilibrium is $p_B = p_H = MC = 12$. The introduction of product differentiation has resulted in a dramatically *increased* price.

That increased product differentiation can result in higher prices does *not* imply that increased product differentiation lowers social welfare, because in return for higher prices consumers receive increased variety. The next section addresses the theoretical impact of increased product differentiation on social welfare.

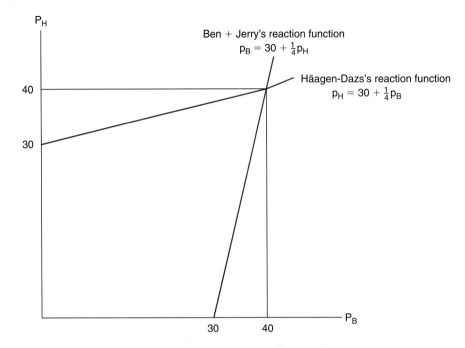

FIGURE 13.1 Bertrand Equilibrium with Product Differentiation

The two Bertrand reaction functions with product differentiation intersect at an equilibrium price of P = 40. In the absence of product differentiation, the Bertrand equilibrium is P = MC = 12. The introduction of product differentiation has dramatically increased the equilibrium price.

13.2.2 The Economics of Monopolistic Competition and the Optimal Amount of Variety

One important theoretical model that incorporates product differentiation is the model of monopolistic competition. The two important characteristics of monopolistic competition are product differentiation and easy entry and exit. Product differentiation gives each monopolistic competitor some degree of market power and implies that it faces a downward-sloping demand curve, rather than the horizontal demand curve faced by a perfectly competitive firm. Short-run equilibrium for a monopolistically competitive firm is shown in Figure 13.2(a). Because the industry contains many firms, each firm's market power is limited and the firm's demand curve is less steeply sloped than the market demand curve. Figure 13.2(a) shows the usual profit-maximizing choice: Produce the quantity of output, q_{SR}, for which marginal revenue equals marginal cost. The corresponding price, P_{SR}, is above average cost, and thus the firm earns a positive economic profit.

As in perfect competition, this positive economic profit cannot persist in the long run. Attracted by profit, new firms will enter the industry. Entry shifts the firm's demand curve to the left, as shown in Figure 13.2(b). Entry continues until economic profits reach zero. In long-run equilibrium, the firm will produce q_{LR}, where marginal

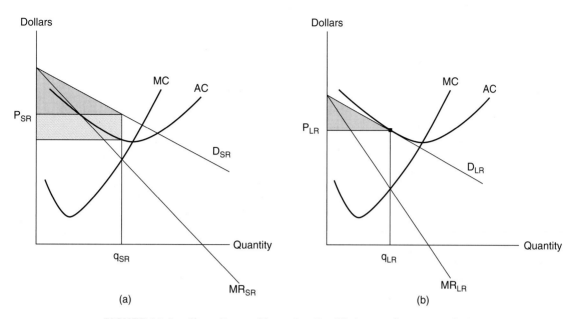

FIGURE 13.2 **Short-Run and Long-Run Equilibrium Under Monopolistic Competition**

Panel (a) shows a firm's profit-maximizing equilibrium with MR = MC. Price is greater than average cost and the firm earns a positive economic profit equal to the red shaded area. With easy entry, positive economic profit attracts entry. Entry shifts the demand curve to the left and entry continues until economic profits reach zero in panel (b). In panel (b) the firm will produce where price equals average cost but is greater than marginal cost. The gray shaded triangles represent consumer surplus.

revenue equals marginal cost *and* where price equals average cost. Even though each firm has market power, the ease of entry and exit drives economic profits to zero.

Economists have identified two sources of inefficiency in a monopolistically competitive market. First, at the firm's profit-maximizing choice of output in both the short and long run, price is greater than marginal cost. Therefore, as in a monopoly, there is a deadweight loss in a monopolistically competitive market. Second, note from Figure 13.2 that in equilibrium the firm does not operate at the minimum of its average cost curve. This situation, in which the monopolistically competitive firm produces a smaller output level than that which minimizes average cost, results in excess capacity. If fewer firms were in the industry, each could operate at a larger scale and a lower average cost. Note, however, that consumers undoubtedly value the opportunity to choose among a variety of products with different characteristics. The "variety" benefits of product differentiation must be considered in addition to the costs of excess capacity.

The Welfare Benefits of Variety with Monopolistic Competition[4]

We now examine the social benefits of variety in a monopolistically competitive industry. Initially assume that only one firm is in the industry and this firm is in short-run equilibrium, as shown in Figure 13.2(a). This firm is the "founding father"

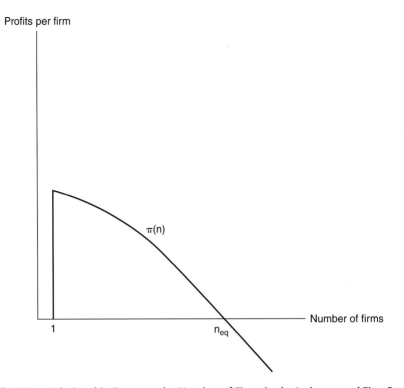

FIGURE 13.3 **Relationship Between the Number of Firms in the Industry and Firm Profits Under Monopolistic Competition**

The function $\pi(n)$ shows the relationship between the number of firms and profits per firm in a monopolistically competitive market. As additional firms enter, profits per firm decline, so there is a negative relationship between the number of firms in the industry and the profits earned by each firm.

firm of the industry, like McDonald's in the fast-food industry. As additional firms enter the industry, the demand curve for the first firm shifts to the left and its profits decline until, in long-run equilibrium, economic profits are zero. In long-run equilibrium, all firms earn zero economic profits as depicted in Figure 13.2(b).

As each additional firm enters, profits per firm decline, so there is a *negative* relationship between the number of firms in the industry and the profits earned by each firm. This relationship is shown by the function $\pi(n)$ in Figure 13.3, where n is the number of firms in the industry. The long-run equilibrium number of firms is n_{eq} where $\pi(n_{eq}) = 0$. In long-run equilibrium, economic profits equal zero for each firm.

Is n_{eq} the socially optimal number of firms? The optimal number of firms must maximize total industry surplus, which equals the sum of consumer surplus and total producer profits.* Total profits are calculated by multiplying the number of

*We simplify the analysis by assuming that the equilibrium number of firms has no impact on the producer surplus of input suppliers, so that the firms' profits measure the producer surplus.

FIGURE 13.4 Relationship Between the Number of Firms in the Industry and Total Industry Profits Under Monopolistic Competition

The total profit function is calculated by multiplying the number of firms, n, by the profits per firm, $\pi(n)$.

firms, n, by the profits per firm, $\pi(n)$. Figure 13.4 shows the total profits function, $n \times \pi(n)$.

Total consumer surplus, CS, is also a function of the number of firms, CS(n). In Figure 13.2(a), consumer surplus with one firm is equal to the gray triangle and consumer surplus per firm with n_{eq} firms is equal to the gray triangle in Figure 13.2(b). With n_{eq} firms in Figure 13.2(b) total consumer surplus would equal [$n_{eq} \times$ (area of the gray triangle)]. Generally, total consumer surplus increases with an increase in the number of firms for two reasons: (1) entry causes total industry output to increase and prices to decline and (2) new firms increase variety and increase the likelihood that a particular consumer will find a product that exactly matches his or her tastes. Figure 13.5 shows CS(n) as a positively sloped curve.*

*It is unlikely, but conceivable, that CS(n) could decrease with increases in n if increased variety enables each firm to cater very closely to the demands of a select group of consumers, thereby enabling firms to dramatically increase prices as variety increases. In our analysis we ignore this possibility.

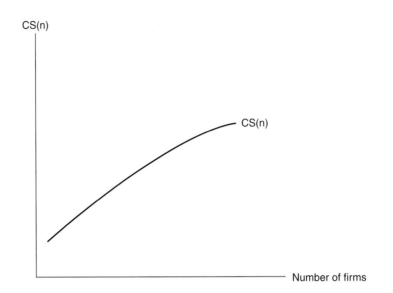

FIGURE 13.5 **Consumer Surplus as a Function of the Number of Firms with Monopolistic Competition**

Total consumer surplus CS is a function of the number of firms CS(n). Total consumer surplus is an increasing function of n because entry causes total industry output to increase and price to decline and because new firms increase variety, which increases the likelihood that consumers will find a product that exactly matches their tastes.

To determine total surplus we add the total producer profits and total consumer surplus so:

$$\text{Total Surplus } (n) = [n \times \pi(n)] + CS(n).$$

In Figure 13.6, the total surplus curve is derived from the sum of the $[n \times \pi(n)]$ curve in Figure 13.4 and the $CS(n)$ curve in Figure 13.5. The socially optimal number of firms is n*. Only with n* firms does the industry maximize total surplus.

In Figure 13.6 the optimal number of firms n* is less than the equilibrium number of firms n_{eq}. In this case, the monopolistically competitive industry will have too many firms and provide too large a variety of goods; therefore, product differentiation is excessive.

This result, however, is not the only possibility. In Figure 13.7 a different monopolistically competitive industry is shown, where $n^* > n_{eq}$ and the industry provides too little variety. There is, therefore, too little product differentiation in the industry represented in Figure 13.7. It is, of course, theoretically possible to construct an industry where $n^* = n_{eq}$. It follows that in a monopolistically competitive industry, product differentiation may be greater than, less than, or equal to the socially optimal level of product differentiation.

The source of this ambiguity lies in the difference between the *private* benefits and the *social* benefits associated with entry. As long as there is some positive economic

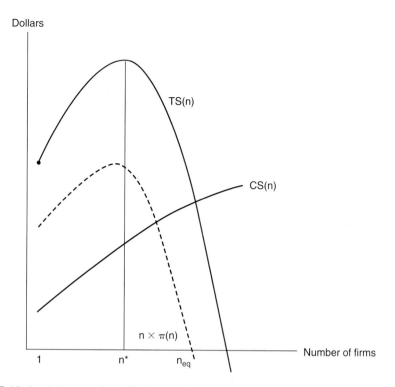

FIGURE 13.6 **A Monopolistically Competitive Industry with Too Many Firms and Too Much Product Differentiation**

The total surplus curve is the sum of the total profit curve $[n \times \pi(n)]$ and consumer surplus curve $CS(n)$. The socially optimal number of firms n^* is the number that maximizes total surplus. Here the socially optimal number of firms n^* is less than the equilibrium number of firms, so the industry will have too many firms and provide too much variety.

profit associated with entry, additional firms will enter the industry. Entry, however, reduces the profits of each of the incumbent firms. The total change in profits for society resulting from entry is, therefore, always less than the private profit of the entering firm, so that from a social viewpoint, the firm has "too much" incentive to enter. This profit effect tends to result in too many firms and too much product differentiation.

Conversely, entry results in an *increase* in consumer surplus, but the entrant ignores this increase in consumer surplus and considers only the increase in profit associated with entry. This consumer surplus effect tends to result in too few firms and too little product differentiation.

The profit effect and the consumer surplus effect work in opposite directions, and therefore, the net effect depends on which effect is dominant. In Figure 13.6, the profit effect is dominant and there is too much product differentiation, whereas in Figure 13.7, the consumer surplus effect is dominant and there is too little product differentiation. Only if the two effects are exactly equal will the socially optimal level of product differentiation be achieved.

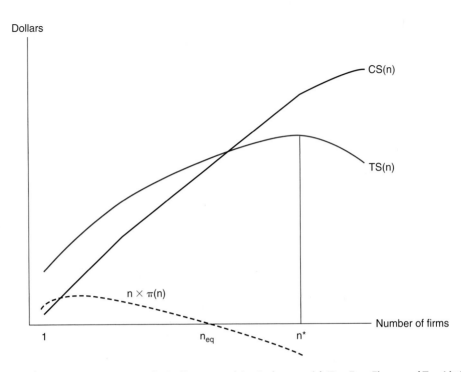

FIGURE 13.7 **A Monopolistically Competitive Industry with Too Few Firms and Too Little Product Differentiation**

Total surplus curve is the sum of the total profit curve $[n \times \pi(n)]$ and consumer surplus curve $CS(n)$. The socially optimal number of firms n^* is the number that maximizes total surplus. Here the socially optimal number of firms n^* is greater than the equilibrium number of firms, so the industry will have too few firms and provide too little variety.

The Waldman Ice Cream Truck Revisited: An Example of Inefficient Product Differentiation

One of the most common methods of differentiation is by geographic location. Recall the Waldman ice cream truck example presented in Chapter 7, in which both Waldman and "Other Truck" located at the middle of the parade route. Middle was a dominant strategy in that simple zero-sum game. Here we ask the question: Was the equilibrium outcome in that game (middle-middle) a socially optimal outcome?

Hotelling first addressed this type of question in 1929.[5] Suppose that a market consists of a 10-mile stretch of road and 100 consumers are distributed uniformly over that 10-mile stretch at one-tenth-of-a mile intervals beginning at the 0.05-mile mark and ending at the 9.95-mile mark. Figure 13.8 shows the 10-mile stretch of road starting with the 0-mile mark on the left and ending with the 10-mile mark on the right. If two duopolists, Exxon and Shell, sell a homogeneous product at the same price, a consumer will select her seller strictly on the basis of which firm is closer, and therefore, which firm minimizes the consumer's transportation costs. Using the logic of the Waldman ice cream truck example from Chapter 7, both firms will locate at the mid-

FIGURE 13.8 Nash Equilibrium and Social Optimum for Exxon and Shell

dle of the road right at the 5-mile mark, and the two firms will divide sales and profits equally, with 50 consumers purchasing from each. The 5-mile mark is a Nash equilibrium because if either firm moved even slightly away from the middle, the firm that remained at the middle would capture a greater share of the market. If Shell moved 1 mile to the left to the 4-mile mark, leaving Exxon alone in the middle, Exxon would capture all 50 of the consumers located to the right of the 5-mile mark *plus* the consumers located at the 4.95-, 4.85-, 4.75-, 4.65- and 4.55-mile marks. Exxon would capture 55 consumers, leaving Shell with only 45 consumers.

With Exxon and Shell each located at the 5-mile mark, a Nash equilibrium has been reached, but is "middle-middle" the optimal choice of locations from the standpoint of society? Society wishes to maximize consumer welfare by minimizing total transportation costs. Suppose transportation costs equal $1 per mile. With both firms located at the 5-mile mark, the average distance of a consumer from a seller is 2.5 miles, so the total transportation costs for the 100 consumers would equal

$$2.5 \times 100 \times \$1 = \$250.^*$$

What locations would minimize transportation costs? Suppose Exxon located at the 2.5-mile mark and Shell located at the 7.5-mile mark. Exxon would now sell to the 50 consumers located between the 0.05- and 4.95-mile marks, and Shell would sell to the 50 consumers located between the 5.05- and 9.95-mile marks. Each firm would still sell to 50 consumers, but consumers would travel an average of only 1.25 miles.[†] In fact, the farthest any consumer would travel would be 2.5 miles, which is equal to the average distance traveled with the Nash equilibrium outcome. Total transportation costs for the 100 consumers would equal $1.25 \times 100 \times \$1 = \125. By moving to the 2.5- and 7.5-mile marks, Exxon and Shell would reduce society's transportation costs by 50 percent with no profit sacrifice to either firm. Clearly, in this example, the Nash equilibrium yields too little product differentiation.

*There are several ways to calculate the average distance traveled by consumers. One could calculate the total miles traveled by all consumers and then divide by 100, as follows:

$$\text{Average Miles Traveled} = \frac{2(0.05 + 0.15 + 0.25 + \cdots + 4.95)}{100} = \frac{250}{100} = 2.5.$$

Using calculus and recognizing that the functional relationship between consumers and miles traveled for the 50 consumers on each side of the 5-mile mark is:

$$\text{Miles Traveled by the xth Consumer} = 0.1x \text{ for } 1 \le x \le 50;$$

the average miles traveled by the 50 consumers located between the 5- and 10-mile marks is:

$$\text{Average Miles Traveled} = \frac{\int_0^{50} \frac{x}{10} \, dx}{50} = \frac{125}{50} = 2.5.$$

†See the previous footnote for details on how to calculate the average miles traveled per customer.

This analysis can be generalized to consider other types of product differentiation besides location. For example, before the widespread introduction of cable TV and satellite TV into the broadcasting industry, most sections of the country received at most three network stations (ABC, CBS, and NBC), and many rural areas received only two stations. If an area received only two stations, both stations would have an incentive to provide very similar "middle-of-the-road" programming with a combination of the same type of shows: some news, some daytime soap operas, prime time comedies and dramas, some sports, and some local programming. If either of the two networks in a rural area had tried to move toward a more specialized format such as all news (CNN), all sports (ESPN), or more intellectual programming (A&E), that station would have lost more viewers than it gained. Therefore, viewers with more extreme tastes, such as current CNN, ESPN, or A&E viewers, were left highly dissatisfied with both stations. The opening up of competition in the industry has resulted in far greater opportunities for those with more extreme tastes.

13.2.3 Product Differentiation with Asymmetric Information

We have already seen how asymmetric information can change market outcomes. For example, in Chapter 11 the existence of asymmetric information made limit pricing a reasonable strategy for an incumbent. In this section we analyze how the existence of asymmetric information in a market with product differentiation can prevent a market from reaching an efficient equilibrium.

The Lemons Model

The seminal article dealing with product differentiation and asymmetric information, entitled "The Market for Lemons: Quality, Uncertainty and the Market Mechanism," was written by George Akerlof in 1970.[6] Akerlof's lemons model can be presented in the form of a simple game. The game has players who are either buyers or sellers of used cars. Sellers offer cars for sale and know the quality of the cars. Buyers are unaware of the quality of specific cars; however, buyers know the probability distribution of good cars and lemons. Nature randomly selects the quality of a specific car, and after nature selects a car, a buyer makes a price offer to buy the car for a price, P. The payoffs to sellers and buyers are levels of utility after the offer is either accepted or rejected by the seller. For convenience, a base value of utility equal to zero is assigned to both buyers and sellers if no trade takes place.

In the simplest version of the model both buyers and sellers have identical tastes. We depict the quality of a given car as θ. If a trade takes place, the buyer's utility payoff is $\theta - P$ and the seller's utility payoff is $P - \theta$.

Product differentiation is brought into the model by assuming the existence of a continuum of different-quality cars. For example, suppose the quality of cars is uniformly distributed between absolute lemons of quality $6000 and good cars of quality $12,000. If 600,100 cars are available for sale, nature can draw from 100 cars of each quality (100 cars valued at $6000, 100 cars valued at $6001, 100 cars valued at $6002 . . . 100 cars valued at $12,000). The average quality is equal to $9000, with 300,000 cars of quality less than $9000 and 300,000 cars of quality greater than $9000 available for nature to draw from. Suppose a buyer considers offering the expected value P = $9000 for a car. The buyer knows that the only cars sellers will be willing to sell for $9000 have quality values less than or equal to $9000. The average quality of the cars

offered for sale at P = $9000, therefore, is only $7500, and buyers know this. Consequently, buyers lower their price offers to $7500, which equals the expected value of the cars offered for sale. Once the price offers are lowered to $7500, sellers only accept the price offer for cars worth between $6000 and $7500, so the average value of the cars sold declines to only $6750. However, if the price offer is lowered to $6750, sellers only accept offers for cars worth between $6000 and $6750, so the average value of the cars sold is only $6375. You should be able to see where this analysis is headed: The price offer keeps declining, until it reaches $6000, and the number of cars sold is a mere 100 absolute lemons. Asymmetric information has caused the entire market for quality cars to collapse!

To this point, despite the absence of good cars being sold, there has been no efficiency loss as a result of the asymmetric information, because buyers and sellers have identical tastes and value cars equally; therefore, from an efficiency standpoint it doesn't matter whether a seller or buyer owns a car. We now expand the model to make it more realistic by assuming that buyers value any given car more highly than sellers. Assume, for example, that buyers place a 20 percent higher value on any car than sellers, so the payoffs to a trade have changed. If a trade takes place, and the seller's quality is still measured by θ, then the buyer's utility payoff is $(1.2)\theta - P$, and the seller's utility payoff is $P - \theta$.

Table 13.1 shows how this inequality would affect the game. The first column shows the quality range to the sellers for cars sold. Now look across the second row where all cars priced between $6000 and $6500 are sold: In this case, the average value of a car to a seller is $\bar{\theta} = \$6250$ and the expected value of a car to a buyer equals $1.2\bar{\theta} = \$7500$. In the price range $6000–$6500, therefore, the expected value of a car to a buyer, $7500, is greater than the price P = $6500 sellers are willing to accept. At P = $6500, buyers would want to purchase more cars than sellers offer for sale and there would be an excess demand for cars. In Table 13.1, the market is in equilibrium

TABLE 13.1 Supply and Demand for Cars in the Lemons Model

Quality Range to the Sellers for Cars Sold	Average Value of the Cars Sold to the Sellers ($\bar{\theta}$)	Price P	Expected Value to a Buyer $(1.2)(\bar{\theta})$	Excess Demand or Excess Supply
6000	6000	6000	7200	Excess demand
6000–6500	6250	6500	7500	Excess demand
6000–7000	6500	7000	7800	Excess demand
6000–7500	6750	7500	8100	Excess demand
6000–8000	7000	8000	8400	Excess demand
6000–8500	7250	8500	8700	Excess demand
6000–9000	**7500**	**9000**	**9000**	**Equilibrium**
6000–9500	7750	9500	9300	Excess supply
6000–10,000	8000	10,000	9600	Excess supply
6000–10,500	8250	10,500	9900	Excess supply
6000–11,000	8500	11,000	10,200	Excess supply
6000–11,500	8750	11,500	10,500	Excess supply
6000–12,000	9000	12,000	10,800	Excess supply

FIGURE 13.9 Equilibrium in the Lemons Model with Continuously Variable Quality

The x-axis measures the expected value of a car to sellers $\bar{\theta}$, and the y-axis measures the price P. The dark red willingness-to-sell curve graphs price P as a function of quality $\bar{\theta}$, and the light red willingness-to-buy curve graphs the price buyers would be willing to pay as a function of quality $\bar{\theta}$. For any value of $\bar{\theta} < \$7500$, the willingness-to-buy curve is above the willingness-to-sell curve, so there is an excess demand. For any value of $\bar{\theta} > \$7500$, the willingness-to-sell curve is above the willingness-to-buy curve, so there is an excess supply. The willingness-to-sell curve equals the willingness-to-buy curve only when P = \$9000 and $\bar{\theta}$ = \$7500, so this is the equilibrium price.

only when all cars in the price range between \$6000 and \$9000 are sold at a price of \$9000. At a price P = \$9000, all cars in the price range between \$6000 and \$9000 are sold and the expected value of a car sold to the seller equals \$7500. The expected value to a buyer equals $1.2\bar{\theta} = 1.2(\$7500) = \9000, so the expected value to the buyer equals price, and equilibrium is achieved.

The equilibrium condition is shown graphically in Figure 13.9. The x-axis measures the expected value of a car to sellers $\bar{\theta}$, and the y-axis measures the price P buyers and sellers are willing to pay or accept, respectively, for a car of quality $\bar{\theta}$. The willingness-to-sell curve graphs price P as a function of $\bar{\theta}$ from Table 13.1, and the willingness-to-buy curve graphs the price buyers are willing to pay as a function of $\bar{\theta}$ from Table 13.1.

The willingness-to-sell curve equals the willingness-to-buy curve only when P = $9000 and $\bar{\theta}$ = $7500. For any value of $\bar{\theta}$ < $7500, the willingness-to-buy curve is above the willingness-to-sell curve, so there is an excess demand; and for any value of $\bar{\theta}$ > $7500, the willingness-to-sell curve is above the willingness-to-buy curve so there is an excess supply. Half the cars are sold—the lower-quality half—and the other half, the better cars, are not.

This equilibrium is inefficient because none of the higher-quality cars, all of which are more highly valued by buyers than sellers, are sold. With symmetric information, buyers and sellers know the value of each and every car and all 600,100 cars are sold. For example, the 100 cars with a value $\bar{\theta}$ = $12,000 to sellers are valued as $1.2\bar{\theta}$ = $14,400 by buyers, and therefore, these cars will all be sold with symmetric information. Furthermore, each sale results in an increase in total social utility and welfare. Asymmetric information in a market with product differentiation results in a large welfare loss.

Adverse Selection

The lemons model is an excellent example of one of the major problems associated with asymmetric information in markets with product differentiation: *adverse selection*. *Adverse selection* refers to any situation where products of different qualities are sold at the same price because buyers or sellers do not have sufficient information to determine the true quality of the products. Based on the lemons model explored in Table 13.1 and Figure 13.9, buyers cannot determine the quality of a car before they purchase the car, and as a result, cars with qualities ranging between $6000 and $9000 to their sellers are all sold at a uniform price of $9000. Some unlucky buyers pay $9000 for lemons worth only $7200 to these buyers. Meanwhile, zero high-quality cars valued by sellers above $9000 are sold. The adverse selection problem causes too few of the high-quality cars to be sold and results in a large welfare loss.

The adverse selection problem is nowhere more apparent than in insurance markets. For example, assume that an individual owns a $200,000 home in an area where the average risk of fire in a given year is known to be 2 percent. Realistically, the probability of having a fire will not be 2 percent for all homeowners. Instead it will vary around the average of 2 percent from house to house. For high-risk homeowners, the risk will be greater than 2 percent and for low-risk homeowners, the risk will be less than 2 percent. As the probability of having a fire increases above 2 percent, a premium based on a 2 percent risk of a fire looks like a good deal for the homeowner. On the other hand, as the probability of having a fire decreases below 2 percent, a premium based on a 2 percent risk of a fire looks like a bad deal. Unless the insurance company can calculate the exact probability of a particular house burning down, it cannot calculate the correct premium to charge for that specific house. Such precise risk calculations are impossible. If the insurance company bases its premium on the assumption that every house has a 2 percent probability of burning down, most homeowners with a probability greater than or equal to 2 percent will purchase insurance, while many homeowners with a probability less than 2 percent will not purchase insurance because the premiums are too high. This outcome is nothing more than the lemons model result in a somewhat different guise. Consequently, only high-risk homeowners purchase insurance. Adverse selection results in a pool of insured homeowners that comes disproportionately from the group of high-risk homeowners. The low-risk homeowners are driven out of the market and the insurance companies are left with a bunch of lemons, in the guise of high-risk customers.

When an insurance company finds itself in the position of insuring a majority of high-risk policyholders, it will have to increase its rates to cover the increased probability of a fire. However, rate increases serve only to drive more of the low-risk homeowners away from the company, thus compounding the firm's problems. This analysis is valid for all types of insurance markets. In each market, the insurance company faces an adverse selection problem that tends to result in a disproportionately large share of high-risk individuals purchasing insurance.

Dealing with the Problems Associated with Product Differentiation, Asymmetric Information, and Adverse Selection

One effective way to solve the adverse selection problem is to obtain more information. Insurance companies attempt to sort out high-risk from low-risk policyholders in a variety of ways. For example, before customers purchase homeowners' insurance, the company typically asks the following questions: Do you have smoke detectors on every floor? Does anyone living in the house smoke? How far is the house from a fire station? Is the local fire department professional or volunteer? How far is the nearest fire hydrant? Do you have a central alarm system? Do you have a sprinkler system? Is the house constructed of wood, brick, cement, or other materials? Is the house located in a wooded area with a high probability of a forest fire?

Similarly, to obtain life insurance, in addition to asking a long list of questions about an applicant's health history and living patterns, insurance companies usually demand a medical examination by a company-approved doctor. Automobile insurance companies look carefully at an applicant's history of accidents and automobile insurance claims, as well as the applicant's age. Young teenagers have the highest risk of serious automobile accidents, and young males in particular are in an extremely high-risk category. Once insurance companies gather all of this information, they place an applicant in a particular risk category and charge policy premiums based on these categories. For example, a 30-year-old nonsmoking female professor will pay far less for health insurance than a 40-year-old male lumberjack smoker.

Another method used by insurance companies is to sell insurance to everyone in a large group. For example, many employers offer health insurance benefits through only one company. Because everyone in the company must enroll in the plan, there is no adverse selection problem within that group of insured individuals; the healthy and the unhealthy are insured together. Similarly, many employers provide life insurance policies for all their employees, which enables the insurance company to overcome its adverse selection problem and offer the group life insurance at relatively low cost.

Consumers have insufficient information to make informed decisions in many other markets besides used cars and insurance. In these markets, the government sometimes attempts to reduce or solve adverse selection problems by mandating the disclosure of information to uniformed parties. For example, in the United States, food manufacturers must conform to food labeling that tells consumers a great deal about the nutritional content of packaged foods. Similarly, the U.S. government requires cigarette manufacturers to divulge the tar and nicotine content of their cigarettes, appliance manufacturers to disclose the energy efficiency of their products, and automobile manufacturers to reveal the fuel mileage of their cars. Furthermore, in the United States, the Federal Trade Commission is authorized to prevent firms from using false or deceptive forms of advertising. As a result, firms producing low-quality prod-

ucts are less likely to attempt to trick consumers, and as a result, firms producing high-quality products can advertise without being accused of hiding the truth. Finally, many states require homeowners to reveal in writing all of their homes' significant defects to potential buyers before selling a house.

APPLICATION 13.1

What Do the Markets for Thoroughbred Racehorses and Baseball Players Have in Common? Product Differentiation, Asymmetric Information, and Adverse Selection

Product differentiation and asymmetric information create adverse selection problems in many markets where sellers have more information about quality than buyers. Consider, for example, the markets for thoroughbred racehorses and baseball players. In both markets sellers know more about quality than buyers. In the market for horses, there are two types of sellers, breeders who breed horses only for sale at auction and racers who breed horses both for racing and for sale. Chezum and Wimmer recognized an adverse selection problem in this market because breeders sell all of their horses while racers keep their best thoroughbreds in house in hopes of racing them to win large purses.* The average quality of horses sold at auction, therefore, should be higher for breeders than racers, and according to the theory of adverse selection, rational buyers would recognize these expected quality differences and pay higher prices for horses sold by breeders than horses sold by racers.

Using data for 304 yearlings sold at auction in Kentucky in September 1994, Chezum and Wimmer developed a measure of racing intensity for each seller and examined the impact of racing intensity on price. They theorized that buyers would offer higher bids for yearlings sold by breeders with low racing intensities than for yearlings sold by racers with high racing intensities. The study controlled for many other factors that could affect prices, including several variables measuring the yearling's pedigree, the yearling's exact age at the time of the auction, and whether the yearling was a colt (male) or a filly (female). In all of the statistical results, racing intensity had a negative and statistically significant impact on yearling auction prices. Buyers recognized the adverse selection problem and adjusted their bids accordingly.

Similarly, adverse selection problems exist in the market for free agent baseball players who can negotiate a contract with any of the 30 Major League Baseball teams. The management of the player's current team should know more information about the player's quality than any of the other 29 teams. Specifically, the player's current team management should know more about his ability, work ethic, and physical conditioning. If a player's current team permits him to become a free agent rather than re-signing him, it suggests that the team has some questions about the player's ability, work ethic, or health. Lehn studied the impact of asymmetric information in the market for Major League Baseball players during the period immediately following the advent of free agency in 1976.[†] Prior to 1976, a team owned the rights to a player for life. Lehn theorized that players eligible for free agency who re-signed with their current teams would be in better physical condition, and therefore, they would be less likely to become hurt and put on the disabled list in the future.

The sample consisted of 155 players and represented all players who were on major league rosters in 1980, "were free agents or would have been eligible to become free agents in the next free agent market, had they not signed a contract with [their

current team]," and had signed a guaranteed contract for at least three years.[‡] The majority of players, 99 of the 155, re-signed with their current teams, while 56 players became free agents and signed with other teams.

The table below shows Lehn's key result: The average number of days a player spent on the disabled list per season increased much more dramatically for free agents than for players re-signing with their current teams, and this difference is statistically significant. The table also breaks down these data between pitchers and nonpitchers, and the breakdown reveals that virtually the entire difference in disability days is because pitchers were much more likely to become disabled if they signed a free agent contract.

Groups of Players	N	Average Age	Pre-Contract Disability	Post-Contract Disability	Percent Change in Disability
All players	155	30.82	4.73	12.55	165.40
Not free agents	99	30.89	4.76	9.68	103.36
Free agents	56	30.68	4.67	17.23	268.95
Pitchers					
Not free agents	33		3.66	9.57	166.94
Free agents	25		5.12	28.07	448.24
Nonpitchers					
Not free agents	66		5.30	9.74	83.77
Free agents	31		4.31	9.83	128.08

Source: Kenneth Lehn, "Information Asymmetries in Baseball's Free Agent Market," *Economic Inquiry,* 22 (January 1984): 40.

Did management learn from these data? One likely response would be to sign fewer free agent pitchers to long-term contracts. The table below shows that this is precisely how management responded to this adverse selection problem. In 1981 and 1982, zero free agent pitchers were signed to five-year contracts. Notice, however, that teams re-signed their own pitchers to long-term contracts in both 1981 and 1982.

Year	Number of Pitchers Signing Five-Year Contracts	Number of Free Agent Pitchers Signing Five-Year Contracts	Number of Other Pitchers Signing Five-Year Contracts
1977	9	4	5
1978	6	3	3
1979	6	2	4
1980	10	5	5
1981	6	0	6
1982	4	0	4

Source: Kenneth Lehn, "Information Asymmetries in Baseball's Free Agent Market," *Economic Inquiry,* 22 (January 1984): 43.

[*]Brian Chezum and Brad Wimmer, "Roses or Lemons: Adverse Selection in the Market for Thoroughbred Yearlings," 79 (*The Review of Economics and Statistics*): 521–26.
[†]Kenneth Lehn, "Information Asymmetries in Baseball's Free Agent Market," *Economic Inquiry,* 22 (January 1984): 37–44.
[‡]*Ibid.,* p. 38. ∎

The Social Benefits and Costs of Advertising

W e have shown that product differentiation can have a positive social impact. Good locations are good for the economy because they minimize the costs of obtaining goods and services and therefore increase consumer welfare. Similarly, given a choice between good and bad service, many consumers willingly pay a premium to receive good service. The premium price that many consumers willingly pay to eat Ben & Jerry's or Häagen-Dazs ice cream instead of lower-quality brands also has social value.[7]

The most controversial aspect of product differentiation is advertising aimed at creating subjective differences between products. These images may border on being fraudulent. Cars and cigarettes do not make one sexy and virile; beer consumption often leads to tragic consequences; and, sadly, students have killed each other over a pair of athletic shoes that may be of no higher quality than an inexpensive pair. These examples have resulted in a call from some to limit or even ban persuasive advertising. The Federal Trade Commission, for example, negotiated a ban on the use of Joe Camel and other cartoon characters to sell cigarettes. Much of the remainder of this chapter concerns the social benefits and costs of advertising.

13.3.1 The Social Benefits of Advertising

We begin by distinguishing between *informational* and *persuasive advertising.* Informational advertising provides consumers with truthful information about price, location, or quality. Most newspaper, magazine, and direct mail advertising is informational. Newspapers in particular are full of advertisements emphasizing price. Grocery stores contend that they are the "low price leader." Department stores announce major sales. Automobile dealers advertise rebates and low-cost credit. These are examples of pro-competitive informational advertising. In 2002, newspaper advertising accounted for 18.6 percent of total advertising expenditures in the United States, magazine advertising accounted for 4.6 percent, direct mail advertising accounted for 19.5 percent, Yellow Pages advertising accounted for 5.8 percent, and Internet advertising accounted for 2.1 percent.[8] These five media accounted for over half of all advertising expenditures, and most of that advertising provided valuable information.

Empirical evidence suggests that advertising about price, referred to as *price advertising,* results in lower prices. Two separate studies found that eyeglass prices were significantly lower in markets that permitted optometrists to advertise than in markets that prohibited advertising.[9] Similarly, prescription drug prices are lower in states that permit price advertising.[10] Porter found that local newspaper advertising has a pro-competitive effect by reducing the profits of convenience goods advertised in newspapers.[11] Arterburn and Woodbury found that magazine advertising tended to increase the level of price competition for *shopping goods* such as furniture and appliances.[12] *Shopping goods* are relatively expensive goods that are purchased intermittently, such as appliances, automobiles, and televisions. Shopping goods are distinguished from *convenience goods,* which are relatively inexpensive items that are purchased on a regular basis, such as soft drinks, cigarettes, and gasoline.

Product differentiation puts pressure on manufacturers to produce high-quality products.[13] Even the simple act of placing a trademark on a product provides some guarantee that the manufacturer believes in the quality of the product and will stand

behind it. In the absence of trademark identification, consumers would not know who produced a product and there would be less incentive for producers to maintain quality.

Advertising may help manufacturers take advantage of economies of scale in production and distribution. In 1990 General Motors sold its first Saturn automobile. GM began advertising the introduction of Saturn well in advance of the production of the first car. If GM had been prevented from advertising, it is doubtful it could have sold enough cars to take advantage of production economies of scale.[14] The Saturn example suggests that advertising may encourage increased investment in research and development by helping manufacturers to rapidly inform consumers of new products and to find a large pool of potential first-time buyers.

Advertising provides a social benefit by subsidizing the mass media. Most of the revenues received by newspapers, magazines, radio, and television are from advertising.[15] Imagine what the Sunday *New York Times* would cost without advertising revenues. The price would be prohibitive to most consumers. In fact, there would not be a Sunday *New York Times* without advertising. Finally, advertising is an entertaining art form, and some of it is quite good. The best, or worst, advertising often becomes part of modern culture. Walter Mondale adapted a Wendy's advertising campaign to be the cornerstone of his 1984 presidential campaign when, in reference to economic policy, he asked Ronald Reagan, "Where's the Beef?" The NFL Super Bowl has even turned into a Super Bowl for commercials.

13.3.2 The Social Costs of Advertising

In 2002 over $236 billion was spent on advertising in the United States.[16] This is over twice as much as federal, state, and local governments spent on all cash assistance programs for the poor in 2002.[17] Table 13.2 lists the 100 leading advertisers in the United States in 2004. General Motors and Procter & Gamble each spent almost $4 billion in 2004 to advertise their cars and soaps, respectively. The opportunity cost of these advertising expenditures is large and raises questions about whether much of this $236 billion would have been better spent on AIDS research, health care, education, or new infrastructure.

Few economists argue that informational advertising creates serious economic waste. The complaints center on persuasive advertising. Persuasive advertising is designed to create a subjective positive reaction to a product. Much of the advertising on television is persuasive.[18] Beautiful people drive fast, good-looking automobiles. Kids love the experience of going to McDonald's. Beer drinkers proclaim "life is good." People who wear Gap jeans look like models and are great dancers. The list of commercials aimed at creating subjective image differences is endless. Many of these advertisements are entertaining but provide relatively little information. Conversely, many television commercials mix information with persuasion, as when Wendy's advertised it was introducing stuffed pitas or when Sprint advertised that it was reducing some long-distance rates to five cents per minute. Furthermore, all advertisements add some information by announcing that the product is available to consumers.

Persuasive advertising may provide valuable information about the quality of *experience goods*. **Experience goods** are those whose qualities can be identified only through trial *after buying the good*. Common examples include consumer nondurable convenience goods such as beer, toothpaste, soap, toiletries, and cereal and consumer durable goods including household appliances such as refrigerators and washing

TABLE 13.2 100 Leading National Advertisers: 2004 (in millions of dollars)

1. General Motors	3,997	35. General Mills	913
2. Procter & Gamble	3,918	36. Target	904
3. Time Warner	3,283	37. Hewlett-Packard	899
4. Pfizer	2,957	38. News Corp.	891
5. SBC Communications	2,687	39. Schering-Plough	853
6. Daimler-Chrysler	2,462	40. Wal-Mart	841
7. Ford	2,459	41. Gillette	837
8. Walt Disney	2,242	42. Wyeth	829
9. Verizon	2,197	43. Anheuser-Busch	817
10. Johnson & Johnson	2,176	44. Cendant	803
11. GlaxoSmithKline	1,828	45. May Department Stores	793
12. Sears Holding	1,823	46. Yum Brands	779
13. Toyota	1,821	47. Bristol-Myers	773
14. General Electric	1,819	48. Dell	756
15. Sony	1,665	49. Federated Department Stores	744
16. Nissan	1,540	50. Mars	740
17. Altria Group	1,399	51. AstraZeneca	723
18. McDonald's	1,389	52. American Express	718
19. L'Oreal	1,341	53. Kroger	686
20. Unilever	1,319	54. Sanofi-Aventis	674
21. Novartis	1,285	55. IAC/InterActiveCorp	648
22. PepsiCo	1,262	56. Kellogg	647
23. Home Depot	1,256	57. IBM	632
24. Merck	1,250	58. Berkshire Hathaway	617
25. U.S. government	1,229	59. Safeway	606
26. Viacom	1,207	60. Deutsche Telekom	604
27. Honda	1,205	61. Diageo	594
28. Sprint	1,114	62. Eli Lilly	587
29. J.C. Penney	1,095	63. Volkswagen	580
30. Estee Lauder	1,057	64. Nextel	576
31. Nestlé	1,028	65. Nike	574
32. Citigroup	1,001	66. Lowe's	542
33. Microsoft	987	67. Burger King	542
34. Best Buy	951	68. Coca-Cola	541

Continued

TABLE 13.2	100 Leading National Advertisers: 2004 (in millions of dollars) *(continued)*		
69. Hyundai	534	85. Mazda	413
70. Kohl's	533	86. BellSouth	405
71. Sara Lee	529	87. Limited	399
72. Gap	526	88. Bank of America	399
73. Clorox	522	89. AT&T	397
74. Albertson's	512	90. Dreamworks	380
75. SC Johnson	511	91. Cadbury Schweppes	375
76. Visa	505	92. Mitsubishi	374
77. Capital One	488	93. Allstate	374
78. Mattel	482	94. United Parcel Service	366
79. SABMiller	471	95. ConAgra	364
80. Doctor's Associates	463	96. Reckitt Benckiser	364
81. Bayer	459	97. Kia	356
82. MasterCard	455	98. Circuit City	350
83. Wendy's	436	99. Kimberly-Clark	342
84. Campbell Soup	425	100. Molson Coors	331

Source: Advertising Age, June 27, 2005.

machines. Experience goods are distinguished from *search goods,* whose qualities can be judged before purchase through prepurchase testing. Search goods include fresh fruits and vegetables, which can be squeezed and smelled to test for freshness; fresh meats, which can be viewed; shoes, which can be tried on; and sofas and chairs, which can be sat on.

Consider two producers of toothpaste. Both toothpastes contain fluoride and have the American Dental Association seal of approval, but the high-quality toothpaste tastes wonderful, and the low-quality toothpaste tastes horrible. The costs of production are equal for both products. Toothpaste is an experience good, so consumers cannot determine quality (taste) unless they buy the toothpaste.

Which firm has a greater incentive to advertise?[19] The horrible-tasting toothpaste producer can induce consumers to buy its product once, but few will buy a second time. The wonderful-tasting toothpaste producer, however, can depend on many repeat purchases. The producer of the high-quality toothpaste has a much greater incentive to advertise because advertising will result not only in initial purchases but in repeat purchases. The low-quality toothpaste manufacturer has little incentive to advertise because advertising will result in initial purchases but few repeat purchases. Large advertising expenditures by the high-quality toothpaste manufacturer signal consumers that it produces a high-quality product, because only high-quality producers would advertise extensively. The low-quality producer would realize that consumers will not buy its toothpaste a second time regardless of their advertising expenditures, and therefore, the low-quality manufacturer would not waste resources on useless advertising.

According to this theory, Philip Morris initially spent a huge amount to advertise Miller Lite beer because Philip Morris knew that Lite was a high-quality product that consumers would be willing to buy again. If Philip Morris had thought that Lite beer was a low-quality product, it would not have wasted its scarce advertising resources on a known "loser." Viewed from a different angle, when Coca-Cola realized most consumers considered New Coke to be of lower quality than Coca-Cola Classic, the company quickly stopped advertising its "low-quality" New Coke and dramatically increased its advertising of "high-quality" Coca-Cola Classic. This advertising strategy signaled consumers that the company believed in the high quality of Coca-Cola Classic but had little faith in the quality of New Coke. It is not surprising, therefore, that only Coca-Cola Classic survived nationally.

Although the social benefits of persuasive advertising may be hard to identify, the private benefits are obvious. Persuasive advertising may increase market power and economic profits. The social costs of persuasive advertising, therefore, may be substantial.

13.4 Advertising and Market Structure

We have seen that advertising can be associated with both positive and negative social effects. In addition, increased advertising can result in either an increase or decrease in market power. This section examines a number of major theories that have been advanced concerning the relationship between market structure and advertising, beginning with the relationship between advertising and monopoly and then examining the relationship between advertising and oligopoly.

13.4.1 Welfare Effects of Advertising

So does advertising increase or decrease welfare? This is a complicated question that economists have attempted to answer for decades. One of the most important and controversial attempts to shed light on the issue was made by Dixit and Norman in 1978.[20] They analyzed the welfare effects of advertising under monopoly, oligopoly, and monopolistic competition. Their conclusions were the same for all three market structures; however, we will analyze only the monopoly case, which is the easiest to present.

In Figure 13.10, suppose that demand curve D is the demand without advertising and that demand curve D_A is the demand curve with advertising expenditures equal to E. Advertising increases demand and also increases the monopolist's profit-maximizing output from q_0 to q_A and price from p_0 to p_A. It is possible to argue that welfare should be calculated based on either the pre-advertising demand curve D or the post-advertising demand curve D_A. Dixit and Norman solved this problem by calculating the change in welfare based on both and then proving that their conclusions did not depend on which demand curve was used.

In Figure 13.10 advertising increases the monopolist's profit by the sum of the three shaded areas A + B + C *minus* the monopolist's advertising expenditures E (E is not shown in the figure), so the change in profits $\Delta\pi = A + B + C - E$. However, the increase in price from p_0 to p_A also results in a decrease in consumer welfare equal to area $A = q_0(p_A - p_0) = q_0(\Delta p)$ on the q_0 units that the consumer purchased for the

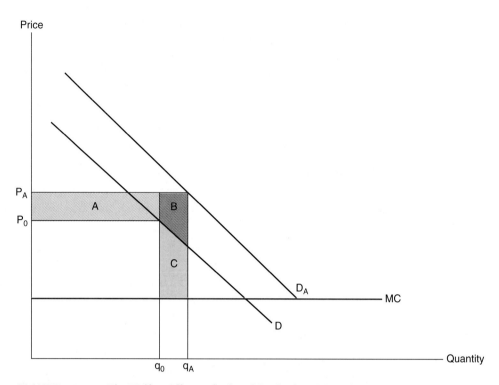

FIGURE 13.10 The Welfare Effects of Advertising in the Dixit and Norman Model

An increase in advertising expenditures of E increases demand from D to D_A and increases the monopolist's profit-maximizing output from q_0 to q_A and profit-maximizing price from p_0 to p_A. If welfare is based on pre-advertising demand curve D, advertising increases the monopolist's profit by the sum of the three shaded areas A + B + C *minus* the monopolist's advertising expenditures E (E is not shown in the figure). The increase in price results in a decrease in consumer surplus equal to area A $= q_0(p_A - p_0) = q_0(\Delta p)$. The total change in welfare is $\Delta W = \Delta \pi - q_0(\Delta p)$. Because $-q_0(\Delta p)$ must be negative and $\Delta \pi = 0$ at the margin, welfare must decrease.

lower price p_0 without advertising but that now must be purchased at the higher price p_A. The change in welfare, therefore, can be expressed as follows:*

$$\Delta W = \Delta \pi - q_0(\Delta p). \qquad [13.6]$$

From Equation 13.6, welfare cannot increase unless profits increase because the second term on the right-hand side, $-q_0(\Delta p)$, must be negative. However, any profit-maximizing monopolist chooses a level of advertising such that the marginal revenue from the last dollar spent on advertising equals the marginal expenditure on advertising (that is, $\Delta(A + B + C) = \Delta E$), so that profit maximization requires that, at the margin, $\Delta \pi = 0$ for the last dollar spent on advertising. But if $\Delta \pi = 0$, then $\Delta W < 0$ because $-q_0(\Delta p) < 0$. At the margin, advertising expenditures contribute nothing to monop-

*Based on the pre-advertising demand D, this is actually a very close approximation to the change in welfare because it includes shaded areas B and C. The true change in welfare equals only area C. Dixit and Norman used this approximation because area B is of "second-order smallness." Avinash Dixit and Victor Norman, "Advertising and Welfare," *Bell Journal of Economics,* 9 (Spring): 1978, p. 4.

oly profits but reduce consumer surplus, and therefore, reduce welfare. This is a rather startling conclusion; all profit-maximizing monopolists spend too much on advertising from a social welfare perspective. Furthermore, as noted earlier, Dixit and Norman also showed that this result holds for oligopoly and monopolistic competition as well.

Dixit and Norman's conclusions have been criticized on a number of grounds, including the following two major criticisms.

1. In the Dixit and Norman model, advertising has no social value; that is, advertising conveys no useful information but is entirely persuasive. We have already shown that informational advertising is likely to have significant positive effects on market performance that are not included in the Dixon and Norman model. Consider, for example, advertising that informs some consumers of the existence of a product but has no impact on previously informed consumers' demand curves, all of which remain unchanged post-advertising.[21] If advertising serves only to bring newly informed consumers into the market, there is an increase in consumer surplus for these consumers that is entirely due to advertising. In this case, advertising must have a positive impact on welfare.

2. Advertising may positively impact the utility consumers derive from purchasing a good.[22] For example, Calvin Klein's advertising can increase consumers' utilities when they wear Calvin Klein clothing. In this case, the pre-advertising demand curve is based on the consumer's lower utility per unit consumed before advertising, but the post-advertising demand curve should accurately measure the consumer's higher utility per unit after advertising. If the measure of welfare is based on the pre-advertising demand curve *before* advertising and the post-advertising demand curve *after* advertising, then the Dixit and Norman conclusions do not necessarily hold because post-advertising, there can be a large increase in consumer surplus on all units of Calvin Klein clothing (all q_A units in Figure 13.10), not just the additional units ($q_A - q_0$ units in Figure 13.10).

13.4.2 The Dorfman-Steiner Model[23]

One of the earlier models of the relationship between market structure and advertising was developed by Dorfman and Steiner. They consider a monopolist characterized by the following demand function:

$$Q = Q(P, A),$$

where Q represents the quantity demanded, P represents price, and A represents advertising expenditures. The monopolist wishes to maximize profits represented by Π as follows:

$$\Pi = TR - TC = P \cdot Q - C(Q) - A = P \cdot Q(P, A) - C(Q(P, A)) - A, \quad [13.7]$$

where $TC = C(Q) + A = C(Q(P, A)) + A$.

In the **Dorfman-Steiner model,** only Q is a function of A, whereas P is independent of the level of advertising expenditures A. Two conditions are necessary for profit maximization in Equation 13.7. First, the monopolist must equate marginal revenue to marginal cost. Recall from Chapter 3 that the MR = MC condition implies:

$$\frac{P - MC}{P} = \frac{1}{|e_D|}, \quad [13.8]$$

where e_D is the price elasticity of demand.

Second, the monopolist must equate the marginal revenue associated with an increase in advertising expenditures, $\Delta TR/\Delta A$, to the marginal cost of the additional advertising expenditures $\Delta TC/\Delta A$. Because Dorfman and Steiner assumed $\Delta P/\Delta A = 0$, this condition can be written as:

$$MR = \frac{\Delta TR}{\Delta A} = P\frac{\Delta Q}{\Delta A} = MC = \frac{\Delta C}{\Delta Q}\frac{\Delta Q}{\Delta A} + \frac{\Delta A}{\Delta A} = \frac{\Delta TC}{\Delta A}. \qquad [13.9]$$

Some algebraic manipulation of Equation 13.9 yields the Dorfman-Steiner result:*

$$\frac{A}{PQ} = \frac{e_A}{|e_D|} = \left(\frac{P - MC}{P}\right)e_A. \qquad [13.10]$$

Equation 13.10 states that the advertising-to-sales ratio, A/PQ, is directly related to the price-cost margin, $(P - MC)/P$; inversely related to the price elasticity of demand, $|e_D|$; and directly related to the advertising elasticity of demand, e_A. The advertising elasticity of demand, e_A, is the percent change in the quantity demanded divided by the percent change in advertising expenditures. Industries in which advertising expenditures have a large impact on sales have high advertising elasticities of demand. For example, RCA and Hughes Electronics introduced the DSS 18-inch satellite TV dish with a tremendous advertising blitz, and the response from consumers was phenomenal.[24] In this case, therefore, the advertising elasticity of demand was very large. Equation 13.10 creates a theoretical link between market structure and advertising because $1/|e_D|$ is the Lerner Index of market power, as discussed in Chapter 3. If the monopolist faces competition from substitute products, e_D is large, its price-cost margin is low, and the advertising-to-sales ratio will be small. As e_D decreases, the price-cost margin increases, and the advertising-to-sales ratio increases.

The basic Dorfman-Steiner model for monopoly suggests a positive link between market power and advertising: As the Lerner Index of market power increases, so does the advertising-to-sales ratio. The Dorfman-Steiner model, however, is a model of

*The algebra is as follows. Equation 13.9 can be written as:

$$P\frac{\Delta Q}{\Delta A} = \frac{\Delta C}{\Delta Q}\frac{\Delta Q}{\Delta A} + 1.$$

First multiply each side by ΔA to yield:

$$P\Delta Q = \frac{\Delta C}{\Delta Q}\Delta Q + \Delta A.$$

The term $\Delta C/\Delta Q$ is simply MC, so we have:

$$(P - MC)\Delta Q = \Delta A.$$

Next multiply each side of the equation by:

$$\frac{A}{PQ\Delta A},$$

which yields:

$$\left(\frac{P - MC}{P}\right)\frac{\Delta Q}{\Delta A}\frac{A}{Q} = \frac{A\Delta A}{PQ\Delta A} = \frac{A}{PQ}.$$

Because $\dfrac{\Delta Q}{\Delta A}\dfrac{A}{Q}$ is the advertising elasticity of demand, it follows that:

$$\frac{A}{PQ} = \left(\frac{P - MC}{P}\right)e_A = \frac{e_A}{|e_D|}.$$

monopoly behavior, not a model of *oligopoly* behavior, and therefore, its implications are limited.

We now extend the model to cases of oligopoly.

13.4.3 Advertising and Oligopoly Behavior

Consider the Dorfman-Steiner model in the case of duopoly with two basically identical manufacturers: Kellogg's and General Mills. Kellogg's output is represented by q_K, its advertising expenditures are represented by A_K, and its market share is represented by $m_K = (q_K/Q)$, where $Q = q_K + q_G$ and q_G represents General Mills' output. To simplify the analysis, we initially assume Cournot behavior with regard to advertising expenditures; that is, both firms assume their rival will maintain its current level of advertising. The advertising elasticity of demand for Kellogg's is denoted by e_{A_K} and is equal to:*

$$e_{A_K} = \left(\frac{\Delta Q}{\Delta A_K}\frac{A_K}{Q}\right) + \left(\frac{\Delta m_K}{\Delta A_K}\frac{A_K}{m_K}\right),$$ [13.11]

where m_K refers to Kellogg's market share.

*The intuitive interpretation of this result is explained in the next paragraph. The technical derivation using calculus is:

$$\Pi = P \cdot q_K - C(q_K) - A_K = P \cdot q_K(P, A_K) - C(q_K(P, A_K)) - A_K.$$

To maximize profit, take the derivative with respect to A_K and set it equal to zero:

$$\frac{d\pi}{dA_K} = P\frac{\partial q_K}{\partial A_K} - \frac{\partial C}{\partial q_K}\frac{\partial q_K}{\partial A_K} - \frac{\partial A_K}{\partial A_K} = (P - MC)\frac{\partial q_K}{\partial A_K} - \frac{\partial A_K}{\partial A_K} = 0.$$

Now substitute the following relationship:

$$q_K = \frac{q_K}{Q}Q = m_K Q$$

to yield:

$$\frac{d\pi}{dA_K} = (P - MC)\frac{\partial(m_K Q)}{\partial A_K} - 1 = 0,$$

recognizing that:

$$\frac{\partial(m_K Q)}{\partial A_K} = m_K\frac{\partial Q}{\partial A_K} + Q\frac{\partial m_K}{\partial A_K}$$

for profit maximization, we obtain:

$$\frac{d\pi}{dA_K} = (P - MC)\left[m_K\frac{\partial Q}{\partial A_K} + Q\frac{\partial m_K}{\partial A_K}\right] = 1,$$

or, multiplying both sides by $\dfrac{A_K}{Pq_K}$:

$$\frac{A_K}{Pq_K} = \left(\frac{P - MC}{P}\right)\left[m_K\frac{\partial Q}{\partial A_K} - Q\frac{\partial m_K}{\partial A_K}\right]\left(\frac{A_K}{q_K}\right)$$

$$\frac{A_K}{Pq_K} = \left(\frac{P - MC}{P}\right)\left[\frac{\dfrac{m_K A_K}{q_K}\dfrac{\partial Q}{\partial A_K} + \dfrac{A_K}{q_K}\dfrac{\partial m_K}{\partial A_K}}{Q}\right]$$

or

$$\frac{A_K}{Pq_K} = \left(\frac{P - MC}{P}\right)\left[\frac{A_K}{Q}\frac{\partial Q}{\partial A_K} + \frac{A_K}{m_K}\frac{\partial m_K}{\partial A_K}\right].$$

The two terms on the right-hand side of Equation 13.11 represent the two effects of an increase in advertising. The first term is the *industry output effect*. Kellogg's increased advertising increases the demand for the generic industry product, not just its own brand. If Kellogg's increases its advertising, consumers will purchase more cereal of all types, including General Mills, Post, and store brands. The second term on the right-hand side represents the *market share effect*. If Kellogg's increases its advertising, its market share will increase relative to that of General Mills, Post, and store brands.*

An example may help to clarify Equation 13.11. If initially $Q = 1000$ and $q_K = 500$, then $m_K = 0.50$. Assume (1) Kellogg's increases its advertising by 1 percent, (2) industry output increases by 1 percent to $Q' = 1010$, and (3) Kellogg's market share increases by 2 percent to $m'_K = 0.51$. According to Equation 13.11, the advertising elasticity of demand for Kellogg's is $e_{A_K} = 1 + 2 = 3$. Kellogg's new output is $m'_K Q' = (0.51)1010 = 515$. The percentage change in q_K is 3 percent.[†] As predicted by Equation 13.11, a 1 percent increase in advertising expenditures results in a 3 percent increase in q_K.

Substituting e_{A_K} from Equation 13.11 into Equation 13.10 yields:[‡]

$$\frac{A_K}{PQ_K} = \left(\frac{P - MC}{P}\right)e_{A_K} = \left(\frac{P - MC}{P}\right)\left[\left(\frac{\Delta Q}{\Delta A_K}\frac{A_K}{Q}\right) + \left(\frac{\Delta m_K}{\Delta A_K}\frac{A_K}{m_K}\right)\right]. \qquad [13.12]$$

Equation 13.12 suggests that oligopolists have an additional incentive to advertise. Not only does advertising increase the total demand for the product, Q, but it increases Kellogg's market share, m_K.

A comparison of Equations 13.11 and 13.12 suggests that for any given price-cost margin, the advertising-to-sales ratio will be larger in oligopoly than in monopoly because the advertising elasticity of demand, e_A, is larger under oligopoly than under monopoly. Intuitively, an increase in advertising does not change the monopolist's 100 percent market share, and this reduces the monopolist's incentive to advertise.

One implication of Equation 13.12 is that firms in competitive environments that face highly elastic demand curves with low price-cost margins will advertise very little. In fact, as the price-cost margin approaches zero, the advertising-to-sales ratio also approaches zero. This helps explain why individual farmers rarely advertise their wheat, milk, or oranges. Advertising in this case makes economic sense only if the farmers advertise collectively through organizations such as the American Dairy Council or the Florida Orange Growers.

There is a potential problem with the formulation of Equations 13.11 and 13.12. Suppose the Cournot assumption concerning advertising is wrong, and General Mills chooses to increase its advertising in response to Kellogg's increased advertising. Equation 13.11 would then have to reflect the impact of General Mills' increased

*Remember that assuming Cournot behavior regarding advertising, the other firm maintains its level of advertising expenditures. We will relax this assumption shortly.

[†]The percentage change in q_K is:

$$\frac{\Delta q_K}{q_K} \times 100 = \frac{15}{500} \times 100 = 3\%.$$

[‡]See the footnote on page 443 for the derivation of this result using calculus.

advertising on total industry output and on Kellogg's market share. The new formulation would be:

$$e_{A_K} = \left[\frac{\Delta(q_K + q_G)}{\Delta(A_K + A_G)}\frac{(A_K + A_G)}{(q_K + q_G)}\right]\frac{A_K}{A_K + A_G} + \left(\frac{\Delta m_K}{\Delta A_K}\frac{A_K}{m_K}\right) + \left(\frac{\Delta m_K}{\Delta A_G}\frac{A_G}{m_K}\right)\left(\frac{\Delta A_G}{\Delta A_K}\frac{A_K}{A_G}\right).$$

[13.13]

Equation 13.13 looks formidable, but it is simply the sum of three straightforward terms. The first term represents the industry output effect and must be positive. It incorporates the elasticity of industry output with respect to a change in total industry advertising expenditures (the term in brackets) and Kellogg's share of industry advertising.* The second term is identical to the second term in Equation 13.11 and is the *market share effect* of Kellogg's advertising on Kellogg's market share. This term must be greater than or equal to zero. The additional third term reflects the impact of General Mills' increased advertising on Kellogg's market share. The third term typically would be less than or equal to zero because $(\Delta m_K/\Delta A_G) \leq 0$ and $(\Delta A_G/\Delta A_K)$ would usually be greater than zero. In theory, however, $(\Delta A_G/\Delta A_K)$ could be negative if General Mills received so much benefit from an increase in Kellogg's advertising that it decided to reduce its own advertising in response.

Which formulation of e_{A_K}, Equation 13.11 with Cournot behavior or Equation 13.13, is closer to reality? We know that under duopoly the prisoner's dilemma makes retaliation in response to price reductions fairly certain, but a response to a new advertising campaign is much more problematic. Price cuts can be matched immediately, whereas a new advertising campaign takes time to devise and implement. When Miller Lite commercials hit the television airwaves, it took quite some time for competitors to respond effectively, and much of Miller's increased market share has remained in place for decades. Until competitors come up with an effective advertising response, the firm that moves first with a successful campaign may significantly increase its market share.

Advertising campaigns, however, are inherently unpredictable. Optimistic firms tend to overestimate the positive second term in Equation 13.13 and underestimate the negative third term. If the negative third term in Equation 13.13 is underestimated or ignored, firms will have a tendency to advertise beyond their profit-maximizing level of advertising.

The possibility of excessive advertising beyond the profit-maximizing level can also be explained by the prisoner's dilemma. Figure 13.11 depicts a possible payoff matrix for high and low levels of advertising. This game has a dominant solution. Regardless of the competitor's choice, it always pays to choose a high level of advertising expenditures, and each firm will earn an economic profit of $100 million. If the two could manage to solve the dilemma, they would reduce their advertising expenditures to a low level and earn a profit of $120 million each. Overspending on advertising costs each firm $20 million in profits.

Evidence suggests that oligopolists often engage in excessive advertising of the type suggested by Figure 13.11. One of the most frequently studied examples is cigarette advertising. When antitrust policy broke up the American Tobacco Company

*An alternative formulation weights the term in brackets by Kellogg's share of industry output.

	General Mills' high advertising expenditures	General Mills' low advertising expenditures
Kellogg's high advertising expenditures	100, 100	130, 80
Kellogg's low advertising expenditures	80, 130	120, 120

FIGURE 13.11 Oligopolistic Advertising and the Prisoner's Dilemma (Kellogg's profits in $million, General Mills' profits in $million)

and turned the industry into an oligopoly, advertising expenditures increased from $4.3 million in 1910 to $13.8 million in 1913.[25] In the 1950s the introduction of king-sized cigarettes caused a sharp escalation in advertising expenditures.[26] More recently the ban on television and then radio advertising in the 1960s and 1970s resulted in a simultaneous decrease in advertising expenditures and increase in profits. This evidence suggests that cigarette advertising has often gone beyond the joint profit-maximizing level.[27]

In a detailed econometric study of advertising in European markets, Lambin found that many industries appeared to advertise beyond the joint profit-maximizing level. These included the gasoline, coffee, yogurt, insecticide, deodorant, detergent, and soft drink industries.[28] Netter found similar results for a sample of American industries.[29]

To summarize the main conclusions concerning advertising to this point:

1. Firms with little market power have low price-cost margins and should have low advertising-to-sales ratios.

2. As a firm's price-cost margin increases, so should its advertising-to-sales ratio.

3. *Ceteris paribus,* oligopolists will have larger advertising-to-sales ratios than monopolists or competitive firms.

4. Oligopolists may tend to engage in excessive advertising.

Figure 13.12 summarizes the expected relationship between market power and advertising expenditures. The relationship is nonlinear. The advertising-to-sales ratio increases with increases in the concentration ratio up to level CR* and decreases with increases in concentration beyond that level. Notice that the monopolist's advertising is significantly greater than the perfectly competitive level of advertising.

So far we have concentrated on the relationship between market structure and product differentiation by emphasizing a theoretical link suggesting that increased concentration causes increased product differentiation; that is, increased market power causes increased advertising. The link between market structure and product differentiation, however, may run in the opposite direction, with increased product differentiation causing increased concentration.[30] The discussion of product proliferation in Chapter 12 suggested such a linkage, as did the discussion of raising rivals' costs through advertising. We now consider this alternative view of the relationship between product differentiation and market structure.

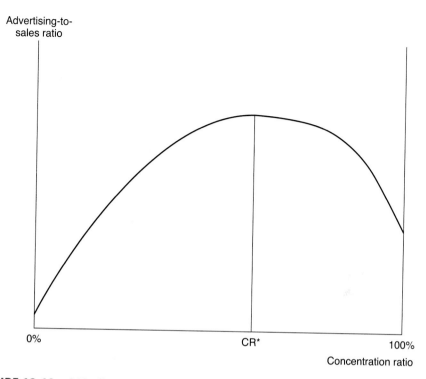

FIGURE 13.12 **A Nonlinear Relationship Between Concentration and the Advertising-to-Sales Ratio**

The expected theroretical relationship between market power and advertising expenditures is nonlinear. The advertising-to-sales ratio increases with concentration up to concentration ratio CR* and decreases with increases in concentration beyond that level.

APPLICATION 13.2

The Variability of the Advertising-to-Sales Ratios Across Industries

The Dorfman-Steiner model suggests that firms with little market power should have lower advertising-to-sales ratios than firms with significant market power and that firms with high advertising elasticities of demand should advertise more than firms with low advertising elasticities of demand. Furthermore, because of the prisoner's dilemma, oligopolists in markets with significant product differentiation may advertise beyond the profit-maximizing level. Putting these theoretical results together, oligopolists in less competitive industries with significant product differentiation should have the highest advertising-to-sales ratios. Furthermore, because competitive conditions, including the advertising elasticity of demand, vary widely across industries, the advertising-to-sales ratio should vary more *across* industries than *within* industries.

Each year *Advertising Age* magazine collects data on the leading 100 advertisers ranked by advertising expenditures in all media in the United States. The following table shows a subsample of the 2004 rankings for which it is possible to calculate U.S.

advertising-to-sales ratios from *Advertising Age* data.* The national average advertising-to-sales ratio for all firms is approximately 2.0 percent; however, because this sample comprises the leading advertisers, the average for this sample is considerably greater than 2.0 percent.

Industry	2004 U.S. Advertising Expenditures ($millions)	2004 U.S. Advertising/Sales (%)
Best Buy	950.5	3.9
Circuit City	350.0	3.5
McDonald's	1,388.9	21.3
Burger King	542.1	7.0
Wendy's	435.8	17.6
Yum Brands (KFC, Pizza Hut, Taco Bell)	779.4	13.5
Dell	756.2	1.5
Hewlett Packard	898.5	3.1
Microsoft	986.6	3.9
IBM	631.9	1.8
General Motors	3,997.4	3.0
Ford	2,458.0	2.5
Daimler-Chrysler	2,462.1	3.1
Honda	1,204.9	2.8
Bell South	404.9	2.0
Verizon	2,197.3	3.2
American Express	717.9	3.1
Capital One	487.9	6.2
General Mills	912.5	9.7
Kellogg	647.1	10.8
Cadbury Schweppes	374.8	7.4
PepsiCo	1,262.2	6.9
Federated Department Stores	744.1	4.8
Gap	525.5	3.7
Sears	1,823.0	3.6
Sara Lee	528.9	4.8
Campbell Soup	425.3	9.3
Bristol-Myers	772.9	7.3
Eli Lilly	586.8	7.7
GlaxoSmithKline	1,828.3	10.8
Merck	1,250.3	9.3
Novartis	1,284.6	11.4
Wyeth	828.7	8.4
News Corp. (Fox)	890.5	5.9
Time Warner	3,283.1	9.8
Viacom	1,207.3	6.4
Nike	573.9	12.0
Sony	1,665.3	8.4

Source: Advertising Age, 100 Leading National Advertisers Supplement, June 27, 2005, www.adage.com/images/random/lna2005.pdf.

Comparing the leading advertisers in each of these markets, with few exceptions, there is far more variability in the advertising-to-sales ratio *across* markets than there is *within* markets (as expected). For example, in automobiles General Motors' advertising-to-sales ratio was 3.0 percent and Ford's was 2.5 percent; in retailing Sears's ratio was 3.6 percent and The Gap's ratio was 3.7 percent; whereas in cereals, General Mills' ratio was 9.7 percent and Kellogg's ratio was 10.8 percent. Among the other industries, the following had relatively low advertising-to-sales ratios: computers and software, retail consumer electronics, and telecommunications. Industries with relatively high advertising-to-sales ratios included pharmaceuticals and fast-food restaurants.

Finally, in several industries, such as fast-food restaurants and cereals, it is hard to imagine that advertising has not exceeded the profit-maximizing level. In 2004, McDonald's spent 21.3 percent of its sales, or almost $1.4 billion, on advertising; Yum Brands (KFC, Pizza Hut, Taco Bell, and Long John Silver's) spent $779 million; Burger King spent $542 million; and Wendy's spent $436 million. In all, these four firms spent more than $3.15 billion on advertising. It seems unlikely that those huge advertising expenditures could increase the demand for hamburgers, chicken patties, pizza, and tacos enough to increase the firms' combined profits. A more likely scenario is that much of McDonald's, Yum's, Burger King's, and Wendy's advertising canceled each other out and had little impact on either the total demand for fast food or the relative market shares of these four firms.

Perhaps a more direct empirical approach to testing the Dorfman-Steiner model is to examine whether less competitive oligopolies with significant product differentiation have the highest advertising-to-sales ratios. This requires market-based rather than firm-based advertising data. Each year Schonfeld & Associates publishes data on advertising-to-sales ratios for more than 300 industries in the United States. Many markets are divided into wholesale and retail markets or producer goods markets and consumer goods markets. The Dorfman-Steiner model suggests that more competitive industries, wholesale markets, and producer goods markets should have lower advertising-to-sales ratios than less competitive industries, retail markets, and consumer goods markets, respectively. In the table below, 2004 advertising-to-sales ratios are shown for industries grouped to show highly competitive, wholesale and producer goods markets juxtaposed with less competitive, retail and consumer goods markets. For example, in keeping with expectations, the advertising-to-sales ratio for the wholesale chemical and allied products industry is 1.0 percent, while the ratio is 3.5 percent for chemical and allied products.

Industry	2004 Advertising/Sales (%)
Chemical & allied products, wholesale	1.0
Chemical & allied products	3.5
Aircraft parts, auxiliary equipment, NEC	1.3
Aircraft	6.4
Amusement & recreation services	2.0
Amusement parks	9.6
Beer, wine & alcoholic beverages, wholesale	2.0
Distilled & blended liquor	15.8
Malt beverages	8.7

Continued

Industry	2004 Advertising/Sales (%)
Wine, brandy & brandy spirits	2.2
Agricultural production—crops	0.3
Cigarettes	4.0
Communications equipment, NEC	1.2
Cable & other pay TV services	6.5
Computer & software, wholesale	0.1
Computer peripheral equipment, NEC	2.9
Computer communication equipment	2.2
Computer & office equipment	1.4
Drugs & proprietary, wholesale	0.0
Pharmaceuticals	4.7
Electric apparatus & equipment, wholesale	0.3
Electrical industrial apparatus	4.6
Television & telegraph apparatus	1.3
TV broadcast stations	11.2
Industrial inorganic chemicals	0.1
Miscellaneous chemical products	1.6
Soaps, detergents & toilet preparations	11.6
Special cleaning, polishing preparations	10.9
Lumber & construction materials, wholesale	0.3
Lumber plywood millwork, wholesale	1.9
Furniture stores	5.9
Lumber & wood products, except furniture	7.3
Motor vehicles supply, new parts, wholesale	0.7
Motor vehicles parts, accessories	0.4
Motor vehicles & car bodies	2.4
Food stores	3.2
Food & kindred products	11.1

Source: Schonfeld & Associates, Advertising Ratios & Budgets—June 2004.

The most striking findings are that wholesale markets consistently have much lower advertising-to-sales ratios than oligopoly markets aimed directly at consumers, producer goods markets have much lower advertising-to-sales ratios than consumer goods markets, and more competitive markets have much lower advertising-to-sales ratios than less competitive markets. Consider a few examples: The advertising-to-sales ratio is 2.0 percent for the wholesale market for beer, wine, and alcoholic beverages but over seven times larger (at 15.8 percent) for the highly oligopolistic distilled and blended liquor market; and the advertising-to-sales ratio is only 1.3 percent for aircraft parts and auxiliary equipment, but 6.4 percent for the oligopolistic aircraft industry.

Overall, the evidence presented from both data sets (from *Advertising Age* and Schonfeld & Associates) is quite consistent with the implications of the Dorfman-Steiner model.

*Many multinational firms (e.g., Coca-Cola, Toyota, Pfizer) report only consolidated worldwide sales or North American sales, but not U.S. sales, and therefore, for these firms it is impossible to calculate a U.S. advertising-to-sales ratio. This greatly limits the data set. ■

13.4.4 The Product Differentiation Advantages of First Movers

Consider the market for a newly introduced experience good such as the provision of Internet services. Recall that experience goods are goods whose qualities can only be identified through trial after buying the good. Examples include beer, toothpaste, soap, toiletries, cereal, refrigerators, and washing machines.

The first mover into the Internet service providers (ISP) market faces a problem because consumers are initially uninformed about Internet service provision. Consumers, therefore, risk being disappointed if they purchase Internet service for the first time. In Figure 13.13, if all consumers were fully informed about Internet service the demand would be:

$$P = 100 - Q.$$

Before their introduction, however, all consumers are uninformed about Internet service and risk buying Internet service and disliking it. Uninformed consumers will be willing to pay less for Internet service than informed consumers, so the demand for

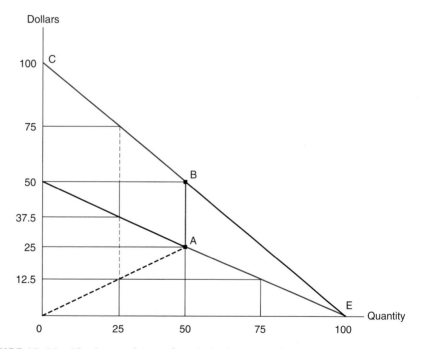

FIGURE 13.13 The Demand Curve for AOL in the ISP Market

At the time of introduction the first mover faces the lower demand curve P = 50 − Q and introduces the service at P = $25 to 50 subscribers. After the introductory offer ends, demand increases to P = 100 − Q for the original 50 subscribers who are informed and the first mover increases price to P = $50 and provides service to 50 subscribers. The new demand curve for the first mover is the red kinky line CBAE.

Internet service before introduction is less than P = 100 − Q. Assume the demand for Internet service if all consumers are uniformed is:[31]

$$P = (100 - Q)(1 - \tau), \qquad\qquad [13.14]$$

where τ represents the risk-cost factor of trying Internet service for the first time. τ measures the risks associated with wasting money on the purchase of a good that the consumer might dislike. The risk-cost factor τ is larger the greater the probability of a bad consumption experience. In addition, τ is larger with less frequent repeat purchases because with infrequent repeat purchases the consumer is "stuck" with a bad decision for a long time. For example, τ is larger for a washing machine than a box of cereal because a mistake in buying a box of cereal can be corrected in a matter of days, whereas a bad washing machine can cause the consumer problems for years.

If $\tau = 0.5$, then the introductory demand for Internet service is:

$$P = (100 - Q)(1 - 0.5) = 50 - \frac{1}{2}Q. \qquad\qquad [13.15]$$

Figure 13.13 depicts both demand curves. At the time of introduction the first mover, AOL, faces the lower demand curve, $P = 50 - \frac{1}{2}Q$. Suppose that AOL decides to introduce Internet service at a low introductory price of P = $25 and sells service to 50 subscribers. After the introductory offer ends, demand increases to P = 100 − Q for the 50 subscribers who are completely informed, and AOL can increase price to P = $50 and continue to provide service to 50 subscribers. After introduction, the new demand curve for AOL is depicted in Figure 13.13 as the red kinky line CBAE, which is composed of part of the informed and part of the uninformed demand curves.

Even if another firm, AT&T for example, provides Internet service that is identical to AOL's service, it faces a different demand curve than line CBAE because consumers cannot be certain that AT&T's Internet service is actually identical to AOL's service. To derive AT&T's demand curve, it is necessary to separate consumers into two groups. Group 1 consists of informed consumers who are already "hooked" on AOL's service. Each of these consumers, except the fiftieth consumer, receives consumer surplus greater than zero from the consumption of Internet service. Consider the twenty-fifth subscriber to AOL's Internet service: That consumer's reservation price is $75 while the price is $50, so for the twenty-fifth subscriber, consumer surplus equals $25 ($75 − $50). What is the highest price this consumer would pay to try AT&T's Internet service? Assume group 1 consumers would pay a maximum price to try AT&T's Internet service of:

$$P = (100 - Q)(1 - \tau) - S, \qquad\qquad [13.16]$$

where S represents the amount of current consumer surplus the consumer receives from the consumption of AOL's service. Consumer surplus enters into the consumer's decision because the consumer risks sacrificing this consumer surplus if he or she tries AT&T's Internet service and does not like it. For the twenty-fifth subscriber in Figure 13.13, S = 25, and therefore, the maximum price this consumer would be willing to pay to try AT&T's Internet service is:

$$P = (100 - Q)(1 - \tau) - S = (100 - 25)(1 - 0.5) - 25 = 75(0.5) - 25 = \$12.5.$$

This creates a large ***first-mover advantage*** for AOL because the twenty-fifth sub-scriber would rather continue to pay $50 for AOL Internet service than try AT&T's Inter-net service at a price greater than $12.5. The fiftieth subscriber receives no consumer surplus and would try AT&T's Internet service at a price of P = (100 − 50)(0.5) − 0 = $25, and the consumer of the tenth unit receives consumer surplus equal to $40 ($90 − $50) and would try AT&T's Internet service at a price of P = (100 − 10) × (0.5) − 40 = $5. In Figure 13.13, the line 0A traces out the maximum price that each group 1 consumer would pay to try AT&T's Internet service.

Group 2 consumers have never tried Internet service because AOL's introductory price of $25 was above the reservation price that they were willing to pay to try Inter-net service. Group 2 consumers lie on the section of the uninformed consumer demand curve depicted by AE. To induce these consumers to try Internet service, AT&T must charge a price below $25.

If AOL continues to charge P = $50, AT&T will have to charge a price below $25 to obtain any subscribers.[32] AT&T's demand curve in Figure 13.14 is derived by taking the horizontal difference between the upward-sloping line segment 0A and the downward-sloping red line segment AE. Consider the points on the demand curve for AT&T's Internet service shown on the next page.

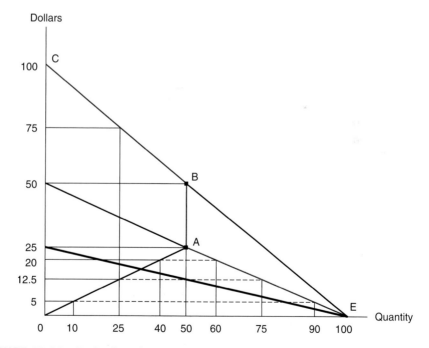

FIGURE 13.14 **Derivation of AT&T'S Demand Curve in the ISP Market**

The second mover's demand curve P = 25 − $\frac{1}{4}$q is derived by taking the horizontal difference between the upward-sloping line segment 0A and the downward-sloping red line segment AE.

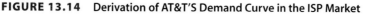

AT&T's Price	(1) Quantity on Line AE in Figure 13.14	(2) Quantity on Line 0A in Figure 13.14	(1) Minus (2) AT&T's Quantity Demanded
$25	50	50	0
$20	60	40	20
$15	70	30	40
$12.5	75	25	50
$10	80	20	60
$5	90	10	80
$0	100	0	100

AT&T's introductory demand curve is:

$$P_{AT} = 25 - \frac{1}{4}q_{AT}. \qquad [13.17]$$

AT&T's demand curve is identified as the heavy black line in Figure 13.14.

This lower demand curve places AT&T at a tremendous disadvantage vis-à-vis AOL. While AOL sells at a price of $50, AT&T will have to sell at a price below $25. For example, recall that the twenty-fifth subscriber would have tried AOL's Internet service at a price of $37.5 but will try AT&T's service only at a price below $12.5. To capture consumers with high reservation prices, AT&T must charge a very low price.

If there are significant sunk costs associated with entry, AT&T may find it impossible to enter and earn a profit. Suppose, for example, that the marginal cost of providing Internet service is constant and equal to $10, and sunk costs are $400. If AT&T enters at its profit-maximizing introductory price of $17.5, it obtains 30 subscribers, and profits would be:*

$$\Pi = Pq_{AT} - mc(q_{AT}) - \text{Sunk Costs} = (\$17.5)(30) - (\$10)(30) - \$400 = -\$175.$$

Under these cost conditions, AT&T cannot enter and earn a profit. However, AOL has already paid its sunk costs and earns a profit of:

$$\Pi = PQ - mcQ = \$50(50) - \$10(50) = \$2000.$$

In response to entry, AOL is capable of responding aggressively and lowering price below $50 while still earning a substantial economic profit. This serves as an additional deterrent to entry.

Empirical evidence of the success of first movers is particularly strong in the pharmaceuticals industry. Several studies have found that first movers in this industry retain a large advantage over late entrants, even when the first mover's price remains well above the entrant's price. Masson and Steiner found that retailers paid far more

*From the "twice-as-steep rule,"

$$MR = 25 - \frac{1}{2}q_{AT}.$$

For profit maximization, MR = MC:

$$25 - \frac{1}{2}q_{AT} = 10 \quad \text{or} \quad q_{AT} = 30.$$

for leading branded drugs than the competitive generic drugs of late entrants.[33] For a sample of 29 drugs, Hurwitz and Caves found that the price of branded leaders was more than twice the price of latecomer generic equivalents.[34] In the Hurwitz and Caves study, the market leaders continued to dominate, despite selling at much higher prices. In addition, the leaders' market shares were positively related to their investment in sales promotion, including advertising.

There are many other documented cases of first movers maintaining dominant shares despite selling at higher prices than late entrants.[35] Some of the well-documented cases were discussed in earlier chapters, including Clorox liquid bleach, Campbell's soups in the United States, Heinz soups in Great Britain, and Coca-Cola soft drinks. More recent examples include Nokia in the cellular phone market, and as in our theoretical example, AOL in the ISP market.

13.5 Advertising as a Barrier to Entry

Recall from Chapter 4 that there may be an *absolute cost advantage* for incumbent firms associated with the *cumulative* effects of advertising. Because advertising generally has an effect on future as well as current demand, it must be viewed as an investment rather than a current expenditure. Successful advertising campaigns have impacts far into the future. Miller Lite's "tastes great, less filling" campaign ended many years ago, yet the impact of that campaign continues into the present. If the impact of advertising is cumulative, entrants have to overcome not only current advertising efforts but also the impact of past campaigns by established firms. If a new cola manufacturer wishes to compete with Coke and Pepsi, it will have to spend far more on advertising in its first few years than the combined amounts spent by Coca-Cola and Pepsico. The cumulative impact of advertising provides a powerful advantage for successful first movers.

Figure 13.15 shows the possible advertising advantage for first movers. Two *advertising response functions* are drawn in Figure 13.15. An advertising response function is $Q = f(A)$, where Q is sales and A is number of advertising messages. The entrant's advertising response function is first horizontal, then rises at an increasing rate, then rises at a decreasing rate, and finally decreases. This assumes a threshold level of advertising messages, AM_1 in Figure 13.15, that the entrant must exceed to have any impact on sales.* Once the threshold level is reached, the marginal impact of additional advertising messages increases, then the marginal impact decreases, and finally the marginal impact becomes *negative* as consumers become tired of the advertising campaign and respond with a negative backlash. An incumbent firm has no threshold level of advertising because the cumulative effect of previous advertising campaigns ensures that current advertising has an immediate impact on sales. Because the impact of previous advertising has not been completely depreciated, the incumbent firm will have a higher level of sales for any given level of advertising expenditures. This results in lower average advertising expenditures for incumbents than for established firms.

The threshold level of advertising expenditures for entrants is a sunk cost associated with entry and creates an entry barrier because incumbent firms have paid this

*Figure 13.15 is based on the assumption that consumers must be saturated with some minimum level of advertising to learn about the existence of the good and be enticed into a trial.

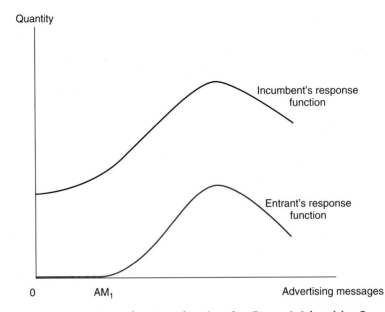

FIGURE 13.15 **Comparison of an Incumbent's and an Entrant's Advertising Response Function**

The entrant's advertising response function is first horizontal, then rises at an increasing rate, then rises at a decreasing rate, and finally decreases. An incumbent firm has no threshold level of advertising because the cumulative effect of previous advertising campaigns ensures that current advertising has an immediate impact on sales; therefore, the incumbent has a higher level of sales for any given level of advertising expenditures.

sunk cost in the past. If the threshold level of advertising is large, the sunk costs of entry will rise significantly and the capital barrier to entry will increase. High sunk costs result in a more or less permanent advantage for first movers over late entrants. The ability of Miller Lite to maintain a large market share in the face of a great deal of entry into the light beer market may be viewed in part as a result of Miller's first-mover advantage. Even a financially strong entrant may find it difficult to overcome the sunk costs of entry. As we discussed earlier, Kodak learned this lesson when it attempted to enter the consumer battery industry.[36]

13.6 Strategic Advantages of Heavily Advertised Brands

Established brands have an ability to respond aggressively to entry by expanding advertising. Recall from Chapter 11 that given asymmetric information, firms might attempt to preempt future entry by cutting price in response to current entry. In markets dominated by heavily advertised brands, established firms may respond to entry by aggressively expanding advertising.

Several examples of aggressive advertising responses to entry have been documented. At the turn of the century when the American Tobacco Company was threatened with a loss of market share to Turkish tobacco brands, it responded by introducing its own Turkish tobacco brands and increasing its advertising expenditures from 0.5 percent to 20.3 percent of sales.[37] When Procter & Gamble introduced a new decaffeinated coffee, "High Point," in 1980, General Foods increased the advertising of its dominant brand, "Sanka," by more than 700 percent to $90 million a year.[38] Minute Maid and Tropicana also responded aggressively to Procter & Gamble's entry into the ready-made orange juice market in 1983.[39]

Cubbin and Domberger found that for a sample of 42 British firms in 18 consumer goods industries, dominant firms were much more likely to respond to entry with a large increase in advertising.[40] Significant retaliation occurred in 61 percent of the markets (11 of 18) and by 38 percent of established firms (16 of 42).

These examples of the strategic use of advertising in response to entry are consistent with the findings of Smiley reported in Chapter 12 that advertising is the most commonly used method of entry deterrence.

13.7 Product Differentiation and Increased Competition

To this point the emphasis of this chapter has been on how product differentiation and advertising result in increased market power. Product differentiation and advertising, however, may result in lower levels of market power. We have already noted that informational advertising is likely to have a procompetitive impact. In addition, numerous case studies show that advertising can lead to a *decrease* in concentration. Advertising may be the only effective method of entering some markets. RCA and Hughes Electronics entered the direct satellite television market with the DSS system through the use of a massive advertising campaign. The small satellite dishes provided new competition to cable systems and large satellite dish systems. Market penetration for the DSS system would undoubtedly have been far lower in the absence of a huge advertising campaign.[41] In the fast-food industry, the entry of Wendy's and Subway on a national level was made possible through extensive advertising campaigns. Advertising also helped Japanese automobile manufacturers enter the United States market on a large scale in the 1960s and 1970s. The success of Korean manufacturers in the U.S. automobile market has also been heavily dependent on advertising. Finally, advertising enabled Pepsi to slowly chip away at Coke's dominant market share. Pepsi's share increased from 10 percent in 1940 to 31 percent in 1987.[42] Pepsi's major market share gains have come during periods when Pepsi's advertising-to-sales ratio was higher than Coke's.

13.8 Empirical Evidence

Advertising and product differentiation, in theory, can have a positive or negative impact on prices, profits, and welfare. Informative advertising tends to have a positive impact, whereas persuasive advertising tends to have a negative impact.

Economists have conducted a vast array of empirical studies to test the relationship among advertising, market structure, and profits. To distinguish between informative and persuasive advertising, most studies have classified goods into different categories based on their characteristics and the way they are marketed.

Recall that experience goods include consumer nondurable convenience goods such as beer, toothpaste, soap, toiletries, and cereal. Search goods include fruits and vegetables, shoes, and sofas and chairs. Theory suggests that much of the advertising associated with experience goods is persuasive, and much of the advertising associated with search goods is informational.

Another important distinction is between manufacturers' advertising and retailers' advertising. Manufacturers' advertising tends to emphasize persuasion and the importance of brand loyalty, whereas retailers' advertising is more likely to emphasize lower prices. A great deal of manufacturers' advertising is through television and radio, whereas most retailers' advertising appears in the print media. Given these characteristics, manufacturers' advertising is more likely to have anticompetitive effects, and retailers' advertising is more likely to have a positive impact.

Empirical attempts to identify the nature of the relationship between advertising and market power are plagued by one serious problem: The direction of the relationship is uncertain. Advertising may erect an entry barrier that enables firms to earn high profits. However, high profits may enable firms to spend large amounts on advertising. Statistical investigations of the relationship between profits and advertising, therefore, may suffer from **simultaneity bias.** The studies noted below generally assume that causation runs *from* advertising *to* profitability; that is, advertising creates an entry barrier that enables firms to earn high profits. It is important to recognize, however, that the direction of causation *from* profitability *to* advertising is equally plausible. Many of the studies apply statistical techniques aimed at correcting for this problem.* Given this important caveat, we proceed to the current state of empirical evidence.

13.8.1 Traditional Studies of the Relationship Between Advertising and Performance Across Industries

Empirical evidence has generally been consistent with expectations.[43] First, a large number of statistical studies in manufacturing industries have attempted to explain the determinants of profitability by using advertising as one of a group of independent variables. Table 13.3 summarizes the results of these studies. Twenty-six of the 34 studies showed some evidence of a positive and statistically significant relationship between profits and advertising. In 10 studies the advertising variable was statistically insignificant in at least some portion of the study, whereas in two studies the sign of the advertising variable was indeterminate because the sign was sometimes positive and sometimes negative. Table 13.3 suggests that advertising is likely to exert a positive influence on profits in manufacturing industries.

The studies in Table 13.3 examined the relationship between profits and advertising; other studies have analyzed the link between prices and advertising. The National Commission on Food Marketing found, for example, that advertised brands consis-

*The technique uses a simultaneous system of equations to estimate the relationship between profits and advertising.

TABLE 13.3 Summary of Studies of the Relationship Between Profits and Advertising in Manufacturing Industries

| | Relationship Between Profits and Advertising | | | |
| | Positive | Negative | Not Significant | Indeterminate |
Author(s)—Year of Study	(+)	(−)	(e)	(?)
B. Imel and P. Helmberger—1971			e	
L. Esposito and F. Esposito—1971	+[1]			
W. Shephard—1972	+[2]			
J. Vernon and R. Nouse—1973	+			
K. Boyer—1974	+			
M. Porter—1974	+[3]		e[4]	
P. Nelson—1975				?
R. Caves, J. Khalilzadeh-Shirazi, and M. Porter—1975	+			
J. Dalton and J. Penn—1976	+			
A. Strickland and L. Weiss—1976	+[5]		e[6]	
R. Stonebraker—1976	+			
P. Hart and E. Morgan—1977	+			
J. Carter—1977	+			
S. Nickell and D. Metcalf—1978	+			
T. Hitris—1978			e	
H. Grabowski and D. Mueller—1978			e[7]	
M. Porter—1979			e	

[1]For consumer goods. [4]For nonconvenience goods. [6]For consumer goods.
[2]For consumer goods. [5]For producer goods. [7]Pharmaceuticals industry only.
[3]For convenience goods.

Sources: B. Imel and P. Helmberger, "Estimation of Structure-Profit Relationships with Application to the Food Processing Sector," *American Economic Review* 61 (1971): 614–627; L. Esposito and F. Esposito, "Foreign Competition and Domestic Industry Profitability," *Review of Economics and Statistics* 53 (1971): 343–353; W.G. Shepherd, "The Elements of Market Structure," *Review of Economics and Statistics* 54 (1972): 25–37; J.M. Vernon and R.E. Nourse, "Profit Rates and Market Structure in Advertising Intensive Firms," *Journal of Industrial Economics* 22 (1973): 1–20; Kenneth D. Boyer, "Informative and Goodwill Advertising," *Review of Economics and Statistics* 56 (November 1974): 541–548; Michael E. Porter, "Consumer Behavior, Retailer Power and Market Performance in Consumer Goods Industries," *Review of Economics and Statistics* 56 (November 1974): 429; Philip Nelson, "The Economic Consequences of Advertising," *Journal of Business* 48 (April 1975): 237; Richard E. Caves, J. Khalilzadeh-Shirazi, and M.E. Porter, "Scale Economies in Statistical Analyses of Market Power," *Review of Economics and Statistics* 57 (May 1975): 133–140; J.A. Dalton and D.W. Penn, "The Concentration-Profitability Relationship: Is There a Critical Concentration Ratio?" *Journal of Industrial Economics* 25 (1976): 133–142; Allyn D. Strickland and Leonard W. Weiss, "Advertising, Concentration, and Price-Cost Margins," *Journal of Political Economy* 85 (October 1976): 1109–1121; John Carter, "In Search of Synergy: A Structure-Performance Test," *Review of Economics and Statistics* 59 (1977): 279–289; R.J. Stonebraker, "Corporate Profits and the Risk of Entry," *Review of Economics and Statistics* 58 (1976): 33–39; P. Hart and E. Morgan, "Market Structure and Economic Performance in the United Kingdom," *Journal of Industrial Economics* 25 (1977): 177–193; S. Nickell and D. Metcalf, "Monopolistic Industries and Monopoly Profits or, Are Kellogg's Cornflakes Overpriced," *Economic Journal* 88 (1978): 254–268; T. Hitiris, "Effective Protection and Economic Performance in UK Manufacturing Industry, 1963 and 1968," *Economic Journal* 88 (1978): 107–120; H.G. Grabowski and D.C. Mueller, "Industrial Research and Development, Intangible Capital Stocks, and Firm Profit Rates," *Bell Journal of Economics* 9 (1978): 328–343; M.E. Porter, "The

TABLE 13.3 Summary of Studies of the Relationship Between Profits and
Advertising in Manufacturing Industries (*continued*)

| | Relationship Between Profits and Advertising | | | |
Author(s)—Year of Study	Positive (+)	Negative (−)	Not Significant (e)	Indeterminate (?)
S. Martin—1979	+			
T. Nakao—1979	+			
S. Martin—1979	+			
P. Geroski—1981	+			
T. Nagle—1981			e	
P. Geroski—1982	+			
R. Bradburd, R. Caves—1982				?
D. Ravenscraft—1983	+			
V. Gupta—1983	+			
R. Clarke—1984			e	
M. Salinger—1984	+			
J. Borthwell, T. Cooley, and T. Hall—1984	+			
R. Connoly, M. Hirschey—1984			e	
J. Kwoka and D. Ravenscraft—1986	+			
W. Shepherd—1986	+			
I. Domowitz, R. Hubbard, and B. Peterson—1986	+			
T. Nakao—1993	+			

Structure Within Industries and Companies' Performance," *Review of Economics and Statistics* 61 (1979): 214–227; Stephen Martin, "Entry Barriers, Concentration and Profits," *Southern Economic Journal* 46 (1979): 471–488; T. Nakao, "Profit Rates and Market Shares of Leading Industrial Firms in Japan," *Journal of Industrial Economics* 27 (1979): 371–383; Stephen Martin, "Advertising, Concentration and Profitability: The Simultaneity Problem," *Bell Journal of Economics* 10 (Autumn 1979): 639–647; P. Geroski, "Specification and Testing the Profits-Concentration Relationship: Some Experiments for the UK," *Economica* 48 (1981): 279–288; T. T. Nagle, "Do Advertising-Profitability Studies Really Show that Advertising Creates a Barrier to Entry," *Journal of Law and Economics* 24 (1981): 333–350; P.A. Geroski, "Simultaneous-Equation Models of the Structure-Performance Paradigm," *European Economic Review* 19 (1982): 145–158; R.M. Bradburd and R.E. Caves, "A Closer Look at the Effect of Market Growth on Industries' Profits," *Review of Economics and Statistics* 64 (1982): 635–645; David Ravenscraft, "Structure-Profits Relationships in Line of Business and Industry Level," *Review of Economics and Statistics* 65 (1983): 22–31; V. Gupta, "A Simultaneous Determination of Structure, Conduct and Performance in Canadian Manufacturing," *Oxford Economic Papers* 35 (1983): 281–301; R. Clarke, "Profit Margins and Market Concentration in UK Manufacturing Industry: 1970–6," *Applied Economics* 16 (1984): 57–71; Michael Salinger, "Tobin's q, Unionization and the Concentration-Profits Relationship," *Rand Journal of Economics* 15 (Summer 1984): 159–170; James L. Bothwell, Thomas F. Cooley, and Thomas E. Hall, "A New View of the Market Structure-Performance Debate," *Journal of Industrial Economics* 32 (June 1984): 397–417; John E. Kwoka Jr. and David J. Ravenscraft, "Cooperation vs. Rivalry: Price-Cost Margins by Line of Business," *Economica* 53 (August 1986): 351–363; William G. Shepherd, "Tobin's q and the Structure-Conduct-Performance Relationship: Comment," *American Economic Review* 76 (December 1986): 1205–1210; Ian Domowitz, R. Glenn Hubbard, and Bruce C. Peterson, "The Intertemporal Stability of the Concentration-Margins Relationship," *Journal of Industrial Economics* 35 (September 1986): 13–33; and Takeo Nakao, "Market Share, Advertising, R&D, and Profitability: An Empirical Analysis of Leading Industrial Firms in Japan," *Review of Industrial Organization* 8 (1993): 315–328.

tently sold at higher prices than nonadvertised distributors' brands.[44] On average, prices were 21 percent higher for the advertised brands. Similarly, Morris found that advertised brands of instant coffee, margarine, and toothpaste were sold at much higher prices than distributors' brands in Britain.[45] For a sample of 133 processed food products, Wills and W. F. Mueller found a strong relationship between advertising outlays and prices.[46] Overall, there is an impressive body of evidence that on average manufacturers' advertising results in higher profits and prices.

With regard to retailing, the evidence is much more limited, but several studies provide valuable insight. The empirical evidence concerning the relationship between retailers' advertising and profits leads to a very different conclusion than the evidence with regard to manufacturers' advertising. Much of this evidence was presented earlier in this chapter. Recall that eyeglass prices were significantly lower in markets that permitted optometrists to advertise than in markets that prohibited advertising, and prescription drug prices were lower in states that permitted price advertising.[47] Furthermore, local newspaper advertising reduced the profits of convenience goods, and magazine advertising tended to increase the level of price competition for shopping goods such as furniture and appliances.[48] Finally, although Boyer found a significant positive relationship between advertising and profits for manufacturing industries, he also found that for retailing there is a significant negative relationship between advertising and profits.[49] Overall, it appears that in retailing, advertising exerts a negative effect on profits.

13.8.2 New Empirical Industrial Organization Studies

Most recent empirical work on the impact of advertising on market structure and performance has used the methodology of the new empirical industrial organization to analyze the impact of advertising on firm behavior in specific markets. For example, Gasmi, Laffont, and Vuong examined the price and advertising competition between Coca-Cola and Pepsi-Cola from 1968 to 1986.[50] They investigated which of four alternative models best explained the behavior of Coke and Pepsi and found that the Stackelberg model with Coke as the Stackelberg leader in both price and advertising worked best. Gasmi, Laffont, and Vuong estimated both the impact of a 1 percent change in Coke's advertising on total market demand and the demand for Pepsi, and the impact of a 1 percent change in Pepsi's advertising on total market demand and the demand for Coke. These estimates indicated: (1) that there was almost no effect of advertising on the total demand for Coke and Pepsi; (2) that a 1 percent increase in Pepsi's advertising resulted in a 0.12 percent decrease in Coke's demand; and (3) that a 1 percent increase in Coke's advertising resulted in a 0.59 percent decrease in Pepsi's demand. Advertising, therefore, was almost entirely predatory because it impacted only the relative market shares of the two firms but had no impact on total demand. Furthermore, Coke's advertising had a much greater negative impact on Pepsi than Pepsi's advertising had on Coke.

Kadiyali examined the price and advertising competition between Kodak and Fuji from 1970 to 1990.[51] She found that in the 1970s, when Kodak was a monopolist in the photographic film industry, Kodak used a combination of heavy advertising and a limit pricing strategy to maintain its monopoly. Kadiyali found that in the 1980s Fuji had both an advertising elasticity and price elasticity advantage compared to Kodak, and therefore, Kodak's best strategy was to accommodate Fuji's entry. According to

Kadiyali, after Fuji's entry the two firms used their combined advertising to help deter further entry. Her most surprising finding was that Kodak's post-entry Lerner Index of 0.62 was significantly higher than its pre-entry monopoly Lerner Index of 0.21. Furthermore, Fuji's Lerner Index of 0.81 was greater than Kodak's post-entry Lerner Index. Kadiyali concluded that "[h]ere incumbents use advertising to strengthen their incumbency advantage, thus endogenizing entry barriers determined by these [advertising] sunk costs."[52]

Slade analyzed the competition in price and advertising between three national brands of saltine crackers (American Brands' Sunshine, Keebler's Zesta, and R.J.R. Nabisco's Premium) and private label brands in isolated small towns during two years, 1984 and 1985.[53] Individual consumers' buying patterns were closely monitored during the study. Slade found that if only one firm advertised, the advertising increased that firm's market share and not only decreased its competitors' market shares but decreased their sales as well. In this case, advertising was predatory and had no effect on total sales. However, if all firms simultaneously increased their advertising, then total industry sales increased and each individual firm's sales increased as well. Slade's results in the cracker market, therefore, were somewhat different from Gasmi, Laffont, and Vuong's results in the Coke-Pepsi market.

SUMMARY

1. A reexamination of the Bertrand model with product differentiation suggests that product differentiation can result in higher prices.

2. Monopolistic competition and oligopoly may result in either too much or too little product differentiation.

3. The lemons model shows the effect of asymmetric information in a market with product differentiation. As a result of asymmetric information, high-quality products are eliminated from the market. The lemons model is an example of adverse selection, where products of different qualities are sold at the same price because buyers or sellers do not have sufficient information to determine the true quality of the products.

4. Insurance companies are constantly faced with problems of adverse selection because the companies cannot identify the true risks associated with insuring an individual client. As a result, high-risk individuals are more likely to purchase insurance than low-risk individuals, and this drives up insurance rates, which further eliminates low-risk individuals from the insurance pool. The best solution to the problem of adverse selection is to gather more information.

5. Product differentiation and advertising can have either a positive or a negative economic impact. Informational advertising, particularly price advertising, tends to have a positive impact, whereas persuasive advertising often has a negative impact.

6. It has been theorized that all monopolists advertise too much from a welfare perspective because at the margin a monopolist's advertising contributes nothing to profit but, assuming constant consumers' utility functions, reduces consumer surplus and, therefore, reduces welfare. This theoretical result has been criticized because it is based on two questionable assumptions: (1) that advertising conveys

no useful information; and (2) that advertising has no positive effect on consumers' utility functions.

7 Theory suggests that advertising intensity should be highest in oligopoly, lowest in highly competitive markets, and somewhere in between in monopolized markets. Furthermore, advertising in oligopoly may exceed the socially optimal level. Persuasive advertising in particular is likely to exceed the social optimum.

8 The first-mover advantage associated with the introduction of a new product may result in persistent market power. If significant sunk costs are also associated with entering the market, entrants will have great difficulty competing effectively against first movers.

9 Advertising may be used strategically to preempt entry and maintain market power. Increased advertising expenditures can be used to raise rivals' costs and deter entry.

10 Empirical evidence supports the position that advertising can have positive or negative effects. Generally, positive effects are associated with retailing and search goods, and negative effects are associated with manufacturing and experience goods. There are, however, many exceptions to this general rule.

KEY TERMS

adverse selection	first-mover advantage	search goods
advertising response function	horizontal product	shopping goods
convenience goods	differentiation	simultaneity bias
Dorfman-Steiner model	informational advertising	vertical product
experience goods	persuasive advertising	differentiation

DISCUSSION QUESTIONS

1. In what type of market structure would you expect the most product differentiation: perfect competition, oligopoly, or monopoly? Why?

2. You are to argue in a debate on the topic, "advertising is a waste of society's resources." Which side of the argument would you prefer to argue: pro or con? Why?

3. In 1964 the United States banned television advertising of cigarettes. Is it possible that the television advertising ban increased the cigarette industry's profits? Explain.

4. Suppose society decided to place an "excess advertising tax" on advertising above 5 percent of a firm's gross sales. Do you believe such a tax would improve economic efficiency?

Would firms such as Coca-Cola and Pepsico fight such a tax? Should they fight such a tax?

5. Which market structure is likely to result in the most advertising: perfect competition, oligopoly, or monopoly? Why?

6. Are oligopolists likely to advertise at the joint profit-maximizing level? Explain why or why not.

7. Does empirical evidence suggest that advertising is a barrier to entry? Why or why not?

8. If the used car market is a lemons market, how would you expect the repair record of used cars that are sold to compare with the repair record of used cars that are not sold? Explain your reasoning.

9. Discuss the application of the lemons model in the insurance market. In what ways do insurance companies deal with adverse selection?

10. Name three specific markets in which adverse selection is present. Explain why there is a problem in each of these markets.

11. In this chapter several different views of the social impact of advertising have been presented. One view is that advertising is informative and has a positive impact on efficiency. A second view is that advertising is primarily persuasive, provides little if any useful information, and has a negative impact on efficiency. Yet a third view is that advertising can be used to erect entry barriers and strategically deter competition. From your knowledge of real-world markets, give an example that seems to support each of these views.

PROBLEMS

1. (You need a calculator to answer this problem.) In the Bertrand model with product differentiation, suppose that the two Bertrand firms face the following symmetric demand curves:

$$q_1 = 96 - 2p_1 + \frac{1}{2}p_2$$

$$q_2 = 96 - 2p_2 + \frac{1}{2}p_1,$$

where $q_1, q_2, \geq 0$ and $p_1, p_2 \leq 48$.
 a. Is product differentiation more or less significant in this example than in the example given in the text in Equations 13.1A and 13.1B? Why?
 b. Given your answer to part (a), would you expect the equilibrium price to be higher or lower than the equilibrium price of 40 given Equations 13.1A and 13.1B?
 c. Find the Bertrand equilibrium.

2. The Waldman ice cream truck example used two trucks. The Nash equilibrium in the absence of collusion was for the two firms to locate at the middle. Interestingly, if there were three trucks competing instead of two, no Nash equilibrium exists. Instead, there is only a mixed strategy equilibrium. Why is there no pure strategy equilibrium with three trucks? [Hint: Try positioning the trucks anywhere along the route. Why does at least one truck always have an incentive to move?]

3. (You need a calculator to answer this problem.) In a monopolistically competitive industry, total profits π are a function of the number of firms n as follows:

$$\pi = p(n) = 10 - \frac{1}{10}n.$$

Furthermore, consumer surplus CS is a function of n where:

$$CS(n) = \sqrt{n}.$$

 a. In long-run equilibrium how many firms will exist in this industry?
 b. In long-run equilibrium what is the sum of profit plus consumer surplus? Is this the socially optimal level of product differentiation? [Hint: What happens to the value of $\pi(n) + CS(n)$ for values of n slightly smaller and slightly larger than the value of n that answers part a?]

c. (Optional: Use calculus.) What is the optimal number of firms in this industry? [Hint: For what value of n is $\pi(n) + CS(n)$ maximized?]

4. (You need a calculator to answer this question.) In the first-mover model of the ISP market presented in this chapter, suppose the risk-cost factor π increased from 0.5 to 0.75.
 a. What would the new introductory demand curve for Internet service be?
 b. If AOL introduced Internet service at a price $P = 12.5$, what would the new demand curve faced by AOL be?
 c. Derive the demand curve for a second-mover firm. What is the highest price at which the second mover can obtain any subscribers?
 d. Has the increase in the risk-cost factor τ made entry more difficult?

5. Consider a monopolist with the following demand curve: $P = 360 - 3Q$ and $MC_m = AC_m = 60$.
 a. Solve for the profit–maximizing level of output, price, and profits for the monopolist.
 b. Let's suppose the monopolist has the opportunity to spend $\$A$ on advertising to raise its demand to $P = 420 - 3Q$. Solve for the most that the monopolist would spend on advertising in this situation.
 c. Calculate the price elasticity of demand at the price and quantity in part b.
 d. Suppose the advertising elasticity of demand is estimated to be 0.25. Using the Dorfman-Steiner model, what is the optimal amount of money the monopolist should spend on advertising?

6. Suppose the elasticity of demand for hotels is 1.9 and the advertising-to-sales ratio for Hilton is 0.097.
 a. Following Dorfman and Steiner, if we assume that Hilton is profit-maximizing, what does Hilton's behavior imply about the value of its advertising elasticity of demand?
 b. Interpret the value of Hilton's advertising elasticity of demand calculated in part a.
 c. Why might the Dorfman-Steiner monopoly model not be the most appropriate to use in this example? Can you think of other effects from advertising that the Dorfman-Steiner model ignores?

7. It has been estimated that McDonald's advertising-to-sales ratio is 0.222. Assume McDonald's can expect an advertising elasticity of demand of 0.20. Using the Dorfman-Steiner model, what does its behavior imply about the value of McDonald's elasticity of demand? As an economist, what do you advise McDonald's to do? Why?

8. Assume there are two players, a buyer and a seller of a used car. The seller knows whether the car is a good car or a lemon and the buyer knows the probability distribution of good cars and lemons. Assume the probability of a good car is 70 percent and the probability of a lemon is 30 percent. Assume that both buyers and sellers have identical tastes and there are only two types of cars. Good cars have a quality value of $20,000 and lemons have a quality value of $10,000.
 a. What is the expected value of a car? Given this information, how will the buyer be informed whether the car is a lemon or not?
 b. What would the Akerlof lemons model predict to be the final outcome of this game? In other words, which cars will be sold and for how much? Explain.

9. Suppose a bank issued credit cards over the Internet at a fixed interest rate to all approved applicants—for example, at 9.9 percent. Explain why this bank would face an adverse selection problem. How might the bank solve this problem? Would your solution make some customers unhappy? Explain your reasoning.

NOTES

1. For a theoretical discussion see André de Palma, Robin Lindsey, Balder von Hohenbalken, and Douglas S. West, "Spatial Price and Variety Competition in an Urban Retail Market: A Nested Logit Analysis," *International Journal of Industrial Organization* 12 (September 1994): 331–357. For empirical evidence see Richard J. Claycombe and Tamara E. Mahan, "Spatial Aspects of Retail Market Structure Beef Pricing Revisited," *International Journal of Industrial Organization* 11 (June 1993): 283–291.

2. *Financial World* (May 10, 1994), p. 1.

3. F.M. Scherer, *Industrial Market Structure and Economic Performance* (Chicago: Rand-McNally, 1980), pp. 381–382.

4. The results obtained in the section draw on Avinash K. Dixit and Joseph E. Stiglitz, "Monopolistic Competition and Optimum Product Diversity," *American Economic Review* 67 (1977): 297–308; and Michael A. Spence, "Product Selection, Fixed Costs, and Monopolistic Competition," *The Review of Economic Studies* 43 (1976): 217–236. For different approaches see John S. Pettingill, "Monopolistic Competition and Optimum Product Diversity: Comment," *American Economic Review* 69 (1979): 957–960; and Roger W. Koenker and Martin K. Perry, "Product Differentiation, Monopolistic Competition, and Public Policy," *The Bell Journal of Economics* 12 (1981): 217–231.

5. Harold Hotelling, "Stability in Competition," *Economic Journal* 39(1929): 41–57.

6. George Akerlof, "The Market for Lemons: Quality Uncertainty and the Market Mechanism," *Quarterly Journal of Economics* 90 (November 1970): 599–617.

7. Products such as Ben & Jerry's and Häagen-Dazs are often priced high on introduction to signal to consumers that the product is of high quality. See Kyle Bagwell and Michael H. Riordan, "High and Declining Prices Signal Product Quality," *American Economic Review* 81 (March 1991): 134–239.

8. *Statistical Abstract of the United States 1999* (Washington: U.S. Bureau of the Census, 1999), p. 592.

9. John E. Kwoka Jr., "Advertising and Price and Quality of Optometric Services," *American Economic Review* 74 (March 1984): 211–216; Lee Benham, "The Effect of Advertising on the Price of Eyeglasses," *Journal of Law and Economics* 15 (October 1972): 337–352. See also John R. Schroeter, Scott L. Smith, and Steven R. Cox, "Advertising and Competition in Routine Legal Services Markets," *Journal of Industrial Economics* 36 (September 1987): 49–60; and Amihai Glazer, "Advertising, Information, and Prices—A Case Study," *Economic Inquiry* 19 (October 1981): 661–671.

10. John F. Cady, "An Estimate of the Price Effects of Restrictions on Drug Price Advertising," *Economic Inquiry* (December 1976): 493–510.

11. Michael E. Porter, "Interbrand Choice, Media Mix and Market Performance," *American Economic Review* (May 1976): 398–406.

12. Alfred Arterburn and John Woodbury, "Advertising, Price Competition, and Market Structure," *Southern Economic Journal* 47 (January 1981): 763–775.

13. See Makoto Mizuno, "Does Advertising Mislead Consumers to Buy Low-Quality Products," *International Journal of Industrial Organization* 8 (December 1990): 545–558.

14. "Saturn Reaches Critical Marketing Strategy Phase," *Automotive News* (March 12, 1990): 32.

15. U.S. Bureau of the Census, *Statistical Abstract of the United States: 1979* (Washington, DC: Government Printing Office, 1979). Unfortunately there are no comparable data for later years.

16. *Statistical Abstract of the United States 1999* (Washington: U.S. Bureau of the Census, 1999), p. 592.

17. *Statistical Abstract of the United States 1999* (Washington: U.S. Bureau of the Census, 1999), Table 613.

18. For more on which products are likely to be advertised on television, see Michael R. Butler, "The Diffusion of Television Advertising," *Review of Industrial Organization* 6 (1991): 283–290.

19. See Phillip Nelson, "Advertising and Information," *Journal of Political Economy* 81 (1970): 729–754; Paul Milgrom and J. Roberts, "Price and Advertising Signals of Product Quality," *Journal of Political Economy* 94 (1986): 796–821; Richard Kihlstrom and Michael Riordin, "Advertising as a Signal," *Journal of Political Economy* 92 (1984): 427–450; and Richard Schmalensee, "A Model of Advertising and Product Quality," *Journal of Political Economy* 86 (1978): 485–503.

20. Avinash Dixit and Victor Norman, "Advertising and Welfare," *Bell Journal of Economics* 9, (Spring 1978): 1–17.

21. Carl Shapiro, "Advertising and Welfare: Comment," *Bell Journal of Economics* 11, (Autumn 1980): 749–752.

22. Franklin M. Fisher and John J. McGowan, "Advertising and Welfare: Comment," *Bell Journal of Economics* 10, (Autumn 1979): 726–727.

23. Robert Dorfman and Peter O. Steiner, "Optimal Advertising and Optimal Quality," *American Economic Review* 44 (December 1954): 826–836.

24. "Sharp, Thompson Switch on $20 M Campaigns," *Advertising Age* (August 28, 1995): 30; "DBS Business Flying High; Direct Broadcasting Satellites; Telemedia Week," *Broadcasting & Cable* 125 (January 9, 1995): 55; and "Ads that Work: Advertising Campaigns that Introduced a Product, Introduced a City and Introduced a Product to a City," *Indiana Business Magazine* (April 1996).

25. Neil Borden, *The Economic Effects of Advertising* (Chicago: Irwin, 1942), pp. 212–216.

26. Lester G. Telser, "Advertising and Cigarettes," *Journal of Law and Economics* 70 (October 1962): 494–498; and Henry G. Grabowski and Dennis C. Mueller, "Imitative Advertising in the Cigarette Industry," *Antitrust Bulletin* 16, (Summer 1971): 257–292.

27. M.A. Alemson, "Advertising and the Nature of Competition in Oligopoly Over Time," *Economic Journal* 80 (June 1970): 293; Henry G. Grabowski and Dennis C. Mueller, "Imitative Advertising in the Cigarette Industry," *Antitrust Bulletin* 16 (Summer 1971): 257–292. See also James L. Hamilton, "The Demand for Cigarettes, Advertising, the Health Scare, and the Cigarette Advertising Ban," *Review of Economics and Statistics* 54 (November 1972): 401–411; Eugene M. Lewit, Douglas Coate, and Michael Grossman, "The Effects of Government Regulation on Teenage Smoking," *Journal of Law and Economics* 24 (December 1981): 545–575; and Lynne Schneider, Benjamin Klein, and Kevin Murphy, "Government Regulation of Cigarette Health Information," *Journal of Law and Economics* 24 (December, 1981): 576–612.

28. Jean Jacques Lambin, *Advertising, Competition, and Market Conduct in Oligopoly over Time* (Amsterdam: North-Holland, 1976).

29. Jeffrey M. Netter, "Excessive Advertising: An Empirical Analysis," *Journal of Law and Economics* 30 (June 1982): 361–373.

30. Bagwell and Ramey have argued that incumbent firms may under-advertise to deter entry if they wish to signal uninformed potential entrants that demand is low. See Kyle Bagwell and Garey Ramey, "Advertising and Pricing to Deter or Accommodate Entry when Demand is Unknown," *International Journal of Industrial Organization* 8 (March 1990): 93–113.

31. Richard Schmalensee, "Product Differentiation Advantages of Pioneering Brands," *American Economic Review* 72 (June, 1982): 349–365.

32. The first mover may want to discriminate in price between new and repeat customers. See Thomas J. Hoerger, "Two-part Pricing for Experience Goods in the Presence of Adverse Selection," *International Journal of Industrial Organization* 11 (December 1993): 451–474.

33. Alison Masson and Robert L. Steiner, *Generic Substitution and Prescription Drug Prices,* Federal Trade Commission staff report (Washington: U.S. Government Printing Office, October 1985). Jung has suggested that entry into the prescription drug industry may result in higher prices being charged by the leading brands because after entry the leading brands mostly have very loyal buyers with highly inelastic demands. See Chao-Shun Jung, "On Monopoly Power in a Differentiated Product Industry," *Review of Industrial Organization* 9 (August 1994): 425–433.

34. Mark A. Hurwitz and Richard E. Caves, "Persuasion or Information? Promotion and the Shares of Brand Name and Generic Pharmaceuticals," *Journal of Law and Economics* 31 (October 1988): 299–320.

35. For additional empirical evidence see William T. Robinson, Gurumurthy Kalyanaram, and Glen L. Urban, "First-Mover Advantages from Pioneering New Markets: A Survey of Empirical Evidence," *Review of Industrial Organization* 9 (February 1994): 1–23.

36. "Battery Power; Kodak Readies New Charge," *Advertising Age* (September 7, 1987); and "Kodak Draws 10% Share of Supermarket Batteries Sales," *Supermarket News* (April 6, 1987).

37. See also Douglas F. Greer, "Some Case History Evidence on the Advertising-Concentration Relationship," *Antitrust Bulletin* 18 (Summer 1973): 307–332. For additional evidence of strategic use of advertising in the cigarette industry see Barry J. Seldon and Khosrow Doroodian, "Does Purely Predatory Advertising Exist?" *Review of Industrial Organization* 5 (1990): 45–70.

38. *Business Week* (January 26, 1981): 65.

39. *Business Week* (October 31, 1983): 50; *Business Week* (January 23, 1989): 38; and *The Wall Street Journal* (August 17, 1984): 14.

40. John Cubbin and Simon Domberger, "Advertising and Post-Entry Oligopoly Behavior," *Journal of Industrial Economics* 37 (December 1988): 123–140.

41. *Supra* note 24.

42. Greer, *Industrial Organization and Public Policy* (New York: Macmillan, 1992), p. 492.

43. For other empirical evidence see Frances F. Esposito, Louis Esposito, and William V. Hogan, "Inter Industry Differences in Advertising in U.S. Manufacturing: 1963–1977," *Review of Industrial Organization* 5 (1990): 53–80; Takeo Nakao, "Market Share, Advertising, R&D, and Profitability: An Empirical Analysis of Leading Industrial Firms in Japan," *Review of Industrial Organization* 8 (June 1993): 315–328.

44. National Commission on Food Marketing, *Special Studies in Food Marketing,* Technical Study 10 (Washington: The Commission, 1966), pp. 66, 70–71.

45. David Morris, "Some Aspects of Large-Scale Advertising," *Journal of Industrial Economics* 24 (December 1975): 119–130.

46. Robert L. Wills and Willard F. Mueller, "Brand Pricing and Advertising," *Southern Economic Journal* 56 (October 1989): 383–395.

47. John E. Kwoka Jr., "Advertising and Price and Quality of Optometric Services," *American Economic Review* 74 (March 1984): 211–216; Lee Benham, "The Effect of Advertising on the Price of Eyeglasses," *Journal of Law and Economics* 15 (October 1972): 337–352. See also John R. Schroeter, Scott L. Smith, and Steven R. Cox, "Advertising and Competition in Routine Legal Services Markets," *Journal*

of Industrial Economics* 36 (September 1987): 49–60; Amihai Glazer, "Advertising, Information, and Prices—A Case Study," *Economic Inquiry* 19 (October 1981): 661–671; and John F. Cady, "An Estimate of the Price Effects of Restrictions on Drug Price Advertising," *Economic Inquiry* 14 (December 1976): 493–510.

48. Michael E. Porter, "Interbrand Choice, Media Mix and Market Performance," *American Economic Review* (May 1976): 398–406; and Alfred Arterburn and John Woodbury, "Advertising, Price Competition, and Market Structure," *Southern Economic Journal* 47 (January 1981): 763–775.

49. Kenneth D. Boyer, "Informative and Goodwill Advertising," *Review of Economics and Statistics* 56 (November 1974): 541–548.

50. F. Gasmi, J.J. Laffont, and Q. Vuong, "Econometric Analysis of Collusive Behavior in a Soft-Drink Market," *Journal of Economics & Management Strategy* 1, no. 2 (Summer 1992): 277–311.

51. Vrinda Kadiyali, "Entry, its Deterrence, and its Accommodation: a Study of the U.S. Photographic Film Industry," *Rand Journal of Economics* 27, no. 3 (Autumn 1996): 452–478.

52. *Ibid.,* p. 477.

53. Margaret E. Slade, "Product Rivalry with Multiple Strategic Weapons: An Analysis of Price and Advertising Competition," *Journal of Economics & Management Strategy* 4, (Fall 1995): 445–476.

INTERNET EXERCISES

Visit **www.aw-bc.com/waldman_jensen** for this chapter's web exercises. Answer our real-world economics problems by searching the Internet for solutions!

Technological Change and Research and Development

The importance of technological change is stressed throughout this text. In Chapter 1 we wrote, "Most economists recognize that even if an industry achieves static efficiency its performance may be poor if it fails to invest in research and development at an optimal rate." Moreover, the current business literature stresses the importance of research and development: Firms become successful by developing either new ways of producing or new products.[1] In this chapter we analyze the theoretical and empirical work in the area of technological change and research and development (R&D), with an emphasis on trying to ascertain whether a relationship exists between market structure and the rate of technological advance. The objective is to determine whether there is an ideal market structure that results in an optimal rate of technological advance. We also examine the United States patent system to determine its impact on the rate of technological advance.

In one of the most influential economic treatises written in this century, Joseph Schumpeter first emphasized the primary importance of dynamic efficiency. We begin with a discussion of Schumpeter's argument. Much of the remaining debate centers on whether Schumpeter was right or wrong.

14.1 Schumpeter and the Process of "Creative Destruction"

In 1942, Joseph Schumpeter's *Capitalism, Socialism, and Democracy* was published.[2] The book mainly examined Marxism and socialism and asked the question: "Can capitalism survive?" To this, Schumpeter answered, "No. I do not think it can."[3] Schumpeter theorized that capitalism would eventually collapse from the weight of its own success. One of the linchpins of his argument was a belief that capital would increasingly be concentrated in a few large-scale, technologically advanced firms.

Because of the historical importance of Schumpeter's hypothesis, we present a rather lengthy excerpt from *Capitalism, Socialism, and Democracy*. The following

passages have had a continuing impact on economic thought for more than 60 years. Schumpeter wrote:

> The essential point to grasp is that in dealing with capitalism we are dealing with an evolutionary process. . . .
>
> Capitalism . . . is by nature a form or method of economic change and not only never is but never can be stationary. . . . The fundamental impulse that sets and keeps the capitalist engine in motion comes from the new consumers' goods, the new methods of production or transportation, the new markets, the new forms of industrial organization that capitalist enterprise creates. . . .
>
> The opening up of new markets, foreign or domestic, and the organizational development from the craft shop and factory to such concerns as U.S. Steel illustrate the same process of industrial mutation—if I may use that biological term—that incessantly revolutionizes the economic structure *from within,* incessantly destroying the old one, incessantly creating a new one. This process of Creative Destruction is the essential fact about capitalism. It is what capitalism consists in and what every capitalist concern has got to live in. This fact bears upon our problem in two ways.
>
> First, because we are dealing with a process whose every element takes considerable time in revealing its true features and ultimate effects, there is no point in appraising the performance of that process *ex visu* of a given point in time; we must judge its performance over time, as it unfolds through decades or centuries. A system—any system, economic or other—that at *every* given point of time fully utilizes its possibilities to the best advantage may yet in the long run be inferior to a system that does so at *no* given point of time, because the latter's failure to do so may be a condition for the level or speed of long-run performance. . . .
>
> The first thing to go is the traditional conception of the *modus operandi* of competition. Economists are at long last emerging from the stage in which price competition was all they saw. As soon as quality competition and sales effort are admitted into the sacred precincts of theory, the price variable is ousted from its dominant position. . . . [I]n capitalist reality as distinguished from its textbook picture, it is not that kind of competition which counts but the competition from the new commodity, the new technology, the new source of supply, the new type of organization (the largest-scale unit of control for instance)—competition which commands a decisive cost or quality advantage and which strikes not at the margins of the profits and the outputs of the existing firms but at their foundations and their very lives. . . .

Having argued that capitalism is driven by *dynamic efficiency,* not *static efficiency,* Schumpeter went on to argue the type of market structure necessary to achieve dynamic efficiency:

> [T]here are superior methods available to the monopolist which either are not available at all to a crowd of competitors or are not available to them so readily: for there are advantages which, though not strictly unattainable on the competitive level of enterprise, are as a matter of fact secured only on the monopoly level . . .

Thus it is not sufficient to argue that because perfect competition is impossible under modern industrial conditions—or because it always has been impossible—the large-scale establishment or unit of control must be accepted as a necessary evil inseparable from the economic progress which it is prevented from sabotaging by the forces inherent in its productive apparatus. What we have got to accept is that [monopoly] has come to be the most powerful engine of that progress and in particular of the long-run expansion of total output not only in spite of, but to a considerable extent through, this strategy which looks so restrictive when viewed in the individual case and from the individual point of time. In this respect, perfect competition is not only impossible but inferior, and has no title to being set up as a model of ideal efficiency.

The implications of Schumpeter's thesis were revolutionary. Perfect competition was not the ideal market structure, but instead large-scale firms with monopoly power became the superior market structure. *Creative destruction* drove a capitalist economy forward in the long run, and large-scale monopolists engaged in research and development led to creative destruction. In the neoclassical world, perfect competition and an increasing capital-labor ratio ensured long-run growth. In the Schumpeterian world large firms with monopoly power ensured long-run growth.

The theory of *creative destruction* raised the following questions: How important is technological change to long-run growth? Do most technological changes originate in large-scale monopoly enterprises? Is monopoly the ideal market structure for dynamic efficiency? Do successful large-scale monopolists inevitably grow to control larger and larger percentages of capital?

In a seminal article Robert Solow investigated the importance of technological change for long-run growth.[4] Examining the 105 percent increase in output of nonfarm labor between 1909 and 1949, Solow found that 87.5 percent of the increase resulted from technological change, whereas only 12.5 percent resulted from an increase in the use of capital relative to labor. Given Solow's findings, it is hard to argue with one of Schumpeter's main points: Technological change drives an economy forward.[5]

APPLICATION 14.1

Examples of Creative Destruction

In his 1939 book *Business Cycles: A Theoretical, Historical and Statistical Analysis of the Capitalist Process*, Schumpeter identified three examples of the types of major technological advances that he was speaking of in his theory of creative destruction.* Schumpeter tied his theory to the work of Russian economist Nikolai Kondratieff on long cycles in which Kondratieff argued that major economic cycles last about 50 to 60 years.† Kondratieff theorized that major depressions occurred at the trough of these long cycles. Unfortunately, Kondratieff offered no theory to explain why these cycles occurred and Joseph Stalin was not very impressed by his work. Stalin had Kondratieff convicted of being a member of a secret society of peasants and he was exiled to Siberia, where he apparently died sometime around 1938 at the age of 46.

Schumpeter saw Kondratieff's long cycles as tied to major innovations that were the great source of growth and entrepreneurial profit. According to Schumpeter, the

first Kondratieff cycle, from 1780 to 1840, was driven by the industrial revolution in textiles. This wave was limited by its reliance on water power as the main source of power. The second wave, from 1840 to 1890, was the modern industrial revolution, driven by the age of steam power and the railroads. This is the period of the large-scale development of the coal and iron industries. The third wave, from 1890 to 1940, was the age of steel and electricity and was driven by the expansion of telecommunications, the large research and development laboratory, and chemicals.

Schumpeter did not live beyond this third wave; however, two more Schumpeterian waves have been identified since his death.[‡] The fourth wave, from 1940 to 1990, was the age of widespread mass production, driven by the interstate highway system, radio and television, and air transportation. Other important factors in this wave were the development of higher education for the masses and large government expenditures on research and development. That brings us to the current wave, which began in the 1990s with the widespread development of computer and microelectronic networks. This is the age of cyberspace and the digital information highway. Power is still mostly dependent on oil and gas.

If we were to speculate on the next wave, we might theorize that around 2040 there will be a new development in energy and transportation that will bring an end to the age of oil and the internal combustion engine. But this, of course, is sheer speculation.

[*]Joseph Schumpeter, *Business Cycles: A Theoretical, Historical and Statistical Analysis of the Capitalist Process,* 2 volumes (New York: McGraw-Hill, 1939).

[†]Nikolai D. Kondratieff, "The Long Waves in Economic Life," English translation, *Review of Economics and Statistics* 17(November 1935): 101–115.

[‡]See Chris Freeman and Luc Soete, *The Economics of Industrial Innovation,* 3rd edition (Cambridge, MA: The MIT Press, 1997), Chapter 1. ■

14.2 The Process of Technological Change

Before proceeding, it is important to distinguish between the different stages of development of a new commercial product or process. Many major technological changes begin with *basic research,* which is research aimed at gaining knowledge for its own sake. The research scientist in a major university laboratory working on quantum physics is engaged in basic research. *Applied research* is aimed at obtaining knowledge with the objective of using that knowledge for commercial purposes. The chemist working on AIDS in a pharmaceutical company's laboratory is doing applied research. The lines between basic and applied research, however, often become blurred. The chemist, for example, may in the course of his or her applied research make a basic research discovery concerning how the immune system works to fight disease. Successful applied research results in *invention* or the discovery of an idea that "should" work. In the invention stage the idea passes through its first rough tests, which indicate that it will indeed work. Invention is an important step in the process of technological development, but it is only a preliminary step. The next stage in the process is *innovation,* which is the first commercial application of the invention. Innovation requires refinement of the invention to "get the bugs out" and develop a marketable product. Large R&D labs spend much time on innovation. Finally, *diffusion* is the stage at which the innovation comes into common use.

Although all of these stages of development are important, this chapter is primarily concerned with invention, innovation, and diffusion. Private firms are primarily engaged in these three stages of technological development. Most basic research, however, is carried out at academic and nonprofit institutions (59.1 percent of total basic research spending in 2000) and by the government (17.9 percent of spending in 2000).[6]

14.3 The Relationship Between Market Structure, Firm Size, and Technological Advance

Schumpeter argued that from the standpoint of dynamic efficiency, monopoly is superior to perfect competition. This argument spurred economists to examine the issue both theoretically and empirically. We begin with the theory.

The following model was developed by Arrow.[7] Suppose two markets have identical demands of $P = 100 - Q$. Industry 1 is a monopoly and Industry 2 is perfectly competitive. Figure 14.1 analyzes the impact of a cost reduction by the monopolist.

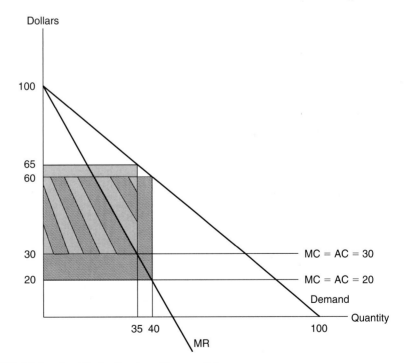

FIGURE 14.1 Cost Reduction by a Monopolist

With demand $P = 100 - Q$, if the monopolist's costs decrease from MC = AC = \$30 to MC = AC = \$20, the price decreases from \$65 to \$60 and profits increase from the sum of the gray and striped areas to the sum of the striped and red areas, or from \$1225 to \$1600, so profits increase by \$375.

Initially MC = AC = $30 and the profit-maximizing monopolist sets Q = 35 and P = $65. Profits are represented by π_M, and:

$$\pi_M = Q(P - AC) = \$35(\$65 - \$30) = \$1225.$$

Suppose a monopolist's innovation produced a cost-saving device that reduced its MC from $30 to $20. The monopolist's new profits would be π_M', where:

$$\pi_M' = Q'(P' - AC') = 40(\$60 - \$20) = \$1600.$$

Profits increase by $375 as a result of the cost-saving device. Notice in Figure 14.1 that consumer surplus also increases because P declines to $60 and Q increases to 40.

Figure 14.2 analyzes the impact of the same cost-saving innovation introduced in a perfectly competitive industry. Initially MC = AC = $30 and the perfectly competitive industry sets Q = 70 and P = $30. Because of perfect competition, profits equal zero, or $\pi_C = 0$, where:

$$\pi_C = Q(P - AC) = 70(\$30 - \$30) = 0.$$

Suppose one firm produced a patented cost-saving innovation that reduced MC from $30 to $20. In a perfectly competitive market, if the innovating firm tried to raise price above $30 it would be unable to sell *any* output. Its best option, therefore, is to

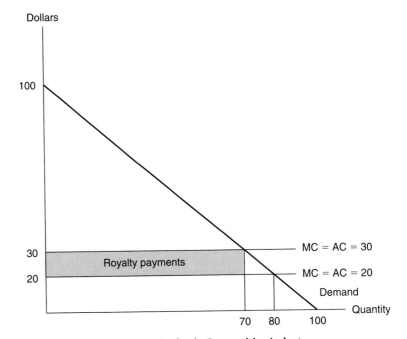

FIGURE 14.2 Cost Reduction in a Perfectly Competitive Industry

With demand P = 100 − Q, if a cost-saving innovation that decreases costs from MC = AC = $30 to MC = AC = $20 is introduced in a perfectly competitive market, the owner of the patent for the innovation can collect royalty payments equal to the shaded red area, or a payment of $700. Price remains at P = $30 and producers continue to earn normal profits.

license the patent for a royalty of 10 per unit of output. The industry's MC continues to equal $30 (including the royalty payment of $10 per unit), and the industry price continues to equal $30. In Figure 14.2, the patent holder's royalties would be $700 ($10Q = $700). The innovator earns an economic rent of $700 as a result of the introduction of the cost-saving device. Notice that consumer surplus does not change because P still equals $30. The entire $700 economic rent accrues to the patent holder. The innovator in the perfectly competitive industry earns almost twice as much ($700 compared to $375) from the new innovation as the monopolist. Therefore, a perfectly competitive firm has a greater economic incentive to develop the cost-saving device. Arrow's conclusion runs contrary to the Schumpeterian view.

What drives Arrow's result? Because the monopolist restricts output compared with the perfectly competitive industry, the monopolist applies the new device to far fewer units than the perfectly competitive industry[8] (40 units in Figure 14.1 compared to 70 units in Figure 14.2).

14.3.1 The Impact of Oligopoly

So far our analysis has centered on whether monopoly or perfect competition is more likely to result in a rapid rate of technological advance. As usual, the introduction of oligopoly makes the analysis more realistic and more complicated. Intuitively, investments in research and development aimed at improvements in technology require both an incentive and an ability to invest. Table 14.1 summarizes the incentive and ability to invest in research and development under perfect competition, oligopoly, and monopoly. Under perfect competition economic profits are normal, and there is little ability to invest in R&D. Few individual farmers, for example, have the time or funds necessary to invest in fertilizer or pesticide research and development. In a monopoly, profits may be greater than zero for long periods, giving the monopolist the ability to invest large sums in R&D. A good example is Microsoft's ability to spend billions of dollars on R&D. In terms of ability, oligopoly lies somewhere in between. Depending on the level of effective competition, oligopolists may or may not have profits available to invest in R&D. Examples of oligopolistic industries that have earned excess profits for long periods include computer equipment, automobiles, electronics, cereals, cigarettes, beer, photographic equipment, electric turbines, and aircraft. High profits in these industries can be channeled into R&D.

With regard to incentives, the monopolist has a low-to-moderate incentive to develop new technologies. Because the monopolist has a 100 percent market share and is protected from competition, it will have little concern about either losing its market share to rivals or gaining market share at its rivals' expense. The monopolist,

TABLE 14.1 Incentives to Invest in Research and Development

	Ability	Incentive
Perfect competition	Low, profits = 0	Moderate
Oligopoly	Moderate, profits ≥ 0	High
Monopoly	High, profits > 0	Low to moderate

therefore, will have limited concern about the time at which it introduces a new technological advance. When AT&T was a regulated monopolist, for example, it continued to supply only black dial telephones for many years beyond the technical necessity of doing so. As long as its monopoly was protected, AT&T would earn few additional profits by offering consumers touch-tone phones in designer colors. Furthermore, because it had no competitors in telephone equipment in its protected markets, AT&T had no reason to worry about competitors gaining market share by introducing color touch-tone phones. As shown by Arrow's model, however, the monopolist can earn additional profits from an innovation, and therefore, it still has some incentive to invest in R&D.

In Arrow's model the perfectly competitive firm has a powerful incentive to invest in R&D. One problem not accounted for in Arrow's model is that diffusion is often rapid in perfectly competitive markets, and profits decline quickly to normal. In retailing, for example, any new technological advance is rapidly duplicated by competitors. The introduction of the supermarket quickly made the small food store obsolete. Similarly, discount stores have virtually eliminated the independent pharmacist and clothing store from America. Because of rapid diffusion in competitive markets, innovation results in lower profits than in less competitive markets, and this reduces the perfectly competitive firm's incentive to invest in R&D.

Table 14.1 shows that an oligopolist has both the ability and the incentive to invest in R&D. Oligopolists have an incentive to invest because they gain vis-à-vis rivals by being the first to develop a new product or process. The expected moderate rate of imitation in oligopoly gives the oligopolist the largest incentive to invest in R&D. For example, when Miller Beer introduced Miller Lite, it initially obtained a large market share from competitors, and competitors only slowly regained their market shares. Similarly, when small tobacco companies introduced king-size cigarettes in the 1950s, they gained a large market share at the expense of the leading firms, who were never able to recapture their entire market. Oligopolists also have the ability to invest: Oligopolies often earn positive economic profits for long periods of time.

Scherer developed a formal model relating the rate of technological advance to market structure.[9] The model compares the present value of costs and benefits associated with a new technological advance under different market structures. Consider the time-cost trade-off associated with a new technological advance. The present value of the cost of development can be identified as:

$$C_{pv} = C_0 + \frac{C_1}{1 + r} + \frac{C_2}{(1 + r)^2} + \frac{C_3}{(1 + r)^3} + \cdots + \frac{C_n}{(1 + r)^n}, \qquad [14.1]$$

where C_{pv} represents the present value of the costs of development, C_i represents the costs of development in time period i, and r represents the firm's discount rate.

If the firm aims at a rapid rate of technological advance, early values such as C_0 and C_1 will be very large because rapid technological advance requires the use of multiple paths of experimentation. The firm aiming at an early technological breakthrough typically proceeds down many scientific avenues at once hoping that one or more will pay off. Rapid technological advance also may require moving on to the next development step before the previous step has been perfected. This too raises costs. Consider, for example, the biological and medical battle against AIDS. If society were truly committed to finding a vaccine or a cure for AIDS in the next three years,

huge resources would have to be devoted to AIDS research. These resources would have to come from other areas of medical research, such as heart disease, cancer, and kidney disease. The opportunity cost of transferring resources to AIDS research, part of the true cost of development, would be very high because it would result in more deaths from heart disease, cancer, and kidney disease. In Equation 14.1, the values for C_0, C_1, C_2, and C_3 would be extremely large compared with a path that has a time horizon measured in decades. The present AIDS research strategy is to invest less in early years, perfect small steps (e.g., protease inhibitors and other antiretroviral agents), and then move on to the next small step. Given the current strategy, the values of C_0, C_1, C_2, and C_3 are relatively low and costs are spread over many years.

The AIDS example suggests that to speed up the rate of technological advance, most of the costs of development must be *front loaded;* that is, most of the costs will be in early periods with high present values. As a project is stretched out over time, the present value of development declines because future costs are discounted, adding less to the present value of costs. In Equation 14.1 the present value C_{pv}, therefore, will be much higher if the time of development is short rather than long. Figure 14.3 shows the present value of the costs of development for any given time by the cost curve C_{pv}.

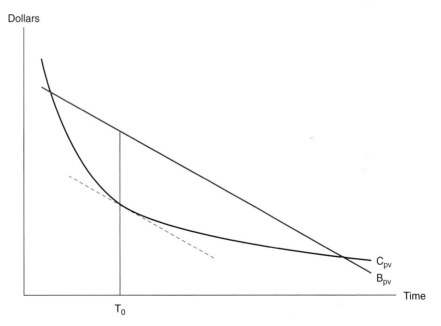

FIGURE 14.3 **The Optimal Time for Technological Development**

The present value of the costs of development of an innovation is depicted by the curve C_{pv}, where the costs decrease as the development time increases. The present value of the benefits of development of an innovation is depicted by the curve B_{pv}, where the benefits decrease as the development time increases. The socially optimal time of development is where the marginal benefit, the slope of the total benefit line, equals the marginal cost, the slope of the total cost curve, at time T_0.

This curve is downward sloping, indicating that the present value of the cost of development decreases as the time of development is lengthened.

Now consider the benefits to the firm of technological development:

$$B_{pv} = B_0 + \frac{B_1}{1 + r} + \frac{B_2}{(1 + r)^2} + \frac{B_3}{(1 + r)^3} + \cdots + \frac{B_n}{(1 + r)^{n'}} \qquad [14.2]$$

where B_{pv} represents the present value of the benefits of development, B_i represents the benefits of development in time period i, and r represents the firm's discount rate.

A more rapid rate of technological advance results in a higher present value of benefits for several reasons. First, if the introduction comes late, most of the benefits will be highly discounted and contribute less to B_{pv}. Early introduction allows the firm to earn benefits when they are most valuable in terms of present value. Second, later development reduces the first-mover advantage for the innovator. Consider AIDS research again. A drug company that introduces a new AIDS drug today will immediately tap into large potential economic benefits. Significant delays in introduction greatly reduce the gains available and greatly increase the probability that another company will introduce a close substitute drug first, which could permanently reduce demand for the innovation.

The present value B_{pv}, therefore, will decrease as the time of development is lengthened. In Figure 14.3, the curve B_{pv} represents the present value of the benefits of development for any period. The curve is downward sloping because the present value of benefits increases as the time of development is shortened.

The optimal development time occurs when benefits exceed costs by the largest amount, or when the marginal benefit of reducing the time of development equals the marginal cost of reducing the time of development. Graphically, this occurs where the slope of the benefit curve equals the slope of the cost curve, or at time T_0 in Figure 14.3.

How would the model be affected by market structure? It is reasonable to assume that the cost function is independent of changes in market structure because it is primarily a function of technological knowledge and inputs.* The benefit function, however, should vary with changes in market structure. Figure 14.4 shows three different benefit curves. The curve B_M represents the present value of benefits for a pure monopolist. The curve B_M is drawn as the highest and flattest curve. Regardless of the time of development, the monopolist gains the most because it has the largest market share and the lowest threat of imitation. Therefore, B_M is always above the other curves. The curve B_M is the flattest curve because the monopolist faces the lowest threat of imitation. The monopolist, therefore, gets to keep most of its gains regardless of when it introduces the innovation.

The curve B_C represents the present value of benefits for a perfectly competitive firm. The curve B_C is the lowest of the three benefit curves because the perfectly competitive firm has the smallest market share and the greatest threat of imitation and, therefore, gains the least from the introduction of a new innovation regardless of the

*Technically, the cost function is independent of market structure only if there are no R&D *spillovers* across firms, that is, if Firm A's technological advance does not lower Firm B's cost of technological advance. Otherwise, a change in market structure that affects Firm A's rate of technological advance could have an impact on Firm B's costs of technological advance.

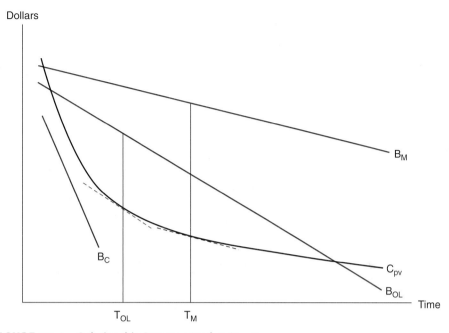

FIGURE 14.4 **Relationship Between Market Structure and the Time of Technological Advance**

The present value of the costs of development of an innovation is depicted by the curve C_{pv}. The present value of the benefits of development of an innovation is depicted under three market structures: B_M for monopoly, B_{OL} for oligopoly, and B_C for perfect competition. The optimal development time with monopoly, T_M, is greater than with oligopoly, T_{OL}. With perfect competition, total costs are always greater than total benefits and there is no development.

time of introduction. The curve B_C slopes rapidly downward because a delay in introduction increases the probability that another firm will imitate the innovation.

Finally, the curve B_{OL} represents the present value of benefits for an oligopolist. The curve lies between the other two curves because the oligopolist has a larger market share than the competitive firm but a smaller market share than the monopolist, and it faces an intermediate threat of imitation. The intermediate threat of retaliation results in a slope that is between the other two benefit curves.

Figure 14.4 shows that innovation will not take place with perfect competition because the present value of benefits is always less than the present value of costs. The monopolist introduces the innovation at time T_M and the oligopolist introduces at time T_{OL}. The most rapid rate of technological advance occurs with oligopoly. Of course, it is possible that higher costs could prevent the oligopolist from introducing the innovation. Figure 14.5 shows a situation in which only the monopolist would introduce the innovation. It is also possible that, with lower costs, the perfectly competitive firm would introduce the innovation first. Such a situation is depicted in Figure 14.6. Scherer's analysis suggests, however, that under a wide variety of cost and benefits conditions, oligopoly will result in the most rapid rate of technological advance.

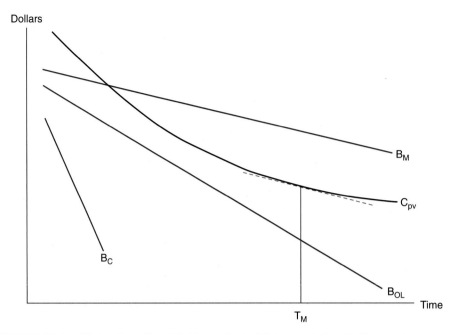

FIGURE 14.5 **Higher Costs Result in Technological Advance Only with Monopoly**

The present value of the costs of development of an innovation is depicted by the curve C_{pv}. The present value of the benefits of development of an innovation is depicted under three market structures: B_M for monopoly, B_{OL} for oligopoly, and B_C for perfect competition. The optimal development time is with monopoly, T_M. With oligopoly and perfect competition, total costs are always greater than total benefits and there is no development. Here the optimal structure for development is monopoly.

14.3.2 Dominant Firms as Fast-Second Innovators

Consider an industry with one dominant firm and one small firm. In Figure 14.7, the benefit curve B_D is the dominant firm's benefit curve, assuming that the smaller firm has not innovated, and the red curve B_S is the small firm's benefit curve, assuming that the dominant firm has yet to innovate.

Which firm will innovate first? In the absence of innovation by either firm, the optimal time for the small firm to innovate is T_S, and the optimal time for the dominant firm to innovate is T_D. Innovation will be undertaken first by the small firm at time $T = T_S$. As soon as the small firm innovates, however, the dominant firm's benefit function shifts down, to B_D', and the dominant firm's optimal time to innovate is dramatically speeded up to T_D'. Once the small firm innovates, the dominant firm has a strong incentive to imitate rapidly to avoid any further erosion in its market share. In this *fast-second* case, the small firm innovates first, but the dominant firm is quick to respond, thereby limiting the small firm's inroads.

Examples of *fast-second innovators* are common. Wilkinson introduced stainless steel shaving blades in the 1960s, but Gillette quickly caught up. Sperry Rand intro-

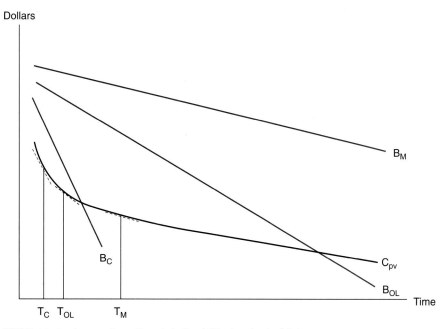

FIGURE 14.6 **Lower Costs Result in Rapid Technological Advance in a Perfectly Competitive Industry**

The present value of the costs of development of an innovation is depicted by the curve C_{pv}. The present value of the benefits of development of an innovation is depicted under three market structures: B_M for monopoly, B_{OL} for oligopoly, and B_C for perfect competition. The optimal development time with monopoly, T_M, is greater than with oligopoly, T_{OL}, which is greater than with perfect competition, T_C. Here the optimal structure for development is perfect competition.

duced the first mainframe computers, but IBM's fast second came to dominate the industry. Similarly, Apple led the way in personal computers in the late 1970s, but IBM took over in the 1980s, although its dominance did not last long. AT&T played the role of the fast second in the development of both microwave relay systems and communication satellites. Kellogg, General Mills, and Quaker Oats lost market share to new granola manufacturers such as Pet and Carnation in the 1970s but quickly regained control, with Quaker Natural Cereal the ultimate winner in this market. Netscape introduced the first Internet browser, but Microsoft now dominates that market. Finally, Snapple's introduction of a line of fruit juice drinks led to a successful response by Coca-Cola with its Frutopia line of juice drinks.

14.3.3 A Contribution of Game Theory

The impact of rapid imitation on the rate of innovation, which is very important in the Scherer model, has been addressed through the use of a simple game theoretic model.[10] The game assumes that duopolists face *constant returns to scale* (a horizontal LRAC) and engage in *Bertrand pricing*. An innovator firm incurs R&D costs equal to 1,

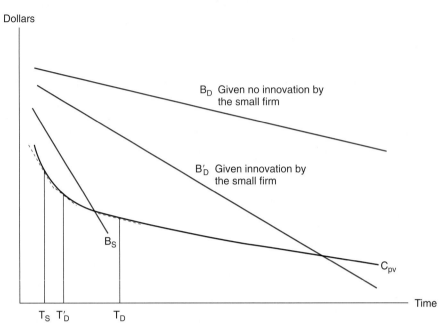

Dollars

B_D Given no innovation by the small firm

B'_D Given innovation by the small firm

B_S

C_{pv}

Time

T_S T'_D T_D

FIGURE 14.7 **The Dominant Firm as a Fast-Second Innovator**

The present value of the costs of development of an innovation is depicted by the curve C_{pv}. The present value of the benefits of development of an innovation is depicted for a small firm, B_S, for a dominant firm if the small firm has not innovated, B_D, and for a dominant firm if the small firm has innovated, B'_D. Here the small firm innovates first, but the dominant firm is quick to respond.

and innovation is immediately imitated at zero cost, so that if GSK (Glaxo-Smith-Kline) innovates first, Merck immediately and costlessly imitates. Furthermore, Bertrand competition always drives price down to marginal cost and average cost. Table 14.2 shows the payoff matrix. If GSK is the innovator and Merck is the imitator, then GSK incurs costs equal to its R&D expenditures and its profits equal −1. By symmetry, if Merck is the innovator and GSK is the imitator, then Merck sustains an economic loss equal to −1. If both innovate, they each sustain an economic loss equal to −1. There is a dominant solution to the game: Both firms *imitate* and the innovation is never developed. Rapid imitation and competitive Bertrand pricing eliminate the innovation altogether.

Suppose that, instead of Bertrand pricing, GSK and Merck collude to charge the joint profit-maximizing price. Once again the cost of innovation equals 1 and imitation is costless. The new payoff matrix is shown in Table 14.3. If both innovate, each firm earns a profit of 2. If one firm innovates and the other imitates, the innovator earns a profit of 2, but the imitator earns a profit of 3. The imitator earns a higher profit because it avoids the cost of innovation. If both imitate, each earns a profit equal to 1. The game has two Nash equilibria (*innovate, imitate*) and (*imitate, innovate*) and a mixed strategy equilibrium in which each firm plays *innovate* half the time and

TABLE 14.2 Innovation Game with Costless Imitation and Bertrand Pricing (GSK's profits, Merck's profits)

imitate the other half of the time.* Recall from Chapter 7 that if each firm plays its optimal mixed strategy, its opponent earns the same profits regardless of its strategy. Given the payoff matrix in Table 14.3, if GSK plays its optimal mixed strategy of *innovate* 50 percent of the time and *imitate* 50 percent of the time, Merck's expected profits equal 2 regardless of Merck's strategy.

The problem with the mixed strategy equilibrium is that it results in an inefficient outcome 50 percent of the time. With each firm playing *innovate* 50 percent of the time and *imitate* 50 percent of the time, there is a 25 percent probability that the result will be (*imitate, imitate*) and a 25 percent probability that the result will be (*innovate, innovate*). Both outcomes are inefficient because (*imitate, imitate*) results in no technological advance, and (*innovate, innovate*) results in a total innovation cost of 2 when society could produce the same innovation for a total cost of 1 with either an (*innovate, imitate*) or an (*imitate, innovate*) outcome.

To prevent the (*imitate, imitate*) outcome in Table 14.3, the government can grant an exclusive license or a patent to the innovator. The next section explores whether patents solve this problem.

14.3.4 The Theoretical Impact of a Patent System

Patents may solve the innovation-imitation game represented by the payoff matrix in Table 14.3. The idea behind the patent system is to increase the incentive to invest in

*To obtain the mixed strategy equilibrium, let ρ equal the probability that GSK innovates and $(1 - \rho)$ equal the probability that GSK imitates, and let τ equal the probability that Merck innovates and $(1 - \tau)$ equal the probability that Merck imitates. If GSK plays its optimal mixed strategy, Merck earns the same profits regardless of its strategy. Therefore, if Merck always plays *innovate*, its profits are equal to its profits if it always plays *imitate*. Mathematically:

$$\rho(2) + (1 - \rho)(2) = \rho(3) + (1 - \rho)(1) \Rightarrow 2\rho + 2 - 2\rho = 3\rho + 1 - \rho$$

$$\Rightarrow 2 = 2\rho + 1 \Rightarrow \rho = \frac{1}{2}.$$

GSK's optimal mixed strategy, therefore, is to play *innovate* 50 percent of the time and *imitate* 50 percent of the time.

If Merck plays its optimal mixed strategy, GSK earns the same profits regardless of its strategy. Therefore, if GSK always plays *innovate* its profits are equal to its profits if it always plays *imitate*. Mathematically:

$$\tau(2) + (1 - \tau)(2) = \tau(3) + (1 - \tau)(1) \Rightarrow 2\tau + 2 - 2\tau = 3\tau + 1 - \tau$$

$$\Rightarrow 2 = 2\tau + 1 \Rightarrow \tau = \frac{1}{2}.$$

Merck's optimal mixed strategy, therefore, is to play *innovate* 50 percent of the time and *imitate* 50 percent of the time.

TABLE 14.3 Innovation Game with Costless Imitation and Collusive Pricing
(GSK's profits, Merck's profits)

research and development by granting a monopoly to the first individual or company to successfully innovate. Ideally, the patent system would result in the optimal amount of spending on research and development. Theoretical work on *patent races* in which firms compete to be the first to receive a patent, however, suggests that patent systems may not result in the optimal level of investment in research and development. Below we present a simple patent race model to analyze this issue. The geometric approach of this model relies on one restrictive assumption. A game based on more realistic assumptions that results in a mixed strategy equilibrium is presented in the appendix. Both approaches reach the same conclusions.

Equation 14.1 and Figure 14.3 showed the time-cost trade-off of a new technological innovation. Figure 14.8 shows this trade-off in a different way with the cost of the innovation identified by expenditures X on the x-axis and the time of innovation $T(X)$ shown on the y-axis. In Figure 14.8, the greater R&D expenditures X, the shorter is the time to development.

Equation 14.2 identified the present value of benefits and Figure 14.3 identified the optimal time of development T_0, where total benefits exceed total costs by the maximum amount. T_0 occurs where the *marginal* benefit of reducing the time of development equals the *marginal* cost of reducing the time of development. In Figure 14.9, the total benefits of an innovation, B_{pv}, are identified as a function of total R&D expenditures X instead of as a function of the time of development.[11] From Figure 14.8, we know that the time of development $T(X)$ is a negative function of R&D expenditures X, and therefore, B_{pv} is a positive function of X. The greater R&D expenditures X, the shorter the development time $T(X)$, and therefore, the greater the total discounted value of benefits $B_{pv}(X)$. $B_{pv}(X)$ is an increasing function of X, but it increases at a decreasing rate because there is a limit to the total benefits from any innovation.

To maximize social surplus, the difference between total benefits and total costs, $B_{pv}(X) - X$, must be maximized. To maximize $B_{pv}(X) - X$, marginal benefit must equal marginal cost or $MB = \Delta B_{pv}(X) = \Delta X = MC$. Dividing both sides of this equation by ΔX yields:

$$\frac{\Delta B_{pv}(X)}{\Delta X} = 1. \qquad [14.3]$$

Equation 14.3 states that profit maximization requires that the slope of the total benefit curve must equal 1. In Figure 14.9, $\dfrac{\Delta B_{pv}(X)}{\Delta X} = 1$ at point a, and therefore, the socially optimal expenditure on R&D is X^*.

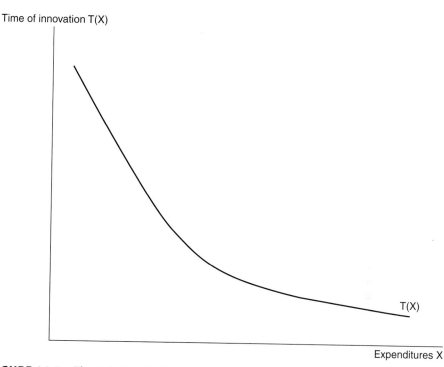

Time of innovation T(X)

Expenditures X

FIGURE 14.8 The Relationship Between Time of Innovation and R&D Expenditures

The time of innovation $T(X)$ is a negative function of R&D expenditures X. Greater expenditures X result in quicker development time $T(X)$.

Now suppose there are multiple firms engaged in a patent race to obtain a monopoly over the innovation by bidding for the right to spend X on R&D. While the winning bidder gains a monopoly, the losing bidders spend nothing on R&D and receive nothing in return. Each firm has an incentive to bid slightly more than X^* on R&D as long as these additional expenditures result in the firm winning the patent race and earning a positive economic profit. Each firm, therefore, has an incentive to increase R&D expenditures up to the point where profit equals zero and total benefits equal total expenditures. That point occurs where the 45-degree line represented by the equation $B_{pv}(X) = X$ intersects point b in Figure 14.9. The winning bid, therefore, is X_e.[†] R&D spending is X_e, which is greater than the socially optimal level X^*.

The model implies that the expected profit for each firm equals zero and that the entire potential surplus from the innovation is lost to society because the firms race to be first to gain the patent, and in so doing, from a social standpoint, spend too much on R&D. Innovation occurs earlier than it would with a monopolist, but the speeding up of the time of innovation is not worth the extra development costs to society.

[†]In this model, we make the simplifying assumption that the firms must bid on the level of expenditure X rather than select a level of X. Without this assumption, there is no Nash equilibrium if the winner spends X_e in Figure 14.9 and the losers spend zero because the winner's best response if the other firms spend zero would be to decrease spending to X^*. One way to view the bidding game is that there is a Stackelberg leader that bids first and commits to spending X_e on R&D before the other firms get to place their bids. Once the leader bids to commit to spending X_e, the other firms' best response is to spend zero on R&D.

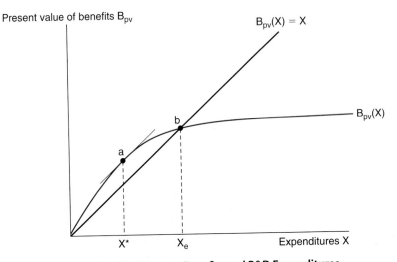

FIGURE 14.9 The Relationship Between Benefits and R&D Expenditures

The total benefits of innovation B_{pv} are a positive function of the total R&D expenditures X. To maximize social surplus, marginal benefit must equal marginal cost or $MB = \Delta B_{pv}(X) =$

$\Delta X = MC$, so $\dfrac{\Delta B_{pv}(X)}{\Delta X} = 1. \dfrac{\Delta B_{pv}(X)}{\Delta X} = 1$ at point a, so the optimal R&D expenditure is X*. When

multiple firms bid for the right to spend X on R&D, each firm has an incentive to bid slightly more than X* if additional expenditures result in the firm obtaining the patent and earning a positive profit. Firms have an incentive to increase expenditures up to the point where profit equals zero, where the 45-degree line $B_{pv}(X) = X$ intersects point b. The winning bid is X, which is greater than the socially optimal level X*.

In the analysis in Figure 14.9, we made the simplifying assumption that firms make bids on their R&D spending and only the winning bidder spends anything on R&D. A more realistic assumption would be that all firms can spend positive amounts on R&D but only one wins the patent race. This model is developed in the appendix.

Both the model in Figure 14.9 and the model in the appendix imply that the patent system results in (1) firms spending more than the socially optimal amount on research and development; (2) too rapid a rate of technological development from a social perspective; and (3) all potential profits associated with research and development being competed away. There is no guarantee, therefore, that a patent system results in the optimal investment in research and development.

14.4 The Impact of Firm Size

Recall that Schumpeter extolled not only the virtues of monopoly, but also the advantages of the "large-scale unit of control." Schumpeter argued that large firms drove the process of creative destruction. John Kenneth Galbraith expanded on

Schumpeter's argument in the 1950s and suggested that large firms were the major force behind modern technological advance:[12]

> A benign Providence . . . has made the modern industry of a few large firms an almost perfect instrument for inducing technical change. . . . There is no more pleasant fiction than that technical change is the product of the matchless ingenuity of the small man forced by competition to employ his wits to better his neighbour. Unhappily, it is a fiction. Technical development has long since become the preserve of the scientist and the engineer. Most of the cheap and simple inventions have, to put it bluntly, been made.

Both Schumpeter and Galbraith argued that technological leaps and bounds are driven almost exclusively by large firms. Subsequent theorists suggested, however, that the relationship between firm size and technological advance is far more complex than Schumpeter and Galbraith hypothesized. First, consider the arguments in favor of large firms. Large firms have greater resources to invest in R&D than smaller firms, and, given the high costs of establishing a modern R&D laboratory, only large firms can set them up. Second, economies of scale are associated with R&D. Large firms can more easily afford to purchase highly specialized equipment, such as high-powered electron microscopes and supercomputers. Large, diversified firms can also employ specialized personnel in many fields. Third, large firms can spread risk over many projects, thereby reducing the overall risk associated with R&D. By contrast, a failed high-cost research and development project can cause the demise of a small firm. Fourth, large firms are often highly diversified, and a technological advance in one area may be useful in another. Finally, large firms may have longer time horizons that enable them to persevere with expensive long-term R&D projects.

At first glance, these points represent an impressive array of arguments in favor of bigness. There is, however, a similar array of arguments in favor of smaller firms. Perhaps the most powerful argument against the large corporation is the tendency for large firms to become bureaucratically inefficient. Successful large corporations often become complacent and refuse to approve new projects or approve them far too slowly.

Consider the experience of IBM in the personal computer market. At the top of the IBM management structure in the 1970s and 1980s was the Management Committee (MC) in Armonk, New York, that consisted of three to six members and which historically decided all matters, even trivial ones. Until 1989, for example, the MC sat in judgment on everything from what a product looked like to whether a salesperson could grant a reduced price to keep a customer.[13] IBM's managerial system was slow, cumbersome, and not suited to the fast-paced personal computer industry of the 1980s. Furthermore, the decision makers typically had only limited technical insight into the personal computer industry, because the CEOs and other top managers were generally drawn from the ranks of the sales department, not from technical areas.

Many of IBM's problems in the 1980s and early 1990s resulted from management's failure to recognize that the personal computer would one day be something more than a home toy. To IBM's senior management in the 1970s and early 1980s, the future was still in mainframes and minicomputers for commercial use. According to one member of the MC, "The general attitude was that you don't have big problems in small markets, and we thought the personal computer was a very small market."[14] In 1985, for example, Don Estridge, the original mastermind of the IBM PC operation,

wanted to produce a new line of PCs based on Intel's fast 80386 microprocessor. Estridge theorized that the way to fight the PC clones was to destroy them by producing much faster and better PCs. The MC, fearing that faster PCs would threaten IBM's mainframe business, which still was the basis for most of IBM's revenues, refused to approve Estridge's plan.

By the 1980s, the MC had become so conservative that it refused to take even moderate risks of damaging or making obsolete some of IBM's product lines. According to Carroll:[15]

> The senior executives, all ex-salesmen, preferred the less disruptive approach that was more conventional around IBM and that had helped it wring such extraordinary profits out of the mainframe business. The executives wanted to milk the existing product line as long as possible. After all, all the expensive work that goes into designing PCs had already been paid for. So why not just sit back and keep producing PCs that cost IBM about half what customers would pay? Only when IBM couldn't delay any longer would it pay to design and bring out products using new technology.

As late as the mid-1980s, IBM's management had completely missed the coming personal computer revolution. Bill Gates, however, had seen the future a full decade earlier. In a 1995 interview Gates noted that:[16]

> [In the mid 1970s] microprocessors were instantly attractive to [Paul Allen and me] because you could build something for a fraction of the cost of conventional electronics. . . .
>
> I remember, from the very beginning, we wondered, "What would it mean for DEC once microcomputers were powerful and cheap enough? What would it mean for IBM?" To us it seemed that they were screwed tomorrow. We were saying, "God, how come these guys aren't stunned? How come they're not just amazed and scared?" . . . The notion was fairly clear to us that computers were going to be a big, big personal tool.

The IBM example appears to undermine the argument that only large firms are willing to take on risky R&D efforts. Any IBM forward movement on a research project required approval at many managerial levels. By comparison, at Microsoft, Google, and other computer hardware and software companies, the decision to move forward on a project rested in the hands of a few creative leaders such as Bill Gates, Sergey Brin, and Larry Page.

Computer technology has also reduced the advantages associated with economies of scale as more and more R&D projects are contracted out to independent R&D companies. It may still be true that one small firm cannot purchase specialized equipment such as wind tunnels, supercomputers, and differential scanning calorimeters, but independent R&D firms working for many small firms and spreading their costs among many projects can purchase such equipment. These independent R&D companies can also employ specialists in many R&D areas.

With regard to the relationship between firm size and technological advance and between market structure and innovation, theory can take us just so far, and it is necessary to examine the empirical evidence.

14.5 Empirical Evidence

S chumpeter's writings and subsequent theoretical work generated an extensive body of empirical work, most of which looked at two hypotheses. The first is that inventive activity increases more than proportionately with firm size. The second is that there is a positive relationship between inventive activity and market concentration. As a result of the focus on these two hypotheses, until recently relatively little work had been done on other determinants of inventive activity.* In this section we review the empirical literature.[17]

14.5.1 Measurement Issues

Measurement issues are particularly difficult in empirical investigations of innovation and technical change. Increases in knowledge clearly contribute to technological progress, yet we do not know how to measure "knowledge." How can innovations from different industries be compared? Should the measure of inventive activity somehow take the value of a discovery into account? All these issues remain unsolved problems, although economists have used a variety of measures of inventive activity in their studies.[18]

The two general classes of measures of innovation are outputs and inputs. The most common measure of innovative outputs across industries is a count of patents.[19] Although patent data has the advantage of being widely available, problems are associated with using counts of patents to measure innovative output. The economic value of patents varies widely; a few patents are highly important and valuable, but many are never used commercially. Also, the propensity to patent varies greatly across industries. In some industries, firms tend to keep discoveries secret rather than patenting them and thereby revealing information to competitors. If a patent count is used to measure innovative output, then an industry with a low propensity to patent will look less innovative than one with a high propensity to patent.[20]

Most studies of innovation, especially the earlier studies, use data on inputs. Expenditures on R&D or the number of R&D personnel are the most commonly used measures of innovative inputs. These measures also have problems. Because of accounting rules, expenditures on R&D include the total amount spent in a given year on equipment, even for equipment that will last several years. Thus, R&D expenditures will be overstated in the year a piece of durable equipment is purchased and understated in the subsequent years.

14.5.2 Testing Schumpeter's Hypotheses

A large number of studies have investigated the relationship between firm size and innovation. Rather than surveying this huge literature in detail, we discuss a few studies,

*Cohen and Levin note that focusing on the two hypotheses has actually worked against gaining an understanding of the fundamental determinants and economic consequences of technological progress, something that Schumpeter was interested in fostering. See Wesley M. Cohen and Richard C. Levin, "Empirical Studies of Innovation and Market Structure," in Richard Schmalensee and Robert D. Willig (eds.), *Handbook of Industrial Organization* (Amsterdam: North-Holland, 1989).

summarize the stylized facts, and consider some methodological problems.* Within this section, we divide our examination of the evidence into two parts: (1) the relationship between firm size and inventive *effort,* or inputs; and (2) the relationship between firm size and inventive *output.*

Firm Size and Inventive Effort

Several early studies examined the relationship between firm size and R&D intensity, typically measured as the ratio of either R&D expenditures or R&D employment to firm size. Comanor, for example, regressed the log of R&D expenditures on firm size using 1955 and 1960 data for 387 firms in 21 groups.[†21] He found evidence of, at most, a very weak positive association between R&D intensity and firm size. Other early studies found similar results.

In two 1965 studies, Scherer criticized both the data and the specification of the estimated regressions in earlier studies.[22] He noted that the samples were biased because only firms with sizable research programs were included. Also, he argued that the specifications used had assumed a linear relationship and that such a specification might not be appropriate. The results of Scherer's studies, in which he employed a larger sample and estimated a nonlinear specification, showed that R&D employment increased more than proportionately with firm size among the smaller firms in his sample but more slowly among the larger firms. In fact, Scherer found that the relationship between R&D employment and firm size might even be *negative* among the very largest firms in some industries. Scherer noted, however, that in some industries, such as chemicals, automobiles, and steel, R&D intensity appeared to increase with firm size.

Scherer's findings were more or less confirmed by other studies, and his results became the consensus opinion in the mid-1970s and early 1980s. In the words of a 1975 review article:

> Thus, it seems that with the possible exception of the chemical industry, there is hardly any support for the hypothesis that the intensity of innovational effort increases with firm size.[23]

More recent work using more disaggregated data sets has shaken this consensus view. Scherer himself contributed to the questioning of the earlier consensus.[24] He used data from the Federal Trade Commission's Line of Business surveys, a data set that reports information on manufacturing companies disaggregated by individual lines of business. For example, consider the activities of General Motors. Recall from Chapter 4 that the standard NAICS data report all of GM's activities in the fields of gas turbines, diesel locomotives, buses, and missile guidance systems under the broad heading "motor vehicle manufacturing." Line of Business data report these activities

*For comprehensive literature surveys of the empirical literature concerning the two Schumpeterian hypotheses, see M.I. Kamien and N.L. Schwartz, *Market Structure and Innovation* (Cambridge: Cambridge University Press, 1982), and W.L. Baldwin and J.T. Scott, *Market Structure and Technological Change* (Chichester: Harwood, 1987).

†Comanor chose the log of R&D intensity rather than R&D intensity as the dependent variable because R&D intensity must, by definition, be nonnegative. See W.S. Comanor, "Market Structure, Product Differentiation, and Industrial Research," *Quarterly Journal of Economics* 81 (November, 1967): 639–657.

under their correct subheadings. Scherer studied *business units* such as GM's unit that manufactures diesel locomotives, and found that for 40 of 196 business units in his sample, R&D intensity increased with business unit size; for most of the remaining lines of business (140 of 196), Scherer's results indicated *no size effect* on R&D intensity.

Another study using the Line of Business data emphasized the need to control for industry effects and to make a distinction between the size of the firm and the size of the business unit.[25] After taking these factors into account, Cohen and colleagues found no effect of size, either of the firm or of the business unit, on R&D intensity. They did find evidence of a threshold effect in the decision to undertake R&D: The likelihood of a business unit engaging in R&D increased as the size of the business unit increased.* Cohen and coworkers also noted that the size variables explained less than one percent of the total variance of R&D intensity and that the magnitude of the effect was very small. Other evidence, however, indicates that R&D intensity is higher among small and large firms than among intermediate-sized firms.[26]

What can we conclude about the relationship between firm size and R&D intensity from the available evidence? The evidence is inconclusive and sometimes contradictory. However, there is certainly no strong support for the claim that R&D intensity increases more than proportionately with firm size.

Firm Size and Inventive Output

Fewer studies have examined the relationship of size to inventive output than of size to inventive inputs. As mentioned earlier, measuring inventive output is particularly difficult. Most studies use patents as a measure of inventive output.

The relatively early evidence about outputs from studies measured at the firm level, rather than at the line of business level, was generally consistent with that about inputs. Given that R&D expenditures and patents are highly correlated, this is not surprising. Kamien and Schwartz summarized the available evidence on innovational output as follows:

> [T]he conclusion about the effect of size on innovational effort tends to be supported and reflected in evidence on size and innovational output. Beyond some magnitude, size does not appear especially conducive to either innovational effort or output in either this country or in European countries where studies have been conducted. However, patterns differ by industry. It seems noteworthy that the chemical industry is cited as an exception both for the United States and abroad.[27]

More recent results support this.[28] Using the Line of Business data, Scherer found that the number of patents increased more than proportionately with size for only 14 of 124, or 11 percent, of the business units. For most industries, 91 of 124, R&D performance as measured by patent counts increased proportionately with size.† Neutrality with regard to the effects of size is the norm.

*Another study also found evidence of a threshold in terms of the decision to engage in R&D along with no effect of firm size beyond that threshold. See Albert N. Link, Terry G. Seaks, and Sabrina R. Woodbery, "Firm Size and R&D Spending: Testing for Functional Form," *Southern Economic Journal* 54 (April 1988): 1027–1038.

†For the remaining 19 industries, there was a disadvantage associated with being large.

Remaining Questions

Some evidence indicates that the inventive process is far too complicated to be described by firm-specific variables such as size. Jewkes, Sawers, and Stillerman compiled a collection of case histories of important inventions of the twentieth century.[29] They described complex interactions of firms in which, for example, large firms sometimes acquire smaller firms to bring an invention to market. It is worth quoting their conclusion about size: "It may well be that there is no optimum size of firm but merely an optimal pattern for any industry, such a distribution of firms by size, character and outlook as to guarantee the most effective gathering together and commercially perfecting of the flow of new ideas."[30] To gain a better understanding of the inventive process, economists need to consider the type of interactions described by Jewkes, Sawers, and Stillerman more fully.

Market Structure and Inventive Activity

In a very early study, Maclaurin compared two rankings of 13 U.S. industries: (1) by important innovations from 1925 to 1950; and (2) by the extent of monopolization.*[31] He found that *some* degree of monopoly power is necessary for technological progress, but that it is not sufficient. Other factors, including ease of entry, entrepreneurial leadership, and the underlying engineering or scientific base, seemed to be much more important.

Maclaurin's results have stood up reasonably well over time. Most studies that look at the relationship between market concentration and industry R&D/sales ratios have found a positive relationship, both for the United States and for other industrialized nations.[32]

A number of studies have examined the specification of the relationship between market concentration and R&D intensity, testing for nonlinearities. Early evidence suggested that the relationship might take the nonlinear form of an "inverted-U," in which R&D intensity increases with concentration at first but then decreases as concentration levels increase still further. Using 1960 data on R&D employment as a percent of total employment, Scherer found a peak in R&D intensity at four-firm concentration levels between 50 and 55.[33] He also found evidence of a threshold: Industries with four-firm concentration ratios below 15 appeared to do almost no research and development.

The inverted-U hypothesis has been tested further using more disaggregated data. Simple tests that regress R&D intensity against the concentration ratio and the square of the concentration ratio support the inverted-U hypothesis. Levin, Cohen, and Mowery found a peak R&D/sales ratio at a four-firm concentration ratio of 52.[34] Similarly, Scott found a peak in R&D intensity at a four-firm concentration ratio of 64.[35]

As long ago as Maclaurin's study, however, economists recognized the importance of industry-specific factors. Including additional explanatory variables to account for some of these factors weakens the empirical support for the inverted-U hypothesis. Examples include indices, based on survey results, that measure the relevance of vari-

*Each ranking was subjective. The ranking by important innovations was based on factors such as the number of patents issued and the presence or absence of a separate research department. The monopolization ranking took into account size of industry price leaders and ease of entry.

ous scientific fields to specific industries' R&D efforts and the importance of contributions from outside an industry to that industry's technological progress.[36] These indices reflect differences in **technological opportunity** or the inherent interindustry differences in ability to make major technological progress. Some industries, such as the computer or the drug industry, have many scientific opportunities to make progress, whereas others, such as the brick industry or the glass bottle industry, have far fewer scientific opportunities. Other indices measure **appropriability**, or the ability of a firm to maintain exclusive control over its technology without seeing that technology lost to competitors. Examples include indices assessing the strength of patents, secrecy, and lead times. Including such measures reduces the statistical significance of market concentration.

Investigations of the relationship between market concentration and inventive activity may suffer from another problem. The analysis considered thus far has assumed that the direction of causation runs *from* concentration *to* R&D. Some economists have suggested, however, that the causation may also run in the opposite direction, with a rapid rate of innovation leading to concentration.[37] If this is the case, statistical techniques that take this into account should be employed in empirical work.

Some studies have attempted to correct for this potential problem.[38] Two tentative conclusions emerge from this work. First, statistical tests find evidence of this causation problem, rejecting the hypothesis that the causal connection between market structure and R&D runs only in one direction. Second, techniques that take this problem into account do not seem to change the empirical findings.

Summary of Empirical Work on the Schumpeterian Hypotheses

Although some stylized facts have emerged from the empirical work on the relationships between firm size and inventive activity and between market structure and inventive activity, the results are not particularly robust. Omitting important variables can bias the estimated coefficients and lead a researcher to draw incorrect conclusions about the relationship of interest. Results seem to be sensitive to industry conditions, making it necessary to think about the fundamental determinants of inventive activity. Economists have recently turned their attention to such fundamental determinants, focusing on three categories: market demand, technological opportunity, and appropriability conditions. Historical literature and case studies make the importance of these factors evident, yet much work remains to be done and little is known at present.*

14.6 The Economics of the Patent System

Since 1995 a United States patent is a twenty-year legal monopoly grant that is awarded to inventors in exchange for their agreement to disclose their inventions to the public.† A valid patent gives an inventor monopoly power to decide on the use, transfer, or withholding of an innovation. The awarding of a patent has an admirable

*See Cohen and Levin in *Handbook of Industrial Organization* (Amsterdam: North-Holland, 1989), pp. 1079–1098, for a discussion of the work that has been done.

†Prior to 1995, patent protection lasted 17 years.

objective, the dissemination of technological knowledge that might otherwise be kept secret, but the patent grant may be abused and come in direct conflict with another economic goal, the reduction of monopoly power.

Patents exist for one economic purpose—to increase the rate of technological advance. Without question, some major technological breakthroughs would never have been developed, or would have been developed much later, in the absence of patent protection. Economic theory suggests, however, that patent protection may not increase the rate of technological advance. In fact, theory suggests that in some cases patent protection *decreases* the rate of technological advance.[39]

To understand the potential dilemma associated with the current system, consider the following three possible scenarios.

Scenario 1

Suppose a weekend garage inventor, hypothetically named Mr. Tinker, is driven to invent, not by money, but by a fairly common character trait—curiosity. One day Mr. Tinker discovers a new method for cheaply harnessing solar energy. Although Mr. Tinker never gave any thought to the patent system as he worked on his invention every weekend, on realizing the importance of his discovery, he runs to a patent attorney, and a few years later receives a patent. He then turns the patent over to a large firm, hypothetically called International Solar Machines (ISM), and on the basis of Mr. Tinker's patent, ISM develops a solar energy device, which it prices well above marginal and average cost. Over the next decade, other firms spend millions of dollars in an unsuccessful attempt to invent around the ISM patent. Finally, after twenty years, the ISM patent is made public, but by then ISM is a virtual monopolist in the solar energy business. Furthermore, during the period of patent protection, ISM patented a number of minor technological advances based on Mr. Tinker's original patent, so that by the time the original patent expires, ISM is firmly entrenched as the leader in the solar energy field, and few firms will consider attempting to challenge ISM's dominance. Mr. Tinker, ISM's management, and ISM's stockholders have all made large fortunes, but the solar energy industry has performed in a very inefficient manner in terms of static efficiency. Furthermore, to protect its investment in Tinker's original device, ISM withheld using some of its improvement patents for several years; therefore, ISM slowed the rate of technological advance on improvements to the Tinker patent. Society has benefited from Mr. Tinker's device but has also paid a price in the form of reduced static efficiency and a slow rate of technological improvement on the basic patent.

Scenario 2

Now consider an alternate scenario to the Mr. Tinker story, one without a patent system. Mr. Tinker develops the same solar energy device and takes the device to ISM. A member of the ISM development department likes the idea, and ISM proceeds with development. Because of a lack of patent protection, ISM decides to introduce the device as quickly as possible before its competitors learn about the existence of the invention (perhaps rumors of the device have already begun to circulate). ISM is first into the market and initially charges a high profit-maximizing price. Within 12 to 24 months, ISM and Mr. Tinker have made a large economic profit, and the first imitations of Mr. Tinker's invention appear on the market. After another 24 months many

imitations are available, but to keep one step ahead of the competition, ISM and some of its competitors have already marketed more advanced devices based on the original Tinker technology. Within five years, the basic Tinker device is obsolete, and many companies are competing for a share of the solar energy harnessing market. Some firms make a profit, others sustain an economic loss and leave the market, but on average the industry is earning normal economic profits. Prices approximate marginal and average cost, and the industry is performing efficiently from a static standpoint. In this scenario, the lack of patent protection has actually increased the rate of technological advance, and the outcome is preferable to that of scenario 1 from both a static and dynamic perspective.

Scenario 3

Now consider another possible scenario in the absence of patent protection. Mr. Tinker develops the same solar energy device and approaches the development department at ISM. After careful consideration, the development department concludes that although the device is technologically sound, development would be too expensive, and therefore, without patent protection ISM could not expect to earn a profit. Mr. Tinker then approaches several other large high-technology firms, but each responds in the same negative manner. Finally, completely discouraged, Mr. Tinker gives up, and the device never becomes a commercial reality. Because of a lack of patent protection, society has lost all of the potential benefits associated with Mr. Tinker's device.

Economic uncertainty surrounding the patent system exists because it is impossible to determine how often the first scenario occurs, as opposed to how often the second or third scenarios *would* occur in the absence of patent protection. Scenario 2, without patent protection, is clearly preferable to scenario 1, with patent protection. However, scenario 1, with patent protection, is clearly preferable to scenario 3, without patent protection.

Another way to think about this dilemma is to recognize that some inventions and innovations are *patent dependent* and others are *not patent dependent;* that is, some technology would become available only with a patent system, but other technology would become available just as quickly, or even more quickly, without a patent system. There are a variety of reasons why many high-technology innovations would be developed without patents. First, many inventions and innovations result from human curiosity and genius. Such inventions are driven primarily by a need to understand. The development of fire and the wheel, for example, were certainly not driven by patents. Second, sufficient economic incentives for invention and innovation often result from first-mover advantages or an ability to move rapidly down a learning curve. Third, complementary investments in marketing and service can provide sufficient protection from competition for new inventions or innovations (e.g., IBM). Finally, secrecy may provide better protection against imitation than patents because with patent protection the new technology is made public, whereas with secrecy competitors are prevented from gaining insight into the new invention or innovation.

Like many economic issues, the patent system involves trade-offs. Some inventions and innovations that are not patent dependent are protected to ensure that society receives the benefits of all patent-dependent inventions and innovations. Because the system involves social costs as well as social benefits, patent holders should not be granted unrestricted rights and privileges.

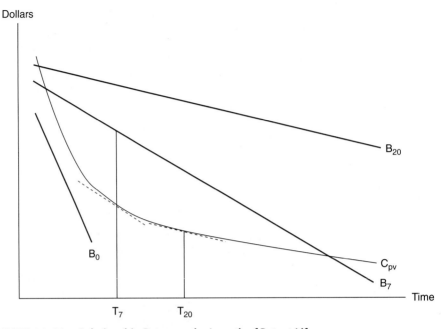

FIGURE 14.10 Relationship Between the Length of Patent Life and the Rate of Technological Advance

The present value of the costs of development of an innovation is depicted by the curve C_{pv}. The present value of the benefits of development of an innovation is depicted with patent protection for 20 years, B_{20}; 7 years, B_7; and zero years, B_0. The optimal development time is with a seven-year patent life. Without patent protection, there is no development.

The impact of the length of time of patent protection on development time can be analyzed using the framework of Figure 14.4. Figure 14.10 reproduces Figure 14.4 except the benefit curves are labeled as B_0, B_7, and B_{20}, where the subscripts 0, 7, and 20 represent the length of patent protection in years. In Figure 14.10, no innovation takes place without patent protection (the B_0 case) because the present value of costs always exceeds the present value of benefits. Patent protection is necessary for innovation to occur, but the time of development is faster with a patent life of seven years rather than twenty years. Of course, every case will be different, but it is possible that a twenty-year patent length could slow down the rate of technological advance.

It is, of course, also possible that a patent life longer than twenty years would be required to induce technological advance. If the cost curve is everywhere above the B_{20} curve, then a patent longer than twenty years is required to obtain the benefits associated with the technological advance.

14.6.1 Empirical Evidence on the Impact of Patents

Patents induce inventions and innovation, but they also increase monopoly power. The patent system *always* results in net social benefits for patent-dependent innovations. The patent system, however, *always* results in net social losses for nonpatent-

dependent innovations because these innovations would be developed without the costs of granting monopoly power.

To try to determine the relative importance of patents compared with other incentives for discovery and development of innovations, Levin and colleagues conducted a survey of 650 high-level R&D executives in 130 lines of business.[40] The R&D executives were asked to rate the importance of patents in protecting the competitive advantages of new processes or products on a scale from 1 = not at all effective to 7 = very effective. The executives were also asked to rate on the same scale the effectiveness of secrecy, lead time, learning curves, and sales or service effort.

Table 14.4 shows Levin and coworkers' major findings. The results were described by the authors as "striking."[41] For new processes, patent protection was the *least* effective method of protection. The executives rated lead time (a first-mover advantage) the most effective method of protecting a new process, followed by learning curve advantages, sales or service effort, and secrecy, respectively. Furthermore, 80 percent of the respondents rated patent effectiveness *below* a 4.0, whereas 80 percent rated lead time above a 4.3 and learning curve advantages above a 4.5. Even secrecy was considered far more effective than patents.

The findings for new products are only slightly more favorable toward patents. With regard to new products, patents were rated less effective than lead time, sales or service effort, and learning curve advantages, but more effective than secrecy. Still, only 20 percent of the executives rated patents above a 5. Compare this with the 80 percent who rated sales or service efforts above a 5.

TABLE 14.4 Effectiveness of Alternative Means of Protecting Advantages of New or Improved Processes and Products

Method of Appropriation	Overall Sample Means		Distribution of Industry Means[1]	
	Processes	*Products*	*Processes*	*Products*
Patents to prevent duplication	3.52	4.33	2.6–4.0	3.0–5.0
Patents to secure royalty income	3.31	3.75	2.3–4.0	2.7–4.8
Secrecy	4.31	3.57	3.3–5.0	2.7–4.1
Lead time	5.11	5.41	4.3–5.9	4.8–6.0
Moving quickly down the learning curve	5.02	5.09	4.5–5.7	4.4–5.8
Sales or service effort	4.55	5.59	3.7–5.5	5.0–6.1

Note. Range: 1 = not at all effective; 7 = very effective.

[1]From the upper bound of the lowest 20 percent to the lower bound of the highest 20 percent.

Source: Richard C. Levin, Alvin K. Klevorick, Richard R. Nelson, and Sidney G. Winter, "Appropriating the Returns from Industrial Research and Development," *Brookings Papers on Economic Activity*, no. 3 (1987): 794.

These findings raise serious questions concerning the extent to which new process and product innovations are patent dependent; they suggest that most inventions and innovations would come into being without patent protection. Taking this implication one step further, the authors noted, "The perceived ineffectiveness of patents in most industries raises the question of why firms use them."[42] Executives in the study noted two motives for patents, each having little to do with protecting innovations.[43] First, firms may obtain patents to measure the productivity of their R&D employees. Second, firms may obtain patents because some foreign governments require patent licensing as a condition of entry into their markets.

More evidence on patent dependency is supplied by Mansfield, who surveyed 100 R&D directors to try to ascertain what proportion of their companies' inventions produced between 1981 and 1983 were patent dependent. Mansfield's results are reported in Table 14.5. The executives rated patents as completely unimportant in six out of 12 industries. Only in pharmaceuticals were more than half the inventions patent dependent, and in only three industries—pharmaceuticals, other chemicals, and petroleum—were 25 percent or more of the inventions patent dependent. Mansfield's results are consistent with Levin and colleagues' findings.

Levin and coworkers also surveyed the executives concerning the impact of patents on the cost and time requirements of imitation. Respondents reported that patents typically increased the costs of imitation and lengthened the time required to duplicate an innovation. These responses suggest that patents may significantly reduce the rate of imitation and thereby slow the rate of technological advance.

These survey findings imply that a relatively small percentage of inventions and innovations are patent dependent. To obtain the benefits associated with this small percentage of patent-dependent inventions and innovations, society pays a price in the form of higher monopoly profits and slower imitation. Is the price worth the benefits associated with patent-dependent inventions and innovations? No definitive answer is possible because the patent-dependent inventions and innovations may be the most valuable technological advances. For example, if technological advances in the pharmaceutical industry are heavily driven by patents, as Mansfield's findings suggest, then one of the greatest benefits of the patent system is saving lives, a benefit that surely should not be taken lightly. As Pakes and Simpson have noted:[44]

> To take an extreme example, a finding that only 0.5 percent of a firm's inventions was dependent on patent protection would not mean that patent protection was unimportant to the firm if that same 0.5 percent accounted for 99.5 percent of the total returns to the firm's R&D program. . . .
> . . . Moreover, half of all the estimated value of patents rights accrues to between 5 and 10 percent of all patents.

All that can be safely concluded is that technological advance would continue even if the patent system were eliminated. Most inventions and innovations would still be developed and effectively protected by some combination of first-mover advantages, learning curves, sales or service efforts, or secrecy. Furthermore, elimination of the patent system would reduce the degree of monopoly power in the economy and increase the rate of imitation. Society, however, might be better or worse off as a result of such a dramatic policy change.

It is unclear from this discussion what policy changes, if any, are called for in the patent system. Proposed changes have included one or more of the following:

TABLE 14.5 Estimated Percentage of Patent-Dependent Inventions by Industry Group, 1981–1983

Industry Group	Percentage of Inventions Whose Existence Depends on Patent Protection
Pharmaceuticals	60
Other chemicals	38
Petroleum	25
Machinery	17
Fabricated metal products	12
Electrical equipment	11
Primary metals	1
Instruments	1
Office equipment	0
Motor vehicles	0
Rubber products	0
Textiles	0

Source: Edwin Mansfield, "Patents and Innovation," 32 *Management Science* (February 1986): 175.

(1) changing the number of years of protection either above or below 20 years; (2) requiring compulsory licensing to all at "reasonable" royalties; (3) expanding the scope of patent protection to include new areas such as university research; (4) tightening the legal requirements to gain patent protection; or (5) speeding up the patent review process so that patents would be granted more quickly. In the last 25 years the legal changes adopted by Congress have moved in the direction of strengthening the value of a patent grant.

In 1980 Congress gave small businesses and universities exclusive patent rights to inventions and innovations developed with the help of federal funding. The 1980 law also reduced the likelihood that the federal courts would find a patent invalid. In 1995, the patent life for all patents was extended from 17 to 20 years. More recently, Congress lengthened the life of drug patents that must receive approval from the Food and Drug Administration (FDA). Congress was addressing the problems associated with the lengthy review period for new drugs, a process that significantly reduces the effective life of most drug patents. Because many inventions and innovations in the drug industry are patent dependent, this extension probably makes economic sense.

14.6.2 Intellectual Property Rights and Copyrights

In recent years issues surrounding intellectual property rights have become at least as important as issues surrounding patents. Today much of what is produced and sold in global markets is a form of intellectual property that is protected by copyright laws, not patent laws. Copyright laws give the creators of art, literature, movies, music, and

computer software the exclusive rights to their works. Under the ***Copyright Term Extension Act*** of 1998 (sometimes called the *Mickey Mouse Protection Act* because it extended Disney's copyright over its famous mouse that was scheduled to expire in 2000), the United States amended its copyright laws to protect an individual's work for life plus 70 years, which represented a 20-year extension from life plus 50 years. Copyrights awarded to businesses last for 95 years or 120 years from the time of creation if that period is shorter than 95 years. The United States has reciprocity agreements with most other countries regarding copyrights. Under these reciprocity agreements, American copyright holders are protected by the laws of the other nation.

Copyright laws vary tremendously from nation to nation. Park and Ginarte developed a measure of intellectual property rights (IPR) across countries.[45] Their IPR index was based on five categories of protection: coverage, membership in international patent agreements, provisions for loss of protection, enforcement mechanisms, and duration. The values within each category varied from a minimum of zero to a maximum of 1. The index was the sum of the values in all five categories. Therefore, the maximum IPR index was 5 and the minimum was zero. Table 14.6 shows the IPR indices for 60 countries. The top six countries with IPR indices over 3.5 are The Netherlands, Austria, Israel, Spain, the United States, and Italy. The four countries with IPR indices under 1 were Nicaragua, Venezuela, Peru, and Indonesia. There is a clear pattern in these two lists: Countries with highly advanced research and development programs provided much better copyright protection.

Park and Ginarte examined the relationship between economic growth and the IPR index. Using data from the complete sample of 60 countries, statistical analysis showed that higher IPR indices were associated with greater total investment and particularly greater investment in research and development. However, when these data were broken down into two groups for developed and less-developed countries, higher IPR indices had an impact on investment and research and development only for the developed countries. This finding is not surprising considering that less-developed countries have few intellectual property rights to protect. As countries become more developed, they have a greater incentive to strengthen their intellectual property rights. In China, for example, for many years there was little, if any, incentive for the government to provide and enforce strong copyright laws. (See Application 14.2.) With greater development and a desire to join the World Trade Organization (WTO), in 2001 China moved to greatly strengthen its copyright laws. Whether or not the Chinese will move to strongly enforce these laws, however, is very much in doubt.

APPLICATION 14.2

Why Bother with Intellectual Property Rights? The Case of China*

China has become the poster child for a nation that all but ignores intellectual property rights. The amount of counterfeiting that takes place in China is astounding. The Hollywood Motion Picture Association estimates that 95 percent of all movies shown in China are counterfeit, resulting in a loss of $178 million a year in potential revenues. In addition, 90 percent of all software running on Chinese computers is pirated. The U.S. Department of Commerce estimates that U.S. companies are losing $20 billion to $24 billion in China because of copyright infringements. Japanese and European losses

TABLE 14.6 Intellectual Property Rights Index Values (average 1960–1990)

Algeria	3.24	Jordan	1.52
Argentina	2.06	Kenya	2.49
Australia	2.84	Korea	3.00
Austria	3.53	Mauritius	2.37
Belgium	3.48	Mexico	1.30
Bolivia	1.48	Netherlands	3.70
Brazil	1.52	New Zealand	2.98
Cameroon	2.04	Nicaragua	0.94
Canada	2.67	Norway	2.92
Central African Republic	2.04	Pakistan	1.70
Chile	1.96	Panama	2.15
Colombia	1.13	Paraguay	1.29
Congo	2.04	Peru	0.65
Costa Rica	1.84	Philippines	2.52
Denmark	3.11	Portugal	1.82
Ecuador	1.60	Rwanda	2.43
El Salvador	1.97	Senegal	1.99
Finland	2.39	Singapore	2.16
France	3.48	South Africa	3.45
Germany	3.29	Spain	3.53
Greece	2.01	Sri Lanka	2.76
Guatemala	1.15	Sweden	2.99
India	1.39	Switzerland	3.23
Indonesia	0.33	Thailand	1.44
Iran	2.00	Trinidads	2.73
Ireland	2.46	Turkey	1.29
Israel	3.53	U.K.	3.26
Italy	3.50	U.S.A.	3.52
Jamaica	2.44	Uruguay	1.63
Japan	3.48	Venezuela	0.75

Source: Walter G. Park and Juan Carlos Ginarte, "Intellectual Property Rights and Economic Growth," *Contemporary Economic Policy* 15(July 1997): 53.

are estimated to be even larger. Counterfeiting may account for a shocking 30 percent of Chinese GDP. The basic problem for highly developed countries is that much of what these countries sell to China is very easy to counterfeit. This includes movies and movie DVDs, music CDs, books, computer software, and pharmaceuticals.

Is the vast Chinese counterfeiting industry bad for China? Despite its rapid growth, China is still a very poor country compared to the United States, Canada, Japan, and other developed countries. For most Chinese factory workers, a full-price DVD movie would cost a third of a month's wages. If you were a political leader of China, would you want to force your relatively poor country to pay high prices for computer software or DVDs or would you ignore your country's copyright laws and permit the use of counterfeit goods? As Ted Fishman, the author of *China Inc.: How the Rise of the Next Superpower Challenges America and the World,* has stated in testimony before the U.S.–China Economic and Security Review Commission:

> Imagine you were the leader of between 1.3 and 1.4 billion people, most of them desperately poor and modestly educated. Suppose you could transfer to your people the jewels of the world's advanced industrialized nations, paying nothing for much of it and pennies on the dollar for some more. Suppose, in other words, you could steal the best technology, copyrighted materials, brand names and top entertainment for your wanting people. And imagine further that you had little expectation of being held to account for that theft. In contrast, you would be rewarded for it. . . . Anyone here would make that choice—the choice which the Chinese government and people made and still do make every day. One of the precepts of good leadership is to make one's people prosperous and capable, and the Chinese practices have followed that hands down.

So the problem of Chinese counterfeiting is exacerbated by the fact that counterfeiting is rational from the standpoint of the leadership in Beijing. This might not be fatal for wealthy multinational firms that produce movies and computer software because these firms can survive on the profits earned in countries that protect intellectual property rights. But there is a more serious problem for industrialized countries: Firms in these countries must pay for the rights to intellectual property that Chinese firms get for free or almost for free. Large American companies spend millions of dollars to acquire and maintain computer software to run their companies. These companies compete directly with Chinese companies that obtain this software for pennies on the dollar compared to their American counterparts. This imbalance in costs exacerbates the trade imbalance between the United States and China. When we think of free trade, we think of countries trading and *paying* for the goods they import, not one country paying for its imports while the other gets its imports for free.

The only long-run solution to this problem is for both countries to pay for the goods they import. In the context of China, this means China must aggressively enforce its intellectual property rights laws. Perhaps the real hope for this to happen is for China to develop its own for-export high technology industries. When that happens, Chinese firms will have a vested interest in protecting their intellectual property rights, and these firms will push the Chinese government to strengthen and enforce intellectual property rights legislation.

*The following is based on Ted C. Fishman, *Hearing on China's High Technology Development* before the U.S. China Economic and Security Review Commission, Stanford University, April 22, 2005, *www.uscc.gov/hearings/ 2005hearings/written_testimonies/05_21_22wrts/fishman_ted_wrts.htm.* ■

14.7 Patents, Intellectual Property Rights, and the Law

S ection 1 of the Sherman Act forbids all restraints of trade. As we have discussed, the courts interpreted this as a per se ban on *all* direct price-fixing agreements. The Constitution, however, explicitly grants a patentee the "exclusive right to make, use, and vend the invention or discovery." Although there is no explicit constitutional right to fix prices, the exclusive right provision can be interpreted as ensuring that a patent holder has the right to fix the sale price on a patented item even if it is produced under license by another manufacturer. Copyrighted materials are also widely protected by the law.

Antitrust and copyright policy has attempted to limit the most obvious patent and copyright abuses while still permitting patent and copyright holders to obtain the basic monopoly benefits associated with the legal system. The first major issue addressed under the antitrust laws was the use of price-fixing clauses in patent licensing agreements. The basic precedent was set in the 1926 *General Electric* case.

THE GENERAL ELECTRIC CASE[46] (1926) General Electric owned the three basic patents for the use of tungsten filaments in light bulbs. Without these patents it was virtually impossible to compete successfully in the light bulb market, and GE could have maintained a monopoly on light bulbs by simply refusing to license its patents. GE, however, granted Westinghouse a license on March 1, 1912. Under the terms of the license, Westinghouse agreed to follow GE's pricing and distribution policy. The licensing agreement explicitly forbade Westinghouse from underpricing GE. In the absence of patent protection, such an agreement would clearly have violated Section 1 of the Sherman Act.

The case presented a classic dilemma in patent antitrust law. If the courts prevented GE from fixing bulb prices, GE could have adopted a nonlicensing policy and produced all tungsten filament bulbs itself. If the Courts permitted price fixing on the patented bulbs, however, it would eliminate some of the incentive for GE's competitors to create improved bulbs, because GE and the licensees would all lose if aggressive competition erupted after the development of a new light bulb. By permitting price fixing and encouraging more licensing, the courts might reduce GE's short-run monopoly power a bit, but they would create an environment that would be less conducive for technological change in the future. Conversely, by strictly enforcing the ban on price fixing, the courts might create an even stronger short-run monopoly for GE, but such a ruling would create an increased incentive for Westinghouse and others to invent around the tungsten filament patents.

The Supreme Court decided in favor of a bit less short-run monopoly power and ruled in favor of permitting price fixing.

> When the patentee licenses another to make and vend, and retains the right to continue to make and vend on his own account, the price at which his licensee will sell will necessarily affect the price at which he can sell his own patented goods. It would seem entirely reasonable that he should say to the licensee, "Yes, you may make and sell articles under my patent, but not so as to destroy the profit that I wish to obtain by making them and selling them myself."

The basic *General Electric* precedent has never been overturned. If a license contains an agreement to abide by the patentee's price, the courts will generally uphold the price-fixing agreement. This ruling can be defended on economic grounds, but it can also be attacked on economic grounds. Because a patentee usually holds a significant cost advantage over any licensee (by virtue of the licensee's royalty payments), a patent holder should be able to compete with its licensees without benefit of a price-fixing clause. In fact, if a licensee elects to charge a lower price than a patentee, the patentee should be able to at least match the lower price, unless the licensee is a more efficient producer. If the licensee is a more efficient producer, there is little economic justification for protecting the inefficient patentee. In other words, in those rare cases in which a licensee can produce a good at a lower social cost than a patentee, it would seem to make economic sense to prevent price fixing and encourage the efficient licensee to charge a lower price. Of course, the licensee would still have to pay royalties to the patentee.

The General Electric precedent provided a sound defense in straightforward cases in which one patentee licensed one patent to a few firms. It quickly became clear, however, that the courts would not permit a group of firms to pool a large number of patents in an obvious attempt to use patent protection to avoid the antitrust laws. The *Hartford-Empire* case is the classic example of such an attempt to monopolize an industry through the use of a ***patent pooling*** arrangement.

THE HARTFORD-EMPIRE CASE[47] **(1945)** The Hartford-Empire case involved one of the most extensive patent pools in United States history. Because patent pooling can be used to solve the prisoner's dilemma, we discussed the case extensively in Chapter 10.48 Recall that by 1938, Hartford had acquired more than 600 glass manufacturing patents.49 Once its control was complete, Hartford allocated each glass manufacturer a strict production quota for each specific type of glass container. As a result of a series of complex quota agreements, in 1938, 94 percent of all glass containers were produced on machines using one or more of Hartford-Empire's patents.50

The Supreme Court ruled against Hartford. The Court ordered the defendants to lease or license glass-making machinery to all on demand at "standard royalties and without discrimination or restrictions."

Despite the 1945 decision, the glass container industry remained highly oligopolistic. Twenty-five years of patent control enabled the leading firms to maintain their market shares well into the future.[51] The case suggests that market power built on patent control is likely to continue long after the patents expire. In the *Hartford-Empire* case, even the remedy of forced licensing had only a limited effect on market structure.

THE NAPSTER CASE[52] **(2001)** The *Napster* case is one of the most important intellectual property rights cases decided by the U.S. courts in the age of digital computer and network technology. In November 1999 Napster began a new Internet service that permitted online registered users of Napster to share music files with other online users. The next month the Recording Industry Association of America (RIAA) and 18 record companies filed a copyright infringement suite against Napster. The facts indicated that the plaintiffs owned copyrights on 87 percent of the files shared

on Napster.[53] Evidence from Napster's internal documents showed that Napster's executives knew they were engaged in unauthorized use of copyrighted materials. For example, Napster's internal documents stated that Napster users "are exchanging pirated music," and "we are not just making pirated music available but also pushing demand."[54]

The District Court ruled that plaintiffs had established a *prima facie* case of copyright infringement. In February 2001, the Ninth Circuit Court of Appeals upheld virtually all of the District Court's opinion and issued an injunction preventing Napster users from exchanging copyrighted materials.[55] Functionally, these decisions shut down Napster and on June 3, 2002, Napster filed for bankruptcy protection.[56]

The Napster story did not end with bankruptcy, however, because Napster had become a well-known brand name, especially among college students. Napster continued to have a cult following and the large digital media company Roxio took advantage of this following by purchasing the Napster brand name, Napster's file-trading software, and its promising T-shirt business for $5 million in November 2002.[57] Roxio then re-launched Napster as a pay service. On October 29, 2003, Roxio offered a Napster service that offered music downloads for a fee. Members could download a song for 99 cents and an album for $9.95.[58] Roxio negotiated copyright agreements with the five largest record labels and paid royalties for all downloaded copyrighted songs. Napster was so successful as a legal pay-for-music service that in September 2004 Roxio decided to drop its Roxio corporate name, change its name to Napster, and take the company public.[59] Napster began trading on Nasdaq in January 2005. In its reincarnation, Napster has been remarkably successful. It ended its fiscal year in May 2005 as the largest brand name in digital music. Napster's 2005 fiscal year ended with 412,000 subscribers and over $46.7 million in revenues.[60]

The Napster case and subsequent company developments show that even in the modern digital technology age, intellectual property rights can be protected and companies can still profit from the legal introduction of new digital technologies that are based on the growing demand to access copyrighted materials.

SUMMARY

1 Schumpeter theorized that technological change came about in dramatic upheavals, which he termed the process of *creative destruction.*

2 For Schumpeter, perfect competition was not the ideal market structure; instead large-scale firms with monopoly power became the superior market structure. Creative destruction drove a capitalist economy forward in the long run, and large-scale monopolists engaged in research and development led to creative destruction.

3 Later theoretical work suggested that either perfect competition or oligopoly was likely to result in a more rapid rate of technological advance than was monopoly.

④ Oligopolists have both the ability and the incentive to invest in R&D. Traditional theories suggested that, under a wide variety of cost and benefit conditions, oligopoly results in the most rapid rate of technological advance.

⑤ Game theorists have suggested, however, that oligopolists may either underinvest or overinvest in R&D.

⑥ The theoretical relationship between firm size and technological advance is complex. Large firms may engage in greater research and development efforts because (1) they have greater resources to invest in R&D; (2) large economies of scale may be associated with R&D; (3) large firms can spread risk over more projects; (4) large firms are often highly diversified and a technological advance in one area may be useful in another; and (5) large firms may have longer time horizons.

⑦ There are arguments in favor of smaller firms. The most powerful argument against the large corporation is the tendency for large firms to become bureaucratically inefficient.

⑧ Empirical studies of the relationship among firm size, market structure, and technological change are burdened by numerous methodological problems.

⑨ Few strong conclusions emerge from a thorough investigation of the available evidence. It appears, however, that no strong empirical support exists for Schumpeter's hypothesis that large firms in concentrated industries are best suited for rapid rates of technological change.

⑩ There is no support for the claim that R&D increases more than proportionally with increases in firm size. R&D output as measured by patents appears to increase proportionally with the size of the firm.

⑪ There is some empirical support for the hypothesis that oligopolists engage in more R&D effort than either competitive firms or monopolists. Recent work suggests, however, that rather than increased concentration leading to increased R&D expenditures, increased R&D expenditures may lead to increased concentration.

⑫ The relationship between concentration and R&D effort is not linear, but rather R&D efforts peak somewhere in the oligopoly range of market structures.

⑬ Although some stylized facts have emerged from the empirical work on the relationship between firm size and inventive activity and between market structure and inventive activity, the results are not particularly robust.

⑭ Economists have recently turned their attention to fundamental determinants of technological change such as product market demand, technological opportunity, and appropriability conditions. Case studies make the importance of these factors clear.

⑮ The patent system sometimes increases the rate of technological advance, yet there are theoretical reasons for suspecting that the system also may slow down the rate of advance.

⑯ In the absence of patents, most inventions would still be made because sufficient economic incentives for invention and innovation often result from first-mover advantages or an ability to move rapidly down a learning curve. In some cases simple secrecy provides better protection against imitation than patents.

17 Several survey findings suggest that a relatively small percentage of inventions and innovations are patent dependent.

18 To obtain the benefits associated with this small percentage of patent-dependent inventions and innovations, society pays a price in the form of higher monopoly profits and slower imitation. Conversely, very important technological advances, for example, in the pharmaceuticals industry, may be heavily driven by patents and result in great benefits for society.

19 Public policy has attempted to limit the most obvious patent and copyright abuses while still permitting patent and copyright holders to obtain the basic monopoly benefits associated with the system.

20 Although the courts have ruled that it is legal for a patent holder to fix the price a licensee may charge for a patented product, any attempt to extend the power of one patent into other areas, such as through a patent-pooling agreement, is on shaky grounds.

21 Strong intellectual property rights laws are associated with increased investment in R&D in developed countries. However, there is little incentive for less-developed countries to enforce such laws.

KEY TERMS

applied research

appropriability

basic research

Copyright Term Extension Act

creative destruction

diffusion

fast-second innovators

innovation

invention

patent pooling

patent race

technological opportunity

DISCUSSION QUESTIONS

1. Would Schumpeter be concerned if an industry were not producing the output for which price equaled marginal cost?

2. Give two examples of creative destruction.

3. Technological progress in agriculture has been remarkable in this century, yet individual farmers invest little in research and development. Why has the industry been able to attain such a high rate of technological advance?

4. How is it possible for patents to slow the rate of technological advance?

5. One difficult question for policymakers has been whether to permit patent holders to license their patents with a price-fixing clause in the license. For example, if I hold a patent on widgets and license you to produce widgets, should I be permitted to fix the price of

your widgets? Discuss the pros and cons of permitting price fixing in this case.

6. Would it be legal for a patent holder to license a single patent to one licensee with a price-fixing clause? Would it be legal for a group of firms to pool their patents, refuse to license an individual patent, and only license the entire group of patents with price-fixing clauses?

7. Some economists have argued that the 1926 *General Electric* precedent is obsolete and should be overturned by the Supreme Court. Do you agree? Explain.

8. What factors are likely to determine a country's level of enforcement of its intellectual property rights laws? Is it probable that countries will become more or less likely to enforce their copyright laws over time? Explain your reasoning.

9. Did the Napster decision make economic sense? Explain your reasoning. Are there any reasonable economic defenses that Napster could have used to argue that its system actually benefited copyright holders' interests?

10. In recent years has the United States been strengthening or weakening its laws concerning patent and copyright protection? Why do you think the United States has decided to move in this direction?

11. What does empirical evidence suggest about the relationship between firm size and the rate of technological innovation? Is this evidence supportive of Schumpeter's theory of technological advance?

12. Explain the problems associated with attempting to measure a society's rate of technological advance.

13. (True or false? Explain your reasoning.) "Based on empirical evidence, the great majority of inventions and innovations are dependent on the existence of patents."

14. (True or false? Explain your reasoning.) "Schumpeter's theory of creative destruction suggests that a market that achieves Pareto efficiency may still be highly inefficient."

15. The rate of technological advance has undoubtedly increased in recent years. What impact might this dramatic increase in the rate of technological advance have on the length of Kondratieff long cycles? Explain your reasoning.

16. What do you think is the optimal market structure for technological advance?

PROBLEMS

1. Using graphs, show how it is possible for an elimination of patent protection to increase the rate of technological advance. Show how it is also possible for the elimination of patent protection to slow down the rate of technological advance.

2. Suppose a monopolist faces a demand curve of $P = 50 - Q$. Currrently LRMC = LRAC = 25. If the monopolist has developed a cost-saving device that lowers its costs to LRMC = LRAC = 20, how much will profits increase after the introduction of the new technology?

 If this industry were perfectly competitive, how much could a patent holder earn on this technology?

 Does a monopolist or a patent holder in a perfectly competitive industry have a greater incentive to introduce this technology?

3. Suppose the payoff matrix for a game of innovation is as follows:

Firm A's Profits, Firm B's Profits

		Firm B's action	
		Innovate	Imitate
Firm A's action	Innovate	4, 4	4, 5
	Imitate	5, 4	1, 1

a. Is there one Nash equilibrium in pure strategies in this game?

b. Are there any Nash equilibria in this game?

c. Show that if Firm A plays *innovate* with a probability of 75 percent and *imitate* with a probability of 25 percent, Firm B earns the same profits regardless of what strategy Firm B selects. What does this suggest about Firm A's strategy of innovating with a probability of 75 percent?

d. If both firms play *innovate* with a probability of 75 percent and *imitate* with a probability of 25 percent, what is the probability of a nonoptimal outcome in the sense that the industry will not maximize joint profits?

4. Consider the patent model presented in Figure 14.9. Suppose that the government placed a sales tax on the output produced in this industry. Would this tax result in an increase or decrease in the time of development of the new innovation? Explain using a graph.

5. In the patent models presented in Section 14.3.4, what are the net profits earned from innovation? In what way is this result similar to the model of monopolistic competition presented in Chapter 13?

6. Use a graph to explain why it is possible to have an innovation that yields *positive net social benefits* under the current patent system, but that always yields *negative net benefits* to any private firm undertaking research and development in this area. In such a case, what policy or policies might solve this problem? Can you think of a real-world example of such a potential innovation?

NOTES

1. See Tom Peters and Robert H. Waterman, *In Search of Excellence: Lessons from America's Best Run Companies* (New York: Harper & Row, 1982); and Michael Porter, *The Competitive Advantage of Nations & Their Firms* (New York: The Free Press, 1990).

2. Joseph A. Schumpeter, *Capitalism, Socialism, and Democracy* (New York: Harper & Brothers Publishers, 1942).

3. *Ibid.,* p. 61.

4. Robert M. Solow, "Technical Change and the Aggregate Production Function," *Review of Economics and Statistics* 39 (August 1957): 312–319.

5. For an updated confirmation of Solow's result, see Edward F. Denison, *Trends in American Economic Growth 1929–1982* (Washington: Brookings, 1985).

6. National Science Foundation, Table B-2A can be accessed at www.nsf.gov/sbe/srs/hsf99335/pdf/appb .pdf.

7. Kenneth J. Arrow, "Economic Welfare and the Allocation of Resources for Invention," in National Bureau of Economic Research conference volume, *The Rate and Direction of Inventive Activity* (Princeton, NJ: Princeton University Press, 1962), pp. 609–625.

8. For a different approach and conclusion, see Harold Demsetz, "Information and Efficiency: Another Viewpoint," *Journal of Law and Economics* 12 (April 1969): 1–22.

9. F.M. Scherer, *Innovation and Growth: Schumpeterian Perspectives* (Cambridge, MA: MIT Press, 1984), pp. 120–129.

10. For early contributions see Glenn C. Loury, "Market Structure and Innovation," *Quarterly Journal of Economics* 93 (August 1979): 395–410; and Tom Lee and Louis L. Wilde, "Market Structure and Innovation," *Quarterly Journal of Economics* 94: (1980): 429–436.

11. The following presentation is based on Partha Dasgupta and Joseph Stiglitz, "Uncertainty, Industrial Structure, and the Speed of R&D," *Bell Journal of Economics* 11, (Spring 1980): 1–28; and Jennifer F. Reinganum, "The Timing of Innovation: Research, Development, and Diffusion," in Richard Schmalensee and Robert D. Willig, eds., *Handbook of Industrial Organization,* vol. 1 (Amsterdam: North-Holland, 1989), pp. 849–905.

12. John Kenneth Galbraith, *American Capitalism* (Boston: Houghton Mifflin, 1956), p. 91.

13. Paul Carroll, *Big Blues: The Unmaking of IBM* (New York: Crown Publishers, 1993), p. 20.

14. *Ibid.,* p. 23.

15. *Ibid.,* p. 123.

16. "Bill Gates & Paul Allen Talk," *Fortune* (October 2, 1995): 70.

17. The organization and discussion in this section draw on that in Wesley M. Cohen and Richard C. Levin, "Empirical Studies of Innovation and Market Structure," in Richard Schmalensee and Robert D. Willig (eds.), *Handbook of Industrial Organization* (Amsterdam: North-Holland, 1989), pp. 1060–1107.

18. Zvi Griliches, "Issues in Assessing the Contribution of Research and Development to Productivity Growth," *Bell Journal of Economics* 10 (1979): 92–116.

19. For early examples, see F.M. Scherer, "Firm Size, Market Structure, Opportunity, and the Output of Patented Inventions," *American Economic Review* 55 (1965): 1097–1125; and H.G. Grabowski, "The Determinants of Industrial Research and Development: A Study of the Chemical, Drug, and Petroleum Industries," *Journal of Political Economy* 76 (1968): 292–306. More recent work includes J. Bound, C. Cummins, Z. Griliches, B.H. Hall, and A. Jaffe, "Who Does R&D and Who Patents?" in Z. Griliches (ed.), *R&D, Patents, and Productivity* (Chicago: University of Chicago Press for the National Bureau of Economic Research, 1984).

20. Z. Griliches, B. Hall, and A. Pakes, "The Value of Patents as Indicators of Inventive Activity," in P. Dasgupta and P. Stoneman (eds.), *Economic Policy and Technological Performance* (Cambridge: Cambridge University Press, 1987).

21. W.S. Comanor, "Market Structure, Product Differentiation, and Industrial Research," *Quarterly Journal of Economics* 81 (November 1967): 639–657.

22. F.M. Scherer, "Size of Firm, Oligopoly, and Research: A Comment," *Canadian Journal of Economics and Political Science* 31 (May 1965): 256–266; and F.M. Scherer, *supra* note 19.

23. Morton L. Kamien and Nancy L. Schwartz, "Market Structure and Innovation: A Survey," *Journal of Economic Literature* 13 (March 1975): 1–37.

24. F.M. Scherer, "Technological Change and the Modern Corporation," in Betty Bock et al. (eds.), *The Impact of the Modern Corporation* (New York: Columbia University Press, 1984).

25. Wesley M. Cohen, Richard C. Levin, and David C. Mowery, "Firm Size and R&D Intensity: A Re-Examination," *Journal of Industrial Economics* 35 (June 1987): 543–565.

26. J. Bound, C. Cummins, Z. Griliches, B.H. Hall, and A. Jaffe, *supra* note 19.

27. Kamien and Schwartz, *supra* note 23, p. 19.

28. In addition to Scherer's work, see David B. Audretsch and Zoltan J. Acs, "Innovation and Size at the Firm Level," *Southern Economic Journal* 57 (January 1991): 739–744.

29. John Jewkes, David Sawers, and Richard Stillerman, *The Sources of Invention,* 2nd edition. (New York: W.W. Norton, 1969).

30. *Ibid.,* p. 168.

31. W.R. Maclaurin, "Technological Progress in Some American Industries," *American Economic Review* 44 (May 1954): 178–189.

32. For a survey, see William L. Baldwin and John T. Scott, *Market Structure and Technological Change* (Chur: Harwood, 1987).

33. F.M. Scherer, "Market Structure and the Employment of Scientists and Engineers," *American Economic Review* 57 (1967): 524–531.

34. Richard C. Levin, Wesley M. Cohen, and David C. Mowery, "R&D, Appropriability, and Market Structure: New Evidence on Some Schumpeterian Hypotheses," *American Economic Review* 75 (May 1985): 20–24.

35. John T. Scott, "Firm versus Industry Variability in R&D Intensity," in Zvi Griliches (ed.), *R&D, Patents, and Productivity* (Chicago: University of Chicago Press, 1984), pp. 200–224.

36. See Levin et al., *supra* note 34.

37. Richard R. Nelson and Sidney G. Winter, "Forces Generating and Limiting Concentration Under Schumpeterian Competition," *Bell Journal of Economics* 9 (1978): 524–548; and Richard R. Nelson and Sidney G. Winter, "The Schumpeterian Tradeoff Revisited," *American Economic Review* 72 (1982): 114–132.

38. J.D. Howe and D.G. McFetridge, "The Determinants of R&D Expenditures," *Canadian Journal of Economics* 9 (1976): 57–61; R.A. Connolly and M. Hirschey, "R&D, Market Structure, and Profits: A Value-Based Approach," *Review of Economics and Statistics* 66 (1984): 682–686; Levin, Cohen, and Mowery, *supra* note 34; R.C. Levin and P.C. Reiss, "Tests of a Schumpeterian Model of R&D and Market Structure," in Z. Griliches (ed.), *R&D, Patents, and Productivity* (Chicago: University of Chicago Press for the National Bureau of Economic Research, 1984); C. Timothy Koeller, "Innovation, Market Structure and Firm Size: A Simultaneous Equations Model," *Managerial and Decision Economics* 16 (May–June 1995): 259–269; Paul A. Geroski, "Innovation, Technological Opportunity, and Market Structure," *Oxford Economic Papers* 42 (July 1990): 586–602; and Zoltan J. Acs and David B. Audretsch, "Innovation, Market Structure, and Firm Size," *Review of Economics and Statistics* 69 (November 1987): 567–574.

39. See William G. Shepherd and Clair Wilcox, *Public Policies Toward Business* (Homewood, IL: Irwin, 1979), p. 506; C.T. Taylor and Z.A. Silberston, *The Economics of the Patent System* (Cambridge, UK:

Cambridge University Press, 1973); and W.D. Nordhaus, *Invention, Growth, and Welfare* (Cambridge, MA: MIT Press, 1969).

40. Richard C. Levin, Alvin K. Klevorick, Richard R. Nelson, and Sidney G. Winter, "Appropriating the Returns from Industrial Research and Development," *Brookings Papers on Economic Activity,* no. 3 (1987), pp. 783–820.
41. *Ibid.,* p. 794.
42. *Ibid.,* p. 798.
43. *Ibid.,* p. 798.
44. Ariel Pakes and Margaret Simpson, "Patent Renewal Date," in *Brookings Papers on Economic Activity: Microeconomics 1989* (Washington, DC: Brookings Institution, 1989), pp. 361–362.
45. Walter G. Park and Juan Carlos Ginarte, "Intellectual Property Rights and Economic Growth," *Contemporary Economic Policy* 15, (July 1997): 51–61.
46. *United States* v. *General Electric Company et al.,* 272 U.S. 476 (1926).
47. *Hartford Empire Company* v. *United States,* 323 U.S. 386 (1945).
48. See *supra,* Chapter 9, pp. 268–269.
49. Don E. Waldman, *The Economics of Antitrust: Causes and Analysis* (Boston: Little, Brown, 1986), p. 218.
50. *Ibid.,* p. 218.
51. Don E. Waldman, *Antitrust Action and Market Structure* (Lexington, MA: D.C. Heath, 1978), pp. 110–111.
52. *A&M Records* v. *Napster,* 114 F.Supp 2d 896 (ND Cal 2000).
53. *A&M Records* v. *Napster,* 114 F.Supp 2d 903 (ND Cal 2000).
54. *Ibid.*
55. *A&M Records* v. *Napster 293,* F.3d 1004 (9th Circuit, 2001).
56. "Napster Files for Bankruptcy," *BBC News,* June 3, 2002, *news.bbc.co.uk/1/hi/business/2023201.stm.*
57. "Roxio Purchases Napster's Remains for $5 Million," November 15, 2002, *playbacktime.com/archives/000088.html.*
58. "Napster's Back," Napster Press Release, October 29, 2003, *www.napster.com/press_releases/pr_031029.html.*
59. "Napster Goes Public with New Napster Name: Out with ROXI, In with NAPS," November 15, 2002, *networks.silicon.com/webwatch/0,39024876, 39126842,00.htm.*
60. "Napster More Than Triples Revenue and Ends Fiscal 2005 with 412,000 Subscribers," Napster Press Release, *investor.napster.com/releasedetail.cfm?Release ID=163134&Version=US.*

INTERNET EXERCISES

Visit **www.aw-bc.com/waldman_jensen** for this chapter's web exercises. Answer our real-world economics problems by searching the Internet for solutions!

Appendix

Game Theory and Patent Races

The analysis in Figure 14.9 made the simplifying assumption that firms make bids on their R&D spending and only the winning bidder spends anything on R&D. A more realistic assumption is that all firms can spend positive amounts on R&D but only one wins the patent race. In the following game, we eliminate the bidding nature of the game in Figure 14.9. Consider, for example, a simple patent race game in an oligopoly with three firms, Firm A, Firm B, and Firm C.* The government grants a patent monopoly to the first firm to innovate. Each firm simultaneously selects a level of R&D spending $X_i \geq 0$ for i = A,B,C.

*See Herve Moulin, *Game Theory for the Social Sciences* (New York: New York University Press, 1986). This patent race is presented in simple form in Eric Rasmusen, *Games and Information: An Introduction to Game Theory* (Oxford, UK: Basil Blackwell, 1989), pp. 294–300.

As in Figure 14.8, the time of innovation, T, is a function of R&D spending. Innovation occurs at time $T(X_i)$ and $\Delta T/\Delta X_i < 0$.* The present value of profits associated with the patent equals $V > 0$, and if two or three firms innovate at the same time, the firms share the profits V. The profit payoffs for Firm i are defined as follows:†

$$\pi_i = V - X_i \quad \text{if} \quad T(X_i) < T(X_j) \quad \text{for } j \neq i \text{ (Firm i innovates first}$$
$$\text{and receives the patent)}$$

$$\pi_i = \frac{V}{1 + m} - X_i \quad \text{if} \quad T(X_i) = T(X_j) \quad \text{(Firm i shares the patent with m = 1}$$
$$\text{or 2 other firms)}$$

$$\pi_i = -X_i \quad \text{if} \quad T(X_i) > T(X_j) \quad \text{for some j (Firm i does not get the patent)}$$

Figure 14.11 depicts the payoffs for Firm A assuming $V = \$100$, $X_B = \$30$, and $X_C = \$20$. If $X_A < \$30$, Firm A does not get the patent and sustains a loss of $-X_A$. If

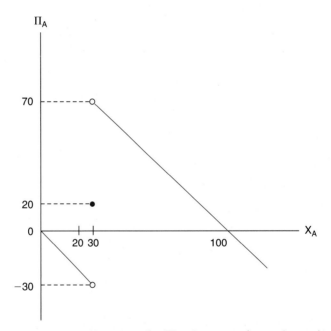

FIGURE 14.11 Patent Race: Firm A's Profits, Π_A, Given $X_B = \$30$ and $X_C = \$20$

Assuming $V = \$100$ is the present value of profits associated with a patent, Firm B spends $X_B = \$30$ on development of the patent, and Firm C spends $X_C = \$20$, then if Firm A spends less than $30 on development, it will lose the patent race and sustain an economic loss equal to its expenditures. If Firm A exactly matches Firm B's spending of $30, the two firms share profits and each earns $20. If Firm A spends more than $30, it wins the patent race and earns a profit of $V - X_A$.

*Using calculus, dT/dX < 0.

†The following two simplifying assumptions are built into the profit payoffs: The firms are risk neutral and have a zero discount rate.

$X_A > \$30$, Firm A gets the patent and earns $\$100 - X_A$. If $X_A = \$30$, Firm A and Firm B innovate simultaneously and share the profit of $100, so Firm A's net earnings then equal $\$50 - \$30 = \$20$.

There is no pure strategy Nash equilibrium in this game because for any values of X_B and X_C less than $V = \$100$, Firm A would maximize profits by spending $\epsilon > 0$ more on R&D than the max $\{X_B, X_C\}$. For example, given $X_B = \$30$ and $X_C = \$20$, Firm A should obtain the patent by spending $X_A = \$30 + \epsilon$ on R&D. If either $X_B = \$100$ or $X_C = \$100$, then Firm A should spend $X_A = 0$ on R&D.

This game has many possible mixed strategy equilibria.* Here we derive one of the possible mixed strategy equilibria. Recall that the game is symmetric. Let $M_i(X)$ represent the probability that Firm i chooses an R&D level less than or equal to X. If Firm B and Firm C play any mixed strategy equilibria, then Firm A is indifferent between any pure or mixed strategy it chooses. If Firm A plays a pure strategy consisting of $X_A = 0$ all of the time or if it plays a pure strategy consisting of $X_A = \$100$ all the time, its expected profits equal zero; therefore, any other mixed strategy equilibria for Firm A must have an expected profit equal to zero. Firm A's expected profit from any R&D spending X_A is the expected value of winning the patent minus the cost, X_A, of its R&D. The probability that Firm A wins the patent race equals the probability that Firm A spends more on R&D than either Firm B or Firm C. For Firm A to win the patent race, therefore, X_A must be greater than *both* X_B and X_C. The probability that Firm A spends more on R&D than both Firm B and Firm C equals the probability that $X_B < X_A$ *times* the probability that $X_C < X_A$, or $M_B(X_A)M_C(X_A)$.† Because any mixed strategy equilibrium for Firm A must have an expected profit of zero, it follows that:

$$V \cdot M_B(X_A)M_C(X_A) - X_A = 0. \qquad [14.4]$$

Algebraic manipulation of Equation 14.4 yields:

$$M_B(X_A)M_C(X_A) = \frac{X_A}{V}. \qquad [14.5]$$

If all three firms select the same mixed strategy, then $M_B(X_A) = M_C(X_A)$, and:

$$M(X_i) = \sqrt{\frac{X_i}{V}} \qquad \text{for } 0 \le X_i \le V. \qquad [14.6]$$

Equation 14.6 represents one possible mixed strategy equilibrium. According to Equation 14.6, the probability of spending less than $100 is $\sqrt{100/100} = 1$ and the probability of spending less than zero is $\sqrt{0/100} = 0$. So unlike the previous model, all firms have positive amounts of R&D spending. Furthermore, the probability of spending less than $25 is $M(25) = \sqrt{25/100} = \sqrt{1/4} = 1/2$, so there is a 50 percent probability that a firm spends less than $25 on R&D and a 50 percent probability that a firm spends more than $25 on R&D. Like the model in Figure 14.9, the expected profit

*For proof that there is a continuum of mixed strategy equilibria in this game, see Michael Baye, Dan Kovenock, and Casper G. de Vries, "Rigging the Lobbying Process: An Application of the All Pay Auction," *American Economic Review* 83 (March 1993): 289–294.

†$M_B(X_A)$ represents the probability that Firm B spends *less* on R&D than does Firm A.

is zero in this game, and therefore, the entire potential profit of V is lost to society because the firms race to be the first to gain the patent, and in so doing spend too much on R&D. Innovation occurs earlier than it would with a monopolist, but the speeding up of the time of innovation is not worth the extra development costs to society.*

*A monopolist by comparison would maximize profits by setting $X = \epsilon$, where ϵ is infinitesimally greater than zero, and the monopolist would earn a profit of $V - \epsilon \cong V$. With monopoly and a zero discount rate, society would receive a net benefit approximately equal to V. The time of innovation, however, would be very slow because $\Delta T / \Delta X_i < 0$. With a patent race the probability that any of the three firms would spend less than ϵ on R&D is:

$$M(\epsilon) = \sqrt{\frac{\epsilon}{V}} \cong 0.$$

The probability that the monopolist would innovate faster than the three firms engaged in a patent race is virtually zero.

Price Discrimination

Price discrimination exists when a firm charges either different consumers different prices for the same product supplied with identical costs or different consumers the same price even though the cost of supplying the good varies between consumers. More generally, price discrimination occurs whenever the difference in prices between consumers is *not proportional* to the difference in costs. In other words, price discrimination exists whenever *the price-cost margin* varies between different consumers.

Consider some examples of price discrimination: two airline passengers paying different fares for coach seats on the same flight; a lawyer charging the same fee for a will that requires 30 minutes of preparation time as a will that requires 8 hours of preparation time; or a department store offering a second pair of jeans at a price 50 percent lower than the first pair. However, two passengers paying different fares for coach seats on different days of the year (e.g., Thanksgiving Day and November 1) may not constitute price discrimination.

There are several important points to understand about price discrimination. Perhaps the most significant point is that discrimination can occur only if market power exists. If two sellers in a perfectly competitive market charge different prices for the same good, consumers will buy only from the lower-priced seller. Also, the existence of most price discrimination implies a lack of *Pareto efficiency;* because different consumers face different marginal rates of substitution, efficiency in exchange is not achieved.*

15.1 Types of Price Discrimination

Economists divide price discrimination into three general categories: *first-degree, second-degree,* and *third-degree price discrimination.*[1] In **first-degree price discrimination,** which is often referred to as **perfect discrimination,** each consumer pays his or

*Recall that Pareto efficiency requires the marginal rate of substitution (MRS) to be equal for all consumers where:

$$MRS = \frac{MU_x}{MU_y} = \frac{P_x}{P_y}.$$

her *reservation price* for the good, which is the highest price he or she is willing to pay for the good. With **second-degree price discrimination,** a firm offers all consumers the same price schedule, and then consumers self-select into the different price categories. **Third-degree price discrimination** depends on the firm's ability to effectively separate consumers into two or more groups according to their elasticities of demand. Unlike second-degree price discrimination, in third-degree discrimination, consumers are put into a group by the firm and cannot self-select into another group. In this section, we consider output and price under each type of price discrimination and pay close attention to the welfare implications of each type of discrimination.

15.1.1 First-Degree Price Discrimination

With first-degree price discrimination, each consumer pays the highest price he or she is willing to pay for the monopolist's good; therefore, monopolists prefer to use first-degree discrimination whenever possible. Figure 15.1 shows a market with a demand curve of $P = 10 - Q$ and production costs of $MC = AC = \$2$. In such a market, first-degree discrimination would require the first unit of the good to be sold at a price of \$9, the second unit at \$8, the third at \$7, and so on, until the eighth unit was sold at $P = MC = \$2$. First-degree discrimination results in total revenue of \$44 (\$9 + \$8 + \$7 + \$6 + \$5 + \$4 + \$3 + \$2 = \$44) on the sale of eight units. The ninth unit would not be sold, because the consumer's reservation price of \$1.00 is less than marginal cost.

To determine the welfare effects of price discrimination, it is necessary to compare the total consumer surplus plus producer surplus with price discrimination versus the total consumer surplus plus producer surplus without price discrimination. With first-

FIGURE 15.1 First-Degree Price Discrimination

With first-degree price discrimination, each unit is sold for the maximum price some consumer is willing to pay. With demand $P = 10 - Q$, the first unit is sold for \$9, the second unit for \$8, the third for \$7, until the eighth unit is sold for \$2. Total revenue equals \$9 + \$8 + \$7 + \$6 + \$5 + \$4 + \$3 + \$2 = \$44. There is no consumer surplus, but producer surplus equals the sum of the light red, gray, and dark red shaded areas X + Y + Z.

degree discrimination, in Figure 15.1, consumer surplus is zero, but producer surplus is the entire shaded area, consisting of the sum of the shaded light red, gray, and dark red areas X + Y + Z. If a firm does not discriminate and charges one price to all buyers, then the profit-maximizing quantity is 4 and price is $6, and therefore, total revenue equals $24. With a one-price policy, consumer surplus is equal to the shaded light red area X and producer surplus is equal to the shaded gray area Y. There is a welfare loss equal to the shaded dark red area Z. Because the elimination of price discrimination results in a welfare loss equal to the dark red area Z, first-degree price discrimination improves welfare. In fact, in the case of first-degree discrimination, allocative efficiency is achieved, because price equals marginal cost for the last unit purchased. Consequently, every consumer who is willing to pay a price greater than or equal to marginal cost receives the good. Pareto efficiency is also achieved with first-degree discrimination, because there is no way to exchange goods in a way that helps one consumer without hurting another.

APPLICATION 15.1
Microsoft's Attempt to Use First-Degree Price Discrimination

Before it signed a consent decree with the Department of Justice in 2002, Microsoft's patent monopoly over Intel-based PC operating systems gave the company the ability to use a form of first-degree price discrimination when it licensed the rights to its operating systems to computer manufacturers such as Dell, Gateway, IBM, and Hewlett Packard. At one time, every Microsoft patent license was individually negotiated and every licensee paid a different price for the right to install the Microsoft operating system on its computers. Microsoft required computer manufacturers to negotiate a fee for a minimum number of licenses, with this minimum number typically greater than or equal to the anticipated total computer shipments of the manufacturer. If a manufacturer expected to ship 100,000 computers in a year, it would agree to pay an individually negotiated license fee, f, on a minimum of 100,000 units. Remarkably, even if it shipped machines with a *non-Microsoft* operating system, the manufacturer paid a royalty to Microsoft! If it shipped fewer than 100,000 units, it still paid Microsoft for 100,000 licenses. If it shipped more than 100,000 units, the licensee paid an additional royalty of f per unit shipped. Once again, the licensee paid the fee regardless of whether or not the units shipped included a Microsoft operating system.

The licenses typically ran for two years. Furthermore, Microsoft tried to negotiate licenses that set a higher minimum number of units than expected shipments by offering a lower per-unit-shipped fee f. At the end of a year the licensee typically had a credit for unused licenses, but Microsoft would only permit the licensee to carry the credit forward into the next year. This created an incentive for computer manufacturers to install Microsoft-based operating systems on the following year's machines.

Microsoft imposed penalties for the installation of non-Microsoft operating systems. A manufacturer using large numbers of non-Microsoft-based systems, for example, might be prohibited from carrying forward unused credits from previous years, or it might be required to agree to a higher minimum number of licenses in future years. In addition, technical support services might be withheld from firms installing non-Microsoft operating systems. Finally, Microsoft was known to increase the price of Windows for firms installing non-MS-DOS operating systems on some of their computers.

The combined effect of all of these policies was that each computer manufacturer paid a different price to install Microsoft's operating systems on its machines. Microsoft's policies were an attempt to obtain the maximum amount of consumer surplus from each computer manufacturer, and therefore, to use first-degree price discrimination. ■

15.1.2 Second-Degree Price Discrimination

Recall that with second-degree discrimination, all consumers are offered the same price schedule, and then consumers self-select into different price categories. Although consumers pay different prices, every consumer who buys within the same price category pays the same price. Firms use second-degree discrimination when they know there are different groups of consumers with different reservation prices, but they are unable to identify, or it is too costly to identify, each type of consumer. Price discrimination in the airline industry is one common example of second-degree discrimination. Airlines typically offer all buyers a large variety of different fares on the same flight depending on a number of restrictions, including when the ticket is purchased and how long the passenger stays at his or her destination before taking a return flight. Pizza Hut, which often charges $10 for the first large pizza but only $5 for the second large pizza, provides another example of second-degree price discrimination. In this case, consumers buying one pizza pay $10 and those buying two pizzas pay only $7.50 per pizza.

Figures 15.2(a) and 15.2(b) illustrate another example of second-degree price discrimination—quantity discounts. Suppose Ralph Lauren produces a pair of designer jeans for MC = AC = $20 and offers a quantity discount. Consumers can purchase one pair for $80, a second pair for $60, a third pair for $40, and a fourth pair for $20. Given this pricing structure, suppose a Ralph Lauren store sells jeans to 10 consumers in each of the four categories each day. All 40 buyers purchase the first pair at $80; 30 buyers purchase the first pair at $80 and a second pair at $60; 20 buyers purchase a first pair at $80, a second pair at $60, and a third pair at $40; and 10 buyers purchase the first pair at $80, a second pair at $60, a third pair at $40, and a fourth pair at $20.

Table 15.1 shows the daily demand for jeans. A total of 100 pairs are sold and total revenue is $6000 ($3200 + $1800 + $800 + $200). Figure 15.2(a) shows the demand curve for Ralph Lauren's designer jeans using second-degree price discrimination. The sum of the shaded areas A + B + C + D represents total revenue and equals $6000.

Bear in mind that the demand curve in Figure 15.2(a) is not comparable to the demand curve for jeans that would exist without price discrimination. Without price discrimination, if Ralph Lauren charged a uniform price of $20 for all of its jeans, the company would sell more than 100 pairs. A demand curve without price discrimination, therefore, would typically lie well to the right of the demand curve in Figure 15.2(a). This makes welfare comparisons in the case of second-degree discrimination difficult.

Figure 15.2(b) identifies the consumer and producer surplus associated with second-degree price discrimination in the Ralph Lauren example. Figure 15.2(b) reproduces Figure 15.2(a), but here the shaded areas have been changed. In Figure 15.2(b), consumer surplus equals the sum of the four shaded dark gray areas W + X + Y + Z while producer surplus equals the sum of the three shaded rectangles A + B + C.

FIGURE 15.2 **Second-Degree Price Discrimination**

In panel (a), consumers purchase one pair of jeans for $80, a second pair for $60, a third pair for $40, and a fourth pair for $20. A total of 100 pairs are sold and total revenue equals the sum of the shaded areas A + B + C + D, or $6000. In panel (b), consumer surplus is the sum of the four shaded areas W + X + Y + Z, and producer surplus is the sum of the three shaded rectangles A + B + C, which equals $4000.

Unlike first-degree discrimination, in the case of second-degree discrimination, there is some consumer surplus. Because the seller cannot identify precisely the demand for each and every consumer, he or she is unable to extract the entire consumer surplus from the market.

TABLE 15.1 The Demand for Ralph Lauren Jeans Using Second-Degree Price Discrimination

Price	Quantity at That Price	Total Quantity Sold
$80	40	40
$60	30	70
$40	20	90
$20	10	100

APPLICATION 15.2
The Use of Coupons and Second-Degree Price Discrimination

One very common example of second-degree price discrimination is the use of discount coupons. In 2003 manufacturers issued over $250 billion worth of coupons.* Consumers redeemed approximately $3 billion worth of these coupons, or roughly 1.2 percent of all the coupons put into circulation. The average face value of a coupon was 85 cents. In addition to manufacturers, retailers are increasingly offering coupons. In fact, 46 percent of all retailers offered some coupons in 2003.

Coupons are available to all buyers, and yet not all buyers use coupons. As noted above, only a small percentage of all the available coupons is redeemed. The explanation for some consumers using coupons far more than others is based on the opportunity cost of time. Using coupons requires a classic economic trade-off of savings obtained from the use of the coupons in return for the opportunity cost of obtaining and using the coupons. These costs include the costs of collecting (for example, looking through magazines, newspapers, and the Internet), organizing, retrieving, and using the coupons. Theoretically, because the savings associated with using a coupon are equal for all users, consumers with lower opportunity costs of time have lower costs of using coupons, and therefore, should use more coupons.

Manufacturers increase their profits only if the users of coupons, who generally pay lower prices than nonusers, have more elastic demands than nonusers. In one of the most thorough and well-known empirical studies of the economics of coupon use, based on approximately 1000 consumers' diary entries for 20 product categories, Narasimhan found that coupon users had more elastic demands than nonusers, and therefore, profits increased when manufacturers were able to use coupons to discriminate between coupon users and nonusers.† Narasimhan also found that higher-priced brands in a product category provided greater coupon savings than lower-priced brands and that larger sizes (larger boxes or cans) provided smaller savings than smaller sizes.

Blattberg, Buesing, Peacock, and Sen studied the degree to which households were likely to take advantage of special deals like coupons to purchase five categories of products: aluminum foil, waxed paper, headache remedies, liquid detergent, and facial tissues.‡ They classified consumers as either deal prone or not deal prone. The tables below show some of their results. In every product category in the first table, unemployed housewives were more likely to be deal prone than employed housewives. This is consistent with the theory that unemployed housewives have a lower opportunity cost of time, and therefore, are more likely to clip coupons and search out bargains.

Somewhat surprisingly, however, the second table shows that there was only a slight increase in deal proneness in families with no small children under the age of six.

Housewife's Employment Status

Employment Status	Product Category				
	Aluminum Foil	Waxed Paper	Headache Remedies	Liquid Detergent	Facial Tissue
Employed	29.0%[a] (62)[b]	17.7% (62)	25.0% (76)	32.6% (92)	22.4% (116)
Unemployed	38.3% (128)	23.5% (153)	28.6% (161)	37.4% (214)	29.2% (226)

[a]The table entry is the percentage of aluminum foil buyers who are employed housewives and are deal prone.
[b]Numbers in parentheses are total within-call sample sizes on which each percentage is based.
Source: Robert Blattberg, Thomas Buesing, Peter Peacock, and Subrata Sen, "Identifying the Deal Prone Segment," *Journal of Marketing Research* 15 (August 1978): 377.

Age of Children

Age of Children	Product Category				
	Aluminum Foil	Waxed Paper	Headache Remedies	Liquid Detergent	Facial Tissue
Children under six	41.5%[a] (41)[b]	21.7% (60)	26.6% (64)	39.8% (83)	24.0% (75)
No children under six	36.0 (89)	25.3 (95)	33.7 (98)	34.0 (141)	28.1 (160)

[a]The table entry is the percentage of aluminum foil buyers who have children under six and are deal prone.
[b]Numbers in parentheses are total within-call sample sizes on which each percentage is based.
Source: Robert Blattberg, Thomas Buesing, Peter Peacock, and Subrata Sen, "Identifying the Deal Prone Segment," *Journal of Marketing Research* 15 (August 1978): 376.

Blattberg et al. theorized that car and home ownership would also impact deal proneness. Because transportation costs are an important element of households' transactions costs, households that own a car have lower transactions costs and can travel more often and to more stores to take advantage of special deals. Compared to renters, home owners living in larger living spaces have lower storage costs, and there-fore, home owners should be more deal prone than renters. Consistent with these theo-ries, Blattberg et al. found that car and home ownership greatly affected deal proneness. Over 35 percent of the families that owned a car and a home were deal prone, compared to only 20.5 percent of the families that did not own a car or a home.

*Promotion Marketing Association, "Promotion Marketing Association Releases 2003 Coupon Stats in Conjunc-tion with National Coupon Month PMA Coupon Council Offers Retail and Manufacturer Usage Information," August 30, 2004, www.pmalink.org/about/press_releases/release69.asp.
†Chakravarthi Narasimhan, "A Price Discrimination Theory of Coupons," *Marketing Science* 3, (Spring 1984): 128–147. However, in a later and more sophisticated statistical study, Nevo and Wolfram found that using coupons in the breakfast cereal industry resulted in lower prices for all consumers, even non–coupon users, and therefore reduced profits. See Aviv Nevo and Catherine Wofram, "Why Do Manufacturers Issue Coupons? An Empirical Analysis of Breakfast Cereals," *Rand Journal of Economics* 33 (Summer 2002): 319–339.
‡Robert Blattberg, Thomas Buesing, Peter Peacock, and Subrata Sen, "Identifying the Deal Prone Segment," *Journal of Marketing Research* 15 (August 1978): 369–377. ■

15.1.3 The Welfare Effects of Second-Degree Price Discrimination

The welfare effects of second-degree price discrimination can be very complex. Consider, for example, second-degree discrimination in the airline industry. Airlines commonly charge different fares for different types of tickets. Carriers discriminate between vacation travelers who stay for a week or longer at their destination and business travelers who stay for one day. Suppose that "Get You There Air" charges two fares for its flights from New York to Los Angeles, an unrestricted round-trip coach fare of $749 and a "vacation special" fare of $400 if you stay in Los Angeles for a minimum of two weeks. A business traveler is willing to pay a maximum of $800 for a round-trip ticket to fly to Los Angeles on Tuesday and return on Wednesday, but this business traveler is willing to pay a maximum of only $450 for a ticket with a minimum stay of two weeks. However, a vacation traveler is willing to pay a maximum of $400 for a ticket with a restriction of a two-week minimum stay and has no interest in staying for one day.

If Get You There Air calculates that the marginal cost per passenger is $100 for the round-trip flight, then by charging $800 for an unrestricted ticket and $400 for a restricted ticket with a two-week minimum stay, Get You There Air earns producer surplus of $1200 − $200 = $1000. Consumer surplus equals zero. The total producer plus consumer surplus with price discrimination, therefore, equals $1000 + $50 = $1000.

If price discrimination were impossible or illegal, then the profit-maximizing strategy would be to charge one price of $800 for all passengers and earn a producer surplus of $800 − $100 = $700.* Only the business traveler flies to Los Angeles by air; the vacation traveler stays home, drives, or takes the train. The total producer plus consumer surplus of $1000 with price discrimination is significantly greater than the total of $700 without price discrimination. Welfare is unambiguously improved by price discrimination in this case.

Second-degree discrimination, however, can reduce welfare compared with a uniform price policy. Suppose the preferences in the above example are changed slightly so that a business traveler is willing to pay a maximum of $800 for a round-trip ticket to fly to Los Angeles on Tuesday and return on Wednesday, but this business traveler is willing to pay a maximum of only $400 for a ticket with a minimum stay of two weeks. A vacation traveler is willing to pay a maximum of $650 for an unrestricted ticket but only $600 for a ticket with a two-week minimum stay restriction.

With discrimination, Get You There Air charges $800 to the business traveler and $600 to the vacation traveler. There is zero consumer surplus and Get You There Air's producer surplus equals ($800 + $600) − $200 = $1200.

Without discrimination, Get You There Air would charge $650 for an unrestricted fare, sell two tickets, and earn a producer surplus of ($650 × 2) − $200 = $1100. In addition, the business traveler would receive consumer surplus equal to $800 − $650 = $150. The sum of producer *plus* consumer surplus would then equal $1100 + $150 = $1250, which is greater than the total producer plus consumer surplus of $1200 with price discrimination. In this case, second-degree price discrimination reduces welfare. The reason for the reduction in welfare of $50 is that with discrimina-

*A price of $800 yields a producer surplus of $700, which is a larger producer surplus than the airline earns by charging a price of $400, selling two tickets, and earning $800 − $200 = $600.

tion, the airline increases the business traveler's fare from $650 to $800. This fare increase eliminates the business traveler's $150 consumer surplus without discrimination. The $150 decrease in the business traveler's consumer surplus is larger than the $100 increase in the airline's producer surplus with discrimination.

15.1.4 Third-Degree Price Discrimination

With third-degree price discrimination, firms are able to separate consumers into two or more groups according to their different elasticities of demand. Consumers are put into a group by the firm and cannot self-select into another group. As long as the firm can distinguish the groups by their different elasticities at any given price, practicing price discrimination increases profit. For example, suppose a large multiplex movie theater in Fort Lauderdale, Florida, recognizes that it faces two distinct demand curves: one for senior citizens age 65 and over and another for adults under age 65. Panel (a) of Figure 15.3 shows the demand curve for adults under age 65 to be $p_a = 10.00 - (1/10)q_a$, where q_a is measured in thousands of tickets. Panel (b) shows the demand curve for senior citizens to be $p_s = 5.00 - (1/30)q_s$, where q_s is measured in thousands of tickets. For any $p > 0$, the demand for adults is more inelastic than the demand for senior citizens. To simplify the analysis, we assume MC = AC = $1.00.

To maximize profit, the theater sets marginal revenue equal to marginal cost for each consumer group. For adults in Figure 15.3(a), $MR_a = MC$ implies that $10.00 - (1/5)q_a = 1.00$, so $q_a = 45$ and $p = \$5.50$. For senior citizens in panel (b), $MR_s = MC$ implies that $5.00 - (1/15)q_s = 1.00$, so $q_s = 60$ and $p = \$3.00$. With price discrimination, adults 65 and under pay $5.50 per ticket and purchase 45,000 tickets and seniors 65 and over pay $3.00 per ticket and purchase 60,000 tickets. The theater sells a total quantity of 105,000 tickets. At their respective equilibrium points, the elasticity of demand for adults is $\epsilon_p = (\Delta q/\Delta p)(p/q) = 10(5.5/45) = 1.22$ at point X, and the elasticity of demand for seniors is $\epsilon_p = (\Delta q/\Delta p)(p/q) = 30(3/60) = 1.5$ at point Y. With third-degree price discrimination, the price is lower in the senior citizen market with the more elastic demand.

15.1.5 Welfare Implications of Third-Degree Price Discrimination

Third-degree price discrimination has the most complicated welfare implications of the three types of discrimination. However, we can draw a few basic points concerning welfare from our Fort Lauderdale theater example. With third-degree price discrimination, we can derive from Figure 15.3 consumer plus producer surplus in each market. In panel (a), consumer surplus for adults equals the area of the red triangle A, which equals $(1/2)(45)(\$10.00 - \$5.50) = (1/2)(45)(\$4.50) = \101.25, and in panel (b), consumer surplus for seniors equals the area of the red triangle C, which equals $(1/2)(60)(\$5.00 - \$3.00) = 1/2(60)(\$2.00) = \60. Therefore, the sum of consumer surplus in both markets equals the sum of areas A + C, or $101.25 + $60 = $161.25. In panel (a), producer surplus equals the area of the gray rectangle B equal to $45(\$4.50) = \202.50, and in panel (b), producer surplus equals the area of the gray rectangle D equal to $60(\$2.00) = \120. Therefore, the sum of producer surplus in both markets equals $202.50 + $120 = $322.50. The sum of consumer and producer surplus with discrimination equals $161.25 + $322.50 = $483.75.

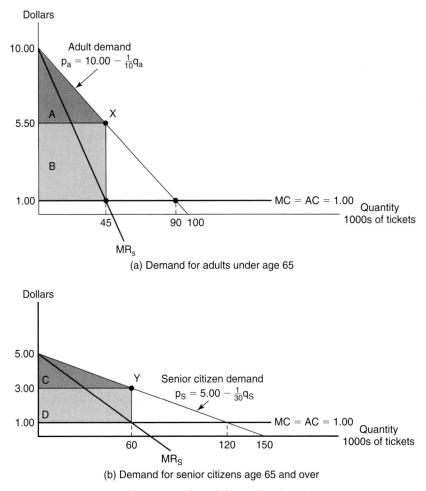

(a) Demand for adults under age 65

(b) Demand for senior citizens age 65 and over

FIGURE 15.3 **The Demand for Movies for Adults and Senior Citizens**

To maximize profit, the theater equates marginal revenue to marginal cost in each market and charges a price of $5.50 per ticket to adults in panel (a) and $3.00 per ticket to seniors in panel (b). Total consumer plus producer surplus in both markets is the sum of shaded areas A + B + C + D, which equals $483.75.

Now suppose the theater was forced by law to charge a uniform price to all buyers. What price would the theater charge? Figure 15.4 shows the result of the horizontal addition of the two demand curves. For prices between $5.00 and $10.00, only the demand for adults under 65 is relevant, so in that price range, the combined demand is p = 10.00 − (1/10)q. For prices between $0 and $5.00, both demands are relevant and the combined demand is the horizontal summation of the two demand curves, which yields the demand curve segment BC. The demand curve becomes much more elastic for prices below $5.00, as the more elastic senior citizen demand is added to the less elastic adults-under-65 demand. The complete demand curve, therefore, is the kinked demand curve ABC.

We can derive the equation of the more elastic portion of the demand curve between points B and C by noting three facts about this segment of the demand curve: (1) The addition of two lines always results in a line, (2) the slope of line BC equals $5.00/200 = 1/40$, and (3) the line goes through the point $q = 250$, $p = 0$. Substituting $q = 250$ and $p = \$0$ into the general linear equation $p = K - (1/40)q$ yields $0 = K - (1/40)(250)$, so $K = 250/40 = \$6.25$. The equation of the demand curve between points B and C, therefore, is $p = \$6.25 - (1/40)q$.

In Figure 15.5, we derive the profit-maximizing uniform price for a non-discriminating theater. For outputs up to 50, the demand curve is the demand curve

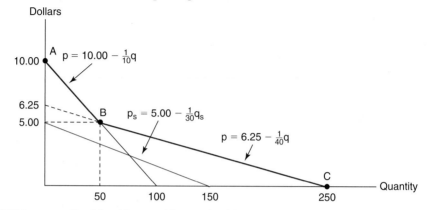

FIGURE 15.4 Combined Demand for Movie Tickets

The sum of the adult and senior demand curves for movie tickets is the horizontal summation of the two demand curves. For prices above $5.00, this consists of only the adults-under-65 demand $p = 10.00 - (1/10)q$. For prices below $5.00, the demand curve is $p = 6.25 - (1/40)q$. The complete demand curve is the kinked dark-red curve ABC.

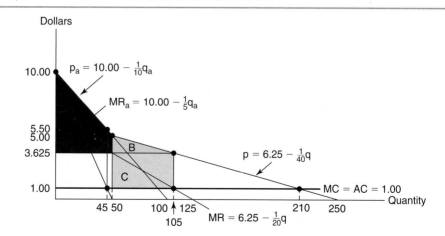

FIGURE 15.5 The Profit-Maximizing Uniform Price

To maximize profit, the theater equates marginal revenue to marginal cost on the second segment of the MR curve at $q = 105$ and sets the price at $3.625. Producer surplus equals the light red shaded area C and consumer surplus equals the sum of the dark red and light gray shaded areas A + B. The sum of consumer and producer surplus equals $507.1875.

for adults under 65: $p_a = 10.00 - (1/10)q_a$, so the marginal revenue curve is $MR_a = 10.00 - (1/5)q_a$. For outputs greater than or equal to 50, the demand curve is $p = 6.25 - (1/40)q$, so the marginal revenue curve is $MR = 6.25 - (1/20)q$.

In Figure 15.5, MC = \$1.00 intersects marginal revenue twice: first at q = 45 along the first segment of the marginal revenue curve; and again at q = 105 along the second segment. Which output, 45 or 105, maximizes profit? If q = 45, the theater sells tickets only to adults under 65 at p = \$5.50, and profit equals 45(\$5.50 − \$1.00) = \$202.50. If the theater sells 105 tickets, price equals p = 6.25 − (1/40)(105) = \$3.625, and profit equals 105(3.625 − 1.00) = \$275.625. The theater therefore maximizes profits by expanding output to 105,000. Recall from Figure 15.3 that without discrimination, adults under 65 purchased 45,000 tickets and seniors purchased 60,000 tickets for a total of 105,000 tickets; therefore, the total output of 105,000 tickets is exactly the same both with and without price discrimination. This is a basic result of price discrimination with linear demand and linear marginal cost curves.[2]

To determine the welfare impact of price discrimination, we compare the total surplus without price discrimination in Figure 15.5 with the total surplus with discrimination in Figure 15.3. In Figure 15.5, total surplus is measured by the sum of consumer surplus equal to the dark red and light gray areas A + B plus producer surplus equal to the light red area C. Geometrically, the dark red area A is a trapezoid, which has an area equal to one-half the altitude times the sum of the bases, or (1/2)(50)(\$6.375 + \$1.375) = \$193.75. The light gray triangle B has an area equal to (1/2)(55)(\$1.375) = \$37.8125. Therefore, consumer surplus equals \$193.75 + \$37.8125 = \$231.5625. Producer surplus equals the area of the light red rectangle C, or 105(\$2.625) = \$275.625. The sum of consumer and producer surplus without discrimination equals \$231.5625 + \$275.625 = \$507.1875.

Table 15.2 shows the welfare comparison with and without price discrimination. Price discrimination increases producer surplus by \$46.875. However, price discrimination reduces consumer surplus by \$70.3125, and therefore, third-degree price discrimination results in a net reduction in total surplus and welfare of \$23.4375. *Generally, with linear demand and linear marginal cost curves, price discrimination reduces welfare.* There is, however, one important exception to this rule: If one group(s) does not consume the good *without* price discrimination, then price discrimination increases total output and results in a net welfare gain.

Unfortunately, as soon as the assumption of linearity in the demand curves is eliminated, the welfare implications of third-degree price discrimination become com-

TABLE 15.2 Welfare Comparison with and Without Third-Degree Price Discrimination

	Consumer Surplus	Producer Surplus	Total Surplus
Without price discrimination Figure 15.5	\$231.5625	\$275.625	\$507.1875
With price discrimination Figure 15.3	\$161.25	\$322.50	\$483.75
Net gain (+) or loss (−) with price discrimination	−\$70.3125	\$46.875	−\$23.4375

plicated and ambiguous.[3] It is possible to show, however, that the change in welfare associated with price discrimination has both a minimum and maximum value (or a lower and upper bound).[4] This result is shown in the appendix.

The appendix also shows that a necessary but not sufficient condition for third-degree price discrimination to increase welfare is that the discrimination increases total output. Intuitively, it may seem that any discrimination that increases total output should increase welfare, but this is not the case because third-degree price discrimination distorts the marginal rate of substitution between consumers, and that distortion always reduces welfare compared to a uniform price policy. If discrimination is to result in a net welfare increase, it must increase output enough to reduce the monopoly price distortion associated with a uniform price policy and more than offset the welfare loss associated with differing marginal rates of substitution.

APPLICATION 15.3
Third-Degree Price Discrimination at Disney World

Families from all over the world travel to Disney World. Once a family has invested in the trip to Disney World, there is then the expense of the four theme parks: Magic Kingdom, Epcot, Disney MGM Studios, and the Animal Kingdom. The family's demand to enter the theme parks at this point is inelastic. They have already spent a thousand dollars or more on transportation and lodging, and therefore, most families are unlikely to let a few hundred more dollars in admission fees prevent them from visiting the theme parks. For these families, the cost of admissions is a relatively small percentage of the total cost of the trip.

By comparison, many local families from Orlando, or elsewhere in Florida, have probably been to Disney World several times and can go for a day trip to the theme parks. For such Florida families, the cost of entering a theme park is a large percentage of the total cost of a day trip to Disney World. These Florida families would have much more elastic demands for theme park entry.

Recognizing these different elasticities, Disney charges Florida residents much less to enter the parks. To ensure that Florida resident tickets are not resold to nonresidents, Disney issues photo IDs with Florida resident passes and checks IDs upon entry. Consider the following examples of some of the pricing schemes that were in effect in 2006:

Type of Admission for Adults	Non–Florida Residents	Florida Residents
Premium annual pass to all theme parks, water parks, and Pleasure Island	$539.00	$429.00
Annual pass to all four theme parks	$415.00	$325.00
Florida resident seasonal pass to all four theme parks during low-demand periods	Not Available	$215.00
Four-day, four-park pass	$195.00	$171.00
One-day, one-park pass	$63.00	$56.70

According to the chart, an Orlando resident could visit a theme park every week for a year for a total of $325.00, or about $6.25 per visit. A nonresident, on the other hand, would have to pay $415.00 for an annual theme park pass and would be less likely to

use it as often. Even to visit each park once, the Florida resident is able to spend $42.75 per visit with a $171.00 pass, compared to $48.75 per visit for nonresidents. The price-cost margins are much higher for nonresidents, who have the more inelastic demand. It is apparent from the different types of admissions listed here that Disney also uses various methods of second-degree price discrimination by offering both Florida residents and nonresidents many different types of passes. In fact, the options listed are a relatively small sample of all the various pricing options available. ■

15.2 Two-Part Tariffs, Tying, and Bundling

Among the most common forms of second-degree price discrimination are two-part tariffs, tying, and bundling. While the three concepts are closely related, they are technically different. A **two-part tariff** consists of a *lump sum* payment for a good or service combined with a *per unit* user charge. Common examples include a rental charge for a copier and a per-copy fee; a golf club that charges a membership fee and a greens fee per round; and an amusement park that charges an entrance fee and a per-attraction charge.

Under a **tie-in sales** agreement consumers can purchase a good only if they agree to purchase another good. Tie-in sales agreements are subdivided into two types: *package tie-in sales,* typically called *bundling,* and *requirements tie-in sales.* Bundling is a tying agreement in which the goods are purchased in *fixed proportions.* The most important recent example is the bundling of Microsoft's Windows operating system with Microsoft's Internet Explorer browser. Another important example is a restaurant that serves only a fixed-price menu including an appetizer, salad, entrée, and dessert.

Requirements tie-in sales consist of a tying agreement in which the goods are purchased in variable proportions. Examples include can manufacturers leasing their can-closing equipment only to customers who agree to purchase all of their cans from the manufacturer; IBM leasing its old punch-card tabulating machines only to customers who agreed to purchase all of their punch-cards from IBM; and McDonald's requiring its franchisees to purchase all of their paper cups from McDonald's.

Because each of these types of price discrimination has different economic impacts, it is useful to analyze them separately.

15.2.1 Two-Part Tariffs[5]

Consider a market for copying machines that consists of equal numbers of two types of consumers. Type A consumers have the following monthly demand for copies:

$$P = 100 - q_A.$$

Type B consumers have the following monthly demand for copies:

$$P = 100 - 2q_B.$$

These monthly demand curves are shown in Figure 15.6(a) and Figure 15.6(b).

Assume the *monthly fixed costs* of renting the machine are 500 and the *marginal cost per copy* is zero. What is the maximum monthly rental each type of consumer

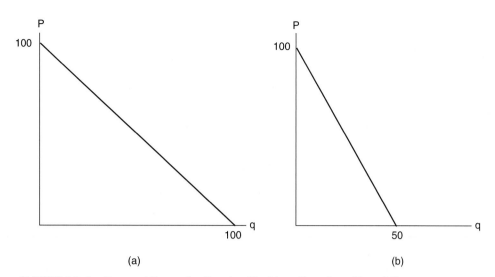

(a) (b)

FIGURE 15.6 Demand Curves for Copying Machines, Type A and Type B Consumers, Respectively

In panel (a) Type A consumers have demand $P = 100 - q_A$ and will pay a maximum monthly rental of $\frac{1}{2}(100)(100) = 5000$. In panel (b) Type B consumers have demand $P = 100 - 2q_B$ and will pay a maximum monthly rental of $\frac{1}{2}(100)(50) = 2500$.

would pay for the copying machine? With first-degree price discrimination each type of consumer would pay a maximum rental fee equal to total consumer surplus obtained if the price per copy was equal to marginal cost, which equals zero in this case. From Figure 15.6(a), Type A consumers would pay a maximum of:

$$CS_A = \frac{1}{2}(100)(100) = 5000.$$

From Figure 15.6(b), Type B consumers would pay a maximum of:

$$CS_B = \frac{1}{2}(100)(50) = 2500.$$

To simplify the analysis, assume there is one consumer of each type. The *single-price* options for the monopolist are either to charge a rental fee of 5000 and rent only to the Type A consumer, or to charge a rental fee of 2500 and rent to both the Type A and Type B consumers. From the monopolist's perspective, which pricing system is best depends on which system maximizes profits.

Consider setting the rental fee equal to 5000 and renting only to the Type A consumer. Profits would be:

$$\Pi_A = 5000 - 500 = 4500.$$

Alternatively, setting the rental fee equal to 2500 and renting to both Type A and Type B consumers results in profits equal to:

$$\Pi_A + \Pi_B = 2(2500 - 500) = 4000.$$

In this case the monopolist maximizes profits by charging the higher rental fee, P = 5000, and renting only to the Type A consumer. The Type B consumer is priced out of the market.

Next we show that by using a two-part tariff, the monopolist's profits can be increased. Suppose the monopolist decides to charge both a fixed monthly rental fee and a per-copy charge to both Type A and Type B consumers. The profit-maximizing combination of a fixed monthly rental fee and a per-copy charge is illustrated in Figure 15.7.* The monopolist should charge a per-copy fee equal to 25 and a fixed fee of 1406.25 to each consumer. This fixed fee equals the consumer surplus for the low-demand Type B consumer if the per-copy charge is 25. Profits then equal:

$$\Pi = 2(\text{fixed fee}) + p(q_A + q_B) - 2(\text{fixed costs})$$
$$= 2(1406.25) + 25(75 + 37.5) - 2(500)$$
$$= (2812.50) + (2812.5) - (1000) = 4625.$$

Using a two-part tariff increases profits from 4500 to 4625 despite the dramatic reduction in the monthly rental fee from 5000 to 1406.25. The reduced rental fee attracts the Type B consumer into the market. The monopolist more than makes up for the reduction in the rental fee by charging a per-copy fee greater than zero.

15.2.2 The Welfare Effects of a Two-Part Tariff

Consider the welfare effects of the two-part tariff above. In the absence of the two-part tariff, the monopolist maximized profits by charging a fixed fee of 5000 and a per-copy fee of zero. In this case, consumer surplus equals zero and profits equal:

$$\Pi = TR - TC = 5000 - 500 = 4500.$$

The sum of consumer surplus plus profit, therefore, equals 4500.

*If both consumers are to rent copiers, the rental fee must be set at the consumer surplus for the low-demand Type B consumer. If p represents the price per copy, then from Figure 15.7(b):

$$CS_B = \frac{1}{2}(100 - p)q = \frac{1}{2}(100 - p)\left(50 - \frac{1}{2}p\right).$$

Summing the two demand curves, the total demand for copies by both consumers can be obtained as follows:

$$p = 100 - q_A \quad \text{and} \quad p = 100 - 2q_B$$

or
$$q_A = 100 - p \quad \text{and} \quad q_B = 50 - \frac{p}{2},$$

so
$$q = (q_A + q_B) = 150 - \frac{3p}{2}.$$

The monopolist's profits, Π, are then:

$$\Pi = TR - TC = [\text{rental fees paid by both consumers} + pq] - 1000$$
$$= \left[(100 - p)\left(50 - \frac{1}{2}p\right) + p\left(150 - \frac{3}{2}p\right)\right] - 1000 = 4000 + 50p - p^2.$$

We can now use calculus to maximize profits. Differentiate profits with respect to p and set equal to zero:

$$\frac{d\Pi}{dp} = 50 - 2p = 0 \Rightarrow p = 25.$$

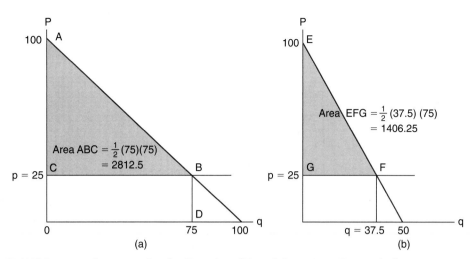

FIGURE 15.7 Consumer Surplus, Type A and Type B Consumers, Respectively

In panel (a) Type A consumers have demand $P = 100 - q_A$ and in panel (b) Type B consumers have demand $P = 100 - 2q_B$. To maximize profit, the monopolist charges a per-copy charge $p = 25$ and a fixed fee equal to 1406.25, which equals the consumer surplus in the low-demand market in panel (b). Total profit is 4625, which is greater than the profit of 4500 associated with charging a fixed fee of 5000 to Type A consumers and pricing Type B consumers out of the market.

The use of a profit-maximizing two-part tariff results in a fixed fee of 1406.25 plus a per-copy charge of 25. The Type B consumer receives no consumer surplus because the fixed fee equals the triangle EFG in Figure 15.7(b). However, the Type A consumer receives consumer surplus because she pays less than the maximum amount she would be willing to pay for 75 copies. With a per-copy charge of 25 and no rental fee, a Type A consumer would receive consumer surplus of $\triangle ABC = 2812.5$. The monopolist is able to capture part of this consumer surplus with the fixed rental fee of 1406.25. Remember that the rental fee cannot be higher than this without driving the Type B consumer out of the market. The Type A consumer, therefore, receives consumer surplus equal to $(2812.5) - (1406.25) = 1406.25$.*

The monopolist's profits were previously calculated to be 4625 under the two-part tariff. Therefore, the sum of consumer surplus and monopoly profits with a two-part tariff equals:

$$CS + \Pi = 1406.25 + 4625 = 6031.25.$$

*The following is an alternative method of calculating the Type A consumer's consumer surplus. In Figure 15.7(a) the maximum amount that the Type A consumer would pay for 75 copies is represented by the trapezoid ABDO, which equals:

$$\text{Area ABDO} = \frac{1}{2}(75)(100 + 25) = 4687.5.$$

The Type A consumer pays a fixed fee of 1406.25 plus a per-copy charge of $pq = (75)(25) = 1875$, or a total payment of 3281.25. The Type A consumer, therefore, receives consumer surplus equal to $(4687.5) - (3281.25) = 1406.25$.

The two-part tariff has increased the sum of consumer surplus plus profits from 4500 to 6031.25, an increase of over 33 percent.

Using a two-part tariff will not improve welfare in all cases. For example, if in the absence of the two-part tariff both Type A and Type B consumers had remained in the market, then welfare would be reduced by a two-part tariff *even if the two-part tariff results in higher profits* for the monopolist. This result follows directly from the fact that in the absence of the two-part tariff, the price per copy equals marginal cost. Because the two-part tariff increases price above marginal cost, welfare would have to be reduced. The major conclusion, therefore, is that a two-part tariff may or may not increase economic welfare.

APPLICATION 15.4

Changing Pricing Strategies at Disneyland and Disney World

When Disneyland opened in Anaheim, California, in 1955, the company used a two-part tariff that included both a fixed fee and a per-ride charge. After paying a fixed-fee admission to enter the park, customers were required to purchase ticket books for the rides. When Disney World opened in Orlando, Florida, in 1971, Disney adopted the same pricing policy for the Magic Kingdom theme park.

By the mid-1970s, Disney decided to change its pricing strategy and began to charge a much higher fixed-fee admission price, but no fee per ride. Disney eliminated the ticket books and replaced them with passports, which entitled the holder to one day of admission that included unlimited rides and attractions. Because the marginal cost to Disney of putting one more customer on a ride is essentially zero, Disney moved from a policy like the one depicted in Figure 15.7, where the price per ride was greater than marginal cost and low-ride- and high-ride-volume consumers were encouraged to enter the parks by a relatively low fixed admission fee, to a policy like the one depicted in Figure 15.6, where the price per ride was set at MC = 0 and the fixed fee was set at a high level that prevented low-ride-volume consumers from entering the theme parks. Disney has maintained this pricing policy for over 25 years now, so it is reasonable to assume that high-ride-volume consumers have a much greater demand for rides than low-ride-volume consumers. ∎

15.2.3 Bundling

Recall that **bundling** is a tying arrangement in which the goods are purchased in fixed proportions. One famous example of bundling occurred in the motion picture industry during the golden years of major studio domination of the industry.[6] The major motion picture producer-distributors, such as MGM, Paramount, and Fox, bundled high-quality and low-quality pictures together and forced theaters to purchase their entire package of films.

To understand why the system increased the studios' profits, consider the following simple example. Table 15.3 shows the maximum rental per film that two theater chains, Regal Cinemas and AMC, are willing to pay for two Disney films, the popular *The Chronicles of Narnia* and the unpopular *Treasure Planet*. Regal Cinemas is willing to pay 800 for *The Chronicles of Narnia* and 250 for *Treasure Planet,* while AMC is willing to pay 700 for *The Chronicles of Narnia* and 300 for *Treasure Planet*. Regal is willing to

TABLE 15.3 Maximum Rentals for Regal Cinemas and AMC

Theater	The Maximum Price per Film		Bundled Price
	The Chronicles of Narnia	*Treasure Planet*	
Regal Cinemas	800	250	1050
AMC Theaters	700	300	1000

pay 1050 for both films bundled together, and AMC is willing to pay 1000. If Disney could discriminate perfectly, it would charge each theater the maximum price the theater would be willing to pay for each film; its revenues would be:

$$TR = 800 + 250 + 700 + 300 = 2050.$$

If Disney must charge the same rental fee for each film to each theater, however, it can either: (a) charge 700 for *The Chronicles of Narnia* and 250 for *Treasure Planet;* or (b) bundle the two films together and charge 1000 for both. With option (a) (without bundling), Disney's revenues equal:

$$TR = 2(700) + 2(250) = 1900.$$

With option (b) (with bundling), Disney's revenues equal:

$$TR = 2(1000) = 2000.$$

In this case, Disney is better off bundling. Bundling is a form of price discrimination because the practice effectively enables Disney to charge a price greater than 700 to Regal for *The Chronicles of Narnia* and a price greater than 250 to AMC for *Treasure Planet.* Bundling, therefore, enables Disney to charge different rental rates to different theaters for the same film.

In this case, bundling works to increase profit because there is a difference in the *relative valuations* of *The Chronicles of Narnia* and *Treasure Planet.* **Relative valuation** refers to how different consumers value different goods in relation to each other. In this case, even though both theaters are willing to pay more for the *The Chronicles of Narnia,* Regal Cinemas is willing to pay more for the *The Chronicles of Narnia* than AMC, while AMC is willing to pay more for *Treasure Planet* than Regal. Therefore, there is a difference in the relative valuations of AMC and Regal for the two movies. In the case of different relative valuations, the demands are said to be *negatively correlated,* meaning that the consumer willing to pay more for one good is willing to pay less for the other good. If the demands were *positively correlated,* one consumer would be willing to pay more for both goods and bundling would not increase total revenues.

15.2.4 Mixed Bundling

It is fairly common for firms to give consumers the choice of paying for products separately or bundled together in packages, a practice known as **mixed bundling.**[7] For example, most restaurants, from McDonald's to *haute cuisine* French restaurants, offer an *á la carte* menu and a bundled *fixed price* complete meal menu. Similarly, all

professional sports teams offer tickets to individual games and season ticket packages of bundled tickets. Presumably, offering consumers this choice maximizes profits of the restaurant or the sports team.

To understand how the firm decides which method of pricing to use, consider the choices facing a fast-food restaurant such as Burger King. Burger King can offer to sell a Whopper and fries either *only* separately (individual pricing of both items), *only* bundled (the consumer can *only* buy a complete meal), or either separately or bundled (mixed bundling). The following analysis assumes that: (1) Burger King faces a downward-sloping demand curve for Whoppers and for fries; (2) Whoppers and fries are not available for resale; and (3) consumers have different tastes for the two products. The first assumption makes sense if we envision the market for fast food as monopolistically competitive. The second assumption is fairly straightforward: Consumers generally do not buy a Whopper and then offer to resell it to another consumer. We examine the third assumption concerning different tastes in detail in the analysis that follows.

First, consider the individual-pricing-only option, that is, charging separate prices for a Whopper and for fries. Figure 15.8(a) identifies the reservation prices for three different consumers for Whoppers and fries. Consumer X will pay a maximum price of $1.75 for a Whopper and $1.75 for fries. Consumer Y will pay a maximum price of $2.50 for a Whopper and $1.75 for fries. Finally, Consumer Z will pay a maximum price of $3.00 for a Whopper and $0.50 for fries. If Burger King charges $2.00 for a

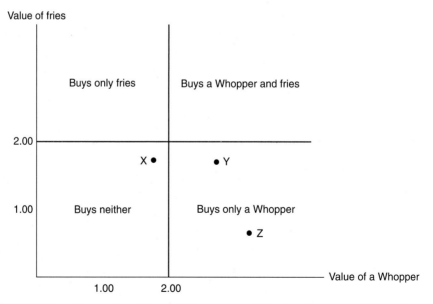

FIGURE 15.8a Reservation Prices for Whoppers and Fries for Consumers X, Y, and Z

Suppose Burger King charges $2.00 for a Whopper and $2.00 for fries. Consumer X has a reservation price of $1.75 for a Whopper and $1.75 for fries and buys neither. Consumer Y has a reservation price of $2.50 for a Whopper and $1.75 for fries and buys only a Whopper. Consumer Z has a reservation price of $3.00 for a Whopper and $0.50 for fries and buys only a Whopper.

Whopper and $2.00 for fries, then Consumer X will purchase nothing (both prices are above Consumer X's respective reservation prices), and Consumers Y and Z will purchase only a Whopper. Note that consumers with reservation prices above $2.00 for each product would buy both a Whopper and fries.

Consider what happens if Burger King bundles its Whopper and fries together by offering *only* a "value meal combo" of a Whopper and fries for $3.50. Figure 15.8(b) shows that Consumer X is now willing to buy the value meal combo at $3.50, which equals his reservation price of $1.75 for a Whopper *plus* $1.75 for fries. Furthermore, Consumer Y and Consumer Z also buy the value combo meal for $3.50. By offering *only* the bundle, Burger King increases its sales from *two* Whoppers and *zero* fries to *three* Whoppers and *three* fries!

Finally, in Figure 15.8(c), we consider *mixed bundling*. In this case, Burger King offers either individual pricing at $2.00 each for a Whopper or for fries, or the bundled combo meal at $3.50. Consumers maximize consumer surplus, and therefore, Consumers X and Y purchase the bundle, but Consumer Z buys only a Whopper. In terms of consumer surplus, Consumer X receives zero consumer surplus since the price of the bundle equals his reservation price. Consumer Y receives consumer surplus equal to $0.75, which equals her reservation price of $4.25 for the bundle ($2.50 + $1.75) *minus* the bundled price of $3.50. This is greater than the $0.50 in consumer surplus she would gain if she bought the Whopper alone for $2.00 (consumer surplus = $2.50 − $2.00). Consumer Z purchases just the Whopper for $2.00 and receives consumer surplus equal to $1.00 ($3.00 − $2.00), which is greater

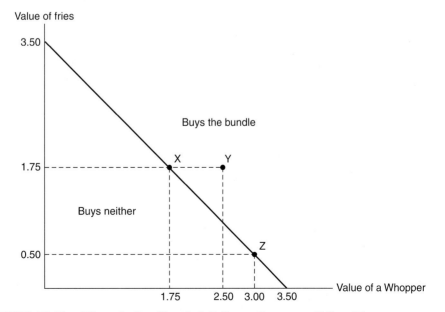

FIGURE 15.8b **Effect of a Bundling-Only Policy on Consumers X, Y, and Z**

Suppose Burger King bundles a Whopper and fries and charges $3.50 for both. Now Consumers X, Y, and Z buy the bundle because $3.50 is less than or equal to the reservation price for the bundle for all three consumers.

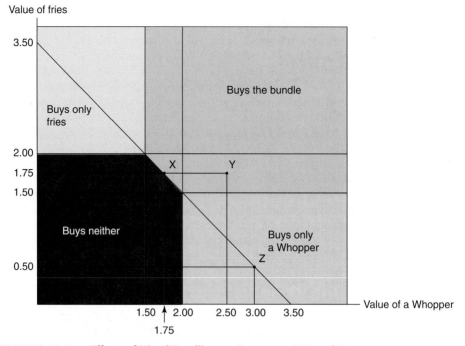

FIGURE 15.8c **Effects of Mixed Bundling on Consumers X, Y, and Z**

Suppose Burger King gives consumers a choice of either the bundle of a Whopper and fries for $3.50 or single-item pricing, with the price for a Whopper or fries equal to $2.00. Now Consumers X and Y maximize consumer surplus by purchasing the bundle, but Consumer Z buys just a Whopper. Consumers with preferences in the dark red area purchase neither a Whopper nor fries; consumers with preferences in the medium red area purchase both a Whopper and fries; consumers with preferences in the light red area purchase only fries; and consumers with preferences in the gray area purchase only a Whopper.

than the $0.00 in consumer surplus he would receive if he purchased the bundle ($3.50 − $3.50 = $0.00).

Summarizing Figure 15.8(c): Consumers with preferences in the medium red area would buy the bundled combo meal; consumers with preferences in the dark red area would buy nothing; consumers with preferences in the light red area would buy only the fries; and consumers with preferences in the gray area would buy only a Whopper.

We have yet to address the most interesting question for Burger King: Which pricing scheme maximizes profits? To determine profits, it is necessary to know not only what prices different consumers are willing to pay for Whoppers and fries, but also Burger King's costs of production. Suppose we have only three types of consumers, as depicted in Figure 15.9. Type A consumers are willing to pay $0.50 for a Whopper and $3.00 for fries. Type B consumers are willing to pay $2.00 for a Whopper and $1.50 for fries. Finally, Type C consumers are willing to pay $3.00 for a Whopper and $0.50 for fries. Assume the average total cost of producing either a Whopper or an order of fries is $1.00.

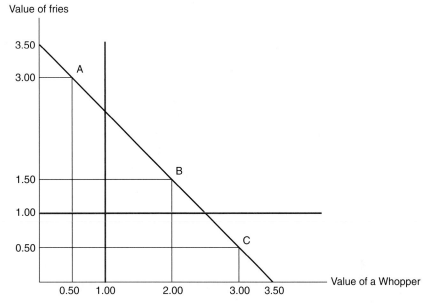

FIGURE 15.9 Comparison of Individual Pricing, Bundling Only, and Mixed Bundling

Suppose the average total cost of producing either a Whopper or fries is $1.00. Type A consumers are willing to pay $0.50 for a Whopper and $3.00 for fries; Type B consumers are willing to pay $2.00 for a Whopper and $1.50 for fries; and Type C consumers are willing to pay $3.00 for a Whopper and $0.50 for fries. Profit maximization with single-item pricing requires charging $2.00 for a Whopper and $3.00 for fries and yields a profit equal to $4. Profit maximization with bundling only requires charging $3.50 for the bundle and yields a profit equal to $4.50. Profit maximization with mixed bundling requires charging $3.50 for the bundle or $2.99 for a Whopper and $2.99 for fries and yields a profit equal to $5.48. Mixed bundling is Burger King's optimal strategy.

Here are the profit-maximizing pricing strategies under each pricing scheme:

Individual pricing only—To maximize profits, Burger King charges $2.00 for a Whopper and $3.00 for fries. Burger King sells two Whoppers (to Consumers B and C) and one order of fries (to Consumer A), and profits equal:

$$\Pi = TR - TC = [2(\$2) + 1(\$3)] - [2(\$1) + 1(\$1)] = \$7 - \$3 = \$4.$$

Bundling only—To maximize profits Burger King charges $3.50 for a value meal combo of a Whopper and fries. Burger King sells three combos (to Consumers A, B, and C), and profits equal:

$$\Pi = TR - TC = 3(\$3.50) - 3(\$2) = \$10.50 - \$6.00 = \$4.50.$$

Mixed bundling—To maximize profits Burger King charges either $3.50 for a value meal combo, *or* an individual price of $2.99 for a Whopper and $2.99 for an order of fries. Burger King would sell one combo to Consumer B, one Whopper to Consumer C, and one order of fries to Consumer A, and profits equal:

$$\Pi = TR - TC = [1(\$3.50) + 1(\$2.99) + 1(\$2.99)] - [1(\$2) + 1(\$1) + 1(\$1)]$$
$$= \$9.48 - \$4.00 = \$5.48.$$

In this case, mixed bundling maximizes profits at $5.48 compared to $4.50 with pure bundling and $4.00 with individual pricing. Despite the fact that Burger King sells more Whoppers and fries with a bundling-only policy, profits are higher with mixed bundling. Profits are lower with a bundling-only policy because under that pricing scheme, Burger King is selling some Whoppers and some fries to consumers who have reservation prices *below* Burger King's costs of production. Consumer A, for example, values the Whopper at only $0.50, which is below Burger King's cost of $1.00. Similarly, Consumer C values the fries at $0.50, which is below Burger King's cost of $1.00. With a bundling-only policy, Burger King earns $1.50 on its sales to Consumers A and C, but with mixed bundling, Burger King earns $1.99 on its sale of fries to Consumer A, and another $1.99 on its sale of a Whopper to Consumer C. Mixed bundling enables Burger King to capture more of the available consumer surplus, and therefore, results in increased profits.

Given the demands in Figure 15.9, if production costs equaled zero, Burger King would be better off with a bundling-only policy. With zero costs of production, Burger King would simply wish to maximize total revenues at $10.50 by using a bundling-only policy. Depending on consumer tastes and the costs of production, any of the various pricing schemes could maximize profits. Because all of the major fast-food chains have adopted a mixed bundling strategy, it is reasonable to conclude that in the fast-food industry a mixed bundling policy maximizes profits.

15.2.5 Requirements Tie-in Sales

Recall that **requirements tie-in sales** consist of a tying agreement in which the goods are purchased in *variable proportions*. In a typical requirements tie-in a firm with market power over good X requires its buyers to purchase all of their requirements of a complementary good, good Y, in order to obtain good X. In one famous example, American Can and Continental Can both adopted a policy of leasing their patented can-closing machines for a minimum of five years with the further restriction that the lessee purchase all of its can requirements during the five-year period from its machinery supplier. Under no circumstances were machines offered for sale. These policies enabled the major can companies to increase their profits by practicing a form of price discrimination in the machinery market. Market power was the result of superior machines, *not* superior cans, yet the companies leased their machines at rentals *below* average cost. This was possible because can prices were kept substantially *above* average cost. The cans were used as a method of metering machine use. The more cans a firm used, the larger were the profits it paid to its can supplier. A purchaser of 1 million cans paid 10 times more for the use of closing machinery than the user of 100,000 cans.

The requirements tie-in used in the can industry had several possible anticompetitive effects. Because American and Continental controlled the machinery market, it was extremely difficult for independent can manufacturers to find a market; the requirements tie-in foreclosed most of the market for cans. *Foreclosure* occurs when upstream firms have difficulty obtaining inputs or when downstream firms have difficulty finding buyers.* In this case, because independent can manufacturers could not

*Examples include Alcoa's control of bauxite ore, foreclosing competitors from the raw material needed to produce virgin aluminum and American automobile producers being foreclosed from Japanese automobile dealers that are controlled by the major Japanese automobile manufacturers.

find buyers, the only way to enter the can market was to produce *both* cans and can-closing machinery. Forcing firms to enter two markets instead of one increased the capital barrier to entry. More important, large R&D expenditures were required to produce non-patent-infringing can-closing machinery capable of competing with American's and Continental's equipment. This proved to be an almost impossible barrier, and American and Continental were able to control both markets.

Requirements tie-in sales have been used in an attempt to extend market power in many industries. Before computers were invented, IBM tied cards to its tabulating machinery. United Shoe Machinery tied shoe machinery supplies, such as nails and tacks, to its shoe machinery. And many franchisors, such as McDonald's, tie several products, such as hamburger patties and buns, to their franchises. Kodak used to tie film processing to its film, and as recently as 1992 the Supreme Court ruled that Kodak had illegally tied its repair parts and maintenance service to its micrographic equipment* and high-volume copiers. Because requirements tie-ins can have anticompetitive effects, they have been the focus of a good deal of antitrust attention; we consider this further in Chapter 16.

15.3 Distribution Effects of Price Discrimination

The distribution effects of price discrimination are straightforward—producers as a group gain and consumers as a group lose. In fact, the producer's incentive to discriminate is a desire to increase profits. First-degree discrimination carries this to an extreme: All of the consumer surplus is transferred to producers.

Is this redistribution of income good or bad? The answer depends entirely on value judgments. Because price discrimination always increases profits, and because much of it is done by large corporations with market power, many believe that this redistribution is bad for society. If price discrimination generally redistributes income from consumers at large to stockholders and managers, it will generate some increase in the degree of inequality in society.

One often-cited example, however, suggests that redistributional effects may have net social benefits. Physicians are among the largest beneficiaries of price discrimination. Doctors routinely discriminate between high- and low-income patients or those with and without good insurance. Discrimination helps explain why doctors have such high incomes. Yet consider the case of a doctor in a small rural community facing the demand and cost situation depicted in Figure 15.10. Because the AC curve is always above the demand curve, no single fee would enable the physician to cover her costs. If she uses second-degree discrimination and charges a group of high-income patients F_H, a group of middle-income patients F_M, and her low-income patients F_L, then she will see a total of Q_3 patients and her average cost per patient will be C_{ALL}. The doctor will earn an excess profit of the light gray area $F_H ADC_{ALL}$ from her high-income patients and an excess profit of the red area BCED from her middle-income patients. These excess profits will offset her loss of the dark gray area EFHG from low-income patients. Only by discriminating is the doctor able to remain in the community. In this case many would argue that the redistributional impact of price discrimination is socially positive.

*Micrographic equipment is used to create, file, retrieve, view, and print microfiche and microfilm.

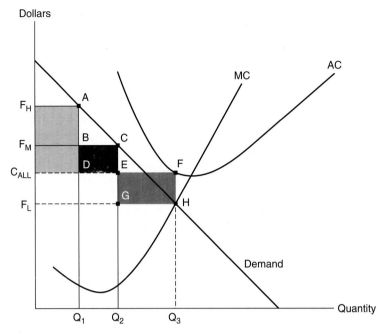

FIGURE 15.10 Price Discrimination by a Doctor in a Small Town

Here the doctor's AC curve is everywhere above the demand curve so no uniform price can cover the doctor's costs. However, the doctor can use price discrimination and charge a fee of F_H to high-income patients, F_M to medium-income patients, and F_L to low-income patients. The doctor treats a total of Q_3 patients at AC $= C_{ALL}$ and earns positive economic profit from treating her high-income and middle-income patients equal to the sum of the light gray and red areas. She sustains an economic loss from treating her low-income patients equal to the dark gray area. Because the sum of the light gray and red areas is greater than the dark gray area, overall she earns positive profit.

15.4 Effect on Competition

Price discrimination can have positive or negative effects on competition. Much depends on whether the discrimination is done by small fringe firms or large dominant firms, and whether it is sporadic or systematic. At one extreme, if discrimination is done by fringe firms in a sporadic attempt to gain additional sales, then the impact is positive. Examples of price discrimination stimulating competition are easy to identify. A firm may temporarily cut its price in one geographic area to find out if demand is elastic. If the firm discovers that demand is more elastic than expected, the discrimination could result in a permanent across-the-board price reduction. Supermarket chains may cut prices in some areas to induce customers to try their stores. Such price cuts are often very deep: Eggs may sell for 29 cents a dozen, or milk may sell for 49 cents a half-gallon. Such "loss-leaders" enhance competition between stores. Hag-

gling with a dealer over the price of a new car is another example of price discrimination that increases competition.

The mobile phone industry provides a good recent example of sporadic price discrimination. Nextel and Cingular seem to change their price structures for each customer in an effort to pry business away from Verizon. Verizon customers know that on any given day Cingular might offer a cash bribe, 5000 frequent-flyer miles, a month of free calls, or a rate reduction to call 10 phone numbers of your choice for a year if you will switch to Cingular. Nextel, of course, is making the same type of offers, and Verizon is trying to match both of them. As a result, many customers of the same company pay different mobile phone rates, and competition through price discrimination drives the general rate schedule down.

Some price discrimination in the airline industry has also been pro-competitive. The major carriers now use sophisticated computer reservation systems to change fares by the hour. If a flight is overbooking, fares are increased, whereas fares can be reduced on empty flights. The result is more competition and fewer empty seats, both of which are positive economic outcomes.[8] It is important to distinguish the airlines' price discrimination to control capacity utilization from predatory fare reductions aimed at eliminating competition (see Chapter 11).

The list of positive examples could go on, but the important point is clear: A good deal of price discrimination is procompetitive and should not be discouraged by public policy.

On the other extreme, systematic price discrimination by dominant firms can reduce competition by entrenching the positions of the dominant firm(s). Chapters 10 and 11 analyzed several examples of this type of price discrimination. In Chapter 10 the basing point pricing system was discussed as a method of solving the prisoner's dilemma. In addition to being a solution to the dilemma, basing point systems are excellent examples of anticompetitive price discrimination because different buyers face vastly different price-cost margins under the system. Figure 10.2 is reproduced here as Figure 15.11. Recall that the buyer in Chicago who purchased steel from a Chicago mill paid a price of $47.60 per ton while the buyer in Pittsburgh paid $40.00. The basing point system discriminated against buyers located close to a steel mill but far from a basing point. This discrimination was systematic and used by all the firms in the industry.

How could the basing point system used in the steel, cement, and plywood industries reduce competition? Consider two small appliance manufacturers, one located in Pittsburgh and the other in Chicago under the Pittsburgh-plus system. The appliance manufacturer located in Pittsburgh purchased one of its important inputs at a much lower price-cost margin than the firm located in Chicago, and as a result the Chicago firm might have a difficult time competing with the Pittsburgh-based manufacturer. This is an example of price discrimination that reduces competition in the *secondary-line market,* by reducing the level of competition between the buyers of the good.

Chapter 10 examined some of the most famous cases of price discrimination that hindered *primary-line* competition. Primary-line competition refers to competition between sellers in the market in which price discrimination is being practiced. The cases in Chapter 11 dealing with predatory pricing included Standard Oil, American Tobacco, IBM, Microsoft, Wal-Mart, Maxwell House, and the airlines. In each case, a dominant firm(s) systematically practiced price discrimination against a particular

FIGURE 15.11 Price Discrimination Under the Basing Point Pricing System
The downward-sloping curve represents the basing point price of steel, which is what buyers actually pay per ton, at locations between Chicago and Pittsburgh. The upward-sloping curve represents the $40-per-ton base price plus true freight costs from Chicago. A buyer located in Chicago and buying from a Chicago mill faced a much higher price-cost margin for steel than a buyer located in Pittsburgh buying from a Pittsburgh mill. This price discrimination hurt buyers in Chicago, who were competing with buyers in Pittsburgh in a secondary market.

competitor(s) in an attempt to reduce competition. For those who read Appendix 11, recall that in the Kreps and Wilson model of predatory pricing the objective of a weak firm behaving like a strong firm was to prevent competition from emerging.

15.5 Antitrust: Price Discrimination and the Robinson-Patman Act

Recall from Chapter 1 that the Robinson-Patman Act is the most controversial of the antitrust statutes. Passed during the Great Depression, its original intention was to prevent large chain store buyers from inducing suppliers to grant price concessions that were unavailable to small retailers. Ironically, Section 2(f), which is the only provision aimed directly at *buyer* behavior, has been ineffective. Instead, the Robinson-Patman Act has been directed almost entirely at sellers who grant discriminatory prices.

Sometimes called the "Magna Carta for small business," the Robinson-Patman Act often turns antitrust policy upside down by protecting small competitors rather than

the competitive process. The problem stems from the statute not adequately recognizing that price discrimination is often procompetitive.

Although most temporary or sporadic price discrimination improves efficiency, some **predatory discrimination** is anticompetitive. This predatory discrimination has the specific aim of weakening or driving competitors from the market, allowing the predator to then raise price above average cost. Most predatory discrimination is systematic and carried out by dominant firms, and it is only this discrimination that offers any serious threat to competition. Unfortunately, the Robinson-Patman Act has rarely been successful in attacking predatory discrimination but, instead, has typically been directed at practices that have few negative effects on competition. Furthermore, at least in theory, true predatory behavior can be attacked under Section 2 of the Sherman Act without reference to the Robinson-Patman Act.

Robinson-Patman Act cases are grouped into either *primary-line* or *secondary-line* cases according to their effects on competition. Recall that **primary-line cases** involve possible injury to a direct competitor. Most primary-line cases involve geographic price discrimination in which a national firm sells in one submarket at prices significantly below its prices elsewhere. For example, if Ben & Jerry's decided to sell ice cream at a much lower price in Montana than in the rest of the country, even though Ben & Jerry's did not manufacture ice cream in Montana, this could cause injury to small Montana dairies. Remember that **secondary-line cases** involve possible injury to a competitor of a buyer who receives a lower discriminatory price. If Ben & Jerry's sold ice cream to Safeway at a lower price than to any other store, it might injure Safeway's competitors, such as Kroeger.

The Robinson-Patman Act forbids price discrimination:

> where the effect of such discrimination may be substantially to lessen competition or tend to create a monopoly in any line of commerce or to injure, destroy, or prevent competition with any person who either grants or knowingly receives the benefit of such discrimination, or with customers of either of them.

Unlike the other antitrust acts, which require some lessening of competition, the Robinson-Patman Act requires injury to either the competitive process or to *specific competitors*. Furthermore, the act requires only that there *may* be a substantial lessening of competition. Any price discrimination that *may* have a negative effect on any competitor at any level of competition, therefore, may be subject to Robinson-Patman Act enforcement.

Recall that the Robinson-Patman Act provided for two major defenses: cost justification and meeting competition. The act, however, left the standards for either defense wide open for judicial interpretation. Most of the major issues in the following cases revolve around the judicial standards for an acceptable defense.

15.5.1 Secondary-Line Cases

Some of the earliest Robinson-Patman Act cases involved **basing point pricing systems.** Two rather obvious questions arise: What does the basing point system have to do with the Robinson-Patman Act? And, why not attack these systems under the Sherman Act? Although basing point systems have been successfully challenged under the Sherman Act, the earliest cases were Robinson-Patman Act cases in which the FTC argued that buyers located close to a seller but far from a basing point paid

higher mill *net* prices and, therefore, were discriminated against. The first ruling handed down was in 1945. It concerned the basing point system in the glucose (corn syrup) industry.

THE CORN PRODUCTS CASE[9] (1945) The Corn Products Refining Company was a large glucose manufacturer that operated plants in Chicago and Kansas City, Missouri. It sold glucose primarily to candy manufacturers, and all sales were made at delivered prices based on a single basing point, Chicago. Candy manufacturers outside Chicago paid a higher price for glucose than Chicago buyers, even if they were located in Kansas City and purchased from Corn Products' Kansas City plant.

In 1939 the Chicago price was $2.09 per hundred pounds, and the Kansas City price was $2.49 ($2.09 + $0.40 *phantom freight* from Chicago). The FTC argued that the system discriminated against candy manufacturers located in Kansas City because the net price (net price = price − actual freight) in Kansas City was $2.49 compared with $2.09 ($2.09 − $0.00) on glucose shipped from Chicago plants to Chicago candy manufacturers.

The Federal Trade Commission argued that candy manufacturers located in Kansas City would be injured by this discrimination, and the Supreme Court agreed. The Court ruled that because glucose is a principal ingredient in low-priced candy, differences of even small fractions of a cent in the price of glucose could divert business from one manufacturer to another, and therefore, there was a "reasonable probability that the effect of the discriminations may be substantially to lessen competition."

THE CEMENT INSTITUTE CASE[10] (1948) The legal death knell for basing point systems came three years after the *Corn Products* decision in the *Cement Institute* case.*

In the *Corn Products* case, the Court held that a single basing point system was illegal, but it reserved judgment on multiple basing point price systems because of the good-faith proviso of Section 2(b) of the Robinson-Patman Act. In the *Cement* case, the Court held that a seller could not justify the adoption of a competitor's basing point price system under Section 2(b) as a good faith attempt to meet the competitor's equally low price. The combined effect of the two decisions, therefore, was to make all basing point pricing systems illegal.

For all practical purposes, the *Cement Institute* case ended legal basing point systems in the United States. The steel industry, for example, voluntarily abandoned its multiple basing point system. Illegal basing point systems, however, still occasionally arise. Recall from Chapter 10 that the plywood industry adopted a basing point system well into the 1970s.[11]

A per se ban on industry-wide systematic basing point systems seems justified. Basing point systems distort market prices and costs. Furthermore, by encouraging firms to enter basing point industries with stable price structures, the systems may encourage excessive entry and a great deal of excess capacity.[12] Although individual producers may, from time to time, be forced to adopt a delivered pricing system to match local competition, this can be accomplished under a uniform F.O.B. pricing system, with freight absorption by the seller permitted to meet a competitor's lower price.† At

*The courts have since upheld basing point systems if freight costs play a very minor role in overall pricing decisions. See *Ethyl Corporation* v. *FTC*, 729 F.2d 128 (1984).

†Under F.O.B. pricing, buyers pay the actual freight costs incurred by the seller.

the very least buyers should have the option of F.O.B. pricing with buyer pickup at the mill. The elimination of most basing point systems has been one of the more positive effects of the Robinson-Patman Act.

MORTON SALT CASE[13] **(1948)** One week after handing down the *Cement Institute* decision, the Supreme Court handed down its first major precedent in a non–basing point case. Morton Salt was the nation's leading producer of table salt. Morton followed a strict quantity-based system of price discrimination. Table 15.4 shows the price schedule used by Morton. Only five large chains, American Stores, National Tea, Kroger, Safeway, and A&P, qualified for the top discount. As a result, these five chains could sell at a retail price below the wholesale price that many independent wholesalers paid for salt. Morton argued that because the discounts were available to all purchasers, they were not discriminatory.

The Supreme Court ruled against Morton. The majority reasoned that the discounts were "theoretically" available to all, but that "functionally" they were available only to the largest chains. In another section of the decision, the Court stated that "the statute does not require that the discriminations must in fact have harmed competition, but only that there is a reasonable possibility that they 'may' have such an effect."

Two important precedents emerged from the *Morton Salt* case. First, only a *reasonable possibility* of injury to competition or competitors was required by the majority. This considerably reduced the burden of proof in Robinson-Patman Act cases because it is often possible to find a reasonable possibility that either competition or a competitor will be injured by price discrimination. Second, the *Morton Salt* case established that pure quantity-based discounts had to be *fully* cost justified.

The *Morton Salt* decision can be criticized on economic grounds. The decision highlighted the basic conflict that arises in so many Robinson-Patman Act cases. If all price discrimination is eliminated, a firm's output is likely to decline, and average costs will rise as long as economies of scale exist. Eliminating all price discrimination is likely, therefore, to raise society's average cost of producing a good. In addition, consumers may well end up paying higher prices.

In the long run, the banning of all quantity discounts may not help even the small retailers—the main focus of Congress's concern when the Robinson-Patman Act was passed. If the banning of discounts on salt encouraged the large chains to produce their own salt (that is, to vertically integrate into salt production), then Morton's output would decline, its average costs might increase, and Morton might increase its price to small retailers that were unable to produce their own salt. Under such circumstances, the difference between what large and small retailers pay for salt might increase.

TABLE 15.4 **Morton Salt's Prices for Different Quantities**

Quantity	Price per Case
Less than carload	$1.60
Carload	$1.50
5000 carloads/year	$1.40
50,000 carloads/year	$1.35

STANDARD OIL OF INDIANA CASE[14] (1958) The next major secondary-line case involved the other major defense established in the Robinson-Patman Act, the good-faith meeting of competition. Standard Oil had followed a policy of charging four large Detroit jobber-retailers prices that were 1.5 cents per gallon less than prices charged its service station customers. Each of the four jobbers sold some of their gasoline at retail, and two of the jobbers charged lower retail prices than generally prevailed for Standard's gasoline. The four jobbers took deliveries in tank-car quantities of 8000 to 12,000 gallons, rather than the typical tank-wagon quantities of 700 to 800 gallons that were delivered to service stations. Some cost savings were associated with these large-quantity purchases; however, the Commission ruled that the *entire* 1.5 cent differential could not be cost justified.

Once its cost justification failed, Standard argued that the reductions were made in a good-faith effort to meet competition. The Commission ruled that meeting competition was not an *absolute* defense under Section 2(b). The FTC's argument was a technical one based on Section 2(a) seeming to make only the cost justification an absolute defense, while the meeting competition defense was relegated to Section 2(b), which dealt primarily with the burden of proof in Robinson-Patman Act cases.

The Supreme Court initially ruled that a good-faith meeting of competition established an absolute defense under the Robinson-Patman Act, and the case was remanded to the FTC for reconsideration of Standard's meeting competition defense. On remand the Commission ruled that Standard had not acted in "good faith," but instead was following a simple pricing system in which purchasers of over 2 million gallons a year received a lower price. The case was then appealed for a second time to the Supreme Court.

This time the Court found for Standard because it was persuaded by evidence that between 1936 and 1941 local suppliers had made numerous attempts to take business away from Standard by reducing prices to the large jobber-retailers. There is a major potential problem with this decision and with the act in general. Suppose Sunoco offered an illegal discriminatory price to one of Standard's jobbers. Should Standard be permitted to undercut Sunoco's price? Under the *Cement Institute* precedent, one would think not. Under the *Standard Oil* precedent, however, it appears to be legitimate to match even an illegal price. Furthermore, if Standard is permitted to undercut Sunoco's price, should Texaco be permitted to cut Standard's price, and then should Shell be permitted to cut Texaco's price? In other words, after one price cut in good faith is permitted, shouldn't every subsequent price cut be permitted? If the answer is yes, then the act becomes meaningless. These are not just hypothetical questions. During the litigation period of the *Standard Oil* case, the FTC had similar suits pending against Gulf, Texaco, and Shell. However, prohibiting good-faith defenses in such cases would tend to make prices more rigid. This suggests another of the many dilemmas raised by Robinson-Patman Act enforcement.

The most important precedent emerging from the two *Standard Oil* Supreme Court decisions was the establishment of the good-faith meeting of competition as an absolute defense in Robinson-Patman Act cases.

TEXACO CASE[15] (1990) Between 1972 and 1981, Texaco sold gasoline to 12 independent retailers in Spokane, Washington. Texaco also sold gasoline to two wholesaler-retailers of gasoline, Gull Oil Company and Dompier Oil Company. Gull

sold gasoline under its own name, but Dompier sold gasoline under the Texaco brand name. Texaco sold gasoline to Gull at prices that ranged from 4 to 6 cents below its prices to the 12 independent retailers, and it sold gasoline to Dompier at prices that ranged from 3.65 to 3.95 cents below its prices to the 12 independents. For several years the independents lost sales to Gull and Dompier; then in July 1976 the 12 independents sued Texaco.

The Supreme Court ruled that Texaco's behavior violated the Robinson-Patman Act. The Court rejected Texaco's argument that Gull and Dompier were wholesalers, not retailers, and therefore that the lower prices were justified to cover the expenses associated with their wholesaler operations. It did not help Texaco's case that both Gull and Dompier generally picked up gasoline from Texaco and immediately resold it to consumers. Neither firm had substantial storage facilities. Another point working against Texaco was the company's refusal to allow the independents to haul their own gasoline from Texaco's storage tanks at lower prices.

MCCORMICK SPICES CASE[16] (2000) On April 27, 2000, the FTC filed a complaint against McCormick & Company, the world's largest supplier of supermarket dry spices. At the time of the filing of the complaint, McCormick had already agreed to a consent decree and that decree was filed simultaneously with the complaint. McCormick held, and still holds, a dominant national market share in dried spices. Burns Philip Food is McCormick's only national competitor. While McCormick had a single national price list for all its products, almost no buyers paid the list price. Instead McCormick individually negotiated prices with each of its customers that included substantial discounts off of McCormick's list prices. These discounts included direct cash payments, free products, off-invoice discounts, rebates, and performance incentives. Furthermore, McCormick sometimes demanded that up to 90 percent of the shelf space allotted to spices in a supermarket had to be devoted to its spices. McCormick's market power left buyers with few alternative suppliers. Its power was so significant that the individually negotiated contracts were an attempt to use first-degree price discrimination.

The FTC charged that on at least five occasions between 1994 and 2000 McCormick discriminated in price by providing preferential payments to some buyers that were not offered to the buyers' direct competitors. As a result, McCormick sold its spices at a lower net price to some firms than others. The FTC charged that McCormick's actions caused secondary-line injury to competition to the firms that paid the higher prices.

The consent decree prohibited McCormick from discriminating in price between buyers unless the discrimination was based on one of the two Robinson-Patman Act defenses, either cost justification or meeting competition. The decree also required McCormick to notify the FTC of any use of price discrimination for 10 years. The *McCormick* case surprised many legal and economic experts by showing that the *Morton Salt* precedent was still relevant in 2000.

VOLVO CASE[17] (2005) In 2005 the Supreme Court agreed to hear another Robinson-Patman Act case on appeal from the Eighth Circuit Court of Appeals. Reeder-Simco (hereafter Reeder) sells heavy-duty trucks in Arkansas. Most heavy-duty trucks are manufactured after a customer has requested bids from several truck retailers and the

customer has accepted one of the bids. During the bidding process it is common practice for the retailers to solicit discounts from the manufacturers so that the retailer can offer lower prices. Reeder claimed that in violation of the Robinson-Patman Act, Volvo systematically offered other Volvo dealers larger discounts and these larger discounts prevented Reeder from obtaining sales.

Reeder argued that these varying discounts were part of Volvo's plan to eliminate many of its dealers. Much of Reeder's evidence was based on an e-mail that Volvo sent to all its dealers in December 1997. The e-mail announced a new policy called "Volvo Vision" and stated that there were too many Volvo heavy-duty truck dealers and many of the current dealers were underperforming. The message went on to state that Volvo's objective was to reduce the number of dealers from 146 to 75. After receiving the Volvo Vision e-mail, Reeder accidentally was sent a number of faxes that showed Volvo offered larger discounts to other Volvo dealers. For example, in 1999, Reeder requested a 12 percent discount on a sale of 12 trucks to Hiland Dairy. Volvo offered Reeder a 7.5 percent discount. Another Volvo dealer, Southwest Missouri Truck Center, was offered an 8.5 percent discount and obtained the Hiland Dairy contract. Reeder also argued that even on bids that it won, it would have earned higher profits if it had received the same discounts that Volvo offered to other dealers. A District Court jury ruled in favor of Reeder and awarded the plaintiff over $5.6 million in treble damages.

Volvo's defense was centered on the issue of whether or not an unsuccessful bidder is a purchaser in the eyes of the law. For example, with regard to the Hiland Dairy contract, the trucks were purchased by Southwest Missouri Truck Center, not Reeder. According to Volvo, if Reeder did not purchase the trucks from Volvo, Volvo could not be held liable for a Robinson-Patman Act violation. The Eighth Circuit Court rejected Volvo's argument for two reasons. First, prior precedent recognized that if a "plaintiff's failure to purchase is directly attributable to the defendant's discriminatory pricing practice," then the defendant is liable to attack under the Robinson-Patman Act.[18] Furthermore, there was evidence that on at least four occasions, Reeder purchased Volvo trucks following successful bids for contracts but received smaller discounts than other Volvo dealers received for the same trucks manufactured and sold at the same time. The smaller discounts harmed Reeder by reducing its profits.

By a 3-2 vote, the Court of Appeals upheld the jury's award against Volvo. The Supreme Court decision will help to define the scope of the Robinson-Patman Act in the early twenty-first century. If the Supreme Court upholds the ruling, it will make manufacturers much less likely to offer widely varying discounts to different buyers in markets where competitive bidding is common.

15.5.2 Primary-Line Cases

Primary-line cases deal with injury to direct competitors and are more likely to involve charges of predatory conduct than secondary-line cases. The cases in this section deal with charges of geographic discrimination where large national firms charged dramatically different prices in different sections of the country. Because competitive conditions can vary greatly across geographic regions, these cases again raise the possibility that the law may protect competitors rather than competition.

THE ANHEUSER-BUSCH CASE[19] (1961) In 1954, Anheuser-Busch lowered the price of Budweiser in St. Louis below the price it charged elsewhere. The FTC ruled that this

violated the Robinson-Patman Act, but the Seventh Circuit Court of Appeals held that "the threshold statutory element of price discrimination had not been established." The Circuit Court argued that because Anheuser-Busch charged the same price to all purchasers in St. Louis, there had been no price discrimination.

The Supreme Court overturned the Appeals Court. Chief Justice Warren stated "it is certain at least that Section 2(a) is violated where there is a price discrimination which deals the requisite injury to primary-line competition, even though secondary-line and tertiary-line competition are unaffected."

Having established that geographic discrimination came within the jurisdiction of the Robinson-Patman Act, the Supreme Court remanded the case to the Appeals Court for further consideration. The facts were straightforward. Before its first price decrease, Anheuser-Busch controlled 12.5 percent of the St. Louis beer market. After two price cuts, which lowered Budweiser's prices to equal its competitors' prices, Budweiser's market share increased to 39.3 percent. The price reductions lifted Budweiser from fourth place (last among the majors) to first place in the St. Louis market, but when Anheuser-Busch increased its prices in March 1955, Budweiser's market share declined to 17.5 percent.

The Circuit Court of Appeals dismissed the case for a second time, ruling that Anheuser-Busch's price discrimination had not caused any injury to competition. The Court of Appeals was persuaded by evidence that Anheuser-Busch's competitors continued to control more than three-fourths of sales in the 12 months after the price of Budweiser was voluntarily increased in St. Louis in March 1955. The Court also noted that the primary beneficiaries of Anheuser-Busch's price reductions were St. Louis consumers.

The Circuit Court recognized that Anheuser-Busch's price reductions improved efficiency by bringing price closer to marginal cost and giving consumers a wider choice of popularly priced beers. Furthermore, the Court implicitly recognized that market competition on a local, rather than national, level determines beer prices. The *Anheuser-Busch* case was not appealed back to the Supreme Court. The 1967 *Utah Pie* Supreme Court decision suggested, however, that the FTC might have won such an appeal during the 1960s.

THE UTAH PIE CASE[20] (1967) The *Utah Pie* decision is one of the most controversial antitrust decisions. Utah Pie was a small company that had been baking fresh pies for 30 years when it entered the frozen pie market in 1957. Utah Pie quickly captured 66.5 percent of the Salt Lake City market. Three large national firms, Pet Milk, Continental, and Carnation, also sold frozen pies in Utah. The case centered on the response of the three national firms to Utah Pie's domination of the Salt Lake City market.

Pet Milk produced frozen pies in California and Pennsylvania, yet its pies sometimes were selling at significantly lower prices in Salt Lake City than in markets located closer to Pet's manufacturing plant in California. Similarly, in June 1961 Continental offered its large apple pies at $2.85 per dozen in Utah, a price well below its apple pie prices in other markets. Evidence suggested that the $2.85 price may have been below "its direct cost plus an allocation for overhead." Finally, in 1959 Carnation cut its price by 60 cents per dozen in Utah, and the Supreme Court concluded that at this price, Carnation was selling pies at prices *below* average total cost.

Some evidence suggested that at some time each of the defendants attempted to cut into Utah Pie's market share by cutting prices. Utah Pie's market share did decline from 66.5 percent in 1958, to 34.3 percent in 1959, 45.5 percent in 1960, and 45.3 percent in 1961. Utah Pie, however, generally remained the leading seller. Furthermore, Utah Pie remained a profitable company throughout the four-year period under investigation.

The Circuit Court of Appeals dismissed the case, holding that the evidence failed to support a finding of *injury to competition*. The Supreme Court overturned the Appeals Court decision because of the evidence of predatory *intent* and a belief that "the Act reaches price discrimination that erodes competition as much as it does price discrimination that is intended to have immediate destructive impact."

It is easy to understand why the *Utah Pie* decision created so much controversy. The case concerned the largely unsuccessful attempt of three competitors to break a firm's 66.5 percent domination of a local market by cutting prices in a temporary and rather sporadic manner. Without question the effect of these price reductions on consumers and short-run welfare was positive, with prices reduced to levels closer to marginal cost.

There is, however, another side to the case. The Supreme Court believed that each of the three national firms showed some evidence of predatory intent. Evidence suggested that Pet Milk went so far as to send an industrial spy into Utah Pie's plant. Furthermore, although prices always covered marginal costs, there was serious doubt that they always covered average total costs. Finally, below-cost pricing can clearly be used by large national firms in local markets to attempt to destroy local competition. If such behavior is always permitted, it might result in long-run problems because a few large national firms could come to dominate many markets by establishing a tough reputation.

The *Utah Pie* decision resulted in a great deal of criticism from economists and was a major impetus for the seminal article by Areeda and Turner in which they argued that only prices below *marginal* cost should be considered predatory. Furthermore, because marginal costs are difficult to calculate, Areeda and Turner advocated using *average variable cost* as a proxy for marginal cost.[21] Areeda and Turner's position was in turn criticized by many economists who argued that it was extreme.[22] Critics noted that carrying Arreda and Turner's recommendation to its logical conclusion, only prices below average variable cost are predatory, which implies that only prices below a firm's short-run shutdown price are predatory. Although such a strict standard may occasionally be breached by a firm obsessed with the destruction of a competitor, virtually all price discrimination takes place at prices well above average variable costs.

GENERAL FOODS CASE[23] (1984) Recall from Chapter 11 that General Foods, the producer of Maxwell House coffee, had responded aggressively to the East Coast entry of Procter & Gamble, the producer of Folgers coffee. Briefly, the facts were as follows. In 1970 General Foods held approximately a 43 percent national market share for noninstant coffee. Most of that share was held by Maxwell House. In 1971 Procter & Gamble began to market Folgers in the East by selling in four test markets. In response to Folgers's entry, General Foods greatly reduced the price of Maxwell House in the test markets. Evidence suggested that Maxwell House was sold at prices below marginal and average variable costs. In the late winter of 1974, for example, Maxwell

House was sold for $2.095 per three-pound can in Pittsburgh, whereas the price of a three-pound can of unroasted green coffee beans was $2.10.

Despite the evidence of below-cost pricing, the Federal Trade Commission dismissed the case because no injury to competition had been proved. The Commission noted, "The principal effect of the heated rivalry between Folgers and Maxwell House has been to reduce the prices consumers pay for coffee and promote product quality. . . . Healthy competition does not violate the Robinson-Patman Act."

The FTC seemed to take a rather limited view of the Robinson-Patman Act in the *General Foods* case. In this case evidence of prices below average variable cost was still not sufficient to result in a finding in support of the FTC staff.

15.5.3 Illegally Induced Price Discrimination

The Robinson-Patman Act was passed in large part to prevent major chain stores with *monopsony* power from inducing lower prices from suppliers. Section 2(f) was aimed directly at this behavior; however, very few successful cases have been filed under Section 2(f). This lack of success can be traced back to the 1953 *Automatic Canteen* precedent.

AUTOMATIC CANTEEN CASE[24] (1953) Automatic Canteen operated more than 230,000 candy vending machines, so it purchased a great deal of candy. It constantly requested lower prices from its candy suppliers under the threat of cutting off its purchases. Furthermore, Automatic Canteen would often estimate its suppliers' cost savings on large-quantity sales to Automatic Canteen and then inform its suppliers of the prices it would find acceptable.

Evidence suggested that this was a classic attempt by a large buyer to induce price concessions from suppliers. In other words, it was precisely the problem Congress had in mind when it passed the Robinson-Patman Act. The Supreme Court, however, ruled in favor of Automatic Canteen.

The Court concluded that a buyer was not liable under the Robinson-Patman Act if the induced lower prices were either "within one of the seller's defenses such as the cost justification or not known by him to be within one of those defenses." In the *Automatic Canteen* case the Court essentially stated that ignorance of the law was a defense.

By placing a heavy burden of proof on the Commission in Section 2(f) cases, the Supreme Court made successful prosecution very difficult. After the *Automatic Canteen* decision, there was little chance of an FTC victory in a Section 2(f) case, unless a seller informed a buyer that the buyer was requesting an illegal discriminatory price. The Supreme Court reinforced this position in 1979 in the A&P case.

THE A&P CASE[25] (1979) In 1965 A&P solicited a bid from Borden to supply A&P's 200 Chicago stores with private-label milk. Borden offered a plan that would have saved A&P $410,000 a year, but A&P was dissatisfied with the offer and solicited a competitive bid from Bowman Dairy. Bowman made a bid that would have saved A&P $737,000 a year. A&P's Chicago buyer then informed Borden, "I have a bid in my pocket. You [Borden] people are so far out of line it is not even funny. You are not even in the ball park." A&P's buyer also told Borden that a $50,000 further reduction "would not be a drop in the bucket." Borden then offered an $820,000-a-year discount. When it made this offer, Borden emphasized that it was only attempting to meet Bowman's offer.

The FTC ruled that because A&P knew that it was the beneficiary of an illegally low price, it had violated Section 2(f). The Second Circuit Court of Appeals affirmed the FTC order, but the Supreme Court overturned it. Justice Stewart wrote that "since Borden had a meeting-competition defense and thus could not be liable under Section 2(b), the petitioner who did no more than accept that offer cannot be liable under Section 2(f)."

One of the ironies of the Robinson-Patman Act is the minuscule number of cases filed under Section 2(f). Between 1936 and 1966, only 30 of 1100 Robinson-Patman Act cases, or 0.03 percent of all cases, were Section 2(f) cases.[26] One of the major Congressional concerns at the time the law was passed, therefore, has not been addressed successfully by enforcement.

Criticism of the Robinson-Patman Act by economists and judges has had a major impact on enforcement, greatly reducing the number of cases filed by the FTC. For example, although the FTC filed 219 Robinson-Patman complaints in 1963 alone, it filed only two cases in 1975, six cases between 1975 and 1982, and one case between 1983 and 1987.[27]

SUMMARY

1. Price discrimination tends to be a complex economic issue. There are so many different types of discrimination with so many possible effects that it is difficult to make many generalizations.

2. Price discrimination requires some market power.

3. The three basic types of discrimination are first, second, and third degree.

4. First-degree price discrimination improves allocative efficiency and increases welfare.

5. With linear demand curves and linear marginal cost, third-degree discrimination has no effect on output but generally reduces welfare.

6. Among the most common forms of second-degree price discrimination are two-part tariffs, tying, and bundling. A two-part tariff consists of a lump sum payment for a good or service combined with a per-unit user charge. Under a tie-in sales agreement consumers can purchase a good only if they agree to purchase another good. Bundling is a tying agreement in which the goods are purchased in fixed proportions.

7. A two-part tariff may improve welfare. However, if in the absence of the two-part tariff both types of consumers consume the product, a two-part tariff will decrease welfare.

8. It is common for firms that bundle goods to used mixed bundling, where the consumer has a choice of whether to buy the goods separately or bundled.

9. Requirements tie-in sales have been used in an attempt to extend market power in many industries.

10. Price discrimination always redistributes income from consumers to producers.

11 Firms use many different types of price discrimination. Most types of discrimination increase profits.

12 Price discrimination may have either positive or negative effects on both competition and welfare; therefore, it is necessary to analyze the effects of price discrimination on a case-by-case basis.

13 Because many types of price discrimination increase total industry output, price discrimination often has a positive effect on welfare.

14 Price discrimination often results in a redistribution of income that makes value judgments inevitable in any analysis of the effects of price discrimination.

15 Robinson-Patman Act cases are grouped into either *primary-line* or *secondary-line* cases according to their effects on competition. Primary-line cases involve possible injury to a direct competitor. Secondary-line cases involve possible injury to a competitor of a buyer who receives a lower discriminatory price.

16 In 1945 the Supreme Court ruled that basing point pricing systems violated the Robinson-Patman Act. This ruling against the basing point pricing system probably marked the high-water mark for Robinson-Patman Act enforcement.

17 There are two defenses in Robinson-Patman Act cases: meeting competition and cost justification. The burden of proof to successfully use these defenses is high. The cost justification requires a penny-for-penny price reduction.

18 Geographic price discrimination often is procompetitive, but the Robinson-Patman Act does not effectively distinguish procompetitive from anticompetitive price discrimination.

19 Areeda and Turner suggested that only prices below average variable cost should violate the Robinson-Patman Act. This will rarely occur because it requires firms to charge a price below the shutdown price. Other economists have suggested that prices below average total cost might violate the Robinson-Patman Act if there is evidence of predatory intent.

20 Despite the government's reluctance to file cases, private suits still abound, and are likely to continue; therefore, legislative action to abolish or change the law could still have a significant impact.

21 The Robinson-Patman Act has not been entirely without its bright moments. The elimination of basing point pricing systems was a positive accomplishment. Nothing in the act prevents a firm from lowering its prices across the board to *all* buyers in response to a competitor's price reduction. In many cases an across-the-board price reduction would result in large increases in consumer welfare.

22 The costs of enforcement have been high, and the Robinson-Patman Act has resulted in far too many costly legal battles over the right of competitors to compete aggressively through the use of lower prices.

23 A pragmatic approach might be to leave the present act on the books but to limit its use to the few cases of truly anticompetitive price discrimination, particularly the use of price discrimination by dominant firms to discipline rivals. The recent reduction in FTC activity indicates a movement in this direction.

KEY TERMS

basing point pricing system

bundling

first-degree price
 discrimination

foreclosure

mixed bundling

perfect discrimination

predatory discrimination

price discrimination

primary-line cases

primary line market

requirements tie-in sales

second-degree price
 discrimination

secondary-line cases

secondary line market

third-degree price
 discrimination

tie-in sales

two-part tariff

DISCUSSION QUESTIONS

1. Consider the following examples of price discrimination. What type of price discrimination, first-degree, second-degree, or third-degree, does each represent?
 a. If you buy one pair of Levi jeans, you can buy a second pair at half price.
 b. Senior citizens receive a cup of coffee for $0.50 at McDonald's, but everyone else pays $0.99.
 c. Five tickets to the Super Bowl are auctioned to the highest bidders. The tickets sell for $12,000, $11,990, $11,980, $11,975, and $11,970, respectively.

2. Suppose Microsoft charges computer manufacturers a fixed fee to place Windows on any of their computers up to 100,000 units per year per company. Is Microsoft practicing a form of price discrimination? Which firms benefit under this system?

 How could Microsoft's policy make it difficult for the manufacturers of competing operating systems to have their operating systems installed on new computers by computer manufacturers?

3. It is common for movie theaters to charge lower admissions for children than for adults, but the theaters do not charge children and adults different prices for popcorn and soft drinks. Can you explain why theaters do not discriminate in popcorn and soft drinks?

4. Does the use of first-degree price discrimination ensure that the allocatively efficient output will be produced? How about second-degree discrimination?

5. Suppose Eat-Em-Up Pie Company produces frozen pies in a small town in Montana. In Montana, Eat-Em-Up has a 75 percent market share, but its market share is zero outside the state. If a large national producer that produced pies in California and held a 50 percent national market share in the frozen pie market entered the Montana market and charged prices in Montana that were 50 percent below the prices charged in California, would this be an example of price discrimination? Could this policy have a negative effect on competition? What factors would you consider in answering this question?

6. Explain how requirements tie-in sales can enable firms to practice price discrimination. Does this price discrimination tend to improve economic efficiency?

7. Give some examples of how professional sports franchises tie products together.

8. Explain the difference between bundling and requirements tie-in sales. Give an example of each.

9. For each of the following scenarios, identify which type of price discrimination is described (first degree, second degree, or third degree).
 a. Although illegal, a local car dealership researches the income, number of children, and debt load of each consumer before negotiating on price. It then offers a price for the car based on each consumer's characteristics.
 b. A local retail store has a "buy one, get the second one at half price" deal on all remaining seasonal clothing items.

c. A phone company charges different rates based on the time of day the phone call is placed (lower rates in the evenings and on weekends than during weekdays).

10. A local department store offers 10 percent discounts on Tuesdays for all senior citizens for any purchase they make. As an economist, you are perplexed by this policy, because you do not believe this method of price discrimination is effective (increases the store's profits). You recommend that the store stop the price discrimination policy. Explain why.

11. One of the original objectives of the Robinson-Patman Act was to protect small retailers from large chain stores. In the long run, has the act protected small retailers from large chain stores? Why or why not?

12. Has the government's decision to file fewer Robinson-Patman Act cases in recent years been a wise decision?

13. Every year a significant number of American college students study in London. Many of these students obtain flats (apartments) from one of a number of rental agencies specializing in finding short-term rentals for American students. Typically, the agency charges every student the same weekly rental, about £120 per week, but the quality of the flats varies greatly, ranging from luxurious flats for two in Kensington to dilapidated flats for five in Bayswa-

ter. Would an economist consider this a form of price discrimination? Would the Robinson-Patman Act consider this price discrimination? Does this suggest a problem with the law?

14. What economic inefficiencies result from successful basing point pricing systems? Why was the basing point pricing system attacked under the Robinson-Patman Act? Did the system violate any other antitrust statutes?

15. What is the difference between a primary-line and a secondary-line Robinson-Patman Act case? What type of case is more likely to result in significant negative effects on competition? Why?

16. Should the Robinson-Patman Act be repealed?

17. How might strict enforcement of the Robinson-Patman Act result in both an increase in vertical integration and a loss of economies of scale?

18. In a 1953 Robinson-Patman Act case, Champion Spark Plug Company was charged with price discrimination in the pricing of its spark plugs to Ford. Champion charged Ford 6 cents for original equipment spark plugs but sold the exact same plugs to wholesalers for 26 cents. Suggest a reason why Champion charged such a low price to Ford for original equipment plugs. The Federal Trade Commission found in favor of Champion in this case. Can you suggest a reason for the Commission's ruling?

PROBLEMS

1. An airplane is about to leave the jetway and take off with 50 empty seats. The regular coach fare is $400 for a seat, and the marginal cost of carrying an extra passenger is $30. Forty standby passengers are hoping to get on the flight. If 10 of those seats can be filled for $200, 25 seats can be filled for $100, and 40 seats can be filled at $40, what is the *socially optimal* fare to charge standby passengers waiting to fill those seats?

 Suppose the profit-maximizing airline must charge all the standby passengers the same price. Should it charge $40, $100, or $200 per ticket? Would the socially optimal result be achieved?

2. Suppose a business traveler is willing to pay $1000 to fly from New York City to Miami on an unrestricted ticket. The business traveler, however, is willing to pay $200 for a ticket with a two-week minimum stay. A vacation traveler is willing to

pay $250 for a ticket with a two-week minimum stay and has no interest in buying a ticket to stay less than a two-week stay. If the marginal cost of the ticket is $100, what is the profit-maximizing pricing policy for the airline? What is total surplus?

What is the profit-maximizing pricing policy if the business traveler is willing to pay $1000 to fly from New York City to Miami on an unrestricted ticket and $200 for a ticket with a two-week minimum stay, and the vacation traveler is willing to pay $250 for a ticket with a two-week minimum stay and $650 for an unrestricted ticket? What is total surplus?

3. Suppose the demand for tickets to the symphony for adults is $P_A = 100 - 2q_A$ and the demand for children is $P_C = 50 - 2q_C$. What is the profit-maximizing pricing policy for the symphony? How many adults and children attend the concert?

If price discrimination were illegal and the symphony had to charge the same ticket price to adults and children, what would be the price of a ticket? How many adults and children would attend the concert?

Which policy results in greater social welfare?

4. Suppose a monopolist sells to two consumers. Consumer 1's demand is $P_1 = 100 - q_1$, and Consumer 2's demand is $P_2 = 50 - q_2$. Marginal cost equals 10. If the monopolist uses a two-part tariff, what will be the maximum fixed fee charged to each consumer? What is the price per unit? What are the monopolist's profits?

5. Suppose that two theaters are willing to pay the following maximum rental fees for *Gladiator* and *Rocky and Bullwinkle*.

The Maximum Price per Film

Theater	Gladiator	Rocky and Bullwinkle
Regal Cinemas	200	140
AMC	120	100

Would it be profitable to bundle the two films together? Explain your reasoning.

6. Suppose that in the two-part tariff example on pages 528–530, everything remained the same except that a government price ceiling prevented the monopolist from charging a per-copy fee above 20. Would the use of a two-part tariff still make sense for the monopolist? What would be the monopolist's profits given the price ceiling?

7. Suppose adults have the following demand curve for a local community theater: $P_A = 30 - \left(\frac{1}{5}\right)q_A$. Children have the demand curve $P_C = 10 - \left(\frac{1}{10}\right)q_C$. Furthermore, $MC = AC = 2$.

 a. Solve for the price charged and number of tickets sold in each separate market. Draw a graph.

 b. Solve for total consumer surplus, total producer surplus, and monopoly profit. Label these areas on your graph from question 7(a).

 c. Now assume the theater wants to charge a single, uniform price in both markets. Solve for the combined demand curve. (Remember: it will have a kink.)

 d. Calculate the uniform price charged and the total amount of tickets sold. Draw a graph of the combined demand, and show the uniform price charged and total amount sold on the graph.

e. Solve for consumer surplus, producer surplus, and monopoly profit with a uniform price. Label these areas on your graph from question 7(d).

f. Compare profit in question 7(b) to profit in question 7(e). Which pricing method does the producer prefer?

g. Prove that, in this case, third-degree price discrimination decreases total welfare.

8. Consider a golf course where each golfer has an identical annual demand function $P = 200 - 4Q$, where P is price per round and Q is rounds per year. MC = AC = \$8. Assume for simplicity that FC = 0.

a. What is the profit-maximizing single price the course should charge each golfer? What is the profit-maximizing level of output? Calculate profit per golfer.

b. Show that the monopolist can make more profit using a two-part tariff with P = MC. Solve for the fixed fee and profit per golfer.

c. Show that even a \$1 increase in price (per round to \$9) would cause profit per golfer to fall from the levels in question 8(b).

9. Consider a monopolist facing two consumers with the following two demand curves for its product: $P_1 = 200 - 4Q_1$ and $P_2 = 122 - 6Q_2$. Assume FC = 0 and MC = \$8.

a. The monopolist decides to use a two-part tariff that permits both consumers to stay in the market. Assume it prices at marginal cost. Solve for each consumer's output and fixed fee under this scenario. What is the monopolist's profit?

b. Show that the monopolist is better off eliminating the low-volume consumer from the market. Solve for the output, fixed fee, and monopolist's profit if the low-volume consumer is eliminated.

10. Nathaniel and Jonathan both love baseball. The minor league team in their town is almost guaranteed to make it to the playoffs. Thus, the following table represents the maximum prices that Nathaniel and Jonathan will pay for regular season tickets and playoff tickets.

	Maximum Price		
	Regular Season	Playoffs	Bundled Price
Nathaniel	\$240	\$60	\$300
Jonathan	\$300	\$40	\$340

a. Compare total revenue for the baseball team under a separate pricing policy and a pure bundled price.

b. Which pricing scheme should the team pick?

c. In what way does your result depend on the way the two demands are correlated? How are Nathaniel's and Jonathan's demand curves correlated? Explain.

11. Consider a situation similar to that in problem 10, but this time, Nathaniel and Jonathan's maximum prices look like this:

	Maximum Price		
	Regular Season	Playoffs	Bundled Price
Nathaniel	\$200	\$40	\$240
Jonathan	\$240	\$48	\$288

a. Compare total revenue for the baseball team under a separate pricing policy and a pure bundled price.

b. Which pricing scheme should the team pick? Explain how your answer is a result of the correlation of the demand curves. How are Nathaniel's and Jonathan's demand curves correlated in this example? Explain.

12. Consider a local fast-food restaurant. The following table shows the maximum price that Alex and Anna will pay for two products: chicken nuggets and fries.

	Maximum Price		
	Chicken Nuggets	Fries	Bundled Price
Alex	$1.50	$1.50	$3.00
Anna	$2.55	$0.45	$3.00

Assume the marginal cost of chicken nuggets is $1.00 and the marginal cost of fries is $0.50.

a. Are Alex and Anna's demands negatively or positively correlated? Explain.

b. Compare all four possible single-item pricing policies to find the profit-maximizing single-item pricing policy.

c. Solve for profit if the restaurant engages in pure bundling.

d. Assume the restaurant engages in mixed bundling and charges $3.00 for a bundle, $2.52 for chicken nuggets, and $1.50 for fries. Show that the profit obtained under mixed bundling will be higher than that under pure bundling or single-item pricing.

13. Consider a local fast-food restaurant. The following table shows the maximum price that Alex and Anna will pay for two products: chicken nuggets and fries. Assume the marginal cost of chicken nuggets is $1.00 and the marginal cost of fries is $0.50.

	Maximum Price		
	Chicken Nuggets	Fries	Bundled Price
Alex	$1.50	$2.00	$3.50
Anna	$2.50	$1.00	$3.50

a. Compare all four possible single-item pricing policies to find the profit-maximizing policy.

b. Solve for profits if the restaurant engages in pure bundling.

c. Assume the restaurant engages in mixed bundling and charges $3.50 for a bundle, $2.45 for chicken nuggets, and $2.00 for fries. Show that the profit obtained under mixed bundling is not higher than that under pure bundling.

d. Explain why mixed bundling does not yield higher profits in this case.

NOTES

1. A.C. Pigou, *The Economics of Welfare* (London: Macmillan, 1920), pp. 240–256.

2. This result was first identified by Joan Robinson. See Joan Robinson, *The Economics of Imperfect Competition* (London: Macmillan, 1933).

3. David A. Malueg, "Bounding the Welfare Effects of Third-Degree Price Discrimination," *American Economic Review* 83 (September 1993): 1011–1021.

4. For a brief derivation see J. Tirole, *The Theory of Industrial Organization* (Cambridge: MIT Press, 1988), pp. 137–139. See also H. Varian, "Price Discrimination and Social Welfare," *American Economic Review* 75: (1985): 870–875.

5. Seminal works include: Walter Y. Oi, "A Disneyland Dilemma: Two-Part Tariffs for a Mickey Mouse Monopoly," *Quarterly Journal of Economics*

85 (1971): 77–96; and Richard Schmalensee, "Monopolistic Two-Part Pricing Arrangements," *The Bell Journal of Economics* 12 (1981): 445–466. See also Michael Katz, "Nonuniform Pricing, Output, and Welfare Under Monopoly," *Review of Economic Studies* 50 (1983): 37–56; Michael A. Spence, "Nonlinear Prices and Welfare," *Journal of Public Economics* 8 (1977): 12–18; and Robert Wilson, *Nonlinear Pricing* (Oxford: Oxford University Press, 1993).

6. George Stigler, "A Not on Block Booking," in George Stigler, *The Organization of Industry* (Homewood, IL: Richard D. Irwin, 1968).

7. The following analysis is based on William J. Adams and Janet L. Yellen, "Commodity Bundling and the Burden of Monopoly," *Quarterly Journal of Economics* 90 (1976): 475–498.

8. See Ian L. Gale and Thomas J. Holmes, "Advance-Purchase Discounts and Monopoly Allocation," *American Economic Review* 83 (March 1993): 135–146.

9. *Corn Products Refining Company et al.* v. *Federal Trade Commission*, 324 U.S. 726 (1945).

10. *Federal Trade Commission* v. *Cement Institute et al.*, 333 U.S. 683 (948).

11. See *In the Matter of Boise Cascade Corporation*, FTC Docket 8958 (1978).

12. Don E. Waldman, "Welfare and Collusion: Comment," *American Economic Review* 72 (March 1982): 268–272.

13. *Federal Trade Commission* v. *Morton Salt Company*, 334 U.S. 37 (1948).

14. *Standard Oil Company* v. *Federal Trade Commission*, 340 U.S. 231 (1951) and *Standard Oil Company* v. *Federal Trade Commission*, 355 U.S. 396 (1958).

15. *Texaco* v. *Hasbrouck*, 496 U.S. 543 (1990).

16. Federal Trade Commission, *In the Matter of McCormick & Company, Incorporated*, Docket No. C-3939, April 27, 2000.

17. *Reeder-Simco* v. *Volvo GM Heavy Truck*, 374 F.3d 701 (2004).

18. *American Can Co.* v. *Bruce's Juices*, 187 F.2d 919 (1951).

19. *Federal Trade Commission* v. *Anheuser-Busch, Inc.*, 363 U.S. 536 (1960); and *Anheuser-Busch, Inc.* v. *Federal Trade Commission*, 289 F.2d 835 (1961).

20. *Utah Pie Company* v. *Continental Baking Company et al.*, 386 U.S. 685 (1967).

21. P. Areeda and D. Turner, "Predatory Pricing and Related Practices Under Section 2 of the Sherman Act," *Harvard Law Review* 88 (February 1975): 697–733.

22. See F.M. Scherer, "Predatory Pricing and the Sherman Act: Comment," *Harvard Law Review* 89 (March 1976): 869–903; O. Williamson, "Predatory Pricing: A Strategic and Welfare Analysis," *Yale Law Journal* 87 (December 1977): 284–340; and R.H. Koller II, "When Is Pricing Predatory," *Antitrust Bulletin* 24 (Summer 1979): 283–306.

23. *In the Matter of General Foods Corp.*, 103 FTC 204 (1984).

24. *Automatic Canteen Company of America* v. *Federal Trade Commission*, 346 U.S. 61 (1953).

25. *Great Atlantic & Pacific Tea Company* v. *Federal Trade Commission*, 440 U.S. 69 (1979).

26. "Robinson-Patman: Dodo or Golden Rule?" *Business Week* (November 12, 1966): 66.

27. Douglas F. Greer, *Business, Government, and Society* (New York: MacMillan, 1983), p. 203; and Richard A. Whiting, "R–P: May It Rest in Peace," *Antitrust Bulletin* 31 (Fall 1986): 711.

INTERNET EXERCISES

Visit **www.aw-bc.com/waldman_jensen** for this chapter's web exercises. Answer our real-world economics problems by searching the Internet for solutions!

Appendix

The Welfare Implications of Price Discrimination with Nonlinear Demand

Consider Figure 15.12, in which panel (a) shows a nonlinear *elastic* demand and panel (b) shows a nonlinear *inelastic* demand. Marginal cost is constant and equal to zero. The optimal prices with discrimination are P_1 and P_2, respectively, and the optimal single price without discrimination is P*. The actual change in welfare, ΔW, with discrimination is identified graphically as follows:

$$\Delta W = \text{Gain} - \text{Loss} = (\text{Areas A} + \text{B}) - (\text{Areas X} + \text{Y}).$$

From Figure 15.12 it is clear that:

$$\Delta W \geq (\text{Area A}) - (\text{Areas X} + \text{Y} + \text{Z})$$

or $$\Delta W \geq (P_1 - MC)\Delta q_1 + (P_2 - MC)\Delta q_2.$$

(Note that with discrimination $\Delta q_1 > 0$ and $\Delta q_2 < 0$.)

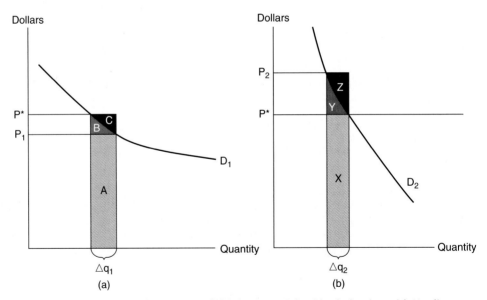

FIGURE 15.12 The Welfare Impact of Third-Degree Price Discrimination with Nonlinear Demand Curves

In panel (a), demand is relatively elastic. In panel (b), demand is relatively inelastic. The optimal price without discrimination is P* and the optimal prices with discrimination are P_1 in panel (a) and P_2 in panel (b). The welfare gain with discrimination is the sum of areas A + B and the welfare loss with discrimination is the sum of areas X + Y or the change in welfare with discrimination, ΔW, equals $(A + B) - (X + Y)$. Therefore, $\Delta W \geq A - (X + Y + Z)$ and $\Delta W \leq (A + B + C) - X$.

In the general case with n different markets:

$$\Delta W \geq \sum_{i=1}^{n} (P_i - MC)\Delta q_i. \qquad \text{[Inequality 15.1]}$$

Inequality 15.1 establishes a *lower bound* for ΔW.

From Figure 15.12 it is also clear that:

$$\Delta W \leq (\text{Areas A} + \text{B} + \text{C}) - (\text{Area X})$$

or

$$\Delta W \leq (P^* - MC)\Delta q_1 + (P^* - MC)\Delta q_2.$$

In the general case with n different markets:

$$\Delta W \leq (P^* - MC)\left(\sum_{i=1}^{n} \Delta q_i\right). \qquad \text{[Inequality 15.2]}$$

This establishes an *upper bound* for ΔW.

In the linear demand example given in Figures 15.3 and 15.5, note that $p_1 = 5.50$, $p_2 = 3.00$, $P^* = 3.625$, $\Delta q_1 = -18.75$, $\Delta q_2 = 18.75$, and $MC = 1.00$. By Inequality 15.1, the lower bound of ΔW is:

$$\Delta W \geq (p_1 - MC)\Delta q_1 + (p_2 - MC)\Delta q_2.$$

or

$$\Delta W \geq (5.50 - 1.00)(-18.75) + (3.00 - 1.00)(18.75) = -84.375 + 37.5 = -46.875,$$

and by Inequality 15.2, the upper bound is:

$$\Delta W \leq (3.625 - 1.00)(-18.75 + 18.75) = 0.$$

In the example in Figures 15.3 and 15.5, it follows that:

$$-46.875 \leq \Delta W \leq 0.$$

The actual change in welfare for the example was calculated in Table 15.2 as -23.4375, which, not surprisingly for linear demand, is right in the middle of the upper and lower bound.

An examination of Inequality 15.2 reveals that any discrimination that results in a reduction in total output (i.e., $\sum \Delta q_i < 0$) *must* lower welfare. Furthermore, even if total output increases so that the upper-bound welfare change is positive, Inequality 15.1 may result in a lower-bound welfare change that is negative, so welfare may still be reduced by price discrimination.

Vertical Integration and Vertical Relationships

C hapter 2 explored the boundaries of the firm. Recall that firms often perform functions internally rather than using the market in an attempt to reduce transactions costs. It is important to bear in mind as you read this chapter that most vertical integration aimed at reducing transactions costs will have positive efficiency and welfare effects.

This chapter examines the theoretical effects of vertical integration and vertical relationships between independent firms, with an emphasis on the conduct and performance implications of vertical relationships. A balancing act is taking place in this chapter. In the first half of the chapter, we show that vertical integration and vertical relationships have a positive economic impact because they solve several potential economic problems. The second half of the chapter examines the potential problems associated with vertical integration and vertical relationships. This balancing act is a delicate one and should be taken seriously.

16.1 Vertical Relationships as a Solution to Economic Problems

C onsider the simplest possible vertical structure, in which an **upstream** wholesaler, perhaps a gasoline jobber, sells to a **downstream** retailer, say, a gasoline retailer, and the retailer simply turns around and sells the product to the final consumer. To simplify this model, it is common to assume that the transactions costs of transferring and delivering the good from one stage to another are zero. This implies that if a competitive gasoline retailer purchases a gallon of gasoline at a wholesale price P_W equal to \$2.50, the retailer will sell the gallon to consumers at a retail price P_R equal to \$2.50, that is, $P_W = MC_R = P_R = \$2.50$.

Any of the following situations is theoretically possible:

Case	Wholesaler is:	Retailer is:
A	Competitive	Competitive
B	Competitive	Monopolist
C	Monopolist	Competitive
D	Monopolist	Monopolist

Under which, if any, of these four competitive environments would vertical integration affect price and profits? In case A, both the wholesaler and retailer operate in perfectly competitive markets; price equals marginal cost everywhere, and vertical integration would have no impact on price.

Figure 16.1 depicts case B with a competitive wholesaler and a monopolist retailer. The downward-sloping demand curve, D_R, and marginal revenue curve, MR_R, represent final retail consumer demand and marginal revenue, respectively. The MC_W curve represents the marginal cost of the product to the wholesalers (for example, the wholesalers' cost per gallon of gasoline). With case B the competitive wholesalers must charge a price equal to marginal cost, so $P_W = MC_W$. The monopolist retailer then takes that price as its marginal cost and charges the profit-maximizing price P_R to consumers. Note that P_R is the joint profit-maximizing price so that a profit-maximizing vertically integrated firm would also charge P_R. In this case the outcome is the same, regardless of whether there is vertical integration.

Figure 16.2 depicts case C with a monopolist wholesaler and a competitive retailer. The downward-sloping retailer demand curve, D_R, is also the demand curve D_W for the monopolist wholesaler, because the quantity along D_R represents the quantity of the good that retailers will sell at any given wholesale price. The marginal revenue curve for the monopolist wholesaler is therefore MR_W. The MC_W curve again represents the marginal cost of the product to the wholesaler. With case C the monopolist

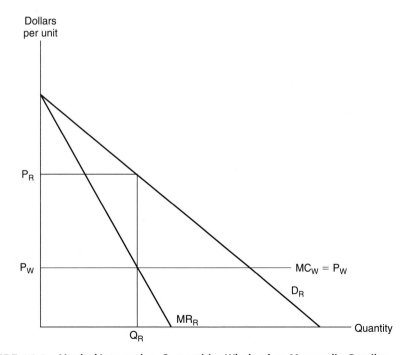

FIGURE 16.1 **Vertical Integration: Competitive Wholesalers, Monopolist Retailer**

With a competitive wholesaler and a monopolist retailer, the wholesaler price P_W equals MC_W and the monopolist retailer maximizes profit by equating MR_R with MC_W; therefore, the market price equals P_R.

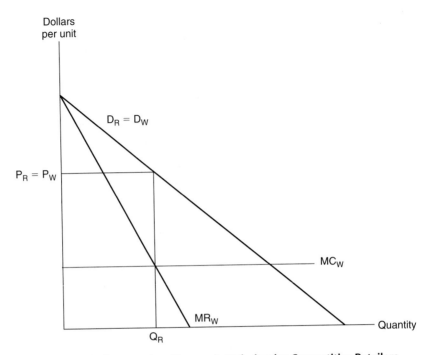

FIGURE 16.2 Vertical Integration: Monopolist Wholesaler, Competitive Retailers

With a monopolist wholesaler and competitive retailers, the monopolist wholesaler faces a demand curve $D_W = D_R$, equates MC_W to MR_W, and charges price P_W to the competitive retailers. The competitive retailers sell the good at the price $P_W = P_R$.

wholesaler sets $MC_W = MR_W$ and charges P_W. The wholesale price P_W becomes the competitive retailers' marginal cost, so $P_W = MC_R = P_R$. Once again, as in case B, P_R is the price that a profit-maximizing vertically integrated firm would charge. Thus, in case C, vertical integration again has no effect on output or price.

16.1.1 The Problem of Double Marginalization

Now consider case D shown in Figure 16.3. Surely with monopoly in both vertical stages, vertical integration must have some effect on price, and it does.[1] The key distinction between Figure 16.3 and Figures 16.1 and 16.2 is that the *marginal revenue* curve of the retailer is now the *demand curve* for the wholesaler. The wholesaler knows that because the retailer will restrict output according to its marginal revenue curve MR_R, the wholesaler's demand at any given wholesale price will be identical to the MR_R curve. If the wholesaler's demand is $D_W = MR_R$, then the wholesaler's marginal revenue curve becomes MR_W. The profit-maximizing wholesaler now sets $MC_W = MR_W$ and charges price P_W. The retailer then takes P_W as its marginal cost, sets $MC_R = MR_R$, and charges a price of P_R. The wholesaler earns an economic profit equal to P_WDFG.

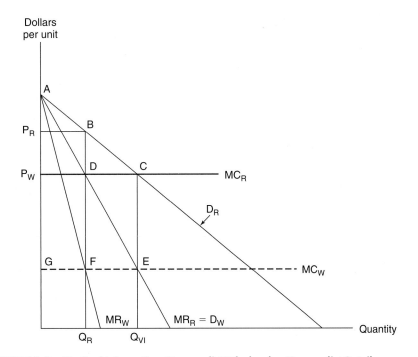

FIGURE 16.3 **Vertical Integration: Monopolist Wholesaler, Monopolist Retailer**

With a monopolist wholesaler and a monopolist retailer, the monopolist wholesaler faces a demand curve $D_W = MR_R$, equates MC_W to MR_W, and charges price P_W to the monopolist retailer. Output is Q_R. The monopolist retailer takes P_W as its marginal cost MC_R, equates MC_R to MR_R, and charges a retail price P_R. If the two monopolists merged, the vertically integrated monopolist would maximize profit by equating MC_W to MR_R and charging a retail price $P_W < P_R$; output would increase to Q_{VI}.

The retailer earns a profit of $P_R BDP_W$, and consumer surplus equals triangle ABP_R. Combined profits are equal to area $P_R BFG$.

If the two monopolists vertically integrated, the firm would maximize profits by considering the internally evaluated marginal cost of the wholesale product to be MC_W, not P_W. As a result the integrated firm would charge a retail price of P_W, joint profits would be maximized and equal to area $P_W CEG$, and consumer surplus would equal triangle ACP_W. Vertical integration is better for the two monopolists because area $P_W CEG$ is larger than area $P_R BFG$ and better for consumers because area ACP_W is larger than area ABP_R. In this case, public policy should do everything possible to encourage vertical integration.

This conclusion is often associated with the Chicago school of economics, even though the model was developed by Joseph Spengler of Duke University.[2] Because of **double marginalization,** each successive stage of monopoly causes a greater price distortion compared with a vertically integrated firm. If the above logic is correct, then in

cases A, B, and C, vertical integration has no welfare implications, and in case D, vertical integration increases output, lowers price, and improves economic welfare. Therefore, public policy should encourage as much vertical integration as possible where successive market power exists.

16.2 Alternative Methods of Achieving Joint Profit Maximization

The Spengler model provides a valuable framework for understanding why certain types of **vertical restraints** are common. *Vertical restraints* refer to a variety of methods used by manufacturers to limit the ways in which retailers can market their product. Three of the most common vertical restraints are **franchise fees,** whereby a manufacturer requires its retailers to pay a fixed fee for the right to sell the product, **resale price maintenance agreements,** whereby the manufacturer sets a minimum or maximum retail price, and **exclusive dealing,** whereby the retailer agrees to purchase its entire supply of a good from one manufacturer, and therefore, the retailer sells only that manufacturer's goods.[3] McDonald's, for example, requires its franchises to pay a franchise fee for the right to open a McDonald's restaurant. For many years Levi Strauss required the retailers of its jeans to abide by a resale price maintenance agreement that set a minimum permissible sale price for its jeans. Suppose that in the two-monopolist case in Figure 16.3, the wholesaler charges the retailer a price per unit equal to MC_W but also charges a fixed franchise fee equal to area P_WCEG. The retailer will then charge the joint profit-maximizing price of P_W but earn only a normal profit because the entire area P_WCEG is transferred to the wholesaler. The franchise fee eliminates the problem of "double marginalization" and improves welfare compared with successive stages of monopoly.

A resale price maintenance agreement could also improve welfare. Suppose the wholesaler sells the good to the retailer at some price between MC_W and P_W in Figure 16.3 and then sets a *maximum* retail price of P_W. Again the joint profit-maximizing result will be achieved. Profits will be divided according to the wholesale price. If the wholesale price is set close to MC_W, the retailer makes the bulk of the profit, whereas if the wholesale price is set close to P_W, the wholesaler makes most of the profit.

Exclusive dealing can improve welfare as well. First, exclusive dealing generally lowers transactions costs because both the manufacturer and retailer spend less time and effort searching for buyers (which lowers manufacturers' transactions costs) and suppliers (which lowers retailers' transactions costs). Second, manufacturers are likely to spend more time and effort training retailers if the manufacturers know that the retailers will sell only their products. This results in improved efficiency on the part of retailers because they know more about the product and can provide better information and service to buyers. Third, manufacturers are likely to spend considerably more on advertising and promotional services that benefit the retailers if the manufacturers know that retailers cannot sell alternative, lower-priced, nonadvertised substitute products to consumers. Exclusive dealing, therefore, is another method manufacturers can use to overcome the potential problems associated with double marginalization.

16.2.1 The Problem of Insufficient Promotional Services[4]

In addition to simply carrying a selection of products, retailers provide pre-sale services to consumers. In fact, in some instances consumers select products primarily on the basis of the quality of pre-sale service. Stride Rite controls a large share of the "high-quality baby shoes" market because it is famous for having retailers who know how to fit baby shoes. Suppose that a monopolist wholesaler, Stride Rite, sells a product through a series of competitive independent retailers. The situation is like case C above with a monopoly at the wholesale level and a competitive retail market.

The demand for Stride Rite shoes is a function not only of price but also of the pre-sale services provided by Stride Rite's retailers. Demand can be represented as:

$$Q = D(P, S), \qquad\qquad [16.1]$$

where the quantity demanded, Q, increases with either a decrease in price, P, or an increase in pre-sale services per unit of output provided by retailers, S.

The situation is identical to that depicted in Figure 16.2. Without vertical restrictions, the competitive retailers have little or no incentive to supply services in this case because no matter what level of service they provide, competitive retailers will earn zero economic profit. In fact, if one retailer tried to provide greater pre-sale services, it would have higher costs and be driven out of the market.* Suppose that initially all retailers provide no service, S = 0. The situation is shown in Figure 16.4, where Q = D(P, 0) because S = 0. Stride Rite's profits are indicated by the shaded red area. This is clearly not an optimal situation for Stride Rite because an increase in S shifts the demand curve to the right and increases Stride Rite's profits by $(P_W - MC_W)\Delta Q$.

There are several possible solutions to the problem of insufficient promotional services. One possible direct solution is increased vertical integration where the manufacturers purchase the retail outlets and then sell only their own products through those outlets. (See Application 16.1.) As noted above, another possible solution is the use of exclusive dealing, which increases the incentive for manufacturers to provide more advertising and promotional services. (Again, see Application 16.1.) In addition to increased vertical integration and exclusive dealing, there must be some combination of price, call it P*, and services per unit, call it S*, that maximizes the wholesaler's profits. In Figure 16.5 it is assumed that D(P, S*) is the demand curve that maximizes Stride Rite's profits. Suppose Stride Rite charged retailers a price $P_W > MC_W$, and in addition used a resale price maintenance agreement to require retailers to charge a price P*. If $P_W = P* - S*$, then the combination of a wholesale price P_W above marginal cost and a *resale price maintenance (RPM)* price set at a maximum price of P* would achieve the joint profit-maximizing result. That combination of policies forces the competitive retailers to provide services, S*, costing $(P* - P_W)$ per unit of sales so that retail profits are driven down to zero.

To understand why the retailers have an incentive to provide services, consider the initial imposition of such a policy in place of a policy of charging price P_W without RPM. Figure 16.5 shows that the imposition of RPM at price P* initially results in

*If one retailer tries to provide services of value to consumers and raises price to cover the costs of these services, then consumers can use the services and buy the good at a lower price from a "no-service," low-price retailer. This is an important case of *free riding*, which is discussed on p. 579.

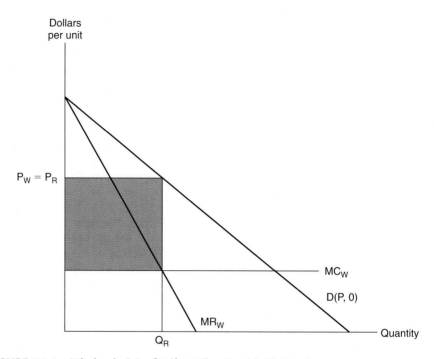

FIGURE 16.4 Wholesaler's Profits if Retailers Provide No Service

With a monopolist wholesaler Stride Rite and competitive retailers, if the retailers provide no service, then Stride Rite faces a demand curve D(P, 0) equates MC_W to MR_W, and charges price $P_W = P_R$ to the competitive retailers. The competitive retailers sell the good at the price $P_W = P_R$ and Stride Rite earns profit equal to the shaded red area.

excess economic profits for the retailers because with no service (the initial situation) $P^* > P_W = AC_R$. The excess profits would encourage established and new retailers to compete by providing better service. The increased provision of services would increase demand and force incumbent competitive retailers to also provide services. In long-run equilibrium all retailers must provide the same level of services and earn zero economic profit.

Consider the welfare implication of the imposition of RPM. In Figure 16.6 combined consumer and producer surplus with no service equals areas B + C + E. With RPM consumer surplus equals areas A + B, producer surplus equals areas E + F, and areas C + D represent the cost of services provided by the retailers. RPM increases consumer surplus by area A, but decreases it by area C; producer surplus increases by area F. It follows that the net welfare effect is ambiguous because we do not know the size of areas A + F relative to area C; it will be different for every case. If (areas A + F) > (area C), then welfare increases; and if (areas A + F) < (area C), then welfare decreases.

In Figure 16.6 welfare increases because (A + F) > C. Although this is one possible outcome, Figure 16.7 shows an example in which welfare decreases because (A + F) < C. Bork has argued that Figure 16.6 is the more likely outcome; in his words, RPM is a "means of increasing distributive efficiency and should be permitted

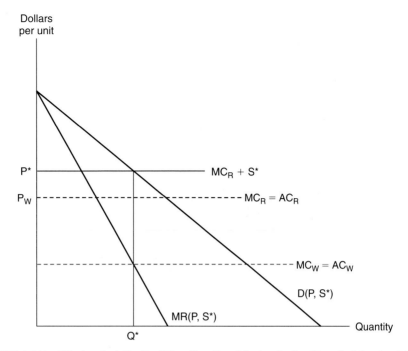

FIGURE 16.5 Wholesaler's Profits if Retailers Provide the Optimal Level of Service, S*

Suppose with monopolist wholesaler Stride Rite and competitive retailers, the combination of price P* and services S* per unit of sales maximizes Stride Rite's profit. Stride Rite's optimal policy is to set an RPM price P* and charge a wholesale price $P_W = P^* - S^*$. The competitive retailers then provide services $S^* = P^* - P_W$ such that demand increases to D(P, S*) and competitive retailers earn zero economic profit.

on grounds of efficient resource allocation."[5] Others have suggested, however, that Figure 16.7 is the more likely outcome because "demand is augmented more by extra service to those with low reservation prices than those who would buy the product even at much higher prices"; as a result, the demand curve is likely to shift *upward* far less for consumers with *high* reservation prices than for consumers with low reservation prices, which is exactly what happens in Figure 16.7.[6] The only definite conclusion is that there is no definite conclusion: RPM agreements aimed at increasing pre-sale services may have either net positive or net negative welfare effects.

APPLICATION 16.1

Vertical Integration, Exclusive Dealing, and the Value of an Upscale Pub's Amenities in Australia

In 2002, Carlton and United Breweries (CUB), which is owned by Foster's Group Ltd., and Lion Nathan dominated the Australian brewing industry with a combined market share of 93 percent. In Australia's second largest regional beer market, Victoria, CUB has been the dominant firm, with more than an 85 percent market share, but Lion Nathan has

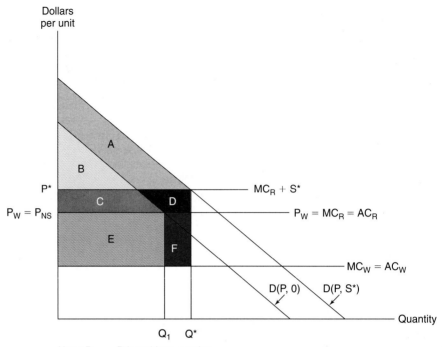

Note: P_{NS} = Price with no service

FIGURE 16.6 **Positive Welfare Effect of Resale Price Maintenance to Induce Service**
With S = 0 and D(P, 0), price equals $P_W = P_{NS}$, consumer surplus equals the sum of areas B + C, and producer surplus equals area E, so total surplus equals the sum of areas B + C + E. With RPM, P = P* and S = S*, and demand is D(P, S*). Consumer surplus equals the sum of areas A + B, producer surplus equals areas E + F, and the sum of areas C + D represents the cost of the retailers' services. Therefore total consumer plus producer surplus equals the sum of areas A + B + E + F. Because (A + F) > C, total welfare increases.

been attempting to make inroads.* The two firms have been competing through a variety of product differentiation strategies including advertising, packaging, and perhaps most importantly, improving the quality of their company-controlled pubs through a rapidly escalating policy of vertical integration and exclusive dealing.

CUB had been vertically integrated into pubs in Victoria for many years; however, in 2000 Lion Nathan began expanding its Victoria pub holdings and its de facto exclusive dealing relationships.[†] In that year, Lion Nathan acquired 45 pubs at a cost of $73 million and invested an additional $40 million in purchasing distribution rights (de facto exclusive dealing rights) for another 260 pubs in Melbourne. In response, CUB expanded its exclusive dealing arrangements with a number of Melbourne pubs. The resulting "quality of pub" competition resulted in the widespread renovation of many of Victoria's pubs.

Donnar and Jakee estimated the economic impact of these increased vertical relationships between the brewers and the pubs by developing a method for measuring the value of the increased pub quality on welfare.[‡] They began by estimating the implicit

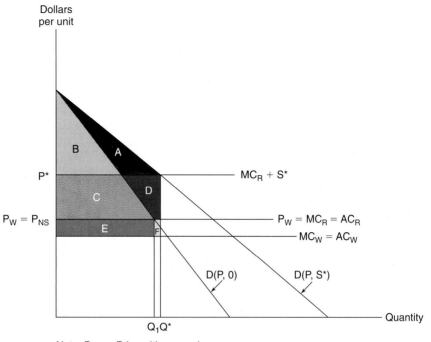

Note: P_{NS} = Price with no service

FIGURE 16.7 **Negative Welfare Effect of Resale Price Maintenance to Induce Serivce**

With S = 0 and D(P, 0), price equals $P_W = P_{NS}$, consumer surplus equals the sum of areas B + C, and producer surplus equals area E, so total surplus equals the sum of areas B + C + E. With RPM, P = P* and S = S*, and demand is D(P, S*). Consumer surplus equals the sum of areas A + B, producer surplus equals area E + F, and the sum of areas C + D represents the cost of the retailers' services. Therefore total consumer plus producer surplus equals the sum of areas A + B + E + F. Because (A + F) < C, total welfare decreases.

value of drinking at a pub as opposed to drinking at home by measuring the difference between the on-premises pub price and the take-away (home consumption) price of alcohol as:

$$P_P = P_O - P_T,$$

where P_P is the value of the pub environment, P_O is the on-premises pub price of alcohol per liter, and P_T is the take-away price per liter. Based on data collected for the year 2001, they estimated $P_P = \$5.96$, $P_O = \$13.32$, and $P_T = \$7.36$. The pub environment, therefore, represented 44.74 percent of total spending.

The total quantity of alcohol consumed in Victoria pubs in 2001 was 134.82 million liters and, combining this figure with the price P_O, Donnar and Jakee estimated the demand for alcohol in Victoria pubs as:[§]

$$P_O = 26.80 - 0.10Q_O.$$

This demand curve is identified as the line D_1 in the figure below. Total expenditures of $1,795.99 million are represented by the area cdhg, and the area cdef represents the $806.53 million expenditure on "pub environment."

The demand curve D_1 includes the value of the renovations to the pubs that, according to an Australian firm specializing in such renovations, averages 10 percent of the value of a typical pub. Donnar and Jakee estimated the total market value of the pub renovations by taking 10 percent of that total market value of the pubs. This figure equaled 10 percent of the $678.1 million total market value of the pubs, or $67.81 million. Next they estimated what the demand curve *would have been* had the $67.81 million renovations *not* taken place. The pre-renovation value of the pub environment per liter was calculated by deducting the $67.81 million total value of the renovations from the $803.53 million total post-renovation value of the pub environment and then dividing this value by the 134.82 million liters of pub alcohol sales; that is, the estimated pre-renovation value of the pub environment per liter was $\dfrac{\$803.53 - \$67.81}{134.82} = \$5.46$ per liter. The price of a take-away liter remained constant at $7.36 both before and after the renovations, and therefore, Donnar and Jakee estimated that the pre-renovation value of a liter at a pub equaled $7.36 + $5.46 = $12.82. In the figure, the pre-renovation

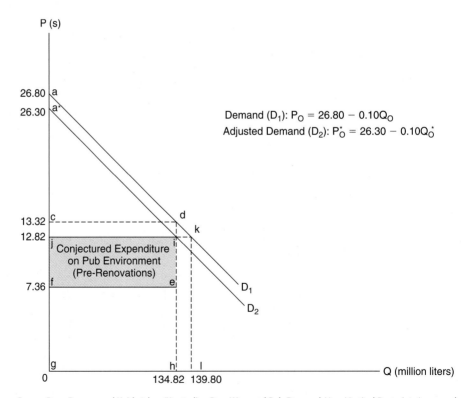

Demand (D_1): $P_O = 26.80 - 0.10Q_O$

Adjusted Demand (D_2): $P_O^* = 26.30 - 0.10Q_O^*$

Source: Ryan Donnar and Keith Jakee, "Australian Beer Wars and Pub Demand: How Vertical Restraints Improved the Drinking Experience," *Applied Economics,* 36 (August 2004): 1620.

demand curve D_2 is estimated to be the linear demand curve $P_O = 26.30 - 0.10Q_O$ that goes through the point i where the price is $12.82 per liter.**

Once the demand curves D_1 and D_2 are identified, it is possible to estimate the welfare change of the improved quality of the pubs by estimating the change in consumer surplus resulting from the renovations *assuming that the price P_O remained constant at the pre-renovation price* of $12.82 per liter. The increase in welfare is the difference between the pre-renovation consumer surplus equal to the area of triangle a*ij, which equals $908.69 million ($\frac{1}{2}(26.30 - 12.82)(134.82) = 908.69$) and post-renovation consumer surplus equal to the area of triangle akj, which equals $977.20 million ($\frac{1}{2}(26.80 - 12.82)(139.80) = 977.20$). In 2001, Donnar and Jakee estimated that consumer welfare increased in Victoria by $67.81 million as a result of the increased vertical integration and exclusive dealing.

*Ryan Donnar and Keith Jakee, "Australian Alcohol Wars and Pub Demand: How Vertical Restraints Improved the Drinking Experience," *Applied Economics*, 36 (August 2004):1615.

†We use the term *de facto* because exclusive dealing in pubs is illegal in Australia even if you own the pub. To get around the prohibition of selling only one's own brands, pubs will stock an unpopular alternative brand and stock very little of it. In addition, the pubs might hide the alternative brew, keeping it completely out of the customers' sight.

‡Donnar and Jakee, "Australian Alcohol Wars and Pub Demand: How Vertical Restraints Improved the Drinking Experience," pp. 1613–1622.

§Donnar and Jakee assumed a linear demand curve $P_O = a + bQ_O$ and, based on previous studies of the elasticity of demand for on-premises alcohol consumption, they assumed an elasticity of demand equal to one. They then derived the demand curve by calculating b from the following equation: $e_p = -1 =$

$\frac{\Delta Q_O}{\Delta P_O} \frac{P_O}{Q_O} = \frac{1}{b} \frac{P_O}{Q_O} = \frac{1}{b} \frac{13.32}{134.82} \Rightarrow b = -0.10$. And then they substituted $b = -0.10$ into $P_O = a + bQ_O$, so

$13.32 = a - 0.10(134.82)$ and $a = 26.80$. The demand curve is then $P_O = 26.80 - 0.10Q_O$.

**The estimated pre-renovation demand curve intercept a* is:

$$12.82 = a^* - 0.10(134.82),$$

and $a^* = 26.30$. And the pre-renovation demand curve for a liter of alcohol in a pub is: $P_O = 26.30 - 0.10Q_O$. ∎

APPLICATION 16.2

The Welfare Effects of Exclusive Dealing in the U.S. Beer Industry

In the U.S. brewing industry, brewers like Anheuser-Busch and Coors sell to independent distributors, who in turn sell to retail outlets. Theory suggests that exclusive dealing can lead to increased promotional investments and efforts by manufacturers and distributors, and these increased promotional efforts can lead to increased costs, higher prices, and increased output. Under this scenario, the welfare effects are ambiguous because demand, price, and output all increase. Exclusive dealing is common in the brewing industry and Anheuser-Busch in particular has used exclusive dealing relationships to market its beers. In 1996, almost 40 percent of Anheuser-Busch's distributors sold only Anheuser-Busch's beers.

Based on data collected in an extensive survey by the National Beer Wholesalers Association, Tim Sass examined the impact of exclusive dealing on the U.S. beer industry

and specifically on brewers' prices, distributors' prices, the dominant firm's output, and total output.* Sass's regressions controlled for many other exogenous factors in addition to the existence of exclusive dealing. These other exogenous variables included the distance from the brewery to the distributor, the height of excise taxes, states' policies toward billboard advertising, income, age, population, stops per distributor's route, years a distributor was owned by its current owner, whether or not a distributor carried imported beer, and each of the individual market shares of Anheuser-Busch, Miller, and Coors.

Using a sample of 203 distributors, Sass found that exclusive dealing had a positive and statistically significant impact on the supplier's average price, the distributor's price of its primary brand, the distributor's per capita sales of the primary brand, and the distributor's per capita sales of all brands. Using a subsample of 109 Anheuser-Busch distributors that included both exclusive and nonexclusive Anheuser-Busch distributors, Sass found identical results. Sass also examined the impact that competing against an Anheuser-Busch exclusive dealer had on rival suppliers' (e.g., Coors', Miller's) average price, rival distributors' price of all brands, and rival distributors' per capita sales of all brands and found that there was *no significant impact* of competing against an Anheuser-Busch exclusive dealer on any of these dependent variables.

Sass concluded that because exclusive dealing (1) increased the sales of the exclusive brand, (2) increased total beer sales, and (3) had no significant impact on the prices of competing brands, it likely had a positive impact on economic welfare. According to Sass, these "empirical results are consistent with the notion that exclusive dealing contracts serve to reduce incentive conflicts between manufacturers and their dealers. . . . As such, [the result] at least casts some doubt on the general applicability of the anticompetitive models of exclusive dealing and suggests that exclusivity may often have net procompetitive impacts in practice."[†]

*Tim R. Sass, "The Competitive Effects of Exclusive Dealing: Evidence from the U.S. Beer Industry," *International Journal of Industrial Organization* 23 (2005): 203–225.

[†]*Ibid.,* pp. 221–222. ∎

16.2.2 Solving the Problem of Input Substitution[7]

In addition to solving the problems of double marginalization and insufficient promotional services, vertical integration and vertical restraints can solve problems associated with inefficient input substitution. Suppose that a monopolist produces good X, using only two inputs, input M and input C. Input M is produced by another monopolist, and input C is produced in a perfectly competitive market. Because the analysis is complex, it is left to an end-of-chapter appendix to show that in the absence of vertical integration or vertical restraints, the monopolist producer of good X would use an inefficient combination of inputs, using "too much" of input C and "too little" of input M, to produce any given output of good X. Vertical integration or vertical restraints can solve this problem.[8]

Thus far most vertical integration and restraints appear to improve economic welfare. The analysis, however, has ignored the possible effects of vertical integration and vertical restraints on market structure and conduct. The next section considers these potential problems.

16.3 The Competitive Effects of Vertical Relationships

16.3.1 Resale Price Maintenance Agreements[9]

Previously, we showed that RPM agreements that fix *maximum* price levels are a possible welfare-improving method of dealing with the problem of double marginalization.* Recall from Figure 16.3 that if the wholesaler sells the good to the retailer at any price between MC_W and P_W and then requires the retailer to sell at a maximum price of P_W, the joint profit-maximizing result will be achieved, and welfare will be increased. In this case RPM is being used to set maximum resale prices, not minimum resale prices. There is little doubt that such maximum resale price fixing improves economic efficiency, even though until recently in the United States the courts have generally frowned on the fixing of maximum prices as a violation of the antitrust laws.[10]

Maximum resale prices have been used in many industries, particularly those in which the product is not physically transformed as it moves from manufacturer to distributor to retailer.[11] Examples include television sets, refrigerators, automobile tires, golf clubs, newspapers, and stereo components.[12] Consider the example of a newspaper publisher with a local monopoly that gives each of its delivery workers an exclusive territory. Each delivery worker has a monopoly in her local territory and, in the absence of a maximum resale price, could exploit her monopoly power. This results in a classic potential double-marginalization problem. In terms of Figure 16.3, the delivery worker wants to set $P = P_R$. If the publisher sets a maximum resale price at P_W, the publisher earns greater profits and improves economic welfare.

Most real-world RPM agreements require the setting of *minimum* rather than *maximum* resale prices. Many studies have shown that, except in rare cases, these RPM agreements result in higher retail prices and, therefore, lower sales for the manufacturer.[13] For example, a study by the Library of Congress concluded that consumers paid between $1.6 billion and $6.2 billion in higher retail prices in states that had legally binding RPM than in states that did not.[14] A study of the impact of RPM on the value of liquor stores compared states with and without RPM between 1974 and 1978, finding that RPM lowered per capita liquor consumption by 8 percent. This study also found that the repeal of RPM lowered liquor store values in California counties that had binding RPM by 23 to 25 percent. This suggests that liquor stores made positive economic profits under RPM and were, therefore, worth more. The study estimated a welfare loss of between $2.5 and $7.5 million as a result of RPM.[15]

It is somewhat surprising that manufacturers would ever set minimum resale prices: Once a manufacturer sets a product's wholesale price, it would normally be in the manufacturer's interest to increase sales by having the product sold at the lowest possible retail price. If RPM generally does not benefit manufacturers, why has it been so commonly used?

Four major arguments have been advanced to explain the adoption of RPM. First, RPM may be the result of collusion among retailers to keep prices high. According to this argument, the most important reason for RPM's popularity has been the desire of

*The Appendix shows that RPM is also a possible welfare-improving method of dealing with the problem of input substitution.

small retailers to compete with large discount stores. Historically, small retailers have put pressure on Congress, and Congress responded by legalizing resale price maintenance with the passage of the ***Miller-Tydings Act*** in 1937. Second, resale price maintenance might make tacit collusion among manufacturers easier to maintain. Third, RPM might prevent retailers from selling high-quality products at low prices or as "loss leaders." According to this theory, if a high-quality product is consistently sold at a low price, consumers will begin to think of it as a low-quality product, and this will hurt the manufacturer in the long run. Finally, RPM has been justified by the argument that some products require high-quality pre-sale service from retailers, and only RPM or vertical integration can ensure the provision of such services. We consider each of these arguments briefly.

Retailer Cartels

RPM agreements may result from collusion among retailers to keep prices high. Suppose, for example, that a group of competitive department stores and drugstores purchases perfume from perfume oligopolists. If the department store and drugstore owners meet at a trade convention and convince all of the perfume manufacturers to set minimum suggested retail prices, the price of perfume can be set above marginal cost.

In this example, RPM is being used by the department stores and drugstores as an effective method of solving the prisoner's dilemma. Price-cutting retailers can be easily identified and punished. Identification will surely be done by competing retailers, and punishment comes in the form of a cutoff of supplies to price cutters. If all the retailers and all the perfume oligopolists abide by the agreement, prices can be increased to the monopoly level and profits divided between the manufacturers and the retailers by charging a wholesale price between the marginal cost of producing the perfume and the profit-maximizing retail price. In this case the vertical restraint is nothing more than an effective method of collusion, and RPM reduces welfare.

One might wonder why the perfume oligopolists do not vertically integrate into retailing, charge the joint profit-maximizing retail price, and capture all of the monopoly profits for themselves. The problem with this solution is that it requires the development of a huge retailing network capable of covering the entire country just to sell perfume. This would be extremely costly, and it is hard to imagine any perfume manufacturer setting up such a national network. Occasionally a manufacturer tries to maintain control over its retail prices by vertically integrating into retailing. Common examples include catalogue companies such as L.L. Bean, Pottery Barn, Williams-Sonoma, and Brookstones that sell exclusively through their catalogues, their Internet sites, or their company-owned stores.

There is reason to believe that few such *retailer cartels* could earn excess profits in the long run. Entry into retailing is typically easy. Even if the RPM results in short-run excess profits, in the long run entry should reduce the retailers' profits by reducing each retailer's volume and increasing the costs of merchandising sales efforts aimed at gaining an advantage over competitors. This probably explains why evidence suggests that relatively few RPM agreements developed primarily because of retailer pressures applied to manufacturers.[16]

Facilitating Manufacturers' Cartels

Resale price maintenance might make it easier for manufacturers to maintain cartel prices. If retail prices are fixed, a manufacturer will have little incentive to reduce prices. Because the price reductions cannot be passed on to consumers, the cuts are likely to have a limited effect on the chiseler's market share.

Empirical evidence is not supportive of this theory. Overstreet found very few industries in which RPM was common and in which concentration was high enough to make a price-fixing conspiracy likely to survive.[17] Telser did find that the American light bulb industry may have used RPM to foster collusion in the early twentieth century, but there are few other documented cases.[18] Overall, facilitating manufacturers' collusion does not appear to explain many RPM agreements.

APPLICATION 16.3

Toys "R" Us as the Facilitator of Toy Manufacturer Collusion

Toys "R" Us is the largest retailer of toys in the United States. In 2000, it sold 20 percent of all the toys sold in the United States. It is critical for major toy manufacturers like Hasbro and Mattel to sell their toys in Toys "R" Us stores. Toys are also sold through other outlets such as Wal-Mart, Target, and retail warehouse clubs Costco and Sam's Club. Until the advent of warehouse clubs, Toys "R" Us was the low-price market leader. During the late 1980s and early 1990s, warehouse clubs began to selectively sell some popular toys at prices 25 to 30 percent below Toys "R" Us prices.

In January 1992, Toys "R" Us responded to the threat from the warehouses by announcing a new policy of restrictive relationships with the toy manufacturers. The policy included the following restrictions on the toy manufacturers:

1. The manufacturers would not supply the warehouse clubs with any new or promoted products unless the clubs carried the entire line.
2. The manufacturers had to give Toys "R" Us the first option to sell all special and exclusive toys before the manufacturers could offer these toys to the clubs.
3. The manufacturers could only sell old and basic toys to the clubs if the toys were sold in special packs.
4. The manufacturers had to give Toys "R" Us the first option to sell all closeouts before the manufacturers could offer these toys to the clubs.

When Toys "R" Us floated this policy with the manufacturers, the manufacturers were reluctant to agree to give up their profitable warehouse club outlets and were concerned that one or more of their rivals would defect from the agreement with Toys "R" Us and sell toys to the clubs. Toys "R" Us then orchestrated an agreement among all of the major toy manufacturers including Mattel, Hasbro, Fisher Price, Tyco, Little Tikes, Today's Kids, and Tiger Electronics not to sell to the clubs on the condition that their competitors would also not sell to the clubs. According to Toys "R" Us President of Merchandising Roger Goddu, "[w]e made a point to tell each of the vendors that we spoke to that we would be talking to our other key suppliers." A Mattel executive stated that Mattel agreed to the Toys "R" Us conditions "based on the fact that competition would do the same," and a Hasbro executive stated it agreed to the policy "because our competitors had agreed not to sell loaded [that is, promoted] products to the clubs[.]"

Once all the manufacturers agreed to the terms of the policy, Toys "R" Us served as a carrier of communications between the manufacturers. Mostly Toys "R" Us communicated manufacturers' complaints that another manufacturer was breaking the agreement. The policy succeeded in reducing the supply of toys for the warehouses and resulted in a decline in the warehouses' market share.

The Federal Trade Commission and the Court of Appeals both ruled that the conduct of Toys "R" Us violated the FTC Act and was an illegal horizontal agreement in restraint of trade. According to the Appeals Court, "[t]hese manufacturers were in effect being asked by [Toys "R" Us] to reduce their output (especially of the popular toys), and as is classically true in such cartels, they were willing to do so only if [Toys "R" Us] could protect them against cheaters."

Source: Toys "R" Us, Inc. v. Federal Trade Commission, 221 F.3d 928 (7th Circuit, 2000). ■

The Establishment of a High-Quality Image

Manufacturers have argued that RPM prevents retailers from damaging their products' images by selling them at low prices or as "loss leaders." Both Levi jeans and Izod alligator shirts may have been victims of this phenomenon when they moved away from RPM.[19] Levi Strauss was persuaded by the FTC to abandon RPM in 1977. Initially Levi's sales increased, but during the early 1980s it lost significant market share to designer jeans such as Gloria Vanderbilt, Ralph Lauren, and Calvin Klein. Similarly, Izod's image and appeal declined as the shirts became widely available.[20]

The welfare implications of the high-quality defense are difficult to assess. If I purchase an alligator shirt, it increases my utility. But if my purchase of an alligator shirt simultaneously decreases your utility, what are the net welfare implications of my purchase? Such circumstances call into question a basic conclusion about the efficiency of markets, because it no longer follows that increased consumption of a good increases consumer surplus. Furthermore, it is important to recognize other ways of dealing with this problem. The manufacturer could simply raise the price of the product, thereby creating an incentive for retailers to charge more. If, for example, Izod increases the price of alligator shirts, retailers almost certainly would charge higher prices. In conclusion, RPM seems like an awkward and indirect method of maintaining a high-quality image.

Ensure Dealer Pre-Sale Services

RPM has been justified by the argument that some products require high-quality pre-sale service from the retailer, and only RPM can ensure such services.* It is certainly true that some products require high-quality pre-sale service from the retailer. For example, high-quality computer manufacturers might require high-quality pre-sale service from their dealers. By imposing RPM on their computer retailers, manufacturers could ensure that the dealers do not compete based on price but, instead, would compete by attempting to provide better service. In the absence of RPM, some computer dealers would provide good, but costly, service and charge high prices, and other dealers would

*The argument does not hold much weight for post-sale services, because a higher-quality service dealership should be able to charge higher prices for post-sale service with little fear of losing significant business to low-quality dealerships.

provide little or no service and charge low prices. Consumers could then shop around at the high-priced, good-service dealers, but purchase their computers at the low-priced dealers. The low-priced dealers would then obtain a *free ride* on the services provided by the high-priced dealers, and over time, the high-priced, good-service dealers might be eliminated from the market.

The prevention of a significant **free rider problem** is the most convincing economic justification for RPM; however, relatively few goods actually require good pre-sale service. The argument may make sense for items such as automobiles, computers, audio and video equipment, and high-quality bicycles, for which in-store pre-sale services are important; it's difficult to believe that Levi's jeans, Izod shirts, Florsheim shoes, or Russell Stover candies, all items commonly sold under RPM, require the provision of good pre-sale service.

Despite the arguments that RPM rarely makes sense for manufacturers, firms continue to use RPM. The continued use of the practice suggests that benefits exist for at least some manufacturers. Perhaps there is a difference between the short-run and long-run effects of RPM. Elimination of RPM may result in short-run gains to manufacturers as more consumers purchase the good, but in the long run the elimination of RPM may result in a serious negative impact on the quality reputation of the good. As we discussed, Levi's jeans and Izod sportswear now have a much less posh reputation than they did under RPM pricing policies.[21]

One final point is that American retailing has become more competitive in the past three decades with the advent of large discount department stores, large outlet malls, and large retail chains such as The Gap and The Limited. With this changing market structure, the potential negative impacts of RPM have declined because manufacturers find it increasingly difficult to refuse to deal with stores in all of these various retail outlets.

16.3.2 Strategic Uses of Vertical Restraints and Integration[22]

Recall from Chapter 12 that entry may be prevented if incumbents are able to raise their rivals' costs. Vertical integration and restraints may be used to raise rivals' costs in a number of ways. Under *exclusive dealing arrangements*, a retailer agrees to carry only one manufacturer's products. One argument in favor of exclusive dealing revolves around the provision of pre-sale services. In the absence of exclusive dealing, a manufacturer may supply a retailer with promotional services, such as advertising and employee training, that increase the flow of consumer traffic into the retail store only to have the retailer, who carries many brands, switch the consumer to a different brand. Classic examples of exclusive dealing include automobile dealerships, Electrolux dealers, and bicycle shops.

Now consider the potential negative effects of exclusive dealing. Under an exclusive dealing arrangement, a manufacturer with market power may be able to prevent entry while still charging a price above the potential entrant's average cost. Consider a monopolist who produces "ABC" brand widgets at $MC = AC = 100$ and sells the widgets at a wholesale price $P = 125$. Assume a potential entrant can produce a similar widget for the same $MC = AC = 100$. To enter effectively, the potential entrant must find dealers willing to take its product. If the monopolist makes it a clear and overtly

stated policy that *any* dealer that accepts another firm's widgets will be immediately cut off from its supply of "ABC" widgets, entry can be deterred while the price of "ABC" widgets can be maintained at a level above average cost. To make the threat credible, any dealer that accepts competitors' widgets must be cut off quickly by the monopolist.

According to Comanor and Frech, this is exactly what happened in the United States market for silicone sealants in the 1970s.[23] Rhodia attempted to enter the sealants market by selling at a much lower price than the dominant firm, General Electric. GE controlled a 75 percent market share and sold its sealants through exclusive dealerships. When one of GE's largest dealers, C. R. Laurence, began to market Rhodia's sealants, GE responded immediately by dropping Laurence from its dealership list. As a result, no other GE dealers marketed Rhodia's sealants and further erosion of GE's market share was prevented.

Vertical integration also may be used strategically to raise the price of inputs for competitors. Suppose that a dominant manufacturer is vertically integrated into an important input and fringe manufacturers are not.[24] Because of economies of scale, the integrated manufacturer can produce the input at a lower cost than it can buy it from small unintegrated input manufacturers. The integrated manufacturer can then purchase enough of the input from independent suppliers to increase the price of the input. This will increase its rivals' costs because the unintegrated rivals must purchase the input from independent suppliers at a higher price.

In this scenario the integrated firm's average costs increase in proportion to its purchase of the input. If, for example, purchases by the integrated manufacturer increase the input price by $1.00 per unit, and the integrated manufacturer produces 75 percent of the input internally and purchases 25 percent from unintegrated input suppliers, the integrated manufacturer's average cost will increase by $(0.25) \times (\$1.00) = \0.25. For the unintegrated fringe manufacturers, however, average costs would increase by the full $1.00 per unit, and the fringe supply would decrease.

Because this policy raises the integrated firm's costs, profits are reduced. The policy makes sense, therefore, only if the reduction in profits caused by the higher input cost is more than offset by an increase in profits that will result from a reduction in the supply of the fringe firms. As the fringe manufacturers reduce output, the integrated firm's output should increase, and this increase in output should result in increased profits. In this case the effect on welfare is unambiguously negative because both costs and price increase.

As discussed in Chapter 4, in some cases a vertically integrated dominant manufacturer of a final good and an important input may be able to strategically create a **price squeeze** on competitors by simultaneously increasing the price of the input and decreasing the price of the finished good. It has been argued, for example, that before 1930 Alcoa increased the price of aluminum ingots (the input) while simultaneously reducing the price of aluminum sheets and fabricated products.[25] Because Alcoa had a monopoly on ingots, this policy resulted in serious problems for unintegrated fabricators, such as Reynolds. Reynolds saw its input prices rising and its fabricated goods' prices falling. Alcoa was able to weather the reduction in profits on fabricated goods because its profits in the ingot market increased. Furthermore, observation of Alcoa's price-squeezing behavior would undoubtedly serve as a strategic reminder to any potential entrants into the fabricating business.

Alcoa's behavior also indicated that vertical integration can be used as an enabling device for price discrimination. In the 1930s and 1940s aluminum was used primarily to produce five manufactured goods: (1) iron and steel (aluminum was an important alloy); (2) cooking utensils; (3) electric cable; (4) automobile parts; and (5) aircraft. Because the availability of substitutes varied widely from one use to another, the elasticity of demand for aluminum varied as well. For example, the demand for aluminum in cooking utensils, for which many potential substitute inputs were available, was much more elastic than the demand for aluminum in aircraft, for which there were no good substitutes. Profit maximization required Alcoa to charge a higher price to aircraft manufacturers than to cooking utensil manufacturers. According to Perry, the demand for aluminum in cooking utensils, electric cable, and automobile parts was relatively elastic, and the demand for aluminum as an iron and steel alloy and in aircraft manufacturing was much more inelastic.[26]

In the absence of vertical integration, Alcoa would be forced to charge one price to all fabricators because otherwise one buyer could transfer the aluminum to another. If, for example, Alcoa attempted to charge aircraft manufacturers a higher price than utensil manufacturers for the same aluminum sheets, arbitrage would be possible between the aircraft and utensil manufacturers; the utensil manufacturer could purchase the aluminum at the low price and resell it to the aircraft manufacturer for a profit.

If Alcoa vertically integrated into utensils, however, it could increase the price to aircraft manufacturers without having to be concerned about the transfer of the good from one buyer to another. Perry has shown that in the early part of the twentieth century Alcoa behaved in just this manner.[27] Alcoa vertically integrated into the three markets with more elastic demands: cooking utensils, electric cables, and automobile parts. This enabled Alcoa to keep the prices it charged to the iron and steel and aircraft industries high. Vertical integration, therefore, enabled Alcoa to practice price discrimination.

16.3.3 Raising the Capital Barrier to Entry

In the preceding section we observed that vertical integration can facilitate the use of certain types of strategic behavior to discourage entry. Recall from Chapter 4 that capital barriers present a formidable barrier to entry in the presence of imperfect capital markets. The existence of significant vertical integration may make it necessary to enter an industry at more than one vertical stage, thereby increasing capital barriers to entry. In aluminum, for example, Alcoa controlled much of the world's bauxite ore supply, the United States' ingot capacity, and a good deal of fabrication capacity. As a result, to compete effectively against Alcoa, it was probably necessary to enter more than one vertical stage of production. This increased the capital barrier to entry tremendously and made it impossible for all but a handful of firms to enter.

16.3.4 Collusion and Vertical Integration

The relationship between vertical integration and the likelihood of effective collusion has troubled economists for many years.[28] Recall from Chapter 9 that two of the most significant factors affecting the probability of effective collusion are the number of firms and concentration. Increased vertical integration is likely to decrease the number

**FIGURE 16.8 An Industry with Four Manufacturers
and 20 Retailers Without Vertical Integration**

With no vertical integration, this industry has four manufacturers and 20 retailers.

of firms in a market and increase concentration. Consider Figure 16.8. In the absence of vertical integration, this industry is characterized by four upstream manufacturers and 20 downstream retailers. Collusion among the retailers will be difficult because 20 is a large number of firms and each firm controls a relatively small 5 percent of the market. Suppose that the manufacturers engage in a vertical merger blitz that transforms the industry structure into that in Figure 16.9. Now only eight retailers remain, and the four-firm concentration ratio in retailing has increased from 20 to 80. Given the structure of Figure 16.9, effective collusion is more likely to occur.

Vertical integration has been shown to help foster collusion in industries as diverse as textiles and pharmaceuticals.[29] Costello found that the key to suppressing price competition in the introduction of new antibiotics in the late 1940s and early 1950s was a combination of patent protection and forward vertical integration into packaging.[30] Telser has suggested that GE and Westinghouse marketed light bulbs only on consignment to eliminate any attempt by the retailers to bargain for better terms with manufacturers.[31] Further evidence is provided by Caves and Porter, who found that increased vertical integration resulted in greater stability of market shares in an industry.[32]

APPLICATION 16.4

The Possible Negative Welfare Impacts of Increasing Vertical Integration: The Case of the Southern California Gasoline Retailing Market

In March 1997, one of the leading branded gasoline retailers in Southern California, ARCO, announced a long-term leasing arrangement with all of the Thrifty Oil Company gasoline stations in the area. The leasing agreements gave ARCO complete control over the stations. Thrifty was by far the largest independent retailer of gasoline in Southern California, where it operated approximately 260 stations. As an independent, Thrifty purchased gasoline from a variety of suppliers. Most of the Thrifty stations became company-operated ARCO stations and some became dealer-operated ARCO stations. After a 60-day waiting period ARCO gained control over the Thrifty stations and by September 1997 all the stations had been converted from Thrifty to ARCO stations.

FIGURE 16.9 An Industry with Four Manufacturers and 20 Retailers and Significant Vertical Integration

After each of the four manufacturers merges with four retailers, the industry is vertically integrated and there are four manufacturers and only eight retailers. Compared to Figure 16.8, the four-firm concentration ratio in retailing has increased from 20 to 80.

Justine Hastings obtained station-specific pricing data for the Los Angeles and San Diego areas for the months of February, June, October, and December 1997; these data covered both the period before and after the conversion of the Thrifty stations.[*] Hastings was able to identify the stations that used to compete with a Thrifty station; she investigated the impact of the increased vertical integration by comparing the pricing patterns of the stations that competed with a Thrifty station before the conversions and those that did not compete with a Thrifty station.

The figures on the next page show an overview of the dramatic results in the Los Angeles and San Diego markets respectively. Before the conversion of the stations, the stations that competed against a Thrifty station had lower average prices than those stations that did not compete against a Thrifty station. After the conversion, the pattern was completely reversed: The stations that competed against a Thrifty station now had *higher* prices than those stations that did not compete against a Thrifty station.

These figures provide some evidence that increased vertical integration resulted in higher gasoline prices; however, Hastings also ran several regressions to test the impact of the change in vertical structure on prices. In one of the regressions, she examined the impact on an individual station's price of the following factors: (1) a competitor becoming a company-operated station; (2) the city; (3) the month; and (4) the station's competing with an independent station. Hastings found a statistically significant *negative* impact on price of a station competing with an independent station. Specifically, if a station competed with an independent station, its price was on average five cents a gallon lower. This meant that if a Thrifty station down the street from a Chevron station converted to an ARCO station, the Chevron station's price would, on average, increase by five cents per gallon.

Hastings concluded that "when independents are replaced by branded integrated stations, price competition in the market is softened, resulting in higher market prices." In this case, increased vertical integration results in higher prices and a welfare loss.

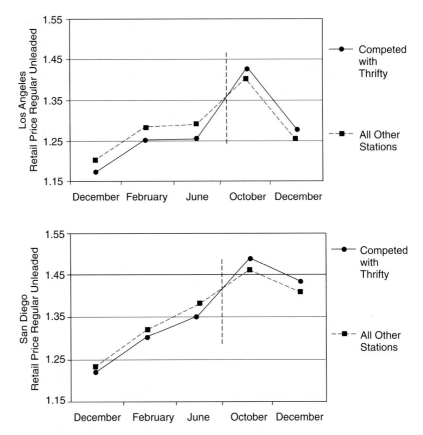

Source: Justine S. Hastings, "Vertical Relationships and Competition in Retail Gasoline Markets: Empirical Evidence from Contract Changes in Southern California," *American Economic Review* 94 (March 2004): 317–328.

*Justine S. Hastings, "Vertical Relationships and Competition in Retail Gasoline Markets: Empirical Evidence from Contract Changes in Southern California," *American Economic Review* 94 (March 2004): 317–328. ■

16.3.5 Foreclosure

As noted previously, *foreclosure* occurs when downstream firms (such as retailers) have difficulty obtaining inputs or when upstream firms (such as manufacturers) have difficulty finding buyers for their products. The United States courts have emphasized foreclosure as the primary problem associated with vertical mergers. Economists, however, have been skeptical that foreclosure has much economic impact unless it increases the capital barrier to entry by virtually requiring an entrant to enter at multiple stages of production.[33] The courts have argued that foreclosure creates potential problems. For example, consider a series of vertical mergers that results in a shift in structure from the one in Figure 16.8 to the one in Figure 16.9. Such a change in structure may force potential entrants to enter both the manufacturing and retailing markets because of a fear of foreclosure. A potential entrant into the manufacturing stage in Figure 16.8 would have 20 possible retail outlets. After the mergers, there are only eight retail outlets, only four

of which are independent of the other manufacturers. If the integrated retailers carry only their manufacturer's brands, then the mergers foreclose the potential entrant from 16 of the 20 retail outlets. The potential entrant may then be forced either to forgo entry altogether or to enter both vertical stages at once. Entry into both vertical stages greatly increases the capital barrier to entry.

The structure shown in Figure 16.9 also may foreclose the four remaining independent retailers from supplies of the manufactured good. This structure leaves the independents in a very precarious position at the mercy of the four integrated manufacturers for supplies. As a result, the independent retailers will probably abide by any demands made regarding vertical restraints, such as RPM or exclusive dealing, made by the manufacturers. The structure of Figure 16.9, therefore, also may make entry into the retailing sector far less likely than the structure of Figure 16.8.

It is important to understand that foreclosure is unlikely to have a major impact on pricing. The potential problem in Figure 16.8 is that there are only four manufacturers. This problem is no worse in Figure 16.9, in which there are still four manufacturers. It follows that except in extreme cases in which foreclosure is virtually complete and the capital barrier to entry is significantly increased, foreclosure is likely to cause few economic problems.

16.4 Antitrust: Public Policy Toward Vertical Restraints of Trade and Group Boycotts

Because each of the restrictions analyzed in this section can be considered as an alternative to increased vertical integration, the economic arguments against these practices are similar to the arguments against vertical integration in Section 16.3. Public policy toward the four most common types of vertical restraints is explored, including tying agreements, exclusive dealing agreements, territorial and customer restrictions, and resale price maintenance.

16.4.1 Tying Agreements

Recall from Chapter 15 that if a firm has market power over good X, it may require that its buyers purchase another good, good Y, to obtain good X. If a film distributor has exclusive rights over a new, popular film, hypothetically entitled *The Matrix 10*, and it also controls a less popular film, hypothetically entitled *The Grasshopper That Ate Cleveland,* then the distributor could require that every theater that shows *The Matrix 10* must also show *The Grasshopper That Ate Cleveland. The Matrix 10*, the film that theaters need to show, is referred to as the ***tying product;*** and *The Grasshopper That Ate Cleveland,* the film that theaters really don't want to show, is referred to as the ***tied product.***

The economic impact of tying has been debated extensively over the past three decades. Opinions vary widely. Some believe that tying is never anticompetitive, and others believe that under certain circumstances tying can be an effective method of increasing monopoly power and monopoly profits.[34] Conventional wisdom rejects the extreme position that tying is never anticompetitive, but accepts that most tying agreements have few anticompetitive effects.

Defendants have advanced two primary arguments to justify tying arrangements. First, they contend that tying is necessary for technological reasons. This argument sometimes makes sense. Often, however, this argument seems almost frivolous, as when International Salt contended that only its salt would prevent its salt dispensing machines from clogging.[35] Second, franchisors such as Carvel and Dunkin' Donuts have argued that it is necessary to tie ingredients together to maintain the high quality associated with their trademarks.[36] As the following cases indicate, these arguments have met with some success in the courts.

AMERICAN CAN CASE[37] (1949) The *American Can* case dealt with the leasing practices of American Can and Continental Can. Recall from Chapter 15 that both firms adopted a policy of leasing can-closing machines for a minimum of five years, with the further restriction that the lessee purchase its entire can requirements during the five-year period exclusively from its machinery supplier. Under no circumstances would American or Continental offer machines for sale. These policies resulted in a two-firm concentration ratio of 80.

The practices had several possible anticompetitive effects. First, by placing approximately 80 percent of all can customers beyond the reach of competitors each year, the long-term leases reduced the potential market available to new can manufacturers. Second, by refusing to sell their machines, American and Continental eliminated any potential competition from a secondhand machinery market. Third, the requirement that lessees purchase their requirements of cans from their machinery supplier established a tie between machinery and cans.

These policies worked because the two firms produced superior closing machinery, and therefore, their market power in machinery was responsible for their power in cans. Recall from Chapter 15 that the tying policy enabled American and Continental to increase profitability by practicing a form of price discrimination that used can purchases to meter machinery use. Under these conditions, potential entrants into the can market were virtually forced to produce closing machinery as well as cans, and this proved to be an almost impossible barrier.

The District Court distinguished between the effect of a tying arrangement and the effect of a requirements contract and ruled that although the tying agreement was illegal, a one-year requirements contract for cans was reasonable.

The District Court's remedy eliminated most of the entry barriers created by American's policies. In addition to a lease or requirements contract being limited to one year, American was required to offer all machines for sale at *reasonable prices*. Buyers were therefore able to purchase machinery, which freed them to deal with any can manufacturer. Furthermore, American was required to charge rental rates above average cost. This encouraged buyers to purchase rather than rent machines and helped ease entry into the machinery market.

The most significant result of the decree was a dramatic increase in backward vertical integration into can production by major can users.[38] Between 1930 and 1946 only Campbell's Soup had integrated backward by purchasing a can facility from Continental Can. After the decision, self-manufacturing of cans became common. Within 10 years of the decree, many large packers had entered the can industry. Backward vertical integration greatly increased the major packers' leverage in dealing with American and Continental, because large vertically integrated packers could fight price increases by threatening to increase their self-manufacturing operations.[39]

JERROLD CASE[40] **(1960)** In December 1950 Jerrold Electronics installed America's first cable TV system in Lansford, Pennsylvania. After a short time the system developed technical problems that required Jerrold to develop new equipment and techniques for cable installations. Because of these problems, Jerrold decided that it would install community-wide systems only if the community agreed to purchase all the necessary equipment from Jerrold and further agreed to purchase a Jerrold service contract.

The District Court ruled that in the early years of the cable TV industry the tie was justified by technological necessity. The Court went on, however, to state that Jerrold could not continue indefinitely to sell only complete cable systems. Before the *Jerrold* decision, it appeared that tying agreements were on the verge of being declared illegal per se. The Supreme Court affirmed the *Jerrold* decision without comment, and thereby established an acceptable technology defense in tying cases.

HYDE CASE[41] **(1984)** In 1984 the Supreme Court further restricted the use of the per se rule in tying cases. Dr. Hyde was a board-certified anesthesiologist who applied to join the staff of Jefferson Parish Hospital in New Orleans in 1976. The medical staff found Dr. Hyde to be a highly qualified anesthesiologist, but the hospital board denied him staff privileges because it had signed an exclusive contract with Roux & Associates, a group of four anesthesiologists, to provide all the hospital's anesthesia services. Hyde then sued Jefferson Parish Hospital.

The District Court ruled in favor of the hospital because the anticompetitive effects were minimal and were outweighed by economic benefits. The Court of Appeals, however, reversed, ruling that the contract involved a tying arrangement that was illegal per se under the Clayton Act. On appeal the Supreme Court reversed the Appeals Court. In its reversal the Supreme Court greatly restricted the use of the per se rule in tying cases and established a significant change in the Court's interpretation of Section 3 of the Clayton Act.

The Supreme Court recognized that the contract between Jefferson Parish Hospital and Roux & Associates established a tie between "hospital operating room services at Jefferson Parish Hospital," the tying product, and "anesthesia services of Roux & Associates," the tied product. The Court ruled, however, that because patients were free to seek services at many other hospitals in the New Orleans area, the hospital did not have sufficient market power in the tying product market, operating room services, to establish a violation of the Clayton Act. In fact, only 30 percent of the patients residing in the Jefferson Parish geographic area used Jefferson Parish Hospital for medical services. The Court noted, "there is no evidence that any patient who was sophisticated enough to know the difference between two anesthesiologists was not also able to go to a hospital that would provide him with the anesthesiologist of his choice."

In the *Hyde* decision, the Supreme Court came precariously close to explicitly overturning the per se rule in all tying cases. Furthermore, in their concurring decision, four Justices—O'Connor, Burger, Powell, and Rehnquist—wanted to explicitly require a Rule of Reason interpretation in tying cases. The majority, however, supported the following "limited per se" rule.

> Our cases have concluded that the essential characteristic of an invalid tying arrangement lies in the seller's exploitation of its control over the tying product to force the buyer into the purchase of a tied product that the buyer either did not

want at all or might have preferred to purchase elsewhere on different terms. When such "forcing" is present, competition on the merits in the market for the tied item is restrained and the Sherman Act is violated.

The *Hyde* ruling is the Supreme Court's most recent pronouncement with regard to tying arrangements, and the decision makes it clear that a tie is illegal per se only if market power in the tying product is significant enough to force buyers to purchase the tied product. It is difficult to understand why this interpretation qualifies as a per se interpretation, because under the *Hyde* precedent defendants always have the right to attempt to prove insufficient market power over the tying product.

16.4.2 Cases Dealing with Franchising Agreements

CARVEL CASE[42] (1964) In 1955 Carvel operated a chain of 400 retail stores that sold soft ice cream. Before 1955 the franchisees were required to purchase their entire requirements of "supplies, machinery, equipment, and paper goods" from Carvel or Carvel-approved sources. In 1955 Carvel changed the standard agreement so that its dealers were required to purchase only supplies "which are a part of the end product" from Carvel. Under the new agreement, franchisees were permitted to purchase machinery, equipment, and paper goods from independent sources. The Court of Appeals ruled that Carvel's tying practices were legal because the agreements protected the Carvel trademark and affected an insubstantial amount of commerce. The *Carvel* case suggested that franchisers could protect their trademark by taking actions to ensure the quality of the products sold at each outlet. In the 1971 *Chicken Delight* case, the Ninth Circuit Court of Appeals further limited the right of the franchiser to restrict its franchisees' behavior.

CHICKEN DELIGHT CASE[43] (1971) The facts in the *Chicken Delight* case varied little from those in the *Carvel* case. Chicken Delight operated several hundred fast food chicken outlets. It required its franchisees to purchase a specified number of chickens and all of their supplies and mixes exclusively from Chicken Delight. Because Chicken Delight received no royalties or fees, its income was completely dependent on the revenues generated from selling the tied products to its dealers.

The Circuit Court ruled that the agreement violated the Clayton Act because Chicken Delight could have effectively specified quality standards for the purchase of cooking equipment and ingredients from independent suppliers.

At first the *Carvel* and *Chicken Delight* decisions might appear to be at odds with each other; however, the two decisions simply reflect a justifiable Rule of Reason approach to franchise agreements. In the *Carvel* decision, the Court majority believed that it was impossible for Carvel to effectively police the quality of ingredients used in its ice cream products, and in the *Chicken Delight* case the Court believed that it was possible for Chicken Delight to set quality standards for chicken and spices.

16.4.3 Exclusive Dealing Agreements

Recall that under an exclusive dealing arrangement, a buyer agrees to purchase its entire requirements of some product or service from one supplier. Applications 16.1 and 16.2

suggested the possible positive effects of exclusive dealing. The potential anticompetitive effects of a requirements contract are highly dependent on the market power of the supplier.[44] If a manufacturer with a small market share entered into a requirements contract, a relatively small share of the market would be foreclosed. However, if a dominant firm followed an exclusive dealing policy, a great deal of foreclosure could occur, and entry barriers might be significantly increased. A Rule of Reason approach, therefore, is justified with respect to exclusive dealing. Unlike tying agreements, which tend to benefit sellers but not buyers, exclusive dealing arrangements provide economic benefits to both buyers and sellers.

STANDARD OIL OF CALIFORNIA CASE[45] (1949) The *Standard Oil* case concerned the use of requirements contracts in the retail gasoline market. Under Standard Oil's contracts, independent service stations agreed to purchase their entire supply of gasoline from Standard. Many of the contracts also required the retailers to purchase their entire supply of tires, tubes, batteries, and accessories from Standard.

Standard Oil had negotiated almost 6000 requirements contracts with independent dealers in the Southwest. The government contended that these contracts foreclosed a substantial amount of the gasoline market, thereby creating a barrier to entry into the oil refining industry. In the Justice Department's view, elimination of the contracts would encourage retailers to become *split pump* stations, that is, stations carrying more than one brand of gasoline. The government hoped that the end of requirements contracts would open the market to new independent refiners, encourage price competition, and give independent retailers more bargaining power vis-á-vis the major refiners.

Although the requirements contracts foreclosed some markets from independent refiners, it is not clear that the overall effect of the contracts was to hinder competition or hurt the independent refiners. The contracts provided both the refiner and the retailer with benefits. They assured small independent retailers of a continuing supply of gasoline and afforded some short-run protection from unforeseen price increases. An independent retailer could therefore plan its competitive strategy on the basis of known costs and avoid the risk of storing a product with a fluctuating demand. From the independent refiners' viewpoint, the contracts lowered selling costs by reducing transaction costs and reduced uncertainty by protecting refiners from a rapid reduction in demand.

The Supreme Court recognized that the requirements contracts might have net economic benefits, but nevertheless ruled that they violated the Clayton Act. According to a slim 5–4 majority, Standard's foreclosure of 6.7 percent of the market indicated a *reasonable probability* that competition would be substantially reduced. The Court majority found against Standard Oil despite a recognition that the decision might result in increased vertical integration by refiners into retailing and that such increased vertical integration might be more anticompetitive than the condemned requirements contracts.

TAMPA ELECTRIC CASE[46] (1961) In 1955 Tampa Electric, a regulated public utility, made plans to construct six additional generating facilities. Although all the existing generating plants in peninsular Florida burned oil, Tampa Electric decided to burn

coal in the first two new generators and contracted with Nashville Coal to supply its entire coal requirements for a period of 20 years. The contract set a minimum price of $6.40 per ton; the future price was to be adjusted with changes in production costs. Tampa Electric spent $3 million more to build the coal-burning plants compared with the cost of building oil-burning facilities, and Nashville spent $7.5 million preparing to meet the conditions of the contract.

In April 1957, immediately before the first scheduled coal delivery, Nashville informed Tampa Electric that the contract violated the Clayton Act, and therefore Nashville would not fulfill its conditions. Tampa Electric was then forced to purchase coal from another company at much higher prices.

Both the District Court and the Circuit Court of Appeals declared the contract void. The Supreme Court, however, overturned the Circuit Court decision. The Court ruled that because the challenged contract preempted less than 1 percent of the relevant market, it did not substantially lessen competition.

The *Tampa Electric* decision established a Rule of Reason with regard to requirements contracts and limited the reach of the 1949 Standard Oil precedent. Wisely, the Supreme Court permitted a requirements contract that had little, if any, anticompetitive effect.

VISA CASE[47] **(2003)** In 2003 in *United States* v. *Visa USA* the Second Circuit Court of Appeals affirmed a district court ruling that Visa and MasterCard had illegally used exclusive dealing arrangements with banks to reduce and eliminate competition from American Express and Discover.[48] Visa and MasterCard work in association with member banks to issue credit cards. The banks are responsible for finding customers and the banks set the terms (annual fees, interest rates, penalties) for the cards. Visa and MasterCard allowed banks to issue both Visa and MasterCard credit cards, but both companies required the expulsion from their credit card and ATM networks of any bank that issued an American Express or a Discover card. Therefore, if a Visa or MasterCard bank issued an American Express or Discover card, the bank would be eliminated from the only two worldwide ATM networks—Visa's Plus and MasterCard's Cirrus. Because virtually every U.S. bank is a member of the Visa, MasterCard, Plus, or Cirrus network, these policies effectively prevented U.S. banks from issuing American Express or Discover cards.

The District Court concluded that Visa's and MasterCard's policies had anticompetitive effects. The Court ordered that the exclusionary rules should be permanently eliminated and the defendants should be prevented from imposing any similar type of restrictions in the future. Deciding the case under the Rule of Reason, to find a violation of the Sherman Act, the Circuit Court required (1) that Visa and MasterCard had to have market power in a particular market; (2) that Visa's and MasterCard's actions had to have substantial adverse negative effects on competition; and (3) that Visa and MasterCard could not provide a pro-competitive effect to justify their conduct. As to point (1), the Circuit Court agreed with the District Court that Visa and MasterCard had substantial market power because "merchants testified that they could not refuse to accept payment by Visa or MasterCard, even if faced with significant price increases, because of customer preferences." As to point (2), the Circuit Court found "[t]he most persuasive evidence for harm to competition is the total exclusion of American Express and Discover from a segment of the market for network services. . . . It is largely undisputed that the exclusionary rules have resulted in the failure of Visa and MasterCard

member banks to become issuers of American Express and Discover-branded cards." As to point (3), the Circuit Court rejected all of the pro-competitive defenses presented by Visa and MasterCard and concluded that "[i]n sum, the defendants have failed to show that the anticompetitive effects of their exclusionary rules are outweighed by pro-competitive benefits."

As a direct result of this decision, on January 29, 2004, MBNA announced that it would begin issuing its own American Express cards.[49] Other companies were quick to follow, including Citibank and Bank of America. This case shows that antitrust decisions can have almost immediate impacts on market structure.[50]

16.4.4 Territorial and Customer Restrictions

Manufacturers sometimes distribute goods through independent dealers who are required to sell only in certain geographic areas or only to certain customers. Although these restrictions often appear to be anticompetitive because they restrict competition among the manufacturer's dealers, they may have redeeming pro-competitive effects.[51] *Territorial restrictions* may enable manufacturers to obtain higher-quality dealers and reduce the costs of providing retailing services. The *net* effect of territorial restrictions is highly dependent on the market power of the manufacturer and whether the restrictions increase the probability of collusion in either manufacturing or retailing. Territorial restrictions, therefore, require a Rule of Reason approach.

WHITE MOTOR CASE[52] (1963) Before the *White Motor* decision, the Justice Department had taken the position that territorial restrictions were illegal per se, and based on this position, the Department had negotiated a large number of consent decrees. The White Motor Company manufactured trucks and truck parts that it distributed through dealers who agreed to abide by a territorial restriction in their contract. The restriction specified that dealers would not sell trucks to any "individual, firm, or corporation" located outside of the dealer's exclusive territory.

White Motor defended the contracts on the grounds that they enabled White to compete against larger truck manufacturers. The District Court found for the Justice Department and declared territorial restrictions a per se violation of the Sherman Act. The court granted a *summary judgment* for the government, which meant that it refused to even consider the evidence.

The Supreme Court overturned the summary judgment and remanded the case to the District Court for a full trial. The Supreme Court ruled that territorial restrictions come within a Rule of Reason because "We need to know more than we do about the actual impact of these arrangements on competition to decide whether they have such a 'pernicious effect on competition and lack . . . any redeeming virtue' . . . and therefore should be classified as per se violations of the Sherman Act."

A full trial based on the evidence was never held in the *White Motor* case because White Motor agreed to a consent decree under which it gave up its exclusive dealerships.

SCHWINN CASE[53] (1967) In 1951 Schwinn was the leading U.S. manufacturer of bicycles, with a 22.5 percent market share. In the next decade Schwinn's share declined

to 12.8 percent, and it lost its leadership position to the Murray Ohio Manufacturing Company. Murray sold primarily private label bicycles to Sears, Montgomery Ward, and other large chain retailers. By contrast, Schwinn sold some of its bikes through 22 wholesale distributors, who in turn sold to a large number of independent retailers, but most of Schwinn's bikes were sold directly to retailers on consignment or under the so-called *Schwinn Plan*. Under the Schwinn Plan, Schwinn shipped its bicycles to retailers but Schwinn maintained *legal* ownership and paid the retailers a commission on each sale.

The case revolved primarily around Schwinn's requirement that its 22 wholesalers sell only to franchised Schwinn dealers located in the wholesaler's exclusive territory. The wholesalers, however, were not restricted to selling only Schwinn bicycles, and many carried other brands. Each franchised Schwinn retailer was authorized to buy from only one wholesaler, and the franchised retailers were forbidden from selling to unfranchised bicycle retailers.

The Supreme Court drew a careful distinction between cases in which Schwinn sold outright to wholesalers and cases in which it sold on consignment or through the Schwinn Plan. In cases of outright sale, a majority held that it was illegal per se for a manufacturer to restrict its distributors' sales territory. In the cases in which Schwinn maintained ownership over the goods, under consignment and the Schwinn Plan, the majority held that Schwinn could impose territorial restrictions under a Rule of Reason interpretation.

The legal and economic implications of the *Schwinn* decision are confusing. The decision was meant to clarify and simplify the law by placing a per se interpretation on most territorial restrictions. However, the *Schwinn* decision created an incentive for firms to avoid a per se ruling by setting up a consignment system of distribution and then hoping the system would pass a Rule of Reason test in court. From an economic perspective, it is hard to see how the Schwinn Plan was any more or less restrictive than the condemned wholesaler–retailer system. In 1977 the Supreme Court came to accept this view and overturned the *Schwinn* decision.

SYLVANIA CASE[54] **(1977)** The confusion created by the *Schwinn* decision was reduced by the *Sylvania* decision. Sylvania manufactured television sets, which before 1962 were marketed through a large number of independent retail stores and company-owned distributors. Prompted by a decline in its market share to between 1 and 2 percent, Sylvania decided to change its distribution system. Sylvania eliminated its wholesale distributors and sold directly to a limited number of franchised dealers. To improve its position vis-á-vis the industry leader RCA, which controlled over 60 percent of the market, Sylvania limited the number of franchisees in any given area and permitted its franchisees to sell only from the location(s) approved by Sylvania. The new system was an effort to attract more aggressive and competent retailers, and the strategy worked. Under the new plan, Sylvania's market share increased to 5 percent.

Continental TV was a San Francisco–based franchisee of Sylvania. In 1965 Sylvania decided to franchise another San Francisco dealer, Young Brothers, which was located approximately one mile from Continental TV. Continental TV protested that this violated Sylvania's marketing policy. When Sylvania went ahead and franchised Young Brothers, Continental TV canceled a large Sylvania order, and instead purchased a supply of televisions from one of Sylvania's competitors.

At approximately the same time that Sylvania franchised Young Brothers, Continental TV wanted to open another store in Sacramento. Sylvania refused to grant Continental TV a franchise in Sacramento because, according to Sylvania, the market was already adequately served by existing franchisees. Continental TV then informed Sylvania that it was going to move some Sylvania televisions from San Francisco to Sacramento and sell them from its Sacramento retail store, regardless of its agreement with Sylvania. Two weeks later Sylvania suddenly reduced Continental TV's credit line from $300,000 to $50,000. In response to the credit reduction, Continental TV withheld payments it owed Sylvania. Sylvania then terminated Continental TV's franchise, and Sylvania's collection agency sued Continental TV in an effort to recover payment for the unpaid Sylvania televisions that were still in Continental TV's possession.

A District Court jury trial resulted in a damage award of $1.77 million to Continental TV. The Ninth Circuit Court of Appeals reversed and held that Sylvania's restrictions were less harmful to competition than the restrictions used by Schwinn.

The Supreme Court ruled in favor of Sylvania, and in the process directly overturned the *Schwinn* decision and returned to the Rule of Reason interpretation of the *White Motor* case.

16.4.5 Resale Price Maintenance Agreements

Resale price maintenance (RPM) is the vertical counterpart of horizontal price fixing. As the following cases indicate, the courts have generally been tougher on resale price maintenance than has Congress. In 1976, however, even Congress turned against RPM and repealed the remaining *"fair trade laws"* that permitted resale price maintenance.

DR. MILES CASE[55] **(1911)** Dr. Miles produced proprietary medicines under a group of secret formulas. The drugs were sold to wholesalers and retailers under a written agreement that they would sell at prices set by Dr. Miles. Park & Sons was a wholesaler that refused to sign the price maintenance agreement. Park induced a number of wholesalers, who had signed the agreement, to supply it with Dr. Miles's medicines at cut-rate prices. When Park advertised and sold these drugs to retailers at reduced prices, Dr. Miles sued Park.

The Supreme Court ruled that the written agreements violated the Sherman Act. Justice Hughes wrote that Dr. Miles, "having sold its product at prices satisfactory to itself, the public is entitled to whatever advantage may be derived from competition in the subsequent traffic."

One of the major determining factors in the *Dr. Miles* decision was the use of a formal written agreement to maintain prices. Eight years later, the Supreme Court handed down a decision that limited the reach of the *Dr. Miles* decision to cases in which a written agreement was used to enforce resale price maintenance.

COLGATE CASE[56] **(1919)** Unlike Dr. Miles, Colgate had not resorted to written agreements to maintain its retail prices. Instead Colgate announced that it would refuse to supply any wholesaler or retailer that did not abide by Colgate's suggested prices. The evidence suggested that Colgate sometimes went beyond simply announcing that it would not deal with price-cutters by using investigations to determine which companies

were reducing prices and soliciting information from dealers regarding which of its retailers were reducing prices. The Supreme Court ruled that Colgate's actions did not violate the Sherman Act. According to the Court, "the act does not restrict the long recognized right of a trader or manufacturer engaged in an entirely private business, freely to exercise his own independent discretion as to parties with whom he will deal."

The *Colgate* decision created a large loophole in the Sherman Act with regard to RPM. Within three years of that decision, however, the Supreme Court twice attempted to clarify its meaning. In both *United States* v. *Schrader's Sons*[57] and *FTC* v. *Beech Nut Packing Company*,[58] the Supreme Court ruled that an express written agreement was not necessary for a resale price maintenance agreement to violate the Sherman Act. In both of these cases, the Court ruled that because the defendants had made elaborate arrangements to police their RPM agreements, the plans violated the antitrust laws. These cases limited, without overturning, the *Colgate* precedent and helped to create a political movement among small retailers to legalize RPM. In 1937 this movement paid off with the passage of the ***Miller-Tydings Act.***

The Miller-Tydings Act amended the Sherman Act to permit states to pass laws legalizing resale price maintenance. The act also prevented the FTC from taking action against RPM as an "unfair method of competition." By 1941 45 of the 48 states had passed so-called fair trade laws permitting RPM. Only Texas, Missouri, Vermont, and the District of Columbia stood as exceptions.

SCHWEGMANN CASE[59] **(1951)** After the Miller-Tydings Act gave states the right to permit written resale price maintenance agreements, Louisiana passed an RPM law. The Louisiana law went beyond merely permitting RPM agreements; it contained a provision that if one firm signed an RPM agreement, all other retailers in Louisiana were forced to abide by the agreement. When Schwegmann Brothers, a large New Orleans retailer, refused to sign an agreement with Calvert Distillers and continued to sell Calvert liquor at cut-rate prices, Calvert took Schwegmann to court.

The Supreme Court sided with Schwegmann and ruled that RPM agreements could not be enforced against nonsigners. According to the Court, if the Louisiana law were upheld, then "once a distributor executed a contract with a single retailer setting the minimum resale price for a commodity in the state, all other retailers could be forced into line." The Court further stated that if Congress had desired to eliminate the consensual element from RPM it would have added a nonsigner provision to the law. Following the Court's lead, Congress voted to overrule the *Schwegmann* decision in 1952 by passing the ***McGuire Act,*** which extended the Miller-Tydings Act to include nonsigners of an RPM agreement.

It was not antitrust policy, but economic pressures that ultimately reduced the incidence of RPM. The emergence of large discount chains and the existence of large mail-order houses in non–fair trade states combined to make the fair trade laws less and less effective. By 1975, only six states had fair trade laws that were enforceable against nonsigners, and in 1976 Congress repealed the Miller-Tydings and McGuire acts.

SHARP CASE[60] **(1988)** Despite the repeal of the fair trade laws by Congress, the issue continued to percolate through the courts. In 1988 the Supreme Court ruled once again that RPM is not illegal per se. The 1988 case involved Sharp Electronics and two of its dealers in Houston, Texas. In 1968 Sharp had granted Business Electronics an exclusive

franchise to market Sharp's electronic calculators (which sold for an average price of approximately $1000 per unit in 1968). In 1972 Sharp granted Hartwell a second Houston franchise. Sharp published a list of suggested retail prices, which Hartwell generally abided by. Business Electronics, however, tended to consistently maintain prices below the suggested level. In June 1973 Hartwell gave Sharp an ultimatum that it would terminate its relationship with Sharp unless Sharp terminated its relationship with Business Electronics. Within a month of the ultimatum, Sharp terminated its relationship with Business Electronics.

A District Court jury found for Business Electronics and awarded $600,000 in damages. The Court of Appeals, however, ordered a new trial because the jury had been given erroneous instructions implying that Sharp's actions could be considered illegal per se. The Supreme Court affirmed the Appeals Court, ordered a new trial, and declared explicitly that vertical restraints including RPM agreements are not to be considered illegal per se unless they include an *explicit* agreement on price between the manufacturer and the retailer.

The *Sharp* decision indicates that manufacturers still have quite a bit of latitude under the *Colgate* precedent. According to the *Sharp* decision, as long as the manufacturer avoids a direct agreement regarding what price a retailer will charge, the manufacturer can unilaterally refuse to supply any retailer.

STATE OIL CASE[61] (1997) In 1968 in *Albrecht* v. *Herald* the Supreme Court ruled that an explicit agreement to set a maximum retail price was illegal per se.[62] In 1997 in *State Oil* v. *Khan,* the Supreme Court did something it rarely does: it overruled this case and ruled that an explicit agreement to set a maximum retail price comes under the Rule of Reason. Khan leased a convenience store from State Oil under an agreement to purchase its gasoline from State Oil at a price equal to a suggested retail price set by State Oil, less 3.25 cents per gallon. Kahn was free to charge any price for gasoline but if its price was greater than State Oil's suggested retail price, Kahn had to rebate any additional revenues it collected to State Oil. Khan quickly fell behind on its lease payments to State Oil and State Oil terminated the agreement and evicted Khan. Kahn then sued State Oil for violating the Sherman Act by preventing Kahn from raising or lowering its retail gas prices. According to the complaint, Kahn would have increased its profits if it had been free to charge any price.

The District Court found for State Oil, but the Court of Appeals for the Seventh Circuit reversed.[63] The Circuit Court ruled that State Oil's policy was a per se violation under the 1968 precedent in *Albrecht* v. *Herald Co.*[64] Despite the fact that the Court of Appeals called the *Albrecht* precedent "unsound when decided," it felt constrained by this precedent. Circuit Judge Posner, however, noted that, "State Oil might want to place a ceiling on the dealers' resale prices in order to prevent them from exploiting that monopoly power fully. [State Oil] would do this not out of disinterested malice, but in its commercial self-interest. The higher the price at which gasoline is resold, the smaller the volume sold, and so the lower the profit to the supplier if the higher profit per gallon at the higher price is being snared by the dealer."

Justice O'Connor wrote for a unanimous Supreme Court:[65]

> After reconsidering *Albrecht's* rationale and the substantial criticism the decision has received, however, we conclude that there is insufficient economic justification

for per se invalidation of vertical maximum price fixing. . . . In overruling *Albrecht,* we of course do not hold that all vertical maximum price fixing is per se lawful. Instead, vertical maximum price fixing, like the majority of commercial arrangements subject to the antitrust laws, should be evaluated under the rule of reason. In our view, rule-of-reason analysis will effectively identify those situations in which vertical maximum price fixing amounts to anticompetitive conduct.

SUMMARY

1 Most vertical integration reduces transactions costs.

2 Vertical integration and vertical relationships can solve several potential economic problems, including the problems of double marginalization, insufficient pre-sale service, and inefficient input substitution.

3 In the case of bilateral monopoly, double marginalization results in a higher price and lower welfare than a vertically integrated monopoly.

4 In the absence of vertical integration, downstream firms may attempt to free ride on the services provided by competitors. The use of resale price maintenance (RPM) may solve this free rider problem.

5 It has been suggested that RPM is used to facilitate collusion among either retailers or manufacturers, but little empirical evidence supports this theory.

6 Manufacturers may use RPM to maintain their products' high-quality images or to ensure that their retailers provide adequate services.

7 Vertical integration and vertical relationships can also be used strategically to increase entry barriers. Such practices include exclusive dealing arrangements and price squeezes.

8 Vertical integration may result in an increased capital barrier to entry if firms are forced to enter more than one vertical stage of an industry.

9 Some economists have suggested that vertical integration may be used to facilitate collusion or foreclose markets.

10 Because of the complexity of analyzing the impact of increased vertical integration, each case of increased vertical integration should be analyzed in detail to determine whether there is a positive or negative effect on economic efficiency.

11 It is safe to conclude that a great deal of existing vertical integration and many vertical relationships have either a positive or a neutral effect on welfare, but public policy should guard against any negative welfare effects.

12 Unlike most horizontal agreements, most vertical restraints of trade are not illegal per se. Tying agreements, requirements contracts, territorial restrictions, and RPM clearly come under a Rule of Reason standard.

13 Until the *Hyde* decision in 1984, tying agreements were illegal per se unless they were initially required for a limited time for technological reasons. In the *Hyde* decision, the Supreme Court moved to make tying illegal only if significant market power exists in the tying product market.

14 Exclusive dealing contracts come under a Rule of Reason and are illegal only if they preempt a significant share of the relevant market demand.

15 The Supreme Court has consistently held that territorial and customer restrictions come under a Rule of Reason interpretation. The courts have permitted small non-dominant firms to use territorial restrictions to acquire dealerships but have forbidden dominant firms from eliminating intraband competition by imposing territorial restrictions.

16 With regard to resale price maintenance (RPM), the basic 1919 *Colgate* doctrine still holds. This gives a manufacturer the right to unilaterally refuse to deal with a distributor. Evidence of an implied conspiracy between the manufacturer and retailer is necessary for RPM to violate the Sherman Act.

17 Current policy recognizes both the potential benefits associated with vertical agreements and the lack of economic justification for many tying and resale price maintenance agreements.

KEY TERMS

double marginalization

downstream

exclusive dealing arrangements

fair trade laws

foreclosure

franchise fees

free rider problem

McGuire Act

Miller-Tydings Act

price squeeze

resale price maintenance agreements

resale price maintenance (RPM)

summary judgement

territorial restrictions

tied product

tying product

upstream

vertical restraints

DISCUSSION QUESTIONS

1. Why might Ralph Lauren refuse to allow retailers to sell its Polo clothing at discount prices?

2. Under what type(s) of market structure is the problem of double marginalization likely to arise? Suggest two solutions to this problem.

3. A manufacturer of shoes purchases a chain of shoe stores. The four-firm concentration ratio in both shoe manufacturing and shoe retailing is low. Would you expect any serious anti-competitive impacts of such a merger?

4. Consumer elecronics and certain brand name clothing (e.g., Liz Claiborne, Ralph Lauren)

are commonly sold under RPM agreements. For which of these two product lines would you expect the provision of improved service to be a more valid justification for RPM? Why?

5. Can you suggest a good that you would be less likely to buy if it was not sold under suggested retail prices? What does this suggest about the relationship between your utility and the total number of units of this good that are sold?

6. A larger and larger percentage of American physicians are becoming employees of HMOs

rather than being self-employed in their own practices. Might there be any anticompetitive effects if HMOs vertically integrated into hospital ownership? If most of America's largest hospitals were owned by HMOs, what do you think would happen to the number of self-employed physicians?

7. Microsoft is basically a monopolist in the production of computer operating systems for PCs, but it produces no computers. Why do you think Microsoft has not vertically integrated into manufacturing computers?

8. Do you agree or disagree with the following statement: The Clayton Act made tying arrangements illegal per se in the United States.

9. Under what circumstances are territorial restrictions economically justified? Have the courts recognized these circumstances?

10. In what ways are exclusive dealing arrangements and tying agreements similar? In what ways do they differ?

11. You are a small retailer of high-quality men's clothing. For years you have sold Ralph Lauren Polo menswear at the company's suggested retail prices. One day you decide to reduce these prices to 20 percent below the suggested retail price. The next month Ralph Lauren informs you that it will no longer supply you with its clothing. There is no evidence that anyone complained to Ralph Lauren about your price cuts. Is Ralph Lauren's behavior a violation of the antitrust laws? Explain your answer.

12. Do you agree with the Court of Appeals ruling in the *Sylvania* case? If RCA, with a 60 percent share of the television market, had tried to use the same territorial restrictions as Sylvania, would a similar court ruling have made economic sense?

13. Would the antitrust laws be violated if KFC announced that henceforth all of its franchisees would be required to purchase all of their paper goods, chickens, and other ingredients from KFC? Would the courts be likely to uphold such an agreement?

14. RPM might be used by manufacturers to prevent low-price, low-service retailers from free riding on the services provided by high-price, high-service retailers. Some of the goods commonly sold under RPM are cosmetics, designer jeans, men's underwear, and boxed candy. What are the services that the manufacturers of these goods are concerned about in these markets? Does this suggest the existence of another motivation for RPM in these cases? What might the motivation be?

PROBLEMS

1. A franchisor is considering whether to charge a franchisee a royalty that is a percentage of the franchisee's profits or a royalty that is a percentage of a franchisee's total revenues. In terms of economic efficiency, does it matter which policy the franchisor adopts?

2. Consider a case of bilateral monopoly in which the demand for the final good is $P = 100 - Q$. The average and marginal cost of producing the monopolized input is $LRAC = LRMC = 20$. Calculate the total gain in consumer plus producer surplus if the two monopolists merged.

3. A monopolist manufacturer sells to competitive retailers. The competitive retailers currently provide no services for the manufacturer's good. Suppose the final consumer demand for the good at the retail level is $P = 100 - Q$ and the costs for the manufacturer of producing the good are represented by:

$$MC_W = AC_W = 20.$$

Currently the monopolist sells the good to retailers at $P = 60$ and does not use RPM. If the manufacturer continues to sell the good to retailers at $P = 60$, but

now uses RPM to set the minimum price at P = 80, demand increases to P = 150 − Q. In this case, does RPM improve economic welfare?

4. Consider a vertically integrated industry with a monopolist manufacturer and competitive retailers. The government is considering placing a per-unit tax of $1.00 on this good at either the manufacturing or retail levels. In terms of economic impact, does it matter whether the unit tax is placed on the manufacturer or the retailer?

5. Consider Application 16.1. Suppose everything in the application remained the same *except* that the elasticity of demand for beer was 1.5 instead of 1.
 a. Calculate the demand curve for beer after the pub renovations have been completed.
 b. Calculate what the demand curve for beer *would have been* without the renovations.
 c. Calculate the change in welfare as a result of the renovations.
 d. Does an increase in the elasticity of demand for beer result in an increase or a decrease in welfare? Can you explain in words why this is the case?

NOTES

1. This result was first identified in Joseph J. Spengler, "Vertical Integration and Antitrust Policy," *Journal of Political Economy* 58 (August 1950): 347–352. This treatment is based on Jean Tirole, *The Theory of Industrial Organization* (Cambridge: MIT Press, 1988), pp. 174–181.

2. Spengler, *supra*. note 1.

3. See Tirole, *supra* note 1, pp. 174–185; Roger D. Blair and David L. Kaserman, "A Note on Incentive Incompatibility Under Franchising," *Review of Industrial Organization* 9 (June 1994): 323–330; Ester Gal-Or, "Optimal Franchising in Oligopolistic Markets with Uncertain Demand," *International Journal of Industrial Organization* 9 (September 1991): 343–364; and Torsten Schmist, "An Analysis of Intrabrand Competition in the Franchise Industry," *Review of Industrial Organization* 9 (June 1994): 293–310.

4. This model is derived from Tirole, *supra* note 1, pp. 181–185. The original idea is based on Lester Telser, "Why Should Manufacturers Want Fair Trade?" *Journal of Law and Economics* 3 (1960): 86–105. See also G. Frank Mathewson and Ralph A. Winter, "The Economic Theory of Vertical Restraints," *Rand Journal of Economics* 15 (1984): 27–38; Martin K. Perry and Robert H. Porter, "Can Resale Price Maintenance and Franchise Fees Correct Sub-optimal Levels of Retail Service?" *International Journal of Industrial Organization* 8 (March 1990): 115–141; and Howard P. Marvel and Stephen McCafferty, "Resale Price Maintenance and Quality Certification," *Rand Journal of Economics* 15 (1984): 346–359. For empirical evidence on the question, see David W. Boyd, "The Choice Between Resale Price Maintenance and Exclusive Territories: Evidence from Litigation," *Review of Industrial Organization* 8 (December 1993): 755–763.

5. Robert H. Bork, "A Reply to Professors Gould and Yamey," *Yale Law Journal* 76 (March 1967): 731; see also Robert H. Bork, "The Rule of Reason and the Per Se Concept: Price Fixing and Market Division," *Yale Law Journal* 75 (January 1966): 402–403, 424; and Robert H. Bork, "Resale Price Maintenance and Consumer Welfare," *Yale Law Journal* 77 (April 1968): 950–960.

6. F.M. Scherer, "The Economics of Vertical Restraints," *Antitrust Law Journal* 52 (1983): 700; and William S. Comanor, "Vertical Price Fixing and Market Restrictions and the New Antitrust Policy," *Harvard Law Review* 98 (March 1985): 990–998.

7. This section is based on John M. Vernon and Daniel A. Graham, "Profitability of Monopolization by Vertical Integration," *Journal of Political Economy* 79 (1971): 924–925. See also: Tirole, *supra* note 1, pp. 179–181; Roger D. Blair and David L. Kaserman, "Vertical Integration, Tying and Antitrust Policy," *American Economic Review* 68 (1978): 397–402; Richard Schmalensee, "A Note on the Theory of Vertical Integration," *Journal of Political Economy* 81 (1973): 442–449; Frederick R. Warren-Boulton, "Vertical Control with Variable Proportions," *Journal of Political Economy* 82 (1974): 783–802; Michael A. Salinger, "Vertical Mergers and Market Foreclosure," *Quarterly Journal of Economics* (1988): 345–356; and James L. Hamilton, "Input Substitutability and Vertical Integration," *Review of Industrial Organization* 7 (1992): 29–38.

8. Blair and Kaserman, *supra* note 7.

9. For an excellent summary of the issues see Thomas R. Overstreet, *Resale Price Maintenance: Economic Theories and Empirical Evidence* (Washington: Federal Trade Commission Bureau of Economics staff report, November 1983). Also see Robert L. Steiner, "The Inverse Association Between the Margins of Manufacturers and Retailers," *Review of Industrial Organization* 8 (December 1993): 717–740.

10. See *Albrecht* v. *Herald Co.*, 390 US 145 (1968) and *State Oil Co.* v. *Khan et al.* 522 US 3(1997).

11. Roger D. Blair and David L. Kaserman, *Antitrust Economics* (Homewood, IL.: Richard D. Irwin, 1985), pp. 342–347.

12. *Ibid.*, p. 342.

13. S.C. Hollander, in B.S. Yamey (ed.), *Resale Price Maintenance* (Chicago: Aldine, 1966), pp. 67–100; Marvin Frankel, "The Effects of Fair Trade: Fact and Fiction in the Statistical Findings," *Journal of Business* 28 (July 1955): 182; and J.F. Pickering, "The Abolition of Resale Price Maintenance in Great Britain," *Oxford Economic Papers* 26 (March, 1975): 120–146.

14. Lawrence Shepherd, "The Economic Effects of Repealing Fair-Trade Laws," *The Journal of Consumer Affairs* 12 (1978): 220–236.

15. Stanley I. Ornstein and Dominique M. Hanssens, "Resale Price Maintenance: Output Increasing or Restricting? The Case of Distilled Spirits in the United States," *Journal of Industrial Economics* 36 (1987): 1–18.

16. Thomas R. Overstreet, *Resale Price Maintenance: Economic Theories and Empirical Evidence* (Washington: FTC Bureau of Economics staff report, November 1983), pp. 13–19, 80, 140–144, 161–163; and Stanley I. Ornstein, "Resale Price Maintenance and Cartels," *Antitrust Bulletin* 30 (1985): 401–432.

17. Overstreet, *supra* note 16, pp. 71–82.

18. Lester G. Telser, "Why Should Manufacturers Want Fair Trade?" *Journal of Law and Economics* 3 (October 1960): 86.

19. Robert L. Steiner, "Jeans: Vertical Restraints and Efficiency," in Larry L. Duetsch (ed.), *Industry Studies* (Englewood Cliffs, NJ: Prentice-Hall, 1993), pp. 182–205; and "Has Izod's Alligator Peaked?" *New York Times* (September 8, 1983): D1.

20. "Has Izod's Alligator Peaked?" *New York Times* (September 8, 1983): D1.

21. For an argument of how RPM worked to benefit Levi Strauss, see Robert L. Steiner, "Jeans: Vertical Restraints and Efficiency," in Larry L. Duetsch (ed.), *Industry Studies* (Englewood Cliffs, NJ: Prentice-Hall, 1993), pp. 182–205.

22. For a game theory model, see Philippe Cyrenne, "Vertical Integration Versus Vertical Separation: An Equilibrium Model," *Review of Industrial Organization* 9 (June 1994): 311–322.

23. William S. Comanor and H.E. Frech III, "The Competitive Effects of Vertical Agreements," *American Economic Review* 75 (1985): 539–546.

24. This argument is based on Steven C. Salop and David T. Scheffman, "Cost-Raising Strategies," *Journal of Industrial Economics* 36 (1987): 19–34.

25. *United States* v. *Aluminum Company of America,* 148 F.2d 416 (1945).

26. Martin K. Perry, "Forward Integration by Alcoa: 1888–1930," *Journal of Industrial Economics* 29 (1980): 37–53.

27. *Ibid.*

28. See R.E. Caves and M.E. Porter, "Market Structure, Oligopoly, and Stability of Market Shares," *Journal of Industrial Economics* 26 (June 1978): 289–313; and Ronald N. Johnson and Allen M. Parkman, "Vertical Mergers and Selective Price Cutting," *Review of Industrial Organization* 10 (October 1995): 533–540.

29. Irwin M. Stelzer, "The Cotton Textile Industry," in Walter Adams (ed.), *The Structure of American Industry* (New York: Macmillan, 1961), pp. 42–73; and Peter M. Costello, "The Tetracycline Conspiracy," *Antitrust Law & Economics Review* 1 (Summer 1968): 13–44. See also Telser, *supra* note 4, pp. 96–104; M.G. Chazeau and Alfred E. Kahn, *Integration and Competition in the Petroleum Industry* (New Haven: Yale University Press, 1959), pp. 428–449; and Walter Adams and Joel Dirlam, "Steel Imports and Vertical Oligopoly Power," *American Economic Review* 54 (September 1964): 626–655.

30. Peter M. Costello, *supra* note 28.

31. Telser, *supra* note 4, pp. 96–104.

32. Caves and Porter, *supra* note 28.

33. There are exceptions, of course; see Roger D. Blair, James M. Fesmire, and Richard E. Romano, "A Note on Vertical Market Foreclosure," *Review of Industrial Organization* 5 (1990): 31–40.

34. For an argument that tying agreements are never anticompetitive, see Dominick T. Armentano, *Antitrust and Monopoly: Anatomy of a Policy Failure* (New York: John Wiley & Sons, 1982), pp. 198–203. For an excellent statement of the position that tying is rarely anticompetitive, see Richard A. Posner, *Antitrust Law: An Economic Perspective* (Chicago: University of Chicago Press, 1976), pp. 171–184. See also William L. Baldwin and David McFarland, "Tying Agreements in Law and Economics," *Antitrust Bulletin* 8 (September 1963); Suchan Chae, "Bundling Subscription TV Channels: A Case of Natural Bundling," *International Journal of Industrial Organization* 10 (June 1992): 213–230.

35. *International Salt Company* v. *United States,* 332 U.S. 392 (1947).

36. *Siegel* v. *Chicken Delight,* 448 F.2d 43 (1971); *Ungar* v. *Dunkin' Donuts of America,* no. 75–1625, CA3.
37. *United States* v. *American Can Company,* 87 F.Supp. 18 (1949).
38. Don E. Waldman, *Antitrust Action and Market Structure* (Lexington, MA: D.C. Heath, 1978), p. 76.
39. Charles H. Hessian, "The Metal Container Industry," in Walter Adams (ed.), *The Structure of American Industry* (New York: Macmillan, 1971), pp. 323–324.
40. *United States* v. *Jerrold Electronics Corporation,* 187 F.Supp. 545 (1960).
41. *Jefferson Parish Hospital District No. 2* v. *Hyde,* 466 U.S. 104 (1984).
42. *Susser et al.* v. *Carvel Corporation,* 332 F.2d 505 (1964).
43. *Siegel et al.* v. *Chicken Delight,* 448 F.2d 43 (1971).
44. See Phillipe Aghion and Patrick Bolton, "Contracts as a Barrier to Entry," *American Economic Review* 77 (June 1987): 388–401; Eric B. Rasmusen, J. Mark Ramseyer, and John S. Wiley, "Naked Exclusion," *American Economic Review* 81 (December 1991): 1137–1145; Robert Innes and Richard J. Sexton, "Strategic Buyers and Exclusionary Contracts," *American Economic Review* 84 (June 1994): 566–584; and David Besanko and Martin K. Perry, "Exclusive Dealing in a Spatial Model of Retail Competition," *International Journal of Industrial Organization* 12, (September 1994): 297–329.
45. *Standard Oil Company of California et al.* v. *United States,* 337 U.S. 293 (1949).
46. *Tampa Electric* v. *Nashville Coal,* 365 U.S. 320 (1961).
47. *United States* v. *VISA USA and MasterCard International,* 344 F.3d 299 (2d Cir. 2003).
48. *Ibid.,* and *United States* v. *VISA USA and MasterCard International* 163 F.Supp. 2d 322 (S.D.N.Y. 2001).
49. "American Express and MBNA Announce Card Issuing Alliance," home3.americanexpress.com/corp/pc/2004/mbna_axp.asp.
50. "Bank of America to Issue American Express," www.creditcards.com/Bank-of-America-Issues-Amex.php.
51. See L.J. White, "Vertical Restraints in Antitrust Law: A Coherent Model," *Antitrust Bulletin* 26 (Summer 1981): 327–345.
52. *White Motor Co.* v. *United States,* 372 U.S. 253 (1963).
53. *United States* v. *Arnold Schwinn & Co. et al.,* 388 U.S. 365 (1967).
54. *Continental T.V.* v. *GTE Sylvania Inc.,* 433 U.S. 36 (1977).
55. *Dr. Miles Medical Company* v. *John Park & Sons Company,* 220 U.S. 373 (1911).
56. *United States* v. *Colgate & Co.,* 250 U.S. 300 (1919).
57. *United States* v. *Schrader's Sons,* 252 U.S. 85 (1920).
58. *FTC* v. *Beech Nut Packing Company,* 257 U.S. 441 (1922).
59. *Schwegmann Brothers et al.* v. *Calvert Distillers Corp.,* 341 U.S. 384 (1951).
60. *Business Electronics Corp.* v. *Sharp Electronics Corp.,* 485 U.S. 717 (1988).
61. *State Oil Co.* v. *Khan et al.,* 522 U.S. 3 (1997).
62. *Albrecht* v. *Herald,* 390 U.S. 145 (1968).
63. *State Oil Co.* v. *Khan et al.,* 93 F.3d 1358 (1996).
64. *State Oil Co.* v. *Khan et al.,* 522 U.S. 3 (1997).
65. *Ibid.*

INTERNET EXERCISES

Visit **www.aw-bc.com/waldman_jensen** for this chapter's web exercises. Answer our real-world economics problems by searching the Internet for solutions!

Appendix

The Problem of Input Substitution

Suppose that a monopolist produces good X, using only two inputs, input M and input C. Input M is produced by a monopolist at marginal cost MC_M, and input C is produced in a perfectly competitive market at marginal cost MC_C. A vertically integrated firm that produced both inputs internally would maximize the following profits:

$$\Pi = TR - TC = P_X Q_X - (MC_M q_M + MC_C q_C).$$

It will be useful to define P_X^*, Q_X^*, q_M^*, and q_C^* as the price and quantities that maximize profits Π.

The profit-maximizing firm must minimize production costs $TC_X = (MC_M q_M + MC_C q_C)$. At this point it is necessary to recall some intermediate microeconomic theory. For any given production function, the *marginal rate of technical substitution* (MRTS) is defined as the rate at which a firm can substitute one input for another input without changing output. Furthermore, the MRTS equals the slope of an isoquant at a point and firms *minimize their long-run costs* by equating the MRTS, given by the slope of an isoquant, to the ratio of input prices, given by the slope of the isocost lines. Given any production function $Q_X = f(q_M, q_C)$, cost minimization, therefore, requires that the vertically integrated firm equate the MRTS between inputs to the ratio of the input prices. In a perfectly competitive world with all prices equal to marginal cost, the ratio of input prices also equals the ratio of the marginal costs of the inputs. Summarizing the theory mathematically, cost minimization requires:

$$MRTS = \frac{MP_M}{MP_C} = \frac{P_M}{P_C} = \frac{MC_M}{MC_C},$$

[16.2]

where MP_M represents the marginal product of input M and MP_C represents the marginal product of input C. The *marginal product* of an input is the change in output associated with a small increase in the quantity of the input. The MP_M, for example, is the change in the quantity of good X (ΔQ_X) associated with a change in the quantity of input M (Δq_M), or $\Delta Q_X / \Delta q_M$.

Suppose the production function for good X, $Q_X = f(q_M, q_C)$, is as follows:*

$$Q_X = q_M^{1/2} q_C^{1/2}.$$

[16.3]

Further assume that $MC_M = MC_C = 1$. For production function 16.3, the cost-minimizing choice of inputs is defined by the following two equations:†

*This production function is of the general form:

$$Q = Ax^\alpha y^\beta,$$

known as a Cobb-Douglas production function.

†Using calculus, the solution is derived by minimizing TC_X with respect to q_M and q_C as follows:

$$TC_X = P_M q_M + P_C q_C \quad (1)$$

subject to the condition that:

$$Q_X = q_M^{1/2} q_C^{1/2}. \quad (2)$$

From (2):

$$q_C = \frac{Q_X^2}{q_M} = Q_X^2 q_M^{-1}. \quad (3)$$

Substituting for q_C from (3) into (1):

$$TC_X = P_M q_M + P_C Q_X^2 q_M^{-1}.$$

Minimizing with respect to q_M yields:

$$\frac{\partial TC_X}{\partial q_M} = P_M - P_C Q_X^2 q_M^{-2} = 0.$$

Solving for q_M:

$$q_M = \frac{\sqrt{P_C} Q_X}{\sqrt{P_M}} = P_M^{-1/2} P_C^{1/2} Q_X.$$

By analogous minimization with respect to q_C:

$$q_C = P_C^{-1/2} P_M^{1/2} Q_X.$$

$$q_M = P_M^{-1/2}P_C^{1/2}Q_X \qquad\qquad [16.4]$$

$$q_C = P_C^{-1/2}P_M^{1/2}Q_X. \qquad\qquad [16.5]$$

The vertically integrated firm would behave as though the input prices equaled marginal cost; that is, for the vertically integrated firm $P_M = MC_M = P_C = MC_C = 1$. Substituting $P_M = 1$ and $P_C = 1$ into Equations 16.4 and 16.5 yields:

$$q_M = 1^{-1/2}1^{1/2}Q_X = Q_X \quad \text{and} \quad q_C = 1^{-1/2}1^{1/2}Q_X = Q_X.$$

Figure 16.10 shows the *isoquants,* which identify input combinations that yield equal outputs, for the production function given by Equation 16.3 and for outputs $Q_X = 2$ and $Q_X = 4$. For $P_M = P_C = 1$, the equilibrium cost-minimizing combinations lie along the input expansion path $q_C = q_M$. The conditions for cost minimization imply that the vertically integrated firm would operate along the input expansion path OA utilizing the input combinations $q_M = q_C = Q_X$.

Now consider the situation with three independent firms (one producing the final good and the other two producing the inputs). Would the monopolist manufacturer of X still operate along the expansion path $q_M = q_C$? Competition would ensure that $P_C = MC_C$. Profit maximization by the monopolist producer of input M, however, would ensure that $P_M > MC_M$. Assume that the monopolist input producer charges $P_M = 2$. From Equations 16.4 and 16.5, with $P_M = 2$ and $P_C = 1$, the monopolist final good producer would now use input combinations:

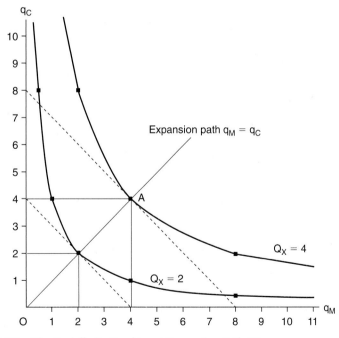

FIGURE 16.10 **The Socially Optimal Input Expansion Path OA**

For the production function $Q_X = q_M^{1/2}q_C^{1/2}$, if the input prices $P_M = P_C = 1$, then the cost-minimizing and socially optimal input expansion path is the 45-degree line $q_C = q_M$.

FIGURE 16.11 Comparison of the Optimal Input Expansion Path OA, with the Nonoptimal Input Expansion Path OB

For the production function $Q_X = q_M^{1/2} q_C^{1/2}$, if the input prices are $P_M = 2$ and $P_C = 1$, then the cost-minimizing, but socially inefficient, input expansion path is the line $q_C = 2q_M$, which is steeper than the socially optimal expansion path $q_C = q_M$.

$$q_M = 2^{-1/2} Q_X = \frac{Q_X}{\sqrt{2}} \tag{16.6}$$

$$q_C = 2^{1/2} Q_X = \sqrt{2} Q_X. \tag{16.7}$$

In Figure 16.11 the profit-maximizing producer of good X would then operate along a steeper input expansion path OB with a slope equal to 2.* As a result, the social costs of producing any given output Q_X would be too high, and economic efficiency in production would not be achieved. In Figure 16.11, for example, at point A the minimum social cost of producing $Q_X = 4$ is $P_C q_C + P_M q_M = 1 \cdot 4 + 1 \cdot 4 = 8$. The nonintegrated producer of good X, however, would produce at point B with social

*The slope of OB is 2 because from Equation 16.6 and 16.7:

$$\frac{q_C}{q_M} = \frac{\sqrt{2} Q_X}{\frac{Q_X}{\sqrt{2}}} = \sqrt{2}\sqrt{2} = 2. \tag{16.8}$$

†Similarly, the minimum social cost of producing $Q_X = 2$ is 4 at point c, but the nonintegrated producer of X would produce at point d with social costs of 5.32.

costs of $P_C q_C + P_M q_M = 1(5.66) + 2(2.83) = 11.32.$[†] Furthermore, because the costs of producing any given Q_X are too high, the monopolist manufacturer restricts output below Q_X^*, the profit-maximizing quantity, and welfare is unambiguously reduced compared with the vertically integrated case.

To eliminate the input substitution problem, the producer of good X need only integrate, perhaps through merger, with the producer of the monopolized input M. The integrated firm would then evaluate the cost of input M as $MC_M = 1$, and because $P_C = MC_C = 1$, the integrated firm would operate along the efficient input expansion path OA in Figure 16.11.

An alternative solution to the problem is for the producer of input M to use a tie combined with RPM to achieve the maximum profit. If the producer of input M purchases input C at $MC_C = 1$ and then ties the two products together for sale at prices such that:

$$\frac{P_M}{P_C} = \frac{MC_M}{MC_C} = 1,$$

the unintegrated monopolist manufacturer of good X will operate along input expansion path OA. Because the prices of the inputs will be greater than marginal cost, the monopolist producer of good X will want to charge a price greater than P_X^*. To guarantee that the profit-maximizing quantity Q_X^* is produced, therefore, the input monopolist uses RPM to set the maximum retail price equal to P_X^*.

Regulation and Deregulation

G overnments enact regulations for a variety of reasons. For example, the Food and Drug Administration (FDA) was established in 1906 to protect consumers. Other agencies, such as the Federal Trade Commission (FTC) and the Consumer Product Safety Commission (CPSC), also protect consumers. The mission of the Environmental Protection Agency (EPA) is to protect the environment and that of the Occupational Safety and Health Administration (OSHA) is to ensure worker safety and health. And Congress created the Transportation Security Administration (TSA) in response to the attacks of 9/11 to protect the nation's transportation systems.

Our focus in this chapter, however, is on economic regulation: regulation that restricts firms' decisions about price, quantity, entry, and exit. Over the past three decades, the extent of direct government regulation of sectors such as public utilities and transportation has declined continually. What was the economic rationale for regulation of industries such as electricity, telecommunications, and airlines? What motivated the recent deregulation? Because a thorough examination of these issues would require an entire book, we address only the most important issues here. However, this is a useful concluding chapter in that it applies a great deal of the knowledge gained throughout the book.

17.1 The Rationale for Regulation: Traditional Public Utility Regulation

T he authority for regulation of private industry comes from no less a source than the Constitution of the United States, which declares that Congress has the right to "regulate commerce . . . among the several states." Despite this constitutional mandate, for the first century of the nation's existence there was virtually no federal regulation over the day-to-day operation of business. In the latter half of the nineteenth century, however, the increasing significance of economies of scale in many sectors resulted in increased market power for some firms.[1] Nowhere was this increase in potential power more dramatic than in the railroad industry in the Midwest and West. Because of the monopoly power of the railroads in sparsely populated areas, farmers

were forced either to pay high shipping rates or to watch their grain spoil. As economic pressures grew, two important agrarian political groups arose: the Populists and the Grangers. These groups were able to support a candidate for President and to win a number of seats in Congress. As the influence of the Populists and Grangers grew, the two major parties were forced to address their economic concerns, and two policies emerged—antitrust and regulation.

The initial economic rationale for regulation was based on the existence of large economies of scale. Previous chapters devoted a great deal of attention to economies of scale, and Chapters 3 and 5 discussed the concept of a ***natural monopoly.*** Recall that in natural monopolies one firm can serve the market more efficiently than more than one firm. Figure 17.1 shows a natural monopoly. The LRAC curve in Figure 17.1 is sloping downward where it intersects the demand curve at an output of q_1. Because the LRAC curve is sloping downward at q_1, LRMC must lie below LRAC at q_1. Allocative efficiency demands that output be expanded as long as price is above LRMC or, as

FIGURE 17.1 **Natural Monopoly as a Justification for Regulation**

This figure depicts a natural monopoly: The LRAC is sloping downward where it intersects the demand curve at q_1. An unregulated monopoly would produce the profit-maximizing output q_m, charge the profit-maximizing price P_m, and earn economic profits equal to the red area $P_m cdC_m$. Allocative efficiency requires that output be expanded to q_2 since price is above LRMC for all output levels less than q_2. The gray area C_2abP_2 shows the economic loss a firm would sustain if it were forced to produce q_2 and charge P_2. Under average cost pricing, regulators would set price equal to P_1 and economic profits would be normal.

in Figure 17.1, until output equals q_2. If a private firm were forced to expand output to q_2 and charge price P_2, price would be below LRAC and the firm would sustain an economic loss equal to the gray area C_2abP_2.

There is a policy dilemma associated with the natural monopoly depicted in Figure 17.1. If an unregulated firm were free to maximize profits, it would produce the profit-maximizing output q_m, charge the profit-maximizing price P_m, and earn excess economic profits equal to the red area P_mcdC_m. Entry would be virtually impossible because the natural monopolist would have a large first-mover advantage and could quickly expand output to q_1 if threatened with entry. The natural monopolist could, therefore, earn excess economic profits for a long period. In fact, in the absence of new technology, it could earn these excess profits indefinitely.

Conversely, if the government attempted to force the natural monopolist to charge the socially optimal price, P_2, at which MC = P, then the monopolist would sustain an economic loss. Under such draconian regulation, no investors would be attracted to the industry, and the industry would have to be subsidized or it would cease to exist.*

There is, however, a middle ground in Figure 17.1. Suppose the regulators set price equal to P_1, where P = LRAC. With price equal to P_1, economic profits are normal, so investors can be attracted into the industry. Furthermore, although output is less than the socially optimal output q_2, it is considerably greater than the profit-maximizing output of q_m. The price P_1 is a compromise price known as a ***Ramsey price.*** The Ramsey price is the price that maximizes total social benefits subject to the requirement that profits cannot be negative. From a welfare perspective, P_1 is significantly better than the profit-maximizing price, but significantly worse than the socially optimal price. In theory, it appears to be a reasonable and workable compromise. In practice, serious problems are associated with such a compromise price. We consider the major problems in the next few sections.

17.2 The Workings of American Regulation

Although the first state regulatory boards were established in 1874, regulation at the national level did not begin until 1887 with the establishment of the Interstate Commerce Commission (ICC). The legal foundation for the ICC was an 1877 Supreme Court decision, *Munn* v. *Illinois*.[2] Illinois had set the maximum price to store grain in warehouses throughout the state. Munn sued, but the Supreme Court ruled in favor of the state. Chief Justice Waite wrote:

> Looking, then, to the common law from whence came the right which the Constitution protects, we find that when private property is "affected with a public interest it ceases to be *juris privati* only."
>
> . . . When, therefore, one devotes his property to a use in which the public has an interest, he, in effect, grants to the public an interest in that use and must

*There is one exception to this conclusion. Price discrimination could enable a monopolist to charge the socially optimal price and still earn an economic profit. This point is discussed later.

submit to be controlled by the public for the common good to the extent of the interest he has thus created.

The *Munn* decision eventually led to the establishment of many regulatory commissions in the United States. Commissioners are appointed by the executive branch of government, the President at the federal level, or the governor at the state level. Most commissions are dominated by lawyers and former politicians and include few, if any, economists. Furthermore, although some commissioners are well trained in economics, most are not.

Public utility commissions have several major tasks. Commissions have the difficult job of simultaneously setting the permitted level of profits, the price level, the price structure, and the rate base. None of these tasks is more important than setting the "correct" level of profits. The target profit level is typically set as a permitted rate of return on invested capital. Profit rates must be high enough to ensure a flow of capital, but not so high as to generate large excess profits. In establishing a price structure, the commission must decide how much price discrimination to permit. Finally, the commission must determine the **rate base,** or the value of the firm's invested capital to be used to calculate profits. As we will see shortly, a decision to allow too much capital into the rate base calculation will result in profits being excessive, and a decision to squeeze the rate base will prevent needed capital from entering the industry.

17.2.1 Setting the Permitted Rate of Return

The commission must set the permitted rate of return r, the permitted price structure p, and the permitted rate base K in the following equation:*

$$r = \frac{TR - TC}{K},$$
[17.1]

where r represents the rate of return on invested capital, TR represents total revenue, TC represents total costs, and K represents the value of the firm's invested capital or the *rate base*.

If r is fixed at "too low" a level, investors will stay away from the utility's stocks and bonds, and capacity may lag behind demand requirements. Insufficient capacity could cause a regulator's worst nightmare—a service interruption. However, if r turns out to be "too high," output will be restricted below a more socially optimal level, and high profits may cause a public outcry against both the commission and the utility.

The value of r goes a long way toward determining the stock value of the company and therefore is extremely important to the firm. Suppose, for example, that a utility's stock is worth 10 times its annual profit flow; that is, the utility's price/earnings ratio equals 10. If the target value of r is set at 10 percent and K = $10 million, then targeted annual profits (TR − TC) are $1 million. The utility's stock value should then be 10 times $1 million, or $10 million. Now suppose the utility convinces

*This equation is often described as:

$$TR = OC + Dep + r(RB),$$

where TR represents total revenues, OC is operating costs, Dep is depreciation, r is the permitted rate of return, and RB is the rate base.

the commission to raise the target r to 11 percent. If K remains fixed at $10 million, permitted target profits increase to $1.1 million, and the value of the utility's stock should increase to 10 times $1.1 million, or $11 million. There is an immediate $1 million capital gain to stockholders because of the increase in the target value of r. It is obviously worth a great deal of time and effort on the part of stockholders to lobby for an increase in r.

How does a commission set the targeted r? Commissions have generally considered three criteria: the cost of raising capital, the utility's capital attraction requirements (that is, whether the utility should be expanding or contracting its capacity), and comparable returns in other "equal risk" industries that would permit the utility to earn a normal economic profit. Historically, commissions have often relied on the third criterion, the concept of comparable returns, which means that the utility should earn a rate of return equal to the average in "similar industries." Although this criterion may initially seem to make economic sense, one realizes on second thought that there are no *unregulated* industries that are comparable to public utilities. Risk to a public utility is so fundamentally different from risk to a firm in an unregulated industry that it is virtually impossible to compare the two. For instance, even if IBM typically earns a 15 percent rate of return, it still runs a risk of sustaining an economic loss in any given year. If Consolidated Edison is targeted to earn a "comparable rate of return" of 15 percent, it runs virtually no risk of sustaining an economic loss in any year.

Because of the problems associated with using comparable returns, economists have argued that it makes more sense to rely on the cost of raising capital and the firm's capital attraction requirements when setting the target r. The cost of capital is calculated as a weighted average of the firm's cost of raising capital through the three standard securities: bonds, preferred stocks, and common stocks. Bonds and preferred stocks pay fixed interest rates, and therefore the cost of capital raised through these instruments is easy to calculate.

The cost of capital raised through the sale of common stocks is more complicated to determine because the cost is directly related to expected future profits. If the utility expects to pay stockholders a fixed dividend per share equal to D every year, and if the price of a share of common stock equals P, then the cost of capital raised by selling a share of common stock is s in the following equation:*

$$P = \frac{D}{(1 + s)} + \frac{D}{(1 + s)^2} + \cdots + \frac{D}{(1 + s)^n}. \qquad [17.2]$$

To understand Equation 17.2, recall from the discussion of present value in Chapter 3 that if $n \to \infty$ in Equation 17.2, then:

$$P = \frac{D}{s} \qquad \text{or} \qquad s = \frac{D}{P}. \qquad [17.3]$$

If, for example, D = $15 and P = $100, then s = 15 percent.

A weighted average of the cost of bonds, preferred stocks, and common stocks is the preferred measure of the cost of capital, but it may not be the optimal permitted rate of return r. The commission also must consider the utility's capital attraction

*The assumption that dividends D are constant is highly questionable, and commissions typically assume some rate of growth in dividend payments over time.

requirements. In a declining industry (e.g., the railroads in 1960), an optimal rate of return should encourage the *withdrawal of capital,* and therefore, the target r should be set below the normal rate of return in the economy. The cost of capital calculation, therefore, is not the optimal way to calculate r in all cases. It is, however, a good first approximation.

17.3 Efficiency Problems Associated with Rate of Return Regulation

17.3.1 X-Inefficiency

Rate of return regulation causes serious efficiency problems. With r guaranteed, there is little incentive for the utility to minimize costs, and this encourages X-inefficiency.[3] Because X-inefficiencies increase total costs and cause r to fall below the permitted level, they may precipitate a request to increase prices. Although a commission can deny a price hike if it determines that X-inefficiencies exist, most price increase requests are approved.

An institutional check against X-inefficiency is **regulatory lag.** Regulatory lag exists whenever costs increase or decrease. If costs increase, the utility cannot immediately raise prices. It must first request a price increase. Until the price hike is approved, the utility will earn a rate of return less than r. Similarly, if costs decrease, the utility will earn a rate of return greater than r until a price reduction is approved. Regulatory lag punishes X-inefficiency and rewards improved efficiency.

17.3.2 The Averch-Johnson Effect

Another efficiency problem associated with public utility regulation was first suggested by Averch and Johnson.[4] They theorized that if r is greater than the market cost of capital, s, the utility has an incentive to use too much capital relative to other inputs. If r = 10 percent and s = 8 percent, for example, then every $1 increase in K costs the utility 8 cents but results in a 10-cent increase in permitted profits. The utility is guaranteed an extra 2 cents in profits for every additional $1 it invests in capital. Averch and Johnson hypothesized that the utility would consider its cost of capital to be approximately 6 percent, 8 percent minus the 2 percent "discount" the utility receives in the form of permitted profits above the market cost of capital. According to Averch and Johnson, therefore:

$$\text{The Utility's Cost of Capital} = s - (r - s) = 2s - r.$$

The **Averch-Johnson effect** is shown in Figure 17.2.* The red **isoquants** labeled Q_1 and Q_2 in Figure 17.2 show the combinations of labor and capital that the regulated firm can use to produce outputs of Q_1 and Q_2, respectively. In the absence of regulation, each dashed red **isocost line** has a negative slope equal to the ratio of the price of labor over the price of capital, $-w/s$. To minimize the cost of producing any quantity,

*It is necessary to have studied intermediate microeconomic theory to understand Figure 17.2.

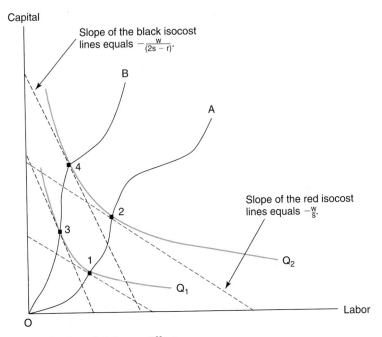

FIGURE 17.2 The Averch-Johnson Effect

In the absence of regulation, each dashed red isocost line has a negative slope equal to the ratio of the price of labor over the price of capital, $-w/s$. The input expansion path OA shows all the possible cost-minimizing combinations of labor and capital for a firm facing these input prices; OA is the socially optimal input expansion path. According to the Averch-Johnson effect, the cost of capital to the utility becomes $2s - r$, which is lower than the social cost of capital, s. Consequently, the isocost lines under regulation are steeper; the black isocost lines have a slope of $-w/(2s - r)$. OB shows the input expansion path under regulation. For any output, a regulated firm uses more capital and less labor than it would along the socially optimal expansion path.

a firm must produce at a point on the relevant isoquant at which the isocost line is tangent to the isoquant. For an output of Q_1 the cost-minimizing point is point 1, and for an output of Q_2 the cost-minimizing point is point 2. The *input expansion path,* OA, shows all the possible cost-minimizing combinations of labor and capital in the absence of regulation. Because the line OA identifies the lowest possible social cost of producing any possible output, it is the *socially optimal input expansion path.*

The Averch-Johnson effect suggests that the cost of capital to the utility is $2s - r$, which is lower than the social cost of capital, s. In Figure 17.2, each black isocost line represents an isocost line faced by a regulated firm. The black isocost lines are steeper than the dashed red isocost lines; the slope of the black lines equals $-w/(2s - r)$. Given the black isocost lines faced by a regulated utility, the optimal input expansion path is OB. For an output of Q_1 the cost-minimizing point is point 3, and for an output of Q_2 the cost-minimizing point is point 4. For any output, a regulated firm uses more capital and less labor along expansion path OB than along the socially optimal expansion path OA. According to Averch and Johnson, the regulated utility will invest in too much capital and select a nonoptimal combination of inputs.

Although testing empirically for the Averch-Johnson effect is difficult, the following evidence suggests that regulated firms attempted to increase their rate bases by using too much capital in the period before the early 1970s:[5]

1. Utilities avoided using ***peak-load pricing***.[6] Under peak-load pricing systems, firms charge higher prices during peak demand periods and lower prices during off-peak periods. Because marginal costs are higher during peak periods, peak-load pricing is efficient. By reducing the quantity demanded during peak periods, peak-load pricing reduces capacity requirements and lowers the utility's rate base. By avoiding peak-load pricing, utilities increase their capital requirements.

2. Utilities invested in capacity that exceeded demand even during peak demand periods.[7]

3. Instead of forming regional power pools to share electricity, power companies preferred to invest in enough capacity to meet their peak requirements.[8]

4. Utilities delayed the introduction of less capital-intensive technologies. In the late 1960s, for example, AT&T continued to invest in capital-intensive transcontinental cables between the United States and Europe when less capital-intensive satellite communications were available.[9] To meet winter peak demand in the northeastern United States, the natural gas industry built capital-intensive pipelines instead of less capital-intensive underground storage facilities.[10]

5. Regulated utilities refused to lease facilities even if leasing reduced costs because leased facilities are not included in a firm's rate base. In the communications industry, common carriers refused to lease satellite communications from Comstat (Communications Satellite Corporation) even though Comstat was established by the government as the official corporation for installing an international satellite communications network.[11] Similarly, electric utilities were hesitant to lease fuel cores for nuclear power plants.[12]

6. Public utilities set too high a standard of service reliability. By attempting to prevent all possible service interruptions, utilities were able to increase their capital expenditures and rate bases.[13]

7. Utilities permitted, even encouraged, outside suppliers to sell inputs at high prices.[14] In the 1950s when the electrical equipment manufacturers were fixing prices, the electric utilities not only failed to identify the conspiracy but also were less than vigorous in pressing damage claims. The utilities had an incentive to be exploited because high input prices increased their rate bases.

8. Utilities invested in capital-intensive areas that increased their rate bases even if the investments resulted in economic losses. In the 1960s, for example, AT&T invested in its TELPAK multichannel business service and its TWX teletype service in competition with Western Union. Its rate of return was very low on both services compared with its return on regulated interstate telephone activities.[15]

As noted, this empirical evidence in support of the Averch-Johnson effect all comes from before the early 1970s. From the end of World War II until the early 1970s, the marginal cost of capital tended to be fairly constant because of relatively low inflation and the Federal Reserve's ***Regulation Q***, which limited the interest rates that banks could pay on all deposits, including large certificates of deposits (CDs). In

the early 1970s two factors changed. First, high energy prices resulted in increased inflation, which increased interest rates and the marginal cost of capital. Second, the Federal Reserve suspended Regulation Q, which caused a dramatic increase in the rate of return on CDs and resulted in a large increase in the marginal cost of capital. With interest rates on CDs rising from 7 percent in 1972 to 12 percent in 1974, the marginal cost of capital suddenly exceeded the permitted rate of return, r, for most utilities.[16] Given this new cost structure, the incentive to invest in excessive capital was eliminated for most utilities.

During the 1950s and 1960s, the Averch-Johnson effect may have had a redeeming feature. Each of these distortions increased costs, but each distortion also increased output. Recall from Figure 17.1 that regulation restricts output below the socially optimal level at which price equals marginal cost. The Averch-Johnson effect encourages regulated utilities to increase output beyond q_1 and to invest in riskier investments. By increasing output and encouraging risk-taking, the Averch-Johnson effect partially offsets two of the major problems associated with regulation. This led Alfred Kahn to suggest that "as an offset to monopoly, the [Averch-Johnson] distortion probably does more good than harm."[17]

Not all economists have accepted the Averch-Johnson hypothesis. Several have theorized that regulation results in the use of too few units of capital relative to other inputs.[18] One alternative hypothesis suggests that firms may underinvest in capital because they fear that future regulations will be tightened. Tighter future regulation would cause a lower permitted rate of return on invested capital.[19] By underinvesting in capital, regulated firms limit the potential damage associated with a lower rate of return in the future. Some empirical studies have failed to find evidence of an Averch-Johnson effect, and at least one study found evidence of undercapitalization.[20]

17.3.3 Setting the Price Structure

The Price Structure with Decreasing Costs

From the end of World War II through the early 1970s, utilities faced declining long-run average cost curves such as those shown in Figure 17.1. Under these cost conditions, commissions used second-degree and third-degree price discrimination to increase output and decrease average costs. In Figure 17.1 if the utility sets price at P_1, profits are normal but output is below the socially optimal level q_2. To increase output toward q_2, commissions permitted the use of second-degree price discrimination. Recall from Chapter 15 that with second-degree price discrimination all buyers are offered the same price schedule and they self-select into different groups.

Figure 17.3 shows how, under conditions of decreasing LRAC, price discrimination can enable a utility to produce the socially optimal output and earn a normal profit. Buyers are offered a price schedule based on their willingness to pay. In response, customers divide themselves into three groups: residential buyers, small commercial buyers, and large commercial buyers. Residential buyers pay the highest price P_1, small commercial buyers pay a lower price P_2, and large commercial buyers pay a price equal to marginal cost P_{mc}. The quantity purchased by residential consumers is q_1, the quantity purchased by small commercial users is $q_2 - q_1$, and the quantity purchased by large commercial users is $q_3 - q_2$. Because total output is q_3, the average cost of production is AC = P_2 for *all* units produced. The utility earns a

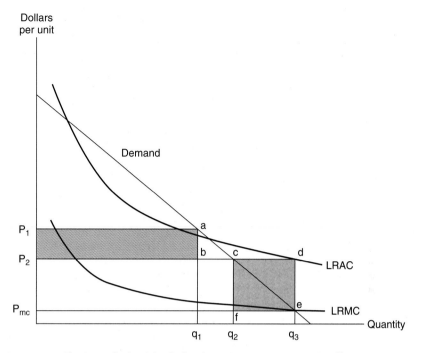

FIGURE 17.3 The Use of Price Discrimination to Improve Economic Efficiency

Under price discrimination, buyers are offered a price schedule based on their willingness to pay. Residential buyers pay the highest price P_1, small commercial buyers pay a lower price P_2, and large commercial buyers pay a price equal to marginal cost P_{mc}. The utility earns a positive economic profit equal to the red area P_1abP_2 on sales to residential users, earns a normal profit on sales to small commercial users, and sustains an economic loss equal to the gray area cdef on sales to large commercial users. If area P_1abP_2 equals area cdef, the utility earns a normal economic profit and output is equal to the socially optimal output.

positive economic profit equal to the red area P_1abP_2 on sales to residential users, earns a normal profit on sales to small commercial users, and sustains an economic loss equal to the gray area cdef on sales to large commercial buyers. If the red area P_1abP_2 equals the gray area cdef, the utility earns a normal economic profit and output is equal to the socially optimal output.

Commissions have also permitted third-degree price discrimination. In the telecommunications industry, for example, customers have been separated into business and residential buyers. Business customers have a more inelastic demand and pay higher rates.

The Price Structure with Increasing Costs

Recall that in the early 1970s cost conditions changed dramatically as the price of oil and other fossil fuels increased and Regulation Q was suspended by the Federal Reserve System. Electric utilities suddenly faced an entirely new cost structure as variable fuel costs became a significant component of total costs and conservation became

a high national priority. In addition, high inflation and interest rates increased the cost of expanding capacity. Almost overnight marginal costs and average costs were *increasing* instead of decreasing, and the optimal pricing structure no longer called for discrimination in favor of large users but, instead, required efforts to reduce demand.

After 1974 the marginal cost of generating electricity was significantly higher during peak demand periods when the last kilowatt-hour of generating capacity had to be brought on line. A typical electric utility, for example, would use only its low-cost hydroelectric or nuclear power capacity during off-peak periods. As demand increased during the day, newer fossil fuel facilities would be used. Finally, as demand reached peak, aging and inefficient facilities would be brought on line. With each increase in demand, therefore, the marginal cost of generating a kilowatt-hour of electricity would increase. The entire cost of operating the last inefficient units of generating capacity, including depreciation, should be allocated to those last units of peak demand.

Figure 17.4 shows the post–1974 cost structure. Suppose demand equals D_P during the peak period from 8:00 a.m. to 10:00 p.m., and demand equals D_{OP} during the off-peak period from 10:00 p.m. to 8:00 a.m. Efficient pricing requires charging P_P during the peak period and P_{OP} during the off-peak period.

The first electric utility to adopt a peak-load pricing system was the Wisconsin Power & Light Company in 1977.* Wisconsin Power & Light charged commercial users 2.03 cents per kilowatt-hour between 8:00 a.m. and 10:00 p.m. and 1.013 cents per kilowatt-hour between 10:00 p.m. and 8:00 a.m.[21] After 1977 many states implemented peak-load pricing schemes into their price structures.[22]

17.4 The Spread of Regulation into Other Markets

17.4.1 The Capture Theory of Regulation

The existence of large economies of scale was used to justify regulation in the railroad industry and the traditional public utilities, such as electricity, gas, and telecommunications. But why did regulation spread to markets in which economies of scale were not significant? Why, for example, did the government regulate trucking rates and airline fares? One possible explanation is that the regulated firms "captured" control of the regulatory commissions. According to this **capture theory**, once the railroads were regulated, the commissions came to view their primary responsibility as protecting the regulated firms from "too much" competition, rather than protecting consumers from monopoly prices. As a result, regulation spread into other transportation industries.

Stigler first suggested that regulation is supplied in response to interest group lobbying pressure to protect the group from competition.[23] Peltzman expanded on Stigler's theory by suggesting that legislators select regulatory policies that maximize the legislators' political support.[24] Interest groups provide votes, campaign contribu-

*Long before the electric utilities moved to a peak-load pricing structure, AT&T charged higher long-distance rates during the peak demand period on weekdays from 8:00 a.m. to 5:00 p.m. In 1984 AT&T offered a 40 percent rate reduction on weekdays from 5:00 p.m. to 11:00 p.m. and a 60 percent reduction on weekends, holidays, and on weekdays from 11:00 p.m. to 8:00 a.m.

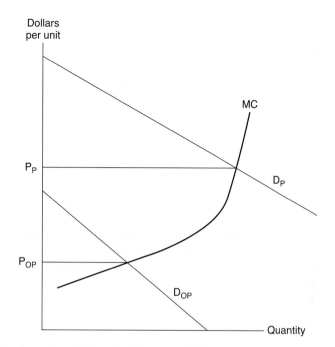

FIGURE 17.4 **Peak-Load Pricing in a Regulated Utility**

D_P shows the demand for electricity during the peak period, say from 8:00 a.m. to 10:00 p.m., while D_{OP} shows the demand during the off-peak period from 10:00 p.m. to 8:00 a.m. Efficient pricing requires charging P_P during the peak period and P_{OP} during the off-peak period.

tions, and other campaign resources to the legislators. In turn, the legislators provide support in the form of wealth transfers to the interest groups that provide the most votes and resources.

To formalize the model, suppose there are n firms in an industry that benefits from regulation. Assume the following:

1. Regulation results in a wealth transfer of T from consumers to the n firms.

2. The cost of organizing firms to lobby is a function of the number of firms n, and equals C(n). The cost function C(n) is a positive function of n because it is more difficult and costly to organize a large group than a small group.

3. The incentive for consumers to lobby against regulation increases with an increase in the total number of consumers negatively impacted by regulation and an increase in the intensity of consumers' feelings.

Given these assumptions, the per capita net benefits of regulation for each firm i, B_i, equal:

$$B_i = \frac{T - C(n)}{n} = \frac{T}{n} - \frac{C(n)}{n}. \qquad [17.4]$$

As n decreases, T/n increases, C(n) decreases, and C(n)/n may increase, decrease, or remain constant. If C(n)/n decreases or remains constant, the net benefits of regulation must increase with a decrease in n. Even if C(n)/n increases, it is likely that the increase in T/n will be greater than the increase in C(n)/n.* Reducing n is likely, therefore, to increase the per capita net benefits associated with regulation and increase the intensity of the groups' lobbying effort.† Application 17.1 illustrates this model, showing how a small group can benefit from regulation.

APPLICATION 17.1

It's More Than Peanuts

From 1949 until 2002, the federal government ran a marketing quota program that limited the number of farmers who could sell peanuts in the domestic market for food uses such as peanut butter, snacks, and peanut candy. At the time the program ended, approximately 70,000 quota owners had the rights to sell these "quota peanuts." If farmers produced more peanuts than the quota limit, these so-called "additional peanuts" had to either be exported or sold in the "crush" market, where they were used to make peanut oil and meal. The price received for peanuts sold to the crush market was well below the price of peanuts sold for food uses. In addition to limiting domestic production, the government also severely restricted imports of peanuts. Finally, price supports guaranteed that the farmers with the peanut quotas could cover their production costs. Not surprisingly, this program led to peanuts selling in the United States at a price above the world price: Estimates indicate that the U.S. price of peanuts was 50 percent higher than the world price.

 Randal Rucker and Walter Thurman estimated the welfare costs of this program. They calculated that for the period 1982 through 1987, the average annual transfer from consumers to producers was $255 million (in 1987 dollars). The program also resulted in an estimated deadweight loss of $34 million. Why did consumers tolerate this loss of surplus? We can use Peltzman's model to answer this question. In 1982 there were 23,046 peanut farmers, so, using Peltzman's notation:

$$\frac{T}{n} = \frac{\$255 \text{ million}}{23,046} = \$11,065.$$

Each peanut farmer gained over $11,000 from the government program. On the other hand, the cost to the average consumer of this program was $1.23. In terms of which group is likely to organize, there is a tremendous asymmetry. Few consumers would spend any time attempting to save $1.23, but peanut farmers were willing to invest a great deal of time, effort, and money to gain $11,000 in benefits.

*In the term T/n, only the denominator declines as n declines. In the term C(n)/n, both the numerator and denominator decline as n declines. If follows that the increase in the term T/n associated with a decrease in n is likely to be greater than any decrease in the term C(n)/n associated with a decrease in n.

†Similarly, as n increases, T/n decreases, whereas C(n)/n may increase, decrease, or remain constant. If C(n)/n increases or remains constant, the net benefits of regulation must decrease with an increase in n. Even if C(n)/n decreases, it is likely that the decrease in T/n will be greater than the decrease in C(n)/n. Increasing n is likely, therefore, to decrease the net benefits associated with regulation and decrease the groups' intensity of lobbying effort.

Sources: Erik Dohlman and Janet Livesey, "Peanut Backgrounder," http://www.ers.usda.gov/Publications/OCS/Oct05/OCS05l01, accessed on March 24, 2006; Randal R. Rucker and Walter N. Thurman, "The Economic Effects of Supply Controls: The Simple Analytics of the U.S. Peanut Program," *Journal of Law and Economics* 33 (October 1990): 483–515. ■

One of the major implications of the Peltzman model is that regulation tends to benefit small, well-organized groups with strong feelings (e.g., regulated firms) at the expense of large, unorganized groups with weak feelings (e.g., consumers). The history of regulation of transportation industries is consistent with the Stigler/Peltzman theory: the railroads were a well-organized, small group with a great deal to gain from expanded regulation into the trucking, busing, water carrier, and airline industries. Ironically, as time passed, regulation came to favor the trucking industry at the expense of the railroads.

Occupational licensing in the professions provides another powerful example of how the regulatory process can be captured and brought under the control of those being regulated. Professional organizations of doctors, lawyers, electricians, engineers, and plumbers have been able to convince state legislatures to establish licensing regulations and to then allow the professional organizations to set the licensing rules themselves. Doctors, for example, decide who can practice medicine, and lawyers decide who can practice law. It should come as no surprise that these self-imposed regulations typically make entry difficult and result in higher incomes for those already licensed.[25]

Additional evidence in support of the capture theory is provided by the aggressive opposition of regulated firms to deregulation. AT&T fought deregulation of the telecommunications industry, and the major air carriers led the fight against airline deregulation.[26] If regulation were detrimental to regulated firms and served the interests of consumers, regulated firms would welcome deregulation. In fact, few regulated firms have supported deregulation.

17.5 The Movement from Regulation to Deregulation

The 1970s and 1980s brought a dramatic move away from regulation. While fully regulated industries produced 17 percent of GNP in 1977, they produced only 6.6 percent by 1988.[27] This move toward deregulation continued into the 1990s. In part, this is due to the development of new technologies that have reduced the incidence of natural monopoly, decreasing the number of justified areas for regulation. Also, supporters of deregulation pointed to the efficiency problems associated with regulation such as those discussed earlier, arguing that deregulation would increase efficiency and lower prices. In this section we consider some of the important movements away from regulation that have occurred in the past 30 years.

17.5.1 Surface Transportation

Despite the efforts of the Interstate Commerce Commission (ICC) to protect the railroads, their competitive position declined after World War II. The development of the interstate highway system combined with the growth of the commercial airline industry destroyed the railroads' passenger business, which declined from 50 billion passenger miles in 1940 to 22 billion in 1960 and 10 billion in 1975.[28] The railroads argued

that the government unfairly subsidized competing modes of transportation. For example, while the government built the interstate highway system and new airports, the railroads had to use their own funds to build and maintain their rail beds. Furthermore, the government permitted truck carriers to use collusion and price discrimination to compete with the railroads, and the ICC was slow to allow the railroads to reduce rates in response to discriminatory price cutting by truckers.*

By 1960 the railroads were in deep financial trouble. The ICC responded by encouraging mergers and permitting service reductions, but the commission still refused to permit major rate cuts. Under pressure from the railroads to deregulate, in 1976 Congress passed the Railroad Revitalization and Regulatory Reform Act, which (1) provided $1.6 billion in government subsidies; (2) increased price flexibility; (3) accelerated the pace of merger approvals; and (4) expedited the closing of low-volume rail routes. The 1976 act did not go far enough, however, and in 1980 Congress passed the Staggers Act, which authorized more subsidies, eliminated antitrust immunity, and permitted greater price flexibility.

Deregulation resulted in immediate improvements in the railroads' economic performance. First, the railroads eliminated many unprofitable routes. Between 1975 and 1982, the railroads abandoned 17.2 percent of their track miles.[29] Deregulation enabled the railroads to increase rates in markets in which they had a comparative advantage, such as the transportation of bulky commodities like coal, and decrease prices in markets in which they faced stiff competition. Overall, rail prices decreased by 17.5 percent between 1975 and 1983.[30]

To level the playing field, in 1980 Congress also passed the Motor Carrier Act, which partially deregulated the trucking industry. This act, which was strongly opposed by the large truck carriers, eased entry and allowed greater price flexibility. Before 1980 regulation prevented entry into trucking if existing truckers could meet demand. Given this restriction, most entry requests were denied. Table 17.1 shows the dramatic impact of the 1980 Motor Carrier Act on entry. Requests for entry authority by truckers increased dramatically after deregulation, and the percentage of requests granted increased as well. One striking figure is the 60.7 percent increase in the number of carriers between 1975 and 1982. Entry caused rates for truckload carriers to decline by 25 percent in this period.[31] As prices fell, profits were squeezed, and the number of trucking bankruptcies increased 400 percent between 1980 and 1985.[32]

Deregulation of surface transportation resulted in improved economic efficiency.[33] Inefficient firms closed down, costs fell, and rates declined. Railroad profits increased, and trucking profits decreased. These results were a direct consequence of increased interindustry competition.

17.5.2 Airline Regulation and Deregulation

Regulation of the airline industry began in the 1920s, when the United States Postal Service was authorized to award mail routes and set rates. In 1934, the ICC took over the regulation of mail carriage and set up a competitive bidding system to allocate routes. To ensure a flow of mail traffic, the airlines continuously bid under cost, and

*The Reed-Bullwinkle Act of 1948 legalized the establishment of cartels, or rate bureaus, in the railroad, trucking, airline, and water carrier industries.

TABLE 17.1 Entry Requests and Approved Requests of Carriers

Year	Entry Authority Applications from Carriers		Percentage of Applications Approved		Number of Carriers
	Existing	New	Existing (%)	New (%)	
1975	2822	276	55	61	16,005
1976	6406	586	61	62	16,462
1977	8622	558	65	72	16,606
1978	12,983	703	69	78	16,874
1979	20,687	974	69	80	17,083
1980	18,788	1490	73	86	18,129
1981	19,135	4576	88	85	22,270
1982	9150	4925	84	55	25,722

Source: Thomas Gale Moore, "Rail and Trucking Deregulation," in Leonard W. Weiss and Michael W. Klass (eds.), *Regulatory Reform: What Actually Happened* (Boston: Little, Brown, 1986), p. 31.

soon many were on the verge of bankruptcy.[34] Congress responded to this threat to the airlines by passing the Civil Aeronautics Act of 1938, which established the Civil Aeronautics Authority. In 1940 the Civil Aeronautics Authority became the Civil Aeronautics Board (CAB). The CAB controlled the industry until the early 1980s and had complete control over rates, entry, exit, and safety. In 1958 the authority over safety was transferred to the Federal Aviation Authority (FAA).

The CAB set fares to earn a target rate of return on investment, and the fares had little relationship to costs. Average costs per passenger mile were significantly higher on short routes than on long routes. Fares, however, were related primarily to distance, so they were maintained well above average cost on long routes. These high fares subsidized below-average-cost fares on short routes. Price changes tended to be across-the-board, and the CAB discouraged price competition. Entry was approved only if it would not harm existing carriers. Finally, inefficient carriers that were in danger of sustaining economic losses were rewarded with new, profitable routes to keep them from going bankrupt.

Between 1949 and 1969, passenger miles increased at an average annual rate of 14 percent, while the average fare per mile decreased by 2 percent.[35] During this period, the Consumer Price Index (CPI) increased by 50 percent.[36] The decline in real air fares resulted from a 22 percent decrease in the average cost per passenger mile.[37] In the late 1960s the impact of regulation first came into serious question when it was discovered that fares on unregulated *intrastate* routes were much lower than fares on comparable regulated routes.[38]

In the absence of price competition, the airlines turned to various forms of nonprice competition, which took the form of increased frequency of flights and more amenities. As the airlines kept adding extra flights, empty seats abounded and load

factors were low. In 1969, for example, only 50.3 percent of available seats were filled.[39] These low load factors increased average costs and reduced profits. (See Application 17.2.)

APPLICATION 17.2

Airline Regulation: Where Did All the Profits Go?

As the discussion in the text indicates, in the era of airline regulation the Civil Aeronautics Board (CAB) closely regulated the fares airlines could charge. Even before deregulation, considerable evidence suggested that the fares permitted by the CAB were well above the level that would have prevailed in an open market. For example, interstate airlines flying between Washington, DC, and Boston charged almost twice as much as intrastate airlines flying between Los Angeles and San Francisco. The flights were approximately the same length, but the interstate fares were regulated by the CAB while the intrastate fares were not. Similar differences in fares existed for the unregulated flights between Dallas and Houston and the regulated flights between Washington and New York City. When some airlines requested reductions in fares, the CAB typically denied them.

Even though airlines were receiving higher-than-market fares because of the CAB's policy, they do not appear to have been earning excess economic profits. Over the 20 years prior to the 1978 deregulation, the average accounting profits for the airline industry were slightly below the national average across all industries. What is the explanation for this seeming paradox?

At least three factors played a role in eating away at airlines' profits. First, as part of its regulation of routes, the CAB required airlines to service some unprofitable routes, typically between sparsely populated areas. On these routes, demand was too low to allow profitable operation. A second factor was payments to employees. Airline employees' unions bargained for and got higher wages, made possible by the above-market fares permitted by the CAB.

The third factor is nonprice competition. In order to make profits at the high prices established by the CAB, airlines had to have passengers. Because they could not cut price, airlines looked for other ways to steal customers from their competitors. They scheduled more frequent flights to reduce waiting times, attracting passengers with the increased convenience. Additionally, airlines competed with each other on the basis of frills: gourmet meals, movies, more flight attendants, complimentary Mickey Mouse ears for passengers traveling to Disney World, and sometimes even live entertainment. Evidence about nonprice competition comes from the period immediately following deregulation. While the Consumer Price Index for food increased 62 percent between 1976 and 1982, the cost of food for airlines increased only 40 percent as airlines cut back on the quality of their food. The number of flight attendants per passenger fell 16 percent during the same period. Overall, the nonprice competition during the period of regulation increased the airlines' costs until the excess economic profits disappeared. Estimates indicated, in fact, that if the airline industry had not been regulated in 1977, industry profits would have been more than $4 billion higher than they actually were.

Source: Steven Morrison and Clifford Winston, *The Economic Effects of Airline Deregulation* (Washington, DC: Brookings Institution, 1986). ∎

In 1976 the CAB took its first tentative steps toward deregulation when it permitted charter flight operators to reduce fares on advance purchase tickets with a minimum stay requirement. In 1977 the CAB allowed certain major carriers to lower fares by 45 percent on "Super Saver" transcontinental flights if the tickets were purchased at least 30 days in advance and were for a minimum seven-day stay. When economist Alfred Kahn became chair of the CAB in June 1977, he announced that his goal was to eliminate all regulation of fares and entry and to ultimately disband the CAB.[40] Under Kahn the CAB began permitting fare reductions of up to 70 percent and fare increases of up to 10 percent.

Over the protests of the major airlines, Congress passed the Airline Deregulation Act (ADA) in October 1978.[41] The ADA ended the CAB's route authority effective December 1980 and its fare authority effective January 1983. The act also abolished the CAB at the end of 1984 and transferred the CAB's remaining authority over antitrust and international matters to the Department of Transportation (DOT).

Deregulating the industry in 1979 proved to be unfortunate. In 1979 the Shah of Iran was overthrown, causing oil prices to increase to $34 a barrel, at the time an all-time high. As a result, the price of jet fuel jumped from 40 cents to over 60 cents per gallon. High oil prices precipitated a severe worldwide recession that greatly reduced the demand for air travel.

Despite these economic problems, entry occurred after deregulation. Midway entered in 1979, New York Air in 1980, and People Express in 1981. Furthermore, several of the larger carriers, such as Pacific Southwest Airlines and Southwest Airlines, entered the interstate market. In addition, most of the major airlines expanded into new territories. The effect was an explosion of new competition.

The new carriers had significantly lower costs than the established airlines and were able to compete effectively based on lower fares. One major advantage for the new airlines was a nonunionized labor force. In 1985, for example, pilots for nonunionized People Express earned between $22,000 and $70,000, compared with an average of $90,000 at the unionized major airlines. The major carriers were also saddled with a large fleet of 747 and DC-10 jumbo jets, which could not be used efficiently on the more price-competitive middle- and short-distance routes. In addition, the entrants reduced maintenance costs by relying on one or two types of aircraft, and they squeezed more seats into their planes. Further cost reductions were achieved by reducing in-flight amenities. People Express even charged for soft drinks and snacks. Between 1976 and 1983, the ratio of flight attendants to passengers decreased by 16 percent. Under deregulation airline travel began to resemble bus travel, with low prices and low amenities.

The increase in competition and reduction in costs led to a sharp decline in fares in those large cities in which a new low-cost airline entered. Between 1975 and 1983, after adjusting for inflation, the average price per passenger-mile declined by 8.5 percent.[42] The major carriers left the smaller markets, and small-market fares tended to increase. The increase in small-market fares was expected because regulation had highly subsidized service to small cities. The overall fare reductions forced several large carriers into bankruptcy. Victims included Braniff and Continental. Continental took advantage of bankruptcy to destroy its unions, reduce costs, and reemerge as a low-cost, low-price carrier.

One of the most dramatic impacts of deregulation was the development of the hub-and-spoke system.[43] Under regulation, many passengers were forced to change

airlines on medium or long trips. Under deregulation the airlines quickly learned that passengers preferred to stay with one carrier. By creating hubs and channeling passengers into and out of these hubs, the airlines could prevent most passengers from changing airlines. The hub-and-spoke system also reduced costs by allowing the airlines to rely on smaller, more efficient planes. Before long, all of the successful airlines were structured around a hub-and-spoke system. The system enabled several regional airlines, such as USAirways and Piedmont, to expand into national carriers.

Deregulation has had many positive effects. Fares have declined, the number of flights has increased, productivity has improved, and capacity utilization has increased.[44] Problems, however, have appeared in recent years as concentration has increased. Recall from Chapter 11 that the major carriers were very aggressive in fighting entry and succeeded in eliminating most of the new firms from the market. Concentration also increased because the Department of Transportation (DOT) failed to prevent a number of anticompetitive mergers even after the Department of Justice (DOJ) opposed them.* In 1986, for example, the TWA–Ozark and Northwest–Republic mergers were both opposed by the Department of Justice but were approved by the Department of Transportation. In just the three short years of 1985 to 1987, 20 mergers were approved. The Department of Transportation consistently acted as though the airline industry is perfectly contestable, yet as we saw in Chapter 5, this is not the case.[45] As Alfred Kahn noted:[46]

> [T]he reconcentration of the industry reflects in part the deplorable failure of the Department of Transportation to disallow even one merger, or, in all but one case, even to set conditions to mitigate potential anticompetitive consequences. The DOT seems to have no appreciation whatever of the dangers our antitrust laws were set up almost a century ago to forestall.

A good deal of empirical evidence indicates that increasing airline concentration is correlated with higher fares.[47] The cost of the DOT's failure to enforce the antitrust laws, therefore, has been substantial. It is now clear that a necessary part of deregulation is strict enforcement of the antitrust laws, which is critical in nurturing competition.

As of early 2006, policy signals are mixed.[48] The Department of Justice did block a merger proposed in May 2000 between United Airlines, the nation's largest carrier at the time, and USAirways, the sixth largest carrier. However, in 2001, it approved the acquisition of TWA and its St. Louis hub monopoly by American Airlines. Additionally, the antitrust agencies and the Department of Transportation have allowed the major carriers to enter into a variety of affiliations and partnerships that have given them considerable control over many of the leading regional and commuter carriers. The agencies have also not been aggressive in attacking barriers to entry identified in Chapter 5 such as slots, gates, and airport ground facilities. On the other hand, the Department of Justice challenged the communication and signaling practices of the airlines' computer reservation systems in the mid-1990s, accusing them of collusive behavior. And government lawyers filed an antitrust suit against American Airlines in 1999, alleging that American used predatory pricing to eliminate new competitors in

*The 1978 deregulation statute gave the Department of Transportation the authority to disapprove anticompetitive mergers. Beginning on January 1, 1989, Congress transferred authority over airline mergers to the Department of Justice.

its Dallas–Fort Worth hub, a practice discussed in Chapter 11.* The future of the airline industry, and of policy toward the industry, remains somewhat up in the air.

17.5.3 Regulation of Telecommunications and Broadcasting

Telecommunications

The history of telecommunications began with the invention of the telephone by Alexander Graham Bell in 1876. Bell founded the American Telephone and Telegraph Company (AT&T) and aggressively attempted to monopolize the communications industry by driving out small local telephone companies.† AT&T refused to sell equipment to independent telephone companies, refused to connect independents to its long-distance lines, and used predatory pricing when necessary. By 1940 AT&T controlled more than 85 percent of the nation's telephones.

There was no federal regulation of the industry until the ICC was given limited authority to regulate telephone service in 1910. The ICC, however, did not control the growth of AT&T. Early in the century, state commissions were established, but they too were passive. The Communications Act of 1934 established the Federal Communications Commission (FCC) to regulate telephone service and radio broadcasting. The FCC studied the industry for four years, and in 1939 issued a report that put the Commission's seal of approval on the existing market structure. Over the next 20 years the FCC undertook few important regulatory actions regarding the telephone industry.

State commissions had no legal authority to regulate interstate commerce, and therefore, state commissions had no authority over long-distance interstate rates and tended to be passive. With a few exceptions, such as California and New York, states spent few resources on telephone regulation. The national Bell system, consisting of a series of regional monopolies that cut across state lines, greatly complicated the state commissions' tasks. Southwestern Bell Telephone, for example, provided service to five states with over 40 million telephones. The interstate composition of the regional Bell companies made it difficult for state commissions to separate intrastate from interstate costs, which made it virtually impossible to regulate effectively.

Early regulation served the interests of AT&T well. The FCC established long-distance rates based on data supplied and interpreted by AT&T. Long-distance rates declined, not because of effective FCC oversight, but because of technological advances and economies of scale. AT&T's profits were high, and it was secure in its monopoly position because the Commission prevented entry.

Under regulation, AT&T kept long-distance rates high to subsidize local service. This pricing policy made entry into long-distance service look particularly attractive. With the development of microwave technology in the 1940s, potential competitors filed with the FCC to enter the long-distance market. The FCC consistently refused to grant licenses to use the microwave radio band for long-distance telecommunications. After a three-year review, the FCC finally ruled in 1959 that it would permit limited

*The court dismissed the case without allowing it to proceed to trial, ruling that American was following a legal, competitive pricing strategy.

†There were actually three conflicting legal claims to invention of the telephone. After many years in court, in 1888 Bell finally won out over the claims of Elisha Gray and Daniel Drawbaugh by a 4–3 Supreme Court decision.

private use of the microwave band.[49] The Commission, however, refused to authorize use of the microwave band by common carriers, and AT&T refused to allow private line users to interconnect with the AT&T system. To compete against the development of private microwave lines, AT&T slashed the price of its TELPAK business service, and the FCC found that AT&T's TELPAK rates were below cost.

In 1963 Microwave Communications Inc. (MCI) filed for common carrier status to build a microwave system for privately leased lines between Chicago and St. Louis. AT&T opposed the request and stated that it would refuse interconnection for the new system. AT&T argued that the proposal was a form of *cream-skimming,* which would allow MCI to steal AT&T's best corporate customers and lead to higher rates for AT&T's subsidized local customers. In 1969 the FCC approved MCI's request, and in 1971 the Commission expanded its ruling to approve interconnection with the AT&T system. AT&T, however, continued to fight interconnection.[50] It was not until 1976 that the FCC granted MCI unlimited interconnection privileges for its private lines.

MCI's legal battle did not end there. In 1975 MCI began to offer limited dial-up long-distance service. Once again AT&T argued this was cream-skimming that would harm local residential customers. This time the FCC agreed with AT&T and refused to permit MCI to offer dial-up service. MCI appealed the FCC ruling to the federal courts, and in 1977 the Court of Appeals overturned the Commission.[51] In 1978 the Supreme Court refused to reconsider the Court of Appeals' decision, and discount long-distance dial-up service became available for many customers.[52] Long-distance rates between cities served by MCI declined dramatically. AT&T's monopoly over long-distance service had been broken by a series of FCC and court decisions, but the major industry changes were yet to come.

Recall from Chapter 3 that in 1974, the Justice Department filed an antitrust suit against AT&T. On January 8, 1982, AT&T signed a consent decree that permitted AT&T to keep Western Electric, Long Lines, and Bell Labs. AT&T's 22 local operating companies, however, had to be divested. Furthermore, AT&T was given permission to enter unregulated markets. This decree resulted in the largest divestiture in antitrust history, over $87 billion in assets.

The combined effect of the 1978 Supreme Court ruling in favor of MCI and the consent decree was a monumental change in market structure. In 1979 AT&T held a 96 percent share of long-distance revenues; by 1987 that share had declined to approximately 70 percent and by 2001 AT&T's market share of long-distance revenues was slightly less than 38 percent.[53] Rates declined dramatically as well. A 10-minute daytime call from New York to Chicago that cost $4.49 in December 1983 was only $2.23 in December 1988, and a 10-minute call from New York to Los Angeles declined from $5.15 to $2.32.[54] Rates for long-distance calls have continued to fall since then. AT&T remained the dominant firm in terms of market share, but it was unable to use this dominance to raise long-distance rates. Furthermore, until 1989 continued regulation made it impossible for AT&T to cut rates in a predatory manner, allowing MCI and Sprint to gain footholds in the long-distance market.[55]

In 1989 the FCC replaced traditional rate of return regulation with *price cap* regulation.[56] Price cap regulation allows firms to raise prices a maximum amount based on the following formula, where X represents expected productivity increases:

$$\text{Permitted Price Increase} = \text{Increase in CPI} - X.$$

In theory, price cap regulation provides an incentive for firms to improve efficiency because they must keep price increases below the increase in the Consumer Price Index (CPI). In the long-distance telecommunications industry, however, the price cap was essentially meaningless because AT&T wanted to *reduce* rates in response to lower costs and increased competition. The 1989 policy change, therefore, effectively deregulated long-distance rates.

The breakup of AT&T resulted in the creation of seven large regional telephone companies to replace the 22 AT&T local operating companies.* Local telephone rates increased immediately after the breakup of AT&T.[57] Three primary factors combined to cause local rate increases. First, after divestiture the local companies could no longer use profits earned on long-distance service to subsidize losses on local service. Second, large users were able to set up their own communications systems, bypassing the local companies entirely. Third, under regulation AT&T had used slow depreciation of its equipment, which left the operating companies greatly underdepreciated at the time of divestiture. After divestiture, the local companies pressed for accelerated depreciation, which increased their short-run costs. Immediately after divestiture, local rates increased dramatically, rising at an 8.7 percent annual rate.[58] In 1985, Pacific Bell requested a 94 percent increase in its basic monthly rate, and Bell of Pennsylvania requested a 66 percent increase.[59] Later in the decade, however, the rate of price increases slowed down considerably.[60] Overall, the prices of local telephone service have increased moderately since 1989.[61]

Broadcasting

Regulation of broadcasting began shortly after the introduction of radio broadcasting in 1920. Because of the limited number of available wavelengths in the radio spectrum, without regulation the airwaves would have turned into a veritable Tower of Babel with stations crowding each other on the spectrum. The Radio Act of 1927 established the Federal Radio Commission to control access to the radio spectrum. With the passage of the Communications Act of 1934, the FCC took over the responsibilities of the Radio Commission. The FCC has had three primary responsibilities: (1) allocating the radio spectrum in a way that maintains a clarity of signals; (2) controlling the ownership structure to achieve a diversity of opinions; and (3) ensuring that broadcasters keep the public informed. Although the FCC was passive in its regulation of telecommunications, it was aggressive in its regulation of the more glamorous broadcasting industry.

No company can operate an over-the-air broadcast station without a license from the FCC. Licenses are terminated automatically after five years, and broadcasters must apply for renewals. It is rare for a renewal request to be denied. The fundamental guideline used by the FCC to allocate licenses is that a licensee must operate for the "public interest, convenience and necessity." To say the least, this is a vague guideline.

The limited number of VHF television stations (channels 2 through 13) available created market power for those companies fortunate enough to obtain a VHF license. In 1975, the average pretax return on invested capital in a VHF television station was 67 percent, and in the largest cities it was generally above 100 percent.[62] In the 1950s

*The seven regional companies were NYNEX, Bell Atlantic, Bell South, Ameritech, Southwestern Bell, U.S. West, and Pacific Telesis. Mergers have since reduced the number.

and 1960s, the FCC protected VHF stations from competition with cable television by limiting cable service to rural areas that could not receive clear over-the-air television signals. When this FCC position became untenable in the late 1960s, the Commission added a series of restrictions on cable services. The FCC limited the number of stations a cable system could carry, required the provision of free public access channels for local government and educational use, and prevented entry into large cities.

With the national movement toward deregulation in the early 1980s, many restrictions on cable television were lifted. The cable industry, however, came under new regulation in 1984, when Congress passed the Cable Communications Act. The 1984 law gave local governments the power to license and control cable companies, which were viewed as natural monopolies. Although the Cable Communications Act of 1984 gave cable companies increased price flexibility, it continued to require cable systems to set aside stations for public and educational access.

To ensure a diversity of opinions in a free and open society, the FCC has ownership restrictions that limit the number of stations any one person or company can own. Until 1996 no one person or company could own more than 12 television stations, 12 AM radio stations, and 12 FM radio stations. Furthermore, the 12 television stations could not reach more than 25 percent of the national population, and no one company could own more than one station in the same market.

The Telecommunications Act of 1996

On February 8, 1996, President Clinton signed into law sweeping changes in the communications industry. The Telecommunications Act of 1996 dramatically reduced regulation in telecommunications, television and radio broadcasting, and cable television. Key provisions of the bill included the following:

1. Local telephone companies, long-distance telephone companies, and cable television companies were allowed to enter each other's markets.

2. Broadcasting ownership regulations were liberalized, permitting television companies to own over-the-air stations reaching up to 35 percent of national viewers. The number of radio stations that could be controlled by one company was also increased, and the ban on ownership of a television station and cable company in the same market was lifted.

3. The bill phased in deregulation of cable television rates by 1999, and many rates were deregulated effective January 8, 1996.

4. Cable and telephone companies were forbidden from acquiring more than a 10 percent interest in each other's operations, except in small communities with a population below 35,000.

5. The bill made it illegal to transmit indecent materials (pornography) across the Internet. This section of the bill came under immediate First Amendment challenge in the courts and was declared unconstitutional.

6. The act expanded FCC jurisdiction to include satellite services.

7. Television manufacturers were required to install a "v-chip" in all new televisions larger than 13 inches. The v-chip allows parents to block out violent or sexually

explicit programming. The television industry was required to develop a rating system within one year warning of violent and sexual content.

The bill has revolutionized telecommunications and broadcasting by blurring the distinctions between markets. AT&T, MCI, and Sprint entered local telephone markets, and some of the Regional Bell Operating Companies (RBOCs) entered the long-distance market. The act opened the door to a huge consolidation merger wave as firms attempted to position themselves for future competition in this vast industry. SBC acquired three former RBOCs: Ameritech, Pacific Bell, and Southwestern Bell. Bell Atlantic, an RBOC, acquired another RBOC, NYNEX, and GTE; AT&T acquired TCI, a cable television provider, and Teleport Communications Group; and AOL acquired Time Warner. The merger activity continues. In October 2005, the FCC approved two mergers involving giants in the telecommunications industry: Verizon acquired MCI and SBC purchased AT&T and changed its name to AT&T. And on March 5, 2006, AT&T announced its intention to acquire BellSouth.

These mergers have only increased the concerns of opponents of the bill that it would result in higher telephone and cable rates as competition decreased. Consumer groups continue to worry that without antitrust enforcement, large mergers will consolidate the industry in the hands of a few large multimedia giants and result in a reduction in competition and a loss of tens of thousands of jobs.

As of this writing, there is no way to know what the final impact of the 1996 Telecommunications Act will be, but the industry is certain to be changed forever. Given the history of telephone deregulation, where we have seen changes such as cell phones and Voice Over Internet Protocol (VOIP) put strong competitive pressure on both local and long-distance phone rates, one virtual certainty is that increased competition will speed up the rate of technological advance in all sectors.

17.5.4 Electricity

In 1935 Congress passed the Public Utility Act, establishing the Federal Power Commission (FPC) to regulate the interstate aspects of the electricity industry. The Department of Energy Organization Act of 1977 transferred authority over interstate electricity regulation to the Federal Energy Regulatory Commission (FERC).

Vertical integration is extremely important in the electricity industry. There are three vertical stages: generation, transmission, and distribution.* Economies of scale are significant at the transmission and distribution stages, but less significant at the generation stage. Unlike the transportation and communications industries, there is a significant amount of government ownership in electricity. The federal government owns facilities that generate approximately 10 percent of all electricity. The Tennessee Valley Authority (TVA) is the most famous of the federal government's operations. State and local governments control approximately 10 percent of distribution services. Nebraska has a statewide distribution utility, and the tiny hamlet of Hamilton, New York, population 3600, has a village electric utility.

Given current cost structures, there is little disagreement that the transmission and distribution sectors are still natural monopolies. The debate over deregulation is

*A fourth function is retailing, which includes metering, billing, and marketing.

centered on the generation stage, in which economies of scale are much less signifi-cant. Generation typically has accounted for over 50 percent of total industry costs, so deregulation of generation would have a significant impact.[63] If vertical integration were dissolved, resulting in independent generation, transmission, and distribution companies, most regions could support multiple generation companies and a reason-able level of competition.[64]

Vertical disintegration and increased competition would likely result in lower industrial rates relative to residential rates because generating companies would com-pete for large commercial accounts. Deregulation also might result in entry by large, private bulk-power users. A lesson learned from the airlines is that for deregulation to benefit residential consumers it would have to be accompanied by watchful antitrust policies aimed at preventing mergers that would increase regional concentration. Generating companies also would have to be guaranteed interconnection to transmis-sion lines.

APPLICATION 17.3
Electricity Restructuring: Lights Out in California?

Recently, several states have moved toward restructuring of electricity. Not surpris-ingly, these states include California, Massachusetts, and New York: states where the regulated rates have been considerably above the cost of generating power using the best available technology and also above the average rates across the country. For example, in California in 1993, the average retail electricity price was 9.7 cents per kilowatt-hour, while the national average was 6.9 cents. In an attempt to improve effi-ciency, California's state legislature passed a bill in 1996 that separated generation from transmission and distribution. Because independent generators were allowed to produce power, the hope was that competition at this level would increase efficiency and lower prices.

Initially, deregulation worked reasonably well: Wholesale prices were low and con-sumer rates were steady. In the summer of 2000, however, a combination of factors hit the California energy market hard. A heat wave caused demand for electricity to soar. Supply was also tight because of a lack of new power plants built over the previous 10 years, because of a drought that reduced the amount of hydroelectric power that could be produced, and because of the inability of outside power generators to supply enough power to the state. In addition, several empirical studies by economists suggest that the generating companies exercised considerable market power in the wholesale market. As a result of these several factors, wholesale energy prices in California rose sharply in June 2000 (to a level more than twice as high as during any month since 1998, when the transition to deregulation began); they increased for almost a year. The average wholesale price of electricity in the spring of 2001 was more than 10 times greater than its price a year earlier.

At the same time as the wholesale price of electricity was soaring, the retail price of electricity was still regulated. Utilities were sometimes forced to sell electricity at a retail price well below the price they were paying in the wholesale market; the distribution companies lost as much as $50 million per day. Because of tight supplies, the lights went out: California experienced rolling blackouts in June 2000 and again on two con-secutive days in January 2001. As utilities accumulated huge debts and faced bank-ruptcy, the state of California took action, becoming the purchaser of wholesale power

for the utilities and regulating retail prices in order to recover the cost of the power the state had purchased during the energy crisis.

What lessons can be learned from California's experience? Some of the problems arose from features of the restructuring plan that can be changed as other states and countries develop plans for their electricity industries. In particular, the distribution companies faced a cap on their retail prices and limits on their ability to enter into forward contracts.* However, some features of the market for electricity—on both the demand and supply sides—imply that restructuring this market is more difficult than deregulating markets such as airlines, trucking, and natural gas. Demand is difficult to forecast; varies widely over the day, over the week, and over the year; and yet is highly price inelastic at any moment. On the supply side, electricity is prohibitively expensive to store, so that producers operate on a just-in-time basis with whatever generating capacity is available. At peak times, capacity is fully utilized; network congestion, combined with nonstorability, keeps remote suppliers from providing power in times of high demand.

Still, economists hold out hope for an improvement over the completely regulated electricity market of the past. Some ideas under consideration include introducing real-time retail pricing and long-term contracting. Real-time pricing would indicate to the final consumer on an hourly basis when electricity is more or less expensive to consume, helping to make short-term demand more responsive to price. Long-term contracting would give utilities more control over wholesale prices while also giving them time to expand transmission capacity.

*A forward contract is an agreement between two parties to buy or sell an asset at an agreed-upon future point in time. This kind of contract is used to control exposure to risk.

Sources: Severin Borenstein, "The Trouble with Electricity Markets: Understanding California's Restructuring Disaster," *Journal of Economic Perspectives* 16 (Winter 2002): 191–211; Paul L. Joskow, "Deregulation and Regulatory Reform in the U.S. Electric Power Sector," in Sam Peltzman and Clifford Winston (eds.), *Deregulation of Network Industries: What's Next?* AEI-Brookings Center for Regulatory Studies (Washington, DC: Brookings Institute): pp. 113–154; and W. Kip Viscusi, Joseph E. Harrington Jr., and John M. Vernon, *Economics of Regulation and Antitrust* (4th edition), (Cambridge, MA: The MIT Press, 2005): pp. 456–461. ∎

17.5.5 Natural Gas Industry

Vertical integration is also very important in the natural gas industry, in which there are also three vertical stages: production at the wellhead, transportation through pipelines, and distribution. Although economies of scale are highly significant in transportation and distribution, they are insignificant at the production stage. Before 1938 the Federal Power Commission had no authority to regulate the price of natural gas, and the Supreme Court had ruled that state and local commissions could not set the price of interstate gas. In 1938 Congress passed the Natural Gas Act, which gave the FPC the power to set interstate pipeline rates but exempted producing and gathering operations at the wellhead from regulation. The FPC was also specifically given control over entry in the transmission segment. In order to build an interstate pipeline that served an area already served by another gas line, a company needed FPC approval.

In 1954 in *Phillips Petroleum* v. *Wisconsin,* the Supreme Court ordered the FPC to begin to regulate the wellhead price of natural gas.[65] Phillips was the largest

nonintegrated gas producer in the county. When Phillips raised its rates to the state of Wisconsin, Wisconsin complained to the FPC. The Commission claimed it had no regulatory authority over gas prices, and Wisconsin then sued Phillips. The Supreme Court ruled that although the 1938 act had exempted producing and gathering operations, it had not exempted the subsequent sale of natural gas across state lines. The Supreme Court ordered the FPC to expand its authority into pricing at the wellhead.

Initially the FPC attempted to regulate gas prices using traditional rate of return regulation, but because gas and oil are usually produced together (gas was actually a wasted by-product of oil production for decades), it was virtually impossible to separate the costs of gas production from the costs of oil production. Rate cases became hopelessly backlogged before the FPC. In desperation the Commission turned to setting regional wellhead prices. The FPC divided the country into 23 producing areas and announced temporary price ceilings in each area. A distinction was made between gas produced from "old" wells and "new" wells. The price ceiling was higher on "new" gas to provide an incentive for exploration.

Regulation of the wellhead price of natural gas never made economic sense, and this became abundantly clear with the onset of the energy crisis of 1973–1974. As OPEC increased oil prices, regulation kept the price of natural gas artificially low. This resulted in an excess demand for natural gas as consumers rationally attempted to switch from expensive oil and electricity to artificially low-priced natural gas. Price controls also reduced the incentive for exploration.

In 1978 Congress passed the Natural Gas Policy Act. The act gradually deregulated the price of natural gas at the wellhead. Price ceilings were removed from deep-well gas (wells more than 5000 feet deep) in November 1979 and from "new" gas in January 1985. "Old" gas remained under price control until July 1989. Today the wellhead price of natural gas is unregulated.

SUMMARY

1 Direct regulation of business began in the United States in markets in which economies of scale were very significant, such as the railroads, electricity and natural gas, and telecommunications.

2 Many government commissions were established to control these industries. Often these commissions were captured by the firms they were meant to regulate.

3 Regulated industries attempted to suppress competition by convincing commissions to expand their regulatory authority into new markets such as trucking, airlines, and cable television.

4 Commissions were primarily concerned with ensuring that service was provided at reasonable rates and with few service interruptions.

5 Regulations centered on establishing a permitted rate of return, a price structure, and a rate base.

6 Effective regulation probably lowered prices, but also resulted in X-inefficiencies and the use of too much capital relative to other inputs.

7. In recent years there has been a movement away from direct regulation of business and toward the use of increased competition to improve economic efficiency.

8. New product technology has tended to create new competition for most regulated industries. Trucking and air travel destroyed the power of the railroads, microwave systems undermined AT&T's control of long-distance telephone service, and cable television weakened the power of over-the-air television stations.

9. More recently, rapid technological change is leading to competition among local telephone, long-distance telephone, and cable television companies in many markets.

10. Although regulation will continue to exist in the few remaining areas of natural monopoly, such as the transmission and local distribution of electricity and gas, the primary lesson from America's history of regulation is that, over time, it is technology and competition that move an economy forward.

11. Creative destruction is a more powerful force than any government policy aimed at protecting consumers from high prices or industries from competition.

KEY TERMS

Averch-Johnson effect	isoquants	rate base
capture theory of regulation	natural monopoly	Regulation Q
cream-skimming	peak-load pricing	regulatory lag
input expansion path	price cap	
isocost lines	Ramsey price	

DISCUSSION QUESTIONS

1. Describe the conditions that result in natural monopoly. What industries remain natural monopolies today? In the past 30 years has the number of natural monopolies in the United States increased or decreased? Why has this change occurred?

2. In what ways can rate of return regulation result in a nonoptimal use of capital? *Ceteris paribus,* would this distortion increase or decrease with an increase in the permitted rate of return r?

3. Under traditional rate of return regulation, would regulated firms prefer rapid rates of depreciation or slow rates of depreciation? Why?

4. Under traditional rate of return regulation, what happens to a firm if it earns too high a rate of return? What happens if a firm earns a rate of return below the target rate? Keeping

your answers to these questions in mind, discuss a firm's incentive to innovate under rate of return regulation.

5. Why do you believe that AT&T agreed to divest most of its assets? Do you think AT&T would have agreed to keep the local operating companies and divest the rest of its operations? Why or why not?

6. Do you think there are economies of scope between local and long-distance telephone service? Why or why not? Why might a regulatory agency want to know if there are economies of scope?

7. When cable television was first introduced, the over-the-air broadcasting industry welcomed the innovation; however, recently the broadcasting industry has opposed deregulation of the cable television industry. Why do you think the industry's position changed?

8. What were the historical similarities and differences in the origins of regulation in the railroads and trucking? In which industry was the economic rationale for regulation greater?

9. Entry restrictions were very important in the regulatory history of the trucking and airline industries, but much less important in the railroad industry. Why?

10. In what ways has airline deregulation been a success? What problems have arisen under deregulation? Do these problems suggest that the industry should be re-regulated?

11. Read Application 17.3. How would the policy proposals under consideration mitigate against the unusual demand and supply conditions of the electricity industry?

12. What problems were caused by the continued regulation of the price of natural gas during the energy crisis of the early 1970s?

PROBLEMS

1. Consider a regulated natural monopoly with the following demand and cost conditions:

$$\text{Demand: } P = 100 - Q$$
$$\text{Total Costs: } TC = 1800 + 10Q$$
$$AC = \frac{TC}{Q} = \frac{1800}{Q} + \frac{10Q}{Q} = \frac{1800}{Q} + 10$$
$$MC = 10.$$

a. If a regulatory commission sets the price at the Ramsey price at which P = AC, what would be the regulated price? Show this result on a graph. [*Hint:* Set AC equal to demand and find the two roots of the quadratic equation. The AC curve "cuts" the demand curve at two outputs, but the Ramsey price is set at the larger quantity.]

b. What is consumer surplus plus profit at the Ramsey price? Show this on your graph.

c. If price were set at marginal cost, what would be the industry output? What would be the value of consumer surplus plus industry profits? Show these areas on your graph.

d. Which price results in greater economic welfare (that is, the sum of consumer surplus plus economic profit)? What area on your graph represents the change in welfare? Explain.

2. Consider the same regulated natural monopoly from problem 1 with the same demand and cost conditions:

$$\text{Demand: } P = 100 - Q$$
$$\text{Total Costs: } TC = 1800 + 10Q$$
$$AC = \frac{TC}{Q} = \frac{1800}{Q} + \frac{10Q}{Q} = \frac{1800}{Q} + 10$$
$$MC = 10.$$

Suppose a regulatory commission established the following price structure: The first 60 units are sold at a price of 40, and the next 30 units are sold at a price of 10.

a. Is this price structure allocatively efficient?

b. What are the profits earned by the regulated firm?

3. Consider a natural monopoly with the following total cost function:

$$LRTC = 0.1q^3 - 10q^2 + 275q.$$

This implies that $LRMC = 0.3q^2 - 20q + 275$ and $LRAC = 0.1q^2 - 10q + 275$. The product demand is $P = 500 - 10q$. Given these conditions, the demand curve cuts the LRAC curve at a point where the LRAC is downward sloping.
 a. Solve for the profit-maximizing unregulated monopoly price and output.
 b. Find the unregulated monopoly's profits.
 c. Now assume this monopoly is regulated. Solve for the output that the monopoly would charge if Ramsey pricing were enforced. What is the price? What is the profit to the monopolist?
 d. Calculate the increase in consumer surplus that results from regulation.

4. Suppose a regulated utility faces the following demand curves:

$$Demand\ Off\text{-}Peak: P = 50 - Q$$
$$Demand\ Peak: P = 110 - Q.$$

Marginal costs are:

$$MC = 20 + \frac{1}{2}Q.$$

 a. What are the socially optimal peak and off-peak prices?
 b. Suppose the regulatory commission sets $P = 30$ during both peak and off-peak periods. What is the social cost of such a pricing policy?
 c. Suppose the regulatory commission sets $P = 40$ during both peak and off-peak periods. What is the social cost of such a pricing policy?

5. Suppose that a heat wave hits. Consequently, both the off-peak (night) and peak (day) demand curves from problem 4 shift out. The new demand curves are as follows:

$$Demand\ Off\text{-}Peak: P = 80 - Q$$
$$Demand\ Peak: P = 140 - Q.$$

Assume marginal cost does not change.
 a. What are the socially optimal peak and off-peak prices now?
 b. Suppose the regulatory commission keeps prices at $P = 40$ during both peak and off-peak periods. Find the social cost of this pricing policy.

NOTES

1. For historical background see I.L. Sharfman, *The Interstate Commerce Commission, A Study in Administrative Law and Procedure* (New York: The Commonwealth Fund, 1931–1937); Gabriel Kolko, *Railroads and Regulation, 1877–1916* (Princeton: Princeton University Press, 1965); Alfred E. Kahn, *The Economics of Regulation: Principles and Institutions* (Cambridge, MA: MIT Press, 1988), particu-

larly vol. II, pp. 26–28. For related background on the passage of the Sherman Act in 1890 see H.B. Thorelli, *The Federal Antitrust Policy: Organization of an American Tradition* (Baltimore: Johns Hopkins Press, 1955); J.D. Clark, *The Federal Trust Policy* (Baltimore: Johns Hopkins Press, 1931); A.H. Walker, *History of the Sherman Law* (New York: Equity Press, 1910); A.D. Neale and D.G. Goyder,

The Antitrust Laws of the U.S.A. (Cambridge, U.K.: Cambridge University Press, 1980).

2. *Munn v. Illinois,* 94 US 113 (1877).

3. Walter J. Primeaux, "An Assessment of X-Efficiency Gained Through Competition," *Review of Economics and Statistics* 59 (February 1977): 105–108; and Rodney E. Stevenson, "X-Efficiency and Interfirm Rivalry: Evidence in the Electric Utility Industry," *Land Economics* 58 (February 1982): 52–66.

4. Harvey Averch and Leland L. Johnson, "Behavior of the Firm Under Regulatory Constraint," *American Economic Review* 52 (December 1962): 1052–1069. Stanislaw Wellisz is often given credit for simultaneously presenting the same theory; see Stanislaw H. Wellisz, "Regulation of Natural Gas Pipeline Companies: An Economic Analysis," *Journal of Political Economy* 71 (February 1963): 30–43.

5. The following list is adapted from Alfred E. Kahn, *supra* note 1, vol. II, pp. 50–54. The empirical evidence has been mixed; see Leland L. Johnson, "The Averch-Johnson Hypothesis after Ten Years," in William G. Shepherd and Thomas G. Gies (eds.), *Regulation in Further Perspective* (Cambridge, MA: Ballinger Publishing Co., 1974), pp. 67–78. For evidence suggesting that the Averch-Johnson effect does not exist, see Charles W. Smithson, "The Degree of Regulation and the Monopoly Firm: Further Empirical Evidence," *Southern Economic Journal* 44 (1978): 568–580; David P. Baron and Robert A. Taggart Jr., "A Model of Regulation Under Uncertainty and a Test of Regulatory Bias," *The Bell Journal of Economics* 8 (1977): 151–167; and W.J. Boyes, "An Empirical Examination of the Averch-Johnson Effect," *Economic Inquiry* 14 (March 1976): 25–35.

6. William G. Shepherd and Thomas G. Gies, *Utility Regulation: New Directions in Theory and Practice* (New York: Random House, 1966), p. 265; William G. Shepherd, "Marginal-Cost Pricing in American Utilities," *Southern Economic Journal* 33 (July 1966): 61–64; Ralph K. Davidson, *Price Discrimination in Selling Gas and Electricity* (Baltimore: Johns Hopkins Press, 1955), pp. 150–151; and Stanislaw H. Wellisz, *supra* note 4.

7. Harold H. Wein, "Fair Rate of Return and Incentives—Some General Considerations," in Harry M. Trebing (ed.), *Performance Under Regulation* (East Lansing, MI: Michigan State University Press, 1968), pp. 42–53.

8. Alfred E. Kahn, *supra* note 1, vol II, pp. 50–51.

9. Merton J. Peck, "The Single-Entity Proposal for International Communications," *American Economic Review* 60 (May 1970): 199–201.

10. Kahn, *supra* note 1, vol. II, p. 51.

11. Kahn, *supra* note 1, vol. II, pp. 51–52.

12. "Utilities' Embrace of Nuclear Fuel Stalled by Its Classification as a Current Asset," *The Wall Street Journal* (November 12, 1968): 4.

13. Kahn, *supra* note 1, vol. II, p. 53.

14. Kahn, *supra* note 1, vol. II, pp. 53–54.

15. 70 *Public Utilities Reports* (3rd series), 129, 143 (November 1967).

16. J.O. Light and William L. White, *The Financial System* (Homewood, IL: Irwin, 1979), p. 268.

17. Kahn, *supra* note 1, vol. II, p. 107.

18. See Elizabeth E. Bailey, *Economic Theory of Regulatory Constraint* (Lexington, MA: Heath, 1973), Chapter 5; Richard J. Gilbert and David M. Newbery, "Regulation Games," Department of Economics Working Paper no. 8879, (1988) Berkeley: University of California, Berkeley; and W. Davis Dechert, "Has the Averch-Johnson Effect been Theoretically Justified?" *Journal of Economic Dynamics and Control* 8 (1984): 1–17.

19. Gilbert and Newbery, *supra* note 18.

20. Smithson found no evidence of a tendency for regulated firms to invest in too much or too little capital; see Charles W. Smithson, "The Degree of Regulation and the Monopoly Firm: Further Empirical Evidence," *Southern Economic Journal* 44 (1978): 568–580. Baron and Taggart found evidence of undercapitalization; see David P. Baron and Robert A. Taggart Jr., *supra* note 5.

21. Sanford Berg (ed.), *Innovative Electric Rates* (Lexington, MA: Lexington Books, 1983).

22. *Ibid,* p. 305.

23. George Stigler, "The Theory of Economic Regulation," *Bell Journal of Economics and Management Science* 2 (Spring 1971): 3–21. Not all economists have accepted this theory. See Clifford Nowell and John Tschirhart, "Testing Theories of Regulatory Behavior," *Review of Industrial Organization* 8 (December 1993): 653–668.

24. Sam Peltzman, "Toward a More General Theory of Regulation," *Journal of Law and Economics* 19 (August 1976): 211–240.

25. William G. Shepherd, *Public Policies Toward Business* (8th edition) (Homewood, IL: Irwin, 1991), pp. 427–428; and Lawrence Shephard, "Licensing Restrictions and the Cost of Dental Care," *Journal of Law and Economics* 21 (April 1971): 187–202.

26. AT&T consistently fought deregulation; see *Allocation of Microwave Frequencies Above 890 Mc.,* 27 FCC 359 (1959); *In the Matter of Microwave Communications Inc.,* 18 FCC 953 (1969); *United States Independent Telephone Association v. MCI Telecommunications Corporation et al.; American Telephone and Telegraph Company v. MCI Telecommunications Corporation et al.;* and *Federal Communication Commission v. MCI Telecommunications Corporation et*

al., 580 F2d 590 (1977). With regard to the airlines, see Pablo T. Spiller, "The Differential Impact of Airline Regulation on Individual Firms and Markets: An Empirical Analysis," *Journal of Law and Economics* 26 (1983): 655–689; and Daniel P. Kaplan, "The Changing Airline Industry," in L.W. Weiss and M.W. Klass, *Regulatory Reform: What Actually Happened* (Boston: Little, Brown, 1986), p. 45.

27. Clifford Winston, "Economic Deregulation: Days of Reckoning for Microeconomists," *Journal of Economic Literature* 31 (September 1993): 1263–1289.

28. William G. Shepherd and Clair Wilcox, *Public Policies Toward Business* (6th edition) (Homewood, IL: Irwin, 1979), p. 377.

29. Theodore E. Keeler, *Railroads, Freight, and Public Policy* (Washington, DC: Brookings Institution, 1983), pp. 105–107.

30. Thomas Gale Moore, "Rail and Trucking Deregulation," in Leonard W. Weiss and Michael W. Klass, *Regulatory Reform: What Actually Happened* (Little, Brown, 1986), p. 25.

31. *Ibid.*, p. 32.

32. Kenneth Labich, "Blessings by the Truckload," *Fortune* (November 11, 1985): 138.

33. For an argument that these gains will be maintained in the long run see James N. Giordano, "Deregulation Without Apology: A Truncated Survivor Analysis of Long-Run Efficiency Gains in the U.S. Trucking Industry," *Review of Industrial Organization* 10 (October 1995): 635–650.

34. W. Kip Viscusi, Joseph E. Harrington Jr., and John M. Vernon, *Economics of Regulation and Antitrust* (4th edition), (Cambridge, MA: The MIT Press, 2005), p. 609.

35. Kaplan, *supra* note 26, p. 41.

36. *Ibid.*

37. *Ibid.*, p. 42.

38. T.E. Keeler, "Airline Regulation and Market Performance," *Bell Journal of Economics* 3 (Autumn 1972): 399–424; Simat, Helliesen and Eichner, Inc., "The Intrastate Air Regulation Experience in Texas and California," in Paul W. MacAvoy and John W. Snow (eds.), *Regulation of Passenger Fares and Competition Among the Airlines* (Washington: American Enterprise Institute for Public Policy Research, 1977): 41–70; and *Civil Aeronautics Board Practices and Procedures,* Report of the Subcommittee on Administrative Practice and Procedure, U.S. Senate, 1975, p. 41.

39. Kaplan, *supra* note 26, p.43.

40. Alfred E. Kahn, "Surprises of Airline Deregulation," *American Economic Review* 78 (May 1988): 316–322; and Alfred E. Kahn, "Airline Deregulation—A Mixed Bag, but a Clear Success Nevertheless," *Transportation Law Journal* 16 (1988): 229–252;

William G. Shepherd, "The Airline Industry," in Walter Adams, ed., *The Structure of American Industry* (New York: Macmillan, 1990), p. 219.

41. Kaplan, *supra* note 26, p. 45.

42. Thomas G. Moore, "U.S. Airline Deregulation: *Its Effects on Passengers, Capitol, and Labor,"* Journal of Law & Economics* 29 (April 1986): 1–28.

43. For a theoretical justification of the hub-and-spoke system as a solution to an optimization problem see Ken Hendricks, Michele Piccione, and Guofu Tan, "The Economics of Hubs: The Case of Monopoly," *Review of Economic Studies* 62 (January 1995): 83–99. The effects of the hub-and-spoke system are analyzed in Robert A. Sinclair, "An Empirical Model of Entry and Exit in Airline Markets," *Review of Industrial Organization* 10 (October 1995): 541–557; and Jan K. Brueckner and Pablo T. Spiller, "Competition and Mergers in Airline Networks," *International Journal of Industrial Organization* 9 (September 1991): 323–342.

44. Alfred E. Kahn, "Surprises of Airline Deregulation," *supra* note 40; Alfred E. Kahn, "Airline Deregulation—A Mixed Bag, but a Clear Success Nevertheless," *supra* note 40; John R. Meyer and Clinton V. Oster Jr., *Deregulation and the Future of Intercity Passenger Travel* (Cambridge, MA: MIT Press, 1987); Steven Morrison and Clifford Winston, *The Evolution of the Airline Industry* (Washington, DC: Brookings Institution, 1994); Douglas W. Caves, Laurtis R. Christensen, Michael W. Tretheway, and Robert J. Windle, "An Assessment of the Efficiency Effects of U.S. Airline Deregulation via an International Comparison," in Elizabeth E. Bailey (ed.), *Public Regulation: New Perspectives on Institutions and Policies* (Cambridge, MA: MIT Press, 1987): 285–320; and Thomas Gale Moore, *supra* note 42.

45. See also Amy D. Abramowitz and Stephen M. Brown, "Market Share and Price Determination in the Contemporary Airline Industry," *Review of Industrial Organization* 8 (August 1993): 419–433; and Andrew S. Joskow, Gregory J. Werden, and Richard L. Johnson, "Entry, Exit, and Performance in Airline Markets," *International Journal of Industrial Organization* 12 (December 1994): 457–471.

46. Alfred E. Kahn, "I Would Do It Again," *Regulation* 2 (1988): 22–28.

47. See E. Han Kim and Vijay Singal, "Mergers and Market Power: Evidence from the Airline Industry," *American Economic Review* 83 (June 1993): 549–569; Thomas G. Moore, *supra* note 42; and Gloria J. Hurdle, Richard L. Johnson, Andrew S. Joskow, Gregory J. Werden, and Michael A. Williams, "Concentration, Potential Entry, and Performance in the Airline Industry," *Journal of Industrial*

Economics 38 (December 1989): 135. See also Severin Borenstein, "Hubs and High Fares: Dominance and Market Power in the U.S. Airline Industry," *Rand Journal of Economics* 20 (Autumn 1989): 344–365; and E.E. Bailey, D.R. Graham, and D.P. Kaplan, *Deregulating the Airlines* (Cambridge, MA: MIT Press, 1985), pp. 169–171.

48. See the discussion on pp. 210–211 of William G. Shepherd and James W. Brock, "Airlines," in Walter Adams and James Brock (eds.), *The Structure of American Industry* (11th edition), (Upper Saddle River, NJ: Pearson Prentice Hall, 2005).

49. *Allocation of Microwave Frequencies Above 890 Mc.,* 27 FCC 359 (1959).

50. *In the Matter of Microwave Communications Inc.,* 18 FCC 953 (1969).

51. *United States Independent Telephone Association v. MCI Telecommunications Corporation et al.; American Telephone and Telegraph Company v. MCI Telecommunications Corporation et al.; and Federal Communication Commission v. MCI Telecommunications Corporation et al.,* 580 F2d 590 (1977).

52. *United States Independent Telephone Association v. MCI Telecommunications Corporation et al.; American Telephone and Telegraph Company v. MCI Telecommunications Corporation et al.; and Federal Communication Commission v. MCI Telecommunications Corporation et al., Certiorari* denied 439 US 980 (1978).

53. See Michael E. Porter, *Competition in the Long Distance Telecommunications Market: An Industry Structure Analysis* (Cambridge, MA: Monitor, October, 1987); Leonard Waverman, "U.S. Interexchange Competition," in Robert W. Crandall and Kenneth Flamm (eds.), *Changing the Rules: Technological Change, International Competition and Regulation in Communications* (Washington, DC: Brookings Institution, 1989) pp. 62–114; and *Statistics of the Long-Distance Telecommunications Industry* (FCC, May 2003).

54. "Cheers, Jeers Still Ringing," *USA Today* (December 30, 1988).

55. Yu Hsing and Franklin G. Mixon Jr., "Price Convergence in Contestable Market Structures: The Impact of Time and Price-Caps on Intercity Telecommunications Rates," *International Journal of Industrial Organization* 9 (December 1994): 813–822.

56. For a discussion of alternatives to traditional rate of return regulation, see David M. Sappington, "Designing Incentive Regulation," *Review of Industrial Organization* 9 (June 1994): 245–272.

57. Fuhr found that although local rates have increased since divestiture, there was no evidence that rural rates had increased more rapidly than the average of all residential rates. Joseph P. Fuhr Jr., "Rural Telephony Since Divestiture," *Review of Industrial Organization* 6 (1991): 89–95.

58. Manley R. Irwin, "The Telecommunications Industry," in Walter Adams (ed.), *The Structure of American Industry* (3rd edition), (New York: Macmillan, 1990), p. 257.

59. Douglas F. Greer, *Business, Government, and Society* (New York: Macmillan, 1987), p. 328.

60. Irwin, *supra* note 58, p. 257.

61. James McConnaughey "Telecommunications," in Adams and Brock, *supra* note 48, p. 184.

62. R.H. Coase, "Payola in Radio and Television Broadcasting," *Journal of Law and Economics* 22 (October 1979): 269–328.

63. Leonard W. Weiss, *Case Studies in American Industry* (New York: John Wiley & Sons, 1980), p. 92.

64. Leonard W. Weiss, "Antitrust in the Electric Power Industry," in A. Phillips (ed.), *Promoting Competition in Regulated Markets* (Washington, DC: Brookings Institution, 1975), pp. 135–173; Paul L. Joskow and Richard Schmalensee, *Markets for Power* (Cambridge, MA: MIT Press, 1983).

65. *Phillips Petroleum Company v. Wisconsin et al.,* 342 US 672 (1954).

INTERNET EXERCISES

Visit www.aw-bc.com/waldman_jensen for this chapter's web exercises. Answer our real-world economics problems by searching the Internet for solutions!

GLOSSARY

abbreviated rule of reason: A limited form of the Rule of Reason which "applies in cases where per se condemnation is inappropriate, but where 'no elaborate industry analysis is required to demonstrate the anticompetitive character' of an inherently suspect restraint."

absolute cost advantage: A cost advantage one firm has over another firm that results in one firm producing any given level of output at a lower average cost.

accounting costs: The costs reported by firms in their financial reports following various bookkeeping conventions. For some inputs, particularly capital and labor, accounting costs and economic costs typically differ considerably, creating problems for the measurement of economic profits.

advertising response function: A function $Q = f(A)$, where Q is sales and A is the number of advertising messages. For a typical entrant, the advertising response function is first horizontal, then rises at an increasing rate, then rises at a decreasing rate, and finally decreases.

aggregate concentration: A measure of the role played by large companies in the economy as a whole, commonly measured by the percentage of total assets controlled by the largest 50, 100, or 200 firms in an economy.

allocative efficiency: A state in which the marginal benefit of producing another unit of output is equal to its marginal cost. If this condition is satisfied, the socially optimal quantity of the good is being produced, meaning that there is no way to reallocate resources to make one consumer or firm better off without hurting another.

applied research: Research aimed at obtaining knowledge with the objective of using that knowledge for commercial purposes. A chemist working on an AIDS vaccine in a pharmaceutical company's laboratory is doing applied research.

appropriability: The ability of a firm to maintain exclusive control over its technology without seeing that technology lost to competitors.

asset specificity: The degree to which some assets are of value primarily to one firm. Asset specificity can arise due to geographic location, physical characteristics, or specialized human capital.

asymmetric information: A situation in which some players in a game know different information than other players.

average cost: Total cost divided by the level of output.

average fixed cost: Fixed cost divided by the level of output.

average variable cost: Variable cost divided by the level of output.

Averch-Johnson effect: A theory suggesting that if a public utility is permitted to earn a rate of return greater than the market cost of capital, the utility will utilize too much capital relative to other inputs and therefore produce inefficiently from a social standpoint.

avoidable cost: The sum of variable cost and the recoverable part of fixed cost. Avoidable costs are those that the firm will not have to pay if it produces zero output in the short run.

barometric price leadership: A form of price leadership in which price changes are initiated by a relatively small firm with no ability to enforce them.

basic research: Research aimed at gaining knowledge for its own sake. For example, a research scientist at a major university working on quantum physics is engaged in basic research.

basing point pricing system: A delivered price system under which one or more geographic locations are established as basing points, and buyers are charged prices that include standard freight charges from the nearest basing point, even if the seller's manufacturing plant is located far from the basing point.

Bertrand model: A model developed by Joseph Bertrand in 1883 that criticized Cournot's result by showing that if firms assumed that all other firms hold their prices constant, Cournot's logic results in an entirely different outcome with price equal to marginal cost.

book value: The value of an asset used in accounting data that is calculated using the historical value of the asset.

bounded rationality: Limits on knowledge based on limited ability of individuals to solve complex problems and envision and understand all future possibilities due to constraints on knowledge, foresight, skill, and time.

bundling: A tying agreement in which the goods are purchased in fixed proportions. See *tying agreements.*

capture theory of regulation: A theory that regulated firms gain control over the regulatory commissions that are supposed to be their regulators. According to the capture theory, once an industry is regulated, the commission comes to view its primary responsibility as protecting the regulated firms from "too much" competition, rather than protecting consumers from monopoly prices.

Celler-Kefauver Act: A 1950 law that amended Section 7 of the Clayton Act to include mergers through asset as well as stock acquisition. The Celler-Kefauver Act also extended Section 7 to reach vertical and conglomerate, as well as horizontal, mergers.

certain information: If a game includes nature, but nature never moves after any other player moves, then the game is said to be of certain information.

chain-store paradox: The paradox that in a repeated prisoner's dilemma game of any number of finite rounds with perfect, complete, certain, and symmetric information, firms defect in every round. See *prisoner's dilemma.*

Chicago School of economics: A school of industrial organization economists who believe that price theory models should be the primary tool for analyzing markets. Followers of the Chicago School rely heavily on price theory models to make predictions about expected conduct and performance and to analyze economic welfare.

Clayton Act: A 1914 law aimed at preventing certain specific types of anticompetitive business conduct, such as price discrimination, tying agreements, exclusive dealing arrangements, mergers reducing competition, and interlocking directorates.

collusive price leadership: A form of price leadership in which a few large firms in an oligopoly lead price changes and expect that all price changes will be followed by competitors.

compatibility: The capability of two or more components or materials to operate together in the same system or environment with no modification or conversion required. An example of compatibility would be a software application such as a word processing program or a computer game written to work on a specific operating system such as Windows.

complements: Two goods or services for which an increase in the price of one good or service results in an increase in the quantity demanded of the other good or service.

complete information: If a game includes nature, but nature does not move first, or nature's first move is observed by all players, the game is of complete information.

concentration ratio: The cumulative share of the K largest firms in the market, where typical values of K are 4, 8, and 20. Thus, the four-firm concentration ratio (CR4) is the sum of the market shares of the four largest firms in the industry. The most common measure of market size is sales, but concentration ratios can also be calculated using other measures of size, such as value added, employment, or assets.

conglomerate mergers: Mergers involving companies that operate in either different product markets or the same product market but different geographic markets.

conscious parallelism: An antitrust law term meaning that a group of oligopolists behave in an identical manner, but there is a lack of proof that the firms ever met to agree on this parallel course of behavior. Conscious parallelism refers to the idea that rational business behavior in a tight oligopoly will lead firms to behave identically with regard to price and other business practices.

consumer surplus: The difference between the maximum amount a consumer is willing to pay for a good and the amount he or she actually pays. Adding consumer surplus over many individuals gives a measure of the aggregate benefit consumers receive from buying a good.

contestable market: A theory developed in the early 1980s which states that potential competi-

tion may be more important than actual competition. According to this theory, even a monopolized market may perform as though it were competitive if there is sufficient potential competition.

convenience goods: Consumer goods that are relatively inexpensive and are purchased on a regular basis, such as soft drinks, cigarettes, and gasoline.

correlation coefficient: A commonly used statistical measure of the strength of the relationship between two variables. The correlation coefficient ranges from 1 to −1. If the coefficient equals 1, a perfect linear relationship exists between the two variables. A correlation coefficient equal to −1 also indicates a perfect linear relationship; in this case the relationship is inverse. If the coefficient equals zero, there is no relationship between the variables.

Cournot-Nash model: A quantity-based model of oligopoly behavior. In the Cournot model, firms assume that the output of all other firms in the industry will remain constant.

cream-skimming: The practice wherein unregulated firms reduce rates to attract the best customers from regulated firms.

creative destruction: The theory of Joseph Schumpeter that capitalism moves forward in major technological leaps that destroy the old economic order and create a new order.

credible threat: A strategy to deter entry that appears rational from the standpoint of the potential entrant.

critical mass: The minimal number of users needed for all potential users to adopt a particular technology.

cross-subsidization: The practice of conglomerate firms attempting to gain an increased market share in one market by using profits earned in another market to subsidize short-run losses.

deadweight loss: Losses of consumer and producer surplus that are not transferred to other parties. Deadweight loss is a measure of the misallocation of resources resulting from problems such as imperfect competition or taxation.

dependent variable: The variable whose values are predicted in a regression equation; the left-hand side variable.

depreciation: A measure of the decrease in economic value that occurs during a period when an asset, such as a machine, is in use.

diffusion: The stage of technological advance in which a technological innovation comes into common use.

discount rate: The rate at which an individual or firm is willing to trade future income for current income. For example, if an individual's discount rate is 10 percent, the individual is willing to trade $1.10 of future income for $1.00 of current income.

discounting: The process of evaluating future dollars as being worth less than their face value today. For example, because X dollars invested today at an interest rate i would increase in value to $X(1 + i)$ dollars in one year, $X(1 + i)(1 + i) = X(1 + i)^2$ in two years, and $X(1 + i)^t$ in t years, the promise to pay X dollars t years from today has a discounted present value of:

$$\text{Discounted Present Value} = \frac{X}{(1 + i)^t}$$

diseconomies of scale: Also called *decreasing returns to scale*. A production function exhibits diseconomies of scale if a proportionate increase in all inputs results in a less than proportionate increase in output. In this case, with constant per-unit input prices, long-run average costs increase as the quantity of output produced increases.

dominant firm price leadership model: A model assuming an industry with one dominant firm and a group of fringe firms, in which the dominant firm maximizes profits subject to the constraint imposed by the fringe firms' output.

dominant strategy: In game theory, a strategy that outperforms any other strategy no matter what strategy an opponent selects.

dominated strategy: In game theory, a strategy that is always worse than some other strategy.

Dorfman-Steiner model: One of the earliest formal models of the relationship between market structure and advertising. The model suggests that the advertising-to-sales ratio in an industry is directly related to the advertising elasticity of demand and inversely related to the price elasticity of demand.

double marginalization: A problem that exists with bilateral monopoly in a vertically structured industry, in which each successive vertical stage of monopoly causes a greater price distortion compared with a vertically integrated firm.

downstream: In a vertically structured industry, a later stage of production.

dynamic games: Games that are sequential, in which Firm 1 moves, then Firm 2 responds, then Firm 1 responds to Firm 2's response, and so on, and so on. . . .

dynamic performance: How an industry performs over time, with an emphasis on whether or not the rate of technological advance is optimal.

economic cost: The payment required to keep a resource in its present employment. Economic cost is closely related to *opportunity cost.*

economic forbearance: An argument against conglomerate mergers between the nation's leading firms, based on the theory that no conglomerate firm will rock the boat in any market because it fears retaliation in another market. For instance, suppose General Motors purchased Dell, and Ford bought Gateway Computers. Ford might discourage Gateway from competing too aggressively against Dell for fear of retaliation by General Motors in the automobile market.

economies of scale: Also called *increasing returns to scale.* A production function exhibits economies of scale if a proportionate increase in all inputs results in a more than proportionate increase in output. In this case, with constant per-unit input prices, long-run average costs decrease as the quantity of output produced increases.

economies of scope: A production function exhibits economies of scope if it is less costly for one firm to perform two activities than it is for two firms to perform the activities separately.

efficiency in production: A cost condition in which firms are producing output at the lowest possible average cost.

endogenous variable: A variable in a model whose numerical value is determined by the model.

engineering studies: An approach to estimate economies of scale in production that uses interviews, questionnaires, and surveys to gather information from engineers who are responsible for designing and planning new plants.

entry barriers: Any factor that prevents long-run entry into a market.

event studies: Statistical studies that examine the impact of a proposed merger on the stock market valuation of the acquired or acquiring firm around the time of the merger.

excess capacity: An industry with more capacity than is required to meet industry demand.

excess return on sales: The ratio of economic profits to sales revenue. Assuming that firms are in long-run equilibrium and operating in the range of their production functions with constant returns to scale, the excess profit rate on sales $\left(\dfrac{TR - TC}{TR}\right)$ will, on average, across all products produced by the firm, equal the Lerner Index.

exclusive dealing: A policy adopted by one firm to sell only the goods or services supplied by another.

exclusive dealing arrangements: An agreement in which a retailer agrees to sell only one manufacturer's products.

exit barriers: Any cost that a firm must incur to leave an industry.

exogenous variable: A variable in a model whose numerical value is determined outside the model, and therefore, is taken as given.

experience goods: Goods whose qualities can be identified only through trial after buying the good. Common examples include consumer nondurable convenience goods such as beer, toothpaste, soap, toiletries, and cereal; and consumer durable goods, including such household appliances as refrigerators and washing machines.

explanatory variable: Also called an *independent variable;* a right-hand-side variable in a regression equation. The values of an explanatory variable are known and are used to predict the value of the *dependent variable.*

explicit collusion: Collusion in which a group of competitors discusses and sets prices and/or quantities. The term is synonymous with *overt collusion.*

extensive form of a game: The game tree representation of a dynamic game.

externalities: Any costs or benefits from an action undertaken by a producer or a consumer that affect other producers or consumers but are not incorporated into the market price for any good or service.

failing firm: A firm on the verge of bankruptcy.

fair trade laws: A euphemistic term referring to laws that permit the use of resale price maintenance.

fast-second innovator: A dominant firm that responds quickly to the technological advances of small competitors.

Federal Trade Commission (FTC): The regulatory commission established by the Federal Trade Commission Act of 1914. The FTC is charged with regulating firms to prevent "unfair methods of competition."

Federal Trade Commission Act: A 1914 law that established the Federal Trade Commission (FTC) as an independent antitrust agency to prevent "unfair methods of competition."

first-degree price discrimination: Price discrimination where each consumer pays his or her reservation price for the good. Often called *perfect discrimination.*

first-mover advantage: An advantage accruing to the first firm to enter an industry that later entrants have great difficulty overcoming. A common example is the product differentiation advantage associated with being the first firm to enter a consumer good industry.

fixed costs: The costs of those inputs, such as land, buildings, and equipment, whose level of usage cannot be changed in the short run. Fixed costs do not vary with the level of output but are the same regardless of whether the firm produces a large or small amount of output.

Folk theorem: A theorem that was part of the oral tradition among game theorists long before it was published. The *grim strategy* is an example.

followship demand curve: A firm's demand curve drawn on the assumption that all firms in an industry charge the same price.

foreclosure: In a vertically structured industry, a situation in which downstream firms have difficulty obtaining inputs or upstream firms have difficulty finding buyers.

franchise fee: A fixed fee charged by a manufacturer for the right to sell its product.

free-rider problem: A situation in which either consumers consume a good but other consumers pay for the good or a group of sellers uses the services provided by another group of sellers without paying for the services. For example, low-priced dealers obtain a free ride on the services provided by high-priced dealers.

gains from trade: The welfare increase in a domestic country associated with a change from a restrictive trade policy to a free trade policy. There are always gains from trade in competitive markets.

game theory: The study of how interdependent decision makers make choices. A game must include players, actions, information, strategies, payoffs, outcomes, and equilibria.

game tree: A diagram that represents a dynamic game as a sequence of possible moves. The game tree representation of a game is also known as the *extensive form* of the game.

geographic extension mergers: A conglomerate merger between companies that produce the same product in different locations. For example, a midwestern beer producer purchases a northeastern beer producer.

grim strategy: A firm's strategy in an infinitely repeated game played with the following behavioral rules: start by cooperating and charging the collusive price; continue to charge the collusive price unless a competitor lowers price, in which case, you charge the Bertrand equilibrium price, $P = MC$, forever. See also *trigger price strategy.*

Hart-Scott-Rodino Act: A 1976 law amending Section 7 of the Clayton Act by requiring advanced notification to the Justice Department and the Federal Trade Commission of any major merger.

Herfindahl-Hirshman Index (HHI): An index of market power that takes into account both the number of firms and the inequality of market shares. The HHI is defined as the sum of the

squares of individual firm's market shares, expressed mathematically as:

$$\text{HHI} = S_1^2 + S_2^2 + S_3^2 + \cdots + S_K^2 = \sum_{i=1}^{K} S_i^2$$

where S_i is the market share of the ith firm and K is the number of firms in the industry.

horizontal merger: A merger involving firms that are direct competitors. The firms must compete in both the same product and geographic markets.

horizontal product differentiation: Differentiation between brands based on different product characteristics but not on different overall quality. For example, a McDonald's Quarter Pounder is somewhat different from a Burger King Whopper or a Wendy's Single, but the overall quality of the three burgers is similar.

incipiency precedent: A legal antitrust precedent that horizontal mergers should be banned even in competitive markets to prevent future increases in concentration.

independent variable: Also called an *explanatory variable;* a right-hand-side variable in a regression equation. The values of an independent variable are known and are used to predict the value of the *dependent variable.*

infinite game: A static game that is repeated an infinite number of times.

informational advertising: Advertising that provides consumers with truthful information about price, location, or quality.

injunction: A court order preventing a person or firm from carrying out a given activity or ordering a given activity to be undertaken.

innovation: The stage in the research and development process consisting of the first commercial application of an invention. Innovation requires refinement of an invention to "get the bugs out" and develop a marketable product.

input expansion path: In an isoquant-isocost diagram, the locus of points showing all the possible cost-minimizing combinations of inputs for producing any possible output.

invention: The discovery of an idea that "should" work. In the invention stage of research and development, the idea passes through its first rough tests, which indicate whether it will work.

isocost lines: In an isoquant-isocost diagram, the lines that represent the input combinations

that it is possible to purchase at the current input prices for a given total cost.

isoquants: Given a production function relating inputs to output, the isoquants are a series of curves that identify input combinations that yield equal outputs.

learning by doing: The process whereby, because of production experience, firms lower their average costs as cumulative output increases.

Lerner Index: Mathematically:

$$\frac{P - MC}{P}$$

The Lerner Index is a measure of the degree of *market power* that a firm possesses.

limit pricing: A strategy of charging a price below the short-run profit-maximizing price to deter entry.

location game: A game in which firms choose between different locations for their manufacturing plants or retail outlets or between different possible characteristics for their products.

low-price guarantees: A promise made to a buyer that the seller "will not be undersold and will match or beat any competitor's price."

marginal cost: The additional cost of producing one more unit of output.

marginal revenue: The change in total revenue resulting from selling one additional unit of output.

market for corporate control: A mechanism by which shirking by managers is limited. If managers use their discretion to further their own interests rather than to maximize profits, an outsider will perceive an opportunity to purchase the poorly run firm, replace the existing managers, and realize a profit.

market power: The ability of a firm to set price above marginal cost.

McGuire Act: A 1952 law that extended the *Miller-Tydings Act* to include nonsigners of a resale price maintenance agreement.

Miller-Tydings Act: A 1937 law that gave the states the right to legalize resale price maintenance in the United States.

minimax strategy: A solution to a zero-sum game in which a firm calculates the maximum outcome for each of its opponent's possible plays

and then selects the strategy that minimizes its opponent's maximum possible outcome.

minimum efficient scale: The lowest level of output for which a firm's long-run average cost is minimized.

mixed bundling: A practice in which firms give consumers the choice of paying for products separately or bundled together in packages.

mixed strategy game: A game with no pure strategy equilibrium in which an optimal strategy is for each player to randomly select its actions with given probabilities that maximize its expected payoff, given the randomly selected strategies being played by its opponents.

mixed strategy Nash equilibrium: The equilibrium in a mixed strategy game. See *mixed strategy game.*

monopolistic competition: A market structure characterized by easy entry, product differentiation, and long-run profits equal to zero.

monopoly: A market controlled by one firm.

most favored customer guarantee: A guarantee made by a firm that if it lowers the price to any one buyer it will retroactively offer that price to any other buyer who purchased the good in the past during some specified period, such as six months or a year. Also known as a *price protection clause.*

multicollinearity: A situation in which two or more of the independent variables in a regression are highly correlated, meaning that they tend to move together. Multicollinearity makes it hard to separate the independent effects of the variables, with the result that estimated coefficients have large standard errors and low t-statistics.

NAICS: the North American Industry Classification System, a new industrial classification system introduced in 1997. This system reflects standardization by Canada, Mexico, and the United States and, unlike the SIC, uses a consistent principle to define markets. The NAICS groups together establishments that use similar production processes.

Nash equilibrium: An equilibrium in a game where both players are doing the best they can given the choice of their opponent(s).

natural monopoly: A market in which one firm can serve the market more efficiently than more than one firm.

nature: A pseudo-player added by the game theorist to take random actions at some point or points in a game.

network externalities: A situation in which the utility that one user derives from consumption of a good increases as the number of other users of the good increases.

node: A point in an extensive form of a game at which a player or nature takes an action or the game ends.

non-followship demand curve: A firm's demand curve drawn on the assumption that all other firms in an industry maintain price.

numbers equivalent: The ratio of 10,000 over the *Herfindahl-Hirshman Index* (*HHI*); that is, N in the following equation:

$$N = \frac{10,000}{HHI}.$$

A measure of the number of equal-sized firms that could "fit" in an industry.

oligopoly: A market structure characterized by the domination of a few firms.

opportunism: The assumption that individuals maximize their utility in a guileful way, misleading, deceiving, and confusing others if it is to their advantage to do so and if such activities cannot be detected easily.

opportunity cost: The value of the resources used to produce a particular good had those resources been used in their best alternative use. Opportunity cost measures foregone possibilities.

overt collusion: A method of collusion in which a group of competitors sits down to discuss and set prices or quantities. The term is synonymous with *explicit collusion.*

overt price-fixing agreement: See *overt collusion.*

parameters: Descriptive measures of a population. In an equation, the coefficients of the independent variables are the parameters; least squares regression is the most common methodology in economics for obtaining estimates of parameters.

parametric price: A price that is considered fixed by sellers or buyers.

patent pooling: An agreement by a group of firms to share a large number of patents in an attempt to monopolize a market.

patent race game: A game in which a group of firms attempts to be the first to obtain a patent. Patent races typically result in too many resources being spent to obtain the patent and a reduction in economic welfare.

peak-load pricing: A pricing system in which firms charge higher prices during high-demand periods and lower prices during low-demand periods.

pecuniary economies: Savings that are purely redistributive, increasing the welfare of one group and reducing the welfare of another.

perfect collusion: Collusion that results in the joint profit-maximizing price.

perfect competition: An economic model that assumes each firm in a market recognizes that its effect on the overall market is insignificant. Therefore, firms do not view other firms as rivals; they make business decisions without considering the actions or reactions of other firms in the industry.

perfect discrimination: Another term for *first-degree price discrimination*. With perfect discrimination, each consumer pays his or her reservation price for the good.

perfect information: A game in which each player knows every move that has been made by the other players before taking any action.

persuasive advertising: Advertising designed to create a subjective positive reaction to a product. Much of the advertising on television is persuasive. For example, beautiful people drive fast, good-looking automobiles.

phantom freight: Under the basing point pricing system, charges for freight that are not incurred as costs by the supplier. These charges are paid by buyers located far from a basing point but close to a seller's manufacturing plant.

phases of the moon system: A collusive pricing system used in the electrical equipment industry in the 1950s. Under the system, each company was awarded a target percentage of the switch-gear market, and the low bidder rotated into the low-bid position based on the current phase of the moon.

potential competition: Competition provided by firms that are not in an industry but may enter the industry if there is a sufficiently large incentive to enter.

predatory discrimination: See *predatory pricing*.

predatory pricing: A strategy of charging a very low price with the objective of driving a competitor(s) out of the market.

present value: The value today of future income. See also *discounting*.

present value of profits: See *present value*.

price cap: Public utility regulation allowing firms to raise price a maximum amount based on the following formula:

Permitted Price Increase = Increase in CPI − X

Under price cap regulation, there is an incentive for firms to improve efficiency because they must keep price increases below the increase in the CPI.

price-cost margin: A measure of performance used in numerous industrial organization studies. The price-cost margin is:

$$\frac{P - AVC}{P}$$

The price-cost margin is typically calculated from data available in the *Census of Manufactures*.

price discrimination: The practice of charging different consumers different price-marginal cost margins for the same product.

(price) elasticity of demand: The percentage change in the quantity demanded of a good in response to a 1 percent change in its price.

price exchange agreement: An agreement among a group of competitors to provide price information to each other.

price squeeze: A pricing policy by a vertically integrated firm in which a firm simultaneously increases the price of an input and decreases the price of a finished good.

primary-line cases: Price discrimination antitrust cases involving injury or possible injury to a direct competitor or competitors of the firm practicing price discrimination.

primary-line discrimination: Price discrimination that involves possible injury to a direct competitor.

prisoner's dilemma game: See *prisoner's dilemma*.

prisoner's dilemma: A game where all the players have a dominant strategy that results in a worse outcome than if they pursued some other strategy or strategies.

producer surplus: The difference between the revenue a producer receives from selling a prod-

uct and the minimum amount the producer would be willing to sell the product for; the amount producers receive for a good in excess of the opportunity costs of producing it.

product extension merger: A conglomerate merger between companies that produce different but related products. For example, a laundry detergent producer purchases a liquid bleach producer.

product proliferation: The strategic decision to preempt potential entrants by creating brands to fill every available product niche.

production function: The mathematical relationship between inputs and outputs indicating the maximum possible output that can be produced from a given set of inputs.

profit rate: A rate of return used to make comparisons across firms. The profit rate is calculated by dividing profits by some base figure, such as stockholders' equity after tax or assets after tax. Earning positive economic profits is equivalent to earning a rate of return that is greater than the competitive rate of return.

profits: Total revenue minus total costs.

pure conglomerate merger: A conglomerate merger between firms operating in entirely separate markets. For example, a telephone company purchases a light bulb company.

raising rivals' costs: Any strategy that attempts to increase rivals' production costs to make entry more difficult.

Ramsey price: The price that maximizes total social benefits subject to the requirement that profits cannot be negative.

rate base: The value of a regulated firm's invested capital, used by a regulatory commission to calculate profits.

rate of return on assets: A measure of profitability calculated as $\dfrac{\pi - T + I}{A}$, where π is profits, T is the tax on profits, I is interest payments to debtholders, and A is total assets.

rate of return on stockholders' equity: A measure of profitability calculated as $\dfrac{\pi - T}{E}$, where π is profits, T is the tax on profits, and E is stockholders' equity. This measure is attractive because it corresponds to what individual investors are trying to maximize. Competitive industries with the same risk will have the same rate of return on equity in the long run.

reaction function: A function that shows the optimal output (price) that one firm will produce (charge) in response to any output (price) produced (charged) by competitors.

real economies: Cost savings that reflect actual savings of resources, such as a reduction in transaction costs.

reciprocity: A practice whereby a large conglomerate encourages its suppliers to purchase inputs from another of the conglomerate's divisions.

regression analysis: The most widely used statistical technique in economics. The technique involves developing a mathematical equation that describes the relationship between a variable to be forecast and the variable(s) believed to be related to the forecast variable.

Regulation Q: The Federal Reserve System's regulation that limited the interest rates banks could pay on all deposits, including large certificates of deposit (CDs).

regulatory lag: When costs increase under regulation, a utility cannot immediately raise prices. Instead, a regulated utility must first request a price increase. Until the price hike is approved, the utility will earn a rate of return less than the permitted rate of return, r. Similarly if costs decrease, the utility will earn a rate of return greater than r until a price reduction is approved. Regulatory lag punishes *X-inefficiency* and rewards improved efficiency.

rental rate: The opportunity cost a firm incurs by using a machine for one hour of production, calculated as the highest amount that another firm would be willing to pay for the use of the machine for an hour.

repeated game: A static game that is played more than once.

replacement cost: A method of evaluating the cost of capital based on the long-run cost of buying a capital asset of comparable quality.

requirements tie-in sales: A tying agreement in which the goods are purchased in variable proportions. See *tying agreements*.

resale price maintenance: A pricing policy in which a manufacturer sets a minimum or

maximum price for which the product may be sold at retail. Also referred to as *RPM*.

resale price maintenance agreements: See *resale price maintenance.*

residual demand curve: A demand curve derived by assuming that a firm faces a demand curve that is left over, or residual, after the other firms in the industry have chosen their outputs.

returns to scale: The rate at which output increases in response to proportional increases in all inputs. If returns to scale are increasing, output increases more than proportionately; with constant returns to scale, output increases at the same rate as inputs. The third case is *decreasing* returns to scale, in which a proportionate increase in all inputs leads to a less than proportionate increase in output.

risk-adjusted rate of return: The return a competitive firm would earn if its projects carried the same level of risk as the firm being examined.

Robinson-Patman Act: A 1936 law that amended Section 2 of the Clayton Act by more strictly limiting the use of price discrimination.

RPM: A pricing policy under which a manufacturer sets a minimum or maximum price for which a product may be sold at retail. Same as *resale price maintenance.*

Rule of Reason: The precedent in antitrust law that only unreasonable attempts to monopolize violate the Sherman Act.

rule-of-thumb pricing: A pricing system under which a firm follows a formula to determine its price. A firm may, for example, set a target rate of return on its invested capital or set price as a fixed mark-up over invoice costs.

sales maximization: An alternative objective of managers, as opposed to profit maximization. Subject to a minimum profit constraint of stockholders, a sales-maximizing manager will choose to produce and sell an additional unit of output as long as marginal revenue is positive.

satisficing: Managerial behavior such that the manager sets a minimum acceptable level of performance below which he or she does not want to fall, rather than trying to maximize profits. Managers might settle for satisficing because of organizational size and complexity.

search goods: Goods whose qualities can be judged before purchase through pre-purchase testing. Search goods include fresh fruits and vegetables, which can be squeezed and smelled to test for freshness; fresh meats, which can be viewed; shoes, which can be tried on; and sofas and chairs, which can be sat upon.

second-degree price discrimination: Price discrimination where all consumers are offered the same price schedule and consumers self-select into the different price categories. Consumers pay different prices, but every consumer who buys within the same price category pays the same price.

secondary-line cases: Price discrimination antitrust cases involving injury or possible injury to a competitor or competitors of a buyer who receives a lower discriminatory price.

secondary-line competition: Competition between the buyers of a good.

secondary line market: See *secondary-line competition.*

separation of ownership and control: A feature of many corporations in which the people who make the day-to-day decisions, the managers, are not the owners, those who receive profits from the firm's operations. Some economists hypothesize that separation of ownership and control results in managers pursuing objectives other than maximizing profits.

Sherman Act: The first national antitrust law passed in 1890. The Sherman Act banned restraints of trade and attempts to monopolize.

shopping goods: Goods that are relatively expensive and are purchased intermittently, such as appliances, automobiles, and televisions.

shutdown cost: See *shutdown price.*

shutdown price: The price below which a firm will choose to produce no output in the short run. Assuming that no fixed costs are recoverable, the shutdown price for a perfectly competitive firm is the minimum of its average variable cost.

SIC code: The Standard Industrial Classification (SIC) code system used by the federal government in the United States prior to 1997 to define manufacturing industries.

simultaneity bias: A statistical bias that may result in studies where it is impossible to identify the direction of the relationship between a dependent variable and an independent variable. For example, advertising may erect an entry barrier that enables firms to earn high

profits, or alternatively, high profits may enable firms to spend large amounts on advertising.

Stackelberg leader: The firm that moves first in the *Stackelberg model.*

Stackelberg model: A quantity-based model that considers what happens if the Cournot model is viewed as a two-stage sequential game in which one firm, the Stackelberg leader, moves first. In equilibrium the Stackelberg leader selects the output on the Stackelberg follower's reaction function that maximizes the Stackelberg leader's profits.

standards: Specifications that ensure that complementary products will operate together. For example, because trains must fit on the tracks, railroads had to reach agreement about the standard gauge in order for traffic to move efficiently from one region of the country to another.

static game: A game in which the players move simultaneously.

static models: Models that deal with a moment in time. For example, when short-run marginal and average cost curves are drawn in a textbook, the curves take a snapshot of the industry at a precise moment in time.

statistical cost analysis: Regression analysis aimed at measuring the significance of economies of scale. In the regression, cost is the dependent variable and output volume is one of the independent variables. To control for the effects of other factors that influence costs, variables such as the age of the equipment, the capacity utilization rate, and input prices must also be included as independent variables in the regression.

stockholder revolt: A decision by stockholders to turn against the management of a company. Some argue that this form of indirect owner control encourages managers to treat stockholders carefully and keep their interests in mind.

straight-line depreciation: An accounting formula that assumes that an asset lasts for some fixed period and decreases in value in equal increments over that fixed period.

strategic barriers to entry: Behavioral barriers to entry based on the notion that existing firms deliberately behave in ways that decrease the probability of entry by other firms.

strong incumbent: An incumbent firm that is always predatory in response to entry.

structural barriers to entry: Elements of basic market structure that act to deter entry. The major structural barriers are economies of scale, absolute cost advantages, capital cost requirements, and product differentiation advantages.

Structure-Conduct-Performance paradigm: An industrial organization paradigm that is primarily empirical in its orientation. The paradigm was developed in the 1940s and 1950s by Professors Mason and Bain, who hypothesized that a direct relationship exists among market structure, market conduct, and market performance.

subgame perfect Nash equilibrium: An equilibrium in which the strategies are a Nash equilibrium, and, within each subgame, the parts of the strategies relevant to the subgame make a Nash equilibrium.

subsidy: A payment from the government to a consumer or firm aimed at encouraging a behavior considered socially beneficial.

summary judgment: A court ruling in favor of one party, where the court believes there is no reason to even consider the evidence.

sunk cost: That portion of fixed costs that is not recoverable.

survivor test: A test of economies of scale based on the idea that, over time, the firms that survive in an industry, supplying constant or increasing fractions of an industry's total output, must be efficient. A decreasing share of output over time is evidence of relative inefficiency; firms or plants of this size are not surviving.

switching costs: The cost for a user of changing from one service to another or of adopting a new technology. Switching costs include the costs of breaking a contract, the costs of training and of learning a new system, the costs of converting data from one software program to another, the costs of searching, and the costs associated with giving up loyalty benefits such as frequent-flyer miles. The higher the switching costs, the more a consumer is locked in to using a specific service or product.

symmetric information: A game in which all players have exactly the same information when each player moves.

tacit collusion: A method of collusion in which firms set identical prices without ever meeting

to discuss prices because of a "meeting of the minds."

tacit price-fixing agreement: See *tacit collusion*.

takeover: A purchase of one firm's stock by another firm or group of investors. The threat of a takeover constrains managers from straying too far from profit-maximizing strategies.

tariff: A tax placed on an imported good.

technological opportunity: The inherent inter-industry differences in ability to make major technological progress. For example, some industries, such as the computer or the drug industry, have many scientific opportunities to make progress, whereas others, such as the brick or the glass bottle industry, have far fewer scientific opportunities.

territorial restrictions: Restrictive agreements under which manufacturers distribute goods through independent dealers who are required to sell only in certain geographic areas or only to certain customers.

third-degree price discrimination: Price discrimination where consumers are separated into two or more groups according to their elasticities of demand, and groups with more inelastic demand face higher price–marginal cost margins.

tied product: In a tying agreement, the product over which the seller does not have market power.

tie-in sales: A tie-in exists when a firm with market power over good X requires its buyers to purchase another good, good Y, in order to obtain good X. Also known as a *tying agreement*.

tit-for-tat strategy: A strategy in a prisoner's dilemma game in which the tit-for-tat player starts off in the first round cooperating, and in every subsequent round $N > 1$, adopts his/her opponent's strategy in the previous round (i.e., the opponent's strategy in round $N - 1$).

Tobin's q: A measure of profitability using the ratio of the market value of the firm to the replacement value of its assets. In a perfectly competitive industry in long-run equilibrium, the value of q would be 1; the market value of the firm would just equal what it would cost to rebuild it.

total cost: In the short run, the sum of fixed costs and variable costs. In the long run, all costs are variable and are included in total cost.

total revenue: The same as sales. Total revenue is equal to price times quantity.

total variable cost: The costs associated with inputs that can be varied in the short run. Often called simply *variable cost*.

transaction costs: The costs of using the market to make a transaction and to gather the information to make those transactions.

tremble: In a game, the small probability that a player makes a mistake and chooses the wrong action.

trigger price strategy: A firm's strategy in an infinitely repeated game played with the following behavioral rules: Start by cooperating and charging the joint profit-maximizing price; continue to charge the joint profit-maximizing price unless a competitor lowers price, in which case, charge the Bertrand equilibrium price, P = MC, forever. See also *grim strategy*.

two-part tariff: A two-part tariff consists of a lump-sum payment (for example, a copier machine rental) combined with a per-unit charge (for example, a per-copy charge).

tying agreements: A tying agreement exists when a firm with market power over good X requires its buyers to purchase another good, good Y, to obtain good X. Also known as a *tie-in sale*.

tying contracts: An agreement that forces a buyer to purchase one good in order to obtain another. See *tying agreements*.

tying product: In a tying agreement, the product over which the seller has market power.

uniform density: A distribution function in which a variable is equally spaced over all possible preferences or locations. For example, consumers are equally spaced over all possible locations.

upstream: In a vertically structured industry, an earlier stage of production.

variable cost: Also known as *total variable cost*.

vertical merger: A merger involving firms that produce at different stages of production in the same industry.

vertical product differentiation: Differentiation in the actual quality of two brands. For example, Ben & Jerry's ice cream and Häagen Dazs ice cream have a higher fat content than Breyers ice cream, which has a higher fat content than the typical store brand of ice cream.

vertical restraints: A variety of methods used by manufacturers to limit the ways in which retail-

ers can market their products. Examples include resale price maintenance, exclusive dealing arrangements, and tying agreements.

weak incumbent: An incumbent firm that will only be predatory in one market if it believes predatory pricing will increase its profits in future markets to compensate for the lost profits as a result of its predatory behavior.

X-inefficiency: A situation in which less than the maximum output is produced from a given set of inputs. X-inefficiency might exist, for example, if managers are interested in living a quiet life and therefore do not continually strive to find the least costly way of doing business.

zero-sum game: A game in which one player's gain is always matched by another player's loss.

ANSWERS TO ODD-NUMBERED PROBLEMS

CHAPTER 2

1. a. Fill in the blanks in the following table.

 b. Draw a graph that shows marginal cost, average variable cost, and average total cost.

Q	FC	TVC	TC	MC	AFC	AVC	ATC
0	40	0	40				
1	40	12	52	12	40	12	52
2	40	22	62	10	20	11	31
3	40	30	70	8	13.3	10	23.3
4	40	40	80	10	10	10	20
5	40	65	105	25	8	13	21

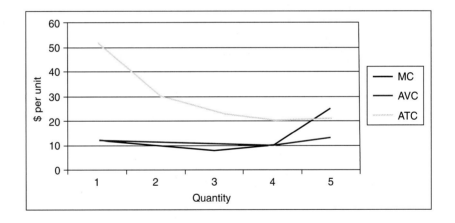

3. A 1-cubic-foot square crate requires 6 square feet of wood; at $1 per square foot, it would cost $6 to build. An 8-cubic-foot square crate (2 ft. × 2 ft. × 2 ft.) requires 12 square feet of wood; at $1 per square foot, it would cost $12 to build. This illustrates economies of scale that result from geometric relationships: Costs increase by a factor of 2 when storage capacity increases by a factor of 8, so the average cost of a cubic foot of storage capacity falls as the crate size increases.

5. The measure of economies of scope is:

$$S_C = \frac{C(q_1, 0) + C(0, q_2) - C(q_1, q_2)}{C(q_1, q_2)}.$$

Substituting $q_C = 20$ and $q_T = 10$ into this formula, we get

$$\frac{50(20) + 60(10) - \left[50(20) + 60(10) - \dfrac{3(20)(10)}{2}\right]}{50(20) + 60(10) - \dfrac{3(20)(10)}{2}} = \frac{300}{1300} = 0.23.$$

Because this number is positive, production of cars and trucks exhibits economies of scope. The magnitude of S_C indicates the degree of the economies.

CHAPTER 3

1. a. The two total cost functions are:

$$TC_1 = 200 + q$$
$$TC_2 = 40 + 5q.$$

b. The two average cost and marginal cost functions are:

$$AC_1 = \frac{200}{q} + \frac{q}{q} = \frac{200}{q} + 1 \qquad MC_1 = 1$$

$$AC_2 = \frac{40}{q} + \frac{5q}{q} = \frac{40}{q} + 5 \qquad MC_2 = 5.$$

c. The smallest number of acres for which she should buy the tractor is identified by the number of acres where $AC_1 = AC_2$.

$$AC_1 = \frac{200}{q} + 1 = \frac{40}{q} + 5 = AC_2$$
$$200 + q = 40 + 5q \Rightarrow 4q = 160 \Rightarrow q = 40$$

She should choose the tractor only if the number of acres mowed is greater than or equal to 40.

d. If the tractor has a positive resale value, this would reduce the AC of using the tractor. If RV represents the tractor's resale value, then:

$$AC_1 = \frac{200}{q} + 1 - \frac{RV}{q}.$$

With lower average costs for the tractor, she would select the tractor to mow fewer than 40 acres. The exact number of acres depends on the value of RV.

3. a. $P = 80 = 4q = MC \Rightarrow q = 20$

b. $\pi = TR - SRTC = (80)(20) - [150 + 2(20)^2] = 1600 - 150 - 800 = 650$

c. $VC = 2q^2 \Rightarrow AVC = 2q$

$MC = 4q = 2q = AVC$ when $q = 0$. This firm will choose to produce rather than shut down for any positive quantity of output.

5. a. $P = MC \Rightarrow P = 2q + 10 \Rightarrow q = \dfrac{P}{2} - 5$

b. $Q_S = nq \Rightarrow Q_S = 100\left(\dfrac{P}{2} - 5\right) \Rightarrow Q_S = 50P - 500$

c. $Q_D = Q_S \Rightarrow \dfrac{12{,}000 - 100P}{9} = 50P - 500 \Rightarrow 12{,}000 - 100P = 450P - 4500 \Rightarrow$
$16{,}500 = 550P \Rightarrow 30 = P.\ Q_D = Q_S = 1000.$

d. Each firm produces 10 units of output. Using the equation of the firm's supply curve from part a, and substituting $P = 30$, $q = \dfrac{30}{2} - 5 = 10$.

e. $\pi = TR - TC = (30)(10) - [(10^2 + 10(10) + 100)] = 0$. Economic profits are equal to zero, which is a necessary condition for long-run equilibrium.

7. a. $MR = 53 - 2Q$

b. $MR = MC \Rightarrow 53 - 2Q = 5 \Rightarrow 48 = 2Q \Rightarrow 24 = Q$
$P = 53 - Q = 29$

c. $\pi = (P - AC)Q = (29 - 5)(24) = 576$

d. $CS_M = \dfrac{(53 - 29)(24)}{2} = 288$

e. Under perfect competition, $P = MC = 5$. $Q = 53 - P = 48$

f. $CS_{PC} = \dfrac{(53 - 5)(48)}{2} = 1152$

g. $DWL = \dfrac{(P_M - P_{PC})(Q_{PC} - Q_M)}{2} = \dfrac{(29 - 5)(48 - 24)}{2} = 288$

h. $288 + 576 + 288 = 1152$

9. a. $MR = 96 - 12Q$

b. $MR = MC \Rightarrow 96 - 12Q = 4Q \Rightarrow 96 = 16Q \Rightarrow 6 = Q$
$P = 96 - 6Q = 60$

c. $\pi = TR - TC = (60)(6) - 2(6)^2 = 360 - 72 = 288$

11. a. The present value of a promise to pay $1000 in two years at a discount rate of 10 percent is:

$$PV = \frac{\$1000}{(1.1)^2} = \frac{\$1000}{1.21} = \$826.45.$$

b. The present value of a promise to pay $1000 for the next 100 years at a discount rate of 10 percent is:

$$PV = \frac{\$1000}{0.10} = \$10{,}000.$$

c. At 5 percent, the present value of a promise to pay $1000 is:

$$PV = \frac{\$1000}{(1.05)^2} = \frac{\$1000}{1.1025} = \$907.03.$$

At 5 percent, the present value of a promise to pay $1000 for the next 100 years is:

$$PV = \frac{\$1000}{0.05} = \$20,000.$$

A lower discount rate gives more weight to dollars received in the future than does a higher discount rate.

13. a. If SO continues its current policy, it will earn profits equal to $200,000 + \frac{200,000}{0.11} = 200,000 + 1,818,182 = \2.018 million.

If SO follows the predatory strategy, it will earn profits equal to $0 + \frac{220,000}{0.11} = \$2.0.$ million

SO will earn slightly more profits by maintaining its current policy.

b. It is unlikely that ABC Oil would be driven from the market forever. If the physical capital, such as pipelines, is still in place, ABC could resume operations once SO raised its price to the monopoly level.

c. Buying ABC Oil for $180,000 and then earning profits of $220,000 makes sense if the discount rate is relatively low. This strategy dominates the predatory strategy for two reasons: (1) The firm may be able to raise price to the monopoly level more quickly; and (2) this strategy ensures that ABC Oil will not be able to resume operations in the future.

CHAPTER 4

1. a. The four-firm concentration ratio is:

$$30 + 20 + 12 + 10 = 72.$$

b. The Herfindahl-Hirshman Index is:

$$(30^2 + 20^2 + 12^2 + 10^2 + 10^2 + 8^2 + 7^2 + 3^2)$$
$$= (900 + 400 + 144 + 100 + 100 + 64 + 49 + 9) = 1766.$$

3. The answers to question 2 are:

a. Four-firm concentration ratio $= 72$

b. The HHI $= 1518$

The concentration ratio suggests that both industries have the same structure, but the HHI indicates a difference. The HHI is much more sensitive to large market shares of the top firms. In this case, the industry in question 1 is identified as being less competitive than the industry in question 2.

5. $N = \dfrac{10,000}{HHI}$

a. $N = \dfrac{10,000}{1000} = 10$

b. $N = \dfrac{10{,}000}{1250} = 8$

c. $N = \dfrac{10{,}000}{1428} = 7$

d. $N = \dfrac{10{,}000}{2500} = 4$

The *numbers equivalent* tells us something about the meaning of a particular HHI by informing us about how many equal-sized firms would "fit" in an industry with a given HHI. Smaller values of N suggest less competition.

The *numbers equivalent* does not convey any information about the distribution of market shares among firms.

7. Under perfect competition, P = MC, so P = 50. Therefore, Q = 200 − 50 = 150. Consumer surplus under perfect competition is 11,250; because MC is constant, there is no producer surplus.

Under monopoly, MR = MC. The MR curve corresponding to the demand is MR = 200 − 2Q. Setting MR = MC yields
200 − 2Q = 40 ⇒ 160 = 2Q ⇒ 80 = Q. P = 200 − 80 = 120. Consumer surplus under monopoly is 3200; the monopolist's profits are 6400. The sum of consumer surplus and profits is 9600, indicating that the mergers reduce welfare in this case. The cost savings are not sufficient to outweigh the deadweight loss.

Now LRMC = LRAC = 20. Setting MR = MC yields 200 − 2Q = 20 ⇒ 180 = 2Q ⇒ 90 = Q. Now P = 200 − 90 = 110. Consumer surplus in this case is 4050; the monopolist's profits are 8100. The sum of consumer surplus and profits is 12,150, indicating that the mergers increase welfare. The cost savings are so large that they outweigh the deadweight loss of monopoly.

CHAPTER 5

1. a. See Figure Problem 5.1. The vertical intercept of the market demand curve is P = 800/3. The vertical intercept of the fringe firms' supply curve is P = 100.

b. The dominant firm's marginal and average costs are equal and constant at MC = AC = 80. See Figure Problem 5.1.

c. To find this price, set the market demand curve equal to the fringe supply curve:

$$800 - 3P_1 = -200 + 2P_1 \Rightarrow 1000 = 5P_1 \Rightarrow 200 = P_1.$$

d. To find this price, set the fringe supply curve equal to zero:

$$Q_F = -200 + 2P_2 = 0 \Rightarrow P_2 = 100.$$

e. To find the dominant firm's residual demand curve, subtract the fringe supply from the market demand:

$$Q_T - Q_F = (800 - 3P) - (-200 + 2P) \Rightarrow Q_D = 1000 - 5P.$$

See Figure Problem 5.1.

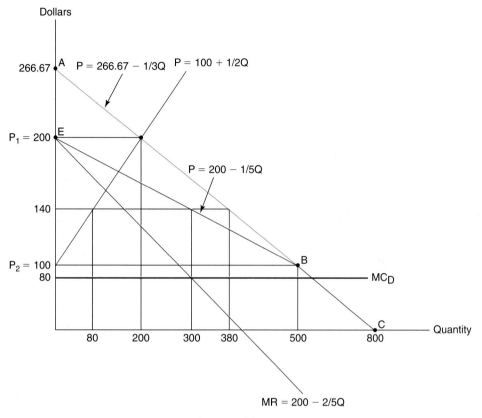

Figure Problem 5.1

f. First, find the MR corresponding to the dominant firm's residual demand:

$$Q_D = 1000 - 5P \Rightarrow P = 200 - \frac{Q_D}{5} \Rightarrow MR = 200 - \frac{2Q_D}{5}.$$

Set MR = MC and solve for Q:

$$200 - \frac{2Q_D}{5} = 80 \Rightarrow 120 = \frac{2Q_D}{5} \Rightarrow 300 = Q_D.$$

g. Substitute the dominant firm's profit-maximizing level of output into its residual demand to get P = 140.

h. The fringe firms know that the dominant firm has the ability to undercut their price and keep them out of the market. Also, the fringe firms earn a profit at the price set by the dominant firm.

i. Profits equal TR − TC = (140)(300) − (80)(300) = 18,000.

j. At a price of 100, the dominant firm will sell 500 units of output. Its profits would equal (100)(500) − (80)(500) = 10,000. Sacrificing current-period profits might make sense if the dominant firm can become a monopoly in the

future by undercutting the fringe firms in the current period. Relevant factors to consider include the discount rate, the amount of profits it could make as a monopolist, and the likelihood of future entry if the dominant firm adopts the monopoly price.

CHAPTER 7

1. Sales would still be split in half with Waldman getting 50 percent and Other Truck getting 50 percent.

This is *not* a Nash equilibrium because each ice cream truck could gain sales by moving toward the middle of the parade route if the other truck remained parked 1/4 mile from the middle.

Society is better off because the total travel time to obtain ice cream is reduced by the action of the local police. With both trucks parked in the middle, some consumers would walk a half mile to obtain ice cream, but with each parked 1/4 mile from one end, the farthest any consumer would walk is 1/4 mile.

3. There is no dominant strategy in this game. There is no Nash equilibrium in this game because there is always an incentive for one of the players to move from a cell. The firms would adopt a mixed strategy.

To solve for the mixed strategy equilibrium, let ρ_{MH} equal the optimal mixed strategy probability for McDonald's to play "High Price." $(1 - \rho_{MH})$ is then the optimal mixed strategy probability for McDonald's to play "Low Price." If McDonald's is playing its optimal mixed strategy, then Burger King will have the same expected value of profits regardless of whether Burger King always plays "High Price" or always plays "Low Price." Mathematically, the following condition must therefore hold:

$$\rho_{MH}(30) + (1 - \rho_{MH})25 = \rho_{MH}(35) + (1 - \rho_{MH})20$$
$$30\rho_{MH} + 25 - 25\rho_{MH} = 35\rho_{MH} + 20 - 20\rho_{MH}$$
$$5 = 10\rho_{MH} \Rightarrow \rho_{MH} = \frac{1}{2} \Rightarrow (1 - \rho_{MH}) = \frac{1}{2}.$$

Let ρ_{BH} equal the optimal mixed strategy probability for Burger King to play "High Price" and $(1 - \rho_{BH})$ the optimal mixed strategy probability for Burger King to play "Low Price." Burger King is playing the optimal mixed strategy when McDonald's has the same expected value of profits regardless of whether McDonald's always plays "High Price" or always plays "Low Price." This yields the following mathematical relationship:

$$\rho_{BH}(40) + (1 - \rho_{BH})30 = \rho_{BH}(35) + (1 - \rho_{BH})32$$
$$40\rho_{BH} + 30 - 30\rho_{BH} = 35\rho_{BH} + 32 - 32\rho_{BH}$$
$$10\rho_{BH} + 30 = 3\rho_{BH} + 32$$
$$7\rho_{BH} = 2 \Rightarrow \rho_{BH} = \frac{2}{7} \Rightarrow (1 - \rho_{BH}) = \frac{5}{7}.$$

5. a. The Nash equilibrium is reached by working backwards. We see that if the entrant stays out, then the incumbent will continue to profit-maximize (the only choice). Also, if the entrant enters, the incumbent is better off choosing to continue to profit-maximize. Thus, the incumbent has a dominant strategy

to "continue to profit-maximize." With this knowledge, the entrant knows if it doesn't enter, it gets 0, but if it does enter, it will get 30. Thus, the entrant chooses to enter, and the incumbent will continue to profit-maximize. The entrant will earn 30 and the incumbent will earn 50.

b. Because the game is played once, the incumbent's threat to fight could not be credible. The possibility of forgoing current profits for future gain is not built into a game played one time.

7. a. Firm A's dominant strategy is to stay open 24 hours. Firm B's dominant strategy is to use double coupons.

b. The Nash equilibrium is in the lower left, where Firm A stays open 24 hours and Firm B uses double coupons.

9. The information structure is imperfect, complete, certain, and asymmetric. Store K has more information than Store D.

11. a.

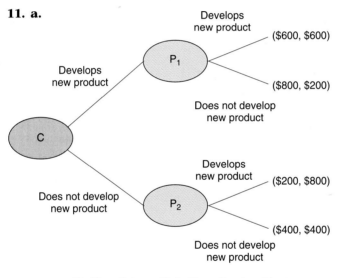

Develops
new product
($600, $600)

P_1

Develops
new product

($800, $200)

Does not develop
new product

C

Develops
new product
($200, $800)

Does not develop
new product

P_2

($400, $400)

Does not develop
new product

($millions Coke profit, $millions Pepsi profit)

b. The Nash equilibrium is Coke *Develops a new product* and Pepsi *Develops a new product.*

13. a. Pepsi does not have a dominant strategy.

b. Coke does not have a dominant strategy.

c. There is no pure Nash equilibrium. The mixed strategy equilibrium is that the probability that Coke will play *Advertises heavily* is 1/3. The probability that Coke will play *Advertises lightly* is 2/3. The probability that Pepsi will play *Advertise heavy* is 2/3. The probability that Pepsi will play *Advertises lightly* is 1/3.

CHAPTER 8

1. There are two methods for solving this problem: using reaction functions, and using the total output rule for two firms with linear demand and marginal cost. We show both solutions below.

Using reaction functions:

$$P = a - b(q_1 + q_2) \quad \text{or} \quad MR_1 = (a - bq_2) - 2bq_1$$

To maximize profits:

$$MR_1 = (a - bq_2) - 2bq_1 = c = MC \Rightarrow 2bq_1 = (a - c) - bq_2$$

solving for q_1

$$q_1 = \frac{(a - c) - bq_2}{2b} = \frac{(a - c)}{2b} - \frac{1}{2}q_2.$$

By symmetry $q_2 = \frac{(a - c)}{2b} - \frac{1}{2}q_1.$

Therefore, $q_1 = \frac{(a - c)}{2b} - \frac{1}{2}\left[\frac{(a - c)}{2b} - \frac{1}{2}q_1\right]$

and $q_1 = \frac{1}{2}\left[\frac{(a - c)}{2b}\right] + \frac{1}{4}q_1 \Rightarrow \frac{3}{4}q_1 = \frac{(a - c)}{4b}$

or $q_1 = \frac{(a - c)}{3b}.$

By symmetry:

$$q_2 = \frac{(a - c)}{3b}.$$

Using the rule that the Cournot-Nash equilibrium with linear demand, linear marginal cost and two firms is equal to 2/3 of the competitive output, we first find the competitive output.

$$P = a - bq = c = MC$$
$$q = \frac{(a - c)}{b}$$

Since the Cournot-Nash total output is 2/3 of q:

$$q_{CN} = \frac{2(a - c)}{3b}.$$

Therefore, $q_1 = q_2 = \frac{(a - c)}{3b}.$

Notice how much simpler it is to use the second method.

3. First identify the follower's reaction function:

$$MR_A = (60 - 2q_B) - 4q_A = 20 = MC_A \Rightarrow 4q_A = 40 - 2q_B$$
$$q_A = 10 - \frac{1}{2}q_B.$$

Next substitute Airbus's reaction function in Boeing's demand curve and maximize profits.

$$P_B = \left[60 - 2\left(10 - \frac{1}{2}q_B\right)\right] - 2q_B = 40 + q_B - 2q_B = 40 - q_B$$
$$MR_B = 40 - 2q_B = 10 = MC_B$$
$$q_B = \frac{30}{2} = 15.$$

Therefore, $q_A = 10 - \frac{1}{2}q_B = 10 - \frac{1}{2}(15) = 10 - (7.5) = 2.5$

$$P = 60 - 2(15 + 2.5) = 25.$$

5. The Cournot-Nash equilibrium for the duopolists is obtained by finding the intersection of the two reaction functions. The American firm's reaction function is:

$$P = 100 - q_J - q_{US} \quad \text{and} \quad MC_{US} = 40$$
$$MR_{US} = (100 - q_J) - 2q_{US} = 40$$
$$q_{US} = 30 - \frac{1}{2}q_J.$$

By symmetry, the Japanese firm's reaction function is:

$$q_J = 30 - \frac{1}{2}q_{US}.$$

The Cournot-Nash equilibrium is:

$$q_{US} = 30 - \frac{1}{2}q_J = 30 - \frac{1}{2}\left(30 - \frac{1}{2}q_{US}\right) = 15 + \frac{1}{4}q_{US}$$
$$q_{US} = \frac{15 \times 4}{3} = 20.$$

By symmetry, $q_J = 20$ and total quantity $q = 40$, and therefore, $P = 60$.

a. With the tariff, the Japanese firm's reaction function changes to:

$$P = 100 - q_{US} - q_J \quad \text{and} \quad MC_J = 50$$
$$MR_J = (100 - q_{US}) - 2q_J = 50$$
$$q_J = 25 - \frac{1}{2}q_{US}.$$

The American firm's Cournot-Nash output is then:

$$q_{US} = 30 - \frac{1}{2}q_J = 30 - \frac{1}{2}\left(25 - \frac{1}{2}q_{US}\right) = 17.5 + \frac{1}{4}q_{US}$$
$$q_{US} = \frac{17.5 \times 4}{3} = 23.33.$$

The Japanese firm's Cournot-Nash output is then:

$$q_J = 25 - \frac{1}{2}q_{US} = 25 - \frac{1}{2}(23.33) = 25 - (11.67) = 13.33.$$

b. Total output with the tariff is 23.33 + 13.33 = 36.66, and price P = 63.34.

c. Before the tariff:

$$CS_{US} = \frac{1}{2}(40)^2 = 800$$

$$\pi_{US} = TR - TC = (20 \times 60) - (250 + 20(40)) = 1200 - 1050 = 150$$
$$\text{and } CS_{US} + \pi_{US} = 800 + 150 = 950.$$

After the tariff:

$$CS_{US} = \frac{1}{2}(36.66)^2 = 671.98$$

$$\pi_{US} = TR - TC = (23.33 \times 64.34) - [250 + 40(23.33)]$$
$$= (1501.05) - (1183.2) = 317.85.$$

In addition, the government gains tax revenue equal to:

$$\text{Tax Revenue} = 10 \times 13.33 = 133.33$$
$$CS_{US} + \pi_{US} + \text{Tax Revenue} = 671.98 + 317.85 + 133.33 = 1123.16.$$

American welfare increases by 1123.16 − 950 = 173.16.

7. a. Q = 6; q_a = q_b = 3. For every additional unit of output a produces, b must produce 1 less in order to keep the collusive agreement. P = 14; profits to Firm a = profits to Firm b = 36. Total profits = 72.

b. Q = 7; q_a = 4. P = 12; profits to Firm a = 40 > 36. Therefore, Firm a has an incentive to cheat. By symmetry, Firm b also has an incentive to cheat.

9. a. Firm a would be expected to be the Stackelberg leader because Firm a has lower costs.

b. q_b = 5.875 − 1/2q_a

c. P_a = 14.25 − q_a

d. q_a = 6.125; q_b = 2.8125; Q = 8.9375; P = 8.125; profits to Firm a = 37.516; profits to Firm b = 15.82; total profits = 53.336

11. All numbers have been rounded to two decimal places.

Model	Price	q_a	q_b	Q	Profits to a	Profits to b	Total Profits
Cournot (6)	10	4	4	8	32	32	64
Collusion (7)	14	3	3	6	36	36	72
Stackelberg (8)	8	6	3	9	36	18	54
Stackelberg with lower costs (9)	8.13	6.13	2.81	8.94	37.52	15.82	53.34
Bertrand (10)	2	6	6	12	0	0	0

From an economic efficiency standpoint, the lower the price, the better the economic performance of the market. The order from best to worst in terms of efficiency, therefore, is Bertrand, Stackelberg, Stackelberg with a cost difference, Cournot, and Collusion.

CHAPTER 9

1. Neither Waldman nor Jensen would ever defect.

3. It would be reasonably easy to maintain effective collusion in this case, because Firm A would always prefer a high price.

Firm A appears to be the dominant firm in this industry.

High price is Firm A's dominant solution. Firm B does not have a dominant strategy; however, Firm B will charge a high price because Firm A always charges a high price.

CHAPTER 11

1. a. The limit price is 60 because the potential entrant's marginal cost and average cost equal 60.

b. Setting MR = MC, the profit-maximizing price is:

$$MR = 200 - 2Q = 50 = MC \Rightarrow Q = 75 \Rightarrow P = 125.$$

Profits equal:

$$\pi = TR - TC = PQ - 50Q = (125)(75) - 50(75) = 9375 - 3750 = 5625.$$

c. At the limit price, profits equal:

$$\pi = TR - TC = PQ - 50Q = (60)(140) - 50(140) = 8400 - 7000 = 1400.$$

3. The Nash equilibrium$(E, \{L, \Pi\})$ is not a subgame perfect Nash equilibrium because it requires that at the node M_1 in Figure 11.4, the monopolist would play limit price (L) if the potential entrant stays out. But playing L is not a Nash equilibrium for the subgame beginning at the node M_1.

5. a. Q = 90; P = 210; profits = 16,200

b. $P = 210 - q_{pe}$

c. $q_{pe} = 42.5$; P = 125; profits = 3612.5; profits to monopolist = 8550

d. P = 40; q = 175; profits = 1750

7. The game is played with perfect, complete, certain, and symmetric information. Therefore, if the game is played a finite number of times, the end result is still the same because of the chain store paradox. By backward induction, at each time period, it is best for the entrant to enter and the monopolist to accommodate entry.

9. Compare the two profit streams.
With predatory pricing:

$$-2 + \frac{-2}{1.1} + \frac{-2}{(1.1)^2} + \cdots + \frac{-2}{(1.1)^9} + \frac{3.5}{(1.1)^{10}} + \frac{3.5}{(1.1)^{11}} + \cdots = \frac{-2}{0.1(1.1)^{-1}} - \frac{-2}{0.1(1.1)^9}$$

$$+ \frac{3.5}{0.1(1.1)^9} = -22 - (-8.49) + 13.51 = 0.31.$$

Without predatory pricing:

$$4 + \frac{3}{1.1} + \frac{2}{(1.1)^2} + \frac{1}{(1.1)^3} + \frac{1}{(1.1)^4} + \cdots = 4 + 2.72 + 1.65 + \frac{1}{0.1(1.1)^2} = 16.63.$$

Predatory pricing makes no sense because profits are much higher without predatory pricing. In fact, profits of $4 million this year are larger than the entire present value of profits with predatory pricing, which are barely above normal profits.

McGee argued that predatory pricing rarely makes sense because the profits that must be sacrificed cannot be made up later. This example is consistent with that theory.

CHAPTER 12

1. The current solution is for the potential entrant to enter and the dominant firm to SR profit-maximize.

The incumbent would have to spend an amount on advertising greater than 250 to prevent entry.

The new solution would be for the potential entrant to stay out and the dominant firm to maximize profits. The dominant firm would earn a profit of just under 2250, which equals 2500 *minus* the amount the dominant firm spends on advertising.

3. a. $q_m = 90$; $p = 120$; profit $= 90(120 - 30) = 8100$

b. $q_m = 67.5$; $p = 97.5$; profit $= 67.5(97.5 - 30) = 4556.25$

$q_{pe} = 45$; $p = 97.5$; profit $= 45(97.5 - 30) - 3000 = 37.5$

c. $q_m = 70$; $p = 95$; profit $= 70(95 - 25) - 1600 = 3300$

$q_{pe} = 45$; $p = 95$; profit $= 45(95 - 30) - 3000 = -75$

d. $q_m = 92.5$; $p = 117.5$; profit $= 92.5(117.5 - 25) - 1600 = 6956.25$

e. In the figure, the Nash equilibrium is for the monopolist at node M_1 to choose capacity $q = 135$, the potential entrant to stay out, and the monopolist to earn a profit equal to 6956.25.

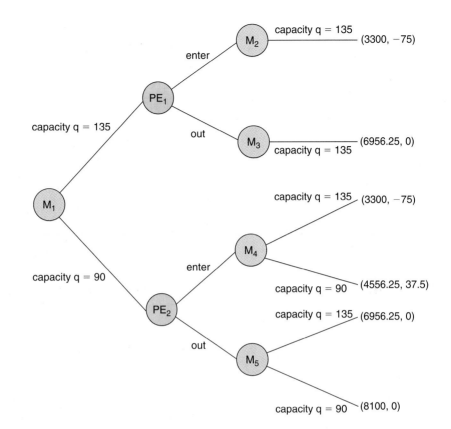

5. a. $q_1 = 3$; $p = 7$; profit $= 3(7 - 4) = 9$

 b. Reaction functions are: $q_1 = 3.75 - (1/2)q_2$; $q_2 = 3 - (1/2)q_1$.

 $q_1 = 3$; $q_2 = 1.5$; $p = 5.5$; monopolist's profits $= 3(5.5 - 2.5) = 9$.

 Profits in the two periods $= 9 + 9 = 18$.

 c. Reaction functions are: $q_1 = 4 - (1/2)q_2$; $q_2 = 3 - (1/2)q_1$.

 $q_1 = 3.33$; $q_2 = 1.23$; $p = 5.44$;

 monopolist's profits in period 2 $= 3.33(5.44 - 2) = 11.46$.

 Profits in period 1 $= 4(6 - 4) = 8$.

 Profits in the two periods $= 8 + 11.46 = 19.46$.

 The monopolist is better off in part c. If learning by doing exists, it may be possible to produce more than the short-run profit-maximizing output in early periods to increase profits in later periods.

CHAPTER 13

1. a. Product differentiation is *less* significant because an increase of 1 in the price of good 2 increases the quantity demanded of good 1 by only 1/2 unit instead of 1 unit.

b. Because product differentiation is less significant, the equilibrium price would be expected to be lower.

c.

$$2p_1 = 96 + \frac{1}{2}p_2 - q_1$$

$$p_1 = \left(48 + \frac{1}{4}p_2\right) - \frac{1}{2}q_1$$

$$MR_1 = \left(48 + \frac{1}{4}p_2\right) - q_1$$

For profit maximization:

$$MR_1 = \left(48 + \frac{1}{4}p_2\right) - q_1 = 12 = MC$$

$$q_1 = 36 + \frac{1}{4}p_2.$$

By symmetry:

$$q_2 = 36 + \frac{1}{4}p_1.$$

To obtain Firm 1's reaction function, solve for p_1:

$$q_1 = 96 - 2p_1 + \frac{1}{2}p_2 = 36 + \frac{1}{4}p_2$$

$$p_1 = 30 + \frac{1}{8}p_2.$$

By symmetry, Firm 2's reaction function is:

$$p_2 = 30 + \frac{1}{8}p_1.$$

To solve for p_1:

$$p_1 = 30 + \frac{1}{8}\left(30 + \frac{1}{8}p_1\right)$$

$$p_1 = 30 + \frac{30}{8} + \frac{1}{64}p_1$$

$$p_1 - \frac{1}{64}p_1 = \frac{63}{64}p_1 = 33.75$$

$$p_1 = \frac{33.75 \times 64}{63} = 34.29.$$

3. a. In long-run equilibrium firms must earn economic profits equal to zero. Therefore,

$$\pi = 0 = 10 - \frac{1}{10}n \Rightarrow n = 100.$$

b. With 100 firms:

$$\pi + CS = 10 - \frac{1}{10}(100) + \sqrt{100} = 10 - 10 + 10 = 10.$$

This is not the socially optimal number of firms, because a decrease in the number of firms increases $\pi + CS$. For example, for $n = 90$:

$$\pi + CS = 10 - \frac{90}{10} + \sqrt{90} = 10 - 9 + (9.49) = 10.49.$$

c. Using calculus, set the first derivative of $\pi + CS$ equal to zero:

$$\pi + CS = 10 - \frac{1}{10}n + n^{1/2}$$

$$\frac{d(\Pi + CS)}{dn} = -\frac{1}{10} + \frac{1}{2}n^{-1/2} = -\frac{1}{10} + \frac{1}{2\sqrt{n}} = 0$$

$$2\sqrt{n} = 10 \Rightarrow \sqrt{n} = 5 \Rightarrow n = 25.$$

5. a. $Q = 50$; $P = 210$; Profits $= 7500$

b. $Q = 60$; $P = 240$; Profits $= 10{,}800 - A$. Would spend at most $3300.

c. $|-1/3\ (240/60)| = |-1.33| = 1.33.$

d. $A/PQ = e_A/|e_p| \rightarrow A/(240)(60) = 0.25/1.33 \rightarrow A = 0.25(14{,}400)/1.33$
$= 2706.77$

7. This implies a price elasticity of demand that is less than one. Therefore, McDonald's cannot be maximizing profit and McDonald's should increase its price.

9. The bank would face an adverse selection problem because only consumers who cannot obtain a credit card at a lower rate would apply online and therefore, the pool of applicants would be relatively high risk. The bank could charge variable interest rates for credit cards to different applicants based on a detailed credit check. High-risk applicants who would have to pay higher interest rates would not be happy with this solution.

CHAPTER 14

1. In Figure Problem 14.1(a) patents slow down the rate of technological advance, but in Figure Problem 14.1(b) the firm's benefits exceed costs only with patent protection. In this figure, the technological advance is developed only with patent protection.

3. a. & b. There is not a unique Nash equilibrium in this game. There are, however, two Nash equilibria (*innovate, imitate*) and (*imitate, innovate*).

Figure Problem 14.1(a)

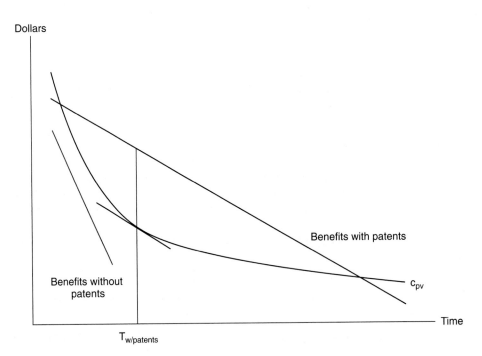

Figure Problem 14.1(b)

c. If Firm A plays *innovate* with a probability of 75 percent and *imitate* with a probability of 25 percent, then Firm B always earns an expected profit equal to 4. For example, consider:

Firm B always plays *innovate:*

$$E(\pi_B) = (0.75)(4) + (0.25)(4) = 3 + 1 = 4.$$

Firm B always plays *imitate:*

$$E(\pi_B) = (0.75)(5) + (0.25)(1) = (3.75) + (0.25) = 4.$$

Firm B plays innovate 50 percent of the time and imitate 50 percent of the time:

$$E(\pi_B) = (0.75)(0.5)(4) + (0.25)(0.5)(4) + (0.75)(0.5)(5) + (0.25)(0.5)(1)$$
$$= (1.5) + (0.5) + 1.875 + (0.125) = 4.$$

No matter what strategy Firm B selects, it always earns an expected profit equal to 4. This suggests an optimal mixed strategy for Firm A.

d. Nonoptimal outcomes are (*innovate, innovate*) and (*imitate, imitate*). The probability of (*innovate, innovate*) equals:

$$\frac{3}{4} \times \frac{3}{4} = \frac{9}{16}.$$

The probability of (*imitate, imitate*) equals:

$$\frac{1}{4} \times \frac{1}{4} = \frac{1}{16}.$$

The probability of a nonoptimal outcome is:

$$\frac{9}{16} + \frac{1}{16} = \frac{10}{16} = \frac{5}{8} = 0.625 = 62.5\%.$$

5. The net economic profits earned from innovation equal zero. This is precisely the same as the profits earned in a monopolistically competitive market. Furthermore, exactly like a monopolistically competitive market, all of the potential positive economic profits are competed away in a race to obtain a patent.

CHAPTER 15

1. The socially optimal fare is 40 because from an economic efficiency perspective, an additional passenger should be allowed on the flight as long as she/he is willing to pay a price greater than or equal to the marginal cost of adding another passenger.

It is first necessary to calculate the marginal revenue of adding stand-by passengers.

Quantity	Price	Total Revenue (PQ)	Marginal Revenue (ΔTR)/(ΔQ)
10	200	2000	2000/10 = 200
25	100	2500	500/15 = 33.33
40	40	1600	(−900)/15 = (−60)

Because the MR of adding the 25th passenger is greater than marginal cost, the airline should charge a price of 100 to maximize profits. The socially optimal result would not be achieved.

3. The marginal cost of an additional patron is zero; therefore, to maximize profits the symphony should equate marginal revenue to zero in each market or:

$$MR_A = 100 - 4q_A = 0 \quad \text{so} \quad q_A = 25$$
$$MR_c = 50 - 4q_c = 0 \quad \text{so} \quad q_c = 12.5.$$

Because it is impossible to seat half a child, the profit-maximizing quantities would be 25 adults and 12 children. Prices would be:

$$p_A = 100 - 2(25) = 50$$
$$p_c = 50 - 2(12) = 26.$$

If price discrimination were illegal, it would be necessary to add the two demand curves to obtain the total demand for tickets, as shown in Figure Problem 15.3. Setting MR = MC = 0:

$$MR = 75 - 2q = 0 \quad \text{so} \quad q = 37.5.$$

Because it is necessary to seat whole people in the theater, the profit-maximizing number of tickets would be 37 and price would equal 38 ($p = 75 - 37 = 38$).

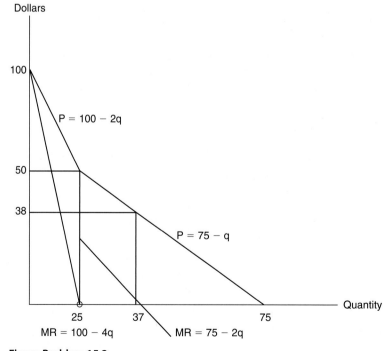

Figure Problem 15.3

With discrimination, total consumer and producer surplus for adults is

$$CS_A + PS_A = \frac{1}{2}(25)(50) + (25)(50) = 1875;$$ and total consumer and producer

surplus for children is $CS_C + PS_C = \frac{1}{2}(12)(24) + (12)(26) = 456.$ Total surplus,

therefore, is $1875 + 456 = 2331.$

Without discrimination, total consumer and producer surplus is the sum of the

two trapezoids in Figure Problem 15.3: $\frac{1}{2}(25)(100 + 50) + \frac{1}{2}(12)(50 + 38) =$

$1875 + 528 = 2403.$ Total surplus and welfare are greater without discrimination.

5. In this case, it would not be profitable to bundle the two films together. If they are bundled, the highest price that can be charged for the bundle is $220 (if both theaters are going to rent the bundle). At any higher price, AMC will not rent the bundle. Thus, revenue from the bundle is $440 ($220 × 2).

 If the films are rented separately, however, $120 is the maximum price that can be charged for *Gladiator* and $100 for *Rocky and Bullwinkle*. Total revenue is the same as with the bundle: $440 ($120 × 2 plus $100 × 2). In this case, bundling is neither more nor less profitable than charging separate fees for each movie.

7. **a.** See the figure below.

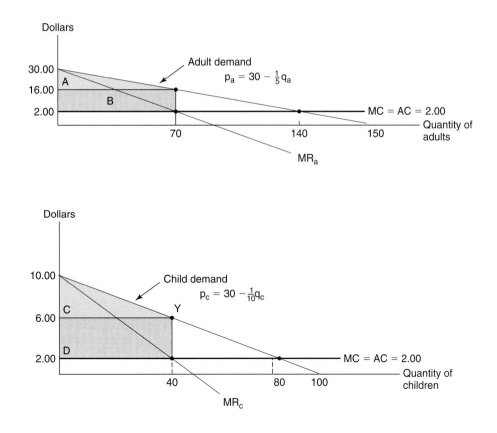

Set MR = MC in each market.

In the adult market: MR = $30 - (2/5)q_a$, using the twice-as-steep rule.

Set MR_a = MC; $30 - (2/5)q_a = 2$; $(2/5)q_a = 28$; $q_a = 70$; $P_a = 30 - (1/5)70 = 16$.

In the child market: MR = $10 - 1/5q_c$.

Set MR_c = MC; $10 - (1/5)q_c = 2$; $(1/5)q_c = 8$; $q_c = 40$; $P_c = 10 - (1/10)40 = 6$.

b. Adult: Consumer surplus = $1/2(30 - 16) \times 70 = 490$ (area A) and producer surplus = $(16 - 2) \times 70 = 980$ (area B).

Children: Consumer surplus = $1/2(10 - 6) \times 40 = 80$ (area C); producer surplus = $(6 - 2) \times 40 = 160$ (area D).

Because MC = AC, profits and producer surplus are equal.

Total: Consumer surplus = 570 and producer surplus/profits = 1140. Total surplus = $570 + 1140 = 1710$.

c. See the figure below.

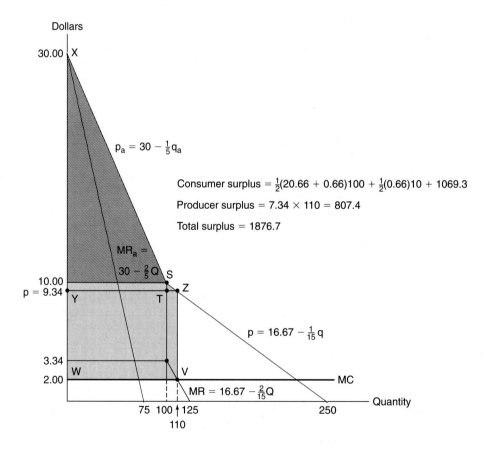

Dollars

30.00 X

$p_a = 30 - \frac{1}{5}q_a$

Consumer surplus = $\frac{1}{2}(20.66 + 0.66)100 + \frac{1}{2}(0.66)10 + 1069.3$

Producer surplus = $7.34 \times 110 = 807.4$

Total surplus = 1876.7

$MR_a = 30 - \frac{2}{5}Q$ S

10.00

p = 9.34 Y T Z

$p = 16.67 - \frac{1}{15}q$

3.34

2.00 W V MC

$MR = 16.67 - \frac{2}{15}Q$

Quantity

75 100 125 250

110

We need to horizontally sum the two demand curves:

$P_a = 30 - (1/5)q_a;$ $(1/5)q_a = 30 - P_a;$ $q_a = 150 - 5P_a$

$P_c = 10 - (1/10)q_c;$ $(1/10)q_c = 10 - P_c$ $q_c = 100 - 10P_c$

$Q = q_a + q_c = 150 - 5P + 100 - 10P$

$Q = 250 - 15P$ for $P \leq 10.$

The kink will occur at $P = 10$. Note that at $P = 10$, $q_a = 150 - 5(10) = 100$ and $Q = 250 - 15(10) = 100$. For prices less than 10, the market demand curve is $Q = 250 - 15P$ or $P = 16.67 - (1/15)Q$ or $P = 16.67 - 0.067Q.$

$MR = 16.67 - (2/15)Q$ or $MR = 16.67 - 0.133Q.$

d. Now, set $MR = MC$ and get: $16.67 - (2/15)Q = 2$; $14.67 = (2/15)Q$; $Q = 110$. (Note that depending on how you round 16 2/3, you might get a small decimal place after 110, but we know from our answer in a that $Q = 110$, so we will round to 110.)

$P = 16.67 - 1/15(110) = 9.34$. Note that at $Q = 100$, MR in the adult market $= -10$. And the MR from the market demand curve $= 3.34$. There is a big jump in the MR curve at $Q = 100$.

e. Producer surplus = Profits = $(9.34 - 2) \times 110 = 807.4$ (area YZVW). Consumer surplus = the area of the trapezoid XSTY + the area of the triangle SZT. Using the formula of $1/2(h_1 + h_2) \times b$, where h_1 and h_2 represent the two bases of the trapezoid, we get consumer surplus $= 1/2(20.66 + 0.66) \times 100 + 1/2(0.66) \times 10 = 1066 + 3.3 = 1069.3$. Total surplus $= 807.4 + 1069.3 = 1876.7.$

f. The producer prefers price discrimination with profit equal to 1140 compared to profit of 807.4 without price discrimination.

g. Total welfare = 1710 under price discrimination. Total welfare = 1876.7 under single-pricing policy. In this case, total welfare is reduced by 166.7 with price discrimination.

9. a. If the monopolist charges $P = MC = 8$, then

$$8 = 200 - 4Q_1; \quad 4Q_1 = 192; \quad Q_1 = 48 \text{ and}$$
$$8 = 122 - 6Q_2; \quad 6Q_2 = 114; \quad Q_2 = 19.$$

The fixed fee can only be equal to what the consumers of the lower demand will pay. Thus, it is equal to $1/2(114) \times 19 = 1083$. Profits are equal to $2 \times 1083 = 2166.$

b. If the monopolist eliminates the low-volume consumer, it can charge a fee that the high-volume user will pay. Consumer surplus for the high demand is equal to $1/2(192)(48) = 4608$. Low-volume users would never pay this fixed fee; thus, they are eliminated. Profits to the firm will be 4608. The monopolist earns more profit by eliminating low-volume users than by charging a low fixed fee to keep them in.

11. a. Total revenue under a separate pricing policy equals $400 + $80 = $480. Total revenue under a pure bundling policy equals $240 + $240 = $480.

b. The team is indifferent between the two pricing policies. The demands are positively correlated so there is no difference in relative valuations; Jonathan is willing to pay more for both types of tickets. Because there is no difference in relative valuations, profits are identical with separate pricing and pure bundling.

13. a. p_{cn} = $1.50 and p_f = $2.00;
profit = ($3.00 − $2.00) + ($2.00 − $0.50) = $2.50

p_{cn} = $1.50 and p_f = $1.00;
profit = ($3.00 − $2.00) + ($2.00 − $1.00) = $2.00

p_{cn} = $2.50 and p_f = $2.00;
profit = ($2.50 − $1.00) + ($2.00 − $0.50) = $3.00

p_{cn} = $2.50 and p_f = $1.00;
profit = ($2.50 − $1.00) + ($2.00 − $1.00) = $2.50

b. Profit = ($7.00 − $4.00) = $3.00

c. Alex buys the bundle and Anna buys chicken nuggets.
Profit = ($3.50 − $2.00) + ($2.45 − $1.00) = $2.95

d. With mixed bundling, the monopolist earns $1.50 from Alex and $1.45 from Anna, but with pure bundling, the monopolist earns $1.50 from each. The monopolist is able to eliminate all of the consumer surplus with pure bundling, but Anna obtains a consumer surplus of $0.05 with mixed bundling.

CHAPTER 16

1. Consider a profit-maximizing franchisee. The royalty on profits will not affect the franchisee's profit-maximizing behavior, because whatever output maximized profits before the royalty on profits will maximize profits, after the imposition of the royalty. Before and after the royalty on profits the franchisee charges the same price and produces the same output. The royalty does not affect consumer surplus or joint profits for the franchisor and franchisee. The royalty affects only the distribution of the profits between the franchisor and franchisee.

To answer the question, we must determine whether a percentage royalty on revenues has an impact on output and price. The percentage revenue royalty reduces the marginal revenue for the franchisee from selling additional units of the good and, therefore, results in a lower marginal revenue curve and reduced output for the franchisee. With lower output, price is increased, and consumer surplus decreases. In addition, combined profits for the franchisee and franchisor are reduced because of the reduction in output.

Because both consumer surplus and combined profits are lower with a royalty based on a percentage of total revenues, economic efficiency is reduced compared with a royalty based on a percentage of profits.

3. The situation is depicted in Figure Problem 16.3. RPM results in an increase in consumer surplus of the red area A, a loss of consumer surplus of the gray area B, and a gain in profits to the manufacturer of the red area C.

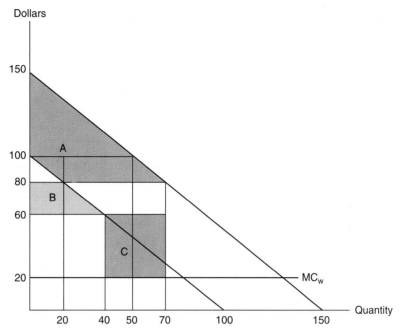

Figure Problem 16.3

The red area A has been broken down into two small triangles, one large triangle, and one rectangle. Area B has been broken down into a rectangle and a triangle. The areas are:

$$\text{Area C} = (40)(30) = 1200$$

$$\text{Area B} = (20)(20) + \frac{1}{2}(20)(20) = 400 + 200 = 600$$

$$\text{Area A} = \frac{1}{2}(50)(50) + (20)(30) + \frac{1}{2}(20)(20) + \frac{1}{2}(20)(20)$$
$$= 1250 + 600 + 200 + 200 = 2250.$$

The net welfare change is: $1200 - 600 + 2250 = 2850$. In this case, RPM improves economic welfare.

5. a. $e_p = -1.5 = \dfrac{\Delta Q_0}{\Delta P_0}\dfrac{P_0}{Q_0} = \dfrac{1}{b}\dfrac{P_0}{Q_0} = \dfrac{1}{b}\dfrac{13.32}{134.82} \Rightarrow b = -0.066$. Substituting $b = -0.066$ into $P_0 = a + bQ_0$, gives $13.32 = a - 0.066(134.82)$ and $a = 22.22$. The demand curve is then $P_0 = 22.22 - 0.066Q_0$.

b. $P = 21.72 - 0.066Q$

c. Consumer surplus without the renovations $= 0.5(21.72 - 12.82)(134.82) = 599.95$. Consumer surplus with the renovations $= 0.5(22.22 - 12.82) \times (142.42) = 669.37$. Renovations increase welfare by $669.37 - 599.95 = 69.42$.

d. The increase in the elasticity of demand decreases welfare. The more elastic the demand, the lower is consumer surplus.

CHAPTER 17

1. a. To find the Ramsey price set AC = Demand:

$$AC = \frac{1800}{Q} + 10 = P = 100 - Q \Rightarrow \frac{1800}{Q} + 10 = 100 - Q$$

$$\frac{1800}{Q} = 90 - Q \Rightarrow Q^2 - 90Q + 1800 = 0$$

$$(Q - 60)(Q - 30) = 0 \Rightarrow Q = 30 \quad \text{and} \quad Q = 60.$$

The regulated quantity would be Q = 60, and the Ramsey price is P = 40.

b. With P = 40 and Q = 60, consumer surplus CS is:

$$CS = \frac{1}{2}(60)^2 = 1800.$$

Profits are zero because P = AC. The triangle A in Figure Problem 17.1 represents the sum of CS plus profits.

c. If P = MC = 10, then Q = 90. Consumer surplus CS equals:

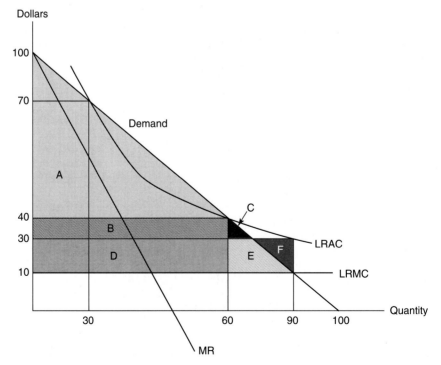

Figure Problem 17.1

$$CS = \frac{1}{2}(90)^2 = 4050.$$

With $Q = 90$, $AC = (1800/90) + 10 = 20 + 10 = 30$. Economic profits, π, are negative and equal to:

$$\pi = Q(P - AC) = 90(10 - 30) = -1800.$$

Total $CS + \pi = 4050 - 1800 = 2250$.

In Figure Problem 17.1, CS is represented by the *sum* of areas A, B, C, D, and E. The economic loss is represented by the *sum* of areas D, E, and F.

d. Price equal to marginal cost results in greater economic welfare by 450 (2250 − 1800).

The change in welfare in Figure Problem 17.1 is represented by the triangle composed of the areas C and E. This is so because the gain in consumer surplus is equal to the sum of areas B, C, D, and E, whereas the economic loss is represented by the sum of areas D, E, and F. The economic loss area equals $90 \times 20 = 1800$. The sum of areas B and D also equals the economic loss, that is, $60 \times 30 = 1800$. It follows that the gain in consumer surplus, equal to the sum of areas B, C, D, and E, *minus* the economic loss equal to the sum of areas B and D, equals the triangle made up of areas C and E.

3. a. $Q = 27.386$; $P = 226.14$

b. Profits = 4107.92

c. $Q = 47.43$; $P = 25.66$; by nature of the Ramsey price, profits = 0.

d. Consumer surplus in part a is 3749.96. Consumer surplus in part c is 11,248.97. The increase in consumer surplus is equal to the difference of those two, or 7499.01. (Due to rounding, if you calculate the actual area of the trapezoid that represents consumer surplus, you may get 7499.56.)

5. a. The socially optimal prices are set where $P = MC$ during each period. During the off-peak period:

$$P = 80 - Q = 20 + \frac{1}{2}Q = MC \Rightarrow \frac{3}{2}Q = 60 \Rightarrow Q = 40 \Rightarrow P = 40.$$

During the peak period:

$$P = 140 - Q = 20 + \frac{1}{2}Q = MC \Rightarrow \frac{3}{2}Q = 120 \Rightarrow Q = 80 \Rightarrow P = 60.$$

b. There is no social cost during the off-peak period because $P = 40$ is the optimal price during the off-peak period.

During the peak period, 100 units of output will be demanded at $P = 40$; $MC = 70$ at $Q = 100$. The social cost $= 1/2(100 - 80)(70 - 40) = 300$.

CASE STUDY INDEX

NAME AND SUBJECT INDEX

Note: Page numbers followed by n indicate footnotes.

A

A&P, 551–552
Abbreviated Rule of Reason, 297
Abere, Andrew E., 16n14
Abernathy, William J., 391n, 407n31, 407n33–n35
Abramowitz, Amy D., 637n45
Absolute cost advantage
 advertising and, 107–108
 capital costs and, 105
 as structural barrier to entry, 103–104
Accounting costs, in single-product firms, 32–33
Accounting profits, 170, 203n5
Accounting rates of return (ARR), 171–172
Acquisitions, mergers and, 115
Acs, Zoltan J., 510n38, 510n28
Adams, Walter, 141n49, 307, 332n11,
 332n12–n13, 333n40, 334n68, 334n76, 391n,
 407n32, 407n45, 407n47, 600n29, 637n40,
 638n48, 638n58, 638n61
Adams, William J., 559n7
Addyston Pipe, 291
Adelphia Communications Corp., 25
Adoption externalities, 154
Advanced Micro Devices (AMD), 143
Adverse selection, 431–433
Advertising
 accounting data and, 171
 by cereal industry, 5
 competition and, 457
 empirical evidence on, 457–462
 as entry barrier, 455–457
 as entry deterrent, 401
 first-mover advantages and, 383
 informational, 435–436
 manufacturers' vs. retailers', 458
 market structure and, 439–455
 oligopoly behavior and, 443–447
 persuasive, 435, 436–439
 product differentiation and, 107–109, 435–462
 profitability and, 458–461
 raising rivals' costs through, 381–382
 social benefits of, 435–436
 social costs of, 436–439
 strategic use of, 456–457

Advertising response function, 455, 456
Advertising-to-sales ratio, 446
 across industries, 447–450
After-tax rate of return, 169n
Aggregate concentration, 90–93
 in manufacturing sector, 91
Aggregate efficiency, collusion and, 301n10
Aghion, Phillipe, 601n44
Aiginger, Karl, 243
Air Atlanta, 357
Airbus, 250, 253
Aircraft manufacturing industry
 Cournot model in, 230–236
 effect of subsidies in, 250–251
 learning by doing as entry barrier in, 388–390
Airline Deregulation Act (ADA, 1978), 623
Airline industry
 Bertrand pricing in, 260
 contestable market hypothesis and, 151–153
 corporate sabotage in, 385
 deregulation of, 622–625
 hub-and-spoke system in, 623–624
 predatory pricing in, 356–358
 price discrimination in, 541
 regulation of, 620–622
 short-run losses in, 56
Air One, 357
AirTran, 358
Ajinomoto Co., 322
Akerlof, George, 428–431, 466n6
Alæk, Svend, 319–321
Alberts, William W., 141–142n53
Alchian, Armen A., 49n3
Alcoa, 76, 104, 122–123, 538n
 excess capacity and, 376–377
 price discrimination by, 581
 price squeeze by, 580
Allen, Beth, 406n1
Allen, Bruce T., 141n37
Allen, Paul, 488
Allis-Chalmers, 309, 312, 326
 pricing and, 321
Allocative efficiency, 58
Allocative inefficiency, 161
 market power and, 88
Almost perfect information, in repeated games, 214

H

CREDITS

Table 4.5, page 124, From David J. Ravenscraft and F.M. Scherer, *Mergers, Sell-offs, and Economic Efficiency* (Washington: Brookings Institution, 1987), p. 60. Reprinted with permission. **Table, page 248,** From Anthony J. Venables, "Trade Policy Under Imperfect Competition," In Paul Krugman and Alasdair Smith (eds.), *Empirical Studies of Strategic Trade Policy,* Chicago, University of Chicago Press, 1994, p. 57. Reprinted with permission. **Table, page 249,** From Anthony J. Venables, "Trade Policy Under Imperfect Competition," In Paul Krugman and Alasdair Smith (eds.), *Empirical Studies of Strategic Trade Policy,* Chicago, University of Chicago Press, 1994, p. 52. Reprinted with permission. **Table, page 251,** From Gernot Klepper, "Industrial Policy in the Transport of Aircraft Industry," In Paul Krugman and Alasdair Smith (eds.), *Empirical Studies of Strategic Trade Policy,* Chicago, University of Chicago Press, 1994, p. 116. **Text, page 322,** From J.G. Fuller, *The Gentle Conspirators,* p. 66 © 1962 by Grove Press, Inc. Renewed © 1990 by John Grant Fuller. Used by permission of Grove/Atlantic, Inc. **Table 11.2, page 357,** From Daniel P. Kaplan, "The Changing Airline Industry," In Leonard W. Weiss and Michael W. Klass (eds.), *Regulatory Reform: What Actually Happened* (Boston: Addison Wesley, 1986), p. 59. **Table 12.2, page 379,** From D. West and B. Von Hoenbalken, "Empirical Tests for Predatory Reputation," *Canadian Journal of Economics* 19 (February 1986): 172. © 1986 Canadian Economics Association. Reprinted with permission. **Table 12.3, page 389,** From David C. Mowery and Nathan Rosenberg, "The Commercial Aircraft Industry," In Richard R. Nelson, ed. *Government and Technical Progress: A Cross-Industry Analysis,* Pergamon Press, 1982, p. 107. Reprinted with permission of Richard R. Nelson. **Table 12.4, page 390,** From David C. Mowery and Nathan Rosenberg, "The Commercial Aircraft Industry," In Richard R. Nelson, ed. *Government and Technical Progress: A Cross-Industry Analysis,* Pergamon Press, 1982, p. 107. Reprinted with permission of Richard R. Nelson. **Table 12.7, page 400,** Reprinted from *International Journal of Industrial Organization* 6 (1980): 172 from Robert Smiley, "Empirical Evidence on Strategic Entry Deterrence," with permission from Elsevier Science. **Table, page 434,** Kenneth Lehn, "Information Asymmetries in Baseball's Free Agent Market," *Economic Inquiry,* 22 (January 1984) 40. Published by permission of Oxford University Press. **Text, pp. 470-471,** From Joseph A. Schumpeter, *Capitalism, Socialism, and Democracy.* © 1950. Reprinted by permission of HarperCollins Publishers, Inc. **Table 14.4, page 497,** From Richard C. Levin et al., "Appropriating the Returns from Industrial Research and Development," *Brookings Papers on Economic Activity,* No. 3 (1987): 794. Reprinted with permission. **Table 14.5, page 499,** Reprinted by permission, from Edwin Mansfield, "Patents and Innovation," *Management Science* (February 1986): 175. Copyright © 1986, the Institute for Management Sciences (currently INFORMS), 901 Elkridge Landing Road, Suite 400, Linthicum, MD 21090-2909 USA. **Table 14.6, page 501,** Walter G. Park and Juan Carlos Ginarte, "Intellectual Property Rights and Economic Growth," *Contemporary Economic Policy,* 15 (July 1997): 53. **Table, page 521,** Robert Blattberg, Thomas Buesing, Peter Peacock, and Subrata Sen, "Identifying the Deal Prone Segment," *Journal of Marketing Research,* Vol. 15, August 1978, p. 377. Reprinted by permission of the American Marketing Association. All rights reserved. **Table, page 521,** Robert Blattberg, Thomas Buesing, Peter Peacock, and Subrata Sen, "Identifying the Deal Prone Segment," *Journal of Marketing Research,* Vol. 15, August 1978, p. 376. Reprinted by permission of the American Marketing Association. All rights reserved.